THE DAVIS EDITION

פירוש בעל הטורים על התורה

BAAL HATURIM CHUMASH

The ArtScroll Series®

Rabbi Nosson Scherman / Rabbi Meir Zlotowitz
General Editors

A PROJECT OF THE

Mesorah Heritage Foundation

פירוש בעל הטורים על התורה

Chumash

ספר במדבר
BAMIDBAR/NUMBERS

The ArtScroll Series®

Published by
Mesorah Publications, ltd

The Davis Edition

BAAL HATURIM

THE TORAH: WITH THE BAAL HATURIM'S CLASSIC COMMENTARY TRANSLATED, ANNOTATED, AND ELUCIDATED

Hebrew text of the *Baal HaTurim* based on Rabbi Yaakov Koppel Reinitz' manuscript edition

Translation of the *Baal HaTurim* by Rabbi Eliyahu Touger

Edited, elucidated and annotated by Rabbi Avie Gold

Designed by Rabbi Sheah Brander

FIRST EDITION
First Impression . . . May 2003
Second Impression . . . November 2006
Third Impression . . . May 2010

Published and Distributed by
MESORAH PUBLICATIONS, Ltd.
4401 Second Avenue
Brooklyn, New York 11232

Distributed in Europe by
LEHMANNS
Unit E, Viking Business Park
Rolling Mill Road
Jarrow, Tyne & Wear NE32 3DP
England

Distributed in Australia & New Zealand by
GOLDS WORLD OF JUDAICA
3-13 William Street
Balaclava, Melbourne 3183
Victoria Australia

Distributed in Israel by
SIFRIATI / A. GITLER — BOOKS
6 Hayarkon Street
Bnei Brak 51127

Distributed in South Africa by
KOLLEL BOOKSHOP
Ivy Common 105 William Road
Norwood 2192, Johannesburg, South Africa

ARTSCROLL SERIES® / THE DAVIS EDITION
BAAL HATURIM CHUMASH
VOL. 4 — BAMIDBAR / NUMBERS

ISBN 10: 1-57819-131-9 / ISBN 13: 978-1-57819-131-4

Typography by CompuScribe at ArtScroll Studios, Ltd.
Custom Bound by **Sefercraft, Inc.,** Brooklyn, N.Y.

The Davis Edition of the Baal HaTurim
is dedicated to the memory of
our beloved son and brother

Simcha ז״ל

שמחה אליעזר דוד ז״ל ב״ר יוסף חיים שיחי׳
נקטף באבי ימיו, א׳ דר״ח תמוז תשס״ד

His name was Simcha and he brought simcha to everyone around him.

Young in years but with the wisdom and sensitivity of a mature man, he radiated warmth and understanding.

When his chaverim needed encouragement, they turned to him. When someone was in trouble, he sensed it and came forward to help. When his yeshiva needed someone to care, to arrange, to organize, it was always Simcha who took the initiative.

He was taken from us so suddenly at the too-young age of sixteen! Who can imagine the extent of the loss, to his family and Klal Yisrael? We can only nurse his glowing legacy of goodness and pray that Hashem Yisbarach will fill the gaping void and comfort all who loved him and cannot forget him.

תנצב״ה

Yosef and Edie Davis

Moshe and Chevie Yehoshua and Elana
Ahuva and Shaul Weinreb Eli and Chasi
Shoni and Shimmy Braun Nesanel and Perl,
and families
and Yisroel Mordechai

◆ Table of Contents

לזכר נשמת אבי מורי

ר׳ יעקב ב״ר אברהם יצחק ז״ל גאלד

נולד ח׳ אדר שני תרע״ג בבאליגראד שבגאליציא

ונפטר בשם טוב שבת קודש י״ג מרחשון תשל״ו

ולזכר נשמת אמי מורתי

האשה החשובה מרים בת ר׳ נחום (האמם) ע״ה

נולדה ד׳ תמוז תרע״ד בעיר ניו יארק

ונפטרה בשם טוב עש״ק כ״ד אדר שני תשס״ג

תנצב״ה

פרשת במדבר

Parashas Bamidbar

א וַיְדַבֵּר יהוה אֶל־מֹשֶׁה בְּמִדְבַּר סִינַי בְּאֹהֶל מוֹעֵד
בְּאֶחָד לַחֹדֶשׁ הַשֵּׁנִי בַּשָּׁנָה הַשֵּׁנִית לְצֵאתָם מֵאֶרֶץ
ב מִצְרַיִם לֵאמֹר: שְׂאוּ אֶת־רֹאשׁ כָּל־עֲדַת בְּנֵי־
יִשְׂרָאֵל לְמִשְׁפְּחֹתָם לְבֵית אֲבֹתָם בְּמִסְפַּר שֵׁמוֹת
ג כָּל־זָכָר לְגֻלְגְּלֹתָם: מִבֶּן עֶשְׂרִים שָׁנָה וָמַעְלָה
כָּל־יֹצֵא צָבָא בְּיִשְׂרָאֵל תִּפְקְדוּ אֹתָם לְצִבְאֹתָם

בעל הטורים

א (א) בְּמִדְבַּר סִינַי. לְעֵיל מִנֵּהּ כְּתִיב "אֵלֶּה הַמִּצְוֹת" וּסְמִיךְ לֵהּ "בְּמִדְבַּר", לוֹמַר, אִם אֵין אָדָם מֵשִׂים עַצְמוֹ כְּמִדְבָּר, אֵינוֹ יָכוֹל לֵידַע תּוֹרָה וּמִצְוֹת:

(ב) שְׂאוּ אֶת רֹאשׁ. לְמַעְלָה כְּתִיב "וְכָל מַעְשַׂר בָּקָר וָצֹאן", וּסְמִיךְ לֵהּ "שְׂאוּ אֶת רֹאשׁ". עַל שֵׁם מַה שֶּׁנֶּאֱמַר "עֹד תַּעֲבֹרְנָה הַצֹּאן עַל יְדֵי מוֹנֶה":

❑ **בְּמִסְפַּר שֵׁמוֹת** כְּתִיב כָּאן. וּבְפָרָשַׁת פִּינְחָס לֹא כְתִיב בְּאוֹתוֹ מִנְיָן "בְּמִסְפַּר שֵׁמוֹת". אֶלָּא כְּתָבוֹ כָּאן, לְהוֹדִיעַ שֶׁלֹּא שִׁנּוּ שְׁמוֹתָם בְּמִצְרַיִם. וּלְכָךְ כְּתִיב "לְבֵית אֲבֹתָם", לוֹמַר לְךָ שֶׁנִּקְרְאוּ בִּשְׁמוֹת אֲבוֹתָם:

BAAL HATURIM ELUCIDATED

I

1. {At *Deuteronomy* 32:48 the Baal HaTurim comments on the phrase וַיְדַבֵּר ה׳ אֶל מֹשֶׁה when it is not followed immediately by לֵאמֹר.}

❑ **בְּמִדְבַּר סִינַי — IN THE WILDERNESS OF SINAI.** In the preceding verse (*Leviticus* 27:34), the Torah states, אֵלֶּה הַמִּצְוֹת, *These are the commandments . . .*, and juxtaposed to that is בְּמִדְבַּר, *in the Wilderness.* This indicates that if a person does not make himself like a wilderness, he will not be able to know Torah[1] and *mitzvos.*[2]

2. שְׂאוּ אֶת רֹאשׁ — TAKE A CENSUS OF. The preceding passage [speaks of the animal tithe. It] begins, וְכָל מַעְשַׂר בָּקָר וָצֹאן, *any tithe of cattle or of the flock* (*Leviticus* 27:32), and juxtaposed to that is the command, שְׂאוּ אֶת רֹאשׁ, *take a census of . . .* This is in accordance with the words of the prophet, עֹד תַּעֲבֹרְנָה הַצֹּאן עַל יְדֵי מוֹנֶה, *The sheep* [i.e., Israel][2a] *will again pass before the hands of the counter* (*Jeremiah* 33:13).[3]

1. *Bamidbar Rabbah* 1:7 — That Midrash reads in full: Whoever does not make himself הֶפְקֵר [*hefker*], *free to all,* like the wilderness, will not be able to acquire wisdom and Torah. The Talmud (*Eruvin* 54a) derives a similar lesson from 21:18 below.

As used in that Midrash, the term *hefker* refers to a modest willingness both to learn from anybody, even from a person whose general knowledge is inferior to one's own (see *Avos* 4:1), and to teach what one knows to anybody who desires to learn (*Tosafos* and *Rosh* to *Nedarim* 55a; *Mattenos Kehunah*). Alternatively: Making oneself *hefker* means making one's knowledge free to all, that is, teaching without charging a fee (pseudo-*Rashi* to *Nedarim* 55a; *Yedei Moshe*).

2. *Peirush HaRokeach.*

2a. Other places where the Baal HaTurim explains צאן as a reference to Israel include *Genesis* 31:6 and *Exodus* 15:13. In his comments to 11:16 below, the Baal HaTurim states that צאן is one of seventy names that Scripture uses for Israel.

3. The Midrash understands the verse from

1 HASHEM *spoke to Moses in the Wilderness of Sinai, in
the Tent of Meeting, on the first of the second month,
in the second year after their exodus from the land of Egypt,
saying:*
2 *"Take a census of the entire assembly of the Children
of Israel according to their families, according to their
fathers' household, by number of the names, every
male according to their head count.* 3 *From twenty years of
age and up — everyone who goes out to the legion in
Israel — you shall count them according to their legions,*

BAAL HATURIM ELUCIDATED

❑ בְּמִסְפַּר שֵׁמוֹת — **BY NUMBER OF THE NAMES.** This phrase is mentioned here, but is omitted from the census ordained in *parashas Pinechas* (*Numbers* 26:2).[4] It is included here to teach that the Jewish people did not change their names during the Egyptian exile.[5] This is also the reason for the phrase לְבֵית אֲבֹתָם, *according to their fathers' household,* [6] i.e., they were given names [based on the traditions] of their fathers.[7]

Jeremiah as a reference to a census of the Children of Israel to be taken in the time of the Messiah. See the Midrash (*Pesikta Rabbasi* 10:14; *Bamidbar Rabbah* 2:11) adduced in note 70 below.

4. That verse reads: שְׂאוּ אֶת רֹאשׁ כָּל עֲדַת בְּנֵי יִשְׂרָאֵל, *Take a census of the entire assembly of the Children of Israel,* מִבֶּן עֶשְׂרִים שָׁנָה וָמַעְלָה, *from twenty years of age and up,* לְבֵית אֲבֹתָם, *according to their fathers' household,* כָּל יֹצֵא צָבָא בְּיִשְׂרָאֵל, *everyone who goes out to the legion in Israel.* Note that that verse includes the phrase לְבֵית אֲבֹתָם, *according to their fathers' household,* as does our verse. However, as the Baal HaTurim points out, it does not contain the phrase בְּמִסְפַּר שֵׁמוֹת, *by number of the names,* which our verse has (see note 6). In his commentary to 26:2 below, the Baal HaTurim explains why the term לְמִשְׁפְּחֹתָם is omitted from that verse.

5. The Midrash teaches that three merits allowed Israel to be redeemed from Egypt: (a) They did not change their language [i.e., they spoke to each other in the Holy Tongue, not in Egyptian]; (b) they did not speak slander [or gossip]; and (c) they retained their Hebrew names (*Pirkei DeRabbi Eliezer* 48; see also *Mechilta* to 12:6 and the Baal HaTurim to *Exodus* 1:1, s.v., וְאֵלֶּה שְׁמוֹת).

6. The phrase לְבֵית אֲבֹתָם, *according to their fathers' household,* appears both here and in *parashas Pinechas* (see note 4 above). There, the phrase לְבֵית אֲבֹתָם is found only once, in the verse that introduces the command to conduct a census; it is not repeated regarding each individual tribe. The term מִשְׁפָּחָה, *family,* however, appears numerous times there [in the forms לְמִשְׁפְּחֹתָם, *according to their families;* מִשְׁפַּחַת, *the family of,* and מִשְׁפְּחֹת, *the families of*] in conjunction with each individual tribal census. Because מִשְׁפָּחָה and בֵּית אֲבֹתָם are never used in the same verse in *parashas Pinechas,* the terms seem to be synonymous: "family" and "father's household" refer to the same group of people. If this is so, the side-by-side use of the two phrases in our verse and with regard to the census of each individual tribe seems redundant. The Baal HaTurim explains that, in our passage, the phrase לְבֵית אֲבֹתָם means *according to their fathers' traditions* and implies that they named their children with the names traditionally used by their fathers. It is repeated in conjunction with each tribe to teach that not only some tribes retained Hebrew names; rather, each tribe named its newborns in the manner of its ancestors (*VeChur LaZahav*).

7. *Peirush HaRokeach.*

א/ד־ה

ד אַתָּ֖ה וְאַהֲרֹֽן׃ וְאִתְּכֶ֣ם יִהְי֔וּ אִ֥ישׁ אִ֖ישׁ לַמַּטֶּ֑ה אִ֛ישׁ
ה רֹ֥אשׁ לְבֵית־אֲבֹתָ֖יו הֽוּא׃ וְאֵ֙לֶּה֙ שְׁמ֣וֹת הָֽאֲנָשִׁ֔ים
אֲשֶׁ֥ר יַֽעַמְד֖וּ אִתְּכֶ֑ם לִרְאוּבֵ֕ן אֱלִיצ֖וּר בֶּן־שְׁדֵיאֽוּר׃

בעל הטורים

(ג) **אַתָּה וְאַהֲרֹן.** וּלְמַעְלָה בְּפָרָשַׁת כִּי תִשָּׂא לֹא סִיַּע אַהֲרֹן בְּאוֹתוֹ מִנְיָן, לְפִי שֶׁעַל יָדוֹ נַעֲשָׂה הָעֵגֶל, שֶׁבִּשְׁבִילוֹ הֻצְרְכוּ לְמִנְיָן. לְכָךְ לֹא מְנָאָם הוּא:

(ד) {**וְאִתְּכֶם.** ג׳ — "וְאִתְּכֶם יִהְיוּ"; "וְאִתְּכֶם בְּנֵי אֲדֹנֵיכֶם, וְאִתְּכֶם הָרֶכֶב וְהַסּוּסִים". שֶׁאֵלּוּ הַשְּׁנֵים עָשָׂר הָיוּ גְדוֹלִין שֶׁבִּשְׁבָטִים, כְּדִכְתִיב "וְאִתְּכֶם בְּנֵי אֲדֹנֵיכֶם", שֶׁהָיוּ אֲדוֹנִים. וְהָיוּ שָׂרֵי אֲלָפִים, כְּדִכְתִיב "וְאִתְּכֶם הָרֶכֶב וְהַסּוּסִים"}:

(ה) **לִרְאוּבֵן אֱלִיצוּר בֶּן שְׁדֵיאוּר.** הַנְּשִׂיאִים מַתְחִיל בֶּ"אֱלִיצוּר" וּמְסַיֵּם בְּ"עֵינָן" עַל שֵׁם

BAAL HATURIM ELUCIDATED

3. אַתָּה וְאַהֲרֹן — YOU AND AARON. [The command to conduct a census here includes both Moses and Aaron.] Earlier, however, in the census commanded in *parashas Ki Sisa* (*Exodus* 30:11-16), Aaron [is not mentioned, indicating that he] did not assist in that count. This is because the golden calf had been made[8] through him, and it was the sin of the calf that necessitated a census at that time.[9] Therefore, he did not participate in counting them.[10]

8. The reading נַעֲשָׂה הָעֵגֶל, *the calf had been made,* follows the majority of manuscripts and printed editions. However, one manuscript version used by *Shoham Yakar* reads עָשׂוּ הָעֵגֶל, *they made the calf.* The pronoun "they" is a reference to the עֵרֶב רַב, *mixed multitude* (*Exodus* 12:38), who were responsible for the manufacture of the golden calf and for its aftermath (see the Baal HaTurim to *Exodus* 32:22; see *Rashi* to *Exodus* 32:4, s.v., **עֵגֶל מַסֵּכָה**, and 32:7, s.v., שִׁחֵת עַמְּךָ).

9. Read simply, the passage in *parashas Ki Sisa* seems to be a statement about how to conduct a census, rather than a specific command to conduct a head count at that particular time. Moreover, that passage (*Exodus* 30:11-16) is recorded in the Torah before the incident of the golden calf (*Exodus,* Ch. 32). Accordingly, the census would seem to be unrelated to the calf. Nevertheless, the Midrash explains the two passages in accordance with the well-known rule, אֵין מֻקְדָּם וּמְאֻחָר בַּתּוֹרָה, *the events of the Torah are not presented in chronological sequence* (*Pesachim* 6b; cited in *Rashi* to 8:2 below). The following parable will explain why God told Moses to count the nation at that time: A king had many sheep which were attacked and decimated by a pack of wolves. He said to his shepherd, "Please count the sheep to determine how many are missing." Similarly, after a large segment of the people had been put to death as a consequence of their participation in the incident of the golden calf, the Holy One, Blessed is He, said to Moses, "Go count the Israelites to determine how many are missing" (*Tanchuma, Ki Sisa* 9; see also *Rashi* to *Exodus* 30:16, 1:1 above, and 26:1 below).

10. The Baal HaTurim's comment may be understood in light of a Talmudic passage regarding the vestments of the Kohen Gadol. Throughout the year and for much of the day on Yom Kippur, the Kohen Gadol wears the eight vestments described in Chapter 28 of *Exodus.* Four of them contain gold (28:6,15,33,36), the other four do not (28:39,42). However, when he enters the Holy of Holies to perform the special Yom Kippur service, the Kohen Gadol wears four linen vestments that do not contain any gold (see *Leviticus* 16:4). The Talmud explains: The Kohen Gadol does not enter the innermost chamber of the Temple, the Holy of Holies, clad in the golden vestments because, אֵין קַטֵּגוֹר נַעֲשֶׂה סַנֵּגוֹר, *an accuser does not serve as a defender.* That is, the gold would serve as a reminder of the golden calf — in whose manufacture the Kohen Gadol, Aaron, was an unwitting participant — and would thereby hinder the attainment of atonement (*Rosh Hashanah* 26a, see *Rabbeinu Chananel* there). Similarly, the purpose of the census of *Ki Sisa* was *to atone for your souls* (*Exodus* 30:16),

you and Aaron. [4] *And with you shall be one man from each tribe; a man who is a leader of his father's household.* [5] *These are the names of the men who shall stand with you: For Reuben, Elizur son of Shedeur.*

BAAL HATURIM ELUCIDATED

4. {**וְאִתְּכֶם — AND WITH YOU.** [The masoretic note, ג׳, means that] this word appears three times in the *Tanach*: (i) here, וְאִתְּכֶם יִהְיוּ, *and with you shall be;* and (ii-iii) twice in the verse, וְאִתְּכֶם בְּנֵי אֲדֹנֵיכֶם וְאִתְּכֶם הָרֶכֶב וְהַסּוּסִים, *and with you are your master's sons, and with you are the chariot force and the horses* (*II Kings* 10:2).[11] This indicates that these twelve men were the most prominent members of their respective tribes, as it is written, *and with you are your master's sons,* i.e., they were [worthy of the title] "masters."[12] Moreover, all of them were "leaders of thousands," as it is written, *and with you are the chariot force and the horses.* [13]}[14]

5. לִרְאוּבֵן אֱלִיצוּר בֶּן שְׁדֵיאוּר — FOR REUBEN, ELIZUR SON OF SHEDEUR. [As listed here,] the roster of the tribal leaders [and their fathers] begins with אֱלִיצוּר, *Elizur,* [15] and concludes with עֵינָן, *Enan* [15a] (v. 15). This recalls the verse, יְצָרֶנְהוּ,

after the golden calf. Thus, Aaron's participation in that counting would have served as a קַטֵּגוֹר, *an accuser,* rather than as a סַנֵּגוֹר, *defender.*

11. Elisha, the successor of Elijah the prophet, dispatched one of his disciples to anoint Jehu son of Jehoshaphat as king over Israel. The disciple anointed Jehu and commanded him to eradicate any remaining members of the House of Ahab (*II Kings* 9:1-10). In fulfilling that charge, Jehu sent intimidating letters to the elders of Jezreel who had been harboring seventy sons of Ahab: *". . . and now, when this letter reaches you* — וְאִתְּכֶם בְּנֵי אֲדֹנֵיכֶם, *and with you are your master's sons,* וְאִתְּכֶם הָרֶכֶב וְהַסּוּסִים, *and with you are the chariot force and the horses, fortified city and weapons — see who is the best and most virtuous of your master's sons and place him upon his father's throne, and fight for the sake of your master's house"* (*II Kings* 10:1-3).

12. See note 11 above. It is clear from the prophet's later words, *see who is the best and most virtuous of your master's sons,* that the earlier phrase, וְאִתְּכֶם בְּנֵי אֲדֹנֵיכֶם, *and with you are your master's sons,* refers to those sons of Ahab displaying the leadership qualities necessary for a successful reign. Thus, the first וְאִתְּכֶם in the verse from *Kings* teaches that the twelve tribal representatives were each worthy of rulership.

13. It is not clear how the words וְאִתְּכֶם הָרֶכֶב וְהַסּוּסִים, *and with you are the chariot force and the horses,* indicate that the tribal leaders under discussion were each שָׂרֵי אֲלָפִים, *leaders of thousands,* the highest of four echelons of officials — *leaders of thousands, leaders of hundreds, leaders of fifties, and leaders of tens* — that Jethro had advised Moses to institute (*Exodus* 18:21). Perhaps another Scriptural passage, the one in which the prophet Samuel describes the prerogatives of royalty, will shed light on the Baal HaTurim's comment. There, the prophet states, *"This is the protocol of the king who will reign over you: He will conscript your sons and place them in his chariot force and in his cavalry . . . and appointing for himself leaders of thousands . . .* (*I Samuel* 8:11-12). Those verses seem to indicate that the king's personal charioteers were worthy of the office "leader of thousands." Thus, the verse in *Kings* that speaks of the would-be king's chariot force may be taken as an allusion to "leaders of thousands" (*VeChur LaZahav*).

14. This comment is not found in the early or later printed editions, but does appear in *Shoham Yakar's* manuscript edition.

15. אֱלִיצוּר may be understood as a compound of אֵלִי, *my God,* and צוּר, [*my*] *Protector,* for the noun צוּר refers to a large, strong rock (e.g., *Exodus* 33:21-22); by extension, it is used for *a fortress* or *protector.*

It is noteworthy that the Baal HaTurim's allusion is taken from the first and last names to appear on the list, in accordance with the term יְסֹבְבֶנְהוּ, *He encircled him* (Y.S.).

15a. עֵינָן is linguistically akin to both עַיִן, *eye,* and עָנָן, *cloud.*

ו־ז לְשִׁמְעוֹן שְׁלֻמִיאֵל בֶּן־צוּרִישַׁדָּי׃ לִיהוּדָה נַחְשׁוֹן
ח־ט בֶּן־עַמִּינָדָב׃ לְיִשָּׂשכָר נְתַנְאֵל בֶּן־צוּעָר׃ לִזְבוּלֻן
י אֱלִיאָב בֶּן־חֵלֹן׃ לִבְנֵי יוֹסֵף לְאֶפְרַיִם אֱלִישָׁמָע
בֶּן־עַמִּיהוּד לִמְנַשֶּׁה גַּמְלִיאֵל בֶּן־פְּדָהצוּר׃
יא־יב לְבִנְיָמִן אֲבִידָן בֶּן־גִּדְעֹנִי׃ לְדָן אֲחִיעֶזֶר בֶּן־
יג־יד עַמִּישַׁדָּי׃ לְאָשֵׁר פַּגְעִיאֵל בֶּן־עָכְרָן׃ לְגָד
טו אֶלְיָסָף בֶּן־דְּעוּאֵל׃ לְנַפְתָּלִי אֲחִירַע בֶּן־
טז עֵינָן׃ אֵלֶּה °קריאי [°קְרוּאֵי ק׳] הָעֵדָה נְשִׂיאֵי
יז מַטּוֹת אֲבוֹתָם רָאשֵׁי אַלְפֵי יִשְׂרָאֵל הֵם׃ וַיִּקַּח
מֹשֶׁה וְאַהֲרֹן אֵת הָאֲנָשִׁים הָאֵלֶּה אֲשֶׁר נִקְּבוּ
יח בְּשֵׁמוֹת׃ וְאֵת כָּל־הָעֵדָה הִקְהִילוּ בְּאֶחָד לַחֹדֶשׁ
הַשֵּׁנִי וַיִּתְיַלְדוּ עַל־מִשְׁפְּחֹתָם לְבֵית אֲבֹתָם
בְּמִסְפַּר שֵׁמוֹת מִבֶּן עֶשְׂרִים שָׁנָה וָמַעְלָה
יט לְגֻלְגְּלֹתָם׃ כַּאֲשֶׁר צִוָּה יְהוָה אֶת־מֹשֶׁה וַיִּפְקְדֵם

בעל הטורים

"יִצְּרֶנְהוּ כְּאִישׁוֹן עֵינוֹ", וְעַל יְדֵי הֶעָנָן:

(טז) קריאי [קְרוּאֵי] הָעֵדָה. וָי"ו קְטִיעָא, וּקְרֵי "קְרוּאֵי" בִּשְׁבִיל שְׁלֻמִיאֵל בֶּן צוּרִישַׁדָּי, שֶׁהוּא זִמְרִי בֶּן סָלוּא. וְכֵן בַּעֲדַת קֹרַח "קְרִאֵי" כְּתִיב חָסֵר וָי"ו. וְשָׁם חָסֵר הַוָּי"ו לְגַמְרֵי, לְפִי שֶׁהָיוּ כֻּלָּם רְשָׁעִים. אֲבָל בְּכָאן הָיוּ הָאֲחֵרִים צַדִּיקִים:

BAAL HATURIM ELUCIDATED

He [*God*] *protected*[16] *him* [*Israel*] כְּאִישׁוֹן עֵינוֹ, *like the pupil of His eye* (*Deuteronomy* 32:10), and [that,][16a] by means of the cloud.[17]

16. קריאי [קְרוּאֵי] הָעֵדָה — THE ONES SUMMONED BY THE ASSEMBLY. The ו of קְרוּאֵי is drawn as ו׳ קְטִיעָה, *a cut off* ו [making it look like a י,[18] as if the word were קְרִיאֵי],

16. The root of יִצְּרֶנְהוּ is נצר, *to guard.* Thus, it is related to the noun צוּר (see note 15).

16a. The text follows the early printed editions. *Shoham Yakar's* manuscript edition omits the prefix וְ־, *and* [*that*].

17. The verse from *Deuteronomy* reads in full: *He* [*God*] *discovered him* [*Israel*] *in a desert land, in desolation, a howling wilderness; He encircled him, He granted him discernment, He protected him like the pupil of His eye.* As explained by *Rashi* there, the term יְסֹבְבֶנְהוּ, *He encircled him,* refers to the Clouds of Glory with which God surrounded the Israelites in the wilderness, and the term יִצְּרֶנְהוּ, *He protected him,* means that He guarded the nation against snakes, fiery serpents and scorpions, as well as against the nations. Elsewhere, *Rashi* explains that the clouds (a) intercepted the arrows and catapult stones that the pursuing Egyptians shot at the fleeing Israelites (*Rashi* to *Exodus* 19:4, s.v., עַל כַּנְפֵי נְשָׁרִים) and (b) killed any snakes or scorpions that were in their path (*Rashi* to *Numbers* 10:34).

18. The masoretic note on this word reads: קְרוּאֵי קְרִי, *The reading is* קְרוּאֵי. The note means that the word is an example of קְרִי וּכְתִיב, *keri uchesiv* [a word spelled one way in the Torah scroll, but

1/6-19 [6] *For Simeon, Shelumiel son of Zurishaddai.* [7] *For Judah,*
Nachshon son of Amminadab. [8] *For Issachar, Nethanel*
son of Zuar. [9] *For Zebulun, Eliab son of Helon.* [10] *For the*
children of Joseph — for Ephraim, Elishama son of
Ammihud; for Manasseh, Gamaliel son of Pedahzur. [11] *For*
Benjamin, Abidan son of Gideoni. [12] *For Dan, Ahiezer son*
of Ammishaddai. [13] *For Asher, Pagiel son of Ochran.*
[14] *For Gad, Eliasaph son of Deuel.* [15] *For Naphtali, Ahira*
son of Enan."

[16] *These were the ones summoned by the assembly, the*
leaders of their fathers' tribes, they are the heads of Israel's
thousands. [17] *Moses and Aaron took these men who had*
been designated by [their] names.

[18] *They gathered together the entire assembly on the*
first of the second month, and they established their
genealogy according to their families, according to their
fathers' household, by number of the names, from twenty
years of age and up, according to their head count.
[19] *As* HASHEM *had commanded Moses, he counted them*

BAAL HATURIM ELUCIDATED

nevertheless, it is pronounced קְרוּאֵי. This is because of Shelumiel son of Zurishaddai — who is also known as Zimri son of Salu[18a] [leader of the tribe of Simeon who later led a rebellion against Moses[19]].[19a]

Similarly, the spelling used with regard to Korah's assembly is קְרִאֵי, *those summoned* (16:2 below), without a ו. Moreover, [although our verse retains a truncated vestige of the ו,] in the other verse the ו is omitted completely, because all of the people involved in that assembly were wicked. Here, however, the [eleven] others were righteous.[20]

pronounced differently]. Although its *kesiv* (spelling) is קריאי, with a י in the middle, its *keri* (pronunciation) is קְרוּאֵי, with a ו. And that is how most commentators describe the word — as a *keri uchesiv* (*Pesikta Zutresa* [*Lekach Tov*]; *Masores Siyag LaTorah* [*Ramah*]; *Peirush HaRokeach; Chizkuni; Rabbeinu Chaim Paltiel; Minchas Shai*). Consequently, various reasons are given for the *keri uchesiv,* all of them related to the number 10, the *gematria* of the letter י. However, the Baal HaTurim describes the middle letter of the word as ו׳׳ו קְטִיעָא, *a cut off letter* ו, that is a ו whose lower half has been truncated so that the letter looks like a י. Accordingly, the Baal HaTurim's comment ignores the י and explains why the foot of the ו has been cut off.

For more about the ו׳׳ו קְטִיעָא, see the Baal HaTurim's comment to 25:12 below, s.v., אֶת בְּרִיתִי שָׁלוֹם.

18a. *Sanhedrin* 52b.

19. See Chapter 25 below, with *Rashi* to 25:6, s.v., וְהִנֵּה, and the Baal HaTurim to 25:14, s.v., הֻכָּה.

19a. The diminished size of the ו reflects the diminished stature of one member of the assembly.

20. *Maharam MiRothenburg,* who also suggests an alternative reason for retaining part of the ו in our verse. Namely, at the time of this census, Zimri had not yet abandoned his righteous ways.

א/כ־כב שני כ בְּמִדְבַּר סִינָי: וַיִּהְיוּ בְנֵי־רְאוּבֵן בְּכֹר יִשְׂרָאֵל
תּוֹלְדֹתָם לְמִשְׁפְּחֹתָם לְבֵית אֲבֹתָם בְּמִסְפַּר שֵׁמוֹת
לְגֻלְגְּלֹתָם כָּל־זָכָר מִבֶּן עֶשְׂרִים שָׁנָה וָמַעְלָה כֹּל
כא יֹצֵא צָבָא: פְּקֻדֵיהֶם לְמַטֵּה רְאוּבֵן שִׁשָּׁה וְאַרְבָּעִים
אֶלֶף וַחֲמֵשׁ מֵאוֹת:
כב לִבְנֵי שִׁמְעוֹן תּוֹלְדֹתָם לְמִשְׁפְּחֹתָם לְבֵית אֲבֹתָם
פְּקֻדָיו בְּמִסְפַּר שֵׁמוֹת לְגֻלְגְּלֹתָם כָּל־זָכָר מִבֶּן

בעל הטורים

(יט) **בְּמִדְבַּר סִינָי.** שְׁנַיִם דִּסְמִיכֵי בס״פ — ״וַיִּפְקְדֵם בְּמִדְבַּר סִינָי״; ״בְּיוֹם צַוֹּתוֹ אֶת בְּנֵי יִשְׂרָאֵל לְהַקְרִיב אֶת קָרְבְּנֵיהֶם לַה׳ בְּמִדְבַּר סִינָי״. לְפִי שֶׁכְּשֶׁהָיוּ נִמְנִין, הָיוּ מַקְרִיבִין קָרְבָּנוֹת עֲלֵיהֶם כְּדֵי שֶׁלֹּא יִשְׁלֹט בָּהֶם דֶּבֶר, כִּדְכְתִיב ״כִּי תִשָּׂא אֶת רֹאשׁ בְּנֵי יִשְׂרָאֵל לִפְקֻדֵיהֶם וְנָתְנוּ אִישׁ כֹּפֶר נַפְשׁוֹ . . .״:

(כב) **לִבְנֵי שִׁמְעוֹן . . . לְגֻלְגְּלֹתָם.** הַלָּמֶ״ד עֲקֻמָּה לְמַטָּה, לְפִי שֶׁהַלָּמֶ״ד שֶׁלּוֹ, זִמְרִי

BAAL HATURIM ELUCIDATED

19. בְּמִדְבַּר סִינָי — IN THE WILDERNESS OF SINAI. The masoretic note,[21] ב׳ דִּסְמִיכֵי בס״פ, means that this phrase appears twice at the end of a *parashah*:[22] (i) here, וַיִּפְקְדֵם בְּמִדְבַּר סִינָי, *he counted them in the Wilderness of Sinai;* and (ii) בְּיוֹם צַוֹּתוֹ אֶת בְּנֵי יִשְׂרָאֵל לְהַקְרִיב אֶת קָרְבְּנֵיהֶם לַה׳ בְּמִדְבַּר סִינָי, *on the day He commanded the Children of*

21. This masoretic note is not known from any source other than *Maharam MiRothenburg,* the apparent source of the Baal HaTurim's comment.

22. The masoretic abbreviation בס״פ usually stands for בְּסוֹף פָּסוּק, *at the end of a verse,* and that is how it is spelled out in all editions of the Baal HaTurim and *Maharam MiRothenburg.* However, that interpretation of בס״פ seems untenable here, for there are two other Scriptural verses (26:64 and 33:15 below) that end with the words בְּמִדְבַּר סִינָי. Accordingly, it is suggested that, in the masoretic note under discussion, the abbreviation בס״פ means בְּסוֹף פָּרָשָׁה, *at the end of a parashah* (see below).

According to masoretic tradition, the text of Scripture is divided into פָּרָשִׁיּוֹת, *parashiyos* (paragraph-like passages), separated from one another by a blank space, and that is how *Tanach* scrolls are written. These spaces appear in one of two forms: פְּתוּחָה, *open,* indicated by ending the previous passage in the middle of a line and then beginning the new passage at the beginning of the next line, or סְתוּמָה, *closed,* indicated by the new passage beginning on the same line on which the previous passage ended, but after a space in which at least nine letters could be written (see illustration). In some printed editions these spaces are indicated by the letters פ and ס. Each of the two verses cited by the Baal HaTurim, *Leviticus* 7:38 and our verse, appears at the end of its respective *parashah* — in *Leviticus* at a פְּתוּחָה, here at a סְתוּמָה. The other two verses (26:64 and 33:15 below), on the other hand, appear in the middle of a *parashah* and are therefore not included in the masoretic note. Following this suggestion, the Baal HaTurim's comment should be emended to שְׁנַיִם דִּסְמִיכֵי בְּסוֹף פָּרָשָׁה, literally, *two [words] forming a phrase at the end of a parashah* (*VeChur LaZahav*).

לעשו לחם ונזיד עדשים ויאכל וישת ויקם
וילך ויבז עשו את הבכרה
ויהי רעב בארץ מלבד הרעב הראשון אשר

פָּרָשָׁה פְּתוּחָה — Open Passage (*Genesis* 25:34-26:1)

את מחלת בת ישמעאל בן אברהם אחות
נביות על נשיו לו לאשה ויצא
יעקב מבאר שבע וילך חרנה ויפגע במקום

פָּרָשָׁה סְתוּמָה — Closed Passage (*Genesis* 28:9-10)

in the Wilderness of Sinai.

20 *These were the sons of Reuben, firstborn of Israel, their offspring according to their families, according to their fathers' household, by number of the names according to their head count, every male from twenty years of age and up, everyone who goes out to the legion.* 21 *Their count, for the tribe of Reuben: forty-six thousand, five hundred.*

22 *For the sons of Simeon, their offspring according to their families, according to their fathers' household, its numbers, by number of the names according to their head count, every male*

BAAL HATURIM ELUCIDATED

Israel to bring their offerings to H*ASHEM*, *in the Wilderness of Sinai* (*Leviticus* 7:38). This indicates that while the Israelites were being counted, they[23] would bring offerings on their behalf, so that a plague would not befall them, in accordance with the verse, כִּי תִשָּׂא אֶת רֹאשׁ בְּנֵי יִשְׂרָאֵל לִפְקֻדֵיהֶם וְנָתְנוּ אִישׁ כֹּפֶר נַפְשׁוֹ, *When you take a head count of the Children of Israel according to their numbers, every man shall give. . . atonement-money for his soul* [*. . . so that there will not be a plague among them when counting them*] (*Exodus* 30:12).[24]

22. לִבְנֵי שִׁמְעוֹן . . . לְגֻלְגְּלֹתָם — FOR THE SONS OF SIMEON . . . ACCORDING TO THEIR HEAD COUNT. [According to a scribal tradition,] the letter ל [of Simeon's tribe] is bent downward.[25] This is because [at a later date] its most exalted

23. The antecedent of the pronoun "they" is unclear: It may refer to the counters, the counted or the ministering Kohanim. It is suggested that "they" are the tribal leaders mentioned earlier (vv. 5-15); and the offerings are those spoken of in Chapter 7 below, as it is stated there (7:2), *The leaders of Israel . . . brought offerings; they were the leaders of the tribes, they were those who stand at the countings* (A.S.).

24. *Maharam MiRothenburg.* The simple meaning of כֹּפֶר in this verse is *atonement-money*, a reference to the atonement attained through the bringing of communal offerings purchased with the half-*shekel* redemption money of that passage (see *Rashi* to *Exodus* 30:15). The Baal HaTurim, however, finds an additional meaning to the word כֹּפֶר, namely, *atonement-offerings*, which were to be brought while the census was being taken (*VeChur LaZahav*). See note 23 above regarding the nature of those offerings.

25. The letter ל appears four times in the Baal HaTurim's rubric. Additionally, none of the extant manuscript Torah scrolls contain a ל that fits the Baal HaTurim's description. Thus, we know neither to which ל the comment refers nor how to draw that letter. Although it has been suggested that the Baal HaTurim refers to the last ל of the four, the latter part of the Baal HaTurim's commentary describes that ל in a different manner, implying that this part of his comment refers to an earlier ל (*VeChur LaZahav*).

Regarding the shape, it is suggested that the term עֲקֻמָּה לְמַטָּה, *bent downward*, refers to the flag-like node that tops the letter (see illustration).

The usual form of the ל is drawn as a כ [with a shortened base] with a ו standing on its upper left corner (*Rokeach; Beis Yosef, Orach Chaim* 36). Halachic literature describes the upright part of the ו as "the neck of the ל" and the node as "the head." Regarding the ו itself, the head must be drawn so that it faces directly to the left, parallel to the line of letters in which it appears (*Beis Yosef*). Similarly, the ו of the ל is drawn with its head facing to the left; and that is how most Torah scrolls are written. However, some [Yemenite] scribes traditionally draw the ל with a slightly bowed head (see illustration, next page). In some hand-written *Chumashim*, particularly the Gaster manuscript known as *The Tittled Bible*, every ל appears with a bowed head. Perhaps, the

כג עֶשְׂרִים שָׁנָה וָמַעְלָה כֹּל יֹצֵא צָבָא: פְּקֻדֵיהֶם
לְמַטֵּה שִׁמְעוֹן תִּשְׁעָה וַחֲמִשִּׁים אֶלֶף וּשְׁלֹשׁ מֵאוֹת:
כד לִבְנֵי גָד תּוֹלְדֹתָם לְמִשְׁפְּחֹתָם לְבֵית אֲבֹתָם
בְּמִסְפַּר שֵׁמוֹת מִבֶּן עֶשְׂרִים שָׁנָה וָמַעְלָה כֹּל יֹצֵא
כה צָבָא: פְּקֻדֵיהֶם לְמַטֵּה גָד חֲמִשָּׁה וְאַרְבָּעִים אֶלֶף
וְשֵׁשׁ מֵאוֹת וַחֲמִשִּׁים:
כו לִבְנֵי יְהוּדָה תּוֹלְדֹתָם לְמִשְׁפְּחֹתָם לְבֵית אֲבֹתָם
בְּמִסְפַּר שֵׁמֹת מִבֶּן עֶשְׂרִים שָׁנָה וָמַעְלָה כֹּל יֹצֵא
כז צָבָא: פְּקֻדֵיהֶם לְמַטֵּה יְהוּדָה אַרְבָּעָה וְשִׁבְעִים
אֶלֶף וְשֵׁשׁ מֵאוֹת:
כח לִבְנֵי יִשָּׂשכָר תּוֹלְדֹתָם לְמִשְׁפְּחֹתָם לְבֵית אֲבֹתָם

בעל הטורים

בֶּן סָלוּא, חָטָא, וְנָפְלוּ מִשִּׁבְטוֹ. וְהַלָּמֶ״ד הִיא גְּבוֹהָה מִכָּל הָאוֹתִיּוֹת, כָּךְ חָסַר מִשִּׁבְטוֹ, שֶׁלֹּא הֶעֱמִיד לֹא מֶלֶךְ וְלֹא שׁוֹפֵט. {הַלָּמֶ״ד הַשֵּׁנִית דְּ״גֻלְגְּלֹתָם״ דְּשִׁמְעוֹן עֲשׂוּיָה כִּמְגֵרָה, וּזְקוּפָה, וְאֵין לָהּ כּוֹבַע בְּרֹאשָׁהּ, לְפִי שֶׁהוֹרָה נְשִׂיא בֵית אָב לַשִּׁמְעוֹנִי זְנוּת בְּיִשְׂרָאֵל, בְּגִלּוּי הָרֹאשׁ וּבְקוֹמָה זְקוּפָה:}

BAAL HATURIM ELUCIDATED

son,[26] Zimri son of Salu, sinned[27] and many members of his tribe fell. [The ל was chosen for this allusion because] the ל is the tallest of all the letters. Moreover, his tribe was diminished [in another manner], for it produced neither king nor judge.[28]

Baal HaTurim's "bent downward" refers to that form of ל (*VeChur LaZahav*).

26. The text reads שֶׁהַלָּמֶ״ד שֶׁלּוֹ, literally, *because its letter* ל, following the early printed editions. It uses the tallest letter of the *aleph-beis* as a metaphor for the exalted position of tribal leadership. This conforms to the Midrash: Why is the ל taller than all the other letters? Because it is in the center of the twenty-two letters [that form the *aleph-beis*], like a king who sits upon his throne of honor with his majesty spread before him. Thus, [in the word מֶלֶךְ, *king,*] the final כ stands for his כִּסֵּא, *throne;* the מ stands for his מַלְכוּת, *majesty,* and he, the ל, is the outstanding letter among them, just as a king [is the outstanding person in his land] (*Osios DeRabbi Akiva, nusach* II).

Most modern editions of the Baal HaTurim have an alternative reading שֶׁהַנָּשִׂיא, *because the leader.* Although the meaning of the allusion is the same, that reading does not explain why the letter ל, rather than any other letter, was chosen for the allusion.

A third version — שהמלמד — appears in *Shoham Yakar's* manuscript version. Clearly, this word also describes the tribal leader; however, its literal meaning is not clear. It may be vowelized in any of three ways: שֶׁהַמְלַמֵּד, *because [its] teacher;* שֶׁהַמְלֻמָּד, *because [its] most learned;* or שֶׁהַמַּלְמָד, *because [its] goad* (*VeChur LaZahav*).

27. See the Baal HaTurim's comment at verse 16 above.

28. The Midrash states: Each of the tribes produced judges and/or kings, except for the tribe of Simeon, from whom arose neither judge nor king, as a consequence of the sin that its leader Zimri committed in Shittim. This teaches you the gravity of lewdness. Thus we find from all the tribes: Othniel from the tribe of Judah; Ehud from Benjamin . . . Eli and Samuel from the tribe of Levi. Those are the Judges of Israel [as listed in the Scriptural סֵפֶר שׁוֹפְטִים, *Book of Judges*]. And these are the kings: Saul from Benjamin; David and

from twenty years of age and up, everyone who goes out to
the legion. [23] *Their count, for the tribe of Simeon: fifty-nine*
thousand, three hundred.
[24] *For the sons of Gad, their offspring according to their*
families, according to their fathers' household, by number of
the names, from twenty years of age and up, everyone who
goes out to the legion. [25] *Their count, for the tribe of Gad:*
forty-five thousand, six hundred and fifty.
[26] *For the sons of Judah, their offspring according to their*
families, according to their fathers' household, by number of
the names, from twenty years of age and up, everyone who
goes out to the legion. [27] *Their count, for the tribe of Judah:*
seventy-four thousand, six hundred.
[28] *For the sons of Issachar, their offspring according*
to their families, according to their fathers' household,

BAAL HATURIM ELUCIDATED

{[According to another scribal tradition,] the second ל of גִּלְגְּלֹתָם, *their head count,* in the verses of Simeon should be drawn like a saw,[29] erect, and without a cap on its head.[30] All this, because a leader of a father's house of the Simeonites[31] taught lewdness in Israel with unabashed brazenness and arrogant pride.[32]}[33]

Solomon from Judah; Jeroboam from Ephraim . . . But Simeon put forth neither king nor judge — because of the sin of lewdness (*Midrash Tadshe* 8).

29. It is not clear what the Baal HaTurim means by this. According to *Or Torah,* in this masoretic note, the word מְגֵרָה does not refer to a *saw,* rather it means *waterspout.* Accordingly, *Or Torah* describes the node at the top of this ל as elongated, looking somewhat like water flowing forth from a spigot. *Minchas Shai,* however, rejects *Or Torah's* view without explaining why. In any case, *Or Torah's* explanation does not seem to fit the Baal HaTurim's comment, for he goes on to say that this ל does not have a node at its top (see note 30 below).

30. In the Gaster manuscript (see note 25 above), the third ל of לגלגלתם was originally drawn like every other ל. However, a later hand emended that letter by deleting its head and adding a one-toothed saw at the upper right corner (see illustration). A marginal note [partially cut off the page] seems to indicate that the erasure was made in accordance with the Baal HaTurim's masoretic note (*R' Yitzhak Ratzabi, HaOsios HaMeshunos BaTorah* in *Torah Sheleimah,* Vol. 29).

31. The Baal HaTurim's description of Zimri appears in 25:14 below.

32. Literally: with uncovered head and an upright posture.

33. Cf. *Peirush HaRokeach.* The passage enclosed in braces is not found in the manuscripts or early printed editions of the Baal HaTurim, but does appear in some early *Mikraos Gedolos* as an independent masoretic note and in some later editions of the Baal HaTurim (see *Shoham Yakar*).

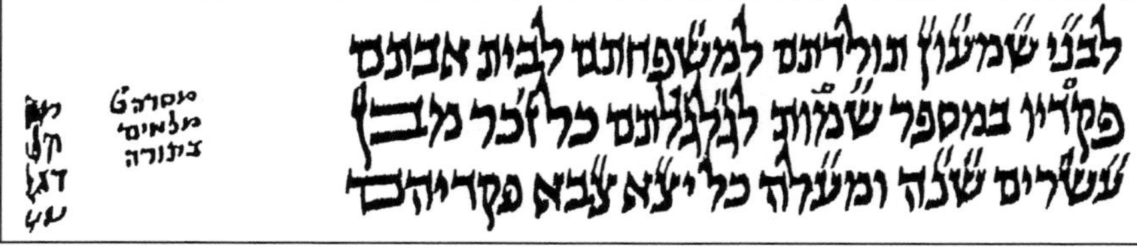
לבני שמעון תולדתם למשפחתם לבית אבתם
פקדיו במספר שמות לגלגלתם כל זכר מבן
עשרים שנה ומעלה כל יצא צבא פקדיהם

בְּמִסְפַּר שֵׁמֹת מִבֶּן עֶשְׂרִים שָׁנָה וָמַעְלָה כֹּל יֹצֵא
כט צָבָא: פְּקֻדֵיהֶם לְמַטֵּה יִשָּׂשכָר אַרְבָּעָה וַחֲמִשִּׁים
אֶלֶף וְאַרְבַּע מֵאוֹת:
ל לִבְנֵי זְבוּלֻן תּוֹלְדֹתָם לְמִשְׁפְּחֹתָם לְבֵית אֲבֹתָם
בְּמִסְפַּר שֵׁמֹת מִבֶּן עֶשְׂרִים שָׁנָה וָמַעְלָה כֹּל יֹצֵא
לא צָבָא: פְּקֻדֵיהֶם לְמַטֵּה זְבוּלֻן שִׁבְעָה וַחֲמִשִּׁים אֶלֶף
וְאַרְבַּע מֵאוֹת:
לב לִבְנֵי יוֹסֵף לִבְנֵי אֶפְרַיִם תּוֹלְדֹתָם לְמִשְׁפְּחֹתָם
לְבֵית אֲבֹתָם בְּמִסְפַּר שֵׁמֹת מִבֶּן עֶשְׂרִים שָׁנָה
לג וָמַעְלָה כֹּל יֹצֵא צָבָא: פְּקֻדֵיהֶם לְמַטֵּה אֶפְרָיִם
אַרְבָּעִים אֶלֶף וַחֲמֵשׁ מֵאוֹת:
לד לִבְנֵי מְנַשֶּׁה תּוֹלְדֹתָם לְמִשְׁפְּחֹתָם לְבֵית אֲבֹתָם
בְּמִסְפַּר שֵׁמוֹת מִבֶּן עֶשְׂרִים שָׁנָה וָמַעְלָה כֹּל יֹצֵא
לה צָבָא: פְּקֻדֵיהֶם לְמַטֵּה מְנַשֶּׁה שְׁנַיִם וּשְׁלֹשִׁים אֶלֶף
וּמָאתָיִם:
לו לִבְנֵי בִנְיָמִן תּוֹלְדֹתָם לְמִשְׁפְּחֹתָם לְבֵית אֲבֹתָם
בְּמִסְפַּר שֵׁמֹת מִבֶּן עֶשְׂרִים שָׁנָה וָמַעְלָה כֹּל יֹצֵא
לז צָבָא: פְּקֻדֵיהֶם לְמַטֵּה בִנְיָמִן חֲמִשָּׁה וּשְׁלֹשִׁים אֶלֶף
וְאַרְבַּע מֵאוֹת:

בעל הטורים

(לב) **לִבְנֵי יוֹסֵף לִבְנֵי אֶפְרַיִם.** וְלֹא אָמַר "לִבְנֵי יוֹסֵף לְאֶפְרַיִם", לְפִי שֶׁיּוֹסֵף לֹא נָשָׂא בְּמִטַּת אָבִיו מִשּׁוּם כְּבוֹד מַלְכוּת. לָכֵן לֹא רָצָה לִמְנוֹתוֹ בַּדְּגָלִים, וְנִקְרָא הַדֶּגֶל עַל שֵׁם בָּנָיו. לָכֵן אָמַר "לִבְנֵי אֶפְרַיִם" כְּדֶרֶךְ שֶׁאוֹמֵר בְּכֻלָּם:

BAAL HATURIM ELUCIDATED

32. לִבְנֵי יוֹסֵף לִבְנֵי אֶפְרַיִם — **FOR THE SONS OF JOSEPH: FOR THE SONS OF EPHRAIM.** The verse does not state merely, "For the sons of Joseph, for Ephraim" [rather, it repeats the word לִבְנֵי, *for the sons of*].[34] This is because, in deference to his royal status, Joseph did not carry his father's bier.[35] Therefore, [the Torah] did not

34. Apparently, the Baal HaTurim's comment is also applicable to the word לִבְנֵי regarding the tribe of Manasseh in verse 34 below.

35. The Midrash teaches: Before Jacob passed away, he instructed his sons [regarding his funeral procession]. "When you carry my remains, carry me with reverence and with respect. Let no other person touch my bier: not any of the Egyptians; not any of your own children, since some of you have taken Canaanite wives" [see *Rashi* to *Genesis* 37:35]. Thus, the Torah repeats the word בָּנָיו, *his sons*, in the passage, *His sons did for him exactly as*

by number of the names, from twenty years of age and up,
everyone who goes out to the legion. 29 *Their count, for the*
tribe of Issachar: fifty-four thousand, four hundred.
30 *For the sons of Zebulun, their offspring according to their*
families, according to their fathers' household, by number of
the names, from twenty years of age and up, everyone who
goes out to the legion. 31 *Their count, for the tribe of Zebulun:*
fifty-seven thousand, four hundred.
32 *For the sons of Joseph: for the sons of Ephraim, their off-*
spring according to their families, according to their fathers'
household, by number of the names, from twenty years of
age and up, everyone who goes out to the legion. 33 *Their*
count, for the tribe of Ephraim: forty thousand, five hundred.
34 *For the sons of Manasseh, their offspring according to*
their families, according to their fathers' household, by
number of the names, from twenty years of age and up,
everyone who goes out to the legion. 35 *Their count, for the*
tribe of Manasseh: thirty-two thousand, two hundred.
36 *For the sons of Benjamin, their offspring according to*
their families, according to their fathers' household, by
number of the names, from twenty years of age and up,
everyone who goes out to the legion. 37 *Their count, for the*
tribe of Benjamin: thirty-five thousand, four hundred.

BAAL HATURIM ELUCIDATED

want to count him among the tribal divisions;[36] rather, the division is called by the names of his sons. Therefore it says, *for "the sons of" Ephraim,* as it does regarding the other tribes [that were included in the divisions].[37]

---

he had commanded them. They — his sons — carried him to the land of Canaan . . . (*Genesis* 50:12-13). The repetition implies, *"his sons" carried him,* and not his grandsons. In what order did he instruct them to carry him? He said to them, "Judah, Issachar and Zebulun shall carry my bier on the eastern side; Reuben, Simeon and Gad shall carry on the south; Dan, Asher and Naphtali shall carry on the north; Benjamin, Ephraim and Manasseh shall carry on the west [and this was the order in which the *degalim* were arranged (see Ch. 2 below)]. But Joseph shall not carry me for he is a king and you are therefore required to afford him honor. As far as Levi is concerned, his tribe is destined to carry the Ark, and it would be unseemly for the one who carries the Ark of the Life-giver of the universe to also carry the coffin of a dead man." [We may ask: Why were his grandsons Ephraim and Manasseh permitted to carry his remains? Because their mother Asenath was the daughter of Poti-phera (*Genesis* 41:50), an Egyptian — not a Canaanite (A.S.).] Jacob continued, "And if you all do this properly and you carry my bier in the manner that I have instructed you, God will rest His Presence upon you in tribal divisions known as דְּגָלִים, *degalim* . . ." (*Tanchuma* 12; *Bamidbar Rabbah* 2:8).

36. Clearly, the exclusion of Joseph, as well as the exclusion of Levi, cannot be understood as a punishment for not having carried Jacob's bier, for in deference to their exalted positions — Joseph's kingship and Levi's priesthood — Jacob had instructed them not to carry him (*VeChur LaZahav*).

37. *Peirush HaRokeach.*

לח לִבְנֵי דָן תּוֹלְדֹתָם לְמִשְׁפְּחֹתָם לְבֵית אֲבֹתָם
בְּמִסְפַּר שֵׁמֹת מִבֶּן עֶשְׂרִים שָׁנָה וָמַעְלָה כֹּל יֹצֵא
לט צָבָא: פְּקֻדֵיהֶם לְמַטֵּה דָן שְׁנַיִם וְשִׁשִּׁים אֶלֶף וּשְׁבַע
מֵאוֹת:
מ לִבְנֵי אָשֵׁר תּוֹלְדֹתָם לְמִשְׁפְּחֹתָם לְבֵית אֲבֹתָם
בְּמִסְפַּר שֵׁמֹת מִבֶּן עֶשְׂרִים שָׁנָה וָמַעְלָה כֹּל יֹצֵא
מא צָבָא: פְּקֻדֵיהֶם לְמַטֵּה אָשֵׁר אֶחָד וְאַרְבָּעִים אֶלֶף
וַחֲמֵשׁ מֵאוֹת:
מב בְּנֵי נַפְתָּלִי תּוֹלְדֹתָם לְמִשְׁפְּחֹתָם לְבֵית אֲבֹתָם
בְּמִסְפַּר שֵׁמֹת מִבֶּן עֶשְׂרִים שָׁנָה וָמַעְלָה כֹּל יֹצֵא
מג צָבָא: פְּקֻדֵיהֶם לְמַטֵּה נַפְתָּלִי שְׁלֹשָׁה וַחֲמִשִּׁים
אֶלֶף וְאַרְבַּע מֵאוֹת:
מד אֵלֶּה הַפְּקֻדִים אֲשֶׁר פָּקַד מֹשֶׁה וְאַהֲרֹן וּנְשִׂיאֵי
יִשְׂרָאֵל שְׁנֵים עָשָׂר אִישׁ אִישׁ־אֶחָד לְבֵית־אֲבֹתָיו
מה הָיוּ: וַיִּהְיוּ כָּל־פְּקוּדֵי בְנֵי־יִשְׂרָאֵל לְבֵית אֲבֹתָם
מִבֶּן עֶשְׂרִים שָׁנָה וָמַעְלָה כָּל־יֹצֵא צָבָא בְּיִשְׂרָאֵל:
מו וַיִּהְיוּ כָּל־הַפְּקֻדִים שֵׁשׁ־מֵאוֹת אֶלֶף וּשְׁלֹשֶׁת
מז אֲלָפִים וַחֲמֵשׁ מֵאוֹת וַחֲמִשִּׁים: וְהַלְוִיִּם לְמַטֵּה
אֲבֹתָם לֹא הָתְפָּקְדוּ בְּתוֹכָם:

בעל הטורים

(מב) בְּנֵי נַפְתָּלִי. בְּכֻלָּן אוֹמֵר "לִבְנֵי", לְבַד מִבְּנַפְתָּלִי שֶׁהוּא אוֹמֵר "בְּנֵי", לְפִי שֶׁבְּשֵׁבֶט נַפְתָּלִי הָיוּ בָנוֹת יוֹתֵר מִבָּנִים. וּלְכָךְ רָמַז בְּבִרְכַּת נַפְתָּלִי אִשָּׁה – "אַיָּלָה שְׁלֻחָה הַנֹּתֵן" רָאשֵׁי תֵבוֹת אִשָּׁה. וּלְפִיכָךְ בְּפָרָשַׁת פִּינְחָס כְּתִיב בְּכֻלָּן "בְּנֵי", לְפִי שֶׁמֵּתוּ הָאֲנָשִׁים וְנִתְרַבּוּ הַנָּשִׁים, וּלְכָךְ לֹא אָמַר "לִבְנֵי":

BAAL HATURIM ELUCIDATED

42. בְּנֵי נַפְתָּלִי — THE SONS OF NAPHTALI. With regard to all [the other tribes], the verse states, לִבְנֵי, *"for" the sons of;* except with regard to Naphtali, where it is stated, בְּנֵי, *the sons of* [without the prefix -לְ, *for*]. The reason [for the omission] is that the tribe of Naphtali had more women [בָּנוֹת, *daughters*] than men [בָּנִים, *sons*].[38] Therefore,

38. *Rabbeinu Bachya; Peirush HaRokeach; Paaneach Raza; Rimzei Rabbeinu Yoel.* A masoretic note to our verse (cited in *Minchas Shai*), however, interprets the absence of the -לְ prefix in the exact opposite way: The term בְּנֵי is used only here, while the other verses state לִבְנֵי, because Naphtali had sons, but not daughters; the others, in contrast, had both sons and daughters.

In either case, the connection between the prefix -לְ and the proportion of men to women is unclear.

[38] *For the sons of Dan, their offspring according to their families, according to their fathers' household, by number of the names, from twenty years of age and up, everyone who goes out to the legion.* [39] *Their count, for the tribe of Dan: sixty-two thousand, seven hundred.*

[40] *For the sons of Asher, their offspring according to their families, according to their fathers' household, by numbers of the names, from twenty years of age and up, everyone who goes out to the legion.* [41] *Their count, for the tribe of Asher: forty-one thousand, five hundred.*

[42] *The sons of Naphtali, their offspring according to their families, according to their fathers' household, by number of the names, from twenty years of age and up, everyone who goes out to the legion.* [43] *Their count, for the tribe of Naftali: fifty-three thousand, four hundred.*

[44] *These are the countings that Moses, Aaron, and the leaders of Israel counted — twelve men, one man for his father's household, were they —* [45] *these were all the countings of the Children of Israel, according to their fathers' households, from twenty years of age and up, everyone who goes out to the legion in Israel:* [46] *All their countings were six hundred and three thousand, five hundred and fifty.*

[47] *The Levites according to their fathers' tribe were not counted among them.*

BAAL HATURIM ELUCIDATED

Jacob's blessing to Naphtali alludes to the word אִשָּׁה, *woman,* in the initial letters of the words, אַיָּלָה שְׁלוּחָה הַנֹּתֵן, *a hind let loose who delivers* (*Genesis* 49:21).[38a] For this same reason, in the census of *parashas Pinechas,* the term בְּנֵי, *the sons of,* without the ל prefix, is used with regard to all the tribes. For many men had died so that the women now outnumbered them.[39] Thus, it does not say לִבְנֵי, *"for" the sons of* [in that census].[40]

38a. The phenomenon of the רָאשֵׁי תֵבוֹת, *initial letters,* spelling אִשָּׁה does not occur anywhere else in the blessings given by Jacob or in the blessings given by Moses at the end of *Deuteronomy.*

39. As a consequence of the incident of the spies, when the male members of the nation believed the evil report about the Holy Land, God decreed: *In this wilderness shall your carcasses drop; all of you . . . from twenty years of age and above . . . you shall not come to the land about which I have raised My hand in an oath to settle you there* (*Numbers* 14:29-30). But that decree affected the men only; the women had not believed the spies' slanderous report and therefore were not included in the decree (*Midrash Tanchuma, Pinechas* 7, cited in *Rashi* to 26:64 below). Accordingly, even in those tribes where the men initially outnumbered the women, the proportions were eventually reversed.

40. *Rabbeinu Bachya; Peirush HaRokeach.*

א/מח־ב/ב

מח־מט וַיְדַבֵּר יְהוָה אֶל־מֹשֶׁה לֵּאמֹר׃ אַךְ אֶת־מַטֵּה לֵוִי לֹא
תִפְקֹד וְאֶת־רֹאשָׁם לֹא תִשָּׂא בְּתוֹךְ בְּנֵי יִשְׂרָאֵל׃
נ וְאַתָּה הַפְקֵד אֶת־הַלְוִיִּם עַל־מִשְׁכַּן הָעֵדֻת וְעַל
כָּל־כֵּלָיו וְעַל כָּל־אֲשֶׁר־לוֹ הֵמָּה יִשְׂאוּ אֶת־
הַמִּשְׁכָּן וְאֶת־כָּל־כֵּלָיו וְהֵם יְשָׁרְתֻהוּ וְסָבִיב לַמִּשְׁכָּן
נא יַחֲנוּ׃ וּבִנְסֹעַ הַמִּשְׁכָּן יוֹרִידוּ אֹתוֹ הַלְוִיִּם וּבַחֲנֹת
נב הַמִּשְׁכָּן יָקִימוּ אֹתוֹ הַלְוִיִּם וְהַזָּר הַקָּרֵב יוּמָת׃ וְחָנוּ
בְּנֵי יִשְׂרָאֵל אִישׁ עַל־מַחֲנֵהוּ וְאִישׁ עַל־דִּגְלוֹ
נג לְצִבְאֹתָם׃ וְהַלְוִיִּם יַחֲנוּ סָבִיב לְמִשְׁכַּן הָעֵדֻת
וְלֹא־יִהְיֶה קֶצֶף עַל־עֲדַת בְּנֵי יִשְׂרָאֵל וְשָׁמְרוּ הַלְוִיִּם
נד אֶת־מִשְׁמֶרֶת מִשְׁכַּן הָעֵדוּת׃ וַיַּעֲשׂוּ בְּנֵי יִשְׂרָאֵל
כְּכֹל אֲשֶׁר צִוָּה יְהוָה אֶת־מֹשֶׁה כֵּן עָשׂוּ׃
ב שלישי א־ב וַיְדַבֵּר יְהוָה אֶל־מֹשֶׁה וְאֶל־אַהֲרֹן לֵאמֹר׃ אִישׁ
עַל־דִּגְלוֹ בְאֹתֹת לְבֵית אֲבֹתָם יַחֲנוּ בְּנֵי יִשְׂרָאֵל

בעל הטורים

(נ) **הַפְקֵד.** ב׳ בַּמָּסוֹרֶת — ״הַפְקֵד אֶת הַלְוִיִּם״; וְאִידָךְ ״הַפְקֵד עָלָיו רָשָׁע״. וְזֶה הוּא שֶׁאָמְרוּ, אֵין אָדָם נַעֲשֶׂה שׁוֹטֵר מִלְּמַטָּה אֶלָּא אִם כֵּן נַעֲשָׂה רָשָׁע מִלְמָעְלָה. וְזֶהוּ ״הַפְקֵד אֶת הַלְוִיִּם״, שֶׁנַּעֲשׂוּ שׁוֹטְרִים, ״הַפְקֵד עָלָיו רָשָׁע״:

ב (ב) אִישׁ עַל דִּגְלוֹ בְאֹתֹת. שֶׁיַּעֲקֹב רָמַז לָהֶם מִי יִהְיֶה רֹאשׁ דֶּגֶל, שֶׁכָּל מִי שֶׁדִּבֵּר עִמּוֹ

BAAL HATURIM ELUCIDATED

50. הַפְקֵד — APPOINT. The masoretic note, ב׳, means that this word appears twice in the *Tanach*: (i) here, הַפְקֵד אֶת הַלְוִיִּם, *appoint the Levites;* and (ii) הַפְקֵד עָלָיו רָשָׁע, *appoint a wicked man over him* (*Psalms* 109:6). This is in accordance with our Sages' statement: A person is not made an officer below [on earth] unless he has been made wicked above [in the eyes of Heaven].[41] Thus, the verse, הַפְקֵד אֶת

41. The Talmud states: כֵּיוָן שֶׁנַּעֲשָׂה אָדָם רָשׁ מִלְּמַטָּה, *Once a person has been made destitute in the lower world* [i.e., on earth], נַעֲשָׂה רָשׁ מִלְמָעְלָה, *he is made destitute in the upper world* [i.e., in heaven] (*Sanhedrin* 103b; see commentaries there). An alternative version of that passage (recorded in part in *Dikdukei Soferim*) reads: כֵּיוָן שֶׁנַּעֲשָׂה אָדָם ראש מִלְּמַטָּה, *Once a person has been made a chief in the lower world,* נַעֲשָׂה רָשָׁע מִלְמָעְלָה, *he is made wicked in the upper world.* Apparently, the *Rambam's* Talmud had this latter version, for in his commentary to the Mishnah (*Avos* 1:10; see R' Kafich's edition, with note 54 there), he writes: By seeking dominion and mastership, one will encounter tribulations and evils in this world, for as a consequence of other people's jealousy they will rebel against him and his faith [in God] will suffer. This is in accord with the Sages' statement: כֵּיוָן שֶׁנִּתְמַנָּה אָדָם פַּרְנָס עַל הַצִּבּוּר מִלְּמַטָּה, *Once a person has been appointed in the lower world as an official over the community,* נַעֲשָׂה רָשָׁע מִלְמָעְלָה, *he is made wicked in the upper world* (*Maharatz Chayus* to *Avos;* see also *Massores HaShas, Avos* 1:10, note 3).

The *Meiri,* who also has the same wording as the *Rambam's* commentary, explains that, generally speaking, one who ascends to power will abuse his

[48] *HASHEM spoke to Moses, saying,* [49] *"But you shall not
count the tribe of Levi, and you shall not take a census of them
among the Children of Israel.* [50] *Now you, appoint the Levites
over the Tabernacle of the Testimony, over all of its utensils
and over everything that belongs to it. They shall carry the
Tabernacle and all its utensils and they shall minister to it; and
they shall encamp around the Tabernacle.* [51] *At the Taberna-
cle's setting out to journey, the Levites shall take it down, and
at the Tabernacle's encamping, the Levites shall erect it; an
alien who approaches shall die.* [52] *The Children of Israel shall
encamp, every man at his camp and every man at his division,
according to their legions.* [53] *The Levites shall encamp around
the Tabernacle of the Testimony so that there shall be no wrath
upon the assembly of the Children of Israel, and the Levites
shall safeguard the watch of the Tabernacle of the Testimony."*
[54] *The Children of Israel did everything that HASHEM com-
manded Moses, so did they do.*

2 [1] *HASHEM spoke to Moses and Aaron, saying,* [2] *"Each
man by his division according to the signs of their pater-
nal household, shall the Children of Israel encamp, at a*

BAAL HATURIM ELUCIDATED

הַלְוִיִּם, *appoint the Levites,* which indicates that they became officers, corresponds to the verse, הַפְקֵד עָלָיו רָשָׁע, *appoint a wicked man over him.*[42]

53. {The Baal HaTurim's comment to this verse appears at 31:19 below.}

II

2. אִישׁ עַל דִּגְלוֹ בְאֹתֹת — EACH MAN BY HIS DIVISION[42a] ACCORDING TO THE SIGNS.[42b] [For Jacob in his farewell blessings to his sons (*Genesis,* Ch. 49)] intimated to them which tribe would be the leader of each of the four tribal divisions. The tribe of

office by instilling excessive fear in the hearts of his subjects, not for the sake of Heaven, but for his personal glory. And the Talmud (*Rosh Hashanah* 17a) classifies such communal leaders among those who "descend to *Gehinnom* [Hell] and are punished there for all eternity."

42. That is, when Moses appoints the Levites to their exalted stations, he should apprise them of the personal spiritual dangers that will surround them.

42a. Unlike other commentators who understand דֶּגֶל as *flag* or *banner, Rashi* understands the noun דֶּגֶל, *degel,* and its verb form דגל as referring to "a division; a disposition of forces or hosts, such as a military formation." Thus, *Rashi* writes, כָּל דֶּגֶל יִהְיֶה לוֹ אוֹת מַפָּה צְבוּעָה תְּלוּיָה בוֹ, *Each "degel" shall have for itself a sign, namely, a colored sheet of cloth hanging in its midst.* Clearly, *degel* cannot mean "flag" in that sentence. Rather, it means "division." See also *Rashi's* comments to *Psalms* 20:6; *Song of Songs* 2:4; and, especially, *Isaiah* 5:26, s.v., נֵס לַגּוֹיִם, where he describes a flag in detail, yet never once uses the word דֶּגֶל. From his comments here and in *Peirush HaTur HaAroch,* it is apparent that the Baal HaTurim agrees with *Rashi's* understanding of the word.

42b. The term אוֹת, *sign,* can be understood as *omen.* Thus, בְּאֹתֹת לְבֵית אֲבֹתָם, *according to the signs of their paternal* [literally, *fathers'*] *household,* may be understood as a reference to the omens that Jacob (אֲבֹתָם) transmitted to his sons (A.S.).

ג מִנֶּ֕גֶד סָבִ֥יב לְאֹֽהֶל־מוֹעֵ֖ד יַחֲנֽוּ׃ וְהַחֹנִ֣ים קֵ֣דְמָה
מִזְרָ֔חָה דֶּ֛גֶל מַחֲנֵ֥ה יְהוּדָ֖ה לְצִבְאֹתָ֑ם וְנָשִׂיא֙ לִבְנֵ֣י
ד יְהוּדָ֔ה נַחְשׁ֖וֹן בֶּן־עַמִּֽינָדָֽב׃ וּצְבָא֖וֹ וּפְקֻדֵיהֶ֑ם אַרְבָּעָ֧ה
ה וְשִׁבְעִ֛ים אֶ֖לֶף וְשֵׁ֥שׁ מֵאֽוֹת׃ וְהַחֹנִ֥ים עָלָ֖יו מַטֵּ֣ה
יִשָּׂשכָ֑ר וְנָשִׂיא֙ לִבְנֵ֣י יִשָּׂשכָ֔ר נְתַנְאֵ֖ל בֶּן־צוּעָֽר׃

בעל הטורים

לְנֹכַח הָיָה רֹאשׁ דֶּגֶל. כְּמוֹ "רְאוּבֵן בְּכֹרִי אַתָּה"; "יְהוּדָה אַתָּה יוֹדוּךָ אַחֶיךָ"; יוֹסֵף "מֵאֵל אָבִיךָ וְיַעְזְרֶךָּ"; דָּן "לִישׁוּעָתְךָ קִוִּיתִי ה'":

❑ **מִנֶּגֶד סָבִיב לְאֹהֶל.** בְּגִימַטְרִיָּא לְאַלְפַּיִם אַמָּה:

(ב־ג) **סָבִיב לְאֹהֶל מוֹעֵד יַחֲנוּ וְהַחֹנִים.** לוֹמַר, כְּשֵׁם שֶׁחֲנָיָתָן לְמַעְלָה אַרְבָּעָה דְגָלִים סָבִיב לְכִסֵּא הַכָּבוֹד, כָּךְ הָיָה לְמַטָּה אַרְבָּעָה דְגָלִים סָבִיב לַמִּשְׁכָּן. וְזֶהוּ "אֲיֻמָּה כַּנִּדְגָּלוֹת". וְזֶהוּ "וְדִגְלוֹ עָלַי אַהֲבָה" שֶׁיִּשְׂרָאֵל רָאוּ בִּשְׁעַת מַתַּן תּוֹרָה הַדְּגָלִים שֶׁל מַעְלָה, וְנִתְאַוּוּ לְאוֹתָם הַדְּגָלִים. וְזֶהוּ "וּבְשֵׁם אֱלֹהֵינוּ נִדְגֹּל":

BAAL HATURIM ELUCIDATED

each son whom he addressed directly [i.e., in the second person][43] became the leading tribe of its division. Thus, [of Reuben it is written,] רְאוּבֵן בְּכֹרִי אַתָּה, *Reuben, **you** are my firstborn* (v. 3 there); [of Judah,] יְהוּדָה אַתָּה יוֹדוּךָ אַחֶיךָ, *Judah — **you** — **your** brothers shall acknowledge **you*** (v. 8); of Joseph [that is, of Ephraim who stood in for Joseph[44]], מֵאֵל אָבִיךָ וְיַעְזְרֶךָּ, *from the God of **your** father and He will help **you*** (v. 25); and of Dan, לִישׁוּעָתְךָ קִוִּיתִי ה׳, *As for **your** salvation,*[45] *I long that it be from Hashem* (v. 18).[45a]

43. The other eight were blessed in the third person only, e.g., *Simeon and Levi are comrades, their weaponry . . .* (v. 5 there); *Zebulun shall settle by seashores. He shall be . . .* (v. 13); *Issachar is a strong-based donkey; he rests . . .* (v. 14); etc.

44. *Ittur Bikkurim;* see the Baal HaTurim to 1:32 above, with note 35.

45. According to *Targum Yonasan, Rashi* and *Ramban,* the verse לִישׁוּעָתְךָ קִוִּיתִי ה׳ means, *For Your salvation do I long, O Hashem;* that is, after blessing Dan, Jacob turned to God and prayed that He provide salvation. And that is certainly the way it is to be understood when it is used in the context of prayer, e.g., in the bedtime *Shema* and in *Tefillas HaDerech* (the Wayfarer's Prayer). However, in the *Peirush HaTur HaAroch,* the Baal HaTurim follows *Rashbam* and *Ibn Ezra* who interpret the verse as a continuation of Jacob's blessing: *As for your* [i.e., *Dan's*] *salvation, I long that it be* [*directly*] *from* [*the hand of*] *Hashem.*

45a. When Jacob blessed his children before his death, he did so in the following order: (i) Reuben, (ii-iii) Simeon and Levi, (iv) Judah, (v) Zebulun, (vi) Issachar, (vii) Dan, (viii) Gad, (ix) Asher, (x) Naphtali, (xi) Joseph, and (xii) Benjamin. Although most of the blessings were couched in the third person, Jacob used the second person for at least a part of each of four blessings — those of Reuben, Judah, Dan and Joseph. According to the Baal HaTurim, the fact that Jacob spoke to them in the second person was equivalent to appointing them as leaders of their respective *degalim*-divisions. If so, we would expect Reuben, whom Jacob blessed first, to lead the first *degel;* Judah, the second; Dan, the third; and Ephraim (standing in for Joseph), the last. Nevertheless, the *degalim* are arranged with Judah first, Reuben second, Ephraim third and Dan last. Perhaps a close analysis of their respective blessings will lead to an explanation of the order of *degalim.* In blessing Reuben, Jacob used the second person five times — אַתָּה, *you;* אַל תּוֹתַר, *do not take more;* עָלִיתָ, *you mounted;* אָבִיךָ, *your father;* and חִלַּלְתָּ, *you desecrated* (*Genesis* 49:3-4). Regarding

distance around the Tent of Meeting they shall encamp.
3 And those who encamp to the front, at the east, shall
be the division of the camp of Judah according to their
legions — and the leader of the children of Judah is
Nachshon son of Amminadab — 4 its legion and their
count are seventy-four thousand, six hundred. 5 And those
who encamp near him are: the tribe of Issachar — and the
leader of the children of Issachar is Nethanel son of Zuar —

BAAL HATURIM ELUCIDATED

❑ מִנֶּגֶד סָבִיב לְאֹהֶל — **AT A DISTANCE AROUND THE TENT.** The *gematria* of this phrase (237) is equal to that of לְאַלְפַּיִם אַמָּה, *for two thousand cubits.*[46]

2-3. סָבִיב לְאֹהֶל מוֹעֵד יַחֲנוּ. וְהַחֹנִים — **AROUND THE TENT OF MEETING THEY SHALL ENCAMP. AND THOSE WHO ENCAMP.** The juxtaposition [of יַחֲנוּ, *they shall encamp,* with וְהַחֹנִים, *and those who encamp*] indicates that just as the heavenly encampment [of angels] consists of four divisions surrounding the Throne of Glory, so too, on earth below, four divisions [of Israelite tribes] surround the Tabernacle. Those [angelic divisions] are referred to in the verses אֲיֻמָּה כַּנִּדְגָּלוֹת, *awe inspiring as the angelic degalim*[46a] (*Song of Songs* 6:4,10). They are also referred to by the verse, וְדִגְלוֹ עָלַי אַהֲבָה, *and His degel was love unto me* (*Song of Songs* 2:4),[46b] for at the Giving of the Torah, the Israelites saw the heavenly *degalim*[46c] and desired [to arrange themselves like] those *degalim.* This is also the implication of the verse, וּבְשֵׁם אֱלֹהֵינוּ נִדְגֹּל, *and in the Name of our God, we shall arrange* [*ourselves in*] *degalim* (*Psalms* 20:6).[47]

Judah, Jacob used the second person eight times — אַתָּה, *you;* יוֹדוּךָ, *they shall acknowledge you;* אַחֶיךָ, *your brothers;* יָדְךָ, *your hand;* אֹיְבֶיךָ, *your enemies;* לְךָ, *to you;* אָבִיךָ, *your father;* and עָלִיתָ, *you elevated yourself* (49:8-9). In Dan's blessing Jacob used the second person only once — לִישׁוּעָתְךָ, *as for your salvation* (49:18). And he blessed Joseph using the second person four times — אָבִיךָ, *your father;* וְיַעְזְרֶךָּ, *and He will help you;* וִיבָרְכֶךָּ, *and He will bless you;* and אָבִיךָ, *your father* (49:25-26). Accordingly, Jacob's use of the second person indicated which tribes would lead their respective *degalim,* and the number of times that he used the second person indicated the order of the *degalim:* Judah with eight second-person words was first; Reuben with five such words was second; Ephraim [who stood in for Joseph] with four was third; and Dan with only one was last (*VeChur LaZahav*).

46. *Peirush HaRokeach.* The Midrash teaches that the distance referred to in our verse was 2000 *amos* [variously reckoned as between six-tenths and seven-tenths of a mile] (*Tanchuma* 9; *Bamidbar Rabbah* 2:9; cited by *Rashi*).

46a. See note 42a above.

46b. That verse reads in full: הֱבִיאַנִי אֶל בֵּית הַיָּיִן, *He brought me to the house of wine,* וְדִגְלוֹ עָלַי אַהֲבָה, *and His degel was love unto me.* The Midrash interprets "the house of wine" as a reference to Mount Sinai. Israel said, "There [at Mount Sinai] I saw [the angel] Michael with his *degel* [and the angel] Gabriel with his *degel.* And my eyes saw the Heavenly arrays and my heart loved them." At that moment, God said to Moses, "Whereas Israel's desire is to be arranged as [those] *degalim,* they shall encamp in *degalim*" (*Shir HaShirim Rabbah* to 2:4).

46c. See *Rashi* to *Deuteronomy* 33:2, s.v., מרבבת קדש.

47. Thus, the juxtaposed words יַחֲנוּ וְהַחֹנִים may be understood as, *They* [the Israelites] *shall encamp* [around the *Mishkan*] *and* [be like] *those who encamp* [around the Throne of Glory].

ו וּצְבָאוֹ וּפְקֻדָיו אַרְבָּעָה וַחֲמִשִּׁים אֶלֶף וְאַרְבַּע
ז מֵאוֹת: מַטֵּה זְבוּלֻן וְנָשִׂיא לִבְנֵי זְבוּלֻן אֱלִיאָב
ח בֶּן־חֵלֹן: וּצְבָאוֹ וּפְקֻדָיו שִׁבְעָה וַחֲמִשִּׁים אֶלֶף
ט וְאַרְבַּע מֵאוֹת: כָּל־הַפְּקֻדִים לְמַחֲנֵה יְהוּדָה מְאַת
אֶלֶף וּשְׁמֹנִים אֶלֶף וְשֵׁשֶׁת־אֲלָפִים וְאַרְבַּע־מֵאוֹת
י לְצִבְאֹתָם רִאשֹׁנָה יִסָּעוּ: דֶּגֶל מַחֲנֵה רְאוּבֵן
תֵּימָנָה לְצִבְאֹתָם וְנָשִׂיא לִבְנֵי רְאוּבֵן אֱלִיצוּר
יא בֶּן־שְׁדֵיאוּר: וּצְבָאוֹ וּפְקֻדָיו שִׁשָּׁה וְאַרְבָּעִים אֶלֶף
יב וַחֲמֵשׁ מֵאוֹת: וְהַחוֹנִם עָלָיו מַטֵּה שִׁמְעוֹן וְנָשִׂיא

בעל הטורים

(ז) מַטֵּה זְבוּלֻן. וְלֹא אָמַר "וּמַטֵּה" כְּדֶרֶךְ שֶׁנֶּאֱמַר בָּאֲחֵרִים, לְפִי שֶׁזְּבוּלֻן הָיָה מְפַרְנֵס לְיִשָּׂשכָר. וְרָאִיתִי בְּתַנְחוּמָא הַטַּעַם שֶׁלֹּא אָמַר "וּמַטֵּה" בִּזְבוּלֻן כְּמוֹ שֶׁאָמַר בְּכֻלָּן. לְלַמֶּדְךָ שֶׁהָיָה זְבוּלֻן עוֹסֵק בִּפְרַקְמַטְיָא וְנוֹתֵן לְתוֹךְ פִּיו שֶׁל יִשָּׂשכָר. לְפִיכָךְ לֹא רָצָה הַכָּתוּב לַעֲשׂוֹתוֹ טָפֵל לוֹ, לוֹמַר שֶׁשְּׂכָרוֹ גָּדוֹל כְּמוֹתוֹ. וְכֵן הוּא אוֹמֵר "עֵץ חַיִּים הִיא לַמַּחֲזִיקִים בָּהּ וְתֹמְכֶיהָ מְאֻשָּׁר", וּכְתִיב "כִּי בְּצֵל הַחָכְמָה בְּצֵל הַכָּסֶף". לָכֵן חָשׁוּב הַכֹּל כְּמַטֶּה אֶחָד, וּכְאִלּוּ אָמַר יִשָּׂשכָר מַטֵּה זְבוּלֻן:

❑ {מַטֵּה. ב׳ רָאשֵׁי פְסוּקִים — "מַטֵּה זְבוּלֻן"; "מַטֵּה עֻזְּךָ יִשְׁלַח ה׳ מִצִּיּוֹן, רְדֵה בְּקֶרֶב אֹיְבֶיךָ". שֶׁהֵם הָיוּ רוֹדִין בְּקֶרֶב אוֹיְבֵיהֶם, דִּכְתִיב "וְכִי נָמֹגוּ כָּל יֹשְׁבֵי הָאָרֶץ מִפְּנֵיכֶם":}

BAAL HATURIM ELUCIDATED

7. מַטֵּה זְבוּלֻן — THE TRIBE OF ZEBULUN. [With regard to Zebulun, the Torah states, מַטֵּה, *the tribe,* without the prefix ־ו, *and*] it does not state וּמַטֵּה, *and the tribe,* as it does regarding the other tribes,[48] because Zebulun would provide sustenance for Issachar.[49] And I have seen in *Midrash Tanchuma* the reason that the Torah does not state וּמַטֵּה with regard to Zebulun as it does with regard to the others:[50] This [omitted conjunctive prefix] teaches that since Zebulun would engage in commerce and provide sustenance for Issachar, the Torah did not wish to write

48. The Torah uses seven verses to describe the makeup of each *degel*: Two verses to describe the leading tribe; the next two verses for the second tribe; and then two verses for the third tribe. A seventh verse, which gives the total census of that *degel,* ends each *degel's* passage. Regarding the two verses for each tribe, the first verse names the tribe, its leader and its location in the *degel* encampment; the second verse gives the tribal census.

With the exception of Zebulun, the second and third tribe of each *degel* is introduced with the conjunctive prefix ־ו or וָ, *and.* Those prefixes indicate that the particular tribe under discussion is secondary or tertiary to the leading tribe of that *degel.* However, with regard to Judah's *degel,* the third tribe's verses begin מַטֵּה זְבוּלֻן, *the tribe of Zebulun,* without the prefix. The Baal HaTurim's comment explains its absence.

49. *Peirush HaRokeach.*

50. Apparently, the Baal HaTurim refers to *Midrash Tanchuma, Vayechi* 11, which explains the relationship between Zebulun and Issachar. However, extant editions of the Midrash (as well as *Bereishis Rabbah* 99:9, which is almost identical to the *Tanchuma*) make no mention of the absent ו prefix in our verse.

[6] *its legion and their count are fifty-four thousand, four hundred;* [7] *the tribe of Zebulun — and the leader of the children of Zebulun is Eliab son of Helon —* [8] *its legion and their count are fifty-seven thousand, four hundred.* [9] *All those counted for the camp of Judah are one hundred and eighty-six thousand, four hundred, according to their legions; they shall be the first to journey.*

[10] *"The division of the camp of Reuben shall be to the south, according to their legions — and the leader of the children of Reuben is Elizur son of Shedeur —* [11] *its legion and their count are forty-six thousand, five hundred.* [12] *And those who encamp near him are: the tribe of Simeon — and the leader of*

BAAL HATURIM ELUCIDATED

anything that would indicate that Zebulun [whose verses follow immediately after Issachar's] was secondary to Issachar, thus it indicates [by the absence of the ו] that Zebulun's reward was as great as Issachar's. This concept is also the theme of the verse, עֵץ חַיִּים הִיא לַמַּחֲזִיקִים בָּהּ וְתֹמְכֶיהָ מְאֻשָּׁר, *It [the Torah] is a tree of life to those who grasp it, and its supporters are praiseworthy*[51] (*Proverbs* 3:18), and of the verse, כִּי בְּצֵל הַחָכְמָה בְּצֵל הַכָּסֶף, *for in the shelter of wisdom, in the shelter of money* (*Ecclesiastes* 7:12).[52] Therefore, the two are considered as if they were one tribe,[52a] as if the verse stated, *Issachar, the tribe of Zebulun.*[53]

❑ {מַטֵּה — THE TRIBE OF. The masoretic note, ב׳ רָאשֵׁי פְסוּקִים, means that the word מַטֵּה appears twice[54] in the *Tanach* at the beginning of a verse: (i) here, מַטֵּה זְבוּלֻן, *the tribe of Zebulun*; and (ii) מַטֵּה עֻזְּךָ יִשְׁלַח ה׳ מִצִּיּוֹן רְדֵה בְּקֶרֶב אֹיְבֶיךָ, *HASHEM will dispatch the staff of your strength from Zion; rule amid your enemies!* (*Psalms* 110:2). [This similarity indicates the military prowess[55] of Zebulun's warriors] that they gain mastery in the midst of their enemies, as it is written, וְכִי נָמֹגוּ כָּל יֹשְׁבֵי הָאָרֶץ מִפְּנֵיכֶם, *and that all the inhabitants of the land have melted because of you*[56] (*Joshua* 2:9).}[57]

51. *Those who grasp it* are the men who study Torah; *its supporters* are the people who sustain the men who study Torah. Thus, the Midrash explains that the verse equates Zebulun with Issachar.

52. See *Yerushalmi, Sotah* 7:4; *Koheles Rabbah* 7:12.

52a. Thus, we find that when Moses blessed the tribes, he mentioned both Zebulun and Issachar in the same blessing (*Deuteronomy* 33:18-19), something that he did not do with regard to any other tribe (A.S.).

53. *R' Yehudah HaChassid.*

54. The noun מַטֶּה can mean *staff* (e.g., 17:17 below) or *tribe* (e.g., 36:7 below). Similarly, the construct form מַטֵּה can mean *the staff of* or *the tribe of*. Indeed, we find the expression מַטֵּה לֵוִי used for both *the staff of Levi* (17:18 below) and *the tribe of Levi* (18:2 below). Similarly, the two appearances of מַטֵּה cited by the Baal HaTurim have different meanings: here the word means *the tribe of*, in *Psalms* it means *the staff of*.

55. See *I Chronicles* 12:34; see also the Baal HaTurim's comment to *Deuteronomy* 33:18.

56. The connection between Zebulun and the verse from *Joshua* is unclear.

57. The passage enclosed in braces is not found in the early or later printed editions, but does appear in *Shoham Yakar's* manuscript edition.

יג לִבְנֵי שִׁמְעוֹן שְׁלֻמִיאֵל בֶּן־צוּרִישַׁדָּי: וּצְבָאוֹ
וּפְקֻדֵיהֶם תִּשְׁעָה וַחֲמִשִּׁים אֶלֶף וּשְׁלֹשׁ מֵאוֹת:
יד־טו וּמַטֵּה גָּד וְנָשִׂיא לִבְנֵי גָד אֶלְיָסָף בֶּן־רְעוּאֵל: וּצְבָאוֹ
וּפְקֻדֵיהֶם חֲמִשָּׁה וְאַרְבָּעִים אֶלֶף וְשֵׁשׁ מֵאוֹת
טז וַחֲמִשִּׁים: כָּל־הַפְּקֻדִים לְמַחֲנֵה רְאוּבֵן מְאַת אֶלֶף
וְאֶחָד וַחֲמִשִּׁים אֶלֶף וְאַרְבַּע־מֵאוֹת וַחֲמִשִּׁים
יז לְצִבְאֹתָם וּשְׁנִיִּם יִסָּעוּ: וְנָסַע אֹהֶל־מוֹעֵד מַחֲנֵה
הַלְוִיִּם בְּתוֹךְ הַמַּחֲנֹת כַּאֲשֶׁר יַחֲנוּ כֵּן יִסָּעוּ אִישׁ
יח עַל־יָדוֹ לְדִגְלֵיהֶם: דֶּגֶל מַחֲנֵה אֶפְרַיִם לְצִבְאֹתָם
יָמָּה וְנָשִׂיא לִבְנֵי אֶפְרַיִם אֱלִישָׁמָע בֶּן־עַמִּיהוּד:
יט־כ וּצְבָאוֹ וּפְקֻדֵיהֶם אַרְבָּעִים אֶלֶף וַחֲמֵשׁ מֵאוֹת: וְעָלָיו
מַטֵּה מְנַשֶּׁה וְנָשִׂיא לִבְנֵי מְנַשֶּׁה גַּמְלִיאֵל בֶּן־
כא פְּדָהצוּר: וּצְבָאוֹ וּפְקֻדֵיהֶם שְׁנַיִם וּשְׁלֹשִׁים אֶלֶף
כב וּמָאתָיִם: וּמַטֵּה בִּנְיָמִן וְנָשִׂיא לִבְנֵי בִנְיָמִן אֲבִידָן

בעל הטורים

(יח) דֶּגֶל מַחֲנֵה אֶפְרַיִם. הַפָּסוּק מַתְחִיל בְּדָלֶ״ת וּמְסַיֵּם בְּדָלֶ״ת, לְפִי שֶׁיַּעֲקֹב הִקְדִּים בְּאַרְבָּעָה מְקוֹמוֹת אֶפְרַיִם לִפְנֵי מְנַשֶּׁה, וּכְנֶגְדּוֹ קָדַם בְּאַרְבָּעָה מְקוֹמוֹת אֶפְרַיִם לִמְנַשֶּׁה — בַּדְּגָלִים וּבַנְּשִׂיאִים וּבַקָּרְבָּנוֹת וּבַשְּׁבָטִים:

BAAL HATURIM ELUCIDATED

18. דֶּגֶל מַחֲנֵה אֶפְרַיִם — THE DIVISION OF THE CAMP OF EPHRAIM. This verse begins with a ד (= 4) and ends with a ד,[58] because on four occasions Jacob mentioned Ephraim before Manasseh[59] and, correspondingly, the Torah mentions Ephraim before Manasseh in four other instances: with regard to (i) the tribal divisions;[60]

58. *Peirush HaRokeach,* the Baal HaTurim's apparent source for this comment, reads, "No verse both begins and ends with a ד, except this one." Clearly, *Peirush HaRokeach* refers to the five *Chumashim,* for we find three other verses in *Tanach* which begin and end with that letter: דִּרְשׁוּ ... תָּמִיד (*Psalms* 105:4 and *I Chronicles* 16:11); and דִּבְרֵי ... אֶחָד (*Ecclesiastes* 12:11).

59. Chapter 48 of *Genesis* describes how Joseph brought his two sons to Jacob to receive the Patriarch's blessing. Although Manasseh was the older son, in each of four verses that describe Jacob's demeanor toward them, Ephraim's name appears first: (i) Jacob said, וְעַתָּה שְׁנֵי בָנֶיךָ... אֶפְרַיִם וּמְנַשֶּׁה... יִהְיוּ לִי, *And now your two sons... Ephraim and Manasseh... shall be mine...* (v. 5); (ii) וַיִּשְׁלַח יִשְׂרָאֵל אֶת יְמִינוֹ... עַל רֹאשׁ אֶפְרַיִם... וְאֶת שְׂמֹאלוֹ עַל רֹאשׁ מְנַשֶּׁה, *But Israel* [*Jacob*] *extended his right hand... on Ephraim's head... and his left hand on Manasseh's head* (v. 14); and (iii-iv) וַיְבָרְכֵם... לֵאמוֹר בְּךָ יְבָרֵךְ יִשְׂרָאֵל לֵאמֹר יְשִׂמְךָ אֱלֹהִים כְּאֶפְרַיִם וְכִמְנַשֶּׁה וַיָּשֶׂם אֶת אֶפְרַיִם לִפְנֵי מְנַשֶּׁה, *[Jacob] blessed them ... saying, "By you shall Israel bless, saying: 'May God make you like Ephraim and Manasseh' " — and he put Ephraim before Manasseh* (v. 20).

60. Ephraim was the primary tribe of the *degel,* as attested to by our verse. Manasseh was secondary (v. 20 below).

the children of Simeon is Shelumiel son of Zurishaddai —
13 its legion and their count are fifty-nine thousand, three
hundred; 14 and the tribe of Gad — and the leader of the
children of Gad is Eliasaph son of Reuel — 15 its legion and
their count are forty-five thousand, six hundred and fifty.
16 All those counted for the camp of Reuben are one hundred
and fifty-one thousand, four hundred and fifty, according to
their legions, they shall be the second to journey.

17 "The Tent of Meeting, the camp of the Levites, shall jour-
ney in the middle of the camps; as they encamp so shall they
journey, everyone at his place according to their divisions.

18 "The division of the camp of Ephraim according to their
legions shall be to the west — and the leader of the children of
Ephraim is Elishama son of Ammihud — 19 its legion and
their count are forty thousand, five hundred. 20 And those
[who encamp] near him are: the tribe of Manasseh —
and the leader of the children of Manasseh is Gamaliel son
of Pedahzur — 21 its legion and their count are thirty-
two thousand, two hundred; 22 and the tribe of Benjamin
— and the leader of the children of Benjamin is Abidan

BAAL HATURIM ELUCIDATED

(ii) the tribal leaders;[61] (iii) the offerings;[62] and the order of the tribes.[63]

61. This refers to verse 1:10 above where Ephraim's leader is listed before Manasseh's.

62. Presumably, this refers to the order in which the leaders of each tribe brought their offerings during the first twelve days following the inauguration of the *Mishkan* and the Kohanim. On that occasion, Elishama son of Ammihud of the tribe of Ephraim brought his offering on the seventh day, while Manasseh's leader, Gamaliel son of Pedahzur, brought his on the eighth day (see Ch. 7 below, especially vv. 48 and 54).

63. The reading וּבַשְּׁבָטִים, *and with regard to the order of the tribes,* follows the later printed editions; and that is how it appears in *Shoham Yakar's* manuscript edition and in the Baal HaTurim's source, *Peirush HaRokeach.* In this version, all four instances of Ephraim preceding Manasseh appear in the Torah, specifically, in the *Book of Numbers.*

The early printed editions, however, read וּבַשֹּׁפְטִים, *and with regard to the judges,* a reference to the fact that during the era of the שׁוֹפְטִים, *Judges,* between the death of Moses and the anointment of Saul as king, Joshua of the tribe of Ephraim was the first leader of the nation after Moses, while the first Judge from the tribe of Manasseh was Gideon (see *Judges* 6:15), some two centuries later. In this version, three of the four incidents appear in the Torah, the fourth, in the Prophets. Accordingly, it is not clear why the Baal HaTurim limited his incidents to four, for there are other times in the Books of the Prophets where Ephraim came before Manasseh: with regard to the lots by which the tribal territories were allotted, the borders of Ephraim's territory (*Joshua* 16:5-10) are given before those of Manasseh's (17:1-13); after the division of the Land of Israel into two kingdoms, Judah and Israel, Jeroboam, the first king of Israel, was from Ephraim (*I Kings* 11:26), then, more than a century later, Jehu of Manasseh ascended the throne (*II Kings,* Chs. 9-10). For further discussion on the verses that speak of Ephraim before Manasseh, see *Pesikta Rabbasi* 3:5, *Bamidbar Rabbah* 14:4 and *Bereishis Rabbah* 97:5.

כג בֶּן־גִּדְעֹנִי׃ וּצְבָאוֹ וּפְקֻדֵיהֶם חֲמִשָּׁה וּשְׁלֹשִׁים
כד אֶלֶף וְאַרְבַּע מֵאוֹת׃ כָּל־הַפְּקֻדִים לְמַחֲנֵה אֶפְרַיִם
מְאַת אֶלֶף וּשְׁמֹנַת־אֲלָפִים וּמֵאָה לְצִבְאֹתָם
כה וּשְׁלִשִׁים יִסָּעוּ׃ דֶּגֶל מַחֲנֵה דָן צָפֹנָה
לְצִבְאֹתָם וְנָשִׂיא לִבְנֵי דָן אֲחִיעֶזֶר בֶּן־עַמִּישַׁדָּי׃
כו וּצְבָאוֹ וּפְקֻדֵיהֶם שְׁנַיִם וְשִׁשִּׁים אֶלֶף וּשְׁבַע
כז מֵאוֹת׃ וְהַחֹנִים עָלָיו מַטֵּה אָשֵׁר וְנָשִׂיא לִבְנֵי
כח אָשֵׁר פַּגְעִיאֵל בֶּן־עָכְרָן׃ וּצְבָאוֹ וּפְקֻדֵיהֶם אֶחָד
כט וְאַרְבָּעִים אֶלֶף וַחֲמֵשׁ מֵאוֹת׃ וּמַטֵּה נַפְתָּלִי
ל וְנָשִׂיא לִבְנֵי נַפְתָּלִי אֲחִירַע בֶּן־עֵינָן׃ וּצְבָאוֹ
וּפְקֻדֵיהֶם שְׁלֹשָׁה וַחֲמִשִּׁים אֶלֶף וְאַרְבַּע מֵאוֹת׃
לא כָּל־הַפְּקֻדִים לְמַחֲנֵה דָן מְאַת אֶלֶף וְשִׁבְעָה
וַחֲמִשִּׁים אֶלֶף וְשֵׁשׁ מֵאוֹת לָאַחֲרֹנָה יִסְעוּ
לְדִגְלֵיהֶם׃
לב אֵלֶּה פְּקוּדֵי בְנֵי־יִשְׂרָאֵל לְבֵית אֲבֹתָם כָּל־פְּקוּדֵי
הַמַּחֲנֹת לְצִבְאֹתָם שֵׁשׁ־מֵאוֹת אֶלֶף וּשְׁלֹשֶׁת
לג אֲלָפִים וַחֲמֵשׁ מֵאוֹת וַחֲמִשִּׁים׃ וְהַלְוִיִּם לֹא

בעל הטורים

(לא) לָאַחֲרֹנָה. ב׳ בַּמָּסוֹרֶת – ״לָאַחֲרֹנָה יִסְעוּ״; וְאִידָךְ ״לֹא יִהְיֶה לָהֶם זִכָּרוֹן עִם שֶׁיִּהְיוּ לָאַחֲרֹנָה״. שֶׁעֲמָלֵק הָיָה מְסָרֵס שֵׁבֶט דָּן בַּעֲוֹן פֶּסֶל מִיכָה שֶׁעִמָּהֶם; ״יִהְיֶה לָהֶם זִכָּרוֹן״ סוֹפֵי תֵבוֹת ״הָמָן״, שֶׁגַּם הוּא בִקֵּשׁ לְאַבֵּד זִכְרָם:

BAAL HATURIM ELUCIDATED

24. {The Baal HaTurim's comment to וּשְׁלֹשִׁים appears at *Genesis* 6:16.}

31. לָאַחֲרֹנָה — AT THE END. The masoretic note, ב׳, means that this word appears twice in the *Tanach*: (i) here, לָאַחֲרֹנָה יִסְעוּ, *they shall journey at the end;* and (ii) לֹא יִהְיֶה לָהֶם זִכָּרוֹן עִם שֶׁיִּהְיוּ לָאַחֲרֹנָה, *there will be no memory of them among those who will be at the end* (*Ecclesiastes* 1:11).[64] [The similarity of expression indicates] that the Amalekites [who followed the Israelites as they traveled away from the Sea of Reeds] would [capture and] castrate members[64a] of the tribe of Dan,[65] as a consequence of the sin regarding Micah's

64. The Midrash (*Koheles Rabbah*) explains this verse as a reference to Amalek.

64a. Thus, *there will be no memory of them,* for they would be unable to bear children to keep their memory alive (A.S.).

65. *Pesikta Rabbasi* 12:13; see also *Tanchuma, Ki Seitzei* 10, cited in *Rashi* and the Baal HaTurim to *Deuteronomy* 25:18.

son of Gideoni — 23 its legion and their count are thirty-five
thousand, four hundred. 24 All those counted for the camp
of Ephraim are one hundred and eight thousand, one
hundred, according to their legions; they shall be the third to
journey.

25 "The division of the camp of Dan shall be to the
north, according to their legions — and the leader of the
children of Dan is Ahiezer son of Ammishaddai — 26 its
legion and their count are sixty-two thousand, seven
hundred. 27 And those who encamp near him are: the tribe
of Asher — and the leader of the children of Asher is Pagiel
son of Ochran — 28 its legion and their count are forty-
one thousand, five hundred; 29 and the tribe of Naphtali —
and the leader of the children of Naphtali is Ahira son of
Enan — 30 its legion and their count are fifty-three thou-
sand, four hundred. 31 All those counted for the camp of
Dan are one hundred and fifty-seven thousand, six hun-
dred; they shall journey at the end, according to their
divisions."

32 These are the countings of the Children of Israel
according to their fathers' households; all the countings
of the camps according to their legions, six hundred and
three thousand, five hundred and fifty.

BAAL HATURIM ELUCIDATED

idol[66] which they [some of the Danites] had carried with them.

The final letters of the three words יִהְיֶה לָהֶם זִכָּרוֹן, of the verse from *Ecclesiastes,* spell the name הָמָן, *Haman,* for he also desired to wipe out their [i.e., Israel's][67] memory.[68]

---

66. Pharaoh had decreed that, if the Israelite slaves would not meet their quota of bricks, their children would be cemented into the walls to complete the structures. When Moses voiced a grievance to God over this, God told him that those who were being killed in this way would have been wicked had they been permitted to live. God then gave Moses permission to save one of those children, so that he might see the truth of God's words. The child that Moses saved was Micah [who made an idol that he carried with him at the splitting of the Sea of Reeds, and according to some sources, made the idol discussed in *Judges,* Chs. 17-18] (*Tanchuma, Ki Sisa* 19; see also *Sanhedrin* 101b, with *Rashi* s.v., נתמכמך בבנין). According to one opinion in *Midrash Tanchuma,* it was this Micah who was responsible for the manufacture of the golden calf.

For other aspects of Micah and his idol see the Baal HaTurim's comments to *Exodus* 2:16, 5:7, 12:11, 14:8, 14:29 and 18:3; *Numbers* 10:25; and *Deuteronomy* 4:24.

67. See *Esther* 3:6, 13; and 9:25.

68. *Peirush HaRokeach;* see also *Maharam MiRothenburg* to 10:28 below.

הָתְפָּקְדוּ בְּתוֹךְ בְּנֵי יִשְׂרָאֵל כַּאֲשֶׁר צִוָּה יהוה
לד אֶת־מֹשֶׁה: וַיַּעֲשׂוּ בְּנֵי יִשְׂרָאֵל כְּכֹל אֲשֶׁר־צִוָּה
יהוה אֶת־מֹשֶׁה כֵּן־חָנוּ לְדִגְלֵיהֶם וְכֵן נָסָעוּ אִישׁ
לְמִשְׁפְּחֹתָיו עַל־בֵּית אֲבֹתָיו:
ג רביעי א וְאֵלֶּה תּוֹלְדֹת אַהֲרֹן וּמֹשֶׁה בְּיוֹם דִּבֶּר יהוה
ב אֶת־מֹשֶׁה בְּהַר סִינָי: וְאֵלֶּה שְׁמוֹת בְּנֵי־אַהֲרֹן
ג הַבְּכֹר ׀ נָדָב וַאֲבִיהוּא אֶלְעָזָר וְאִיתָמָר: אֵלֶּה

בעל הטורים

(לג) **לֹא הָתְפָּקְדוּ בְּתוֹךְ בְּנֵי יִשְׂרָאֵל.** יֵשׁ תָּגִין עַל הַהֵ״א. לוֹמַר, שֶׁבַּחֲמִשָּׁה מְקוֹמוֹת שֶׁנִּמְנוּ יִשְׂרָאֵל, לֹא הָתְפָּקְדוּ בְּתוֹכָם:

ג (ב) **בְּנֵי אַהֲרֹן הַבְּכֹר נָדָב.** עָשָׂה פָּסֵק בֵּין ״הַבְּכֹר״ לְ״נָדָב״, לוֹמַר שֶׁאֵינוֹ חוֹזֵר עַל נָדָב, כִּי נָדָב מֵת בְּלֹא בָנִים וְאֵין נַפְקוּתָא בִּבְכוֹרָה שֶׁלּוֹ. אֶלָּא חוֹזֵר עַל אַהֲרֹן שֶׁהוּא הַבְּכוֹר {לְמֹשֶׁה}:

BAAL HATURIM ELUCIDATED

33. לֹא הָתְפָּקְדוּ בְּתוֹךְ בְּנֵי יִשְׂרָאֵל — [THE LEVITES] WERE NOT COUNTED AMONG THE CHILDREN OF ISRAEL. [According to a Scribal tradition,] the letter ה (= 5) of הָתְפָּקְדוּ is drawn with [extra] *tagin.*[69] This teaches that in five of the censuses in which the Israelites were counted,[70] the Levites were not counted among them.[71]

III

2. בְּנֵי אַהֲרֹן הַבְּכֹר ׀ נָדָב — [Literally,] THE SONS OF AARON, THE FIRSTBORN — NADAB.

69. In the Torah scroll, the letter ה is usually written with one תָּג, *tag* [tittle or crownlet]. However, *Sefer Tagin* lists 360 words in the Torah in which the letter ה is written with four *tagin* instead of the usual one. The word הָתְפָּקְדוּ appears on that list. See illustration and further discussion in note 42 to *parashas Nasso.*

70. The Midrash (*Pesikta Rabbasi* 10:14; *Bamidbar Rabbah* 2:11) enumerates the various censuses of the Israelites that are mentioned in the *Tanach*: The Israelites are counted in ten places — (i) when they descended to Egypt . . . (see *Genesis* 46:27 and *Deuteronomy* 10:22); (ii) when they ascended from Egypt . . . (see *Exodus* 12:37); (iii) after the incident of the golden calf . . . (see *Exodus* 30:16 with *Rashi;* see also the Baal HaTurim to 1:3 above, with note 9); (iv) at the formation of the *degalim* (our passage); (v) with regard to apportioning the Land of Israel [Canaan] (see Ch. 26 below); (vi-vii) twice in the days of King Saul . . . (see *I Samuel* 11:8 and 15:4); (viii) in the days of King David . . . (see *II Samuel* 24:1-2,9); (ix) in the days of Ezra . . . (see *Ezra,* Ch. 2); and (x) in the time of the future, as it is stated, *The sheep will again pass before the hands of the counter* (*Jeremiah* 33:13).

Another Midrash (*Tanchuma, Ki Sisa* 9) has a similar list which excludes the incident of the golden calf [perhaps because the cited verses describe how a census should be taken, but they do not command that such a census be taken at that time (*VeChur LaZahav*)] and has the incident of the spies instead [apparently based on 14:29 below (*VeChur LaZahav*)].

71. The five countings that did not include the Levites are apparently drawn from a list that combines the two versions of the Midrash adduced in note 70. They are: (i) when they ascended from Egypt [that census included the same countees as the census in our passage, except for those who were 18 or 19 years old at the exodus (*Rimzei Rabbeinu Yoel*)]; (ii) at the incident of the golden calf, for the Levites did not take part in that incident (see *Exodus* 32:26 with *Rashi*); (iii) after the incident of the spies, for the Levites had not sent a spy; (iv) the Levites had no part in the formation of the *degalim;* (v) the Levites did not receive portions in the Land of Israel (*VeChur LaZahav*).

[33] *The Levites were not counted among the Children of Israel, as HASHEM had commanded Moses.* [34] *The Children of Israel did everything that HASHEM had commanded Moses — so they encamped according to their divisions and so they journeyed; every man according to his families, by his fathers' household.*

3

[1] *These are the offspring of Aaron and Moses on the day HASHEM spoke with Moses at Mount Sinai:* [2] *These are the names of the sons of Aaron, the firstborn — Nadab; and Abihu, Elazar, and Ithamar.* [3] *These are the*

BAAL HATURIM ELUCIDATED

The cantillation sign פָּסֵק [*paseik*],[72] literally, *pause,* appears between the word הַבְּכֹר and the name נָדָב. This indicates that the term הַבְּכֹר, *the firstborn,* does not refer to Nadab; for Nadab died without children (see v. 4), therefore the fact that he was the firstborn is not significant.[72a] Rather, [הַבְּכֹר, *the firstborn,*] refers to Aaron[73] who was older[74] {than Moses[75]}.[76]

72. Also called פְּסִיק, *pesik.* The cantillation mark appears as an upright line in the space between two words. It is used to indicate a pause after a cantillation note whose usual function is to draw the reading forward. For example, the cantillation note מֻנַּח, *munach,* indicates that the reader should not pause after that word, but should include the following word(s) in the same phrase. The note אֶתְנַחְתָּא, *esnachta,* on the other hand, indicates a pause, like a semicolon. Occasionally, a *pesik* follows a *munach* to indicate that that particular *munach* takes on the role of a pause, like a comma. If our verse were written without a *pesik,* the phrase הַבְּכֹר נָדָב would mean, *the firstborn was Nadab.* However, the insertion of the *pesik* — הַבְּכֹר׀ נָדָב — changes the meaning to, *the firstborn, Nadab.*

The Baal HaTurim also explains the use of the פָּסֵק in his comments to *Genesis* 22:14; *Exodus* 15:18; *Leviticus* 10:6; *Numbers* 3:38, 5:22, 9:10; and *Deuteronomy* 6:4.

72a. A *bechor* inherits a double share of his father's estate. Thus, had Nadab outlived Aaron, he would have inherited forty percent of Aaron's property when Aaron died, while Abihu, Elazar and Ithamar would have each inherited twenty percent. Eventually, Nadab's children would inherit his double-sized share, a very significant reason for the Torah to state that Nadab is Aaron's firstborn. However, both Nadab and Abihu died before Aaron and without children. Accordingly, neither of them inherited anything from Aaron, and their remaining brothers Elazar and Ithamar were Aaron's sole heirs, each of them receiving exactly fifty percent of Aaron's estate. Accordingly, there would be no significant reason for the Torah to label Nadab as Aaron's *bechor* (*VeChur LaZahav*).

73. That is, although the cantillation note under Aaron's name is a *tipcha,* indicating a slight pause that disconnects it from הַבְּכֹר that follows, nevertheless, the *pesik* after הַבְּכֹר indicates that the word may refer back to Aaron.

74. In the context of the Baal HaTurim's comment, the word הַבְּכוֹר, *the firstborn,* cannot be understood in its legal sense — a person's male first child — for Miriam, who was eighty-six at the exodus (*Tanchuma HaYashan, Bo* 7; *Seder Olam Rabbah* 3; *Pesikta Rabbasi* 44:4), was older than Aaron, who was eighty-three at the exodus (*Exodus* 7:7). Rather, in our verse הַבְּכֹר means *the older.* Indeed, *Maharam MiRothenburg,* the Baal HaTurim's apparent source for this comment, reads, זָקֵן מִמֹּשֶׁה, *older than Moses.* For other examples of Scripture using בְּכוֹר in the sense of *older,* see *Rashi's* comments to *Exodus* 12:30, s.v., כִּי אֵין בַּיִת, and *Psalms* 89:28.

75. Moses' name is found in the printed editions, but does not appear in the manuscripts used by *Shoham Yakar.*

76. *Maharam MiRothenburg,* who also explains that the Torah underscores Aaron's seniority at

שְׁמוֹת בְּנֵי אַהֲרֹן הַכֹּהֲנִים הַמְּשֻׁחִים אֲשֶׁר־מִלֵּא
ד יָדָם לְכַהֵן: וַיָּמָת נָדָב וַאֲבִיהוּא לִפְנֵי יהוה
בְּהַקְרִבָם אֵשׁ זָרָה לִפְנֵי יהוה בְּמִדְבַּר סִינַי וּבָנִים
לֹא־הָיוּ לָהֶם וַיְכַהֵן אֶלְעָזָר וְאִיתָמָר עַל־פְּנֵי
אַהֲרֹן אֲבִיהֶם:
ה-ו וַיְדַבֵּר יהוה אֶל־מֹשֶׁה לֵּאמֹר: הַקְרֵב אֶת־מַטֵּה לֵוִי
וְהַעֲמַדְתָּ אֹתוֹ לִפְנֵי אַהֲרֹן הַכֹּהֵן וְשֵׁרְתוּ אֹתוֹ:
ז וְשָׁמְרוּ אֶת־מִשְׁמַרְתּוֹ וְאֶת־מִשְׁמֶרֶת כָּל־הָעֵדָה
לִפְנֵי אֹהֶל מוֹעֵד לַעֲבֹד אֶת־עֲבֹדַת הַמִּשְׁכָּן:
ח וְשָׁמְרוּ אֶת־כָּל־כְּלֵי אֹהֶל מוֹעֵד וְאֶת־מִשְׁמֶרֶת בְּנֵי
ט יִשְׂרָאֵל לַעֲבֹד אֶת־עֲבֹדַת הַמִּשְׁכָּן: וְנָתַתָּה אֶת־
הַלְוִיִּם לְאַהֲרֹן וּלְבָנָיו נְתוּנִם נְתוּנִם הֵמָּה לוֹ מֵאֵת
י בְּנֵי יִשְׂרָאֵל: וְאֶת־אַהֲרֹן וְאֶת־בָּנָיו תִּפְקֹד וְשָׁמְרוּ
אֶת־כְּהֻנָּתָם וְהַזָּר הַקָּרֵב יוּמָת:
יא-יב וַיְדַבֵּר יהוה אֶל־מֹשֶׁה לֵּאמֹר: וַאֲנִי הִנֵּה לָקַחְתִּי
אֶת־הַלְוִיִּם מִתּוֹךְ בְּנֵי יִשְׂרָאֵל תַּחַת כָּל־בְּכוֹר
יג פֶּטֶר רֶחֶם מִבְּנֵי יִשְׂרָאֵל וְהָיוּ לִי הַלְוִיִּם: כִּי לִי
כָּל־בְּכוֹר בְּיוֹם הַכֹּתִי כָל־בְּכוֹר בְּאֶרֶץ מִצְרַיִם
הִקְדַּשְׁתִּי לִי כָל־בְּכוֹר בְּיִשְׂרָאֵל מֵאָדָם עַד־בְּהֵמָה
לִי יִהְיוּ אֲנִי יהוה:
חמישי יד-טו וַיְדַבֵּר יהוה אֶל־מֹשֶׁה בְּמִדְבַּר סִינַי לֵאמֹר: פְּקֹד
אֶת־בְּנֵי לֵוִי לְבֵית אֲבֹתָם לְמִשְׁפְּחֹתָם כָּל־זָכָר
טז מִבֶּן־חֹדֶשׁ וָמַעְלָה תִּפְקְדֵם: וַיִּפְקֹד אֹתָם מֹשֶׁה
יז עַל־פִּי יהוה כַּאֲשֶׁר צֻוָּה: וַיִּהְיוּ־אֵלֶּה בְנֵי־לֵוִי
יח בִּשְׁמֹתָם גֵּרְשׁוֹן וּקְהָת וּמְרָרִי: וְאֵלֶּה שְׁמוֹת בְּנֵי־

BAAL HATURIM ELUCIDATED

6. {The Baal HaTurim's comment to הַקְרֵב appears at *Exodus* 28:1.}

this point in order to explain why Aaron's name precedes that of Moses: When the verse lists names of one's children, they are listed in order of age and not in order of wisdom [or some other trait]. Thus, in *parashas Va'eira* we find, *and she bore him Aaron and Moses* (*Exodus* 6:20), followed by, *this was [the] Aaron and Moses* (6:26) who were mentioned earlier in the order of their

names of the sons of Aaron, the anointed Kohanim, whom he inaugurated to minister. 4 *Nadab and Abihu died before* HASHEM *when they offered an alien fire before* HASHEM *in the Wilderness of Sinai, and they had no children; but Elazar and Ithamar ministered during the lifetime of Aaron, their father.*

5 HASHEM *spoke to Moses, saying,* 6 *"Bring near the tribe of Levi and have it stand before Aaron the Kohen, and they shall serve him.* 7 *They shall safeguard his charge and the charge of the entire assembly before the Tent of Meeting, to perform the service of the Tabernacle.* 8 *They shall safeguard all the utensils of the Tent of Meeting and the charge of the Children of Israel, to perform the service of the Tabernacle.* 9 *You shall present the Levites to Aaron and his sons — presented, presented are they to him — from the Children of Israel.* 10 *You shall appoint Aaron and his sons and they shall safeguard their priesthood; and the alien who approaches will die."*

11 HASHEM *spoke to Moses, saying,* 12 *"Behold! I have taken the Levites from among the Children of Israel, in place of every firstborn, the first issue of every womb among the Children of Israel, and the Levites shall be Mine.* 13 *For every firstborn is Mine: On the day I struck down every firstborn in the land of Egypt I sanctified every firstborn in Israel for Myself, from man to beast; they shall be Mine — I am* HASHEM."

14 HASHEM *spoke to Moses in the Wilderness of Sinai, saying,* 15 *"Count the sons of Levi according to their fathers' household, according to their families, every male from one month of age and up shall you count them."* 16 *Moses counted them according to the word of* HASHEM, *as he had been commanded.*

17 *These were the sons of Levi, by their names: Gershon, Kohath, and Merari.* 18 *These are the names of the sons of*

BAAL HATURIM ELUCIDATED

14. {At *Deuteronomy* 32:48 the Baal HaTurim comments on the phrase וַיְדַבֵּר ה׳ אֶל מֹשֶׁה when it is not followed immediately by לֵאמֹר.}

birth. However, the next verse after that states, *They were the ones who spoke to Pharaoh . . . this was Moses and Aaron* (6:27), i.e., when it comes to pre-eminence regarding appearing as a spokesman before the king and regarding leading Israel out of Egypt, Moses precedes Aaron.

יט גֵּרְשׁ֖וֹן לְמִשְׁפְּחֹתָ֑ם לִבְנִ֖י וְשִׁמְעִֽי׃ וּבְנֵ֥י קְהָ֖ת
כ לְמִשְׁפְּחֹתָ֑ם עַמְרָ֣ם וְיִצְהָ֔ר חֶבְר֖וֹן וְעֻזִּיאֵֽל׃ וּבְנֵ֧י
מְרָרִ֛י לְמִשְׁפְּחֹתָ֖ם מַחְלִ֣י וּמוּשִׁ֑י אֵ֥לֶּה הֵ֛ם מִשְׁפְּחֹ֥ת
כא הַלֵּוִ֖י לְבֵ֥ית אֲבֹתָֽם׃ לְגֵ֣רְשׁ֔וֹן מִשְׁפַּ֙חַת֙ הַלִּבְנִ֔י
וּמִשְׁפַּ֖חַת הַשִּׁמְעִ֑י אֵ֣לֶּה הֵ֔ם מִשְׁפְּחֹ֖ת הַגֵּֽרְשֻׁנִּֽי׃
כב פְּקֻדֵיהֶם֙ בְּמִסְפַּ֣ר כָּל־זָכָ֔ר מִבֶּן־חֹ֖דֶשׁ וָמָ֑עְלָה
כג פְּקֻ֣דֵיהֶ֔ם שִׁבְעַ֥ת אֲלָפִ֖ים וַחֲמֵ֥שׁ מֵאֽוֹת׃ מִשְׁפְּחֹ֖ת
כד הַגֵּֽרְשֻׁנִּ֑י אַחֲרֵ֧י הַמִּשְׁכָּ֛ן יַחֲנ֖וּ יָֽמָּה׃ וּנְשִׂ֥יא בֵֽית־אָ֖ב
כה לַגֵּרְשֻׁנִּ֑י אֶלְיָסָ֖ף בֶּן־לָאֵֽל׃ וּמִשְׁמֶ֤רֶת בְּנֵֽי־גֵרְשׁוֹן֙
בְּאֹ֣הֶל מוֹעֵ֔ד הַמִּשְׁכָּ֖ן וְהָאֹ֑הֶל מִכְסֵ֕הוּ וּמָסַ֕ךְ
כו פֶּ֖תַח אֹ֥הֶל מוֹעֵֽד׃ וְקַלְעֵ֣י הֶֽחָצֵ֗ר וְאֶת־מָסַךְ֙
פֶּ֣תַח הֶֽחָצֵ֔ר אֲשֶׁ֧ר עַל־הַמִּשְׁכָּ֛ן וְעַל־הַמִּזְבֵּ֖חַ סָבִ֑יב
כז וְאֵת֙ מֵֽיתָרָ֔יו לְכֹ֖ל עֲבֹדָתֽוֹ׃ וְלִקְהָ֗ת
מִשְׁפַּ֤חַת הָֽעַמְרָמִי֙ וּמִשְׁפַּ֣חַת הַיִּצְהָרִ֔י וּמִשְׁפַּ֙חַת֙
הַֽחֶבְרֹנִ֔י וּמִשְׁפַּ֖חַת הָֽעָזִּיאֵלִ֑י אֵ֥לֶּה הֵ֖ם מִשְׁפְּחֹ֥ת
כח הַקְּהָתִֽי׃ בְּמִסְפַּר֙ כָּל־זָכָ֔ר מִבֶּן־חֹ֖דֶשׁ וָמָ֑עְלָה
שְׁמֹנַ֤ת אֲלָפִים֙ וְשֵׁ֣שׁ מֵא֔וֹת שֹֽׁמְרֵ֖י מִשְׁמֶ֥רֶת
כט הַקֹּֽדֶשׁ׃ מִשְׁפְּחֹ֖ת בְּנֵֽי־קְהָ֑ת יַחֲנ֕וּ עַ֛ל יֶ֥רֶךְ הַמִּשְׁכָּ֖ן
ל תֵּימָֽנָה׃ וּנְשִׂ֥יא בֵֽית־אָ֖ב לְמִשְׁפְּחֹ֣ת הַקְּהָתִ֑י
לא אֱלִיצָפָ֖ן בֶּן־עֻזִּיאֵֽל׃ וּמִשְׁמַרְתָּ֗ם הָאָרֹ֤ן וְהַשֻּׁלְחָן֙
וְהַמְּנֹרָ֣ה וְהַֽמִּזְבְּחֹ֔ת וּכְלֵ֣י הַקֹּ֔דֶשׁ אֲשֶׁ֥ר יְשָׁרְת֖וּ
לב בָּהֶ֑ם וְהַ֨מָּסָ֔ךְ וְכֹ֖ל עֲבֹדָתֽוֹ׃ וּנְשִׂיא֙ נְשִׂיאֵ֣י הַלֵּוִ֔י
אֶלְעָזָ֖ר בֶּן־אַהֲרֹ֣ן הַכֹּהֵ֑ן פְּקֻדַּ֕ת שֹׁמְרֵ֖י מִשְׁמֶ֥רֶת
לג הַקֹּֽדֶשׁ׃ לִמְרָרִ֕י מִשְׁפַּ֙חַת֙ הַמַּחְלִ֔י וּמִשְׁפַּ֖חַת
לד הַמּוּשִׁ֑י אֵ֥לֶּה הֵ֖ם מִשְׁפְּחֹ֥ת מְרָרִֽי׃ וּפְקֻדֵיהֶם֙
בְּמִסְפַּ֣ר כָּל־זָכָ֔ר מִבֶּן־חֹ֖דֶשׁ וָמָ֑עְלָה שֵׁ֥שֶׁת
לה אֲלָפִ֖ים וּמָאתָֽיִם׃ וּנְשִׂ֤יא בֵֽית־אָב֙ לְמִשְׁפְּחֹ֣ת
מְרָרִ֔י צוּרִיאֵ֖ל בֶּן־אֲבִיחָ֑יִל עַ֣ל יֶ֧רֶךְ הַמִּשְׁכָּ֛ן יַחֲנ֖וּ
לו צָפֹֽנָה׃ וּפְקֻדַּ֣ת מִשְׁמֶ֘רֶת֮ בְּנֵ֣י מְרָרִי֒ קַרְשֵׁי֙ הַמִּשְׁכָּ֔ן
וּבְרִיחָ֖יו וְעַמֻּדָ֣יו וַאֲדָנָ֑יו וְכָל־כֵּלָ֔יו וְכֹ֖ל עֲבֹדָתֽוֹ׃

*Gershon according to their families: Libni and Shimei. [19] The
sons of Kohath according to their families were Amram and
Izhar, Hebron and Uzziel. [20] The sons of Merari according to
their families were Mahli and Mushi. These were the families
of the Levites, according to their fathers' household.*

*[21] Gershon had the family of the Libnites and the family of
the Shimeites; these were the Gershonite families. [22] Their
count according to the number of every male, from one
month of age and up: their count was seven thousand, five
hundred. [23] The Gershonite families would encamp behind the
Tabernacle, to the west. [24] The leader of the father's house-
hold of the Gershonites was Eliasaph son of Lael. [25] The
charge of the sons of Gershon in the Tent of Meeting was the
Tabernacle, the Tent, its Cover, the Screen of the entrance of
the Tent of Meeting; [26] the curtains of the Courtyard, the
Screen of the entrance of the Courtyard that surrounded the
Tabernacle and the Altar, and its ropes — for all its labor.*

*[27] Kohath had the family of the Amramites, the family of the
Izharites, the family of the Hebronites, and the family of the
Uzzielites; these were the Kohathite families. [28] The number of
every male from one month of age and up was eight thou-
sand, six hundred; the guardians of the charge of the sanctity.
[29] The families of the children of Kohath would encamp on the
side of the Tabernacle, to the south. [30] The leader of the
father's household of the Kohathite families was Elizaphan
son of Uzziel. [31] Their charge was the Ark, the Table, the
Menorah, the Altars and the sacred utensils with which they
would minister, the Partition and all its accessories.*

*[32] The leader of the Levite leaders was Elazar son of Aaron
the Kohen, the assignment of the guardians of the charge of
the sanctity.*

*[33] Merari had the family of the Mahlites and the family of the
Mushites; these were the Merarite families. [34] Their count
according to the number of every male from one month of
age and up was six thousand, two hundred. [35] The leader
of the father's household of the Merarite families was Zuriel
son of Abihail; they would encamp on the side of the
Tabernacle, to the north. [36] And the duty of the charge of the
sons of Merari was the planks of the Tabernacle, its bars, its
pillars, its sockets and all its utensils, and all its accessories.*

BAAL HATURIM ELUCIDATED

36. {The Baal HaTurim's comment to וּפְקֻדַּת appears at 16:29 below.}

לז וְעַמֻּדֵ֨י הֶחָצֵ֤ר סָבִיב֙ וְאַדְנֵיהֶ֔ם וִיתֵדֹתָ֖ם וּמֵיתְרֵיהֶֽם׃
לח וְהַחֹנִ֣ים לִפְנֵ֣י הַמִּשְׁכָּ֡ן קֵ֡דְמָה לִפְנֵ֣י אֹֽהֶל־
מוֹעֵ֣ד ׀ מִ֠זְרָחָה מֹשֶׁ֣ה ׀ וְאַהֲרֹ֣ן וּבָנָ֗יו שֹֽׁמְרִים֙
מִשְׁמֶ֣רֶת הַמִּקְדָּ֔שׁ לְמִשְׁמֶ֖רֶת בְּנֵ֣י יִשְׂרָאֵ֑ל וְהַזָּ֥ר
לט הַקָּרֵ֖ב יוּמָֽת׃ כָּל־פְּקוּדֵ֨י הַלְוִיִּ֜ם אֲשֶׁר֩ פָּקַ֨ד מֹשֶׁ֧ה
*וְאַהֲרֹ֛ן עַל־פִּ֥י יְהֹוָ֖ה לְמִשְׁפְּחֹתָ֑ם כָּל־זָכָר֙ מִבֶּן־
מ חֹ֣דֶשׁ וָמַ֔עְלָה שְׁנַ֥יִם וְעֶשְׂרִ֖ים אָֽלֶף׃   וַיֹּ֨אמֶר
יְהֹוָ֜ה אֶל־מֹשֶׁ֗ה פְּקֹ֨ד כָּל־בְּכֹ֤ר זָכָר֙ לִבְנֵ֣י יִשְׂרָאֵ֔ל
מא מִבֶּן־חֹ֖דֶשׁ וָמָ֑עְלָה וְשָׂ֕א אֵ֖ת מִסְפַּ֥ר שְׁמֹתָֽם׃ וְלָקַחְתָּ֨
אֶת־הַלְוִיִּ֥ם לִי֙ אֲנִ֣י יְהֹוָ֔ה תַּ֥חַת כָּל־בְּכֹ֖ר בִּבְנֵ֣י
יִשְׂרָאֵ֑ל וְאֵת֙ בֶּהֱמַ֣ת הַלְוִיִּ֔ם תַּ֣חַת כָּל־בְּכ֔וֹר
מב בְּבֶהֱמַ֖ת בְּנֵ֥י יִשְׂרָאֵֽל׃ וַיִּפְקֹ֣ד מֹשֶׁ֔ה כַּאֲשֶׁ֛ר צִוָּ֥ה יְהֹוָ֖ה
מג אֹת֑וֹ אֶת־כָּל־בְּכֹ֖ר בִּבְנֵ֥י יִשְׂרָאֵֽל׃ וַיְהִ֨י כָל־בְּכ֜וֹר
זָכָ֛ר בְּמִסְפַּ֥ר שֵׁמֹ֖ת מִבֶּן־חֹ֣דֶשׁ וָמַ֑עְלָה לִפְקֻדֵיהֶ֑ם
שְׁנַ֤יִם וְעֶשְׂרִים֙ אֶ֔לֶף שְׁלֹשָׁ֥ה וְשִׁבְעִ֖ים וּמָאתָֽיִם׃

*נקוד על ואהרן

ששי

בעל הטורים

(לח) וְהַחֹנִים . . . לִפְנֵי אֹהֶל מוֹעֵד מִזְרָחָה מֹשֶׁה וְאַהֲרֹן. יֵשׁ פְּסֵק בֵּין ״מֹשֶׁה״ לְ״אַהֲרֹן״, לוֹמַר מֹשֶׁה בְּמָקוֹם אֶחָד לְבַד, וְאַהֲרֹן וּבָנָיו בְּמָקוֹם אֶחָד לְבַד:

(מ) וְשָׂא. ג׳ – ״וְשָׂא אֵת מִסְפַּר שְׁמֹתָם״; ״וְשָׂא עֵינֶיךָ יָמָּה וְצָפֹנָה״; וְאִידָךְ ״רְאֵה עָנְיִי וַעֲמָלִי וְשָׂא לְכָל חַטֹּאותָי״. שֶׁהָיָה דָוִד מִתְפַּלֵּל עַל שֶׁנָּשָׂא אֶת מִסְפַּר בְּנֵי יִשְׂרָאֵל, וְזֶהוּ ״וְשָׂא אֵת מִסְפַּר שְׁמֹתָם״. וְהַמִּתְפַּלֵּל צָרִיךְ שֶׁיִּתֵּן עֵינָיו לְמַטָּה, וְזֶהוּ ״וְשָׂא עֵינֶיךָ יָמָּה״, שֶׁיִּתֵּן עֵינָיו לְמַטָּה וְלֹא יָרִים עֵינָיו לְמַעְלָה:

BAAL HATURIM ELUCIDATED

38. **וְהַחֹנִים . . . לִפְנֵי אֹהֶל מוֹעֵד מִזְרָחָה מֹשֶׁה ׀ וְאַהֲרֹן** — THOSE WHO ENCAMPED . . . BEFORE THE TENT OF MEETING TO THE EAST, WERE MOSES AND AARON. There is a *paseik*[77] between מֹשֶׁה, *Moses,* and וְאַהֲרֹן, *and Aaron,* to indicate that Moses [should camp] in one place, by himself; and Aaron and his [two] sons [should each camp] in one place, by himself.[78]

40. **וְשָׂא** — AND TAKE. [The masoretic note, ג׳, means that] this word appears three times in the *Tanach* [with different meanings[79]]: (i) here, **וְשָׂא אֵת מִסְפַּר שְׁמֹתָם**,

77. See note 72 above.

78. *Peirush HaRokeach;* based on *Tamid* 26a; cf. the Baal HaTurim to *Exodus* 24:2, s.v., יִגָּשׁוּ.

79. The verb root נשא is classified among the חַסְרֵי פ״נ verbs, that is, its first root letter, נ, is dropped in some conjugations. The basic meaning of the word is *to carry* or *to transport* (e.g., וְנָשְׂאוּ, *they shall carry,* 4:25 below); however, it has many secondary meanings. Three of them are: (i) *to*

[37] *The pillars of the Courtyard all around and their sockets, their pegs and their ropes.*

[38] *Those who encamped before the Tabernacle to the front, before the Tent of Meeting to the east, were Moses and Aaron and his sons, guardians of the charge of the Sanctuary, for the charge of the Children of Israel; any alien who approaches shall die.*

[39] *All the countings of the Levites, which Moses and Aaron counted according to the word of HASHEM according to their families, every male from one month of age and up, were twenty-two thousand.*

[40] *HASHEM said to Moses, "Count every firstborn male of the Children of Israel from one month of age and up, and take the count of their names.* [41] *You shall take the Levites for Me — I, HASHEM — in place of every firstborn of the Children of Israel, and the livestock of the Levites in place of every firstborn of the animals of the Children of Israel."* [42] *Moses counted — as HASHEM had commanded him — every firstborn of the Children of Israel.* [43] *Every firstborn male according to the number of their names, from one month of age and up, according to their numbers, was twenty-two thousand, two hundred and seventy-three.*

BAAL HATURIM ELUCIDATED

and take the count of their names; (ii) וְשָׂא עֵינֶיךָ יָמָּה וְצָפֹנָה, *and direct your eyes westward and northward* (*Deuteronomy* 3:27); and (iii) רְאֵה עָנְיִי וַעֲמָלִי וְשָׂא לְכָל חַטֹּאותָי, *See my affliction and my toil, and forgive all my sins* (*Psalms* 25:18). [The same expression is used in each of these verses] because [in *Psalms*] King David was praying [for forgiveness] for having taken an unwarranted census of the Children of Israel.[80] Thus, [וְשָׂא, *and forgive,* of *Psalms* is connected to] the verse וְשָׂא אֵת מִסְפַּר שְׁמֹתָם, *and take the count of their names.* Additionally, one who prays [as in the case of King David] should direct his eyes downward.[81] And that is the allusion of the verse וְשָׂא עֵינֶיךָ יָמָּה, *and direct your eyes westward* [literally, *to the sea*],[82] that one should set his eyes downward, and not raise his eyes upward.

count, e.g., נָשׂא, *take a census* (4:2 below); (ii) *to focus one's eyes,* e.g., וַיִּשָּׂא לוֹט אֶת עֵינָיו (*Genesis* 13:10), usually translated, *Lot raised his eyes* [however, since he was standing on a mountain, looking down on the valley, the expression וַיִּשָּׂא אֶת עֵינָיו is more correctly understood as *he directed his eyes* (see *Radak*)]; and (iii) *to forgive,* e.g., נֹשֵׂא עָוֹן, *Forgiver of iniquity* (14:18 below). Thus, the three meanings of וְשָׂא in the verses cited by the Baal HaTurim are *take a census; direct* [your eyes]; and *forgive.*

80. See *II Samuel* 24:1-17.

81. *Yevamos* 105b.

82. The word יָם means both *sea* and *west,* for the יָם הַגָּדוֹל, *Mediterranean Sea,* literally, *the Great Sea,* lies to the west of the Land of Israel. Thus, directing one's eyes to the יָם implies looking downward, for the sea is lower than the ground (*Shoham Yakar*).

ג/מד־ד/ט

מד־מה וַיְדַבֵּר יְהוָה אֶל־מֹשֶׁה לֵּאמֹר: קַח אֶת־הַלְוִיִּם תַּחַת
כָּל־בְּכוֹר בִּבְנֵי יִשְׂרָאֵל וְאֶת־בֶּהֱמַת הַלְוִיִּם תַּחַת
מו בְּהֶמְתָּם וְהָיוּ־לִי הַלְוִיִּם אֲנִי יְהוָה: וְאֵת פְּדוּיֵי
הַשְּׁלֹשָׁה וְהַשִּׁבְעִים וְהַמָּאתַיִם הָעֹדְפִים עַל־הַלְוִיִּם
מז מִבְּכוֹר בְּנֵי יִשְׂרָאֵל: וְלָקַחְתָּ חֲמֵשֶׁת חֲמֵשֶׁת
שְׁקָלִים לַגֻּלְגֹּלֶת בְּשֶׁקֶל הַקֹּדֶשׁ תִּקָּח עֶשְׂרִים גֵּרָה
מח הַשָּׁקֶל: וְנָתַתָּה הַכֶּסֶף לְאַהֲרֹן וּלְבָנָיו פְּדוּיֵי
מט הָעֹדְפִים בָּהֶם: וַיִּקַּח מֹשֶׁה אֵת כֶּסֶף הַפִּדְיוֹם מֵאֵת
נ הָעֹדְפִים עַל פְּדוּיֵי הַלְוִיִּם: מֵאֵת בְּכוֹר בְּנֵי יִשְׂרָאֵל
לָקַח אֶת־הַכָּסֶף חֲמִשָּׁה וְשִׁשִּׁים וּשְׁלֹשׁ מֵאוֹת
נא וָאֶלֶף בְּשֶׁקֶל הַקֹּדֶשׁ: וַיִּתֵּן מֹשֶׁה אֶת־כֶּסֶף הַפְּדֻיִם
לְאַהֲרֹן וּלְבָנָיו עַל־פִּי יְהוָה כַּאֲשֶׁר צִוָּה יְהוָה
אֶת־מֹשֶׁה:

ד שביעי

א־ב וַיְדַבֵּר יְהוָה אֶל־מֹשֶׁה וְאֶל־אַהֲרֹן לֵאמֹר: נָשֹׂא
אֶת־רֹאשׁ בְּנֵי קְהָת מִתּוֹךְ בְּנֵי לֵוִי לְמִשְׁפְּחֹתָם
ג לְבֵית אֲבֹתָם: מִבֶּן שְׁלֹשִׁים שָׁנָה וָמַעְלָה וְעַד
בֶּן־חֲמִשִּׁים שָׁנָה כָּל־בָּא לַצָּבָא לַעֲשׂוֹת מְלָאכָה
ד בְּאֹהֶל מוֹעֵד: זֹאת עֲבֹדַת בְּנֵי־קְהָת בְּאֹהֶל מוֹעֵד
ה קֹדֶשׁ הַקֳּדָשִׁים: וּבָא אַהֲרֹן וּבָנָיו בִּנְסֹעַ הַמַּחֲנֶה
וְהוֹרִדוּ אֵת פָּרֹכֶת הַמָּסָךְ וְכִסּוּ־בָהּ אֵת אֲרֹן הָעֵדֻת:
ו וְנָתְנוּ עָלָיו כְּסוּי עוֹר תַּחַשׁ וּפָרְשׂוּ בֶגֶד־כְּלִיל
ז תְּכֵלֶת מִלְמָעְלָה וְשָׂמוּ בַּדָּיו: וְעַל ׀ שֻׁלְחַן הַפָּנִים
יִפְרְשׂוּ בֶּגֶד תְּכֵלֶת וְנָתְנוּ עָלָיו אֶת־הַקְּעָרֹת וְאֶת־
הַכַּפֹּת וְאֶת־הַמְּנַקִּיֹּת וְאֵת קְשׂוֹת הַנָּסֶךְ וְלֶחֶם
ח הַתָּמִיד עָלָיו יִהְיֶה: וּפָרְשׂוּ עֲלֵיהֶם בֶּגֶד תּוֹלַעַת שָׁנִי
וְכִסּוּ אֹתוֹ בְּמִכְסֵה עוֹר תָּחַשׁ וְשָׂמוּ אֶת־בַּדָּיו:
ט וְלָקְחוּ ׀ בֶּגֶד תְּכֵלֶת וְכִסּוּ אֶת־מְנֹרַת הַמָּאוֹר

IV

6. {The comment that appears [without a title] at this point in most printed

44 *HASHEM spoke to Moses, saying,* 45 *"Take the Levites in place of every firstborn of the Children of Israel, and the livestock of the Levites in place of their livestock, and the Levites shall be Mine, I am HASHEM.* 46 *And as for the redemptions of the two hundred and seventy-three of the firstborn of the Children of Israel who are in excess of the Levites;* 47 *you shall take five shekels each according to the head count, in the sacred shekel shall you take; the shekel is twenty geras.* 48 *You shall give the money to Aaron and his sons, as redemptions of the additional ones among them."*

49 *Moses took the money of the redemption from those who were in excess of the redemptions of the Levites;* 50 *from the firstborn of the Children of Israel he took the money: one thousand, three hundred and sixty-five in the sacred shekels.* 51 *Moses gave the money of the redemptions to Aaron and his sons according to the word of HASHEM, as HASHEM had commanded Moses.*

4 1 *HASHEM spoke to Moses and Aaron, saying:* 2 *"Take a census of the sons of Kohath from among the sons of Levi, according to their families, according to their fathers' households;* 3 *from thirty years of age and up, until fifty years of age, everyone who comes to the legion to perform work in the Tent of Meeting.*

4 *"This is the work of the sons of Kohath in the Tent of Meeting: the most holy.* 5 *At the camp's setting out to journey, Aaron and his sons shall come and take down the Partition-curtain and cover the Ark of the Testimony with it.* 6 *They shall place upon it a tachash-hide covering, and spread a cloth entirely of turquoise wool over it, and adjust its staves.* 7 *Upon the Table of the show-bread they shall spread a cloth of turquoise wool and place upon it the dishes, the spoons, the pillars, and the shelving-tubes; and the constant bread shall remain on it.* 8 *They shall spread over them a cloth of scarlet wool and cover it with a cover of tachash hide, and emplace its staves.* 9 *They shall take a cloth of turquoise wool and cover the Menorah of illumination,*

editions is presented at verse 11 below.}

וְאֶת־נֵרֹתֶיהָ וְאֶת־מַלְקָחֶיהָ וְאֶת־מַחְתֹּתֶיהָ וְאֵת
י כָּל־כְּלֵי שַׁמְנָהּ אֲשֶׁר יְשָׁרְתוּ־לָהּ בָּהֶם: וְנָתְנוּ
אֹתָהּ וְאֶת־כָּל־כֵּלֶיהָ אֶל־מִכְסֵה עוֹר תָּחַשׁ
יא וְנָתְנוּ עַל־הַמּוֹט: וְעַל ׀ מִזְבַּח הַזָּהָב יִפְרְשׂוּ בֶּגֶד
תְּכֵלֶת וְכִסּוּ אֹתוֹ בְּמִכְסֵה עוֹר תָּחַשׁ וְשָׂמוּ
יב אֶת־בַּדָּיו: וְלָקְחוּ אֶת־כָּל־כְּלֵי הַשָּׁרֵת אֲשֶׁר
יְשָׁרְתוּ־בָם בַּקֹּדֶשׁ וְנָתְנוּ אֶל־בֶּגֶד תְּכֵלֶת וְכִסּוּ
אוֹתָם בְּמִכְסֵה עוֹר תָּחַשׁ וְנָתְנוּ עַל־הַמּוֹט:
יג וְדִשְּׁנוּ אֶת־הַמִּזְבֵּחַ וּפָרְשׂוּ עָלָיו בֶּגֶד אַרְגָּמָן:
יד וְנָתְנוּ עָלָיו אֶת־כָּל־כֵּלָיו אֲשֶׁר יְשָׁרְתוּ עָלָיו בָּהֶם
אֶת־הַמַּחְתֹּת אֶת־הַמִּזְלָגֹת וְאֶת־הַיָּעִים וְאֶת־
הַמִּזְרָקֹת כֹּל כְּלֵי הַמִּזְבֵּחַ וּפָרְשׂוּ עָלָיו כְּסוּי עוֹר
טו תַּחַשׁ וְשָׂמוּ בַדָּיו: וְכִלָּה אַהֲרֹן־וּבָנָיו לְכַסֹּת אֶת
הַקֹּדֶשׁ וְאֶת־כָּל־כְּלֵי הַקֹּדֶשׁ בִּנְסֹעַ הַמַּחֲנֶה
וְאַחֲרֵי־כֵן יָבֹאוּ בְנֵי־קְהָת לָשֵׂאת וְלֹא־יִגְּעוּ אֶל־
הַקֹּדֶשׁ וָמֵתוּ אֵלֶּה מַשָּׂא בְנֵי־קְהָת בְּאֹהֶל מוֹעֵד:

בעל הטורים

ד (יא) {אֶת בַּדָּיו.} בָּאָרוֹן וּבְמִזְבַּח הַנְּחֹשֶׁת כְּתִיב „בַּדָּיו״, וּבַשֻּׁלְחָן וּבְמִזְבַּח הַזָּהָב {כְּתִיב „אֶת בַּדָּיו״. לְפִי שֶׁבַּשֻּׁלְחָן וּבַמִּזְבַּח הַזָּהָב} כְּתִיב „לְבָתִּים לְבַדִּים״, כְּתִיב „אֶת״ לְרַבּוֹת הַבָּתִּים:

BAAL HATURIM ELUCIDATED

11. {אֶת בַּדָּיו — **ITS STAVES.**} With regard to the Ark (v. 6 above) and the Copper Altar (v. 14 below), the Torah states merely בַּדָּיו for *its staves.* With regard to the Table and the Golden Altar, by contrast, the Torah states {**אֶת בַּדָּיו**.[83] This is because with regard to the Table and the Golden Altar, the Torah states}[84] לְבָתִּים לְבַדִּים, *as housings for* [*the*] *staves* (*Exodus* 25:27, 30:4). The

83. Generally, the word אֶת does not have a counterpart in English translation. Its function is to introduce the object of a verb so that it not be confused with the subject; for example, וַתִּקַּח רִבְקָה means *Rebecca took* (*Genesis* 27:15), but וַתִּקַּח אֶת זִלְפָּה means *she took Zilpah* (*Genesis* 30:9). When the noun after a verb is clearly the object of that verb and not its subject, the אֶת is often omitted. Regarding our passage, although it is obvious that וְשָׂמוּ בַּדָּיו does not mean *its staves shall place,* we nevertheless find that the Torah alternates between that formulation and the longer form וְשָׂמוּ אֶת בַּדָּיו. The Baal HaTurim's comment explains why both forms are used in our passage.

84. The passages enclosed in braces are not found in the printed editions or in most manuscripts. They do appear, however, in one of the manuscripts used by *Shoham Yakar.*

and its lamps, and its tongs, and its spoons, and all the
vessels of its oil, with which they minister to it. 10 *They shall*
place it and all its utensils into a cover of tachash-hide, and
place it on the pole. 11 *Upon the Gold Altar they shall spread*
a cloth of turquoise wool, and cover it with a covering of
tachash-hide, and emplace its staves. 12 *They shall take all*
the utensils of service with which they serve in the
Sanctuary and place them on a cloth of turquoise wool, and
cover them with a covering of tachash-hide, and place them
on the pole. 13 *They shall clear the ash from the Altar and*
spread a cloth of purple wool over it; 14 *they shall place*
upon it all the utensils with which they minister upon it: the
fire-pans, the forks, the shovels, and the basins — all the
utensils of the Altar — and spread over it a covering of
tachash hide, and emplace its staves.
15 *"Aaron and his sons shall finish covering the holy and*
all the holy utensils, at the camp's setting out to journey and
then the sons of Kohath shall come to carry, so that they
not touch the Sanctuary and die. These are the burden of
the sons of Kohath in the Tent of Meeting.

word אֶת is added here to include the housings.[85]

85. This comment is difficult, for the almost identical expression בָּתִּים לַבַּדִּים, *housings for the staves* (*Exodus* 38:5), appears regarding the Copper Altar (*Ittur Bikkurim*). Moreover, what difference is there if the verse includes or omits the phrase לְבָתִּים לְבַדִּים? All these vessels had staves and housings, even if the verse does not mention this particular phrase (Y.S.).

Whereas this comment has been corrupted in both the early and later printed editions, it is suggested that, despite *Shoham Yakar's* interpolations, the comment remains incomplete. Perhaps we can explain the difference between וְשָׂמוּ בַּדָּיו and וְשָׂמוּ אֶת בַּדָּיו in another manner and then use that explanation to fill in the missing words. In recording the manufacture of the Ark (*Exodus* 37:4-5) and Copper Altar (*Exodus* 38:6-7), the Torah states, *He made staves . . . he inserted the staves . . .* But with regard to the Table (*Exodus* 37:15) and Golden Altar (*Exodus* 37:28), the Torah states merely, *He made the staves . . .*, without mentioning that he inserted them into the rings. Accordingly, it would seem that those two sets of staves were not inserted until the first time the nation was commanded to travel. If so, the instruction וְשָׂמוּ בַּדָּיו, *they shall emplace its staves,* used regarding the Ark and the Copper Altar required only that they adjust the staves that were already in the rings that served as their housings. However, regarding the Table and the Golden Altar, first the staves had to be inserted, then they had to be adjusted. Therefore, the Torah uses the stronger expression, וְשָׂמוּ אֶת בַּדָּיו, for those two vessels.

If that analysis is correct, we may then apply it to the Baal HaTurim's comment. Our emended version will read as follows: . . . לְפִי שֶׁבַּשֻּׁלְחָן וּבַמִּזְבַּח הַזָּהָב כְּתִיב {רַק} "לְבָתִּים לְבַדִּים" {וְלֹא "וַיָּבֵא אֶת הַבַּדִּים". לְכָךְ} כְּתִיב "אֶת" לְרַבּוֹת {הֲבָאַת הַבַּדִּים אֶל} הַבָּתִּים, . . . *Because with regard to the Table and the Golden Altar the Torah states, "as housings for the staves"* {but not, *"he inserted the staves," therefore*} *the word* אֶת *is written* [*regarding them*], *to include* {*the bringing of the staves into*} *the housings* (*VeChur LaZahav*).

טז וּפְקֻדַּ֞ת אֶלְעָזָ֣ר ׀ בֶּן־אַהֲרֹ֣ן הַכֹּהֵ֗ן שֶׁ֤מֶן הַמָּאוֹר֙
וּקְטֹ֣רֶת הַסַּמִּ֔ים וּמִנְחַ֥ת הַתָּמִ֖יד וְשֶׁ֣מֶן הַמִּשְׁחָ֑ה
פְּקֻדַּ֗ת כָּל־הַמִּשְׁכָּן֙ וְכָל־אֲשֶׁר־בּ֔וֹ בְּקֹ֖דֶשׁ וּבְכֵלָֽיו׃
מפטיר יז־יח וַיְדַבֵּ֣ר יְהוָ֔ה אֶל־מֹשֶׁ֥ה וְאֶֽל־אַהֲרֹ֖ן לֵאמֹֽר׃ אַל־
תַּכְרִ֕יתוּ אֶת־שֵׁ֖בֶט מִשְׁפְּחֹ֣ת הַקְּהָתִ֑י מִתּ֖וֹךְ הַלְוִיִּֽם׃
יט וְזֹ֣את ׀ עֲשׂ֣וּ לָהֶ֗ם וְחָיוּ֙ וְלֹ֣א יָמֻ֔תוּ בְּגִשְׁתָּ֖ם
אֶת־קֹ֣דֶשׁ הַקֳּדָשִׁ֑ים אַהֲרֹ֤ן וּבָנָיו֙ יָבֹ֔אוּ וְשָׂמ֣וּ אוֹתָ֔ם
כ אִ֥ישׁ אִ֛ישׁ עַל־עֲבֹדָת֖וֹ וְאֶל־מַשָּׂאֽוֹ׃ וְלֹא־יָבֹ֧אוּ
לִרְא֛וֹת כְּבַלַּ֖ע אֶת־הַקֹּ֑דֶשׁ וָמֵֽתוּ׃ פפפ

קנ״ט פסוקים. חלקיה״ו סימן.

בעל הטורים

(יט) וְחָיוּ. ב׳ – ״וְחָיוּ וְלֹא יָמֻתוּ״; ״וְחָיוּ אֶת בְּנֵיהֶם וָשָׁבוּ״, בִּתְרֵי עָשָׂר בְּעִנְיַן הַגְּאֻלָּה. מְלַמֵּד שֶׁהַמַּלְאַךְ הַמָּוֶת בָּטֵל לֶעָתִיד לָבֹא. וְזֶהוּ ״וְחָיוּ אֶת בְּנֵיהֶם וָשָׁבוּ״, ״וְחָיוּ וְלֹא יָמֻתוּ״:

BAAL HATURIM ELUCIDATED

16. {The Baal HaTurim's comment to וּפְקֻדַּת appears at 16:29 below.}

19. **וְחָיוּ** — THEY SHALL LIVE. [The masoretic note, ב׳, means that] this word

[16] *"The duty of Elazar son of Aaron the Kohen is the oil of illumination, the incense spices, the meal-offering of the continual offering, and the anointment oil — the charge of the entire Tabernacle and everything in it — of the Sanctuary and its utensils."*

[17] *HASHEM spoke to Moses and Aaron, saying:* [18] *"Do not let the tribe of the Kohathite families be cut off from among the Levites.* [19] *Thus shall you do for them so that they shall live and they shall not die: when they approach the Holy of Holies, Aaron and his sons shall come and assign them, every man to his work and his burden.* [20] *But they shall not come and look as the holy is inserted, lest they die."*

appears twice in the *Tanach*: (i) here, וְחָיוּ וְלֹא יָמֻתוּ, *they shall live and they shall not die;* and (ii) וְחָיוּ אֶת בְּנֵיהֶם וָשָׁבוּ, *they shall live with their children, and they shall return,* in the Book of *Twelve Prophets* (*Zechariah* 10:9), with regard to the redemption. This teaches that the angel of death will be destroyed in the future. Thus, *they shall live with their children, and they shall return;* and, *they shall live and they shall not die.*

פרשת נשא
Parashas Nasso

ד/כא-לז כא-כב וַיְדַבֵּר יְהוָה אֶל־מֹשֶׁה לֵּאמֹר: נָשֹׂא אֶת־רֹאשׁ בְּנֵי
כג גֵרְשׁוֹן גַּם־הֵם לְבֵית אֲבֹתָם לְמִשְׁפְּחֹתָם: מִבֶּן
שְׁלֹשִׁים שָׁנָה וָמַעְלָה עַד בֶּן־חֲמִשִּׁים שָׁנָה תִּפְקֹד
אוֹתָם כָּל־הַבָּא לִצְבֹא צָבָא לַעֲבֹד עֲבֹדָה בְּאֹהֶל
כד מוֹעֵד: זֹאת עֲבֹדַת מִשְׁפְּחֹת הַגֵּרְשֻׁנִּי לַעֲבֹד
כה וּלְמַשָּׂא: וְנָשְׂאוּ אֶת־יְרִיעֹת הַמִּשְׁכָּן וְאֶת־אֹהֶל
מוֹעֵד מִכְסֵהוּ וּמִכְסֵה הַתַּחַשׁ אֲשֶׁר־עָלָיו
כו מִלְמָעְלָה וְאֶת־מָסַךְ פֶּתַח אֹהֶל מוֹעֵד: וְאֵת קַלְעֵי
הֶחָצֵר וְאֶת־מָסַךְ ׀ פֶּתַח ׀ שַׁעַר הֶחָצֵר אֲשֶׁר
עַל־הַמִּשְׁכָּן וְעַל־הַמִּזְבֵּחַ סָבִיב וְאֵת מֵיתְרֵיהֶם
וְאֶת־כָּל־כְּלֵי עֲבֹדָתָם וְאֵת כָּל־אֲשֶׁר יֵעָשֶׂה לָהֶם
כז וְעָבָדוּ: עַל־פִּי אַהֲרֹן וּבָנָיו תִּהְיֶה כָּל־עֲבֹדַת בְּנֵי
הַגֵּרְשֻׁנִּי לְכָל־מַשָּׂאָם וּלְכֹל עֲבֹדָתָם וּפְקַדְתֶּם
כח עֲלֵהֶם בְּמִשְׁמֶרֶת אֵת כָּל־מַשָּׂאָם: זֹאת עֲבֹדַת
מִשְׁפְּחֹת בְּנֵי הַגֵּרְשֻׁנִּי בְּאֹהֶל מוֹעֵד וּמִשְׁמַרְתָּם
כט בְּיַד אִיתָמָר בֶּן־אַהֲרֹן הַכֹּהֵן: בְּנֵי מְרָרִי
ל לְמִשְׁפְּחֹתָם לְבֵית־אֲבֹתָם תִּפְקֹד אֹתָם: מִבֶּן
שְׁלֹשִׁים שָׁנָה וָמַעְלָה וְעַד בֶּן־חֲמִשִּׁים שָׁנָה
תִּפְקְדֵם כָּל־הַבָּא לַצָּבָא לַעֲבֹד אֶת־עֲבֹדַת אֹהֶל
לא מוֹעֵד: וְזֹאת מִשְׁמֶרֶת מַשָּׂאָם לְכָל־עֲבֹדָתָם בְּאֹהֶל
מוֹעֵד קַרְשֵׁי הַמִּשְׁכָּן וּבְרִיחָיו וְעַמּוּדָיו וַאֲדָנָיו:
לב וְעַמּוּדֵי הֶחָצֵר סָבִיב וְאַדְנֵיהֶם וִיתֵדֹתָם וּמֵיתְרֵיהֶם
לְכָל־כְּלֵיהֶם וּלְכֹל עֲבֹדָתָם וּבְשֵׁמֹת תִּפְקְדוּ אֶת־
לג כְּלֵי מִשְׁמֶרֶת מַשָּׂאָם: זֹאת עֲבֹדַת מִשְׁפְּחֹת בְּנֵי
מְרָרִי לְכָל־עֲבֹדָתָם בְּאֹהֶל מוֹעֵד בְּיַד אִיתָמָר
לד בֶּן־אַהֲרֹן הַכֹּהֵן: וַיִּפְקֹד מֹשֶׁה וְאַהֲרֹן וּנְשִׂיאֵי הָעֵדָה
לה אֶת־בְּנֵי הַקְּהָתִי לְמִשְׁפְּחֹתָם וּלְבֵית אֲבֹתָם: מִבֶּן
שְׁלֹשִׁים שָׁנָה וָמַעְלָה וְעַד בֶּן־חֲמִשִּׁים שָׁנָה כָּל־
לו הַבָּא לַצָּבָא לַעֲבֹדָה בְּאֹהֶל מוֹעֵד: וַיִּהְיוּ פְקֻדֵיהֶם
לז לְמִשְׁפְּחֹתָם אַלְפַּיִם שְׁבַע מֵאוֹת וַחֲמִשִּׁים: אֵלֶּה

21 HASHEM spoke to Moses, saying, 22 "Take a census of the sons of Gershon, as well, according to their fathers' household, according to their families. 23 From thirty years of age and up, until fifty years of age shall you count them, everyone who comes to join the legion to perform work in the Tent of Meeting. 24 This is the work of the Gershonite families: to work and to carry. 25 They shall carry the curtains of the Tabernacle and the Tent of Meeting, its Cover and the tachash cover that is over it from above. And the Screen of the entrance of the Tent of Meeting, 26 the lace-hangings of the Courtyard and the Screen of the entrance of the gate of the Courtyard that were around the Tabernacle and the Altar, their ropes and all the utensils of their service, and everything that is made for them, and they shall serve. 27 According to the word of Aaron and his sons shall be all the work of the sons of Gershonites, their entire burden and their entire work; you shall appoint their entire burden as their charge. 28 This is the work of the sons of the Gershonites in the Tent of Meeting; and their charge shall be under the authority of Ithamar, the son of Aaron the Kohen.

29 "The sons of Merari — according to their families, according to their fathers' household shall you count them. 30 From thirty years of age and up, until fifty years of age shall you count them, everyone who comes to the legion to perform the work of the Tent of Meeting. 31 This is the charge of their burden for all of their work in the Tent of Meeting: the planks of the Tabernacle, its bars, its pillars, and its sockets; 32 the pillars of the Courtyard all around and their sockets, their pegs and their ropes for all of their utensils and for all of their work. You shall appoint them by name to the utensils they are to carry on their watch. 33 This is the work of the families of the sons of Merari according to all their work in the Tent of Meeting, under the authority of Ithamar, son of Aaron the Kohen."

34 Moses and Aaron and the leaders of the assembly counted the sons of the Kohathites, according to their families, according to their fathers' household. 35 From thirty years of age and up, until fifty years of age, everyone who comes to the legion for the work in the Tent of Meeting. 36 Their countings according to their families were two thousand, seven hundred and fifty. 37 These are the

פְקוּדֵי֙ מִשְׁפְּחֹ֣ת הַקְּהָתִ֔י כָּל־הָעֹבֵ֖ד בְּאֹ֣הֶל
מוֹעֵ֑ד אֲשֶׁ֨ר פָּקַ֤ד מֹשֶׁה֙ וְאַֽהֲרֹ֔ן עַל־פִּ֥י יְהוָ֖ה
שני לח בְּיַד־מֹשֶֽׁה׃ וּפְקוּדֵ֖י בְּנֵ֣י גֵרְשׁ֑וֹן
לט לְמִשְׁפְּחוֹתָ֖ם וּלְבֵ֥ית אֲבֹתָֽם׃ מִבֶּ֨ן שְׁלֹשִׁ֤ים שָׁנָה֙
וָמַ֔עְלָה וְעַ֖ד בֶּן־חֲמִשִּׁ֣ים שָׁנָ֑ה כָּל־הַבָּא֙ לַצָּבָ֔א
מ לַעֲבֹדָ֖ה בְּאֹ֥הֶל מוֹעֵֽד׃ וַיִּֽהְיוּ֙ פְּקֻ֣דֵיהֶ֔ם לְמִשְׁפְּחֹתָ֖ם
לְבֵ֣ית אֲבֹתָ֑ם אַלְפַּ֕יִם וְשֵׁ֥שׁ מֵא֖וֹת וּשְׁלֹשִֽׁים׃
מא אֵ֣לֶּה פְקוּדֵ֗י מִשְׁפְּחֹת֙ בְּנֵ֣י גֵרְשׁ֔וֹן כָּל־הָעֹבֵ֖ד
בְּאֹ֣הֶל מוֹעֵ֑ד אֲשֶׁ֨ר פָּקַ֥ד מֹשֶׁ֛ה וְאַהֲרֹ֖ן עַל־פִּ֥י
מב יְהוָֽה׃ וּפְקוּדֵ֕י מִשְׁפְּחֹ֖ת בְּנֵ֣י מְרָרִ֑י לְמִשְׁפְּחֹתָ֖ם
מג לְבֵ֥ית אֲבֹתָֽם׃ מִבֶּ֨ן שְׁלֹשִׁ֤ים שָׁנָה֙ וָמַ֔עְלָה וְעַ֖ד
בֶּן־חֲמִשִּׁ֣ים שָׁנָ֑ה כָּל־הַבָּא֙ לַצָּבָ֔א לַעֲבֹדָ֖ה
מד בְּאֹ֥הֶל מוֹעֵֽד׃ וַיִּהְי֥וּ פְקֻדֵיהֶ֖ם לְמִשְׁפְּחֹתָ֑ם שְׁלֹ֥שֶׁת
מה אֲלָפִ֖ים וּמָאתָֽיִם׃ אֵ֣לֶּה פְקוּדֵ֔י מִשְׁפְּחֹ֖ת בְּנֵ֣י
מְרָרִ֑י אֲשֶׁ֨ר פָּקַ֤ד מֹשֶׁה֙ וְאַהֲרֹ֔ן עַל־פִּ֥י יְהוָ֖ה
מו בְּיַד־מֹשֶֽׁה׃ כָּל־הַפְּקֻדִ֡ים אֲשֶׁר֩ פָּקַ֨ד מֹשֶׁ֧ה וְאַהֲרֹ֛ן
וּנְשִׂיאֵ֥י יִשְׂרָאֵ֖ל אֶת־הַלְוִיִּ֑ם לְמִשְׁפְּחֹתָ֖ם וּלְבֵ֥ית
מז אֲבֹתָֽם׃ מִבֶּ֨ן שְׁלֹשִׁ֤ים שָׁנָה֙ וָמַ֔עְלָה וְעַ֖ד בֶּן־
חֲמִשִּׁ֣ים שָׁנָ֑ה כָּל־הַבָּ֗א לַעֲבֹ֨ד עֲבֹדַ֧ת עֲבֹדָ֛ה
מח וַעֲבֹדַ֥ת מַשָּׂ֖א בְּאֹ֥הֶל מוֹעֵֽד׃ וַיִּֽהְי֖וּ פְּקֻדֵיהֶ֑ם
מט שְׁמֹנַ֣ת אֲלָפִ֔ים וַחֲמֵ֥שׁ מֵא֖וֹת וּשְׁמֹנִֽים׃ עַל־פִּ֨י
יְהוָ֜ה פָּקַ֤ד אוֹתָם֙ בְּיַד־מֹשֶׁ֔ה אִ֥ישׁ אִ֛ישׁ עַל־
עֲבֹדָת֖וֹ וְעַל־מַשָּׂא֑וֹ וּפְקֻדָ֕יו אֲשֶׁר־צִוָּ֥ה יְהוָ֖ה
אֶת־מֹשֶֽׁה׃

ה שלישי א-ב וַיְדַבֵּ֥ר יְהוָ֖ה אֶל־מֹשֶׁ֥ה לֵּאמֹֽר׃ צַ֚ו אֶת־בְּנֵ֣י יִשְׂרָאֵ֔ל
וִֽישַׁלְּחוּ֙ מִן־הַֽמַּחֲנֶ֔ה כָּל־צָר֖וּעַ וְכָל־זָ֑ב וְכֹ֖ל
ג טָמֵ֥א לָנָֽפֶשׁ׃ מִזָּכָ֤ר עַד־נְקֵבָה֙ תְּשַׁלֵּ֔חוּ אֶל־מִח֥וּץ

BAAL HATURIM ELUCIDATED

V

2. {The Baal HaTurim's comments to this verse appear at v. 6 below.}

countings of the Kohathite families, all who work in the Tent
of Meeting, whom Moses and Aaron counted, according to
the word of Hashem, *under the authority of Moses.*

38 *The countings of the sons of Gershon according to their*
families, and according to their fathers' household; 39 *from*
thirty years of age and up, until fifty years of age, every-
one who comes to the legion for the work in the Tent of
Meeting. 40 *Their countings according to their families, ac-*
cording to their fathers' household were two thousand, six
hundred and thirty. 41 *These are the countings of the families*
of the sons of Gershon, all who work in the Tent of Meeting,
whom Moses and Aaron counted, according to the word of
Hashem.

42 *The countings of the families of the sons of Merari,*
according to their families, according to their fathers' house-
hold; 43 *from thirty years of age and up, until fifty years of*
age, everyone who comes to the legion, for the work in the
Tent of Meeting. 44 *Their countings according to their families*
were three thousand, two hundred. 45 *These were the count-*
ings of the families of the sons of Merari, whom Moses and
Aaron counted, according to the word of Hashem, *through*
Moses.

46 *All those counted of the Levites, whom Moses and*
Aaron and the leaders of Israel counted, according to their
families and according to their fathers' household; 47 *from*
thirty years of age and up, until fifty years of age, everyone
who comes to perform the work of service and the work of
burden in the Tent of Meeting. 48 *Their countings were eight*
thousand, five hundred and eighty. 49 *He counted them*
according to the word of Hashem, *through Moses, every man*
over his work and over his burden; and his count [was] as
Hashem *had commanded Moses.*

5 1 Hashem *spoke to Moses, saying,* 2 *"Command the Children*
of Israel that they shall expel from the camp every metzora
and every zav, and everyone contaminated by a human
corpse. 3 *Male and female alike shall you expel, to the outside*

BAAL HATURIM ELUCIDATED

3. {The Baal HaTurim's comment to מִזָּכָר עַד נְקֵבָה תְּשַׁלֵּחוּ, which appears at this point in most editions as an independent comment, is presented at verse 6 below, as part of the comment beginning כִּי יַעֲשׂוּ.}

לַמַּחֲנֶה תְּשַׁלְּחוּם וְלֹא יְטַמְּאוּ אֶת־מַחֲנֵיהֶם אֲשֶׁר
ד אֲנִי שֹׁכֵן בְּתוֹכָם: וַיַּעֲשׂוּ־כֵן בְּנֵי יִשְׂרָאֵל וַיְשַׁלְּחוּ
אוֹתָם אֶל־מִחוּץ לַמַּחֲנֶה כַּאֲשֶׁר דִּבֶּר יהוה אֶל־
מֹשֶׁה כֵּן עָשׂוּ בְּנֵי יִשְׂרָאֵל:
ה־ו וַיְדַבֵּר יהוה אֶל־מֹשֶׁה לֵּאמֹר: דַּבֵּר אֶל־בְּנֵי יִשְׂרָאֵל
אִישׁ אוֹ־אִשָּׁה כִּי יַעֲשׂוּ מִכָּל־חַטֹּאת הָאָדָם

בעל הטורים

ה (ג) וְלֹא יְטַמְּאוּ. ב׳ – ״וְלֹא יְטַמְּאוּ אֶת מַחֲנֵיהֶם״; ״וְלֹא יְטַמְּאוּ עוֹד בֵּית יִשְׂרָאֵל שֵׁם קָדְשִׁי״. שֶׁאִם יְטַמְּאוּ אֶת מַחֲנֵיהֶם, מְטַמְּאִין אֶת שֵׁם קָדְשִׁי, כְּדִכְתִיב ״לְמַעַן טַמֵּא אֶת מִקְדָּשִׁי וּלְחַלֵּל אֶת שֵׁם קָדְשִׁי״:

(ו) כִּי יַעֲשׂוּ מִכָּל חַטֹּאת הָאָדָם. סָמַךְ ״חַטֹּאת הָאָדָם״ לְשִׁלּוּחַ טְמֵאִים. שֶׁעַל יְדֵי חַטֹּאת הָאָדָם, שֶׁחָטָא אָדָם הָרִאשׁוֹן שֶׁאָכַל מִן הָעֵץ, וְהַנָּחָשׁ הִטְעָה אֶת הָאִשָּׁה, וְהִיא הוֹצִיאָה שֵׁם רַע עַל אָדָם, לָקוּ שְׁלָשְׁתָּן – הַנָּחָשׁ בְּצָרַעַת; וְהָאִשָּׁה בְּזִיבָה; וְהָאָדָם בְּמִיתָה. וּכְסֵדֶר קִלְלָתָם מוֹנֶה אוֹתָם כָּאן – ״צָרוּעַ״ דְּהַיְנוּ הַנָּחָשׁ; וְ״זָב״ דְּהַיְנוּ הָאִשָּׁה; וְ״טָמֵא לָנָפֶשׁ״

BAAL HATURIM ELUCIDATED

❏ וְלֹא יְטַמְּאוּ — **SO THAT THEY SHOULD NOT DEFILE.** [The masoretic note, ב׳, means that] this word appears twice in the *Tanach*: (i) here, וְלֹא יְטַמְּאוּ אֶת מַחֲנֵיהֶם, *so that they should not defile their camps;* and (ii) וְלֹא יְטַמְּאוּ עוֹד בֵּית יִשְׂרָאֵל שֵׁם קָדְשִׁי, *The House of Israel will no longer defile My holy Name* (*Ezekiel* 43:7). [The similarity of expression indicates] that if they will defile their camps, they would be defiling *My holy Name.* As it is written, לְמַעַן טַמֵּא אֶת מִקְדָּשִׁי וּלְחַלֵּל אֶת שֵׁם קָדְשִׁי, *In order to defile My Sanctuary and to desecrate My holy Name*[1] (*Leviticus* 20:3).[2]

6. כִּי יַעֲשׂוּ מִכָּל חַטֹּאת הָאָדָם — **WHO COMMITS ANY OF THE SINS OF MAN.** The Torah

1. The Midrash explains the implication of *to defile My Sanctuary and to desecrate My holy Name:* It teaches that one who commits the sins mentioned in that passage defiles the Sanctuary, desecrates the Name, causes the *Shechinah* [Immanent Presence of God] to depart, throws Israel at the mercy of the sword and causes them to be exiled from their land (*Toras Kohanim, Kedoshim, parshasa* 10:4 [8:4]).

In that verse, God addresses the sin of Molech worship; such depravity serves *to defile My Sanctuary and to desecrate My holy Name.* In the verse from *Ezekiel,* He broadens this concept to include all forms of idolatry as causing the defilement of *My holy Name.* Based on the similarity of expression in our verse and in *Ezekiel,* the Baal HaTurim expands the concept even further, adding laxity in the observance of the laws regarding *tumah* and *taharah* [spiritual contamination and spiritual purity of the physical aspect] — especially with respect to the *Mishkan* [Tabernacle] and its Courtyard — as causing God's holy Name to be defiled (*VeChur LaZahav,* based on the Baal HaTurim's comment to *Leviticus* 13:44; see note 2 for an alternative interpretation of the Baal HaTurim's comment here).

2. According to *Rashi* (cited by the Baal HaTurim in *Peirush HaTur HaAroch* to *Leviticus* 20:3), the term מִקְדָּשִׁי, literally, *that which is holy unto Me,* of *Leviticus* 20:3, does not refer to the Sanctuary; rather, it refers to כְּנֶסֶת יִשְׂרָאֵל, *the Assembly of Israel,* which is sanctified unto God. Thus, מַחֲנֵיהֶם, *their camps,* of our verse, and מִקְדָּשִׁי, *that which is holy unto Me,* of *Leviticus,* both refer to the same thing, the Assembly of Israel — if they will defile their camps [i.e., themselves], they would be defiling God's holy Name (Y.S.).

of the camp shall you expel them, so that they should not defile their camps, among which I dwell." [4] *The Children of Israel did so: They expelled them to the outside of the camp, as HASHEM had spoken to Moses — so did the Children of Israel do.*

[5] *HASHEM spoke to Moses, saying,* [6] *"Speak to the Children of Israel: A man or woman who commits any of the sins of man,*

BAAL HATURIM ELUCIDATED

juxtaposed the phrase *the sins of man* [which can also be understood as *the sins of Adam*[3]] with the passage concerning the expulsion of the impure. [The reason for this juxtaposition is] that as a consequence of חַטֹּאת הָאָדָם, *the sins of Adam* — that is, whereas Adam, the first man, sinned by eating from the Tree [of Knowledge], and that sin came about because the serpent enticed Eve, and she in turn slandered Adam[4] — all three of them were punished. The serpent was afflicted with *tzaraas*;[5] the woman with menstrual flow;[6] and the man with death.[7] All three of these punishments are mentioned in this passage (v. 2 above) following the order of their curses:[7a] [כָּל] צָרוּעַ, [*every*] *metzora,* i.e., the serpent [is mentioned first]; then וְ[כָל] זָב, *and* [*every*] *zav,* i.e., the woman [Eve];[8] and וְכֹל טָמֵא לָנָפֶשׁ, *and everyone contaminated by a human corpse,* i.e., the man [Adam], who was punished by the fulfillment of the verse, [*But of the Tree of Knowledge of Good and Bad, you must not eat thereof: for on the day you eat of*

3. On a simple level, הָאָדָם of our verse means *the man* and refers to the average person. The phrase חַטֹּאת הָאָדָם, *the sins of man,* is thus understood as any sins that a human being may commit. On a deeper level, however, the *Zohar* (*Nasso* 122a) understands הָאָדָם as a reference to אָדָם קַדְמָאָה, *Adam, the first man,* who is called הָאָדָם, *the man* or *the Adam,* no less than twenty-two times in the story of Creation (see *Genesis* 1:27-4:1). [Indeed, the first Scriptural use of הָאָדָם that refers to humankind in general appears during the life of Noah (*Genesis* 6:1), some 1536 years later.] The Baal HaTurim, also, interprets our verse as referring to Adam.

4. The Midrash records the incident of the serpent's enticing Eve to eat from the Tree of Knowledge: When the evil serpent realized that it would not succeed in tempting Adam to eat from the tree, it thought that Eve might be easier to entice. It sat near Eve and engaged her in conversation. It said, "Although you tell me that God commanded us not to touch this tree, behold, I am touching it and I am not dead. You too, if you touch the tree, you will not die" . . . Eve succumbed and touched the Tree of Knowledge, but did not die. She then slandered Adam in her mind, "All that my teacher [i.e., Adam] instructed me is false." And once she arrived at that conclusion, it was easy for the serpent to get her to eat the forbidden fruit. "Although God commanded us not to eat from this tree, behold, I am eating from it and I am not dead. You too, if you eat from it, you will not die." And so she ate and gave Adam to eat also (*Avos DeRabbi Nosson* 1:5-6).

5. See *Bereishis Rabbah* 20:4; *Shemos Rabbah* 3:13.

6. See *Eruvin* 100b.

7. See *Genesis* 2:17 and 3:3,19.

7a. God first admonished the serpent (*Genesis* 3:14-15), then Eve (v. 16), and finally Adam (vv. 17-19). And that is the order of our passage (A.S.).

Alternatively: The Baal HaTurim refers to the severity of the punishment (*VeChur LaZahav;* see note 9 below).

8. Although the verse uses the masculine form זָב, both זָב and זָבָה are included; for, as the Baal HaTurim points out below, the verse continues, מִזָּכָר עַד נְקֵבָה, *male and female alike* (v. 3 above).

ז לִמְעֹל מַעַל בַּיהוָה וְאָשְׁמָה הַנֶּפֶשׁ הַהִוא: וְהִתְוַדּוּ
אֶת־חַטָּאתָם אֲשֶׁר עָשׂוּ וְהֵשִׁיב אֶת־אֲשָׁמוֹ
בְּרֹאשׁוֹ וַחֲמִישִׁתוֹ יֹסֵף עָלָיו וְנָתַן לַאֲשֶׁר אָשַׁם
ח לוֹ: וְאִם־אֵין לָאִישׁ גֹּאֵל לְהָשִׁיב הָאָשָׁם אֵלָיו
הָאָשָׁם הַמּוּשָׁב לַיהוָה לַכֹּהֵן מִלְּבַד אֵיל הַכִּפֻּרִים
ט אֲשֶׁר יְכַפֶּר־בּוֹ עָלָיו: וְכָל־תְּרוּמָה לְכָל־קָדְשֵׁי
י בְנֵי־יִשְׂרָאֵל אֲשֶׁר־יַקְרִיבוּ לַכֹּהֵן לוֹ יִהְיֶה: וְאִישׁ

בעל הטורים

דְּהַיְנוּ הָאָדָם שֶׁנֶּעֱנַשׁ בְּ״מוֹת תָּמוּת״. {״מִזָּכָר עַד נְקֵבָה תְּשַׁלֵּחוּ״, כְּשֵׁם שֶׁנִּתְגָּרְשׁוּ אָדָם וְחַוָּה וְנָחָשׁ מִגַּן עֵדֶן. וְסָמַךְ פָּרָשַׁת סוֹטָה, לְפִי שֶׁהַנָּחָשׁ בָּא עַל חַוָּה וְנָפְלוּ יְרֵכָיו, דִּכְתִיב ״עַל גְּחֹנְךָ תֵלֵךְ״. וְסָמַךְ פָּרָשַׁת נָזִיר, עַל שֵׁם הַפְּרִי שֶׁאָכַל אָדָם הָרִאשׁוֹן, ״עֲנָבֵמוֹ עִנְּבֵי רוֹשׁ״:}

❑ **לִמְעֹל מַעַל בַּה׳.** לוֹמַר שֶׁכָּל הַמַּטֶּה דִּינוֹ שֶׁל גֵּר, כְּאִלּוּ מַטֶּה דִּינוֹ שֶׁל מָעְלָה:

(ו־ז) **הַנֶּפֶשׁ הַהִוא וְהִתְוַדּוּ.** רֶמֶז שֶׁכָּל הַמּוּמָתִים מִתְוַדִּים בְּעֵת יְצִיאַת הַנֶּפֶשׁ:

(ט) **וְכָל תְּרוּמָה לְכָל קָדְשֵׁי בְנֵי יִשְׂרָאֵל אֲשֶׁר יַקְרִיבוּ לַכֹּהֵן לוֹ יִהְיֶה.** מוֹקֵי לָהּ בְּסִפְרֵי

BAAL HATURIM ELUCIDATED

it,] מוֹת תָּמוּת, *you shall surely die* (*Genesis* 2:17).[9] [The above passage continues,][9a] מִזָּכָר עַד נְקֵבָה תְּשַׁלֵּחוּ, *male and female alike shall you expel* (v. 3), just as Adam, Eve, and the serpent were expelled from the Garden of Eden.

The Torah juxtaposed the passage of a *sotah* [wife suspected of faithlessness (vv. 11-31), with our passage], for the serpent came upon Eve[10] and, as a

9. *Rashi,* following *Pesachim* 67a, explains that the Israelite encampment comprised three concentric areas: (a) The Courtyard of the Tabernacle was מַחֲנֵה שְׁכִינָה, the *camp of the Divine Presence;* (b) the area where the Levites camped was called מַחֲנֵה לְוִיָּה, *the Levite camp;* and (c) the remainder of the national encampment was called מַחֲנֵה יִשְׂרָאֵל, *the Israelite camp.* The *metzora* would be sent out of all three camps (see *Leviticus* 13:46); the *zav* and *zavah* would be permitted to remain in the Israelite camp, but would be sent out of the other two; and the one contaminated by a human corpse would be permitted to remain in the Israelite and Levite camps, but would be sent out of the camp of the Divine Presence.

Accordingly, the types of contamination are listed in the order of descending severity.

9a. The text follows the early printed editions and *Shoham Yakar's* manuscript edition which present the passage enclosed in braces as part of this comment. Most printed editions have "improved' the text by presenting this passage at verse 3 above.

10. *Shabbos* 146a; *Yevamos* 103b — At the moment that the serpent came upon Eve, he cast impurity into her. *Rashi* (to *Shabbos*) explains the expression בָּא הַנָּחָשׁ עַל חַוָּה, *the serpent came upon Eve,* as referring to adulterous cohabitation. This is implied by Eve's response. When God confronted her regarding her eating from the forbidden tree, she said, "הַנָּחָשׁ הִשִּׁיאַנִי, *The serpent deceived me*" (*Genesis* 3:13), using the unusual verb הִשִּׁיאַנִי instead of הִטְעַנִי for *he deceived me,* for that verb is related to the verb הִשִּׂיא, *to marry off.*

This Talmudic passage requires explanation: Man and woman were created as completely pure of spirit. Indeed, *tumah* (impurity) could not attach itself to them in any manner whatever. All this, until the serpent seduced Eve to eat the forbidden fruit. When she succumbed,

by committing a trespass against HASHEM, and that person
shall become guilty — [7] *they shall confess their sin that*
they committed; he shall make restitution for his guilt in
its principal amount and add its fifth to it, and give it to the
one to whom he is indebted. [8] *If the man has no kinsman*
to whom the debt can be returned, the returned debt is
for HASHEM, for the Kohen, aside from the ram of atone-
ment with which he shall provide him atonement. [9] *And*
every portion from any of the holies that the Children
of Israel shall bring to the Kohen shall be his. [10] *A man's*

BAAL HATURIM ELUCIDATED

consequence, his thigh collapsed,[11] as it is written, [*HASHEM God said to the serpent . . .*] עַל גְּחֹנְךָ תֵלֵךְ, *upon your belly shall you go* (*Genesis* 3:14). And to the passage of the *sotah,* the Torah juxtaposed the passage concerning a Nazirite, because the tree from which Adam ate [was a grape vine, as the Midrash derives from the verse,] עֲנָבֵמוֹ עִנְּבֵי רוֹשׁ, *their grapes are grapes of gall* (*Deuteronomy* 32:32).[12]

❑ לִמְעֹל מַעַל בַּה׳ — **BY COMMITTING A TRESPASS AGAINST HASHEM.** This indicates that whoever perverts judgment against a convert[13] is considered as if he perverted judgment against Heaven.[14]

6-7. הַנֶּפֶשׁ הַהִוא. וְהִתְוַדּוּ — **THAT PERSON. THEY SHALL CONFESS.** This is an allusion to the Talmudic teaching that anyone put to death by a court of law should confess at the time of execution.[15]

9. וְכָל תְּרוּמָה לְכָל קָדְשֵׁי בְנֵי יִשְׂרָאֵל אֲשֶׁר יַקְרִיבוּ לַכֹּהֵן לוֹ יִהְיֶה — **AND EVERY PORTION FROM ANY OF THE HOLIES THAT THE CHILDREN OF ISRAEL SHALL BRING TO THE KOHEN SHALL BE HIS.** The halachic Midrash *Sifrei* interprets this verse as referring to the

the serpent's success injected impurity into her, i.e., made her and her descendants susceptible to impurity. The Torah alludes to this with the word הִשִּׁיאַנִי, which may be understood homiletically as "he married me," because the serpent's ultimate intention was to cause Adam to sin and, as a consequence, to die. The serpent hoped that he would then be free to marry Eve (*Maharsha* to *Yevamos* 103b).

11. Part of the *sotah's* punishment (see vv. 21-22,27 below).

12. The Talmud and Midrash record a dispute regarding the species of the Tree of Knowledge. According to one view it was a grapevine, as alluded to by the verse, עֲנָבֵמוֹ עִנְּבֵי רוֹשׁ, *their grapes are grapes of gall,* אַשְׁכְּלֹת מְרֹרֹת, *clusters of bitterness,* i.e., the grapes that Adam and Eve ate were the cause of the bitterness [of death] in the world (*Berachos* 40a; *Bereishis Rabbah* 15:7). The Baal HaTurim finds allusions to the other views in his comments to *Genesis* 1:29 and 3:11; and *Numbers* 20:10.

13. Our passage speaks of one who has sworn falsely in court regarding money he owed to a convert (see *Rashi* to v. 8, s.v., לְהָשִׁיב הָאָשָׁם אֵלָיו).

14. *Chagigah* 5a; see also the Baal HaTurim to *Leviticus* 19:32, s.v., אֲנִי ה׳; see also *Deuteronomy* 10:18 with *Rashi;* and *Deuteronomy* 24:13 and 27:19.

One who steals from a convert profanes God's holy Name in the eyes of the convert who has come to take refuge under His wing. Thus, the person who steals from a convert is guilty of *committing a trespass against HASHEM* (*Sforno*).

15. See *Sanhedrin* 43b.

אֶת־קֳדָשָׁיו לוֹ יִהְיוּ אִישׁ אֲשֶׁר־יִתֵּן לַכֹּהֵן לוֹ יִהְיֶה׃
רביעי יא־יב וַיְדַבֵּר יְהוָה אֶל־מֹשֶׁה לֵּאמֹר׃ דַּבֵּר אֶל־בְּנֵי
יִשְׂרָאֵל וְאָמַרְתָּ אֲלֵהֶם אִישׁ אִישׁ כִּי־תִשְׂטֶה
יג אִשְׁתּוֹ וּמָעֲלָה בוֹ מָעַל׃ וְשָׁכַב אִישׁ אֹתָהּ שִׁכְבַת־
זֶרַע וְנֶעְלַם מֵעֵינֵי אִישָׁהּ וְנִסְתְּרָה וְהִיא נִטְמָאָה
יד וְעֵד אֵין בָּהּ וְהִוא לֹא נִתְפָּשָׂה׃ וְעָבַר עָלָיו
רוּחַ־קִנְאָה וְקִנֵּא אֶת־אִשְׁתּוֹ וְהִוא נִטְמָאָה אוֹ־
עָבַר עָלָיו רוּחַ־קִנְאָה וְקִנֵּא אֶת־אִשְׁתּוֹ וְהִיא
טו לֹא נִטְמָאָה׃ וְהֵבִיא הָאִישׁ אֶת־אִשְׁתּוֹ אֶל־
הַכֹּהֵן וְהֵבִיא אֶת־קָרְבָּנָהּ עָלֶיהָ עֲשִׂירִת הָאֵיפָה
קֶמַח שְׂעֹרִים לֹא־יִצֹק עָלָיו שֶׁמֶן וְלֹא־יִתֵּן
עָלָיו לְבֹנָה כִּי־מִנְחַת קְנָאֹת הוּא מִנְחַת זִכָּרוֹן
טז מַזְכֶּרֶת עָוֺן׃ וְהִקְרִיב אֹתָהּ הַכֹּהֵן וְהֶעֱמִדָהּ

בעל הטורים

בְּבִכּוּרִים. "יַקְרִיבוּ" בְּגִימַטְרִיָּא הֵם הַבִּכּוּרִים׃

(י) וְאִישׁ אֶת קֳדָשָׁיו לוֹ יִהְיוּ. וּסְמִיךְ לֵהּ פָּרָשַׁת סוֹטָה. לוֹמַר שֶׁמִּי שֶׁמַּשְׁהֶה קִנֵּי הַנָּשִׁים וְאֵינוֹ מַקְרִיבָם, כְּדֶרֶךְ שֶׁעָשׂוּ בְּנֵי עֵלִי, הָוֵי כְּאִלּוּ שְׁכָבוּם׃

BAAL HATURIM ELUCIDATED

bikkurim. [16] The *gematria* of יַקְרִיבוּ, [*they*] *shall bring* (328), is equal to that of הֵם הַבִּכּוּרִים, *They are the bikkurim.* [17]

10. וְאִישׁ אֶת קֳדָשָׁיו לוֹ יִהְיוּ — A MAN'S HOLIES SHALL BE HIS.[17a] Juxtaposed to this verse is the passage concerning the *sotah* [wife suspected of faithlessness] (vv. 11-31). This indicates that a *Kohen* who delays, rather than offer in timely fashion, the bird offerings of the women — as the sons of Eli did — is

16. בִּכּוּרִים, *bikkurim* (see *Deuteronomy* 26:1-11), literally, *the early ones,* are the first fruits to ripen from each year's crop of the seven species with which the Torah praises *Eretz Yisrael* — *A land of wheat, barley, grapevine, fig and pomegranate; a land of oil-olives and date-honey* (*Deuteronomy* 8:8). They are taken to the *Beis HaMikdash* where those who bring them are greeted with great festivity and ceremony (see *Mishnayos Bikkurim,* Ch. 3). The Midrash (*Sifrei* 5, cited by *Rashi*) derives from our verse that after the *bikkurim* have been brought to the *Beis HaMikdash* they are presented to the *mishmar* (watch) of Kohanim who are serving on that day. They are then distributed to the individual Kohanim of that *mishmar* and each Kohen's share becomes his personal property. All the restrictions that apply to *terumah* also apply to *bikkurim,* with the added stringency that *bikkurim* may not be removed from Jerusalem (see *Rambam, Hilchos Bikkurim* 3:1-5 and 4:14).

17. *Peirush HaRokeach.*

17a. *Rashi* (citing *Sifrei*) points out that this verse teaches that the owner of the priestly gifts and tithes retains the prerogative regarding which Kohen or Levite they will be presented to.

holies shall be his, and what a man gives to the Kohen shall
be his."
11 *HASHEM spoke to Moses, saying,* 12 *"Speak to the*
Children of Israel and say to them: Any man whose wife
shall go astray and commit a trespass against him; 13 *and*
a man could have lain with her carnally, but it was hidden
from the eyes of her husband, and she became sec-
luded and could have been defiled — but there was no
witness against her — and she had not been forced; 14 *and*
a spirit of jealousy had passed over him and he had warned
his wife, and she had become defiled, or a spirit of jealousy
had passed over him and he had warned his wife and she
had not become defiled. 15 *The man shall bring his wife to*
the Kohen and he shall bring her offering for her, a
tenth-ephah of barley flour; he shall not pour oil over it and
shall not put frankincense upon it, for it is a meal-offering of
jealousies, a meal-offering of remembrance, a reminder of
iniquity.
16 *"The Kohen shall bring her near and have her stand*

BAAL HATURIM ELUCIDATED

considered as if he committed adultery with them.[18]

12. {The Baal HaTurim's comment to תִשְׂטֶה appears at 25:1 below.}

13. {The Baal HaTurim's comment to מֵעֵינֵי appears at *Leviticus* 4:13.}

15. {The Baal HaTurim's comment to וְלֹא יִתֵּן appears at *Exodus* 12:23.}

18. Women from distant places would come to the *Beis HaMikdash* to bring obligatory bird offerings [such as those offered after childbirth (see *Leviticus* 12:8) or upon recovering from *zavah* status (see *Leviticus* 15:29-30)]. The Kohanim were generally alacritous regarding the Altar offerings, so that offerings were almost always completed on the day they were brought to the *Beis HaMikdash.* However, before the *Beis HaMikdash* was built, while the national Altar stood in the *Mishkan* [Tabernacle] at Shiloh, there was a period when the leading Kohanim — Hophni and Phinehas, the sons of Eli the Kohen Gadol — would impose obstacles and would delay bringing any Altar offerings until they had extorted meat from the owner's portion. Moreover, they would ignore any bird offerings as long as animal offerings were being brought. Having no confidence in the Kohanim, the righteous women would remain in Shiloh until they had seen their birds actually offered on the Altar. Sometimes a woman would have to stay there an extra night before she could return home to her family. Because the dishonorable behavior displayed by Eli's sons prevented the women from rejoining their husbands and from procreating, Scripture (*I Samuel* 2:22) regards Hophni and Phinehas' actions as tantamount to adultery (*Shabbos* 55b).

In the juxtaposition of the statement, *and what a man gives to the Kohen shall be his,* with the passage about the *sotah,* the Baal HaTurim sees a reflection of Hophni and Phinehas, who were so concerned with their portion of "shall be his" that they neglected bringing the righteous women's bird offerings. As a result they are considered to have sinned with a *sotah* (*VeChur LaZahav*).

ה/יז-יח

יז לִפְנֵי יהוה: וְלָקַח הַכֹּהֵן מַיִם קְדֹשִׁים בִּכְלִי־חָרֶשׂ
וּמִן־הֶעָפָר אֲשֶׁר יִהְיֶה בְּקַרְקַע הַמִּשְׁכָּן יִקַּח
יח הַכֹּהֵן וְנָתַן אֶל־הַמָּיִם: וְהֶעֱמִיד הַכֹּהֵן אֶת־הָאִשָּׁה
לִפְנֵי יהוה וּפָרַע אֶת־רֹאשׁ הָאִשָּׁה וְנָתַן עַל־כַּפֶּיהָ
אֵת מִנְחַת הַזִּכָּרוֹן מִנְחַת קְנָאֹת הִוא וּבְיַד הַכֹּהֵן

בעל הטורים

(יז) **וּמִן הֶעָפָר אֲשֶׁר יִהְיֶה בְּקַרְקַע הַמִּשְׁכָּן.** בִּירוּשַׁלְמִי – לָמָּה מַיִם וְעָפָר {וּכְתָב}? מַיִם, מִמָּקוֹם שֶׁבָּאת; עָפָר, לְמָקוֹם שֶׁהוֹלֶכֶת; כְּתָב, שֶׁהִיא עֲתִידָה לִתֵּן דִּין וְחֶשְׁבּוֹן:

❑ **בְּקַרְקַע.** ב׳ בַּמָּסוֹרֶת – ״וּמִן הֶעָפָר אֲשֶׁר יִהְיֶה בְּקַרְקַע הַמִּשְׁכָּן״; וְאִידָךְ ״וְאִם יִסָּתְרוּ מִנֶּגֶד עֵינַי בְּקַרְקַע הַיָּם״. פֵּרוּשׁ, ״וְאִם יִסָּתְרוּ מִנֶּגֶד עֵינַי״, שֶׁנִּסְתְּרָה ״וְנֶעְלַם מֵעֵינֵי אִישָׁהּ״, ״בְּקַרְקַע הַיָּם״, יִבְדֹּק אוֹתָהּ עַל יְדֵי קַרְקַע וָיָם, דְּהַיְנוּ מַיִם וְעָפָר:

❑ **בְּקַרְקַע הַמִּשְׁכָּן.** עַ״ן מִדְּלֵי – מִפְּנֵי ״וְעֵין נֹאֵף שָׁמְרָה נֶשֶׁף לֵאמֹר, לֹא תְשׁוּרֵנִי עָיִן״:

BAAL HATURIM ELUCIDATED

17. וּמִן הֶעָפָר אֲשֶׁר יִהְיֶה בְּקַרְקַע הַמִּשְׁכָּן — FROM THE EARTH THAT WILL BE ON THE FLOOR OF THE TABERNACLE. The Talmud Yerushalmi[19] asks: Why [does the *sotah's* ordeal involve] water and earth [as stated in this verse], {and writing[19a]} [see v. 23]? [The Talmud explains that these three substances remind the *sotah* of the three phases of her life — past, present and future:] Water, from where she came;[20] earth, to where she is headed;[21] writing, for she is destined to give an accounting[22] and a reckoning.[23]

❑ **בְּקַרְקַע — ON THE FLOOR.** The masoretic note, ב׳, means that this word appears twice in the *Tanach*: (i) here, וּמִן הֶעָפָר אֲשֶׁר יִהְיֶה בְּקַרְקַע הַמִּשְׁכָּן, *from the earth that will be on the floor of the Tabernacle;* and (ii) וְאִם יִסָּתְרוּ מִנֶּגֶד עֵינַי בְּקַרְקַע הַיָּם, *and if they conceal themselves from My eyes on the floor of the sea* (*Amos* 9:3). The

19. *Sotah* 2:2; cf. *Bamidbar Rabbah* 9:15.

19a. Virtually every printed edition omits this word. It does appear, however, in the Talmud Yerushalmi cited by the Baal HaTurim and in *Shoham Yakar's* manuscript edition.

20. This refers to either the putrid drop (see note 22 below) or the amniotic fluid in which the embryo develops in the womb.

21. With each passing moment she comes closer to the earth in which she will eventually be buried.

22. That is, the writing alludes to the Heavenly book in which all of man's deeds are inscribed (*Avos* 2:1). That book is opened before the Heavenly Tribunal when man is called upon to give his final accounting when his life on earth has ended. As another Mishnah (cited in the *Yerushalmi*) teaches: Consider three things and you will not come into the grip of sin: Know from where you come, to where you are going and before Whom you are destined to give an accounting and a reckoning. From where you came — from a putrid drop [i.e., if the ovum had not been fertilized it would have putrefied and disintegrated]; to where you are going — to a place of dust, worms and maggots; and before Whom you are destined to give an accounting and a reckoning — before the King over kings, the Holy One, Blessed is He (*Avos* 3:1).

Thus, the three substances — water, earth, writing — are an appeal of sorts to the *sotah* to admit her misdeeds, if she is indeed guilty of adultery (*Pnei Moshe*), so that God's Holy Name will not be erased and so that she will be spared the horrific fate of the *sotah's* sentence.

23. *R' Chaim Paltiel;* see also *Tur Yoreh Deah* 376.

before HASHEM. [17] *The Kohen shall take sacred water in an earthenware vessel, and the Kohen shall take from the earth that will be on the floor of the Tabernacle and put it in the water.* [18] *The Kohen shall have the woman stand before HASHEM and uncover the woman's head, and upon her palms he shall put the meal-offering of remembrance — it is a meal-offering of jealousies, and in the hand of the Kohen*

BAAL HATURIM ELUCIDATED

similarity of expression can be explained as follows: If *they conceal themselves from My eyes,* i.e., the *sotah* concealed her deed *and it was hidden from the eyes of her husband* (v. 13 above), then [the resolution will be found] *on the floor of the sea,* i.e., she will be judged through the floor and the sea — water and earth.[23a]

❑ בְּקַרְקַע הַמִּשְׁכָּן — ON THE FLOOR OF THE TABERNACLE. [According to a scribal tradition,] the ע of the word בְּקַרְקַע is [written in Torah scrolls in the enhanced form called] עַיִ״ן מְדֻלֵּי, *a raised letter* ע.[24] This is [an allusion to the *sotah*] because it calls to mind the verse, וְעֵין[25] נֹאֵף שָׁמְרָה נֶשֶׁף לֵאמֹר לֹא תְשׁוּרֵנִי עָיִן, *The adulterer's eye*[25] *awaits the night, saying: "No eye will see me!"* (*Job* 24:15).

23a. At first glance, the Baal HaTurim's allusion adds nothing to what is already explicit in the verses — a wayward wife will be judged through water and earth. But there is a difference. The verse speaks of a woman whose husband suspects her of wrongdoing and tells her of his suspicions. If she ignores his warnings and continues to act suspiciously, she must face the ordeal, the test of water and earth described in the passage. The Baal HaTurim's allusion, on the other hand, extends this concept even to the woman who is very discreet about her wrongdoing so that her husband does not even suspect her. Nevertheless, if she is guilty, her fate will be similar to that of the *sotah* who is indeed guilty (A.S.).

24. According to the ancient *Sefer Tagin,* this ע is one of seventeen in the Torah דְּתְלֵי בָּתַר רֵישֵׁיהוֹן, *that are* [*inscribed*] *suspended behind their heads.*

That is, instead of writing these particular letters ע in the usual manner, the scribes would inscribe them in an enhanced shape (see illustration).

Note that there are three letters ע (מִיַּעַר, *Psalms* 80:14; רְשָׁעִים, *Job* 38:13; and מֵרְשָׁעִים, *Job* 38:15) that the Massorah refers to as תְּלוּיוֹת, *suspended,* but are nevertheless drawn in the usual shape. However, they are called suspended because they are written a bit higher than the other letters of their respective words (see illustration). In the present comment, the Baal HaTurim does not speak of that type of suspended ע.

The Baal HaTurim comments on other unusual shapes of the letter ע at *Exodus* 1:9; *Numbers* 24:6 and 24:8; and *Deuteronomy* 6:4.

25. The Baal HaTurim here plays on the word עַיִן, which means both *eye* and *the letter* ע (see *Rashi* to *Lamentations* 2:16 for a similar word play). It appears twice in the verse from *Job:* the first time, it is in the construct state עֵין, *the eye of;* the second time, it appears at the end of its clause where the *patach* changes to a *kamatz* — עָיִן, in place of עַיִן.

יט יִהְיוּ מֵי הַמָּרִים הַמְאָרְרִים: וְהִשְׁבִּיעַ אֹתָהּ הַכֹּהֵן
וְאָמַר אֶל־הָאִשָּׁה אִם־לֹא שָׁכַב אִישׁ אֹתָךְ
וְאִם־לֹא שָׂטִית טֻמְאָה תַּחַת אִישֵׁךְ הִנָּקִי מִמֵּי
כ הַמָּרִים הַמְאָרְרִים הָאֵלֶּה: וְאַתְּ כִּי שָׂטִית תַּחַת
אִישֵׁךְ וְכִי נִטְמֵאת וַיִּתֵּן אִישׁ בָּךְ אֶת־שְׁכָבְתּוֹ
כא מִבַּלְעֲדֵי אִישֵׁךְ: וְהִשְׁבִּיעַ הַכֹּהֵן אֶת־הָאִשָּׁה
בִּשְׁבֻעַת הָאָלָה וְאָמַר הַכֹּהֵן לָאִשָּׁה יִתֵּן יְהוָה
אוֹתָךְ לְאָלָה וְלִשְׁבֻעָה בְּתוֹךְ עַמֵּךְ בְּתֵת יְהוָה
כב אֶת־יְרֵכֵךְ נֹפֶלֶת וְאֶת־בִּטְנֵךְ צָבָה: וּבָאוּ הַמַּיִם
הַמְאָרְרִים הָאֵלֶּה בְּמֵעַיִךְ לַצְבּוֹת בֶּטֶן וְלַנְפִּל

בעל הטורים

(יח) הַמְאָרְרִים. עוֹלֶה ב׳ פְּעָמִים רמ״ח. לוֹמַר שֶׁבּוֹדְקִין רמ״ח אֵבָרִים שֶׁלָּהּ וְשֶׁלּוֹ. לְכָךְ כְּתִיב ״מִנְחַת קְנָאֹת הוּא״ וְקָרֵינַן ״הִיא״:

BAAL HATURIM ELUCIDATED

18. הַמְאָרְרִים — THAT CAUSE CURSE. The *gematria* of this word (496) equals twice 248 [the number of *eivarim*[26] in the human body]. This implies that [the *sotah's* waters] examine both her 248 *eivarim* and his.[26a, 26b] And that is why the verse

26. *Makkos* 23b; *Yerushalmi, Sotah* 5:1.

An *eiver* [plural, *eivarim*] is a body part containing bone, flesh and cords [i.e., sinews, veins, nerves, etc.] (*Chullin* 102b; *Rambam,* commentary to *Zevachim* 3:4; see *Bartenura* to *Ohalos* 1:7). The Mishnah (*Ohalos* 1:8) enumerates the 248 *eivarim* of the human body. For lack of a precise English equivalent, *eiver* is often translated organ or limb.

26a. The reading רמ״ח אֵבָרִים שֶׁלָּהּ וְשֶׁלּוֹ, *both her 248 eivarim and his,* follows *Shoham Yakar's* manuscript edition. Most printed editions read, רמ״ח אֵבָרִים שֶׁל אִישׁ וְשֶׁל אִשָּׁה, *the 248 eivarim of a man and of a woman. Peirush HaRokeach,* the Baal HaTurim's apparent source for this comment, reads, רמ״ח שֶׁלּוֹ ורמ״ח שֶׁלָּהּ, *his 248 and her 248.* In any case, the comment is based on the words of the Mishnah: Just as the waters test her [i.e., the *sotah*], so do the waters test him [i.e., the suspected adulterer] (*Sotah* 5:1 [27b], cited in *Peirush HaRokeach*). That is, if the woman is indeed guilty and suffers the fate described in our passage, the adulterer, wherever he may be at that time, will suffer the same fate.

The Torah passage mentions only her stomach and her thigh, yet the Baal HaTurim speaks of two hundred and forty-eight *eivarim*! This is in accordance with another Mishnah: According to the measure with which one measures out his actions, with [that same measure] they [the Heavenly Tribunal] measure for him [his recompense]. [For example,] the *sotah* adorned herself for sin, the Omnipresent disgraced her; she revealed herself for sin, the Omnipresent revealed her sin [to all]; she sinned with the thigh first and then with the stomach, therefore the thigh should be struck first and then the stomach — but the rest of the body does not escape [punishment] (*Sotah* 1:7 [8b]).

26b. *Peirush HaRokeach,* the Baal HaTurim's apparent source for this comment, adds a phrase that raises a question regarding the allusion: אַף עַל פִּי שֶׁיֵּשׁ לָהּ ד׳ אֵבָרִים יוֹתֵר, *even though a woman has four eivarim more than a man* (see *Bechoros* 45a). Indeed, the Baal HaTurim himself states that the total number of *eivarim* in a husband and wife are 500, that is, 248 for him and 252 for her (see the Baal HaTurim to *Genesis* 35:11 with note 96). If so,

shall be the bitter waters that cause curse.
19 *"The Kohen shall adjure her and say to the woman, 'If a man has not lain with you, and you have not strayed in defilement with someone other than your husband, then be proven innocent of these bitter waters that cause curse.*
20 *But if you have strayed with someone other than your husband, and if you have become defiled, and a man other than your husband has lain with you — !'*
21 *"The Kohen shall adjure the woman with the oath of the curse, and the Kohen shall say to the woman, 'May HASHEM render you as a curse and as an oath amid your people, when HASHEM causes your thigh to collapse and your stomach to distend.*
22 *These waters that cause curse shall enter your innards to cause stomach to distend and*

BAAL HATURIM ELUCIDATED

writes, מִנְחַת קְנָאֹת הִוא, *it is a meal-offering of jealousies,* [using the masculine spelling הוא, with a ו, as if it were pronounced הוּא] for *it,* yet pronouncing it in the feminine form הִיא [as if it were spelled[26c] with a י].[27]

❑ **18, 19, 22, 23, 24, 27.** {The Baal HaTurim's comment to the words מָרִים and מְאָרְרִים appears at *Deuteronomy* 5:16.}

how can the Mishnah in *Ohalos* (see note 26 above) speak of only 248 *eivarim* in a woman? The *Chida* answers: That Mishnah speaks of the *tumah*-contamination transmitted by the *eivarim* of a corpse. It does not mention the woman's additional four *eivarim,* because they do not convey *tumah* (*Devash LeFi,* cited by *Shoham Yakar*). Although this explains the Mishnah in *Ohalos,* the question remains: Whereas the Baal HaTurim's allusion is speaking of the woman's *eivarim,* why does it include only 248 and not 252? Perhaps the allusion understands the Torah's usage of thigh and stomach as a reference to her four organs of reproduction. Thus, the allusion need only include her remaining 248 *eivarim* (Y.S.).

26c. It is noteworthy that the *gematria* of הוא is 12, while the *gematria* of הִיא is 16, a difference of 4. Thus, it is possible that the spelling הוא is used for the feminine because there are aspects in which man and woman are considered to have the same number of *eivarim* (see note 26b); while the spelling היא is used because there are aspects in which the woman is considered to have four *eivarim* more than a man (*VeChur LaZahav*).

27. It is not clear why the Baal HaTurim chose this particular verse to explain the implication of הוא/היא. For the pronoun היא, *she* or *it,* appears 200 times in the Torah: 189 times spelled הִוא, with a ו; only eleven times spelled הִיא, with a י. The word appears another 284 times in the rest of the *Tanach,* all spelled הִיא.

It is suggested that the Baal HaTurim's comment refers to the fact that our verse reads מִנְחַת קְנָאֹת הִוא, while the same phrase is vowelized מִנְחַת קְנָאֹת הוּא in verse 15 above. Perhaps the comment originally read, לְכָךְ כְּתִיב {"מִנְחַת קְנָאֹת הוּא" וְקָרִינָן "הוּא" וּכְתִיב} מִנְחַת קְנָאֹת "הוּא" וְקָרִינָן "הִיא", *And that is why the [earlier] verse writes* מִנְחַת קְנָאֹת הוּא *and we read it as* הוּא, *while the [later] verse writes* מִנְחַת קְנֹאת הוּא *and we read it* הִיא. A later copyist, who did not understand the Baal HaTurim's intention, thought that an earlier copyist had mistakenly repeated the words that are enclosed in braces, and so he deleted them from his copy (A.S.).

כג יָרֵךְ וְאָמְרָה הָאִשָּׁה אָמֵן | אָמֵן: וְכָתַב אֶת־הָאָלֹת
הָאֵלֶּה הַכֹּהֵן בַּסֵּפֶר וּמָחָה אֶל־מֵי הַמָּרִים:
כד וְהִשְׁקָה אֶת־הָאִשָּׁה אֶת־מֵי הַמָּרִים הַמְאָרְרִים

בעל הטורים

(כב) אָמֵן אָמֵן. פָּסֵק בֵּין שְׁנֵי אֲמֵנִים. לוֹמַר "אָמֵן" מֵאִישׁ זֶה, "אָמֵן" מֵאִישׁ אַחֵר:

(כג) וּמָחָה. ד׳ — "וּמָחָה אֶל מֵי הַמָּרִים"; "וּמָחָה עַל כֶּתֶף יָם כִּנֶּרֶת"; "וּמָחָה אֲדֹנָי אֱלֹהִים דִּמְעָה מֵעַל כָּל פָּנִים"; "וּמָחָה ה׳ אֶת שְׁמוֹ". "וּמָחָה אֶל מֵי הַמָּרִים", הַיְנוּ מַיִם חַיִּים, שֶׁנֶּאֱמַר "מִקֶּדֶם לָעַיִן . . . וּמָחָה עַל כֶּתֶף יָם כִּנֶּרֶת", מָה הָתָם מַיִם חַיִּים, דִּכְתִיב "מִקֶּדֶם לָעַיִן", אַף הָכָא מַיִם חַיִּים. וְאִם נִטְמֵאת, "וּמָחָה ה׳ אֶת שְׁמוֹ"; וְאִם נִמְצֵאת טְהוֹרָה, "וּמָחָה אֲדֹנָי אֱלֹהִים דִּמְעָה", שֶׁאִם הָיְתָה עֲקָרָה, נִפְקֶדֶת, וְאִם הָיְתָה יוֹלֶדֶת בְּצַעַר, יוֹלֶדֶת בְּרֶוַח:

(כד) וְהִשְׁקָה. ג׳ בַּמָּסוֹרֶת — "וְהִשְׁקָה אֶת הָאִשָּׁה"; "וְהִשְׁקָה אֶת נַחַל הַשִּׁטִּים"; "וְאֵד יַעֲלֶה

BAAL HATURIM ELUCIDATED

22. אָמֵן אָמֵן — AMEN, AMEN. The cantillation sign פָּסֵק [*paseik*],[28] literally, *pause,* appears between the two words אָמֵן אָמֵן. This indicates [that the words refer to two different subjects.[29] The *sotah* attests:] "אָמֵן, *it is true,* [that I did not sin] with this man; and אָמֵן, *it is true,* [that I did not sin] with any other man."[30]

23. וּמָחָה — AND ERASE. [The masoretic note, ד׳, means that] this word appears four times in the *Tanach*: (i) here, וּמָחָה אֶל מֵי הַמָּרִים, *and he shall erase* [*it*] *into the bitter waters;* (ii) וּמָחָה[31] עַל כֶּתֶף יָם כִּנֶּרֶת, [*the border shall . . .*] *touch*[31] *upon the bank of the Kinnereth Sea*[32] (below 34:11); (iii) וּמָחָה אֲדֹנָי אֱלֹהִים דִּמְעָה מֵעַל כָּל פָּנִים, *and the Lord, HASHEM/ELOHIM, will erase tears from all faces* (*Isaiah* 25:8); and (iv) וּמָחָה ה׳ אֶת שְׁמוֹ, *and HASHEM will erase his*[32a] *name* (*Deuteronomy* 29:19). [The similarity

28. Also called פְּסִיק, *pesik.* That cantillation mark appears as an upright line in the space between two words. It is used to indicate a pause after a cantillation note whose usual function is to draw the reading forward. For example, the cantillation note *meircha* under the מ of the first אָמֵן indicates that the reader should not pause after that word. Occasionally, a *pesik* follows a *meircha* to indicate that that particular *meircha* takes on the role of a pause, like a comma or semicolon. If our verse were written without a *pesik,* the phrase אָמֵן אָמֵן would be an emphatic statement meaning, *It is absolutely true!* However, the insertion of the *pesik* — אָמֵן | אָמֵן — changes the meaning to, *This is true! That is true!* (*VeChur LaZahav*).

The Baal HaTurim also explains the use of the פָּסֵק in his comments to *Genesis* 22:14; *Exodus* 15:18; *Leviticus* 10:6; *Numbers* 3:2, 3:38, 9:10; and *Deuteronomy* 6:4.

29. From the phrase אָמֵן אָמֵן, the Talmud (*Sotah* 18a; see *Rashi* to our verse) derives at least four laws regarding the *sotah's* oath. *Rashi* there explains that the doubled wording indicates that her oath includes a multiplicity of points. The Baal HaTurim here finds another indication — this one in the cantillation — that her second אָמֵן does not attest to the same point that her first אָמֵן did.

30. *Peirush HaRokeach;* see *Rashi.*

31. The other three appearances of וּמָחָה are forms of the root מחה, *to erase.* However, וּמָחָה in the verse that describes the borders of *Eretz Yisrael* is from the root מחא, *to clap,* that is, *to touch hand to hand* (see *Isaiah* 55:12; *Ezekiel* 25:6), and by extension, the word can refer to any two objects touching each other (*Ibn Ezra* to 34:11 below).

32. The full verse reads: *The border shall descend from Shefam to Riblah,* מִקֶּדֶם לָעַיִן, literally, *east of Ain* (*Targum Onkelos; Rashi*), but which can also be understood as *east of the spring* (*Targum Yerushalmi*); *the border shall descend and touch upon the bank of the Kinnereth Sea to the east.*

32a. According to its simple meaning, that verse

thigh to collapse!' And the woman shall respond, 'Amen, amen.'

23 *"The Kohen shall inscribe these curses on a scroll and he shall erase [it] into the bitter waters.* 24 *He shall cause the woman to drink the bitter waters that cause curse,*

BAAL HATURIM ELUCIDATED

of expression indicates that, like our verse, the other three allude to the ordeal of the *sotah.*] Thus, the water of] *"and he shall erase* [*it*] *into the bitter waters"* must be spring water, as it is stated, *east of the spring . . .* וּמָחָה, *and it shall touch upon the bank of the Kinnereth* Sea; just as that וּמָחָה speaks of spring water, as it is written, *east of the spring,* so, too, here, וּמָחָה refers to spring water.[33]

[The other two verses also allude to the *sotah.*] If she has indeed defiled herself through adultery, *God will erase his name;*[34] but if she is found to be innocent, *the Lord HASHEM/ELOHIM will erase tears from all faces.* For if until now she has been barren, she will now [be cured and] bear children; if until now she has borne children with difficulty, she will now bear them with ease.[35]

24. וְהִשְׁקָה — HE SHALL CAUSE [THE WOMAN] TO DRINK. The masoretic note, ג׳, means that this word appears three times in the *Tanach:*[36] (i) here, וְהִשְׁקָה אֶת הָאִשָּׁה, *He shall cause the woman to drink;* (ii) וְהִשְׁקָה אֶת נַחַל הַשִּׁטִּים, *and it will water the Valley of Shittim* (*Joel* 4:18); and (iii) וְאֵד יַעֲלֶה מִן הָאָרֶץ וְהִשְׁקָה, *A mist would*

speaks of God blotting out the name of the heretic. See note 34 below, for an alternative interpretation in the Baal HaTurim's allusion.

33. The *sotah's* water is drawn from the כִּיּוֹר [*Kiyyor*], *Laver,* in the Temple Courtyard (described in *Exodus* 30:17-18). The Talmud records a dispute regarding the nature of the *Kiyyor's* water: According to one opinion, only spring water could be placed in the *Kiyyor;* thus, the water used for the *sotah's* ordeal was spring water (*Sotah* 15b).

34. That is, the *sotah* will perish. Although the verse speaks of שְׁמוֹ, *his name,* the rules of grammar are sometimes waived for purposes of רֶמֶז, *allusion* (see the Baal HaTurim to *Genesis* 1:1 with note 6a and 14a). Alternatively, the masculine pronoun refers to her partner in adultery, for the Talmud (*Sotah* 27b) teaches that he suffers the same fate as she (*VeChur LaZahav*).

Alternatively: God will hold her responsible for causing His Name (which appears in the curses inscribed on the scroll) to be erased. For she could have prevented the erasure by admitting her sin. If she was innocent, on the other hand, she would not be responsible for the erasure, because there was nothing she could do to prevent it (A.S.).

35. The Talmud records a dispute regarding the interpretation of the verse, *then she shall be absolved, and she shall bear seed* (v. 28 below). One view maintains, "If she had been barren, she would now be cured and bear children." According to the other view the verse does not refer to a barren woman; rather, it means that a woman capable of bearing children would do so under more optimal conditions. For example, "if she had borne children with difficulty, she will henceforth bear them with ease . . ." (*Sotah* 26a). Although both *Rashi* (v. 28 below) and the *Rambam* (*Hilchos Sotah* 2:10) cite only the latter opinion, the Baal HaTurim merges the two.

36. The full note reads: ד׳ ג׳ רָפִין וא׳ מַפִּיק, *Four, three silent and one pronounced.* That is, the spelling והשקה appears four times in the *Tanach.* Three of those times it is vowelized וְהִשְׁקָה, with a silent final ה, and means *he shall cause* [*someone*] *to drink* or *he shall water.* The fourth time it is vowelized וְהִשְׁקָהּ, with a מַפִּיק ה, *mapik* [pronounced] ה, and means, *he shall cause* ***her*** *to drink* (v. 27 below). The Baal HaTurim's comment includes only the three appearances spelled with a silent ה (*Ittur Bikkurim*).

כה וּבָ֥אוּ בָ֛הּ הַמַּ֥יִם הַֽמְאָֽרְרִ֖ים לְמָרִֽים׃ וְלָקַ֣ח הַכֹּהֵ֗ן
מִיַּ֣ד הָֽאִשָּׁ֔ה אֵ֖ת מִנְחַ֣ת הַקְּנָאֹ֑ת וְהֵנִ֤יף אֶת־הַמִּנְחָה֙
כו לִפְנֵ֣י יהוה וְהִקְרִ֥יב אֹתָ֖הּ אֶל־הַמִּזְבֵּֽחַ׃ וְקָמַ֨ץ הַכֹּהֵ֤ן
מִן־הַמִּנְחָה֙ אֶת־אַזְכָּ֣רָתָ֔הּ וְהִקְטִ֖יר הַמִּזְבֵּ֑חָה וְאַחַ֛ר
כז יַשְׁקֶ֥ה אֶת־הָאִשָּׁ֖ה אֶת־הַמָּֽיִם׃ וְהִשְׁקָ֣הּ אֶת־הַמַּ֗יִם
וְהָיְתָ֣ה אִֽם־נִטְמְאָה֮ וַתִּמְעֹ֣ל מַ֣עַל בְּאִישָׁהּ֒ וּבָ֨אוּ בָ֜הּ
הַמַּ֤יִם הַמְאָֽרְרִים֙ לְמָרִ֔ים וְצָבְתָ֥ה בִטְנָ֖הּ וְנָפְלָ֣ה
כח יְרֵכָ֑הּ וְהָיְתָ֧ה הָאִשָּׁ֛ה לְאָלָ֖ה בְּקֶ֥רֶב עַמָּֽהּ׃ וְאִם־לֹ֤א
נִטְמְאָה֙ הָֽאִשָּׁ֔ה וּטְהֹרָ֖ה הִ֑וא וְנִקְּתָ֖ה וְנִזְרְעָ֥ה זָֽרַע׃
כט זֹ֥את תּוֹרַ֖ת הַקְּנָאֹ֑ת אֲשֶׁ֨ר תִּשְׂטֶ֥ה אִשָּׁ֛ה תַּ֥חַת אִישָׁ֖הּ
ל וְנִטְמָֽאָה׃ א֣וֹ אִ֗ישׁ אֲשֶׁ֨ר תַּעֲבֹ֥ר עָלָ֛יו ר֥וּחַ קִנְאָ֖ה
וְקִנֵּ֣א אֶת־אִשְׁתּ֑וֹ וְהֶעֱמִ֤יד אֶת־הָֽאִשָּׁה֙ לִפְנֵ֣י יהוה
לא וְעָ֤שָׂה לָהּ֙ הַכֹּהֵ֔ן אֵ֖ת כָּל־הַתּוֹרָ֥ה הַזֹּֽאת׃ וְנִקָּ֥ה

בעל הטורים

מִן הָאָרֶץ וְהִשְׁקָה״. הַכֹּהֵן נוֹתֵן עָפָר בַּמַּיִם וּמַשְׁקֶה אוֹתָהּ, וְזֶהוּ ״וְאֵד יַעֲלֶה מִן הָאָרֶץ וְהִשְׁקָה״. לָמָּה? בִּשְׁבִיל שֶׁעָשְׂתָה מַעֲשֵׂה שִׁטִּים, שֶׁזָּנְתָה. וְזֶהוּ ״וְהִשְׁקָה אֶת נַחַל הַשִּׁטִּים״:

(כח) וְנִזְרְעָה זָרַע. וּסְמִיךְ לֵהּ ״זֹאת תּוֹרַת״. לוֹמַר שֶׁאִם טְהוֹרָה הִיא, יִהְיוּ לָהּ בָּנִים צַדִּיקִים, בַּעֲלֵי תוֹרָה:

(לא) וְנִקָּה. ג׳ תָּגִין עַל הַהֵ״א. לוֹמַר לְךָ שֶׁנִּקָּה מֵחֲמִשָּׁה עֲוֹנוֹת, וְאֵלּוּ הֵן – עֲוֹן אֵשֶׁת אִישׁ,

BAAL HATURIM ELUCIDATED

ascend from the earth and water (*Genesis* 2:6). [The similarity of expression can be understood as alluding to the *sotah's* folly:] The Kohen places earth into the water and causes her to drink. This is the allusion of, וְאֵד יַעֲלֶה מִן הָאָרֶץ וְהִשְׁקָה, [which can be understood as,] *a disaster*[37] *will ascend from the earth and* [*that which*] *he caused* [*her*] *to drink.*[38] Why [must she undergo this ordeal]? Because she demeaned herself in the manner of the incident at Shittim,[39] i.e., she committed harlotry. This is the allusion of the phrase, *and it will water the Valley of Shittim.*[40]

28. וְנִזְרְעָה זָרַע — AND SHE SHALL BEAR SEED. Juxtaposed to this is the phrase זֹאת . . . תּוֹרַת, literally, *This is the Torah of . . .* (v. 29). This indicates that, if the *sotah* is innocent of harlotry, she will bear righteous sons, masters of the Torah.[41]

37. The word אֵד means *mist* or *vapor.* The similar sounding אֵיד means *disaster* or *catastrophe* (e.g., *Job* 18:12; *Deuteronomy* 32:35). For purposes of the allusion, the Baal HaTurim interprets אֵד as if it read אֵיד (*VeChur LaZahav*).

38. That is, the earth and water that the Kohen causes the *sotah* to drink will be the vehicle by which she is brought to disaster.

39. See 25:1 below, with the Baal HaTurim.

40. *Maharam MiRothenburg;* cf. *Peirush HaRokeach.*

41. *Peirush HaRokeach;* see *Sotah* 17a.

and the waters that cause curse will come into her for bitterness.

[25] *"The Kohen shall take the meal-offering of jealousies from the hand of the woman; he shall wave the meal-offering before* HASHEM, *and he shall offer it on the Altar.* [26] *The Kohen shall scoop up from the meal-offering its remembrance and cause it to go up in smoke on the Altar; after which he shall cause the woman to drink the water.* [27] *He shall cause her to drink the water, and it shall be that if she had become defiled and had committed a trespass against her husband, the waters that cause curse shall come into her for bitterness, and her stomach shall be distended and her thigh shall collapse, and the woman shall become a curse amid her people.* [28] *But if the woman had not become defiled, and she is pure, then she shall be absolved and she shall bear seed.*

[29] *"This is the law of the jealousies, when a woman shall go astray with someone other than her husband and become defiled;* [30] *or of a man over whom passes a spirit of jealousy and he warns his wife, and he causes his wife to stand before* HASHEM, *then the Kohen shall carry out for her this entire law.* [31] *The husband will be absolved of*

BAAL HATURIM ELUCIDATED

31. וְנִקָּה — [THE HUSBAND] WILL BE ABSOLVED. [According to a Scribal tradition,] the ה (= 5) of וְנִקָּה is written with three *tagin* [crownlets].[42] This teaches you that the husband must be innocent of five sins: They are: (a) The sin of adultery;

42. According to the kabbalistic work *Peri Eitz Chaim* (*Shaar Kerias Shema* 1), in the regular Torah script, seven of the twenty-two letters of the *alef-beis,* identified by the mnemonic שַׁעַטְנֵ״ז גָּ״ץ, are adorned with three *tagin,* i.e., crownlets or tittles; six letters, בְּדֶ״ק חַיָ״ה, are adorned with one crownlet; and the remaining nine, מְלָאכֶ״ת סוֹפֵ״ר, have no *tagin.* However, certain specific letters are written with more than the usual number of *tagin,* and those extra *tagin* indicate that there is an allusion hidden in that word or phrase. See illustration.

Sefer Tagin lists 360 words in the Torah in which the letter ה is written with four *tagin* instead of the usual one. The word וְנִקָּה appears on that list. However, there is no mention in that work of any ה that is drawn with three *tagin.* Perhaps the Baal HaTurim understands the three *tagin* to be in addition to the usual one *tag* on the letter ה, for a total of four (*VeChur LaZahav*). See illustration.

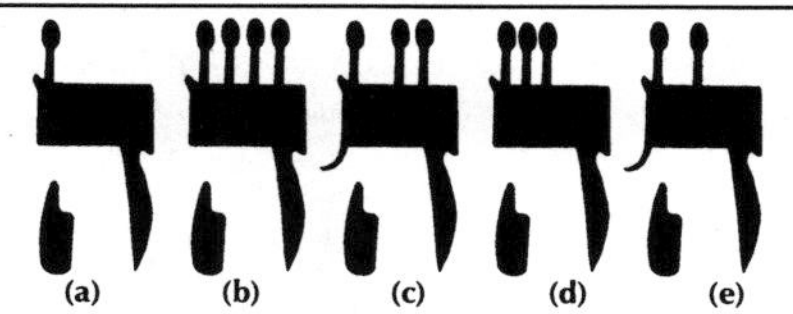

Usual ה with one *tag* (a). ה with four *tagin* according to *Machzor Vitry* (b), *Badei HaAron* (c). Hypothetical ה with three *tagin,* based on *Machzor Vitry* (d), *Badei HaAron* (e).

הָאִישׁ מֵעָוֺן וְהָאִשָּׁה הַהִוא תִּשָּׂא אֶת־עֲוֺנָהּ׃
ו א־ב וַיְדַבֵּר יהוָה אֶל־מֹשֶׁה לֵּאמֹר׃ דַּבֵּר אֶל־בְּנֵי
יִשְׂרָאֵל וְאָמַרְתָּ אֲלֵהֶם אִישׁ אוֹ־אִשָּׁה כִּי יַפְלִא
ג לִנְדֹּר נֶדֶר נָזִיר לְהַזִּיר לַיהוָה׃ מִיַּיִן וְשֵׁכָר יַזִּיר
חֹמֶץ יַיִן וְחֹמֶץ שֵׁכָר לֹא יִשְׁתֶּה וְכָל־מִשְׁרַת
עֲנָבִים לֹא יִשְׁתֶּה וַעֲנָבִים לַחִים וִיבֵשִׁים לֹא
ד יֹאכֵל׃ כֹּל יְמֵי נִזְרוֹ מִכֹּל אֲשֶׁר יֵעָשֶׂה מִגֶּפֶן הַיַּיִן
ה מֵחַרְצַנִּים וְעַד־זָג לֹא יֹאכֵל׃ כָּל־יְמֵי נֶדֶר נִזְרוֹ
תַּעַר לֹא־יַעֲבֹר עַל־רֹאשׁוֹ עַד־מְלֹאת הַיָּמִם

בעל הטורים

עֲוֹן פְּנוּיָה, עֲוֹן שֶׁלֹּא בָא עָלֶיהָ, עֲוֹן בָּנָיו, עֲוֹן בְּנוֹתָיו:

❑ **אֶת עֲוֹנָהּ.** ב׳ בַּמָּסוֹרֶת – הָכָא ״וְהָאִשָּׁה הַהִוא תִּשָּׂא אֶת עֲוֹנָהּ״; וְאִידָךְ בִּנְדָרִים ״וְנָשָׂא אֶת עֲוֹנָהּ״. כִּדְאִיתָא בְּסוֹטָה – שֶׁלֹּא יִדְאַג הַבַּעַל לוֹמַר, גָּרַמְתִּי לָהּ מִיתָה. אֶלָּא הִיא תִּשָּׂא אֶת עֲוֹנָהּ. וְדַוְקָא הָכָא, אֲבָל בִּנְדָרִים, שֶׁהָיָה יָכוֹל לְהָפֵר וְלֹא הֵפֵר לָהּ, ״וְנָשָׂא אֶת עֲוֹנָהּ״:

ו (ב) **יַפְלִא.** ב׳ בַּמָּסוֹרֶת חֲסֵרִים – הָכָא ״כִּי יַפְלִא לִנְדֹּר נֶדֶר נָזִיר״; וְאִידָךְ בַּעֲרָכִין ״אִישׁ כִּי יַפְלִא נֶדֶר״. דְּיָלְפִינַן נְדָרִים מֵעֲרָכִין, מָה הָתָם ״כְּעֶרְכְּךָ הַכֹּהֵן כֵּן יִהְיֶה״, אַף בִּנְדָרִים הַכֹּל תָּלוּי בְּחָכָם. אִם נִרְאֶה לוֹ יַתִּירוֹ, וְאִם לַאו לֹא יַתִּירוֹ:

BAAL HATURIM ELUCIDATED

(b) the sin of consorting with an unmarried woman; (c) the sin of having relations with her [after she had become a *sotah* through his accusation];[43] (d) the sin of his sons; and (e) the sin of his daughters.[44]

❑ {The Baal HaTurim's other comment to וְנִקָּה appears at *Exodus* 21:19.}

❑ **אֶת עֲוֹנָהּ** — HER INIQUITY. The masoretic note, ב׳, means that this phrase appears twice in the *Tanach*: (i) here, וְהָאִשָּׁה הַהִוא תִּשָּׂא אֶת עֲוֹנָהּ, *and that woman will bear her iniquity;* and (ii) with regard to vows, וְנָשָׂא אֶת עֲוֹנָהּ, *he shall bear her iniquity* (*Numbers* 30:16). [The similarity of expression alludes to that] which is written regarding the *sotah*: The husband should not worry, saying, "I caused her death." Rather, she will bear her iniquity.[45] But only here [regarding a *sotah* will

43. It does not matter whether he was guilty of consorting with (a) a married woman, (b) an unmarried woman, or (c) his own wife who had become forbidden to him as a *sotah.* If a man was known to have been guilty of illicit relations, the Kohen would not give the bitter waters to that man's wife. If he did, the examination would be inconclusive (*Sotah* 47b; see *Rambam, Hilchos Sotah* 2:8-9, see *Mishneh LaMelech* there).

44. That is, the fact that a man does not protest the immoral behavior of his children indicates that he himself might be guilty of similar illicit behavior. Thus, the Kohen does not give that man's wife the bitter waters, for the examination will not be conclusive (*Sotah* 47b, as explained by the *Meiri;* see also *Ramban* to our verse).

45. *Sifrei* 21, cited by *Rashi.*

iniquity; and that woman will bear her iniquity."

6

[1] *HASHEM spoke to Moses, saying,* [2] *"Speak to the Children of Israel and say to them: A man or woman who shall articulate a Nazirite vow to become a Nazirite for the sake of HASHEM;* [3] *from new or aged wine shall he abstain, and he shall not drink vinegar of wine or vinegar of aged wine; anything in which grapes have been steeped shall he not drink, and fresh and dried grapes shall he not eat.* [4] *All the days of his abstinence, anything made from wine grapes, even the pips or skin, he shall not eat.* [5] *All the days of his Nazirite vow, a razor shall not pass over his head; until the completion of the days*

the husband be absolved of her iniquity]. With regard to vows, however, where the husband could have revoked the vow, but did not revoke it for her, *he shall bear her iniquity.*[46]

VI

2. יַפְלִא — WHO SHALL ARTICULATE. The masoretic note, ב׳ חֲסֵרִים, means that this word appears twice in the *Tanach* spelled defectively (יַפְלִא, not יַפְלִיא):[47] (i) here, כִּי יַפְלִא לִנְדֹּר נֶדֶר נָזִיר, *who shall articulate a Nazirite vow;* and (ii) with regard to *arachin* [gift evaluations], אִישׁ כִּי יַפְלִא נֶדֶר, *if a man articulates a vow* (*Leviticus* 27:2). [The similarity of expression alludes to the fact] that the laws regarding vows may be derived from the laws of *arachin.* Just as there, כְּעֶרְכְּךָ הַכֹּהֵן כֵּן יִהְיֶה, *like the Kohen's valuation so shall it be*[48] (*Leviticus* 27:12), so too, regarding [the revocation of] vows, all is dependent on a sage. If it appears appropriate to him, he will revoke the vow; if not, he will not revoke it.[49]

46. *Maharam MiRothenburg;* see *Rashi* to 30:16 below.

47. The full note (both here and in *Leviticus*) reads: ד׳ חֲסֵרִים בְּלִישָׁנָא, *four spelled defectively in this form.* It refers to words of the verb root פלא in the *hifil* conjugation that end in ־לִיא. Eight such words appear in the *Tanach*: Four are spelled with the י that separates the second and third root letters; the other four are spelled without the י. The eight words are: (i) הִפְלִא, *Isaiah* 28:29; (ii-iii) הִפְלִיא, *Psalms* 31:22 and *II Chronicles* 26:15; (iv) וּמַפְלִא, *Judges* 13:19; (v-vi) לְהַפְלִיא, *Isaiah* 29:14 and *Joel* 2:26; and (vii-viii) the two appearances of יַפְלִא cited in this comment. The masoretic note cited by the Baal HaTurim includes only the two appearances of יַפְלִא.

48. That is, when one contributes to the Temple treasury an object which cannot be offered on the Altar (e.g., a non-kosher animal), the object may be redeemed by the original owner or anyone else. In either case, the object to be redeemed must first be assessed by a Kohen, and that evaluation determines the amount of the redemption (see *Rashi* to *Leviticus* 27:12).

49. See *Nedarim* 77b.

Scripture sometimes equates the *Kohen* and the Torah sage: *And the man who will act with willfulness, not listening to the Kohen . . . or to the judge* (*Deuteronomy* 9:12); *. . . the two men shall stand before HASHEM, before the Kohanim and the judges* (*Deuteronomy* 19:17); *They shall teach Your ordinances to Jacob and Your Torah to Israel; they shall place incense before Your Presence and burnt-offering on Your Altar* (*Deuteronomy* 33:10); *For the lips of the Kohen shall safeguard knowledge and people should seek Torah from his mouth* (*Malachi* 2:7; Y.S.).

אֲשֶׁר־יַזִּיר לַיהוָה קָדֹשׁ יִהְיֶה גַּדֵּל פֶּרַע שְׂעַר
ו רֹאשׁוֹ: כָּל־יְמֵי הַזִּירוֹ לַיהוָה עַל־נֶפֶשׁ מֵת לֹא
ז יָבֹא: לְאָבִיו וּלְאִמּוֹ לְאָחִיו וּלְאַחֹתוֹ לֹא־יִטַּמָּא
ח לָהֶם בְּמֹתָם כִּי נֵזֶר אֱלֹהָיו עַל־רֹאשׁוֹ: כֹּל יְמֵי
ט נִזְרוֹ קָדֹשׁ הוּא לַיהוָה: וְכִי־יָמוּת מֵת עָלָיו בְּפֶתַע
פִּתְאֹם וְטִמֵּא רֹאשׁ נִזְרוֹ וְגִלַּח רֹאשׁוֹ בְּיוֹם
י טָהֳרָתוֹ בַּיּוֹם הַשְּׁבִיעִי יְגַלְּחֶנּוּ: וּבַיּוֹם הַשְּׁמִינִי
יָבִא שְׁתֵּי תֹרִים אוֹ שְׁנֵי בְּנֵי יוֹנָה אֶל־הַכֹּהֵן
יא אֶל־פֶּתַח אֹהֶל מוֹעֵד: וְעָשָׂה הַכֹּהֵן אֶחָד לְחַטָּאת
וְאֶחָד לְעֹלָה וְכִפֶּר עָלָיו מֵאֲשֶׁר חָטָא עַל־
יב הַנָּפֶשׁ וְקִדַּשׁ אֶת־רֹאשׁוֹ בַּיּוֹם הַהוּא: וְהִזִּיר לַיהוָה
אֶת־יְמֵי נִזְרוֹ וְהֵבִיא כֶּבֶשׂ בֶּן־שְׁנָתוֹ לְאָשָׁם
יג וְהַיָּמִים הָרִאשֹׁנִים יִפְּלוּ כִּי טָמֵא נִזְרוֹ: וְזֹאת תּוֹרַת
הַנָּזִיר בְּיוֹם מְלֹאת יְמֵי נִזְרוֹ יָבִיא אֹתוֹ אֶל־פֶּתַח
יד אֹהֶל מוֹעֵד: וְהִקְרִיב אֶת־קָרְבָּנוֹ לַיהוָה כֶּבֶשׂ
בֶּן־שְׁנָתוֹ תָמִים אֶחָד לְעֹלָה וְכַבְשָׂה אַחַת בַּת־
שְׁנָתָהּ תְּמִימָה לְחַטָּאת וְאַיִל־אֶחָד תָּמִים
טו לִשְׁלָמִים: וְסַל מַצּוֹת סֹלֶת חַלֹּת בְּלוּלֹת בַּשֶּׁמֶן
וּרְקִיקֵי מַצּוֹת מְשֻׁחִים בַּשָּׁמֶן וּמִנְחָתָם וְנִסְכֵּיהֶם:
טז וְהִקְרִיב הַכֹּהֵן לִפְנֵי יְהוָה וְעָשָׂה אֶת־חַטָּאתוֹ
יז וְאֶת־עֹלָתוֹ: וְאֶת־הָאַיִל יַעֲשֶׂה זֶבַח שְׁלָמִים לַיהוָה
עַל סַל הַמַּצּוֹת וְעָשָׂה הַכֹּהֵן אֶת־מִנְחָתוֹ וְאֶת־
יח נִסְכּוֹ: וְגִלַּח הַנָּזִיר פֶּתַח אֹהֶל מוֹעֵד אֶת־רֹאשׁ
נִזְרוֹ וְלָקַח אֶת־שְׂעַר רֹאשׁ נִזְרוֹ וְנָתַן עַל־הָאֵשׁ

בעל הטורים

(ו) **עַל נֶפֶשׁ מֵת לֹא יָבֹא.** לוֹמַר לְךָ, שֶׁאִם תִּשְׁרֶה עָלָיו שְׁכִינָה מֵחֲמַת נִזְרוֹ, שֶׁלֹּא יֹאמְרוּ שֶׁהוּא דוֹרֵשׁ אֶל הַמֵּתִים:

BAAL HATURIM ELUCIDATED

6. עַל נֶפֶשׁ מֵת לֹא יָבֹא — HE SHALL NOT COME NEAR A DEAD PERSON. [This prohibition acts to prevent a misunderstanding.] It tells you that if the Divine Presence rests upon him because of his Nazirite vow, people should not say that he is

*that he will be a Nazirite for the sake of HASHEM, holy shall he
be, the growth of hair on his head shall grow.* 6 *All the days
of his abstinence for the sake of HASHEM he shall not come
near a dead person.* 7 *To his father or to his mother, to his
brother or to his sister — he shall not contaminate himself to
them upon their death, for the crown of his God is upon his
head.* 8 *All the days of his abstinence he is holy to HASHEM.*

9 *"If a person should die near him with quick suddenness
and contaminate his Nazirite head, he shall shave his head
on the day he becomes purified; on the seventh day shall he
shave it.* 10 *On the eighth day he shall bring two turtledoves
or two young doves to the Kohen, to the entrance of the Tent
of Meeting.* 11 *The Kohen shall make one as a sin-offering
and one as a burnt-offering, and he shall provide him
atonement for having sinned regarding the soul; and he shall
sanctify his head on that day.* 12 *He shall dedicate to HASHEM
the days of his abstinence, and he shall bring a sheep in its
first year for a guilt-offering; the first days shall fall aside, for
his abstinence had been contaminated.*

13 *"This shall be the law of the Nazirite: on the day his
abstinence is completed, he shall bring himself to the
entrance of the Tent of Meeting.* 14 *He shall bring his offering
to HASHEM: one unblemished sheep in its first year as a
burnt-offering, one unblemished ewe in its first year as a
sin-offering, and one unblemished ram as a peace-offering;*
15 *a basket of unleavened loaves: loaves of fine flour mixed
with oil and unleavened wafers smeared with oil; and their
meal-offerings and their libations.* 16 *The Kohen shall ap-
proach before HASHEM and perform the service of his
sin-offering and his burnt-offering.* 17 *He shall make the
ram the slaughter of a peace-offering for HASHEM with the
basket of unleavened loaves, and the Kohen shall make
its meal-offering and its libation.* 18 *At the entrance of the
Tent of Meeting the Nazirite shall shave his Nazirite head;
he shall take the hair of his Nazirite head and put it on the fire*

guilty of necromancy.[50]

50. Necromancy, divination through communion with the dead, is specifically prohibited by the Torah (*Deuteronomy* 18:11). The elevated holiness of a Nazirite may cause רוּחַ הַקֹּדֶשׁ, *the Divine Spirit,* i.e., a measure of clairvoyance, to rest upon him. If people saw him in a cemetery, they would suspect that his new-found powers are the result of his practicing necromancy.

יט אֲשֶׁר־תַּחַת זֶבַח הַשְּׁלָמִים: וְלָקַח הַכֹּהֵן אֶת־הַזְּרֹעַ
בְּשֵׁלָה מִן־הָאַיִל וְחַלַּת מַצָּה אַחַת מִן־הַסַּל
וּרְקִיק מַצָּה אֶחָד וְנָתַן עַל־כַּפֵּי הַנָּזִיר אַחַר
כ הִתְגַּלְּחוֹ אֶת־נִזְרוֹ: וְהֵנִיף אוֹתָם הַכֹּהֵן ׀ תְּנוּפָה
לִפְנֵי יהוה קֹדֶשׁ הוּא לַכֹּהֵן עַל חֲזֵה הַתְּנוּפָה
כא וְעַל שׁוֹק הַתְּרוּמָה וְאַחַר יִשְׁתֶּה הַנָּזִיר יָיִן: זֹאת
תּוֹרַת הַנָּזִיר אֲשֶׁר יִדֹּר קָרְבָּנוֹ לַיהוה עַל־נִזְרוֹ
מִלְּבַד אֲשֶׁר־תַּשִּׂיג יָדוֹ כְּפִי נִדְרוֹ אֲשֶׁר יִדֹּר כֵּן
יַעֲשֶׂה עַל תּוֹרַת נִזְרוֹ:
כב־כג וַיְדַבֵּר יהוה אֶל־מֹשֶׁה לֵּאמֹר: דַּבֵּר אֶל־אַהֲרֹן

בעל הטורים

(כא) שְׁלֹשִׁים פְּעָמִים כְּתִיב "נֶדֶר" וּ"נְזִירוּת" בַּפָּרָשָׁה, דִּסְתַם נְזִירוּת שְׁלֹשִׁים יוֹם. וְכֵן גַּם כֵּן "יִהְיֶה" עוֹלֶה שְׁלֹשִׁים:

❑ **זֹאת תּוֹרַת הַנָּזִיר.** וּסְמִיךְ לֵהּ "עַל תּוֹרַת נִזְרוֹ". לוֹמַר, מִי שֶׁשָּׁתָה יַיִן אַל יוֹרֶה. וְסָמַךְ בִּרְכַּת כֹּהֲנִים לְפָרָשַׁת נָזִיר לוֹמַר שְׁתוּיֵי יַיִן פְּסוּלִים לְבִרְכַּת כֹּהֲנִים, שֶׁנִּקְרֵאת עֲבוֹדָה:

BAAL HATURIM ELUCIDATED

21. The passage of the Nazirite (vv. 1-21) uses [a combined total of] thirty words of the roots נדר, *to vow,* and נזר, *to become a Nazirite.* This teaches that a standard term of *nezirus* is thirty days.[51] Additionally: The *gematria* of

51. The Talmud (*Nazir* 5a; *Yerushalmi Nazir* 1:3; *Semachos* 7:20) and Midrash (*Bamidbar Rabbah* 10:10) record a dispute regarding the Scriptural source of the Mishnah's teaching: The standard term of *nezirus* is thirty days (*Nazir* 1:3 [5a]). One view derives this from the fact that this passage mentions twenty-nine words of the roots נדר and נזר, indicating that the standard term contains twenty-nine days and on the thirtieth day the Nazirite brings his offerings, after which he is released from his vows [see note 52 below for the other view]. The twenty-nine appearances are : (i-iv) לִנְדֹּר נֶדֶר נָזִיר לְהַזִּיר — v. 2; (v) יַזִּיר — v. 3; (vi) נִזְרוֹ — v. 4; (vii-ix) נֶדֶר נִזְרוֹ . . . יַזִּיר — v. 5; (x) הַזִּירוֹ — v. 6; (xi) נִזְרוֹ — v. 8; (xii) נִזְרוֹ — v. 9; (xiii-xv) וְהִזִּיר . . . נִזְרוֹ . . . נִזְרוֹ — v. 12; (xvi-xvii) הַנָּזִיר . . . נִזְרוֹ — v. 13; (xviii-xx) הַנָּזִיר . . . נִזְרוֹ . . . נִזְרוֹ — v. 18; (xxi-xxii) הַנָּזִיר . . . נִזְרוֹ — v. 19; (xxiii) הַנָּזִיר — v. 20; (xxiv-xxix) הַנָּזִיר . . . יִדֹּר . . . נִזְרוֹ . . . נִדְרוֹ . . . יִדֹּר . . . נִזְרוֹ — v. 21. The word נֵזֶר in verse 7 is not counted, because it is not related to the root נזר, rather it means *crown* (*Rashi* to *Nazir* 5a). Apparently the Baal HaTurim included that word to arrive at a total of thirty (*Shoham Yakar*). However, it seems difficult to understand why the Baal HaTurim finds it necessary to deviate from the Sages' teaching. Perhaps his intention is to answer another question: Since the terms נדר and נזר appear only twenty-nine times, how do the Sages know that the Torah's intention is for the period of *nezirus* to end on the next day? Maybe the offerings should be brought on the twenty-ninth day? The Baal HaTurim explains that in verse 7 the Torah does not use one of the other words for crown [such as: כֶּתֶר (e.g., *Esther* 1:11); עֲטָרָה (e.g., *Song of Songs* 3:11); צִיץ (e.g., *Exodus* 39:30); or פְּאֵר (e.g., *Isaiah* 61:3, see *Targum* there)], rather it uses the term נֵזֶר as an allusion to a thirtieth day. But whereas that word is not related to נָזִיר etymologically, the Sages do not include it as part of the actual count. If this analysis is correct, then we see that even when allusions are used in the area of דְּרוּשׁ, *derush* [exegesis], to support *halachah,* as in the words of the Talmud, those allusions must be close to the פְּשָׁט, *peshat*

that is under the feast peace-offering. [19] *The Kohen shall*
take the cooked foreleg of the ram and one unleavened loaf from the basket and one unleavened wafer, and place them on the palms of the Nazirite after he has shaved his Nazirite hair.
[20] *The Kohen shall wave them as a wave-service before* HASHEM; *it shall be holy for the Kohen, aside from the breast of the waving and the thigh of the raising-up — afterward the Nazirite may drink wine.*
[21] *"This is the law of the Nazirite who shall pledge his offering to* HASHEM *for his abstinence — aside from what he can afford, according to his vow that he shall pledge, so shall he do in addition to the law of his abstinence."*
[22] HASHEM *spoke to Moses, saying,* [23] *"Speak to Aaron*

BAAL HATURIM ELUCIDATED

יִהְיֶה (v. 5) is thirty.[52,52a]

21. זֹאת תּוֹרַת הַנָּזִיר — THIS IS THE LAW OF THE NAZIRITE. Juxtaposed to this[53] is the phrase עַל תּוֹרַת נִזְרוֹ, *in addition to the law of his abstinence.* This [repetition] indicates that one who has drunk wine may not render *halachic* decisions.[54]

The Torah juxtaposed the passage of the Priestly Blessing (vv. 22-27) with the passage of the Nazirite, to teach that those who have drunk wine may not recite *Bircas Kohanim* [the Priestly Blessing],[55] for it is considered as part of the Temple service[55a] [therefore the one bestowing it must be sober].[56]

[simple meaning of the verse]. In the area of רֶמֶז, *remez* [allusion], on the other hand, as in the Baal HaTurim's comment, allusions are acceptable even if they stray far from the *peshat* of the verse or phrase they explain (*VeChur LaZahav*).

52. The other opinion (see note 51) derives the thirty-day term from the *gematria* of יִהְיֶה in verse 5. Apparently the Talmud interprets that verse: כָּל יְמֵי נֶדֶר נִזְרוֹ, *All the days of his Nazirite vow . . .* אֲשֶׁר יַזִּיר לַה׳ קֹדֶשׁ, *that he will be a Nazirite, holy unto* HASHEM, יהי״ה, *will be thirty* (*VeChur LaZahav*).

52a. There is an additional allusion to the thirty-day term in our verse, for the stich עַל נֶפֶשׁ מֵת לֹא יָבֹא, *he shall not come near a dead person,* may be understood as, עַל נֶפֶשׁ מֵת, *near a dead person,* לֹ״א, [on day] *thirty-one,* יָבֹא, *he may come* (*VeChur LaZahav*).

See the Baal HaTurim to 13:24 below for another allusion.

53. That is, our verse begins with the phrase זֹאת תּוֹרַת הַנָּזִיר and ends redundantly with the phrase עַל תּוֹרַת נִזְרוֹ.

54. Taken together, the two phrases may be understood: זֹאת תּוֹרַת הַנָּזִיר, *This is the circumstance under which the Nazirite may render a decision regarding Torah law,* עַל תּוֹרַת נִזְרוֹ, *he must be in conformity with the laws of his abstinence,* that is, he must not have drunk wine (*VeChur LaZahav*).

See *Kereisos* 13b, cited in *Rashi* to *Leviticus* 10:11; see also the Baal HaTurim to *Leviticus* 10:9, s.v., יַיִן וְשֵׁכָר אֵין פָּסוּק, and 10:11, s.v., וּלְהוֹרֹת.

55. *Taanis* 26b.

55a. A Kohen who drank wine may not perform any Temple service until the effects of the wine have worn off. If such a Kohen does serve, that service is invalid (*Zevachim* 17b).

56. *Peirush HaRosh* cited in *Moshav Zekeinim*; see also *Sotah* 38a; *Rambam, Hilchos Tefillah* 15:4; *Shulchan Aruch, Orach Chaim* 128:28.

ו/כד־כה **וְאֶל־בָּנָיו לֵאמֹר כֹּה תְבָרְכוּ אֶת־בְּנֵי יִשְׂרָאֵל אָמוֹר**
כד־כה **לָהֶם: יְבָרֶכְךָ יהוה וְיִשְׁמְרֶךָ: יָאֵר יהוה | פָּנָיו**

בעל הטורים

(כג) **כֹּה תְבָרְכוּ.** לְהַזְכִּיר זְכוּת "וַאֲנִי וְהַנַּעַר נֵלְכָה עַד כֹּה", וְ"כֹּה יִהְיֶה זַרְעֶךָ". וְזֶהוּ "אֲשֶׁר עַד כֹּה בֵּרְכַנִי ה'":

וְכ"ה אוֹתִיּוֹת בְּפָסוּק "שְׁמַע יִשְׂרָאֵל". וְכ"ה פְּעָמִים לְשׁוֹן בְּרָכָה בַּחֻמָּשׁ; וְכ"ה פְּעָמִים "שָׁלוֹם" בַּחֻמָּשׁ. וּלְכָךְ מַתְחִיל בִּרְכַּת כֹּהֲנִים בִּבְרָכָה וּמְסַיֵּם בְּשָׁלוֹם, וְזֶהוּ "ה' יְבָרֵךְ אֶת עַמּוֹ בַשָּׁלוֹם":

❑ **אָמוֹר לָהֶם.** מָלֵא וָי"ו. כְּנֶגֶד שֵׁשׁ בְּרָכוֹת – יְבָרֶכְךָ, וְיִשְׁמְרֶךָ, יָאֵר, וִיחֻנֶּךָּ, יִשָּׂא, {וְיָשֵׂם לְךָ} שָׁלוֹם. וּכְנֶגֶד שִׁשָּׁה – תּוֹרַת ה' . . . עֵדוּת ה' . . . פִּקּוּדֵי ה' . . . מִצְוַת ה' . . . יִרְאַת ה' . . . מִשְׁפְּטֵי ה':

(כד) **יְבָרֶכְךָ י"י וְיִשְׁמְרֶךָ.** הַתְחָלַת הַתֵּבוֹת עוֹלֶה כ"ו, כְּנֶגֶד הַשֵּׁם שֶׁל אַרְבַּע אוֹתִיּוֹת.

BAAL HATURIM ELUCIDATED

23. כֹּה תְבָרְכוּ — SO SHALL YOU BLESS. [God's commandment regarding *Bircas Kohanim* begins with the word כֹּה, *so* or *this*] in order to recall the merit of [Abraham and Isaac, concerning which the verse states], וַאֲנִי וְהַנַּעַר נֵלְכָה עַד כֹּה, *while I* [*Abraham*] *and the lad* [*Isaac*] *will go this far* (*Genesis* 22:5), and of [God's promise to Abraham], כֹּה יִהְיֶה זַרְעֶךָ, *so shall your offspring be* (*Genesis* 15:5).[57] And this is [the blessing referred to in the verse,] אֲשֶׁר עַד כֹּה בֵּרְכַנִי ה', *for until* ***this*** *point* HASHEM *has blessed me* (*Joshua* 17:14).[58]

[The *gematria* of כֹּה is 25 and] there are 25 letters in the verse שְׁמַע יִשְׂרָאֵל, *Shema Yisrael* (*Deuteronomy* 6:4).[59] Also, the term בְּרָכָה, *blessing,* appears twenty-five times in the Torah;[60] and the term שָׁלוֹם, *peace,* appears twenty-five

57. *Sefer Raaviyah.* It is not clear why *Sefer Raaviyah, Peirush HaRokeach,* and the Baal HaTurim omitted Jacob from this comment. For their apparent source in the Midrash (*Bereishis Rabbah* 43:8) reads: From where did the Children of Israel merit *Bircas Kohanim?* . . . From Abraham, about whom it is written, כֹּה יִהְיֶה זַרְעֶךָ, ***So*** *shall your offspring be;* . . . from Isaac, about whom it is written, וַאֲנִי וְהַנַּעַר נֵלְכָה עַד כֹּה, *I and the lad will go* ***this*** *far;* . . . and from Jacob, about whom it is written, כֹּה תֹאמַר לְבֵית יַעֲקֹב, ***So*** *shall you say to the House of Jacob* (*Exodus* 19:3) . . .

It is noteworthy that the *gematria* of כֹּהֵן, *Kohen,* is 75, equal to that of כֹּה כֹּה כֹּה. Additionally: The suffix ־ן appended to a verb often indicates the person or object engaged in the action described by the verb, e.g., the term רַחֲמָן, *merciful person* (see *Ecclesiastes* 4:10), is derived from the verb רחם, *to be merciful,* and the noun גְּאַיוֹן, *arrogant person* (see *Psalms* 123:4), is derived from גאה, *to be arrogant.* Accordingly, the word כֹּהֵן may be understood as "the one who fulfills the *mitzvah* of כֹּה" (*VeChur LaZahav*).

58. *Peirush HaRokeach;* see also *Rashi* to *Joshua.*

59. The full verse reads, שְׁמַע יִשְׂרָאֵל הוי"ה אֱלֹהֵינוּ הוי"ה אֶחָד, a total of twenty-five letters.

60. *Peirush HaRokeach.* There are at least 140 words in the Torah from the root ברך, including both verbs and nouns. R' Chaim Kanievsky (in his notes to *Peirush HaRokeach*) suggests that the count includes only the noun בְּרָכָה, in its various forms, and only when it does not bear a pronominal suffix. Thus, nouns such as בִּרְכָתִי, *my blessing,* and all verbs are excluded from the list. Following these criteria, *Shoham Yakar* identifies the twenty-five appearances as: (i-v) בְּרָכָה — *Genesis* 12:2, 27:12,

and his sons, saying: So shall you bless the Children of Israel, saying to them: [24] 'May HASHEM bless you and safeguard you. [25] May HASHEM illuminate His countenance

BAAL HATURIM ELUCIDATED

times in the Torah.[61] For this reason, *Bircas Kohanim* begins with blessing[62] and concludes with peace.[63] And this is alluded to in the clause, ה׳ יְבָרֵךְ אֶת עַמּוֹ בַשָּׁלוֹם, *May HASHEM bless His nation with peace*[64] (*Psalms* 29:11).[65]

❑ אָמוֹר לָהֶם — SAYING TO THEM. The word אָמוֹר, *saying,* is spelled in full, with a ו (= 6),[66] corresponding to the six blessings [that comprise *Bircas Kohanim*]:[66a] (i) יְבָרֶכְךָ, *May* [*HASHEM*] *bless you;* (ii) וְיִשְׁמְרֶךָ, *and may He safeguard you;* (iii) יָאֵר, *may He illuminate;* (iv) וִיחֻנֶּךָּ, *and may He be gracious to you;* (v) יִשָּׂא, *may He raise . . .,* and (vi) שָׁלוֹם {וְיָשֵׂם לְךָ}; {*May He establish*} *peace* {*for you*}. And corresponding to the six [terms with which King David refers to the Torah]: תּוֹרַת ה׳, *The Torah of HASHEM;* עֵדוּת ה׳, *the testimony of HASHEM;* פִּקּוּדֵי ה׳, *the orders of HASHEM;* מִצְוַת ה׳, *the command of HASHEM;* יִרְאַת ה׳, *the fear of HASHEM;* and מִשְׁפְּטֵי ה׳, *the judgments of HASHEM* (*Psalms* 19:8-10).[67]

24. יְבָרֶכְךָ י״י וְיִשְׁמְרֶךָ — MAY HASHEM BLESS YOU AND SAFEGUARD YOU. The *gematria* of the initial letters of these words [יי״ו] is 26, equal to that of the Tetragrammaton.

27:36, *Exodus* 32:29 and *Deuteronomy* 11:26; (vi) הַבְּרָכָה — *Genesis* 27:38; (vii-xiii) הַבְּרָכָה — *Genesis* 27:41, *Deuteronomy* 11:27, 11:29, 28:8, 30:1, 30:19 and 33:1; (xiv) לִבְרָכָה — *Deuteronomy* 23:6; (xv-xvii) בִּרְכַּת — *Genesis* 28:4, 39:5 and *Deuteronomy* 33:23; (xviii-xix) כְּבִרְכַּת — *Deuteronomy* 12:15 and 16:17; (xx-xxiv) בִּרְכֹת — *Genesis* 49:25 (three times) and 49:26 (twice); and (xxv) הַבְּרָכוֹת — *Deuteronomy* 28:2.

A parallel comment in *Sefer Raaviyah* reads: כ״ה פְּעָמִים לְשׁוֹן בְּרָכָה בְּמִשְׁנֵה תוֹרָה, *The term* בְּרָכָה *appears twenty-five times in Deuteronomy.* However, the intent of that comment is unclear, for more than forty words of the root ברך appear in *Deuteronomy.*

61. *Sefer Raaviyah; Peirush HaRokeach.* Forms of the word שָׁלוֹם appear 26 times in the Torah. However, if we apply R' Chaim Kanievsky's suggestion (see note 60), the word שְׁלֹמָם (*Deuteronomy* 23:7) is excluded from the count. The twenty-five appearances are then: (i-ix) שָׁלוֹם — *Genesis* 29:6, 43:23, 43:28, *Leviticus* 26:6, *Numbers* 6:26, 25:12, *Deuteronomy* 2:26, 20:11 and 29:18; (x-xi) הֲשָׁלוֹם — *Genesis* 29:6 and 43:27; (xii-xvi) בְּשָׁלוֹם — *Genesis* 15:15, 26:29, 26:31, 28:21 and *Exodus* 18:23; (xvii-xxii) לְשָׁלוֹם — *Genesis* 37:4, 43:27, 44:17, *Exodus* 4:18, 18:7 and *Deuteronomy* 20:10; (xxiii-xxv) שְׁלוֹם — *Genesis* 37:14 (twice) and 41:16 (*VeChur LaZahav*).

Alternatively: The phrase שָׁלוֹם יִהְיֶה לִּי, *Peace will be with me* (*Deuteronomy* 29:18), refers to the imagined peace that a heretic hopes to find in his arrogant defiance. That type of שָׁלוֹם is entirely unrelated to the שָׁלוֹם of the Priestly Blessings. Accordingly, שְׁלֹמָם (*Deuteronomy* 23:7) is the twenty-fifth appearance (A.S.).

62. That is, with the words יְבָרֶכְךָ, *May HASHEM bless you.*

63. That is, with the word שָׁלוֹם, *peace.* It is noteworthy that *Bircas Kohanim* begins with a י (= 10) and ends with a ם (= 40), an allusion to the fifty times that בְּרָכָה and שָׁלוֹם appear in the Torah (*VeChur LaZahav*).

64. This clause also begins and ends with the elements of blessing and peace.

65. *Peirush HaRokeach.*

66. The word appears six times in the *Tanach.* Three times spelled אָמֹר, without a ו (*Exodus* 21:5; *Judges* 15:2; *I Samuel* 20:21); and three times spelled אָמוֹר, with a ו (here; *I Samuel* 2:30; *Jeremiah* 23:17).

66a. *Sefer Raaviyah.*

67. *Peirush HaRokeach.*

וְסוֹף הַתֵּבוֹת רה״ך עוֹלֶה מ״ה, כְּנֶגֶד הַשֵּׁם שֶׁל מ״ה תֵּבוֹת. וְזֶהוּ ״ה׳ יִשְׁמָר צֵאתְךָ וּבוֹאֶךָ״.

וְשָׁלֹשׁ תֵּבוֹת בַּפָּסוּק, כְּדֵי לְהַזְכִּיר זְכוּת אַבְרָהָם יִצְחָק וְיַעֲקֹב. וּבָהֶם ט״ו אוֹתִיּוֹת, עַל שֵׁם הָאָבוֹת, שֶׁרָאוּ זֶה אֶת זֶה ט״ו שָׁנִים. וּזְכוּת הַשְּׁבָטִים עִם הָאָבוֹת, הֵם ט״ו:

❑ **יְבָרֶכְךָ.** בִּזְכוּת אַבְרָהָם דִּכְתִיב בֵּהּ ״וַה׳ בֵּרַךְ אֶת אַבְרָהָם בַּכֹּל״:

וּשְׁלֹשָׁה תֵּבוֹת בַּפָּסוּק כְּנֶגֶד שְׁלֹשָׁה בְּרָכוֹת שֶׁנֶּאֶמְרוּ בוֹ, ״וַאֲבָרֶכְךָ״ ״וֶהְיֵה בְּרָכָה״ ״וַאֲבָרְכָה מְבָרְכֶיךָ״:

❑ **יְבָרֶכְךָ ה׳.** בְּגִימַטְרִיָּא בִּנְכָסִים וּבְגוּף:

(כה) יָאֵר. כְּנֶגֶד יִצְחָק, שֶׁרָאָה בָּעֲקֵדָה וּמֵת. וְהֵאִיר הַקָּדוֹשׁ בָּרוּךְ הוּא אֶת עֵינָיו וְהֶחֱיָהוּ. כִּדְאִיתָא בְּפִרְקֵי רַבִּי אֱלִיעֶזֶר:

❑ **יָאֵר.** לְהֵפֶךְ רא״י, שֶׁהָיָה עוֹלַת רְאִיָּה:

BAAL HATURIM ELUCIDATED

The *gematria* of the final letters of these words — רה״ך — is 45, corresponding to the Divine Name of forty-five words.[68] And this is [alluded to by the verse], ה׳ יִשְׁמָר צֵאתְךָ וּבוֹאֶךָ, *HASHEM will safeguard your departure and arrival*[69] (*Psalms* 121:8).[70]

There are three words in the verse, in order to recall the merit of [the three Patriarchs,] Abraham, Isaac and Jacob.[70a] There are fifteen letters, also referring to the three Patriarchs, for there was a fifteen-year period during which the Patriarchs saw one another.[71] Fifteen also recalls the combined merit of the twelve tribes[72] and three Patriarchs, for a total of fifteen.[73]

❑ יְבָרֶכְךָ — MAY [HASHEM] BLESS YOU in the merit of Abraham[74] of whom it is

68. *Sefer Raaviyah,* the Baal HaTurim's source for this comment, offers the following description of this Divine Name: שֵׁם שֶׁל מ״ה תֵּבוֹת, *that Name which comprises forty-five words,* וְסוֹפוֹ רי״ו, *with the three-letter word* רי״ו at its end, [שֶׁעֲלֵיהֶם הָעוֹלָם עוֹמֵד, *it is upon them that the world stands* (*Peirush HaRokeach*)] תֹּלֶה אֶרֶץ עַל בְּלִימָה, [literally, *He suspends the world on nothingness* (*Job* 26:7), which may also be understood as,] *He suspends the world on* בְּלִי מ״ה, *nothing but* [i.e., on His Divine Name that comprises] *forty-five* [words].

69. The term "departure" refers to the final letters; "arrival," to the initial letters.

70. *Peirush HaRokeach.*

70a. The reading אַבְרָהָם יִצְחָק וְיַעֲקֹב, *Abraham, Isaac and Jacob,* follows *Shoham Yakar's* manuscript edition, and that is how it appears in *Pesikta Zutresa* [*Midrash Lekach Tov*], the Baal HaTurim's apparent source. Most printed editions read ג׳ אָבוֹת, *the three Patriarchs.*

71. Abraham was one hundred when Isaac was born (*Genesis* 21:5). Isaac was sixty [and Abraham was 160] when Jacob was born (*Genesis* 25:26). Abraham lived to 175 (*Genesis* 25:7) at which time Jacob was fifteen years old (see *Rashi* to *Genesis* 25:30). Thus, the Patriarchs saw one another for fifteen years.

Regarding the importance of the three generations of Patriarchs seeing one another, see *Tosafos* to *Kesubos* 62b, s.v., החוט; see also *Bava Basra* 121b, with *Rashbam,* s.v., קפלו.

72. That is, the twelve sons of Jacob, the progenitors of the twelve tribes.

73. *Sefer Raaviyah; Peirush HaRokeach.*

The Midrash speaks of the combined merits of the tribes and the Patriarchs: Moses pleaded, זְכֹר לְאַבְרָהָם לְיִצְחָק וּלְיִשְׂרָאֵל עֲבָדֶיךָ, *Remember for the sake of Abraham, for the sake of Isaac and for the sake of Israel, Your servants* (*Exodus* 32:13). By עֲבָדֶיךָ, Moses meant the tribes, as can be seen from the prophet Isaiah's prayer (*Isaiah* 63:17), שׁוּב לְמַעַן עֲבָדֶיךָ שִׁבְטֵי נַחֲלָתֶךָ, *Return [to us] for the sake of Your servants, the tribes of Your heritage* (*Shemos Rabbah* 44:9; see also *Bamidbar Rabbah* 13:20).

74. See note 57 above.

written, וַה׳ בֵּרַךְ אֶת אַבְרָהָם בַּכֹּל, *and* HASHEM *had blessed Abraham with everything* (*Genesis* 24:1).[75]

There are three words in this verse, corresponding to the three expressions of blessing that are stated regarding Abraham: וַאֲבָרֶכְךָ, *I will bless you*; וֶהְיֵה בְּרָכָה, *and you shall be a blessing;* וַאֲבָרְכָה מְבָרְכֶיךָ, *I will bless those who bless you* (*Genesis* 12:2-3).[75]

❑ יְבָרֶכְךָ ה׳ — **MAY HASHEM BLESS YOU.** The *gematria* of this phrase (278) is equivalent[76] to that of, בִּנְכָסִים וּבְגוּף, *regarding property and regarding your physical person.*[77]

25. יָאֵר — **MAY [HASHEM] ILLUMINATE.** This expression corresponds to the Patriarch Isaac[78] who saw[79] when he was bound as a sacrifice and he died. Then the Holy One, Blessed is He, illuminated Isaac's eyes and brought him back to life, as taught in *Pirkei DeRabbi Eliezer.*[80]

❑ יָאֵר — **MAY [HASHEM] ILLUMINATE.** When reversed, the letters of this word spell ראי, [alluding to רְאִיָּה, *re'iyah*] for Isaac was [placed on the altar as] an עוֹלַת רְאִיָּה, *a re'iyah burnt-offering.*[81]

---

75. *Sefer Raaviyah.*

76. The principle of *im hakollel* allows 278 to be considered equivalent to 279, the *gematria* of the Baal HaTurim's phrase.

77. *Peirush HaRokeach.* The Midrash (*Sifrei*) records a number of opinions regarding the implication of the words יְבָרֶכְךָ and וְיִשְׁמְרֶךָ. According to one view, they mean, יְבָרֶכְךָ בִּנְכָסִים, *May He bless you with property,* וְיִשְׁמְרֶךָ בַּגּוּף, *and may He safeguard your physical person.* In the *gematria* of יְבָרֶכְךָ ה׳, the Baal HaTurim finds an allusion to these two concepts.

78. See note 57 above.

79. The Baal HaTurim states that Isaac saw something, but does not identify what he saw. In *Peirush HaRokeach,* the Baal HaTurim's apparent source, this reads: *May [HASHEM] illuminate* — this expression corresponds to Isaac, who died (see note 80 below) when he was bound as a sacrifice.

80. *Sefer Raaviyah; Peirush HaRokeach.* The Midrash states: As the knife reached his throat, Isaac's soul flew away and left [e.g., he died]. But when a voice went forth from between the angels, saying, *"Do not stretch out your hand against the lad"* (*Genesis* 22:12), his soul returned to his body (*Pirkei DeRabbi Eliezer* 31). However, no mention is made in that Midrash of Isaac seeing and God illuminating his eyes to resurrect him.

Another Midrash states: When our Patriarch Abraham bound his son [Isaac] to the altar, he [Isaac] raised his eyes and gazed at the *Shechinah* [Divine Presence]. God then said to Himself, "[Although Isaac should be put to death in accordance with the verse, *for no human can see Me and live* (*Exodus* 33:20), nevertheless, I will not put him to death now (*VeChur LaZahav*). For] if I put him to death now, I will cause pain to My beloved Abraham. Rather I will decree that Isaac's eyes go blind." [As the Talmud states: Four types of people are considered as if dead: (i) A pauper; (ii) a blind person; . . . (*Avodah Zarah* 5a).] Thus the Torah states (*Genesis* 27:1): *When Isaac had become old, his eyes dimmed from seeing* (*Bereishis Rabbah* 65:10).

The Baal HaTurim's comment seems to merge the two Midrashim into one.

81. *Sefer Raaviyah.* During the pilgrimage festivals — Pesach, Shavuos, Succos — every Jewish male is commanded to appear at the *Beis HaMikdash* (*Exodus* 23:17) where he must bring a burnt-offering (v. 15 there). Both the appearance and the accompanying offering are referred to as רְאִיָּה, *re'iyah,* literally, *appearance.*

When God commanded Abraham to offer his son Isaac on the altar, God said, וְהַעֲלֵהוּ שָׁם לְעֹלָה, *and bring him up there as a burnt-offering* (*Genesis* 22:2). After that incident, Abraham named the mountain on which it took place, ה׳ יִרְאֶה, literally, HASHEM *will see* (v. 14 there). Thus, Isaac became an עֹלַת רְאִיָּה, *re'iyah burnt-offering* (*Peirush HaRokeach*).

כו אֵלֶיךָ וִיחֻנֶּךָּ: יִשָּׂא יהוה | פָּנָיו אֵלֶיךָ וְיָשֵׂם
כז לְךָ שָׁלוֹם: וְשָׂמוּ אֶת־שְׁמִי עַל־בְּנֵי יִשְׂרָאֵל

בעל הטורים

וְיֵשׁ בּוֹ חָמֵשׁ תֵּבוֹת וְעֶשְׂרִים אוֹתִיּוֹת. כְּיִצְחָק שֶׁהָיָה אַחַר עֶשְׂרִים דּוֹרוֹת וְשָׁמַר חֲמִשָּׁה חֻמְשֵׁי תוֹרָה:

(כו) יִשָּׂא. כְּנֶגֶד יַעֲקֹב, דִּכְתִיב בֵּהּ "וַיִּשָּׂא יַעֲקֹב רַגְלָיו", וּכְתִיב בֵּהּ "וְשַׁבְתִּי בְשָׁלוֹם":

וְיֵשׁ בּוֹ שֶׁבַע תֵּבוֹת, כְּנֶגֶד הַשְּׁבָטִים אֲשֶׁר נוֹלְדוּ בְּשֶׁבַע שָׁנִים. וְכ"ה אוֹתִיּוֹת, כְּנֶגֶד "כֹּה תֹאמַר לְבֵית יַעֲקֹב":

❑ **וְיָשֵׂם.** יֵשׁ בּוֹ ז' תָּגִין. שֶׁבְּשִׁבְעָה דְרָכִים "יָשֵׂם לְךָ שָׁלוֹם", עַל שֵׁם "וּבְשִׁבְעָה דְרָכִים יָנוּסוּ לְפָנֶיךָ":

❑ **שָׁלוֹם.** בְּגִימַטְרִיָּא "עֵשָׂו". הֱוֵי מַקְדִּים שָׁלוֹם לְכָל אָדָם, וַאֲפִלּוּ בְּשָׁלוֹם גּוֹי:

(כז) וַאֲנִי אֲבָרְכֵם. בְּגִימַטְרִיָּא אַסְכִּימָה עֲלֵי יְדֵיכֶם:

❑ **וְשָׂמוּ אֶת שְׁמִי . . . וַאֲנִי אֲבָרְכֵם.** וּסְמִיךְ לֵהּ "וַיְהִי בְּיוֹם כַּלּוֹת". וְזֶהוּ "בְּכָל הַמָּקוֹם אֲשֶׁר אַזְכִּיר אֶת שְׁמִי אָבוֹא אֵלֶיךָ וּבֵרַכְתִּיךָ":

BAAL HATURIM ELUCIDATED

There are five words and twenty letters in this verse. This alludes to Isaac who was preceded by twenty generations[82] and who observed the Five Books of the Torah.[83]

26. יִשָּׂא — MAY [HASHEM] LIFT. This blessing corresponds to Jacob, concerning whom it is written, וַיִּשָּׂא יַעֲקֹב רַגְלָיו, *Jacob lifted his feet* (*Genesis* 29:1),[83a] and וְשַׁבְתִּי בְשָׁלוֹם, *and I will return in peace* (*Genesis* 28:21).[83b]

There are seven words in this verse, corresponding to the tribes who were born within a seven-year period.[84] And it contains 25 letters [equal to the *gematria* of the word כֹּה, *so*], thus it corresponds to the verse, כֹּה תֹאמַר לְבֵית יַעֲקֹב,

82. Noah was the tenth generation from Adam (see *Genesis,* Ch. 5; *Avos* 5:2). Abraham was the tenth generation from Noah (see *Genesis* 11:10-26; *Avos* 5:2). Thus, Isaac came into the world after twenty generations.

83. *Sefer Raaviyah* — The Midrash states: Abraham educated his son Isaac; he taught him Torah and guided him in his ways (*Shemos Rabbah* 1:1). This means that Isaac observed the laws of the Five Books of the Torah that he had learned from his father Abraham. And we know that Abraham observed the laws of the Five Books, for the Torah uses five expressions in the verse: (i) עֵקֶב אֲשֶׁר שָׁמַע אַבְרָהָם בְּקֹלִי, *Because Abraham obeyed My voice,* (ii) וַיִּשְׁמֹר מִשְׁמַרְתִּי, *and he observed My safeguard,* (iii) מִצְוֹתַי, *My commandments,* (iv) חֻקּוֹתַי, *My decrees,* (v) וְתוֹרֹתָי, *and My Torahs* (*Genesis* 26:5).

It is not clear why the allusion of the Five Books of the Torah appears with regard to Isaac, especially since the Five Books were taught to him by Abraham.

83a. *Rimzei Rabbeinu Yoel.*

83b. *Sefer Raaviyah.*

84. *Sefer Raaviyah.* This refers to Jacob's first eleven tribes [i.e., sons], all of whom were born while he lived with his father-in-law Laban and within seven years of the time he married Leah and Rachel (*Seder Olam* 2). Neither *Sefer Raaviyah* nor the Baal HaTurim specifies י"א שְׁבָטִים, *eleven tribes,* but a similar comment in *Peirush HaRokeach* reads: And the verse contains seven words because within seven years eleven sons were born to him.

That seven-year period ended with the birth of Rachel's first son Joseph. Until Rachel bore a son, Jacob was unable to return to the Land of Canaan (see *Rashi* to *Genesis* 30:25).

for you and be gracious to you. [26] *May* HASHEM *lift His countenance to you and establish peace for you.'* [27] *Let them place My Name upon the Children of Israel, and I shall bless them."*

BAAL HATURIM ELUCIDATED

So shall you say to the House of Jacob (*Exodus* 19:3).[84a]

❑ וְיָשֵׂם — AND [MAY HE] ESTABLISH. [According to a scribal tradition,] there are seven *tagin* on [the ש of] this word.[85] This is to indicate that through seven paths, God *will establish peace for you,* in accordance with the verse, וּבְשִׁבְעָה דְרָכִים יָנוּסוּ לְפָנֶיךָ, *and on seven roads will they flee before you* (*Deuteronomy* 28:7).[85a]

❑ שָׁלוֹם — PEACE. The *gematria* of this word (376) is equal to that of עֵשָׂו, *Esau.* [This hints at the Mishnaic dictum:] Always be first to greet any person,[86] even to greet a gentile.[87]

❑ {The Baal HaTurim's other comments to the Priestly Blessings appear at *Genesis* 12:2, 3 and *Leviticus* 9:22.}

27. וַאֲנִי אֲבָרְכֵם — AND I SHALL BLESS THEM. The *gematria* of this phrase (330) is equal to that of אַסְכִּימָה עֲלֵי יְדֵיכֶם, *I will endorse [your blessing] at your side.*[88]

❑ וְשָׂמוּ אֶת שְׁמִי ... וַאֲנִי אֲבָרְכֵם — LET THEM PLACE MY NAME ... AND I SHALL BLESS THEM. Juxtaposed to this is [וַיְהִי בְּיוֹם כַּלּוֹת [מֹשֶׁה לְהָקִים אֶת הַמִּשְׁכָּן, *It was on the day that* [*Moses*] *finished* [*erecting the Tabernacle*]. This is in accordance with God's promise, בְּכָל הַמָּקוֹם אֲשֶׁר אַזְכִּיר אֶת שְׁמִי אָבוֹא אֵלֶיךָ וּבֵרַכְתִּיךָ, *Wherever I permit My Name to be mentioned,*[89] *I shall come to you and bless you* (*Exodus* 20:21).[90]

84a. See note 57 above.

85. Regarding *tagin,* see note 42 above. According to *Sefer Tagin,* this is one of 52 times where a ש or ש is written in the Torah with seven *tagin* (see illustration). The Baal HaTurim discusses other instances of the ש with seven *tagin* in his comments to *Genesis* 46:2, *Exodus* 20:7 and *Numbers* 23:9.

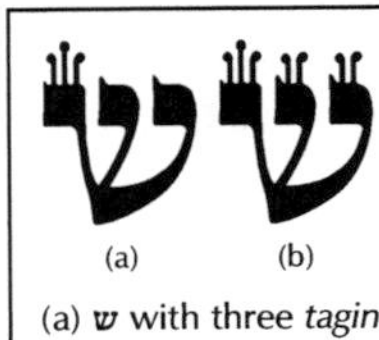

(a) ש with three *tagin*
(b) ש with seven *tagin*

85a. That verse is followed by: יְצַו ה׳ אִתְּךָ אֶת הַבְּרָכָה, HASHEM *will command the blessing for you* (*Deuteronomy* 28:8).

86. *Avos* 4:15, see *Bartenura* there.

87. See *Gittin* 61a; *Berachos* 17a.

88. *Peirush HaRokeach.* The Talmud states: The Torah has taught us the blessing that Israel receives through the mouths of the Kohanim, but it has not taught us which blessing they receive from the mouth [as it were] of the Omnipotent One. therefore, the verse states, וַאֲנִי אֲבָרְכֵם, *and I [God] shall bless them,* that is, the Kohanim bless Israel and the Holy One, Blessed is He, מַסְכִּים עַל יָדָם, *endorses [their blessing] at their side* (*Chullin* 49a; cited by *Rashi* here).

89. This refers to the *Mishkan* and *Beis HaMikdash,* for only there, during *Bircas Kohanim,* did God permit His Name [the Tetragrammaton] to be pronounced as it is written, while at any other time or in any other place it is pronounced as if it were spelled אֲדֹנָי, *Adonai* (*Sotah* 37b-38a). [Note that except during prayer or as part of a blessing or when a Scriptural verse is being read, it is customary to substitute the term הַשֵּׁם, HASHEM, literally, *the Name.*]

90. *Bamidbar Rabbah* 12:2; see also *Sotah* 38a.

ז/א־ג חמישי א וַאֲנִי אֲבָרְכֵם׃ וַיְהִי בְּיוֹם כַּלּוֹת מֹשֶׁה לְהָקִים
אֶת־הַמִּשְׁכָּן וַיִּמְשַׁח אֹתוֹ וַיְקַדֵּשׁ אֹתוֹ וְאֶת־כָּל־
כֵּלָיו וְאֶת־הַמִּזְבֵּחַ וְאֶת־כָּל־כֵּלָיו וַיִּמְשָׁחֵם וַיְקַדֵּשׁ
ב אֹתָם׃ וַיַּקְרִיבוּ נְשִׂיאֵי יִשְׂרָאֵל רָאשֵׁי בֵּית אֲבֹתָם
הֵם נְשִׂיאֵי הַמַּטֹּת הֵם הָעֹמְדִים עַל־הַפְּקֻדִים׃
ג וַיָּבִיאוּ אֶת־קָרְבָּנָם לִפְנֵי יהוה שֵׁשׁ־עֶגְלֹת צָב

בעל הטורים

ז (א) **וַיְהִי בְּיוֹם כַּלּוֹת.** סָמַךְ חֲנֻכַּת מִזְבֵּחַ לְבִרְכַּת כֹּהֲנִים. רֶמֶז לַחַשְׁמוֹנָאִים שֶׁיַּעֲשׂוּ חֲנֻכָּה׃

וְעוֹד, כְּדֵי שֶׁלֹּא תִשְׁלֹט עַיִן רָעָה בִּמְלַאכְתָּם, לְכָךְ בֵּרְכָם תְּחִלָּה.

וְסָמַךְ לַמִּשְׁכָּן. שֶׁבִּזְכוּת הַמִּשְׁכָּן יִהְיֶה שָׁלוֹם. וְכֵן דָּוִד סָמַךְ "ה' יְבָרֵךְ אֶת עַמּוֹ בַשָּׁלוֹם" לְ"מִזְמוֹר שִׁיר חֲנֻכַּת הַבַּיִת"׃

(ב־ג) **הֵם נְשִׂיאֵי הַמַּטֹּת הֵם.** סוֹפֵי תֵבוֹת לְהֵפֶךְ מֵתִים. וְכֵן "הַפְּקֻדִים וַיָּבִיאוּ אֶת קָרְבָּנָם", סוֹפֵי תֵבוֹת מוֹתָם. עַל שֵׁם "וַתִּבְעַר בָּם אֵשׁ ה', וַתֹּאכַל בִּקְצֵה הַמַּחֲנֶה", בַּקְּצִינִים שֶׁבָּהֶם׃

(ג) **שֵׁשׁ עֶגְלֹת.** כְּנֶגֶד שִׁשָּׁה מַזָּלוֹת אֲשֶׁר עוֹלִים בַּגַּלְגַּל וְשִׁשָּׁה יוֹרְדִים. וּכְנֶגֶד שִׁשָּׁה

BAAL HATURIM ELUCIDATED

VII

1. וַיְהִי בְּיוֹם כַּלּוֹת — IT WAS ON THE DAY OF ... FINISHING. The Torah juxtaposed the portion concerning the dedication of the Altar (Ch. 7) with the portion of *Bircas Kohanim* (6:22-27). This is an allusion to the Hasmonean family [of Kohanim] who would perform a [new] dedication.[91]

Additionally: In order that an evil eye not have influence on their work, [Moses] blessed them first.[92]

---

91. The story of the Hasmoneans' miraculous victory over the forces of the Syrian-Greek Antiochus and the subsequent miracle of the oil is well known. But the Menorah and its supply of olive oil were not the only things defiled by the Greeks. The Altar had been defiled with the slaughter of swine that had been offered to pagan deities. Before they were able to bring any Altar offerings, the Hasmoneans had to dismantle the Altar and build a new one on the same spot. Thus, the name חֲנֻכָּה, literally, *dedication,* for they celebrated a new חֲנֻכַּת הַמִּזְבֵּחַ, *dedication of the Altar,* at that time (see *Megillas Taanis* 9:25).

Alternatively: The Baal HaTurim's phrase, שֶׁיַּעֲשׂוּ חֲנֻכָּה, means *who would institute [the festival of] Chanukah* or *who would bring about [the miracle of] Chanukah.*

92. The Midrash relates a parable: A princess was engaged to be married. [In honor of the occasion, her father made a huge banquet. Unfortunately, because of the pomp and publicity surrounding the event,] an evil eye affected her [and she acted in an unseemly manner]. When [the effects of the evil eye had worn off] the king arranged for her wedding, but first he gave her an amulet to ward off another evil eye. And this is what happened when God gave the Torah to Israel with great pomp and publicity: An evil eye affected them . . . and, as a consequence, the *Luchos* [Tablets] were broken . . . Therefore, when they came to erect the *Mishkan,* God first gave them the passage of the blessings, lest an evil eye affect them again. Therefore, *Bircas Kohanim* [precedes the passage about the *Mishkan*] (*Tanchuma* 17).

Now, that Midrash tells us that God gave **the passage** of *Bircas Kohanim,* but the Baal HaTurim's comment reads, בֵּרְכָם, *he blessed them.* To whom does the Baal HaTurim refer? The

[1] *It was on the day of Moses' finishing erecting the Tabernacle that he anointed it, sanctified it and all its utensils, and the Altar and all its utensils, and he had anointed and sanctified them.* [2] *The leaders of Israel, the heads of their fathers' household, brought offerings; they were the leaders of the tribes, they were those who stand at the countings.* [3] *They brought their offering before* HASHEM: *six covered wagons*

BAAL HATURIM ELUCIDATED

Also: The Torah juxtaposed [the passage of *Bircas Kohanim,* which ends with שָׁלוֹם, *peace,* with] the passage of the *Mishkan,* for in the merit of the Sanctuary there will be peace.[93] Similarly, King David juxtaposed the verse, ה׳ יְבָרֵךְ אֶת עַמּוֹ בַשָּׁלוֹם, *HASHEM will bless His nation with peace* (*Psalms* 29:11), with מִזְמוֹר שִׁיר חֲנֻכַּת הַבַּיִת, *A psalm, a song for the dedication of the Temple* (*Psalms* 30:1).

2-3. הֵם נְשִׂיאֵי הַמַּטֹּת הֵם — THEY WERE THE LEADERS OF THE TRIBES, THEY . . . When reversed, the final letters of these words spell the word מֵתִים, *dead ones.* Similarly, the final letters of the words: הַפְּקֻדִים[94] וַיָּבִיאוּ אֶת קָרְבָּנָם, *the appointed officials;*[94] *they brought their offerings,* spell the word מוֹתָם, *their death.* This is in accordance with the verse, וַתִּבְעַר בָּם אֵשׁ ה׳ וַתֹּאכַל בִּקְצֵה הַמַּחֲנֶה, *and a fire of HASHEM burned against them, and it consumed at the edge of the camp* (*Numbers* 11:1) [for the word בִּקְצֵה, *the edge,* in that verse should be understood as] בַּקְּצִינִים, *at the officers* among them.[95]

❑ שֵׁשׁ עֶגְלֹת — **SIX. . .WAGONS.** These correspond to the six constellations of the zodiac that ascend in the heavenly sphere and the six that descend.[96] They also

answer can be found in another Torah passage. Our verse speaks of the first of Nissan (*Gittin* 60a; see *Rashi* here, s.v., בְּיוֹם כַּלּוֹת מֹשֶׁה לְהָקִים). Another passage that speaks about the first of Nissan and discusses the erection of the *Mishkan* (*Exodus* Ch. 40) is preceded by the verse, *And Moses blessed them* (*Exodus* 39:43). The Midrash (*Tanchuma, Pekudei* 11) records his blessing: "May the *Shechinah* [Divine Presence] rest in the work of your hands." Thus, the Baal HaTurim's comment speaks of Moses blessing Israel on that day (*VeChur LaZahav*).

93. *Tanchuma* 25; *Bamidbar Rabbah* 12:1.

94. In the simple meaning of the verse, הַפְּקֻדִים means *the countings.* But it can also mean *the appointed officials* (e.g., 31:14,48 below, see *Rashi* and *Ibn Ezra* there), and that is how the Baal HaTurim's allusion interprets the word. Thus, the three terms נְשִׂיאֵי הַמַּטֹּת, *leaders of the tribes,* הַפְּקֻדִים, *the appointed officials,* and בִּקְצֵה/בַּקְּצִינִים, *at the officers,* all refer to the same people.

95. See 11:1 below, with *Rashi* and the Baal HaTurim, s.v., בִּקְצֵה הַמַּחֲנֶה.

96. The term מַזָּלוֹת, *mazalos* (singular, מַזָּל, *mazal*), can mean *planets,* and that is how the Baal HaTurim uses it in his comments to *Leviticus* 19:15 and to 8:2 below. The noun מַזָּל is related to the verb root נזל, *to flow,* and connotes those heavenly bodies which, in contrast to the fixed stars, can be observed to "flow" or travel through the heavens (*Radak, Shorashim*). For this same reason they are also called כּוֹכְבֵי לֶכֶת, *moving stars.* However, מַזָּלוֹת more often means *constellations,* specifically, the twelve constellations that form the Zodiac (see chart, next page), and that is how the Baal HaTurim uses the term here (and in his comments to *Leviticus* 24:5 and *Deuteronomy* 32:8). They are called מַזָּלוֹת because when God causes His blessings to flow to earth, He uses these constellations as conduits and transformers that bring His infinite beneficence down to the finite world. The varying positions of the *mazalos* with relation to both

וּשְׁנֵי עָשָׂר בָּקָר עֲגָלָה עַל־שְׁנֵי הַנְּשִׂאִים וְשׁוֹר
ד לְאֶחָד וַיַּקְרִיבוּ אוֹתָם לִפְנֵי הַמִּשְׁכָּן: וַיֹּאמֶר יְהוָה
ה אֶל־מֹשֶׁה לֵּאמֹר: קַח מֵאִתָּם וְהָיוּ לַעֲבֹד אֶת־
עֲבֹדַת אֹהֶל מוֹעֵד וְנָתַתָּה אוֹתָם אֶל־הַלְוִיִּם אִישׁ
ו כְּפִי עֲבֹדָתוֹ: וַיִּקַּח מֹשֶׁה אֶת־הָעֲגָלֹת וְאֶת־הַבָּקָר
ז וַיִּתֵּן אוֹתָם אֶל־הַלְוִיִּם: אֵת ׀ שְׁתֵּי הָעֲגָלוֹת וְאֵת
אַרְבַּעַת הַבָּקָר נָתַן לִבְנֵי גֵרְשׁוֹן כְּפִי עֲבֹדָתָם:
ח וְאֵת ׀ אַרְבַּע הָעֲגָלֹת וְאֵת שְׁמֹנַת הַבָּקָר נָתַן לִבְנֵי
מְרָרִי כְּפִי עֲבֹדָתָם בְּיַד אִיתָמָר בֶּן־אַהֲרֹן הַכֹּהֵן:

בעל הטורים

עִתִּים — קֹר וְחֹם וְקַיִץ וְחֹרֶף וְזֶרַע וְקָצִיר:

❑ **וּשְׁנֵי עָשָׂר בָּקָר.** כְּנֶגֶד שְׁנֵים עָשָׂר שְׁבָטִים וּשְׁנֵים עָשָׂר מַזָּלוֹת:

time and earth will affect this heavenly flow in such manner that it can be said that mankind is under the influence or control of the *mazalos.* Nevertheless, the Talmud cites an opinion that אֵין מַזָּל לְיִשְׂרָאֵל, *Mazal does not control Israel. Rashi* explains that since the *mazal* is nothing more than a tool in God's hands, a Jew can overcome his *mazal* through sincere prayer and righteous deeds. God will then rearrange the *mazalos* to be favorable to the petitioner (*Shabbos* 156a; see also *Bereishis Rabbah* 44:10, cited by *Rashi* to *Genesis* 15:5).

As the earth moves in its yearly orbit, it is on different sides of the sun in relation to the fixed stars. As a result, the star background against which the sun appears is constantly changing. Thus, the sun is said to move through the stars during the course of the year. By plotting where among the stars the sun rises each morning, we can map out a great circle along the celestial sphere. This circle is known as the "ecliptic," the path of the sun through the stars. The stars immediately above and below the ecliptic form a band known as the zodiac (literally, circle of animals). This band is divided into twelve equal sections, with a number of the stars in each section being grouped in a constellation (מַזָּל). In the course of a year, the sun makes a complete revolution through the zodiac. Thus, during each of the twelve months, the sun is seen as rising in a different constellation.

For example, the constellation that corre-

מַזָּל / CONSTELLATIONS	ASTRONOMICAL NAME	MONTH
טָלֶה / YOUNG RAM	ARIES (THE RAM)	NISSAN
שׁוֹר / BULL	TAURUS (THE BULL)	IYAR
תְּאוֹמִים / TWINS	GEMINI (THE TWINS)	SIVAN
סַרְטָן / CRAB	CANCER (THE CRAB)	TAMMUZ
אַרְיֵה / LION	LEO (THE LION)	AV
בְּתוּלָה / MAIDEN	VIRGO (THE VIRGIN)	ELUL
מֹאזְנַיִם / SCALES	LIBRA (THE SCALES)	TISHREI
עַקְרָב / SCORPION	SCORPIO (THE SCORPION)	CHESHVAN
קֶשֶׁת / ARCHER'S BOW	SAGITTARIUS (THE ARCHER)	KISLEV
גְּדִי / GOAT OR KID	CAPRICORN (THE GOAT)	TEVES
דְּלִי / BUCKET	AQUARIUS (THE WATER BEARER)	SHEVAT
דָּגִים / FISH	PISCES (THE FISH)	ADAR

and twelve oxen — a wagon for each two leaders and an ox
for each — and they brought them before the Tabernacle.
4 *HASHEM said to Moses, saying,* 5 *"Take from them, and*
they shall be to perform the work of the Tent of Meeting;
you shall give them to the Levites, each man according to
his work."
6 *So Moses took the wagons and the oxen and gave them*
to the Levites. 7 *Two of the wagons and four of the oxen he*
gave to the sons of Gershon, in accordance with their
work. 8 *And four of the wagons and eight of the oxen he*
gave to the sons of Merari, in accordance with their work,
under the authority of Ithamar, son of Aaron the Kohen.

BAAL HATURIM ELUCIDATED

correspond to the six seasons of the year, **קֹר וְחֹם וְקַיִץ וְחֹרֶף וְזֶרַע וְקָצִיר**, *cold and heat, summer and winter, seedtime and harvest.*[97]

❑ **וּשְׁנֵי עָשָׂר בָּקָר** — AND TWELVE OXEN. Corresponding to the twelve tribes and the twelve constellations[98] of the zodiac.[99]

---

sponds to the first month of the year, Nissan, is the Ram (Aries). All through the month of Nissan, the Ram appears on the eastern horizon at daybreak while the seventh constellation, the Scales (Libra), begins to set. At the end of two hours, the Ram has risen completely and the Scales has set completely; the second constellation, the Bull (Taurus), then begins rising and the eighth constellation, the Scorpion (Scorpio), begins to set; and so it proceeds throughout the month of Nissan. During the month of Iyar, the constellation that rises at daybreak is the Bull (Taurus); the Ram, which comes up before the Bull, appears above the horizon during the last two hours of the night.

Accompanying is a chart of these twelve constellations (מַזָּלוֹת) with their corresponding months; note, however, that the rising of a new constellation does not always coincide with the beginning of the month, since the months follow the lunar calendar, while the constellations are tied to the solar cycle.

As the earth rotates on its axis, some stars rise in the east, while others set in the west; as one constellation appears in the east, another slowly disappears in the west. [This is the same phenomenon that causes the sun to rise and set each day.] The process takes two hours; at the end of two hours, the new zodiacal constellation is completely revealed, and another begins rising behind it, while the setting constellation has descended entirely below the western horizon. During the course of twenty-four hours, each of the twelve constellations appears on the horizon for two hours — six constellations by day and six by night [note that the stars that appear during the day are invisible, for they are lost in the glare of the sun]. Consequently, the position of the constellations not only signifies the particular month of the year [caused by the earth's annual revolution around the sun], but also the time of each day [caused by earth's daily rotation on its axis].

97. The verse to which the Baal HaTurim refers actually reads: **וְזֶרַע וְקָצִיר**, *seedtime and harvest,* **וְקֹר וָחֹם**, *cold and heat,* **וְקַיִץ וָחֹרֶף**, *summer and winter* (*Genesis* 8:22). It is not clear why the Baal HaTurim changed the order of the seasons.

The Talmud (*Bava Metzia* 106b) and Midrash (*Bereishis Rabbah* 34:11) correlate the six seasons of that verse with the twelve months: [The latter] half of Tishrei, Cheshvan and [the first] half of Kislev comprise "seedtime"; half of Kislev, Teves and half of Shevat — "winter"; half of Shevat, Adar and half of Nissan — "cold"; half of Nissan, Iyar and half of Sivan — "harvest"; half of Sivan, Tammuz and half of Av — "summer"; half of Av, Elul and half of Tishrei — "heat" (cited in *Rashi* to *Genesis* 8:22).

98. See note 96.

99. *Bamidbar Rabbah* 12:17.

ט וְלִבְנֵי קְהָת לֹא נָתָן כִּי־עֲבֹדַת הַקֹּדֶשׁ עֲלֵהֶם בַּכָּתֵף
י יִשָּׂאוּ: וַיַּקְרִיבוּ הַנְּשִׂאִים אֵת חֲנֻכַּת הַמִּזְבֵּחַ בְּיוֹם
הִמָּשַׁח אֹתוֹ וַיַּקְרִיבוּ הַנְּשִׂיאִם אֶת־קָרְבָּנָם לִפְנֵי
יא הַמִּזְבֵּחַ: וַיֹּאמֶר יהוה אֶל־מֹשֶׁה נָשִׂיא אֶחָד לַיּוֹם
נָשִׂיא אֶחָד לַיּוֹם יַקְרִיבוּ אֶת־קָרְבָּנָם לַחֲנֻכַּת
יב הַמִּזְבֵּחַ: וַיְהִי הַמַּקְרִיב בַּיּוֹם הָרִאשׁוֹן אֶת־
יג קָרְבָּנוֹ נַחְשׁוֹן בֶּן־עַמִּינָדָב לְמַטֵּה יְהוּדָה: וְקָרְבָּנוֹ

בעל הטורים

(יג) **וְקָרְבָּנוֹ.** וָי״ו יְתֵרָה. עַל שֵׁם שִׁשָּׁה בָנִים שֶׁיָּצְאוּ מִמֶּנּוּ, שֶׁכֻּלָּם נִתְבָּרְכוּ בְּשֵׁשׁ בְּרָכוֹת. שִׁשָּׁה בָנִים יָצְאוּ מִנַּחְשׁוֹן, בַּעֲלֵי שֵׁשׁ בְּרָכוֹת, וְאֵלּוּ הֵן – דָּוִד, מָשִׁיחַ, דָּנִיֵּאל, חֲנַנְיָה, מִישָׁאֵל, וַעֲזַרְיָה. דָּוִד – דִּכְתִיב "יֹדֵעַ נַגֵּן, וְגִבּוֹר חַיִל, וְאִישׁ מִלְחָמָה, וּנְבוֹן דָּבָר, וְאִישׁ תֹּאַר, וַה׳ עִמּוֹ". "יֹדֵעַ נַגֵּן" שֶׁיּוֹדֵעַ לִשְׁאוֹל; "וְגִבּוֹר חַיִל" יוֹדֵעַ לְהָשִׁיב; "וְאִישׁ מִלְחָמָה" יוֹדֵעַ לִשָּׂא וְלִתֵּן בְּמִלְחַמְתָּהּ שֶׁל תּוֹרָה; "וּנְבוֹן דָּבָר" מֵבִין דָּבָר מִתּוֹךְ דָּבָר; "וְאִישׁ תֹּאַר" שֶׁמַּרְאֶה פָּנִים בַּהֲלָכָה; "וַה׳ עִמּוֹ" שֶׁהֲלָכָה כְּמוֹתוֹ בְּכָל מָקוֹם.

מָשִׁיחַ – דִּכְתִיב בֵּהּ "וְנָחָה עָלָיו רוּחַ ה׳ – רוּחַ חָכְמָה וּבִינָה, רוּחַ עֵצָה וּגְבוּרָה, רוּחַ דַּעַת, וְיִרְאַת ה׳ ".

דָּנִיֵּאל חֲנַנְיָה מִישָׁאֵל וַעֲזַרְיָה – דִּכְתִיב בְּהוּ "יְלָדִים אֲשֶׁר אֵין בָּהֶם כָּל מְאוּם, וְטוֹבֵי מַרְאֶה, וּמַשְׂכִּלִים בְּכָל חָכְמָה, וְיֹדְעֵי דַעַת, וּמְבִינֵי מַדָּע, וַאֲשֶׁר כֹּחַ בָּהֶם לַעֲמֹד בְּהֵיכַל הַמֶּלֶךְ":

דָּבָר אַחֵר – לָמָּה "וְקָרְבָּנוֹ" עִם וָי״ו יְתֵרָה? כְּנֶגֶד שִׁשָּׁה דְבָרִים שֶׁנִּתְחַדְּשׁוּ בְּאוֹתוֹ הַיּוֹם בָּעוֹלָם – רִאשׁוֹן לִשְׁכִינָה שֶׁשָּׁרְתָה בְּיִשְׂרָאֵל, רִאשׁוֹן לַנְּשִׂיאִים, רִאשׁוֹן לְבִרְכַּת כֹּהֲנִים,

BAAL HATURIM ELUCIDATED

13. וְקָרְבָּנוֹ — HIS OFFERING. The prefix ־וְ (= 6) is superfluous.[100] It alludes to the six descendants of Nahshon who were each blessed with six blessings. [As the Midrash teaches:] Six descendants issued from Nahshon, each of whom was endowed with six blessings. They are David,[101] *Mashiach,* Daniel, Hananiah, Mishael, and Azariah.[102] About David, it is written: (i) יֹדֵעַ נַגֵּן, *he knows how to*

---

100. The offerings brought respectively by the twelve tribal leaders were identical. Moreover, the Torah records each leader's offering in detail in six verses, repeating the same verses for each one, changing only the number of the day and the names of the leader and his tribe. With the exception of the first two tribal leaders, the second verse of each six-verse passage begins with the word קָרְבָּנוֹ, *his offering.* But with regard to the first day, when Nahshon the tribal leader of Judah brought his offerings, the Torah adds the conjunctive prefix ־וְ, *and.* The Baal HaTurim will now offer three explanations for the inclusion of that ו.

101. *Amminadab begot Nahshon; Nahshon begot Salmah; Salmon begot Boaz; Boaz begot Obed; Obed begot Jesse; and Jesse begot David* (*Ruth* 4:20-22).

102. *The king told Ashpenaz, the chief of his officers, to bring from the children of Israel who are from the royal seed* [i.e., from the House of David] . . . *Among them from the children of Judah were Daniel, Hananiah, Mishael and Azariah* (*Daniel* 1:3,6).

[9] *And to the sons of Kohath he did not give; since the sacred
service was upon them, they carried on the shoulder.* [10] *Then
the leaders brought forward offerings for the dedication of the
Altar on the day it was anointed, and the leaders brought their
offering before the Altar.*
[11] *HASHEM said to Moses, "One leader each day, one leader
each day shall they bring their offering for the dedication of the
Altar."*
[12] *The one who brought his offering on the first day was Nah-
shon son of Amminadab, of the tribe of Judah.* [13] *His offering*

BAAL HATURIM ELUCIDATED

play music; (ii) וְגִבּוֹר חַיִל, *and he is a mighty man of valor;* (iii) וְאִישׁ מִלְחָמָה, *and he is a warrior;* (iv) וּנְבוֹן דָּבָר, *and he understands a matter;* (v) וְאִישׁ תֹּאַר, *and he is a handsome man;* and (vi) וַה׳ עִמּוֹ, *and HASHEM is with him* (*I Samuel* 16:18).[102a] [The Midrash explains the six blessings.[103]] *He knows how to play music* means that he knows how to question; *he is a mighty man of valor* means that he knows how to reply; *he is a warrior* means that he knows how to give and take in the wars of the Torah [i.e., he can participate in the discussions and debates of the study hall]; *he understands a matter* means that he can derive one concept from another; *he is a handsome man,* who can explain the fine points of Torah law; and *HASHEM is with him* means that the law follows his opinion in all instances.

About *Mashiach,* it is written: וְנָחָה עָלָיו רוּחַ ה׳, *The spirit of HASHEM will rest upon him* — (i-ii) רוּחַ חָכְמָה וּבִינָה, *a spirit of wisdom and understanding;* (iii-iv) רוּחַ עֵצָה וּגְבוּרָה, *a spirit of counsel and strength;* (v-vi) רוּחַ דַּעַת וְיִרְאַת ה׳, *a spirit of knowledge and fear of HASHEM* (*Isaiah* 11:2).

About Daniel, Hananiah, Mishael and Azariah, it is written: (i) יְלָדִים אֲשֶׁר אֵין בָּהֶם כָּל מאום, *Youths in whom there is no blemish;* (ii) וְטוֹבֵי מַרְאֶה, *they are handsome;* (iii) וּמַשְׂכִּלִים בְּכָל חָכְמָה, *they are skillful in all wisdom;* (iv) וְיֹדְעֵי דַעַת, *they are discerning in knowledge;* (v) וּמְבִינֵי מַדָּע, *they are perceptive in learning;* and (vi) וַאֲשֶׁר כֹּחַ בָּהֶם לַעֲמֹד בְּהֵיכַל הַמֶּלֶךְ, *they have the stamina to stand [and serve] in the king's palace* (*Daniel* 1:4).[104]

Alternatively: Why does וְקָרְבָּנוֹ have a superfluous ו (= 6)? It corresponds to the six new developments that occurred in the world on that day [the first of Nissan]: (i) It was the first day the Divine Presence rested among Israel; (ii) it was the first day of the tribal leaders [bringing offerings]; (iii) it was the first day that *Bircas Kohanim* [the Priestly Blessing] was recited; (iv) it was the

102a. *Midrash Tadshe* 10.

103. Some of the six qualities mentioned in the verse seem trivial. Therefore the Midrash goes on to explain how each refers to another aspect of David's Torah scholarship and his ability to render halachic decisions that cannot be disputed.

104. *Bamidbar Rabbah* 13:11.

ראשון לְמְחִיצַת מַחֲנֵה שְׁכִינָה, רִאשׁוֹן לְאִסּוּר בָּמָה, רִאשׁוֹן לִירִידַת הָאֵשׁ:

יָבוֹא בֶּן נַחְשׁוֹן בְּשֵׁשׁ מִדּוֹת וְיִבְנֶה יְסוֹד בֵּית הַמִּקְדָּשׁ:

וְלָמָּה נִקְרָא שְׁמוֹ נַחְשׁוֹן? עַל שֶׁיָּרַד תְּחִלָּה לְנַחְשׁוֹל שֶׁבַּיָּם:

דָּבָר אַחֵר – "וְקָרְבָּנוֹ" לָמָּה מָלֵא וָי"ו יְתֵרָה? כְּנֶגֶד שִׁשָּׁה דְבָרִים שֶׁנִּטְּלוּ מֵאָדָם הָרִאשׁוֹן, וַעֲתִידִין לַחֲזוֹר כְּשֶׁיָּבוֹא בֶּן נַחְשׁוֹן, הוּא הַמָּשִׁיחַ. וְאֵלּוּ הֵן הַשִּׁשָּׁה דְבָרִים שֶׁנִּטְּלוּ מֵאָדָם הָרִאשׁוֹן – זִיווֹ, דִּכְתִיב "מְשַׁנֶּה פָנָיו וַתְּשַׁלְּחֵהוּ"; חַיָּיו, דִּכְתִיב "כִּי עָפָר אַתָּה וְאֶל עָפָר תָּשׁוּב"; קוֹמָתוֹ, דִּכְתִיב "וַיִּתְחַבֵּא הָאָדָם", מְלַמֵּד שֶׁנִּגְרְעָה קוֹמָתוֹ וְנַעֲשִׂית שֶׁל מֵאָה אַמָּה; פֵּרוֹת הָאָרֶץ וְהָאִילָן, דִּכְתִיב "אֲרוּרָה הָאֲדָמָה בַּעֲבוּרֶךָ, בְּעִצָּבוֹן תֹּאכְלֶנָּה"; מְאוֹרוֹת, דִּכְתִיב "וְחָפְרָה הַלְּבָנָה וּבוֹשָׁה הַחַמָּה". וּמִנַּיִן שֶׁגְּנָזָן? שֶׁנֶּאֱמַר "וְיִמָּנַע מֵרְשָׁעִים אוֹרָם". וּמִנַּיִן שֶׁעֲתִידִים לַחֲזוֹר בִּימֵי הַמָּשִׁיחַ? זִיווֹ, שֶׁנֶּאֱמַר "וְאֹהֲבָיו כְּצֵאת הַשֶּׁמֶשׁ בִּגְבֻרָתוֹ"; חַיָּיו, דִּכְתִיב "כִּי כִימֵי הָעֵץ יְמֵי עַמִּי", ת"ק שָׁנָה, סַדָּן שֶׁל שִׁקְמָה ת"ק שָׁנָה; קוֹמָתוֹ, דִּכְתִיב "וָאוֹלֵךְ אֶתְכֶם קוֹמְמִיּוּת", בְּקוֹמָה זְקוּפָה. פֵּרוֹת הָאָרֶץ וְהָאִילָן, דִּכְתִיב "הַגֶּפֶן תִּתֵּן פִּרְיָהּ וְהָאָרֶץ תִּתֵּן אֶת יְבוּלָהּ"; מְאוֹרוֹת, דִּכְתִיב "וְהָיָה אוֹר הַלְּבָנָה כְּאוֹר הַחַמָּה וְאוֹר הַחַמָּה יִהְיֶה שִׁבְעָתַיִם":

BAAL HATURIM ELUCIDATED

first day that partitions were established around the camp of the Divine Presence; (v) it was the first day of the prohibition against the use of *bamos,* i.e., altars situated outside the precincts of the *Mishkan;* and (vi) it was the first day on which fire descended from heaven [onto the Altar].[105]

[Alternatively:] The superfluous ו (= 6) says, "Let [David], the descendant of Nahshon blessed with six qualities,[106] come and build the foundation[107] of the *Beis HaMikdash.*[108]

Why was he called נַחְשׁוֹן, *Nahshon*? Because he was the first to descend into the [109]נַחְשׁוֹל *waves,* that are in the Sea of Reeds."[110]

105. *Bamidbar Rabbah* 13:10, see *Mattenos Kehunah* there; *Peirush HaRosh,* cited in *Moshav Zekeinim;* cf. *Rashi* to *Leviticus* 9:1.

This same allusion appears in *Midrash Tadshe* 10, but with some differences: (i) It was the first day of the *Kehunah;* (ii) . . . of the tribal leaders' offerings; (iii) . . . of the regular Altar service; (iv) . . . of the exodus from Egypt [i.e., on the first of Nissan, the Israelites were told that they would leave Egypt on the fifteenth (see *Exodus,* Ch. 12)]; (v) . . . the first month; and (vi) . . . the prohibition against *bamos.*

106. See earlier in this comment.

107. When he was settled on his throne, King David complained, *"See now! I am living in a house of cedar while the Ark of God dwells within the curtain!"* (*II Samuel* 7:2; see also *I Chronicles* 17:1). God's reply was that it was not for David to build the Temple, rather, *"When your days are complete and you lie with your forefathers, I will raise after you* [*one of*] *your seed who will issue from your loins, and I will make his kingdom firm. He shall build the Temple for My sake . . ."* (vv. 12-13 there; see also *I Chronicles* 17:11-12). Nevertheless, David dedicated himself to "build the foundation" — i.e., to lay the groundwork by purchasing the site, preparing the materials and organizing the Kohanim and Levites — for the Temple that his son and successor Solomon would build (see *I Chronicles* 21:18—22:19; see also *I Kings* 5:17-19, 6:12 and 8:15-20).

108. *Bamidbar Rabbah* 13:10.

109. The letters נ and ל are sometimes interchanged. Thus, in Chapter 13 of *Nehemiah* we find the words לִשְׁכָּה (vv. 4,5,8) and נִשְׁכָּה (v. 7) used for *chamber,* even though they refer to the same chamber (see *Rashi* to *Nehemiah* 3:30). Similarly, in Chapter 6 of *I Samuel* we find the same place referred to as both הָאֶבֶן הַגְּדוֹלָה (v. 15), אָבֵל הַגְּדוֹלָה (v. 18, see *Rashi* there).

110. *Bamidbar Rabbah* 13:7. The Talmud records what took place at the Sea of Reeds: This one said, "I will not be the first to go down into the sea!" And that one said, "I will not be the first to go down into the sea!" Then Nahshon son

Alternatively: Why is there a superfluous ו (= 6) in the word וְקָרְבָּנוֹ? It corresponds to the six qualities which were taken from Adam the first man [when he sinned,] and will return when *Mashiach,* the descendant of Nahshon, will come. These are the six qualities taken from Adam the first man: (i) the radiance of his countenance,[110a] as it is written, מְשַׁנֶּה פָנָיו וַתְּשַׁלְּחֵהוּ, *You change his countenance and then send him away* (*Job* 14:20); (ii) his life,[111] as it is written, כִּי עָפָר אַתָּה וְאֶל עָפָר תָּשׁוּב, *For you are dust, and to dust shall you return* (*Genesis* 3:19); (iii) his stature,[112] as it is written, וַיִּתְחַבֵּא הָאָדָם, *and Adam hid himself* (*Genesis* 3:8), [which the Midrash[113] interprets] to mean that his stature was reduced, and he became only one hundred cubits tall;[114] (iv-v) the fruits of the earth and of the trees, as it written, אֲרוּרָה הָאֲדָמָה בַּעֲבוּרֶךָ בְּעִצָּבוֹן תֹּאכְלֶנָּה, *accursed is the ground because of you; through suffering shall you eat of it* (*Genesis* 3:17);[115] (vi) the luminaries, as it is written, וְחָפְרָה הַלְּבָנָה וּבוֹשָׁה הַחַמָּה, *The moon will be humiliated and the sun will be shamed* (*Isaiah* 24:23); and how do we know that their light was entombed? For it is said, וְיִמָּנַע מֵרְשָׁעִים אוֹרָם, *and their light will be withheld from the wicked* (*Job* 38:15).

How do we know that these are all going to return in the time of *Mashiach*? (i) His radiance, as it is stated, וְאֹהֲבָיו כְּצֵאת הַשֶּׁמֶשׁ בִּגְבֻרָתוֹ, *Those who love Him will be like the sun going forth in its strength* (*Judges* 5:31); (ii) his life, as it is written, כִּי כִימֵי הָעֵץ יְמֵי עַמִּי, *For the lifetime of My people will be like the lifetime of the tree* (*Isaiah* 65:22),[116] i.e., five hundred years, for the stump of certain wild fig trees[117] can remain alive for five hundred years;[118] (iii) his stature, as it is written, וָאוֹלֵךְ אֶתְכֶם קוֹמְמִיּוּת, *and I shall lead you erect* (*Leviticus* 26:13), i.e., with an upright posture; (iv-v) the fruits of the earth and of the trees, as it is written, הַגֶּפֶן תִּתֵּן פִּרְיָהּ וְהָאָרֶץ תִּתֵּן אֶת יְבוּלָהּ, *The vine will give forth its fruit, the land will give forth its produce* (*Zachariah* 8:12); (vi) the luminaries, as it is written, וְהָיָה אוֹר הַלְּבָנָה כְּאוֹר הַחַמָּה וְאוֹר הַחַמָּה יִהְיֶה שִׁבְעָתַיִם, *The light of the moon will be like the light of the sun, and the light of the sun will be seven times greater* (*Isaiah* 30:26).[119]

---

of Amminadab leaped forward and went into the sea first . . . (*Sotah* 37a).

110a. See *Bava Basra* 58a.

111. That is, death was decreed upon mankind as a result of Adam's sin.

112. At his creation, Adam's height reached to the heavens (*Chagigah* 12a, cited in *Rashi* to *Deuteronomy* 4:32, s.v., וּלְמִקְצֵה הַשָּׁמַיִם).

113. *Bereishis Rabbah* 19:8, see *Peirush Maharzu* there, s.v., אמר ר׳ איבו.

114. The verse in *Genesis* states that *Adam hid . . . among the trees of the garden.* But if Adam reached to the heavens, how could he have hidden among the trees? Thus, this verse teaches that his stature was reduced after his sin (*Peirush Maharzu* to *Bereishis Rabbah* 12:6, s.v., ויתחבא האדם ואשתו).

115. The Baal HaTurim counts the produce of the earth and the produce of the trees as two separate entities, yet he adduces a verse that mentions only הָאֲדָמָה, *the earth,* but not הָאִילָן or הָעֵץ, *the trees!* Perhaps the term בְּעִצָּבוֹן, *through suffering,* can be understood as two words בְּעֵץ בּוֹן, *of the tree of understanding* [בּוֹן is a gerundive form of the verb root בִּין, *to understand*]. Thus, עִצָּבוֹן is a just punishment for having eaten from the עֵץ בּוֹן (*VeChur LaZahav*).

116. See *Radak* there.

117. The translation of סַדָּן שֶׁל שִׁקְמָה follows *Rama, Yoreh Deah* 297:10.

118. The Baal HaTurim's source for the life span of the שִׁקְמָה is unknown. The Midrash states that it remains alive for six hundred years (*Bereishis Rabbah* 12:16 and *Bamidbar Rabbah* 13:12).

119. *Bamidbar Rabbah* 13:12.

ז/יג קַעֲרַת־כֶּסֶף אַחַת שְׁלֹשִׁים וּמֵאָה מִשְׁקָלָהּ
מִזְרָק אֶחָד כֶּסֶף שִׁבְעִים שֶׁקֶל בְּשֶׁקֶל הַקֹּדֶשׁ

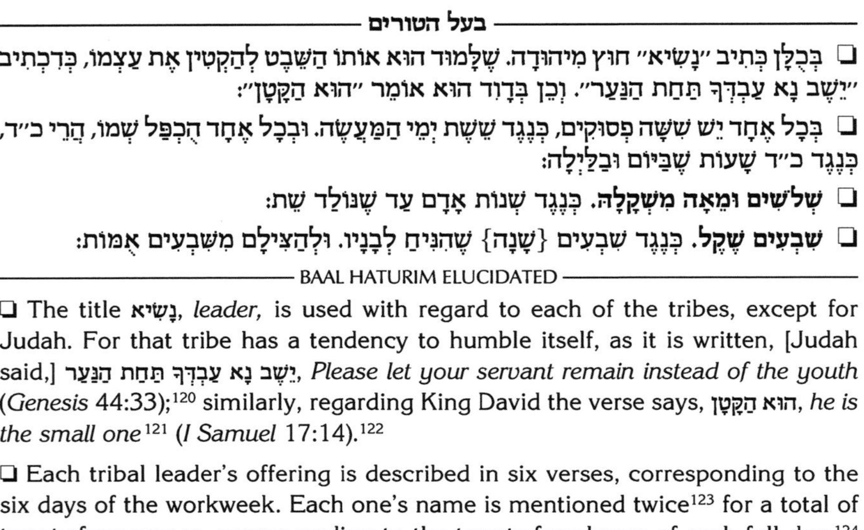

בעל הטורים

❑ בְּכֻלָּן כְּתִיב "נְשִׂיא" חוּץ מִיהוּדָה. שֶׁלָּמוּד הוּא אוֹתוֹ הַשֵּׁבֶט לְהַקְטִין אֶת עַצְמוֹ, כְּדִכְתִיב "יֵשֶׁב נָא עַבְדְּךָ תַּחַת הַנַּעַר". וְכֵן בְּדָוִד הוּא אוֹמֵר "הוּא הַקָּטָן":

❑ בְּכָל אֶחָד יֵשׁ שִׁשָּׁה פְסוּקִים, כְּנֶגֶד שֵׁשֶׁת יְמֵי הַמַּעֲשֶׂה. וּבְכָל אֶחָד הֻכְפַּל שְׁמוֹ, הֲרֵי כ"ד, כְּנֶגֶד כ"ד שָׁעוֹת שֶׁבַּיּוֹם וּבַלַּיְלָה:

❑ **שְׁלֹשִׁים וּמֵאָה מִשְׁקָלָהּ.** כְּנֶגֶד שְׁנוֹת אָדָם עַד שֶׁנּוֹלַד שֵׁת:

❑ **שִׁבְעִים שֶׁקֶל.** כְּנֶגֶד שִׁבְעִים {שָׁנָה} שֶׁהִנִּיחַ לְבָנָיו. וּלְהַצִּילָם מִשִּׁבְעִים אֻמּוֹת:

BAAL HATURIM ELUCIDATED

❑ The title **נָשִׂיא**, *leader,* is used with regard to each of the tribes, except for Judah. For that tribe has a tendency to humble itself, as it is written, [Judah said,] **יֵשֶׁב נָא עַבְדְּךָ תַּחַת הַנַּעַר**, *Please let your servant remain instead of the youth* (*Genesis* 44:33);[120] similarly, regarding King David the verse says, **הוּא הַקָּטָן**, *he is the small one*[121] (*I Samuel* 17:14).[122]

❑ Each tribal leader's offering is described in six verses, corresponding to the six days of the workweek. Each one's name is mentioned twice[123] for a total of twenty-four names, corresponding to the twenty-four hours of each full day.[124]

120. See *Bamidbar Rabbah* 13:3.

121. Although the simple meaning of the verse is that David was the youngest of Jesse's sons, the Talmud (*Megillah* 11b) interprets this phrase as a reference to David's life-long humility and modesty.

122. See *Peirush HaRokeach.*

123. Once in the first verse of his passage; and again in the last.

124. *Peirush HaRokeach.* Neither *Peirush HaRokeach* nor the Baal HaTurim explain the connection between the offerings of the tribal leaders and the days of the workweek or the twenty-four hours of the day.

To understand the link with the six days of work, we will first raise another question: If the tribal leaders brought their offerings on each of twelve contiguous days, then even though no other private offerings ever override the Sabbath restrictions (e.g., slaughtering), nevertheless, at least one of the leaders brought his offering on *Shabbos.* Now, whereas the laws of *Shabbos* were set aside with regard to that offering, we might mistakenly conclude that all the laws of the Sabbath were suspended on that day in honor of the inauguration of the *Mishkan.* Indeed, we find that when King Solomon inaugurated the *Beis HaMikdash,* the celebration and feasting continued right through Yom Kippur (see *I Kings* 8:65; *II Chronicles* 7:8-10; and *Moed Katan* 9a). One might think that something similar happened at the inauguration of the *Mishkan* with regard to *Shabbos.* To prevent such an implication, the Torah uses six verses, alluding to the six days of the work week, as if to say: During the inauguration of the *Mishkan,* even though one tribal leader's offering was brought on *Shabbos,* all other Sabbath laws remained in full force (*VeChur LaZahav*).

The connection between the tribal leaders' offerings and the twenty-four hours of each day may be explained by the kabbalistic teachings that the twelve months of the year correspond to the twelve constellations of the zodiac (*Sefer Yetzirah* 5:2; see note 96 above) and to the twelve tribes of Israel, according to their placement in the *degalim*-divisions, the same order in which the tribal leaders brought their offering, thus: Nissan corresponds to Judah; Iyar to Issachar; Sivan to Zebulun; Tammuz to Reuben; Av to Simeon; Elul to Gad; Tishrei to Ephraim; Cheshvan to Manasseh; Kislev to Benjamin; Teves to Dan; Shevat to Asher; and Adar to Naphtali (*Shaarei Orah* 5 [65b]). Accordingly, we can draw a correspondence between the twelve

was: one silver bowl, its weight a hundred and thirty [shekels]; and one silver basin of seventy shekels in the sacred shekel;

BAAL HATURIM ELUCIDATED

❑ שְׁלֹשִׁים וּמֵאָה מִשְׁקָלָהּ — **ITS WEIGHT A HUNDRED AND THIRTY,** corresponding to the number of years Adam lived before [his son] Seth was born.[125]

❑ שִׁבְעִים שֶׁקֶל — **SEVENTY SHEKELS,** corresponding to the seventy {years} Adam left to his descendants;[126] and to save them[127] from the seventy nations.[128]

מַזָּל / CONSTELLATIONS	TRIBE	MONTH
טָלֶה / YOUNG RAM	JUDAH	NISSAN
שׁוֹר / BULL	ISSACHAR	IYAR
תְּאוֹמִים / TWINS	ZEBULUN	SIVAN
סַרְטָן / CRAB	REUBEN	TAMMUZ
אַרְיֵה / LION	SIMEON	AV
בְּתוּלָה / MAIDEN	GAD	ELUL
מֹאזְנַיִם / SCALES	EPHRAIM	TISHREI
עַקְרָב / SCORPION	MANASSEH	CHESHVAN
קֶשֶׁת / ARCHER'S BOW	BENJAMIN	KISLEV
גְּדִי / GOAT OR KID	DAN	TEVES
דְּלִי / BUCKET	ASHER	SHEVAT
דָּגִים / FISH	NAPHTALI	ADAR

months, the twelve tribes and the twelve constellations: Nissan-Judah-Ram; Iyar-Issachar-Bull; etc. And, as we have seen above (note 96), each of the twelve constellations "rules" for two hours during each day. Thus, the connection between the tribal leaders and the hours of the day. This also explains why each leader's name is mentioned twice — once for each of the two hours that the corresponding constellation "rules" (*VeChur LaZahav*).

125. *Bamidbar Rabbah* 14:12; *Rashi* citing the *Yesod* of R' Moshe HaDarshan.

126. This refers to King David [and the plural form לְבָנָיו, *to his descendants,* refers to the dynasty that he established, because, if not for Adam's largesse, that dynasty would not have come into existence (*VeChur LaZahav*)] and is based on the following Midrash: The Holy One, Blessed is He, showed Adam all future generations . . . When Adam saw David's soul in the Garden of Eden and that it had not been given any years to live on this earth, he was astonished and gave seventy years of his own life to David. Therefore, Adam [who would have lived forever, but because of his sin, was to have lived for only one thousand years] died at age 930. The remaining seventy years of Adam's life were the ones he gave to David (*Zohar* 1:91b, 168a; *Bamidbar Rabbah* 14:12; *Ittur Bikkurim*).

Alternatively: This refers to the seventy-year life span of the average man. It is based on a different Midrash (*Bereishis Rabbah* 19:8) which reads: God said to Adam, "I have told you [regarding the Tree of Knowledge,] that *on the day you eat of it you shall surely die* (*Genesis* 2:17). But you do not know whether I meant one of My days or one of your days. Behold, I am giving you one of My days, which comprises a full millennium" (see *Psalms* 90:4). Yet Adam lived only nine hundred and thirty years (see *Genesis* 5:5), for he left seventy years for his offspring, as it is written (*Psalms* 90:10), *the days of our lifetime are seventy years* (A.S.).

127. According to the first interpretation of the Baal HaTurim's comment (see note 126), the antecedent of the pronoun "them" is King David and his dynasty; i.e., Nahshon intended these offerings as a pre-emptive move so that centuries later their merit could protect "them" from the seventy hostile nations of their respective eras. According to the second interpretation it refers to all of mankind; i.e., Nahshon wished to protect all of Adam's offspring from the evil ways of the seventy hostile nations.

128. See *Rashi.*

יד שְׁנֵיהֶ֣ם ׀ מְלֵאִ֗ים סֹ֛לֶת בְּלוּלָ֥ה בַשֶּׁ֖מֶן לְמִנְחָֽה׃ כַּ֥ף
טו אַחַ֛ת עֲשָׂרָ֥ה זָהָ֖ב מְלֵאָ֥ה קְטֹֽרֶת׃ פַּ֣ר אֶחָ֞ד בֶּן־בָּקָ֗ר
טז אַ֧יִל אֶחָ֛ד כֶּֽבֶשׂ־אֶחָ֥ד בֶּן־שְׁנָת֖וֹ לְעֹלָֽה׃ שְׂעִיר־
יז עִזִּ֥ים אֶחָ֖ד לְחַטָּֽאת׃ וּלְזֶ֣בַח הַשְּׁלָמִים֮ בָּקָ֣ר שְׁנַ֒יִם֒
אֵילִ֤ם חֲמִשָּׁה֙ עַתֻּדִ֣ים חֲמִשָּׁ֔ה כְּבָשִׂ֥ים בְּנֵי־שָׁנָ֖ה
חֲמִשָּׁ֑ה זֶ֛ה קָרְבַּ֥ן נַחְשׁ֖וֹן בֶּן־עַמִּינָדָֽב׃

בעל הטורים

❑ **שִׁבְעִים שֶׁקֶל.** בְּגִימַטְרִיָּא ״שִׁבְעִים נֶפֶשׁ״. בִּשְׁבִיל שִׁבְעִים שֶׁיָּרְדוּ לְמִצְרָיִם:

(יד) **כַּף אַחַת.** כְּנֶגֶד הַתּוֹרָה שֶׁנִּתְּנָה מִכַּף יָדוֹ שֶׁל הַקָּדוֹשׁ בָּרוּךְ הוּא:

❑ **עֲשָׂרָה זָהָב.** כְּנֶגֶד עֲשֶׂרֶת הַדִּבְּרוֹת:

❑ **מְלֵאָה קְטֹרֶת.** תַּחֲלִיף הַקּוּ״ף בְּדָלֶ״ת בְּאַ״תְ בַּ״שׁ וְיַעֲלֶה לְמִנְיַן תרי״ג:

(טו) **פַּר אֶחָד.** כְּנֶגֶד אַבְרָהָם, ״וְאֶל הַבָּקָר רָץ אַבְרָהָם״:

❑ **אַיִל.** כְּנֶגֶד יִצְחָק, ״וַיִּקַּח אֶת הָאַיִל וַיַּעֲלֵהוּ לְעֹלָה תַּחַת בְּנוֹ״:

❑ **כֶּבֶשׂ.** כְּנֶגֶד יַעֲקֹב, ״וְהַכְּשָׂבִים הִפְרִיד יַעֲקֹב״:
״פַּר״ ״אַיִל״ ״כֶּבֶשׂ״ בְּגִימַטְרִיָּא אַבְרָהָם יִצְחָק וְיַעֲקֹב:

(יז) **וּלְזֶבַח הַשְּׁלָמִים בָּקָר שְׁנַיִם.** כְּנֶגֶד מֹשֶׁה וְאַהֲרֹן, שֶׁעָשׂוּ שָׁלוֹם בֵּין יִשְׂרָאֵל לַאֲבִיהֶם שֶׁבַּשָּׁמַיִם:

❑ **אֵילִם . . . עַתּוּדִים . . . כְּבָשִׂים.** שְׁלֹשָׁה מִינִים. כְּנֶגֶד כֹּהֲנִים לְוִיִּם וְיִשְׂרְאֵלִים; וּכְנֶגֶד תּוֹרָה נְבִיאִים וּכְתוּבִים:

BAAL HATURIM ELUCIDATED

❑ **שִׁבְעִים שֶׁקֶל** — SEVENTY SHEKELS. The *gematria* of this phrase (852) is equal to that of [129]**שִׁבְעִים נֶפֶשׁ**, *seventy souls* (*Exodus* 1:5). [It was this weight] because of the seventy souls who descended to Egypt.[130]

14. כַּף אַחַת — ONE LADLE, corresponding to the Torah which was given from the hand[131] of the Holy One, Blessed is He.[132]

❑ **עֲשָׂרָה זָהָב** — GOLD [WEIGHING] TEN [SHEKELS], corresponding to the Ten Commandments.[132]

❑ **מְלֵאָה קְטֹרֶת** — FILLED WITH INCENSE. Exchange the ק [of קְטֹרֶת] for a ד according to the letter exchange system known as [133]**אַ״תְ בַּ״שׁ** and the *gematria*

129. See the Baal HaTurim to *Exodus* 30:13, s.v., שֶׁקֶל.

130. *Peirush HaRokeach* explains that the seventy shekels were offered to give thanks to God for having brought forth the Children of Israel — the descendants of the original seventy souls who descended to Egypt — from their period of slavery in that land.

131. The word כַּף can refer to the *palm* of the hand (e.g., *Leviticus* 14:15); the *sole* of the foot (e.g., *Deuteronomy* 11:24); any body part of similar shape (e.g., *Genesis* 32:25); or any utensil with a depression in which things can be held, such as a spoon or ladle. Thus, כַּף, *ladle,* alludes to כַּף יָד, *the palm of the hand.*

132. *Rashi* to v. 20; see note 134.

133. **אַ״תְ בַּ״שׁ** is a system of letter exchange in which the first letter of the alphabet — **א** — may

both of them filled with fine flour mixed with oil for a meal-offering; 14 *one ladle of gold [weighing] ten [shekels], filled with incense;* 15 *one young bull, one ram, one sheep in its first year for a burnt-offering;* 16 *one he-goat for a sin-offering;* 17 *and for the slaughter of a peace-offering: two cattle, five rams, five he-goats, five sheep in their first year — this is the offering of Nahshon son of Amminadab.*

BAAL HATURIM ELUCIDATED

of that word will be 613.[134]

15. פַּר אֶחָד — ONE BULL, corresponding to Abraham, as the verse states, וְאֶל הַבָּקָר רָץ אַבְרָהָם, *Then Abraham ran to the cattle* (Genesis 18:7) . . .[135]

❑ **אַיִל** — RAM, corresponding to Isaac, as it states, וַיִּקַּח אֶת הָאַיִל וַיַּעֲלֵהוּ לְעֹלָה תַּחַת בְּנוֹ, *and [he] took the ram and offered it up as an offering instead of his son* (Genesis 22:13) . . .[135]

❑ **כֶּבֶשׂ** — SHEEP, corresponding to Jacob, as is written, וְהַכְּשָׂבִים הִפְרִיד יַעֲקֹב, *Jacob segregated the sheep* (Genesis 30:40).[135]

The combined *gematria* of the three words פַּר אַיִל כֶּבֶשׂ, *bull . . . ram . . . sheep,* is 643, equivalent[136] to that of אַבְרָהָם יִצְחָק וְיַעֲקֹב, *Abraham, Isaac, and Jacob.*[137]

17. וּלְזֶבַח הַשְּׁלָמִים בָּקָר שְׁנַיִם — AND FOR THE SLAUGHTER OF A PEACE-OFFERING: TWO CATTLE, corresponding to Moses and Aaron who brought about peace between Israel and their Father in heaven.[138]

❑ **אֵילִם . . . עַתּוּדִים . . . כְּבָשִׂים** — RAMS . . . HE-GOATS . . . SHEEP, three types [of animals] corresponding to [the three divisions of Israel:] Kohanim, Levites and Israelites. And corresponding to [the three divisions of the *Tanach*]: תּוֹרָה, *the Torah,* נְבִיאִים, *the Prophets,* and כְּתוּבִים, *the Writings.*[138a]

כ	י	ט	ח	ז	ו	ה	ד	ג	ב	א
ל	מ	נ	ס	ע	פ	צ	ק	ר	ש	ת

אַ״תְ בַּ״שׁ, in which either letter of a pair may be exchanged for the other.

be exchanged with the last letter — ת; the second letter — ב — with the second to last — ש; and so on. Thus, the name אַ״תְ בַּ״שׁ, after the first two pairs of letter exchanges.

134. *Rashi.* The Baal HaTurim's three comments to this verse should be read together: The כַּף corresponds to the Torah, i.e., the *Luchos* [Tablets] of the Law; it weighed ten shekels, corresponding to the Ten Commandments; and the *gematria* 613 alludes to the 613 *mitzvos,* represented by the first 613 letters on the *Luchos* (see the Baal HaTurim to *Exodus* 20:13 and note 101a there).

135. *Rashi* to v. 21. The three comments — פַּר אֶחָד; אַיִל; כֶּבֶשׂ — should be read as one, for each finds an allusion to another of the three Patriarchs.

136. The principle of *im hakollel* allows 643 to be considered equivalent to 644, the *gematria* of the Baal HaTurim's phrase.

137. *Peirush HaRokeach;* see *Rashi* to verse 21 below.

138. *Rashi* to v. 23.

138a. *Rashi* to v. 23; see also *Bamidbar Rabbah* 14:10. Neither *Rashi* nor the Midrash explain the connection between these three species and the three divisions of either Israel or the *Tanach.*

יח בַּיּוֹם֙ הַשֵּׁנִ֔י הִקְרִ֖יב נְתַנְאֵ֣ל בֶּן־צוּעָ֑ר נְשִׂ֖יא
יט יִשָּׂשכָֽר׃ הִקְרִ֨ב אֶת־קָרְבָּנ֜וֹ קַֽעֲרַת־כֶּ֣סֶף אַחַ֗ת
שְׁלֹשִׁ֣ים וּמֵאָה֮ מִשְׁקָלָהּ֒ מִזְרָ֤ק אֶחָד֙ כֶּ֔סֶף שִׁבְעִ֥ים
שֶׁ֖קֶל בְּשֶׁ֣קֶל הַקֹּ֑דֶשׁ שְׁנֵיהֶ֣ם ׀ מְלֵאִ֗ים סֹ֛לֶת בְּלוּלָ֥ה
כ בַשֶּׁ֖מֶן לְמִנְחָֽה׃ כַּ֥ף אַחַ֛ת עֲשָׂרָ֥ה זָהָ֖ב מְלֵאָ֥ה
כא קְטֹֽרֶת׃ פַּ֣ר אֶחָ֞ד בֶּן־בָּקָ֗ר אַ֧יִל אֶחָ֛ד כֶּֽבֶשׂ־אֶחָ֥ד
כב בֶּן־שְׁנָת֖וֹ לְעֹלָֽה׃ שְׂעִיר־עִזִּ֥ים אֶחָ֖ד לְחַטָּֽאת׃
כג וּלְזֶ֣בַח הַשְּׁלָמִים֮ בָּקָ֣ר שְׁנַ֒יִם֒ אֵילִ֤ם חֲמִשָּׁה֙ עַתֻּדִ֣ים
חֲמִשָּׁ֔ה כְּבָשִׂ֥ים בְּנֵי־שָׁנָ֖ה חֲמִשָּׁ֑ה זֶ֛ה קָרְבַּ֥ן נְתַנְאֵ֖ל
בֶּן־צוּעָֽר׃
כד בַּיּוֹם֙ הַשְּׁלִישִׁ֔י נָשִׂ֖יא לִבְנֵ֣י זְבוּלֻ֑ן אֱלִיאָ֖ב בֶּן־חֵלֹֽן׃
כה קָרְבָּנ֞וֹ קַֽעֲרַת־כֶּ֣סֶף אַחַ֗ת שְׁלֹשִׁ֣ים וּמֵאָה֮ מִשְׁקָלָהּ֒
מִזְרָ֤ק אֶחָד֙ כֶּ֔סֶף שִׁבְעִ֥ים שֶׁ֖קֶל בְּשֶׁ֣קֶל הַקֹּ֑דֶשׁ
כו שְׁנֵיהֶ֣ם ׀ מְלֵאִ֗ים סֹ֛לֶת בְּלוּלָ֥ה בַשֶּׁ֖מֶן לְמִנְחָֽה׃ כַּ֥ף
כז אַחַ֛ת עֲשָׂרָ֥ה זָהָ֖ב מְלֵאָ֥ה קְטֹֽרֶת׃ פַּ֣ר אֶחָ֞ד בֶּן־בָּקָ֗ר
כח אַ֧יִל אֶחָ֛ד כֶּֽבֶשׂ־אֶחָ֥ד בֶּן־שְׁנָת֖וֹ לְעֹלָֽה׃ שְׂעִיר־
כט עִזִּ֥ים אֶחָ֖ד לְחַטָּֽאת׃ וּלְזֶ֣בַח הַשְּׁלָמִים֮ בָּקָ֣ר שְׁנַ֒יִם֒
אֵילִ֤ם חֲמִשָּׁה֙ עַתֻּדִ֣ים חֲמִשָּׁ֔ה כְּבָשִׂ֥ים בְּנֵי־שָׁנָ֖ה
חֲמִשָּׁ֑ה זֶ֛ה קָרְבַּ֥ן אֱלִיאָ֖ב בֶּן־חֵלֹֽן׃

בעל הטורים

❑ וְכֵן "עַתּוּדִים" דִּיהוּדָה מָלֵא וָי"ו. שֶׁדָּוִד שֶׁעָמַד מִמֶּנּוּ, נִתְבָּרֵךְ בְּשֵׁשׁ בְּרָכוֹת. וְאֵין עַתּוּדִים אֶלָּא לְשׁוֹן עֲמִידָה, כְּמָה דְּאַתְּ אָמַר "אֲשֶׁר הִתְעַתְּדוּ לְגַלִּים". וְאוֹמֵר "וְעַתְּדָהּ בַּשָּׂדֶה לָךְ". פֵּרוּשׁ, יָבוֹא בֶּן נַחְשׁוֹן בְּשֵׁשׁ מִדּוֹת וְיִבְנֶה יְסוֹד בֵּית הַמִּקְדָּשׁ:

(יח) בַּיּוֹם הַשֵּׁנִי הִקְרִיב. בְּגִימַטְרִיָּא נָתַן לָהֶם עֵצָה:

BAAL HATURIM ELUCIDATED

❑ In the passage regarding the tribe of Judah, the term עַתּוּדִים, *he-goats,* is spelled in full, with a ו.[139] This is because David, who arose from him, was granted six blessings.[140] The term עַתּוּדִים refers to standing [or arising],[141] as in

139. Regarding each of the other eleven tribes, it is spelled defectively, עַתֻּדִים, without a ו (e.g., in vv. 23, 29, etc.).

140. See the Baal HaTurim to v. 13 above, s.v., וְקָרְבָּנוֹ.

141. In the realm of פְּשָׁט, *peshat* (the simple meaning of the word), the root עתד, like the root עמד, means to stand (see *Ibn Ezra* to the two verses adduced by the Baal HaTurim). In the realm of רֶמֶז, *remez* (allusion), the words עמד and

18 *On the second day, Nethanel son of Zuar the leader*
of Issachar offered. 19 *He brought his offering: one silver*
bowl, its weight a hundred and thirty [shekels]; and one
silver basin of seventy shekels in the sacred shekel; both
of them filled with fine flour mixed with oil for a meal-
offering; 20 *one ladle of gold [weighing] ten [shekels], filled*
with incense; 21 *one young bull, one ram, one*
sheep in its first year for a burnt-offering; 22 *one he-goat*
for a sin-offering; 23 *and for the slaughter of a peace-*
offering: two cattle, five rams, five he-goats, five sheep in
their first year — this is the offering of Nethanel son of
Zuar.

24 *On the third day, the leader of the children of Zebulun,*
Eliab son of Helon. 25 *His offering was: one silver bowl,*
its weight a hundred and thirty [shekels]; and one silver
basin of seventy shekels in the sacred shekel; both of
them filled with fine flour mixed with oil for a meal-
offering; 26 *one ladle of gold [weighing] ten [shekels],*
filled with incense; 27 *one young bull, one ram, one*
sheep in its first year for a burnt-offering; 28 *one he-goat*
for a sin-offering; 29 *and for the slaughter of a peace-*
offering: two cattle, five rams, five he-goats, five sheep
in their first year — this is the offering of Eliab son of
Helon.

BAAL HATURIM ELUCIDATED

the verses, אֲשֶׁר הִתְעַתְּדוּ לְגַלִּים, *that had been made to stand as heaps* (*Job* 15:28); and וְעַתְּדָהּ בַּשָּׂדֶה לָךְ, *and stand it up in the field for yourself* (*Proverbs* 24:27). Thus [the ו is explained as symbolizing a prayer], "Let [David], the descendant of Nahshon[141a] [who was blessed] with six qualities, come, and establish the foundation for the *Beis HaMikdash.*"[142]

18. בַּיּוֹם הַשֵּׁנִי הִקְרִיב — **ON THE SECOND DAY . . . OFFERED.** The *gematria* of this phrase (740) is equal to that of נָתַן לָהֶם עֵצָה, *He gave them the idea.*[143]

19. {The Baal HaTurim's comment to הִקְרִב appears at *Exodus* 14:10.}

עתר are considered equivalent, because in the letter exchange system known as אַיַ״ק בְּכַ״ר (see Introduction), the letters ת and מ may be interchanged (*VeChur LaZahav*).

141a. It is noteworthy that the allusion to David, descendant of Nahshon, is found in the term עַתּוּדִים, for the *gematria* of its singular form — עַתּוּד (480) — is equal to that of דָּוִד בֶּן נַחְשׁוֹן, *David, descendant of Nahshon* (*VeChur LaZahav*).

142. See note 107 above.

143. *Rashi.* It was Nethanel who put forth the suggestion to the tribal leaders to bring the offerings, thus, he merited to bring his offering on the second day, immediately after the leader of the pre-eminent tribe of Judah.

ל בַּיּוֹם֙ הָֽרְבִיעִ֔י נָשִׂ֖יא לִבְנֵ֣י רְאוּבֵ֑ן אֱלִיצ֖וּר בֶּן־
לא שְׁדֵיאֽוּר׃ קָרְבָּנ֞וֹ קַֽעֲרַת־כֶּ֣סֶף אַחַ֗ת שְׁלֹשִׁ֣ים וּמֵאָה֮
מִשְׁקָלָהּ֒ מִזְרָ֤ק אֶחָד֙ כֶּ֔סֶף שִׁבְעִ֥ים שֶׁ֖קֶל בְּשֶׁ֣קֶל
הַקֹּ֑דֶשׁ שְׁנֵיהֶ֣ם ׀ מְלֵאִ֗ים סֹ֛לֶת בְּלוּלָ֥ה בַשֶּׁ֖מֶן לְמִנְחָֽה׃
לב-לג כַּ֥ף אַחַ֛ת עֲשָׂרָ֥ה זָהָ֖ב מְלֵאָ֥ה קְטֹֽרֶת׃ פַּ֣ר אֶחָ֞ד
בֶּן־בָּקָ֗ר אַ֧יִל אֶחָ֛ד כֶּֽבֶשׂ־אֶחָ֥ד בֶּן־שְׁנָת֖וֹ לְעֹלָֽה׃
לד-לה שְׂעִיר־עִזִּ֥ים אֶחָ֖ד לְחַטָּֽאת׃ וּלְזֶ֣בַח הַשְּׁלָמִים֮ בָּקָ֣ר
שְׁנַ֒יִם֒ אֵילִ֤ם חֲמִשָּׁה֙ עַתֻּדִ֣ים חֲמִשָּׁ֔ה כְּבָשִׂ֥ים בְּנֵֽי־
שָׁנָ֖ה חֲמִשָּׁ֑ה זֶ֛ה קָרְבַּ֥ן אֱלִיצ֖וּר בֶּן־שְׁדֵיאֽוּר׃
לו בַּיּוֹם֙ הַֽחֲמִישִׁ֔י נָשִׂ֖יא לִבְנֵ֣י שִׁמְע֑וֹן שְׁלֻֽמִיאֵ֖ל בֶּן־
לז צוּרִֽישַׁדָּֽי׃ קָרְבָּנ֞וֹ קַֽעֲרַת־כֶּ֣סֶף אַחַ֗ת שְׁלֹשִׁ֣ים וּמֵאָה֮
מִשְׁקָלָהּ֒ מִזְרָ֤ק אֶחָד֙ כֶּ֔סֶף שִׁבְעִ֥ים שֶׁ֖קֶל בְּשֶׁ֣קֶל
הַקֹּ֑דֶשׁ שְׁנֵיהֶ֣ם ׀ מְלֵאִ֗ים סֹ֛לֶת בְּלוּלָ֥ה בַשֶּׁ֖מֶן לְמִנְחָֽה׃
לח-לט כַּ֥ף אַחַ֛ת עֲשָׂרָ֥ה זָהָ֖ב מְלֵאָ֥ה קְטֹֽרֶת׃ פַּ֣ר אֶחָ֞ד
בֶּן־בָּקָ֗ר אַ֧יִל אֶחָ֛ד כֶּֽבֶשׂ־אֶחָ֥ד בֶּן־שְׁנָת֖וֹ לְעֹלָֽה׃
מ-מא שְׂעִיר־עִזִּ֥ים אֶחָ֖ד לְחַטָּֽאת׃ וּלְזֶ֣בַח הַשְּׁלָמִים֮ בָּקָ֣ר
שְׁנַ֒יִם֒ אֵילִ֤ם חֲמִשָּׁה֙ עַתֻּדִ֣ים חֲמִשָּׁ֔ה כְּבָשִׂ֥ים בְּנֵֽי־
שָׁנָ֖ה חֲמִשָּׁ֑ה זֶ֛ה קָרְבַּ֥ן שְׁלֻמִיאֵ֖ל בֶּן־צוּרִֽישַׁדָּֽי׃
ששי מב בַּיּוֹם֙ הַשִּׁשִּׁ֔י נָשִׂ֖יא לִבְנֵ֣י גָ֑ד אֶלְיָסָ֖ף בֶּן־דְּעוּאֵֽל׃
מג קָרְבָּנ֞וֹ קַֽעֲרַת־כֶּ֣סֶף אַחַ֗ת שְׁלֹשִׁ֣ים וּמֵאָה֮ מִשְׁקָלָהּ֒
מִזְרָ֤ק אֶחָד֙ כֶּ֔סֶף שִׁבְעִ֥ים שֶׁ֖קֶל בְּשֶׁ֣קֶל הַקֹּ֑דֶשׁ
מד שְׁנֵיהֶ֣ם ׀ מְלֵאִ֗ים סֹ֛לֶת בְּלוּלָ֥ה בַשֶּׁ֖מֶן לְמִנְחָֽה׃ כַּ֥ף
מה אַחַ֛ת עֲשָׂרָ֥ה זָהָ֖ב מְלֵאָ֥ה קְטֹֽרֶת׃ פַּ֣ר אֶחָ֞ד בֶּן־בָּקָ֗ר
מו אַ֧יִל אֶחָ֛ד כֶּֽבֶשׂ־אֶחָ֥ד בֶּן־שְׁנָת֖וֹ לְעֹלָֽה׃ שְׂעִיר־עִזִּ֥ים
מז אֶחָ֖ד לְחַטָּֽאת׃ וּלְזֶ֣בַח הַשְּׁלָמִים֮ בָּקָ֣ר שְׁנַ֒יִם֒ אֵילִ֤ם
חֲמִשָּׁה֙ עַתֻּדִ֣ים חֲמִשָּׁ֔ה כְּבָשִׂ֥ים בְּנֵֽי־שָׁנָ֖ה חֲמִשָּׁ֑ה זֶ֛ה
קָרְבַּ֥ן אֶלְיָסָ֖ף בֶּן־דְּעוּאֵֽל׃
מח בַּיּוֹם֙ הַשְּׁבִיעִ֔י נָשִׂ֖יא לִבְנֵ֣י אֶפְרָ֑יִם אֱלִישָׁמָ֖ע בֶּן־
מט עַמִּיהֽוּד׃ קָרְבָּנ֞וֹ קַֽעֲרַת־כֶּ֣סֶף אַחַ֗ת שְׁלֹשִׁ֣ים וּמֵאָה֮
מִשְׁקָלָהּ֒ מִזְרָ֤ק אֶחָד֙ כֶּ֔סֶף שִׁבְעִ֥ים שֶׁ֖קֶל בְּשֶׁ֣קֶל
הַקֹּ֑דֶשׁ שְׁנֵיהֶ֣ם ׀ מְלֵאִ֗ים סֹ֛לֶת בְּלוּלָ֥ה בַשֶּׁ֖מֶן

*30 On the fourth day, the leader of the children of
Reuben, Elizur son of Shedeur. 31 His offering was: one
silver bowl, its weight a hundred and thirty [shekels];
and one silver basin of seventy shekels in the sacred
shekel; both of them filled with fine flour mixed with oil
for a meal-offering; 32 one ladle of gold [weighing] ten
[shekels], filled with incense; 33 one young bull, one
ram, one sheep in its first year for a burnt-offering; 34 one
he-goat for a sin-offering; 35 and for the slaughter of a
peace-offering: two cattle, five rams, five he-goats, five
sheep in their first year — this is the offering of Elizur son
of Shedeur.*

*36 On the fifth day, the leader of the children of Simeon,
Shelumiel son of Zurishaddai. 37 His offering was: one
silver bowl, its weight a hundred and thirty [shekels]; and
one silver basin of seventy shekels in the sacred shekel;
both of them filled with fine flour mixed with oil for a
meal-offering; 38 one ladle of gold [weighing] ten [shekels],
filled with incense; 39 one young bull, one ram, one sheep
in its first year for a burnt-offering; 40 one he-goat for a
sin-offering; 41 and for the slaughter of a peace-offering:
two cattle, five rams, five he-goats, five sheep in their
first year — this is the offering of Shelumiel son of Zuri-
shaddai.*

*42 On the sixth day, the leader of the children of Gad,
Eliasaph son of Deuel. 43 His offering was: one silver
bowl, its weight a hundred and thirty [shekels]; and one
silver basin of seventy shekels in the sacred shekel; both
of them filled with fine flour mixed with oil for a meal-
offering; 44 one ladle of gold [weighing] ten [shekels],
filled with incense; 45 one young bull, one ram, one
sheep in its first year for a burnt-offering; 46 one he-goat
for a sin-offering; 47 and for the slaughter of a peace-
offering: two cattle, five rams, five he-goats, five sheep in
their first year — this is the offering of Eliasaph son of
Deuel.*

*48 On the seventh day, the leader of the children of Eph-
raim, Elishama son of Ammihud. 49 His offering was: one
silver bowl, its weight a hundred and thirty [shekels]; and
one silver basin of seventy shekels in the sacred shekel;
both of them filled with fine flour mixed with oil for a*

נ־נא לְמִנְחָה: כַּף אַחַת עֲשָׂרָה זָהָב מְלֵאָה קְטֹרֶת: פַּר
אֶחָד בֶּן־בָּקָר אַיִל אֶחָד כֶּבֶשׂ־אֶחָד בֶּן־שְׁנָתוֹ
נב־נג לְעֹלָה: שְׂעִיר־עִזִּים אֶחָד לְחַטָּאת: וּלְזֶבַח הַשְּׁלָמִים
בָּקָר שְׁנַיִם אֵילִם חֲמִשָּׁה עַתֻּדִים חֲמִשָּׁה כְּבָשִׂים
בְּנֵי־שָׁנָה חֲמִשָּׁה זֶה קָרְבַּן אֱלִישָׁמָע בֶּן־עַמִּיהוּד:
נד בַּיּוֹם הַשְּׁמִינִי נָשִׂיא לִבְנֵי מְנַשֶּׁה גַּמְלִיאֵל בֶּן־
נה פְּדָהצוּר: קָרְבָּנוֹ קַעֲרַת־כֶּסֶף אַחַת שְׁלֹשִׁים וּמֵאָה
מִשְׁקָלָהּ מִזְרָק אֶחָד כֶּסֶף שִׁבְעִים שֶׁקֶל בְּשֶׁקֶל
הַקֹּדֶשׁ שְׁנֵיהֶם | מְלֵאִים סֹלֶת בְּלוּלָה בַשֶּׁמֶן לְמִנְחָה:
נו־נז כַּף אַחַת עֲשָׂרָה זָהָב מְלֵאָה קְטֹרֶת: פַּר אֶחָד
בֶּן־בָּקָר אַיִל אֶחָד כֶּבֶשׂ־אֶחָד בֶּן־שְׁנָתוֹ לְעֹלָה:
נח־נט שְׂעִיר־עִזִּים אֶחָד לְחַטָּאת: וּלְזֶבַח הַשְּׁלָמִים בָּקָר
שְׁנַיִם אֵילִם חֲמִשָּׁה עַתֻּדִים חֲמִשָּׁה כְּבָשִׂים בְּנֵי־
שָׁנָה חֲמִשָּׁה זֶה קָרְבַּן גַּמְלִיאֵל בֶּן־פְּדָהצוּר:
ס בַּיּוֹם הַתְּשִׁיעִי נָשִׂיא לִבְנֵי בִנְיָמִן אֲבִידָן בֶּן־גִּדְעֹנִי:
סא קָרְבָּנוֹ קַעֲרַת־כֶּסֶף אַחַת שְׁלֹשִׁים וּמֵאָה מִשְׁקָלָהּ
מִזְרָק אֶחָד כֶּסֶף שִׁבְעִים שֶׁקֶל בְּשֶׁקֶל הַקֹּדֶשׁ
סב שְׁנֵיהֶם | מְלֵאִים סֹלֶת בְּלוּלָה בַשֶּׁמֶן לְמִנְחָה: כַּף
סג אַחַת עֲשָׂרָה זָהָב מְלֵאָה קְטֹרֶת: פַּר אֶחָד בֶּן־בָּקָר
סד אַיִל אֶחָד כֶּבֶשׂ־אֶחָד בֶּן־שְׁנָתוֹ לְעֹלָה: שְׂעִיר־עִזִּים
סה אֶחָד לְחַטָּאת: וּלְזֶבַח הַשְּׁלָמִים בָּקָר שְׁנַיִם אֵילִם
חֲמִשָּׁה עַתֻּדִים חֲמִשָּׁה כְּבָשִׂים בְּנֵי־שָׁנָה חֲמִשָּׁה זֶה
קָרְבַּן אֲבִידָן בֶּן־גִּדְעֹנִי:
סו בַּיּוֹם הָעֲשִׂירִי נָשִׂיא לִבְנֵי דָן אֲחִיעֶזֶר בֶּן־עַמִּישַׁדָּי:
סז קָרְבָּנוֹ קַעֲרַת־כֶּסֶף אַחַת שְׁלֹשִׁים וּמֵאָה מִשְׁקָלָהּ
מִזְרָק אֶחָד כֶּסֶף שִׁבְעִים שֶׁקֶל בְּשֶׁקֶל הַקֹּדֶשׁ
סח שְׁנֵיהֶם | מְלֵאִים סֹלֶת בְּלוּלָה בַשֶּׁמֶן לְמִנְחָה: כַּף
סט אַחַת עֲשָׂרָה זָהָב מְלֵאָה קְטֹרֶת: פַּר אֶחָד בֶּן־בָּקָר
ע אַיִל אֶחָד כֶּבֶשׂ־אֶחָד בֶּן־שְׁנָתוֹ לְעֹלָה: שְׂעִיר־עִזִּים
עא אֶחָד לְחַטָּאת: וּלְזֶבַח הַשְּׁלָמִים בָּקָר שְׁנַיִם אֵילִם
חֲמִשָּׁה עַתֻּדִים חֲמִשָּׁה כְּבָשִׂים בְּנֵי־שָׁנָה חֲמִשָּׁה זֶה

meal-offering; 50 one ladle of gold [weighing] ten [shekels], filled with incense; 51 one young bull, one ram, one sheep in its first year for a burnt-offering; 52 one he-goat for a sin-offering; 53 and for the slaughter of a peace-offering: two cattle, five rams, five he-goats, five sheep in their first year — this is the offering of Elishama son of Ammihud.

54 On the eighth day, the leader of the children of Manasseh, Gamaliel son of Pedahzur. 55 His offering was: one silver bowl, its weight a hundred and thirty [shekels]; and one silver basin of seventy shekels in the sacred shekel; both of them filled with fine flour mixed with oil for a meal-offering; 56 one ladle of gold [weighing] ten [shekels], filled with incense; 57 one young bull, one ram, one sheep in its first year for a burnt-offering; 58 one he-goat for a sin-offering; 59 and for the slaughter of a peace-offering: two cattle, five rams, five he-goats, five sheep in their first year — this is the offering of Gamaliel son of Pedahzur.

60 On the ninth day, the leader of the children of Benjamin, Abidan son of Gideoni. 61 His offering was: one silver bowl, its weight a hundred and thirty [shekels]; and one silver basin of seventy shekels in the sacred shekel; both of them filled with fine flour mixed with oil for a meal-offering; 62 one ladle of gold [weighing] ten [shekels], filled with incense; 63 one young bull, one ram, one sheep in its first year for a burnt-offering; 64 one he-goat for a sin-offering; 65 and for the slaughter of a peace-offering: two cattle, five rams, five he-goats, five sheep in their first year — this is the offering of Abidan son of Gideoni.

66 On the tenth day, the leader of the children of Dan, Ahiezer son of Ammishaddai. 67 His offering was: one silver bowl, its weight a hundred and thirty [shekels]; and one silver basin of seventy shekels in the sacred shekel; both of them filled with fine flour mixed with oil for a meal-offering; 68 one ladle of gold [weighing] ten [shekels], filled with incense; 69 one young bull, one ram, one sheep in its first year for a burnt-offering; 70 one he-goat for a sin-offering; 71 and for the slaughter of a peace-offering: two cattle, five rams, five he-goats, five sheep in their first

קָרְבַּן אֲחִיעֶזֶר בֶּן־עַמִּישַׁדָּי׃
שביעי עב בְּיוֹם עַשְׁתֵּי עָשָׂר יוֹם נָשִׂיא לִבְנֵי אָשֵׁר פַּגְעִיאֵל
עג בֶּן־עָכְרָן׃ קָרְבָּנוֹ קַעֲרַת־כֶּסֶף אַחַת שְׁלֹשִׁים וּמֵאָה
מִשְׁקָלָהּ מִזְרָק אֶחָד כֶּסֶף שִׁבְעִים שֶׁקֶל בְּשֶׁקֶל
הַקֹּדֶשׁ שְׁנֵיהֶם ׀ מְלֵאִים סֹלֶת בְּלוּלָה בַשֶּׁמֶן לְמִנְחָה׃
עד־עה כַּף אַחַת עֲשָׂרָה זָהָב מְלֵאָה קְטֹרֶת׃ פַּר אֶחָד
בֶּן־בָּקָר אַיִל אֶחָד כֶּבֶשׂ־אֶחָד בֶּן־שְׁנָתוֹ לְעֹלָה׃
עו־עז שְׂעִיר־עִזִּים אֶחָד לְחַטָּאת׃ וּלְזֶבַח הַשְּׁלָמִים בָּקָר
שְׁנַיִם אֵילִם חֲמִשָּׁה עַתֻּדִים חֲמִשָּׁה כְּבָשִׂים בְּנֵי־שָׁנָה
חֲמִשָּׁה זֶה קָרְבַּן פַּגְעִיאֵל בֶּן־עָכְרָן׃
עח בְּיוֹם שְׁנֵים עָשָׂר יוֹם נָשִׂיא לִבְנֵי נַפְתָּלִי אֲחִירַע
עט בֶּן־עֵינָן׃ קָרְבָּנוֹ קַעֲרַת־כֶּסֶף אַחַת שְׁלֹשִׁים וּמֵאָה
מִשְׁקָלָהּ מִזְרָק אֶחָד כֶּסֶף שִׁבְעִים שֶׁקֶל בְּשֶׁקֶל
הַקֹּדֶשׁ שְׁנֵיהֶם ׀ מְלֵאִים סֹלֶת בְּלוּלָה בַשֶּׁמֶן לְמִנְחָה׃
פ־פא כַּף אַחַת עֲשָׂרָה זָהָב מְלֵאָה קְטֹרֶת׃ פַּר אֶחָד
בֶּן־בָּקָר אַיִל אֶחָד כֶּבֶשׂ־אֶחָד בֶּן־שְׁנָתוֹ לְעֹלָה׃
פב־פג שְׂעִיר־עִזִּים אֶחָד לְחַטָּאת׃ וּלְזֶבַח הַשְּׁלָמִים בָּקָר
שְׁנַיִם אֵילִם חֲמִשָּׁה עַתֻּדִים חֲמִשָּׁה כְּבָשִׂים בְּנֵי־שָׁנָה
חֲמִשָּׁה זֶה קָרְבַּן אֲחִירַע בֶּן־עֵינָן׃
פד זֹאת ׀ חֲנֻכַּת הַמִּזְבֵּחַ בְּיוֹם הִמָּשַׁח אֹתוֹ מֵאֵת נְשִׂיאֵי
יִשְׂרָאֵל קַעֲרֹת כֶּסֶף שְׁתֵּים עֶשְׂרֵה מִזְרְקֵי־כֶסֶף שְׁנֵים
פה עָשָׂר כַּפּוֹת זָהָב שְׁתֵּים עֶשְׂרֵה׃ שְׁלֹשִׁים וּמֵאָה
הַקְּעָרָה הָאַחַת כֶּסֶף וְשִׁבְעִים הַמִּזְרָק הָאֶחָד כֹּל כֶּסֶף
פו הַכֵּלִים אַלְפַּיִם וְאַרְבַּע־מֵאוֹת בְּשֶׁקֶל הַקֹּדֶשׁ׃ כַּפּוֹת
זָהָב שְׁתֵּים־עֶשְׂרֵה מְלֵאֹת קְטֹרֶת עֲשָׂרָה עֲשָׂרָה הַכַּף
מפטיר פז בְּשֶׁקֶל הַקֹּדֶשׁ כָּל־זְהַב הַכַּפּוֹת עֶשְׂרִים וּמֵאָה׃ כָּל־
הַבָּקָר לָעֹלָה שְׁנֵים עָשָׂר פָּרִים אֵילִם שְׁנֵים־עָשָׂר
כְּבָשִׂים בְּנֵי־שָׁנָה שְׁנֵים עָשָׂר וּמִנְחָתָם וּשְׂעִירֵי עִזִּים
פח שְׁנֵים עָשָׂר לְחַטָּאת׃ וְכֹל בְּקַר ׀ זֶבַח הַשְּׁלָמִים
עֶשְׂרִים וְאַרְבָּעָה פָּרִים אֵילִם שִׁשִּׁים עַתֻּדִים שִׁשִּׁים
כְּבָשִׂים בְּנֵי־שָׁנָה שִׁשִּׁים זֹאת חֲנֻכַּת הַמִּזְבֵּחַ אַחֲרֵי

year — this is the offering of Ahiezer son of Ammishaddai.

72 On the eleventh day, the leader of the children of Asher, Pagiel son of Ochran. 73 His offering was: one silver bowl, its weight a hundred and thirty [shekels]; and one silver basin of seventy shekels in the sacred shekel; both of them filled with fine flour mixed with oil for a meal-offering; 74 one ladle of gold [weighing] ten [shekels], filled with incense; 75 one young bull, one ram, one sheep in its first year for a burnt-offering; 76 one he-goat for a sin-offering; 77 and for the slaughter of a peace-offering: two cattle, five rams, five he-goats, five sheep in their first year — this is the offering of Pagiel son of Ochran.

78 On the twelfth day, the leader of the children of Naphtali, Ahira son of Enan. 79 His offering was: one silver bowl, its weight a hundred and thirty [shekels]; and one silver basin of seventy shekels in the sacred shekel; both of them filled with fine flour mixed with oil for a meal-offering; 80 one ladle of gold [weighing] ten [shekels], filled with incense; 81 one young bull, one ram, one sheep in its first year for a burnt-offering; 82 one he-goat for a sin-offering; 83 and for the slaughter of a peace-offering: two cattle, five rams, five he-goats, five sheep in their first year — this is the offering of Ahira son of Enan.

84 This was the dedication of the Altar, on the day it was anointed, from the leaders of Israel: twelve silver bowls, twelve silver basins, twelve gold ladles; 85 each bowl was one hundred and thirty silver [shekels] and each basin was seventy; all the silver of the vessels was two thousand, four hundred in the sacred shekel. 86 Twelve gold ladles filled with incense, ten [shekels], ten [shekels] each ladle, of the sacred shekels; all the gold of the ladles was one hundred and twenty [shekels]. 87 All the livestock for the burnt-offering: twelve bulls, twelve rams, twelve sheep in their first year, and their meal-offerings; and twelve he-goats for a sin-offering. 88 All the livestock for the slaughter of a peace-offering: twenty-four bulls, sixty rams, sixty he-goats, sixty sheep in their first year — this was the dedication of the Altar after it was anointed.

ז/פט פט הַמָּשַׁח אֹתוֹ: וּבְבֹא מֹשֶׁה אֶל־אֹהֶל מוֹעֵד לְדַבֵּר
אִתּוֹ וַיִּשְׁמַע אֶת־הַקּוֹל מִדַּבֵּר אֵלָיו מֵעַל הַכַּפֹּרֶת
אֲשֶׁר עַל־אֲרֹן הָעֵדֻת מִבֵּין שְׁנֵי הַכְּרֻבִים וַיְדַבֵּר
אֵלָיו: פפפ

קע״ו פסוקים. עמו״ס סימן. עמינד״ב סימן.

בעל הטורים

(פט) מִבֵּין שְׁנֵי הַכְּרֻבִים. רָאשֵׁי תֵבוֹת מֹשֶׁה – לוֹמַר לְךָ שֶׁהוּא חָשׁוּב כִּכְרוּב שֶׁל מָעְלָה:

BAAL HATURIM ELUCIDATED

89. מִבֵּין שְׁנֵי הַכְּרֻבִים — FROM BETWEEN THE TWO CHERUBIM. The initial letters of these words spell the name מֹשֶׁה, Moses. This teaches you that he was

[89] *When Moses arrived at the Tent of Meeting to speak with Him, he heard the Voice speaking to him from atop the Cover that was upon the Ark of the Testimony, from between the two Cherubim, and He spoke to him.*

BAAL HATURIM ELUCIDATED

considered as a heavenly *cherub.* [144, 145]

144. *Peirush HaRokeach;* see the Baal HaTurim to *Exodus* 25:22, s.v., שְׁנֵי הַכְּרֻבִים.

145. The Baal HaTurim's comment may be understood in light of a Talmudic teaching: What is the meaning of the verse, כִּי שִׂפְתֵי כֹהֵן יִשְׁמְרוּ דַעַת, *For the lips of the Kohen shall safeguard knowledge,* וְתוֹרָה יְבַקְשׁוּ מִפִּיהוּ, *and people should seek Torah from his mouth,* כִּי מַלְאַךְ ה׳ צְבָאוֹת הוּא, *for he is an angel of HASHEM, Master of Legions* (*Malachi* 2:7)? It means, if the teacher resembles an angel of God, people should seek Torah from his mouth, but if not, they should not seek Torah from his mouth (*Moed Katan* 17a). Accordingly, the Baal HaTurim finds an allusion that equates Moses, the teacher par excellence, with the angels (A.S.).

פרשת בהעלותך
Parashas Beha'alosecha

ח/א־ג

א־ב וַיְדַבֵּר יהוה אֶל־מֹשֶׁה לֵּאמֹר: דַּבֵּר אֶל־אַהֲרֹן
וְאָמַרְתָּ אֵלָיו בְּהַעֲלֹתְךָ אֶת־הַנֵּרֹת אֶל־מוּל
ג פְּנֵי הַמְּנוֹרָה יָאִירוּ שִׁבְעַת הַנֵּרוֹת: וַיַּעַשׂ כֵּן

בעל הטורים

ח (ב) **בְּהַעֲלֹתְךָ אֶת הַנֵּרֹת.** סָמַךְ נֵרוֹת לַחֲנֻכָּה. {רֶמֶז לַחֲנֻכָּה,} לְפַרְסוּמֵי נִסָּא בְּנֵרוֹת:

❑ **בְּהַעֲלֹתְךָ אֶת.** בְּגִימַטְרִיָּא עֲשֵׂה בָהּ מַעֲלוֹת:

❑ **אֶל מוּל פְּנֵי הַמְּנוֹרָה יָאִירוּ.** כִּי אֲנִי אֵינִי צָרִיךְ לְאוֹרָהּ. "פְּנֵי הַמְּנוֹרָה יָאִירוּ" בְּגִימַטְרִיָּא וְכִי אֲנִי לְאוֹרְךָ צָרִיךְ:

❑ **שִׁבְעַת הַנֵּרוֹת.** כְּנֶגֶד שִׁבְעַת הַמַּזָּלוֹת, חנכ"ל שצ"ם:

BAAL HATURIM ELUCIDATED

VIII

2. **בְּהַעֲלֹתְךָ אֶת הַנֵּרֹת — WHEN YOU KINDLE THE LAMPS.** The Torah juxtaposed [this portion regarding kindling] the lamps with the *chanukah* [dedication of the Altar]. {This is an allusion to [the festival of] Chanukah[1]}[1a] and [the *mitzvah*] to publicize its miracle through kindling lamps.[2]

❑ **בְּהַעֲלֹתְךָ אֶת[2a] — WHEN YOU KINDLE THE . . .** The *gematria* of this phrase (928) is

1. Regarding the connection between the dedication of the Altar and the festival of Chanukah, see the Baal HaTurim to 7:1 above with note 91. The Baal HaTurim's comment on this verse also speaks of Chanukah.

1a. The passage enclosed in braces is not found in the early or later printed editions, but does appear in *Shoham Yakar's* manuscript edition.

2. In *Peirush HaTur HaAroch* the Baal HaTurim explains this concept at length. He writes there: The juxtaposition of the passage regarding the kindling of the Menorah and the passage dealing with the offerings of the tribal leaders may be explained in light of *Rashi's* comment: The Midrash states that when Aaron saw the dedication offerings of the tribal leaders he felt bad, because neither he nor his tribe had been assigned a specific day to bring an offering alongside the other tribes and their leaders. Then God said to Aaron, "By your life! Yours is greater than theirs, for you kindle and prepare the lamps of the Menorah" (*Tanchuma* 5). But, asks the *Ramban,* why did God choose the kindling of the Menorah as the service with which to placate Aaron? Why did He not speak of the twice daily Incense offering or the fact that all offerings are brought to the Altar by Aaron and his sons or the Yom Kippur service which could be performed by none but the Kohen Gadol? Moreover, why did Aaron feel bad; wasn't his offering greater than those of the tribal leaders, for he brought many offerings during the days of the *Mishkan's* inauguration? And if he was distraught because his role in the service did not require any contribution from his personal resources, how was he placated with the Menorah, which did not require any expenditure of his money or possessions? The *Ramban* explains that the Midrash cited by *Rashi* placated him with the prophecy that a great miracle involving the lamp of the Menorah would be performed by his offspring, the Hasmoneans, and that that miracle would be commemorated by the lighting of a Menorah. Moreover, his Chanukah would be greater than theirs, for the Altar they were dedicating would find use only while it and the *Beis HaMikdash* were standing; while the Chanukah (dedication) instituted by his tribe would be celebrated eternally.

2a. The text follows *Shoham Yakar's* manuscript editions. The early printed editions omitted the word אֶת from the Baal HaTurim's rubric. Accordingly, the *gematria* is only 527. To reconcile the *gematriaos, Ittur Bikkurim* suggests emending the Baal HaTurim's phrase to עֲשֵׂה בָהּ מַעֲלָה, *Make a step for it,* a reading that is in accord with *Rashi's* comment on the word בְּהַעֲלֹתְךָ. And that version appears in many of the later printed editions. Nevertheless, both the Talmud and the

[1] HASHEM spoke to Moses, saying, [2] "Speak to Aaron
and say to him: When you kindle the lamps, toward
the face of the Menorah shall the seven lamps cast light."

BAAL HATURIM ELUCIDATED

equal to that of עֲשֵׂה בָהּ מַעֲלוֹת, *Make steps for it.*[3]

❑ אֶל מוּל פְּנֵי הַמְּנוֹרָה יָאִירוּ — **TOWARD THE FACE OF THE MENORAH SHALL [THE SEVEN LAMPS] CAST LIGHT.** For [God says], "I have no need for its[4] light."[5] [An additional allusion is the fact that] the *gematria* of the phrase פְּנֵי הַמְּנוֹרָה יָאִירוּ — 673 — is equivalent[6] to that of וְכִי אֲנִי לְאוֹרָךְ צָרִיךְ, *Am I in need of your light?*[7]

❑ שִׁבְעַת הַנֵּרוֹת — **THE SEVEN LAMPS,** corresponding to the seven celestial bodies[8] known collectively as חנכ״ל שצ״ם [the acronym of: חַמָּה, *the sun;* נֹגַהּ, *Venus;* כּוֹכָב, *Mercury;* לְבָנָה, *the moon;* שַׁבְּתַאי, *Saturn;* צֶדֶק, *Jupiter;* and מַאְדִּים, *Mars*].[9]

Sifrei (see note 3) read מַעֲלוֹת, *steps,* in the plural.

3. *Peirush HaRokeach.* The Mishnah teaches: There was a stone with three steps in front of the Menorah; the Kohen would stand upon it when preparing the lamps (*Tamid* 3:9). Although the Torah makes no mention of such a stone or stairway, the Midrash infers its presence from the word בְּהַעֲלֹתְךָ, *when you kindle,* literally, *when you raise* (*Sifrei,* cited by *Rashi* to our verse and by *Raavad* to *Tamid*). The Baal HaTurim finds an additional allusion to the steps in the *gematria.*

4. Alternatively: The phrase is vowelized לְאוֹרָה, *for light.*

5. *Menachos* 86b. Had the Menorah been needed for its light, the Torah would have placed it closer to the *Shulchan* (Table). By placing these two vessels on opposite sides of the *Mishkan,* the Torah indicates that the Menorah was not needed for illumination (*Rashi* and *Tosafos;* see also the Baal HaTurim's comments to *Exodus* 25:6, s.v., שֶׁמֶן לַמָּאֹר, and 27:20, s.v., וְיִקְחוּ אֵלֶיךָ).

Alternatively: The oil cups of a candelabrum are usually arranged in a circle with their wicks pointed outward, thus spreading their light over a wider area. By placing its cups in a straight line with all their wicks leaning toward the center, the Torah indicates that the Menorah was not in the *Mishkan* for illumination (see *Tanchuma* 5; see also *Rashi* and *Gur Aryeh*).

6. The principle of *im hakollel* allows 673 to be considered equivalent to 674, the *gematria* of the Baal HaTurim's phrase.

7. See *Shabbos* 22b. The phrase there reads as a question: וְכִי לְאוֹרָהּ הוּא צָרִיךְ, *Does He have need of its light?* [The word לְאוֹרָהּ, *of its light,* may also be vowelized לְאוֹרָה, *of light.*]

The Talmud explains its question in more detail: For the forty years that the Israelites traveled through the wilderness, He provided them with light [so it is not possible that He needs their light at this juncture in time]! Rather, the purpose of the Menorah's light is to bear testimony to the people of the world that God rests His Presence among the Israelites. For equal amounts of oil would be placed into each of the seven lamps of the Menorah yet the western lamp would burn for longer than any of the others.

And what is that testimony? The *Amora* Rav explains: It is the נֵר מַעֲרָבִי, *western lamp;* for they would pour precisely the same measure of oil into each lamp and would kindle the western lamp first. Yet that lamp outlasted each of the others [for the others went out in the morning, while the western lamp burned through the day until it was extinguished by the Kohen who came to rekindle the Menorah that evening (*Rashi*)].

8. All the visible stars remain in a fixed position (with respect to one another) on the celestial sphere. There are seven exceptions which are visible to the naked eye. These are known as שִׁבְעָה כּוֹכְבֵי לֶכֶת, *seven moving heavenly bodies.* The Baal HaTurim here refers to them as מַזָּלוֹת, a term usually used for the constellations. Elsewhere, he refers to them as מְשָׁרְתִים, *servants,* and lists them in a different order, שצ״ם חנכ״ל (see the Baal HaTurim to *Genesis* 1:1 with note 35 and 7:3 above with note 96).

9. Pseudo-*Rashi* to *II Chronicles* 4:7; *Bamidbar Rabbah* 15:7. According to this Midrash, the "seven moving heavenly bodies" form the celestial Menorah alluded to as "the eyes of God," in the verse: שִׁבְעָה אֵלֶּה, *these seven,* עֵינֵי ה׳, *the eyes of HASHEM,* הֵמָּה מְשׁוֹטְטִים בְּכָל הָאָרֶץ, *they traverse*

ח/ד אַהֲרֹן אֶל־מוּל֙ פְּנֵ֣י הַמְּנוֹרָ֔ה הֶעֱלָ֖ה נֵרֹתֶ֑יהָ כַּאֲשֶׁ֛ר
ד צִוָּ֥ה יהו֖ה אֶת־מֹשֶֽׁה׃ וְזֶ֨ה מַעֲשֵׂ֤ה הַמְּנֹרָה֙ מִקְשָׁ֣ה
זָהָ֔ב עַד־יְרֵכָ֥הּ עַד־פִּרְחָ֖הּ מִקְשָׁ֣ה הִ֑וא כַּמַּרְאֶ֗ה
אֲשֶׁ֨ר הֶרְאָ֤ה יהוה֙ אֶת־מֹשֶׁ֔ה כֵּ֥ן עָשָׂ֖ה אֶת־הַמְּנֹרָֽה׃

בעל הטורים

❑ כְּתִיב "בְּהַעֲלֹתְךָ אֶת הַנֵּרֹת", וּכְתִיב "לְהַעֲלֹת נֵר תָּמִיד". לְבֵית הִלֵּל {תְּחִלָּה} נֵר וְאַחַר כָּךְ נֵרוֹת – שֶׁמּוֹסִיפִין וְהוֹלְכִין. וְהַיְנוּ "לְהַעֲלֹת נֵר" שֶׁמַּעֲלִין בַּקֹּדֶשׁ. וּלְבֵית שַׁמַּאי תְּחִלָּה נֵרוֹת וְאַחַר כָּךְ נֵר – שֶׁמּוֹרִידִין וְהוֹלְכִין. "לְהַעֲלֹת נֵר תָּמִיד" סוֹפֵי תֵבוֹת תֵּרֵד:

(ד) **וְזֶה מַעֲשֵׂה הַמְּנֹרָה.** "וְזֶה" עוֹלֶה י"ח. שֶׁגָּבְהָהּ שֶׁל מְנוֹרָה י"ח טְפָחִים:

❑ **כַּמַּרְאֶה.** בְּגִימַטְרִיָּא "כְּגַבְרִיאֵל" מְלַמֵּד שֶׁגַּבְרִיאֵל הוּא שֶׁהֶרְאָה לוֹ דְּמוּת הַמְּנוֹרָה:

❑ **כֵּן עָשָׂה.** כֵּ"ן נֵרוֹת עָשָׂה שְׁלֹמֹה בְּעֶשֶׂר הַמְּנוֹרוֹת. "עָשָׂה" בְּגִימַטְרִיָּא שְׁלֹמֹה:

❑ ד' פְּעָמִים הִזְכִּיר "מְנוֹרָה", שֶׁהִיא כְּשֵׁרָה מֵאַרְבָּעָה מִינִין, כִּדְאִיתָא בִּמְנָחוֹת.

BAAL HATURIM ELUCIDATED

❑ It is written, בְּהַעֲלֹתְךָ אֶת הַנֵּרֹת, *when you kindle the lamps* [using the plural form הַנֵּרֹת, *the lamps*]; and it is written [elsewhere] לְהַעֲלֹת נֵר תָּמִיד, *to kindle a continual lamp* (*Exodus* 27:20; *Leviticus* 24:2) [using the singular form נֵר, *a lamp*]. According to the Academy of Hillel[10] [the Chanukah lamps are lit in ascending order], {at the beginning} a single lamp, later on lamps — [for the number of lamps] increases [as the festival of Chanukah progresses]. Thus, [the Torah

---

the entire world (*Zechariah* 4:10). Similarly, the lights of the Menorah are earthly representations of God's eyes, so to speak. And just as God knows what is happening throughout the world without having to rely on the heavenly representation of His eyes, so does He have no need for the light given off by the earthly representation of His eyes (see the Baal HaTurim's preceding comment with notes 5 and 7).

10. See the Baal HaTurim's first comment to this verse with notes 1 and 2. The Talmud records a dispute between Beis Shammai (the Academy of Shammai) and Beis Hillel (the Academy of Hillel) regarding the Chanukah lights. That passage begins with a statement about the essential fulfillment of the commandment to kindle lamps on Chanukah:

The *mitzvah* of Chanukah [is fulfilled with] one lamp [kindled each night] for a man and his entire household; but those who fervently embellish [their performance of *mitzvos* kindle] one light for each and every member of the household [each night]; and regarding those who are even more fervent about embellishing [*mitzvos*, there is a dispute] — Beis Shammai maintains that on the first day of Chanukah one kindles eight lamps, then decreases the number by one on each of the remaining days; Beis Hillel maintains that on the first day one kindles one lamp, then increases the number by one on each of the remaining days . . . (*Shabbos* 21b).

The Talmud then cites a disagreement regarding the rationale for each opinion. All the explanations offered are based on logical reasoning; no Scriptural verses are adduced to support either the concept of lighting a different number of lamps each night or the direction of the changing number of lamps. In the Torah's use of both the singular noun נֵר and the plural form נֵרוֹת, the Baal HaTurim sees an allusion to a changing number of lamps. And that allusion is equally applicable to Beis Shammai's opinion and to Beis Hillel's.

It is noteworthy that the phrase from which the Baal HaTurim draws an allusion to the opinions of both Beis Shammai and Beis Hillel is itself an allusion to those two academies. For the *gematria* of לְהַעֲלֹת נֵר תָּמִיד is 1239, which the principle of *im hakollel* allows to be considered equivalent to 1240, the *gematria* of בֵּית שַׁמַּאי בֵּית הִלֵּל (*VeChur LaZahav*).

[3] *Aaron did so; toward the face of the Menorah he kindled its lamps, as HASHEM had commanded Moses.* [4] *This is the workmanship of the Menorah, hammered-out gold, from its base to its flower it is hammered out; according to the vision that HASHEM showed Moses, so did he make the Menorah.*

BAAL HATURIM ELUCIDATED

states,] לְהַעֲלֹת נֵר, literally, *to raise a lamp* [i.e., to add another lamp], for in holy matters we increase.[11]

But according to the Academy of Shammai [the Chanukah lamps are lit in descending order], at the beginning of the festival [eight] נֵרוֹת, *lamps,* later on [at the end of Chanukah], נֵר, *a single lamp* — for [the number of lamps] decreases [as the festival progresses]. [This is also alluded to by] the final letters of the phrase לְהַעֲלֹת נֵר תָּמִיד, [which] form the word תֵּרֵד, *descend.*[11a]

4. וְזֶה מַעֲשֵׂה הַמְּנֹרָה — THIS IS THE WORKMANSHIP OF THE MENORAH. The *gematria* of וְזֶה, *this is,* is 18, an allusion to the height of the Menorah, 18 handbreadths.[12]

❑ **כַּמַּרְאֶה — ACCORDING TO THE VISION.** The *gematria* of this word, 266, is equal to that of כְּגַבְרִיאֵל, *like Gabriel.* This teaches that it was the angel Gabriel who showed Moses the form of the Menorah.[13]

❑ **כֵּן עָשָׂה — SO DID HE MAKE.** Solomon made 70 lamps [corresponding to the *gematria* of כֵּן] in ten Menoros.[14] And the *gematria* of the word עָשָׂה (375) is equal to that of שְׁלֹמֹה, *Solomon.*[15]

❑ The passage mentions the Menorah four times,[16] for a Menorah is valid if made from any of four substances, as the Talmud states in tractate *Menachos.*[17]

---

11. *Peirush HaRokeach* to *Exodus* 27:20. The Baal HaTurim makes a similar comment at *Leviticus* 24:2.

11a. Perhaps this allusion appears in the final letters of the word as an indication that the number of lights "descends" as the festival approaches its end (Y.S.).

12. *Meiri* to *Succah* 5a; *R' Yehudah HaChassid; Moshav Zekeinim.* See *Menachos* 28b.

13. *Menachos* 29a; see also the Baal HaTurim to *Exodus* 25:9.

14. When King Solomon built the *Beis HaMikdash,* he made ten Menoros in addition to the one Moses made for the *Mishkan.* He placed Moses' in its proper place and adorned it with five replica Menoros on its right and five on its left, as it is written, וַיַּעַשׂ אֶת מְנֹרוֹת הַזָּהָב עֶשֶׂר, *And he made ten golden Menoros,* כְּמִשְׁפָּטָם, *according to their specifications,* חָמֵשׁ מִיָּמִין, *five on the right,* וְחָמֵשׁ מִשְּׂמֹאול, *and five on the left* (*II Chronicles* 4:7; similarly, *I Kings* 7:49). The Talmud records a dispute regarding whether these ten Menoros were strictly decorative or were also kindled each day (*Menachos* 99a). In either case, they were exact copies of Moses' Menorah, as implied by the term כְּמִשְׁפָּטָם, *according to their specifications* (Pseudo-*Rashi* to *II Chronicles* 4:7).

15. *Peirush HaRokeach.* Thus, כֵּן עָשָׂה can be understood as *Solomon made seventy.*

16. That is, the word הַמְּנוֹרָה appears once each in verses 2 and 3 (spelled in full, with a ו); and twice in verse 4 (spelled defectively, without a ו).

17. *Menachos* 28b. Although the Torah clearly prescribes that the Menorah be made of pure gold (*Exodus* 25:31), the Talmud infers from relevant verses that, in the absence of gold, other materials could be used. The Talmud records a dispute regarding which materials are acceptable for this purpose. According to one view, only metal may be used, and that is how the *Rambam* codifies the *halachah* (*Hilchos Beis HaBechirah* 1:18). And, the Talmud explains, that is what the Hasmoneans used when they

ה־ו וַיְדַבֵּר יְהֹוָה אֶל־מֹשֶׁה לֵּאמֹר: קַח אֶת־הַלְוִיִּם
ז מִתּוֹךְ בְּנֵי יִשְׂרָאֵל וְטִהַרְתָּ אֹתָם: וְכֹה־תַעֲשֶׂה לָהֶם
לְטַהֲרָם הַזֵּה עֲלֵיהֶם מֵי חַטָּאת וְהֶעֱבִירוּ תַעַר
ח עַל־כָּל־בְּשָׂרָם וְכִבְּסוּ בִגְדֵיהֶם וְהִטֶּהָרוּ: וְלָקְחוּ פַּר
בֶּן־בָּקָר וּמִנְחָתוֹ סֹלֶת בְּלוּלָה בַשָּׁמֶן וּפַר־שֵׁנִי
ט בֶן־בָּקָר תִּקַּח לְחַטָּאת: וְהִקְרַבְתָּ אֶת־הַלְוִיִּם לִפְנֵי
אֹהֶל מוֹעֵד וְהִקְהַלְתָּ אֶת־כָּל־עֲדַת בְּנֵי יִשְׂרָאֵל:
י וְהִקְרַבְתָּ אֶת־הַלְוִיִּם לִפְנֵי יְהֹוָה וְסָמְכוּ בְנֵי־
יא יִשְׂרָאֵל אֶת־יְדֵיהֶם עַל־הַלְוִיִּם: וְהֵנִיף אַהֲרֹן אֶת־
הַלְוִיִּם תְּנוּפָה לִפְנֵי יְהֹוָה מֵאֵת בְּנֵי יִשְׂרָאֵל וְהָיוּ
יב לַעֲבֹד אֶת־עֲבֹדַת יְהֹוָה: וְהַלְוִיִּם יִסְמְכוּ אֶת־יְדֵיהֶם
עַל רֹאשׁ הַפָּרִים וַעֲשֵׂה אֶת־הָאֶחָד חַטָּאת
וְאֶת־הָאֶחָד עֹלָה לַיהֹוָה לְכַפֵּר עַל־הַלְוִיִּם:
יג וְהַעֲמַדְתָּ אֶת־הַלְוִיִּם לִפְנֵי אַהֲרֹן וְלִפְנֵי בָנָיו וְהֵנַפְתָּ
יד אֹתָם תְּנוּפָה לַיהֹוָה: וְהִבְדַּלְתָּ אֶת־הַלְוִיִּם מִתּוֹךְ

בעל הטורים

וְרֶמֶז לְאַרְבַּע מְנוֹרוֹת בְּשִׂמְחַת בֵּית הַשּׁוֹאֵבָה:

BAAL HATURIM ELUCIDATED

[Additionally:] The fourfold mention of הַמְּנֹרָה is an allusion to the four

---

regained the *Beis HaMikdash* at the miracle of Chanukah: First they made a Menorah of iron rods plated with tin; when their fortunes increased, they replaced those with silver; and when the fortunes increased even more, they replaced them with gold. *Ittur Bikkurim* explains the Baal HaTurim's comment as referring to those four metals — iron, tin, silver, gold.

According to the other view, most substances — specifically: metal, wood, bone or glass [but not earthenware] — may be used. *Shoham Yakar* explains the Baal HaTurim's comment according to that opinion.

Alternatively: The Talmud cites a *baraisa* regarding the composition of the Menorah: If [the artisan] has no gold, he may bring [a Menorah] of silver or of copper or of iron or of tin or of lead. *Dikdukei Soferim* cites a manuscript Talmud that omits the words "or of iron or of tin." According to that second reading, the Talmud names four materials that may be used for the Menorah — gold, silver, copper and lead. Perhaps the Baal HaTurim's Talmud had that version of the *baraisa* (*VeChur LaZahav*).

Two other versions of that *baraisa* are found in the Midrashim, either of which may have been the reading before the Baal HaTurim. *Sifrei* (to 8:4 above) states: If it cannot be of gold, they may make it of silver or of iron or of lead. Accordingly, the four materials are gold, silver, iron and lead (*VeChur LaZahav*).

Finally, *Yalkut Shimoni* (to 8:4 above) reads: If it cannot be of gold, they may make it of silver or of iron or of copper or of lead. Following this version, it is possible that the Baal HaTurim refers to a time when gold is not available. Then there are four other metals that may be used instead — silver, iron, copper and lead (*VeChur LaZahav*).

5 HASHEM spoke to Moses, saying, 6 "Take the Levites
from among the Children of Israel and purify them. 7 So shall
you do to them to purify them: Sprinkle upon them water of
purification, and let them pass a razor over their entire flesh,
and let them immerse their garments, and they shall become
pure. 8 They shall take a young bull and its meal-offering,
fine flour mixed with oil, and a second young bull shall you
take as a sin-offering. 9 You shall bring the Levites before the
Tent of Meeting, and you shall gather together the entire
assembly of the Children of Israel. 10 You shall bring the
Levites before HASHEM, and the Children of Israel shall
lean their hands upon the Levites. 11 Aaron shall wave the
Levites as a wave-service before HASHEM from the Children
of Israel, and they shall remain to perform the service of
HASHEM. 12 The Levites shall lean their hands upon the head
of the bulls; you shall make one a sin-offering and one a
burnt-offering to HASHEM, to provide atonement for the
Levites. 13 You shall stand the Levites before Aaron and
before his sons, and wave them as a wave-offering before
HASHEM. 14 So shall you separate the Levites from among

BAAL HATURIM ELUCIDATED

menoros [that illuminated the Temple Courtyard during the celebration] of the *Simchas Beis HaSho'eivah.* [18]

18. The Mishnah describes the festivities during Succos at the שִׂמְחַת בֵּית הַשּׁוֹאֵבָה, *Simchas Beis HaSho'eivah,* literally, *Rejoicing of the Place of the* [*Water*] *Drawing:* . . . There were [fifty-cubit (80-95 feet) high (*Gemara*)] golden menoros [candelabra] there [in the Women's Courtyard], with golden bowls at their tops. Each menorah had four ladders which were ascended by four young Kohanim holding four pitchers [containing a total] of 120 *log* of oil, which each Kohen poured into his bowl [i.e., each youth carried 30 *log* (3-5 gallons) to the top of his ladder and poured it into one of the four bowls (*Gemara*)] (*Succah* 5:2 [51a]).

The Mishnah does not tell us how many of these menoros there were. Accordingly, it is suggested that the Baal HaTurim's phrase אַרְבַּע מְנוֹרוֹת does not refer to the number of candelabra, but to the number of bowls in each one (*Shoham Yakar*). However, the *Maharil* (*Hilchos Succos*) states that there were four menoros, although he does not adduce a source for his statement (*VeChur LaZahav*).

That Mishnah also does not tell us whether the candelabra stood all year, but were used only during Succos at the *Simchas Beis HaSho'eivah,* or if they were erected especially for the occasion, then dismantled. It is noteworthy that the classic depictions of the Temple Courtyard — such as those of the *Rambam,* R' Moshe Ivier (*talmid HaGra*), *Tosefos Yom Tov* and *Tiferes Yisrael* — do not include any candelabra in the Women's Courtyard. The omission implies that, in the opinion of those commentaries, the candelabra were not permanent fixtures. Although ArtScroll's *Yad Avraham* commentary to the Mishnah states, "In the Women's Court stood candelabra that were used only for the Water Drawing festivities," no inference should be drawn, for an interview with the author of those lines revealed that his research regarding our question was inconclusive (*VeChur LaZahav*).

טו בְּנֵ֣י יִשְׂרָאֵ֑ל וְהָ֥יוּ לִ֖י הַלְוִיִּֽם׃ וְאַחֲרֵי־כֵן֙ יָבֹ֣אוּ הַלְוִיִּ֔ם
לַעֲבֹ֖ד אֶת־אֹ֣הֶל מוֹעֵ֑ד וְטִהַרְתָּ֣ אֹתָ֔ם וְהֵנַפְתָּ֥ אֹתָ֖ם
טז תְּנוּפָֽה׃ כִּי֩ נְתֻנִ֨ים נְתֻנִ֥ים הֵ֨מָּה֙ לִ֔י מִתּ֖וֹךְ בְּנֵ֣י יִשְׂרָאֵ֑ל
תַּ֩חַת֩ פִּטְרַ֨ת כָּל־רֶ֜חֶם בְּכ֥וֹר כֹּל֙ מִבְּנֵ֣י יִשְׂרָאֵ֔ל
יז לָקַ֥חְתִּי אֹתָ֖ם לִֽי׃ כִּ֣י לִ֤י כָל־בְּכוֹר֙ בִּבְנֵ֣י יִשְׂרָאֵ֔ל
בָּאָדָ֖ם וּבַבְּהֵמָ֑ה בְּי֗וֹם הַכֹּתִ֤י כָל־בְּכוֹר֙ בְּאֶ֣רֶץ
יח מִצְרַ֔יִם הִקְדַּ֥שְׁתִּי אֹתָ֖ם לִֽי׃ וָאֶקַּח֙ אֶת־הַלְוִיִּ֔ם תַּ֥חַת
יט כָּל־בְּכ֖וֹר בִּבְנֵ֥י יִשְׂרָאֵֽל׃ וָאֶתְּנָ֨ה אֶת־הַלְוִיִּ֜ם נְתֻנִ֣ים ׀
לְאַהֲרֹ֣ן וּלְבָנָ֗יו מִתּוֹךְ֮ בְּנֵ֣י יִשְׂרָאֵל֒ לַעֲבֹ֞ד אֶת־עֲבֹדַ֤ת
בְּנֵי־יִשְׂרָאֵל֙ בְּאֹ֣הֶל מוֹעֵ֔ד וּלְכַפֵּ֖ר עַל־בְּנֵ֣י יִשְׂרָאֵ֑ל

בעל הטורים

(טז) נְתֻנִים נְתֻנִים הֵמָּה לִי. בְּגִימַטְרִיָּא שֶׁאֵלֶּה לֹא עָשׂוּ עֵגֶל שֶׁל זָהָב:

(יט) וָאֶתְּנָה אֶת הַלְוִיִּם. חָמֵשׁ פְּעָמִים "בְּנֵי יִשְׂרָאֵל" בַּפָּסוּק, כְּנֶגֶד כֹּהֲנִים, לְוִיִּם, יִשְׂרְאֵלִים, גֵּרִים וַעֲבָדִים מְשֻׁחְרָרִים. וְזֶהוּ "קֹדֶשׁ יִשְׂרָאֵל לַה' רֵאשִׁית תְּבוּאָתֹה", תְּבוּאַת ה':

❑ **וּלְכַפֵּר.** ג' — "וּלְכַפֵּר עַל בְּנֵי יִשְׂרָאֵל"; "וְאַהֲרֹן וּבָנָיו מַקְטִירִים וְגוֹ' וּלְכַפֵּר עַל יִשְׂרָאֵל" בְּדִבְרֵי הַיָּמִים; "שָׁבֻעִים שִׁבְעִים נֶחְתַּךְ עַל עַמְּךָ וְגוֹ' וּלְהָתֵם חַטָּאת וּלְכַפֵּר עָוֹן" בְּעִנְיַן הַקֵּץ שֶׁל דָּנִיֵּאל. מְלַמֵּד שֶׁגָּלוּת מְכַפֶּרֶת כְּמוֹ קָרְבָּן:

BAAL HATURIM ELUCIDATED

16. נְתֻנִים נְתֻנִים הֵמָּה לִי — PRESENTED, PRESENTED ARE THEY TO ME. The *gematria* of this phrase (1190) is equal to that of שֶׁאֵלֶּה לֹא עָשׂוּ עֵגֶל שֶׁל זָהָב, *Because these did not make the golden calf.*[19]

19. וָאֶתְּנָה אֶת הַלְוִיִּם — THEN I ASSIGNED THE LEVITES. The phrase, בְּנֵי יִשְׂרָאֵל, *the Children of Israel,* is mentioned five times in this verse,[20] corresponding to [the five categories of people within the nation]: Kohanim, Levites, Israelites, converts and freed slaves.[21] This concept is also alluded to by, קֹדֶשׁ יִשְׂרָאֵל לַה'

19. *Peirush HaRokeach.* The Talmud (*Yoma* 66b) states that not even one member of the tribe of Levi was guilty of sin at the incident of the golden calf.

20. The term בְּנֵי יִשְׂרָאֵל appears in this verse four times without a prefix, and בִּבְנֵי יִשְׂרָאֵל, with a ־ב prefix, appears one time. Generally, when a passage speaks of a particular subject, the first time it is mentioned, the subject is identified by name. After that, the Torah uses a pronoun or a pronominal suffix. Thus, we would expect our verse to read: לַעֲבֹד אֶת עֲבֹדָתָם, *to perform their service* (as in 4:27 above) . . . וּלְכַפֵּר עֲלֵיהֶם, *and to provide atonement for them* (as in v. 21 below), וְלֹא יִהְיֶה בָהֶם נֶגֶף, *so that there will not be a plague among them* (as in *Exodus* 30:12), בְּגִשְׁתָּם אֶל הַקֹּדֶשׁ, *when they approach the Sanctuary* (as in *Exodus* 30:20). Nevertheless, instead of using pronouns, our verse states בְּנֵי יִשְׂרָאֵל, *the Children of Israel,* five times. Grammatically, this is because the verse mentions three groups: the Levites; Aaron and his sons; and the Children of Israel. If the verse were to use a pronoun, we could not be certain to which of those groups it referred. Therefore, בְּנֵי יִשְׂרָאֵל must be repeated several times (*VeChur LaZahav*). The Baal HaTurim finds an additional reason for the fivefold mention of בְּנֵי יִשְׂרָאֵל.

21. Although the Mishnah (*Kiddushin* 4:1 [69a])

the Children of Israel, and the Levites shall remain Mine.
15 *"Thereafter the Levites shall come to serve the Tent of Meeting; you shall purify them and you shall wave them as a wave-service.*
16 *For presented, presented are they to Me from among the Children of Israel; in place of the first issue of every womb, the firstborn of everyone of the Children of Israel, have I taken them to Myself.*
17 *For every firstborn of the Children of Israel became Mine, of man and livestock; on the day I struck every firstborn in the land of Egypt I sanctified them for Myself.*
18 *I took the Levites in place of every firstborn among the Children of Israel.*
19 *Then I assigned the Levites to be presented to Aaron and his sons from among the Children of Israel to perform the service of the Children of Israel in the Tent of Meeting and to provide atonement for the Children of Israel,*

BAAL HATURIM ELUCIDATED

רֵאשִׁית תְּבוּאָתֹה, *Israel is holy to HASHEM, the first of His crop* (*Jeremiah* 2:3). For תְּבוּאָתֹה can be read as two words, תְּבוּאַת ה,[22] *the crop of five.*[23]

❑ **וּלְכַפֵּר — AND TO PROVIDE ATONEMENT.** [The masoretic note, ג׳, means that] this word appears three times in the *Tanach:* (i) here, וּלְכַפֵּר עַל בְּנֵי יִשְׂרָאֵל, *and to provide atonement for the Children of Israel;* (ii) וְאַהֲרֹן וּבָנָיו מַקְטִירִים . . . וּלְכַפֵּר עַל יִשְׂרָאֵל, *Aaron and his sons bring offerings . . . and to provide atonement for Israel,*[23a] in the *Book of Chronicles* (*I* 6:34); and (iii) . . . שָׁבֻעִים שִׁבְעִים נֶחְתַּךְ עַל עַמְּךָ וּלְהָתֵם חַטָּאת וּלְכַפֵּר עָוֹן, *Seventy septets have been decreed upon your people . . . to end sin, and to provide atonement for iniquity,* in the passage regarding the End [of Days] in *Daniel* (9:24). The similarity of expression teaches that exile provides atonement just as an Altar offering does.[24]

---

lists ten categories that ascended to the Land of Israel from Babylon with Ezra at the beginning of the Second Temple era, five of those categories did not exist at the time the Israelites were in the wilderness (A.S.).

22. This word is an example of a *keri uchesiv*, a word spelled one way in the *Tanach*, but pronounced differently. In this case, the *kesiv* (spelling) contains the female possessive suffix ־ָהּ, and the expected pronunciation is תְּבוּאָתָהּ, *her crop* (e.g., *Exodus* 23:10; *Leviticus* 25:3); however, tradition teaches that this word's *keri* (pronunciation) is תְּבוּאָתוֹ, as if it were spelled with the masculine suffix ־וֹ. The Baal HaTurim explains that Scripture uses a ה in place of the ו to allude to the five categories of Israel.

In his comments to בְּרֵעֹה (*Exodus* 32:17) and וּבְנֻחֹה (10:36 below), the Baal HaTurim also explains the use of the suffix ־ה in lieu of the suffix ־ו as an allusion to the number five.

23. Interestingly, the *Zohar* (*Pekudei* 229b) adduces this same verse as a reference to the three classes — Kohanim, Levites and Israelites. Moreover, *Minchas Shai* explains that this verse mentions *Aaron and his sons* once, *the Levites* once, and *the Children of Israel* five times. It thus alludes to the public Torah reading of the Sabbath, at which *aliyos* are given to one Kohen, one Levite and five Israelites.

23a. The verse before this one reads: *And their brethren the Levites are presented for all of the service of the Tabernacle of the House of God.* Together, those two verses echo our verse.

24. Cf. *Sanhedrin* 37b.

At the Covenant Between the Parts (*Genesis* 15:7-21), God showed Abraham [four visions]: the

וְלֹ֨א יִהְיֶ֜ה בִּבְנֵ֤י יִשְׂרָאֵל֙ נֶ֔גֶף בְּגֶ֥שֶׁת בְּנֵֽי־יִשְׂרָאֵ֖ל
כ אֶל־הַקֹּֽדֶשׁ׃ וַיַּ֨עַשׂ מֹשֶׁ֧ה וְאַהֲרֹ֛ן וְכָל־עֲדַ֥ת בְּנֵֽי־
יִשְׂרָאֵ֖ל לַלְוִיִּ֑ם כְּֽכֹל֩ אֲשֶׁר־צִוָּ֨ה יְהוָ֤ה אֶת־מֹשֶׁה֙
כא לַלְוִיִּ֔ם כֵּן־עָשׂ֥וּ לָהֶ֖ם בְּנֵ֥י יִשְׂרָאֵֽל׃ וַיִּֽתְחַטְּא֣וּ הַלְוִיִּ֗ם
וַֽיְכַבְּסוּ֙ בִּגְדֵיהֶ֔ם וַיָּ֨נֶף אַהֲרֹ֥ן אֹתָ֛ם תְּנוּפָ֖ה לִפְנֵ֣י יְהוָ֑ה
כב וַיְכַפֵּ֧ר עֲלֵיהֶ֛ם אַהֲרֹ֖ן לְטַהֲרָֽם׃ וְאַחֲרֵי־כֵ֞ן בָּ֣אוּ
הַלְוִיִּ֗ם לַעֲבֹ֤ד אֶת־עֲבֹֽדָתָם֙ בְּאֹ֣הֶל מוֹעֵ֔ד לִפְנֵ֥י
אַהֲרֹ֖ן וְלִפְנֵ֣י בָנָ֑יו כַּאֲשֶׁר֩ צִוָּ֨ה יְהוָ֤ה אֶת־מֹשֶׁה֙
כג עַל־הַלְוִיִּ֔ם כֵּ֖ן עָשׂ֥וּ לָהֶֽם׃ וַיְדַבֵּ֥ר יְהוָ֖ה
כד אֶל־מֹשֶׁ֥ה לֵּאמֹֽר׃ זֹ֖את אֲשֶׁ֣ר לַלְוִיִּ֑ם מִבֶּ֨ן חָמֵ֤שׁ
וְעֶשְׂרִים֙ שָׁנָה֙ וָמַ֔עְלָה יָבוֹא֙ לִצְבֹ֣א צָבָ֔א בַּעֲבֹדַ֖ת
כה אֹ֥הֶל מוֹעֵֽד׃ וּמִבֶּן֙ חֲמִשִּׁ֣ים שָׁנָ֔ה יָשׁ֖וּב מִצְּבָ֣א
כו הָעֲבֹדָ֑ה וְלֹ֥א יַעֲבֹ֖ד עֽוֹד׃ וְשֵׁרֵ֨ת אֶת־אֶחָ֜יו בְּאֹ֤הֶל
מוֹעֵד֙ לִשְׁמֹ֣ר מִשְׁמֶ֔רֶת וַעֲבֹדָ֖ה לֹ֣א יַעֲבֹ֑ד כָּ֛כָה
תַּעֲשֶׂ֥ה לַלְוִיִּ֖ם בְּמִשְׁמְרֹתָֽם׃

ט שלישי א וַיְדַבֵּ֨ר יְהוָ֤ה אֶל־מֹשֶׁה֙ בְמִדְבַּר־סִינַ֜י בַּשָּׁנָ֨ה הַשֵּׁנִ֜ית
לְצֵאתָ֞ם מֵאֶ֧רֶץ מִצְרַ֛יִם בַּחֹ֥דֶשׁ הָרִאשׁ֖וֹן לֵאמֹֽר׃

בעל הטורים

(כה) וּמִבֶּן. ב׳ — ״וּמִבֶּן חֲמִשִּׁים שָׁנָה יָשׁוּב מִצְּבָא הָעֲבֹדָה״; ״וּמִבֶּן אָדָם חָצִיר יִנָּתֵן״. שֶׁכֵּיוָן שֶׁהִגִּיעַ לִכְלַל חֲמִשִּׁים שָׁנָה אֵין בּוֹ כֹּחַ לַעֲבֹד עֲבוֹדָה, וְכֶחָצִיר יִנָּתֵן:

ט (א) וַיְדַבֵּר ה׳ אֶל מֹשֶׁה וְגוֹ׳. סָמַךְ פָּרָשַׁת פֶּסַח לְטָהֳרַת לְוִיִּם. רֶמֶז שֶׁהַלְוִיִּם מַפְשִׁיטִים:

BAAL HATURIM ELUCIDATED

25. וּמִבֶּן — AND FROM THE AGE OF.[24a] [The masoretic note, ב׳, means that] this word appears twice in the *Tanach:* (i) here, וּמִבֶּן חֲמִשִּׁים שָׁנָה יָשׁוּב מִצְּבָא הָעֲבֹדָה, *and from the age of fifty years he shall withdraw from the legion of work;* and (ii) וּמִבֶּן

Torah, the Altar offerings, *Gehinnom* and Israel's subjugation to the four empires — Babylon, Persia/Medea, Greece and Rome . . . At that time, God said to Abraham, "As long as your offspring engage in [the first] two [i.e., Torah and Altar offerings], they will be saved from [the other] two. Unfortunately, the offerings are destined to cease and the *Beis HaMikdash* is destined to be destroyed. What do you prefer for your descendants at that time, subjugation to *Gehinnom* or to the four empires?" . . . Abraham chose the latter, saying, "Better that my children be subjected to the nations than that a single one of them should descend to *Gehinnom.*" God approved Abraham's choice (*Tanchuma, Pekudei* 9; *Midrash Tehillim* 52:4). Thus, exile stands in place of the Altar offerings as a means of attaining atonement.

24a. The literal meaning of וּמִבֶּן is *and from the son of . . .,* and that is how it is used in the verse from *Isaiah* cited by the Baal HaTurim.

so that there will not be a plague among the Children of Israel
when the Children of Israel approach the Sanctuary."
[20] *Moses, Aaron and the entire assembly of the Children*
of Israel did to the Levites according to everything that
HASHEM had commanded Moses about the Levites, so did
the Children of Israel do to them. [21] *The Levites purified*
themselves and immersed their garments; and Aaron waved
them as a wave-service before HASHEM, and Aaron pro-
vided atonement for them to purify them. [22] *Afterwards*
the Levites came to perform their service in the Tent of
Meeting, before Aaron and before his sons, as HASHEM had
commanded Moses concerning the Levites; so they did for
them.
[23] *HASHEM spoke to Moses, saying,* [24] *"This shall apply to the*
Levites: From the age of twenty-five years and up, he shall join
the legion of the service of the Tent of Meeting; [25] *and from the*
age of fifty years, he shall withdraw from the legion of work
and no longer work. [26] *He shall minister with his brethren in the*
Tent of Meeting to safeguard the charge, but work shall he not
perform. So shall you do to the Levites concerning their
charge."

9 [1] *HASHEM spoke to Moses, in the Wilderness of Sinai, in the sec-*
ond year from their exodus from the land of Egypt, in the first

BAAL HATURIM ELUCIDATED

אָדָם חָצִיר יִנָּתֵן, *and from the son of man who will be made like grass* (*Isaiah* 51:12). This implies that once a Levite reaches the age of fifty, he no longer has adequate strength to perform the Levitic service, and will become [weak] like grass.[25]

IX

1. וַיְדַבֵּר ה׳ אֶל מֹשֶׁה וְגוֹ׳ — HASHEM SPOKE TO MOSES . . . The Torah juxtaposed the passage concerning the *pesach*-offering with the passage concerning the purification of the Levites. This is an allusion to the fact that the process of flaying [the hides of the *pesach*-offerings] was done by the Levites.[26]

❑ {At *Deuteronomy* 32:48 the Baal HaTurim comments on the phrase וַיְדַבֵּר ה׳ אֶל מֹשֶׁה when it is not followed immediately by לֵאמֹר.}

25. This refers to the work of carrying on his shoulder. However, he may be assigned to locking and opening the Temple gates, to the Levite choir, or to unloading the wagons that carried the disassembled *Mishkan* (see *Rashi*).

26. As Scripture relates about the *pesach*-offering of a later generation: *They slaughtered the pesach-offering, the Kohanim threw* [*the blood of the offerings upon the Altar*] *. . . and the Levites were flaying* [*the animals*] (*II Chronicles* 35:11).

ב־ג וְיַעֲשׂוּ בְנֵי־יִשְׂרָאֵל אֶת־הַפָּסַח בְּמוֹעֲדוֹ׃ בְּאַרְבָּעָה
עָשָׂר־יוֹם בַּחֹדֶשׁ הַזֶּה בֵּין הָעַרְבַּיִם תַּעֲשׂוּ אֹתוֹ
בְּמֹעֲדוֹ כְּכָל־חֻקֹּתָיו וּכְכָל־מִשְׁפָּטָיו תַּעֲשׂוּ אֹתוֹ׃
ד וַיְדַבֵּר מֹשֶׁה אֶל־בְּנֵי יִשְׂרָאֵל לַעֲשֹׂת הַפָּסַח׃
ה וַיַּעֲשׂוּ אֶת־הַפֶּסַח בָּרִאשׁוֹן בְּאַרְבָּעָה עָשָׂר יוֹם
לַחֹדֶשׁ בֵּין הָעַרְבַּיִם בְּמִדְבַּר סִינָי כְּכֹל אֲשֶׁר צִוָּה
ו יהוה אֶת־מֹשֶׁה כֵּן עָשׂוּ בְּנֵי יִשְׂרָאֵל׃ וַיְהִי אֲנָשִׁים
אֲשֶׁר הָיוּ טְמֵאִים לְנֶפֶשׁ אָדָם וְלֹא־יָכְלוּ לַעֲשֹׂת־

בעל הטורים

(ב) **בְּמוֹעֲדוֹ.** מָלֵא וָי״ו. לְאַחַר שֵׁשׁ שָׁעוֹת זְמַן שְׁחִיטָה:

❑ **בְּמוֹעֲדוֹ.** בְּאַ״תְּ בַּ״שׁ שיפוזק״ף. בְּמוֹעֲדוֹ שיפוזק״ף בְּגִימַטְרִיָּא בְּשַׁבָּת:

(ד) **לַעֲשׂת הַפָּסַח.** לַעֲשׂת חָסֵר וָי״ו. לוֹמַר לְךָ שֶׁלֹּא עָשׂוּ בַמִּדְבָּר אֶלָּא אוֹתוֹ פֶּסַח בִּלְבָד:

(ו) **אֲנָשִׁים אֲשֶׁר הָיוּ טְמֵאִים לְנֶפֶשׁ אָדָם.** בְּגִימַטְרִיָּא אֵילוּ שֶׁהָיוּ נֹשְׂאִין אֲרוֹנוֹ שֶׁל יוֹסֵף. ״אֲשֶׁר הָיוּ טְמֵאִים״ בְּגִימַטְרִיָּא זֶה לְמֵת מִצְוָה:

BAAL HATURIM ELUCIDATED

2. {The Baal HaTurim's comment on the word וְיַעֲשׂוּ appears at *Exodus* 5:9.}

❑ **בְּמוֹעֲדוֹ — IN ITS APPOINTED TIME.** This word is spelled in full, with a ו [after the מ].[27] [The ו (= 6) indicates that] the appointed time for slaughtering the *pesach* is after six hours[28] of the day have passed.[29]

❑ **בְּמוֹעֲדוֹ — IN ITS APPOINTED TIME.** According to the letter-exchange system

27. The word appears another three times in this passage (vv. 3, 7, 13), each time spelled defectively — בְּמֹעֲדוֹ, with the first ו omitted. The full spelling בְּמוֹעֲדוֹ also appears in 28:2 below, with reference to the daily *tamid*-offering, but the Baal HaTurim does not comment on that word. *Peirush HaRokeach* there explains that the similar full spelling with regard to the *pesach* and the *tamid*-offerings alludes to the Talmudic teaching that just as the word בְּמוֹעֲדוֹ there teaches that the *tamid* is slaughtered every day of the week, overriding the prohibition against slaughtering animals on the Sabbath, so does בְּמוֹעֲדוֹ regarding the *pesach* teach that the *pesach*-offering is slaughtered on the fourteenth of Nissan, even when that date falls on the Sabbath (*Pesachim* 66a; see also the Baal HaTurim's next comment).

28. The *pesach*-offering may not be slaughtered before noon, as the Torah states: *The entire congregation of the assembly of Israel shall slaughter it in the afternoon* (*Exodus* 12:6). Following the terminology of the Talmud, the Baal HaTurim refers to the afternoon as אַחַר שֵׁשׁ שָׁעוֹת, *after six hours*.

The halachic hour is seasonally adjusted. It is found by dividing the daytime (or nighttime) period into twelve equal parts. Thus, a winter daytime hour will be much shorter than a summer daytime hour, and a winter nighttime hour will be much longer than a summer nighttime hour. In this manner, the sixth hour of the day ends at exactly midday, and begins one adjusted hour before that time.

29. *Peirush HaRokeach.* See *Pesachim* 61a. Although the appointed time for the *pesach*-offering is after the sixth hour of the day, in actual practice, it was never offered earlier than an hour and a half after noon. For it was always offered an hour after the *tamid*-offering of the afternoon, and that offering was never brought before a half hour after noon.

month, saying: [2] "The Children of Israel shall make the
pesach-offering in its appointed time. [3] On the fourteenth day
of this month in the afternoon shall you make it, in its
appointed time; according to all its decrees and laws shall
you make it."

[4] Moses spoke to the Children of Israel to make the pesach-
offering. [5] They made the pesach-offering in the first [month],
on the fourteenth day of the month, in the afternoon, in the
Wilderness of Sinai; according to everything that HASHEM had
commanded Moses, so the Children of Israel did.

[6] There were men who had been contaminated through
[contact with] a human corpse and could not make the

BAAL HATURIM ELUCIDATED

known as [30]אַ״תְּ בַּ״שׁ, [the letters of this word may be exchanged for] שיפזקף. And the *gematria* of the two words בְּמוֹעֲדוֹ שיפזקף — 705 — is equivalent[31] to the word בְּשַׁבָּת, *on the Sabbath.*[32]

4. לַעֲשֹׂת הַפָּסַח — TO MAKE THE PESACH-OFFERING. The word לַעֲשֹׂת is spelled defectively, without a ו.[33] This indicates to you that, during their entire sojourn in the wilderness, the nation brought only this one *pesach*-offering.[34]

6. אֲנָשִׁים אֲשֶׁר הָיוּ טְמֵאִים לְנֶפֶשׁ אָדָם — MEN WHO HAD BEEN CONTAMINATED THROUGH [CONTACT WITH] A HUMAN CORPSE. The *gematria* of this phrase (1528) is equal to that of [35]אֵילוּ שֶׁהָיוּ נֹשְׂאִין אֲרוֹנוֹ שֶׁל יוֹסֵף, *These are the ones who were carrying Joseph's coffin.*[36] The *gematria* of the phrase אֲשֶׁר הָיוּ טְמֵאִים, *who had been contaminated* (622), is equivalent[37] to that of זֶה לְמֵת מִצְוָה, *This refers to* [those who had been contaminated through] *a "mes mitzvah."*[38,39]

30. See note 133 to 7:15 above.

31. The principle of *im hakollel* allows 704, the *gematria* of the Baal HaTurim's term, to be considered equivalent to 705.

32. *Peirush HaRokeach.* See *Pesachim* 66a, cited in note 27 above; see also *Rashi* here.

33. This word appears in the Torah seventy-five times; sixty-six times spelled in full, לַעֲשׂוֹת, but only nine times (*Exodus* 35:1, 32; 36:1, 2, 3, 5; *Leviticus* 8:34; and verses 4 and 6 here) spelled defectively, לַעֲשֹׂת. In three places the Baal HaTurim addresses the defective spellings: At *Exodus* 35:1 (see note 8 there), where his comment may be applied to all six verses in *Exodus;* in *Leviticus;* and in our verse, where it also applies to verse 6.

34. *Peirush HaRokeach;* see *Rashi* to v. 1.

35. The wording and spelling of the Baal HaTurim's phrase as it appears in the early printed editions, אֵלּוּ נוֹשְׂאֵי אֲרוֹנוֹ שֶׁל יוֹסֵף, is clearly in error, for its *gematria* does not match that of the verse. The version presented here appears in *Peirush HaRokeach,* the Baal HaTurim's apparent source for this comment.

36. See note 39 below.

37. The principle of *im hakollel* allows 622 to be considered equivalent to 623, the *gematria* of the Baal HaTurim's phrase.

38. A *mes mitzvah,* literally, "a dead person regarding whom there is a commandment," is a corpse whose burial is not being attended to. One who encounters such a corpse is obligated to fulfill the *mitzvah* of burying it (*Toras Kohanim,* beginning of *Emor*).

39. *Peirush HaRokeach.* The Talmud discusses the circumstances through which these men had come in contact with a corpse: According to one view, they were the bearers of the coffin of

הַפֶּסַח בַּיּוֹם הַהוּא וַיִּקְרְבוּ לִפְנֵי מֹשֶׁה וְלִפְנֵי אַהֲרֹן
ז בַּיּוֹם הַהוּא: וַיֹּאמְרוּ הָאֲנָשִׁים הָהֵמָּה אֵלָיו אֲנַחְנוּ
טְמֵאִים לְנֶפֶשׁ אָדָם לָמָּה נִגָּרַע לְבִלְתִּי הַקְרִיב
ח אֶת־קָרְבַּן יהוה בְּמֹעֲדוֹ בְּתוֹךְ בְּנֵי יִשְׂרָאֵל: וַיֹּאמֶר
אֲלֵהֶם מֹשֶׁה עִמְדוּ וְאֶשְׁמְעָה מַה־יְצַוֶּה יהוה לָכֶם:
ט-י וַיְדַבֵּר יהוה אֶל־מֹשֶׁה לֵּאמֹר: דַּבֵּר אֶל־בְּנֵי
יִשְׂרָאֵל לֵאמֹר אִישׁ אִישׁ כִּי־יִהְיֶה טָמֵא ׀ לָנֶפֶשׁ
אוֹ בְדֶרֶךְ *רְחֹקָה לָכֶם אוֹ לְדֹרֹתֵיכֶם וְעָשָׂה
יא פֶסַח לַיהוה: בַּחֹדֶשׁ הַשֵּׁנִי בְּאַרְבָּעָה עָשָׂר יוֹם

*נקוד על ה'

בעל הטורים

(י) טָמֵא לָנֶפֶשׁ. יֵשׁ פָּסֵק בֵּין "טָמֵא" "לָנֶפֶשׁ". לוֹמַר לְךָ שֶׁיֵּשׁ חִלּוּק בֵּין הַטְּמֵאִים – אִישׁ נִדְחֶה וְאֵין צִבּוּר נִדְחִין:

❑ **אוֹ בְדֶרֶךְ רְחֹקָה.** "רְחֹק" בְּגִימַטְרִיָּא זֶה מֵאִיסְקֻפָּה. שֶׁעַל הֵ"א נָקוּד, כְּאִלּוּ לֹא נִכְתַּב:

(י-יא) וְעָשָׂה פֶסַח לַה'. בַּחֹדֶשׁ הַשֵּׁנִי. לְפִי כְּשֶׁמְּעַבְּרִין הַשָּׁנָה, אָז אִיָּר בִּמְקוֹם נִיסָן,

BAAL HATURIM ELUCIDATED

10. טָמֵא לָנֶפֶשׁ — CONTAMINATED THROUGH [CONTACT WITH] A HUMAN CORPSE. The cantillation sign פָּסֵק [*paseik*],[40] literally, *pause,* appears between the words טָמֵא and לָנֶפֶשׁ. This is to indicate to you that there is a distinction between those who have become contaminated: [The *pesach*-offering obligation of] a contaminated individual is postponed [until the next month], but [that of] a contaminated community is not postponed.[41]

❑ **אוֹ בְדֶרֶךְ רְחֹקָה — OR ON A DISTANT ROAD.** The *gematria* of רְחֹק, *distant* (308), is equal to that of זֶה מֵאִיסְקֻפָּה[42], *This* [*means on the other side*] *of the threshold.* [This

Joseph, who had asked his brothers to promise that they would bring his remains to *Eretz Yisrael* for burial (see *Genesis* 50:25 and *Exodus* 13:19); according to another view, they were men who had engaged in burying a dead body (*Succah* 25a-b). In our verse, the Baal HaTurim finds an allusion to each of these opinions.

40. See the Baal HaTurim to 3:2 above and note 72 there.

41. The law stated by the Baal HaTurim is found in the Talmud, where, according to one opinion, it is derived from the phrase אִישׁ אִישׁ, *any man,* literally, *a man, a man,* of our verse, or from verse 5:2 above (*Pesachim* 66b). However, it is not clear how this law is implied by the *paseik* that separates טָמֵא from לָנֶפֶשׁ.

42. The version of this comment found in the early (and in many later) printed editions is problematic. It reads: [By the principle of *im hakollel,*] the *gematria* of רְחוֹקָה (319) is equivalent to that of זֶהוּ מֵאִסְקוּפָּה (310). For there is a dot over the ה, indicating that we expound on the word as if it were spelled without that ה (see note 43).

In this edition, the text has been emended to reconcile the *gematriaos.* As the Baal HaTurim states, the rationale for dropping the final unpronounced ה is that it is dotted, indicating that it is to be ignored (see note 43). Moreover, there is a grammatical phenomenon that sheds a different light on the dotted ה: The word דֶּרֶךְ, *road,* is one of those unusual nouns which can be either masculine or feminine. Thus, we find, וְהוֹדַעְתָּ לָהֶם אֶת הַדֶּרֶךְ, *and you shall make known to them the road,* יֵלְכוּ בָהּ, [*and*] *they shall go in it* (*Exodus* 18:20), with the feminine form of the pronoun בָּהּ, *in it,*

pesach-offering on that day; so they approached Moses and Aaron on that day. [7] *Those men said to him, "We are contaminated through [contact with] a human corpse; why should we be diminished by not offering* HASHEM*'s offering in its appointed time among the Children of Israel?"*

[8] *Moses said to them, "Stand and I will hear what* HASHEM *will command you."*

[9] HASHEM *spoke to Moses, saying,* [10] *"Speak to the Children of Israel, saying: If any man will become contaminated through [contact with] a human corpse or on a distant road, whether you or your generations, he shall make the pesach-offering for* HASHEM, [11] *in the second month, on the fourteenth day,*

BAAL HATURIM ELUCIDATED

gematria ignores the letter ה] for there is a dot over the ה in the word רְחֹקָה,[43] [implying that the word may be interpreted] as if it were spelled without the ה.

10-11. וְעָשָׂה פֶסַח לַה׳. בַּחֹדֶשׁ הַשֵּׁנִי — HE SHALL MAKE THE PESACH-OFFERING FOR HASHEM. IN THE SECOND MONTH. [The juxtaposition of these phrases alludes to the fact that the *pesach*-offering is inherently connected not only to Nissan, the first month, but to Iyar, the second month, as well.] For if the year just ended would have been proclaimed a leap-year, then [the month that has actually been designated as] Iyar is standing in the place of [what would have been] Nissan.[44]

rather than the masculine form בּוֹ. Conversely, we find בְּדֶרֶךְ אֶחָד ... וּבְשִׁבְעָה דְרָכִים, *On one road . . . and on seven roads* (*Deuteronomy* 28:7), using the masculine numbers אֶחָד and שִׁבְעָה, rather than the feminine forms אַחַת and שֶׁבַע (*Kiddushin* 2b). Accordingly, the masculine adjective רָחֹק is appropriate as a modifier of the word דֶּרֶךְ. Thus, the dotted ה changes the feminine form of the adjective רְחֹקָה to the masculine form רָחֹק, and the Baal HaTurim bases his allusion on that form (*VeChur LaZahav*).

It should be noted that in Talmudic and Midrashic literature, there are at least four spellings — אסקופה איסקופה אסקופא איסקופא — for the same word. Note also, that the ו in this word is used in the non-vowelized spelling only, to indicate that the ק is pronounced קֻ and not קָ; it is omitted when the word is spelled with vowel points. Similarly, the י that appears in some versions is there only to indicate that the first letter is vowelized אִ not אַ (as in Modern Hebrew). Nevertheless, for purposes of *gematria*, the letters י and ו are often used in place of the vowels ִ and ֻ and vice versa.

Alternatively: It is possible that the Baal HaTurim's phrase originally read: וְזֶהוּ מֵהָאִסְקֻפָּה, which has a *gematria* of 309. The principle of *im hakollel* then allows 308, the *gematria* of רָחֹק, to be considered equivalent to 309 (*VeChur LaZahav*).

43. Although נְקֻדּוֹת, *vowel signs,* are never written in the Torah scroll, tradition teaches that dots are inscribed over certain letters and words. Such a dot appears over the ה of the word רְחֹקָה. This dot indicates that, in some specific sense, the word רְחֹקָה is to be ignored (see the Baal HaTurim to 21:30 below). The Mishnah explains that the person need not be far from Jerusalem to be included as one who is *on a distant road.* Even a person who is merely on the other side of the threshold of the Temple's Courtyard on the fourteenth of Nissan may delay bringing the *pesach*-offering until the fourteenth of Iyar (*Pesachim* 9:2 [93b]).

44. According to the Torah, Nissan is the first month of the year, as God told Moses on the first of Nissan, *"This month shall be for you the beginning of the months, it shall be the first of the months of the year"* (*Exodus* 12:2). Thus, the phrase *the second month* of our verse refers to Iyar, the month after Nissan. Now, being that the

בֵּין הָעַרְבַּיִם יַעֲשׂוּ אֹתוֹ עַל־מַצּוֹת וּמְרֹרִים
יב יֹאכְלֻהוּ: לֹא־יַשְׁאִירוּ מִמֶּנּוּ עַד־בֹּקֶר וְעֶצֶם לֹא
יג יִשְׁבְּרוּ־בוֹ כְּכָל־חֻקַּת הַפֶּסַח יַעֲשׂוּ אֹתוֹ: וְהָאִישׁ
אֲשֶׁר־הוּא טָהוֹר וּבְדֶרֶךְ לֹא־הָיָה וְחָדַל לַעֲשׂוֹת

בעל הטורים

וּלְפִי שֶׁבַּחֲמִשָּׁה עָשָׂר בּוֹ יָרַד הַמָּן, לְכָךְ עוֹשִׂים בּוֹ פֶּסַח יוֹם אֶחָד:

(יג) **וּבְדֶרֶךְ.** ד׳ בַּמָּסוֹרֶת – ״וּבְדֶרֶךְ לֹא הָיָה״; ״וַיֵּלֶךְ בְּדֶרֶךְ אָבִיו וּבְדֶרֶךְ אִמּוֹ וּבְדֶרֶךְ יָרָבְעָם בֶּן נְבָט״; ״וּבְדֶרֶךְ חַטָּאִים לֹא עָמָד״. וְזֶהוּ ״וּבְדֶרֶךְ לֹא הָיָה וְחָדַל לַעֲשׂוֹת הַפֶּסַח״, שֶׁעוֹשֶׂה כְּדֶרֶךְ שֶׁעָשָׂה יָרָבְעָם, שֶׁהָלַךְ בְּדֶרֶךְ חַטָּאִים, שֶׁבִּטֵּל הַקָּרְבָּנוֹת וְהֶחֱטִיא אֶת יִשְׂרָאֵל. גַּם זֶה שֶׁאֵינוֹ בְדֶרֶךְ וּמְבַטֵּל מִלַּעֲשׂוֹת הַפֶּסַח:

❑ **וְחָדַל.** ב׳ בַּמָּסוֹרֶת – הָכָא ״וְחָדַל לַעֲשׂוֹת הַפֶּסַח״; וְאִידָךְ ״וְחָדַל לְעוֹלָם״. דְּפֶסַח בְּכָרֵת, וְזֶהוּ ״וְחָדַל לְעוֹלָם״, לְעוֹלָמוֹ שֶׁל יוֹבֵל, דְּהַיְנוּ חֲמִשִּׁים שָׁנָה, כְּדִין חַיָּבֵי כְרֵיתוֹת דְּלֹא מַפְּקֵי חֲמִשִּׁים:

BAAL HATURIM ELUCIDATED

Moreover, since on the fifteenth of Iyar the manna began to descend,[45] therefore we celebrate one day of Pesach[45a] during that month.[46]

13. וּבְדֶרֶךְ — AND ON THE ROAD. The masoretic note, ד׳, means that this word

---

year just ended was not a leap year, it comprised twelve months. The thirteenth month was proclaimed as Nissan and the fourteenth as Iyar. However, if the year just ended would have been proclaimed a leap year, then the thirteenth month would have been Adar II and the fourteenth would have been Nissan. Thus, the month that is actually Iyar hypothetically could have been Nissan, and the fourteenth of that month could have been the day of the *pesach*-offering.

The same explanation of why *Pesach Sheini* is celebrated in Iyar is found in *Siddur R' Yaakov Emden:* "For Nissan [of a non-leap year] hypothetically could have been Adar II in a leap year [so that Iyar falls in what could have been Nissan]." There, however, the comment ends by raising an objection: "[The fact that *Pesach Sheini* is celebrated in Iyar even in] a year following a leap year puts this explanation in question."

Perhaps we can resolve the problem by noting that almost two-thirds of all years contain only twelve months. Thus, the Torah ordained *Pesach Sheini* in Iyar for a reason that applies to the majority of years (*VeChur LaZahav*).

45. Actually, the manna began to fall on the sixteenth of Iyar (see *Rashi* to *Exodus* 16:1). On the fifteenth, the nation complained of a lack of food. God responded, *"Behold — I shall rain down for you food from heaven . . ."* (*Exodus* 16:4). Later that evening, God sent the quail, and the next morning the manna. The Baal HaTurim refers to the day on which they were informed about the manna as the day on which the manna began to fall (A.S.).

45a. The manna is intimately connected to the exodus from Egypt, as it is stated (*Exodus* 16:32): *Moses said, "This is the thing that* HASHEM *has commanded: 'A full omer of* [*manna*] *shall be a safekeeping for your generations, so that they shall see the food with which I fed you when I took you out of Egypt'* " (A.S.). Additionally, the Talmud (*Kiddushin* 38a) teaches: The Torah states, *The Children of Israel ate the manna for forty years* (*Exodus* 16:35). Did they not eat it for only thirty days less than forty years? Rather, the verse teaches you that in the cakes that they brought out of Egypt they tasted the flavor of the manna (Y.S.).

46. See Ch. 30 of *II Chronicles* which describes a year in which not only was the fourteenth of Iyar celebrated as *Pesach Sheini,* but the following seven days also were celebrated as the Festival of Matzos.

in the afternoon, shall they make it; with matzos and bitter herbs shall they eat it. 12 *They shall not leave over from it until morning nor shall they break a bone of it; like all the decrees of the pesach-offering shall they make it.* 13 *But a man who is pure and was not on the road yet failed to make*

appears four times in the *Tanach:* (i) here, וּבְדֶרֶךְ לֹא הָיָה, *and he was not on the road;* (ii, iii) וַיֵּלֶךְ בְּדֶרֶךְ אָבִיו וּבְדֶרֶךְ אִמּוֹ וּבְדֶרֶךְ יָרָבְעָם בֶּן נְבָט, *and he went in the path of his father and in the path of his mother, and in the path of Jeroboam son of Nebat* (*I Kings* 22:53); and (iv) וּבְדֶרֶךְ חַטָּאִים לֹא עָמָד, *and stood not in the path of the sinful* (*Psalms* 1:1). [The similarity of expression] indicates [that a person] *who was not on the road, yet had failed to make the pesach-offering,* acted in the way of Jeroboam who went *in the path of the sinful,* for he [Jeroboam] did away with the *korbanos*[47] and caused Israel to sin.[48] Similarly, this one who is not on the road yet does away with making the *pesach*-offering.

❑ וְחָדַל — YET FAILED. The masoretic note, ב׳, means that this word appears twice in the *Tanach:* (i) here, וְחָדַל לַעֲשׂוֹת הַפֶּסַח, *yet had failed to make the pesach-offering;* and (ii) וְחָדַל לְעוֹלָם, *and failed forever* (*Psalms* 49:9). [The similarity of expression can be explained as follows: As stated in this verse,] the punishment for failing to bring the *pesach*-offering is *kares* (excision).[49] Thus, [the word לְעוֹלָם, literally, *forever,* of the phrase] וְחָדַל לְעוֹלָם, *and failed forever,* refers to the word עוֹלָם as applied to the *Yovel* (Jubilee Year), i.e., fifty years,[50] in accordance with the principle that those subject to *kares* do not live out their fiftieth year.[51]

47. *The king* [i.e., Jeroboam] *took counsel and he made two golden calves; and he said to them* [the people]: *"It is too far for you to go to Jerusalem. Behold, your gods, O Israel, who brought you up from the land of Egypt . . ."* (*I Kings* 12:28, see vv. 25-33 there). The Talmud (*Moed Katan* 28b) adds that Jeroboam set sentries along the roads from his territory to Jerusalem in order to prevent any of his subjects from visiting and bringing offerings at the *Beis HaMikdash.* He was apprehensive that they might abandon his breakaway kingdom and become loyal followers of the Kingdom of Judah whose kings were direct descendants of King David (see *I Kings* 12:27). Thus, with regard to his subjects, Jeroboam effectively abolished the Temple service while simultaneously replacing it with idolatry.

48. The expression הֶחֱטִיא אֶת יִשְׂרָאֵל appears eighteen times in the *Tanach,* all in the Book of *Kings* and all with regard to Jeroboam and his idolatry.

49. That is, *That soul shall be cut off from its people,* which, as the Baal HaTurim states further in this comment, implies premature death, before the completion of one's fiftieth year.

50. See *Leviticus* 25:11. The Talmud (*Kiddushin* 15a) explains that וַעֲבָדוֹ לְעֹלָם, literally, *he shall serve him forever* (*Exodus* 21:6), means "he shall serve until *Yovel,*" and refers to the fifty years of each *Yovel* period as עוֹלָמוֹ שֶׁל יוֹבֵל (see *Rashi* to *Exodus* 21:6).

51. *Moed Katan* 28a — According to one opinion there, death in one's fiftieth year is the death of *kares.* According to the other opinion, death in one's fifties is the death of *kares.*

הַפֶּסַח וְנִכְרְתָה הַנֶּפֶשׁ הַהִוא מֵעַמֶּיהָ כִּי ׀ קָרְבַּן יהוה
לֹא הִקְרִיב בְּמֹעֲדוֹ חֶטְאוֹ יִשָּׂא הָאִישׁ הַהוּא: וְכִי־ יד
יָגוּר אִתְּכֶם גֵּר וְעָשָׂה פֶסַח לַיהוה כְּחֻקַּת הַפֶּסַח
וּכְמִשְׁפָּטוֹ כֵּן יַעֲשֶׂה חֻקָּה אַחַת יִהְיֶה לָכֶם וְלַגֵּר
רביעי וּלְאֶזְרַח הָאָרֶץ: וּבְיוֹם הָקִים אֶת־הַמִּשְׁכָּן טו
כִּסָּה הֶעָנָן אֶת־הַמִּשְׁכָּן לְאֹהֶל הָעֵדֻת וּבָעֶרֶב יִהְיֶה
עַל־הַמִּשְׁכָּן כְּמַרְאֵה־אֵשׁ עַד־בֹּקֶר: כֵּן יִהְיֶה תָמִיד טז
הֶעָנָן יְכַסֶּנּוּ וּמַרְאֵה־אֵשׁ לָיְלָה: וּלְפִי הֵעָלֹת הֶעָנָן יז

בעל הטורים

❑ **וְנִכְרְתָה הַנֶּפֶשׁ הַהִוא.** סוֹפֵי תֵבוֹת ״אִשָּׁה״. לוֹמַר לְךָ, אֶחָד הָאִישׁ וְאֶחָד הָאִשָּׁה בִּכְלַל עֳנָשִׁין:

(טו) וּבְיוֹם הָקִים אֶת הַמִּשְׁכָּן. שֶׁבַע פְּעָמִים כְּתִיב {״הַמִּשְׁכָּן״} בַּפָּרָשָׁה, כְּנֶגֶד שִׁבְעָה מִשְׁכָּנוֹת:

❑ **וּבָעֶרֶב.** ד׳ בַּמָּסוֹרֶת – ״וּבָעֶרֶב יִהְיֶה עַל הַמִּשְׁכָּן כְּמַרְאֵה אֵשׁ עַד בֹּקֶר״; ״וּבָעֶרֶב תֹּאמַר מִי יִתֵּן בֹּקֶר״; ״וּמַקְטִרִים לַה׳ וְגוֹ׳ בַּבֹּקֶר וּבָעֶרֶב״; ״וּבָעֶרֶב חָתַרְתִּי לִי בַקִּיר״ בִּיחֶזְקֵאל, שֶׁהָיָה מִתְנַבֵּא עַל הַגָּלוּת. וְזֶהוּ ״וּבָעֶרֶב חָתַרְתִּי לִי בַקִּיר״, כְּשֶׁיָּצְאוּ בַגּוֹלָה ״תֹּאמַר מִי יִתֵּן בֹּקֶר״, כְּהַהוּא עֶרֶב שֶׁנֶּאֱמַר בּוֹ ״וּמַקְטִרִים לַה׳ וְגוֹ׳ בַּבֹּקֶר וּבָעֶרֶב״, וּ״כְמַרְאֵה אֵשׁ עַד בֹּקֶר״:

(יז) הֵעָלֹת. ב׳ בַּמָּסוֹרֶת – ״הֵעָלֹת הֶעָנָן״; ״עִם הֵעָלוֹת הַגּוֹלָה״. זֶהוּ שֶׁאָמְרוּ, רְאוּיִין הָיוּ

BAAL HATURIM ELUCIDATED

❑ **וְנִכְרְתָה הַנֶּפֶשׁ הַהִוא** — THAT SOUL SHALL BE CUT OFF. The final letters of these three words [in reverse order] spell the word אִשָּׁה, *woman.* This indicates to you that both male and female are subject to punishment[51a] [for the non-observance of this *mitzvah*].[52]

15. וּבְיוֹם הָקִים אֶת הַמִּשְׁכָּן — ON THE DAY THE TABERNACLE WAS SET UP. {The word הַמִּשְׁכָּן, *the Tabernacle,*}[52a] is written seven times in this passage (9:15-23),[53] corresponding to the seven Tabernacles.[54]

51a. According to one opinion in the Talmud (*Pesachim* 91b).

52. *Peirush HaRokeach.* In this passage regarding the *pesach sheini* (i.e., the second *pesach*-offering), the Torah's terminology seems to exclude women from the laws of the *korban pesach* (*pesach*-offering): אִישׁ אִישׁ, *any man* (v. 10); וְהָאִישׁ אֲשֶׁר הוּא טָהוֹר, *but a man who is pure . . .*, הָאִישׁ הַהוּא, *that man* (v. 13). In order to include women in the laws of the *korban pesach,* the Torah uses the phrase, וְנִכְרְתָה הַנֶּפֶשׁ הַהִוא, *that soul shall be cut off,* which implies any person, man or woman, rather than וְנִכְרַת הָאִישׁ הַהוּא, *that man shall be cut off* (*Pesachim* 91b with *Tosafos,* s.v., וכתיב; see also *Bava Kamma* 15a). In the final letters of that phrase, the Baal HaTurim finds an additional allusion for the inclusion of women.

52a. The word הַמִּשְׁכָּן is not found in the early printed editions, but appears in *Shoham Yakar's* manuscript edition.

53. Three times in verse 15; once each in verses 18, 19, 20 and 22.

54. *Peirush HaRokeach,* who identifies the seven as: (i) the *Mishkan* that traveled with the Israelites

the pesach-offering, that soul shall be cut off from its people, for he had not offered HASHEM's offering in its appointed time; that man will bear his sin. 14 *When a convert shall dwell with you, and he shall make a pesach-offering to HASHEM, according to the decree of the pesach-offering and its law, so shall he do; one decree shall be for you, for the proselyte and the native of the Land."*

15 *On the day the Tabernacle was set up, the cloud covered the Tabernacle that was a tent for the Testimony, and in the evening there would be upon the Tabernacle like a fiery appearance until morning.* 16 *So it would always be: The cloud would cover it, and an appearance of fire at night.* 17 *And in accord with the lifting of the cloud*

BAAL HATURIM ELUCIDATED

❑ **וּבָעֶרֶב** — AND IN THE EVENING. The masoretic note, ד׳, means that this word appears four times in the *Tanach:* (i) here, וּבָעֶרֶב יִהְיֶה עַל הַמִּשְׁכָּן כְּמַרְאֵה אֵשׁ עַד בֹּקֶר, *and in the evening there would be upon the Tabernacle like a fiery appearance until morning;* (ii) וּבָעֶרֶב תֹּאמַר מִי יִתֵּן בֹּקֶר, *And in the evening you will say, "Who can give back the morning?"* (*Deuteronomy* 28:67);[54a] (iii) וּמַקְטִרִים לַה׳ [עֹלוֹת בַּבֹּקֶר] בַּבֹּקֶר וּבָעֶרֶב [בָּעֶרֶב], *Also, they burn [burnt-offerings] to HASHEM [morning] by morning and evening [by evening]* (*II Chronicles* 13:11); and (iv) וּבָעֶרֶב חָתַרְתִּי לִי בַקִּיר, *and in the evening I tunneled through the wall,* in Ezekiel's prophecy regarding the exile (*Ezekiel* 12:7). The similarity of expression can be interpreted as [a description of the exiles' feelings]: *In the evening* [*when*] *I tunneled through the wall,* [i.e., when the walls of Jerusalem will be destroyed and] its populace will be sent into exile. [On that evening,] *you will say, "Who can give back the morning?"* so that we could return to that [morning and] evening when *they would burn* [*burnt-offerings*] *to HASHEM . . . [morning] by morning and evening* [*by evening*], and when *there would be* [*upon the Tabernacle*] *like a fiery appearance until morning.*

17. הֶעָלוֹת — THE LIFTING. The masoretic note, ב׳, means that this word appears twice in the *Tanach:* (i) here, הֵעָלוֹת הֶעָנָן, *the lifting of the cloud;* and (ii) עִם הֵעָלוֹת הַגּוֹלָה, *with the lifting of the exiles* [*out of their exile*] (*Ezra* 1:11). [The similarity of expression] alludes to our Sages' statement: It would have been proper that a

through the wilderness; (ii-v) those that stood in Gilgal, Shiloh, Nob and Gibeon; (vi-vii) the First and the Second *Beis HaMikdash.*

In his commentary to 24:5 below, the Baal HaTurim mentions only six Tabernacles, omitting the one in the wilderness. There, the comment refers to Balaam's prophecy about Israel's future, and that prophecy did not include the *Mishkan* that had already been established. Our passage, on the other hand, speaks of both the present and the future and therefore includes the *Mishkan* (*Ittur Bikkurim*). Alternatively: Balaam's prophecy referred only to the Tabernacles established within the Land of Israel (*VeChur LaZahav*).

54a. See the Baal HaTurim to that verse.

מֵעַל הָאֹהֶל וְאַחֲרֵי כֵן יִסְעוּ בְּנֵי יִשְׂרָאֵל וּבִמְקוֹם
יח אֲשֶׁר יִשְׁכָּן־שָׁם הֶעָנָן שָׁם יַחֲנוּ בְּנֵי יִשְׂרָאֵל: עַל־פִּי
יהוה יִסְעוּ בְּנֵי יִשְׂרָאֵל וְעַל־פִּי יהוה יַחֲנוּ כָּל־יְמֵי
יט אֲשֶׁר יִשְׁכֹּן הֶעָנָן עַל־הַמִּשְׁכָּן יַחֲנוּ: וּבְהַאֲרִיךְ הֶעָנָן
עַל־הַמִּשְׁכָּן יָמִים רַבִּים וְשָׁמְרוּ בְנֵי־יִשְׂרָאֵל אֶת־
כ מִשְׁמֶרֶת יהוה וְלֹא יִסָּעוּ: וְיֵשׁ אֲשֶׁר יִהְיֶה הֶעָנָן יָמִים
מִסְפָּר עַל־הַמִּשְׁכָּן עַל־פִּי יהוה יַחֲנוּ וְעַל־פִּי יהוה
כא יִסָּעוּ: וְיֵשׁ אֲשֶׁר יִהְיֶה הֶעָנָן מֵעֶרֶב עַד־בֹּקֶר וְנַעֲלָה
הֶעָנָן בַּבֹּקֶר וְנָסָעוּ אוֹ יוֹמָם וָלַיְלָה וְנַעֲלָה הֶעָנָן
כב וְנָסָעוּ: אוֹ־יֹמַיִם אוֹ־חֹדֶשׁ אוֹ־יָמִים בְּהַאֲרִיךְ הֶעָנָן
עַל־הַמִּשְׁכָּן לִשְׁכֹּן עָלָיו יַחֲנוּ בְנֵי־יִשְׂרָאֵל וְלֹא יִסָּעוּ
כג וּבְהֵעָלֹתוֹ יִסָּעוּ: עַל־פִּי יהוה יַחֲנוּ וְעַל־פִּי יהוה יִסָּעוּ
אֶת־מִשְׁמֶרֶת יהוה שָׁמָרוּ עַל־פִּי יהוה בְּיַד־מֹשֶׁה:

בעל הטורים

שֶׁיֵּעָשׂוּ לָהֶם נֵס בִּימֵי עֶזְרָא כְּדֶרֶךְ שֶׁנַּעֲשָׂה לָהֶם בִּימֵי מֹשֶׁה, אֶלָּא שֶׁגָּרַם הַחֵטְא:

❑ **וּבִמְקוֹם.** ב׳ בַּמָּסוֹרֶת – ״וּבִמְקוֹם אֲשֶׁר יִשְׁכָּן שָׁם הֶעָנָן״; ״וּבִמְקוֹם גְּדֹלִים אַל תַּעֲמֹד״. שֶׁלֹּא הָיוּ נִפְנִין לֹא לִפְנֵיהֶם וְלֹא לִצְדָדֵיהֶם, אֶלָּא לַאֲחוֹרֵיהֶם. וְזֶהוּ ״וּבִמְקוֹם אֲשֶׁר יִשְׁכָּן שָׁם הֶעָנָן״, דְּהַיְנוּ לִפְנֵיהֶם אוֹ לִצְדָדֵיהֶם, אַל תַּעֲמֹד לַעֲשׂוֹת שָׁם גְּדוֹלִים:

(כג) **בְּיַד מֹשֶׁה.** וּסְמִיךְ לֵהּ ״עֲשֵׂה לְךָ שְׁתֵּי חֲצוֹצְרֹת כֶּסֶף״ שֶׁלֹּא הָיוּ אֶלָּא בְיָדוֹ, שֶׁבְּחַיָּיו נִגְנְזוּ:

BAAL HATURIM ELUCIDATED

miracle be performed for them [i.e., the Jewish people] in the days of Ezra, just as was done for them in the days of Moses.[55] However, [that did not happen] because sin caused [them to forfeit this reward].[56]

❑ **וּבִמְקוֹם** — AND IN THE PLACE. The masoretic note, ב׳, means that this word appears twice in the *Tanach:* (i) here, וּבִמְקוֹם אֲשֶׁר יִשְׁכָּן שָׁם הֶעָנָן, *and in the place where the cloud would rest;* and (ii) וּבִמְקוֹם גְּדֹלִים אַל תַּעֲמֹד, *and do not stand in the place of great ones* (*Proverbs* 25:6). [The similarity of expression indicates] that they would not relieve themselves in an area in front [of their encampment] or in

55. See *Berachos* 4a where the Talmud uses the phrases "in the days of Ezra" and "in the days of Joshua son of Nun" in lieu of the Baal HaTurim's "in the days of Ezra" and "in the days of Moses." However, the Baal HaTurim's "in the days of Moses" cannot be taken literally, for the entry did not take place during Moses' lifetime. Rather, it is a general statement referring to the generation that entered the Land, virtually all of whom were born before Moses died. A similar statement in *Sotah* 36a and *Sanhedrin* 98b reads, "at the first entry" and "at the second entry."

56. The Baal HaTurim speaks of this same concept in his comment to *Exodus* 12:11, s.v., וְכָכָה.

from atop the Tent, following that the Children of Israel would
journey; and in the place where the cloud would rest, there
the Children of Israel would encamp. 18 *According to the*
word of HASHEM *would the Children of Israel journey, and*
according to the word of HASHEM *would they encamp; all the*
days that the cloud would rest upon the Tabernacle they
would encamp. 19 *When the cloud lingered upon the Taberna-*
cle many days, the Children of Israel would maintain the
charge of HASHEM *and would not journey.* 20 *Sometimes the*
cloud would be upon the Tabernacle for a number of days;
according to the word of HASHEM *would they encamp and*
according to the word of HASHEM *would they journey.* 21 *And*
sometimes the cloud would remain from evening until
morning, and the cloud would be lifted in the morning and
they would journey; or for a day and a night, and the cloud
would be lifted and they would journey. 22 *Or for two days, or*
a month, or a year, when the cloud would linger over the
Tabernacle, resting upon it, the Children of Israel would
encamp and would not journey, but when it was lifted they
would journey. 23 *According to the word of* HASHEM *would*
they encamp, and according to the word of HASHEM *would*
they journey; the charge of HASHEM *would they safeguard,*
according to the word of HASHEM *through the hand of Moses.*

BAAL HATURIM ELUCIDATED

an area alongside of them, but only in an area behind them.[57] Thus *in the place where the cloud would rest,* i.e., to their front or to the sides, *do not stand* to relieve yourself.[58]

18. {The Baal HaTurim explains the words עַל פִּי ה׳ of this verse at *Leviticus* 1:1.}

23. בְּיַד מֹשֶׁה — THROUGH [LIT., IN] **THE HAND OF MOSES.** Juxtaposed to this is the command, עֲשֵׂה לְךָ שְׁתֵּי חֲצוֹצְרֹת כֶּסֶף, *Make for yourself two trumpets of silver* (10:2). This indicates that the silver trumpets were only "in the hand of Moses." They were [not given to anyone else, rather they were] hidden during his lifetime.[59]

57. *Eruvin* 55b. Whereas it was always possible that the cloud leading the Israelites on their way would make its next move to the right, to the left or straight ahead, the Israelites did not know the direction of the next leg of their journey in advance. Therefore, it would have been improper for them to establish a latrine area either in front of or on either side of the wilderness encampment. However, they could safely assume that it would not reverse its previous direction and retrace its earlier steps. Thus, latrine areas were always established behind the camp (*Rashi*).

58. The plural adjectives גְּדוֹלִים, *great ones,* and קְטַנִּים, *small ones,* are often used euphemistically for defecation and urination (see, e.g., *Berachos* 25a). Thus, the Baal HaTurim interprets the term מְקוֹם גְּדֹלִים as an allusion to a latrine.

59. *Peirush HaRokeach; Tanchuma* 10; *Bamidbar Rabbah* 15:15.

א־ב וַיְדַבֵּר יהוה אֶל־מֹשֶׁה לֵּאמֹר: עֲשֵׂה לְךָ שְׁתֵּי
חֲצוֹצְרֹת כֶּסֶף מִקְשָׁה תַּעֲשֶׂה אֹתָם וְהָיוּ לְךָ לְמִקְרָא
ג הָעֵדָה וּלְמַסַּע אֶת־הַמַּחֲנוֹת: וְתָקְעוּ בָּהֵן וְנוֹעֲדוּ
ד אֵלֶיךָ כָּל־הָעֵדָה אֶל־פֶּתַח אֹהֶל מוֹעֵד: וְאִם־בְּאַחַת
יִתְקָעוּ וְנוֹעֲדוּ אֵלֶיךָ הַנְּשִׂיאִים רָאשֵׁי אַלְפֵי יִשְׂרָאֵל:
ה וּתְקַעְתֶּם תְּרוּעָה וְנָסְעוּ הַמַּחֲנוֹת הַחֹנִים קֵדְמָה:
ו וּתְקַעְתֶּם תְּרוּעָה שֵׁנִית וְנָסְעוּ הַמַּחֲנוֹת הַחֹנִים
ז תֵּימָנָה תְּרוּעָה יִתְקְעוּ לְמַסְעֵיהֶם: וּבְהַקְהִיל אֶת־
ח הַקָּהָל תִּתְקְעוּ וְלֹא תָרִיעוּ: וּבְנֵי אַהֲרֹן הַכֹּהֲנִים
יִתְקְעוּ בַּחֲצֹצְרוֹת וְהָיוּ לָכֶם לְחֻקַּת עוֹלָם
ט לְדֹרֹתֵיכֶם: וְכִי־תָבֹאוּ מִלְחָמָה בְּאַרְצְכֶם עַל־הַצַּר

בעל הטורים

י (ב) **לְךָ שְׁתֵּי.** ״לְךָ שְׁתֵּי״ אוֹתִיּוֹת שֶׁלְּךָ, שֶׁמִּשֶּׁלּוֹ עֲשָׂאָם:

❑ **שְׁתֵּי חֲצוֹצְרֹת.** כְּנֶגֶד אַבְרָהָם וְיַעֲקֹב, שֶׁעָשׂוּ מִלְחָמָה בָּאֻמּוֹת וְנִצְּחוּם:

❑ **כֶּסֶף.** וְלֹא זָהָב, שֶׁלֹּא לְהַזְכִּיר ״קוֹל הָעָם בְּרֵעֹה״:

(ח־ט) **לְדֹרֹתֵיכֶם. וְכִי תָבֹאוּ מִלְחָמָה.** רֶמֶז לְמִלְחֶמֶת גּוֹג וּמָגוֹג הָעֲתִידָה לָבוֹא לִימוֹת הַמָּשִׁיחַ. ״תָבֹאוּ מִלְחָמָה״ בְּגִימַטְרִיָּא בְּמִלְחֶמֶת גּוֹג:

❑ **תָבֹאוּ.** אוֹתִיּוֹת ״אָבוֹת״. שֶׁזְּכוּת הָאָבוֹת עוֹמֵד בַּמִּלְחָמָה:

BAAL HATURIM ELUCIDATED

X

2. לְךָ שְׁתֵּי — FOR YOURSELF TWO. The [first three] letters of לְךָ שְׁתֵּי [can be rearranged to] spell the word שֶׁלְּךָ, [*from*] *that which is yours.* Moses made these trumpets from his own resources.[60]

❑ **שְׁתֵּי חֲצוֹצְרֹת — TWO TRUMPETS,** corresponding to the two Patriarchs, Abraham and Jacob, who did battle against the nations[61] and were victorious over them.[62]

---

60. *Peirush HaRokeach; Sifrei* 72; *Tanchuma* 10; *Yoma* 3b.

It is noteworthy that the Talmud expounds on the verse עֲשֵׂה לְךָ שָׂרָף, *make for yourself a fiery serpent* (21:8 below): The word לְךָ implies מִשֶּׁלְּךָ, *from that which is yours* (*Avodah Zarah* 44a), i.e., Moses should make the serpent from his own resources. Accordingly, the Baal HaTurim's comment on the phrase לְךָ שְׁתֵּי here is also applicable to the phrase לְךָ שָׂרָף there (Y.S.).

61. Abraham battled against the combined forces of four kings who, in the course of defeating Sodom and its sister cities, had captured his nephew and brother-in-law, Lot (see *Genesis,* Ch. 14). Jacob prepared himself for battle against Laban (see *Genesis* 31:25), against Esau (see *Rashi* to *Genesis* 32:9, s.v., וְהָיָה) and against the nations of Canaan (see *Bereishis Rabbah* 80:10 and 81:4), but he did not actually engage in battle. Isaac, however, never even had to arm himself for battle (see the Baal HaTurim to *Deuteronomy* 7:21).

62. Whereas one of the purposes for the trumpets was to be used in prayer in time of war, and

10/1-9

[1] *HASHEM spoke to Moses, saying,* [2] *"Make for yourself two trumpets of silver — make them hammered out, and they shall be yours for the summoning of the assembly and to cause the camps to journey.* [3] *When they sound a long blast with them, the entire assembly shall assemble to you, to the entrance of the Tent of Meeting.* [4] *If they sound a long blast with one, the leaders shall assemble to you, the heads of Israel's thousands.* [5] *When you sound short blasts, the camps resting to the east shall journey.* [6] *When you sound short blasts a second time, the camps resting to the south shall journey; short blasts shall they sound for their journeys.* [7] *When you gather together the congregation, you shall sound a long blast, but not a short blast.* [8] *The sons of Aaron, the Kohanim, shall sound the trumpets, and it shall be for you an eternal decree for your generations.* [9] *When you go [to wage] war in your land against the enemy*

BAAL HATURIM ELUCIDATED

❑ כֶּסֶף — SILVER. Gold was not used, so as not to recall [the incident of the golden calf, about which is written,] קוֹל הָעָם בְּרֵעֹה, *the sound of the people in its shouting*[63] (*Exodus* 32:17).

8-9. לְדֹרֹתֵיכֶם. וְכִי תָבֹאוּ מִלְחָמָה — FOR YOUR GENERATIONS. WHEN YOU GO [TO WAGE] WAR. [The juxtaposition of these phrases is] an allusion to the war of Gog and Magog which is destined to occur in the times of *Mashiach* (the Messiah).[64] Indeed, the *gematria* of תָבֹאוּ מִלְחָמָה is 532, equal to that of בְּמִלְחֶמֶת גּוֹג, *in the war of Gog.*[65]

❑ תָבֹאוּ — YOU GO. The letters of this word can be rearranged to spell אָבוֹת, *Patriarchs,* for the merit of the Patriarchs stands guard in time of war.[66]

whereas Israelite victory would come in the merit of the Patriarchs (see the Baal HaTurim to v. 9 below, s.v., תָבֹאוּ), Moses had to fashion two trumpets corresponding to the two Patriarchs who prepared for war.

63. *Peirush HaRokeach; Peirush HaRosh* in *Moshav Zekeinim; Peirush HaTur HaAroch.* The verb root רוע means *to make a loud sound;* it can refer to either shouting, as in the verse from *Exodus,* or trumpeting, as in the words תְּרוּעָה (v. 5 below) and וַהֲרֵעֹתֶם (v. 9). Thus, the תְּרוּעָה of golden trumpets would recall the בְּרֵעֹה of the golden calf.

64. *Peirush HaRokeach; Sifrei.* Scripture tells of a war that will precede the Messianic era. That event is called מִלְחֶמֶת גּוֹג וּמָגוֹג, *the war of Gog and Magog,* because its chief villain will be Gog, the prince of Magog (see *Ezekiel,* Chs. 38 and 39). Although this war is not mentioned specifically in the Five Books of the Torah, the Midrash and the commentaries find many allusions to it.

65. *Peirush HaRokeach.* The early printed editions read מִלְחֶמֶת גּוֹג, without the ־בְּ prefix; the *gematria* is then 530, two less than that of the Scriptural phrase. Therefore, *Ittur Bikkurim* suggests that the principle of *im hateivos* allows two to be added to 530 so that it is considered equivalent to 532. However, many later editions have added the ב, for that is how it appears in *Peirush HaRokeach,* the Baal HaTurim's source for this comment.

66. See the Baal HaTurim above with note 62.

הַצֹּרֵר אֶתְכֶם וַהֲרֵעֹתֶם בַּחֲצֹצְרֹת וְנִזְכַּרְתֶּם לִפְנֵי
י יְהוָה אֱלֹהֵיכֶם וְנוֹשַׁעְתֶּם מֵאֹיְבֵיכֶם: וּבְיוֹם שִׂמְחַתְכֶם
וּבְמוֹעֲדֵיכֶם וּבְרָאשֵׁי חָדְשֵׁכֶם וּתְקַעְתֶּם בַּחֲצֹצְרֹת
עַל עֹלֹתֵיכֶם וְעַל זִבְחֵי שַׁלְמֵיכֶם וְהָיוּ לָכֶם לְזִכָּרוֹן
לִפְנֵי אֱלֹהֵיכֶם אֲנִי יְהוָה אֱלֹהֵיכֶם:
חמישי יא וַיְהִי בַּשָּׁנָה הַשֵּׁנִית בַּחֹדֶשׁ הַשֵּׁנִי בְּעֶשְׂרִים בַּחֹדֶשׁ
יב נַעֲלָה הֶעָנָן מֵעַל מִשְׁכַּן הָעֵדֻת: וַיִּסְעוּ בְנֵי־יִשְׂרָאֵל
לְמַסְעֵיהֶם מִמִּדְבַּר סִינָי וַיִּשְׁכֹּן הֶעָנָן בְּמִדְבַּר
יג פָּארָן: וַיִּסְעוּ בָּרִאשֹׁנָה עַל־פִּי יְהוָה בְּיַד־מֹשֶׁה:
יד וַיִּסַּע דֶּגֶל מַחֲנֵה בְנֵי־יְהוּדָה בָּרִאשֹׁנָה לְצִבְאֹתָם

בעל הטורים

❑ **וַהֲרֵעֹתֶם בַּחֲצֹצְרֹת.** עַל שֵׁם ״רֹעָה הִתְרֹעֲעָה הָאָרֶץ״, ״תְּרֹעֵם בְּשֵׁבֶט בַּרְזֶל״:

(י) שִׂמְחַתְכֶם. בְּגִימַטְרִיָּא גַּם בְּיוֹם הַשַּׁבָּת:

❑ **וּבְמוֹעֲדֵיכֶם.** מָלֵא וָי״ו. כְּנֶגֶד פֶּסַח, עֲצֶרֶת, רֹאשׁ הַשָּׁנָה, יוֹם הַכִּפּוּרִים, סֻכּוֹת, שְׁמִינִי עֲצֶרֶת:

(יד) וַיִּסַּע דֶּגֶל מַחֲנֵה בְּנֵי יְהוּדָה. בְּכֻלָּם כְּתִיב ״וְנָסַע״, וּבִיהוּדָה כְּתִיב ״וַיִּסַּע״ — חָסֵר מ׳.

BAAL HATURIM ELUCIDATED

❑ **וַהֲרֵעֹתֶם בַּחֲצֹצְרֹת — YOU SHALL SOUND SHORT BLASTS OF THE TRUMPETS.** [The term וַהֲרֵעֹתֶם, *you shall sound short blasts,* is] related to [the words רֹעָה הִתְרֹעֲעָה[67] of the verse,] רֹעָה הִתְרֹעֲעָה הָאָרֶץ, *Broken, broken will be the land* (*Isaiah* 24:19),[67a] and to [the word תְּרֹעֵם[67] of the verse,] תְּרֹעֵם בְּשֵׁבֶט בַּרְזֶל, *You will shatter them with an iron rod* (*Psalms* 2:9).[67a, 68]

10. שִׂמְחַתְכֶם — YOUR [DAY OF] GLADNESS. The *gematria* of this word (808) is equal to that of גַּם בְּיוֹם הַשַּׁבָּת, *also on the Sabbath day.*[69]

67. According to the later grammarians, the root of וַהֲרֵעֹתֶם is רוע, *to make a loud sound* (see note 63 above), while the three words רֹעָה הִתְרֹעֲעָה and תְּרֹעֵם are of the root רעע, *to break.* Nevertheless, the Baal HaTurim maintains that they are all forms of the verb root רוע. In this, he agrees with *Radak,* who includes all these words under the entry רוע (*Sefer HaSharashim*).

67a. In his first comment to our verse, the Baal HaTurim relates it to the days of *Mashiach* and the war of Gog and Magog. Here, too, he cites two verses that speak of that period and that war (see *Rashi* to *Isaiah* 24:18; see *Avodah Zarah* 3b; A.S.).

68. That is, the trumpet blasts will shatter the enemies who make war against you (*Shoham Yakar*).

69. *R' Ephraim, MiKesivah Ashkenazis.* According to one opinion in the *Sifrei,* the term וּבְיוֹם שִׂמְחַתְכֶם, *and on your day of gladness,* refers to *Shabbos.* This opinion may be explained in the realm of פְּשַׁט, *peshat,* i.e., according to the simple meaning of the verse: Although the term שִׂמְחָה, *gladness,* is usually used with regard to the festivals, here it cannot be understood as such, for the verse also mentions וּבְמוֹעֲדֵיכֶם, *and on your appointed festivals* (*R' Eliezer Nachum* cited in *Peirush Sifrei DeVei Rav*).

Alternatively: If the term referred to the festivals, the verse would have used the plural form וּבִימֵי, *and on the days of,* rather than the singular וּבְיוֹם, *and on a day.* Although the term

who oppresses you, you shall sound short blasts of the trumpets, and you shall be recalled before HASHEM, *your God, and you shall be saved from your foes.* [10] *And on your day of gladness, and on your appointed festivals, and on your new moons, you shall sound the trumpets over your burnt-offerings and over your feast peace-offerings; and they shall be a remembrance for you before your God; I am* HASHEM, *your God."* [11] *It was in the second year, in the second month, on the twentieth of the month, the cloud was lifted from upon the Tabernacle of the Testimony.* [12] *The Children of Israel journeyed on their journeys from the Wilderness of Sinai, and the cloud rested in the Wilderness of Paran.* [13] *They journeyed for the first time at the bidding of* HASHEM *through Moses.* [14] *The division of the camp of the children of Judah journeyed first according to their legions,*

BAAL HATURIM ELUCIDATED

❑ **וּבְמוֹעֲדֵיכֶם — AND ON YOUR APPOINTED FESTIVALS.** This word is spelled in full, with a ו (= 6) [after the מ].[70] This is an allusion to the six festivals ordained by the Torah: Pesach, Shavuos, Rosh Hashanah, Yom Kippur, Succos and Shemini[70a] Atzeres.[70b, 71]

12. {The Baal HaTurim's comment to וַיִּשְׁכֹּן appears at *Exodus* 24:16.}

14. וַיִּסַּע דֶּגֶל מַחֲנֵה בְנֵי יְהוּדָה — THE DIVISION OF THE CAMP OF THE CHILDREN OF JUDAH JOURNEYED. With regard to all the other tribes, the verse states וְנָסַע [which has a *gematria* of 186], while with regard to Judah, it states וַיִּסַּע,[72] whose *gematria* [146]

שִׂמְחָה is not used explicitly in Scripture with reference to the Sabbath, we nevertheless find the words עֹנֶג, *delight* (e.g., *Isaiah* 58:13), מְנוּחָה, *contentment* (e.g., *Exodus* 23:12), and קְדוּשָׁה, *sanctity* (e.g., *Exodus* 20:3), referring to the Sabbath, and whereas *Shabbos* has these three elements, the term שִׂמְחָה, *joy*, is certainly appropriate to it. And this is the basis for the wording of the *Shabbos* prayer: יִשְׂמְחוּ בְמַלְכוּתְךָ שׁוֹמְרֵי שַׁבָּת וְקוֹרְאֵי עֹנֶג עַם מְקַדְּשֵׁי שְׁבִיעִי . . ., *They shall rejoice in Your kingship — those who observe the Sabbath and call it a delight. The people that sanctifies the Seventh Day . . .* (*Peirush Sifrei DeVei Rav*).

The Baal HaTurim shows that in the realm of רֶמֶז, *remez* [allusion], the term שִׂמְחַתְכֶם also refers to *Shabbos.* For further discussion regarding the שִׂמְחָה of the Sabbath and how it differs from that of *yom tov,* see *Pachad Yitzchak, Shabbos, maamar* 3.

70. The word appears in two other verses in the *Chumash,* both without the prefix -וּ. In 15:3 below, it is spelled defectively, בְּמֹעֲדֵיכֶם, without a ו; while in 29:39 below, it is spelled in full, בְּמוֹעֲדֵיכֶם. The Baal HaTurim does not comment on either of those spellings. See note 70b below.

70a. The Talmud teaches that with respect to six laws, Shemini Atzeres is considered a festival unto itself, independent of Succos (*Succah* 48a).

70b. See note 70 above. Perhaps we may extend the Baal HaTurim's comment to the other appearances of the word: 29:39 is a recapitulation of a long passage that includes the *mussaf* offerings of all the festivals. Thus, בְּמוֹעֲדֵיכֶם is spelled in full, with a ו. But בְּמֹעֲדֵיכֶם of 15:3 refers to the *olas re'iyah* and *shalmei chagigah* (*Menachos* 90b), offerings brought only on Pesach, Shavuos and Succos. Thus, בְּמֹעֲדֵיכֶם is spelled without a ו, indicating that not all the festivals are included (*VeChur LaZahav*).

71. *Peirush HaRokeach.* The Baal HaTurim makes a similar comment about the ו in לְמוֹעֲדָהּ (*Exodus* 13:10).

72. Both words mean *he* [or, *it*] *journeyed.* The word וְנָסַע is composed of two elements: נָסַע, in the

טו וְעַל־צְבָאוֹ נַחְשׁוֹן בֶּן־עַמִּינָדָב׃ וְעַל־צְבָא מַטֵּה
טז בְּנֵי יִשָּׂשכָר נְתַנְאֵל בֶּן־צוּעָר׃ וְעַל־צְבָא מַטֵּה בְּנֵי
יז זְבוּלֻן אֱלִיאָב בֶּן־חֵלֹן׃ וְהוּרַד הַמִּשְׁכָּן וְנָסְעוּ בְנֵי־
יח גֵרְשׁוֹן וּבְנֵי מְרָרִי נֹשְׂאֵי הַמִּשְׁכָּן׃ וְנָסַע דֶּגֶל מַחֲנֵה
רְאוּבֵן לְצִבְאֹתָם וְעַל־צְבָאוֹ אֱלִיצוּר בֶּן־שְׁדֵיאוּר׃
יט וְעַל־צְבָא מַטֵּה בְּנֵי שִׁמְעוֹן שְׁלֻמִיאֵל בֶּן־צוּרִישַׁדָּי׃
כ וְעַל־צְבָא מַטֵּה בְנֵי־גָד אֶלְיָסָף בֶּן־דְּעוּאֵל׃
כא וְנָסְעוּ הַקְּהָתִים נֹשְׂאֵי הַמִּקְדָּשׁ וְהֵקִימוּ אֶת־
כב הַמִּשְׁכָּן עַד־בֹּאָם׃ וְנָסַע דֶּגֶל מַחֲנֵה בְנֵי־אֶפְרַיִם
כג לְצִבְאֹתָם וְעַל־צְבָאוֹ אֱלִישָׁמָע בֶּן־עַמִּיהוּד׃ וְעַל־
צְבָא מַטֵּה בְּנֵי מְנַשֶּׁה גַּמְלִיאֵל בֶּן־פְּדָהצוּר׃
כד וְעַל־צְבָא מַטֵּה בְּנֵי בִנְיָמִן אֲבִידָן בֶּן־גִּדְעוֹנִי׃
כה וְנָסַע דֶּגֶל מַחֲנֵה בְנֵי־דָן מְאַסֵּף לְכָל־הַמַּחֲנֹת

בעל הטורים

שֶׁכָּל מ׳ שָׁנָה שֶׁהָיוּ בַּמִּדְבָּר הָיוּ עַצְמוֹתָיו מְגֻלְגָּלִין בָּאָרוֹן, כְּאִלּוּ לֹא נָסַע:

(כה) מְאַסֵּף. ד׳ בַּמָּסוֹרֶת – ״מְאַסֵּף לְכָל הַמַּחֲנֹת״; {״וְאֵין אִישׁ מְאַסֵּף אוֹתָם הַבַּיְתָה״} וּ״וְאֵין אִישׁ מְאַסֵּף אוֹתִי הַבָּיְתָה״ בְּפִילֶגֶשׁ בְּגִבְעָה; וְאִידָךְ ״וּכְעָמִיר מֵאַחֲרֵי הַקּוֹצֵר וְאֵין מְאַסֵּף״. שֵׁבֶט דָּן, עַל שֶׁהָיָה עִמָּהֶם פֶּסֶל מִיכָה, עַל כֵּן ״אֵין אִישׁ מְאַסֵּף״, שֶׁהֶעָנָן

BAAL HATURIM ELUCIDATED

is forty less. This is because during the entire forty years [that the Israelites sojourned] in the wilderness, Judah's bones were rolling around in his coffin,[73] [as such it is considered] as if he did not[74] journey.[75,75a]

simple past, *he journeyed;* and the conjunctive prefix ־וְ, *and.* The word **וַיִּסַּע** is also composed of two elements: יִסַּע, in the simple future, means, *he* [or, *it*] *will journey;* but the conversive prefix ־וַ changes it to the past tense, *he journeyed.* The Baal HaTurim explains why the Torah uses two forms for the same word. See note 75a below.

73. *Peirush HaRokeach.* Judah had imposed a ban upon himself: *If I do not bring* [*Benjamin*] *back to you . . . I will have sinned to you for all time* (*Genesis* 43:9). Although Judah's ban was conditional to his not returning with Benjamin and his condition was not fulfilled, for he did bring Benjamin back to Jacob, nevertheless, his ban took effect in accordance with the principle: The curse of a sage, even if conditional, is fulfilled (*Makkos* 11a). The Talmud states that as a consequence of Judah's self-imposed ban, his bones were rolling in his coffin [that is, when the Israelites left Egypt, they took the coffins of Jacob's sons, their tribal forebears, with them for burial in *Eretz Yisrael;* with the exception of Judah, whose bones rolled around loosely in his coffin, each of their skeletons remained intact in its coffin (*Rashi*)] during the entire forty-year period in the wilderness, until [at the end of that period] Moses beseeched God . . . then Judah's limbs were reattached at their joints (*Makkos* 11b).

74. It is not clear why Judah's disassembled remains are said not to have journeyed, while his brothers' intact remains are considered to have journeyed. Perhaps an intact skeleton could be

and over its legion was Nahshon son of Amminadab;
15 over the legion of the tribe of the children of Issachar was
Nethanel son of Zuar; 16 and over the legion of the tribe of
Zebulun was Eliab son of Helon. 17 The Tabernacle was
taken down, then journeyed the sons of Gershon and the
sons of Merari, the bearers of the Tabernacle. 18 Then
journeyed the division of the camp of Reuben according to
their legions; and over its legion was Elizur son of Shedeur;
19 over the legion of the tribe of the children of Simeon was
Shelumiel son of Zurishaddai; 20 and over the legion of the
tribe of the children of Gad was Eliasaph son of Deuel.
21 Then journeyed the Kohathites, bearers of the sanctuary;
and they would erect the Tabernacle before their arrival.
22 Then journeyed the division of the camp of Ephraim
according to their legions, and over its legion was Elishama
son of Ammihud; 23 over the legion of the tribe of the
children of Manasseh was Gamaliel son of Pedahzur; 24 and
over the legion of the tribe of the children of Benjamin was
Abidan son of Gideoni. 25 Then journeyed the division of the
camp of the children of Dan, the gatherer for all the camps,

BAAL HATURIM ELUCIDATED

25. מְאַסֵּף — **THE GATHERER** [lit., *the one who brings in*]. The masoretic note, ד׳, means that this word appears four times in the *Tanach:* (i) here, מְאַסֵּף לְכָל הַמַּחֲנֹת, *the gatherer for all the camps;* (ii-iii) with regard to the concubine at Gibeah, {וְאֵין אִישׁ מְאַסֵּף אוֹתָם הַבַּיְתָה, *but not a man is bringing them into the house,* and,}[76] וְאֵין אִישׁ מְאַסֵּף אוֹתִי הַבָּיְתָה, *but not a man is bringing me into the house* (*Judges* 19:15,18); and (iv) וּכְעָמִיר מֵאַחֲרֵי הַקּוֹצֵר וְאֵין מְאַסֵּף, [*a corpse will fall like . . .*] *and like a sheaf behind the harvester, but with no one bringing* [*it*] *in* [*for burial*] (*Jeremiah* 9:21). Because Micah's idol[77] traveled with the tribe of Dan, *not a man is bringing* [*them*] *into the house,*

considered as a person; and even when being carried in a coach or wagon, a person may be said to be journeying. However, a collection of detached bones is not considered as a person, and therefore cannot be said to journey (*VeChur LaZahav*).

75. In both *Peirush HaRosh* (cited in *Moshav Zekeinim*) and *Peirush HaRokeach,* this reads שֶׁלֹּא, *for he did not,* rather than כְּאִלּוּ לֹא, *as if he did not.*

75a. See note 72 above. Perhaps this alludes to another reason for the Torah using the two verb forms וַיִּסַּע and וְנָסַע: Because Judah's remains are not considered to be journeying, his personal journey had not yet begun. Therefore, the Torah uses a basically future tense word, וַיִּסַּע, with regard to him. For the other brothers' remains, however, the journey had already started. Therefore, the Torah uses the basically past tense form וְנָסַע (*VeChur LaZahav*).

76. Despite the masoretic note ד׳, *four,* virtually all the printed editions cite only three verses. It seems obvious that a copyist inadvertently omitted *Judges* 19:15, owing to the fact that it is almost identical with *Judges* 19:18 (*Ittur Bikkurim*).

77. See the Baal HaTurim to 2:31 above and note 66 there.

כו לְצִבְאֹתָם וְעַל־צְבָאוֹ אֲחִיעֶזֶר בֶּן־עַמִּישַׁדָּי: וְעַל־
כז צְבָא מַטֵּה בְּנֵי אָשֵׁר פַּגְעִיאֵל בֶּן־עָכְרָן: וְעַל־צְבָא
כח מַטֵּה בְּנֵי נַפְתָּלִי אֲחִירַע בֶּן־עֵינָן: אֵלֶּה מַסְעֵי
כט בְנֵי־יִשְׂרָאֵל לְצִבְאֹתָם וַיִּסָּעוּ: וַיֹּאמֶר מֹשֶׁה
לְחֹבָב בֶּן־רְעוּאֵל הַמִּדְיָנִי חֹתֵן מֹשֶׁה נֹסְעִים ׀
אֲנַחְנוּ אֶל־הַמָּקוֹם אֲשֶׁר אָמַר יהוה אֹתוֹ אֶתֵּן
לָכֶם לְכָה אִתָּנוּ וְהֵטַבְנוּ לָךְ כִּי־יהוה דִּבֶּר־טוֹב
ל עַל־יִשְׂרָאֵל: וַיֹּאמֶר אֵלָיו לֹא אֵלֵךְ כִּי אִם־אֶל־
לא אַרְצִי וְאֶל־מוֹלַדְתִּי אֵלֵךְ: וַיֹּאמֶר אַל־נָא תַּעֲזֹב
אֹתָנוּ כִּי ׀ עַל־כֵּן יָדַעְתָּ חֲנֹתֵנוּ בַּמִּדְבָּר וְהָיִיתָ לָּנוּ
לב לְעֵינָיִם: וְהָיָה כִּי־תֵלֵךְ עִמָּנוּ וְהָיָה ׀ הַטּוֹב הַהוּא

בעל הטורים

הָיָה פּוֹלֵט אוֹתָם וַעֲמָלֵק הוֹרֵג בָּהֶם, וְנָפְלוּ "כְּעָמִיר מֵאַחֲרֵי הַקּוֹצֵר וְאֵין מְאַסֵּף":

(כח) וַיִּסָּעוּ. ב׳ בַּמָּסוֹרֶת – "לְצִבְאֹתָם וַיִּסָּעוּ"; "וַיִּסָּעוּ וַיְהִי חִתַּת אֱלֹהִים". לוֹמַר, מַה שָּׁם הָיָה חִתַּת אֱלֹהִים עַל כָּל סְבִיבוֹתֵיהֶם, אַף כָּאן:

דָּבָר אַחֵר – "וַיִּסָּעוּ" דְּהָתָם רֹאשׁ פָּסוּק, "וַיִּסָּעוּ" דְּהָכָא סוֹף פָּסוּק. דְּהָתָם לְפִי שֶׁיַּעֲקֹב בִּעֵר עֲבוֹדָה זָרָה מִתּוֹכָם, לְפִיכָךְ נָסְעוּ בְּיָד רָמָה וּשְׁכִינָה לִפְנֵיהֶם. אֲבָל בְּנֵי דָן שֶׁהָיָה בֵּינֵיהֶם עֲבוֹדָה זָרָה, נָסְעוּ לְאָחוֹר וְלֹא לְפָנִים, שֶׁהָיָה הֶעָנָן פּוֹלֵט אוֹתָם וַעֲמָלֵק הָיָה הוֹרֵג בָּהֶם:

(לב) וְהָיָה הַטּוֹב הַהוּא. חָמֵשׁ פְּעָמִים טוֹבָה כְּתִיב כָּאן, כְּנֶגֶד חֲמֵשׁ מֵאוֹת אַמָּה דִּשְׁנָהּ שֶׁל יְרִיחוֹ שֶׁנִּתְּנוּ לְבָנָיו. "וְהֵטַבְנוּ . . . טוֹב . . . הַטּוֹב . . . יֵיטִיב . . . וְהֵטַבְנוּ" בְּגִימַטְרִיָּא בִּירִיחוֹ:

BAAL HATURIM ELUCIDATED

i.e., the clouds of glory[78] expelled them,[79] and Amalek slayed among them, and they fell *like a sheaf behind the harvester, but with no one bringing* [*them*] *in.*

28. וַיִּסָּעוּ — AND THEY JOURNEYED. The masoretic note,[80] ב׳, means that this word appears twice in the *Tanach:* (i) here, לְצִבְאֹתָם וַיִּסָּעוּ, *according to their legions, and they journeyed;* and (ii) וַיִּסָּעוּ וַיְהִי חִתַּת אֱלֹהִים, *They journeyed, and there fell a Godly*

78. The Baal HaTurim implies that the "man" of *not a man is bringing them in* is a metaphor for the clouds of glory. This reflects *Ibn Ezra's* comment to *Exodus* 14:19, which states that an angel traveled before the Israelites. Whenever that angel would travel from one place to the next, the Pillar of Cloud and the Pillar of Fire would travel with that angel. And, as the Baal HaTurim states in his comment to *Genesis* 37:15, the term אִישׁ, *man,* can refer to an angel (A.S.).

79. The Midrash (*Tanchuma, Ki Seitzei* 10) states that the members of the tribe of Dan that the cloud expelled were all idolaters. Cf. the Baal HaTurim to *Exodus* 17:7.

80. The full note reads: ב׳ חַד רֵישׁ פָּסוּק וְחַד סוֹף פָּסוּק, *This appears twice, once at the beginning of its verse, once at the end of its verse.* In *Achlah VeAchlah* (ed. Frensdorff), this word is found on list 90, which is headed, י״ח זוּגִין חַד רֵישׁ פָּסוּק וְחַד סוֹף פָּסוּק, *Eighteen pairs, of which one member appears at the beginning of its verse and one at the end of its verse.* The Baal HaTurim also comments on this phenomenon at *Genesis* 24:29 and 35:5; *Exodus* 19:23 and 21:17; and *Leviticus* 22:11.

according to their legions, and over its legion was Ahiezer
son of Ammishaddai; [26] *over the legion of the tribe of the*
children of Asher was Pagiel son of Ochran; [27] *and over the*
legion of the tribe of the children of Naphtali was Ahira son
of Enan. [28] *These were the journeys of the Children of Israel*
according to their legions, and they journeyed.
[29] *Moses said to Hobab son of Reuel, the Midianite, the*
father-in-law of Moses, "We are journeying to the place of
which HASHEM has said, 'I shall give it to you.' Go with us
and we shall treat you well, for HASHEM has spoken of good
for Israel." [30] *He said to him, "I shall not go; only to my land*
and my family shall I go." [31] *He said, "Please do not forsake*
us, inasmuch as you know our encampments in the wilder-
ness, and you have been as eyes for us. [32] *And it shall be*
that if you come with us, then it will be that that goodness

BAAL HATURIM ELUCIDATED

terror [*on the cities that were around them*] (*Genesis* 35:5).[81] This indicates that just as there was *a Godly terror* [*on the cities that were*] *around them* [when Jacob and his family set forth], so too here [when the Israelites journeyed].[82]

Alternatively: There [in *Genesis*], וַיִּסָּעוּ appears at the beginning of the verse, while here, וַיִּסָּעוּ appears at the conclusion of the verse.[83] Whereas there, Jacob uprooted idol worship from among the midst of his household,[83a] they journeyed with an upraised arm and the Divine Presence went before them. But the tribe of Dan, which had idols among them, journeyed behind, but not within, the camp, for the clouds of glory expelled them, and Amalek slayed among them.[84]

32. וְהָיָה הַטּוֹב הַהוּא — THEN IT WILL BE THAT THAT GOODNESS. Five forms of the word טוֹב, *good,* are written in this passage [regarding Jethro] (vv. 29-32), corresponding to the dimensions of the fertile lands of Jericho, five hundred cubits square, that were given to Jethro's descendants. The *gematria* of these five terms, וְהֵטַבְנוּ ... טוֹב ... הַטּוֹב ... יֵיטִיב ... וְהֵטַבְנוּ — 236 — is equal to that of בִּירִיחוֹ, *in Jericho.*[85]

81. In his comments to our verse, the Baal HaTurim offers two explanations of the masoretic note. In his comments to *Genesis,* he offers a third explanation.

82. *R' Yehudah HaChassid* to *Genesis* 35:5; *Peirush HaRokeach;* see *Shir HaShirim Rabbah* 3:6; see also *Exodus* 15:14-16 and *Joshua* 2:9-11,24 and 5:1.

83. See note 80 above.

83a. See *Genesis* 35:2-4.

84. *Maharam MiRothenburg.* See the Baal HaTurim to v. 25 above.

85. *R' Ephraim, MiKesivah Ashkenazis; Peirush HaRokeach.* The Midrash (*Sifrei,* cited by *Rashi*) describes the goodness to which Moses referred: When Israel was apportioned the land, there was the rich pasture lands of Jericho — five hundred cubits by five hundred cubits — that they set aside and did not assign to any tribe. They said, "In whomever's portion the *Beis HaMikdash* [i.e., the five-hundred-cubit space within which the Temple was erected] will be built, that tribe will be compensated with this area." In the meantime, until the construction of the *Beis HaMikdash,* they gave it to the descendants of Jethro.

י/לג-לה לג אֲשֶׁר יֵיטִיב יהוָה עִמָּנוּ וְהֵטַבְנוּ לָךְ: וַיִּסְעוּ מֵהַר יהוָה
דֶּרֶךְ שְׁלֹשֶׁת יָמִים וַאֲרוֹן בְּרִית־יהוָה נֹסֵעַ לִפְנֵיהֶם
לד דֶּרֶךְ שְׁלֹשֶׁת יָמִים לָתוּר לָהֶם מְנוּחָה: וַעֲנַן יהוָה
ששי לה עֲלֵיהֶם יוֹמָם בְּנָסְעָם מִן־הַמַּחֲנֶה: ׆ וַיְהִי בִּנְסֹעַ

בעל הטורים

(לד) בְּנָסְעָם. ב׳ בַּמָּסוֹרֶת – ״בְּנָסְעָם מִן הַמַּחֲנֶה״; ״בְּנָסְעָם מִקֶּדֶם״. מַה לְּהַלָּן מָרְדוּ, אַף כָּאן מָרְדוּ:

(לה-לו) עָשָׂה נוּנִי״ן הֲפוּכִין. שֶׁרָצָה לְהַעֲבִיר הַשְּׁבָטִים שֶׁאוֹתִיּוֹתֵיהֶם חֲמִשִּׁים, אֶת הַיַּרְדֵּן שֶׁהוּא רֹחַב חֲמִשִּׁים, אֶלָּא שֶׁהַחֵטְא גָּרַם:

טַעַם אַחֵר לְנוּנִי״ן הֲפוּכִין – כִּדְאִיתָא בְּשַׁבָּת, פֶּרֶק כָּל כִּתְבֵי, שֶׁאֵין זֶה מְקוֹמָהּ, וּכְתָבָהּ כָּאן לְהַפְסִיק בֵּין פֻּרְעָנוּת רִאשׁוֹנָה לְפֻרְעָנוּת שְׁנִיָּה. וְעָשָׂה נוּנִי״ן הֲפוּכִין, לוֹמַר שֶׁמְּקוֹמָהּ לִפְנֵי נ׳ פָּרָשִׁיּוֹת לְפָנֶיהָ. וְאִלּוּ לֹא הָיוּ הַנּוּנִי״ן הֲפוּכִין, לֹא הָיִיתִי יוֹדֵעַ אִם לִפְנֵי נ׳ פָּרָשִׁיּוֹת לְפָנֶיהָ אִם לִפְנֵי נ׳ לְאַחֲרֶיהָ, לְכָךְ עֲשָׂאוּם הֲפוּכִים, לוֹמַר לִפְנֵי נ׳ לְפָנֶיהָ. וְהוּא אַחַר ״וְנָסַע אֹהֶל מוֹעֵד מַחֲנֵה הַלְוִיִּם״, בְּפָרָשַׁת בְּמִדְבַּר סִינַי, שֶׁמִּשָּׁם עַד הָכָא נ׳ פָּרָשִׁיּוֹת:

❑ **וַיְהִי בִּנְסֹעַ.** וַי הָיָה לְאֻמּוֹת בִּנְסֹעַ. ״וַיְהִי״ עוֹלֶה ל״א, שֶׁנִּלְחַם עִם ל״א מְלָכִים:

BAAL HATURIM ELUCIDATED

34. בְּנָסְעָם — WHEN THEY JOURNEYED. The masoretic note, ב׳, means that this word appears twice in the *Tanach:* (i) here, בְּנָסְעָם מִן הַמַּחֲנֶה, *when they journeyed from the camp;* and (ii) בְּנָסְעָם מִקֶּדֶם, *When they journeyed from the east* (*Genesis* 11:2). Just as there, the people rebelled, here too, the people rebelled.[86]

35-36. He [God] placed reversed letters נ (= 50) [before and after this pair of verses[87]] for He desired to bring the tribes whose names contain fifty[88] letters across the Jordan River,[88a] which is fifty [cubits] wide.[89] The Jews' sins,[90] however, prevented this from happening.[90a]

---

86. In the Baal HaTurim's comments to *Genesis* 11:2, which speaks of the rebellion leading to the construction of the Tower of Babel, he expounds on this concept: This is in accordance with the Talmudic statement (*Yerushalmi, Taanis* 4:5; *Shabbos* 116a, with *Tosafos,* s.v., פורענות) that on the very day on which they began their journey from Sinai, the Israelites strayed from their commitment to God. They were like a young student fleeing from the book as soon as his lesson is over.

87. The only thing that may be written in a Torah scroll is the unvowelized, unpunctuated text, as God transmitted it to Moses at Mount Sinai. Nevertheless, the Talmud teaches that God instructed Moses to insert signs, in the form of reversed letters נ, before and after verses 35-36 (*Shabbos* 115b; see note 92 below for the continuation of this Talmudic passage).

88. *R' Ephraim, MiKesivah Ashkenazis.* The names of the twelve sons of Jacob, as spelled in the verses that speak of their births, contain exactly fifty letters: רְאוּבֵן (*Genesis* 29:32), שִׁמְעוֹן (v. 33 there), לֵוִי (v. 34), יְהוּדָה (v. 35), דָּן (30:6 there), נַפְתָּלִי (v. 8), גָּד (v. 11), אָשֵׁר (v. 13), יִשָּׂשכָר (v. 18), זְבֻלוּן (v. 20), יוֹסֵף (v. 24) and בִּנְיָמִין (35:19) — (*Sotah* 36a, cited in *Rashi* to *Exodus* 28:10; see also the Baal HaTurim to *Exodus* 28:17 with note 43).

88a. That is, immediately, within three days (*Sifrei* cited in *Rashi* to v. 33; see the Baal HaTurim to 11:4 below).

89. *R' Chaim Paltiel; Sifrei* to *Deuteronomy* 3:26; see the Baal HaTurim to 32:32 below and to *Deuteronomy* 3:25.

90. *R' Chaim Paltiel.* See note 92 below.

90a. This explains why the letters נ are reversed: In order to indicate that the Israelites deviated from the proper path and sinned, the letters are not inscribed in their proper manner (*Ittur Bikkurim*).

with which HASHEM will benefit us, we will do good to you."
33 *They journeyed from the Mountain of HASHEM a three-day distance, and the Ark of the covenant of HASHEM journeyed before them a three-day distance to search out for them a resting place.* 34 *The cloud of HASHEM was over them by day when they journeyed from the camp.*
35 *And it was at the Ark's setting out to journey, Moses*

BAAL HATURIM ELUCIDATED

An alternative reason for the reversed letters נ is offered in tractate *Shabbos,* in the chapter called כָּל כִּתְבֵי:[91] Here [*parashas Beha'alosecha*] is not the proper place for this passage, nevertheless it is written here to interrupt between the first trouble and the second trouble.[92] He placed the reversed letters נ [as signs] to indicate that its proper place is before the preceding fifty *parashiyos.*[93] Now, had the letters נ not been reversed, I would not know whether the intent is before the preceding fifty *parashiyos* or before the fiftieth *parashah* that follows.[94] Therefore, He made them reversed, to indicate [that their place] is before the preceding fifty *parashiyos.*[95] And that is after the verse: וְנָסַע אֹהֶל מוֹעֵד מַחֲנֵה הַלְוִיִּם, *The Tent of Meeting, the camp of the Levites, shall journey . . .* (*Numbers* 2:17), in *parashas Bamidbar,* for there are fifty *parashiyos* from that passage to ours.[96]

❑ וַיְהִי בִּנְסֹעַ — **AND IT WAS AT [THE ARK'S] SETTING OUT TO JOURNEY.** Woe befell[97] the [hostile] nations when [the Ark] would set out to journey.[98] The *gematria* of וַיְהִי equals 31, [alluding to the fact] that it did battle with thirty-one kings.[99]

91. *Shabbos* 116a, in the sixteenth chapter, which begins with the words כָּל כִּתְבֵי.

92. The Talmud continues (see note 87 above): God instructed Moses to insert signs before and after verses 35-36 to indicate that this is not the proper place for this passage . . . If so, why does it appear where it is? To separate between the first trouble and the second. And what is the second trouble? *The people were* [*complaining*] *like those wracked with pain* (11:1). And what is the first? *They journeyed from the Mountain of HASHEM* (10:33), and, within three days, they turned away from God (*Shabbos* 115b-116a).

93. See note 22 to 1:19 above.

94. This is difficult to understand. Fifty *parashiyos* after ours, we find ourselves in *parashas Pinechas* in the middle of a tribal census in which each tribe's count forms a *parashah* by itself; hardly the place for our *parashah.*

95. The letters are reversed, as if they were looking backward.

96. *Rabbeinu Bachya.* In contemporary Torah scrolls, forty-eight *parashiyos* separate our *parashah* from 2:17. And that is how the *Rambam* codifies the *halachah* (*Hilchos Sefer Torah* 8:4). Counting from the end of our passage gives us forty-nine. Nevertheless, *Or Torah* (cited in *Minchas Shai* and *Tikkun Soferim* [Dubna]) reports seeing two ancient Torah scrolls which had a paragraph break (פְּתוּחָה) between 10:21 and 10:22. Perhaps, the Baal HaTurim includes that *parashah* in his count. (See R' C.D. Chavel's notes to *Rabbeinu Bachya* for other ways to reconcile the number of *parashiyos.*)

97. The Talmud (*Megillah* 10b) and Midrash (*Tanchuma, Naso* 12) interpret the term וַיְהִי (of 7:1 above) as two words, וַי הָיָה, *there was woe.* The Baal HaTurim applies that understanding of the word to our verse.

98. The Midrash expounds verse 33: *The Ark of the covenant of HASHEM journeyed before them a three-day distance to search out for them a resting place* — it killed serpents and scorpions [along the way]; it burned any thornbushes; and it killed the enemies of Israel (*Tanchuma, Vayakhel* 7).

Alternatively: When Israel would go to battle, the Ark would be in the vanguard, leading the way and ensuring victory (*Joshua,* Ch. 6; *I Samuel* 4:3-7).

99. In conquering the Land of Canaan, Joshua defeated thirty-one kings (see *Joshua* 12:7-24).

י/לה הָאָרֹ֑ן וַיֹּ֣אמֶר מֹשֶׁ֗ה קוּמָ֣ה ׀ יהוה וְיָפֻ֙צוּ֙ אֹֽיְבֶ֔יךָ

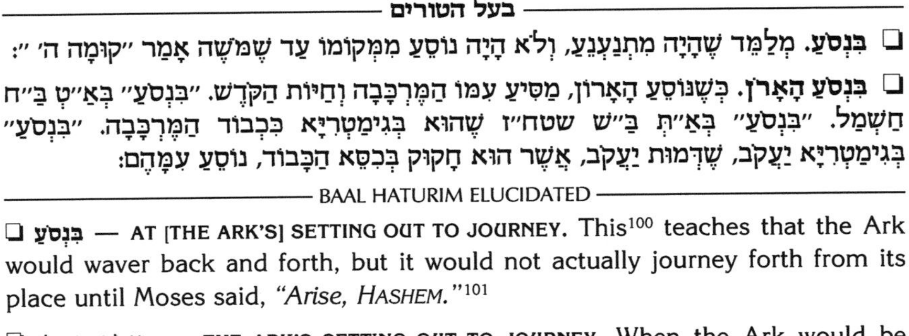

בעל הטורים

❑ **בִּנְסֹעַ.** מְלַמֵּד שֶׁהָיָה מִתְנַעְנֵעַ, וְלֹא הָיָה נוֹסֵעַ מִמְּקוֹמוֹ עַד שֶׁמֹּשֶׁה אָמַר "קוּמָה ה' ":

❑ **בִּנְסֹעַ הָאָרֹן.** כְּשֶׁנּוֹסֵעַ הָאָרוֹן, מַסִּיעַ עִמּוֹ הַמֶּרְכָּבָה וְחַיּוֹת הַקֹּדֶשׁ. "בִּנְסֹעַ" בְּאַ"ט בַּ"ח חַשְׁמַל. "בִּנְסֹעַ" בְּאַ"ת בַּ"שׁ שטח"ז שֶׁהוּא בְּגִימַטְרִיָּא כִּכְבוֹד הַמֶּרְכָּבָה. "בִּנְסֹעַ" בְּגִימַטְרִיָּא יַעֲקֹב, שֶׁדְּמוּת יַעֲקֹב, אֲשֶׁר הוּא חָקוּק בְּכִסֵּא הַכָּבוֹד, נוֹסֵעַ עִמָּהֶם:

BAAL HATURIM ELUCIDATED

❑ **בִּנְסֹעַ** — AT [THE ARK'S] SETTING OUT TO JOURNEY. This[100] teaches that the Ark would waver back and forth, but it would not actually journey forth from its place until Moses said, *"Arise, HASHEM."*[101]

❑ **בִּנְסֹעַ הָאָרֹן** — THE ARK'S SETTING OUT TO JOURNEY. When the Ark would be journeying, the Divine Chariot and the holy *Chayos*[102] would be journeying with it. [Three allusions to this concept are found in the word בִּנְסֹעַ:] (i) In the letter exchange system known as אַ"ט בַּ"ח[103], the letters of בִּנְסֹעַ may be exchanged for the letters of חַשְׁמַל, *Chashmal;*[103a,104] (ii) in the letter exchange system known as

---

100. The form בִּנְסֹעַ is a *makor* (gerund) and indicates ongoing action, literally, *journeying.* But, whereas the verse is relating what happened at that time, we would expect it to say כַּאֲשֶׁר נָסַע, *when it journeyed,* using the simple third person masculine past tense. However, the Torah uses the *makor* instead of the past tense to teach an additional lesson, as the Baal HaTurim explains (*VeChur LaZahav*).

101. *Peirush HaRokeach; Sifrei.*

102. The term מֶרְכָּבָה, *Merkavah* [*chariot*], refers to the Divine Throne described in the first chapter of *Ezekiel.* That Throne is borne by four חַיּוֹת, *Chayos* [literally, *living beings*], a class of heavenly angels, and the general appearance [alternatively, color] of the prophet's vision is described as the appearance of the חַשְׁמַל, *Chashmal,* another class of angel. The Baal HaTurim uses the three terms — *Merkavah, Chayos* and *Chashmal* — in his allusion. Other places where the Baal HaTurim speaks of the Divine Chariot include: *Genesis* 1:7 and 28:12,13; *Exodus* 37:1; *Numbers* 27:20; and *Deuteronomy* 4:36.

103. The Talmud (*Succah* 52b) speaks of a letter exchange known as אַ"ט בַּ"ח which pairs the letters of the *aleph-beis* in a unique manner based on their respective *gematriaos.* As explained by the *Aruch* [*Rashi* (see chart) explains this in another manner (*Hagahos HaBach* and *Maharshal*), one that cannot be reconciled with the Baal HaTurim's comment], the letters א through ט, which represent the units 1 through 9 respectively, are matched so that the total of each pair equals 10; thus: א (= 1) and ט (= 9); ב (= 2) and ח (= 8); ג (= 3) and ז (= 7); ד (= 4) and ו (= 6). The letter ה (= 5), however, has no mate other than itself. Similarly, the letters י through צ, which represent 10 through 90 respectively, are matched to add up to 100; thus: י (= 10) and צ (= 90); כ (= 20) and פ (= 80); ל (= 30) and ע (= 70); מ (= 40) and ס (= 60). Here the letter נ (= 50) has no mate other than itself. In this same manner, the letters representing 100 through 900 are matched in pairs that add up to 1000; thus: ק (= 100) and ץ (= 900); ר (= 200) and ף (= 800); ש (= 300) and ן (= 700); ת (= 400) and ם (= 600). In this grouping ך (= 500) stands alone. See chart.

In this alphabetic formulation, called אַ"ט בַּ"ח after its first two pairs, either letter of a pair may be exchanged for its partner and the three letters הנך may be exchanged for one another.

103a. According to the אַ"ט בַּ"ח formulation, the letter ב of בִּנְסֹעַ may be exchanged for a ח, the ס for a מ, and the ע for a ל. Thus, the first, third and fourth letters of בִּנְסֹעַ form pairs with the corresponding letters of חַשְׁמַל. The second letter of בִּנְסֹעַ, however, presents a problem, for it is the final ן, and not the regular נ, that may be exchanged with the letter ש to spell חַשְׁמַל (*Shoham Yakar*).

To explain the Baal HaTurim's comment, we must turn to the Talmudic passage concerning אַ"ט בַּ"ח. In *Succah* 52b, the Talmud uses אַ"ט בַּ"ח to transform the letters of סַהֲדָה into those of מְנוֹן. But an objection is raised against the *Aruch's* explanation of אַ"ט בַּ"ח, for it is only the regular נ, and not the final ן, that may be exchanged for a ה (*Maharshal*). It is suggested that the letters הנך have a

BAAL HATURIM ELUCIDATED

אַ״תְ בַּ״שׁ[105], the letters of בִּנְסֵעַ may be exchanged for the letters שטח״ז, which have a *gematria* of 324, equal to that of כִּכְבוֹד הַמֶּרְכָּבָה[106], *like the glory of the Chariot;* and (iii) the *gematria* of בִּנְסֹעַ (182) is equal to that of יַעֲקֹב, *Jacob,* for the image of Jacob, which was engraved on the Throne of Glory,[107] traveled with them.[108]

THE אַ״ט־בַּ״ח LETTER EXCHANGE ACCORDING TO *ARUCH*					
THOUSANDS		**HUNDREDS**		**TENS**	
ץ (900)	ק (100)	צ (90)	י (10)	ט (9)	א (1)
ף (800)	ר (200)	פ (80)	כ (20)	ח (8)	ב (2)
ן (700)	ש (300)	ע (70)	ל (30)	ז (7)	ג (3)
ם (600)	ת (400)	ס (60)	מ (40)	ו (6)	ד (4)
ך (500)		נ (50)		ה (5)	

THE אַ״ט־בַּ״ח LETTER EXCHANGE ACCORDING TO *RASHI*					
FIVE HUNDRED		**HUNDREDS**		**TENS**	
ת (400)	ק (100)	צ, ץ (90)	י (10)	ט (9)	א (1)
ש (300)	ר (200)	פ, ף (80)	כ, ך (20)	ח (8)	ב (2)
		ע (70)	ל (30)	ז (7)	ג (3)
		ס (60)	מ, ם (40)	ו (6)	ד (4)
		נ, ן (50)		ה (5)	

unique status in the אַ״ט בַּ״ח formulation beyond the fact that they are the only triplet among twelve pairs. Namely, once the formal arrangement of אַ״ט בַּ״ח has been established [and the kabbalists write at length about the legitimacy of the various letter exchange systems and their ramifications in the Heavenly Spheres], the grouping הנך may be expanded to include כ and ן. Thus, the letter ה can be exchanged with both נ and ן. And so, סְהָדָה and מָנוֹן are the "same" word. Indeed, some of the later kabbalists explain that the three letters הנך that stand alone in אַ״ט בַּ״ח represent three parts of the soul נֶפֶשׁ רוּחַ וּנְשָׁמָה, and that is why the name כֹּהֵן [which contains those three letters] is given to the one who represents the נֶפֶשׁ רוּחַ וּנְשָׁמָה of Israel (*Agra DeChallah, Shemos* 29:1; *Afikei Yam, Pesachim* 109b). Here, too, we find the כ interchanged with the ך and the נ interchanged with the ן with respect to the אַ״ט בַּ״ח formulation. Accordingly, the Baal HaTurim treats the נ of בִּנְסֹעַ as if it were a ן and exchanges it for a ש to spell חַשְׁמַל (*VeChur LaZahav*).

104. *R' Ephraim, MiKesivah Ashkenazis.* See note 102.

105. See note 133 to *parashas Naso.*

106. The text follows *Ittur Bikkur's* emendation. The early printed editions and many contemporary editions read בִּכְבוֹד הַמֶּרְכָּבָה, *in the glory of the Merkavah,* but the *gematria* of that phrase is short by 18.

107. *Bereishis Rabbah* 68:12. In his vision of the Chariot, the prophet Ezekiel describes angels with four faces, one of them being פְּנֵי אָדָם, *the face of a man* (*Ezekiel* 1:10). In his comments to *Exodus* 24:10, the Baal HaTurim states that that face has the visage of Jacob.

108. *R' Ephraim, MiKesivah Ashkenazis; Paaneach Raza.*

It is noteworthy that the tribes traveled with the

י/לו-יא/א לו וְיָנֻסוּ מְשַׂנְאֶיךָ מִפָּנֶיךָ: וּבְנֻחֹה יֹאמַר שׁוּבָה יהוה
רִבְבוֹת אַלְפֵי יִשְׂרָאֵל: ז
יא א וַיְהִי הָעָם כְּמִתְאֹנְנִים רַע בְּאָזְנֵי יהוה וַיִּשְׁמַע
יהוה וַיִּחַר אַפּוֹ וַתִּבְעַר־בָּם אֵשׁ יהוה וַתֹּאכַל

בעל הטורים

❑ **וּבְנֻחֹה.** כְּתִיב בְּהֵ״א. כְּנֶגֶד אַרְבָּעָה דְגָלִים וּמַחֲנֵה לְוִיָּה.

❑ בְּפָסוּק ״וַיְהִי בִּנְסֹעַ״ י״ב תֵּבוֹת כְּמוֹ שֶׁיֵּשׁ בְּפָסוּק ״וּלְכֹל הַיָּד הַחֲזָקָה״ שֶׁהוּא סוֹף הַתּוֹרָה; וּבְפָסוּק ״וּבְנֻחֹה״ יֵשׁ בּוֹ ז׳ תֵּבוֹת כְּמוֹ שֶׁיֵּשׁ בְּפָסוּק ״בְּרֵאשִׁית״ שֶׁהוּא תְּחִלַּת הַתּוֹרָה. לוֹמַר שֶׁהוּא חָשׁוּב סֵפֶר תּוֹרָה בִּפְנֵי עַצְמוֹ. וּמַתְחִיל בְּו׳ וּמְסַיֵּם בְּל׳, עַל שֵׁם ״הֲלִיכוֹת עוֹלָם לוֹ״:

❑ כָּל פָּרָשָׁה שֶׁיֵּשׁ בָּהּ כְּדֵי לְלַקֵּט פ״ה אוֹתִיּוֹת, כְּמוֹ ״וַיְהִי בִּנְסֹעַ״, מַצִּילִין אוֹתָהּ מִפְּנֵי הַדְּלֵקָה. לְכָךְ סָמַךְ לוֹ ״וַתִּבְעַר בָּם אֵשׁ״, לוֹמַר לְךָ שֶׁמַּצִּילִין הַפָּרָשָׁה שֶׁיֵּשׁ בָּהּ פ״ה אוֹתִיּוֹת, מִן הָאֵשׁ. וְעַל כֵּן ״מִילָה״ שֶׁעוֹלָה פ״ה מַצֶּלֶת מִדִּינָהּ שֶׁל גֵּיהִנֹּם:

BAAL HATURIM ELUCIDATED

❑ **וּבְנֻחֹה** — AND AT ITS RESTING. This term is spelled[109] with a ה (=5), corresponding to the four divisions of the Israelite camp,[110] plus the Levite[111] camp.[112]

❑ There are twelve words in the verse [that begins] וַיְהִי בִּנְסֹעַ (v. 35), the same number as in the verse [that begins], וּלְכֹל הַיָּד הַחֲזָקָה, which is the final verse of the Torah. There are seven words in the verse [that begins] וּבְנֻחֹה (v. 36), the same number as in the verse [that begins], בְּרֵאשִׁית, which is the first verse of the Torah. This indicates that this passage is considered a book of the Torah unto itself.[113]

This passage (vv. 35-36) begins with a ו[113a] and concludes with a ל,[113b] the letters of לו, *His,* recalling the verse הֲלִיכוֹת עוֹלָם לוֹ, *for the ways of the world are His* (*Habakkuk* 3:6).[114]

מֶרְכָּבָה on which was engraved Jacob's visage in precisely the same formation as their forebears, the sons of Jacob, carried Jacob's bier (see the Baal HaTurim to 1:32 above, with note 35; Y.S.).

109. This word is a *makor* (gerund) נוּחַ with the conjunctive prefix -ו, the prepositional prefix -בְּ and the third person masculine singular suffix -וֹ. Thus, we would expect it to be spelled וּבְנֻחוֹ, with a final ו.

110. See Ch. 2, above.

111. See 1:50, 53 and 2:17 above.

112. *Peirush HaRokeach.* The word וּבְנֻחֹה can be interpreted as two words, וּבְנֻחַ ה׳, *at the resting of the five,* i.e., the five camps — four Israelite and one Levite.

113. See notes 87 and 92, above. A second view in the Talmud states an altogether different reason for the reversed letters נ. King Solomon describes the Torah as having seven volumes: חָכְמוֹת בָּנְתָה בֵיתָהּ, [*Divine*] *wisdom built its house;* חָצְבָה עַמּוּדֶיהָ שִׁבְעָה, *it carved out its seven pillars* (*Proverbs* 9:1). The נ signs indicate that the Book of *Numbers* is really three Books: The first ends at 10:34; the second contains only two verses, 10:35-36; and the third begins at 11:1 and includes the remainder of *Numbers* (*Shabbos* 116a; see also *Vayikra Rabbah* 11:3).

113a. That is, the ו of וַיְהִי בִּנְסֹעַ (*Rabbeinu Ephraim* [*MiKesivah Ashkenazis*]).

113b. That is, the ל of יִשְׂרָאֵל.

114. *R' Ephraim, MiKesivah Ashkenazis.*

10/36-
11/1 *let those who hate You flee from before You."* [36] *And at its resting, he would say, "Reside tranquilly, O, HASHEM, among the myriad thousands of Israel."*

11 [1] *The people were [complaining] like those wracked with pain: it was evil in the ears of HASHEM, and HASHEM heard and His wrath flared, and a fire of HASHEM burned amongst them, and*

BAAL HATURIM ELUCIDATED

❑ [The Talmud states:] Any Torah passage[115] from which we can gather eighty-five letters, i.e., the number of letters in the passage beginning וַיְהִי בִּנְסֹעַ הָאָרֹן, we may save from a fire [on the Sabbath].[116] Thus the Torah juxtaposed the verse, וַתִּבְעַר בָּם אֵשׁ, *and a fire . . . burned amongst them* (11:1), in order to indicate to you that we may save a passage of 85 letters from a fire.[117] For this reason, too, מִילָה, *circumcision,* which has a *gematria* of 85, saves from the punishment [i.e., the fire] of *Gehinnom.* [117a]

115. The Baal HaTurim's use of פָּרָשָׁה, *passage,* here is difficult. The Talmudic source reads סֵפֶר תּוֹרָה, *Torah scroll,* and that is how the Baal HaTurim codifies the *halachah* (*Tur, Orach Chaim* 334; see also *Rambam, Hilchos Shabbos* 23:28), and that is how it appears in *Peirush HaRokeach,* the Baal HaTurim's apparent source for this comment. Nevertheless, the reading פָּרָשָׁה appears in all the printed editions of the Baal HaTurim as well as in the comments of *R' Ephraim* in *MiKesivah Ashkenazis.*

It is possible that the Baal HaTurim applies the eighty-five-letter rule even to a *parashah* that was never part of a kosher Torah scroll, e.g., a *mezuzah, tefillin* or an unfinished Torah scroll. Indeed, *Rabbeinu Yerucham* codifies the *halachah* in the following manner: And a Torah scroll that has become worn out, but in which there remains at least eighty-five letters that form whole words (see note 116 below) . . . remains in its state of sanctity and we may rescue it from a fire. And the same *halachah* applies regarding a *parashah* that does not have eighty-five letters that form whole words, but does contain the Divine Name, such as the *parashah* of וַיְהִי בִּנְסֹעַ, we may rescue it from a fire (*Toledos Adam* 12:7).

Now, from *Rabbeinu Yerucham's* wording, "And the same . . . a *parashah* that does not have eighty-five words . . . but does contain the Divine Name . . .," we may infer that if eighty-five letters forming full words did remain intact, we may save that *parashah,* even though it is not from a full Torah scroll (*VeChur LaZahav*).

116. Transporting or carrying objects from a public domain to a private domain is forbidden on the Sabbath. Depending upon a number of halachic considerations, the prohibition in a given instance may be of either Scriptural or rabbinic origin. In certain cases, the Sages waived the rabbinic prohibitions, thereby permitting an act of carrying which is not of Scriptural origin. For example, when a Torah scroll is threatened by fire, then, in deference to the sanctity of the Torah, the Sages permitted that scroll to be carried from its present location to a safe haven, if such carrying will not transgress Scriptural law. The Talmud states that even a Torah scroll whose letters have become obliterated may be saved from a fire, provided that some words are still intact and there are at least eighty-five letters in those words, corresponding to the number of letters in the passage beginning וַיְהִי בִּנְסֹעַ (*Shabbos* 116a).

117. *Peirush HaRokeach.*

117a. The Midrash understands *the flame of the ever-turning sword* (*Genesis* 3:24) as an allusion to *Gehinnom.* Adam asked, "What will save my children from this flaming fire?" He was answered, "The sword of circumcision . . ." (*Bereishis Rabbah* 21:9). The Talmud teaches that Abraham sits at the entrance to *Gehinnom* and does not allow anyone who has been circumcised to enter, except . . . (*Eruvin* 19a; see the Baal HaTurim to *Genesis* 1;1, s.v., דָּבָר אַחֵר אוֹתִיּוֹת בְּרִית אֵשׁ, and 18:1, s.v., דָּבָר אַחֵר נִמּוֹלוּ).

יא/ב־ח

ב בִּקְצֵה הַמַּחֲנֶה: וַיִּצְעַק הָעָם אֶל־מֹשֶׁה וַיִּתְפַּלֵּל
ג מֹשֶׁה אֶל־יהוה וַתִּשְׁקַע הָאֵשׁ: וַיִּקְרָא שֵׁם־הַמָּקוֹם
ד הַהוּא תַּבְעֵרָה כִּי־בָעֲרָה בָם אֵשׁ יהוה: וְהָאסַפְסֻף
אֲשֶׁר בְּקִרְבּוֹ הִתְאַוּוּ תַּאֲוָה וַיָּשֻׁבוּ וַיִּבְכּוּ גַּם בְּנֵי
ה יִשְׂרָאֵל וַיֹּאמְרוּ מִי יַאֲכִלֵנוּ בָּשָׂר: זָכַרְנוּ אֶת־הַדָּגָה
אֲשֶׁר־נֹאכַל בְּמִצְרַיִם חִנָּם אֵת הַקִּשֻּׁאִים וְאֵת
הָאֲבַטִּחִים וְאֶת־הֶחָצִיר וְאֶת־הַבְּצָלִים וְאֶת־
ו הַשּׁוּמִים: וְעַתָּה נַפְשֵׁנוּ יְבֵשָׁה אֵין כֹּל בִּלְתִּי
ז אֶל־הַמָּן עֵינֵינוּ: וְהַמָּן כִּזְרַע־גַּד הוּא וְעֵינוֹ כְּעֵין
ח הַבְּדֹלַח: שָׁטוּ הָעָם וְלָקְטוּ וְטָחֲנוּ בָרֵחַיִם אוֹ דָכוּ
בַּמְּדֹכָה וּבִשְּׁלוּ בַּפָּרוּר וְעָשׂוּ אֹתוֹ עֻגוֹת וְהָיָה טַעְמוֹ

בעל הטורים

יא (א) בִּקְצֵה הַמַּחֲנֶה. בְּגִימַטְרִיָּא הַקְּצִינִים:

(ד) מִי יַאֲכִלֵנוּ בָּשָׂר. אַף עַל פִּי שֶׁהָיָה לָהֶם בָּשָׂר הַרְבֵּה, הֵם הָיוּ סְבוּרִים לַעֲבֹר הַיַּרְדֵּן מִיָּד. וְאָמְרוּ, אָנוּ צְרִיכִין לְהִלָּחֵם בַּכְּנַעֲנִי וְלֹא נוּכַל לְהַעֲבִיר מִקְנֵנוּ עִמָּנוּ, וּלְכָךְ אָמְרוּ "מִי יַאֲכִלֵנוּ בָּשָׂר":

(ח) טַעְמוֹ. ד׳ בַּמָּסוֹרֶת – "וְהָיָה טַעְמוֹ כְּטַעַם לְשַׁד הַשָּׁמֶן"; "שַׁאֲנַן מוֹאָב מִנְּעוּרָיו, וְשֹׁקֵט הוּא אֶל שְׁמָרָיו, וְלֹא הוּרַק מִכְּלִי אֶל כֶּלִי, וּבַגּוֹלָה לֹא הָלָךְ, עַל כֵּן עָמַד טַעְמוֹ בּוֹ"; "וַיְשַׁנּוֹ אֶת טַעְמוֹ", "בְּשַׁנּוֹתוֹ אֶת טַעְמוֹ" גַּבֵּי דָּוִד. מוֹאָב שֶׁהָיָה שֹׁקֵט, עָמַד טַעְמוֹ. אֲבָל דָּוִד שֶׁגָּלָה מִמָּקוֹם לְמָקוֹם, "בְּשַׁנּוֹתוֹ אֶת טַעְמוֹ". וְדוֹר הַמִּדְבָּר, אַף עַל פִּי שֶׁגָּלוּ מִמָּקוֹם לְמָקוֹם לֹא שִׁנּוּ אֶת טַעְמָם, בִּשְׁבִיל הַמָּן שֶׁנֶּאֱמַר בּוֹ "טַעְמוֹ". שֶׁלֹּא נִתְּנָה תוֹרָה אֶלָּא לְאוֹכְלֵי הַמָּן:

BAAL HATURIM ELUCIDATED

XI

1. בִּקְצֵה הַמַּחֲנֶה — AT THE EDGE OF THE CAMP. The *gematria* of this phrase (305) is equal to that of הַקְּצִינִים, *the officials.*[118]

4. מִי יַאֲכִלֵנוּ בָּשָׂר — WHO WILL FEED US MEAT? [They made this complaint] even though they had much meat,[119] because they thought they would be crossing the Jordan immediately. They said to themselves, "We will have to fight the Canaanite and we will not be able to bring our livestock across with us." Therefore they said, *"Who will feed us meat?"*[119]

118. *Peirush HaRokeach.* According to one view in the *Sifrei* (as cited by *Rashi*), the term בִּקְצֵה, literally, *at the edge,* means בִּקְצִינִים, *at the officials.* See the Baal HaTurim to 7:2-3 above, s.v., הֵם נְשִׂיאֵי.

119. The Israelites left Egypt with *flock and cattle, very much livestock* (*Exodus* 12:38). Perhaps you will say that, at this point, they had already eaten all those animals, but that cannot be, for when they entered the land forty years later, *the children of Reuven and the children of Gad had abundant livestock* (32:1 below). Thus, their complaint about the lack of meat was merely a pretext to rebel (*Sifrei,* cited by *Rashi*).

it consumed at the edge of the camp. 2 *The people cried out*
to Moses; Moses prayed to HASHEM, *and the fire died down.*
3 *He named that place Taberah [Conflagration], for the fire*
of HASHEM *had burned against them.*

4 *The rabble that was among them cultivated a craving,*
and the Children of Israel also wept once more, and said,
"Who will feed us meat? 5 *We remember the fish that we ate*
in Egypt free of charge; the cucumbers, melons, leeks,
onions and garlic. 6 *But now, our life is parched, there is*
nothing; we have nothing to anticipate but the manna!"

7 *Now the manna was like coriander seed and its color*
was like the color of the bedolach. 8 *The people would stroll*
and gather it, and grind it in a mill or pound it in a mortar
and cook it in a pot or make it into cakes, and its taste was

BAAL HATURIM ELUCIDATED

7. {The Baal HaTurim's comment to הַבְּדֹלַח appears at *Genesis* 2:12.}

8. טַעְמוֹ — ITS TASTE. The masoretic note, ד׳, means that the word טַעְמוֹ[120] appears four times in the *Tanach*: (i) here, וְהָיָה טַעְמוֹ כְּטַעַם לְשַׁד הַשָּׁמֶן, *and its taste was like dough kneaded with oil;* (ii) שַׁאֲנַן מוֹאָב מִנְּעוּרָיו וְשֹׁקֵט הוּא אֶל שְׁמָרָיו {וְלֹא הוּרַק מִכְּלִי אֶל כֶּלִי וּבַגּוֹלָה לֹא הָלָךְ} עַל כֵּן עָמַד טַעְמוֹ בּוֹ, *Moab was complacent from its youth,* [*like wine*] *tranquil on its lees* {*and not poured from container to container, and did not go into exile*};[120a] *therefore its taste/sanity*[121] *remained in it* (*Jeremiah* 48:11); and (iii-iv) twice with regard to King David, וַיְשַׁנּוֹ אֶת טַעְמוֹ, *And he disguised his sanity* (*I Samuel* 21:14), and בְּשַׁנּוֹתוֹ אֶת טַעְמוֹ, *when he disguised his sanity* (*Psalms* 34:1). [The similarity of expression indicates that] because Moab was tranquil, *its sanity remained in it.*[122] But of David, who wandered from place to place, [it is stated,] *when he disguised his sanity.* Nevertheless, the generation of the wilderness, although they wandered from place to place, did not undergo a change of their sanity, due to the manna, concerning which the verse uses the term טַעְמוֹ, *its taste/sanity.* For [as our Sages comment], "The Torah was given solely to the eaters of the manna."[123]

The Baal HaTurim, however, finds a way to mitigate the severity of their wrongdoing.

120. The noun טַעַם refers to a thing's essence, thus, it is used for both *taste* and *sanity.*

120a. The part of the verse enclosed in braces is absent in most editions.

121. In context of Jeremiah's prophecy, the verse refers to the taste of the metaphoric wine. In the Baal HaTurim's allusion, however, it refers to Moab's emotional well-being.

122. See *Shabbos* 145b and *Megillah* 12b.

123. The Midrash states that permission to expound on the Torah was granted solely to those who ate the manna. That is, they were granted the opportunity to delve deeply into the meaning of the words and could thus draw exegetical inferences. This is because those who partook of the manna were not required to labor and toil and devote their time to earning a livelihood. Thus, they were free to spend their time in study (*Mechilta* 16:4; *Tanchuma, Beshalach* 20; see also the Baal HaTurim to *Exodus* 16:4 and 25:2, s.v., תְּרוּמָה; 19:2 below; and *Deuteronomy* 8:3).

ט כְּטַעַם לְשַׁד הַשָּׁמֶן׃ וּבְרֶדֶת הַטַּל עַל־הַמַּחֲנֶה
י לָיְלָה יֵרֵד הַמָּן עָלָיו׃ וַיִּשְׁמַע מֹשֶׁה אֶת־הָעָם בֹּכֶה
לְמִשְׁפְּחֹתָיו אִישׁ לְפֶתַח אָהֳלוֹ וַיִּחַר־אַף יהוה
יא מְאֹד וּבְעֵינֵי מֹשֶׁה רָע׃ וַיֹּאמֶר מֹשֶׁה אֶל־יהוה
לָמָה הֲרֵעֹתָ לְעַבְדֶּךָ וְלָמָּה לֹא־*מָצָתִי חֵן בְּעֵינֶיךָ
יב לָשׂוּם אֶת־מַשָּׂא כָּל־הָעָם הַזֶּה עָלָי׃ הֶאָנֹכִי
הָרִיתִי אֵת כָּל־הָעָם הַזֶּה אִם־אָנֹכִי יְלִדְתִּיהוּ
כִּי־תֹאמַר אֵלַי שָׂאֵהוּ בְחֵיקֶךָ כַּאֲשֶׁר יִשָּׂא הָאֹמֵן

*חסר א׳

בעל הטורים

(יא) וְלָמָּה לֹא מָצָתִי חֵן. חָסֵר אָלֶ״ף. וְאִידָךְ גַּבֵּי אִיּוֹב ״עָרֹם יָצָתִי״ חָסֵר אָלֶ״ף. שֶׁאָמַר, אִם ״לֹא מָצָאתִי חֵן בְּעֵינֶיךָ״, לָמָּה ״יָצָאתִי מִבֶּטֶן אִמִּי״?

(יב) הָאֹמֵן. תָּגִין עַל הֵ״א. שֶׁבַּחֲמִשָּׁה דְבָרִים הָאָב זוֹכֶה לִבְנוֹ, וְאֵלּוּ הֵן: בְּנוֹי, בְּכֹחַ, בְּעֹשֶׁר, בְּחָכְמָה, בְּשָׁנִים. בְּנוֹי – שֶׁנֶּאֱמַר ״יֵרָאֶה אֶל עֲבָדֶיךָ פָעֳלֶךָ וַהֲדָרְךָ עַל בְּנֵיהֶם״; בְּכֹחַ, שֶׁנֶּאֱמַר ״גִּבּוֹר בָּאָרֶץ יִהְיֶה זַרְעוֹ, דּוֹר יְשָׁרִים יְבֹרָךְ״; בְּעֹשֶׁר, שֶׁנֶּאֱמַר ״נַעַר הָיִיתִי גַּם זָקַנְתִּי וְלֹא רָאִיתִי צַדִּיק נֶעֱזָב וְזַרְעוֹ מְבַקֶּשׁ לָחֶם. כָּל הַיּוֹם חוֹנֵן וּמַלְוֶה וְזַרְעוֹ לִבְרָכָה״; בְּחָכְמָה, שֶׁנֶּאֱמַר ״תַּחַת אֲבֹתֶיךָ יִהְיוּ בָנֶיךָ, תְּשִׁיתֵמוֹ לְשָׂרִים בְּכָל הָאָרֶץ״, וּכְתִיב ״לֹא יָמוּשׁוּ מִפִּיךָ וּמִפִּי זַרְעֲךָ וּמִפִּי זֶרַע זַרְעֲךָ״; בְּשָׁנִים, דִּכְתִיב ״לְמַעַן יִרְבּוּ יְמֵיכֶם וִימֵי בְנֵיכֶם עַל הָאֲדָמָה״.

BAAL HATURIM ELUCIDATED

11. {The Baal HaTurim's comment to הֲרֵעֹתָ appears at *Exodus* 5:22.}

☐ **וְלָמָּה לֹא מָצָתִי חֵן** — WHY HAVE I NOT FOUND FAVOR. The word מָצָתִי is spelled defectively, without an א.[124] We find [a parallel anomalous spelling] with regard to Job, [עָרֹם יָצָתִי [מִבֶּטֶן אִמִּי, *Naked did I emerge* [*from my mother's womb*] (*Job* 1:21), with יָצָתִי spelled defectively, without an א.[125] For [it is as if Moses] said,[125a] "If *I did not find favor in Your eyes,* then why *did I emerge from my mother's womb?*"

12. הָאֹמֵן — THE NURSE. [According to a scribal tradition,] there are *tagin*[126] on

124. More than 450 verbs of this root appear in the *Tanach.* In every case, except two — מָצָתִי of our verse; הִמְצִיתִךָ of *II Samuel* 3:8 — the א of the root is present in the word, regardless of whether it is vowelized (e.g., מְצָאָתְנוּ, 20:14 below) or not (e.g., מָצָאתִי, v. 15). Thus, we would expect our verse to use the spelling מָצָאתִי.

125. See note 124. Similarly, of the more than 1000 verbs of the root יצא in the *Tanach,* only two — יָצָתִי of *Job;* הַיּוֹצֵת of *Deuteronomy* 28:57 (which, like the verse from *Job,* refers to emergence from the womb) — are spelled without the א of the root. We would expect *Job* to use the spelling יָצָאתִי, as the word is spelled in 22:32 below.

125a. The reading שֶׁאָמַר, [*as if Moses*] *said,* follows *Shoham Yakar's* manuscript edition. Virtually all other editions read לוֹמַר, literally, *to say,* i.e., to indicate.

126. In the Torah scroll, the letter ה is usually written with one תָּג, *tag* [tittle or crownlet]. However, *Sefer Tagin* lists 360 words in the Torah in which the letter ה is written with four *tagin* instead of the usual one. The word הָאֹמֵן appears on that list. See illustration and further discussion in the *Baal HaTurim's* comment to 5:31 above with note 42.

like the taste of dough kneaded with oil. 9 *When the dew
descended upon the camp at night, the manna would
descend upon it.*

10 *Moses heard the people weeping in their family groups,
each one at the entrance of his tent, and the wrath of*
HASHEM flared greatly; and in the eyes of Moses it was bad.

11 *Moses said to HASHEM, "Why have You brought harm to
Your servant; why have I not found favor in Your eyes, that
You place the burden of this entire people upon me?* 12 *Did I
conceive this entire people or did I give birth to it, that You
say to me, 'Carry them in your bosom, as the nurse carries*

BAAL HATURIM ELUCIDATED

the ה (= 5). [This alludes to a Mishnah:] There are five matters in which the father[127] benefits[128] his sons — (i) in handsomeness of appearance; (ii) in strength; (iii) in wealth; (iv) in wisdom; and (v) in years.[129] [The Talmud[130] adduces the following substantiating verses:] (i) in handsomeness, as the verse states, יֵרָאֶה אֶל עֲבָדֶיךָ פָעֳלֶךָ וַהֲדָרְךָ עַל בְּנֵיהֶם, *Your works shall be visible to Your servants, and Your beauty shall be upon their children* (*Psalms* 90:16); (ii) in strength, as the verse states, גִּבּוֹר בָּאָרֶץ יִהְיֶה זַרְעוֹ דּוֹר יְשָׁרִים יְבֹרָךְ, *His offspring will be mighty in the land, a generation of the upright who shall be blessed* (*Psalms* 112:2); (iii) in wealth, as the verse states, נַעַר הָיִיתִי גַּם זָקַנְתִּי וְלֹא רָאִיתִי צַדִּיק נֶעֱזָב וְזַרְעוֹ מְבַקֶּשׁ לָחֶם, כָּל הַיּוֹם חוֹנֵן וּמַלְוֶה וְזַרְעוֹ לִבְרָכָה, *I have been a youth and have also aged; but I have not seen a righteous man forsaken, nor his children begging for bread; all the day he is gracious and lends, and his children are a blessing* (*Psalms* 37:25-26); (iv) in wisdom, as it is stated, תַּחַת אֲבֹתֶיךָ יִהְיוּ בָנֶיךָ תְּשִׁיתֵמוֹ לְשָׂרִים בְּכָל הָאָרֶץ, *Succeeding your fathers will be your sons; you will appoint them leaders throughout the land* (*Psalms* 45:17), and it is written, לֹא יָמוּשׁוּ מִפִּיךָ וּמִפִּי זַרְעֲךָ וּמִפִּי זֶרַע זַרְעֲךָ, [*My words*] *will not be withdrawn from your mouth nor from the mouth of your offspring nor from the mouth of your offspring's offspring* (*Isaiah* 59:21);[131] and (v) in years, as it is stated, לְמַעַן יִרְבּוּ יְמֵיכֶם וִימֵי בְנֵיכֶם עַל הָאֲדָמָה, *In order to prolong your days and the days of your children upon the land* (*Deuteronomy* 11:21).

127. The term הָאָב, literally, *the father,* should be understood as *the parent.* It is not meant to exclude the mother. Rather, it is used because of the second paragraph of that Mishnah, which speaks of patrilinear generations (*Iggeros Moshe, Yoreh Deah* I, 154).

128. The translation follows the *Rambam's* explanation of the Mishnah: Children usually acquire these traits and assets from their parents. According to R' Ovadiah MiBertinoro, however, the Mishnah means: A deserving parent merits having children in whom these five qualities are found (see *Tosefos Yom Tov* to *Eduyos* 2:9; see also *Radak* to *II Samuel* 3:29).

129. *Eduyos* 2:9.

130. *Yerushalmi, Kiddushin* 1:7.

131. Perhaps the Baal HaTurim had before him a version of the *Yerushalmi* that differs from the extant version. Present-day editions do not include these two verses, but have instead, וְלִמַּדְתֶּם אֹתָם אֶת בְּנֵיכֶם לְדַבֵּר בָּם, *and you shall teach them to your children, to discuss them* (*Deuteronomy* 11:19).

אֶת־הַיֹּנֵק עַל הָאֲדָמָה אֲשֶׁר נִשְׁבַּעְתָּ לַאֲבֹתָיו׃
יג מֵאַיִן לִי בָּשָׂר לָתֵת לְכָל־הָעָם הַזֶּה כִּי־יִבְכּוּ עָלַי
יד לֵאמֹר תְּנָה־לָּנוּ בָשָׂר וְנֹאכֵלָה׃ לֹא־אוּכַל אָנֹכִי
לְבַדִּי לָשֵׂאת אֶת־כָּל־הָעָם הַזֶּה כִּי כָבֵד מִמֶּנִּי׃
טו וְאִם־כָּכָה ׀ אַתְּ־עֹשֶׂה לִּי הָרְגֵנִי נָא הָרֹג אִם־
מָצָאתִי חֵן בְּעֵינֶיךָ וְאַל־אֶרְאֶה בְּרָעָתִי׃
טז וַיֹּאמֶר יהוה אֶל־מֹשֶׁה אֶסְפָה־לִּי שִׁבְעִים אִישׁ

בעל הטורים

וּכְשֵׁם שֶׁהוּא זוֹכֶה לָהֶם, כָּךְ מְחַיֵּב אוֹתָם בַּחֲמִשָּׁה דְבָרִים חִלּוּפָם, דִּכְתִיב ״יָחֻלוּ עַל רֹאשׁ יוֹאָב וְאֶל כָּל בֵּית אָבִיו, וְאַל יִכָּרֵת מִבֵּית יוֹאָב זָב וּמְצֹרָע וּמַחֲזִיק בַּפֶּלֶךְ וְנֹפֵל בַּחֶרֶב וַחֲסַר לָחֶם״ – ״זָב״ תַּחַת הַכֹּחַ, שֶׁהַזִּיבוּת מַתֶּשֶׁת הַכֹּחַ; ״וּמְצֹרָע״ תַּחַת הַנּוֹי, כִּי הַצָּרַעַת מְגֻנָּה עַל הַבְּרִיּוֹת; ״וּמַחֲזִיק בַּפֶּלֶךְ,״ בּוּר שֶׁאֵין בּוֹ חָכְמָה; ״וְנֹפֵל בַּחֶרֶב,״ קְצַר יָמִים; ״וַחֲסַר לָחֶם,״ זֶה עֹנִי תַּחַת הָעֹשֶׁר. נִמְצָא, שֶׁהַצַּדִּיק זוֹכֶה לְבָנָיו בַּחֲמִשָּׁה דְבָרִים, וְהַחַיָּב מְחַיֵּב אוֹתָם בַּחֲמִשָּׁה דְבָרִים חִלּוּפָם׃

(טז) **אֶסְפָה לִי שִׁבְעִים אִישׁ.** כְּנֶגֶד שִׁבְעִים נֶפֶשׁ שֶׁיָּרְדוּ לְמִצְרַיִם.
וּכְנֶגֶד שִׁבְעִים אֻמּוֹת׃
וּכְנֶגֶד שִׁבְעִים שֵׁמוֹת שֶׁיֵּשׁ לוֹ לְהַקָּדוֹשׁ בָּרוּךְ הוּא. וְאֵלּוּ הֵן: אֵל; אֱלֹהִים; ה׳;

BAAL HATURIM ELUCIDATED

Conversely, just as a father can benefit his children in these five matters, so too can he hinder them with five antithetical matters, for it is written, יָחֻלוּ עַל רֹאשׁ יוֹאָב וְאֶל כָּל בֵּית אָבִיו וְאַל יִכָּרֵת מִבֵּית יוֹאָב זָב וּמְצֹרָע וּמַחֲזִיק בַּפֶּלֶךְ וְנֹפֵל בַּחֶרֶב וַחֲסַר לָחֶם, *[The guilt] shall rest upon the head of Joab and upon all his father's house, and may there never cease from Joab's house* (i) *zav,*[132] (ii) *metzora,*[133] (iii) *those who lean on crutches,* (iv) *those who fall by the sword, and* (v) *those who lack food* (*II Samuel* 3:29). The term *zav* represents the antithesis of strength, for the *zav's* condition saps his strength;[133a] *metzora* represents the antithesis of handsomeness, for people consider the malady of *tzaraas* detestable; *those who lean on crutches* [represents the antithesis of wisdom], the intellectually barren person in whom there is no wisdom; *those who fall by the sword* [represents the antithesis of years], a shortening of one's lifetime; and *those who lack food* represents poverty, the antithesis of wealth.

Thus, a righteous person benefits his descendants in five ways, while a corrupt person hinders his descendants in five opposite ways.

16. אֶסְפָה לִי שִׁבְעִים אִישׁ — GATHER TO ME SEVENTY MEN. This number corresponds to the seventy souls who descended into Egypt.[134]

---

132. See *Leviticus* 15:1-15.

133. See *Leviticus,* Ch. 13.

133a. See *Shulchan Aruch, Orach Chayim* 240:14.

134. *Pesikta Zutresa* [*Midrash Lekach Tov*]; see *Genesis* 46:8-27; see also note 135 below.

God told Abraham, "In the merit of circumcision, I shall establish seventy souls for you . . . I shall establish seventy elders from among them . . ." (*Bereishis Rabbah* 49:2).

the suckling, to the land that You swore to its forefathers?
13 Where shall I get meat to give to this entire people when
they weep to me, saying, 'Give us meat that we may eat'? 14 I
alone cannot carry this entire nation, for it is too heavy for
me! 15 And if this is how You deal with me, then kill me now,
if I have found favor in Your eyes, and let me not see my evil!"
16 HASHEM said to Moses, "Gather to Me seventy men

BAAL HATURIM ELUCIDATED

It also corresponds to the seventy nations.[135]

It also corresponds to the seventy Names of God.[136] They are the following:[137] (i) [138]אֵל, *Almighty God;* (ii) [139]אֱלֹהִים,* *Judge;* (iii) [140]ה׳,* *HASHEM;*

135. This refers to the seventy offspring of Noah whose names appear in *Genesis,* Ch. 10 (*Bamidbar Rabbah* 14:12; see also the Baal HaTurim to *Genesis* 25:25-26, with notes 25 and 26). Another Midrash (*Shocher Tov* 9:7) states that precisely seventy souls descended to Egypt with Jacob, corresponding to the seventy nations.

136. *Peirush HaRokeach.*

Although the Baal HaTurim states "seventy names of God," he enumerates only sixty-seven. Similarly, the short commentary to *Song of Songs* that is ascribed to R' Toviyah ben Eliezer (author of *Pesikta Zutresa* [*Midrash Lekach Tov*]), which apparently served as the Baal HaTurim's source for this comment, states that God "is called by seventy Names of praise," then goes on to list only sixty-seven Names. A comparison of the Baal HaTurim's list with that of R' Toviyah reveals that (a) they agree regarding sixty-three Names; (b) each list contains three Names that are absent from the other list; and (c) some of the Names are compounded of two words. [These differences will be pointed out in the footnotes below.] Accordingly, by combining the two lists, we are able to reconstruct what was likely the original list. Thus, the two lists are identical (*VeChur LaZahav;* see note 266a below).

Interestingly, *Midrash Shir HaShirim Zuta* [hereafter called *Midrash Zuta*] gives the number of God's Names as seventy, but enumerates only sixty-six Names. Unlike R' Toviyah's and the Baal HaTurim's lists, which present the Names in alphabetical order [with respect to the first letter only], the list in *Midrash Zuta* follows no apparent order. Additionally, thirty of the Names on the Baal HaTurim's list differ entirely from those in that Midrash, while another five names differ slightly. Moreover, neither the Midrashim nor the Baal HaTurim states the criteria used to determine which words or phrases used in Scripture to describe God are to be considered Divine Names. To add to our confusion, the literature of Kabbalah identifies hundreds of letter combinations that have no obvious meaning yet are described as Divine Names. Thus, it would be presumptuous to try to reconcile the list in *Midrash Zuta* with that of the Baal HaTurim.

There is one more short yet pertinent Midrashic passage: God has seventy Names that are explicit; His other Names, which are not explicit, are beyond calculation, beyond number (*Osios DeRebbe Akiva,* version 1, in *Batei Midrashos,* Vol. 2, cited in *Eitz Yoseph* to *Bamidbar Rabbah* 14:24; *Sefer Chanoch,* in *Otzar HaMidrashim*).

137. *Midrash Zuta* is the source for many of the verses and explanations cited in footnotes 138-267. An asterisk in the translation indicates that the Name appears on the list in that Midrash. Many of these Names also appear in *Shevuos* 35a, as noted in the footnotes. A goodly number of the sources adduced in those footnotes were added by R' Avraham Shereshevsky. We are thankful to him for bringing them to our attention and for all his other learned comments that appear over the initials A.S. throughout the footnotes. His thoughts enhance the quality of this work and we recognize his contributions with humble gratitude.

138. *Exodus* 34:6; see also *Shevuos* 35a.

139. God is called אֱלֹהִים, *Judge,* for He created the world with justice (*Midrash Zuta*). [The term אֱלֹהִים can refer either to God or to a judge (e.g., *Exodus* 21:6). Thus, *Sanhedrin* 66a records a dispute regarding the meaning of אֱלֹהִים in *Exodus* 22:27 (*VeChur LaZahav*).] See also *Rashi* and *Ibn Ezra* to *Exodus* 4:16 and 7:1; see also *Shevuos* 35a.

140. He is Master of the earth and Master of the heavens (*Midrash Zuta*). Although virtually all

אֶחָד; אָדוֹן; אַדִּיר; אֶהְיֶה; אַמִּיץ; אֱמֶת; אֶרֶךְ אַפַּיִם; אַחֲרוֹן — שֶׁאֵינוֹ מוֹסֵר מַלְכוּתוֹ לְאַחֵר; אֱמוּנָה; אֶשְׁכֹּל הַכֹּפֶר; בָּרוּךְ; בּוֹרֵא; גָּדוֹל; גֵּאֶה; גּוֹאֵל; גִּבּוֹר; דָּגוּל; הַיּוֹדֵעַ; וָעֵד; זוֹכֵר; חַי; חָסִיד; חַנּוּן; חוֹקֵר; חֲסִין; חָכָם; טוֹב; טְהוֹר עֵינַיִם; יָשָׁר; יוֹשֵׁב סֵתֶר; כָּבוֹד; מִסְתַּתֵּר; נוֹרָא; נִשְׂגָּב; נֶצַח; נֹצֵר חֶסֶד; נֹשֵׂא עָוֹן; נֹשֵׂא פֶשַׁע; נֹשֵׂא חֵטְא; נוֹקֵם; נוֹטֵר; סֶלָה — "יֹשֵׁב קֶדֶם סֶלָה"; סַלָּח; עֶלְיוֹן; עֹפֶר; עִזּוּז; פּוֹדֶה; צוּר; צְבִי; צְבָאוֹת; קָדוֹשׁ; קַנָּא; קָרוֹב; רַחוּם; רָם; רִאשׁוֹן — שֶׁלֹּא קִבֵּל מַלְכוּתוֹ מֵאַחֵר; רַב חֶסֶד; שׁוֹמֵר; שׁוֹפֵט; שִׁלְטוֹן; שַׂר; שׁוֹכֵן עַד; תָּמִים; תַּקִּיף;

BAAL HATURIM ELUCIDATED

(iv) [141]אֶחָד, *One;* (v) [142]אָדוֹן,* *Lord;* (vi) [143]אַדִּיר,* *Mighty;* (vii) [144]אֶהְיֶה,* *I Shall Be;* (viii) [145]אַמִּיץ, *Strong;* (ix) [146]אֱמֶת, *Truth;* (x) [147]אֶרֶךְ אַפַּיִם, *Slow to Anger;* (xi) [148]אַחֲרוֹן,* *Last,* for He does not hand over His sovereignty to any other being; (xii) [149]אֱמוּנָה, *Faith;* (xiii) [150]אֶשְׁכֹּל הַכֹּפֶר,* *Possessor of Everything, Grantor of Atonement;*[150a] (xiv) [151]בָּרוּךְ, *Blessed;* (xv) [152]בּוֹרֵא,* *Creator;* (xvi) [153]גָּדוֹל,* *Great;* (xvii) [154]גֵּאֶה,* *Proud;* (xviii) [155]גּוֹאֵל,* *Redeemer;* (xix) [156]גִּבּוֹר,* *Mighty;* (xx) [157]דָּגוּל, *Distinguished;* (xxi-xxii) [158]הַיּוֹדֵעַ וָעֵד, *The Knower and Witness;* (xxiii) [159]זוֹכֵר, *Rememberer;* (xxiv) [160]חַי, *Living;* (xxv) [161]חָסִיד,* *Pious;* (xxvi) [162]חַנּוּן,* *Gracious;* (xxvii) [163]חוֹקֵר, *Prober;* (xxviii) [164]חֲסִין, *Powerful;* (xxix) [165]חָכָם, *Wise;* (xxx) [166]טוֹב,* *Good;* (xxxi) טְהוֹר [167]עֵינַיִם,* *Of Pure Eyes;* (xxxii) [168]יָשָׁר,* *Upright;* (xxxiii) [169]יֹשֵׁב סֵתֶר, *He Dwells*

editions read either ה׳ or יי or some other abbreviation usually reserved for the Tetragrammaton, its position on the alphabetic lists among the Names that begin with א implies that the abbreviation, in our case, refers to the Name אֲדֹנָי (*VeChur LaZahav*). See also *Shevuos* 35a.

R' Toviyah's list has ה׳ after אֶחָד.

141. *Zechariah* 14:9.

142. *Exodus* 23:17; *Isaiah* 1:24. He is the Lord of the entire earth (*Midrash Zuta*).

143. *Psalms* 93:4; see also *Shevuos* 35a and *Menachos* 53a.

144. *Midrash Zuta* reads: אֶהְיֶה אֲשֶׁר אֶהְיֶה, *I Shall Be as I Shall Be* (*Exodus* 3:14, see *Targum Onkelos* and *Ramban* there), i.e., He is One, Unique; there is nothing outside of Him. See also *Shevuos* 35a.

145. *Job* 9:4; see also *Shevuos* 35a.

146. *Exodus* 34:6; *Jeremiah* 10:10.

147. *Exodus* 34:6; *Numbers* 14:18; see also *Shevuos* 35a.

148. *Isaiah* 44:6; *Job* 19:25; see Name (lix) below.

149. *Deuteronomy* 32:4.

150. *Song of Songs* 1:14; see *Rashi* there.

150a. The literal meaning of אֶשְׁכֹּל הַכֹּפֶר is *cluster of henna;* the Talmud (*Shabbos* 88b) interprets אֶשְׁכֹּל as, מִי שֶׁהַכֹּל שֶׁלוֹ, *the One to Whom everything belongs;* and הַכֹּפֶר as, *the One Who grants atonement.*

151. *Psalms* 72:19.

152. *Amos* 4:13.

153. *Deuteronomy* 10:17; *Psalms* 147:5; see also *Shevuos* 35a.

154. *Exodus* 15:1. This Name does not appear on R' Toviyah's list.

155. *Isaiah* 47:4; *Jeremiah* 50:34.

156. *Deuteronomy* 10:17; *Psalms* 24:8; see also *Shevuos* 35a.

157. *Song of Songs* 5:10.

158. *Jeremiah* 29:23. Although the Baal HaTurim presents the Names on this list in alphabetical order, these two Names appear with the prefixes הַ־ and וָ־ respectively and are alphabetized accordingly. Apparently, this was done to retain the exact wording of the verse in which they appear (*VeChur LaZahav;* see also note 225 below).

159. *Genesis* 9:15; *Leviticus* 26:42.

160. *Numbers* 14:21; *Deuteronomy* 32:40 (see *Ramban* there); *Joshua* 3:10.

161. *Jeremiah* 3:12.

162. *Exodus* 34:6; *Psalms* 111:4; see also *Shevuos* 35a.

163. *Jeremiah* 17:10.

164. *Psalms* 89:9; this Name does not appear on R' Toviyah's list.

165. *Job* 9:4.

166. *Psalms* 145:9; see also *Menachos* 53b.

167. *Midrash Zuta* reads טָהוֹר, yet adduces *Habakkuk* 1:13, which states טְהוֹר עֵינַיִם.

168. *Psalms* 11:7.

169. *Psalms* 91:1, which reads יֹשֵׁב בְּסֵתֶר עֶלְיוֹן, *He*

Concealed; (xxxiv) [170]כָּבוֹד,* *Glory;* (xxxv) [170a]מִסְתַּתֵּר, *He Who Conceals Himself;* (xxxvi) [171]נוֹרָא, *Awesome;* (xxxvii) [172]נִשְׂגָּב,* *Exalted;* (xxxviii) [173]נֶצַח, *Eternal;* (xxxix) [174]נֹצֵר חֶסֶד, *Preserver of Kindness;* (xl-xlii) [174]נֹשֵׂא עָוֹן, *Forgiver of Iniquity;* נֹשֵׂא פֶשַׁע, *Forgiver of Willful Sin;* [174a]נֹשֵׂא חֵטְא, *Forgiver of Error;* (xliii-xliv) [175]נוֹקֵם,* *Avenger;* נוֹטֵר,* *Bearer of a Grudge;* (xlv) סֶלָה, *Everlasting,* [as it is written,] וְיֹשֵׁב קֶדֶם סֶלָה, *He Who is enthroned from days of old, Selah* (*Psalms* 55:20); (xlvi) [176]סַלָּח, *Pardoner;* (xlvii) [177]עֶלְיוֹן, *Supreme;* (xlviii) [178]עֹפֶר,* *Hart;* (il) [179]עִזּוּז,* *Powerful;* (l) [180]פּוֹדֶה, *Redeemer;* (li) [181]צוּר,* *Rock;* (lii) [182]צְבִי, *Gazelle;* (liii) [183]צְבָאוֹת, *Master of Legions;* (liv) [184]קָדוֹשׁ, *Holy;* (lv) [185]קַנָּא, *Zealous;* (lvi) [186]קָרוֹב,* *Close;* (lvii) [187]רַחוּם,* *Compassionate;* (lviii) [188]רָם,* *Lofty;* (lix) [189]רִאשׁוֹן,* *First,* for He did not receive His sovereignty from any other being; (lx) [190]רַב חֶסֶד, *Abundant in Kindness;* (lxi) [191]שׁוֹמֵר,* *Protector;* (lxii) [192]שׁוֹפֵט,* *Judge;* (lxiii) [193]שִׁלְטוֹן, *Sovereign;* (lxiv) [194]שַׂר, *Ruler;* (lxv) [195]שֹׁכֵן עַד, *He Dwells Forever;* (lxvi) [196]תָּמִים,* *Perfect;* (lxvii) [197]תַּקִּיף, *Strong.*

---

dwells in supreme concealment. Accordingly, R' Toviyah's list reads יֹשֵׁב בַּסֵּתֶר, *He Dwells in Concealment.* The vowelization בְּסֵתֶר indicates that the word סֵתֶר is a construct form, connected to the next word עֶלְיוֹן. [Similarly, the cantillation *dechi* under יֹשֵׁב sets it apart from what follows while the *munach* under בְּסֵתֶר connects that word to עֶלְיוֹן.] However, when the phrase ends with בסתר, that word is not in the construct form and therefore is vowelized בַּסֵּתֶר (A.S.).

170. *Psalms* 29:2, 26:8.

170a. *Isaiah* 45:15. R' Toviyah's list adds the Name מֶלֶךְ, *King* (*Psalms* 145:1; see also *Shevuos* 35a), before מִסְתַּתֵּר.

171. *Deuteronomy* 10:17; *Psalms* 68:36; see also *Shevuos* 35a.

172. *Isaiah* 12:4, 33:5.

173. *I Samuel* 15:29. Alternatively: נִצְחִי, *My Strength* (see *Lamentations* 3:18 with *Targum*).

174. Names xxxviii-xli all appear in *Exodus* 34:7, which reads:. . . נֹצֵר חֶסֶד לָאֲלָפִים נֹשֵׂא עָוֹן וָפֶשַׁע וְחַטָּאָה.

174a. Unlike the Baal HaTurim who uses the masculine noun חֵטְא for *sin,* R' Toviyah's list uses the feminine noun חַטָּאָה as it appears in the verse.

175. *Nahum* 1:2.

176. *Psalms* 86:5.

177. *Genesis* 14:18-22; *Numbers* 24:16; *Psalms* 91:1; 92:2. He is supreme in the heavens (*Midrash Zuta*).

178. *Midrash Zuta* reads עֹפֶר הָאַיָּלִים (*Song of Songs* 2:9).

179. *Psalms* 24:8; see also *Shevuos* 35a.

180. *Psalms* 34:23.

181. *Deuteronomy* 32:4,18; *Psalms* 18:32. R' Toviyah's list adds the Name צַדִּיק, *Righteous,* after צוּר.

182. *Song of Songs* 2:9.

183. *Isaiah* 47:4; see also *Shevuos* 35a.

184. *Isaiah* 57:15.

185. *Exodus* 20:5, 34:14.

186. *Psalms* 145:18.

187. *Exodus* 34:6; *Psalms* 111:4; see also *Shevuos* 35a.

188. *Isaiah* 57:15.

189. *Isaiah* 41:4; see Name (xi) above.

190. *Exodus* 34:6; *Numbers* 14:18; see also *Shevuos* 35a.

191. *Isaiah* 21:11-12; *Psalms* 121:4.

192. *Genesis* 18:25; *Psalms* 7:12.

193. *Ecclesiastes* 8:4, see *Rashi* there.

194. *Isaiah* 9:5. On R' Toviyah's list the Name שַׁדַּי, *Shaddai* (*Exodus* 6:3; see also *Shevuos* 35a), appears in place of שַׂר. Interestingly, according to the *Vilna Gaon,* the Name שַׂר refers to the Name שַׁדַּי, in the following manner: The name of the letter ש is שִׁי״ן. That name may be divided into two parts: the initial ש is the *nigleh* (revealed) part, while the remaining י and ן comprise the *nistar* (concealed) part. Similarly with the letters ד/דָלֶ״ת — the *nigleh* is ד and the *nistar* is לֶ״ת; and י/יו״ד — the *nigleh* is י and the *nistar* is ו״ד. Taken together, the *gematria* of the *nistar* of the three letters, י״ן ל״ת ו״ד, is 500, equal to that of שַׂר (*Beur MeiHaGra* to *Isaiah* 9:5).

195. *Isaiah* 57:15.

196. *Deuteronomy* 32:4.

197. *Ecclesiastes* 6:10, see *Midrash Koheles Rabbah.*

וְשִׁבְעִים שֵׁמוֹת לְיִשְׂרָאֵל, וְאֵלּוּ הֵן: אֵשֶׁת נְעוּרִים; אֵילֵי הַצֶּדֶק; אַלּוּפִים; אַחִים; אֲהוּבִים; אֹם; אֵם; אִישִׁים; אֶפְרַיִם; אַדִּירִים; אֲצִילִים; אֱגוֹז; אֲיֻמָּה; אֲגֻדָּה; בָּנִים; בְּנֵי אֵל חָי; בְּכוֹר; בְּהִירִים; בִּתִּי; בָּרָה; בְּעוּלָה; גּוֹי; גָּדוֹל; גַּן נָעוּל; גַּל נָעוּל; גֶּפֶן; הָעֲמֻסִים; וּנְשֻׂאִים; זֶרַע קֹדֶשׁ; חֲכָמִים; טוֹבִים; יְחִידִים; יַקִּירִים; יִשְׂרָאֵל; יְשֻׁרוּן; יַעֲקֹב;

BAAL HATURIM ELUCIDATED

It also corresponds to the seventy names of Israel.[197a] They are the following: (i) [198]אֵשֶׁת נְעוּרִים,* *Bride of [His] Youth;* (ii) [199]אֵילֵי הַצֶּדֶק,* *Elms of Righteousness;* (iii) [200]אַלּוּפִים, *Chiefs;* (iv) [201]אַחִים,* *Brothers;* (v) [202]אֲהוּבִים,* *Beloved;* (vi) [203]אֹם,* *Nation;* (vii) [204]אֵם,* *Mother;* (viii) [205]אִישִׁים,* *Men of Distinction;* (ix) [206]אֶפְרַיִם, *Ephraim;* (x) [207]אַדִּירִים, *Mighty;* (xi) [208]אֲצִילִים, *Dignitaries;* (xii) [209]אֱגוֹז,* *Nut;* (xiii) [210]אֲיֻמָּה, *Awe-inspiring;* (xiv) [211]אֲגֻדָּה,* *Union;* (xv) [212]בָּנִים,* *Sons* [or, *Children*];

197a. *Peirush HaRokeach.*

Once again (as in note 136 above), the lists presented by the Baal HaTurim and R' Toviyah are almost identical; this time each list contains sixty-nine names, with each having one that does not appear on the other, as well as a few minor variations. Accordingly, the lists complement each other, allowing us to produce a complete list of seventy names. And, once again, a third list appears in *Midrash Zuta* with at least thirty names that differ entirely from those included by the Baal HaTurim and R' Toviyah. Finally, we are again given no indication of the criteria used to determine which words or phrases used in Scripture to describe Israel are to be considered "names."

198. *Isaiah* 54:6.

199. *Isaiah* 61:3.

200. See *Psalms* 144:14 with *Rashi.* When the אַלּוּפִים, *chiefs,* of the nation accept the burden of leadership with patient understanding, the people respond reciprocally, helping to shoulder the leaders' burdens. Thus, they all become worthy of the title אַלּוּפִים (*VeChur LaZahav*). See also *Zechariah* 12:5-6.

201. *Psalms* 122:8.

202. *Malachi* 1:2.

203. The noun אֹם does not appear in the *Tanach* in the singular form; however, it does appear one time in the plural הָאֻמִּים (*Psalms* 117:1) where it refers to the nations of the world. Similarly, the related Hebrew feminine noun אֻמָּה, which has the same meaning, appears only in the plural — לְאֻמֹּתָם (*Genesis* 25:16), which speaks of nations descended from Ishmael; and אֻמּוֹת (*Numbers* 25:15), referring to Midian. The Aramaic form, also אֻמָּה, does appear once in the singular (*Daniel* 3:29) and seven times in the plural, אֻמַּיָּא, each referring to the nations in general. The noun לְאֹם, with the same meaning, appears a total of thirty-five times, including both the singular and the plural לְאֻמִּים. *Midrash Zuta's* list cites that form and adduces *Isaiah* 51:4 as its source (*VeChur LaZahav*; see note 204 below).

204. *Song of Songs* 3:11. *Rashi* (see also *Taanis* 26b) explains אִמּוֹ of that verse as כְּנֶסֶת יִשְׂרָאֵל, *the assembly of Israel. Radak* (*Shorashim,* אם) explains it as synonymous with אֻמּוֹ, except that the א is vowelized with a *chirik* in lieu of a *kubutz* in order to accommodate both the parable אִמּוֹ and the lesson אֻמּוֹ (see also *Proverbs* 1:8 with *Rashi;* see also note 203 above).

205. *Proverbs* 8:4; see *Rashi* to *Yoma* 18a, s.v., אישי. R' Toviyah's list has אִישִׁים after אֶפְרַיִם.

206. See *Jeremiah* 31:19 (20) with *Targum;* and *Ezekiel* 37:16 with *Rashi* and *Radak.*

207. *Psalms* 16:3; see also *Menachos* 53a.

The prophet Jeremiah compares Israel's uninterrupted succession of troubles to the incessant waves of the sea, "כִּי גָדוֹל כַּיָּם שִׁבְרֵךְ, *For your brokenness is as vast as the sea*" (*Lamentations* 2:13). And King David states (*Psalms* 93:4): אַדִּירִים מִשְׁבְּרֵי יָם, which can be understood as, *the* אַדִּירִים *are the broken of the sea.* Thus, Israel, broken as the sea, is identified with אַדִּירִים (*VeChur LaZahav*).

208. See *Exodus* 24:11.

209. *Song of Songs* 6:11. Like its shell protects a nut from the mire and dung into which it may fall, so does the Torah protect Israel from the debauchery of the nations among which it is forced to live during its exile (based on *Chagigah* 15b).

210. *Song of Songs* 6:4,10. R' Toviyah's list has אֲיֻמָּה after אֲגֻדָּה.

211. *Amos* 9:6; see *Menachos* 27a.

212. Although *Midrash Zuta* reads בֵּן in the singular, that Midrash adduces *Deuteronomy* 14:1, which states בָּנִים, in the plural.

(xvi) [213]בְּנֵי אֵל חָי, *Sons* [or, *Children*] *of the Living God;* (xvii) [214]בְּכוֹר,* *Firstborn;* (xviii) [215]בְּהִירִים, *Bright;* (xix) [216]בִּתִּי,* *My Daughter;* (xx) [217]בָּרָה, *Pure;* (xxi) [218]בְּעוּלָה, *Married;* (xxii) [219]גּוֹי,* *Nation;* (xxiii) [220]גָּדוֹל, *Great;* (xxiv) [221]גַּן נָעוּל,* *Locked Garden;* (xxv) [222]גַּל נָעוּל, *Locked Gateway;* (xxvi) [223]גֶּפֶן, *Vine;* (xxvii) [224]הָעֲמֻסִים, *Those Borne;* (xxviii) [225]וְנִשָּׂאִים, *And those Carried;* (xxix) [226]זֶרַע קֹדֶשׁ, *Holy Seed;* (xxx) [227]חֲכָמִים,* *Wise;* (xxxi) [228]טוֹבִים, *Good;* (xxxii) [229]יְחִידִים,* *Solitary;* (xxxiii) [230]יַקִּירִים, *Precious;* (xxxiv) [231]יִשְׂרָאֵל,* *Israel;* (xxxv) [232]יְשֻׁרוּן,* *Jeshurun;* (xxxvi) [233]יַעֲקֹב, *Jacob;*

---

213. *Hosea* 2:1.

214. *Exodus* 4:22.

215. This word appears in Scripture only once, in the singular בָּהִיר (*Job* 37:21) in a context that is not related to Israel. R' Toviyah's list reads בְּחִירִים, *chosen ones — Isaiah* 45:4; *Psalms* 105:6.

216. In *Midrash Zuta* and on R' Toviyah's list this reads בַּת, *daughter* (*Jeremiah* 31:21).

217. *Song of Songs* 6:9,10.

218. *Isaiah* 62:4.

219. *Deuteronomy* 4:6-8.

220. *II Chronicles* 1:10; *Deuteronomy* 4:6-8.

221. *Song of Songs* 4:12. In his comments to that verse, *Rashi* explains this phrase and the next as references to the modest behavior of Jewish women and their refraining from illicit relations. According to the *Targum,* גַּן נָעוּל alludes to married women and גַּל נָעוּל to maidens.

222. *Song of Songs* 4:12. R' Toviyah's list reads גֹּרֶן נָעוּל, *locked threshing floor.* That reading is apparently due to a copyist's error — indeed the printed version reads:

גן נעול · גל (גרן?) נעול · גפן · העמוסים · תשומים ·
זרע קדש · חכמים · טובים · יקרים · יחידים ·

223. *Hosea* 10:1; *Psalms* 80:9,15 (see *Rashi*); see also *Chullin* 92a.

224. *Isaiah* 46:3. See note 225.

225. *Isaiah* 46:3. Although the Baal HaTurim presents the names on this list in alphabetical order, the two terms הָעֲמֻסִים וּנְשֻׂאִים appear with the prefixes הָ־ and וּ־ respectively and are presented in the ה־ו part of the list. Apparently, the הָ־ prefix was used to retain the exact wording of the verse in which it appears. However, that same verse refers to Israel as הַנְּשֻׂאִים, not as וּנְשֻׂאִים, yet the Baal HaTurim uses the prefix וּ־ instead of הַ־! Perhaps the comment originally read הָעֲמֻסִים הַנְּשֻׂאִים, but was emended by a copyist who realized that both names were out of the alphabetical order of the list and appeared in the same verse (*VeChur LaZahav;* see also note 158 above).

The verse in *Isaiah* reads in full: שִׁמְעוּ אֵלַי בֵּית יַעֲקֹב וְכָל שְׁאֵרִית בֵּית יִשְׂרָאֵל, *Listen to Me, O House of Jacob, and all the remnant of the House of Israel,* הָעֲמֻסִים מִנִּי בֶטֶן, *who are borne* [*by Me*] *from the belly,* הַנְּשֻׂאִים מִנִּי רָחַם, *who are carried* [*by Me*] *from the womb.* Although most commentaries explain the repetition [borne/carried; belly/womb] as a literary device to strengthen the concept, the Baal HaTurim seems to understand the two phrases as independent of one another. Thus, he lists הָעֲמֻסִים and הַנְּשֻׂאִים as separate names for Israel. Perhaps the Baal HaTurim interprets the verse in accordance with *Malbim,* who explains מִנִּי בֶטֶן as the period during which the embryo develops in its mother's womb [i.e., Israel's formative years before it reached nationhood], while מִנִּי רָחַם refers to the period after the baby's emergence from its mother's womb [i.e., Israel as a nation] (Y.S.).

The printed version of R' Toviyah's list mistakenly reads ונשומים (see note 222 above) in place of ונשואים.

226. *Isaiah* 6:13.

227. In *Midrash Zuta* this reads חָכָם, in the singular — *Deuteronomy* 4:6.

228. *Psalms* 125:4; see *Menachos* 53b.

229. For they stand alone in this world (*Midrash Zuta*). Alternatively: יְחִידִים means *Gathered Together as One* (see *Rashi* to *Psalms* 68:7). R' Toviyah's list has יְחִידִים after יְקָרִים (see note 230).

230. *Jeremiah* 31:19. R' Toviyah's list reads יְקָרִים — *Lamentations* 4:2 — but the meaning is the same.

231. The name יִשְׂרָאֵל alludes to their יִסּוּרִים, *chastisement* (*Midrash Zuta*), i.e., ישראל is understood as יִסַּר אֵל, *God has chastised* (see *Deuteronomy* 8:5; *VeChur LaZahav*). See note 233 below for a different understanding of יִשְׂרָאֵל.

232. *Deuteronomy* 32:15; 33:26. This name alludes to the fact that they recited שִׁירָה, *song,* at the sea (*Midrash Zuta*).

233. The nation is called both יִשְׂרָאֵל and יַעֲקֹב, many times in the same verse — e.g., *Genesis* 49:7; *Numbers* 24:5; *Isaiah* 48:1. Many a nation is named for the progenitor with whom that nation originated. Thus, for example, the nation of מָדַי, *Media,* began with מָדַי, *Madai,* son of Japheth son

יוֹסֵף; יְהוּדִים; יְלָדִים; יְדִידִים; כַּלָּה; כַּנָּה; כֶּרֶם; כֹּהֲנִים; מְשָׁרְתִים; מְלָכִים; מַעְיָן חָתוּם; נַחֲלָה; נְדִיבִים; נָאוָה; נַעַר; נֶטַע; סְגֻלָּה; עֶלְיוֹנִים; עֲנָוִים; עֵדָה; עִבְרִים; עֲבָדִים; עַמִּים; פְּדוּיִם; פְּרָזִים, צֹאן; צַדִּיקִים; קְדוֹשִׁים; קְנוּיִם; רַבִּים; רַכִּים; שִׁבְטֵי יָהּ; תְּמִימִים; עַד כָּאן: וְשִׁבְעִים שֵׁמוֹת לִירוּשָׁלַיִם:

BAAL HATURIM ELUCIDATED

(xxxvii) [234]יוֹסֵף, *Joseph;* (xxxviii) [235]יְהוּדִים,* *Judeans;* (xxxix) [236]יְלָדִים,* *Children;* (xl) [237]יְדִידִים,* *Friends;* (xli) [238]כַּלָּה,* *Bride;* (xlii) [239]כַּנָּה, *Foundation;* (xliii) [240]כֶּרֶם,* *Vineyard;* (xliv) [241]כֹּהֲנִים, *Priests;* (xlv) [242]מְשָׁרְתִים,* *Servants;* (xlvi) [243]מְלָכִים,* *Kings;* (xlvii) [244]מַעְיָן חָתוּם,* *Sealed Fountain;* (xlviii) [245]נַחֲלָה,* *Inheritance;* (il) [246]נְדִיבִים, *Generous;* (l) [247]נָאוָה, *Comely;* (li) [248]נַעַר,* *Youth;* (lii) [249]נֶטַע,* *Planting;* (liii) [250]סְגֻלָּה,* *Beloved Treasure;* (liv) [251]עֶלְיוֹנִים,* *Uppermost;* (lv) [252]עֲנָוִים,* *Humble;* (lvi) [253]עֵדָה,* *Assembly;* (lvii) [254]עִבְרִים,* *Hebrews;* (lviii) [255]עֲבָדִים,* *Servants;* (lix) [256]עַמִּים,* *Nations;* (lx) [257]פְּדוּיִם,

of Noah; the nation of מִצְרַיִם, *Egypt,* descended from מִצְרַיִם, *Mitzraim,* son of Ham son of Noah; and the forebear of אַשּׁוּר, *Assyria,* was אַשּׁוּר, *Asshur,* son of Shem son of Noah. Accordingly, the Jewish nation is named for its Patriarch Jacob and is referred to as both יַעֲקֹב, *Jacob,* and יִשְׂרָאֵל, *Israel.* The Torah explains why Jacob was called by that name (*Genesis* 25:26, see *Rashi* there) and why his name was changed to יִשְׂרָאֵל, *Israel* (*Genesis* 32:28). However, it does not tell us why the nation is called by both names and whether the two names carry different implications. One of the commentaries who distinguishes between the two national names is the *Malbim.* He explains that יַעֲקֹב, the name the Patriarch was given at his birth, is used as a reference to both Jacob and his descendants in relation to the world of nature [in which the hand of God is often overlooked by mortals]; whereas the name יִשְׂרָאֵל, the name given Jacob after his miraculous encounter with an angel, is used to refer to Israel and his offspring in the realm of the miraculous Divine (*Malbim* to *Genesis* 35:10; for additional explanations see *Malbim* to *Isaiah* 9:7 and *Micah* 1:5, and *Or HaChaim* to *Genesis* 47:28).

234. *Ezekiel* 37:16-19; *Psalms* 80:2, see *Rashi* there. R' Toviyah's list has יוסף after יְהוּדִים.

235. *Esther* 3:6; *Nehemiah* 1:2. They are called יְהוּדִים because they offer מוֹדִים, *thanks* [from the root ידה; see *Genesis* 29:35], to the Holy One, Blessed is He (*Midrash Zuta*).

236. *Midrash Zuta* and R' Toviyah's list read יֶלֶד in the singular as in *Jeremiah* 31:19. *Radak* explains that verse as referring to Israel as a favorite child.

237. *Jeremiah* 11:15, 12:7; see also *Menachos* 53b.

238. *Song of Songs* 4:8-12.

239. *Psalms* 80:16 (see *Ibn Ezra*).

240. *Isaiah* 5:7.

241. *Exodus* 19:6.

242. *Isaiah* 61:6.

243. *Genesis* 17:6; *Judges* 5:3 (see *Radak*). *Midrash Zuta* reads מַמְלֶכֶת כֹּהֲנִים, *a kingdom of priests — Exodus* 19:6.

244. *Song of Songs* 4:12.

245. *Deuteronomy* 4:20, 9:26; *Isaiah* 19:25.

246. *Psalms* 113:8; *Song of Songs* 6:12, 7:2.

247. *Song of Songs* 1:5.

248. *Hosea* 11:1.

249. *Isaiah* 17:10-11.

250. *Exodus* 19:5.

251. *Deuteronomy* 26:19, 28:1. *Daniel* 7:25.

252. *Psalms* 37:11.

253. *Exodus* 12:3; *Leviticus* 8:3. *Midrash Zuta* reads עַם in the singular and adduces *II Kings* 9:6. R' Toviyah's list adds the name עַם after עֵדָה, even though the plural form עַמִּים also appears on that list.

254. *Exodus* 2:6. They are called עִבְרִים because they accepted the Torah that was written in עֵבֶר הַיַּרְדֵּן, *the* [*eastern*] *side of the Jordan* (see *Deuteronomy* 31:2,9; *Midrash Zuta;* see *Rashi* to *Genesis* 10:22 and 14:13 for other interpretations of this name). R' Toviyah's list has עִבְרִים after עֲבָדִים.

255. *Leviticus* 25:55.

256. *Genesis* 28:3, 48:4; *Psalms* 47:10, see *Rashi. Midrash Zuta* reads עַם in the singular — *II Kings* 9:6.

257. *Isaiah* 35:10.

Redeemed; (lxi) [258]פְּרָזִים, *Dwellers in Unwalled Cities;* (lxii) [259]צֹאן, *Flock;* (lxiii) [260]צַדִּיקִים,* *Righteous;* (lxiv) [261]קְדוֹשִׁים,* *Holy;* (lxv) [262]קְנוּיִם, *Acquired;* (lxvi) [263]רַבִּים, *Many;* (lxvii) [264]רַכִּים,* *Gentle;* (lxviii) [265]שִׁבְטֵי יָהּ, *Tribes of God;* (lxix) [266]תְּמִימִים,* *Perfect.* Until here.[266a]

It also corresponds to the seventy names of Jerusalem.[267,268]

---

258. *Esther* 9:19. Some editions of the Baal HaTurim read פְּזוּרִים, *Dispersed — Jeremiah* 50:17; *Joel* 4:2. In what appears to be a copyist's error, R' Toviyah's list reads פִּדְיוֹם, *Redemption Money,* in place of פְּרָזִים.

259. See 27:17 below; *Psalms* 79:13; *Ezekiel* 34:2 etc.

260. *Isaiah* 60:21. The name צַדִּיקִים alludes to the צְדָקָה, *charity,* that they perform (*Midrash Zuta*).

261. *Leviticus* 19:2.

262. *Exodus* 15:16, see *Pesachim* 87b; *Psalms* 74:2.

263. *Exodus* 5:5.

264. *Genesis* 33:13. *Midrash Zuta* reads רַךְ in the singular — *Proverbs* 4:3. This name does not appear on R' Toviyah's list. According to R' Wolff Heidenheim (*Machzor LeShavuos, Shacharis,* day one), the term רַכִּים is a copyist's error, the proper reading being רֵעִים, *companions* (see *Song of Songs* 5:1, with *Sforno*).

265. *Psalms* 122:4.

266. *Proverbs* 2:21.

266a. The abbreviation ע״כ that appears at the end of this list in virtually every edition of the Baal HaTurim stands for עַד כָּאן, *until here.* Its inclusion raises many questions: (i) It is an unusual way of ending a list! (ii) If the Baal HaTurim does end the list of names of Israel with ע״כ, why did he not use it at the end of the list of Names of God? (iii) Why did the Baal HaTurim enumerate the Names of God and the names of Israel, but not those of Jerusalem? To answer these questions, it is suggested that the letters ע״כ do not mean "the list ends here." Rather, they serve their usual function of indicating the end of a quotation or an interpolation from another source, i.e., they act as close quote marks. If so, the two lists were not part of the Baal HaTurim's original manuscript; rather, they were added by a later copyist. But from where were they added? They could not have been added from *Midrash Zuta,* for that work enumerates the seventy names of Jerusalem as well as those of God and of Israel. Moreover, there are too many differences for those lists to have come from the same source as those of the Baal HaTurim. However, as pointed out in notes 136 and 197a above, the Baal HaTurim's list is almost identical with that of R' Toviyah. If this analysis is correct, it becomes clear why the Baal HaTurim does not give the seventy names of Jerusalem. R' Toviyah speaks of three things that have seventy names: "The King of kings, the Holy One, Blessed is He; the Torah; and Israel." But he does not mention Jerusalem. Thus, a copyist familiar with R' Toviyah's commentary inserted the Names of God, from וְאֵלּוּ הֵן, *They are the following,* until תַּקִּיף, *Strong,* and the names of Israel from וְאֵלּוּ הֵן, until ע״כ (*VeChur LaZahav*).

267. *Bamidbar Rabbah* 14:12; *Rabbeinu Ephraim* (*MiKesivah Ashkenazis*).

268. *Midrash Zuta* records approximately sixty-five names for Jerusalem. Whereas that list is not presented in alphabetical order, it is sometimes difficult to determine whether a compound phrase from a single verse is to be considered two names or only one. Moreover, that list is presented in two parts: first, a simple listing, without comments or source verses, in which we could not discern any particular order; second, an annotated list comprising about one quarter of the names on the first list, as well as a few that do not appear there, each followed by either a source verse or a comment or both. Another listing appears in *Midrash HaGadol* (*Vayigash*) with about sixty-eight names, at least ten of which differ entirely from *Midrash Zuta's* listing. For purposes of simplicity, the list that follows has been arranged in alphabetical order. It is drawn from the two that appear in *Midrash Zuta,* with additions from *Midrash HaGadol* enclosed in brackets. As a consequence, more than seventy names appear here: (i) אֶבֶן מַעֲמָסָה — *Zechariah* 12:3; (ii) אֶפְרָתָה — *Psalms* 132:6 [in *Midrash Zuta* this name is followed by שְׂדֵי יָעַר (see name lxxi below), which appears in the same verse]; (iii) אֲרִיאֵל — *Isaiah* 29:1; (iv) [אַרְמוֹן — *Jeremiah* 30:18]; (v) אֵשֶׁת נְעוּרִים — *Isaiah* 54:6; (vi) בֵּית תְּפִלָּה — *Isaiah* 56:7; (vii) בָּמוֹת — *Micah* 1:5; (viii) בְּעוּלָה — *Isaiah* 62:4; it is called בְּעוּלָה, *Married,* for [like a married woman whose sustenance comes only from her husband,] Jerusalem has no sustainer other than the Holy One, Blessed is He (*Midrash Zuta*). (ix) בָּשָׁן — *Psalms* 68:16; (x) גִּבְעַת הַלְּבוֹנָה — *Song of Songs* 4:6; (xi) [גֹּלָה וְסוּרָה — *Isaiah* 49:21]; (xii) גֵּיא

מִזִּקְנֵי יִשְׂרָאֵל אֲשֶׁר יָדַעְתָּ כִּי־הֵם זִקְנֵי הָעָם וְשֹׁטְרָיו וְלָקַחְתָּ אֹתָם אֶל־אֹהֶל מוֹעֵד וְהִתְיַצְּבוּ שָׁם עִמָּךְ׃

בעל הטורים

❑ **אֶסְפָה.** תָּגִין עַל הֵ"א דְאֶסְפָה. לוֹמַר לְךָ שֶׁיִּהְיוּ בְקִיאִין וּזְהִירִין בַּחֲמִשָּׁה חֻמְשֵׁי תוֹרָה:

❑ **עִמָּךְ.** בְּגִימַטְרִיָּא יְהוּ דוֹמִין:

awe of the King Who is on high (*Midrash Zuta*); (xxvi) חֶפְצִי בָהּ — *Isaiah* 62:4; it is called by this name for God says, "חֶפְצִי בָהּ, *I desire her* above all the other countries," as it is written (*Psalms* 87:2), *HASHEM loves the gates of Zion* (*Midrash Zuta*); (xxvii) [טַבּוּר הָאָרֶץ — *Ezekiel* 38:12]; (xxviii) יְבוּס — *Judges* 19:10; (xxix) יְדִידוּת — *Jeremiah* 12:7; (xxx) ה׳ קְדוֹשִׁים — [?]; (xxxi) [ה׳ שָׁמָּה — *Ezekiel* 48:35]; (xxxii) יָם — [about Jerusalem] it is written, . . . *all the nations* (נִקְווּ) *will be gathered . . . to Jerusalem* (*Jeremiah* 3:17); and of the sea is written, *Let the waters . . .* (יִקָּווּ) *be gathered . . . into one area* (*Genesis* 1:9); additionally, just as the יָם, *sea,* took in all the waters of Creation, so is Jerusalem destined to take in all of her children (*Midrash Zuta*); (xxxiii) יָפֶה — *Jeremiah* 11:16; (xxxiv) יְפֵה נוֹף — *Psalms* 48:3 (see name xxiii above); (xxxv) יִרְאֶה — *Genesis* 22:14; it is called יִרְאֶה, literally, *He-is-seen,* for God [looks out] from within it, sees the downtrodden of His nation and extends His mercies to them (*Midrash Zuta*); (xxxvi) יְרֵשָׁה — *Psalms* 61:6 (see *Ibn Ezra* there; see also name xvii above); (xxxvii) יְרוּשָׁלַם — Abraham called the place יִרְאֶה (*Genesis* 22:14), Shem son of Noah called it שָׁלֵם (*Genesis* 14:18; see name lxxii below); the Holy One, Blessed is He, said, "If I call it יִרְאֶה as Abraham did, the righteous Shem will complain; but if I call it שָׁלֵם, the righteous Abraham will complain, so I shall call it יְרוּשָׁלַם, to include both names" (*Bereishis Rabbah* 56:10); (xxxviii) יַרְכְּתֵי צָפוֹן — *Isaiah* 14:13, *Psalms* 48:3 (see name xxiii above); it is called יַרְכְּתֵי צָפוֹן, literally, *the northern flanks,* for all the assets of the north (see *Ezra* 6:8) are destined to be brought there (*Midrash Zuta*); (xxxix) כַּלָּה — *Isaiah* 49:18, 62:5; (xl) כְּלִילַת יֹפִי — *Lamentations* 2:15; (xli) כִּסֵּא ה׳ — *Jeremiah* 3:17; it is called כִּסֵּא ה׳, *HASHEM's Throne,* for within it He will sit on the Throne of Justice and punish the enemies of His people (*Midrash Zuta*); (xlii) לְבָנוֹן — *Deuteronomy* 3:25 (see *Berachos* 48b); (xliii) מִגְדַּל עֵדֶר — *Micah* 4:8; (xliv) [מוֹרְאָה — *Zephaniah* 3:1]; (xlv) מוֹרִיָּה — *Genesis* 22:2; (xlvi) מְנוּחָה — *Deuteronomy* 12:9; (xlvii) מְצוּדָה — *II Samuel* 5:7-9; (xlviii) [מִקְדֶּשֶׁת — *Hosea* 2:21-22 (this term is synonymous with מְאֹרֶסֶת)]; (il) מָרוֹם — *Isaiah* 33:5; (l) מְרוֹמִים —

חִזָּיוֹן — *Isaiah* 22:1; (xiii) גִּילָה — *Isaiah* 65:18; (xiv) גַּן ה׳ — *Jeremiah* 22:6 (see *Radak* there); (xv) גִּלְעָד — *Isaiah* 51:3 [in *Midrash Zuta* this name follows עֵדֶן (see name liv below) which appears in the same verse]; (xvi) דַּלְתוֹת הָעַמִּים — *Ezekiel* 26:2; (xvii) דְּרוּשָׁה — *Isaiah* 62:12 [in the printed edition of *Midrash Zuta* this name appears in brackets following the term יְרֵשָׁה (see name xxxvi below) which appears in parentheses — usually an indication that the editor or printer of that edition emended the text of the manuscript — and is followed by עִיר לֹא נֶעֱזָבָה (see name lxi below), which also appears in *Isaiah* 62:12)]; (xviii) הַר גָּבֹהַּ — *Ezekiel* 40:2; (xix) הַר חָמַד — *Psalms* 68:17; (xx) הַר מוֹעֵד — *Isaiah* 14:13; (xxi) הַר מָרוֹם — [this name does not appear in Scripture; the first appearance seems to be in *Machzor Vitry,* in the *zemer* שְׁעֵה שִׂיחַ for *Motzaei Shabbos;* although it seems to be an abbreviated form of הַר מְרוֹם יִשְׂרָאֵל, it is not, for that name also appears on this list (see next entry); perhaps it is based on the term מְרוֹם הָרִים — *II Kings* 19:23 and *Isaiah* 37:24 (*VeChur LaZahav*); or it may be a copyist's error and should read הַר הַמּוֹרִיָּה — *II Chronicles* 3:1 (A.S.)]; (xxii) הַר מְרוֹם יִשְׂרָאֵל — *Ezekiel* 17:23 and 20:40; (xxiii) הַר צִיּוֹן — *Isaiah* 18:7, *Psalms* 48:3 (see also name lxiv below); [in *Midrash Zuta* this name appears together with four other names from the same verse in *Psalms* — יְפֵה נוֹף (name xxxiv below), מְשׂוֹשׂ כָּל הָאָרֶץ (name li below), יַרְכְּתֵי צָפוֹן (name xxxviii below) and קִרְיַת מֶלֶךְ רָב (name lxvi below)] it is called הַר צִיּוֹן, which can be understood as הַר צִיּוּן, *Monument Mountain,* for [God says], "Just as monuments are erected over gravesites to warn passersby not to tread on them, so have I made known to the entire world that this is [My city] and I am its mate" (*Midrash Zuta*); (xxiv) הַר קֹדֶשׁ — *Daniel* 9:20; (xxv) חַדְרָךְ — *Zechariah* 9:1 [although, on a simple level, that verse speaks of Damascus, the Midrash explains that חַדְרָךְ refers to Jerusalem, for Jerusalem is destined to expand on all sides until it reaches the gates of Damascus (*Shir HaShirim Rabbah* to 7:5; see also *Sifrei, Devarim* 1)]; it is called חַדְרָךְ [which may be interpreted חֶרְדְּךָ, *your awe,* as if the ד and ר changed places] because [its inhabitants] are in

from the elders of Israel, whom you know to be the elders of the people and its officers; take them to the Tent of Meeting and have them stand there with you.

BAAL HATURIM ELUCIDATED

❑ אֶסְפָה — GATHER. According to a scribal tradition, there are *tagin*[269] on the ה (= 5) of the word אֶסְפָה. This teaches you that they [the elders chosen by Moses] must be expert [in knowledge] and heedful [in fulfillment of all that is written] in the five Books of the Torah.[269a]

❑ עִמָּךְ — WITH YOU. The *gematria* of this word (130) is equivalent[270] to that of the phrase יְהוּ דוֹמִין, *They shall be similar* [*to you*].[271]

Isaiah 33:16 (see *Targum* there); (li) מְשׂוֹשׂ כָּל הָאָרֶץ — *Psalms* 48:3 (see xxiii above); (lii) נַחֲלָה — *Deuteronomy* 12:9; (liii) [סַף רַעַל — *Zechariah* 12:2]; (liv) עֵדֶן — *Isaiah* 51:3 (see name xv above); it is called עֵדֶן, *delight,* for its children are destined to be brought into it and find delight there (*Midrash Zuta*); (lv) עִיר דָּוִד — *II Samuel* 5:7; and why is it called by the Name of a mortal being? Because it is known before the Holy One, Blessed is He, that it was built by a mortal and would be destroyed by a mortal; but in Time to Come, it shall be called by the Name of the Holy One, Blessed is He, as it is written (*Isaiah* 60:14), . . . *they will call you, "*עִיר ה׳*, City of* HASHEM*, Zion, Holy One of Israel"* (*Midrash Zuta*); (lvi) עִיר הַיּוֹנָה — *Zephaniah* 3:1; (lvii) עִיר הַנֶּגֶב — *Obadiah* 1:20 [?]; (lviii) עִיר הַצֶּדֶק — *Isaiah* 1:26 [in *Midrash Zuta* this name follows קִרְיָה נֶאֱמָנָה (see name lxv below), which is adjacent to it in the verse]; (lix) עִיר ה׳ — *Isaiah* 60:14; (lx) עִיר יִשְׂרָאֵל — [?]; (lxi) עִיר לֹא נֶעֱזָבָה — *Isaiah* 62:12 (see xvii above); (lxii) עִיר שֶׁחֻבְּרָה לָּהּ — *Psalms* 122:3; (lxiii) עֲקָרָה — *Isaiah* 54:1; (lxiv) צִיּוֹן — *II Samuel* 5:7 (see name xxiii above); (lxv) קִרְיָה נֶאֱמָנָה — *Isaiah* 1:26 (see name lviii above); (lxvi) קִרְיַת מֶלֶךְ רָב — *Psalms* 48:3 (see name xxiii above); it is called קִרְיַת מֶלֶךְ רָב, literally, *City of the Great King,* because it is the city of the King, King of kings, the Holy One, Blessed is He (*Midrash Zuta*); (lxvii) רַבָּתִי בַגּוֹיִם — *Lamentations* 1:1 [in *Midrash Zuta* this name appears between רַבָּתִי עָם (name lxviii below) and שָׂרָתִי בַּמְּדִינוֹת (name lxxiv below) which precede and follow it respectively in the verse]; (lxviii) רַבָּתִי עָם — *Lamentations* 1:1 (see name lxvii above); (lxix) רָמָה (*Midrash Zuta*), רָמַת רָחֵל (*Midrash HaGadol*) — *Jeremiah* 31:14; (lxx) [שגל — (?)]; (lxxi) שְׂדֵי יָעַר — *Psalms* 132:6 (see name ii above); (lxxii) שָׁלֵם — *Genesis* 14:18 (see name xxxvii above); (lxxiii) שֵׁם חָדָשׁ אֲשֶׁר פִּי ה׳ יִקֳּבֶנּוּ — *Isaiah* 62:2; (lxxiv) שָׂרָתִי בַּמְּדִינוֹת — *Lamentations* 1:1 (see name lxvii above).

269. See note 126 above.

269a. *Rashi* explains that when God told Moses, *"Gather to me seventy men from the elders of Israel whom you know . . .,"* He was referring to *the foremen of the Children of Israel . . . who were beaten* by the Egyptians (see *Exodus* 5:14). Accordingly, one may think that the only qualification one needs to be an "elder" is the capacity to stand up for the nation, even against a powerful despot like Pharaoh. But they need not be learned in Torah law; for that, it was sufficient that Moses and Aaron knew *halachah.* The Baal HaTurim teaches that this is a mistake. To be a leader in Israel one must be learned in and heedful of the Torah (A.S.).

270. The principle of *im hakollel* allows 130 to be considered equivalent to 131, the *gematria* of the Baal HaTurim's phrase.

271. *Peirush HaRokeach.* The Mishnah states: All are eligible to judge monetary cases; but not all are eligible to judge capital cases — only Kohanim, Levites and Israelites who are eligible to marry their daughters to Kohanim (*Sanhedrin* 32a). The Gemara explains: A Baraisa teaches — Just as the members of a court must be free from any deficiency in righteousness, so must they be free from any genealogical blemish . . . as it is written, *You are entirely beautiful, my friend, without any blemish in you* (*Song of Songs* 4:7). But perhaps that verse refers to a physical blemish? . . . another verse states וְהִתְיַצְּבוּ שָׁם עִמָּךְ, *and have them stand there with you,* and the term עִמָּךְ, *with you,* implies בְּדוֹמִין לָךְ, *similar to you,* i.e., without genealogical blemish. Perhaps that verse refers only to the first Sanhedrin in the wilderness for they were to experience the Divine Presence? . . . another verse states [regarding the judges that Jethro advised Moses to appoint], וְנָשְׂאוּ אִתָּךְ, *they shall bear* [the burden of judging] *with you* (*Exodus* 18:22), and the term

יז וְיָרַדְתִּי וְדִבַּרְתִּי עִמְּךָ שָׁם וְאָצַלְתִּי מִן־הָרוּחַ אֲשֶׁר
עָלֶיךָ וְשַׂמְתִּי עֲלֵיהֶם וְנָשְׂאוּ אִתְּךָ בְּמַשָּׂא הָעָם
יח וְלֹא־תִשָּׂא אַתָּה לְבַדֶּךָ׃ וְאֶל־הָעָם תֹּאמַר
הִתְקַדְּשׁוּ לְמָחָר וַאֲכַלְתֶּם בָּשָׂר כִּי בְּכִיתֶם בְּאָזְנֵי
יהוה לֵאמֹר מִי יַאֲכִלֵנוּ בָּשָׂר כִּי־טוֹב לָנוּ בְּמִצְרָיִם
יט וְנָתַן יהוה לָכֶם בָּשָׂר וַאֲכַלְתֶּם׃ לֹא יוֹם אֶחָד
תֹּאכְלוּן וְלֹא יוֹמָיִם וְלֹא ׀ חֲמִשָּׁה יָמִים וְלֹא
כ עֲשָׂרָה יָמִים וְלֹא עֶשְׂרִים יוֹם׃ עַד ׀ חֹדֶשׁ יָמִים עַד
אֲשֶׁר־יֵצֵא מֵאַפְּכֶם וְהָיָה לָכֶם לְזָרָא יַעַן כִּי־
מְאַסְתֶּם אֶת־יהוה אֲשֶׁר בְּקִרְבְּכֶם וַתִּבְכּוּ לְפָנָיו

בעל הטורים

(יז) **וְאָצַלְתִּי מִן הָרוּחַ אֲשֶׁר עָלֶיךָ וְשַׂמְתִּי עֲלֵיהֶם.** כִּי אֲנִי לֹא אֶבְחָרֵם וְלֹא אֶתֵּן מֵרוּחִי עֲלֵיהֶם, כִּי אֲנִי אָמַרְתִּי כִּי אַתָּה לְבַדְּךָ תִּשָּׂא אוֹתָם. וְאַתָּה אָמַרְתָּ, לֹא אוּכַל לָשֵׂאת מַשָּׂא כָּל הָעָם הַזֶּה. בְּחַר לְךָ מִי שֶׁיִּשָּׂא עִמְּךָ וְתִתֵּן מֵרוּחֲךָ עֲלֵיהֶם. לְכָךְ כְּתִיב "וַיָּאצֶל מִן הָרוּחַ אֲשֶׁר עָלָיו וַיִּתֵּן עַל שִׁבְעִים אִישׁ":

אֲבָל אֶלְדָּד וּמֵידָד, שֶׁלֹּא הָיוּ מִכְּלַל הַשִּׁבְעִים, נֶאֱמַר בָּהֶם "וַתָּנַח עֲלֵיהֶם הָרוּחַ", פֵּרוּשׁ, הָרוּחַ מֵאֵת ה' וְלֹא מִשֶּׁל מֹשֶׁה. וּכְשֶׁאָמַר לוֹ יְהוֹשֻׁעַ "כְּלָאֵם", אָמַר "וּמִי יִתֵּן כָּל עַם ה' נְבִיאִים" כְּאֵלּוּ הַשְּׁנַיִם, "בְּתֵת ה' אֶת רוּחוֹ עֲלֵיהֶם", וְלֹא כְּשִׁבְעִים זְקֵנִים שֶׁאָצַל מֵרוּחִי וְנָתַן עֲלֵיהֶם:

(כ) **לְזָרָא.** בְּאָלֶ"ף. שֶׁמָּצְאוּ בוֹ כָּל מִינֵי טְעָמִים חוּץ מֵאֶחָד, וְהוּא טַעְמוֹ שֶׁל לִוְיָתָן:

לְזָרָא. בְּגִימַטְרִיָּא לָחֳלִי מֵעַיִם:

BAAL HATURIM ELUCIDATED

17. וְאָצַלְתִּי מִן הָרוּחַ אֲשֶׁר עָלֶיךָ וְשַׂמְתִּי עֲלֵיהֶם — AND I WILL RESERVE[271a] SOME OF THE SPIRIT THAT IS UPON YOU AND PLACE IT UPON THEM. [God was telling Moses,] "I will not choose these elders, nor will I place My spirit upon them; for I have said that you alone shall bear [the entire burden of] the people. But you said, 'I cannot carry the burden of this entire nation' (see v. 14 above). [Therefore,] choose for yourself who shall bear along with you and place some of your spirit upon them." Thus it is written, *And He reserved some of the spirit that was upon him* [Moses] *and gave it to the seventy men* (v. 25 below).

However, regarding Eldad and Medad, who were not among these seventy, it is stated, *and the spirit rested upon them* (v. 26), i.e., the spirit of God, not that of Moses. Thus when Joshua told Moses, *"Incarcerate them!"* (v. 28), Moses

---

אִתְּךָ, *with you,* implies "similar to you" (*Sanhedrin* 36b).

The Baal HaTurim finds an allusion to the concept of דּוֹמִין, [*of*] *similar* [*genealogy*], in the term עִמְּךָ, in accordance with the Talmud's wording.

271a. The translation of וְאָצַלְתִּי as *I will reserve* follows *Ramban,* and that is how the Baal HaTurim explains it in *Peirush HaTur HaAroch.*

[17] *I will descend and speak with you there, and I will reserve some of the spirit that is upon you and place it upon them, and they shall bear the burden of the people with you, and you shall not bear alone.*

[18] *"To the people you shall say, 'Prepare yourselves for tomorrow and you shall eat meat, for you have wept in the ears of HASHEM, saying: Who will feed us meat? for it was better for us in Egypt! So HASHEM will give you meat and you will eat.* [19] *Not for one day shall you eat, nor two days, nor five days, nor ten days, nor twenty days.* [20] *Until an entire month of days, until it comes out of your nose, and becomes nauseating to you, because you have rejected HASHEM Who is in your midst, and you have wept before Him,*

responded, *"Would that the entire people of HASHEM could be prophets* like these two, when Hashem would give *of His own spirit upon them!* (v. 29) — not like the seventy elders for whom He reserved some of my spirit and placed it upon them."[272]

20. לְזָרָא — NAUSEATING. This word is spelled with an א (= 1).[273] This is because they could find in the quail (see vv. 31-33 below) any taste [they desired], except for one — the taste of the Leviathan.[274]

❏ The *gematria* of לְזָרָא (238) is equal to that of the phrase לָחֳלִי מֵעַיִם, *for intestinal disorder.*[275]

272. See *Ramban.* This comment explains the verses in the realm of פְּשָׁט, *peshat* [the simple meaning of the verse]. As such, it is one of the few comments in the Baal HaTurim that are not in the realm of רֶמֶז, *remez* [allusion].

273. The root of this word is זור, *to turn away from, to estrange oneself, to distance oneself.* Hence, זָרָא is used to describe something repulsive that causes a person to recoil in disgust. Accordingly, we would expect the spelling זָרָה, as we find סָרָה, *perversion* (e.g., *Deuteronomy* 13:6), from the root סור, *to go astray,* and צָרָה, *trouble* (e.g., *Genesis* 42:21), which some grammarians ascribe to the root צור, *to beleaguer.* The Baal HaTurim finds two allusions in the anomalous spelling.

274. The Talmud describes the לִוְיָתָן, *Leviathan,* as a gigantic fish that was created on the fifth day of Creation and that rules all the creatures of the sea. Originally, God created two — a male and a female — as with all other species. However, God saw that if these two fish were allowed to mate and multiply, they would destroy the entire world by dint of their great strength and numbers, for the Leviathan is so enormous that all the waters flowing from the Jordan River into the sea can scarcely quench its thirst. God, therefore, killed the female and preserved it in brine, to be served to the righteous at the banquet prepared for them in the time to come (*Bava Basra* 74b; see also the Baal HaTurim to *Leviticus* 23:42 with note 134).

We have been unable to find any source, other than the present comment, which states that any taste except that of Leviathan could be found in the quail.

275. *Peirush HaRokeach.* The Midrash explains verse 33 below: *The meat was still between their teeth, not yet chewed, when the wrath of HASHEM flared among the people* — the Sages explained: As soon as the worst among the complainers tasted of the quail, their bowels turned diarrhetic. The better ones among them suffered only once in thirty days. *The wrath of HASHEM flared among the people* — this teaches that from the day they left Egypt, God did not discipline them as harshly as with the [ailments

כא לֵאמֹר לָמָּה זֶּה יָצָאנוּ מִמִּצְרָיִם: וַיֹּאמֶר מֹשֶׁה
שֵׁשׁ־מֵאוֹת אֶלֶף רַגְלִי הָעָם אֲשֶׁר אָנֹכִי בְּקִרְבּוֹ
וְאַתָּה אָמַרְתָּ בָּשָׂר אֶתֵּן לָהֶם וְאָכְלוּ חֹדֶשׁ יָמִים:
כב הֲצֹאן וּבָקָר יִשָּׁחֵט לָהֶם וּמָצָא לָהֶם אִם אֶת־כָּל־
דְּגֵי הַיָּם יֵאָסֵף לָהֶם וּמָצָא לָהֶם:
כג וַיֹּאמֶר יהוה אֶל־מֹשֶׁה הֲיַד יהוה תִּקְצָר עַתָּה
כד תִרְאֶה הֲיִקְרְךָ דְבָרִי אִם־לֹא: וַיֵּצֵא מֹשֶׁה וַיְדַבֵּר
אֶל־הָעָם אֵת דִּבְרֵי יהוה וַיֶּאֱסֹף שִׁבְעִים אִישׁ
כה מִזִּקְנֵי הָעָם וַיַּעֲמֵד אֹתָם סְבִיבֹת הָאֹהֶל: וַיֵּרֶד
יהוה | בֶּעָנָן וַיְדַבֵּר אֵלָיו וַיָּאצֶל מִן־הָרוּחַ אֲשֶׁר
עָלָיו וַיִּתֵּן עַל־שִׁבְעִים אִישׁ הַזְּקֵנִים וַיְהִי כְּנוֹחַ
כו עֲלֵיהֶם הָרוּחַ וַיִּתְנַבְּאוּ וְלֹא יָסָפוּ: וַיִּשָּׁאֲרוּ שְׁנֵי־
אֲנָשִׁים | בַּמַּחֲנֶה שֵׁם הָאֶחָד | אֶלְדָּד וְשֵׁם הַשֵּׁנִי
מֵידָד וַתָּנַח עֲלֵהֶם הָרוּחַ וְהֵמָּה בַּכְּתֻבִים וְלֹא יָצְאוּ
כז הָאֹהֱלָה וַיִּתְנַבְּאוּ בַּמַּחֲנֶה: וַיָּרָץ הַנַּעַר וַיַּגֵּד לְמֹשֶׁה

בעל הטורים

(כב) אם את כל דגי הים יאסף להם. פֵּרוּשׁ יָמִית לָהֶם, לְשׁוֹן "וַיִּגְוַע וַיָּמָת וַיֵּאָסֶף". וְזֶהוּ בַּאֲסִיפָה בְּעָלְמָא סַגִּי לְהוּ:

(כה) כנוח. ב׳ בַּמָּסוֹרֶת – "וַיְהִי כְּנוֹחַ עֲלֵיהֶם הָרוּחַ"; וְאִידָךְ "כְּנוֹחַ כַּפּוֹת רַגְלֵי הַכֹּהֲנִים נֹשְׂאֵי אֲרוֹן ה׳". לוֹמַר לְךָ, שֶׁנָּחָה עֲלֵיהֶם הַשְּׁכִינָה כְּמוֹ עַל הָאָרוֹן:

(כו) ותנח. ב׳ בַּמָּסוֹרֶת – בְּפָרָשַׁת נֹחַ:

BAAL HATURIM ELUCIDATED

22. **אם את כל דגי הים יאסף להם — IF ALL THE FISH OF THE SEA WILL BE GATHERED FOR THEM.** [The word יֵאָסֵף, here translated *will be gathered,*] means *will be killed,* as in the verse, וַיִּגְוַע וַיָּמָת וַיֵּאָסֶף, *he expired and he died, and he was gathered* (*Genesis* 25:17). This is [an allusion to our Sages' statement]: For fish, אֲסִיפָה, *gathering,* is sufficient.[276]

---

brought on by the] *slav* (*Mechilta DeRashbi* 16:13).

Another Midrash explains why they were punished in this manner: *In the morning you will see the Glory of* HASHEM (*Exodus* 16:7) — this verse teaches that God granted the manna to Israel with a shining countenance [i.e., happily and in a beneficial manner]. But the quail, which they requested while their stomachs were still full, was granted with a darkened countenance [i.e., in an angry, harmful manner] (*Mechilta DeRabbi Yishmael* 16:7; but see the Baal HaTurim to *Exodus* 16:13 with note 134).

276. The Talmud discusses whether fish require *shechitah* [ritual slaughter] before they may be eaten. Our verse is adduced: *Can sheep and cattle be slaughtered for them . . . If all the fish will*

saying: Why did we leave Egypt?' "
21 *Moses said, "Six hundred thousand footsoldiers are the*
people in whose midst I am, yet You say I shall give them
meat, and they shall eat for a month of days! 22 *Can sheep*
and cattle be slaughtered for them and suffice for them? If all
the fish of the sea will be gathered for them, would it suffice
for them?"
23 *HASHEM said to Moses, "Is the hand of HASHEM limited?*
Now you will see whether My word comes to pass or not!"
24 *Moses left and spoke the words of HASHEM to the people;*
and he gathered seventy men from among the elders of the
people and had them stand around the Tent.
25 *HASHEM descended in a cloud and spoke to him, and*
He reserved some of the spirit that was upon him and gave it
to the seventy men, the elders; and it was when the spirit
rested upon them, that they prophesied, but did not do so
again.
26 *Two men remained behind in the camp, the name of one*
was Eldad and the name of the second was Medad, and the
spirit rested upon them; they had been among the recorded
ones, but they had not gone out to the Tent, and they
prophesied in the camp. 27 *The youth ran and told Moses,*

BAAL HATURIM ELUCIDATED

25. כְּנוֹחַ — WHEN [IT] RESTED. The masoretic note, ב׳, means that this word appears twice in the *Tanach*: (i) here, וַיְהִי כְּנוֹחַ עֲלֵיהֶם הָרוּחַ, *and it was when the spirit rested upon them;* and (ii) כְּנוֹחַ כַּפּוֹת רַגְלֵי הַכֹּהֲנִים {נֹשְׂאֵי אֲרוֹן ה׳}, *When the soles of the feet of the Kohanim, {the bearers of the Ark of HASHEM,}*[277] *rested* (*Joshua* 3:13). This indicates to you that the Divine Presence rested upon the seventy men just as it rested upon the Ark.[277a]

26. וַתָּנַח — AND [IT] RESTED. The masoretic note, ב׳, means that this word appears twice in the *Tanach*: [(i) here; and (ii) וַתָּנַח הַתֵּבָה, *And the Ark came to rest* (*Genesis* 8:4). We have commented [on the similarity] in *parashas Noach.*

❑ {The Baal HaTurim's comment to הָאֹהֱלָה appears at *Genesis* 24:67.}

---

be gathered for them . . . Now, if fish require *shechitah,* why does the verse change expression from יִשָּׁחֵט, *will be slaughtered,* to יֵאָסֵף, *will be gathered?* Thus, we learn that "gathering is sufficient for fish" (*Chullin* 27b).

The Baal HaTurim's comment indicates that even though *shechitah* is not required for fish, they may not be eaten when they are still living (see *Chullin* 27b; *Shulchan Aruch, Yoreh Deah* 13:1).

277. The fragment of the verse enclosed in braces is omitted in most printed editions. It appears, however, in *Shoham Yakar's* manuscript edition.

277a. *Peirush HaRokeach.*

כח וַיֹּאמַר אֶלְדָּד וּמֵידָד מִתְנַבְּאִים בַּמַּחֲנֶה: וַיַּעַן
יְהוֹשֻׁעַ בִּן־נוּן מְשָׁרֵת מֹשֶׁה מִבְּחֻרָיו וַיֹּאמַר אֲדֹנִי
כט מֹשֶׁה כְּלָאֵם: וַיֹּאמֶר לוֹ מֹשֶׁה הַמְקַנֵּא אַתָּה לִי וּמִי
יִתֵּן כָּל־עַם יהוה נְבִיאִים כִּי־יִתֵּן יהוה אֶת־רוּחוֹ
ל עֲלֵיהֶם: וַיֵּאָסֵף מֹשֶׁה אֶל־הַמַּחֲנֶה הוּא וְזִקְנֵי שביעי
לא יִשְׂרָאֵל: וְרוּחַ נָסַע ׀ מֵאֵת יהוה וַיָּגָז שַׂלְוִים
מִן־הַיָּם וַיִּטֹּשׁ עַל־הַמַּחֲנֶה כְּדֶרֶךְ יוֹם כֹּה וּכְדֶרֶךְ
יוֹם כֹּה סְבִיבוֹת הַמַּחֲנֶה וּכְאַמָּתַיִם עַל־פְּנֵי
לב הָאָרֶץ: וַיָּקָם הָעָם כָּל־הַיּוֹם הַהוּא וְכָל־הַלַּיְלָה

בעל הטורים

(כז) מִתְנַבְּאִים. קְרִי בֵהּ מֵת נְבִיאָם. שֶׁהָיוּ אוֹמְרִים – מֹשֶׁה מֵת, יְהוֹשֻׁעַ מַכְנִיס אֶת יִשְׂרָאֵל לָאָרֶץ. "מִתְנַבְּאִים" נוֹטָרִיקוֹן "מֹשֶׁה תָּנוּחַ נַפְשׁוֹ בְּגַן אֱלֹהִים, יְהוֹשֻׁעַ מַכְנִיס":

(לא) וַיָּגָז. ב׳ בַּמָּסוֹרֶת – "וַיָּגָז שַׂלְוִים"; וְאִידָךְ "וַיָּגָז אֶת רֹאשׁוֹ" בְּאִיּוֹב. וְזֶהוּ שֶׁיֵּשׁ בַּמִּדְרָשׁ, יוֹתֵר מִמַּה שֶּׁהָרַג בָּהֶם הַשְּׂלָו עַל יְדֵי אֲכִילָה, הָרַג בָּהֶם עַל יְדֵי יְרִידָה וּנְפִילָה, שֶׁנָּפַל עַל רֹאשָׁם. כְּשֵׁם שֶׁנֶּאֱמַר בְּאִיּוֹב "וַיָּגָז אֶת רֹאשׁוֹ" וְהָיָה מִתְאַבֵּל עַל בָּנָיו שֶׁנָּפַל עֲלֵיהֶם הַבַּיִת. גַּם בְּכָאן הָיוּ מִתְאַבְּלִים עַל אוֹתָם שֶׁמֵּתוּ מִנְּפִילַת הַשְּׂלָו עַל רֹאשָׁם:

☐ כְּתִיב "שַׂלְוִים" וְקָרִינַן סַלְוִים – שַׂלְוִים לַצַּדִּיקִים; וְסַלְוִים לָרְשָׁעִים, שֶׁהָיוּ לָהֶם כְּקוֹצִים:

BAAL HATURIM ELUCIDATED

27. מִתְנַבְּאִים — ARE PROPHESYING. This term could be explained as if it read, מֵת נְבִיאָם[277b], *Their prophet is dying.* For, in their prophecy, they were saying, "Moses is dying; Joshua will be bringing Israel into the land." [An additional allusion:] The word מִתְנַבְּאִים can be interpreted as an acronym for the phrase מֹשֶׁה תָּנוּחַ נַפְשׁוֹ בְּגַן אֱלֹהִים יְהוֹשֻׁעַ מַכְנִיס, *Moses — his soul will rest in the Garden of God; Joshua will be bringing* [*the people*] *in.*[278]

31. וַיָּגָז — AND CUT.[278a] The masoretic note,[279] ב׳, means that this word appears

277b. With the letters א and י exchanging their positions.

278. See *Sanhedrin* 17a. The text follows the early printed editions. According to *Shoham Yakar's* manuscript edition, מִתְנַבְּאִים is the acronym for, מֹשֶׁה תָּנוּחַ נַפְשׁוֹ בְּגַן־עֵדֶן, אֲבָל יְהוֹשֻׁעַ מַכְנִיס, *Moses — his soul will rest in the Garden of Eden; but Joshua is bringing* [*the people*] *in.* A third version appears in *Peirush HaRosh*: מֹשֶׁה תָּנוּחַ נַפְשׁוֹ בְּעֵדֶן, אָז יְהוֹשֻׁעַ מַכְנִיס, *Moses — his soul will rest in Eden; then Joshua will be bringing in.*

278a. The translation follows *Ibn Ezra* (see second paragraph of note 279).

279. The full masoretic note reads: ב׳ בִּתְרֵי לִישָׁנֵי, *Twice, with two meanings.* According to that note, in the context of the verse from *Job,* the word וַיָּגָז is from the verb root גזז, *to cut, to shear,* as in לָגֹז צֹאנוֹ, *to shear his sheep* (*Genesis* 38:13). In the context of our verse, it is from the verb root גוז, which *Rashi* interprets in two ways: In his comment to our verse, *Rashi* explains וַיָּגָז as וַיַּפְרִיחַ, *and he made fly,* and adduces the phrase כִּי גָז חִישׁ, *for it flies by fleetingly* (*Psalms* 90:10); but, in his comments to *Psalms, Rashi* explains that וַיָּגָז of our verse implies *bringing across,* thus, וַיָּגָז שַׂלְוִים, *it brought the quail across from the sea.* In either case, the two appearances of וַיָּגָז differ in root and meaning.

In contrast to the masoretic note and to

and he said, "Eldad and Medad are prophesying in the camp."

28 *Joshua son of Nun, the servant of Moses since his youth, spoke up and said, "My lord Moses, incarcerate them!"*

29 *Moses said to him, "Are you being zealous for my sake? Would that the entire people of HASHEM could be prophets, if HASHEM would but place of His own spirit upon them!"*

30 *Moses was brought into the camp, he and the elders of*
Israel. 31 *A wind went forth from HASHEM and cut [a bevy of] quails from the [flock at the] sea and spread them over the camp, a day's journey this way and a day's journey that way, all around the camp, and two cubits above the face of*
the earth. 32 *The people rose up all that day and all the night*

BAAL HATURIM ELUCIDATED

twice in the *Tanach*: (i) here, וַיָּגָז שַׂלְוִים, *and cut [a bevy of] quails;* and (ii) וַיָּגָז אֶת רֹאשׁוֹ, *and he sheared his head* (*Job* 1:20). The similarity of expression alludes to that which is written in the Midrash: [A large number of Israelites died as a result of eating the quail,[280]] but even more than the inundation of quail killed by being eaten, it killed by descending and falling, for it fell on their heads.[281] Thus, just as Job *sheared his head* and mourned for his children who were killed when the house fell upon them (see *Job* 1:18-20), so too, here in the wilderness, they were mourning those who died as a result of the quail falling upon their heads.[282]

❑ The word is spelled שלוים, [as if it were pronounced שְׁלְוִים, *serene,*] but is pronounced [שַׂלְוִים, as if it were spelled] סַלְוִים, *briers.*[283] The righteous [ate the quail] with serenity; but [the quail] were as briers to the wicked among the people, for the quail were [injurious] to them like thorns.[284]

❑ {The Baal HaTurim's comment to כְּדֶרֶךְ appears at *Genesis* 19:31.}

Rashi's comment, *Ibn Ezra* understands both appearances as having the same meaning: A flock of quail as numerous as the sands had gathered at the seashore. God then sent a wind to "cut" a large bevy of birds from the flock and carry them to the Israelite camp. Whereas the Baal HaTurim omitted the second half of the masoretic note — בִּתְרֵי לִישָׁנֵי — it is assumed that he translates both appearances in the same way. Hence, the translation follows *Ibn Ezra.*

280. See the Baal HaTurim to verse 20 above, with note 275.

281. *Sifrei;* see also the Baal HaTurim to 35:23 below.

282. *Maharam MiRothenburg.*

283. The Aramaic word סַלְוָא means *briers* (*Rashi* to *Yoma* 75b; see also *Targum* to *Job* 40:26 where וּבְחוֹחַ, *and with a brier,* is rendered וּבְסַלְוָא in Aramaic).

284. *Yoma* 75b; see the Baal HaTurim to v. 20 above, with note 275. In most of his comments, the Baal HaTurim seeks an allusion in Scripture for a teaching of the Sages of the Talmud and Midrash. In the present comment, the allusion itself appears in the Talmud.

וְכֹל | יוֹם הַמָּחֳרָת וַיַּאַסְפוּ אֶת־הַשְּׂלָו הַמַּמְעִיט
אָסַף עֲשָׂרָה חֳמָרִים וַיִּשְׁטְחוּ לָהֶם שָׁטוֹחַ סְבִיבוֹת
לג הַמַּחֲנֶה: הַבָּשָׂר עוֹדֶנּוּ בֵּין שִׁנֵּיהֶם טֶרֶם יִכָּרֵת וְאַף
יהוה חָרָה בָעָם וַיַּךְ יהוה בָּעָם מַכָּה רַבָּה מְאֹד:
לד וַיִּקְרָא אֶת־שֵׁם־הַמָּקוֹם הַהוּא קִבְרוֹת הַתַּאֲוָה
לה כִּי־שָׁם קָבְרוּ אֶת־הָעָם הַמִּתְאַוִּים: מִקִּבְרוֹת
הַתַּאֲוָה נָסְעוּ הָעָם חֲצֵרוֹת וַיִּהְיוּ בַּחֲצֵרוֹת:
יב א וַתְּדַבֵּר מִרְיָם וְאַהֲרֹן בְּמֹשֶׁה עַל־אֹדוֹת
הָאִשָּׁה הַכֻּשִׁית אֲשֶׁר לָקָח כִּי־אִשָּׁה כֻשִׁית
ב לָקָח: וַיֹּאמְרוּ הֲרַק אַךְ־בְּמֹשֶׁה דִּבֶּר יהוה
ג הֲלֹא גַּם־בָּנוּ דִבֵּר וַיִּשְׁמַע יהוה: וְהָאִישׁ מֹשֶׁה

בעל הטורים

(לד) הַמִּתְאַוִּים. ב׳ — ״כִּי שָׁם קָבְרוּ אֶת הָעָם הַמִּתְאַוִּים״; ״הוֹי הַמִּתְאַוִּים אֶת יוֹם ה׳ לָמָּה״? ״כִּי שָׁם קָבְרוּ אֶת הָעָם הַמִּתְאַוִּים״:

יב (א) הַכֻּשִׁית. בְּגִימַטְרִיָּא יְפַת מַרְאֶה:

(ב) וַיִּשְׁמַע ה׳. וּסְמִיךְ לֵהּ ״וְהָאִישׁ מֹשֶׁה״. שֶׁדִּבְּרוּ עָלָיו בֵּינוֹ וּבֵינָם, וְלֹא שָׁמַע אוֹתָם אָדָם אַחֵר:

BAAL HATURIM ELUCIDATED

32. {The Baal HaTurim's comment to הַשְּׂלָו appears at *Exodus* 16:13.}

❑ {The Baal HaTurim's comment to חֳמָרִים appears at *Exodus* 8:10.}

34. הַמִּתְאַוִּים — WHO HAD BEEN CRAVING. [The masoretic note, ב׳, means that] this word appears twice in the *Tanach*: (i) here, כִּי שָׁם קָבְרוּ אֶת הָעָם הַמִּתְאַוִּים, *because there, they buried the people who had been craving;* and (ii) הוֹי הַמִּתְאַוִּים אֶת יוֹם ה׳ לָמָּה, *Woe to those who "crave" the day of* HASHEM. *Why?*[285] (*Amos* 5:18). Because *there they* [*will have*] *buried the people who had been "craving"* [*for that day*].

285. The text follows *Shoham Yakar's* manuscript edition which includes the words אֶת יוֹם ה׳, *the day of* HASHEM. The early printed editions and most later ones omit these words (see last paragraph of this footnote).

When the prophet Isaiah had warned the sinful people about the impending destruction of the land and the exile of the nation, many of them scoffed, "יְמַהֵר יָחִישָׁה מַעֲשֵׂהוּ לְמַעַן נִרְאֶה, *Let Him hurry, let Him hasten His action so that we may see it*" (*Isaiah* 5:19). To those people, the prophet Amos said, "הוֹי הַמִּתְאַוִּים אֶת יוֹם ה׳, לָמָּה זֶה לָכֶם יוֹם ה׳, הוּא חֹשֶׁךְ וְלֹא אוֹר, *Woe to those who 'crave' the day of* HASHEM*! Why should you [desire] this day of* HASHEM*? [For you] it is darkness and not light!*" The Baal HaTurim cites the first part of the verse from *Amos,* including the interrogative לָמָּה, *Why?* Then he proceeds to cite our verse as the answer to the prophet's question.

According to the reading that omits the words אֶת יוֹם ה׳, the Baal HaTurim's comment reads: . . . (ii) הוֹי הַמִּתְאַוִּים, *Woe to those who crave* (*Amos* 5:18). *Why? Because . . .*

and all the next day and gathered up the quail — the one with the least gathered in ten heaps — and they spread them out all around the camp. [33] *The meat was still between their teeth, not yet chewed, when the wrath of HASHEM flared among the people, and HASHEM struck a very mighty blow against the people.* [34] *He named that place Kibroth-hattaavah, because there they buried the people who had been craving.*

[35] *From Kibroth-hattaavah the people journeyed to Hazeroth; and they were in Hazeroth.*

12

[1] *Miriam and Aaron spoke against Moses regarding the Cushite woman he had married, for he had married a Cushite woman.* [2] *They said, "Was it only to Moses that HASHEM spoke? Did He not speak to us, as well?" And HASHEM heard.* [3] *And the man Moses was*

BAAL HATURIM ELUCIDATED

XII

1. הַכֻּשִׁית — THE CUSHITE. The *gematria* of this word (735) is equivalent[286] to that of יְפַת מַרְאֶה, *beautiful of appearance.*[287]

2. וַיִּשְׁמַע ה׳ — AND HASHEM HEARD. Juxtaposed to this phrase is the phrase וְהָאִישׁ מֹשֶׁה, *and the man Moses* (v. 3). This indicates they [Miriam and Aaron] spoke about Moses between him and themselves, but no other person heard them.[288]

286. The principle of *im hakollel* allows 735 to be considered equivalent to 736, the *gematria* of the Baal HaTurim's phrase. Interestingly, *Rashi,* who does not use the principle of *im hakollel* in any of the *gematriaos* that he uses in his commentary, finds this same allusion in the word כֻּשִׁית, later in the verse. Although that word is spelled defectively, without a ו, for the purpose of his allusion, *Rashi* spells it in full, כּוּשִׁית, with a ו, so that its *gematria* is 736, and that is how this *gematria* is presented in *Midrash Tanchuma, Tzav* 13.

287. *Peirush HaRokeach; R' Ephraim.* The Midrash teaches that "Cushite" cannot be understood in its literal sense, because Moses' wife Zipporah was originally a Midianite (see *Exodus* 2:16-21). Rather, the term Cushite implies just as no one can deny the swarthiness of a Cushite [usually understood as Ethiopian], so was it impossible for anybody to deny Zipporah's beauty. And lest one think that Zipporah was beautiful in her appearance but not in her manner, or beautiful in her manner but not in her appearance, the Torah repeats the term כֻּשִׁית to teach us that she was beautiful in both manner and appearance (*Sifrei; Tanchuma, Tzav* 13, cited by *Rashi* here).

288. *Peirush HaRokeach.* The *Sifrei* records a difference of opinion regarding the interpretation of the phrase, וַיִּשְׁמַע ה׳, *And HASHEM heard,* in our verse: [Since God hears everything, why is this phrase necessary?] One view explains that the phrase וַיִּשְׁמַע ה׳, *and HASHEM heard,* implies that no other creature was present other than Miriam and Aaron when they spoke about Moses. A second view objects: They spoke in the presence of Moses, for it is stated, וַיִּשְׁמַע ה׳, *And HASHEM heard,* וְהָאִישׁ מֹשֶׁה, *and the man Moses* [implying that Moses also heard]. However, since Moses was exceedingly humble, he suppressed the matter, as if he had not heard anything. [If so, why are the two phrases *and HASHEM heard* and *and the man Moses* in different verses? To show that they reacted differently:] Moses ignored the incident [but God acted to protect Moses' honor] (bracketed passages are from *Peirush Sifrei DeVei Rav*).

עָנָו מְאֹד מִכֹּל הָאָדָם אֲשֶׁר עַל־פְּנֵי
ד הָאֲדָמָה: וַיֹּאמֶר יהוה פִּתְאֹם אֶל־
מֹשֶׁה וְאֶל־אַהֲרֹן וְאֶל־מִרְיָם צְאוּ שְׁלָשְׁתְּכֶם
ה אֶל־אֹהֶל מוֹעֵד וַיֵּצְאוּ שְׁלָשְׁתָּם: וַיֵּרֶד יהוה
בְּעַמּוּד עָנָן וַיַּעֲמֹד פֶּתַח הָאֹהֶל וַיִּקְרָא אַהֲרֹן
ו וּמִרְיָם וַיֵּצְאוּ שְׁנֵיהֶם: וַיֹּאמֶר שִׁמְעוּ־נָא דְבָרָי
אִם־יִהְיֶה נְבִיאֲכֶם יהוה בַּמַּרְאָה אֵלָיו אֶתְוַדָּע

בעל הטורים

(ג) **עָנָו.** "עָנָו" כְּתִיב. שֶׁהָיָה ענ"ו יָמִים בָּהָר – "וַיְכַסֵּהוּ הֶעָנָן שֵׁשֶׁת יָמִים", וְאַחַר כָּךְ שָׁלֹשׁ פְּעָמִים אַרְבָּעִים:

❑ **עָנָו.** בְּגִימַטְרִיָּא בְּעֵדֶן. שֶׁנּוֹחֵל גַּן עֵדֶן:

(ו) **בַּמַּרְאָה.** ב׳ בַּמָּסוֹרֶת – "בַּמַּרְאָה אֵלָיו אֶתְוַדָּע"; "בַּמַּרְאָה נֶהֶפְכוּ צִירַי עָלַי". לוֹמַר שֶׁאֲפִלּוּ בַּמַּרְאָה שֶׁאֲנִי נִרְאֶה לַנְּבִיאִים נֶהְפָּךְ צִירָם עֲלֵיהֶם. אֲבָל מֹשֶׁה יוֹשֵׁב כְּתַלְמִיד לִפְנֵי רַבּוֹ:

BAAL HATURIM ELUCIDATED

3. עָנָו — HUMBLE. This term is spelled defectively,[289] ענו (= 126), without a י. Thus, it alludes to the 126 days that Moses was on Mount Sinai. [For he spent six days in preparation, as the verse states,] וַיְכַסֵּהוּ הֶעָנָן שֵׁשֶׁת יָמִים, *And the cloud covered it for a six-day period* (*Exodus* 24:16),[290] and following that were

289. A masoretic note reads: ענו כתיב עניו קרי, *The word is spelled* ענו, *but is pronounced* עָנָיו. [Similar masoretic notes appear on the words שְׂלָו (*Exodus* 16:13) and סְתָו (*Song of Songs* 2:11).] The plural forms עֲנָוִים and עַנְוֵי, *humble people,* appear twenty times in the *Tanach,* but the singular form appears only once — in our verse, with regard to Moses. Now, we may have expected the singular to be spelled עָנָיו — as we find עָבָיו (*Psalms* 18:13), עָדָיו (*Isaiah* 45:24), עָלָיו (*Numbers* 11:25), עָרָיו (*Deuteronomy* 2:34), אֲבֹתָיו (*Numbers* 11:12), סִירֹתָיו (*Exodus* 27:3). Although the ending ־יו of those words is a suffix, while the ו of עָנָיו is part of the basic word, nevertheless, the similarity of sound would dictate a similarity of spelling. The Baal HaTurim explains why the י is omitted (*VeChur LaZahav*).

290. That verse reads in its entirety: וַיִּשְׁכֹּן כְּבוֹד ה׳ עַל הַר סִינַי, *The glory of* HASHEM *rested upon Mount Sinai,* וַיְכַסֵּהוּ הֶעָנָן, *and the cloud covered him* [or, *it*], שֵׁשֶׁת יָמִים, *for a six-day period.* וַיִּקְרָא אֶל מֹשֶׁה בַּיּוֹם הַשְּׁבִיעִי, *And He called to Moses on the seventh day,* מִתּוֹךְ הֶעָנָן, *from the midst of the cloud.* The Talmud (*Yoma* 4b) records a dispute regarding the interpretation of this verse.

According to one view, it means: *The glory of* HASHEM *rested upon Mount Sinai* on Rosh Chodesh Sivan, *and the cloud covered it* [*Mount Sinai*] *for a six-day period. He called to Moses* and spoke the Ten Commandments, *on the seventh day* of Sivan . . . Thus, the object of וַיְכַסֵּהוּ הֶעָנָן, *and the cloud covered it,* is the mountain; the six days of the verse are the first six days of the month of Sivan; on each of those days Moses ascended the mountain and then descended; on the seventh of Sivan Moses ascended and remained upon the mountain for forty days. Consequently, there was no overlap between the six-day period and the forty-day period.

According to the opposing view, the verse means: *The glory of* HASHEM *rested upon Mount Sinai* on the seventh of Sivan, *and the cloud covered him* [*Moses*] *for a six-day period,* from the seventh to the thirteenth of Sivan. *He called to Moses* to emerge from his sequestration *on the seventh day* of that sequestration. Thus, the object of וַיְכַסֵּהוּ הֶעָנָן, *and the cloud covered him,* is Moses; the six days of the verse are the first six days of the forty days that Moses remained on Mount Sinai.

At first glance, the Baal HaTurim's comment seems to follow the first opinion; the six-day period preceded the three forty-day periods.

exceedingly humble, more than any person on the face of the earth!

[4] HASHEM said suddenly to Moses, to Aaron, and to Miriam, "You three, go out to the Tent of Meeting." And the three of them went out. [5] HASHEM descended in a pillar of cloud and stood at the entrance to the Tent, and He summoned Aaron and Miriam; the two of them went out. [6] He said, "Hear now My words. If there shall be prophets among you, in a vision shall I, HASHEM, make Myself known to him;

BAAL HATURIM ELUCIDATED

three forty-day periods.[291]

❑ עָנָו — HUMBLE. The *gematria* of this word (126) is equal to that of בְּעֵדֶן, *in Eden.* This indicates that he[292] is granted a heritage in *Gan Eden.*

6. בַּמַּרְאָה — IN A VISION. The masoretic note, ב׳, means that this word appears twice in the *Tanach*: (i) here, בַּמַּרְאָה אֵלָיו אֶתְוַדָּע, *In a vision shall I make Myself known to him;* and (ii) בַּמַּרְאָה נֶהֶפְכוּ צִירַי עָלַי, *During the vision, my joints shuddered upon me* (*Daniel* 10:16). The similarity of expression implies that [God said], "Even in that [lesser form of] vision by which I appear to the [other] prophets, [the experience overcomes them and] their joints shudder upon them. Moses, by contrast, sits [erect] like a student before his teacher[292a] [even as he receives a greater form of revelation]."[293]

Therefore, he states, וְאַחַר כָּךְ, *and following that* [six-day period] שָׁלֹשׁ פְּעָמִים אַרְבָּעִים, *three forty-day periods* (*VeChur LaZahav*). But, see note 291 for an alternative understanding of the allusion.

291. *Peirush HaRokeach,* presumably the Baal HaTurim's source for this comment, reads: The word עָנָו is spelled without a י to indicate that after the Ten Commandments [were given] there were 126 days, three periods of forty days each *and the cloud covered it* [or, *him*] *for a six-day period.* If so, the number 126 refers to a total of one hundred and twenty days, six of which have a special significance and are therefore counted both as an independent period and as part of a forty-day period. Indeed, we find a similar methodology — an allusion in which two overlapping numbers are added together to yield a total that is greater than the whole — in the Baal HaTurim's comment to *Genesis* 15:8, where the number 122 represents a period of seventy years, as well as the first fifty-two years of that period. Similarly, in *Rashi's* commentary to 7:18-19 above, s.v., מִזְרָק אֶחָד כֶּסֶף, in which the number 520 represents a 500-year period, as well as the last 20 years of that period, for they had a purpose of their own. Similarly, here, the number 126 may represent a 120-day period, as well as the first six days of that period, for they had an added significance (*VeChur LaZahav*).

292. It is not clear whether this refers to Moses in particular, as the Midrash teaches: When God told Moses: *"Behold! Your days are drawing near to die"* (*Deuteronomy* 31:14), He added that Moses would occupy an important position in *Gan Eden.* Moses then made a final plea to be allowed into the Land of Israel, "Master of the Universe, if You do not bring me into *Eretz Yisrael,* then let me remain alive and not die in this world." God replied, "If you will not die in this world, you will not have life in the World to Come" (*Midrash Petiras Moshe Rabbeinu,* cited in *Otzar HaMidrashim*). Lest one think that Moses would be excluded from the afterlife of *Gan Eden,* as he had requested, the Torah spells עָנָו without a י so that its *gematria* should allude to that place.

Or, it may refer to every humble person, as the Talmud (*Sanhedrin* 88b) states: Who is destined for a share in the World to Come? עַנְוְתָן, *One who is humble . . .* (*VeChur LaZahav*).

292a. See *Rambam, Hilchos Yesodei HaTorah* 7:2,6.

293. *Shoham Yakar* cites two Talmud passages

ז בַּחֲלוֹם אֲדַבֶּר־בּוֹ׃ לֹא־כֵן עַבְדִּי מֹשֶׁה בְּכָל־בֵּיתִי
ח נֶאֱמָן הוּא׃ פֶּה אֶל־פֶּה אֲדַבֶּר־בּוֹ וּמַרְאֶה וְלֹא
בְחִידֹת וּתְמֻנַת יהוה יַבִּיט וּמַדּוּעַ לֹא יְרֵאתֶם
ט לְדַבֵּר בְּעַבְדִּי בְמֹשֶׁה׃ וַיִּחַר־אַף יהוה בָּם וַיֵּלַךְ׃
י וְהֶעָנָן סָר מֵעַל הָאֹהֶל וְהִנֵּה מִרְיָם מְצֹרַעַת כַּשָּׁלֶג
יא וַיִּפֶן אַהֲרֹן אֶל־מִרְיָם וְהִנֵּה מְצֹרָעַת׃ וַיֹּאמֶר אַהֲרֹן
אֶל־מֹשֶׁה בִּי אֲדֹנִי אַל־נָא תָשֵׁת עָלֵינוּ חַטָּאת
יב אֲשֶׁר נוֹאַלְנוּ וַאֲשֶׁר חָטָאנוּ׃ אַל־נָא תְהִי כַּמֵּת
אֲשֶׁר בְּצֵאתוֹ מֵרֶחֶם אִמּוֹ וַיֵּאָכֵל חֲצִי בְשָׂרוֹ׃
יג וַיִּצְעַק מֹשֶׁה אֶל־יהוה לֵאמֹר אֵל נָא רְפָא נָא לָהּ׃

בעל הטורים

(ח) וּמַרְאֶה. תָּגִין עַל הֵ״א. לוֹמַר שֶׁמַּבִּיט בַּחֲמִשָּׁה ״נֹגַהּ״ שֶׁנֶּאֱמַר בִּיחֶזְקֵאל, וּבַחֲמִשָּׁה ״אוֹר״ שֶׁנֶּאֱמַר בִּבְרֵאשִׁית׃

(י) וְהֶעָנָן סָר. שֶׁלֹּא יִרְאֶה בְּמַפַּלְתָּהּ. וְזֶהוּ שֶׁאָמְרוּ חֲכָמֵינוּ ז״ל, אַל תִּשְׁתַּדֵּל לִרְאוֹתוֹ בִּשְׁעַת קִלְקָלָתוֹ׃

(יג) רְפָא. ב׳ בַּמָּסוֹרֶת — ״רְפָא נָא לָהּ״; ״רְפָה שְׁבָרֶיהָ כִי מָטָה״. שֶׁמֹּשֶׁה הִתְפַּלֵּל לָאֵל

BAAL HATURIM ELUCIDATED

8. וּמַרְאֶה — [IN] A CLEAR VISION. According to a scribal tradition, there are *tagin*[293a] on the ה (= 5). This implies that Moses saw through[294] the five "brilliances"[295] mentioned in *Ezekiel,* and the five "lights"[296] mentioned in *Genesis.*[297]

that refer to the relationship between Moses and God as that of a student before his Teacher. In the first, the Talmud bisects a verse and explains: The first part of that verse was spoken by the student [Moses], the rest of the verse contains the words of the Teacher [God] . . . Praiseworthy is the student whose Teacher accedes to him (*Berachos* 32a). The second passage records an exchange of words: An established student of Rebbi [Yehudah HaNasi] asked a newcomer to Rebbi's academy why he had come there. The newcomer replied, "I have come to learn Torah from Rebbi." The student continued questioning, "And are you fit to learn Torah from my teacher?" The newcomer responded, "Was Moses fit to learn Torah from the Omnipotent?" The student countered, "But are you Moses?" To which the newcomer replied, "And is your teacher God?" (*Yevamos* 105b).

293a. See note 126 above.

294. The text follows *Shoham Yakar's* manuscript edition. The early printed editions read שֶׁמָּצִינוּ, *that we find,* in place of שֶׁמַּבִּיט, *that he sees.* Some later printed editions follow *Ittur Bikkurim's* emendation, שֶׁמֵּצִיץ, *that he peers* (see *Song of Songs* 2:9).

295. The word נֹגַהּ, *brilliance* or *glow,* appears five times in the vision of the Heavenly Throne (*Ezekiel* 1:4, 13, 27, 28 and 10:4).

296. The word אוֹר, *light,* appears five times in the narrative of the first day of Creation (twice in *Genesis* 1:3, twice in 1:4, and once in 1:5; see the Baal HaTurim's comment at 1:5 there, s.v., ה׳ פעמים אור).

297. The Talmud states: All the [other] prophets saw through an unclear glass; our teacher Moses saw through a clear glass (*Yevamos* 49b). The "glass" is either a mirror or a lens (see *Tosefos Yom Tov* to *Keilim* 30:2); see also *Rambam, Hilchos Yesodei HaTorah* 7:3,6).

The Midrash records two opinions. According to the first, the other prophets saw through nine

in a dream shall I speak with him. 7 *Not so is My servant*
Moses; in My entire house he is the trusted one. 8 *Mouth to*
mouth do I speak to him, in a clear vision and not in riddles,
at the image of HASHEM does he gaze. Why did you not fear
to speak against My servant Moses?"
9 *The wrath of HASHEM flared up against them, and He left.*
10 *The cloud had departed from atop the Tent, and behold!*
Miriam was afflicted with tzaraas, like snow! Aaron turned
to Miriam and behold! she was afflicted with tzaraas.
11 *Aaron said to Moses, "I beg you, my lord, do not cast a*
sin upon us, for we have been foolish and we have sinned.
12 *Let her not be like a corpse, like one who leaves his*
mother's womb with half his flesh having been consumed!"
13 *Moses cried out to HASHEM, saying, "Please, God, heal*
her now."

BAAL HATURIM ELUCIDATED

10. וְהֶעָנָן סָר — THE CLOUD HAD DEPARTED. So that [the Divine Presence manifest in the cloud] would not witness Miriam's disgrace [directly].[298] This reflects our Sages' teaching: Do not endeavor to see your fellow at the time of his degradation.[299]

13. רְפָא — HEAL. The masoretic note, ב׳, means that this word appears twice in the *Tanach*:[300] (i) here, רְפָא נָא לָהּ, *heal her now;* and (ii) רְפָה שְׁבָרֶיהָ כִי מָטָה, *heal its damages, for it totters* (*Psalms* 60:4). For Moses prayed to God that He

---

glasses, while Moses saw through one. According to the second opinion, the others saw through a dirty glass, while Moses saw through a clean glass (*Vayikra Rabbah* 1:14). It is possible that the Baal HaTurim understands the first opinion in the Midrash to mean that there are a total of ten lenses through which a prophet must look in order to see his prophecy clearly. All the other prophets were able to see through as many as nine of those lenses. But Moses saw through another one, i.e., all ten. And five of those ten lenses are represented by the word נֹגַהּ, the other five by the word אוֹר (*VeChur LaZahav*).

298. *Sifrei* — This can be explained through a parable: A king was disturbed by his son's negative attitude toward his studies. When all else failed to effect change, the king authorized his son's tutor to administer corporal punishment at his own discretion. "But," added the king, "do not lift a hand against him in my presence," for such are the mercies of a father to his son.

At first glance, it would seem that the king's mercies were such that, as a father, he could not bear to see his son punished. Therefore, he ordered the tutor to wait until he left before administering any punishment. But that cannot be the meaning of the Midrash, for the king of the parable represents God, Who sees everything, even when His "back" is turned. Accordingly, the Baal HaTurim explains, a father's mercies are such that he does not want his son to be embarrassed by the fact that his father must bear witness to his degradation. Thus, he instructed the tutor not to shame his son in his presence. Similarly, God, Whose Presence rested in the cloud, turned away, so to speak, by having the cloud depart, before the angel assigned to afflict Miriam with *tzaraas* could carry out his charge (*VeChur LaZahav*).

299. *Avos* 4:18.

300. The full note reads: ב׳ חַד כְּתִיב ה׳, *Twice, one time spelled with a* ה. That is, although the verb root רפא, *to heal,* is spelled with an א, in one instance, the imperative form רְפָא is spelled רְפָה with a ה in lieu of an א. Had that word been of the root רפה, *to become weak,* the vowelization would have been רְפֵה [as in רְאֵה, from the root ראה (27:12 below), and קְנֵה, from the root קנה

יב/יד־טז מפטיר יד וַיֹּאמֶר יְהוָה אֶל־מֹשֶׁה וְאָבִיהָ יָרֹק יָרַק בְּפָנֶיהָ
הֲלֹא תִכָּלֵם שִׁבְעַת יָמִים תִּסָּגֵר שִׁבְעַת יָמִים
טו מִחוּץ לַמַּחֲנֶה וְאַחַר תֵּאָסֵף: וַתִּסָּגֵר מִרְיָם מִחוּץ
לַמַּחֲנֶה שִׁבְעַת יָמִים וְהָעָם לֹא נָסַע עַד הֵאָסֵף
טז מִרְיָם: וְאַחַר נָסְעוּ הָעָם מֵחֲצֵרוֹת וַיַּחֲנוּ בְּמִדְבַּר
פָּארָן: פפפ

קל״ו פסוקים. מהללא״ל סימן.

בעל הטורים

שֶׁיִּרְפָּא ״שִׁבְרֶיהָ כִּי מָטָה״, שֶׁאִם לֹא כֵן אֵין מִי שֶׁיְּטַהֲרֶנָּה:

❑ **רְפָא.** תָּגִין עַל הָרֵי״שׁ. אָמַר, הֵסַרְתָּ עֲטֶרֶת רֹאשָׁהּ ״רְפָה שִׁבְרֶיהָ כִּי מָטָה״:

(טו) וְהָעָם לֹא נָסַע. בְּפָסוּק ״וַתֵּתַצַּב אֲחֹתוֹ״ יֵשׁ שֶׁבַע תֵּבוֹת. לְכָךְ הִמְתִּינָה לָהּ שְׁכִינָה שִׁבְעָה יָמִים:

BAAL HATURIM ELUCIDATED

heal Miriam's damages, [i.e., her *tzaraas,*] *for she totters.* Because if not, there would be no one to rule her ritually pure.[301]

(*Genesis* 49:19)], *not* רְפָה. The Baal HaTurim's comment does not address the anomalous spelling.

301. *Sifrei* (cited by *Rashi* to v. 12, s.v., אֲשֶׁר בְּצֵאתוֹ) — Aaron said, *"Let her not be like a corpse"* (v. 12) . . . Aaron meant, "Because of me, my sister will be lost, for I am unable to quarantine her or to pronounce her impure or to pronounce her pure." From this we may infer that Aaron taught that a Kohen may not determine the *tzaraas* status of his relative.

In *Peirush HaTur HaAroch,* the Baal HaTurim asks: On the contrary, if there is no Kohen who is not her relative, then there is no Kohen who may pronounce her impure. And if you will say that, in such a case, she becomes a *metzoraas* without a pronouncement from a Kohen, then she should be able to become pure again without a pronouncement from a Kohen. Perhaps you will say that, in the absence of a Kohen, we may be stringent and pronounce her impure, but we may not be lenient and pronounce her pure. If so, of what benefit was Moses' prayer? Even after she would be cured of her physical manifestation, she would still remain a *metzoraas,* until a Kohen would pronounce her pure! The Baal HaTurim answers: In truth, it is possible that the Midrash does not refer to a true halachic *metzora.* Even if Miriam could not be officially classified as a *metzora,* her physical affliction would cause people to regard her as one and to avoid any social contact with her for the rest of her life, because no Kohen would have pronounced her cured.

The Talmud states: When Miriam contracted *tzaraas,* who confined her? If you would say, "Moses confined her," I would reply, "Moses was not a Kohen, and a non-Kohen does not pronounce a skin affliction to be *tzaraas.*" And if you would say, "Aaron confined her," I would reply, "Aaron was a relative, and a relative does not pronounce *tzaraas.*" Rather, the Holy One, Blessed is He, Himself accorded great honor to Miriam at that time. He said, "I am a Kohen. I am confining her; I am confirming her, and I will release her (*Zevachim* 101b-102a).

12/14-16

[14] *HASHEM said to Moses, "Were her father to spit in her face, would she not be humiliated for seven days? Let her be quarantined outside the camp for seven days, and then she may be brought in."* [15] *So Miriam was quarantined outside the camp for seven days, and the people did not journey until Miriam was brought in.* [16] *Then the people journeyed from Hazeroth, and they encamped in the Wilderness of Paran.*

BAAL HATURIM ELUCIDATED

❑ **רְפָא — HEAL.** [According to a scribal tradition,] there are *tagin*[302] on the ר. [This intimates that] Moses said, "הֵסַרְתָּ עֲטֶרֶת רֹאשָׁהּ, *You have removed the crown of her head;*[303] רְפָה שְׁבָרֶיהָ כִּי מָטָה, *heal her damages, for she totters."*[304]

15. וְהָעָם לֹא נָסַע — AND THE PEOPLE DID NOT JOURNEY. There are seven words in the verse, וַתֵּתַצַּב אֲחֹתוֹ, *His sister stationed herself. . .* (*Exodus* 2:4).[305] Therefore the Divine presence waited seven days for her.[306]

302. See first paragraph of note 42 to *parashas Nasso* above. *Sefer Tagin* disagrees with *Peri Eitz Chaim* regarding the absence of *tagin* on the letter ר (see illustration), for it enumerates one hundred fifty words in the Torah in which the letter ר is written with two *tagin* [including רְפָא of our verse] and ends that list with the statement, "The others have [only] one *tag.*" (Cf. the Baal HaTurim to *Deuteronomy* 3:24.)

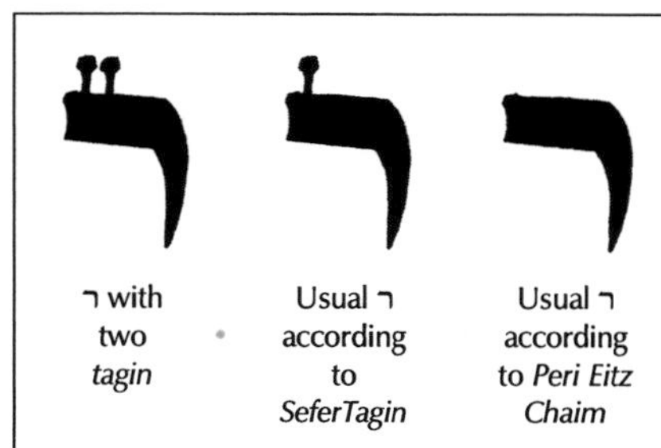

303. The Baal HaTurim borrows this phrase from *Job*: וַיָּסַר עֲטֶרֶת רֹאשִׁי, *He removed the crown of my head* (*Job* 19:9).

Perhaps the statement, "You have removed the crown of her head," is an allusion to the fact that the purification rites of a *metzora* call for a Kohen to shave all of the *metzora's* visible hair, on the first and seventh day of his purification (see *Leviticus* 14:8,9). Alternatively: the phrase עֲטֶרֶת רֹאשָׁהּ, *the crown of her head,* can also be understood as the crown of her letter רֵי״שׁ, i.e., the *tagin* or crownlets on the ר of רְפָא (*VeChur LaZahav*).

304. It has been suggested that the allusion of *tagin* is on the ר, rather than another letter of the word רְפָא, because each of the first five words that the Baal HaTurim attributes to Moses — הֵסַרְתָּ עֲטֶרֶת רֹאשָׁהּ רְפָה שְׁבָרֶיהָ — has that letter in its spelling (*Shoham Yakar*).

305. That verse speaks of Miriam waiting to see the fate of Moses. It reads in full: וַתֵּתַצַּב אֲחֹתוֹ מֵרָחֹק לְדֵעָה מַה יֵּעָשֶׂה לוֹ, *His sister stationed herself at a distance, to know what would be done to him,* a total of seven Hebrew words.

306. See *Sotah* 9b, cited by *Rashi*.

The connection between the number of words in a verse and the number of days is unclear. Nevertheless, the Baal HaTurim uses this same logic at 27:16 below, regarding the number of words in Moses' request that his successor be appointed in his lifetime and the number of years that his successor Joshua would lead Israel.

פרשת שלח

Parashas Shelach

א־ב וַיְדַבֵּר יהוה אֶל־מֹשֶׁה לֵּאמֹר: שְׁלַח־לְךָ אֲנָשִׁים
וְיָתֻרוּ אֶת־אֶרֶץ כְּנַעַן אֲשֶׁר־אֲנִי נֹתֵן לִבְנֵי יִשְׂרָאֵל
אִישׁ אֶחָד אִישׁ אֶחָד לְמַטֵּה אֲבֹתָיו תִּשְׁלָחוּ
ג כֹּל נָשִׂיא בָהֶם: וַיִּשְׁלַח אֹתָם מֹשֶׁה מִמִּדְבַּר

בעל הטורים

יג (ב) **שְׁלַח לְךָ.** סָמַךְ מְרַגְּלִים לְמִרְיָם, בִּשְׁבִיל לָשׁוֹן הָרָע שֶׁסִּפְּרוּ:

❑ **שְׁלַח לְךָ אֲנָשִׁים.** סוֹפֵי תֵבוֹת חָכָם, שֶׁיִּהְיוּ אֲנָשִׁים חֲכָמִים וְצַדִּיקִים:

❑ **שְׁלַח לְךָ.** רֶמֶז לְמִנְיַן שלי״ח שָׁנִים יִשְׁתַּלְּחוּ וְיֵצְאוּ בְגָלוּת. שֶׁבְּג׳ אֲלָפִים וְשלי״ח שָׁנִים חָרַב הַבַּיִת. וְכֵן ״שַׁלַּח מֵעַל פָּנַי וְיֵצֵאוּ״:

(ג) **וַיִּשְׁלַח אֹתָם מֹשֶׁה.** סוֹפֵי תֵבוֹת חַמָּה. שֶׁאָמַר לָהֶם, הַכְנִיסוּ חַמָּה לָעִיר. שֶׁלְּעוֹלָם יִכָּנֵס אָדָם בְּכִי טוֹב וְיֵצֵא בְּכִי טוֹב:

BAAL HATURIM ELUCIDATED

XIII

2. **שְׁלַח לְךָ** — **SEND FORTH FOR YOURSELF.** The Torah juxtaposed the narrative of the spies (Chs. 13-14) with the narrative of Miriam (Ch. 12)[1] because of the *lashon hara*[2] that each of them spoke.[3]

❑ **שְׁלַח לְךָ אֲנָשִׁים** — **SEND FORTH FOR YOURSELF MEN.** The final letters of these three

1. Just before the incident of Miriam, the Torah states: *From Kibroth-hattaavah the people journeyed to Hazeroth; and they were in Hazeroth* (11:35). The story of Miriam ends: *Then the people journeyed from Hazeroth, and they encamped in the Wilderness of Paran* (12:16). And it was from the Wilderness of Paran that Moses sent the spies (see v. 3). Thus, it is clear that the sending of the spies occurred shortly after the incident of Miriam. If so, why does the Baal HaTurim find the need to explain the juxtaposition of the two narratives? Chapter 16 below describes the dispute and rebellion of Korah, but does not state when or where that uprising took place. In fact, *Rashi* presents two views: In his commentary below (16:4), he states that Korah's dispute was "the fourth foulness the Israelites had committed": The first was the incident of the golden calf; the second, that of the מִתְאוֹנְנִים (11:1-3 above); the third, the spies; and the fourth, Korah. According to this view, the incidents of Miriam, the spies and Korah are recorded in chronological order. However, in his comments to *Deuteronomy* 1:1 (s.v., וַחֲצֵרֹת), *Rashi* states that the dispute of Korah took place in Hazeroth. Following this view, the Torah should have juxtaposed the incident of Korah with that of Miriam, for both took place in Hazeroth. Accordingly, in their comments to our verse, *Rashi* and the Baal HaTurim explain why the incidents of the spies and of Korah are not recorded in the sequence in which they occurred (*Mizrachi; Sefer Zikaron*).

2. The literal meaning of לָשׁוֹן הָרָע, *lashon hara,* is evil speech. It includes not merely slander and falsehood, but also any derogatory or unfavorable speech, regardless of whether it is true or false.

3. *Tanchuma* 5 — Why did the Torah follow the story of Miriam with the episode of the spies? Whereas God was aware that the spies would choose to speak *lashon hara* about the Land of Canaan, He said, "I will not give them the opportunity to claim that they were unaware of the consequences of evil speech." Therefore, God juxtaposed the incident of the spies with the incident of Miriam, so that everyone would know that *lashon hara* does not go unpunished. If anyone wishes to speak *lashon hara,* let them look at what happened to Miriam. Despite this, the spies refused to learn from her punishment. [See *Sefer Chafetz Chaim, Asei* 1 and *Lav* 3; *Shemiras HaLashon, Shaar HaTevunah* 12.]

13/1-3

[1] HASHEM spoke to Moses, saying, [2] "Send forth for yourself men, and let them spy out the Land of Canaan that I give to the Children of Israel; one man each from his father's tribe shall you send, every one a tribunal leader among them." [3] Moses sent them forth from the Wilderness

BAAL HATURIM ELUCIDATED

words spell the term חָכָם, *wise man.*[4] For they should be distinguished,[4a] wise[5] and righteous.[6]

❑ שְׁלַח לְךָ — SEND FORTH FOR YOURSELF. The [*gematria* of the] word שְׁלַח [338] is an allusion to the year the nation would be sent out and would go into exile. For the [First] Temple was destroyed[6a] in the year 3,338 [after Creation].[7] This allusion is also reflected in the verse: שַׁלַּח מֵעַל פָּנַי וְיֵצֵאוּ, *Send [them] away from My Presence*[7a] *and let them go!*[7b] (*Jeremiah* 15:1).[8]

3. וַיִּשְׁלַח אֹתָם מֹשֶׁה — **MOSES SENT THEM FORTH.** The final letters of these three words spell חַמָּה, *sun.* This indicates that Moses told the spies, "Escort the sun into the city."[9] For a person should always enter [a city] with [that which the Torah describes as] כִּי טוֹב,[10] and depart with כִּי טוֹב.[11]

4. The word לְךָ, *for yourself,* seems superfluous. *Rashi* explains, in the realm of *peshat* [the simple meaning of the verse], that God told Moses, "I do not command you to send spies; I leave it to your discretion. If you wish to send them, send them לְךָ, *for yourself.*" The Baal HaTurim explains that, in the realm of *remez* [allusion], the word לְךָ is included to describe the criteria for choosing the spies.

4a. See *Rashi* to v. 3, s.v., כֻּלָּם אֲנָשִׁים.

5. *Peirush HaRokeach.*

6. The Baal HaTurim states three criteria: אֲנָשִׁים, *distinguished men,* חֲכָמִים, *wise men,* and צַדִּיקִים, *righteous* men. Now אֲנָשִׁים is explicit in the verse; חֲכָמִים is alluded to in the final letters of שְׁלַח לְךָ אֲנָשִׁים. But where does the verse allude to צַדִּיקִים? It does not. However, if they are not righteous, their wisdom would be to no avail (*Atros Addar*). As the Mishnah (*Avos* 3:9) states: If one sets his fear of sin before his wisdom, his wisdom will remain [with him]. But if one sets his wisdom before his fear of sin, his wisdom will not remain [with him] (Y.S.).

6a. The destruction of the *Beis HaMikdash* took place on the ninth of Av, the anniversary of the night that the nation cried after they accepted the spies' slanderous reports about the Land of Israel (see *Taanis* 29a, cited by *Rashi* to *Lamentations* 1:2; see also the Baal HaTurim to 14:3 below).

7. See *Avodah Zarah* 9a with *Rashi,* s.v., כי מעיינת. Israel left Egypt and received the Torah in the year 2448 after Creation. King Solomon erected the First *Beis HaMikdash* 480 years later (*I Kings* 6:1) and that Temple was destroyed 410 years after it was built (*Yoma* 9a), in the year [2448 + 480 + 410 =] 3338 after Creation.

7a. According to the allusion, that verse means, שַׁלַּח, *in the year [3]338,* מֵעַל פָּנַי, *[they will be removed] from My Presence.*

7b. This verse appears in a series of prophecies regarding the destruction of Jerusalem and the First *Beis HaMikdash* (*Jeremiah* Chs. 14-29).

8. *Peirush HaRokeach.*

9. That is, enter a city when the sun is still shining. When you arrive at a city that is not your final destination, determine first whether you can reach the next city before nightfall. If you cannot, then wait until daybreak before continuing on your journey.

10. In the narrative of Creation, the Torah states, וַיַּרְא אֱלֹהִים אֶת הָאוֹר, *God saw the light,* כִּי טוֹב, *that it was good* (*Genesis* 1:4). Thus, Moses told the spies, "Enter each city with כִּי טוֹב, i.e., during daylight; and leave each city with כִּי טוֹב, i.e., do not travel at night."

Although the Torah states, וַיַּרְא אֱלֹהִים כִּי טוֹב, *God saw that it was good,* five times (1:10, 12, 18, 22, 25), in only one place (1:4) does the verse specify what was "good."

11. *Peirush HaRokeach,* based on *Taanis* 10b,

פָּארָן עַל־פִּי יהוָה כֻּלָּם אֲנָשִׁים רָאשֵׁי בְנֵי־יִשְׂרָאֵל
ד הֵמָּה: וְאֵלֶּה שְׁמוֹתָם לְמַטֵּה רְאוּבֵן שַׁמּוּעַ בֶּן־
ה־ו זַכּוּר: לְמַטֵּה שִׁמְעוֹן שָׁפָט בֶּן־חוֹרִי: לְמַטֵּה יְהוּדָה
ז כָּלֵב בֶּן־יְפֻנֶּה: לְמַטֵּה יִשָּׂשכָר יִגְאָל בֶּן־יוֹסֵף:
ח־ט לְמַטֵּה אֶפְרָיִם הוֹשֵׁעַ בִּן־נוּן: לְמַטֵּה בִנְיָמִן פַּלְטִי
י־יא בֶּן־רָפוּא: לְמַטֵּה זְבוּלֻן גַּדִּיאֵל בֶּן־סוֹדִי: לְמַטֵּה
יב יוֹסֵף לְמַטֵּה מְנַשֶּׁה גַּדִּי בֶּן־סוּסִי: לְמַטֵּה דָן עַמִּיאֵל
יג־יד בֶּן־גְּמַלִּי: לְמַטֵּה אָשֵׁר סְתוּר בֶּן־מִיכָאֵל: לְמַטֵּה
טו נַפְתָּלִי נַחְבִּי בֶּן־וָפְסִי: לְמַטֵּה גָד גְּאוּאֵל בֶּן־
טז מָכִי: אֵלֶּה שְׁמוֹת הָאֲנָשִׁים אֲשֶׁר־שָׁלַח מֹשֶׁה

בעל הטורים

❑ **רָאשֵׁי בְנֵי יִשְׂרָאֵל הֵמָּה.** ״הֵמָּה״ עוֹלֶה חֲמִשִּׁים. מְלַמֵּד שֶׁהָיוּ שָׂרֵי חֲמִשִּׁים:

(י) סוֹדִי. ב׳ בַּמָּסוֹרֶת – ״גַּדִּיאֵל בֶּן סוֹדִי״; ״תְּעֲבוּנִי כָּל מְתֵי סוֹדִי״. הַמְרַגְּלִים שֶׁהָיוּ „מְתֵי סוֹדִי״, שֶׁשְּׁלָחוּ אוֹתָם לָתוּר הָאָרֶץ וּלְגַלּוֹת עַל סוֹדוֹתֶיהָ, ״תִּעֲבוּנִי״, שֶׁהוֹצִיאוּ דִבָּה וְגָרְמוּ שֶׁנִּקְבַּע לִי בְּכִיָּה לְדוֹרוֹת:

(טז) אֵלֶּה שְׁמוֹת הָאֲנָשִׁים. בְּגִימַטְרִיָּא שְׁמוֹתֵיהֶם מְכוֹעָרִים:

BAAL HATURIM ELUCIDATED

❑ **רָאשֵׁי בְּנֵי יִשְׂרָאֵל הֵמָּה** — HEADS OF THE CHILDREN OF ISRAEL WERE THEY. The *gematria* of הֵמָּה is 50.[12] This teaches that the spies were [chosen from among the] leaders of fifty.[13]

---

where the Talmud derives this lesson from the narrative of Joseph sending his brothers back to their father in Canaan: הַבֹּקֶר אוֹר, [literally,] *In the morning, it was light,* וְהָאֲנָשִׁים שֻׁלְּחוּ, *and the men were sent off* (*Genesis* 44:3). Joseph did not allow them to leave until the sun lit up the sky. See also the Baal HaTurim to *Genesis* 37:14, s.v., לֵךְ נָא רְאֵה, and 42:33.

12. Thus, the phrase רָאשֵׁי בְנֵי יִשְׂרָאֵל הֵמָּה may be interpreted: רָאשֵׁי, *heads of,* בְּנֵי יִשְׂרָאֵל הֵמָּה, *fifty Israelites* (*VeChur LaZahav*).

13. At first glance, this seems to refer to the third rank of leaders that Jethro advised Moses to appoint as judges: . . . *leaders of thousands; leaders of hundreds; leaders of fifties; and leaders of tens* (*Exodus* 18:21-25). If that is correct, however, it is difficult to understand why Moses did not seek emissaries from the top-rank leaders. Moreover, our passage describes them as *heads of the Children of Israel* and every one *a tribal leader among them,* titles which identify them as members of the highest echelon of officials. Let us turn to another passage in which Scripture likewise speaks of leaders of fifty. In a dire prophecy regarding the siege and capture of Jerusalem, the prophet Isaiah describes how God will remove all the leaders, heroes, warriors, judges, prophets and teachers from Jerusalem, replacing them with youngsters and scorners. Among those to be driven from the city is the שַׂר חֲמִשִּׁים, *leader of fifty* (*Isaiah* 3:3). But the Talmud does not take that term at face value; rather, it states, אַל תִּקְרֵי חֲמִשִּׁים אֶלָּא חֻמָּשִׁים, *Do not read* [i.e., interpret the word as it is actually vowelized] חֲמִשִּׁים, *fifty, rather* [interpret it as if it were vowelized] חֻמָּשִׁים, *the Five Books of the Torah.* That is, the prophet refers to the sages of Jerusalem who were masters of the Five Books of the Torah (*Chagigah* 14a). It is that verse and the Talmud's interpretation of it to which the Baal HaTurim refers. For as the Baal HaTurim states in his comments to verse 2, the spies were to be men learned in Torah (*Shoham Yakar*).

of Paran at HASHEM*'s command; they were all distinguished men; heads of the Children of Israel were they.*

[4] *These are their names: For the tribe of Reuben, Shammua son of Zaccur.* [5] *For the tribe of Simeon, Shaphat son*
of Hori. [6] *For the tribe of Judah, Caleb son of Jephunneh.*
[7] *For the tribe of Issachar, Yigal son of Joseph.* [8] *For the*
tribe of Ephraim, Hoshea son of Nun. [9] *For the tribe of*
Benjamin, Palti son of Raphu. [10] *For the tribe of Zebulun,*
Gaddiel son of Sodi. [11] *For the tribe of Joseph for the tribe of*
Manasseh, Gaddi son of Susi. [12] *For the tribe of Dan,*
Ammiel son of Gemalli. [13] *For the tribe of Asher, Sethur son*
of Michael. [14] *For the tribe of Naphtali, Nahbi son of Vophsi.*
[15] *For the tribe of Gad, Geuel son of Machi.*
[16] *These are the names of the men whom Moses sent to*

BAAL HATURIM ELUCIDATED

4. {The Baal HaTurim's comment to שְׁמוֹתָם appears at *Exodus* 28:12.}

10. סוֹדִי — SODI. The masoretic note,[14] ב׳, means that this word appears twice in the *Tanach:* (i) here, גַּדִּיאֵל בֶּן סוֹדִי, *Gaddiel son of Sodi;* and (ii) תִּעֲבוּנִי כָּל מְתֵי סוֹדִי, *They displayed disgust with me, all the men privy to my secret* (*Job* 19:19). [The similarity of expression indicates that the verse in *Job* also refers to the spies.[15] As if Israel were saying,] "The spies, who were *the men privy to my counsel,* who were sent to reconnoiter the land and reveal its secrets, *they displayed disgust with me,* for they spoke unfavorably about the land and caused the establishment of a day of weeping for me for all generations."[16]

16. אֵלֶּה שְׁמוֹת הָאֲנָשִׁים — THESE ARE THE NAMES OF THE MEN. The *gematria* of this phrase (1188) is equivalent[17] to that of שְׁמוֹתֵיהֶם מְכוֹעָרִים[18], *Their names are ugly.*[19]

14. This note is not found in the standard editions at either our verse or the verse from *Job.* It does appear, however, in the Codex Hilleli, where it reads: ב׳ בִּתְרֵי לִישָׁנֵי, *Two, with two different meanings;* i.e., once as a man's name, סוֹדִי, *Sodi;* and once as the common noun סוֹד, *secret,* with the possessive suffix ־ִי, *my,* thus, סוֹדִי, *my secret.*

15. Although סוֹדִי was not a spy, but merely the father of one of the spies, his name can be understood as representing all the spies, for the Talmud (*Sanhedrin* 109b) interprets the Patriarch Jacob's blessing to his sons Simeon and Levi — בְּסֹדָם אַל תָּבֹא נַפְשִׁי, *Into their secret conspiracy, do not enter, O my soul!* (*Genesis* 49:6) — as a prophetic reference to the spies. He was asking that his name יַעֲקֹב not appear in the incident of the spies. Thus, the word סוֹד or the name סוֹדִי represents all of the spies (*VeChur LaZahav*).

16. The Talmud relates that the spies returned with their slanderous report on the eighth of Av. *The people wept that night* (14:1, below) and God said, "You wept needlessly, as a consequence, I will establish a weeping for all generations" (*Taanis* 29a).

17. The principle of *im hakollel* allows 1187, the *gematria* of the Baal HaTurim's phrase, to be considered equivalent to 1188.

18. In *Peirush R' Ephraim,* a parallel comment reads, וּשְׁמוֹתָן מְכוֹעָרִים, which means the same as the Baal HaTurim's phrase, but has a *gematria* of 1188, equal to that of the Scriptural phrase.

19. The Talmud and Midrashim often speak of a person's name in relation to that person's deeds. The following three passages speak of the spies' names:

There are four classifications of [people with

לָתוּר אֶת־הָאָרֶץ וַיִּקְרָא מֹשֶׁה לְהוֹשֵׁעַ בִּן־נוּן
יז יְהוֹשֻׁעַ: וַיִּשְׁלַח אֹתָם מֹשֶׁה לָתוּר אֶת־אֶרֶץ כְּנָעַן
וַיֹּאמֶר אֲלֵהֶם עֲלוּ זֶה בַּנֶּגֶב וַעֲלִיתֶם אֶת־הָהָר:
יח וּרְאִיתֶם אֶת־הָאָרֶץ מַה־הִוא וְאֶת־הָעָם הַיֹּשֵׁב
יט עָלֶיהָ הֶחָזָק הוּא הֲרָפֶה הַמְעַט הוּא אִם־רָב: וּמָה
הָאָרֶץ אֲשֶׁר־הוּא יֹשֵׁב בָּהּ הֲטוֹבָה הִוא אִם־רָעָה
וּמָה הֶעָרִים אֲשֶׁר־הוּא יוֹשֵׁב בָּהֵנָּה הַבְּמַחֲנִים אִם
כ בְּמִבְצָרִים: וּמָה הָאָרֶץ הַשְּׁמֵנָה הִוא אִם־רָזָה

בעל הטורים

(יז) אֶת הָהָר. בְּגִימַטְרִיָּא תּוֹרָה, שֶׁתַּעֲמֹד לָהֶם זְכוּת הַתּוֹרָה:

(כ) הַשְּׁמֵנָה. ב׳ בַּמָּסוֹרֶת – "הַשְּׁמֵנָה הִוא אִם רָזָה"; "וְאֶת הַשְּׁמֵנָה וְאֶת הַחֲזָקָה אַשְׁמִיד", בִּיחֶזְקֵאל בְּפָרָשַׁת "הִנְנִי אֶל הָרֹעִים". אִלּוּ לֹא הוֹצִיאוּ דִבָּה, הָיוּ זוֹכִים לְכָל מַה שֶּׁאָמוּר בָּעִנְיָן, "בְּמִרְעֶה טּוֹב אֶרְעֶה אֹתָם . . . וּמִרְעֶה שָׁמֵן תִּרְעֶינָה אֶל הָרֵי יִשְׂרָאֵל". וְעַכְשָׁו שֶׁהוֹצִיאוּ דִבָּה, גָּרְמוּ לְמַה שֶּׁנֶּאֱמַר "וּבְנֵיכֶם יִהְיוּ רֹעִים בַּמִּדְבָּר אַרְבָּעִים שָׁנָה וְגוֹ׳ ":

BAAL HATURIM ELUCIDATED

17. אֶת הָהָר — THE MOUNTAIN. The *gematria* of this phrase (611) is equal to that of תּוֹרָה, *Torah.* [Moses was praying] that the merit of the[ir] Torah [study][20] would stand the spies in good stead.[21]

---

regard to their] names: (i) There are some people whose names are beautiful and whose deeds are beautiful; (ii) some whose names are ugly and whose deeds are ugly; (iii) some whose names are ugly, but whose deeds are beautiful; and (iv) some whose names are beautiful but whose deeds are ugly . . . An example of those whose names and deeds are both ugly is the spies; for the name סְתוּר (v. 13) implies that he was wont to deny [God's deeds (see below)], and the name גַּדִּי (v. 11) implies that they were abrasive and rebellious . . . (*Bereishis Rabbah* 71:3; *Bamidbar Rabbah* 16:10).

Rabbi Yitzchak said: This matter is a tradition that has been transmitted to us by our fathers — the names of the spies were in accordance with their deeds. However, we have retained only one: סְתוּר בֶּן מִיכָאֵל (v. 13) implies that סָתַר, *he denies* [God's ability to conquer Canaan], by describing אֵל, *God,* as מָךְ, *a weakling.* Rabbi Yochanan said: We also have something to say on this topic — נַחְבִּי בֶּן וָפְסִי (v. 14) implies that הֶחְבִּיא, *he concealed,* the matters of the Holy One, Blessed is He, וּפִסֵּעַ, *and stepped on* the attributes of the Holy One, Blessed is He (*Sotah* 34b).

See *Tanchuma, Haazinu* 7, which expounds on the names of nine of the ten spies who returned with a negative report and the names of their fathers, excluding [for unknown reasons] only גְּאוּאֵל בֶּן מָכִי (v. 15), the spy whose name appears last. Perhaps the author of this Midrash relied on the similarity between גְּאוּאֵל and יִגְאָל (v. 7), and that between מָכִי and מִיכָאֵל (v. 13), so that he did not feel the necessity to expound on the twelfth spy's name (*VeChur LaZahav*).

20. See the Baal HaTurim's commentary to verse 3 above, with note 13. The word אֵת refers to the letters of the *alef-beis,* from א through ת, with which the Torah is written; הָהָר, *the mountain,* refers to the elevated status attained by one who studies Torah (see *Avos* 6:2). Thus, the phrase אֶת הָהָר is an apt allusion to the merit of Torah study (*Rimzei Rabbeinu Yoel*).

21. That is, their knowledge of — and faithfulness to — the Torah would give them the proper perspective regarding the Land of Canaan. As the Talmud (*Arachin* 15b) states: What preventive

spy out the land. Moses called Hoshea son of Nun "Joshua."

17 *Moses sent them to spy out the Land of Canaan, and he said to them, "Ascend here in the south and climb the mountain.*
18 *See the land — how is it? and the people that dwells in it — is it strong or weak? is it few or numerous?*
19 *And how is the land in which it dwells — is it good or is it bad? And how are the cities in which it dwells — are they open or are they fortified?*
20 *And how is the land — is it fat or is it lean?*

BAAL HATURIM ELUCIDATED

20. הַשְּׁמֵנָה — IS IT FAT? The masoretic note, ב׳, means that this word appears twice in the *Tanach:* (i) here, הַשְּׁמֵנָה הִוא אִם רָזָה, *Is it fat or is it lean?* and (ii) וְאֶת הַשְּׁמֵנָה וְאֶת הַחֲזָקָה אַשְׁמִיד, *But the fat one and the strong one I will destroy* (*Ezekiel* 34:16), which is contained in Ezekiel's prophecy (Ch. 34) [referred to as] הִנְנִי אֶל הָרֹעִים, *Behold, I am against the shepherds* (34:10).[22] Had the spies not spoken slanderously [about the land], they would have merited all the blessings mentioned in Ezekiel's prophecy, בְּמִרְעֶה טּוֹב אֶרְעֶה אֹתָם . . . וּמִרְעֶה שָׁמֵן תִּרְעֶינָה אֶל הָרֵי יִשְׂרָאֵל, *Upon a good pasture will I graze them . . . and fat pasture will they graze at the mountains of Israel* (34:14). But now that they have spoken slanderously, they have evoked [the curse], וּבְנֵיכֶם יִהְיוּ רֹעִים בַּמִּדְבָּר אַרְבָּעִים שָׁנָה, *Your children will graze in the wilderness for forty years . . .* (14:33 below).

❑ {The Baal HaTurim's comment to הֲיֵשׁ בָּהּ עֵץ אִם אַיִן appears at *Exodus* 17:7.}

measure should one take to control him from speaking *lashon hara* (evil speech)? If he is learned, he should engage in Torah study (see also *Sefer Shemiras HaLashon, Shaar HaTorah,* Ch. 1).

22. *Peirush HaRokeach.*

The commonly used system of chapter numbers does not carry any halachic or exegetic authority. With the exception of *Psalms* and *Lamentations,* that division is not of masoretic origin, nor does it stem from any other Jewish source; rather, it originated with gentile Bible scholars. Chapter divisions were first introduced into *Tanach* by Yaakov ibn Adoniyahu in the 1524 Venice edition, for practical reasons (see his introduction, reprinted in *Mikraos Gedolos,* Warsaw, 1894).

According to masoretic tradition, the text of Scripture is divided into פָּרָשִׁיּוֹת, *parashiyos* (paragraph-like passages), separated from one another by a blank space, and that is how *Tanach* scrolls are written. These spaces appear in one of two forms: פְּתוּחָה, *open,* indicated by ending the previous passage in the middle of a line and then beginning the new passage at the beginning of the next line, or סְתוּמָה, *closed,* indicated by the new passage beginning on the same line on which the previous passage ended, but after a space in which at least nine letters could be written (see illustration at 1:19 above, note 22). [In some printed editions these spaces are indicated by the letters פ and ס.]

Ezekiel's prophecy against the self-serving shepherds — a metaphor for the corrupt kings — comprises four *parashiyos* [(i) 34:1-9, alternatively, 34:1-8; (ii) v. 10, alternatively, vv. 9-10; (iii) vv. 11-19; (iv) vv. 20-31]. Accordingly, it is not clear why the Baal HaTurim identifies this prophecy with a phrase from verse 10, in the second *parashah* of that prophecy. We would expect the prophecy to be identified either as הִנָּבֵא עַל רוֹעֵי יִשְׂרָאֵל, *Prophesy against the shepherds of Israel* (v. 2), the first unique phrase that can identify the passage, or as הִנְנִי אָנִי וְדָרַשְׁתִּי אֶת צֹאנִי, *Behold, I am here, and I will seek out My sheep* (v. 11), from the first verse of the *parashah* in which verse 16, the verse adduced in the Baal HaTurim's allusion, appears.

שני הֲיֵשׁ־בָּהּ עֵץ אִם־אַיִן וְהִתְחַזַּקְתֶּם וּלְקַחְתֶּם מִפְּרִי
כא הָאָרֶץ וְהַיָּמִים יְמֵי בִּכּוּרֵי עֲנָבִים: וַיַּעֲלוּ וַיָּתֻרוּ אֶת־
כב הָאָרֶץ מִמִּדְבַּר־צִן עַד־רְחֹב לְבֹא חֲמָת: וַיַּעֲלוּ
בַנֶּגֶב וַיָּבֹא עַד־חֶבְרוֹן וְשָׁם אֲחִימַן שֵׁשַׁי וְתַלְמַי
יְלִידֵי הָעֲנָק וְחֶבְרוֹן שֶׁבַע שָׁנִים נִבְנְתָה לִפְנֵי צֹעַן
כג מִצְרָיִם: וַיָּבֹאוּ עַד־נַחַל אֶשְׁכֹּל וַיִּכְרְתוּ מִשָּׁם
זְמוֹרָה וְאֶשְׁכּוֹל עֲנָבִים אֶחָד וַיִּשָּׂאֻהוּ בַמּוֹט בִּשְׁנָיִם
כד וּמִן־הָרִמֹּנִים וּמִן־הַתְּאֵנִים: לַמָּקוֹם הַהוּא קָרָא
נַחַל אֶשְׁכּוֹל עַל אֹדוֹת הָאֶשְׁכּוֹל אֲשֶׁר־כָּרְתוּ מִשָּׁם
כה בְּנֵי יִשְׂרָאֵל: וַיָּשֻׁבוּ מִתּוּר הָאָרֶץ מִקֵּץ אַרְבָּעִים יוֹם:
כו וַיֵּלְכוּ וַיָּבֹאוּ אֶל־מֹשֶׁה וְאֶל־אַהֲרֹן וְאֶל־כָּל־עֲדַת
בְּנֵי־יִשְׂרָאֵל אֶל־מִדְבַּר פָּארָן קָדֵשָׁה וַיָּשִׁיבוּ אֹתָם
דָּבָר וְאֶת־כָּל־הָעֵדָה וַיַּרְאוּם אֶת־פְּרִי הָאָרֶץ:
כז וַיְסַפְּרוּ־לוֹ וַיֹּאמְרוּ בָּאנוּ אֶל־הָאָרֶץ אֲשֶׁר שְׁלַחְתָּנוּ
כח וְגַם זָבַת חָלָב וּדְבַשׁ הִוא וְזֶה־פִּרְיָהּ: אֶפֶס כִּי־עַז
הָעָם הַיֹּשֵׁב בָּאָרֶץ וְהֶעָרִים בְּצֻרוֹת גְּדֹלֹת מְאֹד

בעל הטורים

(כא־כב) **חֲמָת. וַיַּעֲלוּ בַנֶּגֶב וַיָּבֹא.** סוֹפֵי תֵבוֹת בְּהֵפֶךְ "אָבוֹת". שֶׁנִּשְׁתַּטֵּחַ עַל קִבְרֵי אָבוֹת:

(כד) **לַמָּקוֹם הַהוּא קָרָא נַחַל אֶשְׁכּוֹל.** הַפָּסוּק מַתְחִיל בְּלָמֶ"ד וּמְסַיֵּם בְּלָמֶ"ד, דִּסְתָם נְזִירוּת שְׁלֹשִׁים יוֹם:

וְהַיַּיִן אִם זָכָה לִשְׁתּוֹתוֹ כָּרָאוּי, אָז חַמְרָא וְרֵיחָנֵי פַּקְחִין, וְזוֹכֶה לִלְמֹד וּלְלַמֵּד:

BAAL HATURIM ELUCIDATED

21-22. חֲמָת. וַיַּעֲלוּ בַנֶּגֶב וַיָּבֹא — HAMATH. THEY ASCENDED IN THE SOUTH AND HE ARRIVED.[23] When their order is reversed, the final letters of these four words spell אָבוֹת, *Patriarchs.* For [Caleb alone went to the Cave of Machpelah in Hebron and] prostrated himself in prayer at the grave of the Patriarchs.[24]

23. Verse 22 begins with a plural verb, וַיַּעֲלוּ, *"they" ascended,* then continues in the singular, וַיָּבֹא, *and "he" arrived.* The Baal HaTurim's comment addresses this apparent contradiction.

24. *Peirush HaRokeach.* When Caleb realized that his fellow spies were planning to return to Moses with an unfavorable report, he separated himself from them and went to the Cave of Machpelah. There, he prostrated himself on the graves of the Patriarchs and requested of them, "My ancestors, plead for mercy on my behalf, that I may be able to save myself from joining in the plot of the other spies." If so, why didn't Joshua also pray at the Cave? Because he was already protected by Moses' blessing, for when Moses changed his disciple's name from הוֹשֵׁעַ, *Hoshea,* to יְהוֹשֻׁעַ, *Joshua* (v. 16 above), he prayed, "יָהּ יוֹשִׁיעֲךָ מֵעֲצַת מְרַגְּלִים, *May God save you from the plot of the spies*" (*Sotah* 34b, cited in *Rashi* to vv. 22 and 16).

are there trees in it or not? You shall strengthen yourselves
and take from the fruit of the land." The days were the
season of the first ripe grapes.
21 *They ascended and spied out the land, from the*
Wilderness of Zin to the expanse at the approach to Hamath.
22 *They ascended in the south and he arrived at Hebron,*
where there were Ahiman, Sheshai, and Talmai, the off-
spring of the giant. Hebron had been built seven years before
Zoan of Egypt. 23 *They arrived at the Valley of Eshcol and*
cut from there a vine with one cluster of grapes, and bore it
on a double pole, and of the pomegranates and of the figs.
24 *They named that place the Valley of Eshcol because of the*
cluster that the Children of Israel cut from there.
25 *They returned from spying out the land at the end of*
forty days. 26 *They went and came to Moses and to Aaron*
and to the entire assembly of the Children of Israel, to the
Wilderness of Paran at Kadesh, and brought back the report
to them and the entire assembly, and they showed them the
fruit of the land.
27 *They reported to him and said, "We arrived at the land*
to which you sent us, and indeed it flows with milk and
honey, and this is its fruit. 28 *But — the people that dwells in*
the land is powerful, the cities are fortified and very great,

BAAL HATURIM ELUCIDATED

24. לַמָּקוֹם הַהוּא קָרָא נַחַל אֶשְׁכּוֹל — THEY NAMED THAT PLACE THE VALLEY OF ESHCOL. This verse begins with the letter ל [= 30] and ends with the letter ל,[25] alluding to the fact that the standard term of a Nazirite vow is thirty days.[26]

[Alternatively:][27] One who drinks wine with proper self-control merits [what one Talmudic Sage describes as], "Wine and fragrances made me wise,"[28] so that he becomes worthy to learn and to teach.[29]

25. The Baal HaTurim discusses this phenomenon in his comments to *Leviticus* 11:47 and 21:22, and *Deuteronomy* 17:20, also.

26. *Peirush HaRokeach;* see *Nazir* 5a; see also the Baal HaTurim to 6:6 above with notes 51 and 52.

Our verse speaks of נַחַל אֶשְׁכּוֹל, literally, *Valley of a Cluster of Grapes,* while the Nazirite is prohibited from partaking of either grapes or the wine derived from them (*VeChur LaZahav*) and, as the Talmud (*Shabbos* 13a) states, we are required to discourage a Nazirite from entering a vineyard (A.S.).

27. This alternative allusion is based upon two aspects of the verse: For one, the letter לָמֶ״ד with which this verse begins represents the verb לִלְמֹד, *to learn* or *to study,* and the לָמֶ״ד with which the verse ends represents the verb לְלַמֵּד, *to teach;* and secondly, the verse speaks of a cluster of grapes, the source of wine.

28. *Sanhedrin* 70a; see also the Baal HaTurim to *Exodus* 30:34, s.v., קַח. If one knows how to control his intake so that he not overindulge, a moderate drink will gladden him and open his heart to wisdom (*Rashi*).

29. *Peirush HaRokeach.*

כט וְגַם־יְלִדֵי הָעֲנָק רָאִינוּ שָׁם: עֲמָלֵק יוֹשֵׁב בְּאֶרֶץ
הַנֶּגֶב וְהַחִתִּי וְהַיְבוּסִי וְהָאֱמֹרִי יוֹשֵׁב בָּהָר וְהַכְּנַעֲנִי
ל יוֹשֵׁב עַל־הַיָּם וְעַל יַד הַיַּרְדֵּן: וַיַּהַס כָּלֵב אֶת־הָעָם
אֶל־מֹשֶׁה וַיֹּאמֶר עָלֹה נַעֲלֶה וְיָרַשְׁנוּ אֹתָהּ כִּי־
לא יָכוֹל נוּכַל לָהּ: וְהָאֲנָשִׁים אֲשֶׁר־עָלוּ עִמּוֹ אָמְרוּ
לֹא נוּכַל לַעֲלוֹת אֶל־הָעָם כִּי־חָזָק הוּא מִמֶּנּוּ:

בעל הטורים

(כט) וְהָאֱמֹרִי יוֹשֵׁב. מָלֵא וָי״ו – שֶׁשָּׁקוּל הוּא כְּשִׁשָּׁה עֲמָמִים, שֶׁנֶּאֱמַר בּוֹ "כְּגֹבַהּ אֲרָזִים גָּבְהוֹ":

(ל) עָלֹה נַעֲלֶה. בְּהֵ״א – לוֹמַר שֶׁאֲפִלּוּ אִם יֹאמַר לָנוּ עֲשׂוּ סֻלָּמוֹת וַעֲלוּ לָרָקִיעַ, שֶׁהוּא מַהֲלַךְ ה׳ מֵאוֹת שָׁנָה, "נַעֲלֶה":

(לא) כִּי חָזָק הוּא מִמֶּנּוּ. אִיתָא בַּגְּמָרָא, אַל תִּקְרֵי "ממנו" אֶלָּא "ממנו". שֶׁאָמְרוּ, שֶׁאֲפִלּוּ בַּעַל הַבַּיִת אֵינוֹ יָכוֹל לְהוֹצִיא כֵּלָיו מִשָּׁם. יֵשׁ מְפָרְשִׁים, אֶלָּא מִמֶּנּוּ, לְשׁוֹן מָנָא, תַּרְגּוּם כְּלִי. וְיֵשׁ מְפָרְשִׁים, לְפִי שֶׁכָּל אוֹתִיּוֹת שֶׁל "מִמֶּנּוּ" כְּפוּלִים, כְּמוֹ מֵ״ם מֵ״ם נֻ״ן וָ״ו, לָכֵן כּוֹלֵל שְׁנֵי דְבָרִים, פְּשׁוּטוֹ וְהַדְּרָשׁ שֶׁלּוֹ:

BAAL HATURIM ELUCIDATED

29. וְהָאֱמֹרִי יוֹשֵׁב — AND THE AMORITE DWELL. [This term is spelled] in full, with a ו (= 6).[30] For the [Amorite] is considered equal to the other six [Canaanite] nations combined, as it is written regarding [the Amorite], [אֲשֶׁר] כְּגֹבַהּ אֲרָזִים גָּבְהוֹ, [*Whose*] *stature was like the stature of cedar trees*[31] (*Amos* 2:9).[32]

30. עָלֹה נַעֲלֶה — WE SHALL SURELY ASCEND. The word is spelled עָלֹה, with a ה (= 5) [rather than עָלוֹ, with a ו] to indicate that Caleb said, "Even if Moses would tell us: 'Build ladders and ascend to the heavens' — a journey of five centuries[33] —

---

30. The Baal HaTurim does not specify to which ו he refers. That letter appears twice in his rubric: once in the word וְהָאֱמֹרִי as the conjunctive prefix וְ־, *and;* the second time in the word יוֹשֵׁב, *it dwells.* Now the conjunctive ו is certainly necessary, for three nations are listed together, *and the Hittite and the Jebusite and the Amorite.* Nor can the ו of יוֹשֵׁב be considered worthy of special mention, for the word appears twenty-four times in the Torah, more than half those times spelled with a ו (see, for example, v. 19 above, where it appears with both spellings). Moreover, a masoretic note to our verse reads: י״ז מְלֵאִים בְּתוֹרָה ג׳ מִנְהוֹן בְּפָסוּק, *This word is spelled in full* [*with a* ו] *seventeen times in the Torah, three of them in this verse.* Thus, the full spelling appears three times in our verse: once regarding Amalek; a second time regarding the Hittite, the Jebusite and the Amorite [although this may seem to be an odd usage for the singular verb יוֹשֵׁב, *"it" dwells,* the same usage appears in 14:25 below]; and a third time, with regard to the Canaanite. It has been suggested that the Baal HaTurim is referring to a variant spelling of וְהָאֱמוֹרִי with a central ו. However, the *Ramah* (*Masores Seyag LaTorah*) cites a masoretic note which states that the name אֱמֹרִי is never spelled with a ו anywhere in the *Tanach.* Thus, the Baal HaTurim's intent remains unclear (*VeChur LaZahav*).

31. The verse reads in full: *Yet I destroyed the Amorite — whose stature was like the stature of cedar trees and who were mighty as oaks — from before them; and I destroyed his fruit from above and his roots from below.*

32. *Peirush HaRokeach;* see *Sifrei, Devarim* 11:23.

33. *Pesachim* 94b. The Baal HaTurim interprets עָלֹה as two words, עַל ה׳, in which עַל can mean either, *he went* (*see Daniel* 2:16) or *a height* (see *Hosea* 11:7). Thus, עָלֹה may be understood as "he

and we also saw there the offspring of the giant. [29] *Amalek*
dwells in the area of the south; and the Hittite and the
Jebusite and the Amorite dwell on the mountain; and the
Canaanite dwells by the Sea and on the bank of the Jordan."
[30] *Caleb silenced the people toward Moses and said, "We*
shall surely ascend and conquer it, for we can surely do it!"
[31] *But the men who had ascended with him said, "We*
cannot ascend to that people for it is stronger than we!"

BAAL HATURIM ELUCIDATED

we would ascend."[34]

31. כִּי חָזָק הוּא מִמֶּנּוּ — FOR IT IS STRONGER THAN WE. The Talmud[34a] states: Do not read ממנו, rather, read ממנו;[35] [for they said] that even the Master could not remove His vessel from there. Some explain [the phrase], "rather, read מִמָּנוּ, *than His vessel,* for מָנָא is the Aramaic word for *vessel.*"[36]

Others explain that the name of each letter of the word מִמֶּנּוּ is double that letter; for the word may be spelled out מֵ״ם מֵ״ם[37] נֻ״ן וָ״ו.[38] Thus, the word מִמֶּנּוּ includes two implications: its simple meaning and its Midrashic meaning.[39]

---

went on a five centuries' journey" or "a height of five centuries' journey" (*VeChur LaZahav*).

34. *Peirush HaRokeach.*

34a. *Sotah* 35a.

35. The Talmud often explains a Scriptural verse with the formula: ... אַל תִּקְרֵי ... אֶלָּא ..., *Do not read ..., rather, read ...;* i.e., do not interpret the verse strictly according to the literal meaning of the spelling and vowelization, rather, interpret the verse as if it were spelled and/or vowelized as herein suggested. In our case, however, the written version and the suggested version seem to be identical — both being read מִמֶּנּוּ — for the term מִמֶּנּוּ has two meanings, *than we* and *than he.* And the spies' statement can be understood as either an acknowledgment that the inhabitants of the land are *stronger than we* [the Israelites], or, the blasphemous claim that the inhabitants of the land are *stronger than He,* referring to God. Accordingly, *Rashi* (in his comment to our verse) follows the second interpretation and explains that they spoke "with regard to the One Above,' and (in his comment to the Talmud) emends the Talmudic passage, eliminating the sentence אַל תִּקְרֵי ממנו אֶלָּא ממנו altogether. He explains that the Talmud merely states that the spies used the term מִמֶּנּוּ to mean *than Him* (see *Tosafos* to *Arachin* 15b, s.v., אַל תִּקְרֵי, and *Minchas Shai* to our verse, for another explanation of אַל תִּקְרֵי). The Baal HaTurim preserves the Talmudic passage.

36. [See, for example, 19:15 below, where *Onkelos* renders כְּלִי, *utensil,* as מָן.] Thus, the Talmud means: Do not explain the word ממנו of our verse only as מִמֶּנּוּ, *than us,* rather, explain it as if it were vowelized מִמָּנוּ, *than His vessel.* And the Talmud continues by quoting the spies, "Even the Master could not remove His vessel from there."

37. The text follows the Fürth edition. Most other editions do not repeat the term מֵ״ם.

38. Every letter has a name, e.g., דָּלֶ״ת is the name of the letter ד. The letter itself — ד — is called the נִגְלֶה, *nigleh* (revealed part), while the other letters of the name — ל״ת — are called the נִסְתָּר, *nistar* (concealed part). The full name of the letter — דל״ת — is called its *millui.* For purposes of an allusion, the value of the letter may be reckoned as the *gematria* of either the *nigleh,* in the case of ד that would be 4; or the *nistar,* in our case ל״ת (= 30 + 400) = 430; or the *millui,* in our case דל״ת = 434. In the word מִמֶּנּוּ, the *nigleh* and *nistar* of each letter is the same: מ״ם מ״ם נ״ן ו״ו.

39. That is, whenever the context allows for two interpretations, the word מִמֶּנּוּ may be understood as connoting both of its meanings. The Talmudic statement should be understood in this manner: אַל תִּקְרֵי מִמֶּנּוּ אֶלָּא מִמֶּנּוּ, *Do not interpret the verse as if the letters of* מִמֶּנּוּ *appear only once, rather, interpret it as if the letters of* מִמֶּנּוּ appear twice — once meaning *than we,* the second time meaning *than He.*

יג/לב-לג לב וַיֹּצִ֜יאוּ דִּבַּ֤ת הָאָ֙רֶץ֙ אֲשֶׁ֣ר תָּר֣וּ אֹתָ֔הּ אֶל־בְּנֵ֥י יִשְׂרָאֵ֖ל
לֵאמֹ֑ר הָאָ֡רֶץ אֲשֶׁר֩ עָבַ֨רְנוּ בָ֜הּ לָת֣וּר אֹתָ֗הּ אֶ֣רֶץ
אֹכֶ֤לֶת יוֹשְׁבֶ֙יהָ֙ הִ֔וא וְכָל־הָעָ֛ם אֲשֶׁר־רָאִ֥ינוּ בְתוֹכָ֖הּ
לג אַנְשֵׁ֥י מִדּֽוֹת׃ וְשָׁ֣ם רָאִ֗ינוּ אֶת־הַנְּפִילִ֛ים בְּנֵ֥י עֲנָ֖ק מִן־
הַנְּפִלִ֑ים וַנְּהִ֤י בְעֵינֵ֙ינוּ֙ כַּֽחֲגָבִ֔ים וְכֵ֥ן הָיִ֖ינוּ בְּעֵינֵיהֶֽם׃

בעל הטורים

(לג) וַנְּהִי. ב׳ בַּמָּסוֹרֶת – הָכָא "וַנְּהִי בְעֵינֵינוּ כַּחֲגָבִים"; "וַנְּהִי כַטָּמֵא כֻּלָּנוּ". לְפִי שֶׁאָז נִגְזַר עֲלֵיהֶם "סוּרוּ טָמֵא":

❑ {וְכֵן הָיִינוּ בְּעֵינֵיהֶם. בְּגִימַטְרִיָּא זֶהוּ נְמָלִים קוֹזִין. "וְכֵן" גַּם נוֹטָרִיקוֹן וּכְמוֹ נְמָלִים. וּבָזֶה יִתְיַשֵּׁב מַה שֶּׁפֵּרֵשׁ רַשִׁ"י, שֶׁמָּעֲנוּ אוֹמְרִים נְמָלִים בַּכְּרָם. כִּי מֵאַן דְּכַר שְׁמָם שֶׁל נְמָלִים? וַהֲלֹא הַפָּסוּק אוֹמֵר "וַנְּהִי בְעֵינֵינוּ כַּחֲגָבִים וְכֵן הָיִינוּ בְּעֵינֵיהֶם", וּמַשְׁמַע כַּחֲגָבִים וְלֹא כִנְמָלִים. אֶלָּא כְּמוֹ שֶׁאָמַרְנוּ נִרְאֶה שֶׁמְּדַקְדֵּק רַשִׁ"י. עַד כָּאן:}

❑ כַּחֲגָבִים. ב׳ בַּמָּסוֹרֶת – "וַנְּהִי בְעֵינֵינוּ כַּחֲגָבִים"; וְאִידָךְ "וְישְׁבֶיהָ כַּחֲגָבִים". כִּדְאִיתָא בַּמִּדְרָשׁ, שֶׁעֲנָק אֶחָד אָכַל רִמּוֹן וְזָרַק הַקְּלִפָּה. וְכָל שְׁנֵים עָשָׂר הַמְרַגְּלִים נִכְנְסוּ לֵישֵׁב בְּתוֹכָהּ מִפְּנֵי הַצֵּל. וְזֶהוּ "וְישְׁבֶיהָ כַּחֲגָבִים", שֶׁיָּשְׁבוּ בָהּ כַּחֲגָבִים:

BAAL HATURIM ELUCIDATED

33. {The Baal HaTurim's comment to אֶת הַנְּפִילִים . . . מִן הַנְּפִלִים appears at *Genesis* 6:4.}

❑ **וַנְּהִי** — AND WE WERE. The masoretic note, ב׳, means that this word appears twice in the *Tanach:* (i) here, וַנְּהִי בְעֵינֵינוּ כַּחֲגָבִים, *and we were like grasshoppers in our eyes;* and (ii) וַנְּהִי כַטָּמֵא כֻּלָּנוּ, *all of us have become like one who is defiled* (*Isaiah* 64:5). The similarity of expression connotes that it was then[40] that [the decree of exile,] סוּרוּ טָמֵא, *Turn away, O defiled one* (*Lamentations* 4:15), was pronounced.[41]

❑ {**וְכֵן הָיִינוּ בְּעֵינֵיהֶם** — AND SO WE WERE IN THEIR EYES. The *gematria* of this phrase (344) is equivalent[41a] to that of זֶהוּ נְמָלִים קוֹזִין, *This* [*refers to*] *"kozin" [!] ants.*[41b]

40. When the spies brought their slanderous report to the people, and they, in turn, accepted the report at face value (see note 16 above).

41. *Peirush HaRokeach.* The text follows *Peirush HaRokeach* and that is how the Baal HaTurim's comment appears in *Shoham Yakar's* manuscript edition. In both the early and later printed editions, the comment is incomplete at this point, with the remainder appearing after the next comment.

41a. The *gematria* of the Baal HaTurim's phrase is 361, seventeen more than that of the Scriptural phrase. The numbers may be reconciled by omitting the word זֶהוּ, thereby subtracting 18 from 361, for a *gematria* of 343, which, by the principle of *im hakollel,* is considered equivalent to 344 (*VeChur LaZahav*).

41b. The text follows the Constantinople and Venice editions. However, the word קוֹזִין is unknown from any other source. The Furth edition reads זֶהוּ נְמָלִים קוֹצִין, *this* [*refers to*] *thorn-like* [or *stinging*] *ants,* which has a *gematria* of 444, one hundred more than that of the Scriptural phrase. Nevertheless, the two *gematriaos* can be reconciled. If the word זֶהוּ is omitted, the Baal HaTurim's phrase reads נְמָלִים קוֹצִין, with a *gematria* of 426, which, by the principle of *im hakollel,* may be considered

[32] *They brought forth to the Children of Israel an evil report on the land that they had spied out, saying, "The land through which we have passed, to spy it out, is a land that devours its inhabitants! All the people that we saw in it were huge!* [33] *There we saw the Nephilim, the sons of the giant from among the Nephilim; and we were like grasshoppers in our eyes, and so we were in their eyes!"*

BAAL HATURIM ELUCIDATED

Similarly, the word וְכֵן, *and so,* can be seen as an abbreviation of וּכְמוֹ נְמָלִים, *like ants.* This explains *Rashi's* commentary, which states: [The spies said,] "We heard them say, 'There are ants in the vineyard [that look like men].' " For [otherwise], who is speaking of ants? The verse states, *and we were like grasshoppers in our eyes, and so we were in their eyes,* which implies, [we were like] grasshoppers — not ants — in their eyes. Therefore, it appears that *Rashi* interprets the verse as we have stated above.[41c] Until here.}[42]

❑ כַּחֲגָבִים — **LIKE GRASSHOPPERS.** The masoretic note, ב׳, means that this word appears twice in the *Tanach:* (i) here, וַנְּהִי בְעֵינֵינוּ כַּחֲגָבִים, *and we were like grasshoppers in our eyes;* and (ii) וְישְׁבֶיהָ כַּחֲגָבִים, *and those who sit in it are like grasshoppers* (*Isaiah* 40:22). The Midrash states that a [Canaanite] giant ate a pomegranate and threw its shell away. Then, all twelve spies entered the shell and sat inside to take shade.[43] Thus, the verse states, *those who sit in it are like grasshoppers,* for they sat in it like grasshoppers.

---

equivalent to 427. Then, extending the Scriptural phrase by one word — כַּחֲגָבִים וְכֵן הָיִינוּ בְּעֵינֵיהֶם — yields a *gematria* of 427 (*VeChur LaZahav*).

Ittur Bikkurim suggests emending the Baal HaTurim's phrase to וְזֶהוּ קֵן נְמָלִים, *and this [refers to] a nest of ants,* which shares the *gematria* 344 with the Scriptural phrase. Many later printed editions follow *Ittur Bikkurim.*

41c. According to *Sforno* the spies meant, *"We were like grasshoppers in our eyes, and so were we [like grasshoppers or smaller] in their eyes."*

42. This comment appears in virtually all printed editions of the Baal HaTurim. *Shoham Yakar* questions the authenticity of this comment on four grounds: (i) It does not appear in any of the extant manuscripts; (ii) the concluding term ע״כ [= עַד כָּאן], *until here,* is a sort of close quote mark used to indicate either the end of a quotation or the end of an editor's insertion [see the Baal HaTurim to 11:16 above, with note 266a]; (iii) it is difficult to believe that *Rashi* would alter the simple meaning of a verse on the basis of a *gematria* or an abbreviation; and (iv) in this entire work, the Baal HaTurim never attempts to resolve a difficulty in *Rashi's* commentary. [Besides the present comment, the Baal HaTurim mentions *Rashi* in six places. In five of them, he cites *Rashi* as a source (*Genesis* 4:10, 16:4 and 47:29; *Exodus* 3:6; and *Deuteronomy* 1:46). In the sixth (*Genesis* 38:24, but see note 83 there), he cites *Ramban's* questions on *Rashi's* comment; however, he presents no answers to them.] To *Shoham Yakar's* objections we can add that the interpretation of וְכֵן as an abbreviated form of וּכְמוֹ נְמָלִים is extremely farfetched and not at all within the purview of the Baal HaTurim's work. Moreover, in those editions in which this comment does appear, it is presented in the middle of another comment, leaving the first half of that comment dangling without an ending. Accordingly, the comment has been placed in braces to indicate its doubtful authenticity.

43. Cited, with somewhat different details, in *Tosefos Shantz* to *Sotah* 35a.

א וַתִּשָּׂא כָּל־הָעֵדָה וַיִּתְּנוּ אֶת־קוֹלָם וַיִּבְכּוּ הָעָם
ב בַּלַּיְלָה הַהוּא: וַיִּלֹּנוּ עַל־מֹשֶׁה וְעַל־אַהֲרֹן כֹּל בְּנֵי
יִשְׂרָאֵל וַיֹּאמְרוּ אֲלֵהֶם כָּל־הָעֵדָה לוּ־מַתְנוּ בְּאֶרֶץ
ג מִצְרַיִם אוֹ בַּמִּדְבָּר הַזֶּה לוּ־מָתְנוּ: וְלָמָה יהוה מֵבִיא
אֹתָנוּ אֶל־הָאָרֶץ הַזֹּאת לִנְפֹּל בַּחֶרֶב נָשֵׁינוּ וְטַפֵּנוּ
ד יִהְיוּ לָבַז הֲלוֹא טוֹב לָנוּ שׁוּב מִצְרָיְמָה: וַיֹּאמְרוּ
אִישׁ אֶל־אָחִיו נִתְּנָה רֹאשׁ וְנָשׁוּבָה מִצְרָיְמָה:

בעל הטורים

יד (ג) **לִנְפֹּל.** ד׳ בַּמָּסוֹרֶת — ״לִנְפֹּל בַּחֶרֶב״; ״דָּחֹה דְחִיתַנִי לִנְפֹּל״; ״אֲשֶׁר הַחִלּוֹתָ לִנְפֹּל לְפָנָיו״; ״גַּם בָּבֶל לִנְפֹּל חַלְלֵי יִשְׂרָאֵל״. שֶׁבַּעֲוֹן זֹאת הַנְּפִילָה דָּחוּנִי, שֶׁגָּרְמוּ לִי עַתָּה נְפִילָה, דִּכְתִיב ״וּפִגְרֵיכֶם אַתֶּם יִפְּלוּ בַּמִּדְבָּר״. וּ״דְחִיתַנִי לִנְפֹּל״ לְדוֹרוֹת, שֶׁגָּרְמוּ שֶׁחָרַב הַבַּיִת וְנָפְלוּ בְּיַד בָּבֶל, וְהַיְנוּ ״גַּם בָּבֶל לִנְפֹּל חַלְלֵי יִשְׂרָאֵל״. וְכֵן בִּימֵי הָמָן, שֶׁכָּתְבוּ שִׂטְנָה עַל בִּנְיַן הַבַּיִת וְלֹא הִנִּיחוּ לִבְנוֹתוֹ:

(ד) **נִתְּנָה רֹאשׁ.** זֶהוּ עֲבוֹדָה זָרָה. וְכֵן בָּעֵגֶל, ״אֲשֶׁר יֵלְכוּ לְפָנֵינוּ״, ״אֲשֶׁר״ אוֹתִיּוֹת ״רֹאשׁ״. וּמָה הָתָם אַחַר אַרְבָּעִים יוֹם, אַף כָּאן אַחַר אַרְבָּעִים יוֹם. ״אִישׁ אֶל אָחִיו נִתְּנָה רֹאשׁ וְנָשׁוּבָה מִצְרָיְמָה״ רָאשֵׁי תֵבוֹת בְּגִימַטְרִיָּא עֲבוֹדָה זָרָה:

BAAL HATURIM ELUCIDATED

XIV

3. **לִנְפֹּל** — TO FALL. The masoretic note, ד׳, means that this word appears four times in the *Tanach:* (i) here, לִנְפֹּל בַּחֶרֶב, *to fall by the sword;* (ii) דָּחֹה דְחִיתַנִי לִנְפֹּל, *You pushed me hard, to* [*make me*] *fall* (*Psalms* 118:13); (iii) אֲשֶׁר הַחִלּוֹתָ לִנְפֹּל לְפָנָיו, *before whom you have begun to fall* (*Esther* 6:13); and (iv) גַּם בָּבֶל לִנְפֹּל חַלְלֵי יִשְׂרָאֵל, *even* [*as*] *the slain of Israel* [*were*] *to fall* [*in*] *Babylonia* (*Jeremiah* 51:49). [The similarity of expression indicates that Israel bemoaned the fact] that as a consequence of the iniquity of this [spiritual] downfall [of our verse], "They pushed me [Israel], for they caused me to fall at this time" — as is written below, וּפִגְרֵיכֶם אַתֶּם יִפְּלוּ בַּמִּדְבָּר, *But your carcasses — yourselves — shall fall in* [*this*] *wilderness* (v. 32). And *you* [*spies*] *pushed me to fall* in future generations," for they caused that the *Beis HaMikdash* be destroyed[44] and that people fall into the hand of Babylonia; and that is [what is meant by the verse,] *even the slain of Israel were to fall in Babylonia.* Similarly, in the days of Haman, for [the enemies of the Jews] *wrote an accusation* (*Ezra* 4:6) against the rebuilding of the *Beis HaMikdash,*[45]

44. See note 16 above.

45. *Ezra* 4:6; *Taanis* 11a, cited in *Rashi's* commentary to *Ezra;* see also the Baal HaTurim to *Genesis* 26:21. That verse reads: *And during the reign of Ahasuerus, at the beginning of his reign,* כָּתְבוּ שִׂטְנָה, *they wrote an accusation against the inhabitants of Judah and Jerusalem. Rashi* (to *Esther* 9:10, citing *Seder Olam* 29) writes that the ten hanged sons of Haman were the ones who had written the accusation. Alternatively: One version of *Yalkut Shimoni* (II, 1045) ascribes the accusation to "the scribe Shimshai son of Haman," while another version of the *Yalkut* reads, "Haman and his son Shimshai the scribe."

[1] *The entire assembly raised up and issued its voice; the people wept that night.* [2] *All the Children of Israel murmured against Moses and Aaron, and the entire assembly said to them, "If only we had died in the land of Egypt, or if only we had died in this wilderness!* [3] *Why is* HASHEM *bringing us to this land to fall by the sword? Our wives and our youngsters will be taken captive! Is it not better for us to return to Egypt?"*

[4] *So they said to one another, "Let us appoint a leader and let us return to Egypt!"*

and they would not permit [the Jews] to rebuild it.[45a]

4. נִתְּנָה רֹאשׁ — LET US APPOINT A LEADER. [The term רֹאשׁ, literally, *head,*] refers to idolatry.[46] And thus, regarding the golden calf we find that the word אֲשֶׁר of the phrase אֲשֶׁר יֵלְכוּ לְפָנֵינוּ, *that will go before us* (*Exodus* 32:1), can be rearranged to spell the word רֹאשׁ. [There is another similarity between the two sins:] Just as the calf was made after a forty-day period [that Moses spent on the mountain], so too here, the spies' sin took place after their return from a forty-day journey. Another allusion to idolatry appears in this verse, for the *gematria* of the initial letters of אִישׁ אֶל אָחִיו נִתְּנָה רֹאשׁ וְנָשׁוּבָה מִצְרָיְמָה, *to one another, "Let us appoint a leader and let us return to Egypt!"* [אאאנרו״מ] is 299, equal to that of עֲבוֹדָה זָרָה, *idol worship.*[47]

❑ {The Baal HaTurim's comment to וְנָשׁוּבָה appears at *Genesis* 22:5.}

45a. Thus, the connection to the verse from *Esther* cited in the masoretic note.

46. The Midrash records: Rabbi Akiva said: These [letters of the *aleph-beis*] are the twenty-two letters with which the Torah was given to the tribes of Israel. And they are engraved with a fiery stylus upon the wondrous and awesome crown of the Holy One, Blessed is He. When He desired to create the world, they all descended [from His crown] and stood before Him. This one said before Him, "Please create the world with me"; and that one said before Him, "Please create the world with me." First the letter ת came before God and said, "Master of the universe, is it Your desire to create Your world with me?" [The ת went on to explain why it felt justified in its request.] But God replied, "No!" [Then the ת asked why its request was refused and God explained His reasons.] Next, the letter ש approached, stood before God and said, "Master of the universe, is it Your desire to create Your world with me?" . . . "No!" . . . Then the letter ר approached and said before God, "Master of the universe, is it Your desire to create Your world with me — as it is written regarding me, 'רֹאשׁ דְּבָרְךָ אֱמֶת, *Your very first utterance is truth'* (*Psalms* 119:160) [which may be interpreted, *the* רֵי״שׁ *of Your utterance is truth,* for רֵישׁ is the Aramaic equivalent of the Hebrew word רֹאשׁ, *head*]." But God replied, "No!" The letter ר asked why its request was refused, and God answered, "Because in the future Israel will use you in the worship of idols, as it is said, נִתְּנָה רֹאשׁ וְנָשׁוּבָה מִצְרָיְמָה, *Let us appoint a* רֹאשׁ *and let us return to Egypt;* and רֹאשׁ means idolatry, as it is said, הוּא צַלְמָא רֵאשֵׁהּ דִּי דְהַב טָב, *This idol, its* רֹאשׁ *of fine gold* (*Daniel* 2:32). Moreover, ר is the initial letter of both רַע, *evil,* and רָשָׁע, *wicked person."* Upon hearing this, the ר departed with dejection . . . (*Midrash Alpha-beta DeRabbi Akiva; Sanhedrin* 107a).

47. *R' Ephraim* (*MiKesivah Ashkenazis*); see also *Rashi.*

ה וַיִּפֹּל מֹשֶׁה וְאַהֲרֹן עַל־פְּנֵיהֶם לִפְנֵי כָּל־קְהַל עֲדַת
ו בְּנֵי יִשְׂרָאֵל׃ וִיהוֹשֻׁעַ בִּן־נוּן וְכָלֵב בֶּן־יְפֻנֶּה מִן־
ז הַתָּרִים אֶת־הָאָרֶץ קָרְעוּ בִּגְדֵיהֶם׃ וַיֹּאמְרוּ אֶל־
כָּל־עֲדַת בְּנֵי־יִשְׂרָאֵל לֵאמֹר הָאָרֶץ אֲשֶׁר עָבַרְנוּ
שלישי ח בָהּ לָתוּר אֹתָהּ טוֹבָה הָאָרֶץ מְאֹד מְאֹד׃ אִם־חָפֵץ
בָּנוּ יהוה וְהֵבִיא אֹתָנוּ אֶל־הָאָרֶץ הַזֹּאת וּנְתָנָהּ
ט לָנוּ אֶרֶץ אֲשֶׁר־הִוא זָבַת חָלָב וּדְבָשׁ׃ אַךְ בַּיהוה
אַל־תִּמְרֹדוּ וְאַתֶּם אַל־תִּירְאוּ אֶת־עַם הָאָרֶץ כִּי
לַחְמֵנוּ הֵם סָר צִלָּם מֵעֲלֵיהֶם וַיהוה אִתָּנוּ
י אַל־תִּירָאֻם׃ וַיֹּאמְרוּ כָּל־הָעֵדָה לִרְגּוֹם אֹתָם
בָּאֲבָנִים וּכְבוֹד יהוה נִרְאָה בְּאֹהֶל מוֹעֵד אֶל־כָּל־
בְּנֵי יִשְׂרָאֵל׃
יא וַיֹּאמֶר יהוה אֶל־מֹשֶׁה עַד־אָנָה יְנַאֲצֻנִי הָעָם
הַזֶּה וְעַד־אָנָה לֹא־יַאֲמִינוּ בִי בְּכֹל הָאֹתוֹת אֲשֶׁר
יב עָשִׂיתִי בְּקִרְבּוֹ׃ אַכֶּנּוּ בַדֶּבֶר וְאוֹרִשֶׁנּוּ וְאֶעֱשֶׂה
יג אֹתְךָ לְגוֹי־גָּדוֹל וְעָצוּם מִמֶּנּוּ׃ וַיֹּאמֶר מֹשֶׁה
אֶל־יהוה וְשָׁמְעוּ מִצְרַיִם כִּי־הֶעֱלִיתָ בְכֹחֲךָ אֶת־
יד הָעָם הַזֶּה מִקִּרְבּוֹ׃ וְאָמְרוּ אֶל־יוֹשֵׁב הָאָרֶץ
הַזֹּאת שָׁמְעוּ כִּי־אַתָּה יהוה בְּקֶרֶב הָעָם הַזֶּה

בעל הטורים

(ט) לַחְמֵנוּ. ד׳ בַּמָּסֹרֶת — ״כִּי לַחְמֵנוּ הֵם״; ״לַחְמֵנוּ נֹאכֵל״; ״זֶה לַחְמֵנוּ חָם הִצְטַיַּדְנוּ {... מֵרֹב הַדֶּרֶךְ מְאֹד}״; ״בְּנַפְשֵׁנוּ נָבִיא לַחְמֵנוּ {מִפְּנֵי חֶרֶב הַמִּדְבָּר}״. אִם ״בַּה׳ אַל תִּמְרֹדוּ . . . לַחְמֵנוּ הֵם״, וְנֹאכְלֵם כַּלֶּחֶם. אֲבָל לְאַחַר שֶׁעָבְרוּ אֶת פִּי ה׳, ״וַיַּכּוּם וַיַּכְּתוּם״. וְזֶהוּ ״בְּנַפְשֵׁנוּ נָבִיא לַחְמֵנוּ מִפְּנֵי חֶרֶב הַמִּדְבָּר״. וְרַב לָהֶם הַדֶּרֶךְ מְאֹד, שֶׁהָלְכוּ אַרְבָּעִים שָׁנָה בַּמִּדְבָּר:

(יג) הֶעֱלִיתָ. ג׳ — בְּפָרָשַׁת כִּי תִשָּׂא:

BAAL HATURIM ELUCIDATED

9. לַחְמֵנוּ — OUR BREAD. The masoretic note, ד׳, means that this word appears four times in the *Tanach:* (i) here, כִּי לַחְמֵנוּ הֵם, *for they are our bread;* (ii) לַחְמֵנוּ נֹאכֵל, *We will consume our bread* (*Isaiah* 4:1); (iii) זֶה לַחְמֵנוּ חָם הִצְטַיַּדְנוּ {. . . מֵרֹב הַדֶּרֶךְ מְאֹד}, *This is our bread: It was hot when we packed it* {*. . . from the very great length of the journey*} (*Joshua* 9:12-13); and (iv) בְּנַפְשֵׁנוּ נָבִיא לַחְמֵנוּ {מִפְּנֵי חֶרֶב הַמִּדְבָּר}, *In mortal danger we shall bring our bread* {*because of the sword of the wilderness*}

[5] *Moses and Aaron fell on their faces before the entire congregation of the assembly of the Children of Israel.*

[6] *Joshua son of Nun and Caleb son of Jephunneh, of the spies of the land, tore their garments.* [7] *They spoke to the entire assembly of the Children of Israel, saying, "The land that we passed through, to spy it out — the land is very, very good!* [8] *If HASHEM desires us, He will bring us to this land and give it to us, a land that flows with milk and honey.* [9] *But do not rebel against HASHEM! You should not fear the people of the land, for they are our bread. Their protection has departed from them; HASHEM is with us. Do not fear them!"*

[10] *But the entire assembly said to pelt them with stones — and the glory of HASHEM appeared in the Tent of Meeting to all the Children of Israel.*

[11] *HASHEM said to Moses, "How long will this people provoke Me, and how long will they not have faith in Me, despite all the signs that I have performed in their midst?* [12] *I will smite them with the plague and annihilate them, and I shall make you a greater and more powerful nation than they."*

[13] *Moses said to HASHEM, "Then Egypt — from whose midst You have brought up this nation with Your power — will hear,* [14] *and they will say about the inhabitants of this land, 'They have heard that You, HASHEM, are in the midst of this people*

BAAL HATURIM ELUCIDATED

(*Lamentations* 5:9). [The similarity of expression indicates that Joshua and Caleb said:] "If you *do not rebel against HASHEM . . .* [*then*] *they are our bread,* and we will consume them like bread." However, after they trespassed on God's word, [*the Amalekite and the Canaanite . . . descended*] *and struck them and pounded them* (v. 45 below). That is the meaning of the verse: *In mortal danger we shall bring our bread, because of the sword of* [*the Amalekite and the Canaanite in*] *the wilderness.* Moreover, their journey became very long,[47a] for [as a result of this sin,] they wandered forty years in the wilderness.

13. {The Baal HaTurim's comment to וְשָׁמְעוּ appears at *Exodus* 3:18.}

❑ הֶעֱלִיתָ — YOU HAVE BROUGHT UP. [The masoretic note, ג׳, means that] this word appears three times in the *Tanach,* [as explained in the Baal HaTurim's comments to] *parashas Ki Sisa* (*Exodus* 33:1).

47a. Thus, the connection to the verse from *Joshua.*

אֲשֶׁר־עַיִן בְּעַיִן נִרְאָה | אַתָּה יהוה וַעֲנָנְךָ עֹמֵד
עֲלֵהֶם וּבְעַמֻּד עָנָן אַתָּה הֹלֵךְ לִפְנֵיהֶם יוֹמָם
טו וּבְעַמּוּד אֵשׁ לָיְלָה: וְהֵמַתָּה אֶת־הָעָם הַזֶּה כְּאִישׁ
אֶחָד וְאָמְרוּ הַגּוֹיִם אֲשֶׁר־שָׁמְעוּ אֶת־שִׁמְעֲךָ
טז לֵאמֹר: מִבִּלְתִּי יְכֹלֶת יהוה לְהָבִיא אֶת־הָעָם הַזֶּה
אֶל־הָאָרֶץ אֲשֶׁר־נִשְׁבַּע לָהֶם וַיִּשְׁחָטֵם בַּמִּדְבָּר:

בעל הטורים

(יד) עַיִן בְּעַיִן. ג׳ בַּמָּסוֹרֶת — ״אֲשֶׁר עַיִן בְּעַיִן נִרְאָה אַתָּה ה׳ ״; ״כִּי עַיִן בְּעַיִן יִרְאוּ בְּשׁוּב ה׳ צִיּוֹן״; וְאִידָךְ ״עַיִן בְּעַיִן שֵׁן בְּשֵׁן״. בָּעוֹלָם הַזֶּה אִי אֶפְשָׁר לִרְאוֹת בַּשְּׁכִינָה, כְּדִכְתִיב ״כִּי לֹא יִרְאַנִי הָאָדָם וָחָי״. וְזֶהוּ שֶׁכָּתוּב כָּאן ״אֲשֶׁר עַיִן בְּעַיִן נִרְאָה״, וּסְמִיךְ לֵהּ ״וְהֵמַתָּה״. אֲבָל לֶעָתִיד לָבוֹא יִרְאוּ, וַעֲתִידִין לוֹמַר ״זֶה ה׳ קִוִּינוּ לוֹ״:

וְכֵן רֶמֶז לְמַה שֶּׁדָּרְשׁוּ, ״עַיִן בְּעַיִן״ מָמוֹן. דִּכְתִיב הָכָא ״עַיִן בְּעַיִן״ וּסְמִיךְ לֵהּ ״וְהֵמַתָּה״, פֵּרוּשׁ, אִם יִהְיֶה עַיִן בְּעַיִן מַמָּשׁ ״וְהֵמַתָּה״, פֵּרוּשׁ, שֶׁמָּא יָמוּת. עַל כֵּן פֵּרוּשׁוֹ מָמוֹן:

(טז) מִבִּלְתִּי. ב׳ בַּמָּסוֹרֶת — ״מִבִּלְתִּי יְכֹלֶת ה׳ ״; וְאִידָךְ ״וַתִּזְנִי אֶל בְּנֵי אַשּׁוּר מִבִּלְתִּי שָׂבְעָתֵךְ״ בְּעִנְיַן תּוֹעֲבוֹת יְרוּשָׁלַיִם. כִּבְיָכוֹל, שֶׁעֲוֹנוֹת יִשְׂרָאֵל עוֹשִׂין לַ״יָּד חֲזָקָה״ כְּאִלּוּ אֵין בָּהּ יְכֹלֶת:

❑ **וַיִּשְׁחָטֵם בַּמִּדְבָּר.** הַחֵי״ת שְׁבוּרָה — לוֹמַר, שֶׁעָבְרוּ עַל הַתּוֹרָה שֶׁכָּרַת עָלֶיהָ ח׳ בְּרִיתוֹת

BAAL HATURIM ELUCIDATED

14. עַיִן בְּעַיִן — EYE TO[48] EYE. The masoretic note, ג׳, means that this phrase appears three times in the *Tanach:* (i) here, אֲשֶׁר עַיִן בְּעַיִן נִרְאָה אַתָּה ה׳, *that eye to eye, You, HASHEM, appeared;* (ii) כִּי עַיִן בְּעַיִן יִרְאוּ בְּשׁוּב ה׳ צִיּוֹן, *for eye by eye* [i.e., each and every eye], *they will see when HASHEM returns to Zion* (*Isaiah* 52:8); and (iii) עַיִן בְּעַיִן שֵׁן בְּשֵׁן, *eye for eye, tooth for tooth* (*Deuteronomy* 19:21). [The similarity of expression in our verse and the verse from *Isaiah* alludes to a Midrashic teaching:] In this world, it is impossible to behold the Divine presence, as it is written, כִּי לֹא יִרְאַנִי הָאָדָם וָחָי, *for no human can see Me and live* (*Exodus* 33:20). This is alluded to by the juxtaposition of [the verse containing the phrase,] אֲשֶׁר עַיִן בְּעַיִן, *that eye to eye* [*You, HASHEM,*] *appeared* [*to them*], with the term וְהֵמַתָּה, *yet You put* [*this people*] *to death* (v. 15). However, in the Time to Come, they will see [God][49] and they will say, זֶה ה׳ קִוִּינוּ לוֹ, *This is HASHEM,*[50] *we*

48. The prepositional prefix בְּ־ usually means "in," e.g., בְּאֹהֶל, *in the tent of* (v. 10), or "with," e.g., בָּאֲבָנִים, *with stones* (v. 10). However, it is also used for other prepositions such as: "at the time of," e.g., בַּלַּיְלָה, *at night* (v. 1); "through" or "by," e.g., בַּחֶרֶב, *by the sword* (v. 3); "against," e.g., בַּה׳, *against HASHEM* (v. 9); ; "despite," e.g., בְּכֹל, *despite all* (v. 11); "to," e.g., בְּקוֹלִי, *to My voice* (v. 22). Thus, each of the three instances of עַיִן בְּעַיִן is translated into English with a different preposition — *to, by* and *for.*

49. As implied by the verse: *For eye by eye they will see when HASHEM returns to Zion.*

50. The Talmud explains this verse: In the future the Holy One, Blessed is He, will make a circle of the righteous people in the Garden of Eden and He will sit in the center of the circle. Each and every one [of the righteous] will point [toward Him] with his finger — as it is stated (*Isaiah* 25:9): *He shall say on that day, "Behold! this is our God; we have hoped to Him and He has saved us; this is HASHEM, we have hoped to Him; let us exult and be*

14/15-16 — *that eye to eye, You,* HASHEM, *appeared and Your cloud stands over them, and that in a pillar of cloud You go before them by day and in a pillar of fire at night —* [15] *yet You put this people to death like a single man!' Then the nations that heard of Your fame will say,* [16] *'Because of the lack of ability on the part of* HASHEM *to bring this people to the land that He had sworn to give them, He slaughtered them in the wilderness.'*

BAAL HATURIM ELUCIDATED

have hoped to Him (*Isaiah* 25:9).[51]

[The similarity of expression] is also an allusion to that which the Sages expounded: The expression עַיִן בְּעַיִן, *eye for eye,* refers [not to inflicting actual physical harm upon a person who injures another, rather it means] the payment of money.[52] Thus, [the verse containing] the phrase עַיִן בְּעַיִן, *eye for eye,* is written here, and juxtaposed to it is the term וְהֵמַתָּה, *yet you put to death,* to indicate that if the court were to carry out *eye for eye* literally, [then וְהֵמַתָּה,] *you might put him to death* [while injuring his eye]. Therefore, the proper interpretation of עַיִן בְּעַיִן is that money must be paid [to compensate for the injured eye].

16. מִבִּלְתִּי — BECAUSE OF THE LACK. The masoretic note, ב׳, means that this word appears twice in the *Tanach:* (i) here, מִבִּלְתִּי יְכֹלֶת ה׳, [*The nations . . . will say,*] *"Because of the lack of ability*[53] *on the part of* HASHEM*";* and (ii) וַתִּזְנִי אֶל בְּנֵי אַשּׁוּר מִבִּלְתִּי שָׂבְעָתֵךְ, *You were licentious with the sons of Assyria, because of the lack of satiation on your part* (*Ezekiel* 16:28), with regard to the abominations [performed by the people] of Jerusalem. [The similarity of expression indicates,] as it were, that the sins of Israel make the *strong hand* (*Exodus* 32:11)[54] [with which God brought Israel out of Egypt] seem to be without the ability [to bring Israel into the Land of Canaan].

❑ **וַיִּשְׁחָטֵם בַּמִּדְבָּר — HE SLAUGHTERED THEM IN THE WILDERNESS.** [According to a scribal tradition,] the ח (= 8) of the word וַיִּשְׁחָטֵם is to be written as ח׳ שְׁבוּרָה, *a "broken" letter* ח.[55] This indicates that they transgressed upon the Torah

glad in His salvation" (*Taanis* 31a). The demonstrative pronoun זֶה, *this,* implies pointing at something that can be seen by the pointer. Thus, when they will say, זֶה ה׳, *This is* HASHEM, they will actually see the Divine Presence (see *Rashi* to *Exodus* 12:2, *Numbers* 8:4 and *I Samuel* 14:1).

51. *Maharam MiRothenburg.*

52. *Bava Kamma* 84a, where the Talmud expounds on the parallel verse *Exodus* 21:24. The Talmud there concludes that the expression עַיִן בְּעַיִן does not mean that an eye must be taken in revenge for an eye; rather, it refers to paying the value of the damaged eye. Although the Talmud records and rejects an argument similar to the one presented here by the Baal HaTurim as proof that that is the Torah's intention, the Talmud nevertheless accepts the interpretation of the verse as a reference to monetary compensation, but relies on other logical arguments to prove the point.

53. Translation follows *Rashi* and the *Targumim.*

54. That verse parallels ours: There Moses is praying that God spare the nation after the sin of the golden calf; here, he prays that God spare the nation after the sin of the spies.

55. According to *Sefer Tagin,* the ח of וַיִּשְׁחָטֵם is one of "37 in the Torah whose legs are פְּתָיִין, *spread wide* [alternatively: *broken*]." *Peirush HaRokeach,* the Baal HaTurim's apparent source for this comment, describes this ח as, "פְּתוּחָה וּשְׁבוּרָה רַגְלָהּ, *its leg is open and broken,*" a

*י׳ רבתי יז וְעַתָּה *יִגְדַּל־נָא כֹּחַ אֲדֹנָי כַּאֲשֶׁר דִּבַּרְתָּ לֵאמֹר:
יח יהוה אֶרֶךְ אַפַּיִם וְרַב־חֶסֶד נֹשֵׂא עָוֺן וָפָשַׁע וְנַקֵּה
לֹא יְנַקֶּה פֹּקֵד עֲוֺן אָבוֹת עַל־בָּנִים עַל־שִׁלֵּשִׁים
יט וְעַל־רִבֵּעִים: סְלַח־נָא לַעֲוֺן הָעָם הַזֶּה כְּגֹדֶל חַסְדֶּךָ

בעל הטורים

בִּכְלָל וְח׳ בְּרִיתוֹת בִּפְרָט. עַל כֵּן נִתַּן רְשׁוּת לְמַלְאֲכֵי חַבָּלָה לִפְרֹעַ עַל חַטָּאתָם:

(יז) **וְעַתָּה יִגְדַּל נָא כֹּחַ.** ״יִגְדַּל״ יוּ״ד גְּדוֹלָה — אָמַר, אִם נִסּוּךְ עֶשֶׂר פְּעָמִים בְּי׳ נִסְיוֹנוֹת, זְכֹר לָהֶם צִדְקַת אֲבִיהֶם, שֶׁנִּסִּיתָ אוֹתוֹ בְּי׳ נִסְיוֹנוֹת:

(יט) **כְּגֹדֶל.** ב׳ בַּמָּסוֹרֶת — ״כְּגֹדֶל חַסְדֶּךָ״; ״כְּגֹדֶל זְרוֹעֲךָ הוֹתֵר בְּנֵי תְמוּתָה״. זֶהוּ שֶׁאָמְרוּ, שְׁנֵי פַּרְנָסִים טוֹבִים עָמְדוּ לְיִשְׂרָאֵל, מֹשֶׁה וְדָוִד, שֶׁיָּדְעוּ לְהִתְפַּלֵּל עֲלֵיהֶם:

BAAL HATURIM ELUCIDATED

regarding which He established eight covenants[56] of a general nature and eight covenants of a particular nature.[57] As a consequence, He granted permission to the מַלְאֲכֵי חַבָּלָה, *destructive angels,* to take retribution for [58]חַטָּאתָם, *their sins.*[58a]

17. וְעַתָּה יִגְדַּל נָא כֹּחַ — AND NOW, MAY THE STRENGTH [OF THE LORD] BE MAGNIFIED. [According to a scribal tradition,] the י (= 10) of יִגְדַּל is to be written larger than usual. [This indicates that Moses] said, "If the people tested You ten times, with ten tests,[59]

---

description that includes both meanings of פַּתְיָין. As the illustration shows, the note does not mean that the leg of the ח is broken off from the rest of the letter. Rather, it refers to the legs being spread wide apart at the bottom, like a person's legs that have been fractured and are in an awkward position so that they cannot support their body. See illustration.

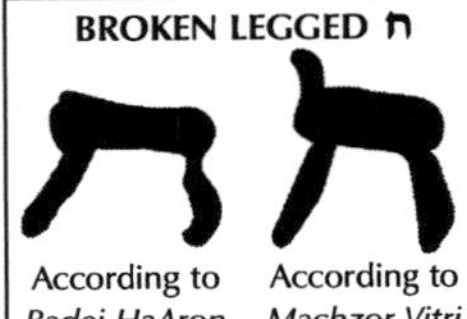

56. The reading בְּרִיתוֹת, *covenants,* follows the manuscripts used by *Shoham Yakar.* It is also found in *Peirush HaRokeach,* the Baal HaTurim's apparent source for this comment, as well as in the Baal HaTurim's comment at *Leviticus* 16:14 (in all editions).

The early printed editions and most later editions read כְּרִיתוֹת, *sealings,* a word derived from the verb root כרת, *to seal a covenant,* e.g., אָנֹכִי כֹּרֵת בְּרִית, *I seal a covenant* (*Exodus* 34:10). Thus, both readings refer to the same thing — the covenants sealed between God and Israel regarding the Torah. (See the Baal HaTurim to *Deuteronomy* 1:1, with note 4.)

57. The Rabbis taught: The term בָּרוּךְ, *blessed,* was stated regarding all the *mitzvos* as a whole, and *blessed* was stated regarding each *mitzvah* in particular; the term אָרוּר, *cursed,* was stated regarding the desecration of all *mitzvos* as a whole, and *cursed* was stated regarding each *mitzvah* in particular. Now the fulfillment of *mitzvos* entails many aspects: לִלְמֹד וּלְלַמֵּד לִשְׁמֹר וְלַעֲשׂוֹת, *to learn, to teach, to observe* and *to do,* thus there are four aspects of each *mitzvah* for which "Blessed" is stated as a generalization and four for which "Blessed" refers to a particular. Four plus four equal eight "Blessed's"; similarly there are eight "Cursed's." Eight plus eight equal sixteen covenants between God and Israel. . . (*Sotah* 37a-b as explained by *Minchas Bikkurim* to *Tosefta Sotah* 8:7). Eight of those covenants [four "Blessed's" and four "Cursed's"] were of a general nature and eight others of a particular nature.

58. The letter ח alludes to חַטָּאת (*Osios DeRabbi Akiva*).

58a. *Peirush HaRokeach,* whose comment ends: וְנָתַן רְשׁוּת לְמַלְאֲכֵי חַבָּלָה לִפְרֹעַ וּלְשַׁבְּרָם, *He granted permission to the destructive angels to take retribution and to break them.* Thus, the allusion of the ח׳ שְׁבוּרָה, *"broken"* ח.

59. See v. 22 below. The Talmud enumerates the ten times that Israel tested God: (i) At the sea, when the Israelites showed a lack of trust in God by complaining, "Were there no graves in Egypt that you took us to die in the wilderness?"

[17] *And now, may the strength of the Lord be magnified as You have spoken, saying,* [18] *'HASHEM, Slow to Anger, Abundant in Kindness, Forgiver of Iniquity and Willful Sin, and Who cleanses — but does not cleanse completely, recalling the iniquity of parents upon children to the third and fourth generations' —* [19] *forgive now the iniquity of this people as befits the greatness of Your kindness*

BAAL HATURIM ELUCIDATED

remember the righteousness of their father [Abraham] whom You tested with ten tests."[60,60a]

❑ {The Baal HaTurim's other comment on the enlarged י of יִגְדַּל appears at *Deuteronomy* 32:18.}

19. כְּגֹדֶל — AS BEFITS THE GREATNESS. The masoretic note, ב׳, means that this word appears twice in the *Tanach:* (i) here, כְּגֹדֶל חַסְדֶּךָ, *as befits the greatness of Your kindness;* and (ii) כְּגֹדֶל זְרוֹעֲךָ הוֹתֵר בְּנֵי תְמוּתָה, *as befits the greatness of Your might, spare those condemned to die* (*Psalms* 79:11). The similarity of expression alludes to the Talmudic statement: Two excellent leaders arose for Israel — Moses and David[61] — for they both knew how to pray on Israel's behalf.[62]

(*Exodus* 14:11); (ii) also at the sea, when *they rebelled about the sea, at the Sea of Reeds* (*Psalms* 106:7) — after the Israelites crossed the sea, they demonstrated a lack of faith by saying, "Just as we are emerging from the sea on this side, so are the Egyptians emerging on the other, and they will pursue us again"; (iii) they were commanded not to leave over any manna until the morning, yet some did (see *Exodus* 16:19-20); (iv) some Israelites went out to gather manna on *Shabbos,* although they had been commanded not to (see *Exodus* 16:27); (v-vi) twice the Israelites asked for meat in an ungrateful manner (see *Exodus* 16:3 and *Numbers* 11:4); (vii-viii) twice they complained of lack of water (see *Exodus* 15:24 and 17:2); (ix) the sin of the Golden Calf (see *Exodus,* Ch. 32); and (x) the sin of the spies in our passage (*Arachin* 15a-b).

60. The Mishnah states that Abraham underwent ten trials (*Avos* 5:3; see also *Pirkei DeRabbi Eliezer* 26). *Rashi* [other *Rishonim* present variant listings of the ten trials; e.g., *Rabbeinu Yonah* to *Avos*] enumerates them in his commentary there [all verse references are to *Genesis*]: (i) Nimrod wanted to kill Abraham, who had to hide underground for thirteen years; (ii) Nimrod cast him into the blazing furnace (see *Rashi* to 11:28); (iii) God exiled him from his birthplace (12:1); (iv) God brought famine during his lifetime (12:10); (v) Sarah was abducted by Pharaoh and Abimelech (12:15, 20:2); (vi) he had to wage war against Chedarlaomer and his allies when they took Lot captive (14:14-15); (vii) at the Covenant Between the Parts, God showed him a vision of the subjugation of his descendants at the hands of the Four Kingdoms (15:12-16; see *Rashi* to 15:14); (viii) God commanded him to circumcise himself and his son Ishmael (17:10); (ix) God told him to send away both his son Ishmael and Ishmael's mother Hagar (21:12); and (x) God commanded him to sacrifice his son, Isaac (22:2).

60a. *R' Yehudah HaChassid.*

61. *Yoma* 86b. Although the Talmud there uses this statement in contrasting Moses and David, the Baal HaTurim (both here and at *Exodus* 4:31) uses it to show that they were cut of the same cloth. (See also *Sefer HaChassidim* 355, which compares Moses and David in many other ways.)

62. The Baal HaTurim's comment seems to be based on the fact that the Book of *Psalms,* in which the second appearance of כְּגֹדֶל occurs, was composed by King David. But this assumption is difficult, for the Talmud states: David wrote the Book of *Psalms* in collaboration with ten elders — with Adam, the first man; with Malchi-zedek; with Abraham; with Moses; with Heman; with Jeduthun; with Asaph; and with the

וְכַאֲשֶׁר נָשָׂאתָה לָעָם הַזֶּה מִמִּצְרַיִם וְעַד־הֵנָּה׃
כ־כא וַיֹּאמֶר יהוה סָלַחְתִּי כִּדְבָרֶךָ׃ וְאוּלָם חַי־אָנִי
כב וְיִמָּלֵא כְבוֹד־יהוה אֶת־כָּל־הָאָרֶץ׃ כִּי כָל־
הָאֲנָשִׁים הָרֹאִים אֶת־כְּבֹדִי וְאֶת־אֹתֹתַי אֲשֶׁר־
עָשִׂיתִי בְמִצְרַיִם וּבַמִּדְבָּר וַיְנַסּוּ אֹתִי זֶה עֶשֶׂר
כג פְּעָמִים וְלֹא שָׁמְעוּ בְּקוֹלִי׃ אִם־יִרְאוּ אֶת־הָאָרֶץ
אֲשֶׁר נִשְׁבַּעְתִּי לַאֲבֹתָם וְכָל־מְנַאֲצַי לֹא יִרְאוּהָ׃
כד וְעַבְדִּי כָלֵב עֵקֶב הָיְתָה רוּחַ אַחֶרֶת עִמּוֹ וַיְמַלֵּא
אַחֲרָי וַהֲבִיאֹתִיו אֶל־הָאָרֶץ אֲשֶׁר־בָּא שָׁמָּה וְזַרְעוֹ
כה יוֹרִשֶׁנָּה׃ וְהָעֲמָלֵקִי וְהַכְּנַעֲנִי יוֹשֵׁב בָּעֵמֶק מָחָר פְּנוּ
וּסְעוּ לָכֶם הַמִּדְבָּר דֶּרֶךְ יַם־סוּף׃
רביעי כו־כו וַיְדַבֵּר יהוה אֶל־מֹשֶׁה וְאֶל־אַהֲרֹן לֵאמֹר׃ עַד־מָתַי
לָעֵדָה הָרָעָה הַזֹּאת אֲשֶׁר הֵמָּה מַלִּינִים עָלָי
אֶת־תְּלֻנּוֹת בְּנֵי יִשְׂרָאֵל אֲשֶׁר הֵמָּה מַלִּינִים עָלַי
כח שָׁמָעְתִּי׃ אֱמֹר אֲלֵהֶם חַי־אָנִי נְאֻם־יהוה אִם־לֹא
כט כַּאֲשֶׁר דִּבַּרְתֶּם בְּאָזְנָי כֵּן אֶעֱשֶׂה לָכֶם׃ בַּמִּדְבָּר הַזֶּה
יִפְּלוּ פִגְרֵיכֶם וְכָל־פְּקֻדֵיכֶם לְכָל־מִסְפַּרְכֶם מִבֶּן
ל עֶשְׂרִים שָׁנָה וָמָעְלָה אֲשֶׁר הֲלִינֹתֶם עָלָי׃ אִם־אַתֶּם
תָּבֹאוּ אֶל־הָאָרֶץ אֲשֶׁר נָשָׂאתִי אֶת־יָדִי לְשַׁכֵּן
אֶתְכֶם בָּהּ כִּי אִם־כָּלֵב בֶּן־יְפֻנֶּה וִיהוֹשֻׁעַ בִּן־נוּן׃

בעל הטורים

(כד) **יוֹרִשֶׁנָּה.** ב׳ בַּמָּסוֹרֶת – ״וְזַרְעוֹ יוֹרִשֶׁנָּה״; ״הִנֵּה אֲדֹנָי יוֹרִשֶׁנָּה״. שֶׁלֹּא הָיָה יָכוֹל לְהוֹרִישָׁם אִלְמָלֵא שֶׁה׳ הוֹרִישָׁם מִפָּנָיו:

BAAL HATURIM ELUCIDATED

24. {Regarding the Baal HaTurim's comment to וַהֲבִיאֹתִיו that appears at this point in some editions, see at v. 31 below.[63]}

three sons of Korah (*Bava Basra* 14b-15a). That is, David included various psalms that had been composed by elders of earlier generations [Adam, Malchi-zedek, Abraham, Moses, the three sons of Korah] and some by his contemporaries, namely, Asaph, Heman and Jeduthun, members of the Levite choir (*Rashi*). Accordingly, psalm 79, which begins, מִזְמוֹר לְאָסָף, *A psalm of Asaph,* was not written by King David. Thus, the Baal HaTurim's ascription of the term כְּגֹדֶל to David is problematic (*VeChur LaZahav*).

63. See note 65.

and as You have forgiven this people from Egypt until now."
20 And HASHEM said, "I have forgiven because of your
words. 21 But as I live — and the glory of HASHEM shall fill the
entire world — 22 that all the men who have seen My glory
and My signs that I performed in Egypt and in the
wilderness, and have tested Me these ten times and have
not hearkened to My voice, 23 if they will see the land that I
have sworn to give their forefathers! — and all who anger
Me shall not see it. 24 But My servant Caleb, because a
different spirit was with him and he followed Me wholeheart-
edly, I shall bring him to the Land to which he came, and his
offspring will drive it[s inhabitant] out. 25 The Amalekite and
the Canaanite dwell in the valley — tomorrow, turn and
journey toward the wilderness in the direction of the Sea of
Reeds."
26 HASHEM spoke to Moses and Aaron, saying, 27 "How
long for this evil assembly that provokes complaints against
Me!? I have heard the complaints of the Children of Israel
whom they provoke against Me. 28 Say to them: As I live —
the word of HASHEM — if I shall not do to you as you have
spoken in My ears . 29 In this wilderness shall your carcasses
drop; all of you who were counted in any of your number-
ings, from twenty years of age and above, whom you
provoked against Me; 30 if you shall come to the land about
which I have raised My hand in an oath to settle you there,
except for Caleb son of Jephunneh and Joshua son of Nun.

BAAL HATURIM ELUCIDATED

❑ **יוֹרִשֶׁנָּה — WILL DRIVE IT[S INHABITANT] OUT.** The masoretic note, ב׳, means that this word appears twice in the *Tanach:*[64] (i) here, וְזַרְעוֹ יוֹרִשֶׁנָּה, *and his offspring will drive it*[*s inhabitant*] *out,* and (ii) [with a different meaning in,] הִנֵּה אֲדֹנָי יוֹרִשֶׁנָּה, *Behold, the Lord will impoverish her* (*Zechariah* 9:4). This indicates that Israel would not have been able to drive out the inhabitants had God not impoverished them first.

64. The full note reads: ב׳ בְּתְרֵי לִישָּׁנֵי, *Twice, with two meanings.* The meaning of the verb root ירש is dependent upon its conjugation. In the simple *kal,* ירש means *to take possession.* In the causative *hifil* it means *to drive out* or *to impoverish.* The form יוֹרִשֶׁנָּה is in the *hifil;* it is composed of the third person masculine future form יוֹרִישׁ, *he will drive out,* or *he will impoverish,* and the suffix ־נָּה, *her* or *it.* According to *Rashi,* וְזַרְעוֹ יוֹרִשֶׁנָּה of our verse means *and his* [i.e., Caleb's] *offspring will drive out* [*the nation that occupies*] *it;* and ה׳ יוֹרִשֶׁנָּה of *Zechariah* means *God will impoverish her,* a reference to the destruction of Tyre. Thus, the masoretic note states that the word is used with two different meanings.

יד/לא־לח

לא וְטַפְּכֶם אֲשֶׁר אֲמַרְתֶּם לָבַז יִהְיֶה וְהֵבֵיאתִי אֹתָם וְיָדְעוּ
לב אֶת־הָאָרֶץ אֲשֶׁר מְאַסְתֶּם בָּהּ: וּפִגְרֵיכֶם אַתֶּם יִפְּלוּ
לג בַּמִּדְבָּר הַזֶּה: וּבְנֵיכֶם יִהְיוּ רֹעִים בַּמִּדְבָּר אַרְבָּעִים
שָׁנָה וְנָשְׂאוּ אֶת־זְנוּתֵיכֶם עַד־תֹּם פִּגְרֵיכֶם בַּמִּדְבָּר:
לד בְּמִסְפַּר הַיָּמִים אֲשֶׁר־תַּרְתֶּם אֶת־הָאָרֶץ אַרְבָּעִים
יוֹם יוֹם לַשָּׁנָה יוֹם לַשָּׁנָה תִּשְׂאוּ אֶת־עֲוֺנֹתֵיכֶם
לה אַרְבָּעִים שָׁנָה וִידַעְתֶּם אֶת־תְּנוּאָתִי: אֲנִי יהוה
דִּבַּרְתִּי אִם־לֹא ׀ זֹאת אֶעֱשֶׂה לְכָל־הָעֵדָה הָרָעָה
הַזֹּאת הַנּוֹעָדִים עָלָי בַּמִּדְבָּר הַזֶּה יִתַּמּוּ וְשָׁם יָמֻתוּ:
לו וְהָאֲנָשִׁים אֲשֶׁר־שָׁלַח מֹשֶׁה לָתוּר אֶת־הָאָרֶץ וַיָּשֻׁבוּ
°וילונו עָלָיו אֶת־כָּל־הָעֵדָה לְהוֹצִיא דִבָּה עַל־ [°וַיַּלִּינוּ ק׳]
לז הָאָרֶץ: וַיָּמֻתוּ הָאֲנָשִׁים מוֹצִאֵי דִבַּת־הָאָרֶץ רָעָה
לח בַּמַּגֵּפָה לִפְנֵי יהוה: וִיהוֹשֻׁעַ בִּן־נוּן וְכָלֵב בֶּן־יְפֻנֶּה חָיוּ

בעל הטורים

(לא) וְהֵבֵיאתִי. יו״ד יְתֵרָה — שֶׁאָבִיא אוֹתָם אֶל הָאָרֶץ שֶׁנִּתְקַדְּשָׁה בְּעֶשֶׂר קְדֻשּׁוֹת:

(לב) וּפִגְרֵיכֶם אַתֶּם. פֵּרוּשׁ, כַּאֲשֶׁר אַתֶּם בִּבְרִיאוּתְכֶם, כֵּן תַּשְׁכִּיבוּ עַצְמְכֶם וְתָמוּתוּ:

(לח) חָיוּ. בְּאַ״תְ בַּ״שׁ סמ״ךְ, שֶׁהוּא בְּגִימַטְרִיָּא בְּחֶלְקָם. שֶׁחָיוּ בְּחֶלְקָם:

BAAL HATURIM ELUCIDATED

31. וְהֵבֵיאתִי — I SHALL BRING.[65] This word is spelled with a superfluous י (= 10). This indicates that [God meant], "I shall bring them to the Land [of Israel,] which has been sanctified with ten levels of holiness."[66]

---

65. One of the manuscripts used by *Shoham Yakar* has this comment under the rubric וַהֲבִיאֹתִיו, which appears in verse 24. That version appears in some later printed editions and seems to have been the reading in the edition used by *Ittur Bikkurim,* even though the version of the Baal HaTurim that appears above *Ittur Bikkurim* reads וְהֵבֵיאתִי. However, it is difficult to consider that י as a superfluous letter, for it appears again in הֲבִיאֹתִיו (*Genesis* 43:9), וַהֲבִיאוֹתִיהוּ (*Ezekiel* 17:20) and וַהֲבִיאוֹתִים (*Isaiah* 56:7, *Ezekiel* 34:13).

All the early printed editions, however, have this comment on the word וְהֵבֵיאתִי of verse 31. Indeed, the verb form הֵבֵאתִי, with and without the prefix ־וְ, appears twenty-nine times. Only here is it spelled with a י after the ב (see *Minchas Shai*). Moreover, this comment appears under וְהֵבֵיאתִי in *Peirush HaRokeach,* the Baal HaTurim's apparent source, and in *Rimzei Rabbeinu Yoel.*

66. *Peirush HaRokeach; Rimzei Rabbeinu Yoel.* The Mishnah discusses the holiness of *Eretz Yisrael* [the Land of Israel]: [Within *Eretz Yisrael*] there are ten enhanced levels of holiness. *Eretz Yisrael* is the holiest of all lands . . . [The enhanced levels are:] (i) Its walled cities have a higher level of holiness . . .; (ii) the area within the walls of Jerusalem is holier . . .; (iii) the Temple Mount is holier . . .; (iv) the *cheil* [a narrow area surrounding the walls of the Temple Courtyard] is holier . . .; (v) the Women's Courtyard is holier . . .; (vi) the Israelites' Courtyard is holier . . .; (vii) the *Kohanim's* Courtyard is holier . . .; (viii) the area between the *Ulam* [Entrance Hall] and the [Outer] Altar is holier . . .; (ix) within the Sanctuary is holier . . .; and (x) the Holy of Holies is holier . . . (*Keilim* 1:6-9).

[31] *And your youngsters of whom you said they will be taken captive, I shall bring them; they shall know the land that you have despised.* [32] *But your carcasses — yourselves — shall fall in this wilderness.* [33] *Your children will graze in the wilderness for forty years and bear your guilt, until the last of your carcasses in the wilderness.* [34] *Like the number of the days that you spied out the land, forty days, a day for a year, a day for a year, shall you bear your iniquities — forty years — and you shall comprehend straying from Me.* [35] *I HASHEM have spoken — if I shall not do this to this entire evil assembly that gathers against Me! In this wilderness shall they cease to be, and there shall they die!"*

[36] *But as for the men whom Moses sent to spy out the land, and who returned and provoked the entire assembly against him by spreading a report against the land —* [37] *the people who spread the evil report about the land died in a plague before HASHEM.* [38] *But [concerning] Joshua son of Nun and Caleb son of Jephunneh, they lived*

BAAL HATURIM ELUCIDATED

32. וּפִגְרֵיכֶם אַתֶּם — literally, **YOUR CARCASSES — YOURSELVES.** This means: When you are yet in your good health,[67] you shall lay down and you shall die.[68]

36. {The Baal HaTurim's explanation of the *keri uchesiv* וילונו/וַיַּלִּינוּ appears at 16:11 below.}

38. חָיוּ — THEY LIVED. In the *aleph-beis* exchange[69] known as אַ״תְּ בַּ״שׁ [the letters of חָיוּ correspond to] סמ״ך, whose *gematria* (180) is equal to that of בְּחֶלְקָם, *in their portion.* This indicates that they [Joshua and Caleb were given and] lived in their [i.e., the other spies'] portions.[70]

67. That is, אַתֶּם, *you,* refers to a time when you are still the same "you" that you have always been, namely, in your full health.

68. The Talmud relates that the spies returned to the camp on the eighth of Av. That night, the ninth of Av, after having heard the evil report, the nation wept. God said, "You wept needlessly; as a consequence, I will establish a weeping for all generations" (*Taanis* 29a). From that time onward, for as long as the Israelites were in the wilderness, on the eighth of Av each year Moses would proclaim, "Go out and dig. Go out and dig." All the men between twenty and sixty years old would go out and dig graves for themselves. Each of them would lie down to sleep in the grave he had dug for himself. In the morning, they would arise to find that [one-fortieth of their number, i.e.,] fifteen thousand of them had died during the night . . . (*Yerushalmi, Taanis* 4:7; *Eichah Rabbasi, Pesichta* 33, cited by *Rashbam* to *Bava Basra* 121a, s.v., שכלו בו מתי מדבר).

69. See note 30 at 9:2 above.

70. *Rimzei Rabbeinu Yoel.* According to the Talmud, in addition to their own portions of land, Joshua and Caleb also received the portions that were designated for the other ten spies. This is derived from our verse, *But Joshua son of Nun and Caleb son of Jephunneh lived from among those men going to spy out the land.* Whereas the Torah states elsewhere, *and not a man was left of them except for Caleb son of Jephunneh and Joshua son of Nun* (26:65 below), our verse is superfluous. It must therefore be understood as implying, *they lived* in land *received from those men going to spy out the land* (*Bava Basra* 118b; cited by *Rashi* here).

מִן־הָאֲנָשִׁים הָהֵם הַהֹלְכִים לָתוּר אֶת־הָאָרֶץ:
לט וַיְדַבֵּר מֹשֶׁה אֶת־הַדְּבָרִים הָאֵלֶּה אֶל־כָּל־בְּנֵי
מ יִשְׂרָאֵל וַיִּתְאַבְּלוּ הָעָם מְאֹד: וַיַּשְׁכִּמוּ בַבֹּקֶר וַיַּעֲלוּ
אֶל־רֹאשׁ־הָהָר לֵאמֹר הִנֶּנּוּ וְעָלִינוּ אֶל־הַמָּקוֹם
מא אֲשֶׁר־אָמַר יהוה כִּי חָטָאנוּ: וַיֹּאמֶר מֹשֶׁה לָמָּה זֶּה
אַתֶּם עֹבְרִים אֶת־פִּי יהוה וְהִוא לֹא תִצְלָח:
מב אַל־תַּעֲלוּ כִּי אֵין יהוה בְּקִרְבְּכֶם וְלֹא תִּנָּגְפוּ לִפְנֵי
מג אֹיְבֵיכֶם: כִּי הָעֲמָלֵקִי וְהַכְּנַעֲנִי שָׁם לִפְנֵיכֶם וּנְפַלְתֶּם
בֶּחָרֶב כִּי־עַל־כֵּן שַׁבְתֶּם מֵאַחֲרֵי יהוה וְלֹא־יִהְיֶה
מד יהוה עִמָּכֶם: וַיַּעְפִּלוּ לַעֲלוֹת אֶל־רֹאשׁ הָהָר וַאֲרוֹן
מה בְּרִית־יהוה וּמֹשֶׁה לֹא־מָשׁוּ מִקֶּרֶב הַמַּחֲנֶה: וַיֵּרֶד
הָעֲמָלֵקִי וְהַכְּנַעֲנִי הַיֹּשֵׁב בָּהָר הַהוּא וַיַּכּוּם וַיַּכְּתוּם
עַד־הַחָרְמָה:

טו

א־ב וַיְדַבֵּר יהוה אֶל־מֹשֶׁה לֵּאמֹר: דַּבֵּר אֶל־בְּנֵי יִשְׂרָאֵל
וְאָמַרְתָּ אֲלֵהֶם כִּי תָבֹאוּ אֶל־אֶרֶץ מוֹשְׁבֹתֵיכֶם
ג אֲשֶׁר אֲנִי נֹתֵן לָכֶם: וַעֲשִׂיתֶם אִשֶּׁה לַיהוה

בעל הטורים

(מ) **וְעָלִינוּ.** ב׳ בַּמָּסוֹרֶת — ״הִנֶּנּוּ וְעָלִינוּ״; ״וְאִם כֹּה יֹאמְרוּ עֲלוּ עָלֵינוּ וְעָלִינוּ״. זֶה שֶׁאָמַר ״כִּי אֵין לַה׳ מַעְצוֹר לְהוֹשִׁיעַ בְּרַב אוֹ בִמְעָט״. אֵלּוּ הָיוּ שִׁשִּׁים רִבּוֹא וְנָפְלוּ, וִיהוֹנָתָן לֹא הָיוּ אֶלָּא הוּא וְנַעֲרוֹ וְנִצְּחוּ:

(מד) **וַיַּעְפִּלוּ.** בְּגִימַטְרִיָּא ״צְלָפְחָד״, דְּאִיכָּא לְמַאן דְּאָמַר מִן הַמַּפְעִילִים הָיָה:

טו (ג) **וַעֲשִׂיתֶם אִשֶּׁה לַה׳.** סָמַךְ פָּרָשַׁת נְסָכִים לְמִלְחָמָה {לְפִי שֶׁדֶּרֶךְ לִידּוֹר בְּמִלְחָמָה}.

BAAL HATURIM ELUCIDATED

40. וְעָלִינוּ — AND WE SHALL GO UP. The masoretic note, ב׳, means that this word appears twice in the *Tanach:* (i) here, הִנֶּנּוּ וְעָלִינוּ, *Here we are, and we shall go up;* and (ii) [with regard to Jonathan's attack on the Philistines], וְאִם כֹּה יֹאמְרוּ עֲלוּ עָלֵינוּ וְעָלִינוּ, *But if they say thus: 'Come up to us!' then we shall go up* (*I Samuel* 14:10). [The similarity of expression] is in accord with another verse [in that passage], כִּי אֵין לַה׳ מַעְצוֹר לְהוֹשִׁיעַ בְּרַב אוֹ בִמְעָט, *For there is no obstacle to* [*prevent*] *Hashem from saving, whether through many or through few* (v. 6 there). These [of our passage] numbered 600,000 men, yet they were defeated. But [in the incident of] Jonathan, none were present except him and his armor-bearer, yet they were victorious.[71]

71. The full story of the miraculous victory and its aftermath appears in *I Samuel,* Chapter 14.

from among those men going to spy out the land.

39 Moses spoke these words to all of the Children of Israel, and the people mourned exceedingly.

40 They awoke early in the morning and ascended toward the mountaintop saying, "Here we are, and we shall go up to the place of which HASHEM *has spoken, for we have sinned!"*

41 Moses said, "Why do you transgress the word of HASHEM*? It will not succeed. 42 Do not ascend, for* HASHEM *is not in your midst! And do not be smitten before your enemies. 43 For the Amalekite and the Canaanite are there before you, and you will fall by the sword, because you have turned away from* HASHEM*, and* HASHEM *will not be with you."*

44 But they were intransigent [in their desire] to ascend to the mountaintop, while the Ark of HASHEM*'s covenant and Moses did not move from the midst of the camp. 45 The Amalekite and the Canaanite who dwelled on that mountain descended and struck them and pounded them until Hormah.*

15 *1* HASHEM *spoke to Moses, saying, 2 "Speak to the Children of Israel and say to them: When you will come to the land of your dwelling places that I give you, 3 and you will make a*

BAAL HATURIM ELUCIDATED

44. וַיַּעְפִּלוּ — BUT THEY WERE INTRANSIGENT. The *gematria* of וַיַּעְפִּילוּ[72] (212) is equal to that of צְלָפְחָד, *Zelophehad.* For there is an opinion that he was one of the intransigent ones.[73]

XV

3. וַעֲשִׂיתֶם אִשֶּׁה לַה' — AND YOU WILL MAKE A FIRE-OFFERING TO HASHEM. The Torah juxtaposed the passage concerning the wine libations with the account of a battle (14:45 above) {for it is proper to vow to bring offerings in time of war[74]}.[74a]

72. Although the verse spells the word without the second י, that י is usually present in the *hifil* conjugation. Thus, the Baal HaTurim uses the full spelling for his allusion.

73. *R' Yehudah HaChassid.* Zelophehad is mentioned in *parashas Pinechas,* in the passage regarding inheritances. He had five daughters and no sons. They approached Moses with the request that they inherit their father's portion in *Eretz Yisrael,* even though *"he had died of his sin"* (27:3 below). The Talmud cites two opinions regarding the nature of Zelophehad's sin: He was either the one who gathered wood on the Sabbath (see 15:32 below) or one of the uncompromising ones of our verse (*Shabbos* 96b-97a). The Baal HaTurim finds an allusion in support of the second opinion.

It is noteworthy that Zelophehad's daughters had inherited their father's uncompromising desire for a portion of the Land of Israel (Y.S.). However, he sought to fulfill his otherwise admirable desire with undisciplined self-righteousness that eventually led to his death. His daughters, on the other hand, approached Moses with dignity and restraint, as they sought to obtain their objective through persuasive halachic reasoning (*VeChur LaZahav*).

74. See *Bereishis Rabbah* 70:1.

74a. The passage enclosed in braces is not found in the printed editions, but does appear in *Shoham Yakar's* manuscript edition.

עֹלָה אוֹ־זֶבַח לְפַלֵּא־נֶדֶר אוֹ בִנְדָבָה אוֹ בְּמֹעֲדֵיכֶם
לַעֲשׂוֹת רֵיחַ נִיחֹחַ לַיהוָה מִן־הַבָּקָר אוֹ מִן־
ד הַצֹּאן: וְהִקְרִיב הַמַּקְרִיב קָרְבָּנוֹ לַיהוָה מִנְחָה סֹלֶת
ה עִשָּׂרוֹן בָּלוּל בִּרְבִעִית הַהִין שָׁמֶן: וְיַיִן לַנֶּסֶךְ
רְבִיעִית הַהִין תַּעֲשֶׂה עַל־הָעֹלָה אוֹ לַזָּבַח לַכֶּבֶשׂ
ו הָאֶחָד: אוֹ לָאַיִל תַּעֲשֶׂה מִנְחָה סֹלֶת שְׁנֵי עֶשְׂרֹנִים
ז בְּלוּלָה בַשֶּׁמֶן שְׁלִשִׁית הַהִין: וְיַיִן לַנֶּסֶךְ שְׁלִשִׁית
חמישי ח הַהִין תַּקְרִיב רֵיחַ־נִיחֹחַ לַיהוָה: וְכִי־תַעֲשֶׂה
בֶן־בָּקָר עֹלָה אוֹ־זָבַח לְפַלֵּא־נֶדֶר אוֹ־שְׁלָמִים
ט לַיהוָה: וְהִקְרִיב עַל־בֶּן־הַבָּקָר מִנְחָה סֹלֶת שְׁלֹשָׁה
י עֶשְׂרֹנִים בָּלוּל בַּשֶּׁמֶן חֲצִי הַהִין: וְיַיִן תַּקְרִיב
יא לַנֶּסֶךְ חֲצִי הַהִין אִשֵּׁה רֵיחַ־נִיחֹחַ לַיהוָה: כָּכָה
יֵעָשֶׂה לַשּׁוֹר הָאֶחָד אוֹ לָאַיִל הָאֶחָד אוֹ־לַשֶּׂה
יב בַכְּבָשִׂים אוֹ בָעִזִּים: כַּמִּסְפָּר אֲשֶׁר תַּעֲשׂוּ כָּכָה
יג תַּעֲשׂוּ לָאֶחָד כְּמִסְפָּרָם: כָּל־הָאֶזְרָח יַעֲשֶׂה־
כָּכָה אֶת־אֵלֶּה לְהַקְרִיב אִשֵּׁה רֵיחַ־נִיחֹחַ לַיהוָה:
יד וְכִי־יָגוּר אִתְּכֶם גֵּר אוֹ אֲשֶׁר־בְּתוֹכְכֶם לְדֹרֹתֵיכֶם
וְעָשָׂה אִשֵּׁה רֵיחַ־נִיחֹחַ לַיהוָה כַּאֲשֶׁר תַּעֲשׂוּ
טו כֵּן יַעֲשֶׂה: הַקָּהָל חֻקָּה אַחַת לָכֶם וְלַגֵּר הַגָּר
חֻקַּת עוֹלָם לְדֹרֹתֵיכֶם כָּכֶם כַּגֵּר יִהְיֶה לִפְנֵי יְהוָה:
טז תּוֹרָה אַחַת וּמִשְׁפָּט אֶחָד יִהְיֶה לָכֶם וְלַגֵּר הַגָּר
אִתְּכֶם:

ששי יז-יח וַיְדַבֵּר יְהוָה אֶל־מֹשֶׁה לֵּאמֹר: דַּבֵּר אֶל־בְּנֵי
יִשְׂרָאֵל וְאָמַרְתָּ אֲלֵהֶם בְּבֹאֲכֶם אֶל־הָאָרֶץ
יט אֲשֶׁר אֲנִי מֵבִיא אֶתְכֶם שָׁמָּה: וְהָיָה בַּאֲכָלְכֶם

בעל הטורים

וְכֵן בְּפִינְחָס "אֲשֶׁר יֵצֵא לִפְנֵיהֶם", סָמַךְ מִיָּד פָּרָשַׁת קָרְבָּנוֹת:

BAAL HATURIM ELUCIDATED

Similarly, in *parashas Pinechas,* the passage containing the verse, *one who will go out* [*to battle*] *before them* (27:17 below), is juxtaposed with the passage of the

fire-offering to HASHEM — a burnt-offering or a [peace-offering]
sacrifice, because of an articulated vow or as a free-will
offering, or on your festivals, to produce a satisfying aroma to
HASHEM, from the cattle or from the flock — 4 *the one who*
brings his offering to HASHEM shall bring a meal-offering of a
tenth[-ephah] fine flour, mixed with a quarter-hin of oil; 5 *and a*
quarter-hin of wine for a libation shall you prepare for the
burnt-offering or the [peace-offering] sacrifice for each sheep.
6 *Or for a ram — you shall prepare a meal-offering, two*
tenth[-ephah] fine flour mixed with a third-hin of oil; 7 *and a*
third-hin of wine for a libation shall you bring as a satisfying
aroma to HASHEM. 8 *When you prepare a young bull as a*
burnt-offering or a [peace-offering] sacrifice, because of an
articulated vow or peace-offering to HASHEM, 9 *one shall bring*
with the young bull a meal-offering: three tenth[-ephah] fine
flour mixed with a half-hin of oil. 10 *You shall bring a half-hin of*
wine for a libation, a fire-offering, a satisfying aroma to
HASHEM. 11 *So shall be done for each bull or for each ram, or*
for a lamb or kid among the sheep or goats. 12 *According to*
the number that you prepare, so shall you do for each one,
according to their number. 13 *Every native shall do so with*
them, to bring a fire-offering, a satisfying aroma to HASHEM.
14 *When a proselyte sojourns with you or one who is among*
you throughout your generations and he shall prepare a
fire-offering, a satisfying aroma to HASHEM — as you do, so
shall he do. 15 *For the congregation — the same decree shall*
be for you and for the proselyte who sojourns, an eternal
decree for your generations; like you like the proselyte shall it
be before HASHEM. 16 *One teaching and one judgment shall be*
for you and for the proselyte who sojourns among you."

17 *HASHEM spoke to Moses, saying,* 18 *"Speak to the Chil-*
dren of Israel and say to them: When you come to the land to
which I bring you, 19 *it shall be that when you will eat of the*

BAAL HATURIM ELUCIDATED

Altar's offerings (Chs. 28-29).[75]

12. {The Baal HaTurim's comment to לְאֶחָד appears at *Exodus* 16:22.}

75. *Ittur Bikkurim,* who was unaware of the interpolated passage, suggests that the Baal HaTurim means: שֶׁבִּזְכוּת הַקָּרְבָּנוֹת הָיוּ נוֹצְחִים בְּמִלְחָמָה, *for in the merit of the offerings they would be victorious in battle* (see the Baal HaTurim to *Exodus* 29:14). Subsequently, some later printed editions included that phrase as if it were part of the Baal HaTurim's comment.

כ מִלֶּחֶם הָאָרֶץ תָּרִימוּ תְרוּמָה לַיהוָה: רֵאשִׁית
עֲרִסֹתֵכֶם חַלָּה תָּרִימוּ תְרוּמָה כִּתְרוּמַת גֹּרֶן כֵּן
כא תָּרִימוּ אֹתָהּ: מֵרֵאשִׁית עֲרִסֹתֵיכֶם תִּתְּנוּ לַיהוָה
כב תְּרוּמָה לְדֹרֹתֵיכֶם: וְכִי תִשְׁגּוּ וְלֹא תַעֲשׂוּ אֵת
כָּל־הַמִּצְוֹת הָאֵלֶּה אֲשֶׁר־דִּבֶּר יהוה אֶל־מֹשֶׁה:
כג אֵת כָּל־אֲשֶׁר צִוָּה יהוה אֲלֵיכֶם בְּיַד־מֹשֶׁה מִן־
כד הַיּוֹם אֲשֶׁר צִוָּה יהוה וָהָלְאָה לְדֹרֹתֵיכֶם: וְהָיָה אִם
מֵעֵינֵי הָעֵדָה נֶעֶשְׂתָה לִשְׁגָגָה וְעָשׂוּ כָל־הָעֵדָה פַּר
בֶּן־בָּקָר אֶחָד לְעֹלָה לְרֵיחַ נִיחֹחַ לַיהוָה וּמִנְחָתוֹ
כה וְנִסְכּוֹ כַּמִּשְׁפָּט וּשְׂעִיר־עִזִּים אֶחָד לְחַטָּת: וְכִפֶּר
הַכֹּהֵן עַל־כָּל־עֲדַת בְּנֵי יִשְׂרָאֵל וְנִסְלַח לָהֶם כִּי־
שְׁגָגָה הִוא וְהֵם הֵבִיאוּ אֶת־קָרְבָּנָם אִשֶּׁה לַיהוָה
כו וְחַטָּאתָם לִפְנֵי יהוה עַל־שִׁגְגָתָם: וְנִסְלַח לְכָל־
עֲדַת בְּנֵי יִשְׂרָאֵל וְלַגֵּר הַגָּר בְּתוֹכָם כִּי לְכָל־הָעָם
כז בִּשְׁגָגָה: וְאִם־נֶפֶשׁ אַחַת תֶּחֱטָא בִשְׁגָגָה שביעי

בעל הטורים

(כ) חַלָּה. תָּגִין עַל הֵ״א. חֲמִשָּׁה דְבָרִים חַיָּבִין בְּחַלָּה. חֲמֵשֶׁת רְבָעִים קֶמַח חַיָּבִין:

(כא) מֵרֵאשִׁית עֲרִסֹתֵיכֶם. הַפָּסוּק מַתְחִיל בְּמֵ״ם וּמְסַיֵּם בְּמֵ״ם. לוֹמַר לְךָ, שֶׁתְּרוּמַת עַיִן יָפָה אֶחָד מֵאַרְבָּעִים:

BAAL HATURIM ELUCIDATED

20. חַלָּה — A LOAF. [According to a scribal tradition,] the ה (= 5) of חַלָּה is written with [extra] *tagin.*[76] They allude both to the five grains[76a] from which *challah*[77]

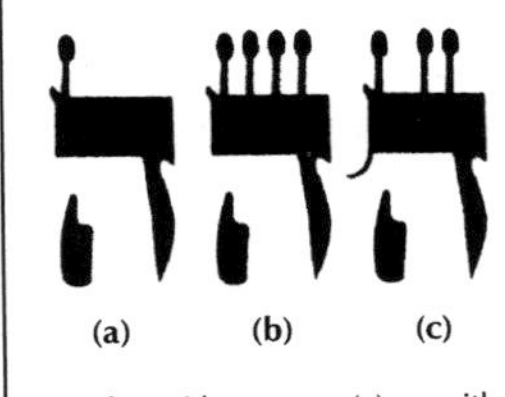

(a) (b) (c)

Usual ה with one *tag* (a). ה with four *tagin* according to *Machzor Vitry* (b), *Badei HaAron* (c).

76. *Sefer Tagin* lists חַלָּה of our verse as one of 360 words in the Torah in which the letter ה is written with four *tagin* instead of the usual one. See illustration.

76a. They are: חִטִּין, *wheat,* שְׂעוֹרִין, *barley,* כֻּסְּמִין or כֻּסֶּמֶת, *spelt,* שִׁבֹּלֶת שׁוּעָל, *oats,* and שִׁפּוֹן, *rye.* In referring to the five grains as חֲמִשָּׁה דְבָרִים, literally, *five things,* rather than חֲמֵשֶׁת הַמִּינִים, *the five species,* a term found more than thirty times in the Talmud, the Baal HaTurim follows the wording of the Mishnah, which never uses the term חֲמֵשֶׁת הַמִּינִים. Indeed, the Talmud asks why the Mishnah uses the general expression *five things* rather than the specific term *five species.* The Talmud answers that, in truth, the five grains comprise only three species, for שִׁפּוֹן is a subspecies of כֻּסְּמִין and שִׁבֹּלֶת שׁוּעָל is a subspecies of שְׂעוֹרִין (*Yerushalmi, Challah* 1:1; see also *Bavli, Pesachim* 35a).

77. The term חַלָּה means *loaf* and refers to the portion of each batch of dough that must be set aside as sanctified and given to a *Kohen.* The laws of *challah* as they apply today may be

bread of the land, you shall set aside a portion for HASHEM.
20 The first of your dough — a loaf — you shall set aside as
a portion, like the portion of the threshing-floor, so shall you
set it aside. 21 From the first of your dough you shall give a
portion to HASHEM, for your generations.
22 "If you err and do not perform all of these command-
ments, which HASHEM has spoken to Moses, 23 everything
that HASHEM commanded you through Moses, from the day
that HASHEM commanded and onward, throughout your
generations. 24 If because of the eyes of the assembly it was
done unintentionally, the entire assembly shall prepare one
young bull as a burnt-offering for a satisfying aroma to
HASHEM, and its meal-offering and its libation according to
the rule, and one he-goat as a sin-offering. 25 The Kohen
shall atone for the entire assembly of the Children of Israel
and it shall be forgiven them, for it was unintentional, and
they have brought their offering, a fire-offering to HASHEM,
and their sin-offering before HASHEM for their unintentional
sin. 26 And it shall be forgiven to the entire assembly of
Israel and to the proselyte who sojourns among them, for it
happened to the entire people unintentionally.
27 "If one person sins unintentionally, he shall offer a

BAAL HATURIM ELUCIDATED

must be taken,[78] and to the [minimum] size from which *challah* must be taken, five *reva'im.*[79]

21. מֵרֵאשִׁית עֲרִסֹתֵיכֶם — FROM THE FIRST OF YOUR DOUGH. This verse begins with a מ (= 40) and ends with a מ. This tells you that [the measure of] a generous person's *terumah*[80] consists of one-fortieth[81] of the crop.[82]

24. {The Baal HaTurim's comments to מֵעֵינֵי appear at *Genesis* 25:25, s.v., אַדְמוֹנִי, and *Leviticus* 4:13.}

found in *Tur* and *Shulchan Aruch, Yoreh Deah* 322-330.

78. *Challah* 1:1.

79. *Challah* 2:6. Opinions regarding the modern-day equivalent of the *rova* (plural, *reva'im*) range between 12 and 21 fluid ounces.

80. The word תְּרוּמָה [*terumah*], *a setting aside,* is a general term for anything set aside for a specific purpose. It is also the name given to the portion of each year's crop that the farmer must set aside for the Kohanim. Although our verse speaks of *challah,* not *terumah,* it nevertheless uses the term *terumah,* and so the Baal HaTurim takes the word out of the context of the verse for purposes of his allusion. Thus, the verse is interpreted as if it were contracted to מֵרֵאשִׁית תְּרוּמָה לְדֹרֹתֵכֶם, *From the first, terumah for your generations* (*VeChur LaZahav*).

81. *Terumos* 4:3 — The [following is the] amount to be set aside as *terumah:* A generous person [sets aside] one-fortieth [of the crop] . . .; an average person, one-fiftieth; and a stingy person, one-sixtieth.

82. *R' Ephraim* (*MiKesivah Ashkenazis*).

טו/כח־לו

כח וְהִקְרִ֛יבָה עֵ֥ז בַּת־שְׁנָתָ֖הּ לְחַטָּֽאת׃ וְכִפֶּ֣ר הַכֹּהֵ֗ן
עַל־הַנֶּ֛פֶשׁ הַשֹּׁגֶ֛גֶת בְּחֶטְאָ֥ה בִשְׁגָגָ֖ה לִפְנֵ֣י יְהוָ֑ה
כט לְכַפֵּ֥ר עָלָ֖יו וְנִסְלַ֥ח לֽוֹ׃ הָֽאֶזְרָח֙ בִּבְנֵ֣י יִשְׂרָאֵ֔ל וְלַגֵּ֖ר
הַגָּ֣ר בְּתוֹכָ֑ם תּוֹרָ֤ה אַחַת֙ יִהְיֶ֣ה לָכֶ֔ם לָעֹשֶׂ֖ה בִּשְׁגָגָֽה׃
ל וְהַנֶּ֜פֶשׁ אֲשֶׁר־תַּעֲשֶׂ֣ה ׀ בְּיָ֣ד רָמָ֗ה מִן־הָֽאֶזְרָח֙
וּמִן־הַגֵּ֔ר אֶת־יְהוָ֖ה ה֣וּא מְגַדֵּ֑ף וְנִכְרְתָ֛ה הַנֶּ֥פֶשׁ
לא הַהִ֖וא מִקֶּ֥רֶב עַמָּֽהּ׃ כִּ֤י דְבַר־יְהוָה֙ בָּזָ֔ה וְאֶת־מִצְוָת֖וֹ
הֵפַ֑ר הִכָּרֵ֧ת ׀ תִּכָּרֵ֛ת הַנֶּ֥פֶשׁ הַהִ֖וא עֲוֺנָ֥ה בָֽהּ׃
לב וַיִּהְי֥וּ בְנֵֽי־יִשְׂרָאֵ֖ל בַּמִּדְבָּ֑ר וַֽיִּמְצְא֗וּ אִ֛ישׁ מְקֹשֵׁ֥שׁ
לג עֵצִ֖ים בְּי֥וֹם הַשַּׁבָּֽת׃ וַיַּקְרִ֣יבוּ אֹת֔וֹ הַמֹּצְאִ֥ים אֹת֖וֹ
מְקֹשֵׁ֣שׁ עֵצִ֑ים אֶל־מֹשֶׁה֙ וְאֶֽל־אַהֲרֹ֔ן וְאֶ֖ל כָּל־
לד הָעֵדָֽה׃ וַיַּנִּ֥יחוּ אֹת֖וֹ בַּמִּשְׁמָ֑ר כִּ֚י לֹ֣א פֹרַ֔שׁ מַה־
לה יֵּעָשֶׂ֖ה לֽוֹ׃ וַיֹּ֤אמֶר יְהוָה֙ אֶל־מֹשֶׁ֔ה מ֥וֹת יוּמַ֖ת
הָאִ֑ישׁ רָג֨וֹם אֹת֤וֹ בָֽאֲבָנִים֙ כָּל־הָ֣עֵדָ֔ה מִח֖וּץ
לו לַֽמַּחֲנֶֽה׃ וַיֹּצִ֨יאוּ אֹת֜וֹ כָּל־הָעֵדָ֗ה אֶל־מִחוּץ֙

בעל הטורים

(לא) הִכָּרֵת תִּכָּרֵת. בְּגִימַטְרִיָּא שֶׁדִּיבְּרָה תוֹרָה כִּלְשׁוֹן בְּנֵי אָדָם:

(לב-לט) סָמַךְ מְקוֹשֵׁשׁ לִמְגַדֵּף לוֹמַר לְךָ שֶׁבִּזְמַן אֶחָד הָיוּ. וּמִפְּנֵי שֶׁשַּׁבָּת חָמוּר כַּעֲבוֹדָה זָרָה, כִּדְאִיתָא בְּחֻלִּין, פֶּרֶק קַמָּא.

BAAL HATURIM ELUCIDATED

30. {The Baal HaTurim's comment to בְּיָד רָמָה appears at *Exodus* 14:8.}

31. {The Baal HaTurim's comment to הֵפַר appears at *Genesis* 17:14.}

❑ הִכָּרֵת תִּכָּרֵת — [THAT PERSON] SHALL SURELY BE CUT OFF. The *gematria* of this phrase (1645) is equal to that of, שֶׁדִּבְּרָה[83] תּוֹרָה כִּלְשׁוֹן בְּנֵי אָדָם, *For the Torah spoke in the language of man.*[84]

83. The text follows *Rimzei Rabbeinu Yoel.* The early printed editions read שֶׁדִּבְּרָה תוֹרָה לְשׁוֹן בְּנֵי אָדָם, but the *gematria* of that phrase is only 1615, thirty less than that of the Scriptural phrase. *Ittur Bikkurim, Matzreif LaKesef* and *Shoham Yakar,* who were unaware of *Rimzei Rabbeinu Yoel,* suggest emendations to reconcile the numbers: One reads, שֶׁדִּבְרֵי הַתּוֹרָה כִּלְשׁוֹן בְּנֵי אָדָם, *For the words of the Torah are in the language of man* (*Ittur Bikkurim*). However, that reading is difficult, for it changes the verb דִּבְּרָה, *it spoke,* of the Baal HaTurim's Talmudic source (see note 84), to the noun דִּבְרֵי, *the words of.* The other reads, שֶׁדִּבְּרָה הַתּוֹרָה כִּלְשׁוֹן בְּנֵי הָאָדָם, which has a *gematria* of 1645 and is in keeping with the Talmud's statement (*Matzreif LaKesef* and *Shoham Yakar*).

84. *Rimzei Rabbeinu Yoel.* In general, the Torah is written in a succinct style that allows for no redundant or otherwise superfluous words or even letters. Thus, every letter of every word of every verse in the Torah is filled with meaning. Indeed, many *halachos* are derived from

she-goat within its first year as a sin-offering. 28 *The Kohen*
shall atone for the erring person when he sins unintentionally
before HASHEM, *to atone for him; and it shall be forgiven him.*
29 *The native among the Children of Israel and the proselyte*
who sojourns among them — there shall be a single teaching
for them, for one who does unintentionally.
30 *"A person who shall act high-handedly, whether native or*
proselyte, he blasphemed HASHEM! *— that person shall be cut*
off from among his people, 31 *for he scorned the word of*
HASHEM *and broke His commandment; that person shall surely*
be cut off, his sin is upon him."
32 *The Children of Israel were in the wilderness and they*
found a man gathering wood on the Sabbath day. 33 *Those*
who found him gathering wood brought him to Moses and
Aaron, and to the entire assembly. 34 *They placed him in cus-*
tody, for it had not been clarified what should be done to him.
35 HASHEM *said to Moses: "The man shall be put to death; the*
entire assembly shall pelt him with stones outside of the camp."
36 *The entire assembly removed him to the outside of the*

BAAL HATURIM ELUCIDATED

32-39. The Torah juxtaposed the passage containing the episode concerning the man who gathered wood on the Sabbath (vv. 32-36) with the passage regarding the man who spoke blasphemy (v. 30),[84a] because the two episodes occurred at the same time.[85] And also to indicate that the Sabbath is of the same severity as idolatry,[86] as we find in tractate *Chullin,* in the first chapter.[87]

---

seemingly extraneous letters or redundant phrases. The Mishnah (*Chagigah* 1:8 [10a]) refers to such laws as "mountains suspended by a hair." Nevertheless, in a discussion regarding תְּחִיַּת הַמֵּתִים, *resurrection of the dead,* the Talmud asks whether the phrase הִכָּרֵת תִּכָּרֵת, literally, *cutting off, he shall be cut off,* implies *cutting off* [*in this world*], *he shall be cut off* [*even after the resurrection*]. If yes, it would then be a Scriptural source for the doctrine of the resurrection of the dead. The Talmud rejects that interpretation because, דִּבְּרָה תוֹרָה כִּלְשׁוֹן בְּנֵי אָדָם, *the Torah spoke in the language of man* (*Sanhedrin* 90b). That is, just as a person will repeat himself to stress a point, in like fashion, the Torah occasionally uses a repetitive expression for emphasis.

84a. That verse alludes to the incident recorded in *Leviticus* 24:10-23.

85. *Peirush HaRokeach.* See *Toras Kohanim, Emor, parshasa* 14:5, cited by *Rashi* in his comments to v. 41 below, s.v., אני ה׳ אלהיכם, and *Leviticus* 24:12. The Baal HaTurim makes the same point in his comments to *Leviticus* 24:10.

86. That is, the severity of desecrating the Sabbath, as in the case of the man who gathered wood on the Sabbath, is as grave as that of idolatry, for blasphemy is equated with idolatry, in that both deny God's supremacy in the world.

87. *Chullin* 5a — One who commits idolatry or desecrates the Sabbath is considered to have transgressed the entire Torah and all its *mitzvos.*

The phrase, כִּדְאִיתָא בְּחֻלִּין פֶּרֶק קַמָּא, *as we find in the first chapter of tractate Chullin,* refers to the Baal HaTurim's comparison of the desecration of Sabbath to idolatry. In the early printed editions, followed by many later printed editions, it erroneously appears after the phrase, שֶׁבִּזְמַן אֶחָד הָיוּ, *because . . . at the same time.*

טו/לז-לח לַמַּחֲנֶה וַיִּרְגְּמוּ אֹתוֹ בָּאֲבָנִים וַיָּמֹת כַּאֲשֶׁר צִוָּה יהוה
אֶת־מֹשֶׁה:
מפטיר לז-לח וַיֹּאמֶר יהוה אֶל־מֹשֶׁה לֵּאמֹר: דַּבֵּר אֶל־בְּנֵי יִשְׂרָאֵל
וְאָמַרְתָּ אֲלֵהֶם וְעָשׂוּ לָהֶם צִיצִת עַל־כַּנְפֵי בִגְדֵיהֶם

בעל הטורים

וְסָמַךְ לָהֶם פָּרָשַׁת צִיצִית שֶׁשְּׁקוּלָה גַם כֵּן כְּכָל הַמִּצְוֹת, דִּכְתִיב ״וּזְכַרְתֶּם אֶת כָּל מִצְוֹת ה׳ ״ – ״כָּל מִצְוֹת ה׳ ״ עוֹלֶה תרי״ב, ״אָנֹכִי״ וְ״לֹא יִהְיֶה לְךָ״ מִפִּי הַגְּבוּרָה שְׁמַעְנוּם:

(לח) וְעָשׂוּ לָהֶם צִיצִת. אָמַר הַקָּדוֹשׁ בָּרוּךְ הוּא, אֲנִי רוֹצֶה שֶׁתִּהְיוּ מְעֻטָּפִים כְּמַלְאָכִים לְבוּשׁ הַבַּדִּים, וְכַאֲשֶׁר רָאִיתָ אוֹתִי מְעֻטָּף. לָכֵן צִוָּה בִּתְכֵלֶת, שֶׁדּוֹמֶה לְרָקִיעַ וּלְכִסֵּא הַכָּבוֹד. צִיצִית בְּאַ״תְ בַּ״שׁ בְּגִימַטְרִיָּא עוֹלֶה כִּסְאִי:

❑ **צִיצִת.** בְּגִימַטְרִיָּא צְדָקוֹת וּבְגִימַטְרִיָּא נְשָׁרִים. לוֹמַר מִי שֶׁהוּא זָהִיר בְּמִצְוַת צִיצִית, זוֹכֶה

BAAL HATURIM ELUCIDATED

The Torah juxtaposes the passage of *tzitzis* (vv. 37-41 below)[87a] to those two passages,[88] for it, too, is equivalent to all the *mitzvos* of the Torah, as it is written, וּזְכַרְתֶּם אֶת כָּל מִצְוֹת ה׳, *and remember all the commandments of HASHEM.* [88a] And the *gematria* of כָּל מִצְוֹת ה׳, *all the commandments of HASHEM* (v. 39), comes to a total of 612. For we heard the commandments, *I am* [*HASHEM, your God*], and *You shall have no* [*other gods*], directly from the Omnipotent.[89]

38. וְעָשׂוּ לָהֶם צִיצִת — THAT THEY SHALL MAKE FOR THEMSELVES TZITZIS. The Holy One, Blessed is He, said: "I desire that you be wrapped as the angels wearing linen,[90] and as you saw[91] Me wrapped in a *tallis.*"[92] For this reason, He

---

87a. See the Baal HaTurim to verse 39 below, s.v., צִיצִית.

88. Those regarding Sabbath desecration and idolatry.

88a. *Menachos* 43b.

89. *Peirush HaRokeach.* The Talmud (*Makkos* 23b) and Midrash (*Pirkei DeRabbi Eliezer* 41; *Tanchuma, Vayeilech* 2) speak of 613 mitzvos, and the Baal HaTurim usually cites that number (in his comments to v. 39 below and to *Genesis* 1:1, 1:4 and 32:5; *Exodus* 20:13; *Numbers* 7:14; *Deuteronomy* 4:2 and 32:1). Nevertheless, the Baal HaTurim sometimes numbers the *mitzvos* at 612 (*Leviticus* 25:36 and 27:34, and here).

The Baal HaTurim himself seems to address this discrepancy by noting that the first two of the Ten Commandments were heard directly from God. His intention may be explained as follows:

The Talmud derives the number 613 from the verse, תּוֹרָה צִוָּה לָנוּ מֹשֶׁה, *Moses commanded the Torah to us* (*Deuteronomy* 33:4). Moses gave us תּוֹרָה (= 611) commandments; two others [the first two of the Ten Commandments] — *I am HASHEM, your God,* and, *You shall have no other gods . . .* (*Exodus* 20:2-6) — were heard directly from God. Thus, there are six hundred and thirteen *mitzvos.*

A passage in the *Zohar* (II, 81b) explains that when God spoke the first two Commandments, He spoke them simultaneously, something that is impossible for any creature to do. Israel, however, heard them as if they were spoken separately. This is the meaning of the verse, *One [statement] has God spoken, these two I have heard* (*Psalms* 62:12).

Accordingly, the Baal HaTurim sometimes reckons the two Commandments heard directly from God as one, for a total of 612 *mitzvos,* and sometimes as two, for a total of 613 *mitzvos* (*Ittur Bikkurim* to *Leviticus* 25:36).

90. Both *Ezekiel* (e.g., 9:2-3) and *Daniel* (10:5; 12:6-7) describe the angels of their visions as לְבוּשׁ בַּדִּים, *wearing linen.*

91. The reading רָאִיתָ, *you* (singular) *saw,* follows virtually all editions. One manuscript used by *Shoham Yakar* reads רְאִיתֶם, *you* (plural) *saw,* a reading that is also found in *Yad Aharon* (see next note).

92. The Talmud expounds on the verse, *HASHEM*

camp; they pelted him with stones and he died, as HASHEM *had commanded Moses.*

37 HASHEM *said to Moses, saying:* 38 *"Speak to the Children of Israel and say to them that they shall make for themselves tzitzis on the corners of their garments,*

BAAL HATURIM ELUCIDATED

commanded [that the *tallis* include threads dyed with] *techeiles,* a color similar to that of the heavens[92a] and to that of the Throne of Glory. Indeed, the *gematria* [of המהמ״א, which] in the *aleph-beis* exchange known as אַ״תְ בַּ״שׁ[93] [corresponds to the word] צִיצִית[94], is 91, equal to that of כִּסְאִי, *My Throne.*[95]

❑ צִיצִת — TZITZIS. The *gematria* of צִיצִית[96] (600) is equal to that of צְדָקוֹת, *acts of righteousness,* and that of נְשָׁרִים, *eagles.* This indicates that one who is careful regarding the *mitzvah* of *tzitzis* will merit to behold the Divine

passed before him and proclaimed (*Exodus* 34:6): This teaches that the Holy One, Blessed is He, wrapped Himself in a *tallis* like a *chazzan* and demonstrated to Moses the order of prayer (*Rosh Hashanah* 17b).

However, according to the reading רְאִיתֶם, in the plural (see note 91), this passage could not be the Baal HaTurim's source, for only Moses was privileged to see that vision. The Midrash, however, records another time that God donned a *tallis:* Moses was unclear about the laws regarding the sanctification of the New Moon by *beis din* upon hearing the testimony of witnesses who saw the emerging moon after its invisible stage. To clarify the laws for Moses, the Holy One, Blessed is He, wrapped Himself in a *tallis* and had Moses stand on one side and Aaron on the other. Then he called for the angels Michael and Gabriel to act as messengers of the court [dispatched the evening before to see whether the moon had emerged or was still invisible. They testified to having seen the moon]. God examined their testimony: In which direction did you see the moon? Were its cusps pointing toward the sun or away from it? Was it north of the sun or south? How high above the horizon was it? Which way was it facing? How wide was it? Then He said to Moses and Aaron, "In this order that you saw [Me, in heaven, sanctify the new moon], thus, shall My children [i.e., Israel] do below." [That is, the *beis din* shall do it] in the presence of an outstanding sage, on the testimony of witnesses, and wearing *tallisos* (*Pesikta Rabbasi* 15:21). In this instance, both Moses and Aaron saw God wrap Himself in a *tallis.* Thus, the plural verb רְאִיתֶם, *you saw* (*VeChur LaZahav*).

92a. Where the angels dwell.

93. See note 30 at 9:2 above.

94. Although the Torah consistently spells צִיצִת without the second י, the Baal HaTurim uses the full spelling צִיצִית for purposes of his *gematria,* a practice not uncommon in the realm of רֶמֶז [*remez*], *allusion* (see *She'ilos Useshuvos Yechaveh Da'as,* Vol. 4, §2). Indeed, the *Zohar* states: צִיצִית, with the second י, has a *gematria* of 600. And even if the Torah has omitted one י, the *chirik* vowel [which is read the same way whether it appears with a י or without a י] is in its place (*Rei'a Mehemna* III, 227a). See also notes 96 and 110 below.

95. The prophet declares: כֹּה אָמַר ה׳, *Thus said* HASHEM, "הַשָּׁמַיִם כִּסְאִי, *The Heavens are My Throne* . . ." (*Isaiah* 66:1). Thus, the Heavens and the Throne of Glory are of the same color (*VeChur LaZahav*).

The Talmud explains the significance of the color turquoise: How does *techeiles* differ from all other types of dyes? *Techeiles* is similar in color to the sea; the sea, to the heavens; the heavens, to the Throne of Glory (*Menachos* 43b; *Chullin* 89a).

96. See note 94 above. Some commentators (e.g., *Ramban*) do not accept *gematriaos* and other allusions that do not conform to the exact spelling used in Scripture. Nevertheless, regarding the term צִיצִית, which appears in the Torah three times (twice in verse 38; and once, with a prefix -לְ, in verse 39), each time without the second י, some of those very commentators consider the prefix ל (= 30) as if it were divided equally among the three appearances, thus adding a י (= 10) to each one. Accordingly, the word may be expounded upon as if it were spelled צִיצִית (*Midrash Lekach Tov* [*Pesikta Zutresa*]; *Tosafos* to *Menachos* 39a, s.v., לא יפחות; *Tur Orach Chaim* 24).

לט לְדֹרֹתָם וְנָתְנוּ עַל־צִיצִת הַכָּנָף פְּתִיל תְּכֵלֶת: וְהָיָה לָכֶם לְצִיצִת וּרְאִיתֶם אֹתוֹ וּזְכַרְתֶּם אֶת־כָּל־מִצְוֹת

בעל הטורים

וְרוֹאֶה פְּנֵי שְׁכִינָה, דִּכְתִיב "אֲנִי בְּצֶדֶק אֶחֱזֶה פָנֶיךָ". וְזוֹכֶה לְמַה שֶּׁנֶּאֱמַר "וָאֶשָּׂא אֶתְכֶם עַל כַּנְפֵי נְשָׁרִים":

(לט) **וּרְאִיתֶם.** בְּגִימַטְרִיָּא צִיצִית בַּיּוֹם:

❑ **וּזְכַרְתֶּם** {אֶת} כְּתִיב זְכִירָה בְּצִיצִית, לָכֵן צִוָּה לַעֲשׂוֹת אַרְבַּע צִיצִיּוֹת בְּאַרְבַּע כַּנְפוֹת בְּגָדָיו, שֶׁבְּכָל מָקוֹם שֶׁיִּפְנֶה יִזְכֹּר:

וּבְכָל אֶחָד חֲמִשָּׁה קְשָׁרִים, כְּדֵי שֶׁיִּזְכֹּר לַחֲמִשָּׁה חֻמְשֵׁי תוֹרָה:

וְיֵשׁ בְּכָל אֶחָד שְׁמוֹנָה חוּטִין, שֶׁיִּמָּנַע מִלַּעֲשׂוֹת עֲבֵרָה בִּשְׁמוֹנָה אֵבָרִים הַמַּרְגִּילִים אֶת הָאָדָם לַעֲבֵרָה, וְאֵלּוּ הֵן – אָזְנַיִם עֵינַיִם פֶּה חֹטֶם יָדַיִם רַגְלַיִם הָעֶרְוָה וְהַלֵּב. וְאִם שָׁמַר עַצְמוֹ מֵעֲבֵרָה, זוֹכֶה לַעֲלוֹת לְמַעְלָה מִשְּׁמֹנָה רְקִיעִים, דִּכְתִיב "וְהָיְתָה נֶפֶשׁ אֲדֹנִי צְרוּרָה בִּצְרוֹר

BAAL HATURIM ELUCIDATED

Presence,[97] as it is written: אֲנִי בְּצֶדֶק[97a] אֶחֱזֶה פָנֶיךָ, *And as for me — In righteousness I shall behold Your countenance* (*Psalms* 17:15). And he will merit the fulfillment of the verse, וָאֶשָּׂא אֶתְכֶם עַל כַּנְפֵי נְשָׁרִים, *I have borne you on the wings of eagles* (*Exodus* 19:4).[98]

39. וּרְאִיתֶם — AND YOU SHALL SEE. The *gematria* of this word (657) is equivalent[99] to that of the phrase, צִיצִית בַּיּוֹם, [the *mitzvah* of] *tzitzis* [applies] *during the day.*[100]

❑ **וּזְכַרְתֶּם {אֶת}**[101] **— AND YOU SHALL REMEMBER.** This term of remembrance is written with regard to *tzitzis,* thus [explaining why] He commanded [each Israelite] to place four *tzitzis* on the four corners of his garments, so that in whichever direction he may turn [east, west, north or south], he will remember [the *mitzvos*].

On each corner are five knots,[102] so that the wearer may remember the five books of the Torah.

And on each corner are eight strands,[103] for one must [remember to] restrain

97. *Menachos* 43b.

97a. Thus the allusion of צְדָקוֹת.

98. *Rashi* to v. 41, s.v., על כנפי בגדיהם.

99. The principle of *im hakollel* allows 657 to be considered equivalent to 658, the *gematria* of the Baal HaTurim's phrase.

100. *Peirush HaRokeach; Rabbeinu Ephraim* (*MiKesivah Ashkenazis*). The Talmud expounds on our verse: וּרְאִיתֶם אֹתוֹ, *and you shall see it,* this excludes night wear (*Menachos* 43a). According to the *Rambam,* the Talmud means that the *mitzvah* of *tzitzis* does not apply at night. According to the *Rosh,* the Baal HaTurim's father, it means that garments made to be worn at night (e.g., sleepwear) are exempt from the *mitzvah* of *tzitzis,* even if they are worn during the day; but garments made to be worn during the day (e.g., business suits) are obligated in the *mitzvah* of *tzitzis,* even if they are worn at night (*Shulchan Aruch, Orach Chaim* 18:1). In the *gematria* of וּרְאִיתֶם, the Baal HaTurim finds an additional allusion to this aspect of the *mitzvah.* (See also *Berachos* 13a with *Rashi,* s.v., ויאמר אינו נוהג אלא ביום.)

101. The early printed editions of Constantinople and Venice erroneously read וּזְכַרְתֶּם אותו. Although the Fürth edition, followed by some later editions, has the corrected reading וּזְכַרְתֶּם אֶת, many later printed editions have nevertheless perpetuated the erroneous version. Some have the word וּזְכַרְתֶּם by itself or the phrase אֹתוֹ וּזְכַרְתֶּם, with the words in the order they appear in the Torah.

102. *Shulchan Aruch, Orach Chayim* 11:14.

103. *Shulchan Aruch, Orach Chayim* 11:12.

throughout their generations. And they shall place upon the tzitzis of each corner a thread of turquoise wool. [39] *It shall constitute tzitzis for you, and you shall see it and you shall remember all the commandments of*

the eight organs that habituate a person to sin. They are his ears, eyes, mouth, nose,[104] hands, feet, genitals and heart.[105] Moreover, if one has guarded himself from sin, he merits to ascend above the eight heavens,[106] as it is written, וְהָיְתָה נֶפֶשׁ אֲדֹנִי צְרוּרָה בִּצְרוֹר הַחַיִּים, *May my lord's soul be bound up in the bond of*

104. According to *Midrash Tadshei* (see note 105), this should read לָשׁוֹן, *tongue.*

105. *Peirush HaRokeach.*

The Midrash states: With regard to every human faculty, the Holy One, Blessed is He, instructed what to do and what not to do. What [has God instructed them] not to do? (i-ii) To the heart and to the eyes [He has said] — *and you shall not explore after your heart and after your eyes* (*Numbers* 15:39); (iii) to the ears — *you shall not bear a false hearing* (*Exodus* 23:1); (iv) to the mouth — *you shall not eat any abomination* (*Deuteronomy* 14:3); (v) to the tongue — *you shall not take the Name of HASHEM, your God, in vain* (*Exodus* 20:7) and *you shall not swear falsely* (*Leviticus* 19:12) and *a man shall not lie to his fellow* (*Leviticus* 19:11) and *you shall not bear false witness* (*Exodus* 20:13); (vi) to the hands — *do not extend your hand with the wicked* (*Exodus* 23:1); (vii) to the genitals — *you shall not commit adultery* (*Exodus* 20:13) and *you shall not make the land lewd lest the land become filled with depravity* (*Leviticus* 19:29); and (viii) to the feet — *you shall not follow after other gods* (*Deuteronomy* 6:14). There you have what not to do . . . And what [has God instructed them] to do? (i) To the heart He has taught — *you shall place these words of Mine upon your heart* (*Deuteronomy* 11:18); (ii) to the eyes — *lest you forget the things that your eyes have beheld* (*Deuteronomy* 4:9); (iii) to the ears — *hear, O Israel, the decrees and the ordinances that I speak into your ears today* (*Deuteronomy* 5:1); (iv) [extant editions of the Midrash inexplicably omit God's instructions to the mouth; perhaps the missing piece speaks of the *mitzvah* of eating the *korban pesach* or *matzah* (*VeChur LaZahav*)]; (v) to the tongue — *you shall teach them to your children and you shall speak of them* (*Deuteronomy* 6:7); (vi) to the hands — *you shall surely open your hand to your brother, to your poor* (*Deuteronomy* 15:11); (vii) to the genitals — *be fruitful and multiply* (*Genesis* 9:7, see *Rashi* there) and *marry wives and bear children* (*Jeremiah* 29:6); and (viii) to the feet — *on the entire way that HASHEM, your God, commanded you, you shall go* (*Deuteronomy* 5:30). Thus, just as God has decreed upon the [heavenly] beings and upon the earthly, instructing them how to act, so has He commanded all the faculties of the human body what they are to do (*Midrash Tadshei* 9).

106. Elsewhere (*Genesis* 1:1; *Exodus* 25:31; *Deuteronomy* 32:1), the Baal HaTurim speaks of ז׳ רְקִיעִים, *seven heavens.* Here, he speaks of eight. The two opinions are found in the words of the Sages.

The Talmud (*Chagigah* 12b; see also *Avos De-Rabbi Nosson* 37:9) names and describes seven heavens, each a higher level than the preceding one. They are:

(i) וִילוֹן, *Vilon* [*curtain*], although nothing happens within this heaven, in the morning it withdraws [like a curtain, allowing the daylight to shine through (*Rashi*)] and in the evening it goes forth [preventing the light of the sun from reaching Earth (*Rashi*)], thus it renews the work of Creation each day;

(ii) רָקִיעַ, *Rakia* [*firmament*], in which the sun, moon, stars and constellations are suspended;

(iii) שְׁחָקִים, *Shechakim* [*powders* or *pulverizers*], in which stand millstones that grind manna for the righteous;

(iv) זְבוּל, *Zevul* [*Temple*], in which stands the heavenly Jerusalem, Temple and Altar upon which the great angelic prince Michael sacrifices offerings;

(v) מָעוֹן, *Maon* [*dwelling*], in which groups of ministering angels recite songs [of praise to God] through the night, but remain silent by day in deference to Israel;

(vi) מָכוֹן, *Machon* [*foundation* or *establishment*], in which are storehouses of snow and of hail, the attics in which harmful dew and heavy rainfall are stored, and the chamber of the whirlwind and the tempest, the grotto of smoke with its

טו/מ־מא

יהוה וַעֲשִׂיתֶם אֹתָם וְלֹא־תָתוּרוּ אַחֲרֵי לְבַבְכֶם
מ וְאַחֲרֵי עֵינֵיכֶם אֲשֶׁר־אַתֶּם זֹנִים אַחֲרֵיהֶם׃ לְמַעַן
תִּזְכְּרוּ וַעֲשִׂיתֶם אֶת־כָּל־מִצְוֺתָי וִהְיִיתֶם קְדֹשִׁים
מא לֵאלֹהֵיכֶם׃ אֲנִי יהוה אֱלֹהֵיכֶם אֲשֶׁר הוֹצֵאתִי
אֶתְכֶם מֵאֶרֶץ מִצְרַיִם לִהְיוֹת לָכֶם לֵאלֹהִים אֲנִי
יהוה אֱלֹהֵיכֶם׃ פפפ קי״ט פסוקים. פל״ט סימן.

בעל הטורים

הַחַיִּים״. וְאִם עָבַר בָּהֶן עֲבֵרָה, נִדּוֹן בִּשְׁמֹנָה דִינִין – בְּחִבּוּט הַקֶּבֶר וּבְשִׁבְעָה מְדוּרוֹת שֶׁל גֵּיהִנֹּם׃

❑ **צִיצִת** עוֹלֶה ת״ר, וּשְׁמֹנָה חוּטִין וַחֲמִשָּׁה קְשָׁרִים עוֹלֶה תרי״ג. לוֹמַר לְךָ שֶׁשְּׁקוּלָה מִצְוַת צִיצִית כְּכָל הַתּוֹרָה כֻּלָּהּ׃

❑ ״בְּכָל עֵת יִהְיוּ בְגָדֶיךָ לְבָנִים״ בְּגִימַטְרִיָּא זֶה צִיצִית לְבִגְדֵיכֶם׃

BAAL HATURIM ELUCIDATED

life (*I Samuel* 25:29).[107] But if he committed sins with them, he becomes subject to eight types of retribution: battering within the grave[108] and the seven chambers of *Gehinnom.*[109]

doors of fire [all of these used for retribution against the wicked (*Rashi*)];

and (vii) עֲרָבוֹת, *Aravos* [*willows* or *darkenings* or *mixtures*], in which are Righteousness, Justice and Charity; caches of Life, Peace and Blessing; the souls of the righteous, the spirits and souls that are destined to be born; and the life-giving dew with which God will resurrect the dead; in that heaven are also the *Ofanim, Serafim, Chayos HaKodesh* and other ministering angels; and the Throne of Glory of the King, God, Life-giver, Exalted One.

Another opinion (*Chagigah* 13a) adds an eighth heaven above the heads of the *Chayos.* Thus, the Baal HaTurim sometimes speaks of seven heavens and sometimes of eight (*Shoham Yakar*).

For other opinions regarding the number and names of the various רְקִיעִים, see *Vayikra Rabbah* 29:11; *Rambam, Hilchos Yesodei HaTorah* 3:1; *Tosefos Yom Tov, Pesachim* 10:5, s.v., להודות; *Eliyahu Rabbah* (*Gra*), *Keilim* 3:4, s.v., אשריך כלים.

107. The Talmud (*Chagigah* 12b) adduces this verse as proof that the souls of the righteous are to be found in the seventh heaven, known as *Aravos* (see note 106, paragraph vii).

108. See the Midrash *Maseches Chibut HaKever* in *Otzar HaMidrashim* [Eisenstein]; see also *Sanhedrin* 47b.

109. *Peirush HaRokeach.* The term מדורות can be read either מְדוּרוֹת or מְדוֹרוֹת. If it is vowelized

HASHEM and you shall perform them; and you shall not explore after your heart and after your eyes after which you stray. 40 *So that you may remember and perform all My commandments and be holy to your God.* 41 *I am HASHEM, your God, Who has removed you from the land of Egypt to be a God unto you; I am HASHEM your God."*

BAAL HATURIM ELUCIDATED

❑ The *gematria* of צִיצִת[110] comes to 600. Together with the eight strands and five knots, it totals 613 [the number of *mitzvos* in the Torah]. This teaches you that the *mitzvah* of *tzitzis* is equivalent to the entirety of the Torah.[111]

❑ The *gematria* of בְּכָל עֵת יִהְיוּ בְגָדֶיךָ לְבָנִים, *At all times, let your garments be white* (*Ecclesiastes* 9:8) — (724) — is equivalent[112] to that of the phrase זֶה צִיצִית לְבִגְדֵיכֶם, *This is* [*a reference to*] *tzitzis for your garments.*[113]

מְדוּרוֹת, it is a variant plural for the masculine noun מָדוֹר, *chamber* or *dwelling area* (see *Daniel* 4:22), which is usually pluralized מְדוֹרִים. If it is vowelized מְדוּרוֹת, it is the plural of the feminine noun מְדוּרָה, *pyre* (see *Ezekiel* 24:9). With regard to *Gehinnom,* the Sages speak of שִׁבְעָה מְדוֹרֵי גֵיהִנֹּם, *the seven chambers of Gehinnom* (*Sotah* 10b; *Midrash Shocher Tov* 11:6; *Zohar, Terumah* 150a; *Tikkunei Zohar* 64), and that terminology is found in the *Rishonim* (*Rashi* and *Radak* to *II Samuel* 19:1; *Rashi* to *Isaiah* 24:22) and the *Acharonim* (*Chasam Sofer,* Vol. 3, *Even HaEzer* 69; *Kitzur Shulchan Aruch* 198:12). Another Midrash (*Maseches Gehinnom* in *Otzar HaMidrashim* [Eisenstein]) speaks of שִׁבְעָה מדורות שֶׁל אֵשׁ, *seven* מדורות *of fire,* which one might be tempted to read מְדוּרוֹת שֶׁל אֵשׁ, *fiery pyres.* However, that reading is untenable for two reasons: (i) It uses the masculine number שִׁבְעָה with the feminine noun מְדוּרוֹת; and (ii) that Midrash continues with the singular form, וּבְכָל מָדוֹר וּמָדוֹר, *and in each and every chamber.* Accordingly, that Midrash speaks of מְדוֹרוֹת שֶׁל אֵשׁ, *fiery chambers,* and thus the Baal HaTurim's comment is vowelized מְדוֹרוֹת שֶׁל גֵּיהִנֹּם (*VeChur LaZahav*).

110. See notes 94 and 96 above.

111. *Rashi* citing *R' Moshe HaDarshan;* see also the Baal HaTurim to verses 32-39 above.

112. The *gematria* of the Baal HaTurim's phrase is 721, and the principle of *im hateivos* allows three more to be added, bringing the total to 724 (*Matzreif LaKesef*).

113. *Shabbos* 153a.

פרשת קרח

Parashas Korach

א וַיִּקַּח קֹרַח בֶּן־יִצְהָר בֶּן־קְהָת בֶּן־לֵוִי וְדָתָן וַאֲבִירָם
ב בְּנֵי אֱלִיאָב וְאוֹן בֶּן־פֶּלֶת בְּנֵי רְאוּבֵן: וַיָּקֻמוּ לִפְנֵי
מֹשֶׁה וַאֲנָשִׁים מִבְּנֵי־יִשְׂרָאֵל חֲמִשִּׁים וּמָאתָיִם

בעל הטורים

טז (א) וַיִּקַּח קֹרַח. סָמַךְ מַחֲלֹקֶת קֹרַח לְפָרָשַׁת צִיצִית, שֶׁעַל עִנְיַן צִיצִית חָלַק עַל מֹשֶׁה:

❑ **וַיִּקַּח קֹרַח.** בְּגִימַטְרִיָּא זֶה בְּמִקָּח רָע. "עֹשֶׁר שָׁמוּר לִבְעָלָיו לְרָעָתוֹ" בְּגִימַטְרִיָּא לְעָשְׁרוֹ שֶׁל קֹרַח לְרָעָתוֹ הָיָה:

(ב) וַיָּקֻמוּ. בְּגִימַטְרִיָּא לַחֲלֹק:

❑ **חֲמִשִּׁים וּמָאתָיִם.** "נֵר רְשָׁעִים יִדְעָךְ":

BAAL HATURIM ELUCIDATED

XVI

1. וַיִּקַּח קֹרַח — KORAH TOOK. The Torah juxtaposed Korah's challenge [of Moses' authority] with the passage concerning *tzitzis* (15:37-41 above), because it was with regard to *tzitzis* that he contended against Moses.[1]

❑ **וַיִּקַּח קֹרַח** — KORAH TOOK. The *gematria* of this phrase (432) is equal to that of זֶה בְּמִקָּח רָע, *This refers to a bad acquisition.*[2] [In a similar vein,] the *gematria* of the verse (*Ecclesiastes* 5:12), עֹשֶׁר שָׁמוּר לִבְעָלָיו לְרָעָתוֹ, *riches hoarded by their owner to*

1. *Tanchuma* 2 — What is written just before this passage of Korah? The passage regarding *tzitzis.* Korah sprang up and said to Moses, "You said, 'And they shall place upon the *tzitzis* of each corner a thread of *techeiles.*' If a garment is woven entirely of *techeiles,* is it not exempt from the obligation of *tzitzis?*" Moses replied, "It requires *tzitzis.*" Korah then said to him, "[How is this possible?] A garment that is woven entirely of *techeiles* does not fulfill the *mitzvah,* yet four strands of *techeiles* [one on each corner] do!" [Korah continued with a similar argument:] "If a house is filled with Torah scrolls, is it not exempt from the obligation of a *mezuzah?*" Moses replied, "It requires a *mezuzah.*" He then said to him, "[How is this possible?] With a complete Torah of 275 [some editions read 278 (see next paragraph below)] *parashiyos* one does not fulfill the *mitzvah,* yet two of these *parashiyos* on the doorpost do! Thus," concluded Korah, "[It is clear that] God did not command you regarding these matters. They are the products of your own imagination." Therefore, the Torah states, וַיִּקַּח קֹרַח, *Korah took,* for the expression וַיִּקַּח implies that his heart took him aside — as it is written, מַה יִּקָּחֲךָ לִבֶּךָ, *To what does your heart take you?* (*Job* 15:12) — and caused him to rebel (cited in part by *Rashi,* s.v., וְדָתָן וַאֲבִירָם; see also note 6 below; see also *Sanhedrin* 110a).

The custom of dividing the Torah into 54 *parashiyos* or *sidros* (weekly portions) and completing the entire Torah each year is universal, but it was not always that way. Other systems existed that divided the Torah into more *parashiyos* which took a much longer time to complete. According to one custom, each *aliyah* would consist of the minimum number of verses required by *halachah,* three. Thus, the seven *olim* would read a total of twenty-one verses each *Shabbos.* And when we divide 5845 (the number of verses in the Torah) by 21, we arrive at 278 1/3. According to that particular custom (cited in *Masores HaTorah VeHaNeviim,* p. 38), it would take about five and a half years to complete the Torah reading.

2. The word וַיִּקַּח can mean *he took* or *he purchased* or *he acquired.* The Talmud explains our verse: The term וַיִּקַּח קֹרַח implies שֶׁלָּקַח מִקָּח רָע לְעַצְמוֹ, *that Korah acquired for himself a bad acquisition* [i.e., he brought on strife (*Rashi*)] (*Sanhedrin* 109b). Korah used his wealth (see note 4 below) in an attempt to wrest the leadership away from Moses, but he made a bad deal. All he acquired in the end was death and dishonor (*Maharsha*).

[1] *Korah son of Izhar son of Kohath son of Levi took [himself] and Dathan and Abiram sons of Eliab and On son of Peleth, sons of [the tribe of] Reuben.* [2] *They stood before Moses with two hundred and fifty men from the Children of Israel,*

BAAL HATURIM ELUCIDATED

his misfortune[3] (1970), is equal to that of לְעָשְׁרוֹ שֶׁל קֹרַח לְרָעָתוֹ הָיָה, [*This refers*] *to Korah's wealth: It was to his misfortune.*[4]

2. וַיָּקֻמוּ — THEY STOOD. The *gematria* of וַיָּקוּמוּ[5] (168) is equal to that of לַחֲלֹק, *to contend.*[6,6a]

❑ **חֲמִשִּׁים וּמָאתָיִם — TWO HUNDRED AND FIFTY.** נֵר רְשָׁעִים יִדְעָךְ, *The lamp of the wicked shall flicker out* (*Proverbs* 24:20; *Job* 21:17).[7]

3. The full verse reads: *There is a sickening evil that I have seen under the sun: riches hoarded by their owner to his misfortune.*

4. The Talmud cites the verse from *Ecclesiastes* as a prelude to a discussion about Korah's wealth, then goes on to explain how he became so rich: [After amassing all the silver and gold of the world (see *Genesis* 47:14 and 41:57)] Joseph concealed three treasures in Egypt: One was later revealed to Korah; one was revealed to Antoninus son of Severus [a Roman emperor who studied Torah under Rabbi Yehudah HaNassi (see *Avodah Zarah* 10b-11a), cited by *Rashi* to *Genesis* 25:23, s.v., שְׁנֵי גוֹיִם)]; and one is hidden away for the righteous [to claim] in the future (*Sanhedrin* 110a; *Pesachim* 119a).

Targum Yonasan ben Uzziel paraphrases verse 19 below: Korah gathered the entire assembly against them [i.e., Moses and Aaron] at the entrance of the Tent of Meeting; he exalted himself with his wealth — for he had found two of the storehouses that Joseph had filled with silver and gold — and he sought to use that wealth to banish Moses and Aaron from the world, [and he may have succeeded] had not the glory of God appeared to the entire assembly.

5. This word appears eight times in the Torah: Twice it is spelled in full וַיָּקוּמוּ (*Genesis* 24:54 and *Numbers* 22:14); the other six times, it is spelled וַיָּקֻמוּ, without the central ו (*Genesis* 18:16, 22:19, 37:35 and 43:15; *Exodus* 32:6; and here). Although our verse uses the defective spelling, for purposes of his allusion, the Baal HaTurim uses the full spelling, a practice not uncommon in the realm of רֶמֶז, *allusion.*

6. *Peirush HaRokeach.*

Targum Yonasan ben Uzziel paraphrases verses 1-2: Korah son of Itzhar . . . took cloaks fabricated entirely of *techeiles.* They stood defiantly and they decided the law regarding the matter of *techeiles* contrary to Moses. Moses said, "I heard directly from the mouth of the Holy One, may His Name be blessed, that the *tzitzis* strands are to be made of white wool, with one strand of *techeiles* among them." Korah and his cohorts fabricated cloaks with their *tzitzis* entirely of *techeiles,* something that God did not command; they were assisted by two hundred and fifty men . . . (see also note 1 above).

6a. Arguments regarding law can take different forms: Honest jurists will discuss conflicting opinions with the intention of determining the truth, each side willing to concede its stand if shown to be wrong; others will insist on the verity of their position, regardless of the weakness of their arguments. The Mishnah (*Avos* 5:17) states regarding the former, that in the end, both opinions will remain valid, and cites the arguments of the *Tannaim* Hillel and Shammai as an example. With regard to the latter, the Mishnah states that the arguments and opinions of the contentious dissidents will not stand and offers the arguments of "Korah and his entire assembly" as an example.

Rashi (to v. 1) teaches that Korah's two hundred and fifty followers were members of the upper echelons of the judicial system. Lest one think that these judges originally entered the dispute in order to ascertain the truth of their own arguments, but later fell in with Korah, in the very first word of the verse that introduces us to these two hundred and fifty men, the Baal HaTurim finds an allusion to their real intention: They arose to contend (A.S.; Y.S.).

7. *Peirush HaRokeach.* This comment interprets the term נֵר, *lamp,* as an allusion to the 250 men who joined with Korah, for the *gematria* of נֵר

ג נְשִׂיאֵי עֵדָה קְרִאֵי מוֹעֵד אַנְשֵׁי־שֵׁם: וַיִּקָּהֲלוּ עַל־
מֹשֶׁה וְעַל־אַהֲרֹן וַיֹּאמְרוּ אֲלֵהֶם רַב־לָכֶם כִּי כָל־
הָעֵדָה כֻּלָּם קְדֹשִׁים וּבְתוֹכָם יהוה וּמַדּוּעַ תִּתְנַשְּׂאוּ
ד-ה עַל־קְהַל יהוה: וַיִּשְׁמַע מֹשֶׁה וַיִּפֹּל עַל־פָּנָיו: וַיְדַבֵּר
אֶל־קֹרַח וְאֶל־כָּל־עֲדָתוֹ לֵאמֹר בֹּקֶר וְיֹדַע יהוה
אֶת־אֲשֶׁר־לוֹ וְאֶת־הַקָּדוֹשׁ וְהִקְרִיב אֵלָיו וְאֵת
ו אֲשֶׁר יִבְחַר־בּוֹ יַקְרִיב אֵלָיו: זֹאת עֲשׂוּ קְחוּ־לָכֶם
ז מַחְתּוֹת קֹרַח וְכָל־עֲדָתוֹ: וּתְנוּ־בָהֵן ׀ אֵשׁ וְשִׂימוּ
עֲלֵיהֶן ׀ קְטֹרֶת לִפְנֵי יהוה מָחָר וְהָיָה הָאִישׁ
אֲשֶׁר־יִבְחַר יהוה הוּא הַקָּדוֹשׁ רַב־לָכֶם בְּנֵי
ח לֵוִי: וַיֹּאמֶר מֹשֶׁה אֶל־קֹרַח שִׁמְעוּ־נָא בְּנֵי לֵוִי:
ט הַמְעַט מִכֶּם כִּי־הִבְדִּיל אֱלֹהֵי יִשְׂרָאֵל אֶתְכֶם
מֵעֲדַת יִשְׂרָאֵל לְהַקְרִיב אֶתְכֶם אֵלָיו לַעֲבֹד אֶת־
עֲבֹדַת מִשְׁכַּן יהוה וְלַעֲמֹד לִפְנֵי הָעֵדָה לְשָׁרְתָם:

בעל הטורים

❑ **קְרִאֵי.** חָסֵר יו״ד, שֶׁעָבְרוּ עַל עֲשֶׂרֶת הַדִּבְּרוֹת:

❑ **אַנְשֵׁי שֵׁם.** בְּחָכְמָה וּבְעֹשֶׁר. וְנִתְחַיְּבוּ כְּדוֹר הַמַּבּוּל, ״אֲשֶׁר מֵעוֹלָם אַנְשֵׁי הַשֵּׁם״:

(ד) **וַיִּשְׁמַע מֹשֶׁה.** בְּגִימַטְרִיָּא מִכָּאן כִּי חֲשָׁדוּהוּ בְּאִשָּׁה:

BAAL HATURIM ELUCIDATED

❑ **קְרִאֵי — THOSE SUMMONED.** This term is spelled defectively,[8] without the central י (= 10), for they transgressed the Ten Commandments.[9]

❑ **אַנְשֵׁי שֵׁם — MEN OF RENOWN,** for their wisdom and honor. Yet they became as deserving of punishment [in *Gehinnom*[10]] as the generation of the flood, who are described with the phrase, אֲשֶׁר מֵעוֹלָם אַנְשֵׁי הַשֵּׁם, *who, from of old, were men of renown*[11]

---

is 250. Thus, the verse is understood as, נֵר רְשָׁעִים, *the* [*assembly of*] *two hundred and fifty wicked,* יִדְעָךְ, *shall die out.*

8. This word appears three times in the *Tanach,* all in the Book of *Numbers,* each time spelled in an irregular manner: (i) In 1:16 above, with reference to the tribal leaders, it is spelled קְרִיאֵי, but pronounced קְרוּאֵי (see the Baal HaTurim there, with note 18); (ii) in 26:9 below, with reference to Korah and his cohorts, it is spelled קְרוּאֵי, but pronounced קְרִיאֵי; (iii) here it is spelled as it is pronounced, קְרִאֵי, but with the central י omitted.

9. *Peirush HaRokeach* to 26:9 below, where it is explained that their defiance against that which God commanded Moses [see note 6 above] was tantamount to denying [the first of] the Ten Commandments.

10. The interpolation is from *Peirush HaRokeach.* According to *R' Chaim Paltiel* this refers to annihilation.

11. Although the literal meaning of אַנְשֵׁי הַשֵּׁם is *men of the name,* i.e., men of renown, Rashi, in a secondary interpretation to *Genesis* 6:4, renders the phrase as אַנְשֵׁי שְׁמָמוֹן, *men of desolation,* for they laid the world desolate. Perhaps the Baal

leaders of the assembly, those summoned for meeting, men of renown. [3] *They gathered together against Moses and against Aaron and said to them, "It is too much for you! For the entire assembly — all of them — are holy and* HASHEM *is among them; why do you exalt yourselves over the congregation of* HASHEM*?"*

[4] *Moses heard and fell on his face.*

[5] *He spoke to Korah and to his entire assembly, saying, "In the morning Hashem will make known the one who is His own and the holy one, and He will draw him close to Himself, and whomever He will choose, He will draw close to Himself.* [6] *Do this: Take for yourselves fire-pans — Korah and his entire assembly —* [7] *and put fire in them and place incense upon them before* HASHEM *tomorrow. Then the man whom* HASHEM *will choose — he is the holy one. It is too much for you, O offspring of Levi!"*

[8] *Moses said to Korah, "Hear now, O offspring of Levi:* [9] *Is it not enough for you that the God of Israel has segregated you from the assembly of Israel to draw you near to Himself, to perform the service of the Tabernacle of* HASHEM*, and to stand before the assembly to minister to them?*

BAAL HATURIM ELUCIDATED

(*Genesis* 6:4).[12]

4. וַיִּשְׁמַע מֹשֶׁה — MOSES HEARD. The *gematria* of this phrase (771) is equivalent[13] to that of מִכָּאן כִּי חֲשָׁדְהוּ בְאִשָּׁה[14], *From here* [the Sages derive] *that they suspected him of* [*adulterous relations with*] *a woman.*[15]

HaTurim interprets אַנְשֵׁי שֵׁם in a similar manner, for these two hundred and fifty men were laid waste (*VeChur LaZahav*).

12. *Peirush HaRokeach; R' Chaim Paltiel.*

13. The principle of *im hakollel* allows 771 to be considered equivalent to 772, the *gematria* of the Baal HaTurim's phrase.

14. The early printed editions read, מִכָּאן שֶׁחֲשָׁדוּהוּ בְאִשָּׁה, with a *gematria* of 1048, and that is what appears in many later printed editions. However, that number cannot be reconciled with the *gematria* of the Scriptural phrase. *Peirush HaRokeach,* the Baal HaTurim's apparent source, reads כְּמוֹ חֲשָׁדוּהוּ לְמֹשֶׁה, whose *gematria* is 770, which, by the principle of *im hakollel,* may be considered equivalent to 771. The present text is based upon *Shoham Yakar's* manuscript edition which reads, מִכָּאן כִּי חֲשָׁדוּהוּ בְּאִשָּׁה (= 778), and to which *Shoham Yakar* comments, "The numbers are not equal." However, the numbers may be reconciled by omitting the central ו, leaving the spelling חֲשָׁדְהוּ (*VeChur LaZahav*).

15. The Talmud explains the implication of this verse: *Moses heard and fell on his face* — What report did Moses hear? . . . He heard that they suspected him of adulterous relations with a woman, as it is stated, וַיְקַנְאוּ לְמֹשֶׁה בַּמַּחֲנֶה, *They were jealous of Moses in the camp* (*Psalms* 106:16) . . . [The word וַיְקַנְאוּ, *they were jealous,* may also be understood as *they warned,* like the similar word וְקִנֵּא, *and he had warned* (5:14 above), regarding the suspected adulteress (*Rashi*).] This implies that each and every husband formally warned his wife against secluding herself with Moses (*Sanhedrin* 110a).

י וַיַּקְרֵב֙ אֹתְךָ֔ וְאֶת־כָּל־אַחֶ֥יךָ בְנֵי־לֵוִ֖י אִתָּ֑ךְ
יא וּבִקַּשְׁתֶּ֖ם גַּם־כְּהֻנָּֽה׃ לָכֵ֗ן אַתָּה֙ וְכָל־עֲדָ֣תְךָ֔
הַנֹּעָדִ֖ים עַל־יְהוָ֑ה וְאַהֲרֹ֣ן מַה־ה֔וּא כִּ֥י °תלונו [°תְּלִ֖ינוּ ק׳]
יב עָלָֽיו׃ וַיִּשְׁלַ֣ח מֹשֶׁ֔ה לִקְרֹ֛א לְדָתָ֥ן וְלַאֲבִירָ֖ם בְּנֵ֣י
יג אֱלִיאָ֑ב וַיֹּאמְר֖וּ לֹ֥א נַעֲלֶֽה׃ הַמְעַ֗ט כִּ֤י הֶֽעֱלִיתָ֙נוּ֙
מֵאֶ֨רֶץ זָבַ֤ת חָלָב֙ וּדְבַ֔שׁ לַהֲמִיתֵ֖נוּ בַּמִּדְבָּ֑ר כִּֽי־
יד תִשְׂתָּרֵ֥ר עָלֵ֖ינוּ גַּם־הִשְׂתָּרֵֽר׃ אַ֗ף לֹ֧א אֶל־אֶ֨רֶץ שני
זָבַ֨ת חָלָ֤ב וּדְבַשׁ֙ הֲבִ֣יאֹתָ֔נוּ וַתִּ֨תֶּן־לָ֔נוּ נַחֲלַ֖ת שָׂדֶ֣ה
וָכָ֑רֶם הַעֵינֵ֞י הָאֲנָשִׁ֥ים הָהֵ֛ם תְּנַקֵּ֖ר לֹ֥א נַעֲלֶֽה׃

בעל הטורים

(י) וּבִקַּשְׁתֶּם. ג׳ בַּמָּסֹרֶת – ״וּבִקַּשְׁתֶּם גַּם כְּהֻנָּה״; ״וּבִקַּשְׁתֶּם מִשָּׁם אֶת ה׳ אֱלֹהֶיךָ״; ״וּבִקַּשְׁתֶּם אֹתִי״ בְּיִרְמְיָה עַל הַגָּלוּת. כְּשֶׁתְּבַקְשׁוּ אוֹתִי בְּגָלוּת בִּתְשׁוּבָה וְתִגָּאֲלוּ, אָז ״וּבִקַּשְׁתֶּם גַּם כְּהֻנָּה״, שֶׁהִיא בְטֵלָה מִכֶּם כָּל זְמַן שֶׁאַתֶּם בְּגָלוּת:

(יא) תַלִּינוּ עָלָיו. ״תִּלוֹנוּ״ כְּתִיב – וַי לָהֶם שֶׁהִרְהֲרוּ עַל רַבָּם:

(יד) הַעֵינֵי. ב׳ בַּמָּסֹרֶת – ״הַעֵינֵי הָאֲנָשִׁים הָהֵם״; וְאִידָךְ ״הַעֵינֵי בָשָׂר לָךְ״. מְלַמֵּד, שֶׁדָּתָן וַאֲבִירָם הֵטִיחוּ דְבָרִים כְּלַפֵּי מַעְלָה, אֶלָּא שֶׁשִּׁנָּה הַכָּתוּב עֲלֵיהֶם. וּלְפִי הַפְּשָׁט, ״הַעֵינֵי הָאֲנָשִׁים הָהֵם תְּנַקֵּר״, שֶׁאַתָּה רוֹצֶה לַעֲשׂוֹת אוֹתָנוּ עִוְרִים, וְעֵינַיִם לָנוּ. שֶׁכְּבָר אָמַרְתָּ לְהָבִיא אוֹתָנוּ אֶל אֶרֶץ זָבַת חָלָב וּדְבַשׁ, וְעַתָּה אַתָּה אוֹמֵר לַהֲמִיתֵנוּ בַּמִּדְבָּר:

BAAL HATURIM ELUCIDATED

10. וּבִקַּשְׁתֶּם — YET YOU SEEK. The masoretic note, ג׳, means that this word appears three times in the *Tanach:* (i) here, וּבִקַּשְׁתֶּם גַּם כְּהֻנָּה, *yet you seek priesthood as well;* (ii) וּבִקַּשְׁתֶּם מִשָּׁם אֶת ה׳ אֱלֹהֶיךָ, *From there*[15a] *you will seek* HASHEM, *your God* (*Deuteronomy* 4:29); and (iii) וּבִקַּשְׁתֶּם אֹתִי, *You will seek Me,* in Jeremiah's prophecy (*Jeremiah* 29:13), [both] concerning the exile.[15b] [The similarity of expression implies that God said,] "When you will seek Me with repentance in the exile and you will be redeemed, then *you will seek priesthood as well,* for it is annulled from you for the entire period that you are in exile."[16]

11. תַלִּינוּ עָלָיו — THAT YOU PROTEST AGAINST HIM. [Although this word is pronounced תַּלִּינוּ,] it is spelled תלונו.[17] This implies: [18]וי, *Woe,* unto them, for

15a. That is, from exile.

15b. That is, the verses from both *Deuteronomy* and *Jeremiah* speak of exile.

16. In his comments at 17:20 below and at *Leviticus* 16:14, s.v., יַזֶּה, the Baal HaTurim also discusses the return of the priesthood to Aaron's family in Messianic times.

17. This word is an example of קְרִי וּכְתִיב, *keri uchesiv,* that is, a Scriptural word whose traditional pronunciation differs from its spelling. Here, we find the *kesiv* (spelling) תִּלוֹנוּ, *you have complained,* with the *keri* (pronunciation) תַּלִּינוּ, *you have incited,* i.e., you have caused others to complain (*Rashi* to *Exodus* 16:7). Understood simply, this *keri uchesiv* teaches that these people not only complained against Moses, they also incited others to join in their complaints.

18. According to the *kesiv,* the middle letter of

[10] *And He drew you near, and all your brethren, the*
offspring of Levi, with you — yet you seek priesthood, as
well! [11] *Therefore, you and your entire assembly that are joining together are against HASHEM! And as for Aaron — what is he that you protest against him?"*

[12] *Moses sent forth to summon Dathan and Abiram, the*
sons of Eliab, but they said, "We shall not go up! [13] *Is it not*
enough that you have brought us up from a land flowing with milk and honey to cause us to die in the wilderness, yet you seek to dominate us, even to dominate further?
[14] *Moreover, you did not bring us to a land flowing with milk and honey nor give us a heritage of field and vineyard! do you hope to gouge out the eyes of those men? We shall not go up!"*

they have misgivings about their teacher.[19]

13. {The Baal HaTurim's comment to הֶעֱלִיתָנוּ appears at *Exodus* 17:3.}

14. **הַעֵינֵי — DO YOU [HOPE] ... THE EYES.** The masoretic note, ב׳, means that this word appears twice in the *Tanach:* (i) here, הַעֵינֵי הָאֲנָשִׁים הָהֵם, *Do you hope [to gouge out] the eyes of those men?*[20]; and (ii) הַעֵינֵי בָשָׂר לָךְ, *Do You* [God] *have eyes of flesh?* (*Job* 10:4). This [similarity of expression] teaches that Dathan and Abiram addressed their complaints against God, but Scripture changed [the implication so that it appears that they were speaking] about themselves.[21]

[Alternatively:] According to its simple meaning, הַעֵינֵי הָאֲנָשִׁים הָהֵם תְּנַקֵּר means:[22] "*You desire to make us*[23] *blind,* but we have eyes [to see the results of your leadership]. Earlier, you promised to bring us *to a land flowing with milk and honey,* but now you are saying [things] that *will cause us to die in the wilderness*" (v. 13).[23a]

this word is ו; according to the *keri,* it is י. The Baal HaTurim combines these two letters to form the word וי, *woe* (*Ittur Bikkurim*).

19. *Peirush HaRokeach.* The Talmud states: Whoever challenges his Torah teacher is considered like one who challenges the Divine Presence, as it is stated (26:9 below), *Dathan and Abiram . . . who contended against Moses and Aaron among the assembly of Korah, when they contended against HASHEM* (*Sanhedrin* 110a).

20. Translation follows the Baal HaTurim's comment in *Peirush HaTur HaAroch.* See note 22.

21. *Nimukei Yosef* to *Moed Katan* 16a, s.v., דכתיב העיני.

It would be unseemly for the Torah to repeat Dathan and Abiram's heresy verbatim (*VeChur LaZahav*).

22. That is, in the context of verses 13-14.

23. A reference to all those who left Egypt during the Exodus (*Peirush HaTur HaAroch*).

23a. *Maharam MiRothenburg.*

טו וַיִּחַר לְמֹשֶׁה מְאֹד וַיֹּאמֶר אֶל־יהוה אַל־תֵּפֶן
אֶל־מִנְחָתָם לֹא חֲמוֹר אֶחָד מֵהֶם נָשָׂאתִי וְלֹא
טז הֲרֵעֹתִי אֶת־אַחַד מֵהֶם: וַיֹּאמֶר מֹשֶׁה אֶל־קֹרַח
אַתָּה וְכָל־עֲדָתְךָ הֱיוּ לִפְנֵי יהוה אַתָּה וָהֵם וְאַהֲרֹן
יז מָחָר: וּקְחוּ ׀ אִישׁ מַחְתָּתוֹ וּנְתַתֶּם עֲלֵיהֶם קְטֹרֶת
וְהִקְרַבְתֶּם לִפְנֵי יהוה אִישׁ מַחְתָּתוֹ חֲמִשִּׁים
יח וּמָאתַיִם מַחְתֹּת וְאַתָּה וְאַהֲרֹן אִישׁ מַחְתָּתוֹ: וַיִּקְחוּ
אִישׁ מַחְתָּתוֹ וַיִּתְּנוּ עֲלֵיהֶם אֵשׁ וַיָּשִׂימוּ עֲלֵיהֶם
קְטֹרֶת וַיַּעַמְדוּ פֶּתַח אֹהֶל מוֹעֵד וּמֹשֶׁה וְאַהֲרֹן:
יט וַיַּקְהֵל עֲלֵיהֶם קֹרַח אֶת־כָּל־הָעֵדָה אֶל־פֶּתַח אֹהֶל
שלישי
כ מוֹעֵד וַיֵּרָא כְבוֹד־יהוה אֶל־כָּל־הָעֵדָה: וַיְדַבֵּר
כא יהוה אֶל־מֹשֶׁה וְאֶל־אַהֲרֹן לֵאמֹר: הִבָּדְלוּ
כב מִתּוֹךְ הָעֵדָה הַזֹּאת וַאֲכַלֶּה אֹתָם כְּרָגַע: וַיִּפְּלוּ עַל־

בעל הטורים

(טו) אל תפן. ג׳ בַּמָּסוֹרֶת — ״אַל תֵּפֶן אֶל מִנְחָתָם״; ״אַל תֵּפֶן אֶל קְשִׁי הָעָם הַזֶּה״; ״אַל תֵּפֶן אֶל אָוֶן״. פֵּרוּשׁ, הֵם קְשִׁי עָם וְדִבְרֵיהֶם דִּבְרֵי אָוֶן, לְפִיכָךְ ״אַל תֵּפֶן אֶל מִנְחָתָם״:

❑ **אחד מהם.** ד׳ בַּמָּסוֹרֶת — ״וְלֹא הֲרֵעֹתִי אֶת אַחַד מֵהֶם״; וְאִידָךְ ״כִּי יֵשְׁבוּ אַחִים יַחְדָּו וּמֵת אַחַד מֵהֶם״; ״יְהִי נָא דְבָרְךָ כִּדְבַר אַחַד מֵהֶם וְדִבַּרְתָּ טּוֹב״; ״[כִּי] כָעֵת מָחָר אָשִׂים אֶת נַפְשְׁךָ כְּנֶפֶשׁ אַחַד מֵהֶם״ בְּאֵלִיָּהוּ. פֵּרוּשׁ, שֶׁמֹּשֶׁה פִּיְּסוֹ לְקֹרַח שֶׁיְּדַבֵּר טוֹבָה וְיַחֲזוֹר בּוֹ. וְכֵיוָן שֶׁלֹּא רָצָה, רָמַז לוֹ שֶׁיָּמוּת כָּעֵת מָחָר:

(יט) ויקהל עליהם קרח. כְּמוֹ שֶׁנַּעֲשָׂה לְאַהֲרֹן כְּשֶׁנִּמְשַׁח, ״וְאֵת כָּל הָעֵדָה הַקְהֵל״:

(כא) כרגע. ג׳ בַּמָּסוֹרֶת — שְׁנַיִם בְּהַאי פָּרָשָׁה; וְאִידָךְ ״אֵיךְ הָיוּ לְשַׁמָּה כְרָגַע״, רֶמֶז לְמַאן

BAAL HATURIM ELUCIDATED

15. אַל תֵּפֶן — DO NOT TURN. The masoretic note, ג׳, means that this word appears three times in the *Tanach:* (i) here, אַל תֵּפֶן אֶל מִנְחָתָם, *Do not turn to their gift-offering;* (ii) אַל תֵּפֶן אֶל קְשִׁי הָעָם הַזֶּה, *Do not turn to the stubbornness of this people* (*Deuteronomy* 9:27); and (iii) אַל תֵּפֶן אֶל אָוֶן, *Do not turn to wrongdoing* (*Job* 36:21). The explanation [for the similarity of expression] is: [Moses said to God,] "They [i.e., Dathan and Abiram[24]] are the [most] stubborn [of the] people; their words are words of wrongdoing. Therefore, *do not turn to their gift-offering.*"

❑ **אַחַד מֵהֶם — ONE OF THEM.** The masoretic note, ד׳, means that this word appears four times in the *Tanach:* (i) here, וְלֹא הֲרֵעֹתִי אֶת אַחַד מֵהֶם, *and I have not wronged* [*even*] *one of them;* (ii) כִּי יֵשְׁבוּ אַחִים יַחְדָּו וּמֵת אַחַד מֵהֶם, *when brothers dwell together and one of them dies* (*Deuteronomy* 25:5); (iii) יְהִי נָא דְבָרְךָ כִּדְבַר אַחַד מֵהֶם וְדִבַּרְתָּ טּוֹב,

24. See *Ibn Ezra* and *Ramban.*

16/15-21

[15] *This distressed Moses greatly, and he said to* HASHEM,
"Do not turn to their gift-offering! I have not taken even one
donkey from them and I have not wronged even one of them."
[16] *Moses said to Korah, "You and your entire assembly, be*
before HASHEM *— you, they, and Aaron — tomorrow.* [17] *Let*
each man take his fire-pan and you shall place incense on
them and you shall bring before HASHEM *each man with his*
fire-pan — two hundred and fifty fire-pans; and you and
Aaron, each man with his fire-pan."
[18] *So they took — each man his fire-pan — and they placed*
fire on them and put incense on them; and they stood at the
entrance of the Tent of Meeting, with Moses and Aaron.
[19] *Korah gathered the entire assembly against them at the*
entrance of the Tent of Meeting, and the glory of HASHEM
appeared to the entire assembly.
[20] HASHEM *spoke to Moses and Aaron, saying,* [21] *"Separate*
yourselves from amid this assembly, and I shall destroy them
in an instant!"

Please let your words be like the word of one of them, and speak favorably! (*I Kings* 22:13); and (iv) [כִּי] כָעֵת מָחָר אָשִׂים אֶת נַפְשְׁךָ כְּנֶפֶשׁ אַחַד מֵהֶם, [*For*] *at this time tomorrow I shall make your soul like the soul of one of them* (*I Kings* 19:2), [in Jezebel's death threat] against Elijah. The explanation [for the similarity of expression] is: Moses endeavored to appease Korah[24a] so that he would speak favorably[24b] and repent. But when Korah refused, Moses intimated to him that he would die[24c] *at this time tomorrow.*[24d]

19. וַיַּקְהֵל עֲלֵיהֶם קֹרַח — **KORAH GATHERED [THE ENTIRE ASSEMBLY] AGAINST THEM.** As was done when Aaron was anointed, [as it is written,] וְאֵת כָּל הָעֵדָה הַקְהֵל, *Gather the entire assembly* (*Leviticus* 8:3).[25]

21. כְּרָגַע — **IN AN INSTANT.** The masoretic note, ג׳, means that this word appears three times in the *Tanach:*[25a] (i-ii) twice in this *parashah* [וַאֲכַלֶּה אֹתָם כְּרָגַע, *and I shall destroy them in an instant*] (here, and in 17:10 below); and (iii) אֵיךְ הָיוּ לְשַׁמָּה כְרָגַע [סָפוּ תַמּוּ], *How have they become desolate in an instant!* [*They perished; they ceased*] (*Psalms* 73:19). This is an allusion to the opinion that

24a. As in our verse.

24b. As in *I Kings* 22:13.

24c. As in *Deuteronomy* 25:5.

24d. As in *I Kings* 19:2.

25. Korah sought to remove the priesthood from Aaron and take it for himself. The Torah therefore uses similar wording for Aaron's anointment and Korah's rebellion (*Shoham Yakar*).

25a. The text follows *Shoham Yakar's* manuscript edition. Most other editions read incorrectly: ב׳ בַּמָּסוֹרֶת בְּהַאי פָּרָשָׁה וְאִידָךְ, *The masoretic note,* ב׳, *means that this word appears twice: In this parashah and another time in . . .*

פְּנֵיהֶם֙ וַיֹּ֣אמְר֔וּ אֵ֕ל אֱלֹהֵ֥י הָרוּחֹ֖ת לְכָל־בָּשָׂ֑ר הָאִ֣ישׁ
כג אֶחָד֙ יֶחֱטָ֔א וְעַ֥ל כָּל־הָעֵדָ֖ה תִּקְצֹֽף׃ וַיְדַבֵּ֥ר
כד יְהוָ֖ה אֶל־מֹשֶׁ֥ה לֵּאמֹֽר׃ דַּבֵּ֥ר אֶל־הָעֵדָ֖ה לֵאמֹ֑ר
כה הֵעָלוּ֙ מִסָּבִ֔יב לְמִשְׁכַּן־קֹ֖רַח דָּתָ֥ן וַאֲבִירָֽם׃ וַיָּ֣קָם
מֹשֶׁ֔ה וַיֵּ֖לֶךְ אֶל־דָּתָ֣ן וַאֲבִירָ֑ם וַיֵּלְכ֥וּ אַחֲרָ֖יו זִקְנֵ֥י
כו יִשְׂרָאֵֽל׃ וַיְדַבֵּ֨ר אֶל־הָעֵדָ֜ה לֵאמֹ֗ר ס֣וּרוּ נָ֡א מֵעַל֩
אָהֳלֵ֞י הָאֲנָשִׁ֤ים הָֽרְשָׁעִים֙ הָאֵ֔לֶּה וְאַֽל־תִּגְּע֖וּ בְּכָל־
כז אֲשֶׁ֣ר לָהֶ֑ם פֶּן־תִּסָּפ֖וּ בְּכָל־חַטֹּאתָֽם׃ וַיֵּעָל֗וּ מֵעַ֧ל
מִשְׁכַּן־קֹ֛רַח דָּתָ֥ן וַאֲבִירָ֖ם מִסָּבִ֑יב וְדָתָ֨ן וַאֲבִירָ֜ם
יָצְא֣וּ נִצָּבִ֗ים פֶּ֚תַח אָהֳלֵיהֶ֔ם וּנְשֵׁיהֶ֥ם וּבְנֵיהֶ֖ם וְטַפָּֽם׃
כח וַיֹּ֣אמֶר מֹשֶׁ֔ה בְּזֹאת֙ תֵּֽדְע֔וּן כִּֽי־יְהוָ֣ה שְׁלָחַ֔נִי
לַעֲשׂ֕וֹת אֵ֥ת כָּל־הַֽמַּעֲשִׂ֖ים הָאֵ֑לֶּה כִּי־לֹ֖א מִלִּבִּֽי׃
כט אִם־כְּמ֤וֹת כָּל־הָֽאָדָם֙ יְמֻת֣וּן אֵ֔לֶּה וּפְקֻדַּת֙ כָּל־

בעל הטורים

דְּאָמַר, עֲדַת קֹרַח אֵין לָהֶם חֵלֶק לָעוֹלָם הַבָּא. וְהַיְנוּ דִּכְתִיב "הָיוּ לְשַׁמָּה כְרָגַע, סָפוּ תַמּוּ", "סָפוּ" בָּעוֹלָם הַזֶּה, "תַּמּוּ" לָעוֹלָם הַבָּא:

(כו) תִּסָּפוּ. ב׳ בַּמָּסוֹרֶת — "פֶּן תִּסָּפוּ בְּכָל חַטֹּאתָם"; "וְאִם הָרֵעַ תָּרֵעוּ גַּם אַתֶּם גַּם מַלְכְּכֶם תִּסָּפוּ". שֶׁאָמַר לָהֶם, שֶׁאִם לֹא יַחְזְרוּ בָהֶם, שֶׁיָּמוּתוּ הֵם וְקֹרַח גְּדוֹלָם:

(כט) יְמֻתוּן. ב׳ בַּמָּסוֹרֶת — "כְּמוֹת כָּל הָאָדָם יְמֻתוּן"; "וְהָאָרֶץ כַּבֶּגֶד תִּבְלֶה וְיֹשְׁבֶיהָ כְּמוֹ כֵן יְמוּתוּן". פֵּרוּשׁ, אָמַר שֶׁתִּבְלֶה, וְיוֹשְׁבֶיהָ יְמוּתוּן שֶׁיִּבָּלְעוּ הֵם תַּחְתָּם:

❑ **וּפְקֻדַּת.** ג׳ בַּמָּסוֹרֶת — "וּפְקֻדַּת כָּל הָאָדָם"; "וּפְקֻדַּת מִשְׁמֶרֶת"; "וּפְקֻדַּת אֶלְעָזָר בֶּן אַהֲרֹן". בִּשְׁבִיל שֶׁרָצוּ לִכָּנֵס בִּפְקֻדַּת אֶלְעָזָר, שֶׁבִּקְשׁוּ כְהֻנָּה, עַל כֵּן "וּפְקֻדַּת כָּל הָאָדָם וְגוֹ׳ ":

BAAL HATURIM ELUCIDATED

Korah's assembly will not receive a portion in the World to Come (*Sanhedrin* 108a-109b). This is the meaning of the verse [from *Psalms*]: *They have become desolate in an instant! They perished; they ceased.* [That is,] *they perished,* in this world; *they ceased,* regarding the World to Come.

26. תִּסָּפוּ — YOU WILL PERISH. The masoretic note, ב׳, means that this word appears twice in the *Tanach:* (i) here, פֶּן תִּסָּפוּ בְּכָל חַטֹּאתָם, *lest you will perish because of all their sins;* and (ii) וְאִם הָרֵעַ תָּרֵעוּ גַּם אַתֶּם גַּם מַלְכְּכֶם תִּסָּפוּ, *But if you act wickedly, both you and your king will perish* (*I Samuel* 12:25). [The similarity of expression indicates] that Moses told them that if they would not repent, they would die — they and Korah, their leader.[25b]

25b. At first glance, the Baal HaTurim seems to add nothing to the simple meaning of the passage: If they do not repent, they will die. At closer look, however, the Baal HaTurim adds an

22 They fell on their faces and said, "O God, God of the spirits of
all flesh, shall one man sin, and You be angry with the entire
assembly?"
23 HASHEM spoke to Moses saying, 24 "Speak to the assembly,
saying, 'Get yourselves up from all around the dwelling places of
Korah, Dathan, and Abiram.' "
25 So Moses stood up and went to Dathan and Abiram, and the
elders of Israel followed him. 26 He spoke to the assembly, saying,
"Turn away now from near the tents of these wicked men, and do
not touch anything of theirs, lest you will perish because of all
their sins." 27 So they got themselves up from near the dwelling of
Korah, Dathan, and Abiram, from all around. Dathan and
Abiram went out erect at the entrance of their tents, with their
wives, their children, and their infants.
28 Moses said, "Through this shall you know that HASHEM sent
me to perform all these acts, that it was not from my heart. 29 If
these will die like the death of all men, and the [final] visitation of all

BAAL HATURIM ELUCIDATED

29. יְמֻתוּן — [THESE] WILL DIE. The masoretic note, ב׳, means that this word appears twice in the *Tanach:* (i) here, כְּמוֹת כָּל הָאָדָם יְמֻתוּן, *[If these] will die like the death of all men;* and (ii) וְהָאָרֶץ כַּבֶּגֶד תִּבְלֶה וְיֹשְׁבֶיהָ כְּמוֹ כֵן יְמוּתוּן, *And the earth will wear thin like a garment and its inhabitants as well will die* (*Isaiah* 51:6). This means: [Moses] said[26] that it would wear thin, and [as a result,] its inhabitants would die, for they would be swallowed up beneath themselves.[27]

❑ **וּפְקֻדַּת**[28] — AND THE [FINAL] VISITATION OF. The masoretic note, ג׳, means that this word appears three times in the *Tanach:* (i) here, וּפְקֻדַּת כָּל הָאָדָם, *the [final] visitation of all men;* (ii) וּפְקֻדַּת מִשְׁמֶרֶת, *and the duty of the charge* (3:36 above); and (iii) וּפְקֻדַּת אֶלְעָזָר בֶּן אַהֲרֹן, *and the duty of Elazar son of Aaron* (4:16 above). Because they sought to usurp פְּקֻדַּת אֶלְעָזָר, *the duty of Elazar* — for they sought the priesthood — therefore, [they were denied] *the final visitation of all men* [i.e., a natural death].[28a]

---

important point: If they [i.e., the assembly] would not repent, they would die — they and Korah [even if he repented, because he was] their leader [and so must suffer the consequence of their action] (A.S.).

26. The text follows the early printed editions and *Shoham Yakar's* manuscript edition. The Furth edition and *Ittur Bikkurim* replace אָמַר, *he said,* with אַחַר, *after,* i.e., after the earth will wear thin, its inhabitants will die, for they will be swallowed up.

27. The Baal HaTurim seems to be describing the mechanism by which God will put the rebels to death: The ground under their feet will attenuate until it can no longer support their weight.

28. The verb root פקד has many meanings, depending upon the context in which it is used. Thus, it can mean *to count* or *to number* (1:44 above); *to appoint* (27:16 below); *to punish* or *to visit upon* (14:18 above). Accordingly, the related noun פְּקֻדָּה can refer to *duty* or *assignment* (4:16 above); *punishment* or *visitation* (*Hosea* 9:7).

28a. The Baal HaTurim's comment shows the connection between our verse and the verse about Elazar. It does not include anything about verse 3:36, which refers to the children of Merari (Y.S.).

ל הָאָדָם יִפָּקֵד עֲלֵיהֶם לֹא יהוה שְׁלָחָנִי: וְאִם־
בְּרִיאָה יִבְרָא יהוה וּפָצְתָה הָאֲדָמָה אֶת־פִּיהָ
וּבָלְעָה אֹתָם וְאֶת־כָּל־אֲשֶׁר לָהֶם וְיָרְדוּ חַיִּים
שְׁאֹלָה וִידַעְתֶּם כִּי נִאֲצוּ הָאֲנָשִׁים הָאֵלֶּה אֶת־
לא יהוה: וַיְהִי כְּכַלֹּתוֹ לְדַבֵּר אֵת כָּל־הַדְּבָרִים הָאֵלֶּה
לב וַתִּבָּקַע הָאֲדָמָה אֲשֶׁר תַּחְתֵּיהֶם: וַתִּפְתַּח הָאָרֶץ

בעל הטורים

❑ **וּפְקֻדַּת כָּל הָאָדָם יִפָּקֵד {עֲלֵיהֶם}.** אָמַר מֹשֶׁה, אִם הַקָּדוֹשׁ בָּרוּךְ הוּא יַעֲשֶׂה לְאֵלּוּ כְּמוֹ שֶׁעוֹשֶׂה לְכָל הָאָדָם, שֶׁהוּא פֹּקֵד עֲוֹן אָבֹת עַל בָּנִים עַל שִׁלֵּשִׁים וְעַל רִבֵּעִים. אֶלָּא שֶׁיַּעֲנִישֵׁם מִיָּד:

(ל) **בְּרִיאָה.** ב׳ בַּמָּסוֹרֶת מִתְּרֵי לִישְׁנֵי — ״וְאִם בְּרִיאָה״; ״וּמַאֲכָלוֹ בְּרִאָה״. שֶׁהֶאֱכִיל קֹרַח לַעֲדָתוֹ עַד שֶׁהִמְשִׁיכָם אַחֲרָיו, כִּדְאִיתָא בְּפֶרֶק אַרְבַּע מִיתוֹת בֵּית דִּין:

❑ **כִּי נִאֲצוּ הָאֲנָשִׁים הָאֵלֶּה.** רָאשֵׁי תֵבוֹת הַכֹּהֵן, עַל שֶׁבִּקְּשׁוּ כְהֻנָּה:

(לא) **וַתִּבָּקַע.** ד׳ בַּמָּסוֹרֶת — ״וַתִּבָּקַע הָאֲדָמָה״; וְאִידָךְ ״וַתִּבָּקַע הָאָרֶץ בְּקוֹלָם״; ״וַתִּבָּקַע הָעִיר״ בְּיִרְמְיָה; וּבִמְלָכִים עַל יְרוּשָׁלַיִם. ״וַתִּבָּקַע הָאָרֶץ בְּקוֹלָם״, וְהַיְנוּ דִּכְתִיב ״וְכָל יִשְׂרָאֵל אֲשֶׁר סְבִיבֹתֵיהֶם נָסוּ לְקֹלָם״. וְרֶמֶז לְהָא דְּאִיתָא בְּעֵרוּבִין, שֶׁפִּתְחָהּ שֶׁל גֵּיהִנֹּם

BAAL HATURIM ELUCIDATED

❑ **וּפְקֻדַּת כָּל הָאָדָם יִפָּקֵד {עֲלֵיהֶם}** — AND THE [FINAL] VISITATION OF ALL MEN IS VISITED {UPON THEM}. Moses said, "If the Holy One, Blessed is He, will do unto them as He does unto all men,[28b] i.e., פֹּקֵד[29] עֲוֹן אָבֹת עַל בָּנִים עַל שִׁלֵּשִׁים וְעַל רִבֵּעִים, [He] *visits the sins of the fathers upon children, upon the third* [*generations*] *and upon the fourth* (*Exodus* 20:5),[29a] [then *He did not send me*]. Rather, He will punish them immediately [for their present rebellion]."[30]

30. בְּרִיאָה — A CREATION. The masoretic note,[31] ב׳ מִתְּרֵי לִישְׁנֵי, means *this word*

28b. That is, unto all men who may be classified by God as שֹׂנְאָי, *those who hate Me* (*Exodus* 20:5).

29. See note 28.

29a. In his commentary to that verse in *Peirush HaTur HaAroch,* the Baal HaTurim cites two interpretations: According to the *Ibn Ezra,* God patiently waits to see whether the succeeding generations will produce a righteous descendant who will break from his forebear's evil ways. Perhaps the second generation will repent; perhaps the third or even the fourth. But that is the last chance. If no descendant has changed, then God brings to mind all the sins of the four generations. Only after the fourth generation does he punish the original sinner with the annihilation of his posterity. According to the *Rambam,* the sins of one man are not sufficient cause to annihilate his posterity. However, if his succeeding generations continue in his ways, their sins are added to his until his cup of iniquities is filled to its brim. At that time, whether it be the second, third, or fourth generation, God decrees the annihilation of his posterity.

Here, however, Moses said that God would not wait even one moment. Rather, He would annihilate them immediately.

30. *Ittur Bikkurim* adds: And that will be the proof that He has sent me.

31. Two masoretic notes appear on this word. The one cited by the Baal HaTurim reads: ב׳ חַד מָלֵא וְחַד חָסֵר, *Two, one spelled in full* (בְּרִיאָה); *and one spelled defectively* (בְּרָאָה).

men is visited upon them, then it is not HASHEM Who has
sent me. 30 But if HASHEM will create a creation, and the
ground will open its mouth and swallow them and all that is
theirs, and they will descend alive to the pit — then you
shall know that these men have provoked HASHEM!"
31 When he finished speaking all these words, the ground
that was under them split open. 32 The earth opened its

BAAL HATURIM ELUCIDATED

appears twice in the Tanach, but with different meanings:[32] (i) here, וְאִם בְּרִיאָה, *and if* [*HASHEM will create*] *a creation;* and (ii) וּמַאֲכָלוֹ בְּרִאָה, *And his food is fat* (*Habakkuk* 1:16). [This similarity of expression indicates] that Korah continued to ply his assembly with food[33] until he had lured them to follow him, as recorded in Chapter *Arba Misos*[34] *Beis Din.*[35]

❑ כִּי נִאֲצוּ הָאֲנָשִׁים הָאֵלֶּה — **THAT THESE MEN HAVE PROVOKED.** The initial letters of these words [can be rearranged to] spell הַכֹּהֵן, *the Kohen.*[35a] [This indicates that the ultimate reason for their provocation was] that they sought to usurp the priesthood.[36]

31. וַתִּבָּקַע — **[THE GROUND . . .] SPLIT OPEN.** The masoretic note ד׳ means that this term appears four times in the *Tanach:* (i) here, וַתִּבָּקַע הָאֲדָמָה, *the ground split open;* (ii) וַתִּבָּקַע הָאָרֶץ בְּקוֹלָם, *the earth split open at their sound* (*I Kings* 1:40); and (iii-iv) וַתִּבָּקַע הָעִיר, *The city* [*wall*] *was split open,* in *Jeremiah* (52:7) and *Kings* (II 25:4) with regard to Jerusalem. [The similarity of expression here and in *I Kings* indicates that here, too,] *the earth split open at their sound,* as it is written וְכָל יִשְׂרָאֵל אֲשֶׁר סְבִיבֹתֵיהֶם נָסוּ לְקֹלָם, *All Israel who were around them fled at their sound* (v. 34 below).

[And the similarity of expression here and in *II Kings* and *Jeremiah* is] an allusion to that which is stated in tractate *Eruvin,* that the portal of *Gehinnom* (Hell)

32. In our verse, בְּרִיאָה is a noun meaning a *creation;* in *Habakkuk* it is an adjective, the feminine form of בָּרִיא, which can mean either *fat* or *nutritious.* Nevertheless, both words derive from the root ברא, which can mean *to create* (as in *Genesis* 1:1) or *to feed* (as in *I Samuel* 2:29).

33. As it appears here, the allusion does not include the key word בְּרִאָה [or בְּרִיאָה]. However, *Maharam MiRothenburg,* the Baal HaTurim's apparent source, reads, בִּשְׁבִיל מַאֲכָלִים בְּרִיאִים שֶׁהֶאֱכִילָם קֹרַח, *because of the fat foods that Korah fed them.* And that is the Baal HaTurim's intention also.

34. The seventh chapter of tractate *Sanhedrin* begins, אַרְבַּע מִיתוֹת נִמְסְרוּ לְבֵית דִּין, and is usually referred to as פֶּרֶק אַרְבַּע מִיתוֹת. Nevertheless, some of the *Rishonim* (medieval authorities) refer to it as פֶּרֶק אַרְבַּע מִיתוֹת בֵּית דִּין omitting the word נִמְסְרוּ from the chapter title (e.g., *Ramban* to 35:29 below; *Ritva* to *Avodah Zarah* 49b).

35. *Maharam MiRothenburg,* based on *Sanhedrin* 52a, cited by the Baal HaTurim in his comments to 17:3 below, s.v., אֵת מַחְתּוֹת הַחַטָּאִים.

35a. It is not clear why the Baal HaTurim reads the initial letters as הַכֹּהֵן, *the Kohen,* rather than the expected כְּהֻנָּה, *priesthood.* In *Paaneach Raza,* this comment reads: רָאשֵׁי תֵבוֹת כְּהֻנָּה וְרָאשֵׁי תֵבוֹת הַכֹּהֵן. Perhaps the term הַכֹּהֵן indicates that Korah's rebels not only sought the priesthood, but each wanted to be "the Kohen," i.e., the *Kohen Gadol* (*VeChur LaZahav*).

36. *Peirush HaRokeach.*

אֶת־פִּ֫יהָ וַתִּבְלַ֣ע אֹתָ֔ם וְאֶת־בָּתֵּיהֶ֑ם וְאֵ֤ת כָּל־הָֽאָדָם֙
לג אֲשֶׁ֣ר לְקֹ֔רַח וְאֵ֖ת כָּל־הָֽרְכֽוּשׁ׃ וַיֵּ֨רְד֜וּ הֵ֣ם וְכָל־אֲשֶׁ֥ר
לָהֶ֛ם חַיִּ֖ים שְׁאֹ֑לָה וַתְּכַ֤ס עֲלֵיהֶם֙ הָאָ֔רֶץ וַיֹּאבְד֖וּ
לד מִתּ֥וֹךְ הַקָּהָֽל׃ וְכָל־יִשְׂרָאֵ֗ל אֲשֶׁ֛ר סְבִיבֹתֵיהֶ֖ם נָ֣סוּ
לה לְקֹלָ֑ם כִּ֣י אָֽמְר֔וּ פֶּן־תִּבְלָעֵ֖נוּ הָאָֽרֶץ׃ וְאֵ֥שׁ יָֽצְאָ֖ה
מֵאֵ֣ת יְהוָ֑ה וַתֹּ֗אכַל אֵ֣ת הַחֲמִשִּׁ֤ים וּמָאתַ֙יִם֙ אִ֔ישׁ
יז א מַקְרִיבֵ֖י הַקְּטֹֽרֶת׃ וַיְדַבֵּ֥ר יְהוָ֖ה אֶל־מֹשֶׁ֥ה
ב לֵּאמֹֽר׃ אֱמֹ֨ר אֶל־אֶלְעָזָ֜ר בֶּן־אַהֲרֹ֣ן הַכֹּהֵ֗ן וְיָרֵ֤ם
אֶת־הַמַּחְתֹּת֙ מִבֵּ֣ין הַשְּׂרֵפָ֔ה וְאֶת־הָאֵ֖שׁ זְרֵה־הָ֑לְאָה
ג כִּ֖י קָדֵֽשׁוּ׃ אֵ֗ת מַחְתּוֹת֩ הַחַטָּאִ֨ים הָאֵ֜לֶּה בְּנַפְשֹׁתָ֗ם

בעל הטורים

בִּירוּשָׁלַיִם. "וַתִּבָּקַע הָעִיר", פֵּרוּשׁ בִּירוּשָׁלַיִם, שָׁם "וַתִּבָּקַע הָאֲדָמָה . . . וַיֵּרְדוּ . . . שְׁאֹלָה":

(לב) הָאָדָם אֲשֶׁר לְקֹרַח. סוֹפֵי תֵבוֹת חֵרֶם. מְלַמֵּד שֶׁעֲשָׂאָן חֵרֶם עַל שֶׁנִּתְחַבְּרוּ לְקֹרַח:

(לג) וַיֹּאבְדוּ. ב׳ בַּמָּסוֹרֶת — "וַיֹּאבְדוּ מִתּוֹךְ הַקָּהָל"; וְאִידָךְ "וַיֹּאבְדוּ כְּלֵי מִלְחָמָה". כֵּיוָן שֶׁנֶּאֶבְדוּ, נֶאֱבַד כְּלֵי מִלְחָמָה:

יז (ג) **אֵת מַחְתּוֹת הַחַטָּאִים הָאֵלֶּה בְּנַפְשֹׁתָם.** שֶׁנִּתְחַיְּבוּ עַל עִסְקֵי נַפְשׁוֹתָם. כִּדְרֵישׁ לָקִישׁ, דְּאָמַר רֵישׁ לָקִישׁ, מַאי דִּכְתִיב "בְּחַנְפֵי לַעֲגֵי מָעוֹג חָרֹק עָלַי שִׁנֵּימוֹ"? בִּשְׁבִיל

BAAL HATURIM ELUCIDATED

is in Jerusalem.[37] Thus, וַתִּבָּקַע הָעִיר, *the city was split open,* i.e., in Jerusalem, *the ground split open . . . and they descended . . . to the pit* (v. 36).[38,39]

---

37. *Eruvin* 19a. The Talmud there discusses the number and the locations of the entrances to *Gehinnom:* There are three portals to *Gehinnom* — one in the wilderness; one in the sea; one in Jerusalem. One is in the wilderness, as it is written, *They and all that was theirs descended alive into the pit* (v. 33 below); one is in the sea, as it is written [in Jonah's prayer from within the fish]. *From the belly of the fish I cried and You heard my voice* (*Jonah* 2:3); and one in Jerusalem, as it is written, *So speaks HASHEM, He Who has a fire in Zion and a furnace in Jerusalem* (*Isaiah* 31:9) . . . "a fire in Zion" refers to *Gehinnom,* and "a furnace in Jerusalem" refers to the portal of *Gehinnom.*

It is noteworthy that the Baal HaTurim finds in our passage an allusion to the portal in Jerusalem, while the *Gemara* states that our passage speaks of the portal in the wilderness. Indeed our verse also alludes to the portal in the sea, for the letters of the word תַּחְתֵּיהֶם, *under them,* may be rearranged to spell תַּחַת הַיָּם, *under the sea.* Then, the statement, וַתִּבָּקַע הָאֲדָמָה אֲשֶׁר תַּחְתֵּיהֶם, may be interpreted, *the ground that is under the sea split open* (*VeChur LaZahav*).

38. According to the Talmud, there are seven names for *Gehinnom:* (i) שְׁאוֹל, *Sheol* or *the Pit* (*Jonah* 2:3); (ii) אֲבַדּוֹן, *Annihilation* (*Psalms* 88:12); (iii) בְּאֵר שַׁחַת, *Well of Destruction* (*Psalms* 16:10); (iv-v) בּוֹר שָׁאוֹן, *Pit of Turbulent Waters,* and טִיט הַיָּוֵן, *Mire* (*Psalms* 40:3); (vi) צַלְמָוֶת, *Shadow of Death* (*Psalms* 107:10); and (vii) אֶרֶץ הַתַּחְתִּית, *Nethermost Earth,* a name known by tradition (*Eruvin* 19a). Although the Talmud does not cite a verse regarding the seventh name, that name does appear in *Ezekiel* 31:14,16,18.

39. *Sanhedrin* 110a — The Talmud there expounds on our verse: What did Moses mean by, *"But if HASHEM will create a creation and the ground will open its mouth"*? Moses said before the Holy One, Blessed is He, "If *Gehinnom* has been created, good. But, if not, let God create it now."

[The Talmud questions this:] To what purpose?

mouth and swallowed them and their households, and all the people who were with Korah, and the entire wealth. 33 They and all that was theirs descended alive to the pit; the earth covered them over and they were lost from among the congregation. 34 All Israel who were around them fled at their sound, for they said, "Lest the earth swallow us!"

35 A flame came forth from HASHEM and consumed the two hundred and fifty men who were offering the incense.

17 1 HASHEM spoke to Moses, saying, 2 "Say to Elazar son of Aaron the Kohen and let him pick up the fire-pans from amid the fire — and he should throw away the flame — for they have become holy. 3 As for the fire-pans of these sinners against their souls —

BAAL HATURIM ELUCIDATED

32. הָאָדָם אֲשֶׁר לְקֹרַח — THE PEOPLE WHO WERE WITH KORAH. The final letters of these words [in reverse order] spell חֵרֶם, *condemned.*[39a] This teaches that they were condemned because they joined with Korah.[40]

33. וַיֹּאבְדוּ — AND THEY WERE LOST. The masoretic note, ב׳, means that this word appears twice in the *Tanach:* (i) here, וַיֹּאבְדוּ מִתּוֹךְ הַקָּהָל, *and they were lost from among the congregation;* and (ii) וַיֹּאבְדוּ כְּלֵי מִלְחָמָה, *and the weapons of war went lost* (*II Samuel* 1:27). [The similarity of expressions indicates that] once Korah and his company were lost to the world, the weapons of war went lost.[41]

XVII

3. אֵת מַחְתּוֹת הַחַטָּאִים הָאֵלֶּה בְּנַפְשֹׁתָם — AS FOR THE FIRE-PANS OF THESE SINNERS AGAINST[41a] THEIR SOULS. They were culpable as a consequence of matters related to [the sustenance of] their souls.[42] As the *Amora* Reish Lakish said: What is the meaning of the verse, בְּחַנְפֵי לַעֲגֵי מָעוֹג חָרֹק עָלַי שִׁנֵּימוֹ, *With flattery and mockery, for the sake of a loaf, he gnashes his teeth at me* (*Psalms* 35:16)? On

If you would say that he wanted God to create a new place called *Gehinnom,* that cannot be, for we have learned, *There is nothing new under the sun* (*Ecclesiastes* 1:9). [Thus, if there were ever to be a *Gehinnom,* it would have been created during the first Six Days of Creation (*Rashi*).] Rather, Moses prayed that the portal of *Gehinnom* be brought near [i.e., God should transport the portal of *Gehinnom* to the spot where Korah and his followers were standing (*Rashi*)].

39a. As used here, the term חֵרֶם can refer to ostracism, destruction or condemnation to death. The Baal HaTurim uses it in the last sense.

40. *Peirush HaRokeach.*

41. Korah was a wise man (*Bamidbar Rabbah* 18:8, cited in *Rashi* to v. 7 above). All two hundred and fifty of his followers were exceptional scholars, heads of courts of law (*Bamidbar Rabbah* 18:3, cited in *Rashi* to v. 1 above, s.v., וְדָתָן וַאֲבִירָם). And whereas the Talmud refers to the give and take, the thrusts and parries of Torah study as מִלְחַמְתָּהּ שֶׁל תּוֹרָה, *the battle of Torah* (see, e.g., *Sanhedrin* 111b; *Chagigah* 14a), Korah and his men can be described as armed for battle, for they possessed the weapons needed in מִלְחַמְתָּהּ שֶׁל תּוֹרָה. When they perished, those weapons — their scholarship, their keenness of thought — perished with them (*VeChur LaZahav,* based on *Maharam MiRothenburg*).

41a. That is, their deaths were a form of suicide, for their willful rebellion was a capital sin (see *Targum Onkelos* and *Gur Aryeh*).

42. The Talmud interprets the verse, מֵאֲשֶׁר חָטָא עַל הַנָּפֶשׁ, literally, *for having sinned regarding the*

וְעָשׂוּ אֹתָם רִקֻּעֵי פַחִים צִפּוּי לַמִּזְבֵּחַ כִּי־הִקְרִיבֻם
ד לִפְנֵי־יהוה וַיִּקְדָּשׁוּ וְיִהְיוּ לְאוֹת לִבְנֵי יִשְׂרָאֵל: וַיִּקַּח
אֶלְעָזָר הַכֹּהֵן אֵת מַחְתּוֹת הַנְּחֹשֶׁת אֲשֶׁר הִקְרִיבוּ
ה הַשְּׂרֻפִים וַיְרַקְּעוּם צִפּוּי לַמִּזְבֵּחַ: זִכָּרוֹן לִבְנֵי
יִשְׂרָאֵל לְמַעַן אֲשֶׁר לֹא־יִקְרַב אִישׁ זָר אֲשֶׁר לֹא
מִזֶּרַע אַהֲרֹן הוּא לְהַקְטִיר קְטֹרֶת לִפְנֵי יהוה
וְלֹא־יִהְיֶה כְקֹרַח וְכַעֲדָתוֹ כַּאֲשֶׁר דִּבֶּר יהוה
בְּיַד־מֹשֶׁה לוֹ:
ו וַיִּלֹּנוּ כָּל־עֲדַת בְּנֵי־יִשְׂרָאֵל מִמָּחֳרָת עַל־
מֹשֶׁה וְעַל־אַהֲרֹן לֵאמֹר אַתֶּם הֲמִתֶּם אֶת־עַם
ז יהוה: וַיְהִי בְּהִקָּהֵל הָעֵדָה עַל־מֹשֶׁה וְעַל־
אַהֲרֹן וַיִּפְנוּ אֶל־אֹהֶל מוֹעֵד וְהִנֵּה כִסָּהוּ הֶעָנָן
ח וַיֵּרָא כְּבוֹד יהוה: וַיָּבֹא מֹשֶׁה וְאַהֲרֹן אֶל־פְּנֵי
רביעי ט אֹהֶל מוֹעֵד: וַיְדַבֵּר יהוה אֶל־מֹשֶׁה
י לֵאמֹר: הֵרֹמּוּ מִתּוֹךְ הָעֵדָה הַזֹּאת וַאֲכַלֶּה אֹתָם

בעל הטורים

חֲנֻפָּה שֶׁהֶחֱנִיפָם קֹרַח עַל עִסְקֵי לְגִימָה, חָרַק עֲלֵיהֶם שַׂר שֶׁל גֵּיהִנֹּם שִׁנָּיו. "חָרַק" אוֹתִיּוֹת קֹרַח:

❑ **הַחַטָּאִים.** ב׳ בַּמָּסוֹרֶת — "הַחַטָּאִים הָאֵלֶּה בְּנַפְשֹׁתָם"; "הַחַטָּאִים אֶת עֲמָלֵק". לוֹמַר לְךָ כְּמוֹ שֶׁאֵלּוּ חָטְאוּ בְּנַפְשׁוֹתָם, כָּךְ חָטָא עֲמָלֵק בְּנַפְשׁוֹ. שֶׁרָאָה כָל הַנִּסִּים שֶׁנַּעֲשׂוּ לְיִשְׂרָאֵל, וְנִזְדַּוֵּג לָהֶם. כִּדְאִיתָא בְּמִדְרָשׁ, מָשָׁל לְמִי שֶׁרָאָה אַמְבַּטִּי רוֹתַחַת וְקָפַץ בְּתוֹכָהּ:

BAAL HATURIM ELUCIDATED

account of the flattery with which Korah flattered them[43] in matters of feast-

soul (6:11 above), as a reference to the nazirite prohibiting himself from drinking wine (*Taanis* 11a). Similarly, the Talmud explains the verse וְעִנִּיתֶם אֶת נַפְשֹׁתֵיכֶם, literally, *and you shall afflict your souls* (*Leviticus* 23:27), as a prohibition against food and drink on Yom Kippur (*Yoma* 74b). Thus, the Talmud refers to sustenance as עִסְקֵי נְפָשׁוֹת, *matters pertaining to the soul* (*Shoham Yakar*).

43. Extant versions of the Talmud read, בִּשְׁבִיל חֲנֻפָּה שֶׁהֶחֱנִיפוּ לְקֹרַח, *On account of the flattery with which they flattered Korah,* i.e., Korah wined and dined them and they flattered him so that he should continue providing them with food and drink. In other words, Korah was the flattered and his followers were the flatterers. And that is the version cited by *Maharam MiRothenburg,* the Baal HaTurim's apparent source for this comment. *Rashi's* comment, however, implies that Korah was the flatterer and his followers were the flattered, for *Rashi* paraphrases the Talmud: On account of the flattery of beverage and loaf that Korah dined and wined his assembly . . . Accordingly, *Rashi's* comment is at odds with the Talmudic text. To reconcile *Rashi* with the words of the Talmud, it is suggested that the Talmud manuscript used by *Rashi* contained the version cited here by the Baal HaTurim, שֶׁהֶחֱנִיפָן קֹרַח, *with which Korah flattered them,* and that version is also cited in *Dikdukei Soferim.* Both

they shall make them hammered-out sheets as a cover-
ing for the Altar, for they offered them before HASHEM,
so they became holy; they shall be for a sign to the
Children of Israel." 4 *Elazar the Kohen took the copper*
fire-pans that the consumed ones had offered and ham-
mered them out as a covering for the Altar, 5 *as a reminder*
to the Children of Israel, so that no alien who is not of
the offspring of Aaron shall draw near to bring up the
smoke of incense before HASHEM, *that he not be like Korah*
and his assembly, as HASHEM *spoke about him through*
Moses.
6 *The entire assembly of the Children of Israel com-*
plained on the morrow against Moses and Aaron, saying,
"You have killed the people of HASHEM*!"* 7 *And it was*
when the assembly gathered against Moses and Aaron,
they turned to the Tent of Meeting and behold! the cloud
had covered it, and the glory of HASHEM *appeared.* 8 *Moses*
and Aaron came before the Tent of Meeting.
9 HASHEM *spoke to Moses, saying,* 10 *"Remove your-*
selves from among this assembly and I shall destroy them

BAAL HATURIM ELUCIDATED

ing,[44] the chief of *Gehinnom* gnashed his teeth at them.[45] [And that verse alludes to Korah, for] the word חָרַק, *gnashed,* is spelled with the same letters as the name קֹרַח, *Korah.*[46]

❑ הַחַטָּאִים — THE SINNERS. The masoretic note, ב׳, means that this word appears twice in the *Tanach:* (i) here, הַחַטָּאִים הָאֵלֶּה בְּנַפְשֹׁתָם, *these sinners against their souls;* and (ii) [אֶת] הַחַטָּאִים אֶת עֲמָלֵק, *the sinners, Amalek* (*I Samuel* 15:18). This indicates to you that just as these [Korah and his cohorts] sinned against their souls,[47] so too, Amalek sinned against its soul. For, despite seeing all the miracles wrought on behalf of the Israelites, Amalek attacked them. As the Midrash states: [Amalek's attack] is comparable to a person who saw a boiling hot bathtub and jumped into it.[48]

---

versions ascribe the underlying cause of Korah's followers' downfall to flattery — either for proffering it or for accepting it (*VeChur LaZahav*).

44. *According to Rashi* (*Sanhedrin* 52a, s.v., בחנפי לעגי מעוג, and *Psalms* 35:16) this refers to the frivolous mockery that often accompanies overindulgence in food and drink.

45. *Sanhedrin* 52a; *Maharam MiRothenburg.*

46. The Talmud does not explain how Reish Lakish infers that the verse from *Psalms* speaks of Korah. The Baal HaTurim finds an allusion to Korah in the word חָרַק.

47. That is, despite seeing all the miracles wrought through the hand of Moses, they chose to dispute his leadership (*Shoham Yakar*).

48. *Tanchuma, Ki Seitzei* 9, cited in *Rashi* to *Deuteronomy* 25:18.

יז/יא-יח

יא כְּרָגַע וַיִּפְּלוּ עַל־פְּנֵיהֶם: וַיֹּאמֶר מֹשֶׁה אֶל־אַהֲרֹן
קַח אֶת־הַמַּחְתָּה וְתֶן־עָלֶיהָ אֵשׁ מֵעַל הַמִּזְבֵּחַ
וְשִׂים קְטֹרֶת וְהוֹלֵךְ מְהֵרָה אֶל־הָעֵדָה וְכַפֵּר
עֲלֵיהֶם כִּי־יָצָא הַקֶּצֶף מִלִּפְנֵי יְהוָה הֵחֵל הַנָּגֶף:
יב וַיִּקַּח אַהֲרֹן כַּאֲשֶׁר ׀ דִּבֶּר מֹשֶׁה וַיָּרָץ אֶל־תּוֹךְ
הַקָּהָל וְהִנֵּה הֵחֵל הַנֶּגֶף בָּעָם וַיִּתֵּן אֶת־הַקְּטֹרֶת
יג וַיְכַפֵּר עַל־הָעָם: וַיַּעֲמֹד בֵּין־הַמֵּתִים וּבֵין הַחַיִּים
יד וַתֵּעָצַר הַמַּגֵּפָה: וַיִּהְיוּ הַמֵּתִים בַּמַּגֵּפָה אַרְבָּעָה
עָשָׂר אֶלֶף וּשְׁבַע מֵאוֹת מִלְּבַד הַמֵּתִים עַל־דְּבַר־
טו קֹרַח: וַיָּשָׁב אַהֲרֹן אֶל־מֹשֶׁה אֶל־פֶּתַח אֹהֶל מוֹעֵד
וְהַמַּגֵּפָה נֶעֱצָרָה:
חמישי טז-יז וַיְדַבֵּר יְהוָה אֶל־מֹשֶׁה לֵּאמֹר: דַּבֵּר ׀ אֶל־בְּנֵי
יִשְׂרָאֵל וְקַח מֵאִתָּם מַטֶּה מַטֶּה לְבֵית אָב מֵאֵת
כָּל־נְשִׂיאֵהֶם לְבֵית אֲבֹתָם שְׁנֵים עָשָׂר מַטּוֹת אִישׁ
יח אֶת־שְׁמוֹ תִּכְתֹּב עַל־מַטֵּהוּ: וְאֵת שֵׁם אַהֲרֹן תִּכְתֹּב

בעל הטורים

(י) וַיִּפְּלוּ עַל פְּנֵיהֶם. וְלֹא הִתְפַּלְּלוּ כְּמוֹ לְמַעְלָה. שֶׁלֹּא הָיְתָה תְפִלָּה שְׁגוּרָה בְּפִיהֶם, וְעַל כֵּן אָמַר "כִּי יָצָא הַקֶּצֶף". כִּדְאָמַר רַבִּי חֲנִינָא בֶּן דּוֹסָא, כְּשֶׁהָיָה מִתְפַּלֵּל עַל הַחוֹלִים, אִם אֵין תְּפִלָּתִי שְׁגוּרָה בְּפִי אֲנִי יוֹדֵעַ שֶׁהוּא מְטֹרָף:

(יב) וַיָּרָץ. בְּאַ"תְּ בַּ"שׁ אוֹתִיּוֹת "מַגֵּפָה", שֶׁרָץ לְהַעֲצִיר הַמַּגֵּפָה:

BAAL HATURIM ELUCIDATED

10. {The Baal HaTuRim's comment to כְּרָגַע appears at 16:21 above.}

❑ וַיִּפְּלוּ עַל פְּנֵיהֶם — **THEY FELL ON THEIR FACES.** They did not pray as they had done earlier,[48a] for [at this time] prayer was not fluent in their mouths; and therefore Moses said, כִּי יָצָא הַקֶּצֶף, *for the fury has gone forth* (v. 11). As the Talmud relates

48a. The phrase וַיִּפְּלוּ עַל פְּנֵיהֶם, *they fell on their faces,* also appears in 16:22 above. There, however, the Torah goes on to quote the words of the prayer they recited in that position. Here, the verse makes no mention of any prayer or of any words being spoken. Thus, the Baal HaTurim understands that they did not utter any prayer at this time. In this point he is at odds with *Targum Yonasan ben Uzziel* who renders both appearances as, וְאִיתְרְכִינוּ בִּצְלוֹ עַל אַפֵּיהוֹן, *they stretched out in prayer upon their faces* (see also *Ibn Ezra*). Interestingly, *Targum Yerushalmi* interpolates the term בִּצְלוֹ, *in prayer,* in our verse, but not in 16:22. Presumably, that *Targum* agrees with *Targum Yonasan;* however, it does not interpolate בִּצְלוֹ in 16:22 because the words of their prayer are explicit in that verse (*VeChur LaZahav*).

Alternatively: The *Targumim* agree with the Baal HaTurim. In both instances Moses and Aaron *fell on their faces* to pray. In 16:22 their prayer was fluent and they completed it. In our verse, their prayer was not fluent and so they did not complete it (Y.S.).

in an instant!" They fell on their faces.
11 Moses said to Aaron, "Take the fire-pan and put on it
fire from upon the Altar and place incense — and go quickly
to the assembly and provide atonement for them, for the
fury has gone forth from the presence of HASHEM*; the*
plague has begun!"
12 Aaron took, as Moses had spoken, and he ran to the
midst of the congregation, and behold! the plague had
begun among the people. He placed the incense and
provided atonement for the people. 13 He stood between the
dead and the living, and the plague was checked. 14 Those
who died in the plague were fourteen thousand, seven
hundred, aside from those who died because of the affair of
Korah. 15 Aaron returned to Moses at the entrance of the
Tent of Assembly, and the plague had been checked.
16 HASHEM *spoke to Moses, saying: 17 "Speak to the Chil-*
dren of Israel and take from them one staff for each father's
house, from all their leaders according to their fathers'
house, twelve staffs; each man's name shall you inscribe on
his staff. 18 And the name of Aaron shall you inscribe on the

BAAL HATURIM ELUCIDATED

regarding Rabbi Chanina ben Dosa when he was praying over the sick: ". . . but if my prayer is not fluent in my mouth, then I know it has been rejected."[49,50]

11. {The Baal HaTurim's comment to וְכִפֶּר appears at *Leviticus* 9:7.}

12. **וַיָּרָץ** — AND HE RAN. In the *aleph-beis* exchange known as אַ״תְ בַּ״שׁ[50a], the letters of וַיָּרָץ correspond to [פמגה, which may be rearranged to spell] מַגֵּפָה, *plague,* for Aaron ran to halt the plague.[51]

❑ {The Baal HaTurim's comment to וַיִּתֵּן אֶת הַקְּטֹרֶת וַיְכַפֵּר עַל הָעָם appears at *Exodus* 30:35.}

49. The Mishnah relates: They said regarding Rabbi Chanina ben Dosa that he would pray for the sick and would then say, "This one will live; that one will die." When they asked him, "How do you know?" he told them, "If my prayer is fluent in my mouth, then I know that it has been well received [and the patient will recover]; but if not, then I know that it has been rejected [and the patient will die]" (*Berachos* 5:5 [34b]).

50. *Peirush HaRokeach.*

50a. See note 133 to 7:14 above.

51. The Talmud records that when Moses ascended to the heavens [at Sinai] the Angel of Death taught him this secret: The Incense stops a plague (*Shabbos* 89a, cited by *Rashi* to v. 11; see also the Baal HaTurim to *Exodus* 30:35).

Once again, the Baal HaTurim seems to present an allusion that adds nothing to the verse, for, like the verse, the allusion tells us that Aaron's purpose was to halt the plague! Perhaps the Baal HaTurim means to explain the implication of the word וַיָּרָץ, *he ran.* Aaron did not follow the natural instinct to run from a dangerous situation. Moreover, he did not hesitate to accept Moses' instruction. Rather, *he ran* with alacrity *to the midst of the congregation,* where *the plague had begun* already (Y.S.).

עַל־מַטֵּה לֵוִי כִּי מַטֶּה אֶחָד לְרֹאשׁ בֵּית אֲבוֹתָם׃
יט וְהִנַּחְתָּם בְּאֹהֶל מוֹעֵד לִפְנֵי הָעֵדוּת אֲשֶׁר אִוָּעֵד
כ לָכֶם שָׁמָּה׃ * וְהָיָה הָאִישׁ אֲשֶׁר אֶבְחַר־בּוֹ מַטֵּהוּ
יִפְרָח וַהֲשִׁכֹּתִי מֵעָלַי אֶת־תְּלֻנּוֹת בְּנֵי יִשְׂרָאֵל אֲשֶׁר
כא הֵם מַלִּינִם עֲלֵיכֶם׃ וַיְדַבֵּר מֹשֶׁה אֶל־בְּנֵי יִשְׂרָאֵל
וַיִּתְּנוּ אֵלָיו ׀ כָּל־נְשִׂיאֵיהֶם מַטֶּה לְנָשִׂיא אֶחָד
מַטֶּה לְנָשִׂיא אֶחָד לְבֵית אֲבֹתָם שְׁנֵים עָשָׂר מַטּוֹת
כב וּמַטֵּה אַהֲרֹן בְּתוֹךְ מַטּוֹתָם׃ וַיַּנַּח מֹשֶׁה אֶת־הַמַּטֹּת
כג לִפְנֵי יהוה בְּאֹהֶל הָעֵדֻת׃ וַיְהִי מִמָּחֳרָת וַיָּבֹא
מֹשֶׁה אֶל־אֹהֶל הָעֵדוּת וְהִנֵּה פָּרַח מַטֵּה־אַהֲרֹן
לְבֵית לֵוִי וַיֹּצֵא פֶרַח וַיָּצֵץ צִיץ וַיִּגְמֹל שְׁקֵדִים׃

*חצי הספר

בעל הטורים

(כ) **יִפְרָח.** ד׳ בַּמָּסוֹרֶת – ״וְהָיָה הָאִישׁ אֲשֶׁר אֶבְחַר בּוֹ מַטֵּהוּ יִפְרָח״; וְאִידָךְ ״צַדִּיק כַּתָּמָר יִפְרָח״; ״יִפְרַח כַּשּׁוֹשַׁנָּה״; ״יִפְרַח בְּיָמָיו צַדִּיק״. ״מַטֵּהוּ יִפְרָח״ זֶהוּ ״צַדִּיק כַּתָּמָר יִפְרָח״. שֶׁכֵּיוָן שֶׁמַּטֵּהוּ יִפְרַח, יֵצֵא צַדִּיק בְּדִינוֹ. וְזֶהוּ ״יִפְרַח כַּשּׁוֹשַׁנָּה . . . וִיהִי כַזַּיִת הוֹדוֹ״. וְזֶהוּ ״כַּשֶּׁמֶן הַטּוֹב עַל הָרֹאשׁ יֹרֵד עַל הַזָּקָן זְקַן אַהֲרֹן״. וְכֵן ״יִפְרַח בְּיָמָיו צַדִּיק״, שֶׁנֶּאֱמַר עַל הַמֶּלֶךְ הַמָּשִׁיחַ, שֶׁבְּיָמָיו תַּחֲזוֹר הַכְּהֻנָּה וְיִפְרַח מַטֵּה אַהֲרֹן:

(כג) **פֶּרַח . . . צִיץ . . . שְׁקֵדִים.** כְּנֶגֶד שְׁלֹשָׁה שֶׁעִרְעֲרוּ עַל הַכְּהֻנָּה, קֹרַח וְיָרָבְעָם וְעֻזִּיָּהוּ:

❑ **שְׁקֵדִים.** בְּגִימַטְרִיָּא חַשְׁמוֹנִים. רֶמֶז לְחַשְׁמוֹנִים שֶׁהֵם מִזֶּרַע אַהֲרֹן, וְתִתְקַיֵּם הַכְּהֻנָּה בְּיָדָם:

BAAL HATURIM ELUCIDATED

20. יִפְרָח — WILL BLOSSOM. The masoretic note,[52] ד׳, means that this word appears four times in the *Tanach:* (i) here, וְהָיָה הָאִישׁ אֲשֶׁר אֶבְחַר בּוֹ מַטֵּהוּ יִפְרָח, *It shall be that the man whom I shall choose — his staff will blossom;* (ii) צַדִּיק כַּתָּמָר יִפְרָח, *A righteous man will blossom like a date palm* (*Psalms* 92:13); (iii) יִפְרַח כַּשּׁוֹשַׁנָּה, *He will blossom like a rosebush*[53] (*Hosea* 14:6); and (iv) יִפְרַח בְּיָמָיו צַדִּיק, *A righteous one will blossom in his days* (*Psalms* 72:7). The one whose *staff will blossom* (of our verse), he is the *righteous man who will blossom like a date palm.* For once his staff will blossom, he will be proven righteous in his cause. And this is also the implication of the verse, *he will blossom like a rosebush . . . his glory will be like* [*that of*] *the olive tree* (*Hosea* 14:6-7), and of the verse, כַּשֶּׁמֶן הַטּוֹב עַל הָרֹאשׁ יֹרֵד עַל הַזָּקָן זְקַן אַהֲרֹן, *Like the precious oil*[54] *upon the head, running down upon the beard, the beard of Aaron* (*Psalms* 133:2). Similarly, *a righteous one will blossom*

52. The full note reads: ד׳ ב׳ פַּתְחִין ב׳ קָמְצִין, *Four: two vowelized with a patach —* ךְ; *two with a kamatz —* ךָ.

53. That verse and the one that follows it read in full: *I shall be to Israel like the dew; he will blossom like a rosebush; his roots will strike out like the* [cedars of] *Lebanon. His tender branches will go forth; his glory will be like* [*that of*] *the olive tree; and his fragrance like* [*that of*] *Lebanon.*

54. The glory of the olive tree is its oil.

staff of Levi, for there shall be one staff for the head of their
fathers' house. [19] *You shall lay them in the Tent of Meeting*
before the Testimony, where I meet with you. [20] *It shall be that*
the man whom I shall choose — his staff will blossom; thus I
shall cause to subside from upon Me the complaints of the
Children of Israel, which they complain against you."
[21] *Moses spoke to the Children of Israel, and all their leaders*
gave him a staff for each leader, a staff for each leader,
according to their fathers' house, twelve staffs; and Aaron's
staff was among their staffs. [22] *Moses laid the staffs before*
HASHEM in the Tent of the Testimony. [23] *On the next day,*
Moses came to the Tent of the Testimony and behold! the
staff of Aaron of the house of Levi had blossomed; it brought
forth a blossom, sprouted a bud and developed — almonds.

BAAL HATURIM ELUCIDATED

in his days refers to the days of the King Messiah,[55] for in his days the priesthood will return and the staff of Aaron[56] will blossom.[57]

21. {The Baal HaTurim's comment to מַטּוֹתָם appears at *Exodus* 7:12.}

23. **פֶּרַח . . . צִיץ . . . שְׁקֵדִים** — A BLOSSOM . . . A BUD . . . ALMONDS. [The verse mentions three facets of the staff's germination,] corresponding to the three individuals who sought to usurp the priesthood: Korah, Jeroboam[58] and Uzziah.[59,60]

❑ **שְׁקֵדִים** — ALMONDS. The *gematria* of this word (454) is equal to that of חַשְׁמוֹנִים, *Hasmoneans.*[61] This is an allusion to the Hasmoneans who were of the seed of Aaron and in whose hand the priesthood endured.

55. See *Targum, Ibn Ezra* and *Radak* to *Psalms* 72:1.

56. The *righteous one* of *Psalms* 72:7.

57. That is, the priesthood will return to the descendants of Aaron (see *Metzudos David* to *Psalms* 92:13; see also the Baal HaTurim to 16:10 above, and to *Leviticus* 16:14, s.v., יַזֶּה).

58. This refers to יָרָבְעָם בֶּן נְבָט, *Jeroboam son of Nebat,* first king of the ten tribes that seceded from the kingdom of the Davidic dynasty. He also tried to usurp the priesthood, as it is written (*I Kings* 13:1): *Just then a man of God came to Beth-el from Judah . . . while Jeroboam was standing atop the altar to burn incense* (*VeChur LaZahav*).

59. This refers to עֻזִּיָּהוּ בֶּן אֲמַצְיָהוּ, *Uzziah son of Amaziah,* eleventh king of the Davidic dynasty. *As he became strong, his heart became haughty to the point of destructiveness and he betrayed HASHEM his God — he entered the Sanctuary of HASHEM to burn incense on the Altar* (*II Chronicles* 26:16; see vv. 17-21 there; see *Rashi* to our verse, s.v., ויגמל שקדים).

60. *Peirush HaRokeach.* It is noteworthy that the *gematria* of the Baal HaTurim's rubric, פֶּרַח צִיץ שְׁקֵדִים (932), is equal to that of קֹרַח יָרָבְעָם עֻזִּיָּהוּ בֶּן אֲמַצְיָהוּ, *Korah, Jeroboam, Uzziah son of Amaziah.* Additionally, the *gematria* of the phrase ג׳ עִרְעֲרוּ עַל הַכְּהֻנָּה, *Three sought to usurp the priesthood* (734), is equal to that of קֹרַח יָרָבְעָם וְעֻזִּיָּהוּ (*VeChur LaZahav*).

61. The more common form of this name — in both Hebrew, חַשְׁמוֹנָאִים, and Aramaic, חַשְׁמוֹנָאֵי — includes an א after the נ, and that is how it appears in the Talmud, Midrash and Targumim. Nevertheless, many *Rishonim* (medieval Torah authorities) use the form חַשְׁמוֹנִים (e.g., the Baal HaTurim here; *Ibn Ezra* to Chs. 9-11 of *Zechariah; Ralbag* to *II Samuel* 24:25). Indeed, some of the later commentaries find an allusion to the Hasmonean victory on the 25th of Kislev

יז/כד־יח/א כד וַיֹּצֵ֨א מֹשֶׁ֤ה אֶת־כָּל־הַמַּטֹּת֙ מִלִּפְנֵ֣י יהוֹה אֶל־כָּל־
בְּנֵ֣י יִשְׂרָאֵ֑ל וַיִּרְא֥וּ וַיִּקְח֖וּ אִ֥ישׁ מַטֵּֽהוּ׃
ששי כה וַיֹּ֨אמֶר יהוֹה אֶל־מֹשֶׁ֗ה הָשֵׁ֞ב אֶת־מַטֵּ֤ה אַהֲרֹן֙ לִפְנֵ֣י
הָֽעֵד֔וּת לְמִשְׁמֶ֥רֶת לְא֖וֹת לִבְנֵי־מֶ֑רִי וּתְכַ֧ל תְּלוּנֹּתָ֛ם
כו מֵעָלַ֖י וְלֹ֥א יָמֻֽתוּ׃ וַיַּ֖עַשׂ מֹשֶׁ֑ה כַּאֲשֶׁ֨ר צִוָּ֧ה יהוֹ֛ה
אֹת֖וֹ כֵּ֥ן עָשָֽׂה׃
כז וַיֹּֽאמְרוּ֙ בְּנֵ֣י יִשְׂרָאֵ֔ל אֶל־מֹשֶׁ֖ה לֵאמֹ֑ר הֵ֥ן גָּוַ֛עְנוּ
כח אָבַ֖דְנוּ כֻּלָּ֥נוּ אָבָֽדְנוּ׃ כֹּ֣ל הַקָּרֵ֧ב ׀ הַקָּרֵ֛ב אֶל־
יח א מִשְׁכַּ֥ן יהוֹ֖ה יָמ֑וּת הַאִ֥ם תַּ֖מְנוּ לִגְוֹֽעַ׃ וַיֹּ֤אמֶר

בעל הטורים

(כד) וַיֹּצֵא מֹשֶׁה אֶת כָּל הַמַּטֹּת. חָסֵר וָי״ו, שֶׁהָיוּ יְבֵשִׁים כְּמוֹ שֶׁהִכְנִיסָם:

(כה) לִבְנֵי מֶרִי. מִכָּאן לָמַד מֹשֶׁה שֶׁקְּרָאָם מַמְרִים:

(כח) הַאִם. ב׳ בַּמָּסוֹרֶת — ״הַאִם תַּמְנוּ לִגְוֹעַ״; וְאִידָךְ בְּאִיּוֹב ״הַאִם אֵין עֶזְרָתִי בִי וְתֻשִׁיָּה נִדְּחָה מִמֶּנִּי״. שֶׁמִּי שֶׁאֵין לוֹ אִשָּׁה, כְּדִכְתִיב ״אֶעֱשֶׂה לוֹ עֵזֶר כְּנֶגְדּוֹ״, וְכֵן מִי שֶׁאֵינוֹ לוֹמֵד תּוֹרָה, כְּדִכְתִיב ״וְתֻשִׁיָּה נִדְּחָה מִמֶּנִּי״, חָשׁוּב כְּמֵת, כְּדִכְתִיב ״הַאִם תַּמְנוּ לִגְוֹעַ״:

BAAL HATURIM ELUCIDATED

24. **וַיֹּצֵא מֹשֶׁה אֶת כָּל הַמַּטֹּת** — MOSES BROUGHT OUT ALL THE STAFFS. The word הַמַּטֹּת, *the staffs,* is spelled defectively here, without a ו,[62] for they were as dry [when Moses took them out] as they were when he brought them in.[63]

25. **לִבְנֵי מֶרִי** — FOR REBELLIOUS ONES. [Based upon God's use of this expression,]

---

in the name of the Israelites' twenty-fifth encampment in the wilderness — חַשְׁמֹנָה (see 33:29-30 below).

Interestingly, we find the name spelled in the Chanukah liturgy both with and without the א: In the *Al HaNissim* prayer, Mattisyahu is referred to as חַשְׁמוֹנָאִי or חַשְׁמוֹנַאי, *the Hasmonean,* while in the *zemer* (song) *Ma'oz Tzur,* the family is called חַשְׁמַנִּים, a word found in *Psalms* 127:32 with reference to high officials (see *Radak* there).

62. In verses 17 and 21, the plural form of מַטֶּה, *staff,* is spelled מַטּוֹת, with a ו. In verses 22 and 24, however, it is spelled הַמַּטֹּת, without the ו. (The definite article prefix הַ־ accounts for the *dagesh* in the מַּ, but not for the absent ו.)

The translation follows *Ittur Bikkurim* and *Shoham Yakar,* who understand that this comment refers to the missing ו of הַמַּטֹּת. Moreover, it is in accord with *Peirush HaRokeach's* comment to verse 22: אֶת הַמַּטֹּת is spelled defectively [without a ו (see note 63 below)] because eleven of them were defective, i.e., dry, and only one blossomed.

Alternatively: The Baal HaTurim refers to the missing ו of וַיֹּצֵא. For the word וַיּוֹצֵא appears seven times in the Torah. Five of those times (*Genesis* 15:5, 24:53, 43:23, 48:12 and *Exodus* 19:17) it is spelled in full, וַיּוֹצֵא. Only here, in verses 23 and 24, is it spelled defectively, וַיֹּצֵא, without the central ו. And this understanding is in accordance with *Peirush HaRokeach's* comment at verse 24: וַיֹּצֵא מֹשֶׁה is spelled defectively [without a central ו], for they were dry (*VeChur LaZahav*).

63. That is, when *Moses laid the staffs before* HASHEM (v. 22), הַמַּטֹּת is spelled defectively; likewise, when *Moses brought out all the staffs* (v. 24), the word is spelled without a ו. Thus, when he brought them out, they were exactly as they had been when he laid them inside, dry (*Shoham Yakar*).

See the Baal HaTurim to *Exodus* 7:12 for another explanation of the defective spelling.

24 *Moses brought out all the staffs from before* HASHEM *to all the*
Children of Israel; they saw and they took, each man his staff.
25 HASHEM *said to Moses: "Bring back the staff of Aaron be-*
fore the Testimony as a safekeeping, as a sign for rebellious
ones; let their complaints cease from Me that they not die."
26 *Moses did as* HASHEM *had commanded him, so he did.*
27 *The Children of Israel said to Moses, saying, "Behold! we*
perish, we are lost, we are all lost. 28 *Everyone who ap-*
proaches closer to the Tabernacle of HASHEM *will die. Will we*
ever stop perishing?"

BAAL HATURIM ELUCIDATED

Moses understood that he could call them מַמְרִים[63a], *rebels.*[64]

28. הַאִם — WILL. The masoretic note, ב׳, means that this word appears twice in the *Tanach:* (i) here, הַאִם תַּמְנוּ לִגְוֹעַ, *Will we ever stop perishing?* and (ii) הַאִם אֵין עֶזְרָתִי בִי וְתֻשִׁיָּה נִדְּחָה מִמֶּנִּי, *Is my helper not with me? Has counsel been thrust away from me?* (*Job* 6:13).[64a] [The similarity of expression indicates] that a man without a wife — [a wife] about whom is written אֶעֱשֶׂה לוֹ עֵזֶר כְּנֶגְדּוֹ, *I will make him a helper corresponding to him*[65] (*Genesis* 2:18) — and one who does not study Torah — [the Torah] about which is written, *Has counsel*[66] *been thrust away from me?* — is considered as dead,[67] as it is written, *Will we ever stop perishing?*

63a. Moses uses the expression, מַמְרִים הֱיִיתֶם עִם ה׳, *You have been rebels against* HASHEM, three times — *Deuteronomy* 9:7 and 24; and 31:27 where הֱיִתֶם is spelled with only one י.

64. *Devarim Rabbah* 2:8 — Moses said to God, "Master of the Universe, why have I been prohibited from entering the Land of Israel? Is it because I addressed them, 'שִׁמְעוּ נָא הַמֹּרִים, *Listen now, O rebels'* (20:10 below)? But You Yourself have said earlier, 'לְמִשְׁמֶרֶת לְאוֹת לִבְנֵי מֶרִי, *as a safekeeping, as a sign for rebellious ones'!"*

Accordingly, it is possible that the Baal HaTurim's comment originally read שֶׁקְּרָאָם מוֹרִים, rather than מַמְרִים.

Moreover, when Moses used the word מַמְרִים for *rebels,* he was admonishing them appropriately for their earlier misdeeds, explaining how they had been rebellious. But when he used the term הַמּוֹרִים for *rebels,* he spoke in anger and consequently erred by smiting the rock instead of speaking to it (*Sifrei* to 31:21 below; cited in *Rashi* there). Thus, it is suggested that the comment be amended to מוֹרִים in lieu of מַמְרִים (*VeChur LaZahav*).

Additionally, according to the *Rashbam* (to 20:10 below), when God told Moses, *"Take the staff . . . and speak to the rock"* (20:8), He was referring to the staff of Aaron that had blossomed and grown almonds. And it was then that Moses said, שִׁמְעוּ נָא הַמֹּרִים (Y.S.).

However, the manuscripts used by *Shoham Yakar,* as well as the early printed editions, read מַמְרִים. Moreover, *Peirush HaRokeach,* the Baal HaTurim's apparent source, reads: שֶׁקְּרָאָן מַמְרִים הֱיִיתֶם עִם ה׳. For he addressed them, *"You have been rebels against* HASHEM*."*

64a. The Talmud (*Yevamos* 62b) derives from this verse that an unmarried man is not able to achieve greatness in Torah [because he is distracted by household matters that are usually the domain of the housewife (*Rashi*)].

65. This verse introduces the creation of Eve as a helpmate for Adam.

66. The word תּוּשִׁיָּה, *counsel,* refers to the Torah (see *Proverbs* 8:14 and *Avos* 6:1 with *Rashi*).

67. The Midrash states regarding an unmarried man: Any man who does not have a wife lodges without life, as it is stated (*Ecclesiastes* 9:9): רְאֵה חַיִּים עִם אִשָּׁה אֲשֶׁר אָהַבְתָּ, *Enjoy life with the woman whom you love* (*Koheles Rabbah* 9:9). The Talmud states that "the woman" of that verse may be understood literally as one's wife or figuratively as the Torah (*Kiddushin* 30b).

יח/ב־ח יהוה אֶל־אַהֲרֹן אַתָּה וּבָנֶיךָ וּבֵית־אָבִיךָ אִתָּךְ תִּשְׂאוּ
אֶת־עֲוֹן הַמִּקְדָּשׁ וְאַתָּה וּבָנֶיךָ אִתָּךְ תִּשְׂאוּ אֶת־עֲוֹן
ב כְּהֻנַּתְכֶם: וְגַם אֶת־אַחֶיךָ מַטֵּה לֵוִי שֵׁבֶט אָבִיךָ הַקְרֵב
אִתָּךְ וְיִלָּווּ עָלֶיךָ וִישָׁרְתוּךָ וְאַתָּה וּבָנֶיךָ אִתָּךְ לִפְנֵי
ג אֹהֶל הָעֵדֻת: וְשָׁמְרוּ מִשְׁמַרְתְּךָ וּמִשְׁמֶרֶת כָּל־הָאֹהֶל
אַךְ אֶל־כְּלֵי הַקֹּדֶשׁ וְאֶל־הַמִּזְבֵּחַ לֹא יִקְרָבוּ וְלֹא־
ד יָמֻתוּ גַם־הֵם גַּם־אַתֶּם: וְנִלְווּ עָלֶיךָ וְשָׁמְרוּ אֶת־
מִשְׁמֶרֶת אֹהֶל מוֹעֵד לְכֹל עֲבֹדַת הָאֹהֶל וְזָר לֹא־
ה יִקְרַב אֲלֵיכֶם: וּשְׁמַרְתֶּם אֵת מִשְׁמֶרֶת הַקֹּדֶשׁ וְאֵת
מִשְׁמֶרֶת הַמִּזְבֵּחַ וְלֹא־יִהְיֶה עוֹד קֶצֶף עַל־בְּנֵי
ו יִשְׂרָאֵל: וַאֲנִי הִנֵּה לָקַחְתִּי אֶת־אֲחֵיכֶם הַלְוִיִּם מִתּוֹךְ
בְּנֵי יִשְׂרָאֵל לָכֶם מַתָּנָה נְתֻנִים לַיהוה לַעֲבֹד
ז אֶת־עֲבֹדַת אֹהֶל מוֹעֵד: וְאַתָּה וּבָנֶיךָ אִתְּךָ תִּשְׁמְרוּ
אֶת־כְּהֻנַּתְכֶם לְכָל־דְּבַר הַמִּזְבֵּחַ וּלְמִבֵּית לַפָּרֹכֶת
וַעֲבַדְתֶּם עֲבֹדַת מַתָּנָה אֶתֵּן אֶת־כְּהֻנַּתְכֶם וְהַזָּר
ח הַקָּרֵב יוּמָת: וַיְדַבֵּר יהוה אֶל־אַהֲרֹן וַאֲנִי הִנֵּה נָתַתִּי

בעל הטורים

יח (ד) וְנִלְווּ. ד׳ בַּמָּסוֹרֶת — ״וְנִלְווּ עָלֶיךָ״; וְאִידָךְ ״וְנִלְווּ עֲלֵיהֶם רַבִּים בַּחֲלַקְלַקּוֹת״; ״וְנִלְווּ גוֹיִם רַבִּים אֶל ה׳ בַּיּוֹם הַהוּא וְהָיוּ לִי לְעָם״; ״צִיּוֹן יִשְׁאָלוּ דֶּרֶךְ הֵנָּה פְנֵיהֶם בֹּאוּ וְנִלְווּ וְגוֹ׳״. פֵּרוּשׁ ״וְנִלְווּ עֲלֵיהֶם רַבִּים בַּחֲלַקְלַקּוֹת״ לְהָצֵר לְיִשְׂרָאֵל, כִּדְכְתִיב ״וּמִן הַמַּשְׂכִּילִים יִכָּשְׁלוּ . . . עַד עֵת קֵץ״. אֲבָל כְּשֶׁיָּבוֹא הַקֵּץ ״וְנִלְווּ גוֹיִם רַבִּים אֶל ה׳ וְגוֹ׳״. וְהַיְנוּ ״וְיִלָּווּ עָלֶיךָ וִישָׁרְתוּךָ״, כִּדְכְתִיב ״וּבְנֵי נֵכָר אִכָּרֵיכֶם וְכֹרְמֵיכֶם״:

(ח) וַאֲנִי הִנֵּה נָתַתִּי. כְּדֶרֶךְ שֶׁכּוֹתְבִין בִּשְׁטַר מַתָּנָה, בְּדַעַת שְׁלֵמָה וּבְנֶפֶשׁ חֲפֵצָה:

BAAL HATURIM ELUCIDATED

XVIII

2. {The Baal HaTurim's comment to הַקְרֵב appears at *Exodus* 28:1.}

4. וְנִלְווּ — THEY SHALL BE JOINED. The masoretic note, ד׳, means that this word appears four times in the *Tanach:* (i) here, וְנִלְווּ עָלֶיךָ, *they shall be joined to you;* (ii) וְנִלְווּ עֲלֵיהֶם רַבִּים בַּחֲלַקְלַקּוֹת, *For many will join themselves to them with glibness* (*Daniel* 11:34); (iii) וְנִלְווּ גוֹיִם רַבִּים אֶל ה׳ בַּיּוֹם הַהוּא וְהָיוּ לִי לְעָם, *Many nations will join themselves to* H*ASHEM* *on that day, and they will become a people unto me* (*Zechariah* 2:15); and (iv) צִיּוֹן יִשְׁאָלוּ דֶּרֶךְ הֵנָּה פְנֵיהֶם בֹּאוּ וְנִלְווּ . . ., *They will ask about Zion; their faces will be turned toward it; [and they will say,] "Come, be joined . . ."*

1 *HASHEM said to Aaron, "You, your sons and your father's
household with you shall bear the iniquity of the Sanctuary;
and you and your sons with you shall bear the iniquity of
your priesthood.* 2 *Also your brethren the tribe of Levi, the
tribe of your father, shall you draw near with you, and they
shall be joined to you and minister to you. You and your
sons with you shall be before the Tent of the Testimony.*
3 *They shall safeguard your charge and the charge of the
entire tent — but to the holy vessels and to the Altar they
shall not approach, that they not die — they as well as you.*
4 *They shall be joined to you and safeguard the charge of the
Tent of Meeting for the entire service of the Tent, and an alien
shall not approach you.* 5 *You shall safeguard the charge of
the Holy and the charge of the Altar, and there shall be no
more wrath against the Children of Israel.* 6 *And I — behold!
I have taken your brethren the Levites from among the
Children of Israel; to you they are presented as a gift for
HASHEM, to perform the service of the Tent of Meeting.* 7 *You
and your sons with you shall safeguard your priesthood
regarding every matter of the Altar and within the Curtain,
and you shall serve; I have presented your priesthood as a
service that is a gift, and any alien who approaches shall
die."*
8 *HASHEM spoke to Aaron: "And I — behold! I have given*

BAAL HATURIM ELUCIDATED

(*Jeremiah* 50:5). The explanation of the similarity of expression: [Before the arrival of the Messiah] *many will join themselves to them with glibness* in order to beleaguer Israel, as it is written, וּמִן הַמַּשְׂכִּילִים יִכָּשְׁלוּ . . . עַד עֵת קֵץ, *Some of the wise men will stumble. . .when the time of the End will be* (*Daniel* 11:35). However, when the End actually arrives, *many nations will join themselves to HASHEM . . .* This is what is meant by וְיִלָּווּ[68] עָלֶיךָ וִישָׁרְתוּךָ, *they shall be joined to you and minister to you* (v. 2 above), as it is written, וּבְנֵי נֵכָר אִכָּרֵיכֶם וְכֹרְמֵיכֶם, *And the sons of the foreigner* [*will be*] *your plowmen and your vineyard workers* (*Isaiah* 61:5).

8. **וַאֲנִי הִנֵּה נָתַתִּי — AND I — BEHOLD! I HAVE GIVEN.** [This[69] is] in the manner that we

---

68. Most editions read וְנִלְווּ; but it seems clear that the Baal HaTurim is citing verse 2 of our passage. In terms of translation, the two words, וְנִלְווּ and וְיִלָּווּ, mean the same thing, *and they shall be joined.* But grammatically they differ. The form וְיִלָּווּ is in the future tense, יִלָּווּ, *they shall be joined,* with the conjunctive prefix -וְ, *and.* The form וְנִלְווּ, on the other hand, is composed of the past tense verb נִלְווּ, *they were joined,* with the conversive prefix -וְ changing it to the future, *they shall be joined* (*VeChur LaZahav*).

69. God's statement.

לְךָ֞ אֶת־מִשְׁמֶ֖רֶת תְּרוּמֹתָ֑י לְכָל־קָדְשֵׁ֣י בְנֵֽי־יִשְׂרָאֵ֗ל
ט לְךָ֨ נְתַתִּ֧ים לְמָשְׁחָ֛ה וּלְבָנֶ֖יךָ לְחָק־עוֹלָֽם׃ זֶ֛ה
יִהְיֶ֥ה לְךָ֛ מִקֹּ֥דֶשׁ הַקֳּדָשִׁ֖ים מִן־הָאֵ֑שׁ כָּל־קָ֠רְבָּנָ֠ם
לְֽכָל־מִנְחָתָ֞ם וּלְכָל־חַטָּאתָ֗ם וּלְכָל־אֲשָׁמָם֙ אֲשֶׁ֣ר
י יָשִׁ֣יבוּ לִ֔י קֹ֣דֶשׁ קָֽדָשִׁ֥ים לְךָ֛ ה֖וּא וּלְבָנֶֽיךָ׃ בְּקֹ֥דֶשׁ
הַקֳּדָשִׁ֖ים תֹּֽאכְלֶ֑נּוּ כָּל־זָכָר֙ יֹאכַ֣ל אֹת֔וֹ קֹ֖דֶשׁ
יא יִֽהְיֶה־לָּֽךְ׃ וְזֶה־לְּךָ֞ תְּרוּמַ֣ת מַתָּנָ֗ם לְכָל־תְּנוּפֹת֮
בְּנֵ֣י יִשְׂרָאֵל֒ לְךָ֣ נְתַתִּ֗ים וּלְבָנֶ֧יךָ וְלִבְנֹתֶ֛יךָ אִתְּךָ֖
יב לְחָק־עוֹלָ֑ם כָּל־טָה֥וֹר בְּבֵיתְךָ֖ יֹאכַ֥ל אֹתֽוֹ׃ כֹּ֚ל
חֵ֣לֶב יִצְהָ֔ר וְכָל־חֵ֖לֶב תִּיר֣וֹשׁ וְדָגָ֑ן רֵֽאשִׁיתָ֛ם
יג אֲשֶׁר־יִתְּנ֥וּ לַֽיהוָ֖ה לְךָ֥ נְתַתִּֽים׃ בִּכּוּרֵ֞י כָּל־אֲשֶׁ֧ר
בְּאַרְצָ֛ם אֲשֶׁר־יָבִ֥יאוּ לַֽיהוָ֖ה לְךָ֣ יִהְיֶ֑ה כָּל־טָה֥וֹר
יד בְּבֵיתְךָ֖ יֹאכְלֶֽנּוּ׃ כָּל־חֵ֖רֶם בְּיִשְׂרָאֵ֥ל לְךָ֥ יִהְיֶֽה׃

בעל הטורים

(ט) מִקֹּדֶשׁ הַקֳּדָשִׁים מִן. סוֹפֵי תֵבוֹת שֶׁמֶן. כְּמוֹ שֶׁדָּרְשׁוּ חֲכָמֵינוּ ז״ל, לְרַבּוֹת לֹ֗ג שֶׁמֶן שֶׁל מְצֹרָע:

(יא) וְזֶה לְּךָ תְּרוּמַת מַתָּנָם. וְכֵן לְמַעְלָה ״זֶה יִהְיֶה לְךָ״. ב׳ פְּעָמִים ״זֶה״ עוֹלֶה עֶשְׂרִים וְאַרְבַּע, רֶמֶז לְעֶשְׂרִים וְאַרְבַּע מַתְּנוֹת כְּהֻנָּה:

BAAL HATURIM ELUCIDATED

write[70] in the title deed of a gift, "with full intent and with willing[70a] spirit."[71]

9. מִקֹּדֶשׁ הַקֳּדָשִׁים מִן — FROM THE MOST HOLY, FROM. The final letters of these words

70. The text follows *Shoham Yakar's* manuscript edition and *Peirush HaRokeach,* the Baal HaTurim's apparent source for this comment. The early printed editions read, כְּדֶרֶךְ שֶׁנּוֹתְנִין בִּשְׁטַר מַתָּנָה . . ., literally, *In the manner that we give in the title deed of a gift . . .* However, because the prepositional prefix ־בּ, *in* or *with,* seems out of place, many later editions dropped it and read, כְּדֶרֶךְ שֶׁנּוֹתְנִין שְׁטַר מַתָּנָה, *In the manner that we give the title deed of a gift,* בְּדַעַת שְׁלֵמָה וּבְנֶפֶשׁ חֲפֵצָה, *with full intent and with willing spirit.*

70a. *Rashi* interprets the word הִנֵּה of our verse as an expression of joy. *Be'er Yitzchak* explains: When a verse begins with הִנֵּה, that word highlights what follows. But, elsewhere in the verse, the word indicates the enthusiasm of the speaker. In our verse, it is an expression of enthusiastic joy.

71. *Peirush HaRokeach,* where the terms are transposed: בְּנֶפֶשׁ חֲפֵצָה וְדַעַת שְׁלֵמָה. The Baal HaTurim uses this expression in *Tur Choshen Mishpat* 222 also, with reference to the Talmudic statement: One must recite a blessing over bad news in the same manner as over good news, i.e., with full intent and with willing spirit.

Regarding title deeds for gifts, he implies that the property must be deeded with an overt display of "willing spirit," such as having the deed written and signed publicly (see, e.g., *Tur Choshen Mishpat* 242). However, he does not write that נֶפֶשׁ חֲפֵצָה or דַּעַת שְׁלֵמָה must be included in the text of the document. Nevertheless, we find that phrases of that ilk are commonly used

you the safeguard of My offerings, of all the sanctities of the
Children of Israel; I have given them to you for distinction
and to your sons as an eternal portion. 9 *This shall be yours*
from the most holy, from the fire: their every offering, their
every meal-offering, their every sin-offering, their every
guilt-offering, that which they return to Me — as most holy
it shall be yours and your sons. 10 *In the most holy shall you*
eat it, every male may eat it, it shall be holy for you. 11 *And*
this shall be yours: what is set aside from their gift, from all
the wavings of the Children of Israel, have I presented them
to you and to your sons and daughters with you as an
eternal portion; every pure person in your household may
eat it. 12 *All the best of your oil and the best of your wine and*
grain, their first, which they give to HASHEM, *to you have I*
given them. 13 *The first fruits of everything that is in their*
land, which they bring to HASHEM, *shall be yours, every*
pure person in your household may eat it. 14 *Every segre-*
gated property in Israel shall be yours.

BAAL HATURIM ELUCIDATED

spell שֶׁמֶן, *oil.* This is in accordance with our Sages' teaching[72] that this verse includes the *lōg*[73] of oil brought by a *metzora.*[74]

11. וְזֶה לְךָ תְּרוּמַת מַתָּנָם — AND THIS SHALL BE YOURS; WHAT IS SET ASIDE FROM THEIR GIFT. [Our verse states, וְ״זֶה״ לְךָ, *and "this" shall be yours,*] similarly, an earlier verse states, ״זֶה״ יִהְיֶה לְךָ, *This shall be yours* (v. 9). [The *gematria* of זֶה is (7 + 5 =) 12, thus,] two times זֶה equals 24, an allusion to the twenty-four priestly gifts.[75]

---

in actual practice (see, e.g., *She'eilos Useshuvos Darchei Noam, Even HaEzer* 21; *She'eilos Useshuvos Noda BiYehudah,* Vol. I, *Choshen Mishpat* 25).

The expression בְּדַעַת שְׁלֵמָה וּבְנֶפֶשׁ חֲפֵצָה is the Baal HaTurim's paraphrase of King David's charge to his son Solomon, "דַּע אֶת אֱלֹהֵי אָבִיךָ, *Know the God of your father,* וְעָבְדֵהוּ, *and serve Him,* בְּלֵב שָׁלֵם וּבְנֶפֶשׁ חֲפֵצָה, *with full heart and with willing spirit"* (*I Chronicles* 28:9). The relationship between knowledge [i.e., דַּע, *know*] and the לֵב, *heart,* is spelled out in the verses: לֵב לָדַעַת, *a heart [with which] to know* (*Deuteronomy* 29:3); לֵב נָבוֹן יִקְנֶה דָּעַת, *An understanding heart will acquire knowledge* (*Proverbs* 18:15). Thus, בְּלֵב שָׁלֵם is synonymous with בְּדַעַת שְׁלֵמָה. And the term בְּלֵב שָׁלֵם also appears regarding gifts: כִּי בְּלֵב שָׁלֵם הִתְנַדְּבוּ לַה׳, *for with full heart they donated gift offerings to* HASHEM (*I Chronicles* 29:9). Accordingly, בְּדַעַת שְׁלֵמָה וּבְנֶפֶשׁ חֲפֵצָה is an apt phrase for the title deed of a gift (*VeChur LaZahav*).

72. The Talmud (*Zevachim* 44b) infers this from the phrase כָּל קָרְבָּנָם, *their every offering,* of our verse.

73. A *lōg* is a measure containing six times the volume of a chicken egg. Opinions regarding the modern-day equivalent of a *lōg* range between 12 and 21 fluid ounces.

74. See *Leviticus* 14:10. That *lōg* of oil is in the category of "most holy" and must be consumed in compliance with the laws of the "most holy" offerings; e.g., only by male Kohanim, within the confines of the Courtyard of the *Mishkan,* or of the *Beis HaMikdash.*

75. *Peirush HaRokeach.* The *Tosefta* (*Challah* 2:8) and the Talmud (*Bava Kamma* 10b; *Chullin* 133b) enumerate the twenty-four gifts. The *Sifrei* explains how each is derived from the verses in our passage. See also *Biyurei HaGra* to *Avos* 6:5.

טו כָּל־פֶּטֶר רֶחֶם לְכָל־בָּשָׂר אֲשֶׁר־יַקְרִיבוּ לַיהוָה
בָּאָדָם וּבַבְּהֵמָה יִהְיֶה־לָּךְ אַךְ ׀ פָּדֹה תִפְדֶּה אֵת
בְּכוֹר הָאָדָם וְאֵת בְּכוֹר־הַבְּהֵמָה הַטְּמֵאָה תִּפְדֶּה׃
טז וּפְדוּיָו מִבֶּן־חֹדֶשׁ תִּפְדֶּה בְּעֶרְכְּךָ כֶּסֶף חֲמֵשֶׁת
יז שְׁקָלִים בְּשֶׁקֶל הַקֹּדֶשׁ עֶשְׂרִים גֵּרָה הוּא׃ אַךְ בְּכוֹר־
שׁוֹר אוֹ בְכוֹר כֶּשֶׂב אוֹ־בְכוֹר עֵז לֹא תִפְדֶּה קֹדֶשׁ
הֵם אֶת־דָּמָם תִּזְרֹק עַל־הַמִּזְבֵּחַ וְאֶת־חֶלְבָּם
יח תַּקְטִיר אִשֶּׁה לְרֵיחַ נִיחֹחַ לַיהוָה׃ וּבְשָׂרָם יִהְיֶה־לָּךְ
יט כַּחֲזֵה הַתְּנוּפָה וּכְשׁוֹק הַיָּמִין לְךָ יִהְיֶה׃ כֹּל ׀ תְּרוּמֹת
הַקֳּדָשִׁים אֲשֶׁר יָרִימוּ בְנֵי־יִשְׂרָאֵל לַיהוָה נָתַתִּי לְךָ

בעל הטורים

(טו) פָּדֹה. ב׳ בַּמָּסוֹרֶת — ״אַךְ פָּדֹה תִפְדֶּה״; וְאִידָךְ ״אָח לֹא פָדֹה יִפְדֶּה״. הַיְנוּ דְּאָמַר רַבִּי יְהוֹשֻׁעַ, רָחֵל שֶׁלֹּא בִכְּרָה וְיָלְדָה שְׁנֵי זְכָרִים, שְׁנֵיהֶם לַכֹּהֵן וְאֵין הָאֶחָד פּוֹטֵר אֶת חֲבֵרוֹ, וְהַיְנוּ ״אָח לֹא פָדֹה יִפְדֶּה״:

(יט) תְּרוּמֹת. ג׳ בַּמָּסוֹרֶת — ״כֹּל תְּרוּמֹת הַקֳּדָשִׁים״; ״הָרֵי בַגִּלְבֹּעַ אַל טַל וְאַל מָטָר עֲלֵיכֶם וּשְׂדֵי תְרוּמֹת״; ״מֶלֶךְ בְּמִשְׁפָּט יַעֲמִיד אָרֶץ, וְאִישׁ תְּרוּמוֹת יֶהֶרְסֶנָּה״. זֶהוּ שֶׁדָּרְשׁוּ חֲכָמֵינוּ ז״ל, אִם דּוֹמֶה הַדַּיָּן לְמֶלֶךְ שֶׁאֵינוֹ צָרִיךְ כְּלוּם, ״יַעֲמִיד אָרֶץ״, וְהַיְנוּ ״וּשְׂדֵי תְרוּמֹת״ שֶׁנֶּאֱמַר גַּבֵּי שָׁאוּל. וְאִם דּוֹמֶה לְכֹהֵן שֶׁמְּחַזֵּר עַל הַגְּרָנוֹת, וְהַיְנוּ ״כֹּל תְּרוּמֹת הַקֳּדָשִׁים״ ״יֶהֶרְסֶנָּה״:

BAAL HATURIM ELUCIDATED

15. פָּדֹה — REDEEM. The masoretic note, ב׳, means that this word appears twice in the *Tanach:* (i) here, אַךְ פָּדֹה תִפְדֶּה, *but you shall surely redeem;* and (ii) אָח לֹא פָדֹה יִפְדֶּה, *yet [a man] would surely not redeem a brother* (*Psalms* 49:8). [The similarity of expression is] an allusion to the opinion of the *Tanna* Rabbi Yehoshua:[76] [If] a ewe that had not given birth previously bore two males . . . both [must be given] to the Kohen.[77] One does not redeem the other. This is alluded to by the verse from *Psalms* [which may be understood as]: אָח לֹא פָדֹה יִפְדֶּה, *a brother shall not redeem.*[78]

19. תְּרוּמֹת — SET-ASIDES. The masoretic note,[79] ג׳, means that this word appears

76. In all extant editions of the Mishnah, Talmud and commentaries, this reads רַבִּי יוֹסֵי הַגְּלִילִי, *Rabbi Yose of Galilee.* Perhaps, the Baal HaTurim used the abbreviation רי״ה, which a copyist interpreted as ר׳ יְהוֹשֻׁעַ (*VeChur LaZahav*).

77. *Bechoros* 2:6 [17a]. The Mishnah there reads: [If] a ewe that had not given birth previously bore two males whose two heads emerged simultaneously — Rabbi Yose of Galilee says: Both are the Kohen's as it is stated, הַזְּכָרִים לַה׳, [*and every first issue . . .*] *the males are* HASHEM'S (*Exodus* 13:12). The Sages, however, say: It is impossible [that both heads emerged at precisely the same instant (*Rashi*)]; rather, one [lamb] is his and one is the Kohen's . . .

78. That is, by giving one of the twin lambs to a Kohen, the owner has not absolved himself from his obligation to give the other twin to a Kohen.

79. The full masoretic note appears in *Samuel* and *Proverbs:* ג׳ בִּקְרִיאָה ב׳ חֲסֵרִים וא׳ מָלֵא . . . וְסִימָן

[15] *"Every first issue of a womb of any flesh that they offer to* HASHEM*, whether man or beast, shall be yours; but you shall surely redeem the firstborn of man, and the firstborn of an impure beast shall you redeem.* [16] *Those that are to be redeemed — from one month shall you redeem according to the valuation, five silver shekels by the sacred shekel; it is twenty gera.* [17] *But the firstborn of an ox or the firstborn of a sheep or the firstborn of a goat you shall not redeem; they are holy; their blood shall you throw upon the Altar and their fat shall you cause to go up in smoke, a fire-offering, a satisfying aroma to* HASHEM*.*
[18] *Their flesh shall be yours; like the breast of the waving and the right thigh shall it be yours.*

[19] *"All set-asides from the sanctities that the Children of Israel have set aside to* HASHEM *have I given to you and your*

three times[80] in the *Tanach:* (i) here, כֹּל תְּרוּמֹת הַקֳּדָשִׁים, *all set-asides from the sanctities;* (ii) הָרֵי בַגִּלְבֹּעַ אַל טַל וְאַל מָטָר עֲלֵיכֶם וּשְׂדֵי תְרוּמֹת, *O mountains in Gilboa — may neither dew nor rain be upon you, nor fields of bounty*[81] (*II Samuel* 1:21) [in David's lament over the deaths of Saul and Jonathan]; and (iii) מֶלֶךְ בְּמִשְׁפָּט יַעֲמִיד אָרֶץ וְאִישׁ תְּרוּמוֹת יֶהֶרְסֶנָּה, *Through justice a king will uphold the land, but a man of haughtiness*[82] *will tear it down* (*Proverbs* 29:4). This [similarity of expression] alludes to the dictum of our Sages, of blessed memory:[83] "If a judge resembles a king who does not require anything, *he will uphold the land*" — as alluded to by *the fields of bounty* mentioned with regard to [King] Saul.[84] If, however, [a judge] resembles a Kohen who goes around to the granaries [collecting *terumah* portions for himself], as alluded to by the verse all *set-asides from the sanctities* [which are given to a Kohen], then *he will tear it down.*[84a]

כָּל טוּרַיָּא דְמַלְכָּא אנ״ך, *Three, in Scripture: two spelled defectively* [תְּרוּמֹת, *without the second* ו] *and one spelled in full* [תְּרוּמוֹת, *with the second* ו]. *A mnemonic* [*for this is the Aramaic phrase*] כָּל טוּרַיָּא דְמַלְכָּא, *all the mountains of the king* [*formed by the first words of the three verses* — כֹּל הָרֵי מֶלֶךְ]. [*The three verses appear one each in*] אוֹרַיְתָא, *Torah* [i.e., *Numbers*], נְבִיאַי, *Prophets* [i.e., *Samuel*], כְּתוּבֵי, *Writings* [i.e., *Proverbs*].

80. In some editions of the Massorah, the note reads ד׳, *four,* and includes לַתְּרוּמוֹת (*Nehemiah* 12:44).

81. The term תְּרוּמָה refers to that which is lifted out or removed from a larger group and set aside for a specific purpose. It is usually used in reference to priestly gifts, such as *terumah,* the portion of each's year's crop set aside for the Kohen. Accordingly, וּשְׂדֵי תְרוּמֹת refers to fields that produce bountiful crops so that substantial portions will be set aside for the Kohanim and Levites (*Rashi*).

82. Here, תְּרוּמוֹת refers to a haughty person who, in his own mind, has raised himself above all others (*Rashi*).

83. *Kesubos* 105b.

84. That is, if a judge is independently wealthy, owning bountiful fields, he will not be beholden to anyone and will render just decisions (*Rashi*).

84a. That is, if a judge has to rely on others for his sustenance, he will be beholden to those who support him. As a consequence, his decisions will be skewed.

וּלְבָנֶיךָ וְלִבְנֹתֶיךָ אִתְּךָ לְחָק־עוֹלָם בְּרִית מֶלַח
כ עוֹלָם הִוא לִפְנֵי יהוה לְךָ וּלְזַרְעֲךָ אִתָּךְ: וַיֹּאמֶר
יהוה אֶל־אַהֲרֹן בְּאַרְצָם לֹא תִנְחָל וְחֵלֶק לֹא־
יִהְיֶה לְךָ בְּתוֹכָם אֲנִי חֶלְקְךָ וְנַחֲלָתְךָ בְּתוֹךְ בְּנֵי
(שביעי) כא יִשְׂרָאֵל: וְלִבְנֵי לֵוִי הִנֵּה נָתַתִּי כָּל־מַעֲשֵׂר
בְּיִשְׂרָאֵל לְנַחֲלָה חֵלֶף עֲבֹדָתָם אֲשֶׁר־הֵם עֹבְדִים
כב אֶת־עֲבֹדַת אֹהֶל מוֹעֵד: וְלֹא־יִקְרְבוּ עוֹד בְּנֵי
כג יִשְׂרָאֵל אֶל־אֹהֶל מוֹעֵד לָשֵׂאת חֵטְא לָמוּת: וְעָבַד
הַלֵּוִי הוּא אֶת־עֲבֹדַת אֹהֶל מוֹעֵד וְהֵם יִשְׂאוּ עֲוֹנָם
חֻקַּת עוֹלָם לְדֹרֹתֵיכֶם וּבְתוֹךְ בְּנֵי יִשְׂרָאֵל לֹא יִנְחֲלוּ
כד נַחֲלָה: כִּי אֶת־מַעְשַׂר בְּנֵי־יִשְׂרָאֵל אֲשֶׁר יָרִימוּ
לַיהוה תְּרוּמָה נָתַתִּי לַלְוִיִּם לְנַחֲלָה עַל־כֵּן אָמַרְתִּי
לָהֶם בְּתוֹךְ בְּנֵי יִשְׂרָאֵל לֹא יִנְחֲלוּ נַחֲלָה:
כה־כו וַיְדַבֵּר יהוה אֶל־מֹשֶׁה לֵּאמֹר: וְאֶל־הַלְוִיִּם תְּדַבֵּר
וְאָמַרְתָּ אֲלֵהֶם כִּי־תִקְחוּ מֵאֵת בְּנֵי־יִשְׂרָאֵל אֶת־
הַמַּעֲשֵׂר אֲשֶׁר נָתַתִּי לָכֶם מֵאִתָּם בְּנַחֲלַתְכֶם
וַהֲרֵמֹתֶם מִמֶּנּוּ תְּרוּמַת יהוה מַעֲשֵׂר מִן־הַמַּעֲשֵׂר:
כז וְנֶחְשַׁב לָכֶם תְּרוּמַתְכֶם כַּדָּגָן מִן־הַגֹּרֶן וְכַמְלֵאָה
כח מִן־הַיָּקֶב: כֵּן תָּרִימוּ גַם־אַתֶּם תְּרוּמַת יהוה מִכֹּל
מַעְשְׂרֹתֵיכֶם אֲשֶׁר תִּקְחוּ מֵאֵת בְּנֵי יִשְׂרָאֵל וּנְתַתֶּם
כט מִמֶּנּוּ אֶת־תְּרוּמַת יהוה לְאַהֲרֹן הַכֹּהֵן: מִכֹּל
מַתְּנֹתֵיכֶם תָּרִימוּ אֵת כָּל־תְּרוּמַת יהוה מִכָּל־חֶלְבּוֹ
(מפטיר) ל אֶת־מִקְדְּשׁוֹ מִמֶּנּוּ: וְאָמַרְתָּ אֲלֵהֶם בַּהֲרִימְכֶם אֶת־
חֶלְבּוֹ מִמֶּנּוּ וְנֶחְשַׁב לַלְוִיִּם כִּתְבוּאַת גֹּרֶן וְכִתְבוּאַת
לא יָקֶב: וַאֲכַלְתֶּם אֹתוֹ בְּכָל־מָקוֹם אַתֶּם וּבֵיתְכֶם

בעל הטורים

(כו) וַהֲרֵמֹתֶם מִמֶּנּוּ. קְרֵי בֵהּ מִמִּנוֹ, שֶׁאֵין תּוֹרְמִין מִמִּין עַל שֶׁאֵינוֹ מִינוֹ, וְלֹא מֵחָדָשׁ עַל הַיָּשָׁן:

BAAL HATURIM ELUCIDATED

26. וַהֲרֵמֹתֶם מִמֶּנּוּ — YOU SHALL SET ASIDE FROM IT. מִמֶּנּוּ, *from it,* can also be read as if

*sons and daughters with you as an eternal portion; it is an
eternal salt-like covenant before HASHEM, for you and your
offspring with you."*
*20 HASHEM said to Aaron, "In their Land you shall have no
heritage, and a share shall you not have among them; I am
your share and your heritage among the Children of Israel.*
*21 "To the sons of Levi, behold! I have given every tithe in
Israel as a heritage in exchange for the service that they
perform, the service of the Tent of Meeting — 22 so that the
Children of Israel shall not again approach the Tent of
Meeting to bear a sin to die. 23 The Levite himself shall
perform the service of the Tent of Meeting, and they shall
bear their iniquity, an eternal decree for your generations;
and among the Children of Israel they shall not inherit a
heritage. 24 For the tithe of the Children of Israel that they set
aside as a portion to HASHEM have I given to the Levites as
a heritage; therefore have I said to them: Among the
Children of Israel they shall not inherit a heritage."*
*25 HASHEM spoke to Moses, saying, 26 "To the Levites shall
you speak and you shall say to them, When you accept
from the Children of Israel the tithe that I have given you
from them as your heritage, you shall set aside from it a
portion to HASHEM, a tithe from the tithe. 27 Your setting
aside shall be reckoned for you like grain from the
threshing-floor and like the ripeness of the vat. 28 So shall
you, too, set aside the portion of HASHEM from all your tithes
that you accept from the Children of Israel, and from it you
shall give HASHEM'S portion to Aaron the Kohen. 29 From all
your gifts you shall set aside HASHEM'S entire portion from
all its best part, its sacred part from it.*
*30 "You shall say to them: 'By your setting aside its
best from it, it shall be considered for the Levites like the
produce of the threshing-floor and the produce of the vat.
31 You may eat it everywhere, you and your household,*

BAAL HATURIM ELUCIDATED

it was written מִמִּנוּ, *of its species.*[85] This alludes to the law[86] that we may not set aside one species as *terumah* for a different species, nor from a new crop for an old crop.[87]

85. Although we do not find any form of the term מִין, *species,* in Scriptures without the י, for purposes of the allusion, the Baal HaTurim omits it.

86. *Sifrei; Terumos* 2:4, see also 1:5 there.

87. *Peirush HaRokeach.*

יח/לב כִּֽי־שָׂכָ֥ר הוּא֙ לָכֶ֔ם חֵ֥לֶף עֲבֹדַתְכֶ֖ם בְּאֹ֥הֶל מוֹעֵֽד׃
לב וְלֹֽא־תִשְׂא֤וּ עָלָיו֙ חֵ֔טְא בַּהֲרִֽימְכֶ֥ם אֶת־חֶלְבּ֖וֹ
מִמֶּ֑נּוּ וְאֶת־קָדְשֵׁ֧י בְנֵֽי־יִשְׂרָאֵ֛ל לֹ֥א תְחַלְּל֖וּ וְלֹ֥א
תָמֽוּתוּ׃ פפפ

צ״ה פסוקים. דניא״ל סימן.

———— BAAL HATURIM ELUCIDATED ————

32. {The Baal HaTurim's comments to this verse appear at 19:2 below.}

18/32

for it is a wage for you in exchange for your service in the
Tent of Meeting. 32 *You shall not bear a sin because of it*
when you set aside its best from it; and the sanctities of the
Children of Israel you shall not desecrate, and you shall not
die.' "

פרשת חקת
Parashas Chukas

יט/א־ב א־ב וַיְדַבֵּר יהוה אֶל־מֹשֶׁה וְאֶל־אַהֲרֹן לֵאמֹר: זֹאת
חֻקַּת הַתּוֹרָה אֲשֶׁר־צִוָּה יהוה לֵאמֹר דַּבֵּר | אֶל־
בְּנֵי יִשְׂרָאֵל וְיִקְחוּ אֵלֶיךָ פָרָה אֲדֻמָּה תְּמִימָה
אֲשֶׁר אֵין־בָּהּ מוּם אֲשֶׁר לֹא־עָלָה עָלֶיהָ עֹל:

בעל הטורים

יט (ב) זאת חֻקַּת הַתּוֹרָה. סָמַךְ "חֻקַּת הַתּוֹרָה" לְ"בַהֲרִימְכֶם אֶת חֶלְבּוֹ מִמֶּנּוּ". רֶמֶז – לֹא נִתְּנָה תוֹרָה אֶלָּא לְאוֹכְלֵי הַמָּן. שְׁנִיָּה לָהּ, לְאוֹכְלֵי תְרוּמָה:

וְעוֹד רֶמֶז – הַמַּחֲזִיקִים בְּתוֹרַת ה׳ יֵשׁ לָהֶם מְנָת, שֶׁאֵין נוֹתְנִין תְּרוּמָה לְכֹהֵן עַם הָאָרֶץ:

❑ "לֹא תְחַלְּלוּ" וּסְמִיךְ לֵהּ "חֻקַּת הַתּוֹרָה". שֶׁתַּלְמִיד חָכָם שֶׁחוֹטֵא הוּא חִלּוּל הַשֵּׁם:

❑ "וְלֹא תָמוּתוּ" וּסְמִיךְ לֵהּ "חֻקַּת הַתּוֹרָה". דִּכְתִיב "עֵץ חַיִּים הִיא לַמַּחֲזִיקִים בָּהּ":

❑ **פָרָה אֲדֻמָּה.** בְּגִימַטְרִיָּא עַל עֲוֹן הָעֵגֶל:

❑ **לֹא עָלָה עָלֶיהָ עֹל.** עֹל כְּתִיב חָסֵר – לוֹמַר שֶׁאֲפִלּוּ לֹא מָשְׁכָה בְעֹל, אֶלָּא עָלָה עָלֶיהָ לְבַד, פְּסוּלָה:

BAAL HATURIM ELUCIDATED

XIV

2. זאת חֻקַּת הַתּוֹרָה — THIS IS THE DECREE OF THE TORAH. The Torah juxtaposed the phrase חֻקַּת הַתּוֹרָה, *the decree of the Torah,* [1] with the phrase, בַּהֲרִימְכֶם אֶת חֶלְבּוֹ מִמֶּנּוּ, *when you set aside its best from it* [2] (18:32 above).[2a] [This is] an allusion to [our Sages' statement]: The Torah was given primarily to those who eat the manna;[3] second to them, those who eat *terumah.* [4]

Another allusion: Those who hold fast to God's Torah are granted a portion. For *terumah* should not be given to an unlearned Kohen.[5]

1. In its context, the phrase זאת חֻקַּת הַתּוֹרָה refers specifically to the laws regarding the red cow. If so, why does the verse state חֻקַּת הַתּוֹרָה, *the decree of the Torah,* rather than חֻקַּת הַפָּרָה, *the decree of the* [*red cow*]?

A precedent for such exegesis appears in the Talmud (*Shabbos* 83b), where the phrase זאת הַתּוֹרָה (v. 16 below) is expounded upon as a reference to the entire Torah, while in context it refers specifically to the laws regarding *tumah* (contamination) contracted through contact with a corpse (A.S.). In the realm of *remez* (allusion), the Baal HaTurim sees the phrase as a reference to the entire Torah (Y.S.).

2. A reference to תְּרוּמָה, *terumah,* the portion of each year's crop that is set aside for the Kohanim.

2a. Although that verse speaks of *terumah* (see note 2 above) it may be explained as an allusion to the manna: The *gematria* of the word חֶלְבּוֹ, *its best,* is 46; and that of מִמֶּנּוּ, *from it,* is 136; and the verse states בַּהֲרִימְכֶם אֶת חֶלְבּוֹ מִמֶּנּוּ, *when you set aside* חֶלְבּוֹ (46) *from* מִמֶּנּוּ (136), i.e., 136 - 46 = 90, the *gematria* of מָן, *manna* (*Sefer Zikaron,* by Rabbi Yaakov Kalichman).

3. The Midrash states that the ability to expound on the Torah was granted primarily to those who ate the manna. That is, they were granted the opportunity to delve deeply into the meaning of the words and could thus draw exegetical inferences. This is because those who partook of the manna were not required to labor and toil and devote their time to earning a livelihood. Thus, they were free to spend their time in study. Likewise, the Kohanim were able to devote the major part of their day to Torah study for their basic needs were provided for them in the form of *terumah* (*Mechilta* 16:4; *Tanchuma, Beshalach* 20; see also note 4 below).

4. *Peirush HaRokeach; Mechilta* to *Beshalach* 16:4; see also the Baal HaTurim to *Exodus* 16:4, 16:16, 25:2; *Numbers* 11:8; and *Deuteronomy* 8:3.

5. *Sanhedrin* 90b — From where do we know that

19/1-2

1 HASHEM spoke to Moses and to Aaron, saying: 2 This is the decree of the Torah, which HASHEM has commanded, saying: Speak to the Children of Israel, and they shall take to you a perfectly red cow, in which there is not a blemish, and upon which a yoke has not come.

BAAL HATURIM ELUCIDATED

❑ [The previous *parashah* ends with the words, לֹא תְחַלְּלוּ וְלֹא תָמוּתוּ, *you shall not desecrate and you shall not die* (18:32).] The Torah juxtaposed חֻקַּת הַתּוֹרָה, *the decree of the Torah,* with לֹא תְחַלְּלוּ, *you shall not desecrate,* for when a Torah scholar sins, it is a desecration of God's Name.[6]

❑ The Torah further juxtaposed חֻקַּת הַתּוֹרָה with וְלֹא תָמוּתוּ, *and you shall not die,* in accordance with that which is written, עֵץ חַיִּים הִיא לַמַּחֲזִיקִים בָּהּ, *It* [*the Torah*] *is a tree of life to those who hold fast to it* (*Proverbs* 3:18).[7]

❑ **פָּרָה אֲדֻמָּה — A RED COW.** The *gematria* of this phrase (335) is equivalent[8] to that of עַל עֲוֹן הָעֵגֶל[9], *for the sin of the calf.*[10]

❑ **לֹא עָלָה עָלֶיהָ עֹל — UPON [WHICH] A YOKE HAS NOT COME.** The word עֹל, *yoke,* is spelled defectively, without a ו.[11] This indicates that even if the cow never pulled with a yoke, rather the yoke was merely placed upon it, it is disqualified.[12]

---

we do not give *terumah* to an unlearned Kohen? For it is stated, *He* [*King Hezekiah*] *said to the people, to the inhabitants of Jerusalem,* [*that they are*] *to give* מְנָת הַכֹּהֲנִים וְהַלְוִיִּם, *the portion of the Kohanim and the Levites, so that they could hold fast in the Torah of HASHEM* (*II Chronicles* 31:4).

6. *Peirush HaRokeach.* The Talmud (*Yoma* 86a) records a number of stories about Torah sages who went out of their way to ensure that their actions and motives would not be misconstrued by the unlearned, who would then cite them as condoning conduct that is in truth inappropriate. For when one's actions cause others to act contrary to the Torah's teachings, the role model is deemed guilty of desecrating God's Name.

7. *Peirush HaRokeach.* There are ten things that are called חַיִּים, *life* or *living:* (i) The Holy One, Blessed is He, [as it is stated,] וַה' אֱלֹהִים אֱמֶת הוּא אֱלֹהִים חַיִּים, *But HASHEM, God, is True; He is the Living God . . .* (*Jeremiah* 10:10); (ii) the Torah, as it is stated, עֵץ חַיִּים הִיא לַמַּחֲזִיקִים בָּהּ וְתֹמְכֶיהָ מְאֻשָּׁר, *It is a tree of life to those who hold fast to it, and its supporters are praiseworthy* (*Proverbs* 3:18) . . . (*Avos DeRabbi Nosson* 34:10).

8. The principle of *im hakollel* allows 334, the *gematria* of the Baal HaTurim's phrase, to be considered equivalent to 335.

9. The text follows *Shoham Yakar's* manuscript edition. The early printed editions read: פָּרָה אֲדוּמָּה בְּגִימַטְרִיָּא, *The gematria of the phrase* פָּרָה אֲדוּמָּה (341) *is equal to that of* זֶה עַל עֲוֹן עֵגֶל, *This is for the sin of the calf.* Note, however, that the word for red, which the verse spells אֲדֻמָּה, without a ו, must be spelled אֲדוּמָּה, with a ו, for purposes of the allusion.

10. See *Tanchuma* 8 (cited by *Rashi* in his comments following verse 22; and *Tosafos* to *Moed Katan* 28a, s.v., מה פרה; see also the Baal HaTurim to *Leviticus* 9:2) — Why must a female of the species be used [i.e., a פָּרָה אֲדֻמָּה, *red cow,* and not a פַּר אָדֹם, *red bull*]? This can be compared to the child of a maidservant who soiled the king's palace. The king said, "Let its mother come and wipe away the excrement." Similarly, the Holy One, Blessed is He, said, "Let the [red] cow come and atone for the incident of the [golden] calf."

11. The noun עֹל, *yoke,* appears twice more in the Torah (*Deuteronomy* 21:3 and 28:48) and eighteen times in the rest of the *Tanach,* each time spelled without a ו. This is in contrast to the nouns חוֹל, *sand* (for example, *Deuteronomy* 33:19), עוֹף, *bird* (*Leviticus* 17:13), and עוֹר, *skin* (31:20 below), which are spelled with a ו whenever they appear; and to the nouns קוֹל, *voice,* and עוֹג, *Og,* which are usually spelled with a ו (e.g., 21:3 and 33 below), but sometimes are spelled defectively (קֹל, *Genesis* 45:16; עֹג, *I Kings* 4:19).

12. *R' Yehudah HaChassid; Peirush HaRokeach.*

ג וּנְתַתֶּם אֹתָהּ אֶל־אֶלְעָזָר הַכֹּהֵן וְהוֹצִיא אֹתָהּ אֶל־
ד מִחוּץ לַמַּחֲנֶה וְשָׁחַט אֹתָהּ לְפָנָיו: וְלָקַח אֶלְעָזָר
הַכֹּהֵן מִדָּמָהּ בְּאֶצְבָּעוֹ וְהִזָּה אֶל־נֹכַח פְּנֵי אֹהֶל־
ה מוֹעֵד מִדָּמָהּ שֶׁבַע פְּעָמִים: וְשָׂרַף אֶת־הַפָּרָה לְעֵינָיו
אֶת־עֹרָהּ וְאֶת־בְּשָׂרָהּ וְאֶת־דָּמָהּ עַל־פִּרְשָׁהּ יִשְׂרֹף:
ו וְלָקַח הַכֹּהֵן עֵץ אֶרֶז וְאֵזוֹב וּשְׁנִי תוֹלָעַת וְהִשְׁלִיךְ
ז אֶל־תּוֹךְ שְׂרֵפַת הַפָּרָה: וְכִבֶּס בְּגָדָיו הַכֹּהֵן וְרָחַץ
בְּשָׂרוֹ בַּמַּיִם וְאַחַר יָבֹא אֶל־הַמַּחֲנֶה וְטָמֵא הַכֹּהֵן
ח עַד־הָעָרֶב: וְהַשֹּׂרֵף אֹתָהּ יְכַבֵּס בְּגָדָיו בַּמַּיִם וְרָחַץ
ט בְּשָׂרוֹ בַּמָּיִם וְטָמֵא עַד הָעָרֶב: וְאָסַף | אִישׁ טָהוֹר

בעל הטורים

(ה) **וְשָׂרַף אֶת הַפָּרָה לְעֵינָיו.** הַפָּסוּק מַתְחִיל וּמְסַיֵּם בִּשְׂרֵפָה. לוֹמַר שֶׁמַּרְבִּים עֵצִים בִּשְׂרֵפָתָהּ:

(ט) **וְאָסַף.** ג׳ בַּמָּסוֹרֶת – הָכָא ״וְאָסַף אִישׁ טָהוֹר״; וְאִידָךְ ״וְאָסַף הַמְּצֹרָע״; ״וְאָסַף נִדְחֵי יִשְׂרָאֵל״. הַמְּצֹרָע אִתְּקַשׁ לְמֵת. וּכְשֵׁם שֶׁאֵפֶר הַפָּרָה מְטַהֶרֶת, כָּךְ תְּפִלַּת הַצַּדִּיקִים גַּם כֵּן מְטַהֶרֶת. ״וְאָסַף נִדְחֵי יִשְׂרָאֵל״ לֶעָתִיד, אָז ״וְאָסַף הַמְּצֹרָע״, דִּכְתִיב ״אָז יְדַלֵּג כָּאַיָּל פִּסֵּחַ״. וְכֵן לֹא יִצְטָרְכוּ לְאֵפֶר פָּרָה, דִּכְתִיב ״בִּלַּע הַמָּוֶת לָנֶצַח״:

BAAL HATURIM ELUCIDATED

5. **וְשָׂרַף אֶת הַפָּרָה לְעֵינָיו — SOMEONE SHALL BURN THE COW BEFORE HIS EYES.** The verse both begins and concludes with the concept of burning.[13] This alludes to the fact that we use much wood for its fire.[14]

9. **וְאָסַף — [HE] SHALL GATHER.** The masoretic note, ג׳, means that this word appears three times in the *Tanach:* (i) here, **וְאָסַף אִישׁ טָהוֹר**, *a pure man shall gather;* (ii) **וְאָסַף הַמְּצֹרָע**, *and the metzora shall gather*[15] (*II Kings* 5:11); (iii) **וְאָסַף נִדְחֵי**

Regarding the red cow, the Mishnah teaches that any burden — no matter how small — placed *upon* the cow renders it invalid (*Parah* 2:3). This rule is derived from the incomplete spelling of עֹל, for the absence of the ו indicates that the word may also be understood as עַל, *upon,* that is, anything placed *upon* an animal may be considered an עֹל (*Midrash Lekach Tov*). However, it should be noted that the Mishnah also states that anything necessary for the animal's comfort, such as a blanket to keep away biting insects, is not considered an עֹל with regard to this rule.

13. The verse begins with וְשָׂרַף and concludes with יִשְׂרֹף, each of which means, *he shall burn.*

14. *Peirush HaRokeach;* see *Parah* 4:4.

15. That verse records Naaman's complaint after he had expected the prophet Elisha to recite a prayer that would miraculously cure his *tzaraas* (a leprous disease; see *Leviticus* Chs. 13-14). Naaman was chagrined when, instead of granting him an audience and praying on his behalf, *Elisha sent him a messenger saying, "Go bathe seven times in the Jordan; your flesh will return to normal and you will be cleansed." Naaman was enraged and left; he said, "Behold, I thought that he would surely come out to me and stand and call [in prayer] in the Name of HASHEM, his God, and wave his hand over the [afflicted] area and the metzora would gather . . ."* (*II Kings* 5:10-11).

The root אסף, *to gather,* as used regarding a *metzora* [one afflicted with the leprous disease

3 *You shall give it to Elazar the Kohen; he shall take it out to the*
outside of the camp and someone shall slaughter it in his
presence. 4 *Elazar the Kohen shall take some of its blood with*
his forefinger, and sprinkle some of its blood toward the front of
the Tent of Meeting seven times. 5 *Someone shall burn the cow*
before his eyes — its hide, and its flesh, and its blood, with its
dung, shall he burn. 6 *The Kohen shall take cedar wood,*
hyssop, and crimson thread, and he shall throw [them] into the
burning of the cow.
7 *The Kohen shall immerse his clothing and immerse himself*
in water, and afterwards he may come into the camp; and the
Kohen shall be impure until evening. 8 *The one who burns it shall*
immerse his clothing in water and immerse himself in water;
and he shall be impure until evening. 9 *A pure man shall gather*

BAAL HATURIM ELUCIDATED

יִשְׂרָאֵל, *And he will gather the castaways of Israel* (*Isaiah* 11:12). [The similarity of expression here and in *Kings* alludes to the Talmudic statement:] A *metzora* is likened to a corpse.[16] Moreover, just as the ashes of the red cow impart purity,[17] so too, the prayers of the righteous impart purity.[18]

[And the similarity of expression in the three verses also alludes to the time of *Mashiach:*] *And he will gather the castaways of Israel,* in the future, at which time *the metzora shall gather,* i.e., will be cured, as it is written, אָז יְדַלֵּג כָּאַיָּל פִּסֵּחַ, *Then the lame man will skip like a gazelle* (*Isaiah* 35:6).[19] And at that time, they will no longer need the ashes of the red cow, as it is written, בִּלַּע הַמָּוֶת לָנֶצַח, *He will have swallowed up death forever*[20] (*Isaiah* 25:8).

tzaraas] refers to healing; for when a *metzora* is healed, he may "gather" with other people, but while he is afflicted, everyone shuns his company (*Rashi* to 12:14 above, s.v., ואחר תאסף, and to *II Kings* 5:6).

16. *Nedarim* 64b — Four are considered as dead: a poor person; a *metzora;* a blind person; and one who is childless. *Tosafos* explains that the point of this teaching is to underscore to others the depth of suffering to which these four are subject, so that people will pray for them.

17. For the entire purpose of the ritual is to cleanse one who has become impure through contact with a corpse (see vv. 11-22 below).

18. As seen from Moses' prayer (12:13 above) for his sister Miriam when she contracted *tzaraas* (A.S.).

19. *Tanchuma, Metzora* 2 — When the Holy One, Blessed is He, said to the serpent, *"Because you have done this, you are accursed beyond every animal . . ."* (*Genesis* 3:14), with what did He curse it? With *tzaraas* . . . The scales of the serpent are a form of *tzaraas.* Moreover, all those who are blemished will be healed in the World to Come, but the serpent will not be healed [of its *tzaraas*], as it is stated, *you are accursed beyond every animal,* from which we learn that everyone will be healed except the serpent: Regarding people, it is written, *Then the lame will skip like a gazelle,* and, *Then the eyes of the blind will be opened . . .* (*Isaiah* 35:6,5); similarly, regarding beast and domestic animal it is written, *Wolf and lamb will graze as one, and a lion — like cattle — will eat straw; but the serpent's food will be dirt* (*Isaiah* 65:25).

20. The ashes of the red cow serve only one purpose, to cleanse the impurity brought about through contact with a corpse, but, in the days of the Messiah, God will swallow up, i.e., destroy, the concept of death and its accompanying impurity.

אֵת אֵפֶר הַפָּרָה וְהִנִּיחַ מִחוּץ לַמַּחֲנֶה בְּמָקוֹם
טָהוֹר וְהָיְתָה לַעֲדַת בְּנֵי־יִשְׂרָאֵל לְמִשְׁמֶרֶת לְמֵי
י נִדָּה חַטָּאת הִוא: וְכִבֶּס הָאֹסֵף אֶת־אֵפֶר הַפָּרָה
אֶת־בְּגָדָיו וְטָמֵא עַד־הָעָרֶב וְהָיְתָה לִבְנֵי יִשְׂרָאֵל
יא וְלַגֵּר הַגָּר בְּתוֹכָם לְחֻקַּת עוֹלָם: הַנֹּגֵעַ בְּמֵת
יב לְכָל־נֶפֶשׁ אָדָם וְטָמֵא שִׁבְעַת יָמִים: הוּא יִתְחַטָּא־
בוֹ בַּיּוֹם הַשְּׁלִישִׁי וּבַיּוֹם הַשְּׁבִיעִי יִטְהָר וְאִם־
לֹא יִתְחַטָּא בַּיּוֹם הַשְּׁלִישִׁי וּבַיּוֹם הַשְּׁבִיעִי לֹא
יג יִטְהָר: כָּל־הַנֹּגֵעַ בְּמֵת בְּנֶפֶשׁ הָאָדָם אֲשֶׁר־יָמוּת
וְלֹא יִתְחַטָּא אֶת־מִשְׁכַּן יהוה טִמֵּא וְנִכְרְתָה
הַנֶּפֶשׁ הַהִוא מִיִּשְׂרָאֵל כִּי מֵי נִדָּה לֹא־זֹרַק עָלָיו
יד טָמֵא יִהְיֶה עוֹד טֻמְאָתוֹ בוֹ: זֹאת הַתּוֹרָה אָדָם
כִּי־יָמוּת בְּאֹהֶל כָּל־הַבָּא אֶל־הָאֹהֶל וְכָל־
טו אֲשֶׁר בָּאֹהֶל יִטְמָא שִׁבְעַת יָמִים: וְכֹל כְּלִי פָתוּחַ

בעל הטורים

(טו) פָּתוּחַ. ד׳ בַּמָּסוֹרֶת – ״וְכֹל כְּלִי פָתוּחַ״; ״שָׁרְשִׁי פָתוּחַ אֱלֵי מָיִם״; ״קֶבֶר פָּתוּחַ גְּרֹנָם״; ״אַשְׁפָּתוֹ כְּקֶבֶר פָּתוּחַ״. הַיְנוּ דְּאָמְרִינַן, אַרְבַּע מִדּוֹת בִּכְלֵי חֶרֶס – נִקַּב בְּכוֹנֵס

BAAL HATURIM ELUCIDATED

15. פָּתוּחַ — OPEN. The masoretic note, ד׳, means that this word appears four times[21] in the *Tanach:* (i) here, וְכֹל כְּלִי פָתוּחַ, *and any open vessel;* (ii) שָׁרְשִׁי פָתוּחַ אֱלֵי מָיִם, *My root will be open to water* (*Job* 29:19); (iii) קֶבֶר פָּתוּחַ גְּרֹנָם, *Their throat is an open grave* (*Psalms* 5:10); and (iv) אַשְׁפָּתוֹ כְּקֶבֶר פָּתוּחַ, *Their garbage heap is like an open grave* (*Jeremiah* 5:16). The similarity of expression alludes to the Talmudic statement:[22]

21. The masoretic note does not differentiate between the initial פ, without a *dagesh,* here and in *Job,* and the initial פּ, with a *dagesh,* in the other two verses. The absence of the *dagesh* in the two verses is in accordance with the grammatical rule known as בֶּגֶ״ד כֶּפֶ״ת, which states in part: When any of the six letters בג״ד כפ״ת appears at the beginning of a word, it takes a *dagesh;* however, if that word is connected by its *ta'am* (cantillation mark) or by a *makaf* (hyphen) to the word before it and the first word ends with one of the letters אהו״י, then the *dagesh* is omitted. Thus, in the phrase כְּלִי פָתוּחַ where the *ta'am munach* under the ל connects the word כְּלִי to the *zakeif katan* of the next word, the פ does not take a *dagesh;* similarly, in the phrase שָׁרְשִׁי פָתוּחַ, the *ta'amim* connect the words, so the פ does not take a *dagesh.* As a general rule, masoretic notes do not differentiate between בג״ד כפ״ת with a *dagesh* and without one.

22. As long as an earthenware vessel can be used for its assigned purpose, it is susceptible to contracting *tumah* (contamination). However, once it has been perforated to such a degree that it cannot serve that purpose, it can no longer contract *tumah.* Moreover, if it had already contracted *tumah* while it was usable, that *tumah* leaves it when it becomes unusable. The Talmud (*Shabbos* 95b) states: There are five categories [see note 23] of perforated earthenware vessels: (i) If it has been perforated with a hole large enough to allow liquid

the ash of the cow and place [it] outside the camp in a pure
place. It shall be for the assembly of Israel as a safekeeping, for
water of sprinkling; it is for purification. 10 *The one who gathers*
the ash of the cow shall immerse his clothing and be impure
until evening. It shall be for the Children of Israel and for the
proselyte who dwells among them as an eternal decree.

11 *Whoever touches the corpse of any human being shall be*
impure for seven days. 12 *He shall purify himself with it on the*
third day and on the seventh day, he will be pure; but if he will
not purify himself on the third day and on the seventh day, he
will not be pure. 13 *Whoever touches a dead body, a human*
being who will have died, and will not have purified himself —
if he has made the Tabernacle of HASHEM *impure, that person*
shall be cut off from Israel; because water of sprinkling has not
been thrown upon him, he shall be impure; his impurity is still
upon him.

14 *This is the teaching regarding a man who would die in a*
tent: Anything that enters the tent and anything that is in the
tent shall be impure for a seven-day period. 15 *Any open vessel*

BAAL HATURIM ELUCIDATED

There are four categories[23] of perforated earthenware vessels [with regard to ritual impurity]: (i) If the vessel has been perforated with a hole large enough to

to escape, it is unfit to be considered a shard [i.e., with regard to the laws of *tumah* and *taharah* (impurity and purity) of earthenware vessels, an otherwise intact vessel that has sprung a tiny leak, thus allowing water to seep out but not in, is still considered a vessel, for it can be used with a shard placed under it to catch the drippings; similarly, a shard that can be placed under a leaky vessel to catch the drippings is considered a vessel, but a shard that leaks is not considered to be a vessel, for one does not place another shard to catch the drippings of the first, rather, he discards the perforated shard and puts another in its place (*Rashi*)], nevertheless, if an intact vessel [springs such a leak], it is still considered a vessel even with regard to *mei chattas* (the water mixed with the ashes of the red cow); (ii) if it has been perforated with a hole large enough to allow liquid to seep in, it has been disqualified as a vessel with regard to sanctifying *mei chattas,* nevertheless, it is still considered a vessel with regard to the purity of seeds growing in it; (iii) if it has been perforated with a hole large enough to allow a small root [of a plant growing in the vessel] to pass through, it is no longer a vessel with regard to seeds, nevertheless, it is still a vessel with regard to olives; (iv) if it has been perforated with a hole large enough to allow an olive to pass through, it is no longer considered a vessel with regard to olives, nevertheless, it is still a vessel with regard to pomegranates; and (v) if it has been perforated with a hole large enough to allow a pomegranate to pass through, it is no longer considered a vessel with regard to *tumah* and *taharah.*

23. The Talmudic passage (see note 22) reads חָמֵשׁ מִדּוֹת, *five categories,* yet the Baal HaTurim states אַרְבַּע מִדּוֹת, *four categories*! In *Maharam MiRothenburg,* the Baal HaTurim's apparent source, the comment concludes: There is yet one other category regarding a perforated earthenware vessel — if a shard has a hole large enough to allow water to leak out — it is unfit to be considered a shard, for one does not say, bring a shard to [catch the drippings of] another shard. But it is not among the categories [included in our allusion] because it refers to a shard and not to an intact vessel.

טז אֲשֶׁר אֵין־צָמִיד פָּתִיל עָלָיו טָמֵא הוּא: וְכֹל
אֲשֶׁר־יִגַּע עַל־פְּנֵי הַשָּׂדֶה בַּחֲלַל־חֶרֶב אוֹ בְמֵת
אוֹ־בְעֶצֶם אָדָם אוֹ בְקָבֶר יִטְמָא שִׁבְעַת יָמִים:
יז וְלָקְחוּ לַטָּמֵא מֵעֲפַר שְׂרֵפַת הַחַטָּאת וְנָתַן עָלָיו
שני יח מַיִם חַיִּים אֶל־כֶּלִי: וְלָקַח אֵזוֹב וְטָבַל בַּמַּיִם אִישׁ
טָהוֹר וְהִזָּה עַל־הָאֹהֶל וְעַל־כָּל־הַכֵּלִים וְעַל־
הַנְּפָשׁוֹת אֲשֶׁר הָיוּ־שָׁם וְעַל־הַנֹּגֵעַ בַּעֶצֶם אוֹ

בעל הטורים

מַשְׁקֶה, נִפְסַל מִלְּקַדֵּשׁ בּוֹ מֵי חַטָּאת, וְהַיְנוּ "כְּלִי פָּתוּחַ" הָאָמוּר כָּאן אֵצֶל מֵי חַטָּאת, שֶׁאֵינוֹ חָשׁוּב כְּלִי, וַעֲדַיִן כְּלִי הוּא לְעִנְיַן זְרָעִים; נִקַּב כְּשֹׁרֶשׁ קָטָן {כְּלוּף, דְּהַיְנוּ מִין קִטְנִית}, טָהוֹר הוּא לְעִנְיַן זְרָעִים, שֶׁאִם הָיוּ זְרָעִים זְרוּעִים בְּעָצִיץ נָקוּב אֵינוֹ מְקַבֵּל טֻמְאָה, וְהַיְנוּ "שָׁרָשַׁי פָּתוּחַ אֱלֵי מָיִם", וַעֲדַיִן כְּלִי הוּא לְעִנְיַן זֵיתִים; נִקַּב כְּמוֹצִיא זַיִת, טָהוֹר מִסְּתָם כְּלִי חֶרֶס הָעוֹמֵד לְזֵיתִים, וְהַיְנוּ "פָּתוּחַ גְּרֹנָם", דִּסְתָם אֲכִילָה בִּכְזַיִת, וַעֲדַיִן כְּלִי הוּא לְרִמּוֹנִים; נִקַּב כְּמוֹצִיא רִמּוֹן, טָהוֹר מִכְּלוּם, וְהַיְנוּ "אַשְׁפָּתוֹ כְּקֶבֶר פָּתוּחַ", כְּלוֹמַר כְּשֶׁנִּקַּב וּפָתוּחַ כְּמוֹצִיא רִמּוֹן, זוֹרְקִין אוֹתוֹ לְאַשְׁפָּה וְאֵין שֵׁם כְּלִי עָלָיו עוֹד:

(יז) אֶל כֶּלִי. ב׳ בַּמָּסוֹרֶת — "וְנָתַן עָלָיו מַיִם חַיִּים אֶל כֶּלִי"; וְאִידָךְ "וְלֹא הוּרַק מִכְּלִי אֶל כֶּלִי". שֶׁצָּרִיךְ שֶׁתְּהֵא חִיּוּתָן בִּכְלִי, וְלֹא שֶׁיְּרִיקֵם מִכְּלִי אֶל כְּלִי:

BAAL HATURIM ELUCIDATED

allow liquid to seep in, it has been disqualified as a vessel with regard to sanctifying *mei chattas* (the water mixed with the ashes of the red cow) [which must be sanctified in a vessel (v. 17 below)] — and that is [the allusion of the phrase], כְּלִי פָּתוּחַ, *an open vessel,* stated here with regard to the *mei chattas,* i.e., it is not considered a vessel[24] — nevertheless, it is still considered as a vessel with regard to seeds [if there are seeds growing in it].

(ii) If it has been perforated with a hole large enough to allow the thin root of a plant {such as *luf,* a species of legume}[25] [that has been planted in it] to pass through, it is no longer considered a vessel with regard to seeds, that is, seeds that have been sown in it are [considered to derive their nourishment from the

24. That is, the term כְּלִי פָּתוּחַ is understood as *a vessel with an* [*unwanted*] *opening,* in other words, a vessel into which water can seep from a perforation in its wall or bottom.

25. The passage enclosed in braces follows *Shoham Yakar's* manuscript edition, but does not appear in either *Maharam MiRothenburg,* the Baal HaTurim's apparent source, or *Moshav Zekeinim,* which probably took this comment from *Maharam MiRothenburg* also. The early printed editions read: נִקַּב כְּשֹׁרֶשׁ קָטָן קָלוּף פֵּרוּשׁ הוּא מַאֲכַל עֲנָבִים דְּהַיְנוּ מִין קִטְנִית . . ., *If it has been perforated with a hole large enough to allow a small peeled root, that is, food of grapes, that is, a species of legume . . .,* but that version does not make much sense. Indeed, *Ittur Bikkurim* states that after much research into the words of the Sages, he was unable to find a reasonable explanation of the Baal HaTurim's words. He ends by citing his teacher's (מורי מהר״י) suggested emendation: נִקַּב כְּשֹׁרֶשׁ קָטָן לוּף פֵּרוּשׁ מַאֲכַל עוֹרְבִים . . ., *If it has been perforated with a hole large enough to allow a small luf root, that is, food for ravens . . .,* in accordance with the Mishnah (*Shabbos* 18:1 [126b]) in which *luf* is described as food for ravens.

that has no cover fastened to it is impure. 16 *Anyone who*
touches on the open field one slain by the sword or one
that died or a human bone or a grave shall be impure
for seven days. 17 *They shall take for the impure person*
some of the ashes of the burning of the purification
[animal], and place upon it spring water in a vessel. 18 *A*
pure man shall take hyssop and dip it in the water, and
sprinkle upon the tent, upon all the vessels, upon the people
who were there, and upon the one who touched the bone or

ground[25a] and, as such, are] not susceptible to *tumah*[26] — and that is [the allusion of the verse], *My roots will be open to water* — nevertheless, it is still considered a vessel with regard to olives.

(iii) If it has been perforated with a hole large enough to allow an olive to pass through, it is no longer considered a standard earthenware food vessel, which usually is used to contain olive-sized pieces of food — and that is [the allusion of the verse], פָּתוּחַ גְּרֹנָם, which can be understood as *open is their throat,* for an ordinary portion of food is the size of an olive[27] — nevertheless, it is still considered a vessel with regard to [being used for storing] pomegranates.

(iv) If it has been perforated with a hole large enough to allow a pomegranate to pass through, it is no longer considered a vessel at all — and that is [the allusion of the verse], *Their garbage heap is like an open grave,* that is, if it is perforated and open enough for a pomegranate to pass through, it is thrown onto the garbage heap, and is no longer identified by the term vessel.

17. אֶל כֶּלִי — IN A VESSEL. The masoretic note, ב׳, means that this phrase appears twice in the *Tanach:* (i) here, וְנָתַן עָלָיו מַיִם חַיִּים אֶל כֶּלִי, *and place upon it spring water* [literally, *living waters*] *in a vessel;* and (ii) וְלֹא הוּרַק מִכְּלִי אֶל כֶּלִי, *and not being poured from vessel to vessel* (*Jeremiah* 48:11). [The similarity of expression indicates] that the waters must still be in the very vessel with which they were removed from their natural state;[28] they may not be poured from one vessel into another.[29]

25a. Foodstuffs are not susceptible to *tumah* as long as they are still attached to their source, e.g., fruit that is still on its tree, vegetables that are still in the ground.

26. See *Demai* 5:10; *Uktzin* 2:10.

27. See Mishnah, *Berachos* 7:1 [45a]; *Rambam, Hilchos Berachos* 3:12; *Tur* and *Shulchan Aruch, Orach Chaim* 210:1.

28. *Sotah* 16b. Elsewhere, the Talmud states that on a Scriptural level, pouring from vessel to vessel does not disqualify the water. Rather, the Rabbis enacted this rule as a stringency to enhance the sanctity of the water (*Pesachim* 34b). Accordingly, both the Talmudic inference from the expression מַיִם חַיִּים אֶל כֶּלִי and the Baal HaTurim's explanation of the similar usage of אֶל כֶּלִי here and in *Jeremiah* are merely Scriptural allusions to a Rabbinic enactment (*Atros Addar*).

29. *Maharam MiRothenburg;* see *Rashi* to *Sotah* 16b and *Pesachim* 34b.

יט בֶחָלָ֔ל א֥וֹ בַמֵּ֖ת א֥וֹ בַקָּֽבֶר׃ וְהִזָּ֤ה הַטָּהֹר֙ עַל־הַטָּמֵ֔א
בַּיּ֥וֹם הַשְּׁלִישִׁ֖י וּבַיּ֣וֹם הַשְּׁבִיעִ֑י וְחִטְּאוֹ֙ בַּיּ֣וֹם הַשְּׁבִיעִ֔י
כ וְכִבֶּ֧ס בְּגָדָ֛יו וְרָחַ֥ץ בַּמַּ֖יִם וְטָהֵ֥ר בָּעָֽרֶב׃ וְאִ֤ישׁ
אֲשֶׁר־יִטְמָא֙ וְלֹ֣א יִתְחַטָּ֔א וְנִכְרְתָ֛ה הַנֶּ֥פֶשׁ הַהִ֖וא
מִתּ֣וֹךְ הַקָּהָ֑ל כִּי֩ אֶת־מִקְדַּ֨שׁ יהוה טִמֵּ֗א מֵ֥י נִדָּ֛ה
כא לֹא־זֹרַ֥ק עָלָ֖יו טָמֵ֥א הֽוּא׃ וְהָיְתָ֥ה לָהֶ֖ם לְחֻקַּ֣ת עוֹלָ֑ם
וּמַזֵּ֤ה מֵֽי־הַנִּדָּה֙ יְכַבֵּ֣ס בְּגָדָ֔יו וְהַנֹּגֵ֙עַ֙ בְּמֵ֣י הַנִּדָּ֔ה

בעל הטורים

(כא) בְּמֵי. ה׳ בַּמָּסוֹרֶת – ״בְּמֵי הַנִּדָּה״; ״אַךְ בְּמֵי נִדָּה יִתְחַטָּא״; ״בְּמֵי מְרִיבַת קָדֵשׁ״; ״בְּמֵי הַיַּרְדֵּן״; ״אִם הִתְרָחַצְתִּי בְמֵי שָׁלֶג״. זֶהוּ מַה שֶּׁדָּרְשׁוּ, ״וַיֹּאמֶר אֶלְעָזָר הַכֹּהֵן אֶל אַנְשֵׁי הַצָּבָא״, שֶׁכֵּיוָן שֶׁבָּא מֹשֶׁה לִכְלַל כַּעַס בָּא לִכְלַל טָעוּת, שֶׁשָּׁכַח לְהוֹרוֹת לָהֶם הִלְכוֹת גִּעוּל – זֶהוּ ״בְּמֵי מְרִיבַת״; כֵּיוָן שֶׁבָּא לִכְלַל מְרִיבָה טָעָה בְמֵי נִדָּה. ״בְּמֵי הַיַּרְדֵּן״ לוֹמַר שֶׁמֵּי הַיַּרְדֵּן דִּינָן כְּמֵי נִדָּה וּצְרִיכִים אַרְבָּעִים סְאָה. וְהַיְנוּ כִּשְׁמוּאֵל, דְּאָסַר לִטְבֹּל בִּנְהָרוֹת שֶׁמָּא יִרְבּוּ הַנּוֹטְפִין עַל הַזּוֹחֲלִין וְאֵינָן מְטַהֲרִין דֶּרֶךְ זְחִילָה.

BAAL HATURIM ELUCIDATED

21. בְּמֵי — WITH THE WATER[30] OF. The masoretic note, ה׳, means that this word appears five times in the *Tanach:* (i) here, בְּמֵי הַנִּדָּה, *with the water of sprinkling;* (ii) אַךְ בְּמֵי נִדָּה יִתְחַטָּא, *but with the water of sprinkling it must be purified*[30a] (*Numbers* 31:23); (iii) בְּמֵי מְרִיבַת קָדֵשׁ, *at the waters of strife at Kadesh* (*Deuteronomy* 32:51); (iv) בְּמֵי הַיַּרְדֵּן, *in the waters of the Jordan* (*Joshua* 3:13); and (v) אִם הִתְרָחַצְתִּי בְמֵי שָׁלֶג, *though I would wash myself in the water of* [*melted*] *snow* (*Job* 9:30). This [similarity of expression] alludes to the Sages' interpretation of the verse, וַיֹּאמֶר אֶלְעָזָר הַכֹּהֵן אֶל אַנְשֵׁי הַצָּבָא, *Elazar the Kohen said to the men of the legion* (31:21 below): Because Moses entered the realm of anger, he entered the realm of error (*Pesachim* 66b), for he forgot to inform the soldiers about the laws concerning the purging [of cooking utensils that have been used by non-Jews][31] — and that is the

30. The word מַיִם is both singular (*water*) and plural (*waters*). Indeed, we find both forms used in the same verse (*Numbers* 24:7): יִזַּל מַיִם מִדָּלְיָו, *Water shall flow from his wells,* where מַיִם is the subject of the singular verb יִזַּל [the plural form would be יִזְּלוּ, as in יִזְּלוּ מָיִם (*Psalms* 147:18)], and is followed by וְזַרְעוֹ בְּמַיִם רַבִּים, *and his seed shall be by abundant waters,* where מַיִם is modified by the plural adjective רַבִּים [the singular form would be רַב, as in כִּי רַב הוּא, *for it is numerous* (22:3 below)].

Likewise, the construct form מֵי is used in both the singular and the plural. Thus, in our passage, where מֵי נִדָּה is the subject of the singular passive verb זֹרַק [the plural form would be זֹרְקוּ], it has been translated in the singular, *water of sprinkling;* but the phrase בְּמֵי מְרִיבַת קָדֵשׁ has been translated in the plural, for we find the expression הֵם מֵי מְרִיבַת קָדֵשׁ, *they are the waters of strife at Kadesh* (27:14 below), with the plural pronoun הֵם, *they,* used for מֵי. Similarly בְּמֵי הַיַּרְדֵּן has been translated in the plural, *in the waters of the Jordan,* for that phrase is followed by מֵי הַיַּרְדֵּן יִכָּרֵתוּן, *the waters of the Jordan will be cut off,* which uses the plural verb יִכָּרֵתוּן [the singular form would be יִכָּרֵת (11:33 above)].

30a. That verse prescribes that the waters of sprinkling be used to purge *tumah* (impurity) that a metal utensil has contracted through contact with a corpse.

31. *Sifrei* to 31:21 below; *Pesachim* 66b. According to the Talmud and Midrash there, Elazar, not

the slain one or the one that died or the grave. [19] *The pure person shall sprinkle upon the impure person on the third day and on the seventh day, and shall purify him on the seventh day; then he shall immerse his clothing and immerse himself in water and be pure in the evening.* [20] *But a man who shall be impure and does not purify himself, that person shall be cut off from the midst of the congregation, if he shall have made the Sanctuary of HASHEM impure; because the water of sprinkling has not been thrown upon him, he is impure.*

[21] *This shall be for them an eternal decree. And the one who sprinkles the water of sprinkling shall immerse his clothing, and one who touches the water of sprinkling*

allusion of the phrase, *at the waters of strife:* because Moses entered the realm of strife, he erred about *the water of sprinkling.*

[The same term in the phrase] בְּמֵי הַיַּרְדֵּן, *in the waters of the Jordan,* indicates that the waters of the Jordan are like מֵי נִדָּה [which may be rendered] *waters* of [the *mikveh* used to purify] a *niddah,*[32] and must contain a volume of forty *se'ah.*[33] And this is in accordance with [the opinion of] the *Amora* Shmuel, who forbids immersion in rivers,[33a] lest the quantity of rainwater be greater than that of the spring water that is the river's source — in such an instance, the river cannot effect purification while its waters are flowing.[34]

Moses, had to teach these laws, because *Moses was angry with the commanders of the legions . . .* (31:14 below). As a consequence of his anger, either Moses forgot the pertinent laws (*Rashi* to 31:21) or he forgot to teach them (Baal HaTurim).

In his comments to 31:21, the Baal HaTurim gives an entirely different interpretation of that verse.

32. *Avodah Zarah* 75b; see also *Tosafos* to *Yevamos* 47b, s.v., במקום. A *niddah* is a woman who has menstruated, but has not yet completed her purification process, which concludes with immersion in a *mikveh,* a reservoir of standing water containing a volume of no less than forty *se'ah* water (see *Leviticus* 15:19-33; see also note 33 below).

33. That is, there must be at least forty *se'ah* of standing water in the area of the immersion. Opinions regarding the modern-day equivalent of a *se'ah* range between 2.25 and 4 gallons. According to the various opinions, the minimum volume of a *mikveh* is between 90 and 160 gallons.

33a. The text follows *Shoham Yakar's* manuscript edition. The early printed editions, as well as some later editions, read, וְהַיְנוּ כִּשְׁמוּאֵל דְּאָסַר בְּשַׁבָּת לְטְבֹּל בִּנְהָרוֹת, literally, *And this is in accordance with [the opinion of] the Amora Shmuel, who forbids — on the Sabbath — immersion in rivers.* However, the word בְּשַׁבָּת there does not refer to the Sabbath; rather, it refers to tractate *Shabbos* (65b), where the Talmud cites Shmuel's words.

34. The *taharah* (purification) of a person or object that has become *tamei* (impure) involves immersion in מִקְוֵה מַיִם, *a gathering of waters* (*Leviticus* 11:36). Specifically, that verse speaks of two such bodies — מַעְיָן, *a spring* [also called מַיִם חַיִּים, literally, *living waters* (see v. 17 above)], and בּוֹר, *a pit* [commonly referred to as a *mikveh*] — and the Sages infer from the word אַךְ, *only,* with which that verse begins, that certain conditions apply only to a spring, but not to a pit, and other conditions apply only to a pit, but not to a spring. Among the differences are these two: (i) Although a spring can effect purification with just enough water to cover the person or object being immersed, a *mikveh* must contain no less

יט/כב־כ/א

כב יִטְמָ֖א עַד־הָעָֽרֶב׃ וְכֹ֨ל אֲשֶׁר־יִגַּע־בּ֤וֹ הַטָּמֵא֙ יִטְמָ֔א
וְהַנֶּ֥פֶשׁ הַנֹּגַ֖עַת תִּטְמָ֥א עַד־הָעָֽרֶב׃

כ *ב׳ טעמים א וַיָּבֹ֣אוּ בְנֵֽי־יִשְׂרָאֵ֣ל *כָּל־הָ֠עֵדָה מִדְבַּר־צִן֙ בַּחֹ֣דֶשׁ
הָרִאשׁ֔וֹן וַיֵּ֥שֶׁב הָעָ֖ם בְּקָדֵ֑שׁ וַתָּ֤מָת שָׁם֙ מִרְיָ֔ם וַתִּקָּבֵ֖ר

בעל הטורים

״בְמֵי שָׁלֶג״ לוֹמַר שֶׁיְּכוֹלִין לַעֲשׂוֹת מִקְוֶה מִשֶּׁלֶג – כִּדְאִיתָא בְּפֶרֶק ז׳ דְּמַסֶּכֶת מִקְוָאוֹת, הֵעִידוּ אַנְשֵׁי מֵידְבָא עַל רַבִּי יִשְׁמָעֵאל שֶׁהָיָה אוֹמֵר לָהֶם צְאוּ וְהָבִיאוּ שֶׁלֶג וַעֲשׂוּ מִקְוֶה בַּתְּחִלָּה:

כ (א) בַּחֹדֶשׁ הָרִאשׁוֹן. סָמַךְ זֶה לְפָרָשַׁת פָּרָה, שֶׁבָּרִאשׁוֹן נִשְׂרְפָה הַפָּרָה. וְגַם כְּמוֹ שֶׁדָּרְשׁוּ חֲכָמֵינוּ זִכְרוֹנָם לִבְרָכָה, שֶׁמִּיתַת צַדִּיקִים מְכַפֶּרֶת כְּמוֹ פָּרָה. פָּרָה אֲדוּמָּה בְּגִימַטְרִיָּא מְכַפֵּר. ״וַתָּמָת שָׁם מִרְיָם וַתִּקָּבֵר שָׁם״ – ״שָׁם״ בְּגִימַטְרִיָּא מְכַפֵּר:

❑ **שָׁם.** בְּגִימַטְרִיָּא אָסוּר בַּהֲנָיָה:

BAAL HATURIM ELUCIDATED

[The fifth verse,] בְמֵי שָׁלֶג, *in the water of [melted] snow,* also alludes to the fact that a *mikveh* can be made from snow, as the Mishnah states in the seventh chapter of tractate *Mikvaos:* The men of Medeba[34a] testified that the *Tanna* Rabbi Yishmael told them, "Go and bring snow and make a new *mikveh.*"[35]

XX

1. בַּחֹדֶשׁ הָרִאשׁוֹן — IN THE FIRST MONTH. The Torah juxtaposed this[36] with the

than forty *se'ah* (see note 33) of rainwater; and (ii) although the waters of a spring effect purification even when they are זוֹחֲלִין, *in motion,* the waters of a *mikveh* must be בְּאַשְׁבֹּרֶן, *standing still* (*Toras Kohanim, Shemini, parashah* 9). [It is noteworthy that leakage is one of the most common problems encountered in building *mikvaos* today, for even a tiny leak can render the *mikveh's* waters זוֹחֲלִין and, as such, invalidate the *mikveh.*]

A river whose source is a spring is regarded as a spring; i.e., it effects purification even with less than forty *se'ah* and even when its water is flowing. But a river fed by rainwater is regarded as a *mikveh,* i.e., it requires forty *se'ah* and its water must be standing still. And the *Tanna* Rabbi Tzadok testified that the earlier *Tannaim* ruled regarding a river in which spring water and rain water flowed together: If the majority of the river's water is springwater, that river is regarded as a spring (*Mikvaos* 5:5). Nevertheless, the Talmud records that, in actual practice, the *Amora* Shmuel ruled that a *niddah* should not immerse in any river, for the volume of rain water may have increased over that of spring water, thereby invalidating the flowing river (*Shabbos* 65b).

Thus, in the Baal HaTurim's comment, we have another instance of a Scriptural allusion to a Rabbinic enactment.

34a. A town in the territory of Reuben on the eastern side of the Jordan (see 21:30 below; *Joshua* 13:16).

35. *Mikvaos* 7:1. That Mishnah does not cite Rabbi Yishmael as saying merely, וַעֲשׂוּ מִקְוֶה, *and make a mikveh.* Rather, it states, וַעֲשׂוּ מִקְוֶה בַּתְּחִלָּה, literally, *and make a mikveh from the beginning,* i.e., he permitted making the entire *mikveh* out of snow. This is because, earlier, the Mishnah had cited Rabbi Akiva's report of a debate he had with Rabbi Yishmael. In the course of that debate, Rabbi Yishmael had said, "Snow cannot complete a *mikveh.*" According to the testimony of the men of Medeba, despite Rabbi Yishmael's academic argumentation with Rabbi Akiva, in actual practice, he allowed snow to be used not only to complete a *mikveh,* he even allowed it to be used as the sole source of water for the *mikveh.*

36. That is, the passage regarding Miriam's death.

shall be impure until evening. [22] *Anything that the impure one shall touch shall be impure, and the person who touches [him] shall be impure until evening.*

20

[1] *The Children of Israel, the entire assembly, arrived at the Wilderness of Zin in the first month and the people settled in Kadesh. Miriam died there and she was buried*

BAAL HATURIM ELUCIDATED

passage concerning the red cow,[37] because it was in the first month [i.e., Nissan] that the cow was burned.[38]

Additionally: It is in accordance with that which our Sages of blessed memory have expounded: The death of the righteous provides atonement, just as does the red cow.[39] Indeed, the *gematria* of פָּרָה אֲדוּמָּה, *red cow* (341), is equivalent[40] to that of מְכַפֵּר, *it atones.*[41] [And similarly in our verse,] וַתָּמָת שָׁם מִרְיָם וְתִּקָּבֵר שָׁם, *Miriam died there and she was buried there,* the *gematria* of שָׁם (340) is equal to that of מְכַפֵּר.[42]

❑ שָׁם — THERE. The *gematria* of שָׁם is equivalent[43] to that of אָסוּר בַּהֲנָיָה[44], *[It is] forbidden regarding deriving benefit.*[45]

37. The laws of the red cow were transmitted to Israel during the second year in the wilderness, on the day that the *Mishkan* (Tabernacle) was erected (*Gittin* 60a-b). The death of Miriam occurred in their fortieth year in the wilderness. If so, why did the Torah juxtapose the two passages? (*Rashi; Mizrachi*).

38. The first red cow was burned on the second day of Nissan, the day after the nation was commanded regarding it (*Talmud Yerushalmi, Megillah* 3:5, cited by *Rashi* to *Megillah* 29a, s.v., ברביעית, and to *Gittin* 60b, s.v., ופרשת פרה אדומה). Miriam's death took place on the tenth of Nissan (see *Tur, Orach Chaim* 580).

39. *Moed Katan* 28a, cited by *Rashi*.

40. The principle of *im hakollel* allows 340, the *gematria* of מְכַפֵּר, to be considered equivalent to 341.

Peirush HaRokeach, the Baal HaTurim's apparent source, and *Rabbeinu Ephraim* (*MiKesivah Ashkenazis*) read, פָּרָה אֲדֻמָּה בְּגִימַטְרִיָּא לְכַפָּרָה, *The gematria of* פָּרָה אֲדֻמָּה (335) *is equal to that of* לְכַפָּרָה, *for atonement.*

41. See note 10 above.

42. *Peirush HaRokeach.*

43. The principle of *im hakollel* allows 339, the *gematria* of the Baal HaTurim's phrase, to be considered equivalent to 340.

44. The text follows *Peirush HaRokeach,* the Baal HaTurim's apparent source for this comment. The early printed editions read, אָסוּר בַּהֲנָאָה הו, *It is forbidden regarding deriving benefit,* which has a *gematria* of 341. The principle of *im hakollel* then allows 340 to be considered equivalent to 341. However, the spelling of הו, *it,* without the final א, is not found in Scripture. Nevertheless, according to *Tosafos* (*Succah* 45a, s.v., אני והו), the kabbalistic Divine Name אני״ והו״ means *I and Him,* thus, הו is an acceptable variant for הוא (*VeChur LaZahav*).

In *Paaneach Raza,* the phrase reads יֵאָסוּר בַּהֲנָאָה, *Let it be prohibited from deriving benefit,* which has a *gematria* of 340. Finally, *Shoham Yakar's* manuscript edition has a fourth reading: אִיסוּר בַּהֲנָאָה, *There is a prohibition against deriving benefit,* likewise with a *gematria* of 340.

45. The Talmud uses the word שָׁם (in our verse and in *Deuteronomy* 21:4) to draw a *gezeirah shavah* [a halachic inference, usually based upon identical wording used in two otherwise unrelated verses; one of the thirteen hermeneutic principles by which Scripture is expounded] between Miriam's death and the decapitated calf (see *Deuteronomy* 21:1-9): Just as it is forbidden to derive benefits from that calf's cadaver, so is it forbidden to derive benefit from a human corpse (*Avodah Zarah* 29b).

כ/ב-ה

ב שָׁם: וְלֹא־הָיָה מַיִם לָעֵדָה וַיִּקָּהֲלוּ עַל־מֹשֶׁה וְעַל־
ג אַהֲרֹן: וַיָּרֶב הָעָם עִם־מֹשֶׁה וַיֹּאמְרוּ לֵאמֹר וְלוּ גָוַעְנוּ
ד בִּגְוַע אַחֵינוּ לִפְנֵי יהוה: וְלָמָה הֲבֵאתֶם אֶת־קְהַל
יהוה אֶל־הַמִּדְבָּר הַזֶּה לָמוּת שָׁם אֲנַחְנוּ וּבְעִירֵנוּ:
ה וְלָמָה הֶעֱלִיתֻנוּ מִמִּצְרַיִם לְהָבִיא אֹתָנוּ אֶל־הַמָּקוֹם
הָרָע הַזֶּה לֹא | מְקוֹם זֶרַע וּתְאֵנָה וְגֶפֶן וְרִמּוֹן

בעל הטורים

(ג) וַיָּרֶב. ב׳ בַּמָּסוֹרֶת – ״וַיָּרֶב הָעָם״; וְאִידָךְ ״וַיָּרֶב בַּנָּחַל״. לוֹמַר שֶׁעָשׂוּ מְרִיבָה עַל עִסְקֵי נַחַל שֶׁפָּסַק מֵהֶם, דְּהַיְנוּ הַבְּאֵר שֶׁהָיָה מוֹשֵׁךְ כְּנַחַל:

(ה) הֶעֱלִיתֻנוּ. חָסֵר וָי״ו – שֶׁעִקַּר הַתַּרְעֹמֶת הָיָה עַל מֹשֶׁה:

❑ **וּתְאֵנָה וְגֶפֶן וְרִמּוֹן.** וּלְהַלָּן הִקְדִּים גֶּפֶן, דִּכְתִיב ״אֶרֶץ חִטָּה וּשְׂעֹרָה וְגֶפֶן וּתְאֵנָה וְרִמּוֹן״. אֶלָּא בְּכָל מָקוֹם הִקְדִּים גֶּפֶן, כִּדְכְתִיב ״אִישׁ תַּחַת גַּפְנוֹ וְתַחַת תְּאֵנָתוֹ״, וְכָאן הִקְדִּים תְּאֵנָה מִשּׁוּם דְּסָלִיק מִפָּרָה. רֶמֶז לְמָה שֶׁאָמְרוּ, בֵּרְרוּ מִשָּׁם עֲצֵי תְאֵנָה:

BAAL HATURIM ELUCIDATED

2. {The Baal HaTurim's comment to וַיִּקָּהֲלוּ עַל מֹשֶׁה וְעַל אַהֲרֹן appears at 33:25 below.}

3. וַיָּרֶב — [THE PEOPLE] QUARRELED. The masoretic note, ב׳, means that this word appears twice[46] in the *Tanach:* (i) here, וַיָּרֶב הָעָם, *The people quarreled;* and (ii) וַיָּרֶב בַּנָּחַל, *he fought [them] in the river valley* (*I Samuel* 15:5).[47] This [similarity of expression] indicates that the people quarreled with Moses regarding the river, i.e., the well that had flowed from a rock like a river,[47a] but had now dried up.[48]

5. הֶעֱלִיתֻנוּ — [AND WHY] HAVE YOU BROUGHT US UP? The term הֶעֱלִיתֻנוּ is spelled defectively, without a ו [after the ת].[49] This implies that their protest was primarily directed against Moses.[50]

---

46. The Baal HaTurim's intention here is unclear, for the word וַיָּרֶב actually appears four times in the *Tanach.* The other two appearances are in *Genesis* 31:36, regarding Jacob's quarrel with Laban; and *Exodus* 17:2, which, like our verse, speaks of the people quarreling because of the lack of water.

47. The translation of that verse follows *Rashi.* According to *Radak,* וַיָּרֶב of that verse is a contraction of וַיֶּאֱרֹב, *he laid an ambush.*

47a. *Tosefta Succah* 3:3 — The waters of the well would flow through the Israelite camp . . . It would form into streams and rivers that would flow into the Mediterranean Sea . . .

48. *Taanis* 9a — The well from a rock was given to Israel in the merit of Miriam. When she died, it was taken from them.

49. The word העליתנו appears four times in the Torah. In *Exodus* 17:3, it is addressed to Moses and is vowelized as a singular verb, לָמָּה זֶּה הֶעֱלִיתָנוּ, *Why is this that you* (singular) *have brought us up;* similarly, in 16:13 above, it is directed at Moses and is vowelized הֶעֱלִיתָנוּ. But in our verse the assembly had *gathered against Moses and against Aaron* (v. 2 above); accordingly the word is vowelized like the plural verb, וְלָמָּה הֶעֱלִיתוּנוּ, *And why have you* (plural) *brought us up,* except that the third syllable is spelled תֻ instead of תוּ. Similarly, in 21:5 below, where the people *spoke against God and against Moses,* the spelling הֶעֱלִיתֻנוּ is used. The Baal HaTurim explains that the ו is omitted in our verse so that the word may be understood as if it were vowelized הֶעֱלִיתָנוּ, in the singular.

50. *Peirush HaRokeach.* Here, the Baal HaTurim finds Scriptural proof in the realm of *remez*

there. [2] *There was no water for the assembly, and they*
gathered against Moses and Aaron. [3] *The people quarreled*
with Moses and spoke up, saying, "If only we had perished
as our brethren perished before HASHEM! [4] *Why have you*
brought the congregation of HASHEM to this wilderness to
die there, we and our animals? [5] *And why havce you*
brought us up from Egypt to bring us to this evil place? It
is not a place of seed and fig and grape and pomegranate;

BAAL HATURIM ELUCIDATED

❑ **וּתְאֵנָה וְגֶפֶן וְרִמּוֹן** — **AND FIG AND GRAPE AND POMEGRANATE.** [Here the Torah mentioned fig before grape.] Further on, it mentioned grape first, as it is written, אֶרֶץ חִטָּה וּשְׂעֹרָה וְגֶפֶן וּתְאֵנָה וְרִמּוֹן, *a land of wheat and barley and grape and fig and pomegranate* (*Deuteronomy* 8:8).[51] Indeed, in most instances[52] it mentioned grape first, as it is written, אִישׁ תַּחַת גַּפְנוֹ וְתַחַת תְּאֵנָתוֹ, *each man under his grapevine and under his fig tree* (*I Kings* 5:5; *Micah* 4:4). But here it mentioned fig first because the Torah has just concluded the passage of the red cow. It is therefore an allusion to the Sages' teaching:[53] They would select fig wood from there.[54]

(allusion) that the thrust of their protest was against Moses. In *Peirush HaTur HaAroch,* he derives this concept from the fact that verse 2 states, *they gathered against Moses and Aaron,* while verse 3 states, *the people quarreled with Moses,* but does not mention Aaron.

51. When Moses later praised the land of Canaan, he mentioned seven species for which that land was noted: wheat, barley, grapes, figs, pomegranates, olives and dates (see *Deuteronomy* 8:8). Here, the people complained of the lack of figs, grapes and pomegranates in the wilderness. Why did they mention those species in particular? At this point, the people were not fully aware of the full variety of fruits growing in Canaan. All they knew about the land's produce was what they had seen of the fruit that the spies brought back to them in the wilderness — *one cluster of grapes . . . pomegranates and figs* (13:23 above). Therefore, they complained only that they had not been taken to the land where those three species grew (*VeChur LaZahav;* see also *Shoham Yakar*).

52. Although the Baal HaTurim writes, אֶלָּא בְּכָל מָקוֹם, *Indeed, in "all" instances,* the translation reads, *in "most" instances,* for in five of the twenty-three passages in which Scripture juxtaposes grapes with figs, figs are mentioned first (here; *Judges* 9:10-13; *Joel* 2:22; *Habakkuk* 3:17; and *Song of Songs* 2:13). In the remaining eighteen verses, grapes are mentioned first (*Numbers* 13:23; *Deuteronomy* 8:8; *I Kings* 5:5; *II Kings* 18:31; *Isaiah* 34:4 and 36:16; *Jeremiah* 5:17 and 8:13; *Hosea* 2:14 and 9:10; *Joel* 1:7 and 12; *Amos* 4:9; *Micah* 4:4; *Haggai* 2:19; *Zechariah* 3:10; *Psalms* 105:33; and *Nehemiah* 13:15).

53. *Tamid* 2:5. This passage, which is part of the Mishnah's description of how the wood was arranged on the Altar pyres, has no apparent connection to the red cow. Indeed, it is not adduced in a similar comment in *Peirush HaRokeach* or *Moshav Zekeinim* (citing *Ramban*), nor does it appear in the Baal HaTurim's comment in *Peirush HaTur HaAroch* (see note 54 below). Accordingly, it is suggested that the last part of this comment has been emended by a copyist who was aware of this Mishnah, but was confused regarding its context (*VeChur LaZahav*).

54. Although the Baal HaTurim was written in the realm of *remez* (allusion) and *Peirush HaTur HaAroch* in the realm of *peshat* (simple meaning of the verse), the same comment occasionally appears in both. In *Peirush HaTur HaAroch,* this comment reads: **וּתְאֵנָה וְגֶפֶן וְרִמּוֹן.** וּלְהַלָּן מַקְדִּים גֶּפֶן כְּדִכְתִיב "אִישׁ תַּחַת גַּפְנוֹ וְתַחַת תְּאֵנָתוֹ." וְכָאן הִקְדִּים תְּאֵנִים. רֶמֶז לְמַה שֶׁאָמְרוּ בְּפָרָה אֲדֻמָּה שֶׁשּׂוֹרְפִין אוֹתָהּ בַּעֲצֵי תְאֵנָה. לְכָךְ הִקְדִּים תְּאֵנָה, מִשּׁוּם דְּסָלִיק מִפָּרָשַׁת פָּרָה — **AND FIG AND GRAPE AND POMEGRANATE.** Further on the verse mentions grape first, as it is written, *each man under his grapevine and under his fig tree* (*I Kings* 5:5; *Micah* 4:4). But here it mentioned fig first. This is an allusion to that which the Sages said regarding the red cow —

כ/ו־י

ו וּמַיִם אַיִן לִשְׁתּוֹת: וַיָּבֹא מֹשֶׁה וְאַהֲרֹן מִפְּנֵי הַקָּהָל
אֶל־פֶּתַח אֹהֶל מוֹעֵד וַיִּפְּלוּ עַל־פְּנֵיהֶם וַיֵּרָא
כְבוֹד־יְהוָה אֲלֵיהֶם:
שלישי [שני] ז־ח וַיְדַבֵּר יְהוָה אֶל־מֹשֶׁה לֵּאמֹר: קַח אֶת־הַמַּטֶּה
וְהַקְהֵל אֶת־הָעֵדָה אַתָּה וְאַהֲרֹן אָחִיךָ וְדִבַּרְתֶּם
אֶל־הַסֶּלַע לְעֵינֵיהֶם וְנָתַן מֵימָיו וְהוֹצֵאתָ לָהֶם מַיִם
ט מִן־הַסֶּלַע וְהִשְׁקִיתָ אֶת־הָעֵדָה וְאֶת־בְּעִירָם: וַיִּקַּח
י מֹשֶׁה אֶת־הַמַּטֶּה מִלִּפְנֵי יְהוָה כַּאֲשֶׁר צִוָּהוּ: וַיַּקְהִלוּ
מֹשֶׁה וְאַהֲרֹן אֶת־הַקָּהָל אֶל־פְּנֵי הַסָּלַע וַיֹּאמֶר לָהֶם
שִׁמְעוּ־נָא הַמֹּרִים הֲמִן־הַסֶּלַע הַזֶּה נוֹצִיא לָכֶם מָיִם:

בעל הטורים

(ח) **וְהַקְהֵל אֶת הָעֵדָה.** אֵלּוּ הַטְּהוֹרִים, הַגְּדוֹלִים שֶׁבָּעֵדָה. וְהוּא לֹא עָשָׂה כֵן, אֶלָּא "וַיַּקְהִלוּ מֹשֶׁה וְאַהֲרֹן אֶת הַקָּהָל", גְּדוֹלִים וּקְטַנִּים:

(י) **פְּנֵי הַסָּלַע.** פֵּ"א כְּפוּלָה. מְלַמֵּד שֶׁהָיוּ כָּל יִשְׂרָאֵל אֶל פְּנֵי הַסֶּלַע פָּנִים אֶל פָּנִים. וְהָיָה הַמּוּעָט מַחֲזִיק אֶת הַמְרֻבֶּה:

❑ **הֲמִן.** ג׳ בַּמָּסוֹרֶת — "הֲמִן הַסֶּלַע"; "הֲמִן הָעֵץ", כְּמוֹ שֶׁלְּשָׁם הֵפֵר הַצִּוּוּי, גַּם כָּאן

BAAL HATURIM ELUCIDATED

8. וְהַקְהֵל אֶת הָעֵדָה — AND GATHER THE ASSEMBLY. The term אֶת הָעֵדָה refers to those who are pure, the prominent members of the assembly.[55] But Moses did not do that, rather, וַיַּקְהִלוּ . . . אֶת הַקָּהָל, *Moses and Aaron gathered the congregation* (v. 10),[56] both the adults and the children.[56a]

10. פְּנֵי הַסָּלַע — BEFORE (literally, at the face of) THE ROCK. The letter פ [of פְּנֵי] is doubled.[57,58] This teaches that all of Israel were present upon the face of the

---

that it is burned on a pyre of fig wood. Therefore, the verse mentioned fig first because the passage of the red cow has just finished.

That version of the comment is based on a Mishnah that describes the pyre on which the red cow was burned: They would set up wood there — any of various species of cedar or smooth fig wood — and arrange it in the form of a tower (*Parah* 3:8). And that may have been the Mishnah adduced by the Baal HaTurim (see note 53 above; *VeChur LaZahav*).

55. Earlier, the Torah speaks of כָּל הָעֵדָה, *the entire assembly* (v. 1 above); here, the word כָּל is omitted. This teaches that God did not command Moses to gather the entire nation at this time (*VeChur LaZahav*).

56. Had the assemblage taken place precisely as God had commanded, that verse would use the same phrase, אֶת הָעֵדָה, as in the command (v. 8). The introduction of new terminology, אֶת הַקָּהָל, indicates that the command was not followed to the letter (*VeChur LaZahav*).

56a. *Peirush HaRokeach* (to v. 10) — The term אֶת הַקָּהָל includes the young, the old and the mixed multitude. But God had commanded Moses only with regard to the עֵדָה, which refers to the adults who have learned to maintain spiritual purity. Yet Moses gathered the entire קָהָל, including children and youth who are not wont to safeguard their spiritual purity.

57. Among the unusual forms used for specific letters in the Torah is the פ׳ כְּפוּלָה, *doubled* פ, which is also known as פ׳ לְפוּפָה (or, פ׳ מְלֻפָּף), *rolled* פ. Unlike the usual פ which is drawn as a י

and there is no water to drink!"

[6] *Moses and Aaron went from the presence of the congregation to the entrance of the Tent of Meeting and fell on their faces. The glory of* HASHEM *appeared to them.*

[7] HASHEM *spoke to Moses, saying,* [8] *"Take the staff and gather the assembly, you and Aaron your brother, and speak to the rock before their eyes that it shall give its waters. You shall bring forth for them water from the rock and give drink to the assembly and to their animals."*

[9] *Moses took the staff from before* HASHEM, *as He had commanded him.* [10] *Moses and Aaron gathered the congregation before the rock and he said to them, "Listen now, O rebels, shall we bring forth water for you from this rock?"*

BAAL HATURIM ELUCIDATED

rock[59] [standing together] face to face.[59a] Thus, this is one of the places where a small place held a great amount.[60]

❑ הֲמִן — FROM? The masoretic note, ג׳, means that this word appears three times in the *Tanach:* (i) here, הֲמִן הַסֶּלַע, *from this rock?;* (ii) . . . הֲמִן הָעֵץ, *from the tree?* (*Genesis* 3:11)[61] [regarding the sin of the Tree of Knowledge] — and just as the Divine command was breached there [when Eve then Adam ate of the forbidden fruit], so, too,

hanging from the roof of a כ, this unusual פ has a miniature פ in place of a י. Thus, the פ of פְּנֵי in our verse is described in *Sefer Tagin* as one of "191 in the Torah whose mouths are on the inside." See illustration.

Usual פ (a). Doubled פ according to *Kiryas Sefer* (b); *Machzor Vitry* (c); *Badei HaAron* (d); and the Gaster ms. (e).

The Baal HaTurim also comments on the פ׳ כְּפוּלָה at *Exodus* 31:17; *Numbers* 23:3; and *Deuteronomy* 1:7, 5:4, 6:25, 7:12, 7:20, 9:7, 13:6, 15:8, 16:16, 17:6 and 17:8.

58. The wording פֵּ״א כְּפוּלָה follows one of the manuscripts used by *Shoham Yakar.* It is based on the passage in *Sefer Tagin* cited in note 57 above. The early (and most later) printed editions read, פְּנֵי בְּגִימַטְרִיָּא כְּפוּלָה, *the gematria of* פְּנֵי (140) *is equivalent* [i.e., by the rule of *im hakollel*] *to that of* כְּפוּלָה, *doubled* (see note 59a). Some later printed editions read, פְּנֵי בְּגִימַטְרִיָּא כְּלַפֵּי, *gematria of* פְּנֵי (140) is equal to that of כְּלַפֵּי, *facing* (see note 59).

59. *Tanchuma* 9 — The verse, *Moses and Aaron gathered the congregation at the face of the rock,* teaches that each and every one saw himself standing upon the face of the rock. Similarly, it is stated, *Gather the entire assembly to the entrance of the Tent of Meeting* (*Leviticus* 8:3; see also note 60).

59a. The word פָּנִים means *face;* its construct form פְּנֵי means *the face of.* The unusual doubled form of the letter פ [or, according to the other version (see note 58), the *gematria* of the word פְּנֵי] in our verse indicates that each Israelite's face appeared to be doubled and redoubled, for each one stood face to face with every other one, as if he were facing in all directions at the same time.

60. *Vayikra Rabbah* 10:9, cited by *Rashi.* The Midrash there and in *Tanchuma* 9 lists other instances of this phenomenon, e.g., *Exodus* 9:8, *Joshua* 3:9.

Under natural circumstances, the nation, which included six hundred thousand adult men, could not have gathered in front of one rock. Thus, the verse can only be describing a miraculous occurrence.

61. See the Baal HaTurim's comment there.

יא וַיָּרֶם מֹשֶׁה אֶת־יָדוֹ וַיַּךְ אֶת־הַסֶּלַע בְּמַטֵּהוּ פַּעֲמָיִם
יב וַיֵּצְאוּ מַיִם רַבִּים וַתֵּשְׁתְּ הָעֵדָה וּבְעִירָם: וַיֹּאמֶר
יהוה אֶל־מֹשֶׁה וְאֶל־אַהֲרֹן יַעַן לֹא־הֶאֱמַנְתֶּם
בִּי לְהַקְדִּישֵׁנִי לְעֵינֵי בְּנֵי יִשְׂרָאֵל לָכֵן לֹא
תָבִיאוּ אֶת־הַקָּהָל הַזֶּה אֶל־הָאָרֶץ אֲשֶׁר־נָתַתִּי
יג לָהֶם: הֵמָּה מֵי מְרִיבָה אֲשֶׁר־רָבוּ בְנֵי־יִשְׂרָאֵל
רביעי יד אֶת־יהוה וַיִּקָּדֵשׁ בָּם: וַיִּשְׁלַח מֹשֶׁה
מַלְאָכִים מִקָּדֵשׁ אֶל־מֶלֶךְ אֱדוֹם כֹּה אָמַר
אָחִיךָ יִשְׂרָאֵל אַתָּה יָדַעְתָּ אֵת כָּל־הַתְּלָאָה
טו אֲשֶׁר מְצָאָתְנוּ: וַיֵּרְדוּ אֲבֹתֵינוּ מִצְרַיְמָה וַנֵּשֶׁב
בְּמִצְרַיִם יָמִים רַבִּים וַיָּרֵעוּ לָנוּ מִצְרַיִם וְלַאֲבֹתֵינוּ:
טז וַנִּצְעַק אֶל־יהוה וַיִּשְׁמַע קֹלֵנוּ וַיִּשְׁלַח מַלְאָךְ

בעל הטורים

נִמְּי הֵפֵר הַצִּוּוּי; וְאִידָךְ ״הֲמִן הַגֹּרֶן אוֹ מִן הַיָּקֶב״, כְּמוֹ שֶׁהָיָה שָׁם רָעָב, גַּם כָּאן ״אֶרֶץ צִיָּה . . . בְּלִי מָיִם״:

וְסֶמֶךְ לְמַאן דְּאָמַר עֵץ שֶׁאָכַל מִמֶּנּוּ אָדָם הָרִאשׁוֹן חִטָּה הָיָה, וְזֶהוּ ״הֲמִן הָעֵץ״ ״הֲמִן הַגֹּרֶן״. וּלְמַאן דְּאָמַר אֶשְׁכּוֹל הָיָה, דִּכְתִיב ״אוֹ מִן הַיָּקֶב״:

(יא) וַיַּךְ אֶת הַסֶּלַע. הוּא הִכָּה לְסֶלַע אֶחָד, וְנִבְקְעוּ כָּל הַצּוּרִים שֶׁבַּמִּדְבָּר, שֶׁנֶּאֱמַר ״יְבַקַּע צֻרִים בַּמִּדְבָּר״:

(יב) לָכֵן. בְּגִימַטְרִיָּא מִדָּה בְּמִדָּה:

BAAL HATURIM ELUCIDATED

here, the Divine command was breached [when Moses smote the rock]; and (iii) הֲמִן הַגֹּרֶן אוֹ מִן הַיָּקֶב, *from the threshing floor or from the winepress?* (*II Kings* 6:27) — just as there was a famine at that time,[62] so, too, here, they were in *a parched land . . . without water.*[63]

The masoretic note also lends support to the opinion that the tree from which Adam ate was in actuality wheat:[64] thus, *from the tree, from the threshing floor.* And it lends support to the opinion that the tree was a grapevine, as it is written, *or from the winepress.*[64]

11. **וַיַּךְ אֶת הַסֶּלַע** — AND [HE] STRUCK THE ROCK. He struck one rock and all the rocks

62. The passage in which that verse appears begins: *It happened after that . . . There was a great famine in Samaria* (*II Kings* 6:24-25).

63. *Peirush HaRokeach.*

The Baal HaTurim's wording is borrowed from King David's description of the Wilderness of Judah in *Psalms* 63:2.

64. *Berachos* 40a; *Sanhedrin* 71b; *Bereishis Rabbah* 15:7. According to the first opinion cited here, in certain respects wheat is considered a tree (see *Rashi* to *Rosh Hashanah* 16a, s.v., שתי הלחם).

[11] *Then Moses raised his arm and struck the rock with his staff twice; abundant water came forth and the assembly and their animals drank.*

[12] *HASHEM said to Moses and to Aaron, "Because you did not believe in Me to sanctify Me in the eyes of the Children of Israel, therefore you will not bring this congregation to the land that I have given them."* [13] *They are the waters of strife, where the Children of Israel contended with HASHEM, and He was sanctified through them.*

[14] *Moses sent emissaries from Kadesh to the king of Edom: "So said your brother Israel: You know all the hardship that has befallen us.* [15] *Our forefathers descended to Egypt and we dwelled in Egypt many years, and the Egyptians did evil to us and to our forefathers.* [16] *We cried out to HASHEM and He heard our voice; He sent an angel*

BAAL HATURIM ELUCIDATED

in the wilderness split, as the verse states, יְבַקַּע צֻרִים בַּמִּדְבָּר, *He split rocks in the wilderness* (*Psalms* 78:15).[65]

12. {The Baal HaTurim's comments to יַעַן לֹא הֶאֱמַנְתֶּם בִּי appear at *Exodus* 8:1 and *Deuteronomy* 31:14.}

❏ לָכֵן — **THEREFORE.** The *gematria* of this word (100) is equal to that of מִדָּה בְּמִדָּה, *measure for measure.*[66]

❏ {The Baal HaTurim's comment to לָכֵן לֹא תָבִיאוּ appears at *Deuteronomy* 3:26.}

65. *Bamidbar Rabbah* 19:9 — Each and every rock and stone in that area gave forth water, as it is stated: *He split rocks in the wilderness.*

Note that our verse uses the singular form הַסֶּלַע, *rock,* while the verse from *Psalms* uses צֻרִים, the plural form of צוּר, a synonym for סֶלַע. Nevertheless, they refer to the same incident as alluded to by the *milui* of הַסֶּלַע, i.e., ה״י סמ״ך למ״ד עי״ן, which has a *gematria* of 339, equivalent (by the principle of *im hakollel*) to 340, the *gematria* of צֻרִים (*VeChur LaZahav*).

66. The Baal HaTurim uses this same *gematria* in his comments to *Genesis* 30:15 and *Numbers* 25:12. It explains that the term לָכֵן indicates a direct causal relationship between an action and its consequence. The Baal HaTurim, however, does not spell out that relationship.

Perhaps God's plan called for Moses to sanctify God's Holy Name in two ways: First, Moses was to sanctify God's Name by causing water to flow from a rock at God's verbal command delivered through the mouth of Moses; and that act of sanctification would, in turn, provide Moses with the merit that would permit him to sanctify God's Name again by bringing the Children of Israel into the Holy Land. However, Moses nullified the first opportunity by striking the rock instead of speaking to it, and two consequences followed, measure for measure: Moses lost the opportunity to sanctify God's Name a second time by leading the nation into the Land of Israel; and God Himself would sanctify His own Name in this particular place by denying Moses the right to enter the Holy Land (see *Rashi* to v. 13 and to *Leviticus* 10:3). Thus, both Moses' fate and God's execution of that fate are examples of the Divine attribute of מִדָּה בְּמִדָּה, *measure for measure* (*VeChur LaZahav,* based on *Yad Aharon*).

וַיֹּצִאֵנוּ מִמִּצְרָיִם וְהִנֵּה אֲנַחְנוּ בְקָדֵשׁ עִיר קְצֵה
יז גְבוּלֶךָ: נַעְבְּרָה־נָּא בְאַרְצֶךָ לֹא נַעֲבֹר בְּשָׂדֶה
וּבְכֶרֶם וְלֹא נִשְׁתֶּה מֵי בְאֵר דֶּרֶךְ הַמֶּלֶךְ נֵלֵךְ לֹא
יח נִטֶּה יָמִין וּשְׂמֹאול עַד אֲשֶׁר־נַעֲבֹר גְּבֻלֶךָ: וַיֹּאמֶר
אֵלָיו אֱדוֹם לֹא תַעֲבֹר בִּי פֶּן־בַּחֶרֶב אֵצֵא לִקְרָאתֶךָ:

בעל הטורים

(טז) **וַיֹּצִאֵנוּ.** חָסֵר יו״ד – עַל יְדֵי עֶשֶׂר מַכּוֹת הוֹצִיאָנוּ מִשָּׁם:

(יז) **נַעְבְּרָה נָּא בְאַרְצֶךָ.** וּבְסִיחוֹן אָמַר, ״אֶעְבְּרָה״. אֶלָּא אָמַר, זְכֹר מַה שֶּׁאָמַר עֵשָׂו ״נִסְעָה וְנֵלֵכָה״, וּלְכָךְ אָמַר ״אָחִיךָ יִשְׂרָאֵל״:

(יח) **פֶּן בַּחֶרֶב אֵצֵא לִקְרָאתֶךָ.** וְהַיְנוּ דִּכְתִיב ״אֲנִי שָׁלוֹם וְכִי אֲדַבֵּר הֵמָּה לַמִּלְחָמָה״:

BAAL HATURIM ELUCIDATED

16. וַיֹּצִאֵנוּ — AND HE TOOK US OUT. This word is spelled defectively,[67] without a י (= 10). [This alludes to the fact that] He took us from there by means of ten plagues.[68]

17. נַעְבְּרָה נָּא בְאַרְצֶךָ — LET US PLEASE PASS THROUGH YOUR LAND. [Here, speaking to

67. A masoretic note reads: ג׳ וּמִשְׁתַּנִּין בִּכְתָבְהוֹן, *Three, and they differ in their spelling:* In *Numbers* 20:16, it is spelled doubly defective, וַיֹּצִאֵנוּ, with neither a ו between the י and the צ nor a י between the צ and the א; in *Deuteronomy* 6:21, it is spelled defective, yet full, וַיֹּצִיאֵנוּ, without a ו between the י and the צ, but with a י between the צ and the א; and in *Deuteronomy* 26:8, it is spelled full, yet defective, וַיּוֹצִאֵנוּ, with a ו between the י and the צ, but without a י between the צ and the א (*Minchas Shai* citing *Ramah*).

68. At face value, this comment states that the omitted י (= 10) alludes to the ten plagues with which God smote Egypt; the word מִשָּׁם, *from there,* means from Egypt. *Rimzei Rabbeinu Yoel* seems to interpret the allusion in this manner, for there the comment reads: He did not take us out until after ten plagues.

In *Peirush HaRokeach* and *Rabbeinu Ephraim* (*MiKesivah Ashkenazis*), however, the comment reads: It is spelled defectively, without a י, for ten plagues were visited [upon the Egyptians] at the sea. According to that interpretation, the Baal HaTurim's term מִשָּׁם, *from there,* means from the sea [as we find the Sea of Reeds referred to by the term שָׁם, *there;* e.g., in the verse, הָפַךְ יָם לְיַבָּשָׁה, *He changed the sea into dry land,* שָׁם נִשְׂמְחָה בּוֹ, *there we rejoiced in Him* (*Psalms* 66:6; see also *Amos* 9:3, *Psalms* 104:25 and *Ecclesiastes* 1:7; *VeChur LaZahav*)], and refers to the Mishnaic teaching: The Holy One, Blessed is He, brought ten plagues upon the Egyptians in Egypt and ten at the sea (*Avos* 5:4). But such an interpretation is difficult, for the verse reads מִמִּצְרָיִם, *from Egypt,* and not מִן הַיָּם, *from the sea!*

To understand why *Peirush HaRokeach* understands this verse to allude to the plagues at the sea, rather than to those in Egypt, as the simple meaning of the verse indicates, we must compare our verse with *Deuteronomy* 26:8. There we are told, וַיּוֹצִאֵנוּ ה׳ מִמִּצְרַיִם, *HASHEM took us out of Egypt,* which the Sages explain to mean, לֹא עַל יְדֵי מַלְאָךְ, *not by the hands of an angel* (*Sifrei,* cited in the *Haggadah*). Yet our verse reads, וַיִּשְׁלַח מַלְאָךְ וַיֹּצִאֵנוּ מִמִּצְרָיִם, *He sent an angel and he took us out of Egypt,* which seems to contradict the Sages. To resolve this contradiction, *Peirush HaRokeach* explains our verse as referring to the plagues at the sea; and that is why the Baal HaTurim substitutes מִשָּׁם, *from there,* for מִמִּצְרַיִם, *from Egypt.* If this analysis is correct, the term מִמִּצְרַיִם of our verse does not refer to the land of Egypt, rather it refers to the Egyptians, for the Torah refers to both the land and its people as מִצְרַיִם [e.g., see v. 15 where it is used with both meanings; see also *Rashi* to *Exodus* 14:25, s.v., נלחם להם במצרים] (*VeChur LaZahav*).

Alternatively: מִמִּצְרָיִם may be interpreted as if it were two words, מִמֵּצַר יָם, *from the border of the sea* (*VeChur LaZahav*).

and he took us away from Egypt. Now, behold! We are in Kadesh, a city at the edge of your border. [17] *Let us please pass through your land; we shall not pass through field or vineyard, and we shall not drink well water; on the king's road shall we travel — we shall not veer right or left — until we pass through your border."*

[18] *Edom said to him, "You shall not pass through me — lest I come out against you with the sword!"*

BAAL HATURIM ELUCIDATED

the king of Edom/Esau, Moses spoke in the plural, "*Let us . . .*,"][68a] but to the Amorite king Sihon, he said [in the singular],[68a] "אֶעְבְּרָה, *Let me pass through* (21:22 below)." As if to say, remember the offer made by your ancestor, Esau, נִסְעָה וְנֵלֵכָה, *Let us travel*[69] *and let us go*[70] (*Genesis* 33:12). For this same reason, Moses used the expression *your brother*[71] *Israel*[72] (v. 14 above).

❑ {The Baal HaTurim's other comment to נָא appears at 21:22 below.}

18. פֶּן בַּחֶרֶב אֵצֵא לִקְרָאתֶךָ — LEST I COME OUT AGAINST YOU WITH THE SWORD. This reflects the verse, אֲנִי שָׁלוֹם וְכִי אֲדַבֵּר הֵמָּה לַמִּלְחָמָה, *I am peace; but when I speak, they threaten war* (*Psalms* 120:7).[73]

68a. Note 70 below explains the Baal HaTurim's comment in two ways. The interpolated bracketed passages follow *Shoham Yakar.* According to *Ittur Bikkurim:* The interpolation should read: [. . . Moses used נַעְבְּרָה and the added word נָא] but to the Amorite king Sihon, he said [only one word], אֶעְבְּרָה.

69. The translation of נִסְעָה as *let us travel* is based on *Ibn Ezra's* second explanation of the word. If so, the נ of נִסְעָה is not the נ of the verb root נסע, for that נ falls away in conjugation. Rather, like the נ of נֵלֵכָה (root — הלך), it is a prefix that indicates first person plural in the future tense. According to *Rashi,* however, the נ of נִסְעָה is not a prefix, rather it is the נ of the root נסע, and the word is in the imperative — *Travel on.*

70. Whereas Esau spoke to Jacob in the plural, Jacob's descendant Moses spoke to Esau's descendant, the king of Edom, in the plural (*Shoham Yakar*).

Alternatively: Whereas Esau said נִסְעָה וְנֵלֵכָה, two words that begin with נ, Moses said נַעְבְּרָה נָא, two words that begin with נ (*Ittur Bikkurim*).

71. Moses said, אָחִיךָ יִשְׂרָאֵל, *your brother Israel,* to recall that at the time Esau met Jacob [who had recently been given the name Israel (*Genesis* 32:28)] and told him, נִסְעָה וְנֵלֵכָה, *Let us travel and let us go,* Esau addressed Jacob/Israel as אָחִי, *my brother* (*Genesis* 33:9; *VeChur LaZahav*).

72. *Peirush HaRokeach.*

73. In the context of *Psalms,* King David speaks of the belligerence of Meshech (Greece) and Kedar (Arabia) who interpret his overtures of peace as signs of weakness. The Midrash, however, interprets the verse and the one that precedes it as referring to Edom/Esau: *Long has my soul dwelt with those who hate peace. I am peace; but when I speak, they threaten war* (*Psalms* 120:6-7). Is there a person who hates peace? Yes! Esau hates peace. And so is it written — *I will provide peace in the land . . .* And when will that be? When *I will cause the wildness of beasts to cease from the land* (*Leviticus* 26:6). For the term "wildness of beasts" refers to none but Esau (*Midrash Shocher Tov*).

Another Midrash interprets the verse, *I am peace . . .,* as God's explanation of why Edom refused Israel's request and threatened to go to war to prevent Israel from passing through its land. "It is not merely their will to keep you out. Rather, it is My will that you not pass through their land. Thus, I told Moses to command you regarding Edom, *'You shall not provoke them, for I shall not give you of their land even the right to set foot'* (*Deuteronomy* 2:5). Thus [the verse in *Psalms* means], *I,* [HASHEM,] *am peace,* i.e., I do not want you to encroach on their territory even one step, *and because I speak thus, they threaten war,* for they know that you will not violate My will" (*Tanchuma* 13; *Bamidbar Rabbah* 19:15, see *Maharzu*).

כ/יט־כו

יט וַיֹּאמְרוּ אֵלָיו בְּנֵי־יִשְׂרָאֵל בַּמְסִלָּה נַעֲלֶה וְאִם־
מֵימֶיךָ נִשְׁתֶּה אֲנִי וּמִקְנַי וְנָתַתִּי מִכְרָם רַק אֵין־דָּבָר
כ בְּרַגְלַי אֶעֱבֹרָה: וַיֹּאמֶר לֹא תַעֲבֹר וַיֵּצֵא אֱדוֹם
כא לִקְרָאתוֹ בְּעַם כָּבֵד וּבְיָד חֲזָקָה: וַיְמָאֵן | אֱדוֹם נְתֹן
אֶת־יִשְׂרָאֵל עֲבֹר בִּגְבֻלוֹ וַיֵּט יִשְׂרָאֵל מֵעָלָיו:
חמישי [שלישי] כב וַיִּסְעוּ מִקָּדֵשׁ וַיָּבֹאוּ בְנֵי־יִשְׂרָאֵל כָּל־הָעֵדָה הֹר
כג הָהָר: וַיֹּאמֶר יְהוָה אֶל־מֹשֶׁה וְאֶל־אַהֲרֹן בְּהֹר הָהָר
כד עַל־גְּבוּל אֶרֶץ־אֱדוֹם לֵאמֹר: יֵאָסֵף אַהֲרֹן אֶל־עַמָּיו
כִּי לֹא יָבֹא אֶל־הָאָרֶץ אֲשֶׁר נָתַתִּי לִבְנֵי יִשְׂרָאֵל עַל
כה אֲשֶׁר־מְרִיתֶם אֶת־פִּי לְמֵי מְרִיבָה: קַח אֶת־אַהֲרֹן
כו וְאֶת־אֶלְעָזָר בְּנוֹ וְהַעַל אֹתָם הֹר הָהָר: וְהַפְשֵׁט
אֶת־אַהֲרֹן אֶת־בְּגָדָיו וְהִלְבַּשְׁתָּם אֶת־אֶלְעָזָר בְּנוֹ

בעל הטורים

(יט) מִכְרָם. ג׳ בַּמָּסוֹרֶת – ״וְאִם מֵימֶיךָ נִשְׁתֶּה . . . וְנָתַתִּי מִכְרָם״; ״וָאָעִיד בְּיוֹם מִכְרָם צָיִד״; ״עַל מִכְרָם בַּכֶּסֶף צַדִּיק״. בִּשְׁבִיל שֶׁמָּכְרוּ בַכֶּסֶף צַדִּיק, וְצָדוּ אֶת אֲבִיהֶם בְּיוֹם מִכְרָם בְּפִיהֶם, וְאָמְרוּ לוֹ ״חַיָּה רָעָה אֲכָלַתְהוּ״, עַל כֵּן ״וְנָתַתִּי מִכְרָם״, וְהֻצְרְכוּ לִשְׁתּוֹת מֵימֵיהֶם בַּכֶּסֶף:

(כה) וְהַעַל. ב׳ בַּמָּסוֹרֶת – הָכָא וּבְפָרָשַׁת וָאֵרָא:

(כו) וְהִלְבַּשְׁתָּם. ב׳ בַּמָּסוֹרֶת – ״וְהִלְבַּשְׁתָּם אֶת אֶלְעָזָר בְּנוֹ״; ״וְהִלְבַּשְׁתָּם כֻּתֳּנֹת״.

BAAL HATURIM ELUCIDATED

19. {The Baal HaTurim's comment to מֵימֶיךָ appears at *Exodus* 23:25.}

❑ **מִכְרָם — THEIR PRICE.** The masoretic note, ג׳, means that this word appears three times in the *Tanach:*[74] (i) here, וְאִם מֵימֶיךָ נִשְׁתֶּה . . . וְנָתַתִּי מִכְרָם, *and if we drink your waters . . . I shall give their price;* (ii) וָאָעִיד בְּיוֹם מִכְרָם צָיִד, *I warned them on the day of their selling game* [*that they had*] *trapped* (*Nehemiah* 13:15);[75] and (iii) עַל מִכְרָם בַּכֶּסֶף צַדִּיק, *for their selling a righteous man for money* (*Amos* 2:6). [The similarity of expression alludes to the consequence of the sale of Joseph by his brothers:] Because they sold a righteous man [Joseph] for money and, *on the day of their*

---

74. The note ends with the abbreviation אנ״ך, meaning that one of the three appearances is in אוֹרַיְתָא, Aramaic for *Torah;* one in נְבִיאֵי, *Prophets;* and one in כְּתוּבַיָּא, *Hagiographa* or *Writings.*

Although the spellings and vowelizations of these words are identical, they are not all of the same part of speech. In our verse, מִכְרָם is a noun form composed of מֶכֶר, *a price* or *a sale,* with the pronominal suffix ־ָם, *their,* referring to the waters; thus, מִכְרָם means *their* [i.e., your waters'] *price.* But in the other two verses מִכְרָם is a verb form composed of the *makor* (gerundive infinitive) מְכֹר, *selling,* with the pronominal suffix ־ָם referring to the people who are doing the selling; thus, in those verses, מִכְרָם means *their* [action of] *selling.*

75. In that passage, Nehemiah admonishes the people regarding their flagrant desecration of the Sabbath by engaging in commerce and other forbidden activities.

*19 The Children of Israel said to him, "We shall go up on the
highway, and if we drink your waters — I or my flock — I shall
give their price. Only nothing will happen; let me pass through
on foot."*

*20 He said, "You shall not pass through!" Then Edom went
out against him with a massive throng and a strong hand.
21 So Edom refused to permit Israel to pass through his border,
and Israel turned away from near him.*

*22 They journeyed from Kadesh and the Children of Israel
arrived — the entire assembly — at Mount Hor. 23 HASHEM said
to Moses and Aaron at Mount Hor by the border of the land of
Edom, saying, 24 "Aaron shall be gathered to his people, for he
shall not enter the Land that I have given to the Children of
Israel, because you defied My word at the waters of strife.
25 Take Aaron and Elazar his son and bring them up to Mount
Hor. 26 Strip Aaron of his vestments and dress Elazar his son in*

BAAL HATURIM ELUCIDATED

selling, they entrapped their father with their mouth by saying, *"A savage beast devoured him"* (*Genesis* 37:20,33), as a consequence [God said], "וְנָתַתִּי מִכְרָם, *I shall give* [*them*] *their price,*" and they had to pay money to drink their water.[76]

25. וְהַעַל — AND BRING [THEM] UP. The masoretic note, ב׳, means that this word appears twice in the *Tanach:* (i) here; and (ii) in *Parashas Va'eira* (*Exodus* 8:1). [See the Baal HaTurim's commentary to that verse.]

26. וְהִלְבַּשְׁתָּם — AND DRESS [ELAZAR HIS SON] IN THEM. The masoretic note, ב׳, means that this word appears twice in the *Tanach:* (i) here, וְהִלְבַּשְׁתָּם אֶת אֶלְעָזָר בְּנוֹ, *and dress Elazar his son with them*[77]; and (ii) [regarding the inauguration of Aaron's sons as Kohanim,] וְהִלְבַּשְׁתָּם כֻּתֳּנֹת, *and dress them in tunics* (*Exodus* 29:8).[78]

---

76. The Baal HaTurim's intention here is not clear, for there seems to be no connection between the incidents. Moreover, the Israelites did not actually pay out any money, for Edom refused them passage. *Atros Addar* suggests that it was the sale of Joseph that led to the Israelites moving to Egypt and becoming enslaved there. Had that sale not taken place, they would never have left Canaan and would not have had to offer to pay for their water now.

Alternatively: Before the Israelites would be allowed to return to Canaan, they would have to exhibit their willingness to divest themselves of any financial benefit accrued to them as a result of having sold Joseph. They would accomplish this by spending those ill-gotten gains on drinking water (*VeChur LaZahav*).

77. Literally, *and you shall dress them onto Elazar his son.* Note that the suffix ם־ of וְהִלְבַּשְׁתָּם is the direct object of the verb and means *them.* In our verse, ם־, *them,* refers to the vestments — *and you shall dress them,* i.e., you shall place the vestments — and not to the one being dressed in them. In the verse from *Exodus,* however, the suffix refers to the people who are being dressed, for that verse reads: וְאֶת בָּנָיו תַּקְרִיב וְהִלְבַּשְׁתָּם כֻּתֳּנֹת, *You shall cause his sons to come near; and you shall dress them in tunics.* In that case, ם־, *them,* refers to the sons of Aaron — *and you shall dress them,* i.e., his sons — and not to the vestments.

78. The Baal HaTurim's comment here echoes his comment to that verse.

כז וְאַהֲרֹן יֵאָסֵף וּמֵת שָׁם: וַיַּעַשׂ מֹשֶׁה כַּאֲשֶׁר צִוָּה יהוה
כח וַיַּעֲלוּ אֶל־הֹר הָהָר לְעֵינֵי כָּל־הָעֵדָה: וַיַּפְשֵׁט מֹשֶׁה
אֶת־אַהֲרֹן אֶת־בְּגָדָיו וַיַּלְבֵּשׁ אֹתָם אֶת־אֶלְעָזָר בְּנוֹ
וַיָּמָת אַהֲרֹן שָׁם בְּרֹאשׁ הָהָר וַיֵּרֶד מֹשֶׁה וְאֶלְעָזָר מִן־
כט הָהָר: וַיִּרְאוּ כָּל־הָעֵדָה כִּי גָוַע אַהֲרֹן וַיִּבְכּוּ אֶת־
כא א אַהֲרֹן שְׁלֹשִׁים יוֹם כֹּל בֵּית יִשְׂרָאֵל: וַיִּשְׁמַע
הַכְּנַעֲנִי מֶלֶךְ־עֲרָד יֹשֵׁב הַנֶּגֶב כִּי בָּא יִשְׂרָאֵל
דֶּרֶךְ הָאֲתָרִים וַיִּלָּחֶם בְּיִשְׂרָאֵל וַיִּשְׁבְּ ׀ מִמֶּנּוּ
ב שֶׁבִי: וַיִּדַּר יִשְׂרָאֵל נֶדֶר לַיהוה וַיֹּאמַר אִם־נָתֹן
תִּתֵּן אֶת־הָעָם הַזֶּה בְּיָדִי וְהַחֲרַמְתִּי אֶת־עָרֵיהֶם:
ג וַיִּשְׁמַע יהוה בְּקוֹל יִשְׂרָאֵל וַיִּתֵּן אֶת־הַכְּנַעֲנִי
וַיַּחֲרֵם אֶתְהֶם וְאֶת־עָרֵיהֶם וַיִּקְרָא שֵׁם־הַמָּקוֹם
חָרְמָה:
ד וַיִּסְעוּ מֵהֹר הָהָר דֶּרֶךְ יַם־סוּף לִסְבֹב אֶת־אֶרֶץ אֱדוֹם

בעל הטורים

דְּאִיכָּא מַאן דְּאָמַר, כֹּהֵן גָּדוֹל בֶּן כֹּהֵן גָּדוֹל טָעוּן מְשִׁיחָה. כְּשֵׁם דְּ״וְהִלְבַּשְׁתָּם כֻּתֳּנֹת״ דְּהָתָם הָיָה בִּמְשִׁיחָה, אַף ״וְהִלְבַּשְׁתָּם״ דְּהָכָא הָיָה בִּמְשִׁיחָה:

(כח) וַיָּמָת אַהֲרֹן שָׁם. בְּגִימַטְרִיָּא מְלַמֵּד כִּי מֵת בִּנְשִׁיקָה:

(כט) וַיִּרְאוּ. בְּגִימַטְרִיָּא בָּעֲנָנִים:

BAAL HATURIM ELUCIDATED

[The similarity of expression is] in accordance with the Talmudic opinion[78a] that a newly appointed Kohen Gadol, [even one] who is the son of the previous Kohen Gadol, must be anointed [when he assumes his office].[79] Thus, just as [the fulfillment of] *you shall dress them in tunics* was accompanied by anointment,[80] so too was [the fulfillment of] *you shall dress* [*Elazar his son*] *in them* accompanied by anointment.[81]

28. וַיָּמָת אַהֲרֹן שָׁם — THEN AARON DIED THERE. The *gematria* of this phrase (1052) is

78a. *Atros Adar* notes that there is no conflicting opinion in the Talmud or Midrash.

79. *Horayos* 11b. In this the Kohen Gadol differs from the king. A king's son who succeeds his father to the throne need not be anointed, except when there are other claimants to the throne. Thus, Solomon son of David was anointed king by Zadok the Kohen in the face of David's other son Adonijah's claim to the throne (see *I Kings* 1:5-10; 32-39).

80. See *Exodus* 29:21; 30:30; see also *Kereisos* 5b.

81. *Maharam MiRothenburg;* see also *Maharsha* to *Taanis* 5b, s.v., משה.

them; Aaron shall be gathered in and die there."*
[27] *Moses did as HASHEM commanded, and they ascended Mount Hor before the eyes of the entire assembly.* [28] *Moses stripped Aaron's garments from him and dressed Elazar his son in them; then Aaron died there on the top of the mountain, and Moses and Elazar descended from the mountain.* [29] *The entire assembly saw that Aaron had perished; they wept for Aaron thirty days, the entire House of Israel.*

21 [1] *The Canaanite king of Arad, who dwelled in the south, heard that Israel had come by the route of the spies, and he warred against Israel and took a captive from it.* [2] *Israel made a vow to HASHEM and said, "If You will deliver this people into my hand, I will consecrate their cities."* [3] *HASHEM heard the voice of Israel, and He delivered the Canaanite, and it consecrated them and their cities. It named the place Hormah.*
[4] *They journeyed from Mount Hor by way of the Sea of Reeds to go around the land of Edom, and the*

BAAL HATURIM ELUCIDATED

equivalent[81a] to that of מְלַמֵּד כִּי מֵת בִּנְשִׁיקָה, *This teaches that he died by a kiss.*[82]

29. וַיִּרְאוּ — THEY SAW. The *gematria* of this word (223) is equivalent[83] to that of בָּעֲנָנִים, *in the clouds.*[84]

XXI

2. {The Baal HaTurim's comment to וַיִּדַּר appears at *Genesis* 28:20.}

81a. The principle of *im hakollel* allows 1051, the *gematria* of the Baal HaTurim's phrase, to be considered equivalent to 1052.

82. *Bava Basra* 17a; see *Rashi* to 20:1 above and 33:38 below; see also the Baal HaTurim to 27:13 below and *Deuteronomy* 32:50.

מִיתַת נְשִׁיקָה, *death by a kiss* [*of God*], as it were, means death directly through God, without the intercession of the Angel of Death (see *Bava Basra* 17a; *Rabbeinu Bachye*). The Talmud describes this as the most desirable form of death, likening it to pulling a hair from milk; that is, the soul leaves the body without resistance (*Berachos* 8a). This means that to the extent that people sin in life and establish a bond between their souls and the pleasures of this world, it becomes increasingly more difficult for them to part from physical life. For those who have become totally attached to physicality, the Sages liken death to pulling embedded thistles from sheep's wool. But for those of the stature of Moses, Aaron and Miriam, whose souls remained pure throughout their earthly sojourn, there is no effort and no pain when the soul returns to its source (*Resisei Laylah* 56).

83. The principle of *im hakollel* allows 222, the *gematria* of the Baal HaTurim's phrase, to be considered equivalent to 223.

84. *Peirush HaRokeach.* The Talmud states that when Aaron died, the Clouds of Glory departed from Israel. It goes on to interpret the word וַיִּרְאוּ, *they saw,* of our verse as if it read וַיֵּירָאוּ, *they appeared,* and כִּי, *that,* with its alternative meaning *because.* The verse is then rendered: *The entire assembly appeared,* i.e., they were no longer covered and hidden by the Clouds, *because Aaron had perished* (*Taanis* 9a). In the *gematria* of וַיִּרְאוּ, the Baal HaTurim finds a second allusion to those Clouds.

כא/ה ה וַתִּקְצַר נֶפֶשׁ־הָעָם בַּדָּרֶךְ: וַיְדַבֵּר הָעָם בֵּאלֹהִים
וּבְמֹשֶׁה לָמָה הֶעֱלִיתֻנוּ מִמִּצְרַיִם לָמוּת בַּמִּדְבָּר כִּי
אֵין לֶחֶם וְאֵין מַיִם וְנַפְשֵׁנוּ קָצָה בַּלֶּחֶם הַקְּלֹקֵל:

בעל הטורים

כא (ד) וַתִּקְצַר נֶפֶשׁ הָעָם. מְלַמֵּד שֶׁרָאוּ כָּל הַצָּרוֹת שֶׁיָּבוֹאוּ עֲלֵיהֶם בְּגָלוּת אֱדוֹם, וְאֵיךְ יִמָּשֵׁךְ גָּלוּת אֱדוֹם:

❏ **וַתִּקְצַר.** ד' בַּמָּסוֹרֶת – "וַתִּקְצַר נֶפֶשׁ הָעָם"; "וַתִּקְצַר נַפְשׁוֹ בַּעֲמַל יִשְׂרָאֵל"; "וַתִּקְצַר נַפְשׁוֹ לָמוּת"; "וַתִּקְצַר נַפְשִׁי בָּהֶם". כֵּיוָן שֶׁבָּאוּ לִגְבוּל אֱדוֹם "וַתִּקְצַר נֶפֶשׁ הָעָם" – וְדִבְּרוּ בַּה' וּבְמֹשֶׁה; וְקָצְרָה נַפְשׁוֹ בַּעֲמַל יִשְׂרָאֵל – שֶׁחָטְאוּ; "וַתִּקְצַר נַפְשׁוֹ לָמוּת" – שֶׁמֵּת אַהֲרֹן בִּגְבוּל אֱדוֹם. וְכֵן "וַתִּקְצַר נַפְשִׁי בָּהֶם", דְּרֵישֵׁיהּ דִּקְרָא "וָאַכְחִד אֶת שְׁלֹשֶׁת הָרֹעִים בְּיֶרַח אֶחָד", שֶׁדָּרְשׁוּ אוֹתוֹ עַל אַהֲרֹן וּמִרְיָם וּמֹשֶׁה, שֶׁמֵּתוּ שְׁלָשְׁתָּן בְּחֹדֶשׁ אֶחָד:

(ה) קְלֹקֵל. בְּגִימַטְרִיָּא זֶה רמ"ח, שֶׁנִּבְלַע בְּרמ"ח אֵבָרִים:

BAAL HATURIM ELUCIDATED

4. וַתִּקְצַר נֶפֶשׁ הָעָם — AND THE PEOPLE BECAME EXASPERATED.[85] This teaches that they [were granted prophetic vision and] saw all the troubles that would come upon them during the Edomite exile,[85a] and how protracted the Edomite exile would be.[86]

❏ **וַתִּקְצַר — [AND THE PEOPLE] BECAME EXASPERATED.** The masoretic note, ד', means that this word appears four times in the *Tanach:* (i) here, וַתִּקְצַר נֶפֶשׁ הָעָם, *and the people became exasperated;* (ii) וַתִּקְצַר נַפְשׁוֹ בַּעֲמַל יִשְׂרָאֵל, *then He became impatient*[87] *regarding the travail of Israel*[88] (*Judges* 10:16); (iii) וַתִּקְצַר נַפְשׁוֹ לָמוּת, *and he became anxious*[87] *to die* (*Judges* 16:16); and (iv) וַתִּקְצַר נַפְשִׁי בָּהֶם, *I became impatient with them* (*Zechariah* 11:8). [The similarity of expression indicates that] when the nation arrived at the border of Edom, *the people grew impatient* — they spoke against God and against Moses; consequently, *He grew impatient*

85. The expression קֹצֶר נֶפֶשׁ, literally, *shortness of spirit,* is an idiom for a negative emotion. It may refer to anxiety, impatience, exasperation or any other undesirable feeling (see *Rashi,* s.v., ותקצר נפש העם). Thus, the expression has not been translated uniformly in the four verses adduced by the Baal HaTurim in his next comment.

85a. Our verse describes the journey during which the Israelites had *to go around the land of Edom.*

86. The nation had been traveling through the wilderness for almost forty years. Why, then, does the Torah mention their exasperation at this particular point? The Baal HaTurim explains that they were exasperated with *galus Edom* (the Edomite exile) of which they were given prophetic vision. But where in the phrase וַתִּקְצַר נֶפֶשׁ הָעָם do we see a hint of that exile which would not begin until more than a thousand years later? In both *Rabbeinu Ephraim* (*MiKesivah Ashkenazis*) and *Rimzei Rabbeinu Yoel,* this same concept appears under the rubric וַתִּקְצַר נֶפֶשׁ הָעָם בַּדָּרֶךְ. Accordingly, the superfluous word בַּדָּרֶךְ, usually translated *on the way,* or *on the road,* indicates that the cause of the nation's exasperation was *the road,* not the road upon which they traveled in the wilderness, but rather, the prolonged road of the Wandering Jew during the Edomite exile (*VeChur LaZahav*).

87. See note 85 above.

88. The word עָמָל can mean either *agony, travail* or *evil, sinfulness.* In the context of the verse in *Judges,* עֲמַל יִשְׂרָאֵל refers to *the travail of Israel* suffered at the hand of Ammon. In the Baal HaTurim's allusion, however, it refers to *the sinfulness of Israel* and the agony, so to speak, that that sinfulness caused God.

people became exasperated regarding the way. [5] *The people spoke against God and Moses: "Why have you brought us up from Egypt to die in this wilderness, for there is no food and no water, and our soul is disgusted with the insubstantial food?"*

BAAL HATURIM ELUCIDATED

regarding the sinfulness of Israel[88a] — for they had sinned; *and He became impatient to death* — for Aaron died at the border of Edom. Similarly, the verse, *I* [*God*] *became impatient with them,* begins, וָאַכְחִד אֶת שְׁלֹשֶׁת הָרֹעִים בְּיֶרַח אֶחָד, *I removed the three shepherds in one month,* which the Sages explain as referring to Aaron, Miriam and Moses, for the three of them died in [the course of] one month.[89]

5. {The Baal HaTurim's comment to וּבְמֹשֶׁה appears at *Exodus* 14:31.}

❑ **הַקְּלֹקֵל — INSUBSTANTIAL.** The *gematria* of קְלֹקֵל (260) is equal to that of זֶה רמ״ח, *This* [*refers to*] *248.*[90] For the manna would become absorbed into the 248 *eivarim*[91] of the body.[92]

88a. *Taanis* 9a.

89. The Talmud explains that, actually, Miriam died in the month of Nissan (see 20:1 above); Aaron, in Av (see 33:38 below); and Moses, in Adar, eleven months after his sister (see *Kiddushin* 38a). However, three excellent gifts were bestowed upon Israel in the merit of those three leaders, but only while they were alive. Thus, the well was provided in the merit of Miriam; the pillar of cloud in the merit of Aaron; and the manna in the merit of Moses. When Miriam died, the well disappeared (see 20:1-2 above, with *Rashi,* s.v., ולא היה מים); nevertheless, it returned in the merit of the other two [Moses and Aaron]. When Aaron died, the Clouds of Glory disappeared and the king of Arad heard that the protective Clouds of Glory had disappeared, so he attacked Israel (see 20:28-21:1 and note 84 above); yet, both the well and the clouds returned in the merit of Moses. When Moses died, all three gifts disappeared. Thus, the verse in *Zechariah* means that the gifts bestowed due to the merits of these three leaders all ended in the same month, the month in which Moses died (*Taanis* 9a).

Now, we may ask: Why does the verse state that the three gifts were removed in one month; if they all disappeared with Moses' death, the verse should have said "in one day"? Although the Torah forbade the people to save the manna from one day to the next (see *Exodus* 16:19-20), the Talmud (*Kiddushin* 38a) proves that the manna that fell on the last day of Moses' life nourished the nation for thirty-nine days. Presumably, the well's water, which they were not enjoined from saving from one day to the next, also lasted for a period of time. Accordingly, the nation would have felt the disappearance of the clouds on the day of Moses' death, but they would not feel the loss of the manna and the well until sometime later, when they would realize that their depleting supplies were not being replenished and would soon give out. When this realization hit them, they felt fully the loss of the three gifts and the three leaders in whose merit they had been bestowed, all this in the course of one month (*VeChur LaZahav*).

This also explains the order used by the Baal HaTurim at the end of his comment, an order that does not follow the order of their birth or of their passing, both of which were Miriam, Aaron and Moses. The absence of the clouds at the death of Aaron was immediate; thus, Aaron's death was felt first. Presumably, the well's water gave out before the manna, and so Miriam's death was felt second. Finally, the full impact of the loss came when the people realized the impact of Moses' passing as the stores of manna began to dwindle (*VeChur LaZahav*).

90. A parallel comment in *Rimzei Rabbeinu Yoel* reads: The *gematria* of הַקְּלֹקֵל (265) is equal to that of בָּאֵיבָרִים, *in the eivarim.*

91. An *eiver* is a body part containing bone, flesh and sinews (*Chullin* 102b; see *Bartenura* to *Ohalos* 1:7). For lack of a precise English word, *eiver* is often translated organ or limb. The Mishnah (*Ohalos* 1:8) enumerates the two hundred and forty-eight *eivarim* of the human body.

92. *R' Ephraim;* see *Sifrei* 88; *Tanchuma Yashan, Beshalach* 22; *Yoma* 75b; see also the Baal

ו וַיְשַׁלַּ֨ח יְהוָ֜ה בָּעָ֗ם אֵ֚ת הַנְּחָשִׁ֣ים הַשְּׂרָפִ֔ים וַיְנַשְּׁכ֖וּ
ז אֶת־הָעָ֑ם וַיָּ֥מָת עַם־רָ֖ב מִיִּשְׂרָאֵֽל׃ וַיָּבֹא֩ הָעָ֨ם
אֶל־מֹשֶׁ֜ה וַיֹּאמְר֣וּ חָטָ֗אנוּ כִּֽי־דִבַּ֤רְנוּ בַֽיהוָה֙ וָבָ֔ךְ
הִתְפַּלֵּל֙ אֶל־יְהוָ֔ה וְיָסֵ֥ר מֵעָלֵ֖ינוּ אֶת־הַנָּחָ֑שׁ
ח וַיִּתְפַּלֵּ֥ל מֹשֶׁ֖ה בְּעַ֥ד הָעָֽם׃ וַיֹּ֨אמֶר יְהוָ֜ה אֶל־מֹשֶׁ֗ה
עֲשֵׂ֤ה לְךָ֙ שָׂרָ֔ף וְשִׂ֥ים אֹת֖וֹ עַל־נֵ֑ס וְהָיָה֙ כָּל־
ט הַנָּשׁ֔וּךְ וְרָאָ֥ה אֹת֖וֹ וָחָֽי׃ וַיַּ֤עַשׂ מֹשֶׁה֙ נְחַ֣שׁ נְחֹ֔שֶׁת
וַיְשִׂמֵ֖הוּ עַל־הַנֵּ֑ס וְהָיָ֗ה אִם־נָשַׁ֤ךְ הַנָּחָשׁ֙ אֶת־אִ֔ישׁ
ששי י וְהִבִּ֛יט אֶל־נְחַ֥שׁ הַנְּחֹ֖שֶׁת וָחָֽי׃ וַיִּסְע֖וּ בְּנֵ֣י יִשְׂרָאֵ֑ל
יא וַֽיַּחֲנ֖וּ בְּאֹבֹֽת׃ וַיִּסְע֖וּ מֵאֹבֹ֑ת וַֽיַּחֲנ֞וּ בְּעִיֵּ֣י הָעֲבָרִ֗ים
בַּמִּדְבָּר֙ אֲשֶׁר֙ עַל־פְּנֵ֣י מוֹאָ֔ב מִמִּזְרַ֖ח הַשָּֽׁמֶשׁ׃
יב-יג מִשָּׁ֖ם נָסָ֑עוּ וַֽיַּחֲנ֖וּ בְּנַ֥חַל זָֽרֶד׃ מִשָּׁם֮ נָסָ֒עוּ֒ וַֽיַּחֲנ֗וּ

בעל הטורים

(ו) **הַנְּחָשִׁים.** לְפִי שֶׁעָשׂוּ מַעֲשֵׂה נָחָשׁ, שֶׁהוֹצִיאוּ לָשׁוֹן הָרָע עַל הַמָּן:

❑ **אֶת הַנְּחָשִׁים.** לְרַבּוֹת כְּלָבִים וְחַיּוֹת רָעוֹת:

(ט) **וַיְשִׂמֵהוּ עַל הַנֵּס.** כְּדֶרֶךְ הַמְיַסֵּר אֶת בְּנוֹ, שֶׁמֵּשִׂים הַשּׁוֹט שֶׁמַּכֵּהוּ בוֹ בְּמָקוֹם גָּבוֹהַּ, כְּדֵי שֶׁיִּרְאֶה אוֹתוֹ בְּכָל פַּעַם וְיִזָּכֵר:

(יג) **מִשָּׁם נָסָעוּ.** וְלֹא אָמַר "וַיִּסְעוּ מִנַּחַל זָרֶד", כְּדֶרֶךְ הַכָּתוּב בְּכָל הַמַּסָּעוֹת, לְפִי שֶׁעַל נַחַל זֶרֶד הָיוּ מְקוֹמוֹת רַבִּים – דִּיבוֹן גָּד וְעַלְמוֹן דִּבְלָתָיְמָה – וְנָסְעוּ הַכֹּל עַל הַנַּחַל מִמָּקוֹם לְמָקוֹם:

BAAL HATURIM ELUCIDATED

6. הַנְּחָשִׁים — THE SERPENTS. [They were punished with serpents,] because they had acted in the manner of the serpent, for they had spoken malicious slander about the manna.[93]

❑ **אֶת הַנְּחָשִׁים — THE SERPENTS.** The word אֵת is used to include[94] dogs and wild beasts.[95]

HaTurim to *Exodus* 16:14. The Talmud and Midrash explain that the manna was totally absorbed by their *eivarim,* leaving no waste to be excreted. The people panicked, "This manna will eventually cause our innards to explode. Is it possible that a human being who ingests should not excrete?" (cited by *Rashi*).

93. *Tanchuma* 19, cited by *Rashi.* The serpent in the Garden of Eden had spoken against God's words in order to convince Eve to rebel against God's command regarding that which He had forbidden Adam and his wife to eat. And now, the people complained against the food that God gave them in the wilderness.

94. The word אֵת (or אֶת) is sometimes translated *with* (see, e.g., *Targum Onkelos* to *Exodus* 1:1). Sometimes it is understood by the Sages as an inclusionary term that adds something not stated explicitly by the verse (see, e.g., *Sotah* 17a; *Menachos* 11b).

95. *Peirush HaRokeach;* see *Bamidbar Rabbah* 19:23, cited by *Rashi.* The Midrash expounds on

6 *God sent the fiery serpents against the people and they*
bit the people. A large multitude of Israel died. 7 *The people*
came to Moses and said, "We have sinned, for we have
spoken against HASHEM *and against you! Pray to* HASHEM
that He remove from us the serpent." Moses prayed for the
people.
8 HASHEM *said to Moses, "Make yourself a fiery [serpent]*
and place it on a pole, and it will be that anyone who was
bitten will look at it and live." 9 *Moses made a serpent of*
copper and placed it on the pole; so it was that if the serpent
bit a man, he would stare at the copper serpent and live.
10 *The Children of Israel journeyed and encamped at Oboth.*
11 *They journeyed from Oboth and encamped in the ruins of*
the passes in the wilderness facing Moab, toward the rising
sun. 12 *From there they journeyed and encamped in the*
valley of Zered. 13 *From there they journeyed and encamped*

BAAL HATURIM ELUCIDATED

7. {The Baal HaTurim's commentary to וַיָּסֵר appears at *Exodus* 10:17.}

9. וַיְשִׂמֵהוּ עַל הַנֵּס — AND [HE] PLACED IT ON THE POLE, in the manner of a father who disciplines his son: He places the rod with which he would strike him in a high [and obvious] place, so that the son will continuously see it and remember [his punishment].[96]

13. מִשָּׁם נָסָעוּ — FROM THERE THEY JOURNEYED. The Torah does not use the formula, וַיִּסְעוּ מִנַּחַל זָרֶד, *And they journeyed from the valley of Zered,* as it does with regard to all the [other] journeys,[97] for there were several [encampment] places along the valley of Zered — e.g., Dibon-gad and Almon-diblathaimah[98] — and they journeyed from place to place along the valley.[99]

---

the phrase, וְהָיָה כָּל הַנָּשׁוּךְ, *anyone who was bitten will . . .* (v. 8): The Torah does not specify *anyone bitten by a serpent;* this teaches that the miraculous antidote of looking up at the copper serpent would be effective even for those bitten by other reptiles, scorpions, wild beasts or dogs.

A question may be raised: The Midrash (*Sifrei* 83, cited by *Rashi* to *Numbers* 10:34) teaches that the Clouds of Glory would clear a path through the wilderness, killing any potential threats, such as serpents and scorpions, in Israel's way. Now, even though the clouds had departed with Aaron's death, they returned in the merit of Moses (see note 89 above). If so, how could Israel have been bitten by any animal other than the serpents sent against them? The Baal HaTurim explains that the superfluous אֶת indicates that the visitation was not limited to serpents; rather, it included other dangerous biting animals (*VeChur LaZahav*).

96. *Peirush HaRokeach;* see *Bamidbar Rabbah* 16:18. Torah law permits corporal punishment when it is used wisely and after other means of discipline have failed. Indeed, under certain circumstances, a parent or teacher can be faulted for sparing the rod (see, e.g., *Proverbs* 13:24 and 29:15,17; see also *Makkos* 2:2 [8a]).

97. See 20:22; 21:4, 11 above; and throughout Ch. 33 below.

98. See 33:45-46 below. *Peirush HaRokeach* adds הָרֵי הָעֲבָרִים, *the mountains of the passes* (33:47).

99. *Peirush HaRokeach.*

מֵעֵבֶר אַרְנוֹן אֲשֶׁר בַּמִּדְבָּר הַיֹּצֵא מִגְּבֻל הָאֱמֹרִי כִּי
יד אַרְנוֹן גְּבוּל מוֹאָב בֵּין מוֹאָב וּבֵין הָאֱמֹרִי: עַל־כֵּן
יֵאָמַר בְּסֵפֶר מִלְחֲמֹת יהוה אֶת־וָהֵב בְּסוּפָה וְאֶת־
טו הַנְּחָלִים אַרְנוֹן: וְאֶשֶׁד הַנְּחָלִים אֲשֶׁר נָטָה לְשֶׁבֶת

בעל הטורים

(יד) **אֶת וָהֵב בְּסוּפָה.** כְּמוֹ "יָהֵב", וְכֵן "הֱוֵה גְבִיר" כְּמוֹ "הֱיֵה". פֵּרוּשׁ, אֲשֶׁר נָתַן לָנוּ בְּסוּפָה. כְּלוֹמַר בִּמְהִירוּת, כְּמוֹ "כַּעֲבוֹר סוּפָה", שֶׁבִּמְהֵרָה לָקַחְנוּ הוֹן רָב. וְזֶהוּ שֶׁכָּתוּב "בְּ{סֵפֶר} מִלְחֲמֹת ה'", דִּכְתִיב "רַק הַבְּהֵמָה בָּזַזְנוּ לָנוּ וּשְׁלַל הֶעָרִים":

❑ **בְּסוּפָה.** ב' בַּמָּסוֹרֶת – "אֶת וָהֵב בְּסוּפָה"; "ה' בְּסוּפָה וּבִשְׂעָרָה דַּרְכּוֹ". וְזֶהוּ שֶׁתִּרְגֵּם אֻנְקְלוֹס "בְּסוּפָה" כְּשֶׁיַּזְכִּירוּ נִסִּים שֶׁל יַם סוּף, כְּדִכְתִיב "ה' בְּסוּפָה וְגוֹ'", וְסֵיפֵהּ דִּקְרָא "גּוֹעֵר בַּיָּם וַיַּבְּשֵׁהוּ", הָכָא נַמִּי אַיְרֵי בִּיבֹשֶׁת יַם סוּף:

(טו) **וְאֶשֶׁד הַנְּחָלִים.** סוֹפֵי תֵבוֹת דָּם. שֶׁהַדָּם הָיָה יוֹרֵד מִן הַהֲרוּגִים שֶׁנֶּהֶרְגוּ בַּנָּחַל:

❑ **לְשֶׁבֶת.** ב' בַּמָּסוֹרֶת – "לְשֶׁבֶת עָר"; "לְשֶׁבֶת אַבְרָם". שֶׁבִּזְכוּת אַבְרָהָם זָכוּ לָזֶה:

BAAL HATURIM ELUCIDATED

14. {The Baal HaTurim's comment to יֵאָמַר appears at *Genesis* 10:9.}

❑ **אֶת וָהֵב בְּסוּפָה** — HE HAS GIVEN WITH TEMPEST-LIKE SPEED. [The word וָהֵב is] identical in meaning with יָהֵב, *he gives* (*Daniel* 2:21).[100] Similarly, [the word הֱוֵה of the phrase] הֱוֵה גְבִיר, *Be a lord!* (*Genesis* 27:29), is identical in meaning with the imperative form הֱיֵה, *Be!* (e.g., *Exodus* 18:19). The meaning [of the phrase אֶת וָהֵב בְּסוּפָה is then], "that which He has given to us[101] with a tempest," i.e., hurriedly,[102] as we find the expression כַּעֲבוֹר סוּפָה, *as the tempest passes*[103] (*Proverbs* 10:25). [In other words, our verse means] that we speedily acquired a vast fortune. And this is what is written in the *Book of the wars of HASHEM:*[104] as it is written, רַק הַבְּהֵמָה בָּזַזְנוּ לָנוּ וּשְׁלַל הֶעָרִים[105], *Only the animals did we loot for ourselves, and the booty of the cities* (*Deuteronomy* 2:35).[106]

❑ **בְּסוּפָה** — AT THE SEA OF REEDS.[107] The masoretic note, ב', means that this word

100. *Rashi;* cf. *Ibn Ezra.* That is, the letters י and ו are interchangeable in this word.

101. Some editions read, אֲשֶׁר נִיתַּן לָנוּ, *which has been given to us.*

102. The word סוּפָה, *tempest,* is often used in Scripture as a metaphor for something done suddenly or with great speed, like the winds of a tempest (see *Ibn Ezra* to *Isaiah* 5:28 and *Nahum* 1:3).

103. Suddenly (*Rashi*); swiftly (*Ibn Ezra*).

104. In this comment, the Baal HaTurim follows *Targum Yonasan Ben Uzziel's* Aramaic paraphrase of סֵפֶר מִלְחֲמֹת ה' as *the Book of the Torah in which the wars of HASHEM are recorded.*

105. The text follows *Peirush HaRokeach,* the Baal HaTurim's apparent source for this comment. The early printed editions, as well as most later editions, read: רַק הַבְּהֵמָה וּשְׁלַל הֶעָרִים בָּזוֹנוּ לָנוּ, *Only the animals and the booty of the cities did we loot for ourselves.* However, no such verse exists in Scripture. Rather, that "verse" is a confusion between *Deuteronomy* 2:35 (cited in the Baal HaTurim's comment) and 3:7, which reads: וְכָל הַבְּהֵמָה וּשְׁלַל הֶעָרִים בַּזּוֹנוּ לָנוּ.

106. *Peirush HaRokeach.* The Baal HaTurim's intent in adducing this verse is not clear, for the verse does not seem to have any relation to his comment.

107. The translation here differs from that of the previous comment because, in this comment, the Baal HaTurim translates the verse quite differently from the way he does in the earlier one.

on the other side of Arnon — which is in the wilderness — that juts out from the border of the Amorite; for Arnon is the border of Moab, between Moab and the Amorite.
14 *Therefore it is said in the Book of the Wars of* HASHEM: *He has given with tempest-like speed; and the rivers of Arnon,*
15 *the outpouring of the rivers when it veered to dwell*

BAAL HATURIM ELUCIDATED

appears twice in the *Tanach:* (i) here, אֶת וָהֵב בְּסוּפָה [the Baal HaTurim translates this below]; and (ii) ה׳ בְּסוּפָה וּבִשְׂעָרָה דַּרְכּוֹ, HASHEM — *His path is in a tempest and in a storm* (*Nahum* 1:3). This [similarity of expression can be explained] in accordance with *Targum Onkelos:*[108] בְּסוּפָה refers to [the Israelites'] mentioning of the miracles[109] of יַם סוּף, *the Sea of Reeds,* as indicated by the verse from *Nahum:* ה׳ בְּסוּפָה, HASHEM *at the Sea of Reeds . . .,* for that passage continues, גּוֹעֵר בַּיָּם וַיַּבְּשֵׁהוּ, *He roars at the sea and makes it dry* (v. 4).[110] Here, too, בְּסוּפָה refers to the drying of the Sea of Reeds.

15. וְאֶשֶׁד הַנְּחָלִים — THE OUTPOURING OF THE RIVERS. The final letters of these words spell דָּם, *blood.* This implies that the blood from the corpses of those killed at the gorge flowed down [into the river].[111]

❑ **לְשֶׁבֶת** — TO DWELL. The masoretic note, ב׳, means that this word appears twice in the *Tanach:* (i) here, לְשֶׁבֶת עָר, *to dwell at Ar;* and (ii) לְשֶׁבֶת אַבְרָם, *of Abram's dwelling* (*Genesis* 16:3).[112] [This indicates that] it was in the merit of Abraham that they were found worthy of this [miracle].[113]

108. *Targum Onkelos* (as recorded in the Sabioneta edition of the *Chumash,* 1557) paraphrases our verse: עַל כֵּן יִתְאֲמַר בְּסִיפְרָא, *Therefore it will be stated in the book,* קְרָבִין עֲבַד יְיָ עַל יַמָּא דְסוּף, HASHEM *waged wars at the Sea of Reeds,* וּגְבוּרָן עַל נַחֲלֵי אַרְנוֹן, *and* [*performed*] *powerful deeds along the rivers of Arnon.* (See also *Rashi,* s.v., ואת הנחלים.)

109. Although extant editions of *Targum Onkelos* mention only קְרָבִין, *wars,* at the Sea of Reeds, the Baal HaTurim uses the term נִסִּים, *miracles.* Perhaps the Baal HaTurim's copy of *Targum Onkelos* read, קְרָבִין וְנִסִּין עֲבַד יְיָ, HASHEM *waged wars and* [*performed*] *miracles.* Indeed, the phrase, בְּסֵפֶר מִלְחֲמֹת ה׳, literally, *in the book of the wars of* HASHEM, is paraphrased by *Targum Yerushalmi* as: בְּסֵפֶר קְרָבַיָּא נִיסַיָּא וּגְבוּרָתָא דַּעֲבַד יְיָ לְעַמֵּיהּ, *In the book of the wars, the miracles and the powerful deeds that* HASHEM *performed for His people.*

110. See *Radak* to that verse. The early printed editions of the Baal HaTurim, as well as many later editions, erroneously read גּוֹעֵר בְּיַם סוּף וַיַּבְּשֵׁהוּ, which confuses the verse from *Nahum* with another verse, וַיִּגְעַר בְּיַם סוּף וַיֶּחֱרָב, *He roared at the Sea of Reeds and it became dry* (*Psalms* 106:9).

111. *Peirush HaRokeach.* The Amorites had planned to ambush the Israelites as they passed through a narrow gorge near the Moabite border. The Amorite army hid in caves over the pass, ready to push huge boulders down upon the unsuspecting Israelites. God, however, caused the upper parts of the two facing cliffs to come together. Stone outcroppings of one side moved into the caves of the other side where the Amorites were hiding, crushing them to death in the process. The Israelites would never have known about this miracle. To inform them, God caused the well that accompanied them in the wilderness to enter the gorge and swallow up the blood and bones of the Amorite army. The well then spewed forth all that it had swallowed. And thus the nation learned of the miracle that saved them from certain death (*Tanchuma* 20, cited by *Rashi;* see also *Berachos* 54a-b).

112. The Baal HaTurim's comment there is an expanded version of his alternative comment here.

113. *Peirush HaRokeach.*

כא/טז־כא טז עָר וְנִשְׁעַן לִגְבוּל מוֹאָב: וּמִשָּׁם בְּאֵרָה הוּא הַבְּאֵר
אֲשֶׁר אָמַר יהוה לְמֹשֶׁה אֱסֹף אֶת־הָעָם וְאֶתְּנָה
יז לָהֶם מָיִם: אָז יָשִׁיר יִשְׂרָאֵל אֶת־הַשִּׁירָה
יח הַזֹּאת עֲלִי בְאֵר עֱנוּ־לָהּ: בְּאֵר חֲפָרוּהָ שָׂרִים כָּרוּהָ
נְדִיבֵי הָעָם בִּמְחֹקֵק בְּמִשְׁעֲנֹתָם וּמִמִּדְבָּר מַתָּנָה:
יט־כ וּמִמַּתָּנָה נַחֲלִיאֵל וּמִנַּחֲלִיאֵל בָּמוֹת: וּמִבָּמוֹת
הַגַּיְא אֲשֶׁר בִּשְׂדֵה מוֹאָב רֹאשׁ הַפִּסְגָּה וְנִשְׁקָפָה
עַל־פְּנֵי הַיְשִׁימֹן:
שביעי [רביעי] כא וַיִּשְׁלַח יִשְׂרָאֵל מַלְאָכִים אֶל־סִיחֹן מֶלֶךְ־הָאֱמֹרִי

בעל הטורים

דָּבָר אַחֵר — הַיְנוּ דְּאָמְרִינַן, נָשָׂא אִשָּׁה וְשָׁהָה עִמָּהּ עֶשֶׂר שָׁנִים וְלֹא יָלְדָה, שֶׁהוּא יָכוֹל לְהוֹצִיאָהּ. וְיָלְפִינַן לָהּ מִדִּכְתִיב "מִקֵּץ עֶשֶׂר שָׁנִים לְשֶׁבֶת אַבְרָם בְּאֶרֶץ כְּנָעַן", שֶׁלָּקַח הָגָר. וְהַיְנוּ "לְשֶׁבֶת עָר", שֶׁיָּשַׁב עֲרִירִי, יָכוֹל לִשָּׂא אַחֶרֶת. וְכַמָּה, "מִקֵּץ עֶשֶׂר שָׁנִים":

❑ **וְנִשְׁעַן.** ב׳ בַּמָּסוֹרֶת — "וְנִשְׁעַן לִגְבוּל מוֹאָב"; "וְנִשְׁעַן עַל ה׳ קְדוֹשׁ יִשְׂרָאֵל בֶּאֱמֶת". כֵּיוָן שֶׁבָּאוּ לִגְבוּל מוֹאָב וְרָאוּ הַנִּסִּים שֶׁנַּעֲשׂוּ לָהֶם "וְנִשְׁעַן עַל ה׳ קְדוֹשׁ יִשְׂרָאֵל בֶּאֱמֶת":

(יז) עֲלִי בְאֵר עֱנוּ לָהּ. כְּשֶׁחָזְרוּ מִן הַמִּלְחָמָה, חָנוּ עַל הַבְּאֵר וְאָמְרוּ שִׁירָה בִּמְקוֹם טָהֳרָה, דִּכְתִיב "בֵּין מַשְׁאַבִּים שָׁם יְתַנּוּ צִדְקוֹת ה׳":

❑ **עֱנוּ.** ב׳ בַּמָּסוֹרֶת — "עֲלִי בְאֵר עֱנוּ לָהּ"; "עֱנוּ לַה׳ בְּתוֹדָה". שֶׁעַל הַבְּאֵר עָנוּ לַה׳ בְּתוֹדָה וְאָמְרוּ שִׁירָה:

(כ) וּמִבָּמוֹת הַגַּיְא. קְרֵי בָּא מָוֶת בַּגַּיְא, דִּכְתִיב "וַיִּקְבֹּר אֹתוֹ בַגַּי":

BAAL HATURIM ELUCIDATED

Alternatively: This [similarity of expression] alludes to that which the Sages taught: If a man married a woman and lived with her for ten years during which she did not bear any children, he is permitted to divorce her.[114] And they derive this concept from the verse, מִקֵּץ עֶשֶׂר שָׁנִים לְשֶׁבֶת אַבְרָם בְּאֶרֶץ כְּנָעַן, *after ten years of Abram's living in the Land of Canaan,* [without having children,] he married Hagar.[114a] Thus [we may interpret עָר of] לְשֶׁבֶת עָר [as if it read עֲרִירִי, *childless,* and the phrase means], *when he has dwelt without children,* he is permitted to marry another woman. When? *After ten years.*[115]

114. Or take another wife. The Talmud restricts this ruling to an otherwise healthy couple who have had normal marital relations for ten years while dwelling in *Eretz Yisrael* (see the Baal HaTurim to *Genesis* 16:3). However, if one or the other of them was sick or if the two were confined in prison, even though they had normal relations, we assume that whichever iniquity caused Heaven to punish them with sickness or imprisonment also caused them to be barren, and therefore the ruling does not apply (see *Rosh* to *Yevamos* VI, 11, cited in *Tur Even HaEzer* 154).

114a. *Yevamos* 64a.

115. *R' Yehudah HaChassid.*

at Ar, and leaned against the border of Moab. [16] And from there to the well — it is the well of which HASHEM said to Moses, "Assemble the people and I shall give them water."

[17] Then Israel would sing this song: Go up, O well! Call out to it! [18] Well that the princes dug, that the nobles of the people excavated, through a lawgiver, with their staffs. A gift from the wilderness — [19] the gift went to the valley, and from the valley to the heights, [20] and from the heights to the valley in the field of Moab, at the top of the peak, overlooking the surface of the wilderness.

[21] Israel sent emissaries to Sihon, king of the Amorite,

BAAL HATURIM ELUCIDATED

❑ **וְנִשְׁעַן** — AND LEANED AGAINST. The masoretic note, ב׳, means that this word appears twice in the *Tanach:* (i) here, וְנִשְׁעַן לִגְבוּל מוֹאָב, *and leaned against the border of Moab;* and (ii) וְנִשְׁעַן עַל ה׳ קְדוֹשׁ יִשְׂרָאֵל בֶּאֱמֶת, *but relied on HASHEM, the Holy One of Israel, in truth* (*Isaiah* 10:20). When the Israelites came to the border of Moab and saw the miracles performed for them, *they relied on HASHEM, the Holy One of Israel, in truth.*

17. {The Baal HaTurim's comment to אָז יָשִׁיר appears at *Exodus* 15:1.}

❑ **עֲלִי בְאֵר עֱנוּ לָהּ** — GO UP, O WELL, CALL OUT TO IT! When they returned from the war, they encamped at the well and recited a song of praise at a place of purity. This is also implied by the verse, בֵּין מַשְׁאַבִּים שָׁם יְתַנּוּ צִדְקוֹת ה׳, *between water holes, there they will recount the righteous deeds of HASHEM* (*Judges* 5:11).[116]

❑ **עֱנוּ** — CALL OUT. The masoretic note, ב׳, means that this word appears twice in the *Tanach:* (i) here, עֲלִי בְאֵר עֱנוּ לָהּ, *Go up, O well, call out to it;* and (ii) עֱנוּ לַה׳ בְּתוֹדָה, *Call out to HASHEM in thanksgiving* (*Psalms* 147:7). [The similarity of expression indicates] that at the well, they called out to God with thanksgiving and recited a song [of praise].

20. וּמִבָּמוֹת הַגַּיְא — AND FROM THE HEIGHTS TO THE VALLEY. This phrase may be interpreted as [a contraction of] בָּא מָוֶת[117] בַּגַּיְא, *Death came into the valley,*[118] as the verse states [regarding the death of Moses], וַיִּקְבֹּר אֹתוֹ בַגַּי, *He buried him in the valley* (*Deuteronomy* 34:6).[119]

116. See the Baal HaTurim to *Genesis* 16:7.

117. *Shoham Yakar's* manuscript edition reads: הַמָּוֶת, *the death.*

118. That is, it was decreed that Moses would die (*Rimzei Rabbeinu Yoel*).

119. *Tanchuma* 21 — Moses said, "Master of the Universe, after all the miracles that You performed for them, am I to die under their hands? וּמִמִּדְבָּר מַתָּנָה — From the wilderness You gave them the Torah. וּמִמַּתָּנָה נַחֲלִיאֵל — Through me it was bestowed upon them as a Godly heritage. וּמִנַּחֲלִיאֵל בָּמוֹת — Once they took it as a heritage, You decreed death upon me." וּמִבָּמוֹת הַגַּיְא אֲשֶׁר בִּשְׂדֵה מוֹאָב ... — This refers to Moses' burial place, as it is stated, *He buried him in the valley, in the land of Moab* (*Deuteronomy* 34:6).

כב לֵאמֹר: אֶעְבְּרָה בְאַרְצֶךָ לֹא נִטֶּה בְּשָׂדֶה וּבְכֶרֶם
לֹא נִשְׁתֶּה מֵי בְאֵר בְּדֶרֶךְ הַמֶּלֶךְ נֵלֵךְ עַד
כג אֲשֶׁר־נַעֲבֹר גְּבֻלֶךָ: וְלֹא־נָתַן סִיחֹן אֶת־יִשְׂרָאֵל
עֲבֹר בִּגְבֻלוֹ וַיֶּאֱסֹף סִיחֹן אֶת־כָּל־עַמּוֹ וַיֵּצֵא
לִקְרַאת יִשְׂרָאֵל הַמִּדְבָּרָה וַיָּבֹא יָהְצָה וַיִּלָּחֶם
כד בְּיִשְׂרָאֵל: וַיַּכֵּהוּ יִשְׂרָאֵל לְפִי־חָרֶב וַיִּירַשׁ אֶת־
אַרְצוֹ מֵאַרְנֹן עַד־יַבֹּק עַד־בְּנֵי עַמּוֹן כִּי עַז גְּבוּל
כה בְּנֵי עַמּוֹן: וַיִּקַּח יִשְׂרָאֵל אֵת כָּל־הֶעָרִים הָאֵלֶּה
וַיֵּשֶׁב יִשְׂרָאֵל בְּכָל־עָרֵי הָאֱמֹרִי בְּחֶשְׁבּוֹן וּבְכָל־
כו בְּנֹתֶיהָ: כִּי חֶשְׁבּוֹן עִיר סִיחֹן מֶלֶךְ הָאֱמֹרִי הִוא
וְהוּא נִלְחַם בְּמֶלֶךְ מוֹאָב הָרִאשׁוֹן וַיִּקַּח אֶת־כָּל־
כז אַרְצוֹ מִיָּדוֹ עַד־אַרְנֹן: עַל־כֵּן יֹאמְרוּ הַמֹּשְׁלִים
כח בֹּאוּ חֶשְׁבּוֹן תִּבָּנֶה וְתִכּוֹנֵן עִיר סִיחוֹן: כִּי־אֵשׁ
יָצְאָה מֵחֶשְׁבּוֹן לֶהָבָה מִקִּרְיַת סִיחֹן אָכְלָה עָר
כט מוֹאָב בַּעֲלֵי בָּמוֹת אַרְנֹן: אוֹי־לְךָ מוֹאָב אָבַדְתָּ
עַם־כְּמוֹשׁ נָתַן בָּנָיו פְּלֵיטִם וּבְנֹתָיו בַּשְּׁבִית לְמֶלֶךְ
ל אֱמֹרִי סִיחוֹן: וַנִּירָם אָבַד חֶשְׁבּוֹן עַד־דִּיבֹן וַנַּשִּׁים

בעל הטורים

(כב) אֶעְבְּרָה בְאַרְצֶךָ. וְלֹא אָמַר "נָא" כְּדֶרֶךְ שֶׁאָמַר בֶּאֱדוֹם, שֶׁלֹּא רָצָה לְפַיְּסוֹ כָּל כָּךְ. וְלֹא שָׁלַח לוֹ אֶלָּא כְּדֵי לִפְתֹּחַ לוֹ בְּשָׁלוֹם. וְעַל כֵּן לֹא הֵשִׁיב לוֹ תְשׁוּבָה כְּמוֹ שֶׁעָשָׂה מֶלֶךְ אֱדוֹם, אֶלָּא מִיָּד יָצָא לִקְרָאתוֹ לַמִּלְחָמָה:

(כז) עַל כֵּן יֹאמְרוּ הַמֹּשְׁלִים. בְּגִימַטְרִיָּא אֵלֶּה הֵמָּה הַמֹּשְׁלִים בְּיִצְרָם:

BAAL HATURIM ELUCIDATED

22. אֶעְבְּרָה בְאַרְצֶךָ — LET ME PASS THROUGH YOUR LAND. Here Moses did not say נָא, *please,* as he had said to Edom (20:17 above), for he was not that interested in placating Sihon. He sent the messengers merely as a gesture of peace.[120] Therefore, Sihon did not send Moses a response, as the king of Edom had, rather, he immediately set out to war against him.

❑ {The Baal HaTurim's other comment to אֶעְבְּרָה appears at 20:17 above.}

120. *Tanchuma* 22 — God had said to Moses, *"See! I have delivered into your hand Sihon king of Heshbon, the Amorite, and his land: Begin to drive* [*him*] *out, provoke war against him"* (*Deuteronomy* 2:24). Nevertheless, Moses took into consideration God's great love of peace, and so he first fulfilled the precept, *Turn from evil and do good; seek peace and pursue it* (*Psalms* 34:15), even though he knew that Sihon would refuse his peace overture.

saying, [22] *"Let me pass through your land; we shall not turn off to field or vineyard; we shall not drink well water; on the king's road shall we travel, until we pass through your border."*

[23] *But Sihon did not permit Israel to pass through his border, and Sihon assembled his entire people and went out against Israel to the wilderness. He arrived at Jahaz and waged war against Israel.* [24] *Israel smote him with the edge of the sword and took possession of his land, from Arnon to Jabbok to the children of Ammon — for the border of the children of Ammon was powerful.* [25] *Israel took all these cities, and Israel settled in all the Amorite cities, in Heshbon and all its suburbs.* [26] *For Heshbon — it was the city of Sihon, king of the Amorite; and he had warred against the first king of Moab and took all his land from his control, until Arnon.* [27] *Regarding this the proverbialists would say: Come to Heshbon — it will be built and established as the city of Sihon.* [28] *For a fire has come forth from Heshbon, a flame from the city of Sihon. It consumed Ar of Moab, the masters of Arnon's heights.* [29] *Woe to you, O Moab, you are lost, O people of Chemosh! He made his sons fugitives and his daughters captives of the king of the Amorite, Sihon.* [30] *Their sovereignty over Heshbon was lost, it was removed from Dibon, and we laid waste*

BAAL HATURIM ELUCIDATED

27. עַל כֵּן יֹאמְרוּ הַמֹּשְׁלִים — REGARDING THIS THE PROVERBIALISTS[121] WOULD SAY. The *gematria* of this phrase (852) is equivalent[122] to that of אֵלֶּה הֵמָּה הַמֹּשְׁלִים בְּיִצְרָם, *These are the people who rule*[121] *over their inclinations.*[123]

121. The term מוֹשֵׁל (plural, מוֹשְׁלִים) has two meanings: (i) *ruler* — e.g., *Genesis* 24:2; *Isaiah* 14:5; and (ii) *proverbialist* — e.g., *Ezekiel* 16:44 and 18:2. In the context of our passage הַמֹּשְׁלִים means *the proverbialists,* i.e., those who write proverbs, but in the homiletic interpretation of the Sages, it means *those who rule.*

122. The principle of *im hakollel* allows 852 to be considered equivalent to 853, the *gematria* of the Baal HaTurim's phrase.

123. *Bava Basra* 78b. The Talmud there explains our verse homiletically as a lesson in how to control one's desires and inclinations: עַל כֵּן יֹאמְרוּ הַמֹּשְׁלִים . . ., *Regarding this the "moshelim" would say . . .* — the *moshelim* are the ones who rule over their inclinations. They advise others, "בֹּאוּ חֶשְׁבּוֹן, *Come into 'cheshbon'* " — the term *cheshbon* means *accounting,* i.e., they say, "Come let us take an accounting of this world [by following the advice of the Mishnah (*Avos* 2:1)], weighing the present cost of a *mitzvah* against its future reward and the fleeting gain of a sin against its far greater loss in the future. If you make this accounting and act upon it, תִּבָּנֶה, *you will be built up* in this world, וְתִכּוֹנֵן, *and you will be established* in the World to Come. [Note that תִּבָּנֶה is used in both the second person masculine singular, *you will be built,* and the third person feminine singular, *she* (or, *it*) *will be built.* Similarly, וְתִכּוֹנֵן.]

כא/לא־כב/א

לא עַד־נֹ֫פַח *אֲשֶׁר֙ עַד־מֵֽידְבָֽא׃ וַיֵּ֙שֶׁב֙ יִשְׂרָאֵ֔ל בְּאֶ֖רֶץ
לב הָֽאֱמֹרִֽי׃ וַיִּשְׁלַ֤ח מֹשֶׁה֙ לְרַגֵּ֣ל אֶת־יַעְזֵ֔ר וַֽיִּלְכְּד֖וּ
לג בְּנֹתֶ֑יהָ °ויירש אֶת־הָֽאֱמֹרִ֖י אֲשֶׁר־שָֽׁם׃ וַיִּפְנוּ֙ וַֽיַּעֲל֔וּ
דֶּ֖רֶךְ הַבָּשָׁ֑ן וַיֵּצֵ֣א עוֹג֩ מֶֽלֶךְ־הַבָּשָׁ֨ן לִקְרָאתָ֜ם ה֧וּא
לד וְכָל־עַמּ֛וֹ לַמִּלְחָמָ֖ה אֶדְרֶֽעִי׃ וַיֹּ֨אמֶר יְהוָ֤ה אֶל־
מֹשֶׁה֙ אַל־תִּירָ֣א אֹת֔וֹ כִּ֣י בְיָדְךָ֞ נָתַ֧תִּי אֹת֛וֹ וְאֶת־
כָּל־עַמּ֖וֹ וְאֶת־אַרְצ֑וֹ וְעָשִׂ֣יתָ לּ֔וֹ כַּאֲשֶׁ֣ר עָשִׂ֔יתָ
לה לְסִיחֹן֙ מֶ֣לֶךְ הָֽאֱמֹרִ֔י אֲשֶׁ֥ר יוֹשֵׁ֖ב בְּחֶשְׁבּֽוֹן׃ וַיַּכּ֨וּ
אֹת֤וֹ וְאֶת־בָּנָיו֙ וְאֶת־כָּל־עַמּ֔וֹ עַד־בִּלְתִּ֥י הִשְׁאִֽיר־
כב א לֹ֖ו שָׂרִ֑יד וַיִּֽירְשׁ֖וּ אֶת־אַרְצֽוֹ׃ וַיִּסְע֖וּ בְּנֵ֣י יִשְׂרָאֵ֑ל
וַֽיַּחֲנוּ֙ בְּעַֽרְב֣וֹת מוֹאָ֔ב מֵעֵ֖בֶר לְיַרְדֵּ֥ן יְרֵחֽוֹ׃ ססס

*נָקוּד עַל ר׳

[°וַיּוֹרֶשׁ ק׳]

מפטיר

פ״ז פסוקים. למידב״א סימן. ימוא״ל סימן. עז״י סימן.

בעל הטורים

(ל) אֲשֶׁר עַד מֵידְבָא. רֵי״שׁ נְקוּדָה, וְנִשְׁאַר ״אֵשׁ״ — כִּי שְׂרָפָה בָּאֵשׁ, וְנִטַּל רֹאשׁ שֶׁלָּהּ:
(לב) וַיּוֹרֶשׁ. כְּתִיב וַיִּירַשׁ, שֶׁלֹּא הֻצְרְכוּ לְהוֹרִישָׁם, אֶלָּא בָּרְחוּ מֵעַצְמָם:

BAAL HATURIM ELUCIDATED

30. אֲשֶׁר עַד מֵידְבָא — WHICH REACHES UNTIL MEDEBA. [According to a masoretic tradition] there is a dot over the ר of אֲשֶׁר, leaving the word אֵשׁ, *fire.*[124] This alludes to the fact that it was burnt in fire and its head[125] was taken from it.[126]

124. Although נְקֻדּוֹת, *vowel signs,* are never written in a Torah scroll, the Massorah teaches that dots are inscribed above certain letters and words. One such dot appears above the ר of אֲשֶׁר in our verse (see illustration). Usually, the dot is taken as an indication that the word may also be interpreted as if that letter were not there (see the Baal HaTurim to 9:10 above, with note 43). Thus, the word אֲשֶׁר may be understood as אֵשׁ, *fire.* The verse can then be explained, *and we laid waste to Nophah,* אֵשׁ, *with fire,* until Medeba.

ונירם אבד חשבון עד דיבן ונשים
עד נפח אשר עד מידבא וישב
ישראל בארץ האמרי וישלח

125. The word אֲשֶׁר alludes to sovereignty, for its letters can be rearranged to spell ראש, *head* or *chief* (see the Baal HaTurim to 14:4 above, with note 46). Since the dotted ר is considered as if it were removed, it intimates that the city's ראש was lost to the אֵשׁ (*Shoham Yakar*).

Alternatively: The name of the letter ר is spelled רֵישׁ, which is the Aramaic equivalent of ראש, *head* or *chief* (see 1:4 above with *Targum Onkelos*). Thus, the dot implies that they lost their ר, that is, their role as chief among the nations (see *Rashi* to 22:2 below) when their city was burned in אֵשׁ, *fire* (*VeChur LaZahav*).

126. *Peirush HaRokeach.*

to Nophah, which reaches until Medeba.
[31] Israel settled in the land of the Amorite. [32] Moses sent
[spies] to spy out Jazer and they conquered its suburbs;
and he drove out the Amorite who was there. [33] They turned
and ascended by way of Bashan; Og, king of Bashan, went
out against them, he and his entire people, to do battle at
Edrei. [34] HASHEM said to Moses, "Do not fear him, for into
your hand have I given him, his entire people and his land;
you shall do to him as you did to Sihon, king of the Amorite,
who dwells in Heshbon." [35] They smote him, his sons and
all his people, until there was no survivor left of him, and
they took possession of his land.

22 [1] The Children of Israel journeyed and encamped in the plains of Moab, on the bank of the Jordan, opposite Jericho.

BAAL HATURIM ELUCIDATED

32. וַיּוֹרֶשׁ — AND HE DROVE OUT. [Although this word is pronounced וַיּוֹרֶשׁ, according to the masoretic tradition] it is spelled ויירש [in the Torah scroll].[127] This indicates that they did not have to drive out the Amorites; rather, they fled on their own[128] initiative.[129]

127. This is an example of a קְרִי וּכְתִיב, *keri uchesiv*. The *kesiv* (spelling) of the word is וַיִּירַשׁ, *he took possession,* while the *keri* (pronunciation) is וַיּוֹרֶשׁ, *he drove out.*

128. The *keri* indicates that Moses' intention was to send spies to scout for ways to drive the Amorites out of Jazer. The *kesiv* teaches that this was an unnecessary step, for when the Amorites in Jazer heard that Israel was coming, they fled on their own. Therefore all that was left for Israel to do was to take possession.

129. *Peirush HaRokeach.* This comment seems to contradict the Midrash which states: These spies sent by Moses were alacritous. They said to themselves, "We take assurance in Moses' blessing. We are aware that Moses has sent out spies in the past, and those spies brought misfortune. We shall not do the same. Rather, we have faith in God and we shall enter into battle." They did so and killed *the Amorite who was there . . .* (*Tanchuma* 24; cited by *Rashi*). How then can the Baal HaTurim state that the Amorites ran away on their own accord? The verse does not say that the spies conquered Jazer; it says that they conquered its suburbs. The Midrash explains that they accomplished this by killing *the Amorite who was there* in those suburbs. But they did not have to kill any of the residents of Jazer, for when they heard that the suburbs had been conquered they fled the city on their own initiative (*VeChur LaZahav*).

פרשת בלק
Parashas Balak

ב וַיַּרְא בָּלָק בֶּן־צִפּוֹר אֵת כָּל־אֲשֶׁר־עָשָׂה יִשְׂרָאֵל
ג לָאֱמֹרִי: וַיָּגָר מוֹאָב מִפְּנֵי הָעָם מְאֹד כִּי רַב־

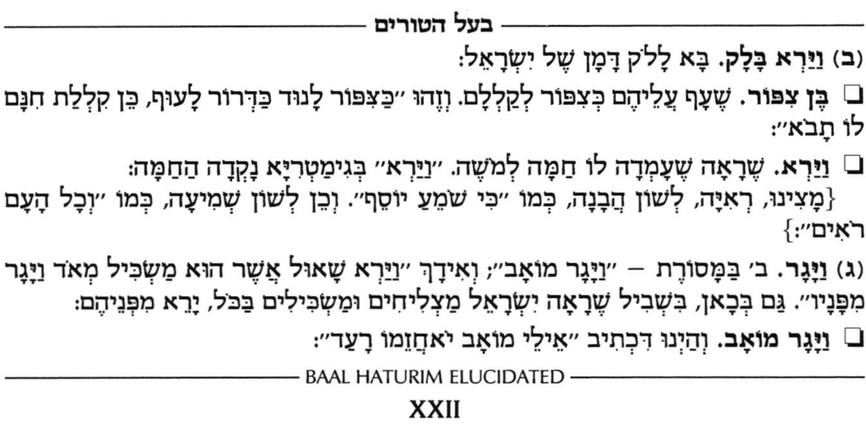

בעל הטורים

(ב) וַיַּרְא בָּלָק. בָּא לָלֹק דָּמָן שֶׁל יִשְׂרָאֵל:

❑ **בֶּן צִפּוֹר.** שֶׁעָף עֲלֵיהֶם כְּצִפּוֹר לְקַלְּלָם. וְזֶהוּ "כַּצִּפּוֹר לָנוּד כַּדְּרוֹר לָעוּף, כֵּן קִלְלַת חִנָּם לוֹ תָבֹא":

❑ **וַיַּרְא.** שֶׁרָאָה שֶׁעָמְדָה לוֹ חַמָּה לְמֹשֶׁה. "וַיַּרְא" בְּגִימַטְרִיָּא נָקְדָה הַחַמָּה:
{מָצִינוּ, רְאִיָּה, לְשׁוֹן הֲבָנָה, כְּמוֹ "כִּי שֹׁמֵעַ יוֹסֵף". וְכֵן לְשׁוֹן שְׁמִיעָה, כְּמוֹ "וְכָל הָעָם רֹאִים":}

(ג) וַיָּגָר. ב׳ בַּמָּסוֹרֶת — "וַיָּגָר מוֹאָב"; וְאִידָךְ "וַיַּרְא שָׁאוּל אֲשֶׁר הוּא מַשְׂכִּיל מְאֹד וַיָּגָר מִפָּנָיו". גַּם בְּכָאן, בִּשְׁבִיל שֶׁרָאָה יִשְׂרָאֵל מַצְלִיחִים וּמַשְׂכִּילִים בַּכֹּל, יָרֵא מִפְּנֵיהֶם:

❑ **וַיָּגָר מוֹאָב.** וְהַיְנוּ דִּכְתִיב "אֵילֵי מוֹאָב יֹאחֲזֵמוֹ רָעַד":

BAAL HATURIM ELUCIDATED

XXII

2. וַיַּרְא בָּלָק — BALAK . . . SAW. The name בָּלָק implies[1] בָּא לָלֹק, *he came to lap up*[2] the blood of the Israelites.[3]

❑ **בֶּן צִפּוֹר — SON OF ZIPPOR.** The name צִפּוֹר, literally, *a bird,* implies that Balak swooped down upon them like a bird to curse them.[4] This is the implication of the verse, כַּצִּפּוֹר לָנוּד כַּדְּרוֹר לָעוּף[5] כֵּן קִלְלַת חִנָּם לוֹ תָבֹא[6], *As a bird to be wandering, as a wild bird to be flying* [*back to its nest*], *so will an unwarranted curse come* [*back*] *to him* (*Proverbs* 26:2).[6a]

1. Throughout the Torah we find that a name is not merely an identification tag; rather, it is a description of the nature and role of the person or object that it names [see, e.g., how the Torah explains the name given to each of Jacob's children (*Genesis* 29:32—30:24)]. Thus, various Midrashim expound on the names of Scriptural characters, equating their personalities or deeds with those particular names. Here, the Baal HaTurim explains the aptness of Balak's name.

Alternatively: Why must the Torah identify Balak as the son of Zippor? Nowhere else in *Tanach* do we find anyone named Balak, and we know nothing about Zippor, except that he was Balak's father! Accordingly, בֶּן צִפּוֹר, *son of Zippor,* must be a description of Balak; and if that name begs exposition (see the Baal HaTurim's next comment), then his own name does, too (*VeChur LaZahav*).

2. לֹק is a *makor* (gerundive) form of the verb root לקק, *to lap up* or *to lick* (see, e.g., *I Kings* 21:19). Thus, בָּא לָלֹק means, *he came with the intention of lapping up.* An alternative analysis of the name Balak explains it as בָּא לָק, *He came; he smote,* using לָק, a shortened variant of לָקָה, of the root לקה, *to smite* or *to beat* (*Zohar III,* 199b).

3. *Pesikta Zutresa* [*Midrash Lekach Tov*]; see also *Tanchuma, Ki Seitzei* 9, where the name עֲמָלֵק is similarly explained as עַם שֶׁבָּא לָלֹק, *a nation that came to lap up,* the blood of the Israelites.

4. *Peirush HaRokeach.*

5. The text follows *Rimzei Rabbeinu Yoel* and that is how it appears in *Shoham Yakar's* manuscript edition. The early printed editions, as well as many later ones, mistakenly begin the verse with, כְּצִפּוֹר נוֹדֶדֶת מִן קִנָּהּ, *As a bird wandering from its nest,* a fragment of *Proverbs* 27:8 which ends, כֵּן אִישׁ נוֹדֵד מִמְּקוֹמוֹ, *so is a man who wanders from his place.*

6. This verse contains a קְרִי וּכְתִיב, *keri uchesiv,* i.e., a word spelled one way in the *Tanach,* but pronounced differently or, as in this case, understood differently. The *kesiv* (spelling) is לֹא תָבֹא, *it will not come,* but the *keri* (reading) is לוֹ תָבֹא, *it will come* [*back*] *to him.* The Baal HaTurim's allusion utilizes the *keri* rather than the *kesiv.*

6a. *Metzudos David* paraphrases that verse: Just as a bird flies from its nest to navigate the heavens, then returns to its nest, so does an

2 Balak son of Zippor saw all that Israel had done to the Amorite. 3 Moab was very intimidated by the nation, for

BAAL HATURIM ELUCIDATED

❑ **וַיַּרְא** — [BALAK. . .] SAW. He saw[7] that the sun stood still for Moses [in the war against Sihon].[8] [This is alluded to by the fact that] the *gematria* of וַיַּרְא (217) is equal to that of נָקְדָה הַחַמָּה, *The sun stood in place.*[9]

{[Alternatively:] We find the root ראה, *to see,* used in the sense of understanding,[9a] [just as the root שמע, *to hear,* is used in the sense of understanding][9b] e.g., in the verse, כִּי שֹׁמֵעַ יוֹסֵף, *that Joseph understood* (*Genesis* 42:23).[10] Additionally, it can be interpreted as hearing, e.g., in the verse, וְכָל הָעָם רֹאִים [אֶת הַקּוֹלֹת], *The entire people saw* [*the noises*] (*Exodus* 20:15).[11]}[12]

3. וַיָּגָר — [MOAB] WAS INTIMIDATED. The masoretic note, ב׳, means that this word appears twice in the *Tanach*: (i) here, וַיָּגָר מוֹאָב, *Moab was intimidated;* and (ii) וַיַּרְא שָׁאוּל אֲשֶׁר הוּא מַשְׂכִּיל מְאֹד וַיָּגָר מִפָּנָיו, *Saul saw that he* [*David*] *was very successful, and he was intimidated by him* (*I Samuel* 18:15). [Just as Saul was intimidated by David's success,] so, too, here, because [Moab] saw Israel succeeding in all matters, they cringed before them.

❑ **וַיָּגָר מוֹאָב** — MOAB WAS INTIMIDATED. Thus it is written, אֵילֵי מוֹאָב יֹאחֲזֵמוֹ רָעַד, *trembling will grip the powers of Moab* (*Exodus* 15:15).[13]

---

unwarranted curse return to the curser himself — it went forth from his lips and it will come [back] into his innards.

7. The verse tells us that Balak saw what Israel had done to the Amorite. But Balak was in Moab, too far from the scene to have witnessed the war against Sihon and his nation! Therefore, the Baal HaTurim offers two interpretations of the word וַיַּרְא, *he saw* (*Atros Addar*).

8. *Avodah Zarah* 25a — Just as the sun stood still for Joshua (see *Joshua* 10:13), so did it stand still for Moses [in the war against Sihon (*Rashi*)]. Our verse tells us that Balak was frightened when he saw the sun standing still, for when the sun stood still for Moses and for Joshua, it was not just an illusion perceived by those who were in the vicinity of the respective battle. Rather, the heavenly bodies ceased their motions, and that phenomenon could be seen throughout the world.

9. The text, ״וַיַּרְא״ בְּגִימַטְרִיָּא נָקְדָה הַחַמָּה, *the gematria of* וַיַּרְא (217) *is equal to that of* נָקְדָה הַחַמָּה [literally, *the sun had pierced* (*the heavens*), see *Gittin* 56a], follows *Shoham Yakar's* manuscript edition and *Peirush HaRokeach.* The early printed editions, as well as many later ones, read, ״וַיַּרְא״ שֶׁנִּתְקַדְּרָה חַמָּה, which can mean either, *He saw that the sun had pierced,* or *he saw that the sun had darkened;* they make no mention of *gematria.* That reading is difficult because it is merely a restatement of the Baal HaTurim's first sentence.

9a. *R' Chaim Paltiel,* who adduces *Ecclesiastes* 1:16.

9b. See note 12 below.

10. See *Rashi* to *Genesis* 41:15.

11. In *Peirush HaTur HaAroch* to that verse, the Baal HaTurim explains that, in the realm of *peshat* (the simple meaning of Scripture), we find the root ראה, *to see,* used in place of the root שמע, *to hear,* as in the verse, וַיַּרְא יַעֲקֹב כִּי יֶשׁ שֶׁבֶר בְּמִצְרָיִם, *Jacob* [who was in Canaan] *saw that there were provisions in Egypt* (*Genesis* 42:1).

By expanding on the root ראה in light of the root שמע, the Baal HaTurim teaches that the same verbs that describe the functions of the senses on a physical level also describe those senses on an intellectual level (Y.S.).

12. *R' Chaim Paltiel.* The passage enclosed in braces appears in the early printed editions, but not in the manuscripts used by *Shoham Yakar.* Without the bracketed interpolation, this comment is hardly understandable, consequently, various emendations have been made in the later printed editions, many of which interchange the adduced verses: מָצִינוּ רְאִיָּה לְשׁוֹן הֲבָנָה, כְּמוֹ ״וְכָל הָעָם רֹאִים״. וְכֵן לָשׁוֹן שְׁמִיעָה, כְּמוֹ ״כִּי שֹׁמֵעַ יוֹסֵף״.

13. *Peirush HaRokeach.* That verse reads in full: *Then the chieftains of Edom were confounded;*

ד הָוּא וַיָּקָץ מוֹאָב מִפְּנֵי בְּנֵי יִשְׂרָאֵל: וַיֹּאמֶר מוֹאָב
אֶל־זִקְנֵי מִדְיָן עַתָּה יְלַחֲכוּ הַקָּהָל אֶת־כָּל־סְבִיבֹתֵינוּ
כִּלְחֹךְ הַשּׁוֹר אֵת יֶרֶק הַשָּׂדֶה וּבָלָק בֶּן־צִפּוֹר מֶלֶךְ
ה לְמוֹאָב בָּעֵת הַהִוא: וַיִּשְׁלַח מַלְאָכִים אֶל־בִּלְעָם
בֶּן־בְּעוֹר פְּתוֹרָה אֲשֶׁר עַל־הַנָּהָר אֶרֶץ בְּנֵי־עַמּוֹ
לִקְרֹא־לוֹ לֵאמֹר הִנֵּה עַם יָצָא מִמִּצְרַיִם הִנֵּה כִסָּה
ו אֶת־עֵין הָאָרֶץ וְהוּא יֹשֵׁב מִמֻּלִי: וְעַתָּה לְכָה־נָּא

בעל הטורים

(ד) יְלַחֲכוּ. ב׳ בַּמָּסוֹרֶת — ״עַתָּה יְלַחֲכוּ הַקָּהָל״; ״יְלַחֲכוּ עָפָר כַּנָּחָשׁ״ בִּתְרֵי עָשָׂר, בְּפָרָשַׁת ״רְעֵה עַמְּךָ בְשִׁבְטֶךָ״ שֶׁמְּדַבֵּר בְּעִנְיַן הַגְּאֻלָּה. וְהַיְנוּ דִּכְתִיב ״כַּאֲשֶׁר שֵׁמַע לְמִצְרָיִם יָחִילוּ כְּשֵׁמַע צֹר״, לוֹמַר, כַּאֲשֶׁר נָפַל פַּחְדָּם עַל כָּל הָאֻמּוֹת כֵּן יִהְיֶה לֶעָתִיד:

(ה) אֶל בִּלְעָם בֶּן בְּעוֹר פְּתוֹרָה. בְּגִימַטְרִיָּא ״זֶהוּ פּוֹתֵר חֲלוֹמוֹת״:

❑ **הִנֵּה עַם יָצָא.** ״הִנֵּה״ עוֹלֶה שִׁשִּׁים. לוֹמַר, שִׁשִּׁים רִבּוֹאוֹת יָצָא:

❑ **יֹשֵׁב מִמֻּלִי.** שֶׁיּוֹשֵׁב כְּנֶגְדִּי וְרוֹאֶה אוֹתִי. וַאֲנִי אֵינִי יָכוֹל לִרְאוֹתוֹ מִפְּנֵי הָעֲנָנִים שֶׁמַּקִּיפִים אוֹתוֹ:

(ו) לְכָה נָא. בְּהֵ״א — כִּי אַרְבָּעָה דְגָלִים הֵם, וְעֵרֶב רַב יוֹצֵא אַחֲרֵיהֶם זָנָב:

BAAL HATURIM ELUCIDATED

4. יְלַחֲכוּ — [THEY] WILL LICK UP. The masoretic note, ב׳, means that this word appears twice in the *Tanach*: (i) here, עַתָּה יְלַחֲכוּ הַקָּהָל, *Now the congregation will lick up;* and (ii) יְלַחֲכוּ עָפָר כַּנָּחָשׁ, *They will lick dirt like the snake* (*Micah* 7:17), in the *Twelve Prophets,* in the passage beginning רְעֵה עַמְּךָ בְשִׁבְטֶךָ, *Shepherd Your people with Your staff* (v. 14), which discusses the future Redemption of Israel. This is in accord with the verse, כַּאֲשֶׁר שֵׁמַע לְמִצְרָיִם יָחִילוּ כְּשֵׁמַע צֹר, *Just as* [*they did*] *at the tidings of Egypt, so will they tremble at the tidings of Tyre*[14] (*Isaiah* 23:5). This indicates that just as awe [of Israel] fell upon all the nations [then], so will it be in the future.

5. אֶל בִּלְעָם בֶּן בְּעוֹר פְּתוֹרָה — TO BALAAM SON OF BEOR TO PETHOR. The *gematria* of this phrase (1194) is equal to that of, זֶהוּ פּוֹתֵר חֲלוֹמוֹת, *This* [*refers to*] *an interpreter of dreams.*[15]

---

trembling gripped [literally, *will grip*] *the powers of Moab; all the dwellers of Canaan dissolved.* Regarding Edom and Canaan, the verse speaks in the past tense; but with regard to Moab, it uses the future. The Baal HaTurim sees this as an allusion to a future fear that would engulf Moab some forty years later, as described in our verse (*Atros Addar*).

14. Tyre in that verse does not refer to the city of that name; rather, it is a metaphor for Edom and for Israel's millennia-long exile under its hand (*Mahari Kara*). *Rashi* to that verse draws a parallel between the ten plagues visited upon Egypt and the plagues prophesied to be visited upon Tyre at the time of the ultimate Redemption.

15. *Peirush HaRokeach.* The translation of פְּתוֹרָה as a place name follows *Targum Onkelos,* who renders it לִפְתוֹר, *to Pethor.* According to *Targum Yonasan ben Uzziel,* Balaam's city was named after the profession of its favorite son, for that

it was numerous, and Moab was disgusted because of the Children of Israel. [4] *Moab said to the elders of Midian, "Now the congregation will lick up our entire surroundings, as an ox licks up the greenery of the field." Balak son of Zippor was king of Moab at that time.*

[5] *He sent messengers to Balaam son of Beor to Pethor, which is by the River of the land of the members of his people, to summon him, saying, "Behold! a people has come out of Egypt, behold! it has covered the surface of the earth and it sits opposite me.* [6] *So now — please come*

BAAL HATURIM ELUCIDATED

❑ הִנֵּה עַם יָצָא — **BEHOLD! A PEOPLE HAS COME OUT [OF EGYPT].** The *gematria* of הִנֵּה, *Behold,* is 60. This is an allusion to the sixty myriads who came out of Egypt.[16]

❑ יֹשֵׁב מִמֻּלִי — **[IT] SITS OPPOSITE ME.** That nation sits opposite me and sees me, but I cannot see it because of the clouds that surround it.[17]

6. לְכָה נָא — **PLEASE COME.** [The word לְכָה is spelled[18]] with a ה (= 5). [This is an allusion to the nation that Balak wanted Balaam to curse.] For there are four[18a] tribal divisions (see Ch. 2 above), plus [a fifth,] the mixed multitude that protruded behind them like a tail.[19]

Targum's Aramaic paraphrase of פְּתוֹרָה reads, וּבֵית מוֹתְבֵהּ בְּפַדַּן הִיא פְתוֹר עַל שְׁמֵהּ פָּתִיר חֶלְמַיָּא, *And the house of his residence was in Padan which was* [*called*] *Pethor in his honor* [*for he was*] *an interpreter of dreams.*

16. *Peirush HaRokeach.* Sixty myriad equals 600,000, and that is the number of adult Israelite men who left Egypt (see *Exodus* 12:37). Thus, the phrase הִנֵּה עַם יָצָא can be understood as, הִנֵּה עַם, *a people of sixty* [*myriads*], יָצָא, *has come out.*

17. The connection between the Baal HaTurim's rubric, יֹשֵׁב מִמֻּלִי, and his comment seems tenuous at best. It is difficult to see how that phrase implies that Israel could see him but he could not see them. In *Pesikta Zutresa* [*Midrash Lekach Tov*], presumably the Baal HaTurim's source, this comment appears under a different rubric. That work first explains the preceding phrase, הִנֵּה כִסָּה אֶת עֵין הָאָרֶץ, *it has covered the surface* [literally, *the eye*] *of the earth.* Then it states: וְהוּא יֹשֵׁב מִמֻּלִי means מִמֻּל הָרוֹאֶה, *opposite the viewer.* דָּבָר אַחֵר, *Alternatively,* הִנֵּה כִסָּה אֶת עֵין הָאָרֶץ, *it has covered the eye* [*of the inhabitants*] *of the land . . .* הוּא רוֹאֶה אוֹתִי, *it sees me,* וַאֲנִי אֵינִי יָכוֹל לִרְאוֹת אוֹתוֹ, *but I am unable to see it,* מִפְּנֵי הָעֲנָנִים שֶׁמַּקִּיפִין אוֹתוֹ, *because of the clouds that surround it.*

It is possible that the Baal HaTurim's original comment was longer, like the comment of *Pesikta Zutresa* [*Midrash Lekach Tov*], but an early copyist inadvertently omitted some words. Alternatively, the original rubric may have read, הִנֵּה כִסָּה אֶת עֵין הָאָרֶץ וְהוּא יֹשֵׁב מִמֻּלִי, which a copyist shortened to just the last two words (*VeChur LaZahav*).

18. In the simple imperative, the masculine singular form of הלך, *to go* or *to come,* is usually given as לֵךְ [or, when hyphenated, לֶךְ] and that form appears 107 times in *Tanach.* The variant form לְכָה [or לְךָ] appears another 33 times. It is noteworthy that the term appears ten times in our passage: When the speaker is either God (22:20) or an angel (22:35), the form לֵךְ is used; when the speaker is either Balak (22:6,17; 23:13,27) or Balaam (22:11; 23:7 twice; 24:14), the variant לְכָה [in 23:13 spelled לְךָ] is used (*VeChur LaZahav*).

18a. The reading אַרְבָּעָה, *four,* follows *Shoham Yakar's* manuscript edition and *Peirush HaRokeach,* the Baal HaTurim's apparent source. The early printed editions, followed by many later editions, read ה׳, *five.*

19. *Peirush HaRokeach,* who adds, "Two opposite

כב/ו אָרָה־לִּי אֶת־הָעָם הַזֶּה כִּי־עָצוּם הוּא מִמֶּנִּי
אוּלַי אוּכַל נַכֶּה־בּוֹ וַאֲגָרְשֶׁנּוּ מִן־הָאָרֶץ כִּי
יָדַעְתִּי אֵת אֲשֶׁר־תְּבָרֵךְ מְבֹרָךְ וַאֲשֶׁר תָּאֹר יוּאָר:

בעל הטורים

❑ **אָרָה לִּי.** פִּיו הִכְשִׁילוֹ, שֶׁלְּבַסּוֹף קִלֵּל אוֹתוֹ:

❑ **מְבֹרָךְ.** ג׳ בַּמָּסוֹרֶת – ״אֲשֶׁר תְּבָרֵךְ מְבֹרָךְ״; ״יְהִי שֵׁם ה׳ מְבֹרָךְ״; וְאִידָךְ דְּאִיּוֹב ״יְהִי שֵׁם ה׳ מְבֹרָךְ״. מְלַמֵּד שֶׁהָיָה יוֹדֵעַ לְכַוֵּן הַשָּׁעָה שֶׁהַקָּדוֹשׁ בָּרוּךְ הוּא כּוֹעֵס בָּהּ. וְהָיָה מְקַלֵּל וּמְבָרֵךְ בַּה׳, וְזֶהוּ ״יְהִי שֵׁם ה׳ מְבֹרָךְ״:

❑ **תָּאֹר.** ג׳ בַּמָּסוֹרֶת – ״וַאֲשֶׁר תָּאֹר״; ״לֹא תָאֹר אֶת הָעָם״; ״וְנָשִׂיא בְעַמְּךָ לֹא תָאֹר״ –

BAAL HATURIM ELUCIDATED

❑ **אָרָה לִּי — CURSE . . . FOR ME.**[20] Balak's mouth tripped him up,[20a] for, in the end, Balaam cursed him.[21]

❑ **מְבֹרָךְ — IS BLESSED.** The masoretic note, ג׳, means that this word appears three times in the *Tanach*: (i) here, אֲשֶׁר תְּבָרֵךְ מְבֹרָךְ, *that whomever you will bless is blessed;* (ii) יְהִי שֵׁם ה׳ מְבֹרָךְ, *Blessed be the Name of HASHEM* (*Psalms* 113:2); and (iii) again in *Job* (1:21), יְהִי שֵׁם ה׳ מְבֹרָךְ, *Blessed be the Name of HASHEM.* This teaches that Balaam was able to focus precisely on the moment when God would become angry.[22] Then he would curse or bless by [the Name of] God. This is the connection to the verse: *Blessed be the Name of HASHEM.*[23]

---

two and [another] one protruding like a tail." That phrase is borrowed from the Mishnah (*Kilayim* 4:6) that discusses the configuration in which five vines constitute a vineyard [see illustration]. Why did *Peirush HaRokeach* find it necessary to add this phrase?

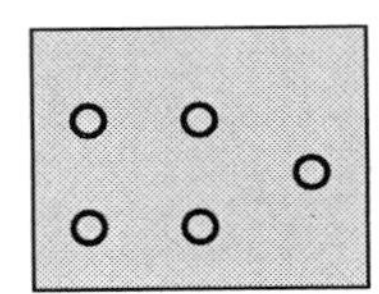

Two vines opposite two vines and another one protruding like a tail (*Mishnah, Kilayim* 4:6).

The Talmud records a dispute regarding the travel formation used by the Israelites. One opinion holds that they traveled like a box, i.e., they would travel in the same four-sided formation, in which they would encamp. The other opinion states that they traveled like a beam, i.e., the tribes following one another in a single line (*Yerushalmi, Eruvin* 5:1, cited by *Rashi* to *Numbers* 10:25). Now, according to the view that the Israelites traveled in a single line, the mixed multitude did not "protrude like a tail," they were merely at the tail end of the line. Therefore, the allusion of לְכָה is in accordance with the view that the nation traveled in a square formation (*Atros Addar*). To emphasize this, *Peirush HaRokeach* added, "Two opposite two and [another] one protruding like a tail" (*VeChur LaZahav*).

20. When taken by itself, the phrase אָרָה לִּי can mean either *utter a curse on my behalf* or *utter a curse against me* (see *Rashi* to *I Samuel* 3:13, s.v., כי מקללים להם).

20a. *Pesikta Zutresa* [*Midrash Lekach Tov*].

21. *Peirush HaRokeach.* See 24:9,17 below.

22. See *Berachos* 7a where the Talmud derives this from the verse וְיֹדֵעַ דַּעַת עֶלְיוֹן, *and he knows the mind of the Supreme One* (24:16 below, see *Rashi* there).

23. The Baal HaTurim's intent is unclear. For one, his words imply that Balaam would not recite blessings or curses except at the time of

and curse this people for me, for it is too powerful for me; perhaps I will be able to strike it and drive it away from the land. For I know that whomever you will bless is blessed and whomever you will curse will be cursed."

BAAL HATURIM ELUCIDATED

❑ תָּאֹר — YOU WILL CURSE.[24] The masoretic note, ג׳, means that this word appears three times in the *Tanach*: (i) here, וַאֲשֶׁר תָּאֹר, *and whomever you will curse;* (ii) לֹא תָאֹר אֶת הָעָם, *you shall not curse the people* (v. 12 below); and (iii) וְנָשִׂיא בְעַמְּךָ לֹא תָאֹר, *And you shall not curse a leader among your people* (*Exodus* 22:27), which, the Talmudic Sages explain in tractate *Sanhedrin,*[25]

Divine wrath; but the Talmudic source (see note 22) makes no mention of Balaam's blessings, only his curses! Additionally, all the verses adduced in this comment speak of blessing, not curse, yet the Baal HaTurim relates them to both blessing and curse!

Perhaps the following two prefaces — one Scriptural, one Talmudic — will lead to an understanding of the comment. Verbs of the root ברך appear more than 260 times in the *Tanach.* The vast majority of those verbs refer to *blessing.* Four of them (*Genesis* 24:11; *Psalms* 95:6; *Daniel* 6:11; and *II Chronicles* 6:13) refer to *kneeling* (from בֶּרֶךְ, *knee*). In at least seven other verses (*I Kings* 21:10,13; *Psalms* 10:3; *Job* 1:5,11 and 2:5,9) the root is used euphemistically with regard to cursing. Accordingly, it is possible to interpret the word מְבֹרָךְ (in *Job* 1:21) in a euphemistic sense — cursed, not blessed — even though that is not its contextual meaning. If so, we may interpret the word מְבֹרָךְ in *Psalms* 113:2 (where it is part of the joyous Hallel prayer) in its literal meaning, *blessed,* and the same word in *Job* in an opposite manner. Thus, the Baal HaTurim adduces identical phrases for both curse and blessing.

The Talmud states: From the blessing of the righteous, you may deduce a curse for the wicked; and from the curse of the wicked, you may deduce a blessing for the righteous (*Yoma* 38b). This means that the righteous and the wicked are inversely related. When one succeeds, the other fails. Thus, when blessings are showered upon the righteous, curses befall the wicked. Conversely, when adversity strikes the wicked, the righteous meet with blessing (*Maharal* of Prague, *Nesivos Olam, Nesiv HaTzedek,* Ch. 2). We may carry this logic one step further: When one pronounces a blessing upon the wicked, he is casting a curse on the righteous. And that was how Balaam operated. He would curse his intended victim in one of two ways. He would either curse the intended party, or bless that party's adversary. Nevertheless, whichever method he would choose at any particular time, his words would be effective only at the instant of Divine wrath (*VeChur LaZahav*).

24. The order in which the next four comments appear — (1) תָּאֹר, *You will curse,* from verse 6; (2) וַאֲשֶׁר תָּאֹר יוּאָר, *And whomever you will curse is cursed,* also from verse 6; (3) לֹא תָאֹר אֶת הָעָם, *You shall not curse the people,* from verse 12; and (4) מֵאֵן, *He has refused,* from verse 13 — follows the order of the verses and that is the order used by *Shoham Yakar* and many other editions. However, the early printed editions (as well as some later ones) present these comments in a variety of orders, some logical, some illogical. Thus, for example, the Constantinople and Venice editions place מֵאֵן from verse 13 between the two comments to verse 6, while the Fürth edition and the Netter *Chumash* have מֵאֵן before comment to verse 12. The Kamarna *Chumash* also follows the order of the verses, but sets the comment תָּאֹר after וַאֲשֶׁר תָּאֹר יוּאָר. According to that arrangement, it is possible that the comment beginning תאר is not on the word תָּאֹר of verse 6, but on the word תָּאֹר of verse 12 (*VeChur LaZahav*).

25. *Sanhedrin* 66a.

ז וַיֵּלְכוּ זִקְנֵי מוֹאָב וְזִקְנֵי מִדְיָן וּקְסָמִים בְּיָדָם וַיָּבֹאוּ
ח אֶל־בִּלְעָם וַיְדַבְּרוּ אֵלָיו דִּבְרֵי בָלָק׃ וַיֹּאמֶר אֲלֵיהֶם
לִינוּ פֹה הַלַּיְלָה וַהֲשִׁבֹתִי אֶתְכֶם דָּבָר כַּאֲשֶׁר יְדַבֵּר
ט יהוה אֵלָי וַיֵּשְׁבוּ שָׂרֵי־מוֹאָב עִם־בִּלְעָם׃ וַיָּבֹא
אֱלֹהִים אֶל־בִּלְעָם וַיֹּאמֶר מִי הָאֲנָשִׁים הָאֵלֶּה עִמָּךְ׃
י וַיֹּאמֶר בִּלְעָם אֶל־הָאֱלֹהִים בָּלָק בֶּן־צִפֹּר מֶלֶךְ
יא מוֹאָב שָׁלַח אֵלָי׃ הִנֵּה הָעָם הַיֹּצֵא מִמִּצְרַיִם וַיְכַס
אֶת־עֵין הָאָרֶץ עַתָּה לְכָה קָבָה־לִּי אֹתוֹ אוּלַי אוּכַל
יב לְהִלָּחֶם בּוֹ וְגֵרַשְׁתִּיו׃ וַיֹּאמֶר אֱלֹהִים אֶל־בִּלְעָם
לֹא תֵלֵךְ עִמָּהֶם לֹא תָאֹר אֶת־הָעָם כִּי בָרוּךְ הוּא׃

בעל הטורים

וְדָרְשִׁינַן מִנֵּהּ בְּסַנְהֶדְרִין, הוּא הַדִּין לְכָל אָדָם. עַל כֵּן "לֹא תָאֹר", שֶׁאָסוּר לְקַלֵּל לְכָל אָדָם:

☐ **וַאֲשֶׁר תָּאֹר יוּאָר.** בְּגִימַטְרִיָּא שֶׁקִּלַּלְתָּ אֶת מוֹאָב:

(יב) לֹא תָאֹר אֶת הָעָם. בִּלְעָם אָמַר "קָבָה לִּי", וְהַקָּדוֹשׁ בָּרוּךְ הוּא הֱשִׁיבוֹ "לֹא תָאֹר", אֲפִילוּ חֶסְרוֹן כָּל דְּהוּ:

BAAL HATURIM ELUCIDATED

applies [not only to cursing a leader, but] also to cursing any person. Therefore,[26]

26. The text and translation follow the Constantinople edition (see illustration). In that version, the abbreviation ע׳ כ׳ seemingly begins a new thought. Accordingly, it has been written out as עַל כֵּן, *therefore,* and that is how *Shoham Yakar* presents this comment. In the Venice and Fürth editions, however, the abbreviation ע״כ seemingly ends a thought. If that is not a typographical error, the abbreviation stands for עַד כָּאן, *until here,* i.e., the quotation from tractate *Sanhedrin* ends at this point. However, the Baal HaTurim does not use that term — abbreviated or written in full — at the end of any other Talmudic citation.

תאור ג׳ ואשר תאר · לא תאור את העם · ונשיא בעמך לא תאור · ודרשינן מיניה
בסנהדרין הוא הדין לכל אדם · ע׳כ׳ לא תאור שאסור לקלל כל אדם · מאן ג׳ מאן יי׳
לתתי · מאן בלעם הלוך עמנו · אשר מאן לתתי לך בכסף · מלמד שכונתו לי רבות

Constantinople, 1514 — קושטא, רע״ד

מבורך · תאור ג׳ ואשר תאר · לא תאור את העם · ונשיא בעמך לא תאור · ודרשינן מיניה
בסנהדרין הוא הדין לכל אדם ע״כ · לא תאור שאסור לקלל כל אדם · מאן ג׳ מאן יי׳ לתתי ·
מאן בלעם הלוך עמנו · אשר מאן לתתי לך בכסף · מלמד שכונתו לחרבות לו שכרו · וזהו

Venice, 1544 — ויניציא, ד״ש

והק״בה בועט בה והיה מקלל ומברך ביי׳ וזהו יהי ישב יי׳ מבורך · תאור ג׳ ואשר תאר ، לא תאור
את העם · ונשיא בעמך לא תאור ודרשינן מיני׳ בסנהדרין הוא הדין לכל אדם ע״כ · לא תאור שאסור
לקלל כל אדם (תתלז) ואשר תאר יואר בגימ׳ שקללת את מואב (תתלח) מאן ג׳ מאן יי׳ לתתי מאן

Fürth, 1752 — פיורדא, תקי״ב

[7] *The elders of Moab and the elders of Midian went with
charms in their hand; they came to Balaam and spoke to him
the words of Balak.* [8] *He said to them, "Spend the night here
and I shall give you a response, as HASHEM shall speak to me."
So the officers of Moab stayed with Balaam.*

[9] *God came to Balaam and said, "Who are these men with
you?"*

[10] *Balaam said to God, "Balak son of Zippor, king of Moab,
sent to me:* [11] *'Behold! the people coming out of Egypt has
covered the surface of the earth. Now go and curse it for me;
perhaps I will be able to make war against it and drive it away.' "*

[12] *God said to Balaam, "You shall not go with them! You
shall not curse the people, for it is blessed!"*

BAAL HATURIM ELUCIDATED

You shall not curse, for it is forbidden to curse any person.[26a]

❑ וַאֲשֶׁר תָּאֹר יוּאָר — **AND WHOMEVER YOU WILL CURSE WILL BE CURSED.** The *gematria* of this phrase (1325) is equivalent[27] to that of שֶׁקִּלַּלְתָּ אֶת מוֹאָב, *for you cursed Moab.*[28]

12. לֹא תָאֹר אֶת הָעָם — **YOU SHALL NOT CURSE THE PEOPLE.** Balaam had used the term קָבָה[29] לִי (v. 11). God responded, "לֹא תָאֹר[30], *you shall not curse,*" implying that he could not pronounce even the most minimal curse.[31]

26a. The verse from *Exodus* teaches that it is forbidden to curse a leader; verse 12 below teaches that it is forbidden to curse the entire nation; verse 6 adds that those prohibitions are not restricted to the nation as a whole or to its king, rather they include וַאֲשֶׁר תָּאֹר, *whomever you will* [*intend to*] *curse* (Y.S.).

27. The *gematria* of the Baal HaTurim's phrase is 1310, fifteen less than that of the Scriptural phrase. Nevertheless, this comment appears verbatim in *Rabbeinu Ephraim* (*MiKesivah Ashkenazis*) and *Rimzei Rabbeinu Yoel.* Various emendations have been suggested to reconcile the *gematriaos*: (i) Using the variant spelling שֶׁקִּילַּלְתָּ, with a י, adds 10 and the principle of *im haosios* allows 12 more to be added, bringing the *gematria* of the Baal HaTurim's phrase to 1332; then the spelling תָּאוֹר, with a ו, adds 6 and the principle of *im hakollel* allows one more to be added, bringing the *gematria* of the Scriptural phrase to 1332 (based on *Ittur Bikkurim*); (ii) some editions of the Baal HaTurim use the ungrammatical spelling שֶׁקִּילַּלְתָּה, with an extraneous י and ה, to bring the *gematria* of the Baal HaTurim's phrase to 1325, equal to that of the Scriptural phrase; (iii) the annotators of *R' Ephraim* (note 54) suggest using the spelling תָּאוֹר, which brings the *gematria* of the Scriptural phrase to 1331, and emending the Baal HaTurim's phrase to, כְּשֶׁקִּלַּלְתָּ אֶת מוֹאָב, *when you cursed Moab,* with the כ adding 20 and the principle of *im hakollel* allowing one more to be added, for a total of 1331; (vi) the annotator of *Rimzei Rabbeinu Yoel* suggests emending the Baal HaTurim's phrase to וְזֶהוּ שֶׁקִּלַּלְתָּ אֶת מוֹאָב, which has a *gematria* of 1328, and invoking the principle of *im hateivos* to add three more to the *gematria* of the Scriptural verse for a total of 1328.

28. See *Tanchuma, Chukas* 24, cited by *Rashi* to 21:27, s.v., הַמֹּשְׁלִים; *Zohar* 199a; *Rabbeinu Ephraim* (*MiKesivah Ashkenazis*); *Rimzei Rabbeinu Yoel.*

29. An imperative form of the root נקב, which implies a clearly stated and specific curse (see *Rashi* to v. 11, s.v., קָבָה לִי).

30. A future tense verb of the root ארר, which implies a milder, non-specific curse (see *Rashi* to v.11).

31. The verb קבה implies a more virulent form of cursing than does the verb ארה (*Tanchuma* 5; cited by *Rashi* to v. 11, s.v., קָבָה לִי).

כב/יג־כ שני יג וַיָּקָם בִּלְעָם בַּבֹּקֶר וַיֹּאמֶר אֶל־שָׂרֵי בָלָק לְכוּ אֶל־
[חמישי]
יד אַרְצְכֶם כִּי מֵאֵן יהוה לְתִתִּי לַהֲלֹךְ עִמָּכֶם: וַיָּקוּמוּ
שָׂרֵי מוֹאָב וַיָּבֹאוּ אֶל־בָּלָק וַיֹּאמְרוּ מֵאֵן בִּלְעָם הֲלֹךְ
טו עִמָּנוּ: וַיֹּסֶף עוֹד בָּלָק שְׁלֹחַ שָׂרִים רַבִּים וְנִכְבָּדִים
טז מֵאֵלֶּה: וַיָּבֹאוּ אֶל־בִּלְעָם וַיֹּאמְרוּ לוֹ כֹּה אָמַר בָּלָק
יז בֶּן־צִפּוֹר אַל־נָא תִמָּנַע מֵהֲלֹךְ אֵלָי: כִּי־כַבֵּד
אֲכַבֶּדְךָ מְאֹד וְכֹל אֲשֶׁר־תֹּאמַר אֵלַי אֶעֱשֶׂה וּלְכָה־
יח נָּא קָבָה־לִּי אֵת הָעָם הַזֶּה: וַיַּעַן בִּלְעָם וַיֹּאמֶר
אֶל־עַבְדֵי בָלָק אִם־יִתֶּן־לִי בָלָק מְלֹא בֵיתוֹ כֶּסֶף
וְזָהָב לֹא אוּכַל לַעֲבֹר אֶת־פִּי יהוה אֱלֹהָי לַעֲשׂוֹת
יט קְטַנָּה אוֹ גְדוֹלָה: וְעַתָּה שְׁבוּ נָא בָזֶה גַּם־אַתֶּם
כ הַלָּיְלָה וְאֵדְעָה מַה־יֹּסֵף יהוה דַּבֵּר עִמִּי: וַיָּבֹא
אֱלֹהִים ׀ אֶל־בִּלְעָם לַיְלָה וַיֹּאמֶר לוֹ אִם־לִקְרֹא
לְךָ בָּאוּ הָאֲנָשִׁים קוּם לֵךְ אִתָּם וְאַךְ אֶת־הַדָּבָר

בעל הטורים

(יג) **מֵאֵן.** ג׳ — ״מֵאֵן ה׳ לְתִתִּי״; ״מֵאֵן בִּלְעָם הֲלֹךְ עִמָּנוּ״; ״אֲשֶׁר מֵאֵן לָתֶת לְךָ בְּכֶסֶף״. מְלַמֵּד שֶׁכַּוָּנָתוֹ לְהַרְבּוֹת לוֹ שְׂכָרוֹ. {וְזֶהוּ ״מֵאֵן״, כְּדֵי לְתִתּוֹ בְּכֶסֶף פִּדְיוֹם לְהַרְבּוֹת שְׂכָרוֹ}:

(כ) **וְאַךְ אֶת הַדָּבָר.** יָכוֹל אִם יִרְצֶה לְקַלֵּל הָאֻמּוֹת יְקַלֵּל יִשְׂרָאֵל עִמָּהֶם, אוֹ אִם יִרְצֶה לְבָרֵךְ יִשְׂרָאֵל יְבָרֵךְ הָאֻמּוֹת עִמָּהֶם. תַּלְמוּד לוֹמַר ״אַךְ״ — חִלֵּק:

BAAL HATURIM ELUCIDATED

13. מֵאֵן — HE HAS REFUSED. This word appears three times:[32] (i) here, מֵאֵן ה׳ לְתִתִּי, *HASHEM has refused to give me [permission]*; (ii) מֵאֵן בִּלְעָם הֲלֹךְ עִמָּנוּ, *Balaam has refused to go with us* (v. 14); and (iii) [in Jezebel's statement regarding Naboth's refusal to sell his ancestral land to Ahab] אֲשֶׁר מֵאֵן לָתֶת לְךָ בְּכֶסֶף, *which he has refused to give you for money* (*I Kings* 21:15). This [similarity of expression] teaches that Balaam's intent in refusing was to increase his wages.[33] {Thus,

32. The Baal HaTurim's intention here is unclear, for the word מֵאֵן actually appears five times in the *Tanach*: (i-iii) the three adduced by the Baal HaTurim; (iv) כָּבֵד לֵב פַּרְעֹה מֵאֵן לְשַׁלַּח הָעָם, *Pharaoh's heart is stubborn; he has refused to send [out] the people* (*Exodus* 7:14); and, (v) with regard to levirate marriage, וְאָמְרָה מֵאֵן יְבָמִי לְהָקִים לְאָחִיו שֵׁם בְּיִשְׂרָאֵל, *[the widow] shall say, "My brother-in-law has refused to establish a name for his brother in Israel"* (*Deuteronomy* 25:7). It has been suggested that the Baal HaTurim did not intend his ג׳ to be construed as a masoretic note, indeed, he does not include the word בַּמָּסוֹרֶת, as he usually does when he cites masoretic notes. Rather, he cites only those appearances of מֵאֵן that can be linked together (*Ittur Bikkurim;* but see note 33).

33. Balaam's greed inspired him to seek God's permission to curse Israel (*Tanchuma* 6, cited by *Rashi* to v. 18 below, s.v., מְלֹא בֵיתוֹ), even though he knew it was improper to do so (see the Baal HaTurim to 23:7 below, s.v., מִן אֲרָם).

The connection between these verses may be expanded to include the verses from *Exodus* and

[13] *Balaam arose in the morning and said to the officers of
Balak, "Go to your land, for HASHEM has refused to give me
[permission] to go with you."*
[14] *The officers of Moab arose and came to Balak and said,
"Balaam has refused to go with us."*
[15] *Balak kept on sending officers — more, and higher ranking
than these.*
[16] *They came to Balaam and said to him, "So said Balak son of
Zippor, 'Do not refrain from going to me,* [17] *for I shall honor you
greatly, and everything that you say to me I shall do; so go now
and curse this people for me.' "*
[18] *Balaam answered and said to the servants of Balak, "If
Balak will give me his houseful of silver and gold, I cannot
transgress the word of HASHEM, my God, to do anything small
or great.* [19] *And now, you, too, stay here for the night, and I will
know what more HASHEM will speak with me."*
[20] *God came to Balaam at night and said to him, "If the men
came to summon you, arise and go with them, but only the thing*

BAAL HATURIM ELUCIDATED

[Jezebel's words may be understood as a false accusation:[34]] מֵאֵן, *he has refused,* in order to give it to you for monetary redemption, i.e., to increase his take.}[35]

❑ {The Baal HaTurim's comment to לַהֲלֹךְ appears at *Exodus* 3:19.}

20. וְאַךְ אֶת הַדָּבָר — BUT ONLY THE THING. It is possible for one to think that if [Balaam] would desire[35a] to curse the [other] nations, he would be able to curse Israel along with them, or if he would desire to bless Israel, he would be able to bless the other nations along with them. [To prevent this mistake,] the verse has stated "אַךְ, *but,*" and has thus created a distinction.[36]

❑ {The Baal HaTurim's other comment to וְאַךְ appears at *Genesis* 9:5.}

Deuteronomy, for Pharaoh's refusal was based on the profitability of slave labor. Similarly, the Talmud speaks of a brother-in-law who either is not a proper match for his brother's widow or is suspected of wanting to perform *yibum* (levirate marriage) only for monetary gain (for when a man dies without children, his father — or, if his father is deceased, his brothers — inherit his estate; but in the case of *yibum,* the brother who marries the widow becomes the sole heir). In either of those cases, it is permissible to trick the brother-in-law into refusing to perform *yibum* by making him think that his refusal will bring him financial gain (*Yevamos* 106a). Thus, as in the case of Balaam, their refusals were intended to earn them greater financial reward (*Shoham Yakar*).

34. *VeChur LaZahav.*

35. The passage in brackets does not appear in the manuscripts used by *Shoham Yakar.* It does appear, however, in the early and later printed editions.

35a. Alternatively: The vowelization both here and below is יִרְצֶה, *He* [i.e., God] *would consent.* If so, the comment reads: It is possible for one to think that if He would consent [to allow Balaam] to curse the [other] nations, he would be able to curse Israel along with them, or if He would consent [to allow Balaam] to bless Israel, he would be able to bless the [other] nations along with them.

36. The statement, תַּלְמוּד לוֹמַר אַךְ חִלֵּק, *the verse has stated "אַךְ, but," and has thus created a*

כב/כא־כז
שלישי

כא אֲשֶׁר־אֲדַבֵּר אֵלֶיךָ אֹתוֹ תַעֲשֶׂה׃ וַיָּקָם בִּלְעָם
בַּבֹּקֶר וַיַּחֲבֹשׁ אֶת־אֲתֹנוֹ וַיֵּלֶךְ עִם־שָׂרֵי מוֹאָב׃
כב וַיִּחַר־אַף אֱלֹהִים כִּי־הוֹלֵךְ הוּא וַיִּתְיַצֵּב מַלְאַךְ
יְהוָה בַּדֶּרֶךְ לְשָׂטָן לוֹ וְהוּא רֹכֵב עַל־אֲתֹנוֹ
כג וּשְׁנֵי נְעָרָיו עִמּוֹ׃ וַתֵּרֶא הָאָתוֹן אֶת־מַלְאַךְ יְהוָה
נִצָּב בַּדֶּרֶךְ וְחַרְבּוֹ שְׁלוּפָה בְּיָדוֹ וַתֵּט הָאָתוֹן
מִן־הַדֶּרֶךְ וַתֵּלֶךְ בַּשָּׂדֶה וַיַּךְ בִּלְעָם אֶת־הָאָתוֹן
כד לְהַטֹּתָהּ הַדָּרֶךְ׃ וַיַּעֲמֹד מַלְאַךְ יְהוָה בְּמִשְׁעוֹל
כה הַכְּרָמִים גָּדֵר מִזֶּה וְגָדֵר מִזֶּה׃ וַתֵּרֶא הָאָתוֹן
אֶת־מַלְאַךְ יְהוָה וַתִּלָּחֵץ אֶל־הַקִּיר וַתִּלְחַץ
כו אֶת־רֶגֶל בִּלְעָם אֶל־הַקִּיר וַיֹּסֶף לְהַכֹּתָהּ׃ וַיּוֹסֶף
מַלְאַךְ־יְהוָה עֲבוֹר וַיַּעֲמֹד בְּמָקוֹם צָר אֲשֶׁר אֵין־
כז דֶּרֶךְ לִנְטוֹת יָמִין וּשְׂמֹאול׃ וַתֵּרֶא הָאָתוֹן אֶת־
מַלְאַךְ יְהוָה וַתִּרְבַּץ תַּחַת בִּלְעָם וַיִּחַר־אַף בִּלְעָם

בעל הטורים

(כב) **בַּדֶּרֶךְ לְשָׂטָן.** מִכָּאן שֶׁכָּל הַדְּרָכִים בְּחֶזְקַת סַכָּנָה׃

(כג) **וַתֵּט.** ג׳ בַּמָּסוֹרֶת – בְּהַאי עִנְיָנָא תְּרֵי; וְחַד ״וַתֵּט אֲשֻׁרֵינוּ מִנִּי אָרְחֶךָ״. לָמָּה ״וַתֵּט הָאָתוֹן״? בִּשְׁבִיל ״וַתֵּט אֲשֻׁרֵינוּ״, שֶׁבִּלְעָם נָטָה ״מִנִּי אָרְחֶךָ״, שֶׁהָיָה חָפֵץ לְקַלְּלָם, וְהַקָּדוֹשׁ בָּרוּךְ הוּא רָצָה לְבָרְכָם׃

BAAL HATURIM ELUCIDATED

22. {The Baal HaTurim's comment to מַלְאַךְ ה׳ בַּדֶּרֶךְ appears at v. 32 below.}

❑ **בַּדֶּרֶךְ לְשָׂטָן** — ON THE ROAD AS AN ADVERSARY. From this [phrase we can find support for the Sages' teaching[37]] that all roads are presumed to be dangerous.[38]

---

distinction, appears more than a dozen times in the Talmud (e.g., *Pesachim* 71a; *Bechoros* 15a). Some vowelize the phrase, תַּלְמוּד לוֹמַר אַךְ חַלֵּק, *the verse has stated "*אַךְ*, but," as if to say, "Make a distinction!"*

As used in Scriptures, the terms אַךְ, *but* or *however,* and רַק, *only,* imply the exclusion of something not explicit in the verse; and the terms אֶת (used either to introduce the object of a verb or as an untranslatable linguistic embellishment) and גַּם, *also,* imply the inclusion of something not explicit in the verse (*Yerushalmi, Berachos* 9:7). Thus, the word אַךְ serves to limit the application of God's words to Balaam, as if to say, "Do not add anything that I have not explicitly instructed you."

37. *Yerushalmi, Berachos* 4:4 — The Mishnah states: One traveling in a dangerous place recites a short prayer [i.e., rather than placing oneself at risk of being attacked by highwaymen or wild animals while concentrating on the recitation of *Shemoneh Esrei,* one need recite only a short prayer, as specified in the Mishnah, and then continue to his destination, where he

that I shall speak to you — that shall you do."
21 Balaam arose in the morning and saddled his she-
donkey and went with the officers of Moab. 22 God's
wrath flared because he was going, and an angel of HASHEM
stood on the road as an adversary against him. He was
riding on his she-donkey and his two young men were
with him. 23 The she-donkey saw the angel of HASHEM
standing on the road with his sword drawn in his hand,
so the she-donkey turned away from the road and went
into the field; then Balaam smote the she-donkey to turn
her back onto the road. 24 The angel of HASHEM *stood in*
the path of the vineyards, a fence on this side and a
fence on that side. 25 The she-donkey saw the angel of
HASHEM *and pressed against the wall, and she pressed*
Balaam's leg against the wall — and he continued to
smite her. 26 The angel of HASHEM *again passed ahead*
and stood in a narrow place, where there was no room to
turn right or left. 27 The she-donkey saw the angel of
HASHEM *and crouched beneath Balaam. Balaam's anger*

BAAL HATURIM ELUCIDATED

23. וַתֵּט — [SHE] TURNED AWAY. The masoretic note, ג׳, means that this word appears three times in the *Tanach*: (i-ii) twice in this passage (here and v. 33) [with the reference to the she-donkey turning off the path]; and (iii) וַתֵּט אֲשֻׁרֵינוּ מִנִּי אָרְחֶךָ, *our footsteps have turned away from Your path* (*Psalms* 44:19). Why is it that *the she-donkey turned away?* Because *our footsteps*[39] *have turned away,* i.e., Balaam turned away *from Your* [i.e., God's] *path,* for he desired to curse [Israel], while the Holy One, Blessed is He, desired to bless them.

will recite the entire *Shemoneh Esrei* in safety]. The *Gemara* adds axiomatically: All roads are presumed to be dangerous. In our verse, the Baal HaTurim finds a Scriptural source for that statement.

38. *Peirush HaRokeach.* The verse could have stated, *An angel of* HASHEM *stood as an adversary against him,* omitting the word בַּדֶּרֶךְ, *on the road,* for it is clear from the next verse that they had been traveling on the road. By including that word, the Torah implies a connection between roads and adversaries, thus, roads are dangerous places (*VeChur LaZahav*).

39. The text — אֲשֻׁרֵינוּ, *our footsteps,* first person plural — follows the later printed editions. The early printed editions read אֲשׁוּרְךָ, *your footsteps,* second person singular. And *Shoham Yakar's* manuscript edition has אֲשׁוּרַי, *my footsteps,* first person singular. From a grammatical standpoint, none of the three versions seems to be accurate, for the comment speaks about Balaam in the third person. The expected form is therefore אֲשׁוּרוֹ, *his footstep,* or אֲשׁוּרָיו, *his footsteps.* Perhaps the manuscript copyist, who did not use vowel signs, inadvertently omitted the final ו of אשוריו or truncated the final ו of אשורו leaving אשורי. In any case, whereas none of the extant versions are preferred grammatically, the text uses the wording of the verse from *Psalms* (*VeChur LaZahav*).

כח וַיַּ֥ךְ אֶת־הָאָת֖וֹן בַּמַּקֵּֽל׃ וַיִּפְתַּ֥ח יהוה אֶת־פִּ֣י הָאָת֑וֹן
וַתֹּ֤אמֶר לְבִלְעָם֙ מֶֽה־עָשִׂ֣יתִֽי לְךָ֔ כִּ֣י הִכִּיתַ֔נִי זֶ֖ה
כט שָׁל֥שׁ רְגָלִֽים׃ וַיֹּ֤אמֶר בִּלְעָם֙ לָֽאָת֔וֹן כִּ֥י הִתְעַלַּ֖לְתְּ
ל בִּ֑י ל֤וּ יֶשׁ־חֶ֙רֶב֙ בְּיָדִ֔י כִּ֥י עַתָּ֖ה הֲרַגְתִּֽיךְ׃ וַתֹּ֨אמֶר
הָאָת֜וֹן אֶל־בִּלְעָ֗ם הֲל֨וֹא אָנֹכִ֣י אֲתֹֽנְךָ֡ אֲשֶׁר־רָכַ֣בְתָּ
עָלַ֩י מֵעֽוֹדְךָ֙ עַד־הַיּ֣וֹם הַזֶּ֔ה הַהַסְכֵּ֣ן הִסְכַּ֔נְתִּי
לא לַעֲשׂ֥וֹת לְךָ֖ כֹּ֑ה וַיֹּ֖אמֶר לֹֽא׃ וַיְגַ֣ל יהוה֮ אֶת־עֵינֵ֣י
בִלְעָם֒ וַיַּ֞רְא אֶת־מַלְאַ֣ךְ יהוה֗ נִצָּ֣ב בַּדֶּ֔רֶךְ וְחַרְבּ֥וֹ

בעל הטורים

(כז) וַיַּךְ {בִּלְעָם} אֶת הָאָתוֹן. וְלֹא קִלֵּל אוֹתָהּ, לְפִי שֶׁהָיָה דַעְתּוֹ לְקַלֵּל אֶת יִשְׂרָאֵל, וְאֵין שְׁתֵּי קְלָלוֹת בְּיוֹם אֶחָד, דִּכְתִיב ״לֹא אֹסִף לְקַלֵּל {עוֹד . . . וְלֹא אֹסִף עוֹד לְהַכּוֹת}״:

אִי נַמִּי – מִפְּנֵי שֶׁלֹּא הִגִּיעַ הָרֶגַע שֶׁל הַזַּעַם:

(ל) הֲלוֹא אָנֹכִי אֲתֹנְךָ. מָלֵא וָי״ו – שִׁשָּׁה דְבָרִים אָמְרָה לוֹ. לְטְעִינָה בְּעָלְמָא, אַקְרַאי בְּעָלְמָא . . . כִּדְאִיתָא בְּפֶרֶק קַמָּא דַּעֲבוֹדָה זָרָה:

❑ **רָכַבְתָּ עָלַי.** בְּגִימַטְרִיָּא רְבַעְתַּנִי:

BAAL HATURIM ELUCIDATED

27. וַיַּךְ {בִּלְעָם} אֶת הָאָתוֹן — THEN {BALAAM}[39a] **SMOTE THE SHE-DONKEY.** He did not curse it,[40] for his intent was to curse Israel, and two curses cannot be effective in one day, as it is written, לֹא אֹסִף לְקַלֵּל {עוֹד . . . וְלֹא אֹסִף עוֹד לְהַכּוֹת}, *I will not continue to curse {again . . . nor will I again continue to smite}*[40a]

39a. The text follows the early printed editions (followed by most later editions) which omit the word בִּלְעָם, thus assigning the comment to verse 27. Note 40a below offers support for this version. *Shoham Yakar's* manuscript edition includes the word בִּלְעָם in the rubric, thus assigning the comment to verse 23.

40. Whereas Balaam's power lay in his mouth — *whomever you will bless is blessed and whomever you will curse will be cursed* (v. 6 above) — we would expect him to have cursed the donkey. Alternatively, it is the manner of donkey drivers to train their animals to follow verbal commands [e.g., the English interjections "Gee!" and "Haw!" are used to turn the animal to the right and to the left respectively]. Nevertheless, Balaam struck his donkey. The Baal HaTurim explains why (*VeChur LaZahav*).

40a. The part of the verse enclosed in braces is not found in the early or later printed editions, but does appear in *Shoham Yakar's* manuscript edition.

The inclusion of both bracketed passages seems paradoxical. For, as stated in note 39a, if Balaam's name is included in the rubric, then the comment belongs to verse 23 and refers to the first time that Balaam smote his donkey. Accordingly, the statement, *nor will I again continue to smite,* seems out of place, for Balaam did smite his donkey again, twice. However, if Balaam's name is not included in the rubric, then the comment belongs to verse 27 and refers to the third and last time that Balaam smote his donkey. Accordingly, the statement, *nor will I again continue to smite,* is in place in this comment.

Additionally, the verb וַיַּךְ, *he smote* (from the root נכה, *smite*), can also apply to verbal abuse [see *Deuteronomy* 27:24 where אָרוּר מַכֵּה רֵעֵהוּ בַּסָּתֶר, literally, *Cursed is one who smites his fellow in secret,* is explained as one who speaks slanderously against his fellow (see *Rashi* and the Baal HaTurim there)]. Thus, from verses 23 and 25, it is not clear whether Balaam smote the donkey with a stick or with his mouth. Verse 27, on the other

flared and he smote the she-donkey with the stick.
[28] Hashem opened the mouth of the she-donkey and she
said to Balaam, "What have I done to you that you struck
me these three times?"
[29] Balaam said to the she-donkey, "Because you mocked
me! If only there were a sword in my hand I would now
have killed you!"
[30] The she-donkey said to Balaam, "Am I not your
she-donkey, that you have ridden upon me all your life until
this day? Have I regularly been doing such a thing to you?"
He said, "No."
[31] Then Hashem uncovered Balaam's eyes and he saw
the angel of Hashem standing on the road with his sword

BAAL HATURIM ELUCIDATED

(*Genesis* 8:21).[41]

Alternatively: He did not curse it, because the moment of [Divine] wrath had not yet arrived.[42]

30. הֲלוֹא אָנֹכִי אֲתֹנְךָ — AM I NOT YOUR SHE-DONKEY. [The word הֲלוֹא is spelled] in full,[43] with a ו (= 6). [This indicates that] the donkey told Balaam six things:[43a] [Regarding his claims that he used her] only for carrying burdens; only occasionally; . . . as it is stated in the first chapter of tractate *Avodah Zarah.*[44]

❑ **רָכַבְתָּ עָלַי** — YOU HAVE RIDDEN UPON ME. The *gematria* of this expression (732) is equal to that of רְבַעְתַּנִי, *you have committed bestiality with me.*[45]

31. {The comment to מַלְאַךְ ה׳ בַּדֶּרֶךְ, that is found at this point in many editions, appears below, as part of the Baal HaTurim's comment to v. 32.}

hand, states explicitly, וַיַּךְ אֶת הָאָתוֹן בַּמַּקֵּל, *he smote the she-donkey with the stick* (*VeChur LaZahav*).

41. *Sefer Chasidim* (409) states that a court may not declare two bans on the same day and adduces *Genesis* 8:21, *Malachi* 3:6,9 and *Nahum* 1:9 as support for that rule (*Shoham Yakar;* see also *Eliyahu Rabbah, Orach Chaim* 306:28).

42. See the Baal HaTurim to v. 6 above, s.v., מְבֹרָךְ.

43. The full spelling — הֲלוֹא — appears twelve times in the Torah; the defective spelling — הֲלֹא — appears seventeen times. Only here does the Baal HaTurim discuss the significance of the spelling.

43a. *Peirush HaRokeach;* see also the Baal HaTurim to v. 33 below, s.v., וְאוֹתָהּ הֶחֱיֵיתִי.

44. *Avodah Zarah* 4b (the numbering of the donkey's statements follows *Yad Aharon*) — Balaam claimed to be one *who knows the mind of the Supreme One* (24:16 below), yet he did not even know the mind of his animal! For when the Moabite emissaries saw Balaam riding on a donkey, they said, "Why are you not riding a horse [which travels faster than a donkey, so that you would fulfill Balak's request expeditiously (*Maharsha*)]?" He replied to them, "[I usually do, but today] I put it in the marshland [to graze]." Immediately, *the she-donkey said to Balaam,* (i) *"Am I not your [regular] she-donkey?"* Balaam said to her, "Only for carrying burdens." She said further, (ii) *"that you have ridden upon me . . ."* Then Balaam [interrupted her and] said, "Only occasionally [have I ridden on you]," but she continued, (iii) *"all your life* [i.e., in the past] (iv) *until this day* [i.e., in the present]. Moreover, (v) I furnish you with transportation by day and (vi) conjugality at night," as implied by the dual meaning of the phrase הַהַסְכֵּן הִסְכַּנְתִּי [related to the word סֹכֶנֶת in *I Kings* 1:2; see also the Baal HaTurim's next comment].

45. *Peirush HaRokeach;* see note 44 (vi) above.

כב/לב-לג

לב שְׁלְפָה בְּיָדוֹ וַיִּקֹּד וַיִּשְׁתַּחוּ לְאַפָּיו: וַיֹּאמֶר אֵלָיו מַלְאַךְ
יהוה עַל־מָה הִכִּיתָ אֶת־אֲתֹנְךָ זֶה שָׁלוֹשׁ רְגָלִים הִנֵּה
לג אָנֹכִי יָצָאתִי לְשָׂטָן כִּי־יָרַט הַדֶּרֶךְ לְנֶגְדִּי: וַתִּרְאַנִי
הָאָתוֹן וַתֵּט לְפָנַי זֶה שָׁלֹשׁ רְגָלִים אוּלַי נָטְתָה
מִפָּנַי כִּי עַתָּה גַּם־אֹתְכָה הָרַגְתִּי וְאוֹתָהּ הֶחֱיֵיתִי:

בעל הטורים

(לב) הִנֵּה אָנֹכִי יָצָאתִי לְשָׂטָן. יָצָאתִי מִמִּדָּתִי, מִמִּדַּת רַחֲמִים. שֶׁמַּלְאַךְ רַחֲמִים הָיָה. "מַלְאַךְ ה' בַּדֶּרֶךְ" בְּגִימַטְרִיָּא גַּבְרִיאֵל הַמַּלְאָךְ:

(לג) אֹתְכָה. כְּתִיב בְּהֵ' – בַּחֲמִשָּׁה דְבָרִים חָטָאת:

❑ **וְאוֹתָהּ הֶחֱיֵיתִי.** מָלֵא וָי"ו – שֶׁהֱשִׁיבָהּ אוֹתוֹ שִׁשָּׁה דְבָרִים. וְנִבְרֵאת בְּיוֹם שִׁשִּׁי בֵּין הַשְּׁמָשׁוֹת:

BAAL HATURIM ELUCIDATED

32. הִנֵּה אָנֹכִי יָצָאתִי לְשָׂטָן — BEHOLD! I WENT OUT TO BE AN ADVERSARY. [The angel meant,] "I departed from my usual character, that of mercy."[46] For it was an angel of mercy.[47] The *gematria* of the phrase (v. 22 above), מַלְאַךְ ה' בַּדֶּרֶךְ, *an angel of HASHEM on the road* (343), is equivalent[48] to that of the phrase, גַּבְרִיאֵל הַמַּלְאָךְ, *the angel Gabriel.*[49,49a]

46. *Tanchuma* 8, cited by *Rashi* to v. 22 above.

47. The Tetragrammaton, i.e., the Divine Name spelled with the four letters י־ק־ו־ק, here translated as *HASHEM,* is associated with God's attribute of mercy. The Name אֱלֹהִים, on the other hand, is associated with His attribute of strict judgment (*Sifrei, Deuteronomy* 3:24). Accordingly, the term מַלְאַךְ ה', *an angel of HASHEM,* implies an angel of mercy (*Rashi* to v. 22 above, as explained by *Amar Nekai*).

48. The principle of *im hakollel* allows 342, the *gematria* of the Baal HaTurim's phrase, to be considered equivalent to 343.

49. Many Midrashim (e.g., *Bereishis Rabbah* 1:3; *Pirkei DeRabbi Eliezer* 4; *Tanchuma, Vayigash* 6) and many of the kabbalistic writings (e.g., *Zohar, Bereishis* 40b; *Vayechi* 235b; *Pekudei* 239a; *Pinechas* 225a) depict מִיכָאֵל, *Michael,* as a watery angel standing to the right (south) of the Heavenly Throne and representing the Divine Attribute of Mercy and Loving-kindness, while גַּבְרִיאֵל, *Gabriel,* is a fiery angel standing to the left (north) of the Heavenly Throne and representing the Divine Attribute of Strict Judgment (see *Maharsha, Berachos* 4b, *Aggados,* s.v., מיכאל גו'). Accordingly, the Baal HaTurim's assertions that the angel who confronted Balaam was an angel of mercy and that the angel was named Gabriel seem to contradict one another.

Although angelic nomenclature, especially as it relates to kabbalistic concepts, is beyond the purview of the present work, the remarks that follow seem to be in place. True, the name גַּבְרִיאֵל implies the Attribute of Strict Justice, nevertheless, we find various missions of mercy assigned to the angel Gabriel: (i) Gabriel assisted Raphael in saving Lot and his family from the destruction of Sodom (see *Bereishis Rabbah* 50:11 with *Mattenos Kehunah*); (ii) when Joseph *was blundering in the field* (*Genesis* 37:16), it was the angel Gabriel who gave him directions (see *Rashi* and the Baal HaTurim to *Genesis* 37:15); (iii) Gabriel acted to protect Tamar, from whom would descend King David (see *Sotah* 10b); (iv) Gabriel taught Joseph seventy languages and therefore Joseph succeeded in whatever he did (*Sotah* 33a; see the Baal HaTurim to *Genesis* 39:4); (v) when Jerusalem was about to be destroyed, God sent an angel to *pass through the midst of the city, through the midst of Jerusalem and make a sign on the foreheads of* the righteous people so that the destructive angels shall have no power over them (*Ezekiel* 9:4; *Shabbos* 55a); the Talmud (there) identifies that angel as Gabriel; (vi) Gabriel cooled the coals that would have destroyed all of Israel along with the *Beis HaMikdash* (*Ezekiel* 10:7; *Yoma* 77a); and (vii) Gabriel saved Hananiah, Mishael and Azariah from Nebuchadnezzar's flaming furnace (see *Daniel* 3:19-29; *Pesachim* 118a).

drawn in his hand. He bowed his head and prostrated himself
on his face.
32 *The angel of* HASHEM *said to him, "For what reason did*
you strike your she-donkey these three times? Behold! I went
out to be an adversary, for you hastened on a road to oppose
me. 33 *The she-donkey saw me and turned away from me*
these three times. Had she not turned away from me, I would
now even have killed you and I would have let her live!"

BAAL HATURIM ELUCIDATED

33. אֹתְכָה — YOU. [This word is] spelled[50] with a ה (= 5). [The angel intimated to Balaam,] "You have committed five sins."[51]

❑ **וְאוֹתָהּ הֶחֱיֵיתִי** — AND I WOULD HAVE LET HER LIVE. [The word וְאוֹתָהּ, *and it,* is] spelled in full,[51a] with a ו (= 6) [between the א and the ת]. This indicates that the donkey replied [to Balaam regarding] six things.[52] [Additionally: As the Mishnah[53] teaches,] it[54] was created during twilight on the sixth day [of creation].[55]

Indeed, the Talmud states: מִיכָאֵל בְּאַחַת גַּבְרִיאֵל בִּשְׁתַּיִם, *[The angel] Michael [completes his mission] with one [flutter of his wings] and [the angel] Gabriel with two . . .* (*Berachos* 4b). The kabbalistic work *Sefer HaPeliah* (Vol. I, 49b, s.v., ויברא אלהים את התנינים; see also *Maharsha*) explains that Michael needs to exert only half the effort that Gabriel requires because Michael is כֻּלּוֹ רַחֲמִים, *entirely mercy,* while Gabriel is קָשֶׁה וְרַפֶּה, *hard and soft* [i.e., judgmental, yet merciful].

Based on the above, it is suggested that just as Michael and the angels under him are responsible for carrying out God's missions of mercy, so are Gabriel and the angels under him. Both groups are מַלְאֲכֵי הַשָּׁרֵת, *ministering angels,* מִסִּטְרָא דִימִינָא, *from the right side,* as opposed to מַלְאֲכֵי חַבָּלָה, *destructive angels,* מִסִּטְרָא דִשְׂמָאלָא, *from the left side.* Therefore, when the Divine Will calls for Mercy, either Michael or Gabriel may be charged with its fulfillment. However, when the Divine Will calls for Strict Judgment, Gabriel's function is changed from מִדַּת הָרַחֲמִים, *the Attribute of Mercy,* to מִדַּת הַדִּין, *the Attribute of Strict Judgment,* as it is here (*VeChur LaZahav*).

49a. The text follows *Shoham Yakar's* manuscript edition. In most other editions, however, the latter half of this note, beginning מַלְאַךְ ה׳ בַּדֶּרֶךְ, appears as an independent comment and is assigned to verse 31. But that reading seems to be in error, for in that verse, the word נִצָּב, *[it is] standing,* separates מַלְאַךְ ה׳ from בַּדֶּרֶךְ, and the Baal HaTurim does not usually skip over words in formulating his gematraic allusions (*VeChur LaZahav*).

50. The term אוֹתְךָ, *you* (masculine, singular, objective case), appears forty-nine times in the *Tanach.* Fifteen of those appearances are spelled in full — אוֹתְךָ — with a ו (e.g., *Deuteronomy* 9:14); another thirty-three times it is spelled defectively — אֹתְךָ — without a ו (e.g., 16:10 above). Only here is it spelled אֹתְכָה with a ה at the end. [The unusual variant form אֹתְכָה appears at *Exodus* 29:35, but the Baal HaTurim does not comment on that word.]

51. Two of the five sins are found in verse 12 and three in verse 21: (i-ii) [Although God had told him,] *"You shall not go with them!"* and *"You shall not curse the people!"* [he nonetheless sought ways to defy God's words]; (iii) *Balaam arose in the morning* [i.e., the zeal with which he set out to perpetrate evil is reckoned as a sin unto itself]; (iv) *he saddled his she-donkey* [i.e., due to his fierce hatred of Israel, even though he had two young male servants with him (see v. 22), he saddled his donkey by himself (*Rashi*)]; and (v) *he went with the officers of Moab* [despite his awareness that God was not favorable to his going] (*Rabbeinu Ephraim* [*MiKesivah Ashkenazis*]).

51a. The pronoun אֹתָהּ, *her,* spelled defectively, without a ו, appears ninety-three times in the Torah; the full spelling appears only once (30:9 below), but the Baal HaTurim does not comment on the ו of that word. With the conjunctive ו, it appears twice: once spelled defectively, וְאֹתָהּ (*Leviticus* 10:17); and in our verse spelled in full, וְאוֹתָהּ.

52. See note 44 above.

53. *Avos* 5:6.

54. This refers to the donkey's ability to speak.

55. *Peirush HaRokeach.*

כב/לד־כג/א

לד וַיֹּאמֶר בִּלְעָם אֶל־מַלְאַךְ יהוה חָטָאתִי כִּי לֹא
יָדַעְתִּי כִּי אַתָּה נִצָּב לִקְרָאתִי בַּדָּרֶךְ וְעַתָּה אִם־רַע
לה בְּעֵינֶיךָ אָשׁוּבָה לִּי׃ וַיֹּאמֶר מַלְאַךְ יהוה אֶל־בִּלְעָם
לֵךְ עִם־הָאֲנָשִׁים וְאֶפֶס אֶת־הַדָּבָר אֲשֶׁר־אֲדַבֵּר
אֵלֶיךָ אֹתוֹ תְדַבֵּר וַיֵּלֶךְ בִּלְעָם עִם־שָׂרֵי בָלָק׃
לו וַיִּשְׁמַע בָּלָק כִּי־בָא בִלְעָם וַיֵּצֵא לִקְרָאתוֹ אֶל־עִיר
מוֹאָב אֲשֶׁר עַל־גְּבוּל אַרְנֹן אֲשֶׁר בִּקְצֵה הַגְּבוּל׃
לז וַיֹּאמֶר בָּלָק אֶל־בִּלְעָם הֲלֹא שָׁלֹחַ שָׁלַחְתִּי אֵלֶיךָ
לִקְרֹא־לָךְ לָמָּה לֹא־הָלַכְתָּ אֵלָי הַאֻמְנָם לֹא אוּכַל
לח כַּבְּדֶךָ׃ וַיֹּאמֶר בִּלְעָם אֶל־בָּלָק הִנֵּה־בָאתִי אֵלֶיךָ
עַתָּה הֲיָכֹל אוּכַל דַּבֵּר מְאוּמָה הַדָּבָר אֲשֶׁר יָשִׂים
רביעי [ששי] לט אֱלֹהִים בְּפִי אֹתוֹ אֲדַבֵּר׃ וַיֵּלֶךְ בִּלְעָם עִם־בָּלָק
מ וַיָּבֹאוּ קִרְיַת חֻצוֹת׃ וַיִּזְבַּח בָּלָק בָּקָר וָצֹאן וַיְשַׁלַּח
מא לְבִלְעָם וְלַשָּׂרִים אֲשֶׁר אִתּוֹ׃ וַיְהִי בַבֹּקֶר וַיִּקַּח בָּלָק
אֶת־בִּלְעָם וַיַּעֲלֵהוּ בָּמוֹת בָּעַל וַיַּרְא מִשָּׁם קְצֵה
כג א הָעָם׃ וַיֹּאמֶר בִּלְעָם אֶל־בָּלָק בְּנֵה־לִי בָזֶה שִׁבְעָה
מִזְבְּחֹת וְהָכֵן לִי בָּזֶה שִׁבְעָה פָרִים וְשִׁבְעָה אֵילִים׃

בעל הטורים

כג (א) שִׁבְעָה פָּרִים וְשִׁבְעָה אֵילִים. וְכֵן עָשָׂה אִיּוֹב. כִּי כֵן מִנְהַג בְּנֵי נֹחַ לְהַקְרִיב שִׁבְעָה שִׁבְעָה כְּנֶגֶד שֶׁבַע מִצְוֹת שֶׁלָּהֶם׃

BAAL HATURIM ELUCIDATED

38. {The Baal HaTurim's comment to בְּפִי, that is found at this point in many editions, appears at 23:5 below.}

XXIII

1. שִׁבְעָה פָּרִים וְשִׁבְעָה אֵילִים — SEVEN BULLS AND SEVEN RAMS. And thus did [God instruct the three companions of] Job [to] do (see *Job* 42:8), for such was the practice of the Noahides,[55a] to make offerings consisting of seven animals each, corresponding to their seven commandments.[56]

55a. The Talmud (*Bava Basra* 15b-16a) records a dispute regarding when Job lived. According to some opinions there, Job must have been Jewish; according to others, he was not. The Baal HaTurim's comment here reflects the opinion that Job was not Jewish (*VeChur LaZahav*). Indeed, according to *Ramban,* Job and his companions were all descendants of Abraham, either through Esau or through Keturah.

56. *Peirush HaRokeach.*

Shoham Yakar first suggests that this custom arose from the fact that Noah was commanded

34 *Balaam said to the angel of* HASHEM, *"I have sinned,*
for I did not know that you were standing opposite
me on the road. And now, if it is evil in your eyes, I shall
return."

35 *The angel of* HASHEM *said to Balaam, "Go with the*
men, but only the word that I shall speak to you — that
shall you speak." So Balaam went with the officers of
Balak.

36 *Balak heard that Balaam had come, so he went out*
toward him to the city of Moab, which is on the border of
Arnon, which is at the edge of the border. 37 *Balak said to*
Balaam, "Did I not urgently send to you to summon you?
Why did you not go to me? Am I not capable of honoring
you?"

38 *Balaam said to Balak, "Behold! now I have come to*
you — am I empowered to say anything? Whatever word
God puts into my mouth, that shall I speak!"

39 *Balaam went with Balak and they came to Kiriath-*
huzoth. 40 *Balak slaughtered cattle and sheep and sent to*
Balaam and to the officers who were with him. 41 *And it*
was in the morning: Balak took Balaam and brought him up
to the heights of Baal, and from there he saw the edge of the
people.

23 1 *Balaam said to Balak, "Build for me here seven altars and*
prepare for me here seven bulls and seven rams."

---

to bring seven pairs of each kosher animal into the ark in order to be able to make offerings of them after the flood will have ended. However, he rejects this explanation on the basis of *Ramban's* comment (*Genesis* 7:8): Two of each species, a male and a female, came to the ark on their own, in order to preserve the species; Noah then sought an additional six pairs of each kosher animal to bring as altar offerings after the flood. Thus, argues *Shoham Yakar,* Noah's offerings could not have been the basis for his descendants' custom of bringing seven, for he brought only six.

Nevertheless, *Shoham Yakar's* initial suggestion remains viable. For God commanded Adam regarding only six mitzvos: the prohibition against (i) idolatry, (ii) blessing [a euphemism for the opposite] God, (iii) murder, (iv) adultery, and (v) stealing; and (vi) the precept to establish law and order. And until the flood these were the only six commandments that God had issued to mankind. After the flood, God added a seventh commandment, when He forbade Noah and his descendants to eat the flesh of a living animal (see *Rambam, Hilchos Melachim* 9:1; *Rashi* to *Genesis* 9:4). Accordingly, it is possible that before the flood Noah prepared and subsequently brought only six pairs of animals as offerings, corresponding to the six commandments to which he was subject, and that would have become the precedent for his offspring to offer groups of six animals. However, soon after Noah built an altar and offered his animals (*Genesis* 8:20), God added the seventh commandment (9:4), and from then on the Noahides would bring altar offerings of seven animals each (*VeChur LaZahav*).

כג/ב־ג

ב וַיַּעַשׂ בָּלָק כַּאֲשֶׁר דִּבֶּר בִּלְעָם וַיַּעַל בָּלָק
ג וּבִלְעָם פָּר וָאַיִל בַּמִּזְבֵּחַ: וַיֹּאמֶר בִּלְעָם לְבָלָק
הִתְיַצֵּב עַל־עֹלָתֶךָ וְאֵלְכָה אוּלַי יִקָּרֶה יהוה
לִקְרָאתִי וּדְבַר מַה־יַּרְאֵנִי וְהִגַּדְתִּי לָךְ וַיֵּלֶךְ שֶׁפִי:

בעל הטורים

(ג) **עַל עֹלָתֶךָ.** חָסֵר וָי״ו – כִּי לֹא חָפֵץ בָּהּ הַקָּדוֹשׁ בָּרוּךְ הוּא. שֶׁאָמַר לוֹ ״טוֹב פַּת חֲרֵבָה וְשַׁלְוָה בָהּ מִבַּיִת מָלֵא זִבְחֵי רִיב״ רָאשֵׁי תֵבוֹת ״מַמְזֵר״. פֵּרוּשׁ, מִ״שִּׁבְעָה פָרִים וְשִׁבְעָה אֵילִים״, שֶׁהִקְרִיבוּ הַמּוֹאָבִים שֶׁבָּאוּ מִמַּמְזֵרוּת:

❑ **יַרְאֵנִי.** ב׳ בַּמָּסוֹרֶת – ״וּדְבַר מַה יַּרְאֵנִי״; וְאִידָךְ ״אֱלֹהִים יַרְאֵנִי בְשֹׁרְרָי״. מְלַמֵּד שֶׁהָיָה בִּלְעָם שׂוֹנֵא אוֹתָם וְחָפֵץ לְקַלְּלָם יוֹתֵר מִבָּלָק, וְהָיָה מִתְפַּלֵּל עֲלֵיהֶם ״אֱלֹהִים יַרְאֵנִי בְשֹׁרְרָי״:

❑ **וַיֵּלֶךְ שֶׁפִי.** בְּגִימַטְרִיָּא חִיגֵּר בְּרֶגֶל. דָּבָר אַחֵר – מִלְּשׁוֹן שָׁף מְדוּכְתֵּיהּ. מִשּׁוּם שֶׁנֶּאֱמַר ״וַתִּלְחַץ אֶת רֶגֶל בִּלְעָם אֶל הַקִּיר״:

❑ **שֶׁפִי.** פֵּ״א כְפוּלָה – שֶׁפִּשְׁפֵּשׁ וְחִפֵּשׂ, בְּאֵיזֶה שָׁעָה טוֹב לְקַלֵּל אֶת יִשְׂרָאֵל:

BAAL HATURIM ELUCIDATED

3. עַל עֹלָתֶךָ — NEAR YOUR BURNT-OFFERING. [The word עֹלָתֶךָ is] spelled defectively, without a ו,[57] for God did not desire it. For He said to him,[58] טוֹב פַּת חֲרֵבָה וְשַׁלְוָה בָהּ מִבַּיִת מָלֵא זִבְחֵי רִיב, *Better dry bread, but with serenity in it, than a house full of contentious sacrifices* (*Proverbs* 17:1).[58] The initial letters [of the last four words in that verse, מִבַּיִת מָלֵא זִבְחֵי רִיב,] form the acronym מַמְזֵר, *mamzer* [one born from an adulterous union]. The verse thus means [that dry bread is preferable] to *seven bulls and seven rams*[59] offered by the Moabites who

57. It is not clear why the Baal HaTurim chose to expound on the defective spelling of עֹלָתֶךָ, for that word appears three times in the *Tanach* (*Leviticus* 9:7 and twice in our passage, vv. 3 and 15), each time with the same spelling. Now it is true that the Baal HaTurim's comment can be applied to verse 15 as well as to our verse. But it certainly cannot be applied to the verse in *Leviticus,* which speaks of the inauguration offerings that God had commanded Aaron to bring! Even less clear is why the Baal HaTurim would speak of the absent ו in any form of the noun עוֹלָה, for that word appears in the Torah, with and without prefixes and suffixes, 147 times, only four of them spelled with a ו (*Numbers* 28:24 and 27; *Deuteronomy* 12:11 and 27:6). Accordingly, we would expect comments that explain why those verses use the full spelling. And, indeed, the Baal HaTurim comments on the full spelling in *Numbers* 28:27, but not at the other three verses.

58. The Midrash relates that when Balaam had the seven altars constructed, he said to God, "You favor Israel because of their altar service. Would it not be more fitting that all seventy nations serve at Your altar, rather than just one nation?" God's response was to quote the verse from *Proverbs, "Better dry bread* [i.e., a meal-offering from Israel, even if it is only a dry offering of flour without oil], *but with serenity in it* [for that offering fosters serenity and peace between Israel and its Maker], *than a house full of contentious sacrifices,* i.e., your offerings, that are an attempt to drive a wedge between Israel and Me (*Bamidbar Rabbah* 20:18).

59. It is noteworthy that after removing the initial letters of the phrase מִבַּיִת מָלֵא זִבְחֵי רִיב, to form the word מַמְזֵר, the *gematria* of the remaining letters of the phrase, בי״ת ל״א בח״י י״ב — 475 — is the same as that of מז׳ פָּרִים ז׳ אֵילִים, *than seven bulls* [and] *seven rams* (*VeChur LaZahav*).

[2] *Balak did as Balaam had spoken, and Balak and Balaam brought up a bull and a ram on each altar.* [3] *Balaam said to Balak, "Stand near your burnt-offering while I go; perhaps* HASHEM *will happen toward me and He will show me something that I can tell you." He went with injured gait.*

BAAL HATURIM ELUCIDATED

descended from an incestuous union.[60]

❑ יַרְאֵנִי — HE WILL SHOW ME. The masoretic note, ב׳, means that this word appears twice in the *Tanach*: (i) here, וּדְבַר מַה יַּרְאֵנִי, *and He will show me something;* and (ii) אֱלֹהִים יַרְאֵנִי בְשֹׁרְרָי, *May God show me* [*what will befall*] *my watchful foes* (*Psalms* 59:11). This [similarity of expression] teaches that Balaam hated Israel and desired to curse them even more than Balak did,[61] and so he would pray regarding them: *May God show me* [*what will befall*] *my watchful foes.*

❑ וַיֵּלֶךְ שֶׁפִי — HE WENT WITH INJURED GAIT.[62] The *gematria* of this phrase (456) is equal to that of חִיגֵּר בְּרֶגֶל, *with a crippled foot.*[63] Alternatively: [The word שֶׁפִי] is akin to [שָׁף in the phrase] שָׁף מְדוּכְתֵּהּ, *it was dislocated from its place.*[64] [His foot became dislocated,] as it is stated, *she* [*his donkey*] *pressed Balaam's leg against the wall* (22:25 above).[65]

❑ שֶׁפִי — TO A HIGH PLACE.[65a] The letter פ [of this word] is doubled.[66] [This indicates that Balaam] פִּשְׁפֵּשׁ, *sought,* and חִפֵּשׂ, *searched,*[67] [to learn] which hour would be propitious to curse Israel.[68]

60. *Peirush HaRokeach.* For the circumstances of Moab's birth, see *Genesis* 19:30-37.

61. *Tanchuma* 5 and *Bamidbar Rabbah* 20:9, cited in *Rashi* to 22:11 above, s.v., וְגֵרַשְׁתִּיו.

62. Unlike *Targum Onkelos* and *Rashi,* who render שֶׁפִי, *alone,* the Baal HaTurim (see *Peirush HaTur HaAroch*) understands שֶׁפִי in the realm of *peshat* (simple meaning) as the singular of שְׁפָיִים, *high places* (see *Ibn Ezra;* see also *Jeremiah* 3:21 with *Radak*). In this comment, however, he explains it to mean *with injured gait,* both in the realm of *remez* (allusion) and in the realm of *peshat.*

63. See *Sanhedrin* 105a. Thus in the realm of *remez,* וַיֵּלֶךְ שֶׁפִי indicates that Balaam had a lame leg.

64. *Rashi* to *Sanhedrin* 105a, s.v., שפי. The phrase שָׁף מְדוּכְתֵּהּ appears in *Chullin* (42b, 54a-b) with regard to an animal whose hind thighbone became dislocated from its socket. Thus, even in the realm of *peshat,* וַיֵּלֶךְ שֶׁפִי indicates that Balaam had a lame leg.

65. *Peirush HaRokeach.*

65a. See note 62 above.

66. See the Baal HaTurim to 20:10 above, with note 57.

67. The doubled פ alludes to the abundance of letters פ in the phrase פִּשְׁפֵּשׁ וְחִפֵּשׂ (*Shoham Yakar*). Alternatively: The doubled פ indicates that the root letters of שפי, i.e., שפ, should be read as if each appeared twice — thus, פִּשְׁפֵּשׁ. The Baal HaTurim adds the term וְחִפֵּשׂ to intensify the meaning of פִּשְׁפֵּשׁ, i.e., he sought and searched, scrutinizing every possible moment for an opportune time to pronounce his curse (*VeChur LaZahav*).

68. *Sanhedrin* 105a, cited by *Rashi* to v. 8 below, s.v., לא זעם, and to 24:16 below; see also the Baal HaTurim to 22:6 above, s.v., מְבֹרָךְ, and 22:23.

ד וַיִּקָּר אֱלֹהִים אֶל־בִּלְעָם וַיֹּאמֶר אֵלָיו אֶת־
שִׁבְעַת הַמִּזְבְּחֹת עָרַכְתִּי וָאַעַל פָּר וָאַיִל בַּמִּזְבֵּחַ׃
ה וַיָּשֶׂם יהוה דָּבָר בְּפִי בִלְעָם וַיֹּאמֶר שׁוּב אֶל־
ו בָּלָק וְכֹה תְדַבֵּר׃ וַיָּשָׁב אֵלָיו וְהִנֵּה נִצָּב עַל־
ז עֹלָתוֹ הוּא וְכָל־שָׂרֵי מוֹאָב׃ וַיִּשָּׂא מְשָׁלוֹ וַיֹּאמַר

בעל הטורים

(ד) **עָרַכְתִּי.** ב׳ בַּמָּסֹרֶת – ״אֶת שִׁבְעַת הַמִּזְבְּחֹת עָרַכְתִּי״; וְאִידָךְ ״הִנֵּה נָא עָרַכְתִּי מִשְׁפָּט״. כְּלוֹמַר, שֶׁעָרַךְ הַמִּזְבְּחוֹת כְּדֵי לַעֲרֹךְ מִשְׁפָּט עִם יִשְׂרָאֵל:

(ה) **בְּפִי.** בְּגִימַטְרִיָּא מַלְאָךְ. ״בְּפִי״ בְּגִימַטְרִיָּא הַזְּמָם. שֶׁמַּלְאָךְ נָתַן זְמָם לְתוֹךְ פִּיו לְהַחֲזִירוֹ אֶל בָּלָק:

(ז) **וַיִּשָּׂא מְשָׁלוֹ.** שֶׁהֵרִים קוֹלוֹ שֶׁיִּשְׁמְעוּהוּ כָּל שִׁבְעִים אֻמּוֹת, כְּדֵי שֶׁיְּקַנְאוּ בְיִשְׂרָאֵל. וְזֶהוּ ״מְבָרֵךְ רֵעֵהוּ בְּקוֹל גָּדוֹל . . . קְלָלָה תֵּחָשֶׁב לוֹ״:

BAAL HATURIM ELUCIDATED

4. {The Baal HaTurim explains the word וַיִּקָּר in his comments to *Leviticus* 1:1.}

❑ **עָרַכְתִּי — I HAVE PREPARED.** The masoretic note, ב׳, means that this word appears twice in the *Tanach*:[69] (i) here, אֶת שִׁבְעַת הַמִּזְבְּחֹת עָרַכְתִּי, *I have prepared the seven altars;* and (ii) הִנֵּה נָא עָרַכְתִּי מִשְׁפָּט, *Behold, I have prepared [my] argument* (*Job* 13:18). [Similar expressions are used] to imply that he prepared the altars in order to arrange arguments against Israel.[70,71]

5. בְּפִי — IN THE MOUTH OF.[72] The *gematria* [of this word] (92) is equiva-

69. The Baal HaTurim's citation of the masoretic note is difficult, for the word עָרַכְתִּי appears a third time in the *Tanach* — שָׁם אַצְמִיחַ קֶרֶן לְדָוִד, *There I shall cause sovereignty to sprout for David;* עָרַכְתִּי נֵר לִמְשִׁיחִי, *I have prepared a lamp for My anointed one* (*Psalms* 132:17). Indeed, the masoretic note, ג׳, appears at each of the three verses. Perhaps the Baal HaTurim's comment originally included that verse (as suggested in note 71 below), but a later copyist inadvertently omitted a few words. Subsequent copyists, seeing that the Baal HaTurim cited only two verses, assumed that the ג׳, *three,* should read ב׳, *two* (*VeChur LaZahav*).

70. The Midrash explains why Balaam said, שִׁבְעַת הַמִּזְבְּחֹת, ***the** seven altars,* rather than שִׁבְעָה מִזְבְּחֹת, *seven altars.* Balaam was saying to God, "Israel's ancestors built a combined total of seven altars: Abraham built four (see *Genesis* 12:7, 12:8, 13:18 and 22:9); Isaac built one (see *Genesis* 26:25); and Jacob built two (see *Genesis* 33:20 and 35:7). But I, Balaam, have built seven, corresponding to ***the** seven altars* that they built" (*Tanchuma, Tzav* 1, cited by *Rashi;* see also *Maharal, Nesivos Olam, Nesiv HaAvodah,* Ch. 1).

71. *Ittur Bikkurim* suggests how the third appearance of עָרַכְתִּי (see note 69 above) fits into this comment: Although Balaam's purpose in preparing the seven altars was his attempt to prepare an argument against them, in the end, he was forced to speak prophecies that bode well for Israel and especially for David and the Messiah (see *Rashi* and the Baal HaTurim to 24:17 and 19 below).

72. Because בְּפִי in our verse and בְּפִי in 22:38 above are identical in spelling and vowelization, many editions present this comment at that verse, the first time the word בְּפִי appears. That

[4] *God happened upon Balaam and he said to Him, "I have prepared the seven altars and brought up a bull and ram on each altar."*

[5] *HASHEM put something in Balaam's mouth, and said, "Go back to Balak, and thus shall you say."*

[6] *He returned to him and behold! he was standing by his burnt-offering, he and all the officers of Moab.*

[7] *He declaimed his parable and said:*

BAAL HATURIM ELUCIDATED

lent[73] to that of מַלְאָךְ, *angel;* and the *gematria* of בְּפִי is equal to that of הַזְּמָם, *the muzzle.* For He [God] placed an angel, [to serve as] a muzzle in [Balaam's] mouth,[74] in order to make him return to Balak.[74a]

7. וַיִּשָּׂא מְשָׁלוֹ — HE DECLAIMED [literally, **HE RAISED**] **HIS PARABLE.** He raised his voice so that all the seventy nations would hear, in order to make them envious of Israel. This exemplifies [King Solomon's statement], מְבָרֵךְ רֵעֵהוּ בְּקוֹל גָּדוֹל ... קְלָלָה תֵּחָשֶׁב לוֹ, *If one blesses his friend loudly . . . it will be considered a curse to him* (*Proverbs* 27:14).[75]

is incorrect, however, for all the sources adduced in note 74 below cite our verse. Moreover, the two appearances of בְּפִי differ in meaning. Here, as indicated by the cantillation signs *munach* and *esnachta,* it is in the construct form, connected to the next word, forming the phrase, בְּפִי בִלְעָם, *in the mouth of Balaam.* In 22:38, however, as indicated by the cantillation sign *tipcha,* it stands independently, and means בְּפִי, *in my mouth.* Now, we can be quite sure that Balaam did not have the Baal HaTurim's allusion in mind when he spoke this word (*VeChur LaZahav*).

73. The principle of *im hakollel* allows 91, the *gematria* of מַלְאָךְ, to be considered equivalent to 92.

74. The Talmud records two opinions regarding what it was that God placed in Balaam's mouth. According to one view it was an angel [that would speak through Balaam's mouth (*Midrash Tanchuma* 12; that would prevent Balaam from cursing Israel (*Rashi*)]; according to the other, it was a חַכָּה, *fishhook* [that would serve as a bit with which to lead him (*Aruch,* cited in *Etz Yosef* to *Tanchuma* 12); that would prevent Balaam from opening his mouth to curse (*Rashi*)] (*Sanhedrin* 105b). The *Zohar* (III, 210a) states that a מַחְסוֹם, *muzzle* [synonymous with זְמָם], was placed in Balaam's mouth. The Baal HaTurim follows *Yalkut Shimoni* (cited by *Shoham Yakar* in *Harchavas HaDaas*), which combines the two views: God placed an angel in Balaam's mouth to serve as a bit.

74a. As our verse continues: [God said,] "*Go back to Balak . . .*"

75. Balaam raised his voice to bless Israel loudly, but his true intentions came to the fore when he advised Balak how to turn God against Israel. "The God of Israel hates promiscuity and idolatry . . ." (*Sanhedrin* 106a, cited by *Rashi* in his comments to *Proverbs* 27:14 and 24:14 below; see also *Tanchuma* 15; see *Sanhedrin* 105b regarding Balaam's intended curses).

Alternatively: The verse from *Proverbs* means that when one blesses, i.e., speaks in praise of, another person, lauding his kindness and hospitality, then others who do not have that person's best interests in mind will take advantage of his largesse or government officials will reassess his wealth and raise his taxes. Thus, the loud blessing becomes a curse (*Arachin* 16a, cited in *Rashi* to *Proverbs* 27:14). Therefore, Balaam raised his voice, hoping to incite the nations against Israel (*Yalkut Shimoni*).

מִן־אֲרָם יַנְחֵנִי בָלָק מֶלֶךְ־מוֹאָב מֵהַרְרֵי־קֶדֶם

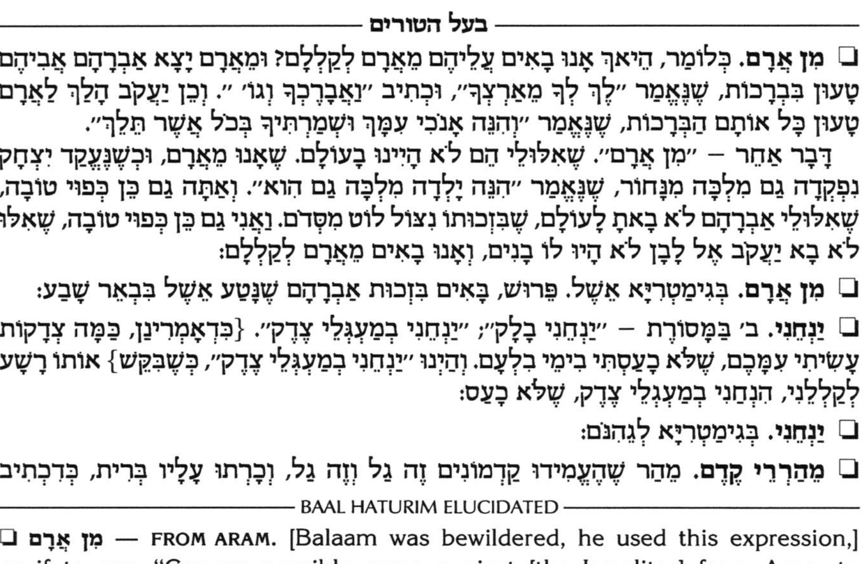

בעל הטורים

❑ **מִן אֲרָם.** כְּלוֹמַר, הֵיאךְ אָנוּ בָּאִים עֲלֵיהֶם מֵאֲרָם לְקַלְּלָם? וּמֵאֲרָם יָצָא אַבְרָהָם אֲבִיהֶם טָעוּן בִּבְרָכוֹת, שֶׁנֶּאֱמַר "לֶךְ לְךָ מֵאַרְצְךָ", וּכְתִיב "וַאֲבָרֶכְךָ וְגוֹ'". וְכֵן יַעֲקֹב הָלַךְ לַאֲרָם טָעוּן כָּל אוֹתָם הַבְּרָכוֹת, שֶׁנֶּאֱמַר "וְהִנֵּה אָנֹכִי עִמָּךְ וּשְׁמַרְתִּיךָ בְּכֹל אֲשֶׁר תֵּלֵךְ".

דָּבָר אַחֵר – "מִן אֲרָם". שֶׁאִלּוּלֵי הֵם לֹא הָיִינוּ בָּעוֹלָם. שֶׁאָנוּ מֵאֲרָם, וּכְשֶׁנֶּעֱקַד יִצְחָק נִפְקְדָה גַּם מִלְכָּה מִנָּחוֹר, שֶׁנֶּאֱמַר "הִנֵּה יָלְדָה מִלְכָּה גַם הִוא". וְאַתָּה גַּם כֵּן כְּפוּי טוֹבָה, שֶׁאִלּוּלֵי אַבְרָהָם לֹא בָאתָ לָעוֹלָם, שֶׁבִּזְכוּתוֹ נִצּוֹל לוֹט מִסְּדֹם. וַאֲנִי גַם כֵּן כְּפוּי טוֹבָה, שֶׁאִלּוּ לֹא בָא יַעֲקֹב אֶל לָבָן לֹא הָיוּ לוֹ בָנִים, וְאָנוּ בָּאִים מֵאֲרָם לְקַלְּלָם:

❑ **מִן אֲרָם.** בְּגִימַטְרִיָּא אֵשֶׁל. פֵּרוּשׁ, בָּאִים בִּזְכוּת אַבְרָהָם שֶׁנָּטַע אֵשֶׁל בִּבְאֵר שָׁבַע:

❑ **יַנְחֵנִי.** ב' בַּמָּסוֹרֶת – "יַנְחֵנִי בָלָק"; "יַנְחֵנִי בְמַעְגְּלֵי צֶדֶק". {כִּדְאָמְרִינַן, כַּמָּה צְדָקוֹת עָשִׂיתִי עִמָּכֶם, שֶׁלֹּא כָעַסְתִּי בִּימֵי בִלְעָם. וְהַיְנוּ "יַנְחֵנִי בְמַעְגְּלֵי צֶדֶק", כְּשֶׁבִּקֵּשׁ} אוֹתוֹ רָשָׁע לְקַלְּלֵנִי, הִנְחַנִי בְמַעְגְּלֵי צֶדֶק, שֶׁלֹּא כָעַס:

❑ **יַנְחֵנִי.** בְּגִימַטְרִיָּא לְגֵהִנֹּם:

❑ **מֵהַרְרֵי קֶדֶם.** מֵהַר שֶׁהֶעֱמִידוּ קַדְמוֹנִים זֶה גַל וְזֶה גַל, וְכָרְתוּ עָלָיו בְּרִית, כִּדְכְתִיב

BAAL HATURIM ELUCIDATED

❑ **מִן אֲרָם** — FROM ARAM. [Balaam was bewildered, he used this expression,] as if to say, "Can we possibly come against [the Israelites] from Aram to curse them? It was from Aram that their ancestor Abraham went forth laden with blessings, as it is stated, [*God said to Abram,*] "לֶךְ לְךָ מֵאַרְצְךָ, *Go for yourself from your land*" (*Genesis* 12:1), and it is written, [God said,] "וַאֲבָרֶכְךָ, *I will bless you . . .*" (*Genesis* 12:2). Similarly, Jacob journeyed to Aram laden with all those very blessings, as it is stated, וְהִנֵּה אָנֹכִי עִמָּךְ וּשְׁמַרְתִּיךָ בְּכֹל אֲשֶׁר תֵּלֵךְ, *Behold, I am with you; I will guard you wherever you go* (*Genesis* 28:15).[76]

Alternatively: *From Aram* [implies] that [Balaam was telling Balak,] "Were it not for them [the Israelites], we would not exist in the world. For we are from Aram [a grandson of Abraham's brother Nahor],[77] and it was when Isaac was bound [as an offering] that Milcah, Nahor's wife, conceived,[77a] as it is stated, *Behold! Milcah too has borne* [— thus, we are both being ungrateful to Abraham in our respective ways]. Even you are ungrateful, because were it not for Abraham, you would not have come into the world, for it was in his merit that [your ancestor] Lot was saved from [the destruction of] Sodom.[78]

"And even I am ungrateful. For if Jacob had not come to live with Laban,[79] Laban would not have had any sons.[80] Yet, we are coming from Aram to

---

76. *Yalkut Shimoni* 766.

77. See *Genesis* 22:20-21.

77a. Thus suggesting that Milcah conceived in the merit of Abraham and Isaac at the *Akeidah* (binding of Isaac).

78. Lot was saved from the destruction of Sodom in Abraham's merit (see *Genesis* 19:29). That very night, he cohabited with his daughter, who conceived and bore a son whom she named Moab (see *Genesis* 19:31-37).

79. The Talmud identifies Beor the father of Balaam with Laban (*Sanhedrin* 105a). *Targum Yonasan ben Uzziel* (22:5 above) identifies Balaam himself with Laban. (But see note 87a below.)

80. See *Rashi* to *Genesis* 30:27.

According to the Talmud (see note 79) Balaam

BAAL HATURIM ELUCIDATED

curse [Jacob's descendants]."[81]

[Moreover:] The *gematria* of מִן אֲרָם (331) is equal to that of אֶשֶׁל, *eshel-tree.* That is, [Balaam said,] "We are coming [only] due to the merit of Abraham, who planted an *eshel*-tree in Beer-sheba" (see *Genesis* 21:33).[82]

❑ יַנְחֵנִי — BALAK LED ME. The masoretic note, ב׳, means that this word appears twice in the *Tanach*: (i) here, יַנְחֵנִי בָלָק, *Balak led me;* and (ii) יַנְחֵנִי בְמַעְגְּלֵי צֶדֶק, *He would lead me on paths of righteousness* (*Psalms* 23:3). {[The similarity of expression can be explained] on the basis of the Talmudic statement: [God said,] "How many acts of righteousness did I perform for you when I did not become angry during the days of Balaam."[83] Thus, [Israel responded,] "*He would lead me on paths of righteousness.* When}[84] that wicked man {sought}[84] to curse me, God led me on paths of righteousness, for He did not become angry."[85]

❑ יַנְחֵנִי — LED ME. The *gematria* of this word (128) is equal to that of לְגֵהִנֹּם, *to Gehinnom.*[86]

❑ מֵהַרְרֵי קֶדֶם — FROM THE MOUNTAINS OF YORE,[87] that is, [Balaam was saying,] "From the mountain upon which [our] forebears [Laban and Jacob][87a] each set up a mound of rocks[87b] and upon which they entered into a covenant, as it is written,

was saying, "If not for Jacob, I would not have been born." According to *Targum Yonasan* he was saying, "Until Jacob came, I did not have any sons." (But see note 87a below.)

81. *Yalkut Shimoni* 765.

82. Had it not been for the merit of Abraham's hospitality, [as exemplified by the *eshel*-tree that Abraham planted many years later in Beer-sheba and under which he would serve his guests,] we would not be here today. For it was in the merit of Abraham's hospitality that the angels were dispatched to save Lot from Sodom (*VeChur LaZahav*).

83. *Sanhedrin* 105b, cited by *Rashi* to v. 8 below; see the Baal HaTurim to 22:6 above and to 23:3 with note 67.

84. The passage enclosed in braces does not appear in either the earlier or later printed editions, but is found in *Shoham Yakar's* manuscript edition. Many later editions have interpolated the word כְּשֶׁבָּא, *when he came,* to the beginning of the comment — "When that wicked man came to curse me" — in order to lend meaning to it.

85. *Maharam MiRothenburg.*

86. *Rabbeinu Ephraim* (*MiKesivah Ashkenazis*); see also the Baal HaTurim to 24:25 below. The Midrash interprets the phrase מִן אֲרָם יַנְחֵנִי as: *He led me down from the heights* [אֲרָם, akin to רָם, *lofty*] into eternal *Gehinnom* (*Tanchuma, Metzora* 1).

87. The word קֶדֶם means *before* or *in front of,* either in space or in time. In the Holy Tongue, directions are often expressed from the vantage point of a person facing east. Accordingly, the direction before him, i.e., east, is called קֶדֶם (e.g., *Genesis* 2:8, 10:30, 29:1); the direction to his rear, i.e., west, is called אָחוֹר, literally *behind* or *in back of* (e.g., *Isaiah* 9:11); the south is to his right side and is called יָמִין, literally *right* (e.g., *Psalms* 89:13); and the north, to his left, is called שְׂמֹאל, literally, *left* (e.g., *Genesis* 14:15). Thus, *Targum Onkelos* translates מֵהַרְרֵי קֶדֶם as מִטּוּרֵי מַדִּינְחָא, *from the mountains of the east.* But the Baal HaTurim interprets קֶדֶם of that phrase as referring to time not space. Thus, the phrase means *from the mountains of yore,* a reference to the days of old when Laban and Jacob, the ancestors of Moab and Israel respectively, met on those mountains.

87a. This comment is not in accordance with either of the two opinions cited in note 70 above (Y.S.).

87b. That is, although there was only one mountain, our verse uses the plural form הַרְרֵי, *mountains of,* as a reference to the two mounds set up there by Jacob and Laban (A.S.).

ח לְכָה֙ אָֽרָה־לִּ֣י יַעֲקֹ֔ב וּלְכָ֖ה זֹעֲמָ֥ה יִשְׂרָאֵֽל׃ מָ֣ה
אֶקֹּ֔ב לֹ֥א קַבֹּ֖ה אֵ֑ל וּמָ֣ה אֶזְעֹ֔ם לֹ֥א זָעַ֖ם יהוָֽה׃
ט כִּֽי־מֵרֹ֤אשׁ צֻרִים֙ אֶרְאֶ֔נּוּ וּמִגְּבָע֖וֹת אֲשׁוּרֶ֑נּוּ הֶן־עָם֙

בעל הטורים

"אִם אָנִי לֹא אֶעֱבֹר אֵלֶיךָ אֶת הַגַּל הַזֶּה וְגוֹ'", וְהוּא שָׁלַח אֵלַי לַעֲבֹר הַבְּרִית לְקַלְלָם.

דָּבָר אַחֵר – "מֵהַרְרֵי קֶדֶם" אֲנִי רוֹאֶה שֶׁלֹּא לְקַלְלָם. כִּי הֶהָרִים נָהֲגוּ בָהֶם כָּבוֹד, דִּכְתִיב "הֶהָרִים רָקְדוּ כְאֵילִים" לִכְבוֹדָם, וַאֲנִי אֲקַלְלֵם:

❑ **מֵהַרְרֵי קֶדֶם.** בְּגִימַטְרִיָּא מֵאֲבוֹת הָעוֹלָם:

❑ **אָרָה לִּי יַעֲקֹב וּלְכָה זֹעֲמָה יִשְׂרָאֵל.** הִזְכִּירָם בִּשְׁנֵי שְׁמוֹתֵיהֶם. אָמַר, בְּאֵיזֶה שֵׁם אֲקַלְלֵם? הַקָּדוֹשׁ בָּרוּךְ הוּא בֵּרְכוֹ כְּשֶׁהָיָה שְׁמוֹ יַעֲקֹב, וְשׁוּב בֵּרְכוֹ בְשֵׁם יִשְׂרָאֵל, אִם כֵּן, בְּאֵיזֶה שֵׁם אֲקַלְלֵם? וְהַקָּדוֹשׁ בָּרוּךְ הוּא לֹא רָצָה לְיַחֵד שְׁמוֹ עַל קִלְלָתָם. שֶׁבִּקְלָלוֹת כְּתִיב "וּבָאוּ עָלֶיךָ כָּל הַקְּלָלוֹת", וּבִבְרָכוֹת כְּתִיב "יְצַו ה' אִתְּךָ אֶת הַבְּרָכָה בַּאֲסָמֶיךָ וּבְכֹל מִשְׁלַח יָדֶךָ" – וְהֵיאָךְ אֲקַלְלֵם?

(ט) **כִּי מֵרֹאשׁ צֻרִים אֶרְאֶנּוּ.** אֲנִי רוֹאֶה שֶׁנִּבְרְאוּ קֹדֶם שֶׁנִּבְרָא הָעוֹלָם וְהַצּוּרִים:

❑ **כִּי מֵרֹאשׁ.** בְּגִימַטְרִיָּא עַל הַר הַמּוֹרִיָּה:

❑ **מֵרֹאשׁ צֻרִים.** בְּגִימַטְרִיָּא מִזְּכוּת הָאָבוֹת:

❑ **וּמִגְּבָעוֹת.** בְּגִימַטְרִיָּא הֵן הָאִמָּהוֹת:

BAAL HATURIM ELUCIDATED

אִם אָנִי לֹא אֶעֱבֹר אֵלֶיךָ אֶת הַגַּל הַזֶּה, *that I may not cross over to you past this mound . . .* (*Genesis* 31:52). Nevertheless, Balak has sent for me to abrogate this covenant in order to curse Israel."[88]

Alternatively: מֵהַרְרֵי קֶדֶם, *from the mountains of yore,* I see that it is wrong to curse Israel, for the mountains accorded them honor, as it is written, [*When Israel left Egypt . . .*] הֶהָרִים רָקְדוּ כְאֵילִים, *the mountains danced like rams* (*Psalms* 114:4), in their honor. Shall I, then, curse them?

[Alternatively: The phrase alludes to their exalted forebears, for] the *gematria* of מֵהַרְרֵי קֶדֶם is 599, equivalent[88a] to that of מֵאֲבוֹת הָעוֹלָם, *from the Patriarchs of the world.*[89]

❑ **אָרָה לִּי יַעֲקֹב וּלְכָה זֹעֲמָה יִשְׂרָאֵל — CURSE JACOB FOR ME, COME BRING ANGER UPON ISRAEL.** Balaam called them by both of their names [Jacob and Israel]. He said, "By what name shall I curse them? God has blessed their Patriarch when his name was Jacob, and blessed him again when he was renamed Israel

88. According to the Midrash, the wall against which Balaam's donkey pressed his leg (see 22:25 above) was the very mound built by Laban and Jacob. Laban himself (whom *Targum Yonasan* identifies with Balaam) assigned that mound to the role of witness. And then when Balaam (Laban) was breaking his covenant in which he promised not to cross the mound to cause evil to Jacob (see *Genesis* 31:46-53), the witness, i.e., the mound/wall, punished him by crippling his leg (*Tanchuma, Vayeitzei* 13).

88a. The principle of *im hakollel* allows 599 to be considered equivalent to 600, the *gematria* of the Baal HaTurim's phrase.

89. *Peirush HaRokeach.* That is, Balaam said, "Being that they are descended from the Patriarchs of the world, how can I curse them?" (*Rimzei Rabbeinu Yoel*).

of yore, 'Come curse Jacob for me, come bring anger upon Israel.'

8 *"How can I curse? — God has not cursed. How can I anger? — HASHEM is not angry.*

9 *"For I see it ahead of the rocks, and from the hills do I see it. Behold! it is a nation that will dwell in*

BAAL HATURIM ELUCIDATED

(see *Genesis* 28:14 and 35:9). If so, by which name can I curse them?[90]

"Moreover," [Balaam continued,] "[even when] God [threatened them with a curse, He] did not identify His name with their curse. Thus, regarding the curses it is written, וּבָאוּ עָלֶיךָ כָּל הַקְּלָלוֹת [הָאֵלֶּה], *Then all* [*these*] *curses will come upon you* (*Deuteronomy* 28:15).[91] But with regard to the blessings, the verse states, יְצַו ה׳ אִתְּךָ אֶת הַבְּרָכָה בַּאֲסָמֶיךָ וּבְכֹל מִשְׁלַח יָדֶךָ, *HASHEM will command the blessing for you in your storehouses and your every undertaking* (*Deuteronomy* 28:8). How, then, can I curse them?"[92]

9. כִּי מֵרֹאשׁ צֻרִים אֶרְאֶנּוּ — FOR I SEE IT AHEAD OF THE ROCKS. [Balaam said,] "I see that they were created before the world and the rocks were created."[93]

❑ **כִּי מֵרֹאשׁ — FOR AHEAD OF.** [This phrase can also be understood as *on top of.* Indeed,] its *gematria* (571) is equal to that of עַל הַר הַמּוֹרִיָּה, *upon Mount Moriah.*[94]

❑ **מֵרֹאשׁ צֻרִים — AHEAD OF THE ROCKS.** The *gematria* of מֵרֹאשׁ צֻרִים (881) is equivalent[95] to that of מִזְּכוּת אָבוֹת, *from the merit of the Patriarchs.*[96]

❑ **וּמִגְּבָעוֹת — AND FROM THE HILLS.** The *gematria* of this word (527) is equivalent[97] to that of הֵן הָאִמָּהוֹת, *They are the Matriarchs.*[98]

90. Cf. *Rashi.*

91. Rather than, "God will bring these curses upon you." See the Baal HaTurim to *Genesis* 1:5, s.v., וְלַחֹשֶׁךְ קָרָא לָיְלָה.

92. *Tanchuma* 12; *Bamidbar Rabbah* 20:19.

93. *Yalkut Shimoni* 766 — When God decided to create the world, He looked into the future and saw the idolatry of the generation of Enosh and the evils of the generation of the Flood. He said, "How can I create a world for these wicked ones?" But, when He saw that Abraham would arise from them, He said, "I have found the foundation stone upon which to build and establish the world."

94. *Peirush HaRokeach.* Balaam was saying, "How can I curse them? The merit of Abraham and Isaac on Mount Moriah (see *Genesis* Ch. 22) will protect them from my words" (*Yad Aharon*).

95. The principle of *im hakollel* allows 881 to be considered equivalent to 882, the *gematria* of the Baal HaTurim's phrase.

In some editions, the Baal HaTurim's phrase reads מִזְּכוּת הָאָבוֹת, which has a *gematria* of 887. To reconcile the *gematriaos,* these editions use the full spelling צוּרִים, with a ו, thus bringing the *gematria* of the Scriptural phrase to 887.

96. *Rabbeinu Ephraim* (*MiKesivah Ashkenazis*); *Rimzei Rabbeinu Yoel.* The Midrash states: מֵרֹאשׁ צֻרִים אֶרְאֶנּוּ refers to the Patriarchs; וּמִגְּבָעוֹת אֲשׁוּרֶנּוּ refers to the Matriarchs (*Tanchuma* 12).

97. The *gematria* of הֵן הָאִמָּהוֹת is only 512, fifteen less than that of וּמִגְּבָעוֹת. And, indeed, *Shoham Yakar* cites one manuscript that omits the word בְּגִימַטְרִיָּא; nevertheless, virtually all the printed editions have that word. The *gematriaos* may be reconciled by adding a י to הֵן הָאִימָּהוֹת, raising its *gematria* to 522; and dropping the prefix -ו from וּמִגְּבָעוֹת, reducing its *gematria* to 521, which the principle of *im hakollel* allows to be considered equivalent to 522. And that is how this comment appears in *Peirush HaRokeach* and *Rimzei Rabbeinu Yoel.* Alternatively: The -ו should be retained in וּמִגְּבָעוֹת keeping its *gematria* at 527; but the Baal HaTurim's phrase should be emended to הִנֵּה הָאִימָּהוֹת, which raises its *gematria* to 527, without changing its meaning (*Yad Aharon*).

98. *Peirush HaRokeach.* See note 96 above.

י לְבָדָד יִשְׁכֹּן וּבַגּוֹיִם לֹא יִתְחַשָּׁב: מִי מָנָה עֲפַר יַעֲקֹב

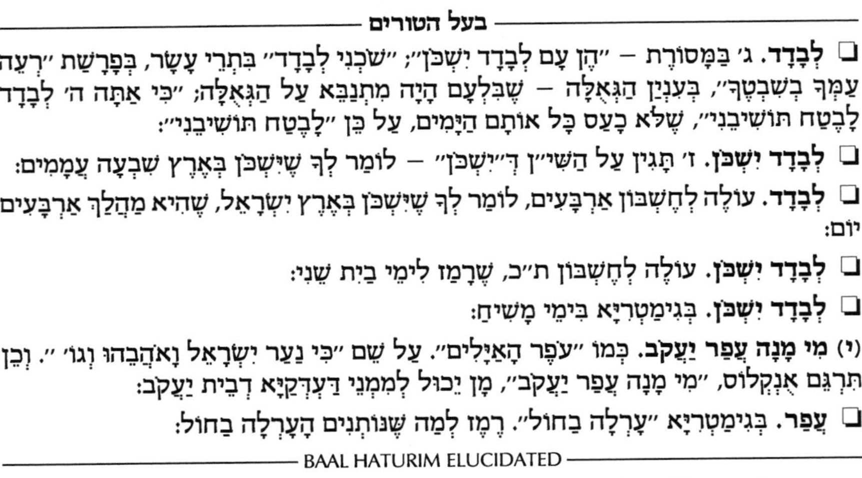

בעל הטורים

❑ **לְבָדָד.** ג׳ בַּמָּסוֹרֶת – ״הֶן עָם לְבָדָד יִשְׁכֹּן״; ״שֹׁכְנִי לְבָדָד״ בִּתְרֵי עָשָׂר, בְּפָרָשַׁת ״רְעֵה עַמְּךָ בְשִׁבְטֶךָ״, בְּעִנְיַן הַגְּאֻלָּה – שֶׁבִּלְעָם הָיָה מִתְנַבֵּא עַל הַגְּאֻלָּה; ״כִּי אַתָּה ה׳ לְבָדָד לָבֶטַח תּוֹשִׁיבֵנִי״, שֶׁלֹּא כָעַס כָּל אוֹתָם הַיָּמִים, עַל כֵּן ״לָבֶטַח תּוֹשִׁיבֵנִי״:

❑ **לְבָדָד יִשְׁכֹּן.** ז׳ תָּגִין עַל הַשִּׁי״ן דְ״יִשְׁכֹּן״ – לוֹמַר לְךָ שֶׁיִּשְׁכֹּן בְּאֶרֶץ שִׁבְעָה עֲמָמִים:

❑ **לְבָדָד.** עוֹלֶה לְחֶשְׁבּוֹן אַרְבָּעִים, לוֹמַר לְךָ שֶׁיִּשְׁכֹּן בְּאֶרֶץ יִשְׂרָאֵל, שֶׁהִיא מַהֲלַךְ אַרְבָּעִים יוֹם:

❑ **לְבָדָד יִשְׁכֹּן.** עוֹלֶה לְחֶשְׁבּוֹן ת״כ, שֶׁרָמַז לִימֵי בַּיִת שֵׁנִי:

❑ **לְבָדָד יִשְׁכֹּן.** בְּגִימַטְרִיָּא בִּימֵי מָשִׁיחַ:

(י) מִי מָנָה עֲפַר יַעֲקֹב. כְּמוֹ ״עֹפֶר הָאַיָּלִים״. עַל שֵׁם ״כִּי נַעַר יִשְׂרָאֵל וָאֹהֲבֵהוּ וְגוֹ׳ ״. וְכֵן תִּרְגֵּם אֻנְקְלוֹס, ״מִי מָנָה עֲפַר יַעֲקֹב״, מָן יַכוּל לְמִמְנֵי דַּעְדְקַיָּא דְבֵית יַעֲקֹב:

❑ **עֲפַר.** בְּגִימַטְרִיָּא ״עָרְלָה בַחוֹל״. רֶמֶז לְמָה שֶׁנּוֹתְנִים הָעָרְלָה בַּחוֹל:

BAAL HATURIM ELUCIDATED

❑ **לְבָדָד** — IN SOLITUDE. The masoretic note, ג׳, means that this word appears three times in the *Tanach*: (i) here, הֶן עָם לְבָדָד יִשְׁכֹּן, *Behold! It is a nation that will dwell in solitude;* (ii) שֹׁכְנִי לְבָדָד, *let them dwell in* [*secure*] *solitude* (*Micah* 7:14), which appears in the *Twelve Prophets,* in the passage [that begins], רְעֵה עַמְּךָ בְשִׁבְטֶךָ, *Shepherd Your people with Your staff,* which refers to the Redemption — for Balaam, too, is prophesying regarding the Redemption;[98a] and (iii) כִּי אַתָּה ה׳ לְבָדָד לָבֶטַח תּוֹשִׁיבֵנִי, *for You, HASHEM, alone — You would make me dwell in security* (*Psalms* 4:9), for God did not become wrathful all those days [that Balaam sought to curse Israel].[99] In that manner, *You would make me*[99a] *dwell in security.*

❑ **לְבָדָד יִשְׁכֹּן** — WILL DWELL IN SOLITUDE. [According to a scribal tradition,] there are seven *tagin*[100] on the ש of יִשְׁכֹּן. This indicates to you that [the Israelites] will dwell in the land of the seven [Canaanite] nations.

❑ **לְבָדָד** — IN SOLITUDE. The *gematria* of this word is 40, to indicate to you that Israel will dwell in *Eretz Yisrael* which measures the distance of a forty-day march [in each direction].[101]

❑ **לְבָדָד יִשְׁכֹּן** — WILL DWELL IN SOLITUDE. The *gematria* of this phrase is 420,

98a. For example, at 24:14 below.

99. See the Baal HaTurim's comments to 22:6 above, s.v., מְבֹרָךְ, and 23:7, s.v., יַנְחֵנִי.

99a. The text follows the Constantinople edition, and that is how it appears in most printed editions. The Furth edition and *Shoham Yakar's* manuscript edition read תּוֹשִׁיבֵנוּ, *You would make us dwell.*

100. See 6:26 above, with note 85 and illustration.

101. *R' Ephraim.* The dimensions of *Eretz Yisrael* are given as 400 *parsah* by 400 *parsah* (see *Rashi* to 13:25 above; *Tosafos, Rosh Hashanah* 23b, s.v., כמה; *Tosafos, Bava Metzia* 28a, s.v., חמשה עשר), and an average person can cover ten *parsah* in one day (*Pesachim* 93b). Thus, to traverse *Eretz Yisrael* (either north-south or east-west) would take forty days. Opinions regarding the modern-day equivalent of a *parsah* range between 2.386 and 2.863 miles. 400 *parsah* would then measure between 954 and 1145 miles.

solitude and not be reckoned among the nations.
[10] *"Who has counted the youth of Jacob or [assigned] a*

alluding to the number of years the Second Temple stood.[102]

❑ לְבָדָד יִשְׁכֹּן — WILL DWELL IN SOLITUDE. The *gematria* of this phrase (420) is equal to that of בִּימֵי מָשִׁיחַ, *in the days of the Messiah.* [103]

10. מִי מָנָה עֲפַר יַעֲקֹב — WHO HAS COUNTED THE YOUTH OF JACOB? [The word עֲפַר (usually rendered *the dust of*[104])[105] means *the youth of*] as in the verse, לְעֹפֶר הָאַיָּלִים, *to the young of the harts* (*Song of Songs* 2:9,17 and 8:14). This is in accordance with the verse, . . . כִּי נַעַר יִשְׂרָאֵל וָאֹהֲבֵהוּ, *for Israel is a youth and I have loved him . . .* (*Hosea* 11:1). Similarly, *Onkelos* renders the phrase מִי מָנָה עֲפַר יַעֲקֹב as מַן יְכוֹל לְמִמְנֵי דַּעְדְקַיָּא דְבֵית יַעֲקֹב, *Who is able to count the youngsters of the House of Jacob?*[106]

❑ עֲפַר — literally, THE DUST OF. The *gematria* of עֲפַר (350) is equivalent[107] to that of עָרְלָה בַּחוֹל, *the foreskin in the sand,* an allusion to the [custom of] placing the foreskin in sand [after the circumcision.[108]][109]

102. *Peirush HaRokeach; R' Ephraim.* For further allusions to this number, see the Baal HaTurim to *Genesis* 1:2; *Exodus* 6:4, 25:8, 27:20; and *Leviticus* 26:11.

103. *Peirush HaRokeach.* According to the Midrash, this phrase refers to the ultimate Redemption in the time of *Mashiach* (*Yalkut Shimoni* 768).

104. See, for example, *Genesis* 28:14, *Exodus* 8:13.

105. And that is how the word is understood in our verse according to *Targum Yonasan ben Uzziel, Rashi* (second interpretation), *Ibn Ezra, Ramban* and the Baal HaTurim's next comment.

106. According to the Midrash our verse means: Who is able to count the youth of Israel who engage themselves in Torah study and thereby assume the role of protective armament for Israel (*Tanna DeVei Eliyahu* 21).

107. The principle of *im hakollel* allows 350 to be considered equivalent to 351, the *gematria* of the Baal HaTurim's phrase.

108. The relationship between our verse and circumcision is unclear. A suggested connection between the two is based on the Midrash which states: Because of the pain involved in moving about following circumcision [but see *Yevamos* 71b-72a for another reason], the Children of Israel did not circumcise their children during their forty-year journey in the wilderness, as it is stated, *All the people who were born in the wilderness on the way during their exodus from Egypt were not circumcised* (*Joshua* 5:5) . . . But is it possible that those Israelites who were uncircumcised were able to hear God's voice at Mount Sinai? Or that He gave the Torah to the uncircumcised, Heaven forbid? Rather, the nation did circumcise the newborns in the wilderness, but they only performed the first step of the circumcision, מִילָה, *milah* [i.e., the excision of the foreskin]. However, they omitted the second step, פְּרִיעָה, *uncovering* [i.e., the removal of the thin membrane that usually adheres to the glans, in order that the entire glans be uncovered], and any circumcision that does not include פְּרִיעָה is not a valid circumcision (see *Shabbos* 137b). When Israel entered *Eretz Yisrael,* God told Joshua that they had not been circumcised properly, so he should now *return and circumcise the Children of Israel a second time* (*Joshua* 5:2) [this time including the second step, פְּרִיעָה. Thus, in one respect Israel performed circumcision in the wilderness, but in another respect, they did not.]

The Midrash continues: The Israelites would cover the foreskins with the earth of the wilderness. So that when Balaam came [to curse them], he said, *"Who has counted the dust of Jacob?"* Based on this the Sages decreed that the bloody foreskin be covered with the dust of the ground (*Pirkei DeRabbi Eliezer* 29).

In truth, Balaam could have used the more specific word חול, *sand,* which the Torah uses elsewhere as a metaphor for the children of Israel (see *Genesis* 22:17), and which according to some opinions is preferable to earth for covering the foreskin (see *Radal* to *Pirkei DeRabbi*

וּמִסְפָּר אֶת־רֹבַע יִשְׂרָאֵל תָּמֹת נַפְשִׁי מוֹת יְשָׁרִים
יא וּתְהִי אַחֲרִיתִי כָּמֹהוּ: וַיֹּאמֶר בָּלָק אֶל־בִּלְעָם מֶה
עָשִׂיתָ לִי לָקֹב אֹיְבַי לְקַחְתִּיךָ וְהִנֵּה בֵּרַכְתָּ בָרֵךְ:
יב וַיַּעַן וַיֹּאמַר הֲלֹא אֵת אֲשֶׁר יָשִׂים יהוה בְּפִי אֹתוֹ
חמישי יג אֶשְׁמֹר לְדַבֵּר: וַיֹּאמֶר אֵלָיו בָּלָק לְךָ־נָּא אִתִּי
אֶל־מָקוֹם אַחֵר אֲשֶׁר תִּרְאֶנּוּ מִשָּׁם אֶפֶס קָצֵהוּ

בעל הטורים

❏ **תָּמֹת.** ג׳ בַּמָּסוֹרֶת – ״תָּמֹת נַפְשִׁי מוֹת יְשָׁרִים״; וְאִידָךְ ״תָּמֹת נַפְשִׁי עִם פְּלִשְׁתִּים״; וְאִידָךְ ״תָּמֹת בַּנֹּעַר נַפְשָׁם״. הוּא בִקֵּשׁ שֶׁתָּמוּת נַפְשׁוֹ עִם הַיְשָׁרִים, וְלֹא הָיָה כֵן. אֶלָּא אַדְּרַבָּה, מֵת מוֹת פְּלִשְׁתִּים, כְּלוֹמַר מוֹת רְשָׁעִים, וּבַנֹּעַר, כִּדְאִיתָא, ״אַנְשֵׁי דָמִים וּמִרְמָה לֹא יֶחֱצוּ יְמֵיהֶם״, שֶׁבֶּן ל״ד שָׁנִים הָיָה כְּשֶׁהֲרָגוּ פִּינְחָס:

❏ **יְשָׁרִים.** בְּגִימַטְרִיָּא אֲבוֹת הָעוֹלָם. סוֹפֵי תֵבוֹת שֶׁל שְׁמוֹת הָאָבוֹת {אַבְרָהָם יִצְחָק יַעֲקֹב} בְּגִימַטְרִיָּא בִּלְעָם, וְזֶהוּ ״וּתְהִי אַחֲרִיתִי כָּמֹהוּ״:

BAAL HATURIM ELUCIDATED

❏ **תָּמֹת — . . . DIE.** The masoretic note, ג׳, means that this word appears three times[110] in the *Tanach*: (i) here, תָּמֹת נַפְשִׁי מוֹת יְשָׁרִים, *O that my soul would die the death of the upright;* (ii) תָּמֹת נַפְשִׁי עִם פְּלִשְׁתִּים, *Let my soul die with the Philistines!* (*Judges* 16:30); and (iii) תָּמֹת בַּנֹּעַר נַפְשָׁם, *Their soul will die in* [*its*] *youth* (*Job* 36:14). [Balaam] desired that his soul die the death of the righteous. But that did not happen. Rather, to the contrary, he died the death of the Philistines, i.e., the death of the wicked; moreover, he died as a young man, as [the Talmud] states: [The verse,] *Men of bloodshed and deceit shall not live out half their days* (*Psalms* 55:24), means that Balaam was only thirty-four years old[111]

Eliezer 29, note 51), rather than the more general עָפָר, *earth* or *dust.* Perhaps he used the word עָפָר because its letters can be rearranged to spell פָּרַע, *he uncovered,* i.e., Balaam, whose desire was to curse Israel, meant to say, "Who has counted the number of circumcisions that lacked the essential step of פְּרִיעָה?" Thus did he hope to cause Israel to lose favor with God. But God turned Balaam's words from a curse into a blessing. For, after all, they did perform whatever part of the circumcision they were able to, as attested to by the foreskins lying in the sands of the wilderness (*VeChur LaZahav*).

109. See *Pirkei DeRabbi Eliezer* 29 (cited in note 108); *Zohar, Lech Lecha* 95a; *Tur* and *Shulchan Aruch, Yoreh Deah* 265:10; *Hagahos Maimonios* to *Hilchos Milah* 3:9:5; the Baal HaTurim to *Genesis* 26:15.

110. The noun נֶפֶשׁ, *soul,* is a feminine noun. The usual form of the verb מוּת, *to die,* in third person feminine singular future tense is תָּמוּת, and that form appears six times in the *Tanach* (*Exodus* 7:18; *Isaiah* 66:24; *Ezekiel* 18:4, 20; *Zechariah* 11:9; and *Job* 12:2). The masoretic note reads in full: ג׳ חָסֵר וְחַד וְתָמֹת, *The* [*variant*] *form* תָּמֹת appears three times [without a prefix], each time spelled defectively [without a ו after the מ]; and one more time as וְתָמֹת, with the prefix וְ־ (*Isaiah* 50:2).

111. The Talmud discusses Balaam's age at his death: A certain heretic asked Rabbi Chanina, "Have you heard how old Balaam was [when he was killed]?" Rabbi Chanina replied, "Nothing is written [in Scripture] about this matter. Nevertheless, [we can make an inference] from that which is written, *Men of bloodshed and deceit shall not live out half their days* (*Psalms* 55:24);

number [to] one of [the] four [degel-divisions] of Israel? O
that my soul would die the death of the upright, and that
my end be like his!"
11 *Balak said to Balaam, "What have you done to me! To*
curse my enemy have I brought you — but behold! you
have even blessed!"
12 *He spoke up and said, "Is it not so that whatever HASHEM puts in my mouth, that I must take heed to speak?"*
13 *Balak said to him, "Please come with me to a different place from which you will see them; however, you*

BAAL HATURIM ELUCIDATED

when Phinehas killed him.[112]

❑ יְשָׁרִים — OF THE UPRIGHT. The *gematria* of this word (560) is equal to that of אֲבוֹת הָעוֹלָם, *the Patriarchs of the world.* [113] [Thus, too,] the *gematria* of the final letters of the names of the Patriarchs {— [the ם (=40) of] אַבְרָהָם, *Abraham,* [the ק (=100) of] יִצְחָק, *Isaac,* and [the ב (=2) of] יַעֲקֹב, *Jacob,* a total of 142 —}[113a] is equal to that of בִּלְעָם, *Balaam.* This is alluded to by the phrase, *and that my end be like his.* [114]

he must have lived [less than half the duration of a normal life span of seventy years (see *Psalms* 90:10)] — thirty-three or thirty-four years." The heretic then said, "You have spoken well! For I have seen the Chronicle of Balaam, and it is written there: Balaam the lame was thirty-three years old when he was killed by Phinehas the outlaw" (*Sanhedrin* 106b).

A question has been raised regarding this comment: Whereas the Talmud cites the Chronicle of Balaam, which gives his age as thirty-three, why does the Baal HaTurim use the number thirty-four? (*Shoham Yakar*). Perhaps, when Rabbi Chanina said that Balaam lived thirty-three or thirty-four years, he meant that Balaam had already passed his thirty-third birthday but had not yet reached his thirty-fourth. If so, the Chronicle of Balaam records the number of full years that Balaam lived; the Baal HaTurim, however, reckons the number of the year of Balaam's life in which he died. In doing so, the Baal HaTurim teaches an important lesson: The inference that Rabbi Chanina made from a verse in *Psalms* bears more credence than anything recorded in a secular annal of history. Had the Baal HaTurim cited the words of the heretic, it would appear that he found the heretic to be more precise than Rabbi Chanina. By citing the number thirty-four, the Baal HaTurim displays his preference for Rabbi Chanina's inferences and his skepticism regarding the heretic's Chronicle (*VeChur LaZahav*).

112. According to *Rashi* (*Sanhedrin* 106b), Phinehas may not have actually killed Balaam. Rather, as general of the Israelite army during the battle in which Balaam was killed (see 31:1-8 below), any enemy killed in that battle would be ascribed to Phinehas.

According to others, however, Phinehas actually drew his sword and slew Balaam (see *Targum Yonasan ben Uzziel* to 31:8 below).

113. *Peirush HaRokeach.* The Talmud identifies the סֵפֶר הַיָּשָׁר, *Book of the Upright* (*Joshua* 10:13), as the book of Abraham, Isaac and Jacob [i.e., the *Book of Genesis,* which records their lives (*Rashi*)] who are called יְשָׁרִים, *upright ones,* by Balaam in our verse.

113a. The passage enclosed in braces does not appear in the printed editions, but is found in *Shoham Yakar's* manuscript edition.

114. *Peirush HaRokeach.*

יד תִּרְאֶה וְכֻלּוֹ לֹא תִרְאֶה וְקָבְנוֹ־לִי מִשָּׁם: וַיִּקָּחֵהוּ
שְׂדֵה צֹפִים אֶל־רֹאשׁ הַפִּסְגָּה וַיִּבֶן שִׁבְעָה מִזְבְּחֹת
טו וַיַּעַל פָּר וָאַיִל בַּמִּזְבֵּחַ: וַיֹּאמֶר אֶל־בָּלָק הִתְיַצֵּב
טז כֹּה עַל־עֹלָתֶךָ וְאָנֹכִי אִקָּרֶה כֹּה: וַיִּקָּר יהוה
אֶל־בִּלְעָם וַיָּשֶׂם דָּבָר בְּפִיו וַיֹּאמֶר שׁוּב אֶל־בָּלָק
יז וְכֹה תְדַבֵּר: וַיָּבֹא אֵלָיו וְהִנּוֹ נִצָּב עַל־עֹלָתוֹ וְשָׂרֵי
יח מוֹאָב אִתּוֹ וַיֹּאמֶר לוֹ בָּלָק מַה־דִּבֶּר יהוה: וַיִּשָּׂא
מְשָׁלוֹ וַיֹּאמַר קוּם בָּלָק וּשְׁמָע הַאֲזִינָה עָדַי בְּנוֹ
יט צִפֹּר: לֹא אִישׁ אֵל וִיכַזֵּב וּבֶן־אָדָם וְיִתְנֶחָם הַהוּא
כ אָמַר וְלֹא יַעֲשֶׂה וְדִבֶּר וְלֹא יְקִימֶנָּה: הִנֵּה בָרֵךְ
כא לָקָחְתִּי וּבֵרֵךְ וְלֹא אֲשִׁיבֶנָּה: לֹא־הִבִּיט אָוֶן בְּיַעֲקֹב
וְלֹא־רָאָה עָמָל בְּיִשְׂרָאֵל יהוה אֱלֹהָיו עִמּוֹ

בעל הטורים

(יג) **וְכֻלּוֹ.** ב׳ בַּמָּסוֹרֶת – ״וְכֻלּוֹ לֹא תִרְאֶה״; וְאִידָךְ ״וְכֻלּוֹ מַחֲמַדִּים״. הַיְנוּ דְּאָמְרִינַן בְּמַסֶּכֶת נִדָּה, ״מִי מָנָה עֲפַר יַעֲקֹב וּמִסְפָּר אֶת רֹבַע יִשְׂרָאֵל״, עַל דָּבָר זֶה נִסְמֵית עֵינוֹ שֶׁל בִּלְעָם, שֶׁאָמַר, הַקָּדוֹשׁ בָּרוּךְ הוּא, שֶׁהוּא קָדוֹשׁ וּמְשָׁרְתָיו קְדוֹשִׁים, יִסְתַּכֵּל בְּדָבָר זֶה? וְהַיְנוּ ״וְכֻלּוֹ לֹא תִרְאֶה״. בִּשְׁבִיל שֶׁדִּבֵּר כְּנֶגֶד הַקָּדוֹשׁ בָּרוּךְ הוּא, שֶׁ״כֻּלּוֹ מַחֲמַדִּים״, נִסְמֵית עֵינוֹ, ״וְכֻלּוֹ לֹא תִרְאֶה״:

(כא) **לֹא הִבִּיט אָוֶן בְּיַעֲקֹב.** שֶׁאֵין אוֹתִיּוֹת חֵ״ט בִּשְׁמוֹתָם שֶׁל שְׁבָטִים:

BAAL HATURIM ELUCIDATED

13. וְכֻלּוֹ — ALL OF IT. The masoretic note ב׳ means that this term appears twice in the *Tanach*: (i) here, וְכֻלּוֹ לֹא תִרְאֶה, *but you will not see all of it;* and (ii) וְכֻלּוֹ מַחֲמַדִּים, *and He is all delight* (*Song of Songs* 5:16). This [similarity of expression] alludes to the Sages' statement in tractate *Niddah*: As a consequence of Balaam's statement — "*Who has counted the youth of Jacob or numbered the 'rova'*[115] *of Israel?*" — one of Balaam's eyes became blind, for he said [to himself], "[Is it proper that] the Holy One, Blessed is He, Who is holy and Whose ministers are holy, should gaze at such a thing?" Thus, [our verse states,] *but you will not see* ***all*** *of it,* [i.e., your sight will fail]. Because [Balaam] spoke against God Who *is* ***all***

115. According to the simple meaning of the verse, the term רֹבַע means *one-fourth* and refers to one of the four *degalim*-divisions of Israel (*Targum Onkelos; Peirush HaTur HaAroch*). According to the Talmud (*Niddah* 31a) and Midrash (*Tanchuma* 12), רֹבַע refers to רְבִיעוֹתֵיהֶן, *their cohabitations.* Thus, the Talmud explains Balaam's statement: This verse indicates that God sits and counts the cohabitations of Israel in anticipation of the droplet from which a righteous person will be created. And it was over this matter that one of Balaam's eyes became blind. For Balaam [meant to ridicule when he spoke this verse; he] said, "He Who is pure and holy, and Whose ministers are pure and holy, should He gaze at such a thing?" Immediately, his eye became blind.

will see its edge but you will not see all of it — and you will curse it for me from there." [14] *He took him to the field of the lookouts, to the top of the peak, and he built seven altars and brought up a bull and a ram on each altar.* [15] *He said to Balak, "Stand here near your burnt-offering, and I will be happened upon here."*

[16] *HASHEM happened upon Balaam and put an utterance in his mouth; and said, "Go back to Balak and so shall you say."*

[17] *He came to him and — behold! he was standing by his burnt-offering and the officers of Moab were with him. Balak said to him, "What did HASHEM speak?"*

[18] *He declaimed his parable and said: "Stand erect, O Balak, and hear; give ear to me, O son of Zippor.*

[19] *"God is not a man that He should be deceitful, nor a son of man that He should relent.*

Would He say and not do, or speak and not confirm?

[20] *"Behold! to bless have I received — He has blessed, and I shall not contradict it.*

[21] *"He perceived no iniquity in Jacob, and saw no perversity in Israel. HASHEM his God is with him, and the*

BAAL HATURIM ELUCIDATED

delight, one of his eyes became blind, [in fulfillment of the verse,] *you will not see all of it.* [116]

21. לֹא הִבִּיט אָוֶן בְּיַעֲקֹב — HE PERCEIVED NO INIQUITY IN JACOB, for the letters ח and ט[116a] [the primary letters of the word חֵטְא, *sin*] do not appear in the names of the tribes.[117]

116. *Maharam MiRothenburg.*

116a. The early printed editions, followed by many later ones, read, שֶׁאֵין אוֹתִיּוֹת חֲטוּפוֹת בִּשְׁמוֹתָם שֶׁל שְׁבָטִים, *for there are no letters vowelized with a chataf* [אֱ אֳ אֲ] *in the names of the tribes.* That reading is based on the fact that the vowels called *chataf* [literally, *snatched* or *hurried*] are not full vowel sounds; rather they are used to strengthen the *sheva* in situations where the *sheva* cannot stand on its own. As such, they may be considered semivowels, i.e., incomplete vowels. Accordingly, they may be understood as alluding to incompleteness and imperfection. Conversely, the absence of any *chataf*-vowel from the names of the tribes may be seen as an allusion that *He perceived no iniquity* [i.e., imperfection] *in Jacob* (*Ittur Bikkurim* citing an anonymous source). However, that reading is difficult for the verse refers to the tribes collectively as יַעֲקֹב, in which the letter ע is vowelized with a *chataf-patach* (*VeChur LaZahav*).

The reading אוֹתִיּוֹת ח״ט appears in the manuscripts used by *Shoham Yakar.* It is also cited by *Ittur Bikkurim* as an emendation suggested by his in-law R' Sender Mimitz of Furth, who certainly had no access to [or knowledge of] the manuscript version.

117. Thus, the verse means, לֹא הִבִּיט אָוֶן, *He did not perceive any sin,* בְּיַעֲקֹב, *in* [*the offspring of*] *Jacob* (see the Baal HaTurim to *Genesis* 49:1; *Exodus* 28:17 with note 43; and 10:35-36 above with note 88).

כב וּתְרוּעַת מֶלֶךְ בּוֹ: אֵל מוֹצִיאָם מִמִּצְרָיִם כְּתוֹעֲפֹת
כג רְאֵם לוֹ: כִּי לֹא־נַחַשׁ בְּיַעֲקֹב וְלֹא־קֶסֶם בְּיִשְׂרָאֵל
כד כָּעֵת יֵאָמֵר לְיַעֲקֹב וּלְיִשְׂרָאֵל מַה־פָּעַל אֵל: הֶן־עָם
כְּלָבִיא יָקוּם וְכַאֲרִי יִתְנַשָּׂא לֹא יִשְׁכַּב עַד־יֹאכַל
כה טֶרֶף וְדַם־חֲלָלִים יִשְׁתֶּה: וַיֹּאמֶר בָּלָק אֶל־בִּלְעָם
כו גַּם־קֹב לֹא תִקֳּבֶנּוּ גַּם־בָּרֵךְ לֹא תְבָרְכֶנּוּ: וַיַּעַן בִּלְעָם
וַיֹּאמֶר אֶל־בָּלָק הֲלֹא דִּבַּרְתִּי אֵלֶיךָ לֵאמֹר כֹּל
ששי [שביעי] כז אֲשֶׁר־יְדַבֵּר יהוה אֹתוֹ אֶעֱשֶׂה: וַיֹּאמֶר בָּלָק אֶל־
בִּלְעָם לְכָה־נָּא אֶקָּחֲךָ אֶל־מָקוֹם אַחֵר אוּלַי יִישַׁר
כח בְּעֵינֵי הָאֱלֹהִים וְקַבֹּתוֹ לִי מִשָּׁם: וַיִּקַּח בָּלָק אֶת־
כט בִּלְעָם רֹאשׁ הַפְּעוֹר הַנִּשְׁקָף עַל־פְּנֵי הַיְשִׁימֹן: וַיֹּאמֶר
בִּלְעָם אֶל־בָּלָק בְּנֵה־לִי בָזֶה שִׁבְעָה מִזְבְּחֹת וְהָכֵן לִי
ל בָּזֶה שִׁבְעָה פָרִים וְשִׁבְעָה אֵילִם: וַיַּעַשׂ בָּלָק כַּאֲשֶׁר
כד א אָמַר בִּלְעָם וַיַּעַל פָּר וָאַיִל בַּמִּזְבֵּחַ: וַיַּרְא בִּלְעָם כִּי
טוֹב בְּעֵינֵי יהוה לְבָרֵךְ אֶת־יִשְׂרָאֵל וְלֹא־הָלַךְ
כְּפַעַם־בְּפַעַם לִקְרַאת נְחָשִׁים וַיָּשֶׁת אֶל־הַמִּדְבָּר
ב פָּנָיו: וַיִּשָּׂא בִלְעָם אֶת־עֵינָיו וַיַּרְא אֶת־יִשְׂרָאֵל שֹׁכֵן
ג לִשְׁבָטָיו וַתְּהִי עָלָיו רוּחַ אֱלֹהִים: וַיִּשָּׂא מְשָׁלוֹ
וַיֹּאמַר נְאֻם בִּלְעָם בְּנוֹ בְעֹר וּנְאֻם הַגֶּבֶר שְׁתֻם הָעָיִן:

בעל הטורים

(כד) הֶן עָם. הַפָּסוּק מַתְחִיל בְּהֵ״א וּמְסַיֵּם בְּהֵ״א – שֶׁלֹּא יָמוּת מֹשֶׁה עַד שֶׁיַּהֲרֹג לַחֲמֵשֶׁת מַלְכֵי מִדְיָן:

כד (ג) וּנְאֻם הַגֶּבֶר. כְּמָא דְּאַתְּ אָמַר קָרָא גֶבֶר, שֶׁדּוֹמֶה בִלְעָם לְתַרְנְגוֹל. כְּמוֹ שֶׁהַתַּרְנְגוֹל הוּא

BAAL HATURIM ELUCIDATED

22. {The Baal HaTurim's comment to אֵל מוֹצִיאָם מִמִּצְרָיִם appears at 24:8 below.}

24. הֶן עָם — BEHOLD! A PEOPLE. This verse begins with a ה (= 5) and ends with a ה.[117a] [Balaam was prophesying that] Moses would not die until he would kill the five kings of Midian.[118]

❑ {The Baal HaTurim's comment to כְּלָבִיא יָקוּם וְכַאֲרִי יִתְנַשָּׂא appears at 2:49 below, s.v., כָּרַע שָׁכַב כַּאֲרִי.}

117a. This phenomenon appears twenty-six times in the Torah. The Baal HaTurim comments upon it in four places: *Genesis* 19:23; here; *Deuteronomy* 10:14 and 11:30.

118. See *Tanchuma* 14, cited by *Rashi*, s.v., וְדַם חֲלָלִים יִשְׁתֶּה.

friendship of the King is in him.
22 *"God took them out of Egypt according to the power of*
His loftiness,
23 *"for there is no divination in Jacob and no sorcery in Israel.*
Even now it is said to Jacob and Israel what God has wrought.
24 *"Behold! A people that will arise like a lion cub and raise*
itself like a lion; it will not lie down until it will consume [its]
prey, and drink the blood of the slain."
25 *Balak said to Balaam, "Neither shall you curse them at all,*
nor shall you bless them at all!"
26 *Balaam answered and said to Balak, "Have I not spoken to you,*
saying, 'Whatever HASHEM shall speak, that I shall do'? "
27 *Balak said to Balaam, "Go, now, I shall take you to a*
different place, perhaps it will be proper in God's eyes that you
will curse them for me from there." 28 *Balak took Balaam to the*
summit of the height that overlooks the face of the wasteland.
29 *Balaam said to Balak, "Build for me here seven altars and*
prepare for me here seven bulls and seven rams." 30 *Balak did*
as Balaam said, and he brought up a bull and a ram on each
altar.

24 1 *Balaam saw that it was good in HASHEM'S eyes to bless Israel,*
so he did not go as every other time toward divinations, but he
set his face toward the wilderness. 2 *Balaam raised his eyes*
and saw Israel dwelling according to its tribes, and the spirit of
God was upon him. 3 *He declaimed his parable and said:*
"The word of Balaam son of Beor, the word of the man with
the open eye;

BAAL HATURIM ELUCIDATED

XXIV

3. וּנְאֻם הַגֶּבֶר — THE WORD OF THE MAN. [The term הַגֶּבֶר, *the man,* may be understood] as in the [Talmudic] expression קָרָא גֶבֶר, *the rooster has called,* [119] for Balaam is like a rooster. Just as the rooster is the most promiscuous of all [fowl],[120]

119. For example, קְרִיאַת הַגֶּבֶר, *the crowing of the rooster* (*Yoma* 20a); קָרָא הַגֶּבֶר, *the rooster crowed* (*Succah* 51b).

120. Two species of bird may be offered on the Temple's Altar: תֹּרִים, *mature turtledoves,* and בְּנֵי יוֹנָה, *young doves.* Because turtledoves are loyal and mate for life, they are offered on the Altar in their adulthood. Doves, however, although they are also loyal to their mates, sometimes quarrel and separate, each seeking another mate. Thus, they are permitted on the Altar only before they are old enough to mate. Chickens, on the other hand, are promiscuous creatures and therefore may never be offered on the Altar (*Ramban* to *Leviticus* 1:14 cited by the Baal HaTurim in *Peirush HaTur HaAroch;* see also the Baal HaTurim to *Leviticus* 12:6 with note 16).

*בראש עמוד
בי״ה שמ״ו סימן

ד נְאֻ֗ם שֹׁמֵ֙עַ֙ אִמְרֵי־אֵ֔ל אֲשֶׁ֨ר מַחֲזֵ֤ה שַׁדַּי֙ יֶֽחֱזֶ֔ה נֹפֵ֖ל
ה וּגְל֥וּי עֵינָֽיִם׃ *מַה־טֹּ֥בוּ אֹהָלֶ֖יךָ יַֽעֲקֹ֑ב מִשְׁכְּנֹתֶ֖יךָ
ו יִשְׂרָאֵֽל׃ כִּנְחָלִ֣ים נִטָּ֔יוּ כְּגַנֹּ֖ת עֲלֵ֣י נָהָ֑ר כַּאֲהָלִים֙ נָטַ֣ע
ז יְהוָ֔ה כַּאֲרָזִ֖ים עֲלֵי־מָֽיִם׃ יִזַּל־מַ֙יִם֙ מִדָּ֣לְיָ֔ו וְזַרְע֖וֹ

בעל הטורים

נוֹאֵף מִכֹּל, כֵּן בִּלְעָם רָבַע אֲתוֹנוֹ. וּכְמוֹ שֶׁהַתַּרְנְגוֹל יוֹדֵעַ הָעִתִּים, כֵּן בִּלְעָם יָדַע לְכַוֵּן הַשָּׁעָה שֶׁהַקָּדוֹשׁ בָּרוּךְ הוּא כּוֹעֵס. וּכְמוֹ שֶׁהַתַּרְנְגוֹל דַּרְכּוֹ לַעֲמֹד עַל רֶגֶל אַחַת, כֵּן בִּלְעָם חִגֵּר בְּאַחַת מֵרַגְלָיו:

(ד) נֹפֵל. בִּשְׁבִיל הָעָרְלָה, שֶׁהִיא מְאוּסָה בִּפְנֵי הַקָּדוֹשׁ בָּרוּךְ הוּא. ״יֶחֱזֶה נֹפֵל וּגְלוּי עֵינָיִם״ סוֹפֵי תֵבוֹת מִילָה:

(ה) מַה טֹּבוּ אֹהָלֶיךָ. לְפִי שֶׁיַּעֲקֹב הוּא בְּאֹהֶל שֶׁל מַטָּה וּבְאֹהֶל שֶׁל מַעְלָה, בְּכִסֵּא הַכָּבוֹד. שֵׁשׁ תֵּבוֹת בַּפָּסוּק, כְּנֶגֶד שִׁשָּׁה אֹהָלִים – נֹב, וְגִבְעוֹן, גִּלְגָּל, שִׁילֹה וּבֵית עוֹלָמִים שְׁנַיִם:

(ו) כַּאֲהָלִים נָטַע ה׳. עַיִ״ן שֶׁל נָטַע עֲקֻמָּה. כִּי בְּזֶה הָעוֹלָם אֵין לְיִשְׂרָאֵל נְטִיעָה קַיֶּמֶת, רַק לֶעָתִיד לָבוֹא:

(ז) יִזַּל מַיִם. בְּגִימַטְרִיָּא יִגְדַּל מֶלֶךְ, שֶׁאֵין מוֹשְׁחִין הַמְּלָכִים אֶלָּא עַל הַנָּהָר:

BAAL HATURIM ELUCIDATED

so did Balaam commit bestiality with his donkey.[121] And just as the rooster knows the hours,[122] so did Balaam know the hour when God is angry.[123] And just as a rooster is wont to stand on just one foot, so was Balaam crippled in one of his feet.[124]

4. נֹפֵל — [HE SHALL SEE,] WHILE HE IS FALLEN, because of his foreskin,[124a] which is deemed detestable by God.[125] [This is also alluded to by] the final letters of the words יֶחֱזֶה נֹפֵל וּגְלוּי עֵינָיִם, *he shall see while he is fallen and with uncovered eyes,* [which, in reverse order,] spell the word מִילָה, *circumcision.*[126]

5. מַה טֹּבוּ אֹהָלֶיךָ יַעֲקֹב — HOW GOODLY ARE YOUR TENTS, O JACOB. [The plural form אֹהָלֶיךָ, *your tents,*[127] is used] because Jacob is in an earthly tent [i.e., dwelling][128] and in a heavenly tent, on the Throne of Glory.[129,129a]

---

121. See the Baal HaTurim to 22:30 above, with note 44.

122. Thus, the blessing each morning, . . . אֲשֶׁר נָתַן לַשֶּׂכְוִי בִינָה לְהַבְחִין בֵּין יוֹם וּבֵין לָיְלָה, . . . *Who has given the rooster understanding to distinguish between night and day* (see *Berachos* 60a).

123. See the Baal HaTurim to 23:3 above, s.v., שֶׁפִי.

124. See the Baal HaTurim to 23:3 above, s.v., וַיֵּלֶךְ שֶׁפִי.

124a. That is, he was not circumcised.

125. Because Balaam was uncircumcised, he was unable to receive words or visions of prophecy while standing erect (*Rashi;* see also *Pirkei De-Rabbi Eliezer* 29, cited in *Rashi* to *Genesis* 17:3).

126. *Peirush HaRokeach.*

127. Whereas the verse addresses the nation in the singular — *O Jacob* — we would expect it to use the singular noun אָהָלְךָ, *your tent* (as in *Psalms* 61:5). The Baal HaTurim explains the implication of the plural *tents.*

128. According to the Talmud: יַעֲקֹב אָבִינוּ לֹא מֵת, *Our Patriarch Jacob did not die* (*Taanis* 5b; cited in *Rashi* and *Ramban* to *Genesis* 49:33; see also the Baal HaTurim to *Genesis* 50:5). Thus, he is still living in his earthly "tent" (*VeChur LaZahav*).

129. *Rabbeinu Ephraim* (*MiKesivah Ashkenazis*). In his vision of the Chariot, the prophet Ezekiel describes angels with four faces, one of them being פְּנֵי אָדָם, *the face of a man* (*Ezekiel* 1:10). In his comments to *Exodus* 24:10, the Baal HaTurim states that that face had the visage of Jacob. See also the

24/4-7

[4] *"the word of the one who hears the sayings of God —*
who the vision of SHADDAI *he shall see — while he is fallen*
and with uncovered eyes:
[5] *"How goodly are your tents, O Jacob, your dwelling*
places, O Israel;
[6] *"stretching out like brooks, like gardens by a river, like*
aloes planted by HASHEM, *like cedars by water.*
[7] *"Water shall flow from his wells, and his seed shall be*

BAAL HATURIM ELUCIDATED

[Alternatively: The plural form alludes to the six Sanctuaries.[130] Thus] there are six words in this verse, corresponding to the six Sanctuaries: Nob, Gibeon, Gilgal, Shiloh, and the First and Second Temples in Jerusalem.[130a]

❑ {The Baal HaTurim comments further on this verse at *Genesis* 49:8 and *Deuteronomy* 33:4.}

6. כַּאֲהָלִים נָטַע ה׳ — LIKE ALOES PLANTED BY HASHEM. [According to a scribal tradition,] the ע of the word נָטַע, *planted,* is to be [written in the Torah scrolls in the enhanced form[131] called] עַיִ״ן עֲקֻמָּה, *a bent letter* ע.[132] [This unusual ע implies] that Israel is not permanently planted in this world,[133] but will be [permanently planted] in the time to come.

7. יִזַּל מַיִם — WATER SHALL FLOW. The *gematria* of this phrase (137) is equal to that of יִגְדַּל מֶלֶךְ, *May [the] king become great.* [133a] [This alludes to the law] that a king is anointed only near a stream. [134]

Baal HaTurim to 10:35 above, s.v., בִּנְסֹעַ הָאָרֹן.

129a. On the phrase, וְיַעֲקֹב אִישׁ תָּם יֹשֵׁב אֹהָלִים, *but Jacob was a wholesome man, dwelling in tents* (*Genesis* 25:27), the Midrash comments: [אֹהָלִים, *tents,* in the plural, implies] two tents, i.e., the study hall of Shem and the study hall of Eber (*Bereishis Rabbah* 63:10, cited by *Rashi*). Perhaps the plural form of that verse can also be explained with the Baal HaTurim's comment here (Y.S.).

130. In his commentary to 9:15 above, the Baal HaTurim speaks of seven Tabernacles; here he numbers them at six! There, the comment discusses both the present and the future, thus, that verse alludes to the six future Tabernacles as well as the *Mishkan* of the wilderness. Here, the comment refers to Balaam's prophecy about Israel's future, and that prophecy did not include the *Mishkan* that had already been established (*Ittur Bikkurim*). Alternatively: The earlier passage refers to every Tabernacle, regardless of where it stood. Our passage, on the other hand, refers only to the Tabernacles established in the Land of Israel (*VeChur LaZahav*).

130a. *Peirush HaRokeach.*

131. The Baal HaTurim comments on other unusual forms of the letter ע in his comments to *Exodus* 1:9; *Numbers* 5:17 and 24:8; and *Deuteronomy* 6:4.

132. That is, instead of writing this particular ע in the usual way, the scribes would adorn it with curlicue tittles (see illustration). According to the ancient *Sefer Tagin* (Paris ed.) this ע is one of six in the Torah which are written with their tails bent behind them.

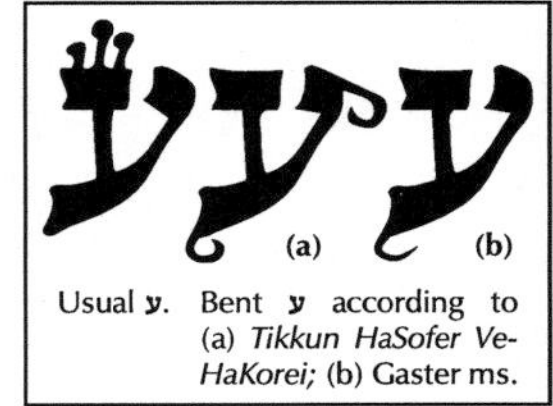

Usual ע. Bent ע according to (a) *Tikkun HaSofer VeHaKorei;* (b) Gaster ms.

133. The ע stands for עוֹלָם, *world;* its unusual form indicates non-permanence, i.e., this world (*VeChur LaZahav*).

133a. The Baal HaTurim's phrase is a literal translation into Hebrew of *Targum Onkelos'* Aramaic paraphrase of יִזַּל מַיִם, which *Onkelos* renders, יִסְגֵּי מַלְכָּא, *May the king become great* (*Yad Aharon*).

134. *Peirush HaRokeach.* The Talmud states: We do not anoint kings anywhere except at a

בְּמַיִם רַבִּים וְיָרֹם מֵאֲגַג מַלְכּוֹ וְתִנַּשֵּׂא מַלְכֻתוֹ:
ח אֵל מוֹצִיאוֹ מִמִּצְרַיִם כְּתוֹעֲפֹת רְאֵם לוֹ יֹאכַל
גּוֹיִם צָרָיו וְעַצְמֹתֵיהֶם יְגָרֵם וְחִצָּיו יִמְחָץ:
ט כָּרַע שָׁכַב כַּאֲרִי וּכְלָבִיא מִי יְקִימֶנּוּ מְבָרְכֶיךָ

בעל הטורים

(ח) **אֵל מוֹצִיאוֹ מִמִּצְרַיִם.** אָמַר זֶה שְׁתֵּי פְעָמִים. לוֹמַר, כְּשֵׁם שֶׁהוֹצִיאָם מִמִּצְרַיִם, כֵּן יוֹצִיאָם לֶעָתִיד לָבוֹא מִבֵּין הָאֻמּוֹת:

❑ **וְעַצְמֹתֵיהֶם.** עַיִ״ן תְּלוּיָה. לוֹמַר לְךָ כִּי יַעֲקֹר שִׁבְעָה עֲמָמִים. וְלֶעָתִיד לָבוֹא, ס״ג אֻמּוֹת. וְזֶהוּ ״כֻּלּוֹ סָג יַחְדָּו נֶאֱלָחוּ״:

(ט) **כָּרַע שָׁכַב כַּאֲרִי וּכְלָבִיא מִי יְקִימֶנּוּ.** וּלְמַעְלָה אָמַר ״הֶן עָם כְּלָבִיא יָקוּם וְכַאֲרִי יִתְנַשָּׂא״. לְמַעְלָה הִקְדִּים לָבִיא. כִּי כֵן דֶּרֶךְ, מִתְּחִלָּה יִתְגַּבֵּר מְעַט כְּלָבִיא, וְאַחַר כָּךְ יִתְנַשֵּׂא וְהוֹלֵךְ כְּמוֹ הָאֲרִי שֶׁהוּא מִתְגַּבֵּר וְהוֹלֵךְ. וְכָאן הִקְדִּים אֲרִי לְלָבִיא, שֶׁרָמַז גַּם כֵּן, ״שָׁכַב כַּאֲרִי״ בִּימֵי מֹשֶׁה, ״וּכְלָבִיא״ בִּימֵי יְהוֹשֻׁעַ; שֶׁפְּנֵי מֹשֶׁה כִּפְנֵי חַמָּה, וּפְנֵי יְהוֹשֻׁעַ כִּפְנֵי לְבָנָה:

BAAL HATURIM ELUCIDATED

8. אֵל מוֹצִיאוֹ מִמִּצְרַיִם — GOD TOOK HIM OUT OF EGYPT. [Balaam] said this twice.[135] The repetition indicates that just as God took them out of Egypt, so will He take them out from [their exile] among the gentile nations in time to come.[136]

❑ **וְעַצְמֹתֵיהֶם — THEIR BONES.** [According to a scribal tradition,] the ע of this word is to be [written in the Torah scrolls in the enhanced form[137] called] עַיִ״ן תְּלוּיָה, *a suspended letter* ע.[138] This [unusual ע (=70) refers to the seventy gentile

spring, in order that their kingdom stretch forth [like a river whose source is a spring] (*Horayos* 12a).

Additionally: The *gematria* of מַיִם, *water,* is 90, equal to that of מֶלֶךְ, *king.*

135. The beginning of our verse is also identical with that of 23:22 above, except that in the earlier verse Balaam spoke of the Israelites as a group of individuals — אֵל מוֹצִיאָם, *God took them out.* In our verse, however, he speaks of Israel as a unit — אֵל מוֹצִיאוֹ, *God took him* [or *it*] *out.* The Baal HaTurim's comment addresses the repetition, but not the minor change of expression.

Interestingly, each of these suffixes — וֹ — and ָם — can be understood as an allusion to the number of Israelites who left Egypt. The Torah rounds out that number to 600,000 (see *Exodus* 12:37). Now, the *gematria* of ו is six. Thus, מוֹצִיאוֹ may be understood as מוֹצִיא ו׳, *He brought out six* [*hundred thousand*]. The *gematria* of the final ם is usually reckoned as the same as that of the regular מ, *forty.* However, the final letters are sometimes assigned values of their own: ך = 500; ם = 600; ן = 700; ף = 800; and ץ = 900. According to that system, מוֹצִיאָם may be understood as מוֹצִיא ם׳, *He brought out six hundred* [*thousand*] (*Peirush HaRokeach,* as explained by R' Chaim Kanievsky).

136. *Peirush HaRokeach.* When God took Israel out of Egypt, *also a mixed multitude* [*of foreigners*] *went up with them* (*Exodus* 12:38). But when God takes Israel out of its present exile, *it is a nation that will dwell in solitude* (23:9 above). Thus, when speaking of the exodus from Egypt, the verse uses the plural suffix — מוֹצִיאָם, *he took them* [Israel and the mixed multitude] *out.* But with reference to the future exodus, the singular is used — מוֹצִיאוֹ, *He took him* [Israel alone] *out* (*VeChur LaZahav,* based on *Ittur Bikkurim*).

137. See note 131 above.

138. *Sefer Tagin* lists וְעַצְמֹתֵיהֶם of our verse as

by abundant waters. His king shall be exalted over Agag, and his kingdom shall be upraised.

8 *"God took him out of Egypt according to the power of His loftiness. He will consume the nations that oppress him and crush their bones, and his arrows shall pierce them.*

9 *"He crouched and lay down like a lion, and, like a lion cub — who can stand him up? Those who bless you are*

BAAL HATURIM ELUCIDATED

nations[139] and] indicates to you that the seven Canaanite nations would be uprooted [now, when Israel enters the Land of Canaan]; and, in time to come, the other sixty-three [will be uprooted].[140] This is [alluded to by the verse], כֻּלּוֹ סָג יַחְדָּו נֶאֱלָחוּ, *All of it* [*mankind*] *is dross* (סָג = 63), *together they have become depraved* (*Psalms* 53:4).[141]

9. כָּרַע שָׁכַב כַּאֲרִי וּכְלָבִיא מִי יְקִימֶנּוּ — HE CROUCHED AND LAY DOWN LIKE A LION, AND LIKE A LION CUB[141a] — WHO CAN STAND HIM UP? Earlier, [Balaam] had said, *"Behold! A people that will arise like a lion cub and raise itself like a lion"* (23:24 above). There he mentioned lion cub first [before lion]. For that is how it will be, at the outset, [Israel] will become [slightly] more powerful, like a lion cub; then it will continue to grow, like a lion who continuously becomes stronger with time. In our verse, [by contrast,] he mentioned lion before lion cub, to make an additional allusion: *He lay down like a lion,* in the days of Moses; *and like a lion cub,* in the days of Joshua. For [Moses was a greater leader than Joshua, as the Talmud states:] Moses' countenance is like that of the sun, and Joshua's countenance is like that of the moon.[142]

---

one of seventeen words in which the letters ע are inscribed תְּלֵי בָתַר רֵישֵׁיהוֹן, *suspended behind their heads* (see illustration at note 24 to *parashas Nasso*).

139. For the Baal HaTurim's opinion regarding the identities of the seventy nations, see his comment to *Genesis* 25:25 with note 25.

140. The unusual shape of the ע indicates that it may be considered as a word unto itself. Accordingly, the letters of the word וְעַצְמֹתֵיהֶם may be anagrammed to read, וְע׳ צְמִתֵיהֶם, *and their seventy annihilations* (see *Psalms* 94:23) [seven of them immediately; sixty-three in the time to come] (*Rimzei Rabbeinu Yoel*).

141. See the Baal HaTurim to *Genesis* 25:23, s.v., גוֹיִם. The reading הַכֹּל סָג that appears in the early printed edition and in many later editions is the result of a confusion between two verses, as explained below.

Psalms 53:4 reads in its entirety: כֻּלּוֹ סָג, *All of it* [i.e., all of mankind (see v. 3 there)] *is dross,* יַחְדָּו נֶאֱלָחוּ, *they have all become depraved,* אֵין עֹשֵׂה טוֹב, *there is no doer of good,* אֵין גַּם אֶחָד, *there is not even one.* Now, in psalm 14 (which, except for a few minor differences, parallels psalm 53), verse 3 reads the same as 53:4 except for the first two words; there the verse begins with הַכֹּל סָר, *The entirety* [*of mankind*] *has gone astray.* The Baal HaTurim's comment explains the implication of the change from סָר to סָג (*VeChur LaZahav*).

It is noteworthy that in the letter exchange known as אַ״תְ בַּ״שׁ, the letters ג and ר are exchanged for one another (*VeChur LaZahav*).

141a. The translation follows *Ramban* to 23:24 above.

142. *Bava Basra* 75a.

י בָּר֑וּךְ וְאֹרְרֶ֖יךָ אָרֽוּר׃ וַיִּֽחַר־אַ֤ף בָּלָק֙ אֶל־בִּלְעָ֔ם
וַיִּסְפֹּ֖ק אֶת־כַּפָּ֑יו וַיֹּ֨אמֶר בָּלָ֜ק אֶל־בִּלְעָ֗ם לָקֹ֤ב
אֹֽיְבַי֙ קְרָאתִ֔יךָ וְהִנֵּה֙ בֵּרַ֣כְתָּ בָרֵ֔ךְ זֶ֖ה שָׁלֹ֥שׁ פְּעָמִֽים׃
יא וְעַתָּ֖ה בְּרַח־לְךָ֣ אֶל־מְקוֹמֶ֑ךָ אָמַ֙רְתִּי֙ כַּבֵּ֣ד אֲכַבֶּדְךָ֔
יב וְהִנֵּ֛ה מְנָעֲךָ֥ יהוה מִכָּבֽוֹד׃ וַיֹּ֥אמֶר בִּלְעָ֖ם אֶל־בָּלָ֑ק
הֲלֹ֗א גַּ֧ם אֶל־מַלְאָכֶ֛יךָ אֲשֶׁר־שָׁלַ֥חְתָּ אֵלַ֖י דִּבַּ֥רְתִּי
יג לֵאמֹֽר׃ אִם־יִתֶּן־לִ֨י בָלָ֜ק מְלֹ֣א בֵיתוֹ֮ כֶּ֣סֶף וְזָהָב֒
לֹ֣א אוּכַ֗ל לַעֲבֹר֙ אֶת־פִּ֣י יהוה לַעֲשׂ֥וֹת טוֹבָ֛ה א֥וֹ
יד רָעָ֖ה מִלִּבִּ֑י אֲשֶׁר־יְדַבֵּ֥ר יהוה אֹת֥וֹ אֲדַבֵּֽר׃ וְעַתָּ֕ה שביעי
הִנְנִ֥י הוֹלֵ֖ךְ לְעַמִּ֑י לְכָה֙ אִיעָ֣צְךָ֔ אֲשֶׁ֨ר יַעֲשֶׂ֜ה הָעָ֥ם
טו הַזֶּ֛ה לְעַמְּךָ֖ בְּאַחֲרִ֥ית הַיָּמִֽים׃ וַיִּשָּׂ֥א מְשָׁל֖וֹ וַיֹּאמַ֑ר
נְאֻ֤ם בִּלְעָם֙ בְּנ֣וֹ בְעֹ֔ר וּנְאֻ֥ם הַגֶּ֖בֶר שְׁתֻ֥ם הָעָֽיִן׃

בעל הטורים

❑ **מְבָרְכֶיךָ בָרוּךְ וְאֹרְרֶיךָ אָרוּר.** בִּלְעָם שֶׁהָיָה בְלִבּוֹ לְקַלְּלָם, לְכָךְ סִיֵּם בִּקְלָלָה. וְיִצְחָק סִיֵּם בְּבִרְכוֹתָיו שֶׁל "וְיִתֶּן לְךָ" בְּבָרוּךְ, "אֹרְרֶיךָ אָרוּר וּמְבָרְכֶיךָ בָּרוּךְ":

❑ **וְאֹרְרֶיךָ אָרוּר.** עַל כֵּן לֹא אָמַר לוֹ בָלָק לְקַלְּלָם יוֹתֵר, אֶלָּא אָמַר לוֹ "בְּרַח לְךָ אֶל מְקוֹמֶךָ":

(יא) מְנָעֲךָ. ב׳ בַּמָּסוֹרֶת – "וְהִנֵּה מְנָעֲךָ ה׳ מִכָּבוֹד"; "אֲשֶׁר מְנָעֲךָ ה׳ מִבּוֹא בְדָמִים". בִּשְׁבִיל שֶׁמְּנָעֲךָ מִבּוֹא בְדָמִים, שֶׁלֹּא לְקַלְּלָם, עַל כֵּן מְנָעֲךָ מִכָּבוֹד:

(טו) בְּנוֹ בְעֹר. "בְּעֹר" כְּתִיב, חָסֵר וָי"ו, כִּי נִבְעַר מִדַּעַת. שֶׁמֵּאָז לֹא דִבְּרָה עִמּוֹ שְׁכִינָה:

BAAL HATURIM ELUCIDATED

❑ מְבָרְכֶיךָ בָּרוּךְ וְאֹרְרֶיךָ אָרוּר — **THOSE WHO BLESS YOU ARE BLESSED AND THOSE WHO CURSE YOU ARE CURSED.** [These words were spoken by] Balaam — whose intention was to curse them — therefore, he concluded with a curse.[143] Isaac [whose intention was to bless them] concluded his blessings [to Jacob] which began, וְיִתֶּן לְךָ . . ., *And may God give you . . .* (*Genesis* 27:28), [in the reverse order,] אֹרְרֶיךָ אָרוּר וּמְבָרְכֶיךָ בָּרוּךְ, *Those who curse you are cursed, and those who bless you are blessed* (v. 29 there).[143a]

❑ וְאֹרְרֶיךָ אָרוּר — **AND THOSE WHO CURSE YOU ARE CURSED.** Because of this [statement], Balak did not ask him to curse [Israel] another time. Rather, he told him, "בְּרַח לְךָ אֶל מְקוֹמֶךָ, *Flee to your place*" (v. 11 below).[144]

---

143. Balaam wanted those who would curse Israel to have the final say. Alternatively: He wanted the curses to prevail over the blessings (*VeChur LaZahav*).

143a. Jacob wanted those who would bless Israel to have the final say. Alternatively: He wanted the blessings to prevail over the curses (*VeChur LaZahav*).

144. Balak feared that even if he merely remained in the proximity of Balaam, he would become

24/10-15 *blessed and those who curse you are cursed."*
10 *Balak's anger flared against Balaam and he clapped his*
hands. Balak said to Balaam, "To curse my enemies did I sum-
mon you, and behold! you have continually blessed them
these three times! 11 *Now, flee to your place. I said I would*
honor you, but — behold! HASHEM *has prevented you from*
[receiving] honor."
12 *Balaam said to Balak, "Did I not speak to your emissaries*
whom you sent to me, saying, 13 *'If Balak were to give me his*
houseful of silver and gold, I cannot transgress the word of HA-
SHEM *to do good or bad on my own. Whatever* HASHEM *speaks,*
that shall I speak.' 14 *And now, behold! I go to my people.*
Come, I shall advise you what this people will do to your people
in the End of Days." 15 *He declaimed his parable and said:*
"The word of Balaam son of Beor, the word of the man with
the open eye.

BAAL HATURIM ELUCIDATED

11. מְנָעֲךָ — [HE] HAS PREVENTED YOU. The masoretic note, ב׳, means that this word appears twice in the *Tanach*: (i) here, וְהִנֵּה מְנָעֲךָ ה׳ מִכָּבוֹד, *But, behold!* HASHEM *has prevented you from* [*receiving*] *honor;* and (ii) אֲשֶׁר מְנָעֲךָ ה׳ מִבּוֹא בְדָמִים, *as* HASHEM *has prevented you from coming to bloodshed* (*I Samuel* 25:26). Because He has prevented you *from coming to bloodshed,* i.e., that you not curse them, therefore, *He has prevented you from* [*receiving*] *honor.*

14. {The Baal HaTurim's comment to לְכָה אִיעָצְךָ appears at *Exodus* 18:19.}

15. בְּנוֹ בְעֹר — SON OF BEOR. The name Beor is spelled defectively, without a ו,[145] [as if it were בַּעַר, *an ignoramus,*] for he was made ignorant, devoid of knowledge. From this time onward, the Divine Presence did not communicate with him.[146,147]

subject to, *and those who curse you are cursed* (*VeChur LaZahav;* see also the Baal HaTurim to 22:2 above, s.v., בֶּן צִפּוֹר).

145. The name of Balaam's father is usually spelled בְּעוֹר, with a ו (e.g., 22:5 above; 31:8 below; *Joshua* 24:9). Here and in verse 3 above, however, it is spelled defectively, בְּעֹר, without a ו. The Baal HaTurim's comment explains the absence of the ו in our verse, but not in verse 3. See note 147 below.

146. It seems clear from our *parashah* that Balaam was a genuine prophet (see, e.g., v. 16). Nevertheless, he is later referred to as, *Balaam the sorcerer* (*Joshua* 13:22). The Talmud explains that when Balaam decided to curse Israel, God stripped him of his prophetic powers. Thus deprived, he turned to sorcery instead (*Sanhedrin* 106a, see *Rashi* and *Yad Ramah* there).

147. As mentioned in note 145, the defective spelling בְּעֹר appears twice. Similarly, the name of Balak's father is usually spelled צִפּוֹר, with a ו (e.g., 22:2,4 above; *Joshua* 24:9), except in two verses (22:10 and 23:18 above), where it is spelled defectively, צִפֹּר, without a ו. It is noteworthy that each time one of these names appears without the ו, it is spoken by Balaam; and, conversely, each time Balaam mentions either of these names it is spelled defectively. It would seem that, like some of today's generation, Balaam held little regard for the past generation, "They are so old fashioned and backwards. We are up to date and advanced." Therefore, to demonstrate Balaam's contempt for צִפּוֹר and בְּעוֹר, whenever Balaam mentions either of those names, the Torah uses the defective spelling — צִפֹּר or בְּעֹר (*VeChur LaZahav*).

טז נְאֻ֗ם שֹׁמֵ֙עַ֙ אִמְרֵי־אֵ֔ל וְיֹדֵ֖עַ דַּ֣עַת עֶלְי֑וֹן מַחֲזֵ֤ה שַׁדַּי֙
יז יֶֽחֱזֶ֔ה נֹפֵ֖ל וּגְל֥וּי עֵינָֽיִם׃ אֶרְאֶ֙נּוּ֙ וְלֹ֣א עַתָּ֔ה אֲשׁוּרֶ֖נּוּ
וְלֹ֣א קָר֑וֹב דָּרַ֨ךְ כּוֹכָ֜ב מִֽיַּעֲקֹ֗ב וְקָ֥ם שֵׁ֙בֶט֙ מִיִּשְׂרָאֵ֔ל
יח וּמָחַץ֙ פַּאֲתֵ֣י מוֹאָ֔ב וְקַרְקַ֖ר כָּל־בְּנֵי־שֵֽׁת׃ וְהָיָ֨ה
אֱד֜וֹם יְרֵשָׁ֗ה וְהָיָ֧ה יְרֵשָׁ֛ה שֵׂעִ֖יר אֹיְבָ֑יו וְיִשְׂרָאֵ֖ל
יט עֹ֥שֶׂה חָֽיִל׃ וְיֵ֖רְדְּ מִֽיַּעֲקֹ֑ב וְהֶֽאֱבִ֥יד שָׂרִ֖יד מֵעִֽיר׃
כ וַיַּרְא֙ אֶת־עֲמָלֵ֔ק וַיִּשָּׂ֥א מְשָׁל֖וֹ וַיֹּאמַ֑ר רֵאשִׁ֤ית גּוֹיִם֙
כא עֲמָלֵ֔ק וְאַחֲרִית֖וֹ עֲדֵ֥י אֹבֵֽד׃ וַיַּרְא֙ אֶת־הַקֵּינִ֔י וַיִּשָּׂ֖א
מְשָׁל֑וֹ וַיֹּאמַ֗ר אֵיתָן֙ מֽוֹשָׁבֶ֔ךָ וְשִׂ֥ים בַּסֶּ֖לַע קִנֶּֽךָ׃

בעל הטורים

(טז) **וְיֹדֵעַ דַּעַת עֶלְיוֹן.** אָמַר כָּאן "וְיֹדֵעַ דַּעַת עֶלְיוֹן", לְפִי שֶׁרָצָה לְגַלּוֹת יְמוֹת הַמָּשִׁיחַ:

(יז) **וּמָחַץ פַּאֲתֵי מוֹאָב וְקַרְקַר כָּל בְּנֵי שֵׁת.** "קַרְקַר" בְּאַ"תְּ בַּ"שׁ דגדג, בְּגִימַטְרִיָּא דָּוִד:

(יט) **וְיֵרְדְּ מִיַּעֲקֹב.** ב׳ בַּמָּסוֹרֶת — הָכָא; וְאִידָךְ "וְיֵרְדְּ מִיָּם עַד יָם", דְּהַיְנוּ מֶלֶךְ הַמָּשִׁיחַ. שֶׁהִתְנַבֵּא עַל מֶלֶךְ הַמָּשִׁיחַ:

(כ) **וַיַּרְא אֶת עֲמָלֵק וַיִּשָּׂא מְשָׁלוֹ וַיֹּאמַר רֵאשִׁית גּוֹיִם עֲמָלֵק וְאַחֲרִיתוֹ עֲדֵי אֹבֵד.** "רֵאשִׁית גּוֹיִם" בְּגִימַטְרִיָּא שֶׁנִּלְחַם בְּיִשְׂרָאֵל:

(כא) **מוֹשָׁבֶךָ.** ג׳ בַּמָּסוֹרֶת — "אֵיתָן מוֹשָׁבֶךָ"; "מִשְׁמַנֵּי הָאָרֶץ יִהְיֶה מוֹשָׁבֶךָ"; "וְנִפְקַדְתָּ כִּי

BAAL HATURIM ELUCIDATED

16. וְיֹדֵעַ דַּעַת עֶלְיוֹן — AND WHO KNOWS THE MIND OF THE SUPREME ONE. Here, the verse states, *and who knows the mind of the Supreme One,*[148] for he desired to reveal the time of the era of *Mashiach.*[149]

17. {The Baal HaTurim's comment to דָּרַךְ כּוֹכָב מִיַּעֲקֹב appears at *Deuteronomy* 2:5.}

❑ **וּמָחַץ פַּאֲתֵי מוֹאָב וְקַרְקַר כָּל בְּנֵי שֵׁת** — AND HE SHALL SMASH THE CORNERS OF MOAB AND PIERCE ALL THE CHILDREN OF SETH. In [the *aleph-beis* exchange known as] אַ"תְּ בַּ"שׁ[150], the letters of קַרְקַר, *undermine,* correspond to דגדג, which has a *gematria* of 14, equal to that of דָּוִד, *David.*[151]

19. וְיֵרְדְּ מִיַּעֲקֹב — ONE FROM JACOB SHALL RULE. The masoretic note, ב׳, means that the word וְיֵרְדְּ appears twice in the *Tanach*: (i) here; and (ii) וְיֵרְדְּ מִיָּם עַד יָם, *May he rule from sea to sea* (*Psalms* 72:8), which refers to *Mashiach.*[152] Similarly,

148. Our verse is a repetition of verse 4 above, but with the additional phrase וְיֹדֵעַ דַּעַת עֶלְיוֹן, *and who knows the mind of the Supreme One,* and without the word אֲשֶׁר.

149. As Balaam himself stated: *"Come, I shall advise you what this people will do to your people in the End of Days"* (v. 14 above; see also the Baal HaTurim's comment to v. 19 below).

150. See note 133 at 7:14 above.

151. *Peirush HaRokeach.* According to *Rashi,* this prophecy will be carried out by King David, and has its fulfillment in *II Samuel* 8:2.

152. See *Ibn Ezra* and *Radak* to *Psalms* 72:1.

16 *"The word of one who hears the sayings of God, and who knows the mind of the Supreme One, the vision of SHADDAI he shall see, while he is fallen and with uncovered eyes.*

17 *"I shall see him, but not now, I shall look at him, but it is not near. A star has issued from Jacob and a scepter-bearer has risen from Israel, and he shall smash the corners of Moab and pierce all the children of Seth.*

18 *"Edom shall be a conquest and Seir shall be the conquest of his enemies — and Israel will attain success.*

19 *"One from Jacob shall rule and destroy the remnant of the city."*

20 *He saw Amalek and declaimed his parable and said: "Amalek is the first among nations, but its end will be eternal destruction."*

21 *He saw the Kenite and declaimed his parable and said: "Strong is your dwelling, and set in a rock is your nest.*

BAAL HATURIM ELUCIDATED

Balaam prophesied about the Messianic king.[153]

20. וַיַּרְא אֶת עֲמָלֵק וַיִּשָּׂא מְשָׁלוֹ וַיֹּאמַר רֵאשִׁית גּוֹיִם עֲמָלֵק וְאַחֲרִיתוֹ עֲדֵי אֹבֵד — HE SAW AMALEK AND DECLAIMED HIS PARABLE AND SAID: "AMALEK IS THE FIRST AMONG NATIONS, BUT ITS END WILL BE ETERNAL DESTRUCTION."[153a] The *gematria* of רֵאשִׁית גּוֹיִם, *the first among nations,* (970) is equivalent[154] to that of שֶׁנִּלְחַם בְּיִשְׂרָאֵל, *who went to battle against Israel.*[155]

21. מוֹשָׁבֶךָ — YOUR DWELLING.[156] The masoretic note, ג׳, means that this word appears three times in the *Tanach*: (i) here, אֵיתָן מוֹשָׁבֶךָ, *Strong is your dwelling;* (ii) מִשְׁמַנֵּי הָאָרֶץ יִהְיֶה מוֹשָׁבֶךָ, *Of the fatness of the earth shall be your dwelling* (*Genesis* 27:39); and (iii) וְנִפְקַדְתָּ כִּי יִפָּקֵד מוֹשָׁבֶךָ, *And you will be missed because*

153. *Peirush HaRokeach.*

153a. The Baal HaTurim uncharacteristically cites the entire verse as his rubric. He does this in order to avoid beginning his comment with a statement that might be construed as favorable to Amalek, for רֵאשִׁית גּוֹיִם can be understood as *the premier nation.* After having belied that interpretation by citing the end of the verse, *but its end will be eternal destruction,* the Baal HaTurim repeats the words רֵאשִׁית גּוֹיִם and explains their pejorative connotation (A.S.).

154. The principle of *im hakollel* allows 970 to be considered equivalent to 971, the *gematria* of the Baal HaTurim's phrase.

155. *Peirush HaRokeach;* see *Targum Onkelos,* cited by *Rashi.* The verse cannot mean that the Amalekites were the first group of people who formed a nation; for most of the Biblical nations were founded earlier than Amalek (see note 139 above). Nor could רֵאשִׁית refer to nobility of birth, for the progenitor of Amalek was the son of a concubine (see *Genesis* 36:12). Thus, "first" in this verse must refer to an unprecedented incident, namely, Amalek's attack (see *Exodus* 17:8-16) against Israel (*Mizrachi; Sifsei Chachamim*).

156. The term מוֹשָׁב is related to the verb root ישב, *to sit, to seat, to dwell,* and can mean *a seat* (e.g., *I Samuel* 20:25) or *a dwelling place* (e.g., 31:10; 35:29 below).

כב כִּ֥י אִם־יִהְיֶ֖ה לְבָ֣עֵֽר קָ֑יִן עַד־מָ֖ה אַשּׁ֥וּר תִּשְׁבֶּֽךָּ׃
כג־כד וַיִּשָּׂ֥א מְשָׁל֖וֹ וַיֹּאמַ֑ר א֕וֹי מִ֥י יִחְיֶ֖ה מִשֻּׂמ֥וֹ אֵֽל׃ וְצִים֙
מִיַּ֣ד כִּתִּ֔ים וְעִנּ֥וּ אַשּׁ֖וּר וְעִנּוּ־עֵ֑בֶר וְגַם־ה֖וּא עֲדֵ֥י
כה אֹבֵֽד׃ וַיָּ֣קָם בִּלְעָ֔ם וַיֵּ֖לֶךְ וַיָּ֣שָׁב לִמְקֹמ֑וֹ וְגַם־בָּלָ֖ק
הָלַ֥ךְ לְדַרְכּֽוֹ׃

כה
א וַיֵּ֤שֶׁב יִשְׂרָאֵל֙ בַּשִּׁטִּ֔ים וַיָּ֣חֶל הָעָ֔ם לִזְנ֖וֹת אֶל־בְּנ֥וֹת

בעל הטורים

יִפָּקֵד מוֹשָׁבֶךָ״. אַף עַל פִּי שֶׁאֵיתָן וּמִשְׁמַנֵּי אֶרֶץ מוֹשָׁבֶךָ, ״יִפָּקֵד מוֹשָׁבֶךָ״, כִּי יָבוֹא אַשּׁוּר וְיִשְׁבֶּךָ:

(כב) **עַד מָה.** ד׳ בַּמָּסוֹרֶת – ״עַד מָה אַשּׁוּר תִּשְׁבֶּךָּ״; ״עַד מָה ה׳ תֶּאֱנַף לָנֶצַח״; ״עַד מָה ה׳ תִּסָּתֵר לָנֶצַח״; ״וְלֹא אִתָּנוּ יוֹדֵעַ עַד מָה״ עַל גָּלוּת אַשּׁוּר. ״עַד מָה ה׳ תֶּאֱנַף לָנֶצַח״ וְ״תִּסָּתֵר לָנֶצַח״, כִּי אֵין ״אִתָּנוּ יוֹדֵעַ עַד מָה״, שֶׁיֹּאמַר לִי מָה יָשׁוּבוּ גָּלוּת אַשּׁוּר. כִּי אַף כְּשֶׁחָזְרוּ גָּלוּת יְהוּדָה וּבִנְיָמִין, לֹא חָזְרוּ עֲשֶׂרֶת הַשְּׁבָטִים:

(כה) **וַיָּשָׁב לִמְקֹמוֹ.** וְלֹא אָמַר ״הָלַךְ לְדַרְכּוֹ״, שֶׁנִּטְרַד מִדַּרְכּוֹ וְיָרַד לְגֵיהִנֹּם:

כה (א) בַּשִּׁטִּים. לְשׁוֹן ״כִּי תִשְׂטֶה אִשְׁתּוֹ״:

❑ **וַיָּחֶל הָעָם.** מְלַמֵּד שֶׁנִּתְחַלְּלוּ מִקְדֻשָּׁתָם. ״רַבִּים חֲלָלִים״ בְּגִימַטְרִיָּא ״זֶה שִׁטִּים״:

BAAL HATURIM ELUCIDATED

your seat will be empty (*I Samuel* 20:18). [Balaam was saying,] even though your dwelling is strong and of the fatness of the earth, nevertheless *your dwelling place will be empty,* because Assyria will come and take you captive.[157]

22. עַד מָה — UNTIL WHEN.[158] The masoretic note, ד׳, means that this phrase appears four times in the *Tanach*:[158a] (i) here, עַד מָה אַשּׁוּר תִּשְׁבֶּךָּ, *Until when can Assyria take you captive?* (ii) עַד מָה ה׳ תֶּאֱנַף לָנֶצַח, *Until when, HASHEM, will You be angry forever?* (*Psalms* 79:5); (iii) עַד מָה ה׳ תִּסָּתֵר לָנֶצַח, *Until when, HASHEM, will You hide Yourself* [*? Will it be*] *forever?*[158b] (*Psalms* 89:47); *and* (iv) וְלֹא אִתָּנוּ יוֹדֵעַ עַד מָה, *and there is none among us who knows until when* (*Psalms* 74:9), which speaks of the Assyrian exile.[159] [The similarity of expression recalls the fate of the Ten Tribes exiled by Assyria.[160] We plead to God:] *Until when, HASHEM, will You be angry forever,* and *will You hide Yourself forever?* For *there is none among us who knows until when,* i.e., who can tell me when they will return from the Assyrian exile. For even when

157. See verses 21-22 below with *Targum Yonasan ben Uzziel* and *Rashi.*

158. Unlike *Rashi,* who understands the phrase עַד מָה of our verse as עַד הֵיכָן, *until where,* the Baal HaTurim (both here and in *Peirush HaTur HaAroch*) follows *Ibn Ezra* and *Ramban* who render it as עַד מָתַי, *until when.*

158a. The text of this comment follows *Shoham Yakar's* manuscript edition. The version that appears in the early printed editions is rife with misquoted verses and omissions. Most of the later printed editions attempted to correct the errors, but in doing so deleted a large part of the comment.

158b. Translation follows *Metzudas David.*

159. See *Midrash Tehillim* 79:1.

160. See *II Kings,* Ch. 17.

22 *"For if the Kenite should be laid waste, until when can Assyria take you captive?"*
23 *He declaimed his parable and said: "Oh! Who will survive when He imposes these!*
24 *"Big ships from the coast of Kittim will afflict Assyria and afflict the other bank — but it, too, will be forever destroyed."*
25 *Then Balaam rose up and went and returned to his place, and Balak also went on his way.*

1 *Israel settled in the Shittim and the people became debased, committing harlotry with the daughters of Moab.*

BAAL HATURIM ELUCIDATED

the tribes of Judah and Benjamin [which had been exiled by the Babylonians] returned from exile, the Ten Tribes [exiled by the Assyrians] did not return.

25. וַיָּשָׁב לִמְקֹמוֹ — AND HE RETURNED TO HIS PLACE. [With regard to Balaam,] the verse does not say הָלַךְ לְדַרְכּוֹ, *he went on his way* [as it does regarding Balak]. For he was driven from his way and descended to *Gehinnom.*[161]

XXV

1. בַּשִּׁטִּים — IN THE SHITTIM. [The name שִׁטִּים is related to the verb root שטה, *to stray,*] as the verb in the phrase, [אִישׁ אִישׁ] כִּי תִשְׂטֶה אִשְׁתּוֹ, [*any man*] *whose wife shall go astray* (5:12 above).[162]

❑ **וַיָּחֶל הָעָם** — AND THE PEOPLE BECAME DEBASED. This teaches that they defiled themselves from their state of holiness.[163] [An allusion to this is found in] the *gematria* of the phrase רַבִּים חֲלָלִים, [*she has brought down*] *many defiled ones*[163a] (*Proverbs* 7:26, which speaks of a harlot) — 370 — which is equivalent[164] to that of זֶה שִׁטִּים, *This refers to Shittim.*

161. See the Baal HaTurim to 23:7 above, with note 86.

162. *Peirush HaRokeach.* Like the root שטה, the root סטה means *to stray* (see *Psalms* 101:3; עֲשֹׂה סֵטִים, *doing wayward deeds*). If so, why does the Torah prefer the term כִּי תִשְׂטֶה regarding a wayward wife, rather than כִּי תִסְטֶה, which has the same meaning? Whereas the Torah prefers the שׂ to the ס in this word, the Talmud explains it as if it were spelled כִּי תִשְׁטֶה, with a שׁ instead of a שׂ; it then means *if she becomes foolish.* From this the Talmud generalizes: A person does not sin [with immorality] unless a spirit of foolishness (שְׁטוּת) enters into that person (*Sotah* 3a; cited in *Rashi* to 5:12 above). [The Midrash states that כִּי תִשְׂטֶה only teaches regarding a woman. How do we know that a man does not commit adultery unless a spirit of foolishness enters into him? From the verse, נֹאֵף אִשָּׁה חֲסַר לֵב, *One who commits adultery with a woman is missing an understanding heart* (*Proverbs* 6:32; *Tanchuma, Naso* 5).] Elsewhere, the Talmud explains the place name שִׁטִּים: it was so named because Israel engaged in matters of foolishness (שְׁטוּת) [i.e., immorality] (*Sanhedrin* 106a; see also *Targum Yonasan ben Uzziel*).

163. *Peirush HaRokeach.* The verb root חלל can mean *to begin* or *to defile, debase.* Unlike *Targum Onkelos,* who renders וַיָּחֶל הָעָם, *and the people began,* the Baal HaTurim understands the phrase, as *the people became debased* (see *Genesis* 9:20 with *Rashi; Leviticus* 21:9 with *Rashi* and *Ibn Ezra;* see also *Targum Yonasan ben Uzziel* to our verse).

163a. Alternatively: *many corpses.*

164. The principle of *im hakollel* allows 370, the

ב מוֹאָב: וַתִּקְרֶאןָ לָעָם לְזִבְחֵי אֱלֹהֵיהֶן וַיֹּאכַל הָעָם
ג וַיִּשְׁתַּחֲווּ לֵאלֹהֵיהֶן: וַיִּצָּמֶד יִשְׂרָאֵל לְבַעַל פְּעוֹר
ד וַיִּחַר־אַף יהוה בְּיִשְׂרָאֵל: וַיֹּאמֶר יהוה אֶל־מֹשֶׁה
קַח אֶת־כָּל־רָאשֵׁי הָעָם וְהוֹקַע אוֹתָם לַיהוה נֶגֶד
ה הַשָּׁמֶשׁ וְיָשֹׁב חֲרוֹן אַף־יהוה מִיִּשְׂרָאֵל: וַיֹּאמֶר
מֹשֶׁה אֶל־שֹׁפְטֵי יִשְׂרָאֵל הִרְגוּ אִישׁ אֲנָשָׁיו
ו הַנִּצְמָדִים לְבַעַל פְּעוֹר: וְהִנֵּה אִישׁ מִבְּנֵי יִשְׂרָאֵל
בָּא וַיַּקְרֵב אֶל־אֶחָיו אֶת־הַמִּדְיָנִית לְעֵינֵי מֹשֶׁה
וּלְעֵינֵי כָּל־עֲדַת בְּנֵי־יִשְׂרָאֵל וְהֵמָּה בֹכִים פֶּתַח
מפטיר ז אֹהֶל מוֹעֵד: וַיַּרְא פִּינְחָס בֶּן־אֶלְעָזָר בֶּן־אַהֲרֹן
ח הַכֹּהֵן וַיָּקָם מִתּוֹךְ הָעֵדָה וַיִּקַּח רֹמַח בְּיָדוֹ: וַיָּבֹא
אַחַר אִישׁ־יִשְׂרָאֵל אֶל־הַקֻּבָּה וַיִּדְקֹר אֶת־שְׁנֵיהֶם
אֵת אִישׁ יִשְׂרָאֵל וְאֶת־הָאִשָּׁה אֶל־קֳבָתָהּ וַתֵּעָצַר
ט הַמַּגֵּפָה מֵעַל בְּנֵי יִשְׂרָאֵל: וַיִּהְיוּ הַמֵּתִים בַּמַּגֵּפָה
אַרְבָּעָה וְעֶשְׂרִים אָלֶף: פפפ ק״ד פסוקים. מנו״ח סימן.

בעל הטורים

(ג) לְבַעַל פְּעוֹר. ״בַּעַל״ בְּגִימַטְרִיָּא צוֹאָה. וּבְגִימַטְרִיָּא ״הַהֶבֶל וַיֶּהְבָּלוּ״:

(ז) וַיִּקַּח רֹמַח. אוֹתִיּוֹת חֵרֶם, שֶׁעֲשָׂאָן חֵרֶם:

BAAL HATURIM ELUCIDATED

3. לְבַעַל פְּעוֹר — TO BAAL-PEOR. The *gematria* of בַּעַל (102) is equal to that of צוֹאָה, *feces.*[165] It is also equivalent[166] to that of הַהֶבֶל וַיֶּהְבָּלוּ, [*they pursued*] *futility,*

gematria of the Scriptural phrase, to be considered equivalent to 371, the *gematria* of the Baal HaTurim's phrase.

165. *R' Chaim Paltiel; Paaneach Raza.* The comment refers to the disgusting manner of Peor worship. The idolaters would expose themselves and defecate in front of it (*Sanhedrin* 106a, cited by *Rashi*).

Additionally: צוֹאָה is a fitting description of idolatry, for the prophet (*Isaiah* 30:22) speaks

2 *They invited the people to the feasts of their gods; the*
people ate and prostrated themselves to their gods. 3 *Israel*
became attached to Baal-peor, and the wrath of HASHEM
flared up against Israel.
4 *HASHEM said to Moses, "Take all the leaders of the*
people. Hang them before HASHEM against the sun — and
the flaring wrath of HASHEM will withdraw from Israel."
5 *Moses said to the judges of Israel, "Let each man kill his*
men who were attached to Baal-peor."
6 *Behold! a man of the Children of Israel came and*
brought a Midianite woman near to his brothers in the sight
of Moses and in the sight of the entire assembly of the
Children of Israel; and they were weeping at the entrance of
the Tent of Meeting.
7 *Phinehas son of Elazar son of Aaron the Kohen saw,*
and he stood up from amid the assembly and took a spear
in his hand. 8 *He followed the Israelite man into the tent and*
pierced them both, the Israelite man and the woman into
her stomach — and the plague was halted from upon the
Children of Israel. 9 *Those who died in the plague were*
twenty-four thousand.

BAAL HATURIM ELUCIDATED

and became futile[167] (*Jeremiah* 2:5).

7. וַיִּקַּח רֹמַח — HE TOOK A SPEAR. The letters of רֹמַח may be rearranged to spell חֵרֶם, *a waste,* for Phinehas laid them waste.

---

about the end of days and how the idolaters will discard their former objects of worship: . . . *your silver idols . . . your molten golden images, you will cast each of them away like someone unclean; you will say to it,* צֵא, *you are feces* (*Yerushalmi, Shabbos* 9:1, cited in *Ramban* to *Exodus* 32:20 and *Radak* to *Isaiah* 30:22).

166. The principle of *im hakollel* allows 101, the *gematria* of the Baal HaTurim's phrase, to be considered equivalent to 102.

167. That verse speaks of idolatry. It reads in full: *Thus said HASHEM, "What wrong did your forefathers find in Me, that they distanced themselves from Me? They pursued futility and became futile."*

פרשת פינחס

Parashas Pinechas

כה/י־יא

י־יא וַיְדַבֵּר יְהוָה אֶל־מֹשֶׁה לֵּאמֹר: פִּינְחָס בֶּן־אֶלְעָזָר
בֶּן־אַהֲרֹן הַכֹּהֵן הֵשִׁיב אֶת־חֲמָתִי מֵעַל בְּנֵי־
יִשְׂרָאֵל בְּקַנְאוֹ אֶת־קִנְאָתִי בְּתוֹכָם וְלֹא־כִלִּיתִי

בעל הטורים

כה (יא) הֵשִׁיב אֶת חֲמָתִי מֵעַל. בְּגִימַטְרִיָּא זֶהוּ אֶת הַמַּלְאָךְ שֶׁל אַף וְשֶׁל חֵמָה:

☐ **בְּקַנְאוֹ אֶת קִנְאָתִי.** תָּגִין עַל הַקוּ״ף, לוֹמַר שֶׁעִטְּרוֹ עַל שֶׁקִּנֵּא לַה׳:
שָׁלֹשׁ פְּעָמִים ״קִנְאָה״ כְּנֶגֶד שָׁלֹשׁ עֲבֵרוֹת שֶׁעָשׂוּ. ״לִזְנוֹת״ ״וַיִּשְׁתַּחֲווּ״ ״וַיִּצָּמֶד״:

BAAL HATURIM ELUCIDATED

11. הֵשִׁיב אֶת חֲמָתִי מֵעַל — [PHINEHAS . . .] HAS TURNED BACK MY WRATH FROM UPON. The *gematria* of this phrase (1316) is equivalent[1] to that of זֶהוּ אֶת הַמַּלְאָךְ שֶׁל אַף וְשֶׁל חֵמָה, *This [refers to] the angel of wrath and of fury.*[2]

☐ **בְּקַנְאוֹ אֶת קִנְאָתִי — WHEN HE ZEALOUSLY AVENGED ME.** [According to a scribal tradition, there should be] *tagin* on the ק,[3] to indicate that [Phinehas] was crowned[4] because he took zealous vengeance for the sake of God.

---

1. The principle of *im hakollel* allows 1315, the *gematria* of the Baal HaTurim's phrase, to be considered equivalent to 1316.

A parallel comment in *Peirush HaRokeach* uses the phrase, אֶת הַמַּלְאָךְ שֶׁל הָאַף וְשֶׁל הַחֵימָה, *the angel of the wrath and of the fury,* which has a *gematria* of 1317. The principle of *im hakollel* allows 1316, the *gematria* of the Scriptural phrase, to be considered equivalent to 1317.

2. The expression אֶרֶךְ אַפַּיִם (*Exodus* 34:6) is usually rendered *slow to anger* or *long-suffering.* However, according to one opinion in the Talmud, it means *distancing anger.* This concept is best understood through the following parable: A king [who loved his people] had two legions of elite troops. He thought, "I do not wish them to remain camped near me in the capital lest the populace anger me and I command my legions to attack them. Rather, I am sending them to a distant location. In that case, if the populace were to anger me, then even before I am able to send for my troops, the people will have appeased me and I will have forgiven them." Similarly, the Holy One, Blessed is He, said, "אַף, *Wrath,* and חֵמָה, *Fury,* are My destructive angels. Therefore, I am sending them to a distant location. Thus, if Israel were to anger Me, then even before I send for those angels and bring them [against Israel], Israel will have repented and I will have accepted their repentance" (*Yerushalmi Taanis* 2:1).

Both אַף and חֵמָה play a role in the incident under discussion: (i) וַיִּחַר אַף ה׳, *the wrath of* H*ASHEM flared up* (25:3 above); and (ii) here, הֵשִׁיב אֶת חֲמָתִי, *turned back My fury.* When Phinehas acted against the sinners, God sent אַף and חֵמָה to a distant location, and וַתֵּעָצַר הַמַּגֵּפָה, *the plague was halted* (25:8 above.). It is noteworthy that the *gematria* of הַמַּגֵּפָה is 133, which the principle of *im hakollel* allows to be considered equivalent to 134, the *gematria* of אַף חֵמָה (*VeChur LaZahav*).

ק with one *tag* ק with three *tagin*

3. See note 42 to 5:31 above regarding *tagin.* Although the letter ק is usually crowned with only one *tag,* according to the ancient *Sefer Tagin,* the letters ק of בְּקַנְאוֹ אֶת קִנְאָתִי are two of 185 (one version lists only 181) in the Torah which are uncharacteristically crowned with three *tagin* (see illustration).

Although all of the printed editions of the Baal HaTurim read, תָּגִין עַל הַקוּ״ף, *[there should be] tagin on the* ק, which implies only one ק of the two that appear in this phrase, nevertheless, the list in *Sefer Tagin* includes both. Additionally, one of the manuscripts used by *Shoham Yakar* reads, שְׁנֵי הַקוּפִי״ן מְתֻיָּגִין, *both letters* ק *are crowned with tagin.*

4. According to the Talmud, even though *kehunah* (priesthood) had already been given to Aaron and his offspring, it had been given only to his sons who were anointed along with him, and to the children they would beget after their anointment. But Phinehas, who had already been born before that time, but had not been anointed [with his father and grandfather], had not been granted the *kehunah* until after he had slain Zimri (*Zevachim* 101b, as explained by *Rashi* here).

[10] HASHEM spoke to Moses, saying: [11] Phinehas son of
Elazar son of Aaron the Kohen has turned back My
fury from upon the Children of Israel, when he zealously
avenged My vengeance among them, so I did not consume

BAAL HATURIM ELUCIDATED

The root קנא, *to take zealous vengeance,* appears three times [in this verse],[5] corresponding to the three sins the people committed: לִזְנוֹת, *committing harlotry* (25:1 above); וַיִּשְׁתַּחֲווּ, *and they prostrated themselves* (25:2); and וַיִּצָּמֶד, [*Israel*] *became attached* [*to Baal-peor*] (25:3).[6]

The Mishnah speaks of three crowns: the crown of the Torah; the crown of the *kehunah;* and the crown of *royalty* (*Avos* 4:13). Accordingly, Phinehas was now crowned with the crown of *kehunah.* The Baal HaTurim explains that the extra *tagin* or crownlets on the letters ק allude to that crown. However, it is not clear why the letter ק was chosen for the honor.

Three approaches are suggested regarding the relevance of the letter ק to the crown of *kehunah.* The first is based on the difference between the anointments of Kings David and Solomon, and those of Kings Saul and Jehu. David and Solomon were anointed with a קֶרֶן, *horn,* of oil (see *I Samuel* 16:13 and *I Kings* 1:39); Saul and Jehu, with a פַּךְ, *flask,* of oil (see *I Samuel* 10:1 and *II Kings* 9:3). Whereas the dynasty of David was prolonged [more than four centuries, and will be reinstated with the coming of *Mashiach*], while those of Saul [four years] and Jehu [about one hundred years] were not, the Sages state that a king should be anointed exclusively with a קֶרֶן (*Tosefta, Sanhedrin* 4:6; *Yerushalmi, Shekalim* 6:1). Accordingly, the ק was chosen as an allusion to the anointment of Phinehas, because it is the initial letter of קֶרֶן, the ideal utensil for anointment (A.S.).

Alternatively: The Sages only speak of the קֶרֶן with regard to kings. They do not state which utensil should be used for anointing Kohanim. Accordingly, it is possible that Phinehas was anointed with a פַּךְ. If so, the ק was chosen to allude to Phinehas' anointment, for the *gematria* of ק is 100, equal to that of פַּךְ (*VeChur LaZahav*).

Alternatively: What separates the Kohanim from the rest of Israel is their level of קְדוּשָׁה, *sanctity.* Thus, all the Israelites are קְדֹשִׁים, *holy* (see *Leviticus* 19:2), but the Kohanim are קֹדֶשׁ קָדָשִׁים, *holy of holies* (see *I Chronicles* 23:13). And, as the Talmud (*Shabbos* 104a) states [in another regard], the letter ק stands for קָדוֹשׁ, *holy.* Accordingly, the ק is an appropriate symbol for the *kehunah* (Y.S.).

5. (i) בְּקַנְאוֹ, *when he zealously avenged;* (ii) קִנְאָתִי, *My vengeance;* and (iii) בְּקִנְאָתִי, *in My vengeance.*

6. The three sins are: (i) consorting with Moabite women, a transgression that is not mentioned explicitly in the Torah, but was taught orally by Moses at Mount Sinai (see *Avodah Zarah* 36b) — לִזְנוֹת alludes to that sin; (ii) worshiping an idol by bowing to it — a form of worship reserved for the service of God (see *Sanhedrin* 60b) — וַיִּשְׁתַּחֲווּ alludes to that sin; and (iii) worshiping an idol by performing its formal ritual (see *Sanhedrin* 60b) — וַיִּצָּמֶד alludes to that sin (*VeChur LaZahav*).

It is noteworthy that the Baal HaTurim does not include וַיֹּאכַל הָעָם, *the people ate,* as one of the sins. This is in accord with the Midrash that describes the wiles used by the Moabite girls to lure the Israelites to sin. An older Moabitess would sit in front of a food store in the marketplace. She would display some of her culinary delights and invite Israelite men into the store to see the rest of her wares. Once the Israelite had entered, the shopkeeper's youthful daughter would engage him in conversation, only to "discover" that they were cousins — descendants of Terah, father of Israel's patriarch Abraham and grandfather of Moab's patriarch Lot. She would invite him to join them for a meal. When he would refuse on the grounds that he is not permitted to eat their meat, she would reply, "We have calves and chickens. Slaughter some according to your own ritual and eat with us." When he had succumbed to this ploy, she would ply him with wine [at that time, such wine had not yet become forbidden] until he submitted to her harlotry (*Bamidbar Rabbah* 20:23). Thus, the act of eating was not done with any sinful intention on the Israelite's part, nor was the food he ate forbidden to him (*VeChur LaZahav*).

יב אֶת־בְּנֵי־יִשְׂרָאֵל בְּקִנְאָתִי: לָכֵן אֱמֹר הִנְנִי נֹתֵן
יג לוֹ אֶת־בְּרִיתִי שָׁלוֹם: וְהָיְתָה לּוֹ וּלְזַרְעוֹ אַחֲרָיו

בעל הטורים

(יב) **לָכֵן.** שְׁנֵי פְּסוּקִים מַתְחִילִין "לָכֵן אֱמֹר" – הָכָא; וְאִידָךְ "לָכֵן אֱמֹר לִבְנֵי יִשְׂרָאֵל". וְזֶהוּ שֶׁאָמַר הַקָּדוֹשׁ בָּרוּךְ הוּא, בְּמִצְרַיִם "גַּן נָעוּל אֲחֹתִי כַלָּה", וְעַתָּה אַתֶּם קְרוֹבִים לָאָרֶץ וְאַתֶּם פְּרוּצִים בַּעֲרָיוֹת:

❑ **לָכֵן.** בְּגִימַטְרִיָּא מִדָּה בְּמִדָּה:

❑ **אֶת בְּרִיתִי שָׁלוֹם.** שלים כְּתִיב, וְהִיא וָי"ו קְטִיעָא – בְּפֶרֶק ג' דְקִדּוּשִׁין, כְּשֶׁהוּא שָׁלֵם: דָּבָר אַחֵר – מַתָּנָה שְׁלֵמָה אֲנִי נוֹתֵן לוֹ. עֶשֶׂר מַתָּנוֹת בַּמִּקְדָּשׁ, עֶשֶׂר בַּמְּדִינָה:

BAAL HATURIM ELUCIDATED

12. לָכֵן — THEREFORE. There are two verses [in the Torah[7]] that begin with the phrase [7a]לָכֵן אֱמֹר, *therefore say,* (i) this verse; and (ii) לָכֵן אֱמֹר לִבְנֵי יִשְׂרָאֵל, *therefore, say to the Children of Israel* (*Exodus* 6:6)[8] [regarding the exodus from Egypt]. This [similarity of expression] alludes to what God said [to Israel]: "In Egypt, [you upheld the standards of morality, as alluded to in the verse,] גַּן נָעוּל אֲחֹתִי כַלָּה, [*You are chaste as*] *a locked garden, My sister, O bride* (*Song of Songs* 4:12).[8a] Yet, now, you are approaching the [Holy] Land and you are breaching [those standards, mired] in immorality."[9]

❑ **לָכֵן — THEREFORE.** The *gematria* of this word (100) is equal to that of מִדָּה בְּמִדָּה, *Measure for measure.*[10]

7. The full note, which appears in some editions of the Massorah, reads: ב׳ רֵישׁ פָּסוּק בַּתּוֹרָה, *Twice at the beginning of a verse in the Torah.* The phrase also appears at the beginning of eight other verses, all in the *Book of Ezekiel* (11:16 and 17, 12:23 and 28, 14:6, 20:30, 33:25, and 36:22).

7a. The text follows *Shoham Yakar's* manuscript edition. The printed editions read either לָכֵן ב׳ רֵישׁ פָּסוּק, *The word* לָכֵן *appears twice at the beginning of a verse;* or, לָכֵן ב׳ פְּסוּקִים מַתְחִילִין, *Two verses begin with* לָכֵן. However, that cannot be the intent of the masoretic note, for *Numbers* 16:11 also begins with the word לָכֵן (*VeChur LaZahav*).

8. The Baal HaTurim there explains this masoretic note in a different manner.

8a. See *Yoma* 75a; see also *Targum* and *Rashi* to that verse.

9. The Midrash states: There are wells whose waters raise strong people and those that raise weak ones; those that raise handsome people and those that raise ugly ones; those that raise modest people and those that raise people sunken in licentiousness. The well of Shittim was a fountain of immorality . . . Thus you find that from the days of Abraham, not one of his offspring breached the rules of morality. But as soon as they arrived at Shittim and drank its waters, they breached [their standards and became mired] in immorality, as it is stated, [*Israel settled in Shittim*] *and the people became debased, committing harlotry.* Come and see! What is written regarding the exodus from Egypt? *Speak to the Children of Israel and let them . . . encamp before Pi-hahiroth* [literally, "the mouth of libertinism"] (*Exodus* 14:2). And what does the name Pi-hahiroth connote? It was a place dedicated to immorality, but whereas Israel guarded their morals when leaving Egypt, the place was called "The Mouth of Libertinism" [i.e., the place where Israel sealed itself against immorality like a mouth sealed against the entry of any unwanted substances (*VeChur LaZahav*)]. But there [in the passage about Shittim], because they sinned with the women of Moab, of them is written, *The people became debased, committing harlotry with the daughters of Moab* (*Tanchuma, Balak* 17).

10. The Baal HaTurim uses this same *gematria* in his comments to *Genesis* 30:15 and *Numbers* 20:12. He explains that the term לָכֵן indicates a direct causal relationship between an action and its consequence.

the Children of Israel in My vengeance. 12 *Therefore, say: Behold! I give him My covenant of peace,* 13 *and it shall be for him*

BAAL HATURIM ELUCIDATED

❑ **אֶת בְּרִיתִי שָׁלוֹם** — MY COVENANT OF PEACE. [The word שָׁלוֹם is] spelled שלים, for the ו [of that word] is a ו׳ קְטִיעָא, *a cut-off* ו.[10a] [This is explained] in the third chapter of tractate *Kiddushin,* [as the source of the law that] only [the Temple service performed by] a complete, i.e., unblemished [Kohen is valid].[11]

Alternatively: [God was telling Phinehas:] "I am granting you a complete gift, [which includes] ten gifts [given to you] in the Sanctuary and ten[11a] in the province."[11b]

By slaying the perpetrator who caused God's wrath to descend upon Israel, Phinehas appeased God and fostered peace between Him and Israel. As a consequence, he was rewarded with God's covenant of peace (*Shoham Yakar;* see *Rashi* and *Radak* to *Malachi* 2:5).

10a. See the Baal HaTurim to 1:16 above, with note 18.

11. *Kiddushin* 66b — The Talmud there states: How do we know that if the Temple service is performed by a physically blemished Kohen it is invalid? [That is, the Torah states that a blemished Kohen may not perform the service (*Leviticus* 21:16-24). But it does not tell us whether such service — if performed unintentionally, i.e., when the Kohen did not realize that he had a disqualifying blemish — is valid or invalid.] For the verse states, *Therefore say . . . Behold I give him My covenant of* שָׁלוֹם, *peace.* This means, [only] when he is שָׁלֵם, *whole,* [is a Kohen's service in the *Mishkan* valid,] but not when he is incomplete [i.e., blemished]. [An objection is raised:] But the Torah states שלום, with a ו, which is vowelized שָׁלוֹם and means *peace* [and not שלם, without a ו, which would be vowelized שָׁלֵם, meaning *whole*]? . . . [The Talmud answers:] The ו of שלום is קְטִיעָה, *cut off* [as if it were a י or as if it were absent altogether; thus the word could be interpreted as שָׁלֵם/שָׁלִים, *whole*].

Similarly, the masoretic note on the word שלום reads: ו׳ זוּטָא וְהוּא חַד מֵא״ב מֵאוֹתִיּוֹת קְטַנּוֹת, *the* ו *is diminutive and is one of the items on the list called "Aleph-Beis of Diminutive Letters."* And it also appears on list 84 — "Diminutive Letters in Scripture, in Aleph-Beis Order" — in the masoretic anthology *Ochlah VaOchlah* (Frensdorff ed.).

There is an unresolved centuries-old dispute regarding the shape of the "cut-off ו." Indeed, in extant Torah scrolls this ו is found in a variety of forms, among them: (i) a ו of regular shape, but diminutive in size; (ii) a ו of regular size, but with

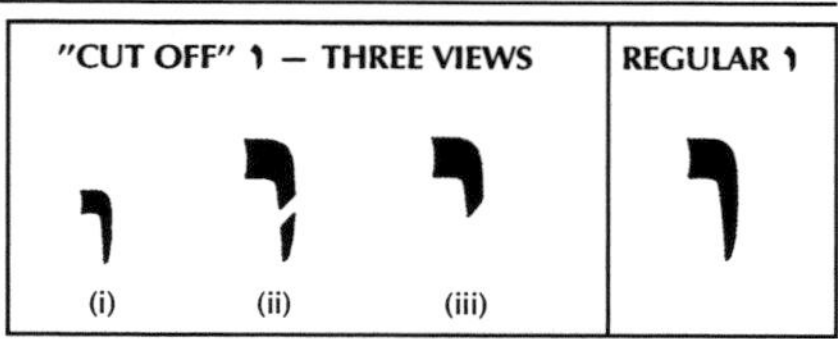

the leg severed from the head; (iii) a ו of regular proportion, but with the bottom of its leg missing, so that it can be read as a י. From the Baal HaTurim's comment to 1:16 above (see note 18 there), it is clear that he follows (iii) above.

11a. The letter י alludes to 20, for the name of the letter is spelled יו״ד, which has a *gematria* of 20 (*Ittur Bikkurim*). Alternatively: According to the opinion that a ו׳ קְטִיעָה is made of two pieces, each piece may be considered as a י; thus it alludes to two times ten (*Shoham Yakar*).

11b. See the Baal HaTurim to 18:11 above, with note 75.

The Talmud states: Twenty-four priestly gifts were given to Aaron and his sons . . . They are: Ten in the Sanctuary [i.e., they must be consumed within the Temple Courtyard]; four in Jerusalem [i.e., they must be consumed within the walls of the city or are given to the Kohanim within Jerusalem]; and ten in the provinces [i.e., everywhere else in the Land of Israel, some even outside of the land] (*Bava Kamma* 110b; *Chullin* 133b). It is not clear why the Baal HaTurim omits any mention of the other four gifts. In a parallel comment, *Peirush HaRokeach* mentions only the ten gifts in the Sanctuary.

It is possible that the Baal HaTurim's comment was originally longer and containing an allusion to the other four gifts as well, but a part of the comment was omitted due to a copyist's oversight (A.S.). Another question may lead us to an explanation of the missing four gifts: According to the Baal HaTurim's understanding

בְּרִית כְּהֻנַּת עוֹלָם תַּחַת אֲשֶׁר קִנֵּא לֵאלֹהָיו
יד וַיְכַפֵּר עַל־בְּנֵי יִשְׂרָאֵל: וְשֵׁם אִישׁ יִשְׂרָאֵל הַמֻּכֶּה
אֲשֶׁר הֻכָּה אֶת־הַמִּדְיָנִית זִמְרִי בֶּן־סָלוּא נְשִׂיא

בעל הטורים

דָּבָר אַחֵר – וָי״ו קְטִיעָא כִּי פִּינְחָס הוּא אֵלִיָּהוּ, וְכֵן ״אֵלִיָּה״ כְּתִיב חָסֵר וָי״ו, וְיַעֲקוֹב מָלֵא וָי״ו. שֶׁנָּטַל וָי״ו מֵאֵלִיָּהוּ לְמַשְׁכּוֹן, עַד שֶׁיָּבוֹא עִם הַמָּשִׁיחַ וְיִגְאַל אֶת בָּנָיו. וְזֶהוּ ״יָגֵל יַעֲקֹב יִשְׂמַח יִשְׂרָאֵל״ – ״יִשְׂמַח״ אוֹתִיּוֹת ״מָשִׁיחַ״ – שֶׁיִּשְׂמַח לִימוֹת הַמָּשִׁיחַ וְיַחֲזִיר הַוָּי״ו וִיהֵא אֵלִיָּהוּ שָׁלֵם. ״שָׁלוֹם״ בְּגִימַטְרִיָּא זֶהוּ מָשִׁיחַ:

(יג) וַיְכַפֵּר. ״לְכַפֵּר״ לֹא נֶאֱמַר אֶלָּא ״וַיְכַפֵּר״ – שֶׁעוֹמֵד וּמְכַפֵּר עַל יִשְׂרָאֵל עַד סוֹף כָּל הַדּוֹרוֹת:

(יד) שְׁלֻמִיאֵל בְּגִימַטְרִיָּא זֶה זִמְרִי בֶּן סָלוּא:

BAAL HATURIM ELUCIDATED

Alternatively: The letter ו (= 6) is cut off because Phinehas is identical with [the prophet] אֵלִיָּהוּ, *Elijah.*[12] And Elijah's name is [sometimes] spelled, אֵלִיָּה, without a ו,[13] while Jacob's name is [sometimes] spelled, יַעֲקוֹב, with a ו.[14] [This indicates] that Jacob took the ו from Elijah as security until Elijah would come with *Mashiach*[15] and redeem [Jacob's] descendants.[16] This is also [intimated by the verse], יָגֵל יַעֲקֹב יִשְׂמַח יִשְׂרָאֵל, *Jacob will exult, Israel will rejoice* (*Psalms* 14:7),[17]

of ו׳ קטיעה (see note 11 above), why does the Talmud identify the letter as a cut off ו, rather than calling it simply a י, [i.e., the word is a קְרִי וּכְתִיב, it is spelled שָׁלִים, but pronounced שָׁלוֹם] as we find in *Genesis* 24:33, where the word is spelled וַיִּישַׂם, but read ויוּשַׂם (see the Baal HaTurim there). Perhaps, by calling it a ו even though it appears as a י, the Talmud hints at the difference between the two letters, i.e., the *gematria* of י is 10, while the *gematria* of ו is 6, a difference of four. Thus, we have an allusion to the other four gifts (*VeChur LaZahav*).

12. *Pirkei DeRabbi Eliezer* 47; *Zohar* II 190a, III 215a; see *Rashi* to *Bava Metzia* 114b, s.v., לאו כהן מר, but see *Tosafos* there for other opinions regarding the genealogy of Elijah. See also the Baal HaTurim to 26:15 below, with note 44.

13. The shortened spelling appears five times: *II Kings* 1:3, 1:4, 1:8, 1:12; and *Malachi* 3:23.

It is noteworthy that the *gematria* of חָסֵר וָי״ו, *without a* ו, is 290, equal to that of כִּי פִּינְחָס אֵלִיָּהוּ (*VeChur LaZahav*).

14. The enhanced spelling appears five times: *Leviticus* 26:42; *Jeremiah* 30:18, 33:26, 46:27 and 51:19.

15. The prophet declared: *The first one* [*to come*] *to Zion* [*will announce*], *"Behold! They are here!" For I will send* מְבַשֵּׂר, *a herald, to Jerusalem* (*Isaiah* 41:27). Although the context of the verse refers to the return from the Babylonian exile seventy years after the destruction of the First Temple, the Talmud assigns this prophecy to the coming of *Mashiach* (*Pesachim* 5a). Elsewhere, the Talmud identifies the מְבַשֵּׂר, *herald,* as Elijah the prophet, as it is written (*Malachi* 3:23), *Behold, I send you* אֵלִיָּה, *Elijah, the prophet, before the coming of the great and awesome day of* HASHEM (*Eruvin* 43b; see *Rashi,* s.v., לפני בא, and *Tosafos,* s.v., דלא אתא, there). Thus, Jacob took a ו from Elijah's name as security, to ensure that Elijah would faithfully fulfill his mission as the מְבַשֵּׂר, *herald.*

16. *Rashi* to *Leviticus* 26:42. This may be understood on a deeper level. King Solomon taught that security guarantees are sealed with a handshake (see *Proverbs* 6:1). The letter ו is long and narrow like a finger so that the five letters ו that Jacob took from Elijah represent the five fingers of a handshake. Thus, Jacob holds on to Elijah's hand and will not release it until Elijah comes to herald the coming of *Mashiach* (*Gur Aryeh;* for another interpretation of Jacob's purpose in taking the letter ו as security, see *She'eilos Useshuvos Sho'eil Umeishiv,* I 3:88).

17. The beginning of that verse reads: *O, that out of Zion will come Israel's salvation! When* HASHEM

and his offspring after him a covenant of eternal priesthood, because he took zealous vengeance for his God, and he brought atonement for the Children of Israel.

14 *The name of the smitten Israelite man who was smitten with the Midianitess was Zimri son of Salu, leader of a*

BAAL HATURIM ELUCIDATED

for the letters of יִשְׂמַח are the same as those of מָשִׁיחַ. For [Jacob] will rejoice [at Israel's redemption] in the time of *Mashiach,* and he will return the ו so that Elijah's name will be complete.[18] [This is all alluded to by the word שָׁלוֹם, for] the *gematria* of שָׁלוֹם is 376, equal to that of וְזֶהוּ מָשִׁיחַ, *This is* [*a reference to*] *Mashiach.*

13. וַיְכַפֵּר — AND HE BROUGHT ATONEMENT. The verse does not state לְכַפֵּר, *to atone,* but וַיְכַפֵּר, *he brought atonement,* [which may be interpreted as if it read וִיכַפֵּר, *he will bring atonement,*[19]] for Phinehas stands ready and brings atonement for Israel, until the end of all generations.[20]

14. The *gematria* of שְׁלֻמִיאֵל, *Shelumiel,*[21] (411) is equivalent to that of זֶה זִמְרִי בֶּן סָלוּא, *This* [*person*] *is Zimri son of Salu.*[22]

restores the captivity of His people, Jacob will . . .

The words יָגֵל יַעֲקֹב, *Jacob will exult,* refer explicitly to Jacob. Elijah is alluded to in the name יִשְׂרָאֵל, *Israel:* For the *gematria* of יִשְׂרָאֵל is 541, which, by the principle of *im hakollel,* may be considered equivalent to 542, the *gematria* of מְבַשֵּׂר, *herald* (see note 15 above), an allusion to Elijah. And *Mashiach* is alluded to in the words יַעֲקֹב and יִשְׂרָאֵל: For the Talmud records a four-pronged dispute regarding the given name of *Mashiach* — (i) שִׁילֹה; (ii) יִנּוֹן; (iii) חֲנִינָה; or (iv) מְנַחֵם (*Sanhedrin* 98b). The combined *gematria* of these four names is 722, which, by the principle of *im hakollel,* is considered equivalent to 723, the *gematria* of יַעֲקֹב יִשְׂרָאֵל (*VeChur LaZahav*).

18. In one of the manuscripts used by *Shoham Yakar* this reads, וִיהֵא אֵלִיָּהוּ שָׁלֵם וְשָׁלוֹם שָׁלֵם, *The name* אֵלִיָּהוּ *will be complete and the word* שָׁלוֹם *will be complete.*

19. The word לְכַפֵּר, *to atone,* would imply that Phinehas' deed served to bring atonement for Israel's lapse regarding the daughters of Moab and the Peor idol. After that, Phinehas' role as the one who brings atonement for Israel was completed. But the term וַיְכַפֵּר, *he brought atonement,* has a different implication: The word יְכַפֵּר is a future tense verb meaning *he will bring atonement;* which the conversive prefix -וַ changes to the past tense — *he brought atonement.* However, since the Torah scroll is written without vowels, that word may be read וִיכַפֵּר, that is, וְיְכַפֵּר, with the conjunctive prefix -וְ [a combination that requires a change from -וְיְ to וִי, because two *sheva* vowels cannot appear together at the beginning of a word], which means *and he will bring atonement,* i.e., in the future. Thus, the verses may be understood: *Behold, I give him My covenant of peace, and it shall be . . . a covenant of eternal priesthood . . . so that he will bring atonement for the Children of Israel* (*Peirush Sifrei D'Vei Rav*).

20. *Sifrei.*

21. The leader of the tribe of Simeon (see 1:6 above) whom the Talmud (*Sanhedrin* 82b) identifies as Zimri of our verse.

22. *Peirush HaRokeach.* The *gematria* of זֶה זִמְרִי בֶּן סָלוּא is actually 418, seven more than that of שְׁלֻמִיאֵל. Various approaches have been suggested to resolve this discrepancy: (a) Although the name שְׁלֻמִיאֵל is spelled defectively, without a ו, each of the five times that it appears in the Torah (1:6, 2:12, 7:36, 7:41 and 10:19 above), for purposes of the allusion, the Baal HaTurim uses the full spelling שְׁלוּמִיאֵל, with a ו (= 6). The *gematria* is then 417, which, by the principle of *im hakollel,* is considered equivalent to 418 (*Ittur Bikkurim*).

(b) The name שְׁלֻמִיאֵל should be spelled as it appears in the Torah, without a ו, leaving its *gematria* at 411, which the principle of *im hakollel* allows to be considered equivalent to 412. The name of Zimri's father, however, should be spelled defectively, סָלָא, without a ו, even though it is spelled with a ו in the verse; the *gematria* of זֶה זִמְרִי בֶּן סָלָא is then 412 (see *Paaneach Raza*). [It is noteworthy that we find a

טו בֵּית־אָב לַשִּׁמְעֹנִי: וְשֵׁם הָאִשָּׁה הַמֻּכָּה הַמִּדְיָנִית
כָּזְבִּי בַת־צוּר רֹאשׁ אֻמּוֹת בֵּית־אָב בְּמִדְיָן הוּא:
טז־יז וַיְדַבֵּר יהוה אֶל־מֹשֶׁה לֵּאמֹר: צָרוֹר אֶת־הַמִּדְיָנִים

בעל הטורים

❑ **הֻכָּה.** ג׳ בַּמָּסוֹרֶת – הָכָא "אֲשֶׁר הֻכָּה אֶת הַמִּדְיָנִית"; וְאִידָךְ "הוּכָּה כָעֵשֶׂב וַיִּבַשׁ לִבִּי"; "הֻכָּה אֶפְרַיִם". עַל יְדֵי הַמִּדְיָנִית "הוּכָּה כָעֵשֶׂב וְגוֹ׳ ", שֶׁהָיְתָה בָהֶם הַמַּגֵּפָה. וְסֵיפֵהּ דִּקְרָא "כִּי שָׁכַחְתִּי מֵאֲכֹל לַחְמִי", שֶׁעַל יְדֵי אֲכִילַת לַחְמִי טָעִיתִי וְנִצְמַדְתִּי לְבַעַל פְּעוֹר. כִּדְאִיתָא בַּמִּדְרָשׁ, שֶׁהוֹשִׁיבוּ לָהֶם פֻּנְדְּקָאוֹת שֶׁהָיוּ מוֹכְרִים לָהֶם מִינֵי מַאֲכָל וּמַשְׁקֶה. וְכֵן "הֻכָּה אֶפְרַיִם" עַל יְדֵי פְּעוֹר, כִּדְאִיתָא בִּתְחִלַּת הַפָּרָשָׁה "הֵמָּה בָּאוּ בַעַל פְּעוֹר וַיִּנָּזְרוּ לַבֹּשֶׁת וְגוֹ׳":

(יז) **צָרוֹר אֶת הַמִּדְיָנִים.** לְשׁוֹן יָחִיד, "וְהִכִּיתֶם" לְשׁוֹן רַבִּים! "צָרוֹר", כִּי עַל יָדְךָ הָיָה, שֶׁאָמַר לָהּ אָבִיהָ, אַל תִּבָּעֲלִי אֶלָּא לַגָּדוֹל שֶׁבָּהֶם, וְזֶהוּ מֹשֶׁה. "וְהִכִּיתֶם" לְשׁוֹן רַבִּים, וְלֹא מֹשֶׁה, כִּי נִתְגַּדֵּל בְּמִדְיָן:

BAAL HATURIM ELUCIDATED

❑ **הֻכָּה — WAS SMITTEN.** The masoretic note, ג׳, means that this word appears three times in the *Tanach:*[23] (i) here, אֲשֶׁר הֻכָּה אֶת הַמִּדְיָנִית, *who was smitten with the Midianitess;* (ii) הוּכָּה כָעֵשֶׂב וַיִּבַשׁ לִבִּי, *smitten like grass until my heart is withered*[24] (*Psalms* 102:5); and (iii) הֻכָּה אֶפְרַיִם, *Ephraim*[24a] *was smitten* (*Hosea* 9:16). [The similarity of expression indicates that] because of the Midianitess, [Israel] was *smitten like grass* etc.,[25] for the plague was in their midst. Moreover, the conclusion of the verse [from *Psalms*] reads: כִּי שָׁכַחְתִּי מֵאֲכֹל לַחְמִי, *for I have forgotten to eat my food,* [as if Israel were saying,] "For it was through eating my food, that I strayed and I became attached to *Baal-peor.*"[26] As the Midrash

Benjaminite mentioned twice in the *Tanach,* one time as סַלָּא (*Nehemiah* 11:7), the second time as סַלּוּא (*I Chronicles* 9:7). Although the nouns סָלוּא and סַלָּא are vowelized differently, it is possible that just as סָלוּא can be spelled סַלָּא, so can סָלוּא be spelled סַלָּא (*VeChur LaZahav*).]

(c) Using the exact spellings found in the Torah, we find the *gematria* of שְׁלֻמִיאֵל to be 411, to which the principle of *im haosios* allows us to add 6, for a total of 417. And the *gematria* of זִמְרִי בֶּן סָלוּא is 406, to which the principle of *im haosios* allows us to add 10, bringing the *gematria* to 416, and the principle of *im hakollel* allows one more to be added, for a total of 417 (*VeChur LaZahav*).

23. The full note reads: ג׳ ב׳ חֲסֵרִים וא׳ מָלֵא, *Three, twice spelled defectively* [*without a* ו] *and once spelled in full* [with a ו].

24. The full verse reads: [*I am*] *smitten like grass* [*by the sun*] *and my heart is withered,* כִּי שָׁכַחְתִּי מֵאֲכֹל לַחְמִי, *for I have forgotten to eat my bread.*

24a. In this passage, אֶפְרַיִם, *Ephraim,* does not refer to the tribe of that name. Rather, it refers to the ten tribes that had broken away from the Kingdom of Judah and become the Kingdom of Israel (see *Ibn Ezra* to *Hosea* 5:3). Thus, *Targum Yonasan ben Uzziel* renders אֶפְרַיִם of that verse as בֵּית יִשְׂרָאֵל, *the house of Israel* (similarly, *Targum* to many other verses in *Hosea*).

25. The reading, "עַל יְדֵי הַמִּדְיָנִית "הוּכָּה כָעֵשֶׂב וְגוֹ׳ שֶׁהָיְתָה בָהֶם הַמַּגֵּפָה, *because of the Midianitess,* [*Israel*] *was "smitten like grass etc.," for the plague was in their midst,* follows one of the manuscripts used by *Shoham Yakar.* In the Constantinople and Venice editions, the phrase הוּכָּה כָעֵשֶׂב is absent and the word וְגוֹמֵר is abbreviated וג׳ instead of וגו׳, which the printers of the Furth edition understood as וְג׳, *and three,* and spelled out as וּשְׁלֹשָׁה. *Shoham Yakar's* edition follows another manuscript which reads, עַל יְדֵי הַמִּדְיָנִית "הוּכָּה כָעֵשֶׂב" וְגַם שֶׁהָיְתָה בָהֶם הַמַּגֵּפָה, *Because of the Midianitess, [Israel] was "smitten like grass," and also the plague was in their midst.*

26. The verse is to be understood: כִּי שָׁכַחְתִּי, *If I have forgotten* [*God, and I have sinned*], מֵאֲכֹל לַחְמִי, [*it comes*] *from eating my food* (*VeChur LaZahav*).

father's house of the Simeonites. [15] *And the name of the slain Midianitess was Cozbi daughter of Zur, who was head of the peoples of a father's house in Midian.*

[16] *HASHEM spoke to Moses, saying:* [17] *"Harass the Midianites*

BAAL HATURIM ELUCIDATED

relates, the Midianites set up their women as shopkeepers, who sold the Israelites food and drink . . .[27] Similarly, *Ephraim was smitten* because of Baal-peor, as that paragraph begins, הֵמָּה בָּאוּ בַעַל פְּעוֹר וַיִּנָּזְרוּ לַבֹּשֶׁת, *They came to Baal-peor and dedicated themselves to shamefulness* etc. (*Hosea* 9:10).

17. צָרוֹר אֶת הַמִּדְיָנִים — HARASS THE MIDIANITES. [The command צָרוֹר, *harass,* is] a singular verb form,[28] while וְהִכִּיתֶם, *and you shall smite them,* is a plural verb![29] [The subject of צָרוֹר is Moses. God said to him,] *"Harass . . .,* for it was on your account [that Cozbi came]. For her father had told her, 'Do not engage in relations with anyone other than their leader,' and that is Moses."[30] The verb וְהִכִּיתֶם is in the plural [as it was addressed to the nation in general,] not to Moses.[30a] [It would have been improper for Moses to smite Midian] for he had been nurtured in Midian.[31]

27. *Bamidbar Rabbah* 20:23, cited in note 6 above.

28. That is, the word צָרוֹר is a *makor* [gerundive] (see *Rashi* and *Ibn Ezra*). As such, it indicates ongoing action and its literal meaning is "be harassing." In this verse it is used as an imperative, in which case it can be either singular or plural. Thus we find the parallel *makor* זָכוֹר used both for the singular [e.g., זָכוֹר אֵת אֲשֶׁר עָשָׂה לְךָ עֲמָלֵק, *Remember what Amalek did to you* (*Deuteronomy* 25:17), which uses the singular pronoun לְךָ, *to you*] and for the plural [e.g., זָכוֹר אֶת הַיּוֹם הַזֶּה אֲשֶׁר יְצָאתֶם, *Remember this day on which you departed,* which uses the plural form יְצָאתֶם, *you departed*]. Accordingly, when the Baal HaTurim calls it a singular verb, he means a verb that may be either singular or plural.

29. Whereas צָרוֹר is a *makor* (see note 28), we might expect the verse to use the *makor* הַכּוֹת in the second stich of the verse. Nevertheless, the verse switches to the plural verb form וְהִכִּיתֶם, *you shall smite.* The Baal HaTurim explains why.

30. *Sanhedrin* 82a — The Talmud there states: She said, "My father told me that since I am the daughter of a king [according to the Midrash, Zur and Balak were one and the same. He was called Zur while he was a chieftain in Midian; later, he became a king over Midian (see 31:8 below), where he retained the name Zur; subsequently, he was appointed king of Moab where he was known as Balak (*Bamidbar Rabbah* 20:7 with *Maharzu*)], I should not become involved with any Israelite but the leader." Zimri responded, "Like your father in Midian, I too am a chieftain of a father's house in Israel." She then acceded to Zimri (see also *Bamidbar Rabbah* 20:24).

This Talmudic passage also answers another question: If Zur's name was changed to Balak, as stated in the Midrash cited above, why is his daughter called בַּת צוּר, rather than בַּת בָּלָק, in our verse? The Torah refers to צוּר, the head of a father's house in Midian, because that particular phase of his life was the crux of Zimri's persuasive argument (Y.S.).

30a. In the battles against Sihon and Og, Moses himself led the Israelite army against the enemy (see *Rashi* to 27:17 below, s.v., אשר יצא). Here, however, in the battle against Midian, Moses sent Phinehas in his place (see *Rashi* to 31:6 below, s.v., אתם ואת פינחס). The Baal HaTurim explains why Moses did not lead the army in this battle (A.S.).

31. *Peirush HaRokeach; Moshav Zekeinim.* The trait of הַכָּרַת הַטּוֹב, *recognition and thankful acknowledgment of kindness,* is a major tenet of ethical living. Therefore, one must never harm anybody or anything that had once been beneficial to him. As the Talmud states: Do not throw stones into the well from which you drank (*Bava Kamma* 92b; see also *Rashi* to *Exodus* 7:19).

יח וְהִכִּיתֶ֖ם אוֹתָֽם׃ כִּ֣י צֹרְרִ֥ים הֵם֙ לָכֶ֔ם בְּנִכְלֵיהֶ֛ם
אֲשֶׁר־נִכְּל֥וּ לָכֶ֖ם עַל־דְּבַ֣ר פְּע֑וֹר וְעַל־דְּבַ֞ר כׇּזְבִּ֨י
בַת־נְשִׂ֤יא מִדְיָן֙ אֲחֹתָ֔ם הַמֻּכָּ֥ה בְיוֹם־הַמַּגֵּפָ֖ה
*פסקא באמצע פסוק
כו א עַל־דְּבַר־פְּעֽוֹר׃ וַיְהִ֖י אַחֲרֵ֣י הַמַּגֵּפָ֑ה *
וַיֹּ֤אמֶר יהוה֙ אֶל־מֹשֶׁ֔ה וְאֶ֧ל אֶלְעָזָ֛ר בֶּן־אַהֲרֹ֥ן
ב הַכֹּהֵ֖ן לֵאמֹֽר׃ שְׂא֞וּ אֶת־רֹ֣אשׁ ׀ כׇּל־עֲדַ֣ת בְּנֵֽי־
יִשְׂרָאֵ֗ל מִבֶּ֨ן עֶשְׂרִ֥ים שָׁנָ֛ה וָמַ֖עְלָה לְבֵ֣ית אֲבֹתָ֑ם
ג כׇּל־יֹצֵ֥א צָבָ֖א בְּיִשְׂרָאֵֽל׃ וַיְדַבֵּ֨ר מֹשֶׁ֜ה וְאֶלְעָזָ֧ר
הַכֹּהֵ֛ן אֹתָ֖ם בְּעַרְבֹ֣ת מוֹאָ֑ב עַל־יַרְדֵּ֥ן יְרֵח֖וֹ
ד לֵאמֹֽר׃ מִבֶּ֛ן עֶשְׂרִ֥ים שָׁנָ֖ה וָמָ֑עְלָה כַּאֲשֶׁ֨ר צִוָּ֤ה
יהוה֙ אֶת־מֹשֶׁה֙ וּבְנֵ֣י יִשְׂרָאֵ֔ל הַיֹּצְאִ֖ים מֵאֶ֥רֶץ
ה מִצְרָֽיִם׃ רְאוּבֵ֖ן בְּכ֣וֹר יִשְׂרָאֵ֑ל בְּנֵ֣י רְאוּבֵ֗ן חֲנוֹךְ֙ שני
מִשְׁפַּ֣חַת הַחֲנֹכִ֔י לְפַלּ֕וּא מִשְׁפַּ֖חַת הַפַּלֻּאִֽי׃
ו לְחֶצְרֹ֕ן מִשְׁפַּ֖חַת הַחֶצְרוֹנִ֑י לְכַרְמִ֕י מִשְׁפַּ֖חַת

בעל הטורים

כו (א) וַיְהִי אַחֲרֵי הַמַּגֵּפָה. פָּרָשָׁה זוֹ פְּתוּחָה. שֶׁעָשָׂה הֶפְסֵק בֵּין הַמַּגֵּפָה לַמִּנְיָן, שֶׁלֹּא תִשְׁלֹט הַמַּגֵּפָה בִּפְקֹד אוֹתָם:

(ב) **לְבֵית אֲבֹתָם.** וְלֹא אָמַר "לְמִשְׁפְּחֹתָם" כְּמוֹ לְמַעְלָה. לְפִי שֶׁאָמַר בְּכָל אֶחָד "מִשְׁפַּחַת הַחֲנֹכִי", "מִשְׁפַּחַת הַפַּלֻּאִי", וְכֵן בְּכֻלָּם:

(ו) **לְכַרְמִי.** ב׳ — הָכָא "לְכַרְמִי מִשְׁפַּחַת הַכַּרְמִי"; וְאִידָךְ "מַה לַּעֲשׂוֹת עוֹד לְכַרְמִי". מִי הוּא

BAAL HATURIM ELUCIDATED

XXVI

1. וַיְהִי אַחֲרֵי הַמַּגֵּפָה — IT WAS AFTER THE PLAGUE. [According to the Massorah,] this passage is open,[32] for an interruption is made between the plague and the

32. According to masoretic tradition, the text of Scripture is divided into פָּרָשִׁיּוֹת, *parashiyos* (paragraph-like passages), separated from one another by a blank space (see note 22 to 1:19 above).

Our verse is one of three in the Torah, each of which is divided between two *parashiyos,* a phenomenon known as פִּסְקָא בְּאֶמְצַע פָּסוּק, *a new paragraph in the middle of a verse.* [The other two are *Genesis* 35:22 and *Deuteronomy* 2:8; however, the Baal HaTurim does not comment on those verses; there are also twenty-five such verses in the Prophets.] In explaining our verse, we treat it as if it were two separate verses, with the first, וַיְהִי אַחֲרֵי הַמַּגֵּפָה, belonging to the previous narrative and the second, from וַיֹּאמֶר until לֵאמֹר, belonging to the next. But when it is read, the passage is treated as one long verse.

Grammatically, the entire verse should be part of the following paragraph. For even though it speaks of the plague, the topic of the previous narrative, nevertheless, it serves as an introduction to the following narrative — the census after the plague. The Baal HaTurim explains why the paragraph break comes in the middle of a verse.

and smite them; [18] for they harassed you through their conspir-
acy that they conspired against you in the matter of Peor, and in
the matter of Cozbi, daughter of a leader of Midian, their sister,
who was slain on the day of the plague, in the matter of Peor."

26

[1] It was after the plague — HASHEM spoke to Moses and to
Elazar son of Aaron the Kohen, saying: [2] Take a census of the
entire assembly of the Children of Israel, from twenty years of
age and up, according to their fathers' houses, all who go out to
the legion in Israel.

[3] Moses and Elazar the Kohen spoke to them in the plains of
Moab, by the Jordan near Jericho, saying: [4] "From twenty years
of age and up, as HASHEM had commanded Moses and the
Children of Israel, who were coming out of the land of Egypt."

[5] Reuben the firstborn of Israel — the sons of Reuben: [of]
Hanoch, the family of the Hanochite; of Pallu, the family of the
Palluite; [6] of Hezron, the family of the Hezronite; of Carmi, the

BAAL HATURIM ELUCIDATED

census, in order that the plague not affect them[33] when they are counted.[34]

2. לְבֵית אֲבֹתָם — **ACCORDING TO THEIR FATHERS' HOUSES.** The verse does not say, לְמִשְׁפְּחֹתָם, *according to their families,* as does an earlier verse [regarding another tribal census] (*Numbers* 1:2). This is because [here] each verse states [the word מִשְׁפַּחַת, *the family of,* e.g.,] מִשְׁפַּחַת הַחֲנֹכִי, *the family of the Hanochite;* מִשְׁפַּחַת הַפַּלְּאִי, *the family of the Palluite;*[35] and so on for all of them.[36]

❑ {The Baal HaTurim's other comment to this verse appears at 1:2 above.}

6. לְכַרְמִי — **OF CARMI.** This word appears twice:[37] (i) here, לְכַרְמִי מִשְׁפַּחַת הַכַּרְמִי, *of Carmi, the family of the Carmite* [as a proper noun]; and (ii) מַה לַּעֲשׂוֹת עוֹד לְכַרְמִי, *What more could have been done for My vineyard?* (*Isaiah* 5:4) [as a common noun]. [This similarity of expression indicates that God said,] "Who is referred to

33. The Baal HaTurim's words here paraphrase *Exodus* 30:12. Counting the Children of Israel is not a simple matter. If the census is not conducted properly, it could result in a death plague (see *Exodus* 30:12). Thus, we find that when King David ordered his general Joab to take a census of Israel, seventy thousand people died in an ensuing plague. Both King David and Gad the prophet blamed those deaths on the improperly conducted census (see *II Samuel* 24:1-15; see also *Rashi* to *Exodus* 30:12, s.v., ולא יהיה).

34. *Peirush HaRokeach.*

35. The Baal HaTurim uses these two as examples because they are the first two families mentioned in this census (v. 5).

36. *Peirush HaRokeach.* This comment is one of the few found in the Baal HaTurim which are in the realm of *peshat* (simple meaning of the verse) rather than *remez* (allusion).

37. In the standard version of the Massorah, no note appears on this word, either here or in *Isaiah.* In fact, the word לְכַרְמִי appears a third time, in *Isaiah,* in the verse following the one cited by the Baal HaTurim. Perhaps the Baal HaTurim's ב׳ means merely that the word לְכַרְמִי appears with two meanings: (i) *of Carmi* son of Reuben; and (ii) *for My vineyard,* i.e., the noun כֶּרֶם, *vineyard,* with the prepositional prefix -לְ, *to* or *for,* and the possessive suffix ־ִי, *my.*

ז הַכַּרְמִי: אֵלֶּה מִשְׁפְּחֹת הָרְאוּבֵנִי וַיִּהְיוּ פְקֻדֵיהֶם
שְׁלֹשָׁה וְאַרְבָּעִים אֶלֶף וּשְׁבַע מֵאוֹת וּשְׁלֹשִׁים:
ח־ט וּבְנֵי פַלּוּא אֱלִיאָב: וּבְנֵי אֱלִיאָב נְמוּאֵל וְדָתָן
וַאֲבִירָם הוּא־דָתָן וַאֲבִירָם °קרואי הָעֵדָה °קְרִיאֵי ק׳
אֲשֶׁר הִצּוּ עַל־מֹשֶׁה וְעַל־אַהֲרֹן בַּעֲדַת־קֹרַח
י בְּהַצֹּתָם עַל־יהוה: וַתִּפְתַּח הָאָרֶץ אֶת־פִּיהָ
וַתִּבְלַע אֹתָם וְאֶת־קֹרַח בְּמוֹת הָעֵדָה בַּאֲכֹל
הָאֵשׁ אֵת חֲמִשִּׁים וּמָאתַיִם אִישׁ וַיִּהְיוּ לְנֵס:

בעל הטורים

כַּרְמִי? זֶה שֶׁנֶּאֱמַר בּוֹ ״לְכַרְמִי מִשְׁפַּחַת הַכַּרְמִי״, כְּדִכְתִיב ״כִּי כֶרֶם ה׳ צְבָאוֹת בֵּית יִשְׂרָאֵל״:

(י) **וַיִּהְיוּ לְנֵס.** שֶׁמַּחְתּוֹתָם הָיוּ לְאוֹת וּלְזִכָּרוֹן:

❑ **לְנֵס.** ג׳ בַּמָּסוֹרֶת – ״וַיִּהְיוּ לְנֵס״ {כו׳}; ״שֹׁרֶשׁ יִשַׁי אֲשֶׁר עֹמֵד לְנֵס עַמִּים״; ״שֵׁשׁ בְּרִקְמָה מִמִּצְרַיִם הָיָה מִפְרָשֵׂךְ לִהְיוֹת לָךְ לְנֵס״. זֶהוּ שֶׁאָמְרוּ, מָקוֹם נִתְבַּצֵּר לָהֶם. כְּשֶׁנִּפְתְּחָה הָאָרֶץ נִשְׁאַר מָקוֹם בְּאֶמְצַע. כְּמוֹ הַנֵּס שֶׁהוּא בְּרֹאשׁ הַתֹּרֶן, כָּךְ נִשְׁאַר מָקוֹם כְּמוֹ תֹּרֶן:

וּמִכָּאן רֶמֶז לְמַאן דְּאָמַר שֶׁהִיא אֲבֵדָה הַמִּתְבַּקֶּשֶׁת, שֶׁיַּעַמְדוּ לִתְחִיַּת הַמֵּתִים, לִימוֹת הַמָּשִׁיחַ. וְהַיְנוּ ״שֹׁרֶשׁ יִשַׁי אֲשֶׁר עֹמֵד לְנֵס {עַמִּים}״:

BAAL HATURIM ELUCIDATED

as כַּרְמִי, *My vineyard*? The one of whom it it is said, לְכַרְמִי מִשְׁפַּחַת הַכַּרְמִי, *of Carmi, the family of the Carmite.*" For thus is it written, כִּי כֶרֶם ה׳ צְבָאוֹת בֵּית יִשְׂרָאֵל, *For the House of Israel is the vineyard of HASHEM, Master of Legions* (*Isaiah* 5:7).[38]

10. וַיִּהְיוּ לְנֵס — AND THEY BECAME AS AN ENSIGN. For their fire-pans became a sign and a reminder.[39]

38. The Baal HaTurim's intention is unclear. He seems merely to be interpreting the term לְכַרְמִי, *for My vineyard,* of *Isaiah* 5:4-5 as a reference to Israel. But if that were so, the allusion would be entirely superfluous, for the prophet states that explicitly in verse 7 there, and the Baal HaTurim cites that verse also!

Rashi (v. 5) cites the Midrash that explains why the Torah forms a family's name by adding the prefix ־הַ and the suffix ־ִי to the name of the progenitor of that family: The other nations would humiliate the Israelites by saying, "Why are these people tracing their genealogy according to their tribes? They must think that the Egyptians did not hold sway over their mothers! But if the Egyptians ruled over the Israelites' bodies, they certainly ruled over their wives!" God responded by adding His Name — יָהּ — to their names, the letter ה at the beginning and the letter י at the end. Thus, He testified that they are the legitimate children of their fathers. And that is the meaning of King David's statement (*Psalms* 122:4): שִׁבְטֵי יָהּ עֵדוּת לְיִשְׂרָאֵל, [*They are*] *the tribes of* יָהּ, [*Who bears*] *testimony* [*that they are from the nation*] *of Israel* (*Shir HaShirim Rabbah* 4:12; *Pesikta DeRav Kahana, Beshalach*).

It is possible that the Baal HaTurim alludes to that Midrash: God said, "Who is referred to as כַּרְמִי, *My vineyard?*" And He continued, "*The House of Israel is the vineyard of HASHEM.* But only when they fulfill the verse לְכַרְמִי מִשְׁפַּחַת הַכַּרְמִי, i.e., they must meet the criteria needed לְכַרְמִי, *for Carmi,* to be called, מִשְׁפַּחַת הַכַּרְמִי, with My signature testifying to their purity" (*VeChur LaZahav;* see also *Kiddushin* 70b with *Maharsha,* s.v., ואין מעיד).

39. *Peirush HaRokeach.* The narrative of Korah's rebellion is the subject of Chapter 16 above. In

family of the Carmite. 7 *These are the families of the*
Reubenite; their count was forty-three thousand, seven
hundred and thirty. 8 *The sons of Pallu: Eliab.* 9 *And the sons*
of Eliab: Nemuel and Dathan and Abiram, the same Dathan
and Abiram who were summoned by the assembly, who
contended against Moses and Aaron among the assembly
of Korah, when they contended against HASHEM. 10 *Then the*
earth opened its mouth and swallowed them and Korah with
the death of the assembly, when the fire consumed two
hundred and fifty men — and they became as an ensign.

BAAL HATURIM ELUCIDATED

❑ לְנֵס — AS AN ENSIGN. The masoretic note,[40] ג׳, means that this word appears three times in the *Tanach:* (i) here, [40a]{כֻּלְהוּ} וַיִּהְיוּ לְנֵס, *they became as an ensign* {*etc.* }; (ii) שֹׁרֶשׁ יִשַׁי אֲשֶׁר עֹמֵד לְנֵס עַמִּים, *the descendant of Jesse who stands as an ensign for the peoples* (*Isaiah* 11:10); and (iii) שֵׁשׁ בְּרִקְמָה מִמִּצְרַיִם הָיָה מִפְרָשֵׂךְ לִהְיוֹת לָךְ לְנֵס, *Embroidered Egyptian linen was your sail, to be as an ensign for you* (*Ezekiel* 27:7). This [similarity of expression] alludes to the Sages' statement: A place was set up high [in *Gehinnom*] for them [i.e., Korah's sons].[41] When the earth opened, a place in the center remained. Like the ensign atop the mast, so did a mastlike high place remain [for them].

This [similarity of expression here and in the verse from *Isaiah*] is an allusion to the [Talmudic] opinion: It [the congregation of Korah] is like a lost object being sought by its owner. That is, they will arise with the Resurrection of the Dead, in the era of *Mashiach.*[42] And that is the meaning of the verse, [*Mashiach is*] *the descendant of Jesse who stands as an ensign* {*for the peoples*[42a]}.

---

the aftermath, the copper fire-pans used by the rebels were beaten into sheets which were used to plate the Altar (see 17:1-5 above). There they were to serve לְאוֹת, *as a sign* (17:3), and זִכָּרוֹן, *a reminder* (17:5), that a non-Kohen should never even attempt to serve at the Altar.

40. The note is found at *Isaiah* 11:10.

40a. In the early printed editions, the multipurpose preposition כִּי appears between the first two verses adduced by the Baal HaTurim. However, none of the various meanings of כִּי seem to be appropriate there. Accordingly, most later editions, including *Shoham Yakar's* manuscript edition, omit that word. The text here is emended to read כֻּלְהוּ כו׳ [*etc.*] as suggested by R' Avraham Shereshevsky, for the gist of the Baal HaTurim's comment connects the words וַיִּהְיוּ לְנֵס with the verse that follows.

41. *Sanhedrin* 110a. The word לְנֵס of our verse is followed by the verse: *But the sons of Korah did not die.* The Midrash explains that when the ground opened to swallow up Korah and his followers, the sons of Korah filled their hearts with thoughts of repentance (*Midrash Shocher Tov* 45). Consequently, the Talmud explains, a place was set up high in *Gehinnom* and they sat there reciting songs of praise to God (*Sanhedrin* 110a, cited by *Rashi;* see also *Midrash Shocher Tov* 1:15). As attested to by their opening verses, psalms 45-49, 84-85, 87-88 were composed by the sons of Korah.

42. *Sanhedrin* 109b.

42a. The text follows *Shoham Yakar's* manuscript edition. The early printed editions, as well as most later editions, omit the word עַמִּים from the comment.

יא־יב וּבְנֵי־קֹרַח לֹא־מֵתוּ: בְּנֵי שִׁמְעוֹן לְמִשְׁפְּחֹתָם
לִנְמוּאֵל מִשְׁפַּחַת הַנְּמוּאֵלִי לְיָמִין מִשְׁפַּחַת
יג הַיָּמִינִי לְיָכִין מִשְׁפַּחַת הַיָּכִינִי: לְזֶרַח מִשְׁפַּחַת
יד הַזַּרְחִי לְשָׁאוּל מִשְׁפַּחַת הַשָּׁאוּלִי: אֵלֶּה מִשְׁפְּחֹת
טו הַשִּׁמְעֹנִי שְׁנַיִם וְעֶשְׂרִים אֶלֶף וּמָאתָיִם: בְּנֵי
גָד לְמִשְׁפְּחֹתָם לִצְפוֹן מִשְׁפַּחַת הַצְּפוֹנִי לְחַגִּי
טז מִשְׁפַּחַת הַחַגִּי לְשׁוּנִי מִשְׁפַּחַת הַשּׁוּנִי: לְאָזְנִי

בעל הטורים

(טו) הַצְּפוֹנִי. ב׳ בַּמָּסוֹרֶת – ״לִצְפוֹן מִשְׁפַּחַת הַצְּפוֹנִי״; וְאִידָךְ ״וְאֶת הַצְּפוֹנִי אַרְחִיק מֵעֲלֵיכֶם״. זֶה מִבְּנֵי גָד. {וְכֵן כְּשֶׁיָּבוֹא אֵלִיָּהוּ שֶׁהוּא מִבְּנֵי גָד,} שֶׁבְּדִבְרֵי הַיָּמִים מְיַחֵס אוֹתוֹ מִבְּנֵי גָד, ״וְאֶת הַצְּפוֹנִי אַרְחִיק מֵעֲלֵיכֶם״, שֶׁיִּתְבַּטֵּל יֵצֶר הָרָע:

❑ **לִצְפוֹן.** הוּא ״צִפְיוֹן״. וּכְתִיב שָׁם ״צִפְיוֹן״, עַל שֵׁם שֶׁמֹּשֶׁה שֶׁקִּבֵּל י׳ הַדִּבְּרוֹת צָפוּן בְּחֶלְקוֹ:

BAAL HATURIM ELUCIDATED

15. הַצְּפוֹנִי — THE ZEPHONITE. The masoretic note, ב׳, means that this word appears twice in the *Tanach:*[43] (i) here, לִצְפוֹן מִשְׁפַּחַת הַצְּפוֹנִי, *of Zephon, the family of the Zephonite;* and (ii) וְאֶת הַצְּפוֹנִי אַרְחִיק מֵעֲלֵיכֶם, *I will distance the hidden one from you* (*Joel* 2:20). [The similarity of expression alludes to the time of *Mashiach:*] This [family הַצְּפוֹנִי of our verse] is from the tribe of Gad. {And so [God says,] "When Elijah — who is from the children of Gad,[44]}[44a] for in *Chronicles*[45] he is ascribed to the children of Gad — will come [to herald the *Mashiach*], *I will distance the hidden one from you,* for the evil inclination[46]

43. The note, as it appears in *Joel,* reads: ב׳ בִּתְרֵי לִישְׁנֵי, *Two, with two different meanings.* In our verse it is a proper noun, the name of a family; in *Joel* it is a common noun, from the root צפן, *to hide,* and means *the hidden one.*

44. Earlier (at 25:12 above, s.v., דָּבָר אַחֵר וָי״ו קְטִיעָא, see note 12 there), the Baal HaTurim found an allusion to the Midrashic view that Elijah was identical with Phinehas. If so, Elijah was a Kohen and a member of the tribe of Levi. Nevertheless, there are other Midrashim which trace Elijah's ancestry to either Gad or Benjamin (*Tanchuma, Ki Sisa* 13; *Bereishis Rabbah* 71:9 and 99:11; *Tanna DeVei Eliyahu Rabbah* 18; *Tanna DeVei Eliyahu Zuta* 15; see also *Tosafos* to *Bava Metzia* 114b, s.v., מהו, and *Rashbam* to *Bava Basra* 121b, s.v., אחיה השילוני, and *Tosafos* there; see also *Radak* to *I Kings* 17:1).

44a. The passage enclosed in braces is not found in the early printed editions or in most later editions. However, it does appear in *Shoham Yakar's* manuscript edition.

45. The Baal HaTurim's source for this statement is unclear. For the Midrashim that speak of Elijah being from the tribe of Gad (see note 44) do not adduce any verses from *Chronicles.* Rather, they cite *I Chronicles* 8:27 to prove that Elijah is a Benjaminite. Consequently, many later editions emend the comment to read מְלָכִים, *Kings* (see *I Kings* 17:1), in place of דִּבְרֵי הַיָּמִים, *Chronicles.* Nevertheless, the Baal HaTurim's statement cannot be dismissed as a copyist's error, for many of the Midrashim that interpret the genealogical lists in *Chronicles* are no longer extant, but may have been in the Baal HaTurim's time.

46. The Talmud states that the evil inclination is called by seven names: (i) God called it רַע, *Evil* (*Genesis* 8:21); (ii) Moses called it עָרֵל, *Uncircumcised* (*Deuteronomy* 10:16); (iii) King David

[11] *But the sons of Korah did not die.*

[12] *The sons of Simeon according to their families: of Nemuel, the family of the Nemuelite; of Jamin, the family of the Jaminite; of Jachin, the family of the Jachinite;* [13] *of Zerah, the family of the Zerahite; of Shaul, the family of the Shaulite.* [14] *These are the families of the Simeonite: twenty-two thousand, two hundred.*

[15] *The sons of Gad according to their families: of Zephon, the family of the Zephonite; of Haggi, the family of the Haggite; of Shuni, the family of the Shunite;* [16] *of Ozni,*

BAAL HATURIM ELUCIDATED

will be brought to naught[47] [at that time].[48]

❑ לְצְפוֹן — OF ZEPHON. [Elsewhere] he is [called] צִפְיוֹן, *Ziphion*[48a] (*Genesis* 46:16).[48b] There [his name is] spelled צִפְיוֹן, [with a י (= 10)] as an allusion that Moses, who received the Ten Commandments, is צָפוּן, *hidden,*[48c] in his portion[49] [of the land].[49a]

called it טָמֵא, *Unclean* (*Psalms* 51:12); (iv) King Solomon called it שׂוֹנֵא, *Foe* (*Proverbs* 25:21); and the prophets called it (v) מִכְשׁוֹל, *Stumbling Block* (*Isaiah* 57:14); (vi) אֶבֶן, *Stone* (*Ezekiel* 36:26), and צְפוֹנִי, *Hidden* (*Joel* 2:20). The Rabbis taught: *I will distance the hidden one from you* refers to the evil inclination that is hidden and lurks in the heart of man (*Succah* 52a).

47. The Talmud teaches that the evil inclination will cease to exist [or, at least, have no power] in the World to Come (*Succah* 52a).

48. *Maharam MiRothenburg.*

48a. The text follows *Shoham Yakar's* manuscript edition. The comment means: Although Gad named his son צְפוֹן, without a י, as it appears here, nevertheless, in *Genesis* the Torah adds a י to his name as an allusion to the Ten Commandments. The early printed editions read: לְצְפוֹן הוּא צְפוֹן וּכְתִיב צִפְיוֹן, OF ZEPHON. *He is* [i.e., his real name is] *Zephon, yet* [*in Genesis*] *it is spelled Ziphion.* And that version has the same meaning as the one in the manuscript edition.

According to *Ittur Bikkurim,* however, Gad named his son צִפְיוֹן, with a י, as it appears in *Genesis,* but, in our *parashah,* the Torah shortened that name, hiding the י to indicate that the one who had received the Ten Commandments was hidden in this tribe's territory. He therefore emends the comment to read: לְצְפוֹן הוּא צִפְיוֹן וּכְתִיב צְפוֹן, OF ZEPHON. *He is* [i.e., his real name is] *Ziphion, yet* [*here*] *it is spelled Zephon.* And that is the version that appears in many of the later editions.

48b. *Pesikta Zutresa* [*Midrash Lekach Tov*].

48c. That is, buried in an unidentifiable grave (see *Deuteronomy* 34:6).

49. *Peirush HaRokeach.* The Talmud cites the words of Moses' blessing to the tribe of Gad, *He chose the finest for himself, for that is where the lawgiver's portion is* סָפוּן, *hidden* (*Deuteronomy* 33:21), as proof that Moses was buried in the territory of Gad (*Sotah* 13b). [Note that the three verb roots ספן (e.g., *Haggai* 1:4), צפן (e.g., *Exodus* 2:3), and שׂפן (e.g., *Deuteronomy* 33:19) are synonymous and mean *to hide* or *to be hidden.*]

It is not clear whether the Baal HaTurim means (a) that Moses was buried in Zephon/Ziphion's portion in the territory of Gad, thus the allusive י appears in his name, or (b) that we do not know in which Gadite family's portion Moses is buried; the י then appears in Zephon/Ziphion for some other reason, perhaps because, as Gad's firstborn, he represents the entire tribe (*VeChur LaZahav*); or (c) because the name צְפוֹן is related to סָפוּן, *hidden,* as stated earlier in this note (Y.S.).

49a. It is suggested that the allusions in each of the Baal HaTurim's comments regarding the family names [לְצְפוֹן (v. 15); לְפֻוָּה, (v. 23); יָשׁוּב (v. 24); לִשְׁפוּפָם (v. 39)] refer to the respective family's entire tribe (A.S.).

יז מִשְׁפַּחַת הָאׇזְנִי לְעֵרִי מִשְׁפַּחַת הָעֵרִי: לַאֲרוֹד
מִשְׁפַּחַת הָאֲרוֹדִי לְאַרְאֵלִי מִשְׁפַּחַת הָאַרְאֵלִי:
יח אֵלֶּה מִשְׁפְּחֹת בְּנֵי־גָד לִפְקֻדֵיהֶם אַרְבָּעִים אֶלֶף
יט וַחֲמֵשׁ מֵאוֹת: בְּנֵי יְהוּדָה עֵר וְאוֹנָן וַיָּמׇת עֵר
כ וְאוֹנָן בְּאֶרֶץ כְּנָעַן: וַיִּהְיוּ בְנֵי־יְהוּדָה לְמִשְׁפְּחֹתָם
לְשֵׁלָה מִשְׁפַּחַת הַשֵּׁלָנִי לְפֶרֶץ מִשְׁפַּחַת הַפַּרְצִי
כא לְזֶרַח מִשְׁפַּחַת הַזַּרְחִי: וַיִּהְיוּ בְנֵי־פֶרֶץ לְחֶצְרֹן
כב מִשְׁפַּחַת הַחֶצְרֹנִי לְחָמוּל מִשְׁפַּחַת הֶחָמוּלִי: אֵלֶּה
מִשְׁפְּחֹת יְהוּדָה לִפְקֻדֵיהֶם שִׁשָּׁה וְשִׁבְעִים אֶלֶף
כג וַחֲמֵשׁ מֵאוֹת: בְּנֵי יִשָּׂשכָר לְמִשְׁפְּחֹתָם תּוֹלָע
כד מִשְׁפַּחַת הַתּוֹלָעִי לְפֻוָּה מִשְׁפַּחַת הַפּוּנִי: לְיָשׁוּב
כה מִשְׁפַּחַת הַיָּשֻׁבִי לְשִׁמְרֹן מִשְׁפַּחַת הַשִּׁמְרֹנִי: אֵלֶּה
מִשְׁפְּחֹת יִשָּׂשכָר לִפְקֻדֵיהֶם אַרְבָּעָה וְשִׁשִּׁים אֶלֶף
כו וּשְׁלֹשׁ מֵאוֹת: בְּנֵי זְבוּלֻן לְמִשְׁפְּחֹתָם לְסֶרֶד
מִשְׁפַּחַת הַסַּרְדִּי לְאֵלוֹן מִשְׁפַּחַת הָאֵלֹנִי לְיַחְלְאֵל
כז מִשְׁפַּחַת הַיַּחְלְאֵלִי: אֵלֶּה מִשְׁפְּחֹת הַזְּבוּלֹנִי
כח לִפְקֻדֵיהֶם שִׁשִּׁים אֶלֶף וַחֲמֵשׁ מֵאוֹת: בְּנֵי
כט יוֹסֵף לְמִשְׁפְּחֹתָם מְנַשֶּׁה וְאֶפְרָיִם: בְּנֵי מְנַשֶּׁה
לְמָכִיר מִשְׁפַּחַת הַמָּכִירִי וּמָכִיר הוֹלִיד אֶת־גִּלְעָד
ל לְגִלְעָד מִשְׁפַּחַת הַגִּלְעָדִי: אֵלֶּה בְּנֵי גִלְעָד אִיעֶזֶר
מִשְׁפַּחַת הָאִיעֶזְרִי לְחֵלֶק מִשְׁפַּחַת הַחֶלְקִי:

בעל הטורים

(כג) לְפֻוָּה מִשְׁפַּחַת הַפּוּנִי. הָיָה לוֹ לוֹמַר ״הַפֻּוָּהִי״. וּכְתִיב ״הַפּוּנִי״. לוֹמַר שֶׁכׇּל יִשְׂרָאֵל פּוֹנִים אֵלָיו לִלְמֹד מִתּוֹרָתוֹ:

(כד) יָשׁוּב. הוּא ״יוֹב״, וְקוֹרֵא אוֹתוֹ יָשׁוּב, בִּשְׁבִיל שֶׁבַּעֲלֵי יְשִׁיבָה הָיוּ:

BAAL HATURIM ELUCIDATED

23. לְפֻוָּה מִשְׁפַּחַת הַפּוּנִי — OF PUVAH, THE PUNITE. [Following the manner of naming the other families,] this family should have been called הַפֻּוָּהִי, the *Puvahite.*[50] But

50. In assigning family names to the Children of Israel, the Torah usually places a ה at the beginning of the name of the family's founding father and a י at the end (see note 38 above for an explanation). Accordingly, in the case of פֻּוָּה, we would expect the family to be called הַפֻּוָּהִי (or, perhaps, הַפּוּהִי). Why does the Torah use a נ instead of a ה to form the family name הַפּוּנִי?

the family of the Oznite; of Eri, the family of the Erite; [17] *of Arod, the family of the Arodite; of Areli, the family of the Arelite.* [18] *These are the families of the sons of Gad according to their count forty thousand, five hundred.*

[19] *The sons of Judah, Er and Onan; Er and Onan died in the land of Canaan.* [20] *The sons of Judah according to their families were: of Shelah, the family of the Shelanite; of Perez, the family of the Perezite; of Zerah, the family of the Zerahite.* [21] *The sons of Peretz were: of Hezron, the family of the Hezronite; of Hamul, the family of the Hamulite.* [22] *These are the families of Judah according to their count: seventy-six thousand, five hundred.*

[23] *The sons of Issachar according to their families were: [of] Tola, the family of the Tolaite; of Puvah, the family of the Punite;* [24] *of Jashub, the family of the Jashubite; of Shimron, the family of the Shimronite.* [25] *These are the families of Issachar according to their count: sixty-four thousand, three hundred.*

[26] *The sons of Zebulun according to their families: of Sered, the family of the Seredite; of Elon, the family of the Elonite; of Jahleel, the family of the Jahleelite.* [27] *These are the families of the Zebulunite according to their count: sixty thousand, five hundred.*

[28] *The sons of Joseph according to their families: Manasseh and Ephraim.* [29] *The sons of Manasseh: of Machir, the family of the Machirite, and Machir begat Gilead; of Gilead, the family of the Gileadite.* [30] *These are the sons of Gilead: [of] Iezer, the family of the Iezerite; of Helek, the family of the Helekite;*

BAAL HATURIM ELUCIDATED

the Torah states הַפּוּנִי, *the Punite,* to indicate that all of Israel פּוֹנִים, *would turn,* to it, to learn its Torah teachings.[51]

24. יָשׁוּב — [OF] JASHUB. [Elsewhere] he is [called] יוֹב, *Iov* (*Genesis* 46:13).[52] Here he is referred to as יָשׁוּב, *Jashub,* for they were בַּעֲלֵי יְשִׁיבָה, *members of the court.*[53]

51. *Peirush HaRokeach.* Whoever was unsure of the proper *halachah* would ask members of the tribe of Issachar, who would in turn explain the *halachah* to them (*Bamidbar Rabbah* 13:15; see also the Baal HaTurim to *Genesis* 49:14, s.v., בֵּין הַמִּשְׁפְּתָיִם). That Midrash does not specify either Puvah or his family as this tribe's scholars. Indeed, the only family name singled out as scholars is that of יָשׁוּב (see the Baal HaTurim's next comment; see also note 49a above).

52. *Rashi.*

53. *Bamidbar Rabbah* 13:15 — The term יָשׁוּב refers to courts of law, as it is stated: [*The children of your people . . . speak to one another . . . saying, "Come now and hear what is the word that issues forth from* HASHEM."] *They will come to you as a people comes, and My nation will sit* (וְיֵשְׁבוּ) *before you and they will hear your words . . .* (*Ezekiel* 33:30-31).

לא וְאַשְׂרִיאֵל מִשְׁפַּחַת הָאַשְׂרְאֵלִי וְשֶׁכֶם מִשְׁפַּחַת
לב הַשִּׁכְמִי: וּשְׁמִידָע מִשְׁפַּחַת הַשְּׁמִידָעִי וְחֵפֶר
לג מִשְׁפַּחַת הַחֶפְרִי: וּצְלָפְחָד בֶּן־חֵפֶר לֹא־הָיוּ לוֹ
בָּנִים כִּי אִם־בָּנוֹת וְשֵׁם בְּנוֹת צְלָפְחָד מַחְלָה
לד וְנֹעָה חָגְלָה מִלְכָּה וְתִרְצָה: אֵלֶּה מִשְׁפְּחֹת
מְנַשֶּׁה וּפְקֻדֵיהֶם שְׁנַיִם וַחֲמִשִּׁים אֶלֶף וּשְׁבַע
לה מֵאוֹת: אֵלֶּה בְנֵי־אֶפְרַיִם לְמִשְׁפְּחֹתָם
לְשׁוּתֶלַח מִשְׁפַּחַת הַשֻּׁתַלְחִי לְבֶכֶר מִשְׁפַּחַת
לו הַבַּכְרִי לְתַחַן מִשְׁפַּחַת הַתַּחֲנִי: וְאֵלֶּה בְּנֵי שׁוּתָלַח
לז לְעֵרָן מִשְׁפַּחַת הָעֵרָנִי: אֵלֶּה מִשְׁפְּחֹת בְּנֵי־אֶפְרַיִם
לִפְקֻדֵיהֶם שְׁנַיִם וּשְׁלֹשִׁים אֶלֶף וַחֲמֵשׁ מֵאוֹת
לח אֵלֶּה בְנֵי־יוֹסֵף לְמִשְׁפְּחֹתָם: בְּנֵי בִנְיָמִן
לְמִשְׁפְּחֹתָם לְבֶלַע מִשְׁפַּחַת הַבַּלְעִי לְאַשְׁבֵּל
מִשְׁפַּחַת הָאַשְׁבֵּלִי לַאֲחִירָם מִשְׁפַּחַת הָאֲחִירָמִי:
לט לִשְׁפוּפָם מִשְׁפַּחַת הַשּׁוּפָמִי לְחוּפָם מִשְׁפַּחַת

בעל הטורים

(לד) מְנַשֶּׁה נִתְרַבָּה בְּזֶה הַמִּנְיָן עֶשְׂרִים אֶלֶף וַחֲמֵשׁ מֵאוֹת. וְזֶהוּ שֶׁאָמְרוּ בְּנֵי יוֹסֵף "עַד כֹּה בֵּרְכַנִי ה׳ ":

(לה) **אֵלֶּה בְנֵי אֶפְרַיִם.** בִּבְנֵי אֶפְרַיִם כְּתִיב "אֵלֶּה", עַל שֵׁם "אֵלֶּה אֱלֹהֶיךָ יִשְׂרָאֵל". שֶׁיָּצָא מִמֶּנּוּ יָרָבְעָם שֶׁעָשָׂה שְׁנֵי עֲגָלִים. וְלָכֵן כְּתִיב גַּם כֵּן "אֵלֶּה" בִּבְנֵי דָן, עַל שֵׁם "וְאֶת הָאֶחָד נָתַן בְּדָן":

(לט) **לִשְׁפוּפָם מִשְׁפַּחַת הַשּׁוּפָמִי.** הָיָה לוֹ לוֹמַר "הַשְּׁפוּפָמִי". רֶמֶז שֶׁמֵּת בִּנְיָמִין בְּעֶטְיוֹ שֶׁל

BAAL HATURIM ELUCIDATED

34. In this census, the population of the tribe of Manasseh increased by 20,500.[54] The children of Joseph alluded to this increase when they said, עַד כֹּה בֵּרְכַנִי ה׳, *HASHEM has blessed me until* כֹּה (*Joshua* 17:14).[55]

35. אֵלֶּה בְּנֵי אֶפְרַיִם — THESE ARE THE SONS OF EPHRAIM. With regard to the tribe of Ephraim, the Torah uses the expression אֵלֶּה, *these are,*[56] a reference to the

54. In the earlier census (1:35 above), the population of Manasseh is given as 32,200. Here it is given as 52,700, an increase of 20,500.

55. *Rashi* to *Joshua* 17:14 — The word כֹּה, literally, *here,* alludes to 20,500, for the *gematria* of כ is 20 and the *gematria* of ה is 5. Thus, כֹּה may be understood as כ thousand and ה hundred; the phrase from *Joshua* then means, *HASHEM has blessed me with* [*an increase of*] *twenty thousand and five hundred offspring.*

56. Regarding the other tribes, the census report begins, "the sons of So-and-so." However, the counts of Ephraim and Dan are introduced with the extra word אֵלֶּה, *these are.*

 31 *and [of] Asriel, the family of the Asrielite; and [of] Shechem,
the family of the Shechemite; 32 *and [of] Shemida, the family*
of the Shemidaite; and [of] Hepher, the family of the Hepherite.
33 *Zelophehad son of Hepher had no sons, only daugh-*
ters; and the names of Zelophehad's daughters: Mahlah,
Noah, Hoglah, Milcah, and Tirzah. 34 *These are the families of*
Manasseh, and their count: fifty-two thousand, seven hun-
dred.

35 *These are the sons of Ephraim according to their fami-*
lies: of Shuthelah, the family of the Shuthelahite; of Becher,
the family of the Becherite; of Tahan, the family of the
Tahanite. 36 *And these are the sons of Shuthelah: of Eran, the*
family of the Eranite. 37 *These are the families of the sons of*
Ephraim according to their count: thirty-two thousand, five
hundred. These are the sons of Joseph according to their
families.

38 *The sons of Benjamin according to their families: of Bela,*
the family of the Belaite; of Ashbel, the family of the Ashbelite;
of Ahiram, the family of the Ahiramite; 39 *of Shephupham,*
the family of the Shuphamite; of Hupham, the family of the

BAAL HATURIM ELUCIDATED

verse, אֵלֶּה אֱלֹהֶיךָ יִשְׂרָאֵל, *These are your gods, O Israel* (*Exodus* 32:4) [which speaks of the idolatry of the golden calf]. [This expression is used with regard to Ephraim,] because Jeroboam, who set up two [golden] calf idols (*I Kings* 12:28), descended from this tribe (*I Kings* 11:26).

Similarly the term אֵלֶּה is used with regard to the tribe of Dan (v. 42 below), in accordance with the verse,[57] אֶת הָאֶחָד נָתַן בְּדָן, *And the* [*other*] *one he placed in Dan*[57a] (*I Kings* 12:29).[58]

39. לִשְׁפוּפָם מִשְׁפַּחַת הַשּׁוּפָמִי — OF SHEPHUPHAM, THE FAMILY OF THE SHUPHAMITE. We would expect the Torah to use the term, הַשְּׁפוּפָמִי, *the Shephuphamite.* [The elision of שפופ into שופ is] an allusion to the fact that Benjamin died because of

57. The text of the Baal HaTurim has been emended here to agree with the text of the verse in *Kings*. Virtually all previous editions read, וַיִּתֵּן אֶת הָאֶחָד בְּדָן, a misquote that does not change the meaning of the verse (*VeChur LaZahav*).

57a. It is understandable that the passage of Ephraim, whose leading member (a few centuries later) — Jeroboam — introduced calf-idol worship into Israel, is introduced with an allusion to idolatry. But just because Jeroboam placed one of his golden calves in the territory of Dan, why should that tribe be identified as idolaters? Jeroboam was aware of Dan's inclination toward idolatry (see *Sanhedrin* 103b; see also the Baal HaTurim to 2:31 and 10:25 above), therefore he selected that tribe's territory as the site of his second calf's temple. Accordingly, the Torah alludes to idolatry in Dan's passage (A.S.). Alternatively: Micah, of the tribe of Dan, was responsible for the original golden calf idol (see *Tanchuma, Ki Sissa* 19, cited by *Rashi* to *Exodus* 34:2). Thus, Jeroboam set his calf idol in Dan (Y.S.).

58. *R' Yehudah HaChassid; Rabbeinu Bachya* to v. 12 above.

מ הַחוּפָמִי: וַיִּהְיוּ בְנֵי־בֶלַע אַרְדְּ וְנַעֲמָן מִשְׁפַּחַת
מא הָאַרְדִּי לְנַעֲמָן מִשְׁפַּחַת הַנַּעֲמִי: אֵלֶּה בְנֵי־בִנְיָמִן
לְמִשְׁפְּחֹתָם וּפְקֻדֵיהֶם חֲמִשָּׁה וְאַרְבָּעִים אֶלֶף וְשֵׁשׁ
מב מֵאוֹת: אֵלֶּה בְנֵי־דָן לְמִשְׁפְּחֹתָם לְשׁוּחָם מִשְׁפַּחַת
מג הַשּׁוּחָמִי אֵלֶּה מִשְׁפְּחֹת דָּן לְמִשְׁפְּחֹתָם: כָּל־
מִשְׁפְּחֹת הַשּׁוּחָמִי לִפְקֻדֵיהֶם אַרְבָּעָה וְשִׁשִּׁים אֶלֶף
מד וְאַרְבַּע מֵאוֹת: בְּנֵי אָשֵׁר לְמִשְׁפְּחֹתָם לְיִמְנָה
מִשְׁפַּחַת הַיִּמְנָה לְיִשְׁוִי מִשְׁפַּחַת הַיִּשְׁוִי לִבְרִיעָה
מה מִשְׁפַּחַת הַבְּרִיעִי: לִבְנֵי בְרִיעָה לְחֶבֶר מִשְׁפַּחַת
מו הַחֶבְרִי לְמַלְכִּיאֵל מִשְׁפַּחַת הַמַּלְכִּיאֵלִי: וְשֵׁם בַּת־
מז אָשֵׁר שָׂרַח: אֵלֶּה מִשְׁפְּחֹת בְּנֵי־אָשֵׁר לִפְקֻדֵיהֶם
מח שְׁלֹשָׁה וַחֲמִשִּׁים אֶלֶף וְאַרְבַּע מֵאוֹת: בְּנֵי
נַפְתָּלִי לְמִשְׁפְּחֹתָם לְיַחְצְאֵל מִשְׁפַּחַת הַיַּחְצְאֵלִי
מט לְגוּנִי מִשְׁפַּחַת הַגּוּנִי: לְיֵצֶר מִשְׁפַּחַת הַיִּצְרִי
נ לְשִׁלֵּם מִשְׁפַּחַת הַשִּׁלֵּמִי: אֵלֶּה מִשְׁפְּחֹת נַפְתָּלִי
לְמִשְׁפְּחֹתָם וּפְקֻדֵיהֶם חֲמִשָּׁה וְאַרְבָּעִים אֶלֶף
נא וְאַרְבַּע מֵאוֹת: אֵלֶּה פְּקוּדֵי בְּנֵי יִשְׂרָאֵל שֵׁשׁ־מֵאוֹת
אֶלֶף וָאָלֶף שְׁבַע מֵאוֹת וּשְׁלֹשִׁים:

בעל הטורים

נָחָשׁ, שֶׁנֶּאֱמַר בּוֹ, ״הוּא יְשׁוּפְךָ רֹאשׁ״:
וְיֵשׁ פ׳ בְּכָל תֵּבָה וְתֵבָה, לוֹמַר שֶׁהָיָה לוֹ פֶּה וְלֹא גִּלָּה עַל אֶחָיו בִּמְכִירַת יוֹסֵף:

BAAL HATURIM ELUCIDATED

the counsel of the serpent,[59] about whom it is stated, הוּא יְשׁוּפְךָ[59a] רֹאשׁ, *He will*

59. *Peirush HaRokeach.* The Talmud states: Four people [were completely unsullied by sin and did not deserve to die; nevertheless, they] died as a result of the serpent's counsel [to Eve, which was the ultimate cause of the decree of death for all of mankind]. They are: Benjamin son of Jacob; Amram father of Moses; Jesse father of David; and Chileab son of David.

The Talmud goes on to state that the fates of Benjamin, Amram and Chileab are known by tradition [rather than from any Scriptural source], while that of Jesse is derived from the verse that refers to his daughter as אֲבִיגַל בַּת נָחָשׁ, *Abigal daughter of Nachash* (*II Samuel* 17:25). But was she the daughter of Nachash? Was she not the daughter of Jesse? Rather, the verse means that she was the daughter of one who died only as a result of the counsel of the נָחָשׁ, *serpent* (*Bava Basra* 17a).

In our verse, the Baal HaTurim finds an allusion to the fate of Benjamin.

59a. It is noteworthy that the word יְשׁוּפְךָ, *he will bruise you,* alludes to Benjamin, for the *gematria* of בִּנְיָמִין בֶּן יַעֲקֹב, *Benjamin son of Jacob,* is 396, equal to that of יְשׁוּף, *he will bruise* (*VeChur LaZahav*).

Huphamite. 40 *And the sons of Bela were Ard and Naaman:*
the family of the Ardite; of Naaman, the family of the
Naamite. 41 *These are the sons of Benjamin according to*
their families, and their count: forty-five thousand, six
hundred.

42 *These are the sons of Dan according to their families: of*
Shuham, the family of the Shuhamite. These are the
families of Dan according to their families. 43 *All the*
Shuhamite families according to their count: sixty-four
thousand, four hundred.

44 *The sons of Asher according to their families: of Imnah,*
the family of the Imnite; of Ishvi, the family of the Ishvite; of
Beriah, the family of the Beriite; 45 *of the sons of Beriah: of*
Heber, the family of the Heberite; of Malchiel, the family of
the Malchielite. 46 *The name of Asher's daughter: Serah.*
47 *These are the families of the sons of Asher according to*
their count: fifty-three thousand, four hundred.

48 *The sons of Naphtali according to their families: of*
Jahzeel, the family of the Jahzeelite; of Guni, the family of
the Gunite; 49 *of Jezer, the family of the Jezerite; of Shillem,*
the family of the Shillemite. 50 *These are the families of*
Naphtali according to their families, and their count:
forty-five thousand, four hundred.

51 *These are the countings of the sons of Israel: six*
hundred and one thousand, seven hundred and thirty.

bruise your head[60] (*Genesis* 3:15).

The letter פ appears [at least once] in each word [of this verse].[61] This indicates that [Benjamin] had the [opportunity to open his] פֶּה, *mouth,*[62] yet he did not reveal what his brothers had done regarding the sale of Joseph.[63]

60. The Baal HaTurim seems to relate the name הַשּׁוּפָמִי to the verb root שׁוּף, *to bruise.* God's statement to the serpent, *"He* [i.e., man] *will bruise your head,"* implies that any man who will be undeserving of death because he is sinless will pound the serpent's head with complaints, because it is the cause of his being subject to dying (*VeChur LaZahav*).

61. *Peirush HaRokeach* points out that this is the only verse in which this phenomenon appears.

62. The name of the letter פ can be spelled in any of three ways: פֵּ״א פֵּ״ה פֵּ״י. The spelling פֵּ״ה is reminiscent of the word פֶּה, *mouth.*

The Midrash states that Benjamin's stone on the *Kohen Gadol's* breastplate was the יָשְׁפֵה, *yashfeh,* for the name of that stone alludes to the expression יֵשׁ פֶּה, *There is a mouth,* i.e., Benjamin had the opportunity to open his mouth and tattle on his brothers, but due to their ban, he kept his mouth closed (*Bereishis Rabbah* 79:5; see also the Baal HaTurim to *Exodus* 28:20).

63. *Peirush HaRokeach;* see *Midrash Shocher Tov* to *Tehillim* 15:3.

נב־נג שלישי וַיְדַבֵּר יהוה אֶל־מֹשֶׁה לֵּאמֹר: לָאֵלֶּה תֵּחָלֵק הָאָרֶץ
נד בְּנַחֲלָה בְּמִסְפַּר שֵׁמוֹת: לָרַב תַּרְבֶּה נַחֲלָתוֹ וְלַמְעַט
תַּמְעִיט נַחֲלָתוֹ אִישׁ לְפִי פְקֻדָיו יֻתַּן נַחֲלָתוֹ:
נה אַךְ־בְּגוֹרָל יֵחָלֵק אֶת־הָאָרֶץ לִשְׁמוֹת מַטּוֹת־
נו אֲבֹתָם יִנְחָלוּ: עַל־פִּי הַגּוֹרָל תֵּחָלֵק נַחֲלָתוֹ בֵּין רַב
נז לִמְעָט: וְאֵלֶּה פְקוּדֵי הַלֵּוִי לְמִשְׁפְּחֹתָם
לְגֵרְשׁוֹן מִשְׁפַּחַת הַגֵּרְשֻׁנִּי לִקְהָת מִשְׁפַּחַת הַקְּהָתִי
נח לִמְרָרִי מִשְׁפַּחַת הַמְּרָרִי: אֵלֶּה ׀ מִשְׁפְּחֹת לֵוִי
מִשְׁפַּחַת הַלִּבְנִי מִשְׁפַּחַת הַחֶבְרֹנִי מִשְׁפַּחַת
הַמַּחְלִי מִשְׁפַּחַת הַמּוּשִׁי מִשְׁפַּחַת הַקָּרְחִי וּקְהָת
נט הוֹלִד אֶת־עַמְרָם: וְשֵׁם ׀ אֵשֶׁת עַמְרָם יוֹכֶבֶד
בַּת־לֵוִי אֲשֶׁר יָלְדָה אֹתָהּ לְלֵוִי בְּמִצְרָיִם וַתֵּלֶד
לְעַמְרָם אֶת־אַהֲרֹן וְאֶת־מֹשֶׁה וְאֵת מִרְיָם אֲחֹתָם:
ס וַיִּוָּלֵד לְאַהֲרֹן אֶת־נָדָב וְאֶת־אֲבִיהוּא אֶת־אֶלְעָזָר
סא וְאֶת־אִיתָמָר: וַיָּמָת נָדָב וַאֲבִיהוּא בְּהַקְרִיבָם
סב אֵשׁ־זָרָה לִפְנֵי יהוה: וַיִּהְיוּ פְקֻדֵיהֶם שְׁלֹשָׁה
וְעֶשְׂרִים אֶלֶף כָּל־זָכָר מִבֶּן־חֹדֶשׁ וָמָעְלָה כִּי ׀ לֹא
הָתְפָּקְדוּ בְּתוֹךְ בְּנֵי יִשְׂרָאֵל כִּי לֹא־נִתַּן לָהֶם נַחֲלָה
סג בְּתוֹךְ בְּנֵי יִשְׂרָאֵל: אֵלֶּה פְּקוּדֵי מֹשֶׁה וְאֶלְעָזָר
הַכֹּהֵן אֲשֶׁר פָּקְדוּ אֶת־בְּנֵי יִשְׂרָאֵל בְּעַרְבֹת מוֹאָב
סד עַל יַרְדֵּן יְרֵחוֹ: וּבְאֵלֶּה לֹא־הָיָה אִישׁ מִפְּקוּדֵי
מֹשֶׁה וְאַהֲרֹן הַכֹּהֵן אֲשֶׁר פָּקְדוּ אֶת־בְּנֵי יִשְׂרָאֵל
סה בְּמִדְבַּר סִינָי: כִּי־אָמַר יהוה לָהֶם מוֹת יָמֻתוּ

בעל הטורים

(סה) מוֹת יָמֻתוּ. כְּתִיב חָסֵר. קְרֵי בֵהּ יָמֻתוּ מִיתוֹת הַרְבֵּה, מִתְלוֹנְנִים וַעֲדַת קֹרַח:

BAAL HATURIM ELUCIDATED

55. {The Baal HaTurim's comment to יִנְחָלוּ appears at 35:8 below.}

65. מוֹת יָמֻתוּ — THEY WILL SURELY DIE [literally, DYING, THEY WILL DIE]. [The word יָמֻתוּ is] spelled defectively [without the first ו].[64] Spelled as it is, it could be

64. The singular form יָמוּת, *he will die,* appears twenty times in the Torah and another forty-six times in the rest of the *Tanach,* each time spelled in full. Accordingly, we would expect the

52 *HASHEM spoke to Moses, saying:* 53 *To these shall the Land be divided as an inheritance, according to the number of names.* 54 *For the numerous one you shall increase its inheritance, and for the fewer one you shall lessen its inheritance; each one according to his count shall his inheritance be given.* 55 *Only by lot shall the Land be divided, according to the names of their fathers' tribes shall they inherit.* 56 *According to the lot shall one's inheritance be divided, between the numerous and the few.*

57 *These are the countings of the Levites, according to their families: of Gershon, the family of the Gershonite; of Kohath, the family of the Kohathite; of Merari, the family of the Merarite.* 58 *These are the Levite families: the family of the Libnite; the family of the Hebronite; the family of the Mahlite; the family of the Mushite; the family of the Korahite; and Kohath begat Amram.* 59 *The name of Amram's wife was Jochebed, daughter of Levi, who was born to Levi in Egypt; and she bore to Amram Aaron, Moses, and their sister Miriam.* 60 *To Aaron were born Nadab and Abihu, Elazar and Ithamar.* 61 *Nadab and Abihu died when they brought an alien fire before HASHEM.* 62 *Their counts were twenty-three thousand, every male from one month of age and above, for they did not count themselves among the Children of Israel, for an inheritance was not given them among the Children of Israel.*

63 *These are the ones counted by Moses and Elazar the Kohen, who counted the Children of Israel in the plains of Moab, by the Jordan, near Jericho.* 64 *And of these, there was no man of those counted by Moses and Aaron the Kohen, who counted the Children of Israel in the Wilderness of Sinai.* 65 *For HASHEM had said of them, "They will surely die in the*

BAAL HATURIM ELUCIDATED

vowelized יָמֻתוּ,[65] which implies various types of deaths,[65a] [for example,] those

plural form to be spelled יָמוּתוּ, *they will die.* The Baal HaTurim explains why our verse uses the defective spelling יָמֻתוּ, without the central ו.

However, it is noteworthy that the plural form appears thirteen times in the Torah [four of them with the conversive prefix -וַ], each time with the defective spelling יָמֻתוּ. Accordingly, it is not clear why the Baal HaTurim has chosen to comment on the absence of the ו in this verse only.

65. A defective form of יוּמְתוּ, *they shall be put to death* (*Leviticus* 20:11), in the causative passive *hufal* conjugation.

65a. The Talmud states that the singular *hufal* form מוֹת יוּמָת, literally, *dying, he shall be put to death* (35:21 below), implies that if the court is unable to apply the particular type of death prescribed by the Torah for the capital sin committed, the sinner should nevertheless be put to death in any way possible (*Sanhedrin* 45b, 53a, 72b; see also *Rambam, Hilchos Sanhedrin*

בַּמִּדְבָּר וְלֹא־נוֹתַר מֵהֶם אִישׁ כִּי אִם־כָּלֵב בֶּן־יְפֻנֶּה

כז א וִיהוֹשֻׁעַ בִּן־נוּן: וַתִּקְרַבְנָה בְּנוֹת צְלָפְחָד בֶּן־
חֵפֶר בֶּן־גִּלְעָד בֶּן־מָכִיר בֶּן־מְנַשֶּׁה לְמִשְׁפְּחֹת מְנַשֶּׁה
בֶן־יוֹסֵף וְאֵלֶּה שְׁמוֹת בְּנֹתָיו מַחְלָה נֹעָה וְחָגְלָה
ב וּמִלְכָּה וְתִרְצָה: וַתַּעֲמֹדְנָה לִפְנֵי מֹשֶׁה וְלִפְנֵי אֶלְעָזָר
הַכֹּהֵן וְלִפְנֵי הַנְּשִׂיאִם וְכָל־הָעֵדָה פֶּתַח אֹהֶל־מוֹעֵד
ג לֵאמֹר: אָבִינוּ מֵת בַּמִּדְבָּר וְהוּא לֹא־הָיָה בְּתוֹךְ
הָעֵדָה הַנּוֹעָדִים עַל־יְהוָֹה בַּעֲדַת־קֹרַח כִּי־בְחֶטְאוֹ
ד מֵת וּבָנִים לֹא־הָיוּ לוֹ: לָמָּה יִגָּרַע שֵׁם־אָבִינוּ מִתּוֹךְ
מִשְׁפַּחְתּוֹ כִּי אֵין לוֹ בֵּן תְּנָה־לָּנוּ אֲחֻזָּה בְּתוֹךְ אֲחֵי
רביעי *ך רבתי ה אָבִינוּ: וַיַּקְרֵב מֹשֶׁה אֶת־מִשְׁפָּטָן* לִפְנֵי יְהוָֹה:
ו־ז וַיֹּאמֶר יְהוָֹה אֶל־מֹשֶׁה לֵּאמֹר: כֵּן בְּנוֹת צְלָפְחָד
דֹּבְרֹת נָתֹן תִּתֵּן לָהֶם אֲחֻזַּת נַחֲלָה בְּתוֹךְ אֲחֵי

בעל הטורים

כז (ז) דֹּבְרֹת. ב׳ בַּמָּסוֹרֶת — ״כֵּן בְּנוֹת צְלָפְחָד דֹּבְרֹת״; ״וַאֲנִי אֲשִׂימֵם דֹּבְרוֹת בַּיָּם״. שֶׁהָיוּ מְלֵאוֹת רוּחַ אֱלֹהִים וְחָכְמָה כַּיָּם שֶׁהוּא מָלֵא. כְּמוֹ שֶׁדָּרְשׁוּ רַבּוֹתֵינוּ ז״ל, חַכְמָנִיּוֹת הָיוּ, דַּרְשָׁנִיּוֹת הָיוּ:

BAAL HATURIM ELUCIDATED

who complained[66] and the congregation of Korah.[67,68]

12:8). Thus, the Baal HaTurim understands the absence of the ו in יָמֻתוּ to allow the word to be interpreted as יוּמְתוּ, *they will be put to death,* implying various forms of death (*VeChur LaZahav*).

66. And died by fire (see 11:1-2 above).

67. Some of them were swallowed up by the earth (see 16:28-33 above); others were consumed by fire (see 16:35); still others died in a plague (see 17:9-15).

68. *Peirush HaRokeach.*

The allusion appears in the form of an omitted letter ו (=6) because there were six communal death sentences in the wilderness: (i) at the incident of the golden calf [where some died by the sword, others in a plague, and still others through *hydrokan,* a stomach disease (*Yoma* 66b, cited in *Rashi* to *Exodus* 32:20)]; (ii) at the incident of the complainers [who were killed by a heavenly fire (11:1-2 above)]; (iii) the rabble who craved [meat and were slain when HASHEM *struck a very mighty blow against the people* (11:33 above)]; (iv) the spies [who died in a plague (14:37 above)]; (v) the congregation of Korah [who were swallowed up by the earth (see note 67 above)]; and (vi) in Shittim [where the followers of Zimri died in a plague (25:3-9 above) or were stoned and hanged by *beis din* (see *Rashi* to 25:4-5 above)] (*Rabbeinu Ephraim* [*MiKesivah Ashkenazis*]).

There was one other incident — that of the serpents — about which the Torah states וַיָּמָת עַם רָב מִיִּשְׂרָאֵל, *A large multitude of Israel died* (21:6 above). If so, why is that incident not included on the roster of communal death sentences? The kabbalistic work *Eitz HaDaas Tov* asks another question: Why does the Torah include the word מִיִּשְׂרָאֵל, *of Israel?* Wouldn't וַיָּמָת עַם רָב, *a large multitude died,* suffice? Or, perhaps, וַיָּמֻתוּ רַבִּים מִיִּשְׂרָאֵל, *many of the Israelites died?* One of the answers given in that work is that the term עַם רָב, *a large multitude,* refers to the עֵרֶב רַב, *mixed multitude,* that mingled with Israel when they departed from Egypt. [Indeed, within the words

wilderness," and not a man was left of them, except for Caleb son of Jephunneh, and Joshua son of Nun.

27

[1] *The daughters of Zelophehad, son of Hepher, son of Gilead, son of Machir, son of Manasseh, of the families of Manasseh son of Joseph drew near — and these are the names of his daughters: Mahlah, Noah, Hoglah, Milcah, and Tirzah —* [2] *and they stood before Moses, before Elazar the Kohen, and before the leaders and the entire assembly at the entrance to the Tent of Meeting, saying:* [3] *"Our father died in the wilderness, but he was not among the assembly that was gathering against* H*ASHEM in the assembly of Korah, but he died of his own sin; and he had no sons.* [4] *Why should the name of our father be omitted from among his family because he had no son? Give us a possession among our father's brothers."* [5] *And Moses brought their claim before* H*ASHEM.*

[6] H*ASHEM said to Moses, saying,* [7] *"The daughters of Zelophehad are speaking properly. You shall surely give them a possession of inheritance among the brothers of*

XXVII

7. דֹּבְרֹת — ARE SPEAKING. The masoretic note, ב׳, means that this word appears twice in the *Tanach:*[69] (i) here, כֵּן בְּנוֹת צְלָפְחָד דֹּבְרֹת, *The daughters of Zelophehad are speaking properly;* and (ii) [with a different meaning in,] וַאֲנִי אֲשִׂימֵם דֹּבְרוֹת בַּיָּם, *I will make them into rafts on the sea* (*I Kings* 5:23). [The similarity of expression indicates] that [Zelophehad's daughters] were filled as full with a Godly spirit and wisdom as the sea is full [of water].[69a] Thus our Sages of blessed memory state: They were wise women; they were expositors.[70]

עַם רָב we find all the letters of מֵעֵרֶב רַב (*Degel Machaneh Ephraim*).] Accordingly, that incident is not included in the list of communal death sentences against the Israelites (*VeChur LaZahav*).

Alternatively: In his comments to 27:2 below, the *Shelah* interprets the term עֵרֶב רַב as a reference to Zelophehad who was עַם, i.e., an עַם הָאָרֶץ, *unlearned person,* yet רַב, a *rav,* i.e., a tribal leader. He was the only one who had spoken *against God and against Moses* (21:5), hence that verse begins, וַיְדַבֵּר, *he spoke,* rather than וַיְדַבְּרוּ, *they spoke;* and he is the only one who died from the snakebite, hence the singular וַיָּמָת, *he died,* rather than וַיָּמוּתוּ, *they died.* Accordingly, the incident of the serpents has no place on the list of communal punishments (*VeChur LaZahav*).

69. Some editions of the Massorah read: ב׳ בִּתְרֵי לִישָׁנֵי, *Two, with two different meanings.* In our verse דֹּבְרֹת is a present tense plural feminine verb and means *speak* or *are speaking;* in the other, it is a common noun and means *rafts.*

Other editions read: ב׳ חַד חָסֵר וְחַד מָלֵא, *Two, one spelled defectively and one spelled in full.* Our verse uses the defective spelling דֹּבְרֹת; the verse in *Kings* reads דֹּבְרוֹת, with a ו. [In *Psalms* 31:19 this word appears with the definite article prefix הַ-, and is spelled הַדֹּבְרוֹת, with a ו after the ר.]

69a. The Baal HaTurim's metaphor is borrowed from *Isaiah* 11:9.

70. *Bava Basra* 119b — The daughters of Zelophehad were wise; they were expositors; and they were righteous. They were wise, for

ח אֲבִיהֶם וְהַעֲבַרְתֶּם אֶת־נַחֲלַת אֲבִיהֶן לָהֶן׃ וְאֶל־בְּנֵי
יִשְׂרָאֵל תְּדַבֵּר לֵאמֹר אִישׁ כִּי־יָמוּת וּבֵן אֵין לוֹ
ט וְהַעֲבַרְתֶּם אֶת־נַחֲלָתוֹ לְבִתּוֹ׃ וְאִם־אֵין לוֹ בַּת
י וּנְתַתֶּם אֶת־נַחֲלָתוֹ לְאֶחָיו׃ וְאִם־אֵין לוֹ אַחִים
יא וּנְתַתֶּם אֶת־נַחֲלָתוֹ לַאֲחֵי אָבִיו׃ וְאִם־אֵין אַחִים
לְאָבִיו וּנְתַתֶּם אֶת־נַחֲלָתוֹ לִשְׁאֵרוֹ הַקָּרֹב אֵלָיו
מִמִּשְׁפַּחְתּוֹ וְיָרַשׁ אֹתָהּ וְהָיְתָה לִבְנֵי יִשְׂרָאֵל
לְחֻקַּת מִשְׁפָּט כַּאֲשֶׁר צִוָּה יהוה אֶת־מֹשֶׁה׃
יב וַיֹּאמֶר יהוה אֶל־מֹשֶׁה עֲלֵה אֶל־הַר הָעֲבָרִים הַזֶּה
וּרְאֵה אֶת־הָאָרֶץ אֲשֶׁר נָתַתִּי לִבְנֵי יִשְׂרָאֵל׃
יג וְרָאִיתָה אֹתָהּ וְנֶאֱסַפְתָּ אֶל־עַמֶּיךָ גַּם־אָתָּה כַּאֲשֶׁר
יד נֶאֱסַף אַהֲרֹן אָחִיךָ׃ כַּאֲשֶׁר מְרִיתֶם פִּי בְּמִדְבַּר־
צִן בִּמְרִיבַת הָעֵדָה לְהַקְדִּישֵׁנִי בַמַּיִם לְעֵינֵיהֶם
טו הֵם מֵי־מְרִיבַת קָדֵשׁ מִדְבַּר־צִן׃ וַיְדַבֵּר

בעל הטורים

(יא) נַחֲלָתוֹ לִשְׁאֵרוֹ. אוֹתִיּוֹת נַחֲלַת שְׁאֵרוֹ לוֹ, וְאֵין שְׁאֵרוֹ אֶלָּא אִשְׁתּוֹ. וְהַיְנוּ מַה שֶּׁאָמְרוּ חֲכָמֵינוּ ז״ל, גּוֹרְעִין וּמוֹסִיפִין וְדוֹרְשִׁין. פֵּרוּשׁ, גּוֹרְעִין הַוָּי״ו מִ„נַחֲלָתוֹ״, וּמוֹסִיפִין אוֹתָהּ עַל הַלָּמֶ״ד שֶׁל ״לִשְׁאֵרוֹ״, הֲרֵי נִשְׁאַר ״לוֹ״. הֲרֵי „נַחֲלַת שְׁאֵרוֹ לוֹ״. וְדוֹרְשִׁין, נַחֲלַת שְׁאֵרוֹ, שֶׁהִיא אִשְׁתּוֹ, לוֹ. וְהַיְנוּ מַה שֶּׁאָמְרוּ חֲכָמֵינוּ ז״ל, שֶׁהַבַּעַל יוֹרֵשׁ אֶת אִשְׁתּוֹ׃

(יג) וְרָאִיתָה. כְּתִיב בְּהֵ״א. מְלַמֵּד שֶׁהֶרְאָהוּ כָּל הָאָרֶץ, הַמְּעָרוֹת וְהַמְּחִלּוֹת וְאוֹצְרוֹת כֶּסֶף וְזָהָב שֶׁבָּהּ׃

❑ **נֶאֱסַף אַהֲרֹן אָחִיךָ.** בְּגִימַטְרִיָּא זֶהוּ בִּנְשִׁיקָה׃

BAAL HATURIM ELUCIDATED

11. נַחֲלָתוֹ לִשְׁאֵרוֹ — HIS INHERITANCE TO HIS RELATIVE. The letters [of these two words can be rearranged to] read, נַחֲלַת שְׁאֵרוֹ לוֹ, *The inheritance of his relative belongs to him,* and שְׁאֵרוֹ, *his relative,* refers to none but his wife. Thus our Sages, of blessed memory, state: We subtract and add [letters within a verse] and then expound [on the anagrammed phrase]. That means, we subtract the ו from נַחֲלָתוֹ and add it to the ל of לִשְׁאֵרוֹ, producing the word לוֹ, *to him.* It now reads נַחֲלַת שְׁאֵרוֹ לוֹ, *the inheritance of his relative belongs to him.* And we expound: נַחֲלַת שְׁאֵרוֹ, *the estate left by his relative,* i.e., his wife, לוֹ, *belongs to him.* From this exegesis, our Sages, of blessed memory, derive the law: A husband inherits his wife['s estate].[71]

they spoke in timely fashion . . . they were expositors [for they were familiar with laws derived through Scriptural exegesis] . . . they were righteous, for they would not marry unless the man would be a fitting husband for them.

71. *Bava Basra* 111b.

their father, and you shall cause the inheritance of their
father to pass over to them. 8 *And to the Children of Israel*
you shall speak, saying: If a man will die and he has no son,
you shall cause his inheritance to pass over to his daughter.
9 *If he has no daughter, you shall give his inheritance to his*
brothers. 10 *If he has no brothers, you shall give his*
inheritance to the brothers of his father. 11 *If there are no*
brothers of his father, you shall give his inheritance to his
relative who is closest to him of his family, and he shall
inherit it. This shall be for the Children of Israel as a decree
of justice, as HASHEM commanded Moses."
12 *HASHEM said to Moses, "Go up to this mountain of*
Abarim and see the land that I have given to the Children of
Israel. 13 *You shall see it and you shall be gathered unto*
your people, you, too, as Aaron your brother was gathered
in; 14 *because you rebelled against My word in the*
Wilderness of Zin, in the assembly's strife, to sanctify Me at
the water before their eyes. They were the waters of strife at
Kadesh, in the Wilderness of Zin."

BAAL HATURIM ELUCIDATED

13. וְרָאִיתָה — YOU SHALL SEE IT. [This word is] spelled with a ה.[72] This teaches that [God] showed [Moses] the entire land, [including] the caves, the underground caverns, and the stores of silver and gold that are within it.[73]

❑ **נֶאֱסַף אַהֲרֹן אָחִיךָ** — AARON YOUR BROTHER WAS GATHERED IN. The *gematria* of this phrase (486) is equivalent[74] to that of וְזֶהוּ בִנְשִׁיקָה, *This* [refers to death] *by a kiss* [from God].[75]

72. The word רָאִיתָ, *you saw,* with and without the conversive prefix ־וְ, appears six more times in the Torah. Only in our verse is it spelled with a superfluous ה. Thus, the masoretic note, לֵית מְלָא, *There is none other* [*in the Torah*] *that is spelled in full* [with a ה]. [In the rest of the *Tanach* it appears sixteen times without the ה and five times with it.]

73. *Sifrei* 135-136 — The Omnipresent showed Moses the distant [parts of the land as clearly] as the near; the hidden [as clearly] as the revealed; everything that is called the Land of Israel . . . The Omnipresent showed Moses all the chambers of the Land of Israel as if it were a set table, as it is written, וַיַּרְאֵהוּ ה׳ אֶת כָּל הָאָרֶץ, *HASHEM showed him the "entire" land* (*Deuteronomy* 34:1).

The Baal HaTurim finds an allusion to this in the superfluous ה. However, he does not explain how the letter ה alludes to the entire land. Perhaps the ה (=5) alludes to five directions: west, east, north, south and down, i.e., all that lies beneath the surface of the earth, which includes the caves, caverns and stores of precious metals enumerated by the Baal HaTurim (A.S.). An additional allusion to this fifth direction can be found in the *gematria* of וְרָאִיתָה אֹתָהּ — 1028 — which by the principle of *im hakollel* is considered equivalent to 1029, equal to that of רְאֵה תַחְתֶּיהָ, *See* [*what is*] *under it* (*VeChur LaZahav*).

74. The principle of *im hakollel* allows 485, the *gematria* of the Baal HaTurim's phrase, to be considered equivalent to 486.

75. See the Baal HaTurim to 20:28 above, with note 82 there.

טז מֹשֶׁה אֶל־יהוָה לֵאמֹר: יִפְקֹד יהוָה אֱלֹהֵי הָרוּחֹת
יז לְכָל־בָּשָׂר אִישׁ עַל־הָעֵדָה: אֲשֶׁר־יֵצֵא לִפְנֵיהֶם
וַאֲשֶׁר יָבֹא לִפְנֵיהֶם וַאֲשֶׁר יוֹצִיאֵם וַאֲשֶׁר יְבִיאֵם
וְלֹא תִהְיֶה עֲדַת יהוָה כַּצֹּאן אֲשֶׁר אֵין־לָהֶם רֹעֶה:
יח וַיֹּאמֶר יהוָה אֶל־מֹשֶׁה קַח־לְךָ אֶת־יְהוֹשֻׁעַ בִּן־נוּן
אִישׁ אֲשֶׁר־רוּחַ בּוֹ וְסָמַכְתָּ אֶת־יָדְךָ עָלָיו:
יט וְהַעֲמַדְתָּ אֹתוֹ לִפְנֵי אֶלְעָזָר הַכֹּהֵן וְלִפְנֵי כָּל־
כ הָעֵדָה וְצִוִּיתָה אֹתוֹ לְעֵינֵיהֶם: וְנָתַתָּה מֵהוֹדְךָ

בעל הטורים

(טו) וַיְדַבֵּר מֹשֶׁה אֶל ה׳ לֵאמֹר. אֵין פָּסוּק אַחֵר כָּזֶה בַּתּוֹרָה. אָמַר לוֹ, לֹא תִזְכֹּר כַּמָּה ״וַיְדַבֵּר״ שֶׁדִּבַּרְתָּ אֵלַי:

(טז־יז) יִפְקֹד ה׳ אֱלֹהֵי הָרוּחֹת לְכָל בָּשָׂר אִישׁ עַל הָעֵדָה. אֲשֶׁר יֵצֵא לִפְנֵיהֶם וַאֲשֶׁר יָבֹא לִפְנֵיהֶם וַאֲשֶׁר יוֹצִיאֵם וַאֲשֶׁר יְבִיאֵם וְלֹא תִהְיֶה עֲדַת ה׳ כַּצֹּאן אֲשֶׁר אֵין לָהֶם רֹעֶה. בְּאֵלּוּ שְׁנֵי הַפְּסוּקִים יֵשׁ כ״ח תֵּבוֹת. וּלְכָךְ פִּרְנֵס יְהוֹשֻׁעַ אֶת יִשְׂרָאֵל כ״ח שָׁנִים. וְזֶהוּ שֶׁאָמַר ״וְזָכַרְתָּ אֶת ה׳ אֱלֹהֶיךָ כִּי הוּא הַנֹּתֵן לְךָ כֹּחַ לַעֲשׂוֹת חָיִל״:

❑ **וַאֲשֶׁר יָבֹא.** ב׳ בַּמָּסוֹרֶת — הָכָא ״וַאֲשֶׁר יָבֹא לִפְנֵיהֶם״; וְאִידָךְ ״וַאֲשֶׁר יָבֹא אֶת רֵעֵהוּ בַיַּעַר לַחְטֹב עֵצִים״. לוֹמַר לְךָ בֵּין בַּיִּשּׁוּב בֵּין בַּיַּעַר, בְּכָל פַּעַם צָרִיךְ לָבוֹא לִפְנֵיהֶם:

(יט) וְצִוִּיתָה. כָּתוּב בְּהֵ״א. לוֹמַר לְךָ שֶׁלִּמְּדוֹ חֲמִשָּׁה חֻמְשֵׁי תוֹרָה:

(כ) מֵהוֹדְךָ. בְּגִימַטְרִיָּא הַסּוֹד. לוֹמַר לְךָ שֶׁמָּסַר לוֹ סוֹד הַמֶּרְכָּבָה וּמַעֲשֵׂה בְרֵאשִׁית:

BAAL HATURIM ELUCIDATED

15. וַיְדַבֵּר מֹשֶׁה אֶל ה׳ לֵאמֹר — MOSES SPOKE TO HASHEM, SAYING. There is no other such verse in the Torah.[76] [Moses] said to [God], "Do You not remember how many [passages beginning] וַיְדַבֵּר, You have spoken to me?"[76a]

16-17. יִפְקֹד ה׳ אֱלֹהֵי הָרוּחֹת לְכָל בָּשָׂר אִישׁ עַל הָעֵדָה. אֲשֶׁר יֵצֵא לִפְנֵיהֶם וַאֲשֶׁר יָבֹא לִפְנֵיהֶם וַאֲשֶׁר יוֹצִיאֵם וַאֲשֶׁר יְבִיאֵם וְלֹא תִהְיֶה עֲדַת ה׳ כַּצֹּאן אֲשֶׁר אֵין לָהֶם רֹעֶה — MAY HASHEM GOD OF THE SPIRITS OF ALL FLESH, APPOINT A MAN OVER THE ASSEMBLY, WHO SHALL GO OUT BEFORE THEM AND WHO SHALL COME IN BEFORE THEM, WHO SHALL TAKE THEM OUT AND

76. *Sifrei Zuta* — There is not another verse in the entire Torah that states, וַיְדַבֵּר מֹשֶׁה אֶל ה׳ לֵאמֹר, *Moses spoke to HASHEM, saying.*

[That Midrash continues (similarly *Sifrei*) by interpreting לֵאמֹר as *to say,* i.e., Moses asked God to say something to him:] In truth, Moses said here, "Inform me whether You will [fulfill my request and] appoint a successor in my place." And this is one of the [five] matters about which Moses said before the Omnipresent, "Inform me if You will do [this] or if You will not do [this] on my behalf." [In each case,] the Omnipresent said to him, "I will do [as you have requested]."

The Midrash then cites the other four verses in which Moses said לֵאמֹר to God, they are: *Exodus* 6:12, where Moses asked God whether He would redeem the Israelites from Egyptian bondage; *Exodus* 17:4, where Moses asked God whether the contentious assembly would stone him; *Numbers* 12:13, where Moses asked God whether He would heal Miriam's affliction; and *Deuteronomy* 3:23, where Moses asked God whether he would be permitted to enter the Land of Israel.

76a. The Baal HaTurim's intent is unclear.

[15] *Moses spoke to HASHEM, saying,* [16] *"May HASHEM, God of the spirits of all flesh, appoint a man over the assembly,* [17] *who shall go out before them and who shall come in before them, who shall take them out and who shall bring them in; and not let the assembly of HASHEM be like sheep that have no shepherd."*

[18] *HASHEM said to Moses, "Take to yourself Joshua son of Nun, a man in whom there is spirit, and lean your hand upon him.* [19] *You shall stand him before Elazar the Kohen and before the entire assembly, and you shall command him before their eyes.* [20] *You shall place some of your majesty*

BAAL HATURIM ELUCIDATED

WHO SHALL BRING THEM IN; AND LET NOT THE ASSEMBLY OF HASHEM BE LIKE SHEEP THAT HAVE NO SHEPHERD. These two verses contain [a total of] twenty-eight words. Thus, Joshua served as the leader of Israel for twenty-eight years.[77] This is what is alluded to in the verse, וְזָכַרְתָּ אֶת ה׳ אֱלֹהֶיךָ כִּי הוּא הַנֹּתֵן לְךָ כֹּחַ לַעֲשׂוֹת חָיִל, *Then you shall remember HASHEM, your God: that it was He Who gives you* כֹּחַ[77a] *to accomplish greatly* (*Deuteronomy* 8:18).

❑ {The Baal HaTurim's comment to אֲשֶׁר יֵצֵא לִפְנֵיהֶם appears at 15:3 above.}

❑ וַאֲשֶׁר יָבֹא — **AND WHO SHALL COME IN.** The masoretic note, ב׳, means that this phrase appears twice in the *Tanach:* (i) here, וַאֲשֶׁר יָבֹא לִפְנֵיהֶם, *and who shall come in before them;* and (ii) וַאֲשֶׁר יָבֹא אֶת רֵעֵהוּ בַיַּעַר לַחְטֹב עֵצִים, *or who will come with his fellow into the forest to hew trees* (*Deuteronomy* 19:5). [The similarity of expression is] to indicate to you that whether they are in the settlement or in the forest, he must always lead them.[78]

19. וְצִוִּיתָה — **AND YOU SHALL COMMAND.** This word is spelled with a ה (= 5).[78a] This is to tell you that Moses taught him the five Books of the Torah.[79]

20. מֵהוֹדְךָ — **SOME OF YOUR MAJESTY.** The *gematria* of this word (75) is equal to that of הַסּוֹד, *the secret.* This is to tell you that Moses transmitted to him the secret of the Divine Chariot and the Work of the Creation.[80]

77. *Peirush HaRokeach; Rabbeinu Ephraim* (*Mi-Kesivah Ashkenazis*). See *Seder Olam* 12, cited in *Rashi* to *Judges* 11:26. The two verses form a sort of prayer, and the length of the prayer determined the length of the reign of the successor for whom Moses prayed (see *R' Ephraim*). The Baal HaTurim introduces a similar concept in his comment to 12:15 above.

77a. The *gematria* of כֹּחַ, literally, *strength,* is 28.

78. *Sifrei Zuta.*

78a. In its only other appearance in the *Tanach,* this word is spelled וְצִוִּיתָ, without a final ה (*Jeremiah* 27:4). The word also appears without the conjunctive prefix ־וְ, eight times without the ה (*Psalms* 7:7, 71:3, 119:138; *Job* 38:12; *Ezra* 9:11; *Nehemiah* 1:7 and 8, 9:14) and three times with the ה (*Jeremiah* 32:23; *Psalms* 119:4; *Lamentations* 1:10).

79. *Peirush HaRokeach;* see *Avos* 1:1; see also the Baal HaTurim to 11:16 above, with note 269a.

80. *Rimzei Rabbeinu Yoel.* On a simple level, the Divine Chariot refers to the first chapter of *Ezekiel* and the Work of Creation refers to the first chapter of *Genesis.* On a more lofty plane,

כז/כא־כח/ג כא עָלָיו לְמַעַן יִשְׁמְעוּ כָּל־עֲדַת בְּנֵי יִשְׂרָאֵל: וְלִפְנֵי
אֶלְעָזָר הַכֹּהֵן יַעֲמֹד וְשָׁאַל לוֹ בְּמִשְׁפַּט הָאוּרִים
לִפְנֵי יהוה עַל־פִּיו יֵצְאוּ וְעַל־פִּיו יָבֹאוּ הוּא
כב וְכָל־בְּנֵי־יִשְׂרָאֵל אִתּוֹ וְכָל־הָעֵדָה: וַיַּעַשׂ מֹשֶׁה
כַּאֲשֶׁר צִוָּה יהוה אֹתוֹ וַיִּקַּח אֶת־יְהוֹשֻׁעַ וַיַּעֲמִדֵהוּ
כג לִפְנֵי אֶלְעָזָר הַכֹּהֵן וְלִפְנֵי כָּל־הָעֵדָה: וַיִּסְמֹךְ
אֶת־יָדָיו עָלָיו וַיְצַוֵּהוּ כַּאֲשֶׁר דִּבֶּר יהוה בְּיַד־
מֹשֶׁה:

כח חמישי א־ב וַיְדַבֵּר יהוה אֶל־מֹשֶׁה לֵּאמֹר: צַו אֶת־בְּנֵי יִשְׂרָאֵל
וְאָמַרְתָּ אֲלֵהֶם אֶת־קָרְבָּנִי לַחְמִי לְאִשַּׁי רֵיחַ
ג נִיחֹחִי תִּשְׁמְרוּ לְהַקְרִיב לִי בְּמוֹעֲדוֹ: וְאָמַרְתָּ לָהֶם

בעל הטורים

(כג) וַיְצַוֵּהוּ כַּאֲשֶׁר דִּבֶּר ה׳ בְּיַד מֹשֶׁה. צִוָּהוּ שֶׁלֹּא לְבַטֵּל תּוֹרָה וְתָמִיד מִפְּנֵי הַמִּלְחָמָה. וּלְכָךְ סָמַךְ כָּאן פָּרָשַׁת תְּמִידִין:

כח (א־ב) מֹשֶׁה לֵּאמֹר צַו אֶת. סוֹפֵי תֵבוֹת תּוֹרָה. לוֹמַר שֶׁהָעוֹסֵק בַּתּוֹרָה כְּאִלּוּ הִקְרִיב קָרְבָּן:

BAAL HATURIM ELUCIDATED

22. {The Baal HaTurim's comment to וַיַּעֲמִדֵהוּ appears at *Genesis* 47:7.}

23. וַיְצַוֵּהוּ כַּאֲשֶׁר דִּבֶּר ה׳ בְּיַד מֹשֶׁה — AND HE COMMANDED HIM,[81] AS HASHEM HAD SPOKEN THROUGH MOSES. Moses commanded Joshua not to abandon Torah study or the daily Altar offerings,[82] [even] in the face of the war [he was to wage]. For this reason, the Torah juxtaposed the passage concerning the daily offerings[83] to our verse.

---

these terms are kabbalistic nomenclature for certain esoteric, even mystical, concepts derived from those chapters. The Talmud presents many teachings related to these subjects (*Chagigah* 11b-16a; for further discussion, see *Chagigah* 11b, note 33, in the Schottenstein edition).

81. In verse 19 above we are told that God ordered Moses to command Joshua, and in our verse we are told that he did. But neither verse tells us the nature of that command! The Baal HaTurim explains what it was.

82. The Talmud fills in the gaps in the conversation between Joshua and the angel menacing him with a drawn sword as it is recorded in the *Book of Joshua* (5:13-15): The angel said to Joshua, "This afternoon you neglected to bring the daily Altar offering, and now you have neglected Torah study." Joshua asked, "For which of these two misdeeds have you come?" The angel replied, "I have come now [i.e., for the current sin of neglecting Torah study]." Immediately . . . Joshua delved into the profundities of Torah law (*Megillah* 3a-b).

Now, it stands to reason that in the course of battle, the nation must have neglected other *mitzvos* also. If so, why did the angel mention only these two? It must be that Moses had commanded Joshua specifically with regard to these *mitzvos*. The Baal HaTurim adduces Scriptural support for this concept (*VeChur LaZahav*).

83. Which begins with an allusion to Torah study (see the Baal HaTurim's next comment).

upon him, so that the entire assembly of the Children of
Israel will pay heed. 21 *Before Elazar the Kohen shall he*
stand, who shall inquire for him of the judgment of the Urim
before HASHEM*; at his word shall they go out and at his*
word shall they come in, he and all the Children of Israel
with him, and the entire assembly.

22 *Moses did as* HASHEM *had commanded him. He took*
Joshua and stood him before Elazar the Kohen and before
the entire assembly. 23 *He leaned his hands upon him, and*
he commanded him, as HASHEM *had spoken through*
Moses.

28 1 HASHEM *spoke to Moses, saying:* 2 *Command the Children*
of Israel and say to them: My offering, My food for My fires,
My satisfying aroma, shall you be scrupulous to offer to Me
in its appointed time. 3 *And you shall say to them: This is*

BAAL HATURIM ELUCIDATED

XXVIII

1-2. מֹשֶׁה לֵּאמֹר. צַו אֶת — MOSES, SAYING: COMMAND THE. [When read in reverse order,] the final letters [of these four words] spell תּוֹרָה, *Torah.*[83a] This indicates that a person who engages in Torah study is considered as if he has brought an Altar offering.[84]

❑ {The Baal HaTurim's comment to צַו appears at *Exodus* 27:20.}

❑ {The Baal HaTurim's comment to לַחְמִי appears at *Leviticus* 6:1-2.}

83a. See the Baal HaTurim to *Deuteronomy* 21:16 with note 42.

84. *Rimzei Rabbeinu Yoel;* cf. the Baal HaTurim to *Leviticus* 6:1-2.

The Talmud (*Menachos* 110a) expounds on the phrase זאת תורת, *This is the law of,* which begins many passages in *Leviticus: This is the law of the burnt-offering* (6:2): . . . *of the meal-offering* (6:7); . . . *of the sin-offering* (6:18); . . . *of the guilt-offering* (7:1); . . . *of the peace-offering* (7:11). The phrase teaches that whoever occupies himself with studying the laws of the burnt-offering (. . . the meal-offering, . . . the sin-offering, etc.) is considered as if he had brought that particular offering.

The Talmud (*Shabbos* 30a) relates: David requested of the Holy One, Blessed is He, "Master of the universe, *Let me know, O* HASHEM, *my end*" (*Psalms* 39:5). God replied, "I have already established a rule that no creature of flesh and blood shall be told his end." But David persisted, asking, *"The measure of my days, what is it?"* Again God replied, "I have already established a rule that no man will be informed of the measure of his days." Finally David pleaded, *"Let me know when I will be deficient* [i.e., *dead*]." God answered, "You will die on a Sabbath day." David asked, "Let me die on the day after the Sabbath" [so that there will be ample time to make funeral preparations and proper eulogies (*Rashi*)]. God denied this request saying, "By then, the reign of your son Solomon will have commenced, and one kingdom may not encroach on another one by even as little as a hairsbreadth." David then asked, "Let me die on the day before the Sabbath," and God answered him, *"One day in your courtyard is worth more than one thousand"* (*Psalms* 84:11), i.e., one day of your Torah study is worth more to Me than a thousand burnt-offerings that your son Solomon will offer before Me on the Altar (see *I Kings* 3:4).

זֶה הָאִשֶּׁה אֲשֶׁר תַּקְרִיבוּ לַיהוָה כְּבָשִׂים בְּנֵי־שָׁנָה
ד תְּמִימִם שְׁנַיִם לַיּוֹם עֹלָה תָמִיד׃ אֶת־הַכֶּבֶשׂ
אֶחָד תַּעֲשֶׂה בַבֹּקֶר וְאֵת הַכֶּבֶשׂ הַשֵּׁנִי תַּעֲשֶׂה
ה בֵּין הָעַרְבָּיִם׃ וַעֲשִׂירִית הָאֵיפָה סֹלֶת לְמִנְחָה

בעל הטורים

(ג) **זֶה הָאִשֶּׁה.** ג׳ תָּגִין עַל הֵ״א אַחֲרוֹנָה שֶׁל ״הָאִשֶּׁה״. לוֹמַר לְךָ חֲמִשָּׁה מִינֵי קָרְבָּנוֹת נָתַתִּי לָכֶם, וְהָעוֹלָה חֲבִיבָה מִכֻּלָּם. וְעִסְקוּ בַּחֲמִשָּׁה חֻמְשֵׁי תוֹרָה, וּמַעֲלֶה אֲנִי עֲלֵיכֶם כְּאִלּוּ הִקְרַבְתֶּם חֲמִשָּׁה מִינֵי קָרְבָּנוֹת׃

❑ **תְּמִימִם שְׁנַיִם לַיּוֹם.** רָאשֵׁי תֵבוֹת תשׁ״ל. שֶׁכָּל כָּךְ תְּמִידִין קְרֵבִין לְשָׁנָה׃

❑ **לַיּוֹם עֹלָה תָמִיד.** קְרֵי בֵהּ ״לַיּוֹם עוֹלֶה״. לוֹמַר לְךָ שֶׁשּׁוֹחֲטִים אוֹתוֹ בְּמָקוֹם שֶׁהַיּוֹם עוֹלֶה׃

BAAL HATURIM ELUCIDATED

3. **זֶה הָאִשֶּׁה** — THIS IS THE FIRE-OFFERING. [According to a scribal tradition,] there should be three *tagin* on the final ה (= 5) of the word הָאִשֶּׁה, *the fire-offering.*[85] This is to tell you [that God said], "I gave you five types of Altar-offerings,[86] and

---

85. *Sefer Tagin* lists 360 words in the Torah in which the letter ה is written with four *tagin* instead of the usual one. Both letters ה of הָאִשֶּׁה appear on that list. See note 42 to *parashas Nasso.*

86. The list חַטָּאת עוֹלָה אָשָׁם שְׁלָמִים תּוֹדָה that appears in parentheses in many editions does not appear in the manuscripts or in the early printed editions. Later printers added that list to the Baal HaTurim's text, based upon *Ittur Bikkurim's* commentary. Accordingly, as *Ittur Bikkurim* points out, the Baal HaTurim is in disagreement with the *Rambam,* who states: There are four types of *korbanos* — (i) הַחַטָּאת, *the sin-offering;* (ii) וְהָאָשָׁם, *and the guilt-offering;* (iii) וְהָעוֹלָה, *and the burnt-offering;* (iv) וְהַשְּׁלָמִים או הַדּוֹמֶה לִשְׁלָמִים, *and the peace-offering or that which is similar to the peace-offering.* And there is no other *korban* of any type mentioned in our Torah, neither as the offering of an individual nor as a communal offering, except any of these four types or a combination of them (*Rambam's* introduction to tractate *Zevachim* [incorrectly entitled הקדמת הרמב״ם לסדר קדשים in many editions, see *Rambam* to *Zevachim* 5:8]).

Based on this passage, *Ittur Bikkurim* suggests that the *Rambam* includes the תּוֹדָה, *thanksgiving-offering,* in the phrase, "or that which is similar to the peace-offering." However, this suggestion is contradicted by the *Rambam* himself, who writes elsewhere (commentary to *Zevachim* 5:8): And know that what we said at the beginning of our commentary to this tractate, "the peace-offering or that which is similar to the peace-offering," our intention was the following three offerings — הַבְּכוֹר, the *first-born-offering;* וְהַמַּעֲשֵׂר, and the *animal-tithe-offering;* וְהַפֶּסַח, *and the pesach-offering* — for they are similar to the *peace-offering* with regard to . . . [*Rambam* goes on to list several similarities and explains why he did not enumerate each of these three by itself for a total of seven types of offering].

Rambam makes no mention of the תּוֹדָה, for he considers it in the category of שְׁלָמִים, *peace-offering* (see *Hilchos Maaseh HaKorbanos* 9:3,5). Moreover, this concept is borne out by the wording of the verse: *This is the law of the peace-offering sacrifice . . . If he shall offer it as a thanksgiving offering . . .* (*Leviticus* 7:11-12), which implies that the תּוֹדָה is a modified version of the peace-offering, not merely something similar to it (*VeChur LaZahav*).

There is one more passage in the *Rambam's* commentary that may shed light on the identity of the Baal HaTurim's fifth type of offering. His commentary to *Zevachim* 5:8 continues: Additionally, it is only to these offerings that the Torah applies the expression זֹאת הַתּוֹרָה, *This is the law,* as it is written, זֹאת הַתּוֹרָה, *This is the law,* לָעֹלָה, *of the burnt-offering,* לַמִּנְחָה, *of the meal-offering,* וְלַחַטָּאת, *and of the sin-offering,* וְלָאָשָׁם, *and of the guilt-offering,* וְלַמִּלּוּאִים, *and of the inauguration offerings,* וּלְזֶבַח הַשְּׁלָמִים, *and of the peace-offering sacrifice* (*Leviticus* 7:37). Thus, we see that there is no other offering except these.

the fire-offering that you are to offer to HASHEM: male lambs in their first year, unblemished, two a day, as a continual burnt-offering. 4 *The one lamb shall you make in the morning and the second lamb shall you make in the afternoon,* 5 *with a tenth-ephah of fine flour as a meal-offering,*

BAAL HATURIM ELUCIDATED

the *olah* [burnt-offering] is most cherished among them.[87] So if you will occupy yourselves with the study of the five Books of the Torah, I will consider it as if You brought the five types of offerings."[88]

❑ תְּמִימִם שְׁנַיִם לַיּוֹם — UNBLEMISHED, TWO A DAY. The initial letters of these words, תש״ל, have a *gematria* of 730, [alluding to] the number of *tamid* offerings brought during each [solar] year.[89]

❑ לַיּוֹם עֹלָה תָמִיד — A DAY, AS A CONTINUAL BURNT-OFFERING. This phrase can be vowelized, לַיּוֹם עוֹלֶה, *as the day ascends,* to indicate to you that it is slaughtered in the place where the sun[90] ascends.[91]

4. {The Baal HaTurim's comment to אֶחָד appears at *Exodus* 29:39.}

5. {The Baal HaTurim's comment to וַעֲשִׂירִית appears at *Exodus* 29:40, s.v., וְעִשָּׂרֹן.}

❑ {In his comments to *Exodus* 29:39, the Baal HaTurim compares the wording of our passage with the wording of that passage. See note 87 there.}

However, we have not included the inauguration offerings [in the four mentioned in our introduction] because we only mention those that are applicable in all generations. And [we have omitted the] meal-offering, because its laws will be explained in the next tractate [*Menachos*].

Now *Rambam's* reason for omitting the meal-offering from his list does not apply to the Baal HaTurim's comment. Accordingly, the Baal HaTurim's number includes the four offerings listed by the *Rambam,* as well as the מִנְחָה, *meal-offering* (*VeChur LaZahav*).

87. *Avos DeRabbi Nosson* 4:1 — The prophet declares, [God says:] *I desire kindness, not sacrificial offerings; and knowledge of God more than burnt-offerings* (*Hosea* 6:6). [Now, the term עלות, *burnt-offerings,* should have been included in the collective noun זֶבַח, *sacrificial offering.* Why then is it used as a parallel expression? (*Binyan Yehoshua*).] This indicates that the burnt-offering is the most cherished of all.

88. See *Menachos* 110a.

89. Two lambs were offered each day. Thus, in three hundred and sixty-five days, there were seven hundred and thirty lambs offered (see the Baal HaTurim to *Exodus* 29:38, s.v., שְׁנַיִם לַיּוֹם).

90. The term יוֹם, literally, *day,* is sometimes used as a reference to the sun (see *Rashi* here; *Genesis* 3:8, s.v., לְרוּחַ הַיּוֹם; *Genesis* 18:1, s.v., כְּחֹם הַיּוֹם; *Malachi* 3:19, s.v., כִּי הִנֵּה; and *Avodah Zarah* 4a, s.v., היום בא).

91. See the Baal HaTurim to *Exodus* 29:38, s.v., שָׁנָה שְׁנַיִם. The Torah could have omitted the word עֹלָה from our verse, for we know from verse 6 that this offering is an עֹלָה. Indeed, that is what we find in the parallel passage in *Exodus* 29:38-42 (*Ittur Bikkurim*).

See *Tamid* 31b. *Olah*-offerings, such as the *tamid,* were slaughtered in the area of the Courtyard to the north of the Altar. At the time of the slaughter of the morning *tamid,* the sun was still relatively low in the eastern sky, and the eastern end of the Courtyard was still in shadow. Therefore, the lamb was slaughtered "opposite the sun," i.e., toward the western end of the area in which it may be slaughtered, so that the sun would illuminate the slaughter area. Conversely, the afternoon *tamid* was offered when the sun was already well into its western descent, and the western area of the Courtyard was in shadow. Therefore, that offering was slaughtered "opposite the sun," i.e., in the eastern portion on the north side of the Altar.

ו בְּלוּלָ֥ה בְּשֶׁ֛מֶן כָּתִ֖ית רְבִיעִ֥ת הַהִֽין׃ עֹלַ֖ת תָּמִ֑יד
ז הָעֲשֻׂיָה֙ בְּהַ֣ר סִינַ֔י לְרֵ֣יחַ נִיחֹ֔חַ אִשֶּׁ֖ה לַיהוָֽה׃ וְנִסְכּוֹ֙
רְבִיעִ֣ת הַהִ֔ין לַכֶּ֖בֶשׂ הָאֶחָ֑ד בַּקֹּ֗דֶשׁ הַסֵּ֛ךְ נֶ֥סֶךְ שֵׁכָ֖ר
ח לַיהוָֽה׃ וְאֵת֙ הַכֶּ֣בֶשׂ הַשֵּׁנִ֔י תַּעֲשֶׂ֖ה בֵּ֣ין הָעַרְבָּ֑יִם
כְּמִנְחַ֨ת הַבֹּ֤קֶר וּכְנִסְכּוֹ֙ תַּעֲשֶׂ֔ה אִשֵּׁ֛ה רֵ֥יחַ נִיחֹ֖חַ
לַיהוָֽה׃
ט וּבְיוֹם֙ הַשַּׁבָּ֔ת שְׁנֵֽי־כְבָשִׂ֥ים בְּנֵֽי־שָׁנָ֖ה תְּמִימִ֑ם וּשְׁנֵ֣י
י עֶשְׂרֹנִ֗ים סֹ֧לֶת מִנְחָ֛ה בְּלוּלָ֥ה בַשֶּׁ֖מֶן וְנִסְכּֽוֹ׃ עֹלַ֥ת
שַׁבַּ֖ת בְּשַׁבַּתּ֑וֹ עַל־עֹלַ֥ת הַתָּמִ֖יד וְנִסְכָּֽהּ׃
יא וּבְרָאשֵׁי֙ חָדְשֵׁיכֶ֔ם תַּקְרִ֥יבוּ עֹלָ֖ה לַיהוָ֑ה פָּרִ֨ים
בְּנֵֽי־בָקָ֤ר שְׁנַ֙יִם֙ וְאַ֣יִל אֶחָ֔ד כְּבָשִׂ֧ים בְּנֵֽי־שָׁנָ֛ה
יב שִׁבְעָ֖ה תְּמִימִֽם׃ וּשְׁלֹשָׁ֣ה עֶשְׂרֹנִ֗ים סֹ֤לֶת מִנְחָה֙
בְּלוּלָ֣ה בַשֶּׁ֔מֶן לַפָּ֖ר הָאֶחָ֑ד וּשְׁנֵ֣י עֶשְׂרֹנִ֗ים סֹ֤לֶת
יג מִנְחָה֙ בְּלוּלָ֣ה בַשֶּׁ֔מֶן לָאַ֖יִל הָאֶחָֽד׃ וְעִשָּׂרֹ֣ן עִשָּׂר֗וֹן
סֹ֤לֶת מִנְחָה֙ בְּלוּלָ֣ה בַשֶּׁ֔מֶן לַכֶּ֖בֶשׂ הָאֶחָ֑ד עֹלָה֙
יד רֵ֣יחַ נִיחֹ֔חַ אִשֶּׁ֖ה לַיהוָֽה׃ וְנִסְכֵּיהֶ֗ם חֲצִ֣י הַהִין֩ יִהְיֶ֨ה
לַפָּ֜ר וּשְׁלִישִׁ֧ת הַהִ֣ין לָאַ֗יִל וּרְבִיעִ֥ת הַהִ֛ין לַכֶּ֖בֶשׂ
יָ֑יִן זֹ֣את עֹלַ֥ת חֹ֙דֶשׁ֙ בְּחָדְשׁ֔וֹ לְחָדְשֵׁ֖י הַשָּׁנָֽה׃
טו וּשְׂעִ֨יר עִזִּ֥ים אֶחָ֛ד לְחַטָּ֖את לַיהוָ֑ה עַל־עֹלַ֧ת
ששי טז הַתָּמִ֛יד יֵעָשֶׂ֖ה וְנִסְכּֽוֹ׃ וּבַחֹ֣דֶשׁ הָֽרִאשׁ֗וֹן
יז בְּאַרְבָּעָ֥ה עָשָׂ֛ר י֖וֹם לַחֹ֑דֶשׁ פֶּ֖סַח לַיהוָֽה׃ וּבַחֲמִשָּׁ֨ה
עָשָׂ֥ר י֛וֹם לַחֹ֥דֶשׁ הַזֶּ֖ה חָ֑ג שִׁבְעַ֣ת יָמִ֔ים מַצּ֖וֹת
יח יֵאָכֵֽל׃ בַּיּ֥וֹם הָרִאשׁ֖וֹן מִקְרָא־קֹ֑דֶשׁ כָּל־מְלֶ֥אכֶת
יט עֲבֹדָ֖ה לֹ֥א תַעֲשֽׂוּ׃ וְהִקְרַבְתֶּ֨ם אִשֶּׁ֤ה עֹלָה֙ לַיהוָ֔ה
פָּרִ֧ים בְּנֵֽי־בָקָ֛ר שְׁנַ֖יִם וְאַ֣יִל אֶחָ֑ד וְשִׁבְעָ֤ה
כ כְבָשִׂים֙ בְּנֵ֣י שָׁנָ֔ה תְּמִימִ֖ם יִהְי֥וּ לָכֶֽם׃ וּמִ֨נְחָתָ֔ם
סֹ֖לֶת בְּלוּלָ֣ה בַשָּׁ֑מֶן שְׁלֹשָׁ֨ה עֶשְׂרֹנִ֜ים לַפָּ֗ר וּשְׁנֵ֧י
כא עֶשְׂרֹנִ֛ים לָאַ֖יִל תַּעֲשֽׂוּ׃ עִשָּׂר֤וֹן עִשָּׂרוֹן֙ תַּעֲשֶׂ֔ה
כב לַכֶּ֖בֶשׂ הָאֶחָ֑ד לְשִׁבְעַ֖ת הַכְּבָשִֽׂים׃ וּשְׂעִ֥יר חַטָּ֖את
כג אֶחָ֑ד לְכַפֵּ֖ר עֲלֵיכֶֽם׃ מִלְּבַד֙ עֹלַ֣ת הַבֹּ֔קֶר אֲשֶׁ֖ר

mixed with a quarter-hin of crushed oil. 6 It is the continual
burnt-offering that was done at Mount Sinai, for a satisfying
aroma, a fire-offering to Hashem. 7 And its libation is a
quarter-hin for the one lamb, to be poured on the holy [Altar],
an intoxicating libation for Hashem. 8 The second lamb you
shall make in the afternoon; like the meal-offering of the
morning and like its libation shall you make, a fire-offering for
a satisfying aroma to Hashem.

9 And on the Sabbath day: two male lambs in their first year,
unblemished, two tenth-ephah of fine flour for a meal-offering,
mixed with oil, and its libation. 10 The burnt-offering of each
Sabbath on its own Sabbath, in addition to the continual
burnt-offering and its libation.

11 On your New Moons, you shall bring a burnt-offering to
Hashem: two young bulls, one ram, seven male lambs in their
first year, unblemished. 12 And three tenth-ephah of fine flour
for a meal-offering mixed with oil, for each bull; and two
tenth-ephah of fine flour mixed with oil, for the one ram; 13 and
a tenth-ephah of fine flour for a meal-offering, mixed with oil,
for each lamb — a burnt-offering, a satisfying aroma, a
fire-offering to Hashem. 14 And their libations: a half-hin for
each bull, a third-hin for the ram, a quarter-hin for each lamb
— of wine. This is the burnt-offering of each month in its own
month for the months of the year. 15 And one male of the goats
for a sin-offering to Hashem. In addition to the continual
burnt-offering shall it be made, and its libation.

16 In the first month, on the fourteenth day of the month, shall
be a pesach-offering to Hashem. 17 And on the fifteenth day of
this month is a festival; for a seven-day period matzos shall be
eaten. 18 On the first day is a holy convocation; you shall not do
any laborious work. 19 You shall offer a fire-offering, a burnt-
offering to Hashem: two young bulls, one ram, seven male
lambs within their first year, unblemished shall they be for you.
20 And their meal-offering: fine flour mixed with oil; you shall
make three tenth-ephah for each bull and two tenth-ephah for
the ram. 21 One tenth-ephah shall you make for each lamb of
the seven lambs. 22 And one he-goat for a sin-offering, to atone
for you. 23 Aside from the burnt-offering of the morning that is

BAAL HATURIM ELUCIDATED

14. {The Baal HaTurim's comment to לְחָדְשֵׁי הַשָּׁנָה appears at *Exodus* 12:2.}

כד לְעֹלַת הַתָּמִיד תַּעֲשׂוּ אֶת־אֵלֶּה: כָּאֵלֶּה תַּעֲשׂוּ
לַיּוֹם שִׁבְעַת יָמִים לֶחֶם אִשֵּׁה רֵיחַ־נִיחֹחַ לַיהוָה
כה עַל־עוֹלַת הַתָּמִיד יֵעָשֶׂה וְנִסְכּוֹ: וּבַיּוֹם הַשְּׁבִיעִי
מִקְרָא־קֹדֶשׁ יִהְיֶה לָכֶם כָּל־מְלֶאכֶת עֲבֹדָה לֹא
כו תַעֲשׂוּ: וּבְיוֹם הַבִּכּוּרִים בְּהַקְרִיבְכֶם מִנְחָה
חֲדָשָׁה לַיהוָה *בְּשָׁבֻעֹתֵיכֶם מִקְרָא־קֹדֶשׁ יִהְיֶה
כז לָכֶם כָּל־מְלֶאכֶת עֲבֹדָה לֹא תַעֲשׂוּ: וְהִקְרַבְתֶּם
עוֹלָה לְרֵיחַ נִיחֹחַ לַיהוָה פָּרִים בְּנֵי־בָקָר שְׁנַיִם
כח אַיִל אֶחָד שִׁבְעָה כְבָשִׂים בְּנֵי שָׁנָה: וּמִנְחָתָם סֹלֶת
בְּלוּלָה בַשָּׁמֶן שְׁלֹשָׁה עֶשְׂרֹנִים לַפָּר הָאֶחָד שְׁנֵי
כט עֶשְׂרֹנִים לָאַיִל הָאֶחָד: עִשָּׂרוֹן עִשָּׂרוֹן לַכֶּבֶשׂ
ל הָאֶחָד לְשִׁבְעַת הַכְּבָשִׂים: שְׂעִיר עִזִּים אֶחָד לְכַפֵּר
לא עֲלֵיכֶם: מִלְּבַד עֹלַת הַתָּמִיד וּמִנְחָתוֹ תַּעֲשׂוּ
תְּמִימִם יִהְיוּ־לָכֶם וְנִסְכֵּיהֶם:

*ב׳ טעמים

בעל הטורים

(כז) כָּל "עֹלָה" הַכְּתוּבוֹת בַּמּוֹעֲדוֹת כֻּלָּם חֲסֵרִים, חוּץ מֵעוֹלַת עֲצֶרֶת שֶׁהוּא מָלֵא. רֶמֶז שֶׁבְּשִׁשָּׁה בְּסִיוָן נִתְּנָה בוֹ תּוֹרָה:

❑ בְּכָל הַמּוֹעֲדוֹת נֶאֱמַר "חַג". חוּץ מִשָּׁבוּעוֹת, כִּי פְּעָמִים נִדְחֶה, אִם הוּא בְשַׁבָּת, לְבֵית שַׁמַּאי יוֹם טְבוֹחַ לְמָחָר. אֲבָל בְּפֶסַח וְסֻכּוֹת יָבִיא בְּחֻלּוֹ שֶׁל מוֹעֵד. אֲבָל שָׁבוּעוֹת תַּשְׁלוּמִין שֶׁלוֹ אֵינוֹ בְחַג:

(ל) בְּכֻלָּם נֶאֱמַר "לְחַטָּאת", חוּץ מֵעֲצֶרֶת. בִּשְׁבִיל שֶׁנִּתְּנָה בוֹ תוֹרָה, שֶׁמְּכַפֶּרֶת עַל לוֹמְדֶיהָ:

BAAL HATURIM ELUCIDATED

27. Whenever the word[91a] עֹלָה appears with regard to the festivals, it is spelled defectively, without a ו, with the exception of the *olah*-offering of Shavuos, where it is spelled in full — עוֹלָה, with a ו. The letter ו (= 6) is an allusion to the sixth of Sivan, the day on which the Torah was given to Israel.[92]

91a. Most editions read עֹלַת, but that reading is difficult, for the word עֹלַת appears sixteen times in this passage, all with reference to the *tamid,* the *mussaf* of *Shabbos* or the *mussaf* of Rosh Chodesh.

The text follows some of the later printed editions (e.g., the *Karmarna Chumash*) that have עֹלָה in place of עֹלַת.

92. *Paaneach Raza* to 29:11. Regarding each of the other festivals, the Torah gives the month and date: Pesach on the fifteenth day of the first month [Nissan] (28:16-7); Rosh Hashanah on the first day of the seventh month [Tishrei] (29:1); Yom Kippur on the tenth of the seventh month (29:7); and Succos on the fifteenth day of that month (29:12). However, no date is given for Shavuos. Elsewhere (*Leviticus* 23:15-21) we are taught that Shavuos is to be celebrated on the fiftieth day after the *Omer* offering is brought on the second day of Pesach. In ancient times, there was no fixed calendar such as we use today. The *Sanhedrin* [high court] would declare

for the continual burnt-offering shall you make these. 24 Like these shall you make each day of the seven-day period: food, a fire-offering, a satisfying aroma to HASHEM; in addition to the continual burnt-offering shall it be made, and its libation. 25 The seventh day shall be a holy convocation for you; you shall not do any laborious work.

26 On the day of the first-fruits, when you offer a new meal-offering to HASHEM on your Festival of Weeks, it shall be a holy convocation to you; you shall not do any laborious work. 27 You shall offer a burnt-offering for a satisfying aroma to HASHEM: two young bulls, one ram, seven lambs within their first year. 28 And their meal-offering: fine flour mixed with oil — three tenth-ephah for each bull; two tenth-ephah for the one ram; 29 one tenth-ephah for each lamb of the seven lambs. 30 One male of the goats to atone for you. 31 Aside from the continual burnt-offering and its meal-offering shall you offer [them] — unblemished shall they be for you — and their libations.

BAAL HATURIM ELUCIDATED

❑ Regarding the other festivals (Passover and Succos), we find the term חַג [or חָג], *a festival.*[93] But not with regard to Shavuos, because according to the School of Shammai, when Shavuos would fall on the Sabbath, the חֲגִיגָה, *festive offering,* is postponed to the next day,[94] which is already after the festival. On Pesach and Succos, by contrast [even when the first day of the festival is on the Sabbath, and the חֲגִיגָה is postponed to the next day], it is still brought during *Chol HaMoed* [which is an integral part of the festival]. But the make-up days of Shavuos are not during the festival.

30. Regarding the other holidays, the Torah uses the term לְחַטָּאת, *for a sin-offering,* [or חַטָּאת, *a sin-offering,*][95] but not with regard to Shavuos. Because on that day the Torah was given, and it brings atonement for those who study it.[96]

the beginning of a new month based on the testimony of witnesses who actually saw the *molad* (birth) of the newly emerging moon. Until witnesses appeared, nobody would know which day would begin the new month — the thirtieth of the previous month or the thirty-first. Thus, depending on how many days there are in Nissan and Iyar of any particular year, the festival of Shavuos could fall on the fifth of Sivan [when both Nissan and Iyar have thirty days], on the sixth of Sivan [when one has twenty-nine and the other thirty], or on the seventh of Sivan [when each month has only twenty-nine days]. But, Shavuos is also the day on which we celebrate receiving the Torah on the sixth of Sivan (but see *Shabbos* 86b). Therefore, even though the Torah cannot give a date for Shavuos, it hints at the sixth of the month by adding a ו [= 6] to the word עוֹלָה.

93. Pesach, 28:17; Succos, 29:12.

94. See *Chagigah* 17a.

95. Rosh Chodesh, 28:15; Pesach, 28:22; Rosh Hashanah, 29:5; Yom Kippur, 29:11; Succos, 29:16,19,22,25,28,31,34; Shemini Atzeres 29:38.

96. *Talmud Yerushalmi, Rosh Hashanah* 4:8.

א וּבַחֹדֶשׁ הַשְּׁבִיעִי בְּאֶחָד לַחֹדֶשׁ מִקְרָא־קֹדֶשׁ יִהְיֶה
לָכֶם כָּל־מְלֶאכֶת עֲבֹדָה לֹא תַעֲשׂוּ יוֹם תְּרוּעָה
ב יִהְיֶה לָכֶם: וַעֲשִׂיתֶם עֹלָה לְרֵיחַ נִיחֹחַ לַיהוה פַּר
בֶּן־בָּקָר אֶחָד אַיִל אֶחָד כְּבָשִׂים בְּנֵי־שָׁנָה שִׁבְעָה
ג תְּמִימִם: וּמִנְחָתָם סֹלֶת בְּלוּלָה בַשָּׁמֶן שְׁלֹשָׁה
ד עֶשְׂרֹנִים לַפָּר שְׁנֵי עֶשְׂרֹנִים לָאָיִל: וְעִשָּׂרוֹן אֶחָד
ה לַכֶּבֶשׂ הָאֶחָד לְשִׁבְעַת הַכְּבָשִׂים: וּשְׂעִיר־עִזִּים
ו אֶחָד חַטָּאת לְכַפֵּר עֲלֵיכֶם: מִלְּבַד עֹלַת הַחֹדֶשׁ
וּמִנְחָתָהּ וְעֹלַת הַתָּמִיד וּמִנְחָתָהּ וְנִסְכֵּיהֶם
ז כְּמִשְׁפָּטָם לְרֵיחַ נִיחֹחַ אִשֶּׁה לַיהוה: וּבֶעָשׂוֹר
לַחֹדֶשׁ הַשְּׁבִיעִי הַזֶּה מִקְרָא־קֹדֶשׁ יִהְיֶה לָכֶם
וְעִנִּיתֶם אֶת־נַפְשֹׁתֵיכֶם כָּל־מְלָאכָה לֹא תַעֲשׂוּ:
ח וְהִקְרַבְתֶּם עֹלָה לַיהוה רֵיחַ נִיחֹחַ פַּר בֶּן־בָּקָר
אֶחָד אַיִל אֶחָד כְּבָשִׂים בְּנֵי־שָׁנָה שִׁבְעָה תְּמִימִם
ט יִהְיוּ לָכֶם: וּמִנְחָתָם סֹלֶת בְּלוּלָה בַשָּׁמֶן שְׁלֹשָׁה
י עֶשְׂרֹנִים לַפָּר שְׁנֵי עֶשְׂרֹנִים לָאַיִל הָאֶחָד: עִשָּׂרוֹן
יא עִשָּׂרוֹן לַכֶּבֶשׂ הָאֶחָד לְשִׁבְעַת הַכְּבָשִׂים: שְׂעִיר־
עִזִּים אֶחָד חַטָּאת מִלְּבַד חַטַּאת הַכִּפֻּרִים וְעֹלַת
יב הַתָּמִיד וּמִנְחָתָהּ וְנִסְכֵּיהֶם: וּבַחֲמִשָּׁה שביעי
עָשָׂר יוֹם לַחֹדֶשׁ הַשְּׁבִיעִי מִקְרָא־קֹדֶשׁ יִהְיֶה
לָכֶם כָּל־מְלֶאכֶת עֲבֹדָה לֹא תַעֲשׂוּ וְחַגֹּתֶם
יג חַג לַיהוה שִׁבְעַת יָמִים: וְהִקְרַבְתֶּם עֹלָה אִשֵּׁה

בעל הטורים

כט (ב) בְּרֹאשׁ הַשָּׁנָה כְּתִיב "וַעֲשִׂיתֶם עֹלָה לְרֵיחַ נִיחֹחַ לַה׳ וְגוֹ׳". לוֹמַר עֲשׂוּ תְּשׁוּבָה, וַאֲנִי מַעֲלֶה עֲלֵיכֶם כְּאִלּוּ הִקְרַבְתֶּם כָּל הַקָּרְבָּנוֹת. וּבִפְסִיקְתָּא דּוֹרֵשׁ כְּאִלּוּ נַעֲשָׂה בְּרִיָּה חֲדָשָׁה:

(יא) בְּיוֹם הַכִּפּוּרִים כְּתִיב "שְׂעִיר עִזִּים אֶחָד חַטָּאת", וְלֹא כְתִיב "לְכַפֵּר". לְפִי שֶׁיּוֹם הַכִּפּוּרִים מְכַפֵּר:

BAAL HATURIM ELUCIDATED

XXIX

2. With regard to Rosh Hashanah, our verse states . . . וַעֲשִׂיתֶם עֹלָה לְרֵיחַ נִיחֹחַ לַה׳,

1 *In the seventh month, on the first day of the month, there
shall be a holy convocation for you; you shall do no
laborious work, it shall be a day of shofar sounding for you.*
2 *You shall make a burnt-offering for a satisfying aroma to
HASHEM: one young bull, one ram, seven male lambs in their
first year, unblemished.* 3 *And their meal-offering: fine flour
mixed with oil — three tenth-ephah for the bull; two
tenth-ephah for the ram;* 4 *and one tenth-ephah for each lamb
of the seven lambs.* 5 *One male of the goats for a sin-offering
to provide you atonement.* 6 *Aside from the burnt-offering of
the New Moon and its meal-offering, the continual burnt-
offering and its meal-offering, and their libations according to
their law — for a satisfying aroma, a fire-offering to HASHEM.*
7 *On the tenth day of this seventh month there shall be a
holy convocation for you and you shall afflict yourselves;
you shall not do any work.* 8 *You shall offer a burnt-offering
to HASHEM for a satisfying aroma — one young bull, one ram,
seven male lambs in their first year; unblemished shall they
be for you.* 9 *And their meal-offering: fine flour mixed with oil
— three tenth-ephah for the bull; two tenth-ephah for the one
ram;* 10 *and one tenth-ephah for each lamb of the seven
lambs.* 11 *One male of the goats for a sin-offering, aside from
the sin-offering of the atonement and the continual burnt-
offering, with its meal-offering, and their libations.*
12 *On the fifteenth day of the seventh month, there shall be
a holy convocation for you; you shall do no laborious work;
you shall celebrate a festival to HASHEM for a seven-
day period.* 13 *You shall offer a burnt-offering, a fire-offering,*

BAAL HATURIM ELUCIDATED

You shall "make"[96a] *a burnt-offering for a satisfying aroma to HASHEM . . .* This indicates [that God says], "עֲשׂוּ תְשׁוּבָה, *Make penance,* and I will consider it as if you have brought all the offerings." The *Pesikta*[97] expounds [on this phrase, that one who repents sincerely] is considered as a new creation.[98]

11. Regarding Yom Kippur is written, שְׂעִיר עִזִּים אֶחָד חַטָּאת, *one male of the goats for a sin-offering,* but it does not include the term לְכַפֵּר, *to provide atonement.* For it is the essence of Yom Kippur that brings the atonement.[99]

96a. In contrast with all the other festivals, regarding which the Torah states תַּקְרִיבוּ or וְהִקְרַבְתֶּם, *you shall offer.*

97. *Pesikta Rabbasi* 41:5; quoted in *Yalkut Shimoni* to *Emor* 645.

98. That is, free of sin.

99. See *Yoma* 85b.

רֵ֤יחַ נִיחֹ֙חַ֙ לַֽיהוָ֔ה פָּרִ֧ים בְּנֵי־בָקָ֛ר שְׁלֹשָׁ֥ה עָשָׂ֖ר
אֵילִ֣ם שְׁנָ֑יִם כְּבָשִׂ֧ים בְּנֵי־שָׁנָ֛ה אַרְבָּעָ֥ה עָשָׂ֖ר
יד תְּמִימִ֥ם יִהְיֽוּ׃ וּמִ֙נְחָתָ֔ם סֹ֖לֶת בְּלוּלָ֣ה בַשָּׁ֑מֶן שְׁלֹשָׁ֨ה
עֶשְׂרֹנִ֜ים לַפָּ֣ר הָֽאֶחָ֗ד לִשְׁלֹשָׁ֤ה עָשָׂר֙ פָּרִ֔ים שְׁנֵ֤י
טו עֶשְׂרֹנִים֙ לָאַ֣יִל הָֽאֶחָ֔ד לִשְׁנֵ֖י הָאֵילִֽם׃ *וְעִשָּׂר֣וֹן
עִשָּׂר֔וֹן לַכֶּ֖בֶשׂ הָאֶחָ֑ד לְאַרְבָּעָ֥ה עָשָׂ֖ר כְּבָשִֽׂים׃
טז וּשְׂעִיר־עִזִּ֥ים אֶחָ֖ד חַטָּ֑את מִלְּבַד֙ עֹלַ֣ת הַתָּמִ֔יד
יז מִנְחָתָ֖הּ וְנִסְכָּֽהּ׃ וּבַיּ֣וֹם הַשֵּׁנִ֗י פָּרִ֧ים בְּנֵי־
בָקָ֛ר שְׁנֵ֥ים עָשָׂ֖ר אֵילִ֣ם שְׁנָ֑יִם כְּבָשִׂ֧ים בְּנֵי־שָׁנָ֛ה
יח אַרְבָּעָ֥ה עָשָׂ֖ר תְּמִימִֽם׃ וּמִנְחָתָ֣ם וְנִסְכֵּיהֶ֡ם לַ֠פָּרִים
יט לָאֵילִ֧ם וְלַכְּבָשִׂ֛ים בְּמִסְפָּרָ֖ם כַּמִּשְׁפָּֽט׃ וּשְׂעִיר־
עִזִּ֥ים אֶחָ֖ד חַטָּ֑את מִלְּבַד֙ עֹלַ֣ת הַתָּמִ֔יד וּמִנְחָתָ֖הּ
כ וְנִסְכֵּיהֶֽם׃ וּבַיּ֧וֹם הַשְּׁלִישִׁ֛י פָּרִ֥ים עַשְׁתֵּי־עָשָׂ֖ר
אֵילִ֣ם שְׁנָ֑יִם כְּבָשִׂ֧ים בְּנֵי־שָׁנָ֛ה אַרְבָּעָ֥ה עָשָׂ֖ר
כא תְּמִימִֽם׃ וּמִנְחָתָ֣ם וְנִסְכֵּיהֶ֡ם לַ֠פָּרִים לָאֵילִ֧ם
כב וְלַכְּבָשִׂ֛ים בְּמִסְפָּרָ֖ם כַּמִּשְׁפָּֽט׃ וּשְׂעִ֥יר חַטָּ֖את אֶחָ֑ד
כג מִלְּבַד֙ עֹלַ֣ת הַתָּמִ֔יד וּמִנְחָתָ֖הּ וְנִסְכָּֽהּ׃ וּבַיּ֧וֹם
הָרְבִיעִ֛י פָּרִ֥ים עֲשָׂרָ֖ה אֵילִ֣ם שְׁנָ֑יִם כְּבָשִׂ֧ים בְּנֵי־
כד שָׁנָ֛ה אַרְבָּעָ֥ה עָשָׂ֖ר תְּמִימִֽם׃ מִנְחָתָ֣ם וְנִסְכֵּיהֶ֡ם
לַ֠פָּרִים לָאֵילִ֧ם וְלַכְּבָשִׂ֛ים בְּמִסְפָּרָ֖ם כַּמִּשְׁפָּֽט׃
כה וּשְׂעִיר־עִזִּ֥ים אֶחָ֖ד חַטָּ֑את מִלְּבַד֙ עֹלַ֣ת הַתָּמִ֔יד
כו מִנְחָתָ֖הּ וְנִסְכָּֽהּ׃ וּבַיּ֧וֹם הַחֲמִישִׁ֛י פָּרִ֥ים
תִּשְׁעָ֖ה אֵילִ֣ם שְׁנָ֑יִם כְּבָשִׂ֧ים בְּנֵי־שָׁנָ֛ה אַרְבָּעָ֥ה
כז עָשָׂ֖ר תְּמִימִֽם׃ וּמִנְחָתָ֣ם וְנִסְכֵּיהֶ֡ם לַ֠פָּרִים לָאֵילִ֧ם
כח וְלַכְּבָשִׂ֛ים בְּמִסְפָּרָ֖ם כַּמִּשְׁפָּֽט׃ וּשְׂעִ֥יר חַטָּ֖את אֶחָ֑ד
כט מִלְּבַד֙ עֹלַ֣ת הַתָּמִ֔יד וּמִנְחָתָ֖הּ וְנִסְכָּֽהּ׃ וּבַיּ֧וֹם
הַשִּׁשִּׁ֛י פָּרִ֥ים שְׁמֹנָ֖ה אֵילִ֣ם שְׁנָ֑יִם כְּבָשִׂ֧ים בְּנֵי־
ל שָׁנָ֛ה אַרְבָּעָ֥ה עָשָׂ֖ר תְּמִימִֽם׃ וּמִנְחָתָ֣ם וְנִסְכֵּיהֶ֡ם
לַ֠פָּרִים לָאֵילִ֧ם וְלַכְּבָשִׂ֛ים בְּמִסְפָּרָ֖ם כַּמִּשְׁפָּֽט׃
לא וּשְׂעִ֥יר חַטָּ֖את אֶחָ֑ד מִלְּבַד֙ עֹלַ֣ת הַתָּמִ֔יד מִנְחָתָ֖הּ

*נקוד על ו' בתרא של ועשרון

a satisfying aroma to HASHEM: thirteen young bulls, two
rams, fourteen male lambs in their first year; they shall
be unblemished. 14 And their meal-offering: fine flour
mixed with oil — three tenth-ephah for each bull of the
thirteen bulls; two tenth-ephah for each ram of the two
rams; 15 and one tenth-ephah for each lamb of the fourteen
lambs. 16 One male of the goats for a sin-offering, aside
from the continual burnt-offering with its meal-offering and
its libation.

17 And on the second day: twelve young bulls, two rams,
fourteen male lambs within their first year, unblemished.
18 And their meal-offering and their libations for the bulls,
the rams, and the lambs, in their proper numbers, as
required. 19 One male of the goats for a sin-offering; aside
from the continual burnt-offering, its meal-offering and their
libations.

20 And on the third day: eleven bulls, two rams, fourteen
male lambs within their first year, unblemished. 21 And their
meal-offering and their libations for the bulls, the rams, and
the lambs, in their proper numbers, as required. 22 One
he-goat for a sin-offering; aside from the continual burnt-
offering, its meal-offering and its libation.

23 And on the fourth day: ten bulls, two rams, four-
teen male lambs within their first year, unblemished. 24 And
their meal-offering and their libations for the bulls, the
rams, and the lambs, in their proper numbers, as re-
quired. 25 One male of the goats for a sin-offering; aside
from the continual burnt-offering, its meal-offering and its
libation.

26 And on the fifth day: nine bulls, two rams, fourteen
male lambs within their first year, unblemished. 27 And their
meal-offering and their libations for the bulls, the rams, and
the lambs, in their proper numbers, as required. 28 One
he-goat for a sin-offering; aside from the continual burnt-
offering, its meal-offering and its libation.

29 And on the sixth day: eight bulls, two rams, fourteen
male lambs within their first year, unblemished. 30 And their
meal-offering and their libations for the bulls, the rams, and
the lambs, in their proper numbers, as required. 31 One
he-goat for a sin-offering; aside from the continual burnt-
offering, its meal-offering and its libations.

כט/לב-ל/א לב וְנִסְכֶּֽהָ׃ וּבַיּ֣וֹם הַשְּׁבִיעִ֗י פָּרִ֥ים שִׁבְעָ֛ה אֵילִ֥ם
שְׁנָ֑יִם כְּבָשִׂ֧ים בְּנֵי־שָׁנָ֛ה אַרְבָּעָ֥ה עָשָׂ֖ר תְּמִימִֽם׃
לג וּמִנְחָתָ֣ם וְנִסְכֵּהֶ֡ם לַ֠פָּרִ֠ים לָאֵילִ֧ם וְלַכְּבָשִׂ֛ים
לד בְּמִסְפָּרָ֖ם כְּמִשְׁפָּטָֽם׃ וּשְׂעִ֥יר חַטָּ֖את אֶחָ֑ד מִלְּבַד֙
מפטיר לה עֹלַ֣ת הַתָּמִ֔יד מִנְחָתָ֖הּ וְנִסְכָּֽהּ׃ בַּיּוֹם֙ הַשְּׁמִינִ֔י
עֲצֶ֖רֶת תִּהְיֶ֣ה לָכֶ֑ם כָּל־מְלֶ֥אכֶת עֲבֹדָ֖ה לֹ֥א תַעֲשֽׂוּ׃
לו וְהִקְרַבְתֶּ֨ם עֹלָ֜ה אִשֵּׁ֨ה רֵ֤יחַ נִיחֹ֙חַ֙ לַֽיהוָ֔ה פַּ֥ר אֶחָ֖ד
אַ֣יִל אֶחָ֑ד כְּבָשִׂ֧ים בְּנֵי־שָׁנָ֛ה שִׁבְעָ֖ה תְּמִימִֽם׃
לז מִנְחָתָ֣ם וְנִסְכֵּיהֶ֗ם לַפָּ֛ר לָאַ֥יִל וְלַכְּבָשִׂ֖ים בְּמִסְפָּרָ֥ם
לח כַּמִּשְׁפָּֽט׃ וּשְׂעִ֥יר חַטָּ֖את אֶחָ֑ד מִלְּבַד֙ עֹלַ֣ת הַתָּמִ֔יד
לט וּמִנְחָתָ֖הּ וְנִסְכָּֽהּ׃ אֵ֛לֶּה תַּעֲשׂ֥וּ לַיהוָ֖ה בְּמוֹעֲדֵיכֶ֑ם
לְבַ֨ד מִנִּדְרֵיכֶ֜ם וְנִדְבֹתֵיכֶ֗ם לְעֹלֹתֵיכֶם֙ וּלְמִנְחֹ֣תֵיכֶ֔ם
ל א וּלְנִסְכֵּיכֶ֖ם וּלְשַׁלְמֵיכֶֽם׃ וַיֹּ֥אמֶר מֹשֶׁ֖ה אֶל־בְּנֵ֣י
יִשְׂרָאֵ֑ל כְּכֹ֛ל אֲשֶׁר־צִוָּ֥ה יְהוָ֖ה אֶת־מֹשֶֽׁה׃ פפפ

קס״ח פסוקים. לחל״ק סימן. ואל״י פלה״ו סימן.

BAAL HATURIM ELUCIDATED

33. {The Baal HaTurim's comment to this verse appears at *Genesis* 32:15.}

32 And on the seventh day: seven bulls, two rams, fourteen lambs within their first year, unblemished. 33 And their meal-offering and their libations for the bulls, the rams, and the lambs, in their proper numbers, in their requirements. 34 One he-goat for a sin-offering; aside from the continual burnt-offering, its meal-offering and its libation.

35 The eighth day shall be a restriction for you; you shall not do any laborious work. 36 You shall offer a burnt-offering, a fire-offering, a satisfying aroma to HASHEM*; one bull, one ram, seven lambs within their first year, unblemished. 37 Their meal-offering and libations for the bull, the ram, and the lambs shall be in their proper numbers, as required. 38 One he-goat for a sin-offering; aside from the continual burnt-offering, its meal-offering and its libation.*

39 These are what you shall make for HASHEM *on your appointed festivals, aside from your vows and your free-will offerings for your burnt-offerings, your meal-offerings, your libations, and your peace-offerings.*

30 *1 Moses said to the Children of Israel according to everything that* HASHEM *had commanded Moses.*

BAAL HATURIM ELUCIDATED

39. {The Baal HaTurim's comment to לְבַד מִנִּדְרֵיכֶם וְנִדְבֹתֵיכֶם appears at 30:2 below.}

פרשת מטות

Parashas Mattos

ב וַיְדַבֵּר מֹשֶׁה אֶל־רָאשֵׁי הַמַּטּוֹת לִבְנֵי יִשְׂרָאֵל

בעל הטורים

(ב) **רָאשֵׁי הַמַּטּוֹת.** סָמַךְ רָאשֵׁי הַמַּטּוֹת לִנְדָרִים וּנְדָבוֹת דִּכְתִיב לְעֵיל, "לְבַד מִנִּדְרֵיכֶם וְנִדְבֹתֵיכֶם", לוֹמַר לְךָ שֶׁרָאשֵׁי הַמַּטּוֹת כּוֹפִין לְהָבִיא הַנְּדָרִים וְהַנְּדָבוֹת, כִּדְאָמְרִינַן, אַזְהָרָה לְבֵית דִּין שֶׁיְּעַשׂוּךָ. וְכֵן רְגָלִים, עַל פִּי רָאשֵׁי הַמַּטּוֹת נִקְבָּעִים. וְעוֹד, כְּשֶׁיִּשְׂרָאֵל בְּצָרָה, רָאשֵׁיהֶם נוֹדְרִים, כְּמוֹ בְיִפְתָּח, וְכֵן בְּשָׂרֵי הָאֲלָפִים, "וַנַּקְרֵב אֶת קָרְבַּן ה' ":

BAAL HATURIM ELUCIDATED

XXX.

2. **רָאשֵׁי הַמַּטּוֹת** — THE HEADS OF THE TRIBES. The Torah juxtaposed the term רָאשֵׁי הַמַּטּוֹת, *heads of the tribes,* with the verse regarding vow and free-will offerings, לְבַד מִנִּדְרֵיכֶם וְנִדְבֹתֵיכֶם, *aside from your vows*[1] *and your free-will offerings,* that appears above (29:39), to indicate to you that the heads of the tribes compel [those who have pledged] to bring their vow and free-will offerings [in fulfillment of their commitments]. As [the Talmudic Sages] state: [This[2]

1. The term נֶדֶר, *vow* (plural, נְדָרִים), may refer either to a vow offering [i.e., an item that one obligates oneself to bring as an offering in the *Beis HaMikdash*] or to a personal prohibition that one has accepted upon oneself or one's possessions in the form of a vow. Vows of the first type are mentioned at the end of the previous *parashah* (29:39); while the present passage deals with the הֲקָמָה, *validation,* הַתָּרָה, *annulment,* and הֲפָרָה, *deferment,* of the latter type of vows. Whereas it is the tribal leaders, in their role as judges, who are given the authority to annul vows, it is obvious why they are mentioned in our passage. But why does this passage appear at this particular place in the Torah? Let us examine the flow of the passages from the end of *parashas Balak* until here: After the narrative of Zimri and the Midianitess (25:6-15), God commanded Moses to smite Midian (25:16-18). But before going to battle, Moses was to conduct a census (26:1-51), to determine how many Israelites had survived the plague that had been brought about by the sin of Zimri and the Midianitess (*Rashi*) and to determine the number of men eligible to serve in the Israelite army (*Abarbanel*). After the census, we would expect the Torah to continue with the narrative of the war; however, the Torah digresses by stating that God told Moses that the Land of Israel would be divided among those counted in that census (26:52-56). The count of the Levites, who were not to be granted private holdings in Israel, follows (26:57-65). When Moses informed the Israelites regarding the apportionment of the land, the daughters of Zelophehad stepped forward to make their claim to their father's portion (27:1-5), and that leads to the passage regarding inheritance of land (27:6-11). God then reasserted to Moses that he would not enter the Holy Land, but would pass away in the wilderness (27:12-14). As a consequence, Moses asked God to appoint his successor in his own lifetime, and God appointed Joshua (27:15-23). But God also said, "Rather than you commanding Me about My children [i.e., who would lead them into the land], you must command My children about Me [i.e., about My Altar offerings]" (see *Rashi* to 28:2). God then proceeded to enumerate the daily, Sabbath and festival offerings (28:1-30:1). After all these digressions, we would expect the Torah to return to the war against Midian, but such is not the case. Rather, the passage of personal vows and prohibitions appears first (Ch. 30), with the narrative of the war against Midian following (Ch. 31). The Baal HaTurim explains why our passage appears first.

2. *Rosh Hashanah* 6a — The Talmud there refers to the verse: מוֹצָא שְׂפָתֶיךָ תִּשְׁמֹר וְעָשִׂיתָ, *The issuance of your lips, you shall observe and you shall do* (*Deuteronomy* 23:24). That verse is interpreted as containing three commandments: (a) The phrase מוֹצָא שְׂפָתֶיךָ, *the issuance of your lips,* is a positive commandment [to fulfill your vow]; (b) the term תִּשְׁמֹר, *you shall observe,* is a negative commandment, i.e., do not neglect to fulfill your vow [as the Talmud teaches

[2] **M**oses spoke to the heads of the tribes of the Children of

BAAL HATURIM ELUCIDATED

is] an admonition to [the justices of] the court that they should compel[3] you.[4]

And similarly: [The preceding passages deal with] the festivals,[5] which are also established by the leaders[6] of the tribes.[7]

Additionally: When Israel is in distress, their leaders are wont to take vows, as Jephthah did.[8] Similarly, regarding the officers of thousands who said, "וַנַּקְרֵב אֶת קָרְבַּן ה׳, *So we have brought an offering for* HASHEM" (31:50 below) [indicating that they had made vows during the battle[9]].[10]

elsewhere: As used in the Torah, forms of the verb שמר in the *nifal* conjugation indicate a negative commandment (*Eruvin* 96a; *Makkos* 13b)]; and (c) the term וְעָשִׂיתָ, *and you shall do,* is an admonition to [the justices of] the court that they should compel you [to fulfill your vow].

3. The translation of שֶׁיְּעַשּׂוּךָ as *they shall compel you* follows *Rashi* to *Kesubos* 77a, s.v., אין מעשין; *Tosafos Rid* to *Gittin* 88b, s.v., פי׳ גט מעושה.

4. *Peirush HaRokeach.*

5. The reading רְגָלִים, *festivals,* follows *Peirush HaRokeach,* the Baal HaTurim's apparent source, and that is the reading in *Shoham Yakar's* manuscript edition, as well as in most of the later printed editions. The early printed editions read, וְכֵן דְּגָלִים, *and similarly, the tribal divisions,* a reading which seems to be a scribal or a typographical error.

6. As the ranking scholars of their respective tribes, each of the tribal leaders was worthy of a seat on the *Sanhedrin* that declared each new month. And the declaration of the new month would fix the festivals; e.g., if the Sanhedrin declared Sunday to be the first day of Nissan, then the festival of Pesach would begin two Sundays later, on the fifteenth of Nissan; if Monday were declared the first of Tishrei, then Yom Kippur, the tenth of that month, would fall on Wednesday of the following week (see *Chagigah* 18a).

7. *Peirush HaRokeach.*

8. *Jephthah declared a vow to* HASHEM, *and he said, "If you will indeed deliver the Children of Ammon into my hand . . ."* (*Judges* 11:30).

9. Although the Torah does not make explicit mention of the officers of the thousands undertaking any vows, it is understood from their statement that they were now prepared to fulfill vows that they had previously undertaken (*VeChur LaZahav*).

There are at least two other narratives in which the Torah speaks explicitly about vows made during times of distress: The first was when *Jacob took a vow, saying, "If God will be with me, and He will guard me on this way that I am going . . ."* (*Genesis* 28:20, see the Baal HaTurim and note 46 there); the second, when *Israel made a vow to* HASHEM, *and said, "If you will deliver this people into my hand, I will consecrate their cities"* (21:2 above). Nevertheless, the Baal HaTurim adduces a verse from Prophets rather than one of those Torah verses, because his comment stresses the role of the tribal leaders and army officers vowing to bring Altar offerings. Those two verses, however, involve either an individual — Jacob (see the Baal HaTurim to 31:2 below, with note 21) — or the entire nation undertaking vows (*VeChur LaZahav*). Alternatively: The Baal HaTurim does not cite Jacob's vow because it did not pertain to an Altar offering (*Shoham Yakar; see Rambam, Hilchos Arachin* 6:32-33).

Another verse in Prophets relates that the sailors on Jonah's ship made vows to bring offerings when they would arrive in port (see *Jonah* 1:16 with *Targum Yonasan ben Uzziel*). The Baal HaTurim does not cite that incident because their vows were not made at the time of their distress; rather they were undertaken after the storm had subsided and the sea had stopped its raging (v. 15 there). Alternatively: He does not cite it because at that time it was the entire crew that undertook vows, not just the ship's officers (*VeChur LaZahav*).

10. *Peirush HaRokeach.*

ג לֵאמֹ֑ר זֶ֣ה הַדָּבָ֔ר אֲשֶׁ֖ר צִוָּ֥ה יהוָֽה׃ אִישׁ֩ כִּֽי־יִדֹּ֨ר
נֶ֜דֶר לַֽיהוָ֗ה אֽוֹ־הִשָּׁ֤בַע שְׁבֻעָה֙ לֶאְסֹ֤ר אִסָּר֙ עַל־
נַפְשׁ֔וֹ לֹ֥א יַחֵ֖ל דְּבָר֑וֹ כְּכָל־הַיֹּצֵ֥א מִפִּ֖יו יַעֲשֶֽׂה׃
ד וְאִשָּׁ֕ה כִּֽי־תִדֹּ֥ר נֶ֖דֶר לַֽיהוָ֑ה וְאָסְרָ֥ה אִסָּ֛ר בְּבֵ֥ית
ה אָבִ֖יהָ בִּנְעֻרֶֽיהָ׃ וְשָׁמַ֨ע אָבִ֜יהָ אֶת־נִדְרָ֗הּ וֶֽאֱסָרָהּ֙
אֲשֶׁ֣ר אָסְרָ֣ה עַל־נַפְשָׁ֔הּ וְהֶחֱרִ֥ישׁ לָ֖הּ אָבִ֑יהָ

בעל הטורים

(ג) נְדָרִים בְּגִימַטְרִיָּא רוֹצֵחַ. שֶׁהַנּוֹדֵר חָשׁוּב כְּרוֹצֵחַ אִם אֵינוֹ מְשַׁלֵּם, דִּבַעֲוֹן נְדָרִים הַבָּנִים מֵתִים:

(ה) **וְהֶחֱרִישׁ לָהּ.** ב׳ בַּמָּסוֹרֶת – ״וְהֶחֱרִישׁ לָהּ אָבִיהָ וְקָמוּ כָּל נְדָרֶיהָ״, וְאִידָךְ בַּפָּרָשָׁה עַצְמָהּ ״וְשָׁמַע אִישָׁהּ בְּיוֹם שָׁמְעוֹ וְהֶחֱרִישׁ לָהּ וְקָמוּ נְדָרֶיהָ״. הַיְנוּ דְּאִיתָא בִנְדָרִים, ״וְשָׁמַע אִישָׁהּ״, פְּרָט אִם חֵרֵשׁ שֶׁהוּא מְדַבֵּר וְאֵינוֹ שׁוֹמֵעַ, שֶׁאֵינוֹ מֵפֵר. וְיָלְפִינַן אָב מִבַּעַל:

BAAL HATURIM ELUCIDATED

3. The *gematria* of the word נְדָרִים, *vows,* (304) is equal to that of רוֹצֵחַ, *murderer.* [This intimates] that a person who makes vows and does not fulfill them is considered as a murderer, for [as the Talmud states], children die as a consequence of the[ir parents'] sin of [failure to carry out their] vows.[11]

5. **וְהֶחֱרִישׁ לָהּ — AND HE WAS SILENT ABOUT HER.** The masoretic note,[12] ב׳, means that this phrase appears twice in the *Tanach:* (i) here, וְהֶחֱרִישׁ לָהּ אָבִיהָ וְקָמוּ כָּל נְדָרֶיהָ, *and her father was silent about her, then all her vows shall stand;* and (ii) [later] in this very passage, וְשָׁמַע אִישָׁהּ בְּיוֹם שָׁמְעוֹ וְהֶחֱרִישׁ לָהּ וְקָמוּ נְדָרֶיהָ, *And her husband heard, and on the day of his hearing he was silent about her, then her vows shall stand* (v. 8). This [similarity of expression] indicates that which our Sages teach in tractate *Nedarim:* The verse states, וְשָׁמַע אִישָׁהּ, *And her husband heard,* excluding a deaf person,[12a] [it teaches] that [even] one who can speak but cannot

11. The Talmud derives this from a verse that appears in a passage regarding vows: *Let not your mouth bring guilt upon your flesh, and do not tell the gabbai* [who comes to collect what you have pledged (*Rashi*)] *that it was an error. Why should God be angered by your speech and destroy your handiwork?* (*Ecclesiastes* 5:5). And what is a man's "handiwork"? You must say that it refers to a man's sons and daughters (*Shabbos* 32b).

12. *Maharam MiRothenburg's* parallel comment (see note 14 below) cites a fuller version of the masoretic note: ב׳ חֲסֵירֵי יו״ד, [*This word appears*] *twice with a defective spelling, without a* י. And *Minchas Shai* (*Genesis* 34:5) reports seeing such a masoretic note in a manuscript *Chumash.* In truth, the word וְהֶחֱרִישׁ appears four times in the Torah: (i-ii) Twice in our *parashah,* spelled in full, וְהֶחֱרִישׁ, with a י (vv. 5 and 8); (iii) once more in our *parashah,* that time spelled defectively, וְהֶחֱרִשׁ, without a י (v. 12); and (iv) again with the defective spelling, וְהֶחֱרִשׁ יַעֲקֹב, *Jacob was silent* (*Genesis* 34:5).

12a. The Baal HaTurim's wording פְּרָט אִם חֵרֵשׁ, literally, *excluding if a deaf person,* is puzzling, for the word אִם, *if,* seems out of place. Indeed, many later editions have therefore added the word הוּא after אִם, thus, the comment reads: *excluding if he is a deaf person.* However, the Talmudic passage adduced by the Baal HaTurim does not include the word אִם. Rather, it reads, וְשָׁמַע אִישָׁהּ פְּרָט לְאֵשֶׁת חֵרֵשׁ, [*The verse states,*] *and her husband heard, excluding the wife of a deaf man.* Perhaps that is the proper reading here too (A.S.).

Israel, saying: This is the thing that HASHEM has com-
manded: 3 *If a man takes a vow to HASHEM or swears an*
oath to establish a prohibition upon himself, he shall not
desecrate his word; according to whatever comes from his
mouth shall he do.
4 *But if a woman will take a vow to HASHEM or establish a*
prohibition in her father's home in her youth; 5 *and her*
father heard of her vow or the prohibition that she estab-
lished upon herself, and her father was silent about her,

BAAL HATURIM ELUCIDATED

hear may not defer [her vows].[13] And we derive [the laws regarding] the father from [the laws regarding] the husband.[14]

---

13. *Nedarim* 73a.

14. *Atros Addar* raises a question: Whereas the same words are written regarding the father — וְשָׁמַע אָבִיהָ, *and her father heard* (v. 5) — and regarding the husband — וְשָׁמַע אִישָׁהּ, *and her husband heard* (v. 8) — why does the Talmud not expound the exclusion of one who is deaf yet can speak from the first וְשָׁמַע rather than from the second? Moreover, what does the Baal HaTurim mean when he says that we derive the laws regarding a deaf father from the laws regarding a deaf husband? Does the first וְשָׁמַע not imply the same law as the second וְשָׁמַע? *Atros Addar* leaves these questions unanswered.

A parallel comment by *Maharam MiRothenburg* interprets the Talmudic passage in a different manner, one that anticipates *Atros Addar's* questions. It reads: A masoretic note states, ב׳ חֲסֵירֵי יו״ד בְּלִישָׁנֵי, [*This word appears*] *twice with a defective spelling, without a* י, both with the same meaning. One of them appears here [וְשָׁמַע אִישָׁהּ וְהֶחֱרִשׁ לָהּ, *and her husband heard and he was silent about her* (v. 12)]; and the second is, וְהֶחֱרִשׁ יַעֲקֹב עַד בֹּאָם, *Jacob kept silent until their arrival* (*Genesis* 34:5), regarding [his daughter] Dinah. [This similarity of expression is needed to derive the laws regarding a deaf father from the laws regarding a deaf husband] for in tractate *Nedarim* (73a) the Talmud teaches: The verse states, וְשָׁמַע אִישָׁהּ אֶת נִדְרָהּ, *and her husband heard her vow,* excluding a deaf person, i.e., if her husband could speak but could not hear he is not able to defer [her vows]. Now with regard to her father it is also stated וְשָׁמַע אָבִיהָ, *and her father heard,* [yet the Talmud does not expound on that verse,] therefore, the masoretic note finds an allusion to intimate that if her father is deaf, even if he can speak, he cannot defer her vows. For our passage regarding her husband states, וְהֶחֱרִשׁ, without a י (v. 12), which may be interpreted as if it were vowelized וְהַחֵרֵשׁ, *and the deaf man* [verse 12 would then be understood: וְשָׁמַע אִישָׁהּ, *and her husband heard,* וְהֶחֱרִשׁ, *and was silent,* וְהַחֵרֵשׁ, *or he was a deaf man* . . . וְקָמוּ כָּל נְדָרֶיהָ, *all her vows shall stand*], and there, with regard to the incident of Dinah, it is stated about her father Jacob, וְהֶחֱרִשׁ יַעֲקֹב עַד בֹּאָם, *Jacob kept silent until their arrival.* [Thus, we learn the laws regarding the father from the laws regarding the husband.]

Following *Maharam MiRothenburg's* comment, it is possible to explain that the Talmud does not infer the exclusion of a deaf husband from the words וְשָׁמַע אִישָׁהּ of verse 8; rather that law is derived from the phrase וְשָׁמַע אִישָׁהּ וְהֶחֱרִשׁ לָהּ of verse 12, with the gist of the derivation coming from the defective spelling of וְהֶחֱרִשׁ. If so, *Atros Addar's* questions are resolved (*VeChur LaZahav*).

Alternatively: The phrase וְשָׁמַע אָבִיהָ, *and her father heard,* appears only once in this passage (v. 5). But the phrase וְשָׁמַע אִישָׁהּ, *and her husband heard,* appears twice (v. 8 and v. 12). Whereas the Torah repeats the phrase, the Talmud sees the second appearance (v. 12) as redundant. It is from that verse that the Talmud expounds the law regarding a deaf husband (Y.S.).

It is noteworthy that although the Talmud cites only the verse וְשָׁמַע אִישָׁהּ, the *Sifrei* expounds, לְהוֹצִיא אֶת הַחֵרֵשׁ, *to exclude the deaf one,* at each of the three verses under discussion (vv. 5,8,12).

וְקָמוּ כׇּל־נְדָרֶיהָ וְכׇל־אִסָּר אֲשֶׁר־אָסְרָה עַל־נַפְשָׁהּ
ו יָקוּם: וְאִם־הֵנִיא אָבִיהָ אֹתָהּ בְּיוֹם שׇׁמְעוֹ כׇּל־
נְדָרֶיהָ וֶאֱסָרֶיהָ אֲשֶׁר־אָסְרָה עַל־נַפְשָׁהּ לֹא יָקוּם
ז וַיהוה יִסְלַח־לָהּ כִּי־הֵנִיא אָבִיהָ אֹתָהּ: וְאִם־הָיוֹ
תִהְיֶה לְאִישׁ וּנְדָרֶיהָ עָלֶיהָ אוֹ מִבְטָא שְׂפָתֶיהָ אֲשֶׁר
ח אָסְרָה עַל־נַפְשָׁהּ: וְשָׁמַע אִישָׁהּ בְּיוֹם שׇׁמְעוֹ
וְהֶחֱרִישׁ לָהּ וְקָמוּ נְדָרֶיהָ וֶאֱסָרֶהָ אֲשֶׁר־אָסְרָה
ט עַל־נַפְשָׁהּ יָקֻמוּ: וְאִם בְּיוֹם שְׁמֹעַ אִישָׁהּ יָנִיא
אוֹתָהּ וְהֵפֵר אֶת־נִדְרָהּ אֲשֶׁר עָלֶיהָ וְאֵת מִבְטָא
שְׂפָתֶיהָ אֲשֶׁר אָסְרָה עַל־נַפְשָׁהּ וַיהוה יִסְלַח־לָהּ:
י וְנֵדֶר אַלְמָנָה וּגְרוּשָׁה כֹּל אֲשֶׁר־אָסְרָה עַל־נַפְשָׁהּ
יא יָקוּם עָלֶיהָ: וְאִם־בֵּית אִישָׁהּ נָדָרָה אוֹ־אָסְרָה אִסָּר
יב עַל־נַפְשָׁהּ בִּשְׁבֻעָה: וְשָׁמַע אִישָׁהּ וְהֶחֱרִשׁ לָהּ לֹא
הֵנִיא אֹתָהּ וְקָמוּ כׇּל־נְדָרֶיהָ וְכׇל־אִסָּר אֲשֶׁר־
יג אָסְרָה עַל־נַפְשָׁהּ יָקוּם: וְאִם־הָפֵר יָפֵר אֹתָם ׀
אִישָׁהּ בְּיוֹם שׇׁמְעוֹ כׇּל־מוֹצָא שְׂפָתֶיהָ לִנְדָרֶיהָ
וּלְאִסַּר נַפְשָׁהּ לֹא יָקוּם אִישָׁהּ הֲפֵרָם וַיהוה
יד יִסְלַח־לָהּ: כׇּל־נֵדֶר וְכׇל־שְׁבֻעַת אִסָּר לְעַנֹּת נָפֶשׁ

בעל הטורים

(יד) לְעַנֹּת. ב׳ בַּמָּסוֹרֶת – ״לְעַנֹּת נָפֶשׁ״; ״עַל מָחֲלַת לְעַנּוֹת״, וְהוּא עִנְיַן כְּלֵי שִׁיר. לוֹמַר שֶׁאִם נָדְרָה שֶׁלֹּא לִשְׁמֹעַ כְּלֵי שִׁיר, שֶׁבַּעְלָהּ מֵפֵר לָהּ, שֶׁחָשׁוּב כְּנֶדֶר עִנּוּי נֶפֶשׁ. כִּדְאִיתָא בְּמוֹעֵד קָטָן, שֶׁאַף הַזְּקֵנוֹת נֶהֱנוֹת מִכְּלֵי שִׁיר, בַּת שִׁתִּין כְּבַת שִׁית לְקָל טַבְלָא רִיהֲטָא {כָּךְ הוּא הַלָּשׁוֹן שָׁם}:

BAAL HATURIM ELUCIDATED

14. לְעַנֹּת — TO CAUSE AFFLICTION. The masoretic note,[15] ב׳, means that this word appears twice in the *Tanach:* (i) here, לְעַנֹּת נָפֶשׁ, *to cause personal affliction;* and (ii) [with a different meaning in,] עַל מָחֲלַת לְעַנּוֹת, *on the mahalath-le'annoth* (*Psalms* 88:1), where it refers to a musical instrument. [The similarity of expression] indicates that if a woman vowed not to listen to musical instruments, her

15. The full note is found in *Psalms* and reads: ב׳ בִּתְרֵי לִישָׁנֵי חַד חָסֵר, *Twice, with two meanings; one is spelled defectively.* That is, the word appears twice in the *Tanach:* once as a verb, *to afflict,* and spelled defectively, לְעַנֹּת, without a ו; the other time as a noun, the name of a musical instrument, and spelled in full, לְעַנּוֹת, with a ו.

The masoretic note at our verse ignores the different meanings. It reads: לֵית חָסֵר וְחַד מָלֵא, *There is no other* [*appearance of this word that is*] *spelled defectively; but there is one that is spelled in full.*

then all her vows shall stand, and any prohibition that she established upon herself shall stand. [6] *But if her father restrained her on the day of his hearing, all her vows or prohibitions that she established upon herself shall not stand; and* HASHEM *will forgive her, for her father had restrained her.*

[7] *If she shall be married to a man and her vows were upon her, or an utterance of her lips by which she had prohibited something upon herself,* [8] *and her husband heard, and on the day of his hearing he was silent about her, then her vows shall stand and her prohibition that she established upon herself shall stand.* [9] *But if on the day of her husband's hearing he shall restrain her and he shall defer the vow that is upon her or the utterance of her lips by which she had prohibited something upon herself — then* HASHEM *will forgive her.*

[10] *The vow of a widow or a divorcee — anything she had prohibited upon herself — shall remain upon her.*

[11] *But if she vowed in her husband's home, or she established a prohibition upon herself through an oath,* [12] *and her husband heard and was silent about her — he did not restrain her — then all her vows shall stand and any prohibition she established upon herself shall stand.* [13] *But if her husband shall defer them on the day of his hearing, anything that came out of her mouth regarding her oaths or the prohibition upon herself shall not stand; her husband had deferred them and* HASHEM *will forgive her.* [14] *Any vow and any oath-prohibition to cause personal affliction,*

BAAL HATURIM ELUCIDATED

husband may defer her vow,[15a] for [her vow] is considered a vow that causes personal affliction.[15b] For it is taught in tractate *Moed Katan*[16] that even older women enjoy [listening to the sounds of] musical instruments. [Thus, the adage:] A sixty-year-old woman, like a six-year-old girl, will run to the sound of wedding bells[17] {that is the [proper] wording there[18]}.

15a. *Shulchan Aruch, Yoreh Deah* 234:62.

15b. The only *nedarim* that a husband may defer are those that are either in the realm of matters affecting their relationship or are matters concerning personal affliction of the wife.

16. *Moed Katan* 9b.

17. *Maharam MiRothenburg.*

18. The passage enclosed in braces appears in the early printed editions, but is not found in all of the manuscripts. Moreover, it is hardly the style of the Baal HaTurim to authenticate the text of Talmudic passages. We cannot determine whether these four words were written by the Baal HaTurim or were inserted by some copyist. Nevertheless, the author of *Mekorei Baal HaTurim* suggests a possible reason for their inclusion in this comment: The halachic compendium *Kol Bo* (whose author was a contemporary of the Baal HaTurim) quotes *Maharam MiRothenburg's* ruling about women's vows of abstention from listening to music, but

ל/טו-לא/ב טו אִישָׁהּ יְקִימֶנּוּ וְאִישָׁהּ יְפֵרֶנּוּ: וְאִם־הַחֲרֵשׁ יַחֲרִישׁ
לָהּ אִישָׁהּ מִיּוֹם אֶל־יוֹם וְהֵקִים אֶת־כָּל־נְדָרֶיהָ אוֹ
אֶת־כָּל־אֱסָרֶיהָ אֲשֶׁר עָלֶיהָ הֵקִים אֹתָם כִּי־
טז הֶחֱרִשׁ לָהּ בְּיוֹם שָׁמְעוֹ: וְאִם־הָפֵר יָפֵר אֹתָם אַחֲרֵי
יז שָׁמְעוֹ וְנָשָׂא אֶת־עֲוֺנָהּ: אֵלֶּה הַחֻקִּים אֲשֶׁר צִוָּה
יהוה אֶת־מֹשֶׁה בֵּין אִישׁ לְאִשְׁתּוֹ בֵּין־אָב לְבִתּוֹ
בִּנְעֻרֶיהָ בֵּית אָבִיהָ:
לא שני א-ב וַיְדַבֵּר יהוה אֶל־מֹשֶׁה לֵּאמֹר: נְקֹם נִקְמַת בְּנֵי

בעל הטורים

(יז) בִּנְעֻרֶיהָ. אוֹתִיּוֹת "נַעֲרָה י"ב" – לוֹמַר לְךָ, בַּת י"ב שָׁנִים {וְיוֹם אֶחָד} נְדָרֶיהָ נִבְדָּקִין:

לא (ב) נְקֹם נִקְמַת בְּנֵי יִשְׂרָאֵל. סָמַךְ זֶה לְפָרָשַׁת נְדָרִים, לוֹמַר לְךָ שֶׁנּוֹדְרִין בְּעֵת צָרָה וּמִלְחָמָה. וְעוֹד {אָמְרוּ} הַמַּחֲרִישׁ לְבִתּוֹ וּלְאִשְׁתּוֹ וְלֹא הֵפֵר לָהֶן, הוּא נִכְנָס תַּחְתֵּיהֶן –

BAAL HATURIM ELUCIDATED

16. {The Baal HaTurim's comment to אֶת עֲוֺנָהּ appears at 5:31 above.}

17. בִּנְעֻרֶיהָ — IN HER YOUTH. The letters of this word can be rearranged to spell נַעֲרָה י"ב, *a maiden*[19] [*of*] *12.* This teaches that the vows of a maiden in her twelfth year[20] are examined.

---

with one minor difference. In that work, the Talmudic citation reads, כְּבַת שֶׁב, *like a seven-year-old girl,* in place of כְּבַת שִׁית, *like a six-year-old girl.* Perhaps the phrase "that is the proper reading there" is meant to correct that citation.

19. With regard to all the *mitzvos* of the Torah (but see next paragraph), *halachah* distinguishes between two ages of a man: Before he has reached י"ג שָׁנִים וְיוֹם אֶחָד, *thirteen* [*full*] *years and one day,* i.e., his thirteenth birthday, he is a קָטָן, *minor;* and from his thirteenth birthday onward, he is a גָּדוֹל, *adult,* and is obligated to observe all the *mitzvos.* But *halachah* also recognizes the fact that girls generally mature earlier than boys and thus distinguishes between three ages of a woman: Before she has reached י"ב שָׁנִים וְיוֹם אֶחָד, *twelve* [*full*] *years and one day,* i.e., her twelfth birthday, she is a קְטַנָּה, *minor;* from her twelfth birthday onward, for the next six months, she is a נַעֲרָה, *na'arah,* in some respects she is still under the jurisdiction of her father, in others, she is independent; after twelve years and six months she is considered independent in all respects.

However, this schedule is altered with regard to the obligation to fulfill one's vows and oaths. During one's last year as a minor — a boy at age twelve, a girl at age eleven — vows and oaths are regarded more seriously than are other points of *halachah*. The child is interrogated to determine whether he or she understands to Whom the vow is being made. If the child understands, the vow is valid and must be adhered to; if not, the vow is invalid. However, at reaching full maturity (a girl at twelve, a boy at thirteen) this interrogation is no longer made, rather their *nedarim* are fully and unconditionally valid (see *Niddah* 5:6 [45b]; *Rashi,* v. 4 above).

20. The words וְיוֹם אֶחָד enclosed in braces appear in the early printed editions and in some of the manuscripts used by *Shoham Yakar.* Nevertheless, their inclusion is troublesome. With those words, the Baal HaTurim's comment reads: This teaches that the vows of a twelve-year-old girl are examined — a statement that is in direct conflict with the Mishnah (see note 19 above). It is noteworthy that *Peirush HaRokeach* (to v. 4 above), the Baal HaTurim's apparent source for this comment, reads: The letters of בִּנְעֻרֶיהָ can be rearranged to spell נַעֲרָה י"ב, for the vows of a twelve-year-old girl, קַיָּמִין, *stand valid.* And *Atros Addar* suggests emending the Baal HaTurim to

her husband may let it stand and her husband may defer it.
[15] If her husband shall be silent about her from day to day —
he will have let stand all her vows; or all the prohibitions that
are upon her, he will have let them stand, for he was silent
about her on the day of his hearing. [16] But if he shall defer
them after his having heard, he shall bear her iniquity.
[17] These are the decrees that HASHEM commanded Moses,
between a man and his wife, between a father and his
daughter in her youth, in her father's house.

31 *[1] HASHEM spoke to Moses, saying, [2] "Take vengeance for the*

BAAL HATURIM ELUCIDATED

XXXI.

2. נְקֹם נִקְמַת בְּנֵי יִשְׂרָאֵל — TAKE VENGEANCE FOR THE CHILDREN OF ISRAEL. This passage is juxtaposed with the passage concerning vows to indicate to you that vows should be made in a time of distress or war.[21]

Additionally: {They have stated:[22]} When a man remains silent regarding the vows of his daughter or his wife and does not defer [their vows] for them, he

---

that version. An alternative suggestion would retain the words נְדָרֶיהָ נִבְדָּקִין, but prefaced with the word אֵין, *are not,* i.e., the vows of a twelve-year-old are not investigated (*Ittur Bikkurim*). A third suggested emendation is that the words וְיוֹם אֶחָד be deleted, leaving בַּת י״ב שָׁנִים, *a maiden in her twelfth year,* i.e., between her eleventh and twelfth birthday (*Ittur Bikkurim; Yad Aharon*). Our translation follows this last suggestion. Indeed, the omission of וְיוֹם אֶחָד is verified by *Meleches Shlomo* (*Niddah* 5:6, s.v., בת י״א שנה), who quotes the Baal HaTurim's passage verbatim, yet excludes those two words (*VeChur LaZahav*).

21. *Bereishis Rabbah* 70:1.

Earlier (30:2 above), the Baal HaTurim stated that in times of distress the tribal leaders are obligated to make vows to bring Altar offerings when the danger has passed. Here, he speaks of each individual (*Ittur Bikkurim*).

In times of distress, everyone should sanctify himself by vowing to undertake some meritorious deed or to change his lifestyle, e.g., Jacob vowed, *"This stone which I have set up as a pillar shall become a House of God; and whatever You will give me, I will certainly tithe it to You"* (*Genesis* 28:22).

22. The term אָמְרוּ, *They have stated,* enclosed in braces, is the product of an interesting series of metamorphoses. According to *Shoham Yakar,* it is completely absent in one manuscript; and, being that only half of what follows is found in the writings of the Talmudic Sages [the usual subjects of the Baal HaTurim's אָמְרוּ, *they said*], that is the preferred reading. However, another manuscript (one that *Shoham Yakar* found after having declared his preference) reads אִם, *if* or *whereas,* i.e., the comment states: Whereas when a man remains silent . . .

In the first printed edition (Constantinople) the word אִם has been transformed into the contraction אמ׳, which the Venice edition spells out as אָמַר, *he said,* while the Fürth edition offers אָמְרוּ, *they said,* and that is how the comment reads in most later editions.

לפרשת נדרים לו׳ ר לך שנודרין בעת צרה ומלחמה · ועוד אמ׳ המחריש לבתו

Constantinople, 1514 — קושטא, רע״ד

בעת צרה ומלחמה · ועוד אמר המחריש לבתו ולאשתו ולא הפר להן הוא נכנס תחתיהן ·

Venice, 1544 — ויניציא, ד״ש

לפרשת נדרים (תתצב) לומר לך שנודרין בעת צרה ומלחמה ، ועוד אמרו המחריש לבתו ולאשתו ולא הפר

Fürth, 1752 — פיורדא, תקי״ב

יִשְׂרָאֵל מֵאֵת הַמִּדְיָנִים אַחַר תֵּאָסֵף אֶל־עַמֶּיךָ:
ג וַיְדַבֵּר מֹשֶׁה אֶל־הָעָם לֵאמֹר הֵחָלְצוּ מֵאִתְּכֶם
אֲנָשִׁים לַצָּבָא וְיִהְיוּ עַל־מִדְיָן לָתֵת נִקְמַת־יהוה
ד בְּמִדְיָן: אֶלֶף לַמַּטֶּה אֶלֶף לַמַּטֶּה לְכֹל מַטּוֹת

בעל הטורים

מִדְיָנִים שֶׁהֶחֱטִיאוּ אֶת יִשְׂרָאֵל, לֹא כָל שֶׁכֵּן שֶׁיֵּעָנְשׁוּ:

❑ **אַחַר תֵּאָסֵף.** לְפִי שֶׁרָאָה מַעֲשֵׂה מִדְיָנִית וְלֹא קִנֵּא לַשֵּׁם, לְכָךְ נִתְלוּ חַיָּיו בְּנִקְמַת מִדְיָנִים:

❑ **אֶל עַמֶּיךָ.** מָלֵא יוּ״ד — לוֹמַר לְךָ שֶׁבַּעֲשָׂרָה מְקוֹמוֹת הֻזְכְּרָה מִיתָתוֹ בַּתּוֹרָה:

(ד) **אֶלֶף לַמַּטֶּה אֶלֶף לַמַּטֶּה.** לְכָל מַטֶּה שְׁנֵי אֲלָפִים. הֲרֵי עֶשְׂרִים וְאַרְבָּעָה אֲלָפִים הָלְכוּ עֲלֵיהֶם לַמִּלְחָמָה, כְּנֶגֶד עֶשְׂרִים וְאַרְבָּעָה אֲלָפִים שֶׁהִפִּילוּ מִיִּשְׂרָאֵל:

❑ הַפָּסוּק מַתְחִיל בְּאָלֶ״ף וּמְסַיֵּם בְּאָלֶ״ף, לוֹמַר לְךָ שֶׁכֻּלָּם הָיָה לָהֶם לֵב אֶחָד לַאֲבִיהֶם שֶׁבַּשָּׁמַיִם:

BAAL HATURIM ELUCIDATED

stands in their stead.[23] If so, the Midianites who caused the Israelites to sin will certainly be punished.[24]

❑ **אַחַר תֵּאָסֵף — AFTERWARD YOU WILL BE BROUGHT IN.** Whereas Moses witnessed the incident of the Midianitess and did not act zealously on God's behalf,[25] his life[26] was made dependent on exacting vengeance from the Midianites.[27]

❑ **אֶל עַמֶּיךָ — UNTO YOUR PEOPLE.** The word עַמֶּיךָ is spelled with the י (= 10) of the plural,[27a] to indicate to you that in ten different places Scripture[27b] mentions

23. *Sifrei* to 30:16, cited by *Rashi* to that verse; see also the Baal HaTurim to 5:31 above, s.v., אֶת עֲוֹנָהּ.

24. If the father's or husband's passivity in not revoking his daughter's or wife's vows causes him to be considered responsible for her not fulfilling her vows, then certainly the active role that the Midianites played in causing Israel to sin makes them culpable for Israel's sins (*Atros Addar*).

25. See *Rashi* to 25:6, s.v., וְהֵמָּה בֹכִים, and 25:7 above.

26. When Zimri sinned with the Midianite princess Cozbi, Moses should have acted by putting the two to death. However, Heaven concealed the law from Moses so that he did not know how to react. The reason God concealed the law from Moses was so that Phinehas would have the opportunity to rise to the occasion and thus gain the priesthood as his reward (*Tanchuma, Balak* 20, cited by *Rashi* to 25:6 above, s.v., והמה בכים). Nevertheless, Moses was given a second chance to exact vengeance against Midian. Indeed, he was allowed to remain alive [even after the time appointed for his demise, if such time were needed] until he had inflicted God's vengeance upon Midian (A.S.).

27. *Paaneach Raza.*

27a. The word עַם is usually translated *people.* However, this leads to confusion, for the word "people" is used as a singular noun (plural: peoples) meaning a group of persons with a common background, e.g., a nation, a race; but it is also used as a plural noun meaning persons (it has no singular form in that usage). Similarly, in Hebrew: The word עַמְּךָ/עַמֶּךָ, spelled without a י, is a singular noun and means *your people,* i.e., your nation; however עַמֶּיךָ, with a י, is a plural noun and means *your people,* i.e., the individual persons who comprise your nation.

27b. Although the Baal HaTurim writes בַּתּוֹרָה, *in the Torah,* two of the ten verses are found in the Book of *Joshua* (see note 28 below).

Children of Israel against the Midianites; afterward you will be brought in unto your people."

[3] Moses spoke to the people, saying, "Arm men from among yourselves for the legion that they may be against Midian to inflict HASHEM's *vengeance against Midian. [4] A thousand per tribe, a thousand per tribe, for all the tribes of*

BAAL HATURIM ELUCIDATED

the death[27c] of [Moses].[28]

4. אֶלֶף לַמַּטֶּה אֶלֶף לַמַּטֶּה — A THOUSAND PER TRIBE, A THOUSAND PER TRIBE, i.e., two thousand from each tribe.[29] Thus, twenty-four thousand [Israelites] went to war against them, corresponding to the twenty-four thousand Israelites[30] whose death they caused.[31]

❑ The verse begins with an א (= 1) and concludes with an א,[32] to indicate to you that all [the warriors] were of one heart,[33] dedicated to their Father in Heaven.[34]

27c. That is, ten Scriptural verses (enumerated in note 28) contain words of the root מות, *to die,* with regard to Moses. The death of Moses is mentioned in other verses (e.g., here and in 27:13 above), but verbs of the root מות do not appear in those verses.

28. *Peirush HaRokeach.* The Midrash enumerates the ten verses regarding Moses' death [in an apparently haphazard order (*Maharzu*)]. The first eight verses are in *Deuteronomy:* (i) הֵן קָרְבוּ יָמֶיךָ לָמוּת — 31:14; (ii) וּמֻת בָּהָר — 32:50; (iii) כִּי אָנֹכִי מֵת — 4:22; (iv) כִּי יָדַעְתִּי אַחֲרֵי מוֹתִי — 31:29; (v) וְאַף כִּי אַחֲרֵי מוֹתִי — 31:27; (vi) לִפְנֵי מוֹתוֹ — 33:1; (vii) וּמֹשֶׁה בֶּן מֵאָה וְעֶשְׂרִים שָׁנָה בְּמֹתוֹ — 34:7; (viii) וַיָּמָת שָׁם מֹשֶׁה עֶבֶד ה׳ — 34:5; and two more in the Book of *Joshua,* (ix) וַיְהִי אַחֲרֵי מוֹת מֹשֶׁה — 1:1; and (x) מֹשֶׁה עַבְדִּי מֵת — 1:2 (*Pesikta DeRav Kahana; Devarim Rabbah* 11:10). *Devarim Rabbah* continues: This teaches that the decree that Moses not enter into the Land of Israel was handed down on ten occasions, but was not sealed until [the tenth time].

It is not clear why *Peirush HaRokeach* and the Baal HaTurim chose to wait for this verse for this comment. The phrase אֶל עַמֶּיךָ appears earlier, with the same spelling and in the same context, in 27:13, and that is where this same comment appears in *Midrash Chaseiros Viseiros* and in *Rimzei Rabbeinu Yoel.*

29. The Midrash records a dispute regarding the interpretation of the double expression, אֶלֶף לַמַּטֶּה אֶלֶף לַמַּטֶּה, *a thousand per tribe, a thousand per tribe.* According to R' Yishmael it means *a thousand from each tribe and a [second] thousand from each tribe,* for a total of 24,000. According to R' Akiva it means *a thousand from each and every tribe,* for a total of 12,000 (*Sifrei*).

Another Midrash states: Some say there were two thousand from each tribe, some say there were three thousand, as the verse mentions אֶלֶף לַמַּטֶּה a third time (v. 5) — twelve thousand to do battle; twelve thousand to guard the supplies; and twelve thousand to pray (*Tanchuma* 3, cited in *Bamidbar Rabbah* 22:3).

30. See 25:9 above.

31. *Peirush HaRokeach.*

32. There are forty-three such verses in the *Tanach,* eight of which are in the Torah: (i) *Genesis* 24:45; (ii-iii) *Exodus* 21:19 and 21; (iv-vi) *Leviticus* 4:28, 11:36 and 27:26; (vii) our verse; and (viii) *Deuteronomy* 18:20. In addition to our verse, the Baal HaTurim also comments on this phenomenon at each of the two verses in *Exodus.*

33. This is the implication of the first א (= 1).

34. This is the implication of the second א; it stands for אֲבִיהֶם, *their Father,* i.e., God. Moreover, we find that the letter א alludes to God, as the Sages teach: Why was the world created with the letter ב [i.e., why does the narrative of creation open with the phrase בְּרֵאשִׁית בָּרָא אֱלֹהִים, which begins with a ב, instead of אֱלֹהִים בָּרָא בְּרֵאשִׁית, which has God's Name as the first word (*Tanna DeVei Eliyahu* 31) and which begins with the first letter of the *aleph-beis* (*Tanchuma, Bereishis* 5)]? Because the ב has two serifs, one pointing upward and one pointing behind it. When we say to the ב, "Who created you?" it points heavenward, saying, "The One Above

ה יִשְׂרָאֵל תִּשְׁלְחוּ לַצָּבָא: וַיִּמָּסְרוּ מֵאַלְפֵי יִשְׂרָאֵל
ו אֶלֶף לַמַּטֶּה שְׁנֵים־עָשָׂר אֶלֶף חֲלוּצֵי צָבָא: וַיִּשְׁלַח
אֹתָם מֹשֶׁה אֶלֶף לַמַּטֶּה לַצָּבָא אֹתָם וְאֶת־פִּינְחָס
בֶּן־אֶלְעָזָר הַכֹּהֵן לַצָּבָא וּכְלֵי הַקֹּדֶשׁ וַחֲצֹצְרוֹת
ז הַתְּרוּעָה בְּיָדוֹ: וַיִּצְבְּאוּ עַל־מִדְיָן כַּאֲשֶׁר צִוָּה יהוה
ח אֶת־מֹשֶׁה וַיַּהַרְגוּ כָּל־זָכָר: וְאֶת־מַלְכֵי מִדְיָן הָרְגוּ
עַל־חַלְלֵיהֶם אֶת־אֱוִי וְאֶת־רֶקֶם וְאֶת־צוּר וְאֶת־
חוּר וְאֶת־רֶבַע חֲמֵשֶׁת מַלְכֵי מִדְיָן וְאֵת בִּלְעָם
ט בֶּן־בְּעוֹר הָרְגוּ בֶּחָרֶב: וַיִּשְׁבּוּ בְנֵי־יִשְׂרָאֵל אֶת־נְשֵׁי
מִדְיָן וְאֶת־טַפָּם וְאֵת כָּל־בְּהֶמְתָּם וְאֶת־כָּל־מִקְנֵהֶם

בעל הטורים

(ה) וַיִּמָּסְרוּ מֵאַלְפֵי יִשְׂרָאֵל. שֶׁמָּסְרוּ עַצְמָם עַל קְדֻשַּׁת הַשֵּׁם לְהַצָּלַת יִשְׂרָאֵל:

(ו) וַיִּשְׁלַח אֹתָם מֹשֶׁה אֶלֶף לַמַּטֶּה לַצָּבָא . . . וְאֶת פִּינְחָס. וְהַנְּשִׂיאִים לֹא שָׁלַח עִמָּהֶם, כְּדֵי שֶׁלֹּא יִתְבַּיֵּשׁ שֵׁבֶט שִׁמְעוֹן, שֶׁנֶּהֱרַג נְשִׂיאוֹ:

(ח) וְאֵת בִּלְעָם בֶּן בְּעוֹר הָרְגוּ בֶּחָרֶב. בִּיהוֹשֻׁעַ אוֹמֵר "וְאֶת בִּלְעָם בֶּן בְּעוֹר הַקּוֹסֵם {הָרְגוּ בְנֵי יִשְׂרָאֵל בַּחֶרֶב}". מְלַמֵּד שֶׁהֱבִיאוּהוּ לִפְנֵי מֹשֶׁה וְדָנוּהוּ כְּדִין "מְכַשֵּׁפָה לֹא תְחַיֶּה":

"יֵשׁ דֶּרֶךְ יָשָׁר לִפְנֵי אִישׁ, וְאַחֲרִיתָהּ דַּרְכֵי מָוֶת" — "יֵשׁ דֶּרֶךְ יָשָׁר" רָאשֵׁי תֵבוֹת עוֹלֶה כ"ד, וְסוֹפֵי תֵבוֹת שָׂכָר. {שֶׁנָּתְנוּ לוֹ שְׂכַר} כ"ד אֶלֶף שֶׁהִפִּיל מִיִּשְׂרָאֵל בַּעֲצָתוֹ:

BAAL HATURIM ELUCIDATED

5. וַיִּמָּסְרוּ מֵאַלְפֵי יִשְׂרָאֵל — SO THEY WERE DELIVERED, FROM AMONG THE THOUSANDS OF THE CHILDREN OF ISRAEL. This implies that they delivered themselves [prepared to die] for the Sanctification of His Name,[35] for the salvation of Israel.[36]

6. וַיִּשְׁלַח אֹתָם מֹשֶׁה אֶלֶף לַמַּטֶּה לַצָּבָא . . . וְאֶת פִּינְחָס — MOSES SENT THEM, A THOUSAND PER TRIBE FOR THE LEGION . . . AND PHINEHAS. He did not send the tribal leaders with

---

created me." And when we ask, "What is His Name?" it points back to the א, saying, "אָדוֹן, *Lord,* is His Name" (*Yerushalmi, Chagigah* 2:1; *Bereishis Rabbah* 1:10).

Alternatively: The opening א and the closing א each alludes to the single-minded purpose of the warriors. Their respective positions in the verse indicate that the warriors were single-minded from the onset of their mission until its conclusion (*Atros Addar*).

35. *Sifrei.* The term וַיִּמָּסְרוּ could also be understood as implying מְסִירַת נֶפֶשׁ, *self-sacrifice,* thus, וַיִּמָּסְרוּ, *they delivered themselves,* i.e., they were aware of the dangers of going into battle, yet were prepared to deliver their souls in self-sacrifice if they had to.

36. At this point, Israel was not under attack by any enemy. The purpose of this battle was to punish Midian for causing the death of 24,000 Israelites (see v. 2 above). If so, what does the Baal HaTurim mean by "salvation of Israel"? (*Atros Addar*). Indeed, where the Baal HaTurim reads, "for the salvation of Israel," *Sifrei* has, "over this matter"! Perhaps the Baal HaTurim refers to spiritual salvation. If the Midianites were permitted to remain alive, they would hatch other plots to entice Israel into sinning. The warriors went to save Israel's future from this insidious enemy (*VeChur LaZahav*).

Israel shall you send to the legion."
[5] *So they were delivered, from among the thousands of the Children of Israel, a thousand per tribe, twelve thousand armed for the legion.* [6] *Moses sent them — a thousand from each tribe for the legion — them and Phinehas son of Elazar the Kohen to the legion, and the sacred vessels and the trumpets for sounding in his hand.* [7] *They massed against Midian, as HASHEM had commanded Moses, and they killed every male.* [8] *They killed the kings of Midian along with their slain ones: Evi, Rekem, Zur, Hur, and Reba, the five kings of Midian; and Balaam son of Beor they slew with the sword.* [9] *The Children of Israel took captive the women of Midian and their youngsters; and all their cattle and flocks*

BAAL HATURIM ELUCIDATED

them, in order not to embarrass the tribe of Simeon, for its leader had been put to death.[37]

8. וְאֵת בִּלְעָם בֶּן בְּעוֹר הָרְגוּ בֶּחָרֶב — **AND BALAAM SON OF BEOR THEY SLEW WITH THE SWORD.** In the Book of *Joshua* is stated, וְאֶת בִּלְעָם בֶּן בְּעוֹר הַקּוֹסֵם {הָרְגוּ בְנֵי יִשְׂרָאֵל בַּחָרֶב}[38], *and Balaam son of Beor, the sorcerer, {the Children of Israel slew with the sword}* (*Joshua* 13:22). This teaches that they brought him before Moses, who judged him in accordance with the commandment, מְכַשֵּׁפָה לֹא תְחַיֶּה, *You shall not allow a sorceress*[39] *to live* (*Exodus* 22:17).

[King Solomon taught:] יֵשׁ דֶּרֶךְ יָשָׁר לִפְנֵי אִישׁ וְאַחֲרִיתָהּ דַּרְכֵי מָוֶת, *There is a way that seems right to a man, but at its end are the ways of death* (*Proverbs* 14:12; 16:25). The initial letters of יֵשׁ דֶּרֶךְ יָשָׁר have a *gematria* of 24, and the final letters spell שָׂכָר, *reward.* {They gave him a just reward}[40] for causing the death of 24,000 Jews through his advice.[41]

37. The text follows *Shoham Yakar's* manuscript edition and is in accordance with *Paaneach Raza* (25:14 above and 34:19 below) and *Or HaChaim* (34:19 below). After Zimri was put to death, there was never again a נָשִׂיא, *leader,* in the tribe of Simeon (see also the Baal HaTurim to 1:22 above, with note 28).

Virtually all other editions read, שֶׁנֶּהֱרַג נָשִׂיא מִשִּׁבְטוֹ, *for a leader of its tribe had been put to death,* implying that the tribe of Simeon had more than one נָשִׂיא. This is in accordance with *Rashi's* comment at 25:14.

38. This part of the verse from *Joshua* is not found in the early printed editions of the Baal HaTurim, but does appear in some later printed editions and in *Shoham Yakar's* manuscript edition. The verse reads in full: *And Balaam son of Beor, the sorcerer, the Children of Israel slew with the sword, among the [other Midianites who were] slain.*

39. Although that verse speaks of a sorceress, the law applies to a sorcerer as well. The Torah uses the feminine noun because women are more prone to practice sorcery (*Sanhedrin* 67a, cited by *Rashi* to that verse; see also the Baal HaTurim there).

40. The phrase enclosed in braces does not appear in the early printed editions or in many later editions (some of which omit שֶׁנָּתְנוּ לוֹ, but include שָׂכָר). It does appear in *Shoham Yakar's* manuscript edition.

41. *Rabbeinu Ephraim* (*MiKesivah Ashkenazis*); see *Sifrei.*

י וְאֶת־כָּל־חֵילָם בָּזָזוּ׃ וְאֵת כָּל־עָרֵיהֶם֙ בְּמֽוֹשְׁבֹתָ֔ם
יא וְאֵ֖ת כָּל־טִֽירֹתָ֑ם שָׂרְפ֖וּ בָּאֵֽשׁ׃ וַיִּקְחוּ֙ אֶת־כָּל־
יב הַשָּׁלָ֔ל וְאֵ֖ת כָּל־הַמַּלְק֑וֹחַ בָּאָדָ֖ם וּבַבְּהֵמָֽה׃ וַיָּבִ֡אוּ
אֶל־מֹשֶׁה֩ וְאֶל־אֶלְעָזָ֨ר הַכֹּהֵ֜ן וְאֶל־עֲדַ֣ת בְּנֵֽי־
יִשְׂרָאֵ֗ל אֶת־הַשְּׁבִ֛י וְאֶת־הַמַּלְק֥וֹחַ וְאֶת־הַשָּׁלָ֖ל
אֶל־הַֽמַּחֲנֶ֑ה אֶל־עַרְבֹ֣ת מוֹאָ֔ב אֲשֶׁ֖ר עַל־יַרְדֵּ֥ן
שלישי [שני] יג יְרֵחֽוֹ׃ וַיֵּ֨צְא֜וּ מֹשֶׁ֨ה וְאֶלְעָזָ֧ר הַכֹּהֵ֛ן וְכָל־
נְשִׂיאֵ֥י הָעֵדָ֖ה לִקְרָאתָ֑ם אֶל־מִח֖וּץ לַֽמַּחֲנֶֽה׃
יד וַיִּקְצֹ֣ף מֹשֶׁ֔ה עַ֖ל פְּקוּדֵ֣י הֶחָ֑יִל שָׂרֵ֤י הָאֲלָפִים֙ וְשָׂרֵ֣י
טו הַמֵּא֔וֹת הַבָּאִ֖ים מִצְּבָ֥א הַמִּלְחָמָֽה׃ וַיֹּ֥אמֶר אֲלֵיהֶ֖ם
טז מֹשֶׁ֑ה הַֽחִיִּיתֶ֖ם כָּל־נְקֵבָֽה׃ הֵ֣ן הֵ֜נָּה הָי֨וּ לִבְנֵ֤י
יִשְׂרָאֵל֙ בִּדְבַ֣ר בִּלְעָ֔ם לִמְסָר־מַ֥עַל בַּֽיהוָ֖ה עַל־
יז דְּבַר־פְּע֑וֹר וַתְּהִ֥י הַמַּגֵּפָ֖ה בַּעֲדַ֥ת יהוָֽה׃ וְעַתָּ֖ה הִרְג֣וּ
כָל־זָכָ֖ר בַּטָּ֑ף וְכָל־אִשָּׁ֗ה יֹדַ֥עַת אִ֛ישׁ לְמִשְׁכַּ֥ב זָכָ֖ר

בעל הטורים

(יז) ידעת איש. בְּגִימַטְרִיָּא אֵין בְּתוּלֶיהָ חוֹזְרִין׃

❑ **ידעת.** ג׳ בַּמָּסוֹרֶת — ״וְכָל אִשָּׁה יֹדַעַת אִישׁ״; וְאִידָךְ דְּיָבֵשׁ גִּלְעָד ״וְכָל אִשָּׁה יֹדַעַת מִשְׁכַּב זָכָר״; ״נִפְלָאִים מַעֲשֶׂיךָ וְנַפְשִׁי יֹדַעַת מְאֹד״. וְהַיְנוּ דְּאִיתָא בִּיבָמוֹת שֶׁהֶעֱבִירוּם לִפְנֵי צִיץ. כֹּל שֶׁפָּנֶיהָ מוֹרִיקוֹת בְּיָדוּעַ שֶׁנִּבְעֲלָה. וְהַיְנוּ ״נִפְלָאִים מַעֲשֶׂיךָ״, שֶׁעַל יְדֵי נִפְלְאוֹת מַעֲשֶׂיךָ נוֹדַע אִם הִיא יוֹדַעַת אִישׁ׃

❑ **וכל אשה ידעת איש למשכב.** בְּגִימַטְרִיָּא אִם בַּת שָׁלֹשׁ שָׁנִים וְיוֹם אֶחָד׃

BAAL HATURIM ELUCIDATED

17. {The Baal HaTurim's comment to וְכָל אִשָּׁה appears at *Exodus* 35:25.}

❑ **ידעת איש** — WHO KNOWS INTIMACY WITH A MAN. The *gematria* of this phrase (795) is equal to that of אֵין בְּתוּלֶיהָ חוֹזְרִין, *Her signs of virginity do not return.*[42]

❑ **ידעת** — WHO KNOWS. The masoretic note, ג׳, means that this word appears three times in the *Tanach:* (i) here, וְכָל אִשָּׁה יֹדַעַת אִישׁ, *and every woman who knows intimacy with a man;* (ii) with regard to [the execution of the inhabitants of] Jabesh-Gilead, וְכָל אִשָּׁה יֹדַעַת מִשְׁכַּב זָכָר, *and every woman who knows intimacy, lying with a man* (*Judges* 21:11); and (iii) נִפְלָאִים מַעֲשֶׂיךָ וְנַפְשִׁי יֹדַעַת מְאֹד, *Wondrous are Your works, and my soul knows it very well* (*Psalms* 139:14). This [similarity

42. *Peirush HaRokeach.* This means that she is fit to have carnal intimacy with a man, even if she has not actually had such intimacy, i.e., she has reached the age at which signs of virginity would be lost forever if she were to have intimate relations with a man (*Sifrei; Yevamos* 60b; see *Rashi* here). The Talmud states that those signs do not return if she is intimate with a man after her third birthday (*Yevamos* 60b; *Niddah* 45a; see the Baal HaTurim's last comment to this verse).

and all their wealth they took as spoils. 10 *All the cities of*
their habitations and all their palaces they burned in fire.
11 *They took all the booty and all the captives of people and*
animals. 12 *They brought to Moses, and to Elazar the*
Kohen, and to the assembly of the Children of Israel the
captives, the animals, and the booty to the camp, at the
plains of Moab, which was by the Jordan near Jericho.

13 *Moses, Elazar the Kohen, and all the leaders of the*
assembly went out to meet them outside the camp.
14 *Moses was angry with the commanders of the army, the*
officers of the thousands and the officers of the hundreds,
who came from the legion of the battle.

15 *Moses said to them, "Did you let every female live?*
16 *Behold! — it was they who caused the Children of Israel,*
by the word of Balaam, to commit a trespass against
HASHEM regarding the matter of Peor; and the plague oc-
curred in the assembly of HASHEM. 17 *So now, put to death*
every male among the youngsters, and every woman who
knows intimacy with a man, to be lying with a male, you

BAAL HATURIM ELUCIDATED

of expression] alludes to what is taught in tractate *Yevamos:* They [the officers] made the Midianite women pass before the *Tzitz.*[43] Anyone whose face turned sallow had certainly been[44] intimate.[45] Thus, [the connection to the verse,] *Wondrous are Your works,* for through the wonders of Your works it was revealed whether a girl [was fit] to know intimacy with a man.

❑ וְכָל אִשָּׁה יֹדַעַת אִישׁ לְמִשְׁכַּב — **AND EVERY WOMAN WHO KNOWS INTIMACY WITH A MAN, TO BE LYING.** The *gematria* of this phrase (1549) is equivalent[46] to that of אִם בַּת שָׁלֹשׁ שָׁנִים וְיוֹם אֶחָד[47], *If she was three years and one day old*[48] [i.e., she has reached her third birthday].[49]

43. The golden Head-plate of the Kohen Gadol (see *Exodus* 28:37-38).

44. That is, was fit to be intimate (see note 42 above).

45. *Yevamos* 60b.

46. The principle of *im hakollel* allows 1548, the *gematria* of the Baal HaTurim's phrase, to be considered equivalent to 1549.

47. The reading follows *Peirush HaRokeach,* the Baal HaTurim's apparent source, and that reading is also suggested by *Yad Aharon, Shoham Yakar* and *Mekorei Baal HaTurim.* The manuscripts used by *Shoham Yakar,* the early printed editions, as well as many later ones, read: וָהוּ אִם הִיא בַּת ג׳ [=שָׁלֹשׁ] שָׁנִים וְיוֹם א׳ [=אֶחָד], *This applies if she was three years and one day old,* with the two words וָהוּ and הִיא adding 34 to the *gematria* of the phrase. To further complicate matters, those editions all omit the ל of לְמִשְׁכַּב, leaving a gap of 73 between the two *gematriaos. Yosef Daas* and *Ittur Bikkurim,* who never saw the *Peirush HaRokeach,* suggest imaginative emendations that were not generally accepted by the later printers. As a result, the Baal HaTurim's phrase appears in a variety of forms that attempt, usually unsuccessfully, to reconcile the two *gematriaos.*

48. See the Baal HaTurim above, with note 42.

49. *Peirush HaRokeach.*

יח הָרְגוּ: וְכֹל הַטַּף בַּנָּשִׁים אֲשֶׁר לֹא־יָדְעוּ מִשְׁכַּב זָכָר
יט הַחֲיוּ לָכֶם: וְאַתֶּם חֲנוּ מִחוּץ לַמַּחֲנֶה שִׁבְעַת יָמִים
כֹּל הֹרֵג נֶפֶשׁ וְכֹל ׀ נֹגֵעַ בֶּחָלָל תִּתְחַטְּאוּ בַּיּוֹם
כ הַשְּׁלִישִׁי וּבַיּוֹם הַשְּׁבִיעִי אַתֶּם וּשְׁבִיכֶם: וְכָל־
בֶּגֶד וְכָל־כְּלִי־עוֹר וְכָל־מַעֲשֵׂה עִזִּים וְכָל־כְּלִי־עֵץ
כא תִּתְחַטָּאוּ: וַיֹּאמֶר אֶלְעָזָר הַכֹּהֵן אֶל־אַנְשֵׁי הַצָּבָא

בעל הטורים

❑ **וְלֹא נִפְקַד מִמֶּנּוּ אִישׁ.** בְּגִימַטְרִיָּא לַעֲבֵירוֹת:

(יט) חֲנוּ. ב׳ בַּמָּסוֹרֶת — ״חֲנוּ מִחוּץ לַמַּחֲנֶה״; ״חֲנוּ עָלֶיהָ סָבִיב״. פֵּרוּשׁ, אַף עַל פִּי שֶׁאָמַר ״חֲנוּ מִחוּץ לַמַּחֲנֶה״, ״חֲנוּ . . . סָבִיב״, דְּהַיְנוּ בְּמַחֲנֶה לְוִיָּה, כִּדְכְתִיב ״וְהַלְוִיִּם יַחֲנוּ סָבִיב לְמִשְׁכַּן הָעֵדֻת״. דְּטְמֵא מֵת מֻתָּר לִכָּנֵס בְּמַחֲנֶה לְוִיָּה:

(כא) וַיֹּאמֶר אֶלְעָזָר הַכֹּהֵן. מֹשֶׁה דִּבֵּר לְרָאשֵׁי הָאֲלָפִים פָּרָשַׁת טָהֳרָה. וְהֵם לֹא הָיוּ בְיָדָם כְּלֵי מַתָּכוֹת אֶלָּא בְּגָדִים חֲשׁוּבִים. אֲבָל אֶלְעָזָר הַכֹּהֵן דִּבֵּר לְאַנְשֵׁי הַצָּבָא, וְרָאָה בְיָדָם כֵּלִים שֶׁל תַּשְׁמִישׁ הַנִּמְצָאִים בַּבָּתִּים. לְכָךְ הוֹרָה לָהֶם דִּינֵי גִעוּל:

אִי נַמִּי — לְפִי שֶׁהָיְתָה הַהֲזָאָה עַל יָדוֹ, לְכָךְ הוֹרָה לָהֶם גַּם כֵּן דִּינֵי גִעוּל:

BAAL HATURIM ELUCIDATED

❑ וְלֹא נִפְקַד מִמֶּנּוּ אִישׁ[49a] — AND NOT A MAN OF US WAS MISSING. The *gematria* of this phrase (718) is equal to that of לַעֲבֵירוֹת, [*due*] *to sins.*[49b]

19. חֲנוּ — MAKE CAMP. The masoretic note, ב׳, means that this word appears twice in the *Tanach:* (i) here, חֲנוּ מִחוּץ לַמַּחֲנֶה, *Make camp outside the* [*main*] *camp;* and (ii) חֲנוּ עָלֶיהָ סָבִיב, *Make camp against her all around* (*Jeremiah* 50:29). The explanation [for the similarity of expression] is: Although Moses said, *"Make*

49a. Although the rubric of this comment is taken from verse 49 below, and that is where the comment appears in *Shoham Yakar's* manuscript edition, nevertheless, it appears at this point in virtually all other editions. The unusual placement of this comment is explained in note 49b.

49b. *Peirush HaRokeach.* The Talmud (*Yevamos* 61a) records two possible interpretations of the phrase, וְלֹא נִפְקַד מִמֶּנּוּ אִישׁ: It can mean that not a single Israelite was lost in the fighting. Or it can mean that despite the wiles of the Midianite daughters who tried to seduce the Israelite soldiers into sinning with them, not one soldier succumbed to them. By placing the comment at verse 17, which speaks of the woman old enough to have intimate relations with a man, the Baal HaTurim indicates that the allusion supports the second opinion (A.S.).

But according to the manuscripts that place the comment at verse 49, the allusion can also support the first Talmudic opinion. Elsewhere, the Talmud records a dispute concerning the meaning of הַיָּרֵא וְרַךְ הַלֵּבָב, *the fearful and the fainthearted,* who are permitted to return from the battlefield (*Deuteronomy* 20:8). According to one view, that verse is to be taken literally; it refers to one who is afraid to stand in the front lines. According to the other opinion, however, it refers to a person who is apprehensive that, as a consequence of his sins, he will not be afforded Divine protection in battle (*Sotah* 44a, cited by *Rashi*). Thus, the Baal HaTurim's comment teaches that not even one of the twelve thousand men sent to fight Midian had reason to fear, for, as the Baal HaTurim has stated earlier (v. 4 above), these warriors were all totally dedicated to their Father in Heaven (Y.S.).

shall put to death. [18] *But all the youngsters among the women who have not known lying with a male, you may keep alive for yourselves.* [19] *And as for you, make camp outside the [main] camp for a seven-day period; whoever killed a person or touched a corpse shall purify yourselves on the third day and on the seventh day — you and your captives.* [20] *And every garment, every vessel of hide, everything made of that which comes from goats, and every vessel of wood, you shall purify."*

[21] *Elazar the Kohen said to the men of the legion who*

camp outside the [*main*] *camp,"* the intent was [that they] *make camp . . . all around,* i.e., in the Camp of the Levites,[50] as it is written, וְהַלְוִיִּם יַחֲנוּ סָבִיב לְמִשְׁכַּן הָעֵדֻת, *The Levites shall encamp around the Tabernacle of the Testimony* (1:53 above), for one who has contracted *tumah* (impurity) through contact with a corpse[50a] is permitted to enter the Camp of the Levites.

21. וַיֹּאמֶר אֶלְעָזָר הַכֹּהֵן — ELAZAR THE KOHEN SAID. Moses addressed the leaders of the thousands, teaching them the passage regarding purification [of people, garments and wooden utensils after contact with a corpse].[51] [But he did not teach them about *kashering*[52] metal utensils because] they did not have booty of metal utensils in their hands, only valuable garments. Elazar the Kohen, on the other hand, spoke to the warriors and he saw booty of household utensils in their hands. Therefore he instructed them in the laws regarding *kashering* utensils.[53]

Alternatively: Whereas the sprinkling[54] was performed through Elazar,[54a] therefore he instructed them with regard to the laws of *kashering.*[55]

❑ {The Baal HaTurim's other comment to this verse appears at 19:21 above.}

50. In the wilderness, the Israelite encampment was formed by three concentric camps: In the center stood the *Mishkan* (Tabernacle) which, with its Courtyard, was called the מַחֲנֵה שְׁכִינָה, *Camp of the Divine Presence;* surrounding that camp on four sides was the מַחֲנֵה לְוִיָּה, *Camp of the Levites;* and surrounding that was מַחֲנֵה יִשְׂרָאֵל, *Camp of the Israelites.*

Those who have contracted *tumah* through contact with a corpse, such as the warriors who had just returned from the battle against Midian, may not enter the Camp of the Divine Presence, but are permitted to enter the Camp of the Levites and the Camp of the Israelites (*Pesachim* 66b, cited by *Rashi* here and at v. 24 below).

50a. The subject of our verse.

51. Verses 19 and 20 are an abridged version of 19:11-22 above.

52. That is, purging utensils of any remnant of non-kosher foodstuffs — even their intangible taste — that may have adhered to them during cooking. The laws of *kashering* are the subject of verses 21-24.

53. *Peirush HaRokeach;* see also *Rashi* to v. 22.

54. See Ch. 19 above.

54a. Elazar was charged with overseeing the procedure of preparing the ashes of the red cow and the sprinkling waters (19:4 above), a responsibility that included deciding all halachic questions regarding their use.

55. *Pesikta Zutresa* [*Midrash Lekach Tov*] to v. 24.

הַבָּאִים לַמִּלְחָמָה זֹאת חֻקַּת הַתּוֹרָה אֲשֶׁר־צִוָּה יהוה
כב אֶת־מֹשֶׁה: אַךְ אֶת־הַזָּהָב וְאֶת־הַכָּסֶף אֶת־הַנְּחֹשֶׁת
כג אֶת־הַבַּרְזֶל אֶת־הַבְּדִיל וְאֶת־הָעֹפָרֶת: כָּל־דָּבָר
אֲשֶׁר־יָבֹא בָאֵשׁ תַּעֲבִירוּ בָאֵשׁ וְטָהֵר אַךְ בְּמֵי נִדָּה
יִתְחַטָּא וְכֹל אֲשֶׁר לֹא־יָבֹא בָּאֵשׁ תַּעֲבִירוּ בַמָּיִם:
כד וְכִבַּסְתֶּם בִּגְדֵיכֶם בַּיּוֹם הַשְּׁבִיעִי וּטְהַרְתֶּם וְאַחַר
רביעי כה תָּבֹאוּ אֶל־הַמַּחֲנֶה: וַיֹּאמֶר יהוה אֶל־מֹשֶׁה
כו לֵּאמֹר: שָׂא אֵת רֹאשׁ מַלְקוֹחַ הַשְּׁבִי בָּאָדָם וּבַבְּהֵמָה
כז אַתָּה וְאֶלְעָזָר הַכֹּהֵן וְרָאשֵׁי אֲבוֹת הָעֵדָה: וְחָצִיתָ
אֶת־הַמַּלְקוֹחַ בֵּין תֹּפְשֵׂי הַמִּלְחָמָה הַיֹּצְאִים לַצָּבָא
כח וּבֵין כָּל־הָעֵדָה: וַהֲרֵמֹתָ מֶכֶס לַיהוה מֵאֵת אַנְשֵׁי
הַמִּלְחָמָה הַיֹּצְאִים לַצָּבָא אֶחָד נֶפֶשׁ מֵחֲמֵשׁ הַמֵּאוֹת
מִן־הָאָדָם וּמִן־הַבָּקָר וּמִן־הַחֲמֹרִים וּמִן־הַצֹּאן:
כט מִמַּחֲצִיתָם תִּקָּחוּ וְנָתַתָּה לְאֶלְעָזָר הַכֹּהֵן תְּרוּמַת
ל יהוה: וּמִמַּחֲצִת בְּנֵי־יִשְׂרָאֵל תִּקַּח | אֶחָד | אָחֻז

בעל הטורים

(כד) **וּטְהַרְתֶּם.** ב׳ בַּמָּסוֹרֶת – ״וְכִבַּסְתֶּם בִּגְדֵיכֶם בַּיּוֹם הַשְּׁבִיעִי וּטְהַרְתֶּם״; ״וְזָרַקְתִּי עֲלֵיכֶם מַיִם טְהוֹרִים וּטְהַרְתֶּם״. שֶׁעִם הִלְכוֹת גִּעוּל, הוֹרָה לָהֶם גַּם כֵּן טָהֳרַת הַכֵּלִים שֶׁהִיא בְּהַזָּאָה:

(כו) **מַלְקוֹחַ.** ב׳ בַּמָּסוֹרֶת – ״שָׂא אֵת רֹאשׁ מַלְקוֹחַ״; ״הֲיֻקַּח מִגִּבּוֹר מַלְקוֹחַ״. פֵּרוּשׁ, ״הֲיֻקַּח מִגִּבּוֹר מַלְקוֹחַ?״ וְאַתֶּם לְקַחְתֶּם מִגִּבּוֹר מַלְקוֹחַ! לָכֵן ״שָׂא אֵת רֹאשׁ מַלְקוֹחַ״ וְתִתֵּן מִמֶּנּוּ ״מֶכֶס לַה׳ ״:

(ל) **אָחֻז.** ד׳ בַּמָּסוֹרֶת – ״אֶחָד אָחֻז מִן הַחֲמִשִּׁים״; וְאִידָךְ ״אָחֻז לְאֶלְעָזָר וְאָחֻז אָחֻז

BAAL HATURIM ELUCIDATED

23. {The Baal HaTurim's comment to בְּמֵי appears at 19:21 above.}

24. **וּטְהַרְתֶּם** — AND YOU SHALL BECOME PURIFIED. The masoretic note, ב׳, means that this word appears twice in the *Tanach:* (i) here, וְכִבַּסְתֶּם בִּגְדֵיכֶם בַּיּוֹם הַשְּׁבִיעִי וּטְהַרְתֶּם, *You shall immerse your garments on the seventh day and become purified;* and (ii) וְזָרַקְתִּי עֲלֵיכֶם מַיִם טְהוֹרִים וּטְהַרְתֶּם, *Then I will sprinkle pure water upon you, that you may become cleansed* (*Ezekiel* 36:25). [The similarity of expression implies] that together with the laws of *kashering,*[56] Elazar also taught them the laws of purifying utensils [from the impurity contracted by contact with a human corpse] which requires sprinkling.[57]

26. **מַלְקוֹחַ** — SPOILS. The masoretic note, ב׳, means that this word appears twice

56. See note 52 above.

57. See Ch. 19 above.

came to the battle, "This is the decree of the Torah, which
HASHEM commanded Moses: 22 Only the gold and the silver,
the copper, the iron, the tin and the lead — 23 everything that
comes into the fire — you shall pass through the fire and it
will be purified; but it must be purified with the water of
sprinkling; and everything that would not come in the fire,
you shall pass through the water. 24 You shall immerse your
garments on the seventh day and you shall become purified;
afterward you may enter the camp.

25 HASHEM said to Moses, saying: 26 Take a count of the
spoils that were captured, of people and animals, you, Elazar
the Kohen, and the heads of the fathers of the assembly.
27 Divide the spoils in half, between those who undertook the
battle, who go out to the legion, and the entire assembly.
28 You shall raise up a tribute to HASHEM from the men of war
who go out to the legion, one living being of five hundred,
from the people, from the cattle, from the donkeys, and
from the flock. 29 You shall take it from their half and give it
to Elazar the Kohen, as a portion of HASHEM. 30 And from
the half of the Children of Israel you shall take one share

BAAL HATURIM ELUCIDATED

in the *Tanach:* (i) here, שָׂא אֵת רֹאשׁ מַלְקוֹחַ, *take a count of the spoils;* and (ii) הֲיֻקַּח מִגִּבּוֹר מַלְקוֹחַ, *Can spoils be taken from a mighty warrior?* (*Isaiah* 49:24). The explanation [for the similarity of expression] is as follows: [God said,] *"Can spoils be taken from a mighty warrior* [under normal circumstances]? Yet [through My intervention] you have taken spoils from a mighty warrior. Therefore *take a count of the spoils,* and give of them *a tribute unto HASHEM"* (v. 28).

30. אָחֻז — SHARE.[58] The masoretic note,[59] ד׳, means that this word appears four times in the *Tanach:* (i) here, אֶחָד אָחֻז מִן הַחֲמִשִּׁים, *one share from fifty;* (ii-iii) אָחֻז לְאֶלְעָזָר וְאָחֻז אָחֻז לְאִיתָמָר, *a share for Elazar, and a share, a share for*

---

58. The verb root אחז means *to hold, to grasp.* Accordingly, the term אָחֻז (or אָחוּז) can mean *being held, being supported,* or it can refer to something held, such as *a share* or *a portion.* In *Esther,* it has the former meaning (see *Targum* there), while here and in *Chronicles* it has the latter meaning (see *Ibn Ezra* here).

59. At least seven versions of this masoretic note appear in the various manuscripts: (i) ד׳, *Four;* (ii) ד׳ א׳ מָלֵא וג׳ חָסֵר, *Four, one spelled* אָחוּז, *in full* [*with a* ו] *and three spelled* אָחֻז, *defectively* [*without a* ו]; *(iii)* ד׳ וְחַד וְאָחֻז, *Four, and one* [*more*] *with a conjunctive prefix* וְ־; (iv) ד׳ חָסֵר וא׳ מָלֵא, *Four spelled defectively and one spelled in full;* (v) ה׳, *Five;* (vi) ה׳ א׳ מָלֵא, *Five, one spelled in full;* and (vii) ה׳ ג׳ בְּחַד פָּסוּק, *Five, three of them in one verse.*

Nevertheless, the different versions are not at odds with one another. The full spelling אָחוּז appears once; the defective spelling אָחֻז appears three times by itself and a fourth time with the conjunctive prefix וְ־. The masoretic notes that read ד׳, *four,* refer to the appearances without a prefix; those that speak of five include וְאָחֻז. Alternatively: Some of the versions include הָאָחֻז (v. 47 below), but not וְאָחֻז.

מִן־הַחֲמִשִּׁים מִן־הָאָדָם מִן־הַבָּקָר מִן־הַחֲמֹרִים
וּמִן־הַצֹּאן מִכָּל־הַבְּהֵמָה וְנָתַתָּה אֹתָם לַלְוִיִּם שֹׁמְרֵי
לא מִשְׁמֶרֶת מִשְׁכַּן יהוה: וַיַּעַשׂ מֹשֶׁה וְאֶלְעָזָר הַכֹּהֵן
לב כַּאֲשֶׁר צִוָּה יהוה אֶת־מֹשֶׁה: וַיְהִי הַמַּלְקוֹחַ יֶתֶר
הַבָּז אֲשֶׁר בָּזְזוּ עַם הַצָּבָא צֹאן שֵׁשׁ־מֵאוֹת אֶלֶף
לג וְשִׁבְעִים אֶלֶף וַחֲמֵשֶׁת אֲלָפִים: וּבָקָר שְׁנַיִם וְשִׁבְעִים
לד־לה אָלֶף: וַחֲמֹרִים אֶחָד וְשִׁשִּׁים אָלֶף: וְנֶפֶשׁ אָדָם
מִן־הַנָּשִׁים אֲשֶׁר לֹא־יָדְעוּ מִשְׁכַּב זָכָר כָּל־נֶפֶשׁ
לו שְׁנַיִם וּשְׁלֹשִׁים אָלֶף: וַתְּהִי הַמֶּחֱצָה חֵלֶק הַיֹּצְאִים
בַּצָּבָא מִסְפַּר הַצֹּאן שְׁלֹשׁ־מֵאוֹת אֶלֶף וּשְׁלֹשִׁים
לז אֶלֶף וְשִׁבְעַת אֲלָפִים וַחֲמֵשׁ מֵאוֹת: וַיְהִי הַמֶּכֶס
לח לַיהוה מִן־הַצֹּאן שֵׁשׁ מֵאוֹת חָמֵשׁ וְשִׁבְעִים: וְהַבָּקָר
שִׁשָּׁה וּשְׁלֹשִׁים אָלֶף וּמִכְסָם לַיהוה שְׁנַיִם וְשִׁבְעִים:
לט וַחֲמֹרִים שְׁלֹשִׁים אֶלֶף וַחֲמֵשׁ מֵאוֹת וּמִכְסָם לַיהוה
מ אֶחָד וְשִׁשִּׁים: וְנֶפֶשׁ אָדָם שִׁשָּׁה עָשָׂר אָלֶף וּמִכְסָם
מא לַיהוה שְׁנַיִם וּשְׁלֹשִׁים נָפֶשׁ: וַיִּתֵּן מֹשֶׁה אֶת־מֶכֶס
תְּרוּמַת יהוה לְאֶלְעָזָר הַכֹּהֵן כַּאֲשֶׁר צִוָּה יהוה
חמישי מב אֶת־מֹשֶׁה: וּמִמַּחֲצִית בְּנֵי יִשְׂרָאֵל אֲשֶׁר חָצָה מֹשֶׁה
מג מִן־הָאֲנָשִׁים הַצֹּבְאִים: וַתְּהִי מֶחֱצַת הָעֵדָה מִן־
הַצֹּאן שְׁלֹשׁ־מֵאוֹת אֶלֶף וּשְׁלֹשִׁים אֶלֶף שִׁבְעַת

בעל הטורים

"לְאִיתָמָר", בְּדִבְרֵי הַיָּמִים בְּעִנְיַן הַמִּשְׁמָרוֹת; "חוּר כַּרְפַּס וּתְכֵלֶת אָחוּז". בִּשְׁבִיל שֶׁנַּעֲשׂוּ מִשְׁמָרוֹת לַעֲמֹד עַל הַשִּׁיר, נָטְלוּ אֶחָד אָחוּז מִן הַחֲמִשִּׁים. "כַּרְפַּס וּתְכֵלֶת אָחוּז", מְלַמֵּד שֶׁאַף עַל פִּי שֶׁלֹּא נִצְטַוּוּ לִתֵּן מֶכֶס אֶלָּא מִן הָאָדָם וְהַבְּהֵמָה, מֵעַצְמָם נָתְנוּ מִבִּזַּת הַמִּטַּלְטְלִין, דְּיָלְפִינַן "אָחֻז" דְּהָכָא מֵ"אָחוּז" דְּהָתָם:

BAAL HATURIM ELUCIDATED

Ithamar, in *Chronicles* (*I* 24:6) with regard to the priestly watches; and [with a different meaning,] (iv) חוּר כַּרְפַּס וּתְכֵלֶת אָחוּז, [*hangings of*] *white, green, and turquoise being held . . .* (*Esther* 1:6). [The similarity of expression indicates that] because they were made [members of the] watches[60] that would stand in song[61] [at

60. These watches are alluded to in our verse, for the phrase שֹׁמְרֵי מִשְׁמֶרֶת may be understood as *keepers of the watch.*

61. The Talmud (*Taanis* 26a-27b) teaches that the early prophets — King David and the prophet Samuel — established twenty-four מִשְׁמָרוֹת כְּהֻנָּה,

from fifty, from the people, from the cattle, from the
donkeys, from the flock — from all the animals — and you
shall give them to the Levites, the guardians of the charge of
HASHEM's Tabernacle.

31 *Moses and Elazar the Kohen did as HASHEM had*
commanded Moses. 32 *The animal booty, beyond the spoils*
that the people of the legion looted: the flock, six hundred
and seventy-five thousand; 33 *and cattle, seventy-two thou-*
sand; 34 *and donkeys, sixty-one thousand;* 35 *and human*
beings, the women who had not known lying with a male,
all the souls, thirty-two thousand. 36 *The half, which was the*
share of those who went out to the legion, was: the count of
the flock, three hundred and thirty-seven thousand, five
hundred — 37 *the tribute of HASHEM from the flock, six*
hundred and seventy-five; 38 *and the cattle, thirty-six thou-*
sand — and their tribute to HASHEM, seventy-two; 39 *and the*
donkeys, thirty thousand, five hundred — and their tribute
to HASHEM, sixty-one; 40 *and the human beings, sixteen*
thousand — and their tribute to HASHEM, thirty-two people.
41 *Moses gave the tribute that was raised up for HASHEM to*
Elazar the Kohen, as HASHEM had commanded Moses.

42 *From the half of the Children of Israel that Moses had*
divided from the men of the legions, 43 *the half of the*
assembly was: of the flock, three hundred and thirty-seven

BAAL HATURIM ELUCIDATED

the daily *tamid* offerings], they were granted a one-fiftieth share [of the spoils].[62]

[The use of the word אָחוּז in the verse,] *hangings of white, green and turquoise,* אָחוּז, *being held . . .*, teaches that even though they were not commanded to give tribute from any spoils other than from the humans and the animals, nevertheless, on their own initiative they volunteered to give tribute from the inanimate chattel. For we interpret the word אָחֻז in our verse [as a reference to nonliving chattel], similar to the word אָחוּז in *Esther* [which refers to curtains].[63]

---

priestly watches, to scrupulously perform the Temple service, and twenty-four מִשְׁמְרוֹת לְוִיָּה, *Levite watches,* consisting of the gatekeepers and the orchestra. The "watches" would serve in a regular rotation so that each watch would serve once every twenty-four weeks. The formation of the watches of the First Temple along with their names and order of rotation appear in *I Chronicles:* the watches of Kohanim in 24:1-19; the Levite watches in 24:20-25:31.

62. The Baal HaTurim does not explain how the fraction one-fiftieth pertains to the Levite watches. Perhaps that number is related to the fact that each watch would serve a week at a time, that is, one-fiftieth of the lunar year (A.S.).

63. The Baal HaTurim's source for this comment is unknown. Although *Rashi* (to v. 32 below) mentions that there was inanimate chattel among the spoils, he does not state that any part of them was given to the Levites.

לא/מד־לב/א

מד אַלְפַּיִם וַחֲמֵשׁ מֵאוֹת: וּבָקָר שִׁשָּׁה וּשְׁלֹשִׁים אָלֶף:
מה-מו וַחֲמֹרִים שְׁלֹשִׁים אֶלֶף וַחֲמֵשׁ מֵאוֹת: וְנֶפֶשׁ אָדָם
מז שִׁשָּׁה עָשָׂר אָלֶף: וַיִּקַּח מֹשֶׁה מִמַּחֲצִת בְּנֵי־יִשְׂרָאֵל
אֶת־הָאָחֻז אֶחָד מִן־הַחֲמִשִּׁים מִן־הָאָדָם וּמִן־
הַבְּהֵמָה וַיִּתֵּן אֹתָם לַלְוִיִּם שֹׁמְרֵי מִשְׁמֶרֶת מִשְׁכַּן
מח יהוה כַּאֲשֶׁר צִוָּה יהוה אֶת־מֹשֶׁה: וַיִּקְרְבוּ אֶל־
מֹשֶׁה הַפְּקֻדִים אֲשֶׁר לְאַלְפֵי הַצָּבָא שָׂרֵי הָאֲלָפִים
מט וְשָׂרֵי הַמֵּאוֹת: וַיֹּאמְרוּ אֶל־מֹשֶׁה עֲבָדֶיךָ נָשְׂאוּ
אֶת־רֹאשׁ אַנְשֵׁי הַמִּלְחָמָה אֲשֶׁר בְּיָדֵנוּ וְלֹא־נִפְקַד
נ מִמֶּנּוּ אִישׁ: וַנַּקְרֵב אֶת־קָרְבַּן יהוה אִישׁ אֲשֶׁר מָצָא
כְלִי־זָהָב אֶצְעָדָה וְצָמִיד טַבַּעַת עָגִיל וְכוּמָז לְכַפֵּר
נא עַל־נַפְשֹׁתֵינוּ לִפְנֵי יהוה: וַיִּקַּח מֹשֶׁה וְאֶלְעָזָר הַכֹּהֵן
נב אֶת־הַזָּהָב מֵאִתָּם כֹּל כְּלִי מַעֲשֶׂה: וַיְהִי ׀ כָּל־זְהַב
הַתְּרוּמָה אֲשֶׁר הֵרִימוּ לַיהוה שִׁשָּׁה עָשָׂר אֶלֶף
שְׁבַע־מֵאוֹת וַחֲמִשִּׁים שָׁקֶל מֵאֵת שָׂרֵי הָאֲלָפִים
נג וּמֵאֵת שָׂרֵי הַמֵּאוֹת: אַנְשֵׁי הַצָּבָא בָּזְזוּ אִישׁ לוֹ:
נד וַיִּקַּח מֹשֶׁה וְאֶלְעָזָר הַכֹּהֵן אֶת־הַזָּהָב מֵאֵת שָׂרֵי
הָאֲלָפִים וְהַמֵּאוֹת וַיָּבִאוּ אֹתוֹ אֶל־אֹהֶל מוֹעֵד
זִכָּרוֹן לִבְנֵי־יִשְׂרָאֵל לִפְנֵי יהוה:
לב ששי [שלישי] א וּמִקְנֶה ׀ רַב הָיָה לִבְנֵי רְאוּבֵן וְלִבְנֵי־גָד עָצוּם מְאֹד

בעל הטורים

לב (א) וּמִקְנֶה רַב הָיָה לִבְנֵי רְאוּבֵן וְלִבְנֵי גָד — הִקְדִּים רְאוּבֵן. "וַיֹּאמֶר בְּנֵי גָד וּבְנֵי רְאוּבֵן" — הִקְדִּים בְּנֵי גָד. אֶלָּא תְּחִלָּה הִקְדִּים רְאוּבֵן שֶׁהָיָה הַגָּדוֹל, וְאַחַר כָּךְ הִקְדִּים גָּד, שֶׁהָיוּ גִבּוֹרִים וַהֲרוּגֵיהֶם נִכָּרִים, דִּכְתִיב "וְטָרַף זְרוֹעַ אַף קָדְקֹד".

BAAL HATURIM ELUCIDATED

49. {The Baal HaTurim's comment to וְלֹא נִפְקַד מִמֶּנּוּ אִישׁ appears at verse 17 above.}

50. {The Baal HaTurim's comment to וַנַּקְרֵב אֶת קָרְבַּן ה׳ appears at 30:2 above.}

XXXII.

1. וּמִקְנֶה רַב הָיָה לִבְנֵי רְאוּבֵן וְלִבְנֵי גָד — THERE WAS A GREAT AMOUNT OF LIVESTOCK BELONGING TO THE CHILDREN OF REUBEN AND THE CHILDREN OF GAD. [This verse] placed *the children of Reuben* first. [Another verse], **וַיֹּאמֶר בְּנֵי גָד וּבְנֵי רְאוּבֵן**, *the*

thousand, five hundred — 44 *and the cattle, thirty-six thousand;* 45 *and the donkeys, thirty thousand five hundred;* 46 *and the human beings, sixteen thousand.* 47 *Moses took from the half of the Children of Israel the one drawn from the fifty, from the people and the animals, and gave them to the Levites, the guardians of the charge of* HASHEM*'s Tabernacle, as* HASHEM *had commanded Moses.*

48 *The commanders of the thousands in the legions, the officers of the thousands and the officers of the hundreds, approached Moses.* 49 *They said to Moses, "Your servants took a census of the men of war under our command, and not a man of us was missing.* 50 *So we have brought an offering for* HASHEM*: what any man found of gold vessels, anklet and bracelet, ring, earring and clasp, to atone for our souls before* HASHEM*."* 51 *Moses and Elazar the Kohen took the gold from them, every fashioned vessel.* 52 *All the gold that was raised up, which they set apart for* HASHEM*, was sixteen thousand, seven hundred and fifty shekel, from the officers of the thousands and the officers of the hundreds.* 53 *As for the men of the legion, each man looted for himself.* 54 *Moses and Elazar the Kohen took the gold from the officers of the thousands and the hundreds and brought it to the Tent of Meeting, a remembrance for the Children of Israel before* HASHEM*.*

32 1 *There was a great amount of livestock belonging to the children of Reuben and the children of Gad — very great.*

BAAL HATURIM ELUCIDATED

children of Gad and the children of Reuben said . . . (v. 25 below), placed *the children of Gad* first.[64] Our passage placed Reuben first, for he was the older brother. After that, it placed Gad first, because its men were mighty warriors whose victims were identifiable, as it is written, וְטָרַף זְרוֹעַ אַף קָדְקֹד, *he would tear off an arm as well as a head*[65] *(Deuteronomy* 33:20).[66]

64. It is not clear why the Baal HaTurim assigned this comment to verse 25, when two earlier verses (2 and 6) also mention Gad's tribe before Reuben's.

It is noteworthy that the early printed editions read וַיֹּאמְרוּ בְּנֵי גָד וּבְנֵי רְאוּבֵן, using the plural וַיֹּאמְרוּ in place of the singular וַיֹּאמֶר of verse 25. Perhaps the Baal HaTurim's comment originally adduced verse 2, וַיָּבֹאוּ בְּנֵי גָד וּבְנֵי רְאוּבֵן וַיֹּאמְרוּ, which a copyist inadvertently miswrote as ויאמרו בני גד . . . But whereas no such verse exists, a later copyist "corrected" that verse by dropping the final ו, leaving ויאמר (*VeChur LaZahav*).

65. *Rashi* to that verse explains: Those whom they killed were identifiable, for they would cut off the head and the arm [of their opponent in battle] with a single mighty blow. (See also *Rashi* to v. 17 above, s.v., לפני בני ישראל.)

66. *Peirush HaRokeach.*

וַיִּרְאוּ אֶת־אֶרֶץ יַעְזֵר וְאֶת־אֶרֶץ גִּלְעָד וְהִנֵּה
ב הַמָּקוֹם מְקוֹם מִקְנֶה: וַיָּבֹאוּ בְנֵי־גָד וּבְנֵי רְאוּבֵן
וַיֹּאמְרוּ אֶל־מֹשֶׁה וְאֶל־אֶלְעָזָר הַכֹּהֵן וְאֶל־נְשִׂיאֵי
ג הָעֵדָה לֵאמֹר: עֲטָרוֹת וְדִיבֹן וְיַעְזֵר וְנִמְרָה וְחֶשְׁבּוֹן
ד וְאֶלְעָלֵה וּשְׂבָם וּנְבוֹ וּבְעֹן: הָאָרֶץ אֲשֶׁר הִכָּה יהוה
לִפְנֵי עֲדַת יִשְׂרָאֵל אֶרֶץ מִקְנֶה הִוא וְלַעֲבָדֶיךָ
ה מִקְנֶה: וַיֹּאמְרוּ אִם־מָצָאנוּ חֵן בְּעֵינֶיךָ יֻתַּן אֶת־
הָאָרֶץ הַזֹּאת לַעֲבָדֶיךָ לַאֲחֻזָּה אַל־תַּעֲבִרֵנוּ אֶת־
ו הַיַּרְדֵּן: וַיֹּאמֶר מֹשֶׁה לִבְנֵי־גָד וְלִבְנֵי רְאוּבֵן
ז הַאַחֵיכֶם יָבֹאוּ לַמִּלְחָמָה וְאַתֶּם תֵּשְׁבוּ פֹה: וְלָמָּה
°תנואון אֶת־לֵב בְּנֵי יִשְׂרָאֵל מֵעֲבֹר אֶל־הָאָרֶץ [תְנִיאוּן ק׳]
ח אֲשֶׁר־נָתַן לָהֶם יהוה: כֹּה עָשׂוּ אֲבֹתֵיכֶם בְּשָׁלְחִי
ט אֹתָם מִקָּדֵשׁ בַּרְנֵעַ לִרְאוֹת אֶת־הָאָרֶץ: וַיַּעֲלוּ
עַד־נַחַל אֶשְׁכּוֹל וַיִּרְאוּ אֶת־הָאָרֶץ וַיָּנִיאוּ אֶת־לֵב
בְּנֵי יִשְׂרָאֵל לְבִלְתִּי־בֹא אֶל־הָאָרֶץ אֲשֶׁר־נָתַן
י לָהֶם יהוה: וַיִּחַר־אַף יהוה בַּיּוֹם הַהוּא וַיִּשָּׁבַע
יא לֵאמֹר: אִם־יִרְאוּ הָאֲנָשִׁים הָעֹלִים מִמִּצְרַיִם מִבֶּן
עֶשְׂרִים שָׁנָה וָמַעְלָה אֵת הָאֲדָמָה אֲשֶׁר נִשְׁבַּעְתִּי
לְאַבְרָהָם לְיִצְחָק וּלְיַעֲקֹב כִּי לֹא־מִלְאוּ אַחֲרָי:
יב בִּלְתִּי כָּלֵב בֶּן־יְפֻנֶּה הַקְּנִזִּי וִיהוֹשֻׁעַ בִּן־נוּן כִּי מִלְאוּ
יג אַחֲרֵי יהוה: וַיִּחַר־אַף יהוה בְּיִשְׂרָאֵל וַיְנִעֵם

בעל הטורים

❑ ח׳ פְּעָמִים הֻזְכְּרוּ בְּנֵי גָד וּבְנֵי רְאוּבֵן בְּפָרָשָׁה זוֹ – וְזֶהוּ "נַחֲלָה מְבֹהֶלֶת בָּרִאשׁוֹנָה, וְאַחֲרִיתָהּ לֹא תְבֹרָךְ". "מְבֹחֶלֶת" כְּתִיב בְּחֵי"ת, בִּשְׁבִיל ח׳ פְּעָמִים שֶׁהֻזְכְּרוּ עַל נַחֲלָתָן לִקַּח בָּרִאשׁוֹנָה. "אַחֲרִיתָהּ לֹא תְבֹרָךְ", שֶׁגָּלוּ ח׳ שָׁנִים קֹדֶם לִשְׁאָר הַשְּׁבָטִים:

BAAL HATURIM ELUCIDATED

❑ The children of Gad and the children of Reuben are mentioned eight times in this passage.[67] This is [what is stated in the verse,] נַחֲלָה מְבֹהֶלֶת[68] בָּרִאשׁוֹנָה וְאַחֲרִיתָהּ

67. They are mentioned together seven times, in verses 1, 2, 6, 25, 29, 31 and 33. Each tribe is mentioned one more time, Gad in verse 34 and Reuben in verse 37.

68. This word appears in the verse as a קְרִי וּכְתִיב, *keri uchesiv,* i.e., it is spelled one way, but pronounced differently. In this case, the *kesiv* (spelling) is מְבֹחֶלֶת, *disgusting,* while the *keri*

They saw the land of Jazer and the land of Gilead, and behold! — the place was a place for livestock. ²*The children of Gad and the children of Reuben came and said to Moses, to Elazar the Kohen, and to the leaders of the assembly, saying,* ³*"Ataroth, and Dibon, and Jazer, and Nimrah, and Heshbon, and Elealeh, and Sebam, and Nebo and Beon —* ⁴*the land that HASHEM smote before the assembly of Israel — it is a land for livestock, and your servants have livestock."*

⁵*They said, "If we have found favor in your eyes, let this land be given to your servants as a heritage; do not bring us across the Jordan."*

⁶*Moses said to the children of Gad and the children of Reuben, "Shall your brothers go out to battle while you settle here?* ⁷*Why do you dissuade the heart of the Children of Israel from crossing to the land that HASHEM has given them?* ⁸*This is what your fathers did, when I sent them from Kadesh-barnea to see the land.* ⁹*They went up to the valley of Eshcol and saw the land and they dissuaded the heart of the Children of Israel, not to come to the land that HASHEM has given them.* ¹⁰*The wrath of HASHEM burned on that day, and He swore saying,* ¹¹*'If these men who came up from Egypt — from the age of twenty years and above — will see the ground that I swore to Abraham, to Isaac and to Jacob . . . for they have not followed Me fully,* ¹²*except for Caleb son of Jephunneh, the Kenizzite, and Joshua son of Nun, for they followed HASHEM fully.'* ¹³*The wrath of HASHEM burned against Israel and He made them wander*

BAAL HATURIM ELUCIDATED

לֹא תְבֹרָךְ, *An inheritance taken hastily at its beginning, will not be blessed at its end* (*Proverbs* 20:21). [Although the word is pronounced מְבֹהֶלֶת, with a ה] it is spelled מְבֹחֶלֶת[68], with a ח (=8), alluding to the eight times that these [two tribes] are mentioned regarding their inheritance, which they were the first [among the tribes] to take.[69] [As a consequence,] *it was not blessed at its end,* for these [two tribes] were exiled [from their inheritance] eight years before[70] the other tribes.[71]

4. {The Baal HaTurim's comment to וְלַעֲבָדֶיךָ appears at *Exodus* 8:5.}

(pronunciation) is מְבֹהֶלֶת, *hasty.*

69. They were hasty in requesting their inheritance before any of the other tribes had been granted theirs.

70. See *Rashi* to *Isaiah* 8:23.

71. *Peirush HaRokeach;* see *Rashi* to *Proverbs* 20:21.

בַּמִּדְבָּר אַרְבָּעִים שָׁנָה עַד־תֹּם כָּל־הַדּוֹר הָעֹשֶׂה
יד הָרַע בְּעֵינֵי יהוה׃ וְהִנֵּה קַמְתֶּם תַּחַת אֲבֹתֵיכֶם
תַּרְבּוּת אֲנָשִׁים חַטָּאִים לִסְפּוֹת עוֹד עַל חֲרוֹן אַף־
טו יהוה אֶל־יִשְׂרָאֵל׃ כִּי תְשׁוּבֻן מֵאַחֲרָיו וְיָסַף עוֹד
טז לְהַנִּיחוֹ בַּמִּדְבָּר וְשִׁחַתֶּם לְכָל־הָעָם הַזֶּה׃ וַיִּגְּשׁוּ
אֵלָיו וַיֹּאמְרוּ גִּדְרֹת צֹאן נִבְנֶה לְמִקְנֵנוּ פֹּה וְעָרִים
יז לְטַפֵּנוּ׃ וַאֲנַחְנוּ נֵחָלֵץ חֻשִׁים לִפְנֵי בְּנֵי יִשְׂרָאֵל עַד
אֲשֶׁר אִם־הֲבִיאֹנֻם אֶל־מְקוֹמָם וְיָשַׁב טַפֵּנוּ בְּעָרֵי
יח הַמִּבְצָר מִפְּנֵי יֹשְׁבֵי הָאָרֶץ׃ לֹא נָשׁוּב אֶל־בָּתֵּינוּ
יט עַד הִתְנַחֵל בְּנֵי יִשְׂרָאֵל אִישׁ נַחֲלָתוֹ׃ כִּי לֹא נִנְחַל
אִתָּם מֵעֵבֶר לַיַּרְדֵּן וָהָלְאָה כִּי בָאָה נַחֲלָתֵנוּ אֵלֵינוּ
מֵעֵבֶר הַיַּרְדֵּן מִזְרָחָה׃
שביעי [רביעי] כ וַיֹּאמֶר אֲלֵיהֶם מֹשֶׁה אִם־תַּעֲשׂוּן אֶת־הַדָּבָר הַזֶּה
כא אִם־תֵּחָלְצוּ לִפְנֵי יהוה לַמִּלְחָמָה׃ וְעָבַר לָכֶם כָּל־
חָלוּץ אֶת־הַיַּרְדֵּן לִפְנֵי יהוה עַד הוֹרִישׁוֹ אֶת־אֹיְבָיו
כב מִפָּנָיו׃ וְנִכְבְּשָׁה הָאָרֶץ לִפְנֵי יהוה וְאַחַר תָּשֻׁבוּ

בעל הטורים

(יז) חֻשִׁים. ב׳ בַּמָּסוֹרֶת, מִתְּרֵי לִישָׁנֵי – "וַאֲנַחְנוּ נֵחָלֵץ חֻשִׁים"; וְאִידָךְ "וּבְנֵי דָן חֻשִׁים". וְהַיְנוּ דְאִיתָא בְּפֶרֶק מִי שֶׁמֵּת, וְדִלְמָא כְּחוּשִׁים שֶׁל קָנֶה. פֵּרוּשׁ, הַרְבֵּה קָנִים יוֹצְאִים מִשֹּׁרֶשׁ אֶחָד וּלְמַעְלָה נִפְרָדִים זֶה מִזֶּה. כָּךְ פֵּרוּשׁ: נֵחָלֵץ כְּמוֹ חוּשִׁים שֶׁל קָנֶה שֶׁנֶּאֱחָזִים זֶה בָּזֶה. כָּךְ נֵחָלֵץ לַמִּלְחָמָה. כִּי כֵן דֶּרֶךְ הַנִּלְחָמִים לְהִתְקָרֵב זֶה אֶל זֶה, כְּדֵי שֶׁלֹּא יַפְרִידוּם הָאוֹיְבִים:

(כ) לִפְנֵי ה׳. בַּפָּרָשָׁה שֶׁבַע פְּעָמִים, כְּנֶגֶד שֶׁבַע שָׁנִים שֶׁל כִּבּוּשׁ:

BAAL HATURIM ELUCIDATED

17. חֻשִׁים — SWIFTLY. The masoretic note, ב׳ מִתְּרֵי לִישָׁנֵי, means that this word appears twice in the *Tanach,* with two different meanings: (i) here [as an adverb], וַאֲנַחְנוּ נֵחָלֵץ חֻשִׁים, *we shall arm ourselves swiftly;* and (ii) [as a proper noun,] וּבְנֵי דָן חֻשִׁים, *Dan's sons: Hushim* (*Genesis* 46:23).[72] And this [similarity of expression] alludes to that which is taught in chapter *Mi Shemais*[73]: Perhaps [Dan's offspring were] like חוּשִׁים, *clusters of reeds.*[74] That is, many reeds emerge [packed in a dense mass] from a single root base, but at their tops split into individual reeds.

72. The Baal HaTurim makes this same comment at that verse.

73. The ninth chapter of tractate *Bava Basra.*

74. Although this usage does not appear elsewhere in the *Tanach,* the Talmud (*Bava Basra* 143b) interprets the name חֻשִׁים as an allusion to חוּשִׁים of reeds, which *Rashi* translates into Old French as *troches,* "clusters."

in the wilderness for forty years, until the end of the entire
generation that did evil in the eyes of HASHEM. 14 *Behold! —*
you have risen up in place of your fathers, a society of sinful
people, to add more to the burning wrath of HASHEM *against*
Israel. 15 *For if you will turn away from after Him, He will*
again let it rest in the wilderness, and you will destroy this
entire people."

16 *They approached him and said, "Pens for the flock*
shall we build here for our livestock and cities for our
youngsters. 17 *We shall arm ourselves swiftly in the van-*
guard of the Children of Israel until we will have brought
them to their place, and our youngsters will dwell in the
fortified cities before the inhabitants of the land. 18 *We shall*
not return to our homes until the Children of Israel will have
inherited — every man his inheritance — 19 *for we shall not*
inherit with them across the Jordan and beyond, for our
inheritance has come to us on the east bank of the Jordan."

20 *Moses said to them, "If you do this thing, if you arm*
yourselves before HASHEM *for the battle,* 21 *and every armed*
man among you shall cross the Jordan before HASHEM, *until*
He drives out His enemies before Him, 22 *and the land will*
be conquered before HASHEM, *and then you shall return —*

BAAL HATURIM ELUCIDATED

Thus, [the Danites and the Reubenites were saying,] *"We will arm ourselves like clusters of reeds,* clinging to one another.[75] That is how we will arm ourselves for battle." For it is the manner of warriors to group themselves together so that the enemies will not separate them.[76]

20. לִפְנֵי ה׳ — BEFORE HASHEM. [This phrase appears] seven times in our passage,[77] corresponding to the seven years of conquest [of the Land of Canaan].[78]

21. {The Baal HaTurim's comment, s.v., חָלוּץ, that appears at this point in most editions, is presented at verse 27 below, s.v., חָלוּץ; see note 80 there.}

75. *Bava Basra* 143b.

76. *Maharam MiRothenburg.*

77. In verses 20, 21, 22 (twice), 27, 29 and 32.

78. *Rashi* (v. 24) points out that the tribes of Gad and Reuven actually remained in the Land of Canaan for fourteen years. For Moses imposed the condition וְנִכְבְּשָׁה הָאָרֶץ, *and the land will be conquered* (v. 22), but the two tribes had already accepted a more strident condition upon themselves, עַד הִתְנַחֵל בְּנֵי יִשְׂרָאֵל, *until the Children of Israel will have inherited* (v. 18). If so, why does the Baal HaTurim speak of only seven years? Perhaps the Baal HaTurim understands the term לִפְנֵי ה׳, literally, *before* HASHEM, in the manner of *Targum Onkelos,* who [six of the seven times] paraphrases, קֳדָם עַמָּא דַיְיָ, *before the people of* HASHEM. Accordingly, that phrase refers to the time during which Gad and Reuben were before, i.e., in front of Israel, leading the battle against the Canaanite inhabitants of the land — a total of seven years (Y.S.).

וִהְיִיתֶם נְקִיִּם מֵיהוָה וּמִיִּשְׂרָאֵל וְהָיְתָה הָאָרֶץ
כג הַזֹּאת לָכֶם לַאֲחֻזָּה לִפְנֵי יהוָה: וְאִם־לֹא תַעֲשׂוּן
כֵּן הִנֵּה חֲטָאתֶם לַיהוָה וּדְעוּ חַטַּאתְכֶם אֲשֶׁר
כד תִּמְצָא אֶתְכֶם: בְּנוּ־לָכֶם עָרִים לְטַפְּכֶם וּגְדֵרֹת
כה לְצֹנַאֲכֶם וְהַיֹּצֵא מִפִּיכֶם תַּעֲשׂוּ: וַיֹּאמֶר בְּנֵי־גָד
וּבְנֵי רְאוּבֵן אֶל־מֹשֶׁה לֵאמֹר עֲבָדֶיךָ יַעֲשׂוּ כַּאֲשֶׁר
כו אֲדֹנִי מְצַוֶּה: טַפֵּנוּ נָשֵׁינוּ מִקְנֵנוּ וְכָל־בְּהֶמְתֵּנוּ
כז יִהְיוּ־שָׁם בְּעָרֵי הַגִּלְעָד: וַעֲבָדֶיךָ יַעַבְרוּ כָּל־חֲלוּץ
צָבָא לִפְנֵי יהוָה לַמִּלְחָמָה כַּאֲשֶׁר אֲדֹנִי דֹּבֵר:
כח וַיְצַו לָהֶם מֹשֶׁה אֵת אֶלְעָזָר הַכֹּהֵן וְאֵת יְהוֹשֻׁעַ
בִּן־נוּן וְאֶת־רָאשֵׁי אֲבוֹת הַמַּטּוֹת לִבְנֵי יִשְׂרָאֵל:
כט וַיֹּאמֶר מֹשֶׁה אֲלֵהֶם אִם־יַעַבְרוּ בְנֵי־גָד וּבְנֵי־
רְאוּבֵן ׀ אִתְּכֶם אֶת־הַיַּרְדֵּן כָּל־חָלוּץ לַמִּלְחָמָה
לִפְנֵי יהוָה וְנִכְבְּשָׁה הָאָרֶץ לִפְנֵיכֶם וּנְתַתֶּם לָהֶם

בעל הטורים

(כה) וַיֹּאמֶר בְּנֵי גָד. הָיָה לוֹ לוֹמַר ״וַיֹּאמְרוּ״. אֶלָּא הַגָּדוֹל שֶׁבָּהֶם דִּבֵּר בִּשְׁבִיל כֻּלָּם:

(כז) חֲלוּץ. ב׳ בַּמָּסוֹרֶת – ״כָּל חֲלוּץ {צָבָא}״; ״חֲלוּץ הַנָּעַל״. וְהַיְנוּ דְּאָמְרִינָן, כָּל הַיּוֹצֵא לְמִלְחֶמֶת בֵּית דָּוִד, גֵּט כְּרִיתוּת כּוֹתֵב לְאִשְׁתּוֹ, שֶׁלֹּא תִזָּקֵק לַיָּבָם וְלֹא תִצְטָרֵךְ לַחֲלֹץ נַעַל הַיָּבָם. וְשָׁמְעִינַן מִכָּאן שֶׁגַּם מֹשֶׁה עָשָׂה כֵן, וּמִמֶּנּוּ לָמַד דָּוִד. וְזֶהוּ ״כָּל חָלוּץ {צָבָא}״, פֵּרוּשׁ, ״חֲלוּץ הַנָּעַל״:

BAAL HATURIM ELUCIDATED

25. וַיֹּאמֶר בְּנֵי גָד — THE CHILDREN OF GAD SAID. The verse should have used [the plural form] וַיֹּאמְרוּ, *they said* [rather than the singular form וַיֹּאמֶר, *he said*]. [The singular indicates that] the senior representative of the two tribes spoke on behalf of all of them.[79]

27. חֲלוּץ[80] — ARMED. The masoretic note,[81] ב׳, means that this word appears

79. *Peirush HaRokeach.* Although this form is not grammatically precise, it is not uncommon for Scripture to use a singular noun with a plural subject, e.g., וַיֹּאמֶר אֲבִימֶלֶךְ וּפִיכֹל שַׂר צְבָאוֹ (*Genesis* 21:22); וַיֵּלֶךְ מֹשֶׁה וְאַהֲרֹן (*Exodus* 4:29); וַיִּקַּח מֹשֶׁה וְאַהֲרֹן (1:17 above). In each of those cases, the first mentioned is the primary subject [as if to say: Moses, as well as Aaron]. In our verse, however, even if בְּנֵי גָד is the primary subject, it is a plural term and should have a plural verb.

80. The note appears in the ancient compendium of masoretic notes, *Achlah VeAchlah.* List 59 there is an alphabetical catalogue of one hundred words, each of which appears exactly twice in the *Tanach,* but with two different meanings. The fifty-fourth pair on that list is וְנִקְרָא שְׁמוֹ בְּיִשְׂרָאֵל בֵּית and וַעֲבָדֶיךָ יַעַבְרוּ כָּל חֲלוּץ חֲלוּץ.

Virtually all editions of the Baal HaTurim present this comment on the word חָלוּץ of verse 21 above, and adduce the phrase וְעָבַר לָכֶם כָּל

then you shall be vindicated from HASHEM and from Israel,
and this land shall be a heritage for you before HASHEM.
23 But if you do not do so, behold! — you will have sinned to
HASHEM; know your sin that will encounter you. 24 Build for
yourselves cities for your youngsters and pens for your
flock, and what has come from your mouth shall you do."
25 The children of Gad and the children of Reuben said to
Moses, saying, "Your servants shall do as my lord com-
mands. 26 Our youngsters, our wives, our livestock, and all
our animals will be there in the cities of the Gilead. 27 And
your servants shall cross over — every man armed for the
legion — before HASHEM, to do battle, as my lord speaks."
28 Concerning them, Moses commanded Elazar the Ko-
hen, Joshua son of Nun, and the heads of the fathers of the
tribes of the Children of Israel. 29 Moses said to them, "If the
children of Gad and children of Reuben will cross the Jordan
with you — every man armed for battle before HASHEM,
and the land is conquered before you — you shall give them

twice in the *Tanach:* (i) here, {כָּל חֲלוּץ {צָבָא, *every man armed {for the legion};* and (ii) חֲלוּץ הַנָּעַל, *the one whose shoe was removed* (*Deuteronomy* 25:10). This [similarity of expression] alludes to [the Sages' teaching]: Every man who would go out to the wars of the House of David would [first] write a bill of divorce for his wife, so that [if he would be killed in the war,] she would be subject neither to marrying her brother-in-law [in *yibum* (levirate marriage)[81a]] nor to having to remove her brother-in-law's shoe.[81b] Our verse indicates that Moses had also followed this practice, and David had learned it from him. Thus, {כָּל חֲלוּץ {צָבָא refers to [everyone who took measures regarding the passage of] חֲלוּץ הַנָּעַל, *the one whose shoe was removed.*[82]

חֲלוּץ of that verse. However, that reading is untenable for various reasons, among them: (i) that verse reads חָלוּץ, while the verse from *Deuteronomy* reads חֲלוּץ; (ii) even if the masoretic note ignored the different vowelizations, each of the words חָלוּץ and חֲלוּץ appears twice in Scripture — חֲלוּץ in our verse and *Deuteronomy* 25:10; חָלוּץ in verses 21 and 29 of our passage; thus, the masoretic note should have read ד׳ rather than ב׳. Moreover, *Maharam MiRothenburg,* the Baal HaTurim's source for this comment, adduces the two phrases כָּל חֲלוּץ צָבָא (v. 27) and חֲלוּץ הַנָּעַל. The passages that appear in braces have been emended in accordance with *Maharam MiRothenburg's* comment.

81. The full note reads, ב׳ בִּתְרֵי לִישָׁנֵי, *Two, with two different meanings.*

81a. See *Deuteronomy* 25:5-10.

81b. The reading נַעַל הַיָּבָם, *the brother-in-law's shoe,* follows *Maharam MiRothenburg.* The early printed editions, as well as most later editions, have עַל הַיָּבָם, *upon the brother-in-law,* which seems to be a typographical or scribal error. Some later editions have emended that to מִן הַיָּבָם, *from the brother-in-law,* or לְהַיָּבָם, *for the brother-in-law,* i.e., she would not have to remove [a shoe] from the brother-in-law['s foot].

82. *Maharam MiRothenburg.*

ל אֶת־אֶרֶץ הַגִּלְעָד לַאֲחֻזָּה: וְאִם־לֹא יַעַבְרוּ חֲלוּצִים
לא אִתְּכֶם וְנֹאחֲזוּ בְתֹכְכֶם בְּאֶרֶץ כְּנָעַן: וַיַּעֲנוּ בְנֵי־גָד
וּבְנֵי רְאוּבֵן לֵאמֹר אֵת אֲשֶׁר דִּבֶּר יהוה אֶל־עֲבָדֶיךָ
לב כֵּן נַעֲשֶׂה: נַחְנוּ נַעֲבֹר חֲלוּצִים לִפְנֵי יהוה אֶרֶץ
לג כְּנָעַן וְאִתָּנוּ אֲחֻזַּת נַחֲלָתֵנוּ מֵעֵבֶר לַיַּרְדֵּן: וַיִּתֵּן לָהֶם ׀
מֹשֶׁה לִבְנֵי־גָד וְלִבְנֵי רְאוּבֵן וְלַחֲצִי ׀ שֵׁבֶט ׀ מְנַשֶּׁה
בֶן־יוֹסֵף אֶת־מַמְלֶכֶת סִיחֹן מֶלֶךְ הָאֱמֹרִי וְאֶת־
מַמְלֶכֶת עוֹג מֶלֶךְ הַבָּשָׁן הָאָרֶץ לְעָרֶיהָ בִּגְבֻלֹת עָרֵי
לד הָאָרֶץ סָבִיב: וַיִּבְנוּ בְנֵי־גָד אֶת־דִּיבֹן וְאֶת־עֲטָרֹת
לה וְאֵת עֲרֹעֵר: וְאֶת־עַטְרֹת שׁוֹפָן וְאֶת־יַעְזֵר וְיָגְבְּהָה:
לו וְאֶת־בֵּית נִמְרָה וְאֶת־בֵּית הָרָן עָרֵי מִבְצָר וְגִדְרֹת
לז צֹאן: וּבְנֵי רְאוּבֵן בָּנוּ אֶת־חֶשְׁבּוֹן וְאֶת־אֶלְעָלֵא
לח וְאֵת קִרְיָתָיִם: וְאֶת־נְבוֹ וְאֶת־בַּעַל מְעוֹן מוּסַבֹּת שֵׁם
וְאֶת־שִׂבְמָה וַיִּקְרְאוּ בְשֵׁמֹת אֶת־שְׁמוֹת הֶעָרִים
לט אֲשֶׁר בָּנוּ: וַיֵּלְכוּ בְּנֵי מָכִיר בֶּן־מְנַשֶּׁה גִּלְעָדָה
מפטיר מ וַיִּלְכְּדֻהָ וַיּוֹרֶשׁ אֶת־הָאֱמֹרִי אֲשֶׁר־בָּהּ: וַיִּתֵּן מֹשֶׁה
מא אֶת־הַגִּלְעָד לְמָכִיר בֶּן־מְנַשֶּׁה וַיֵּשֶׁב בָּהּ: וְיָאִיר
בֶּן־מְנַשֶּׁה הָלַךְ וַיִּלְכֹּד אֶת־חַוֹּתֵיהֶם וַיִּקְרָא אֶתְהֶן

בעל הטורים

(לב) **נַחְנוּ נַעֲבֹר חֲלוּצִים.** הַפָּסוּק מַתְחִיל וּמְסַיֵּם בְּנוּ"ן – כְּלוֹמַר, נַעֲבֹר הַיַּרְדֵּן שֶׁהוּא רָחָב נ' אַמָּה. וְיֵשׁ בּוֹ י"ב תֵּבוֹת, לוֹמַר שֶׁכָּל י"ב שְׁבָטִים יַעַבְרוּ:

❑ **נַחְנוּ.** ג' בַּמָּסוֹרֶת – "נַחְנוּ נַעֲבֹר"; "כֻּלָּנוּ בְּנֵי אִישׁ אֶחָד נָחְנוּ"; "נַחְנוּ פָשַׁעְנוּ וּמָרִינוּ". "נַחְנוּ נַעֲבֹר". לָמָּה? כִּי "כֻּלָּנוּ בְּנֵי אִישׁ אֶחָד נָחְנוּ". וְאִם לֹא, "נַחְנוּ פָשַׁעְנוּ וּמָרִינוּ", כִּדְכְתִיב "וּדְעוּ חַטַּאתְכֶם אֲשֶׁר תִּמְצָא אֶתְכֶם":

BAAL HATURIM ELUCIDATED

32. נַחְנוּ נַעֲבֹר חֲלוּצִים — WE SHALL CROSS OVER, ARMED. This verse begins with a נ (= 50) and concludes with a נ,[83] as if to say, we shall cross the Jordan River which is fifty cubits wide.[84] And the verse contains twelve words, indicating that all twelve tribes will cross over.[84a]

83. There are eleven such verses in the *Tanach,* three of them in the Torah: (i) *Leviticus* 13:9; (ii) here; and (iii) *Deuteronomy* 18:15. The Baal HaTurim comments on this phenomenon here and in *Deuteronomy.*

84. See the Baal HaTurim to 10:35 above and *Deuteronomy* 3:25.

84a. *R' Yehudah HaChassid.*

the land of Gilead as a heritage. [30] *But if they do not cross*
over, armed, with you, then they will take [their] heritage
among you in the Land of Canaan."
[31] *The children of Gad and the children of Reuben spoke*
up, saying, "As HASHEM *has spoken to your servants, so*
shall we do. [32] *We shall cross over, armed, before* HASHEM
to the Land of Canaan, and ours shall be the heritage of our
inheritance across the Jordan."
[33] *So Moses gave to them — to the children of Gad, and*
the children of Reuben, and half the tribe of Manasseh son
of Joseph — the kingdom of Sihon king of the Amorite, and
the kingdom of Og king of the Bashan; the land with its
cities in the boundaries, and the cities of the surrounding
land.
[34] *The children of Gad built Dibon, and Ataroth, and*
Aroer; [35] *and Atroth-shophan, and Jazer, and Jogbehah;*
[36] *and Beth-nimrah, and Beth-haran — fortified cities and*
pens for the flock. [37] *The children of Reuben built Heshbon,*
and Elealeh, and Kiriathaim; [38] *and Nebo and Baal-*
meon with altered names, and Sibmah; and they called
[them] by [other] names [instead of] the names of the
cities that they built. [39] *The children of Machir son of*
Manasseh went to Gilead and captured it, and drove out
the Amorite who were in it. [40] *Moses gave the Gilead to*
Machir son of Manasseh and he settled in it. [41] *Jair son of*
Manasseh went and captured their villages, and called them

BAAL HATURIM ELUCIDATED

❑ **נַחְנוּ** — WE. The masoretic note,[85] ג׳, means that this word appears three times in the *Tanach:* (i) here, נַחְנוּ נַעֲבֹר, *we shall cross;* (ii) כֻּלָּנוּ בְּנֵי אִישׁ אֶחָד נָחְנוּ, *All of us, sons of one man are we* (*Genesis* 42:11);[86] and (iii) נַחְנוּ פָשַׁעְנוּ וּמָרִינוּ, *We have transgressed and rebelled* (*Lamentations* 3:42). [The similarity of expression implies that they said,] "*We shall cross over,* and why? Because *all of us, sons of one man are we.*[86a] But if we do not,[86b] then *we will have transgressed and rebelled,*" as it is written, וּדְעוּ חַטַּאתְכֶם אֲשֶׁר תִּמְצָא אֶתְכֶם, *Know your sin that will encounter you* (v. 23 above).

33. {The Baal HaTurim's comment to מַמְלֶכֶת appears at *Exodus* 32:33.}

85. The full note reads: ג׳ תְּרֵי פַּתָּח וְחַד קָמַץ, *Three, two with a patach* (נַחְנוּ) *and one with a kamatz* (נָחְנוּ).

86. See the Baal HaTurim to that verse for another interpretation of the masoretic note.

86a. That is, we are responsible for one another.

86b. That is, if we were to cross over for ulterior motives, rather than to fulfill our filial and fraternal duties, then *we will have transgressed* against our father and our brothers *and rebelled* against our obligations.

מב חַוֹּת יָאִיר: וְנֹבַח הָלַךְ וַיִּלְכֹּד אֶת־קְנָת וְאֶת־בְּנֹתֶיהָ
וַיִּקְרָא לָה נֹבַח בִּשְׁמוֹ: פפפ

קי״ב פסוקים. בקי״י סימן. יק״ב סימן. עיב״ל סימן.

בעל הטורים

(מב) וַיִּקְרָא לָה נֹבַח. "לָה", ג׳ לֹא מַפִּיק הֵ״א – "וַיִּקְרָא לָה נֹבַח בִּשְׁמוֹ", שֶׁלֹּא נִתְקַיֵּם לָהּ שֵׁם זֶה; "וַיֹּאמֶר אֵלַי לִבְנוֹת לָה בַיִת בְּאֶרֶץ שִׁנְעָר", שֶׁבִּקֵּשׁ לִבְנוֹת וְלֹא בָנָה; "וַיֹּאמֶר לָה בֹעַז", שֶׁלֹּא דִבֵּר עִמָּהּ הוּא בְּעַצְמוֹ אֶלָּא עַל יְדֵי שָׁלִיחַ. "לָה" כְּמוֹ "לָא":

BAAL HATURIM ELUCIDATED

42. וַיִּקְרָא לָה נֹבַח — AND HE NAMED IT NOBAH. This word appears three times without a *mapik* (pronounced) ה:[87] (i) וַיִּקְרָא לָה נֹבַח בִּשְׁמוֹ, *and he named it Nobah, after his own name,* for that name did not last; (ii) וַיֹּאמֶר אֵלַי לִבְנוֹת לָה בַיִת בְּאֶרֶץ שִׁנְעָר, *He said to me, "To build her* (לָה) *a house in the land of Shinar"* (*Zechariah* 5:11),

87. The word לָהּ, *to her* or *to it,* appears more than 200 times in the *Tanach,* each time spelled with a dot in the הּ (e.g., 21:17 and 30:13 above), to indicate that, unlike other words with a silent final ה, the final הּ of this word is to be pronounced — not לָה, *lo,* but לָהּ, *loh.* Three times, however, לָה appears without the dotted ה. When spelled that way, the word is pronounced exactly the same way as לָא, Aramaic for לֹא, *not.* Indeed, the Hebrew word לֹא appears with a ה in place of the א in the word הֲלֹה [= הֲלֹא], *is it not,* or *behold!* (*Deuteronomy* 3:11), and the Aramaic word לָא appears with a ה in place of the א in the word כְּלָה, *as nothing* (*Daniel* 4:32). Accordingly, the use of לָה with an undotted ה allows the word to be interpreted as two words — לָהּ, *to her,* and לָא, *not.* Thus, our verse means: וַיִּקְרָא לָהּ נֹבַח, *he named it Nobah,* [*but*], לָא נֹבַח, *it was not Nobah,* for people continued to use the former name (*Rabbi Moshe HaDarshan,* cited by *Rashi*).

Havvoth-jair. [42] *Nobah went and captured Kenath and its suburbs, and he named it Nobah, after his own name.*

for he sought to build this house, but did not actually build it;[88] and (iii) וַיֹּאמֶר לָה בֹעַז, *Boaz said to her* (*Ruth* 2:14), for he did not speak to her personally, rather he communicated through a messenger.[89] Thus, [in all three cases] לָה is equivalent to לָא, *no.*[90]

88. *Rashi* to our verse states: "But I am puzzled regarding how Rabbi Moshe HaDarshan would explain the two words לָה in the verses וַיֹּאמֶר לָה בֹעַז and לִבְנוֹת לָה בַיִת." Nevertheless, in his commentary to *Kiddushin* 49b (see also *Tosafos,* s.v., לבנות לה בית), *Rashi* offers two explanations of לִבְנוֹת לָה, the second reads, "Alternatively: He wanted them to build, but they did not build" (see also *Ramban* to our verse).

89. *Peirush HaRokeach,* the Baal HaTurim's apparent source for this comment, reads מְתַרְגְּמָן, *translator,* in place of שָׁלִיחַ, *messenger.*

90. The Midrash expounds upon the conversation between Boaz and Ruth (*Ruth* 2:13-14). *She said, "May I continue to find favor in your eyes, my lord . . . though I am not even as worthy as one of your maidservants."* וַיֹּאמֶר לָה, *And he said, "No!* God forbid [i.e., do not speak of yourself that way]. You are not of the אֲמָהוֹת, *maidservants,* rather, you are of the אִמָּהוֹת, *matriarchs."* Similarly: [The word לָה in the verse,] *Nobah went and captured Kenath and its suburbs* [וַיִּקְרָא לָה נֹבַח, *and he named it* (לָה) *Nobah,*] teaches that that name did not last. Similarly: [לָה in the verse,] *He said to me, "To build her* (לָה) *a house in the land of Shinar,"* teaches that falsehood [i.e., ingratiating flattery and pretentious vainglory (*Mattenos Kehunah*)] cannot endure (*Rus Rabbah* to 2:13).

פרשת מסעי
Parashas Masei

לג/א־ד א אֵלֶּה מַסְעֵי בְנֵי־יִשְׂרָאֵל אֲשֶׁר יָצְאוּ מֵאֶרֶץ מִצְרַיִם
ב לְצִבְאֹתָם בְּיַד־מֹשֶׁה וְאַהֲרֹן׃ וַיִּכְתֹּב מֹשֶׁה אֶת־
מוֹצָאֵיהֶם לְמַסְעֵיהֶם עַל־פִּי יהוה וְאֵלֶּה מַסְעֵיהֶם
ג לְמוֹצָאֵיהֶם׃ וַיִּסְעוּ מֵרַעְמְסֵס בַּחֹדֶשׁ הָרִאשׁוֹן בַּחֲמִשָּׁה
עָשָׂר יוֹם לַחֹדֶשׁ הָרִאשׁוֹן מִמָּחֳרַת הַפֶּסַח יָצְאוּ
ד בְנֵי־יִשְׂרָאֵל בְּיָד רָמָה לְעֵינֵי כָּל־מִצְרָיִם׃ וּמִצְרַיִם

בעל הטורים

(ב) **מוֹצָאֵיהֶם לְמַסְעֵיהֶם.** וּבָתַר הָכֵי הָפַךְ וְכָתַב "מַסְעֵיהֶם לְמוֹצָאֵיהֶם". לוֹמַר שֶׁהַכֹּל הָיָה עַל פִּי ה׳, בֵּין מַסָּע בֵּין מוֹצָא:

(ג) **וַיִּסְעוּ מֵרַעְמְסֵס.** וּבָתַר הָכֵי כְּתִיב "וַיִּסְעוּ בְנֵי יִשְׂרָאֵל מֵרַעְמְסֵס". מִתְּחִלָּה נָסְעוּ בְּעִרְבּוּבְיָא, עֵרֶב רַב בֵּינֵיהֶם. וּבָתַר הָכֵי, כְּשֶׁמְּסַפֵּר הַמַּסָּעוֹת כֻּלָּם, הִזְכִּיר "בְּנֵי יִשְׂרָאֵל", כִּי הִפְרִידוּ עֵרֶב רַב מִבֵּינֵיהֶם:

❑ **יָצְאוּ בְּנֵי יִשְׂרָאֵל בְּיָד רָמָה לְעֵינֵי כָּל מִצְרָיִם** {**וּמִצְרַיִם**}. לוֹמַר שֶׁגַּם עֵרֶב רַב, שֶׁהֵם מִצְרִים, יָצְאוּ בְּיָד רָמָה לְעֵינֵי שְׁאָר מִצְרִים:

(ד) **וּמִצְרַיִם.** ב׳ רָאשֵׁי פְסוּקִים — "וּמִצְרַיִם מְקַבְּרִים"; "וּמִצְרַיִם יָלַד אֶת לוּדִים". לוֹמַר שֶׁאֲפִלּוּ אוֹתָם שֶׁכְּבָר מֵתוּ, רֻבָּם נֶחְטְטוּ:

BAAL HATURIM ELUCIDATED

XXXIII.

2. מוֹצָאֵיהֶם לְמַסְעֵיהֶם — THEIR SETTINGS FORTH TO THEIR JOURNEYS. [The verse used this expression first,] but then, it reversed [the order of the words] and wrote, מַסְעֵיהֶם לְמוֹצָאֵיהֶם, *their journeys to their settings forth.* This indicates that everything was done עַל פִּי ה׳, *according to the word of* HASHEM *— both* the journey and the setting forth.[1]

3. וַיִּסְעוּ מֵרַעְמְסֵס — THEY JOURNEYED FROM RAMESES. Later on, the Torah states: וַיִּסְעוּ בְנֵי יִשְׂרָאֵל מֵרַעְמְסֵס, *The Children of Israel journeyed from Rameses* (v. 5). [The phrase *Children of Israel* was omitted the first time because] at the outset [when they departed from Egypt], they journeyed as a conglomeration with the mixed multitude[2] traveling among them. But later on, when the Torah relates all of the

1. During the nation's forty-year sojourn in the wilderness, they encamped in forty-two places. Earlier, we have been told that each מַסָּע, *journey,* and each חֲנָיָה, *encampment,* was עַל פִּי ה׳, *according to the word of* HASHEM, i.e., at God's bidding (e.g., 9:18, 20 above). Here, the Torah teaches us that there was a third phase for each journey and it preceded the other two: First there was a מוֹצָא, *setting forth,* i.e., decampment and preparation for the journey; then there was the actual journey (see *Sforno*), and finally, the encampment. Now, based on what we have learned earlier, we might think that the Israelites would decide when they wished to set out on their next journey, and God would then inform them regarding the route they should take. Or, conversely, God would tell them when to depart, but they would choose their own route. Therefore, our verse reverses the order of מוֹצָאֵיהֶם, *their settings forth,* and מַסְעֵיהֶם, *their journeys,* to teach that both phases were undertaken עַל פִּי ה׳, *according to the word of* HASHEM.

2. According to *Rashi* (*Exodus* 12:38), the עֵרֶב רַב, *mixed multitude,* consisted of a large number of non-Israelites from many nations who joined

[1] *These are the journeys of the Children of Israel, who went*
forth from the land of Egypt according to their legions,
under the hand of Moses and Aaron. [2] *Moses wrote their set-*
tings forth to their journeys according to the word of HASHEM,
and these were their journeys to their settings forth: [3] *They*
journeyed from Rameses in the first month, on the fifteenth
day of the first month — on the day after the pesach-offering
— the Children of Israel went forth with upraised hand,
before the eyes of all the Egyptians. [4] *And the Egyptians*

BAAL HATURIM ELUCIDATED

journeys, it specifies *the Children of Israel,* for they had separated the mixed multitude from among them.[3]

❑ **יָצְאוּ בְנֵי יִשְׂרָאֵל בְּיָד רָמָה לְעֵינֵי כָּל מִצְרָיִם {וּמִצְרַיִם} — THE CHILDREN OF ISRAEL WENT FORTH WITH UPRAISED HAND, BEFORE THE EYES OF ALL THE EGYPTIANS. {AND THE EGYPTIANS}**[4] [The Torah juxtaposes וּמִצְרַיִם, *and the Egyptians,* with the verse about the Children of Israel leaving Egypt] to indicate that even the mixed multitude — who were themselves Egyptians[5] — went forth with an upraised hand before the eyes of the other Egyptians.[6]

4. וּמִצְרַיִם — AND THE EGYPTIANS. The masoretic note, ב׳ רָאשֵׁי פְסוּקִים, means that this word appears twice in the Torah at the beginning of a verse:[7] (i) here, וּמִצְרַיִם מְקַבְּרִים, *and the Egyptians were burying;* and (ii) וּמִצְרַיִם יָלַד אֶת לוּדִים, *And Mizraim* [the progenitor of Egypt] *begot Ludim* (*Genesis* 10:13). This [similarity of expression] indicates that even the majority of those who had already died [and been buried] were dug up [from their graves].[8]

---

the Children of Israel when they left Egypt. *Ibn Ezra* describes them as Egyptian nationals who mingled with the Israelites. In the Baal HaTurim's next comment, he follows *Ibn Ezra's* opinion. Without first consulting God, Moses converted that multitude and accepted them into the nation. However, their conversion was not sincere and they eventually became degenerate and dragged others along with them (see *Rashi* to *Exodus* 32:7, s.v., שִׁחֵת עַמְּךָ).

3. See the Baal HaTurim to 22:6 above.

4. The word וּמִצְרַיִם, *and the Egyptians,* which is the first word of verse 4, is not found in the early printed editions or in most later printed editions. However, it appears in the manuscripts used by *Shoham Yakar.*

5. See note 2 above.

6. The passage cited in the rubric of this comment is interpreted as: *The Children of Israel went forth with upraised hand, before the eyes of all those Egyptians* that remained in their land, *and so did those Egyptians* who had joined the Israelites.

7. The masoretic note to our verse reads, ה׳ רָאשֵׁי פְּסוּקִים, *Five at the beginning of a verse.* But the masoretic note at *Genesis* 10:13 reads, ב׳ רָאשֵׁי פְּסוּקִים, *Two at the beginning of a verse.* The note in *Genesis* refers to the Five Books of the Torah and counts only the two verses cited by the Baal HaTurim. The note to our verse refers to the entire *Tanach* and includes three other verses as well: *Isaiah* 30:7 and 31:3; and *I Chronicles* 1:11.

8. The Midrash records the ancient Egyptian custom of burying their dead within their homes. During the plague of the firstborn, even those firstborn who had died before the plague were afflicted, for dogs [or, rodents (*Tashbeitz*)] pulled them from their graves into the houses. This served as a double punishment for the Egyptians. Not only did the oldest living child in each family die, but the family was also reminded in vivid fashion of their earlier losses

מְקַבְּרִים אֵת אֲשֶׁר הִכָּה יהוָה בָּהֶם כָּל־בְּכוֹר
ה וּבֵאלֹהֵיהֶם עָשָׂה יהוָה שְׁפָטִים: וַיִּסְעוּ בְנֵי־יִשְׂרָאֵל
ו מֵרַעְמְסֵס וַיַּחֲנוּ בְּסֻכֹּת: וַיִּסְעוּ מִסֻּכֹּת וַיַּחֲנוּ בְאֵתָם
ז אֲשֶׁר בִּקְצֵה הַמִּדְבָּר: וַיִּסְעוּ מֵאֵתָם וַיָּשָׁב עַל־
פִּי הַחִירֹת אֲשֶׁר עַל־פְּנֵי בַּעַל צְפוֹן וַיַּחֲנוּ לִפְנֵי
ח מִגְדֹּל: וַיִּסְעוּ מִפְּנֵי הַחִירֹת וַיַּעַבְרוּ בְתוֹךְ־הַיָּם
הַמִּדְבָּרָה וַיֵּלְכוּ דֶּרֶךְ שְׁלֹשֶׁת יָמִים בְּמִדְבַּר אֵתָם
ט וַיַּחֲנוּ בְּמָרָה: וַיִּסְעוּ מִמָּרָה וַיָּבֹאוּ אֵילִמָה וּבְאֵילִם

בעל הטורים

❑ **מְקַבְּרִים.** ב׳ — ״וּמִצְרַיִם מְקַבְּרִים״; ״מְקַבְּרִים אֶת הָעֹבְרִים״, בְּפָרָשַׁת גּוֹג. וְהַיְנוּ דִכְתִיב ״כַּאֲשֶׁר שֵׁמַע לְמִצְרָיִם יָחִילוּ כְּשֵׁמַע צֹר״:

(ה) בְּסֻכֹּת. שֶׁשָּׁם נִסְתּוֹכְכוּ בְּעַנְנֵי כָבוֹד:

(ז) וַיָּשָׁב עַל פִּי הַחִירֹת. וְאֵינוֹ אוֹמֵר ״וַיָּשׁוּבוּ״. מְלַמֵּד שֶׁכֻּלָּם הָיָה לָהֶם לֵב אֶחָד לַעֲשׂוֹת כֵּן עַל פִּי צִוּוּיוֹ שֶׁל מֹשֶׁה:

❑ **עַל פִּי הַחִירֹת.** {וּבְפָרָשַׁת וַיְהִי בְּשַׁלַּח אוֹמֵר ״לִפְנֵי פִּי הַחִירוֹת״.} מְלַמֵּד שֶׁאָמַר לָהֶם מֹשֶׁה, עַל פִּי ה׳ אֲנִי אוֹמֵר לָכֶם שֶׁתִּהְיוּ בְנֵי חוֹרִין:

(ח) וַיִּסְעוּ מִפְּנֵי הַחִירֹת. הָיָה לוֹ לוֹמַר ״מִפִּי הַחִירֹת״. אֶלָּא ״וַיִּסְעוּ . . . בְּיָד רָמָה . . . מִפְּנֵי״ שֶׁהִבְטִיחָן שֶׁיִּהְיוּ בְּנֵי חוֹרִין:

(ט) וַיָּבֹאוּ אֵילִמָה. וְלֹא אָמַר ״וַיַּחֲנוּ בְּאֵילִם״. מְלַמֵּד שֶׁלֹּא הָיָה דַעְתָּם לַחֲנוֹת שָׁם, עַד

BAAL HATURIM ELUCIDATED

❑ **מְקַבְּרִים — WERE BURYING.** The masoretic note, ב׳, means that this word appears twice in the *Tanach:* (i) here, וּמִצְרַיִם מְקַבְּרִים, *and the Egyptians were burying;* and (ii) מְקַבְּרִים אֶת הָעֹבְרִים, *burying, together with the passersby* (*Ezekiel* 39:14), in the passage regarding [the wars of] Gog [and Magog].[8a] This [similarity of expression] recalls the verse, כַּאֲשֶׁר שֵׁמַע לְמִצְרָיִם יָחִילוּ כְּשֵׁמַע צֹר, *Just as* [*they did*] *at the tidings of Egypt, so will they tremble at the tidings of Tyre* (*Isaiah* 23:5).[9]

5. בְּסֻכֹּת — IN SUCCOTH. [The place was called סֻכֹּת[9a]] because that was where they became covered by the Clouds of Glory.[10]

7. וַיָּשָׁב עַל פִּי הַחִירֹת — AND IT TURNED BACK NEAR TO PI-HAHIROTH. [The verse uses the singular verb form וַיָּשָׁב, *he* (or, *it*) *turned back,*] but it does not use the

(*Yalkut Shimoni* I:186, cited in *Teshuvos Tashbeitz* II:246 with minor differences). The Baal HaTurim finds an allusion to this Midrash in the similarity of expression: The Egyptians witnessed the disinterment of their long-buried firstborns and felt as if their children were being reborn [thus, the allusion of וּמִצְרַיִם יָלַד, which can be understood as, *the Egyptians begot*] and dying right before their eyes, for they had to rebury them that very day (*Ittur Bikkurim*).

8a. See the Baal HaTurim to 10:8-9 above with note 64.

9. Cf. *R' Yehudah HaChassid; R' Ephraim.* See the Baal HaTurim to 22:4 above with note 14.

9a. From the verb root סכך, *to cover.*

10. *Mechilta* to *Exodus* 13:20; *Targum Yonasan ben Uzziel,* here.

were burying those among them whom HASHEM had struck,
every firstborn; and on their gods HASHEM had inflicted
punishments. 5 *The Children of Israel journeyed from*
Rameses and encamped in Succoth. 6 *They journeyed from*
Succoth and encamped in Etham, which is at the edge of
the wilderness. 7 *They journeyed from Etham and it turned*
back near to Pi-hahiroth, which is before Baal-zephon, and
they encamped before Migdol. 8 *They journeyed from be-*
fore Hahiroth and passed through the midst of the sea
toward the wilderness; they went on a three-day trip in the
Wilderness of Etham, and they encamped in Marah. 9 *They*
journeyed from Marah and they came to Elim; in Elim

BAAL HATURIM ELUCIDATED

[plural] form וַיָּשׁוּבוּ, *they turned back.*[11] This teaches that all of them were united, with one heart, ready to do so[12] in accordance with Moses' instruction.[13]

❑ עַל פִּי הַחִירֹת — NEAR TO PI-HAHIROTH. {In [a parallel verse in] *parashas Beshalach* this reads, לִפְנֵי פִּי הַחִירֹת, *before Pi-hahiroth* (*Exodus* 14:2).}[13a] This teaches that Moses said to them, "It is in accordance with the word of HASHEM that I tell you that you will be free men."[14]

8. וַיִּסְעוּ מִפְּנֵי הַחִירֹת — THEY JOURNEYED FROM BEFORE HAHIROTH. The verse should have stated, מִפִּי הַחִירֹת [as in the previous verse]. But [the word מִפְּנֵי[15] is used to imply that] *they journeyed . . . with upraised hand . . . because* he promised them that they would be free men.[15a]

9. וַיָּבֹאוּ אֵילִמָה — AND THEY CAME TO ELIM. [This verse uses the term וַיָּבֹאוּ אֵילִמָה, *and they came to Elim*] but does not use the formula, וַיַּחֲנוּ בְּאֵילִם, *and they encamped in Elim* [as it does regarding the other encampments]. This teaches that they did not originally intend to encamp there,[16] until a miracle

11. As it does in *Exodus* 14:2.

12. That is, not one Israelite rebelled against Moses' instruction to turn back in the direction of Egypt (*Yad Aharon*). Unfortunately, their unison was short-lived, for as soon as they saw the Egyptian army pursuing them, they split into a number of factions. And that was the first of the ten times that they "tested" God (*Arachin* 15a).

13. *Peirush HaRokeach;* see also *Rashi* to *Exodus* 14:4, s.v., ויעשו כן, and 19:2, s.v., ויחן שם, and to 32:25 above.

13a. The passage enclosed in braces has been inexplicably omitted in many later editions.

14. The two words עַל פִּי of the phrase עַל פִּי הַחִירֹת are interpreted as [an abridgment of עַל פִּי ה׳ (v. 3)], *according to the word of HASHEM* (*VeChur LaZahav*); and הַחִירֹת is considered synonymous with הַחֵרוּת, *the freedom* (*Rashi* to *Exodus* 14:2).

15. The term מִפְּנֵי can mean either *from the face of* [i.e., *from in front of, from before*] or *because of.* The translation follows the former meaning, while the allusion follows the latter.

15a. הַחִירֹת is understood as הַחֵרוּת, *the freedom.*

16. The Baal HaTurim's statement, "they did not intend to encamp there," seems in direct conflict with verses 9:18 and 20 above (see note 1 to this *parashah*). Earlier, the Torah teaches us that there were three signs that the Israelites should begin a new journey: (i) the word of God, i.e., when God commanded the clouds to move, the next journey would commence (see 9:18 above with *Rashi,* s.v., עַל פִּי ה׳ יִסְעוּ); (ii) the word of

לג/י-יח שְׁתֵּים עֶשְׂרֵה עֵינֹת מַיִם וְשִׁבְעִים תְּמָרִים וַיַּחֲנוּ־
*שני י-יא שָׁם: וַיִּסְעוּ מֵאֵילִם וַיַּחֲנוּ עַל־יַם־סוּף: * וַיִּסְעוּ מִיַּם־
יב סוּף וַיַּחֲנוּ בְּמִדְבַּר־סִין: וַיִּסְעוּ מִמִּדְבַּר־סִין וַיַּחֲנוּ
יג-יד בְּדָפְקָה: וַיִּסְעוּ מִדָּפְקָה וַיַּחֲנוּ בְּאָלוּשׁ: וַיִּסְעוּ מֵאָלוּשׁ
וַיַּחֲנוּ בִּרְפִידִם וְלֹא־הָיָה שָׁם מַיִם לָעָם לִשְׁתּוֹת:
טו-טז וַיִּסְעוּ מֵרְפִידִם וַיַּחֲנוּ בְּמִדְבַּר סִינָי: וַיִּסְעוּ מִמִּדְבַּר
יז סִינָי וַיַּחֲנוּ בְּקִבְרֹת הַתַּאֲוָה: וַיִּסְעוּ מִקִּבְרֹת הַתַּאֲוָה
יח וַיַּחֲנוּ בַּחֲצֵרֹת: וַיִּסְעוּ מֵחֲצֵרֹת וַיַּחֲנוּ בְּרִתְמָה:

בעל הטורים

שֶׁנַּעֲשָׂה לָהֶם נֵס שֶׁיָּצְאוּ שְׁתֵּים עֶשְׂרֵה עֵינוֹת מַיִם, וְאָז חָנוּ שָׁם:

(יא) בְּמִדְבַּר סִין. מִתְּחִלָּה נִקְרָא "מִדְבַּר סִין", וּלְבַסּוֹף נִקְרָא "מִדְבַּר סִינַי". שֶׁנִּתּוֹסְּפָה לוֹ יוּ"ד כְּנֶגֶד יוּ"ד דִּבְּרוֹת:

❑ **סי"ן** יָמִים הָיָה מֹשֶׁה בָּהָר:

(יב) בְּדָפְקָה. שָׁם דָּפַק לִבָּם, שֶׁלֹּא הָיָה לָהֶם לֶחֶם:

(יג) בְּאָלוּשׁ. נִתַּן לָהֶם הַמָּן, בִּזְכוּת "לוּשִׁי וַעֲשִׂי עֻגוֹת":

(יח) בְּרִתְמָה. עַל שֵׁם הַמְרַגְּלִים, שֶׁנֶּאֱמַר "חִצֵּי גִבּוֹר שְׁנוּנִים עִם גַּחֲלֵי רְתָמִים":

BAAL HATURIM ELUCIDATED

occurred for them and twelve springs of water emerged.[16a] Only then did they encamp there.

11. בְּמִדְבַּר סִין — IN THE WILDERNESS OF SIN. At the beginning [of our passage], the place is called מִדְבַּר סִין, *the Wilderness of Sin,* and at the end [i.e., in vv. 15-16], it is called מִדְבַּר סִינַי, *the Wilderness of Sinai.* For the letter י (= 10) was added to it, corresponding[17] to the Ten Commandments.[18]

Moses (see 10:35 above); and (iii) the sound of the trumpets (see 10:2 above with *Rashi,* s.v., וּלְמַסַּע אֶת הַמַּחֲנוֹת). Similarly, when they were to encamp, it would be at the word of God and the word of Moses (see *Rashi* to 9:18 above, s.v., וְעַל פִּי ה׳ יַחֲנוּ). It is possible that God sometimes displayed His will through some heavenly sign other than the clouds. If so, when the Israelites left Marah, a place where the water was too bitter for human consumption or for irrigating fruits and vegetables, they did not think that they would be able to encamp again until they would have traveled a considerable distance from Marah. Nevertheless, when they arrived at Elim, which is very close to Marah, and found a spring of fresh water and date palm trees, they took that as a sign עַל פִּי ה׳, that they were to make camp there (*Shoham Yakar*).

16a. The Baal HaTurim's statement, "until a miracle occurred for them and twelve springs of water emerged," seems in direct conflict with the Midrash that states that the twelve wells were there from the time of Creation (*Mechilta* 15:27; adduced by the Baal HaTurim in *Peirush HaTur HaAroch* to *Exodus*). Perhaps, at the time of Creation, God prepared twelve subterranean water sources in Elim, but did not permit them to spout forth from underground until after the Israelites arrived there (*VeChur LaZahav*).

17. The text follows the printed editions. However, the manuscripts used by *Shoham Yakar* read, לְאַחַר שֶׁנִּתְּנוּ לוֹ י׳ דִּבְּרוֹת, *after the Ten Commandments were given to him,* i.e., to Moses [or לְאַחַר שֶׁנִּתְּנוּ עָלָיו י׳ דִּבְּרוֹת, *after the Ten Commandments were given upon it*], in place of כְּנֶגֶד יוּ"ד

were twelve springs of water and seventy date palms, and
they encamped there. 10 *They journeyed from Elim and*
encamped by the Sea of Reeds. 11 *They journeyed from the*
Sea of Reeds and encamped in the Wilderness of Sin. 12 *They*
journeyed from the Wilderness of Sin and encamped in
Dophkah. 13 *They journeyed from Dophkah and encamped in*
Alush. 14 *They journeyed from Alush and encamped in*
Rephidim, and there was no water there for the people to
drink. 15 *They journeyed from Rephidim and encamped in*
the Wilderness of Sinai. 16 *They journeyed from the Wilderness*
of Sinai and encamped in Kibroth-hattaavah. 17 *They jour-*
neyed from Kibroth-hattaavah and encamped in Hazeroth.
18 *They journeyed from Hazeroth and encamped in Rithmah.*

BAAL HATURIM ELUCIDATED

❏ [The *gematria* of] סִין (120) is equal to the number of days that Moses was on Mount Sinai.[19]

12. בְּדָפְקָה — IN DOPHKAH. [It was called דָּפְקָה, from the root דפק, *to knock*[20]] because their hearts throbbed there, for they did not have bread.[21,21a]

13. בְּאָלוּשׁ — IN ALUSH.[22] [It was called אָלוּשׁ, from the root לוּשׁ, *to knead,* because] the manna was given to them [there] in the merit of Abraham's request to Sarah,] לוּשִׁי וַעֲשִׂי עֻגוֹת, *Knead and make cakes* (*Genesis* 18:6).[23]

15. {The Baal HaTurim's comment to בְּמִדְבַּר סִינָי appears at v. 11 above.}

18. בְּרִתְמָה — IN RITHMAH.[24] [It was called רִתְמָה] because of [the malicious report] of the spies, as it is said, חִצֵּי גִבּוֹר שְׁנוּנִים עִם גַּחֲלֵי רְתָמִים, *the sharp arrows of a*

דִּבְּרוֹת, *corresponding to the Ten Commandments.*

The Baal HaTurim's comment implies that Sin and Sinai are one and the same. But that is difficult, for another verse locates the *Wilderness of Sin . . . between Elim and Sinai* (*Exodus* 16:1), implying that Sin and Sinai are different places. It has been suggested that the Wilderness of Sin was a vast area that stretched from Elim on one side to Mount Sinai on the other. Somewhere between those points were Dophkah, Alush and Rephidim. Thus, verse 12 of our passage speaks of the Israelites encamping in the Wilderness of Sin near its border with Elim. When the nation received the Torah at Mount Sinai, the name of the entire area was changed from מִדְבַּר סִין to מִדְבַּר סִינַי to commemorate the giving of the Ten Commandments (*Atros Addar*).

18. *Peirush HaRokeach.* The Baal HaTurim makes a similar comment at *Exodus* 16:1.

19. See the Baal HaTurim to 12:3 above, with notes 290 and 291.

20. See *Song of Songs* 5:2.

21. As the Psalmist (104:15; see also *Genesis* 18:5) writes, וְלֶחֶם לְבַב אֱנוֹשׁ יִסְעָד, *and bread to sustain the heart of man* (Y.S.).

21a. *Peirush HaRokeach;* see *Ramban* to *Exodus* 16:1, cited by the Baal HaTurim in *Peirush HaTur HaAroch* there.

22. Literally, אָלוּשׁ means *I shall knead.*

23. *Peirush HaRokeach;* see *Bava Metzia* 86b; *Yerushalmi, Beitzah* 2:1; *Ramban* to *Exodus* 16:1.

24. The only two appearances of the term רִתְמָה in the *Tanach* are in verses 18 and 19 here. The name is generally understood as a form of רֹתֶם, *rotem,* a wilderness shrub/tree that *Rashi* (*I Kings* 19:4) renders *juniper.* According to *Targum Yonasan ben Uzziel,* the place was called רִתְמָה because it is "a place where rotem-trees grow in abundance." The Baal HaTurim shows that the name also alludes to that which occurred when the Israelites encamped there.

לג/יט־לג

יט־כ וַיִּסְעוּ מֵרִתְמָה וַיַּחֲנוּ בְּרִמֹּן פָּרֶץ: וַיִּסְעוּ מֵרִמֹּן פָּרֶץ
כא־כב וַיַּחֲנוּ בְּלִבְנָה: וַיִּסְעוּ מִלִּבְנָה וַיַּחֲנוּ בְּרִסָּה: וַיִּסְעוּ
כג מֵרִסָּה וַיַּחֲנוּ בִּקְהֵלָתָה: וַיִּסְעוּ מִקְּהֵלָתָה וַיַּחֲנוּ
כד־כה בְּהַר־שָׁפֶר: וַיִּסְעוּ מֵהַר־שָׁפֶר וַיַּחֲנוּ בַּחֲרָדָה: וַיִּסְעוּ
כו מֵחֲרָדָה וַיַּחֲנוּ בְּמַקְהֵלֹת: וַיִּסְעוּ מִמַּקְהֵלֹת וַיַּחֲנוּ
כז־כח בְּתָחַת: וַיִּסְעוּ מִתָּחַת וַיַּחֲנוּ בְּתָרַח: וַיִּסְעוּ מִתָּרַח
כט וַיַּחֲנוּ בְּמִתְקָה: וַיִּסְעוּ מִמִּתְקָה וַיַּחֲנוּ בְּחַשְׁמֹנָה:
ל־לא וַיִּסְעוּ מֵחַשְׁמֹנָה וַיַּחֲנוּ בְּמֹסֵרוֹת: וַיִּסְעוּ מִמֹּסֵרוֹת
לב וַיַּחֲנוּ בִּבְנֵי יַעֲקָן: וַיִּסְעוּ מִבְּנֵי יַעֲקָן וַיַּחֲנוּ בְּחֹר
לג הַגִּדְגָּד: וַיִּסְעוּ מֵחֹר הַגִּדְגָּד וַיַּחֲנוּ בְּיָטְבָתָה:

בעל הטורים

(כא) וַיַּחֲנוּ בְּרִסָּה. שֶׁנִּתְרוֹסְסוּ שָׁם:

(כב) בִּקְהֵלָתָה. עַל שֵׁם "וַיַּקְהֵל עֲלֵיהֶם קֹרַח אֶת כָּל הָעֵדָה":

(כה) בְּמַקְהֵלֹת. עַל שֵׁם "וַיִּקָּהֲלוּ עַל מֹשֶׁה וְעַל אַהֲרֹן":

❑ **בְּמַקְהֵלֹת.** ב' – "וַיִּסְעוּ מֵחֲרָדָה וַיַּחֲנוּ בְּמַקְהֵלֹת"; "בְּמַקְהֵלוֹת בָּרְכוּ אֱלֹהִים", דְּדָרְשִׁינַן מִנֵּהּ, שֶׁאֲפִלּוּ עֻבָּרִים שֶׁבִּמְעֵי אִמָּן אָמְרוּ שִׁירָה עַל הַיָּם. וְזֶהוּ "וַיִּסְעוּ מֵחֲרָדָה", פֵּרוּשׁ, מֵחֶרְדַּת מִצְרַיִם שֶׁהָיָה "נֹסֵעַ אַחֲרֵיהֶם". "וַיַּחֲנוּ בְּמַקְהֵלֹת", מְלַמֵּד שֶׁנַּעֲשׂוּ קְהִלּוֹת קְהִלּוֹת לוֹמַר שִׁירָה:

BAAL HATURIM ELUCIDATED

warrior, with coals of rotem-wood[25] (*Psalms* 120:4).[26]

21. וַיַּחֲנוּ[27] **בְּרִסָּה** — AND THEY ENCAMPED[27] IN RISSAH. [It was called רִסָּה, related to רְסִיסִים, *fragments* (*Amos* 6:11)] because they were crushed there.[28]

25. This verse must be read together with the preceding verse: *What will a treacherous tongue give to you? What will it gain for you? The sharp arrows of a warrior, with coals of rotem-wood* (*Psalms* 120:3-4). These verses refer to the malicious report (see 13:27-33 above) of the spies (*Rashi*).

The Midrash explains why malicious speech is compared to arrows and rotem-wood coals: Arrows differ from other weapons, for the others are effective only at close range, while the arrow is effective even from afar. So it is with malicious speech that may be spoken in Rome, yet can slay [someone who is far away, e.g.,] in Syria. Similarly, rotem-wood coals are different from those of other woods, for the embers of other woods cool off on the inside as well as on the outside, while rotem coals, even though they cool on the outside, nevertheless remain burning on the inside. So it is with malicious speech: One may appease the person who believes it; nevertheless, its effects remain burning within him (*Bereishis Rabbah* 98:19).

26. *Rashi.*

27. The text follows the Constantinople and Venice editions. Most later editions follow that of Furth, in which the word וְהַיְנוּ, *and that is* [*what is meant by*], appears in place of וַיַּחֲנוּ, *and they encamped,* and it is a continuation of the previous comment. But it is difficult to find any meaning to that version.

28. *Peirush HaRokeach.* This refers either to the death of the spies (*Yad Aharon*); or to the intransigent ones (*Shoham Yakar;* see 14:44 above); or to the decree that the entire generation would die in the wilderness (A.S.).

[19] *They journeyed from Rithmah and encamped in Rim-*
mon-perez. [20] *They journeyed from Rimmon-perez and*
encamped in Libnah. [21] *They journeyed from Libnah and*
encamped in Rissah. [22] *They journeyed from Rissah and*
encamped in Kehelathah. [23] *They journeyed from Kehe-*
lathah and encamped in Mount Shepher. [24] *They journeyed*
from Mount Shepher and encamped in Haradah. [25] *They*
journeyed from Haradah and encamped in Makheloth.
[26] *They journeyed from Makheloth and encamped in*
Tahath. [27] *They journeyed from Tahath and encamped in*
Terah. [28] *They journeyed from Terah and encamped in*
Mithkah. [29] *They journeyed from Mithkah and encamped in*
Hashmonah. [30] *They journeyed from Hashmonah and*
encamped in Moseroth. [31] *They journeyed from Moseroth*
and encamped in Bene-jaakan. [32] *They journeyed from*
Bene-jaakan and encamped in Hor-haggidgad. [33] *They jour-*
neyed from Hor-haggidgad and encamped in Jotbathah.

BAAL HATURIM ELUCIDATED

22. בְּקְהֵלָתָה — IN KEHELATHAH.[29] [It was called קְהֵלָתָה, from the root קהל, *to gather*] because of [the event associated with it, as is written]: וַיַּקְהֵל עֲלֵיהֶם קֹרַח אֶת כָּל הָעֵדָה, *Korah gathered the entire assembly against them* (16:19 above).[30]

25. בְּמַקְהֵלֹת — IN MAKHELOTH.[31] [It was called מַקְהֵלֹת, from קהל, *to gather*] because of [the event associated with it, as it is written]: וַיִּקָּהֲלוּ עַל מֹשֶׁה וְעַל אַהֲרֹן, *They gathered against Moses, and against Aaron* (20:2 above).[32]

❑ **בְּמַקְהֵלֹת** — IN MAKHELOTH. The masoretic note, ב׳, means that this word appears twice in the *Tanach:*[33] (i) here, וַיִּסְעוּ מֵחֲרָדָה וַיַּחֲנוּ בְּמַקְהֵלֹת, *They journeyed from Haradah and encamped in Makheloth;* and (ii) בְּמַקְהֵלוֹת בָּרְכוּ אֱלֹהִים, *In congregations bless God* (*Psalms* 68:27). Our Sages infer from the verse from *Psalms* that even the fetuses in their mothers' womb recited songs of praise at the Sea of Reeds.[34] And that is the implication of our verse: וַיִּסְעוּ מֵחֲרָדָה, *they journeyed from trepidation,*[35] i.e., from the dread of Egypt which was *traveling after them* [toward the sea] (*Exodus* 14:10). [But then, after their miraculous salvation,] *they encamped in congregations;* this teaches that they formed groups to recite songs of praise.

29. Literally, קְהֵלָתָה means *gathering place.*

30. *Targum Yonasan ben Uzziel.*

31. Literally, מַקְהֵלֹת means *gatherings* or *congregations.*

32. *Peirush HaRokeach.*

33. Two masoretic notes appear on this word: (i) ב׳ חַד חָסֵר וְחַד מָלֵא, *Two, one spelled defectively* [בְּמַקְהֵלֹת, without a ו] *and one spelled in full* [בְּמַקְהֵלוֹת, with a ו]; (ii) ב׳ בִּתְרֵי לִישָּׁנֵי, *Two, with two different meanings,* i.e., in our verse it is a proper noun, the name of a place; in *Psalms,* it is a common noun meaning *in congregations.*

34. *Sotah* 30b-31a.

35. Literally חֲרָדָה means *trepidation, perplexity* (see *Genesis* 27:33).

לג/לד־נב לד־לה וַיִּסְעוּ מִיָּטְבָתָה וַיַּחֲנוּ בְּעַבְרֹנָה: וַיִּסְעוּ מֵעַבְרֹנָה
לו וַיַּחֲנוּ בְּעֶצְיֹן גָּבֶר: וַיִּסְעוּ מֵעֶצְיֹן גָּבֶר וַיַּחֲנוּ
לז בְמִדְבַּר־צִן הִוא קָדֵשׁ: וַיִּסְעוּ מִקָּדֵשׁ וַיַּחֲנוּ בְּהֹר
לח הָהָר בִּקְצֵה אֶרֶץ אֱדוֹם: וַיַּעַל אַהֲרֹן הַכֹּהֵן אֶל־הֹר
הָהָר עַל־פִּי יהוה וַיָּמָת שָׁם בִּשְׁנַת הָאַרְבָּעִים
לְצֵאת בְּנֵי־יִשְׂרָאֵל מֵאֶרֶץ מִצְרַיִם בַּחֹדֶשׁ
לט הַחֲמִישִׁי בְּאֶחָד לַחֹדֶשׁ: וְאַהֲרֹן בֶּן־שָׁלֹשׁ וְעֶשְׂרִים
מ וּמְאַת שָׁנָה בְּמֹתוֹ בְּהֹר הָהָר: וַיִּשְׁמַע
הַכְּנַעֲנִי מֶלֶךְ עֲרָד וְהוּא־יֹשֵׁב בַּנֶּגֶב בְּאֶרֶץ כְּנָעַן
מא בְּבֹא בְּנֵי יִשְׂרָאֵל: וַיִּסְעוּ מֵהֹר הָהָר וַיַּחֲנוּ בְּצַלְמֹנָה:
מב־מג וַיִּסְעוּ מִצַּלְמֹנָה וַיַּחֲנוּ בְּפוּנֹן: וַיִּסְעוּ מִפּוּנֹן וַיַּחֲנוּ
מד בְּאֹבֹת: וַיִּסְעוּ מֵאֹבֹת וַיַּחֲנוּ בְּעִיֵּי הָעֲבָרִים בִּגְבוּל
מה־מו מוֹאָב: וַיִּסְעוּ מֵעִיִּים וַיַּחֲנוּ בְּדִיבֹן גָּד: וַיִּסְעוּ מִדִּיבֹן
מז גָּד וַיַּחֲנוּ בְּעַלְמֹן דִּבְלָתָיְמָה: וַיִּסְעוּ מֵעַלְמֹן
מח דִּבְלָתָיְמָה וַיַּחֲנוּ בְּהָרֵי הָעֲבָרִים לִפְנֵי נְבוֹ: וַיִּסְעוּ
מֵהָרֵי הָעֲבָרִים וַיַּחֲנוּ בְּעַרְבֹת מוֹאָב עַל יַרְדֵּן יְרֵחוֹ:
מט וַיַּחֲנוּ עַל־הַיַּרְדֵּן מִבֵּית הַיְשִׁמֹת עַד אָבֵל הַשִּׁטִּים
שלישי [חמישי] נ בְּעַרְבֹת מוֹאָב: וַיְדַבֵּר יהוה אֶל־מֹשֶׁה
נא בְּעַרְבֹת מוֹאָב עַל־יַרְדֵּן יְרֵחוֹ לֵאמֹר: דַּבֵּר אֶל־בְּנֵי
יִשְׂרָאֵל וְאָמַרְתָּ אֲלֵהֶם כִּי אַתֶּם עֹבְרִים אֶת־הַיַּרְדֵּן
נב אֶל־אֶרֶץ כְּנָעַן: וְהוֹרַשְׁתֶּם אֶת־כָּל־יֹשְׁבֵי הָאָרֶץ
מִפְּנֵיכֶם וְאִבַּדְתֶּם אֵת כָּל־מַשְׂכִּיֹּתָם וְאֵת כָּל־
צַלְמֵי מַסֵּכֹתָם תְּאַבֵּדוּ וְאֵת כָּל־בָּמוֹתָם תַּשְׁמִידוּ:

בעל הטורים

(נב) וְאִבַּדְתֶּם. ב׳ בַּמָּסוֹרֶת – הָכָא ״וְאִבַּדְתֶּם אֵת כָּל מַשְׂכִּיֹּתָם״; וְאִידָךְ ״וְאִבַּדְתֶּם אֶת שְׁמָם״. ״מַשְׂכִּיֹּתָם״ הַיְנוּ בֵּית עֲבוֹדָה זָרָה שֶׁלָּהֶם. וְהַמְאַבֵּד עֲבוֹדָה זָרָה צָרִיךְ לְשָׁרֵשׁ אַחֲרֶיהָ, דִּכְתִיב ״וְאִבַּדְתֶּם אֶת שְׁמָם״:

BAAL HATURIM ELUCIDATED

52. וְאִבַּדְתֶּם — AND YOU SHALL OBLITERATE. The masoretic note, ב׳, means that this word appears twice in the *Tanach:* (i) here, וְאִבַּדְתֶּם אֵת כָּל מַשְׂכִּיֹּתָם, *and you shall obliterate all their temples;* and (ii) וְאִבַּדְתֶּם אֶת שְׁמָם, *And you shall obliterate their*

34 *They journeyed from Jotbathah and encamped in
Abronah.* 35 *They journeyed from Abronah and encamped
in Ezion-geber.* 36 *They journeyed from Ezion-geber and
encamped in the Wilderness of Zin, which is Kadesh.*
37 *They journeyed from Kadesh and encamped in Mount
Hor, at the edge of the land of Edom.* 38 *Then Aaron the
Kohen went up to Mount Hor according to the word of
HASHEM and died there, in the fortieth year after the exodus
of the Children of Israel from the land of Egypt, in the fifth
month on the first of the month.* 39 *Aaron was one hun-
dred and twenty-three years old at his death on Mount Hor.*

40 *The Canaanite king of Arad heard — he was dwelling
in the south, in the Land of Canaan — of the approach of
the Children of Israel.* 41 *They journeyed from Mount Hor
and encamped in Zalmonah.* 42 *They journeyed from
Zalmonah and encamped in Punon.* 43 *They journeyed
from Punon and encamped in Oboth.* 44 *They journeyed
from Oboth and encamped in the ruins of the passes, at the
border of Moab.* 45 *They journeyed from the ruins and
encamped in Dibon-gad.* 46 *They journeyed from Dibon-
gad and encamped in Almon-diblathaimah.* 47 *They jour-
neyed from Almon-diblathaimah and encamped in the
mountains of the passes before Nebo.* 48 *They journeyed
from the mountains of the passes and encamped in the
Plains of Moab by the Jordan, at Jericho.* 49 *They en-
camped by the Jordan, from Beth-jeshimoth until the
Plains of Shittim, in the Plains of Moab.*

50 *HASHEM spoke to Moses in the plains of Moab, by
the Jordan, at Jericho, saying:* 51 *Speak to the Children
of Israel and say to them: When you cross the Jordan
to the Land of Canaan,* 52 *you shall drive out all the
inhabitants of the land before you; and you shall obli-
terate all their temples; all their molten images shall you
destroy; and all their high places shall you demolish.*

BAAL HATURIM ELUCIDATED

names (*Deuteronomy* 12:3). The term מַשְׂכִּיֹּתָם refers to the temples of their idolatry.[36] And one who destroys idols must uproot them, as it is written: *And you shall obliterate their names.*[37]

36. As *Targum Onkelos* renders: בֵּית סְגֻדַּתְהוֹן, *the temple of their worship* (see *Rashi*).

37. *Avodah Zarah* 45b.

נג וְהוֹרַשְׁתֶּ֤ם אֶת־הָאָ֙רֶץ֙ וִֽישַׁבְתֶּם־בָּ֑הּ כִּ֥י לָכֶ֛ם נָתַ֥תִּי
נד אֶת־הָאָ֖רֶץ לָרֶ֥שֶׁת אֹתָֽהּ׃ וְהִתְנַחַלְתֶּם֩ אֶת־הָאָ֨רֶץ
בְּגוֹרָ֜ל לְמִשְׁפְּחֹֽתֵיכֶ֗ם לָרַ֞ב תַּרְבּ֤וּ אֶת־נַחֲלָתוֹ֙
וְלַמְעַט֙ תַּמְעִ֣יט אֶת־נַחֲלָת֔וֹ אֶל֩ אֲשֶׁר־יֵ֨צֵא ל֥וֹ שָׁ֛מָּה
נה הַגּוֹרָ֖ל ל֣וֹ יִהְיֶ֑ה לְמַטּ֥וֹת אֲבֹתֵיכֶ֖ם תִּתְנֶחָֽלוּ׃ וְאִם־לֹ֨א
תוֹרִ֜ישׁוּ אֶת־יֹשְׁבֵ֣י הָאָ֘רֶץ֮ מִפְּנֵיכֶם֒ וְהָיָ֗ה אֲשֶׁ֤ר
תּוֹתִ֙ירוּ֙ מֵהֶ֔ם לְשִׂכִּים֙ בְּעֵ֣ינֵיכֶ֔ם וְלִצְנִינִ֖ם בְּצִדֵּיכֶ֑ם
וְצָרְר֣וּ אֶתְכֶ֔ם עַל־הָאָ֕רֶץ אֲשֶׁ֥ר אַתֶּ֖ם יֹשְׁבִ֥ים בָּֽהּ׃
נו וְהָיָ֗ה כַּאֲשֶׁ֥ר דִּמִּ֛יתִי לַעֲשׂ֥וֹת לָהֶ֖ם אֶעֱשֶׂ֥ה לָכֶֽם׃

בעל הטורים

(נד) **וְהִתְנַחַלְתֶּם.** ב׳ – הָכָא ״וְהִתְנַחַלְתֶּם אֶת הָאָרֶץ״; וְאִידָךְ גַּבֵּי עֶבֶד, ״וְהִתְנַחַלְתֶּם אֹתָם״. דְּעֶבֶד אִתְּקַשׁ לְקַרְקָעוֹת:

❑ **וְהִתְנַחַלְתֶּם.** אַרְבַּע פְּעָמִים נַחֲלָה בַּפָּסוּק, שֶׁכָּל אֶחָד {וְאֶחָד} הָיָה לוֹ בְּאַרְבָּעָה מְקוֹמוֹת, בָּהָר וּבַמִּישׁוֹר וּבַשְּׁפֵלָה וּבְחוֹף הַיָּם:

❑ וְהַפָּסוּק מַתְחִיל וּמְסַיֵּם בְּנַחֲלָה, לוֹמַר שֶׁבְּמָקוֹם שֶׁיָּצָא הַגּוֹרָל, אֲפִלּוּ רָחוֹק זֶה מִזֶּה, אֵין לְשַׁנּוֹת:

(נה) **וְלִצְנִינִם.** לָשׁוֹן צִנָּה, שֶׁיָּבֹאוּ עֲלֵיהֶם בְּמָגֵן וְצִנָּה:

BAAL HATURIM ELUCIDATED

54. וְהִתְנַחַלְתֶּם — YOU SHALL TAKE HOLD [OF THE LAND] AS AN INHERITANCE. The masoretic note, ב׳, means that this word appears twice in the *Tanach:* (i) here, וְהִתְנַחַלְתֶּם אֶת הָאָרֶץ, *You shall take hold of the land as an inheritance;* and (ii) with regard to a Canaanite servant, וְהִתְנַחַלְתֶּם אֹתָם, *You shall hold them as a heritage* (*Leviticus* 25:46).[38] [The similarity of expression implies] that a slave is compared to real property.[39]

❑ **וְהִתְנַחַלְתֶּם — YOU SHALL TAKE HOLD [OF THE LAND] AS AN INHERITANCE.** Four [forms of the word] נַחֲלָה, *inheritance,* appear in this verse.[39a] For each {and every one}[39b] had [an inheritance] in four types of terrain: on the mountain, in the plain, in the lowland and on the seacoast.[40]

38. The Baal HaTurim's comment to that verse is similar to his comment here.

39. *Kiddushin* 22b. The Talmud there derives from the word אֲחֻזָּה, *ancestral heritage,* used in *Leviticus* 25:46 with regard to Canaanite slaves, that such slaves are acquired as a possession through the same three legal means as real property, which is also referred to as אֲחֻזָּה (*Leviticus* 25:25), is acquired. The three means are: (i) the transfer of money; (ii) a document of transfer; or (iii) a proprietary act performed by the new owner (see *Kiddushin* 26a).

39a. (i) וְהִתְנַחַלְתֶּם, *you shall take hold as an inheritance;* (ii-iii) twice, נַחֲלָתוֹ, *its inheritance;* and (iv) תִּתְנֶחָלוּ, *you shall inherit.*

39b. The word וְאֶחָד, *and* (*even*) *one,* is not found in any of the early or later printed editions but does appear in *Shoham Yakar's* manuscript edition.

40. *Peirush HaRokeach.*

In two places, the Talmud speaks of the various types of terrain included in each ancestral heritage — one regarding the tribal heritages, one regarding the individual heritage of each person. With regard to the tribal territories assigned by

[53] *You shall possess the land and you shall settle in it, for to you have I given the land to possess it.* [54] *You shall take hold of the land as an inheritance by lot to your families; to the many you shall increase its inheritance and to the few shall you decrease its inheritance; wherever its lot shall fall, his shall it be, according to the tribes of your fathers you shall inherit.* [55] *But if you do not drive out the inhabitants of the land before you, those of them whom you leave shall be as pins in your eyes and as sieges at your flanks, and they will harass you upon the land in which you dwell.* [56] *And it shall be that what I had meant to do to them, I shall do to you.*

BAAL HATURIM ELUCIDATED

❑ The verse begins and ends with forms of the word נַחֲלָה, *inheritance,*[41] to indicate that whichever place the lot appointed — even if two parts were far from one another[42] — it should not be changed.[43]

55. וְלִצְנִינִם — AND AS SIEGES. [This word is] related to צִנָּה, *a besieging encampment,*[43a] [indicating] that [the nations] will come against [Israel] with [defensive] shield and [offensive] siege.[44,44a]

Joshua, the Talmud states: וְאֵין לְךָ כָּל שֵׁבֶט וְשֵׁבֶט מִיִּשְׂרָאֵל, *And you do not have a single tribe from the nation of Israel,* שֶׁאֵין לוֹ, *that does not have* [*some part of its portion*], בָּהָר, *on the mountain,* וּבַשְּׁפֵלָה, *and in the lowland,* וּבַנֶּגֶב, *and in the dry land* [i.e., the treeless plain (*Rashi*)], וּבָעֵמֶק, *and in the valley* [i.e., the seacoast (*Maharsha*)] (*Bava Kamma* 81b).

Elsewhere, the Talmud speaks of the individual heritages of each Israelite that will be assigned in the time of *Mashiach:* Unlike the division of the Land of Israel in this world [i.e., in the time of Joshua], will be the division in the world to come . . . In the World to Come, אֵין לְךָ כָּל אֶחָד וְאֶחָד, *there will not be a single one,* שֶׁאֵין לוֹ, *who does not have* [*some part of his portion*], בָּהָר, *on the mountain,* וּבַשְּׁפֵלָה, *and in the lowland,* וּבָעֵמֶק, *and in the valley* [i.e., the seacoast] (*Bava Basra* 122a).

Now, at first glance, the Baal HaTurim seems to have combined these two Talmudic passages, for he begins with {כָּל אֶחָד {וְאֶחָד, as does the statement about the future division that appears in *Bava Basra.* But he goes on to enumerate four types of terrain, as in the statement about Joshua's division that appears in *Bava Kamma*!

It is probable, however, the Baal HaTurim's comment refers to the original division of the land by Joshua. Thus, he states, הָיָה לוֹ, *he had,* rather than יִהְיֶה לוֹ, *he will have.* Moreover, *Tosafos* (s.v., אין לך כל שבט; see also *Dikdukei Soferim*) records an alternative reading of the passage in *Bava Kamma,* which has וְאֵין לְךָ כָּל אֶחָד וְאֶחָד, *And you do not have a single one,* in place of, וְאֵין לְךָ כָּל שֵׁבֶט וְשֵׁבֶט, *And you do not have a single tribe.* Even though that reading is rejected by *Tosafos,* it may have been the version in the Baal HaTurim's copy of *Bava Kamma* (*VeChur LaZahav*).

41. That is, it begins with וְהִתְנַחַלְתֶּם, *you shall take hold as an inheritance,* and ends with תִּתְנֶחָלוּ, *you shall inherit.*

42. This seems to imply that the lot may assign a non-contiguous territory to a tribe, a concept that is difficult to comprehend. Why would the original division of the land [into territories that were to be assigned to the tribes by lot] allow a tribal heritage that is not contiguous? Perhaps the Baal HaTurim's comment refers specifically to the tribe of Manasseh — half of which received its territory on the other side of the Jordan, along with the tribes of Reuben and Gad. The Baal HaTurim's allusion teaches that if the lot assigns to the other half of Manasseh a territory that is not contiguous with its first half, that assignment should not be changed (*VeChur LaZahav*).

43. *Peirush HaRokeach.*

43a. See *Rashi* to *Ezekiel* 23:24.

44. The expression מָגֵן וְצִנָּה appears in *Jeremiah* 46:3, *Ezekiel* 39:9 and *Psalms* 35:2.

44a. *Targum Onkelos* renders the expression

לד/א-יז א-ב וַיְדַבֵּר יְהוָה אֶל־מֹשֶׁה לֵּאמֹר: צַו אֶת־בְּנֵי יִשְׂרָאֵל
וְאָמַרְתָּ אֲלֵהֶם כִּי־אַתֶּם בָּאִים אֶל־הָאָרֶץ כְּנָעַן זֹאת
הָאָרֶץ אֲשֶׁר תִּפֹּל לָכֶם בְּנַחֲלָה אֶרֶץ כְּנַעַן
ג לִגְבֻלֹתֶיהָ: וְהָיָה לָכֶם פְּאַת־נֶגֶב מִמִּדְבַּר־צִן עַל־יְדֵי
אֱדוֹם וְהָיָה לָכֶם גְּבוּל נֶגֶב מִקְצֵה יָם־הַמֶּלַח קֵדְמָה:
ד וְנָסַב לָכֶם הַגְּבוּל מִנֶּגֶב לְמַעֲלֵה עַקְרַבִּים וְעָבַר צִנָה
[°וְהָיוּ ק׳] °והיה תּוֹצְאֹתָיו מִנֶּגֶב לְקָדֵשׁ בַּרְנֵעַ וְיָצָא חֲצַר־אַדָּר
ה וְעָבַר עַצְמֹנָה: וְנָסַב הַגְּבוּל מֵעַצְמוֹן נַחְלָה מִצְרָיִם
ו וְהָיוּ תוֹצְאֹתָיו הַיָּמָּה: וּגְבוּל יָם וְהָיָה לָכֶם הַיָּם
ז הַגָּדוֹל וּגְבוּל זֶה־יִהְיֶה לָכֶם גְּבוּל יָם: וְזֶה־יִהְיֶה לָכֶם
ח גְּבוּל צָפוֹן מִן־הַיָּם הַגָּדֹל תְּתָאוּ לָכֶם הֹר הָהָר: מֵהֹר
הָהָר תְּתָאוּ לְבֹא חֲמָת וְהָיוּ תּוֹצְאֹת הַגְּבֻל צְדָדָה:
ט וְיָצָא הַגְּבֻל זִפְרֹנָה וְהָיוּ תוֹצְאֹתָיו חֲצַר עֵינָן
י זֶה־יִהְיֶה לָכֶם גְּבוּל צָפוֹן: וְהִתְאַוִּיתֶם לָכֶם לִגְבוּל
יא קֵדְמָה מֵחֲצַר עֵינָן שְׁפָמָה: וְיָרַד הַגְּבֻל מִשְּׁפָם
הָרִבְלָה מִקֶּדֶם לָעָיִן וְיָרַד הַגְּבֻל וּמָחָה עַל־כֶּתֶף
יב יָם־כִּנֶּרֶת קֵדְמָה: וְיָרַד הַגְּבוּל הַיַּרְדֵּנָה וְהָיוּ
תוֹצְאֹתָיו יָם הַמֶּלַח זֹאת תִּהְיֶה לָכֶם הָאָרֶץ
יג לִגְבֻלֹתֶיהָ סָבִיב: וַיְצַו מֹשֶׁה אֶת־בְּנֵי יִשְׂרָאֵל לֵאמֹר
זֹאת הָאָרֶץ אֲשֶׁר תִּתְנַחֲלוּ אֹתָהּ בְּגוֹרָל אֲשֶׁר צִוָּה
יד יְהוָה לָתֵת לְתִשְׁעַת הַמַּטּוֹת וַחֲצִי הַמַּטֶּה: כִּי לָקְחוּ
מַטֵּה בְנֵי הָרְאוּבֵנִי לְבֵית אֲבֹתָם וּמַטֵּה בְנֵי־הַגָּדִי
טו לְבֵית אֲבֹתָם וַחֲצִי מַטֵּה מְנַשֶּׁה לָקְחוּ נַחֲלָתָם: שְׁנֵי
הַמַּטּוֹת וַחֲצִי הַמַּטֶּה לָקְחוּ נַחֲלָתָם מֵעֵבֶר לְיַרְדֵּן
יְרֵחוֹ קֵדְמָה מִזְרָחָה:
רביעי [ששי] טז-יז וַיְדַבֵּר יְהוָה אֶל־מֹשֶׁה לֵּאמֹר: אֵלֶּה שְׁמוֹת הָאֲנָשִׁים

בעל הטורים

לד (יז) אֵלֶּה שְׁמוֹת הָאֲנָשִׁים. וּלְמַטָּה פַּעַם אַחֶרֶת, ״וְאֵלֶּה שְׁמוֹת הָאֲנָשִׁים״. לוֹמַר שֶׁנָּאִים בִּשְׁמוֹתָם וְנָאִים בְּמַעֲשֵׂיהֶם:

וּלְמַשְׁרְיָן מַקְּפָנְכוֹן as וְלִצְנִינִם בְּצִדֵּיכֶם, *and like encampments surrounding you.*

34/1-17 1 *HASHEM spoke to Moses, saying:* 2 *Command the Children of*
Israel and say to them: When you come to the land of Canaan, this
is the land that shall fall to you as an inheritance, the land of
Canaan according to its borders. 3 *Your southern side shall be from*
the Wilderness of Zin at the side of Edom, and your southern border
shall be from the edge of the Salt Sea to the east. 4 *The border shall*
go around south of Maaleh-akrabbim, and shall pass toward Zin;
and its outskirts shall be south of Kadesh-barnea; then it shall go
out to Hazar-addar and pass to Azmon. 5 *The border shall go*
around from Azmon to the stream of Egypt, and its outskirts shall
be toward the sea. 6 *The western border: It shall be for you the*
Great Sea and the district; this shall be for you the western border.
7 *This shall be for you the northern border: from the Great Sea*
you shall turn to Mount Hor. 8 *From Mount Hor you shall turn to the*
approach to Hamath, and the outskirts of the border shall be
toward Zedad. 9 *The border shall go forth toward Zifron and its*
outskirts shall be Hazar-enan; this shall be for you the northern
border. 10 *You shall draw yourselves as the eastern border from*
Hazar-enan to Shefam. 11 *The border shall descend from Shefam to*
Riblah, east of Ain; the border shall descend and touch upon the
bank of the Kinnereth Sea to the east. 12 *The border shall descend to*
the Jordan, and its outskirts shall be the Salt Sea; this shall be the
land for you, according to its borders all around.
13 *Moses commanded the Children of Israel, saying: This is the*
land that you shall divide as an inheritance by lot, which HASHEM
has commanded to give to the nine-and-a-half tribes. 14 *For the tribe*
of the children of Reuben have taken according to their fathers'
house, and the tribe of the children of Gad according to their fathers'
house, and half the tribe of Manasseh have taken their inheritance.
15 *Two-and-a-half tribes have taken their inheritance on the bank of*
the Jordan by Jericho, eastward toward the sunrise.
16 *HASHEM spoke to Moses, saying:* 17 *These are the names of the*

BAAL HATURIM ELUCIDATED

XXXIV.

17. אֵלֶּה שְׁמוֹת הָאֲנָשִׁים — **THESE ARE THE NAMES OF THE MEN.** This phrase is repeated below — וְאֵלֶּה שְׁמוֹת הָאֲנָשִׁים, *and these are the names of the men* (v. 19)[45] — to indicate that they are becoming in their names and becoming in their deeds.[46]

45. The second verse could have used the shorter form וְאֵלֶּה שְׁמוֹתָם, *And these are their names,* as in 13:4 above.

46. *Peirush HaRokeach.* The Midrash teaches: There are some people whose names are becoming, but whose deeds are loathsome; and some

אֲשֶׁר־יִנְחֲלוּ לָכֶם אֶת־הָאָרֶץ אֶלְעָזָר הַכֹּהֵן
יח וִיהוֹשֻׁעַ בִּן־נוּן: וְנָשִׂיא אֶחָד נָשִׂיא אֶחָד מִמַּטֶּה
יט תִּקְחוּ לִנְחֹל אֶת־הָאָרֶץ: וְאֵלֶּה שְׁמוֹת הָאֲנָשִׁים
כ לְמַטֵּה יְהוּדָה כָּלֵב בֶּן־יְפֻנֶּה: וּלְמַטֵּה בְּנֵי שִׁמְעוֹן
כא שְׁמוּאֵל בֶּן־עַמִּיהוּד: לְמַטֵּה בִנְיָמִן אֱלִידָד בֶּן־
כב-כג כִּסְלוֹן: וּלְמַטֵּה בְנֵי־דָן נָשִׂיא בֻּקִּי בֶּן־יָגְלִי: לִבְנֵי
יוֹסֵף לְמַטֵּה בְנֵי־מְנַשֶּׁה נָשִׂיא חַנִּיאֵל בֶּן־אֵפֹד:
כד וּלְמַטֵּה בְנֵי־אֶפְרַיִם נָשִׂיא קְמוּאֵל בֶּן־שִׁפְטָן:
כה-כו וּלְמַטֵּה בְנֵי־זְבוּלֻן נָשִׂיא אֱלִיצָפָן בֶּן־פַּרְנָךְ: וּלְמַטֵּה
כז בְנֵי־יִשָּׂשכָר נָשִׂיא פַּלְטִיאֵל בֶּן־עַזָּן: וּלְמַטֵּה בְנֵי־
כח אָשֵׁר נָשִׂיא אֲחִיהוּד בֶּן־שְׁלֹמִי: וּלְמַטֵּה בְנֵי־
כט נַפְתָּלִי נָשִׂיא פְּדַהְאֵל בֶּן־עַמִּיהוּד: אֵלֶּה אֲשֶׁר צִוָּה
יְהוָה לְנַחֵל אֶת־בְּנֵי־יִשְׂרָאֵל בְּאֶרֶץ כְּנָעַן:
לה חמישי א וַיְדַבֵּר יְהוָה אֶל־מֹשֶׁה בְּעַרְבֹת מוֹאָב עַל־יַרְדֵּן
ב יְרֵחוֹ לֵאמֹר: צַו אֶת־בְּנֵי יִשְׂרָאֵל וְנָתְנוּ לַלְוִיִּם
מִנַּחֲלַת אֲחֻזָּתָם עָרִים לָשָׁבֶת וּמִגְרָשׁ לֶעָרִים
ג סְבִיבֹתֵיהֶם תִּתְּנוּ לַלְוִיִּם: וְהָיוּ הֶעָרִים לָהֶם לָשָׁבֶת
וּמִגְרְשֵׁיהֶם יִהְיוּ לִבְהֶמְתָּם וְלִרְכֻשָׁם וּלְכֹל חַיָּתָם:

בעל הטורים

(כא) אֱלִידָד בֶּן כִּסְלוֹן. הוּא אֶלְדָּד. וְהוֹסִיפוּ לוֹ יוּ״ד עַל שֵׁם הַנְּבוּאָה, שֶׁנִּקְרֵאת בַּעֲשָׂרָה לְשׁוֹנוֹת:

BAAL HATURIM ELUCIDATED

21. אֱלִידָד בֶּן כִּסְלוֹן — ELIDAD SON OF CHISLON. He is Eldad (see 11:26-27

whose names are loathsome, but whose deeds are becoming; some whose names and deeds are both loathsome; and some whose names and deeds are both becoming. Examples of people whose names are becoming but whose deeds are loathsome are Ishmael and Esau, for יִשְׁמָעֵאל implies שׁוֹמֵעַ אֵל, *he listens* [*to*] *God,* but he did not listen, and עֵשָׂו implies עוֹשֶׂה רְצוֹן עוֹשָׂיו, *he does the will of his Maker,* but he did not do God's will; examples of people whose names are loathsome but whose deeds are becoming are those who returned from the Babylonian exile . . . and built the *Beis HaMikdash;* examples of those whose names and deeds are both loathsome are the spies . . . (see the Baal HaTurim to 13:16 above, with note 19); and of those whose names and deeds are both becoming are the tribes . . . (*Tanchuma, Shelach* 6; see also *Bereishis Rabbah* 71:3). The Baal HaTurim adds the tribal leaders listed in our passage to the category of people whose names and deeds are both becoming.

The letters of the word אֲנָשִׁים can be rearranged to spell שֶׁנָּאִים, *for they are becoming.* With the repetition of the term הָאֲנָשִׁים, the Torah alludes to the fact that they were becoming in deed as well as in name (*VeChur LaZahav*).

men who are to take possession of the land for you: Elazar
the Kohen and Joshua son of Nun, [18] *and one leader*
from each tribe shall you take to possess the Land. [19] *And*
these are the names of the men: for the tribe of Judah,
Caleb son of Jephunneh; [20] *and for the tribe of the children*
of Simeon, Shemuel son of Ammihud; [21] *for the tribe of*
Benjamin, Elidad son of Chislon; [22] *and for the tribe of*
the children of Dan, as leader, Bukki son of Jogli; [23] *for*
the children of Joseph, for the tribe of the children of
Manasseh, as leader, Hanniel son of Ephod; [24] *and for*
the tribe of the children of Ephraim, as leader, Kemuel
son of Shiftan; [25] *and for the tribe of the children of Zebu-*
lun, as leader, Elizaphan son of Parnach; [26] *and for the*
tribe of the children of Issachar, as leader, Paltiel son
of Azzan; [27] *and for the tribe of the children of Asher,*
as leader, Ahihud son of Shelomi; [28] *and for the tribe*
of the children of Naphtali, as leader, Pedahel son of
Ammihud. [29] *These are the ones whom* HASHEM *com-*
manded to apportion to the Children of Israel in the Land of
Canaan.

35 [1] HASHEM *spoke to Moses in the plains of Moab, by the*
Jordan, at Jericho, saying: [2] *Command the Children of*
Israel that they shall give to the Levites, from the heritage of
their possession, cities for dwelling, and open space for the
cities all around them shall you give to the Levites. [3] *The*
cities shall be theirs for dwelling, and their open space shall
be for their animals, for their wealth and for all their needs.

BAAL HATURIM ELUCIDATED

above).[47] [Whereas he prophesied,] they[47a] added a י (= 10) to his name as an allusion to prophecy, which is referred to by ten different names[48] [in the *Tanach*].[49]

47. The Midrash identifies Eldad and Medad (11:26-27 above) with Elidad son of Chislon (v. 21 here) and Kemuel son of Shiftan (v. 24 here) respectively (*Tanchuma, Beha'alosecha* 12).

47a. The text follows *Shoham Yakar's* manuscript edition; the plural "they" refers to either the nation in general or the tribe of Benjamin. Virtually all other editions have the singular form וְהוֹסִיף, *he added,* and refers to either God or Moses.

48. According to the Midrash, prophecy is called by ten names: (i) נְבוּאָה — e.g., *II Chronicles* 15:8; (ii) חָזוֹן — e.g., *Ezekiel* 7:26; (iii) הַטָּפָה — e.g., *Ezekiel* 21:2; (iv) דִּבּוּר — e.g., *Hosea* 1:1; (v) אֲמִירָה — e.g., *Ezekiel* 21:33; (vi) צִוּוּי — e.g., *Ezekiel* 37:7; (vii) מַשָּׂא — e.g., *Nahum* 1:1; (viii) מָשָׁל — e.g., *Ezekiel* 17:2; (ix) מְלִיצָה — e.g., *Habbakuk* 2:6; and (x) חִידָה — e.g., *Ezekiel* 17:2 (*Bereishis Rabbah* 44:6; also *Avos DeRabbi Nosson* with minor differences).

49. *Peirush HaRokeach.*

לה/ד-י

ד וּמִגְרְשֵׁי֙ הֶעָרִ֔ים אֲשֶׁ֥ר תִּתְּנ֖וּ לַלְוִיִּ֑ם מִקִּ֤יר הָעִיר֙
ה וָח֔וּצָה אֶ֥לֶף אַמָּ֖ה סָבִֽיב׃ וּמַדֹּתֶ֞ם מִח֣וּץ לָעִ֗יר
אֶת־פְּאַת־קֵ֣דְמָה אַלְפַּ֪יִם בָּֽאַמָּ֟ה וְאֶת־פְּאַת־נֶ֜גֶב
אַלְפַּ֨יִם בָּאַמָּ֜ה וְאֶת־פְּאַת־יָ֣ם ׀ אַלְפַּ֣יִם בָּאַמָּ֗ה וְאֵ֨ת
פְּאַ֥ת צָפ֛וֹן אַלְפַּ֥יִם בָּאַמָּ֖ה וְהָעִ֣יר בַּתָּ֑וֶךְ זֶ֚ה יִהְיֶ֣ה
ו לָהֶ֔ם מִגְרְשֵׁ֖י הֶעָרִֽים׃ וְאֵ֣ת הֶעָרִ֗ים אֲשֶׁ֤ר תִּתְּנוּ֙ לַלְוִיִּ֔ם
אֵ֚ת שֵׁשׁ־עָרֵ֣י הַמִּקְלָ֔ט אֲשֶׁ֣ר תִּתְּנ֔וּ לָנֻ֥ס שָׁ֖מָּה
ז הָרֹצֵ֑חַ וַעֲלֵיהֶ֣ם תִּתְּנ֔וּ אַרְבָּעִ֥ים וּשְׁתַּ֖יִם עִֽיר׃ כָּל־
הֶֽעָרִ֗ים אֲשֶׁ֤ר תִּתְּנוּ֙ לַלְוִיִּ֔ם אַרְבָּעִ֥ים וּשְׁמֹנֶ֖ה עִ֑יר
ח אֶתְהֶ֖ן וְאֶת־מִגְרְשֵׁיהֶֽן׃ וְהֶעָרִ֗ים אֲשֶׁ֤ר תִּתְּנוּ֙ מֵאֲחֻזַּ֣ת
בְּנֵֽי־יִשְׂרָאֵ֔ל מֵאֵ֤ת הָרַב֙ תַּרְבּ֔וּ וּמֵאֵ֥ת הַמְעַ֖ט תַּמְעִ֑יטוּ
אִ֗ישׁ כְּפִ֤י נַחֲלָתוֹ֙ אֲשֶׁ֣ר יִנְחָ֔לוּ יִתֵּ֥ן מֵעָרָ֖יו לַלְוִיִּֽם׃
ששי [שביעי] ט-י וַיְדַבֵּ֥ר יְהֹוָ֖ה אֶל־מֹשֶׁ֥ה לֵּאמֹֽר׃ דַּבֵּר֙ אֶל־בְּנֵ֣י
יִשְׂרָאֵ֔ל וְאָמַרְתָּ֖ אֲלֵהֶ֑ם כִּ֛י אַתֶּ֥ם עֹבְרִ֥ים אֶת־הַיַּרְדֵּ֖ן

בעל הטורים

לה (ה) וּמַדֹּתֶם מִחוּץ לָעִיר . . . אַלְפַּיִם בָּאַמָּה. שֶׁאַלְפַּיִם אַמָּה יִהְיוּ חוּץ מִשִּׁבְעִים אַמָּה וְשִׁירַיִם. וְזֶהוּ "וּמַדֹּתֶם מִחוּץ לָעִיר {. . . אַלְפַּיִם בָּאַמָּה}":

(ח) יִנְחָלוּ. ג' בַּמָּסוֹרֶת – הָכָא "כְּפִי נַחֲלָתוֹ אֲשֶׁר יִנְחָלוּ"; וְאִידָךְ "לִשְׁמוֹת מַטּוֹת אֲבֹתָם יִנְחָלוּ"; "כָּבוֹד חֲכָמִים יִנְחָלוּ". "אֲשֶׁר יִנְחָלוּ", "לִשְׁמוֹת מַטּוֹת אֲבֹתָם יִנְחָלוּ", כִּי לְיוֹצְאֵי מִצְרַיִם נִתְחַלְּקָה הָאָרֶץ. וְכֵן "לִשְׁמוֹת מַטּוֹת אֲבֹתָם" יִנְחֲלוּ חֲכָמִים, דְּבַחֲמִשָּׁה דְבָרִים הָאָב זוֹכֶה לִבְנוֹ, וְקָתָנֵי בְּחָכְמָה:

BAAL HATURIM ELUCIDATED

XXXV.

5. וּמַדֹּתֶם מִחוּץ לָעִיר . . . אַלְפַּיִם בָּאַמָּה — YOU SHALL MEASURE FROM OUTSIDE THE CITY. . . TWO THOUSAND CUBITS. [This teaches] that the two thousand cubits are beyond the seventy plus cubits[50] [after the last dwelling]. This is implied by the phrase: *You shall* [*begin to*] *measure from outside the city,* {*. . . two thousand cubits*}.[51]

8. יִנְחָלוּ — THEY SHALL INHERIT. The masoretic note, ג׳, means that this word appears three times in the *Tanach:* (i) here, כְּפִי נַחֲלָתוֹ אֲשֶׁר יִנְחָלוּ, [*each*] *according to his inheritance that they shall inherit;* (ii) לִשְׁמוֹת מַטּוֹת אֲבֹתָם יִנְחָלוּ, *According to the*

50. Halachically, a city ends approximately seventy and two-third (the square root of 5000) cubits past its last house (see *Eruvin* 57a with *Rashi,* s.v., נותנין קרפף).

51. The words enclosed in braces are not found in the early printed editions but do appear in the manuscripts used by *Shoham Yakar.*

4 *The open spaces of the cities that you shall give to the*
Levites, from the wall of the city outward: a thousand
cubits all around. 5 *You shall measure from outside the city*
on the eastern side two thousand cubits; on the southern
side two thousand cubits; on the western side two thou-
sand cubits; and on the northern side two thousand cubits,
with the city in the middle; this shall be for them the open
spaces of the cities. 6 *The cities that you shall give to the*
Levites: the six cities of refuge that you shall provide for
a murderer to flee there, and in addition to them you shall
give forty-two cities. 7 *All the cities that you shall give to*
the Levites: forty-eight cities, them and their open spaces.
8 *The cities that you shall give from the possession of the*
Children of Israel, from the many you shall increase and
from the few you shall decrease, each according to his
inheritance that they shall inherit shall he give of his cities to
the Levites.

9 *HASHEM spoke to Moses, saying:* 10 *Speak to the Chil-*
dren of Israel and say to them: When you cross the Jordan

BAAL HATURIM ELUCIDATED

names of their fathers' tribes shall they inherit (*Numbers* 26:55); and (iii) כָּבוֹד חֲכָמִים יִנְחָלוּ, *The wise shall inherit honor* (*Proverbs* 3:35). [The similarity of expression connects the two passages from *Numbers:*] Regarding *that* [*which*] *they shall inherit,* it shall be *according to the names of their father's tribes that they shall inherit,* for the land was apportioned to those who went forth from Egypt [and had subsequently died].[52]

Similarly, [the verse from *Proverbs* is connected to the verse about the fathers:] *According to the names of their fathers they shall inherit* [the wisdom of] the wise, for a father benefits his son in five ways,[53] and wisdom is listed among them.[54]

❑ {The comment beginning בְּפָרָשַׁת that appears at this point in most editions appears at verse 25 below.}

52. *Bava Basra* 117a; see *Rashi* to 26:55 above, s.v., לשמות מטות. The Torah made the laws regarding the initial inheritance of land different from the regular laws of inheritance. Normally, the living inherit the estates of the dead, but here, the dead inherited from the living. For example: Two brothers went forth from Egypt, one had one son, the other had three. The one's son took one portion of the land; the other's sons took three portions . . . Their four portions reverted to their [deceased] grandfather and were subsequently reapportioned to them in equal shares, i.e., each of the two original brothers received half of the four portions and bequeathed them to his son[s]. Thus, the one grandson received half of the total inheritance, while each of the three grandsons received only one-sixth.

53. *Eduyos* 2:9.

54. The Baal HaTurim cites and elaborates on that Mishnah in his comments to 11:12 above.

יא אַרְצָה כְּנָעַן: וְהִקְרִיתֶם לָכֶם עָרִים עָרֵי מִקְלָט
יב תִּהְיֶינָה לָכֶם וְנָס שָׁמָּה רֹצֵחַ מַכֵּה־נֶפֶשׁ בִּשְׁגָגָה: וְהָיוּ
לָכֶם הֶעָרִים לְמִקְלָט מִגֹּאֵל וְלֹא יָמוּת הָרֹצֵחַ
יג עַד־עָמְדוֹ לִפְנֵי הָעֵדָה לַמִּשְׁפָּט: וְהֶעָרִים אֲשֶׁר תִּתֵּנוּ
יד שֵׁשׁ־עָרֵי מִקְלָט תִּהְיֶינָה לָכֶם: אֵת | שְׁלֹשׁ הֶעָרִים
תִּתְּנוּ מֵעֵבֶר לַיַּרְדֵּן וְאֵת שְׁלֹשׁ הֶעָרִים תִּתְּנוּ בְּאֶרֶץ
טו כְּנָעַן עָרֵי מִקְלָט תִּהְיֶינָה: לִבְנֵי יִשְׂרָאֵל וְלַגֵּר
וְלַתּוֹשָׁב בְּתוֹכָם תִּהְיֶינָה שֵׁשׁ־הֶעָרִים הָאֵלֶּה לְמִקְלָט
טז לָנוּס שָׁמָּה כָּל־מַכֵּה־נֶפֶשׁ בִּשְׁגָגָה: וְאִם־בִּכְלִי
יז בַרְזֶל | הִכָּהוּ וַיָּמֹת רֹצֵחַ הוּא מוֹת יוּמַת הָרֹצֵחַ: וְאִם
בְּאֶבֶן יָד אֲשֶׁר־יָמוּת בָּהּ הִכָּהוּ וַיָּמֹת רֹצֵחַ הוּא
יח מוֹת יוּמַת הָרֹצֵחַ: אוֹ בִּכְלִי עֵץ־יָד אֲשֶׁר־יָמוּת
יט בּוֹ הִכָּהוּ וַיָּמֹת רֹצֵחַ הוּא מוֹת יוּמַת הָרֹצֵחַ: גֹּאֵל
הַדָּם הוּא יָמִית אֶת־הָרֹצֵחַ בְּפִגְעוֹ־בוֹ הוּא יְמִתֶנּוּ:
כ וְאִם־בְּשִׂנְאָה יֶהְדָּפֶנּוּ אוֹ־הִשְׁלִיךְ עָלָיו בִּצְדִיָּה
כא וַיָּמֹת: אוֹ בְאֵיבָה הִכָּהוּ בְיָדוֹ וַיָּמֹת מוֹת־יוּמַת הַמַּכֶּה
רֹצֵחַ הוּא גֹּאֵל הַדָּם יָמִית אֶת־הָרֹצֵחַ בְּפִגְעוֹ־בוֹ:

בעל הטורים

(יז) בְּאֶבֶן. ג׳ — הָכָא "וְאִם בְּאֶבֶן יָד אֲשֶׁר יָמוּת בָּהּ"; וְאִידָךְ "וְהִכָּה אִישׁ אֶת רֵעֵהוּ בְּאֶבֶן"; "בְּאֶבֶן הַמֶּלֶךְ". "וְהִכָּה אִישׁ אֶת רֵעֵהוּ בְּאֶבֶן" — אִם הוּא בְּאֶבֶן יָד צָרִיךְ אֹמֶד שֶׁיְּהֵא בוֹ כְּדֵי לְהָמִית, שֶׁנֶּאֱמַר "אֲשֶׁר יָמוּת בָּהּ". אֲבָל אִם הוּא גָדוֹל כְּאֶבֶן הַמֶּלֶךְ, אֵין צָרִיךְ אֹמֶד. מִמֵּילָא יֵשׁ בּוֹ כְּדֵי לְהָמִית:

BAAL HATURIM ELUCIDATED

17. בְּאֶבֶן — WITH A STONE. The masoretic note, ג׳, means that this word appears three times in the *Tanach:* (i) here, וְאִם בְּאֶבֶן יָד אֲשֶׁר יָמוּת בָּהּ, *or if with a hand-sized stone by which one could die;* (ii) וְהִכָּה אִישׁ אֶת רֵעֵהוּ בְּאֶבֶן, *and a man strikes his fellow with a stone* (*Exodus* 21:18); and (iii) בְּאֶבֶן הַמֶּלֶךְ, *by the king's weighing stone* (*II Samuel* 14:26). If *a man strikes his fellow with a stone,* [then,] if it is a hand-sized stone, it must be assessed to ascertain whether it is of sufficient size to kill a person,[55] as it is stated, אֲשֶׁר יָמוּת בָּהּ, *by which one could die.* If, however,

55. That is, we must assess whether the death actually was caused by the blow with the stone, taking into account all the circumstances surrounding the incident, including the strength of the killer, the size and weight of the stone, the health of the victim and his strength to withstand the blow, the distance from which the rock was thrown (*Rambam, Hilchos Rotzeach* 3:1-3).

to the Land of Canaan, 11 *you shall designate cities for*
yourselves, cities of refuge shall they be for you, and a
murderer shall flee there — one who takes a life unintention-
ally. 12 *The cities shall be for you a refuge from the avenger,*
so that the murderer will not die until he stands before the
assembly for judgment. 13 *As to the cities that you shall*
designate, there shall be six cities of refuge for you. 14 *Three*
cities shall you designate on the other side of the Jordan,
and three cities shall you designate in the Land of Canaan;
they shall be cities of refuge. 15 *For the Children of Israel and*
the proselyte and resident among them shall these six cities
be a refuge, for anyone who kills a person unintentionally to
flee there.

16 *If he had struck him with an iron implement and he*
died, he is a murderer; the murderer shall surely be put to
death. 17 *Or if with a hand-sized stone by which one could*
die did he strike him, and he died, he is a murderer; the
murderer shall surely be put to death. 18 *Or if he struck him*
with a hand-sized wood implement through which one
could die, and he died, he is a murderer; the murderer shall
surely be put to death. 19 *The avenger of the blood, he shall*
kill the murderer; when he encounters him, he shall kill him.
20 *If he pushed him out of hatred or hurled upon him from*
ambush, and he died; 21 *or in enmity struck him with his*
hand and he died, the assailant shall surely be put to death,
he is a murderer; the avenger of the blood shall kill the
murderer when he encounters him.

the stone is as large as *the king's weighing stone,*[56] it does not require assessment, for it is obvious that it is large enough to kill.[56a]

56. The verse containing the phrase בְּאֶבֶן הַמֶּלֶךְ speaks of King David's son Absalom's annual haircut [for as a נְזִיר עוֹלָם, *permanent nazir,* Absalom was permitted to cut his hair no more than once a year (*Nazir* 4b)]. That verse ends: . . . *he weighed the hair of his head at two hundred shekels by the king's weighing stone.* However, neither the verse nor the Baal HaTurim tells us the weight of the king's stone or the difference between the king's stone and any other weighing stone. *Ittur Bikkurim* assumes that since the verse mentions אֶבֶן הַמֶּלֶךְ in conjunction with two hundred *shekel*-weight of hair, the Baal HaTurim speaks of a stone of that weight. [In modern-day terminology a 200-*shekel* weight is equal to a little under two pounds.]

56a. The Baal HaTurim seems to mean that once it has been established that the stone meets the criteria of אֶבֶן הַמֶּלֶךְ, the remainder of the assessment (described in note 55) need not be completed. Regardless of any other circumstances, the stone is considered one *by which one could die.* However, there is no other source known for this law.

לה/כב־כה כב וְאִם־בְּפֶתַע בְּלֹא־אֵיבָה הֲדָפוֹ אוֹ־הִשְׁלִיךְ עָלָיו כָּל־
כג כְּלִי בְּלֹא צְדִיָּה׃ אוֹ בְכָל־אֶבֶן אֲשֶׁר־יָמוּת בָּהּ בְּלֹא
רְאוֹת וַיַּפֵּל עָלָיו וַיָּמֹת וְהוּא לֹא־אוֹיֵב לוֹ וְלֹא מְבַקֵּשׁ
כד רָעָתוֹ׃ וְשָׁפְטוּ הָעֵדָה בֵּין הַמַּכֶּה וּבֵין גֹּאֵל הַדָּם עַל
כה הַמִּשְׁפָּטִים הָאֵלֶּה׃ וְהִצִּילוּ הָעֵדָה אֶת־הָרֹצֵחַ מִיַּד
גֹּאֵל הַדָּם וְהֵשִׁיבוּ אֹתוֹ הָעֵדָה אֶל־עִיר מִקְלָטוֹ

בעל הטורים

(כב) הֲדָפוֹ. ב׳ בַּמָּסוֹרֶת — ״בְּלֹא אֵיבָה הֲדָפוֹ״; ״לֹא עָמַד כִּי ה׳ הֲדָפוֹ״. וְהַיְנוּ דְּאָמְרִינַן, ״וְהָאֱלֹהִים אִנָּה לְיָדוֹ״, מָשָׁל לִשְׁנֵי בְנֵי אָדָם, אֶחָד הָרַג שׁוֹגֵג וְאֶחָד הָרַג מֵזִיד. הַקָּדוֹשׁ בָּרוּךְ הוּא מְזַמְּנָן לְפֻנְדָּק אֶחָד. זֶה שֶׁהָרַג שׁוֹגֵג, עוֹלֶה בַסֻּלָּם וְנוֹפֵל עַל זֶה שֶׁהָרַג מֵזִיד. וְנִמְצָא הוֹרְגוֹ בְשׁוֹגֵג וְנִתְחַיֵּב גָּלוּת. וְזֶהוּ ״בְּלֹא אֵיבָה הֲדָפוֹ״, וְרוֹצֶה לְהִתְחַזֵּק וְלַעֲמֹד, וְלֹא יוּכַל לַעֲמֹד, ״כִּי ה׳ הֲדָפוֹ״:

(כג) וַיַּפֵּל. ג׳ — ״וַיַּפֵּל עָלָיו וַיָּמֹת״; ״וַיַּפֵּל בְּקֶרֶב מַחֲנֵהוּ״; ״וַיַּפֵּל ה׳ אֱלֹהִים תַּרְדֵּמָה״. כִּדְאִיתָא בְּמִדְרָשׁ, יוֹתֵר מִמַּה שֶּׁהָרַג בָּהֶם הַשְּׂלָו עַל יְדֵי אֲכִילָה, הָרַג בָּהֶם עַל יְדֵי יְרִידָה, שֶׁיָּרַד וְנָפַל עַל רֹאשָׁם. וְזֶהוּ ״וַיַּפֵּל עָלָיו וַיָּמֹת״.

״וַיַּפֵּל ה׳ אֱלֹהִים תַּרְדֵּמָה״, כִּדְאִיתָא בְּמִדְרָשׁ, צַדִּיקִים אוֹכְלִים וּמֵתִים מִיָּד, רְשָׁעִים יוֹרְדִים לְמִטָּתָם וּמִתְנַוְּנִים וְהוֹלְכִים עַד שְׁלֹשִׁים יוֹם. וְזֶהוּ ״וַיַּפֵּל ה׳ אֱלֹהִים תַּרְדֵּמָה״, שֶׁתַּרְדֵּמָה נָפְלָה עֲלֵיהֶם ״וְיָשְׁנוּ שְׁנַת עוֹלָם״:

(כה) בְּפָרָשַׁת מִגְרָשׁ כְּתִיב חָמֵשׁ פְּעָמִים ״מִקְלָטוֹ״. שֶׁיִּקָּלֵט, וְלֹא יֵהָרֵג הַנֶּפֶשׁ, שֶׁיֵּשׁ לוֹ חֲמִשָּׁה שֵׁמוֹת:

BAAL HATURIM ELUCIDATED

22. הֲדָפוֹ — HE PUSHED HIM. The masoretic note, ב׳, means that this word appears twice in the *Tanach:* (i) here, בְּלֹא אֵיבָה הֲדָפוֹ, *without enmity he pushed him;* and (ii) לֹא עָמַד כִּי ה׳ הֲדָפוֹ, *he could not stand, because* H*ASHEM had pushed him* (*Jeremiah* 46:15). This [similarity of expression] alludes to the Talmudic statement [explaining the verse about the accidental killer]: The verse, וְהָאֱלֹהִים אִנָּה לְיָדוֹ, *and God had caused it to come to his hand* (*Exodus* 21:13), [may be understood through] a parable regarding two people, one of whom had killed a person unintentionally, and one of whom had killed intentionally [and there were no witnesses to either incident]. The Holy One, Blessed is He, summons them to the same inn. The one who had killed unintentionally ascends the ladder and falls upon the person who had killed intentionally. It thus happens that he has killed him unintentionally [before witnesses] and is sentenced to exile.[57] Thus, *without enmity he pushed him,* for the one who fell tried to support himself and maintain his balance, but he could not remain standing, *because* H*ASHEM had pushed him.*[58]

57. *Makkos* 10b, cited in *Rashi* to *Exodus* 21:13; see also the Baal HaTurim to *Genesis* 2:21. Thus, the intentional killer receives his just deserts — he is put to death by "stoning"; and the unintentional killer, whose second unintentional killing has been witnessed by the other guests at the inn, is sentenced to flee to a city of refuge.

58. *Maharam MiRothenburg.*

[22] *But if with suddenness, without enmity, he pushed him, or
he hurled any implement upon him without ambush;* [23] *or
with any stone through which one could die, without having
seen, and he caused it to fall upon him and he died — but he
was not his enemy and did not seek his harm —* [24] *then the
assembly shall judge between the assailant and the avenger
of the blood, according to these laws.* [25] *The assembly shall
rescue the murderer from the hand of the avenger of the
blood, and the assembly shall return him to his city of refuge*

BAAL HATURIM ELUCIDATED

23. וַיַּפֵּל — AND HE CAUSED IT TO FALL. The masoretic note, ג׳, means that this word appears three times in the *Tanach:* (i) here, וַיַּפֵּל עָלָיו וַיָּמֹת, *and he caused it to fall upon him and he died;* (ii) וַיַּפֵּל בְּקֶרֶב מַחֲנֵהוּ, *and He caused it to fall amid His camp* (*Psalms* 78:28);[58a] and (iii) וַיַּפֵּל ה׳ אֱלֹהִים תַּרְדֵּמָה, *and HASHEM God caused a deep sleep to fall* [*upon Adam*] (*Genesis* 2:21).[59] [The similarity of expression] alludes to that which is written in the Midrash: [A large number of Israelites died as a result of eating the quail (see 11:31-33 above), but] even more than the inundation of quail killed through eating, it killed through descending, for it descended and fell on their heads. Thus, *He* [God] *caused it to fall upon him and he died.*[60]

The phrase *and HASHEM God caused a deep sleep to fall* alludes to the statement of the Midrash: The [relatively] righteous ate [of the quail] and died immediately; the wicked had to lie in their bed where they deteriorated for a period of thirty days [and then died]. This is the implication of *and HASHEM God caused a deep sleep to fall,* for a very deep sleep fell upon them and *they slept the sleep*[61] *of eternity.*[62]

25.[63] In the passage [whose opening verses speak] about the open spaces [around the Levite cities (i.e., Ch. 11)],[64] the word מִקְלָטוֹ, *his refuge,*[65] is written five times.[66] [This indicates that the purpose of the cities of refuge is] so that the soul — which has five names[67] — should be given refuge and should not be killed.

58a. That verse appears in a passage (*Psalms* 78:26-31) that recounts the incident of the שְׂלָו, *quails* (see 11:4-5, 18-23, 31-34 above).

59. See the Baal HaTurim there for a different interpretation of the masoretic note.

60. See the Baal HaTurim to 11:31 above.

61. The reading שְׁנַת עוֹלָם, *the sleep of eternity,* appears in the early printed editions and is based upon *Jeremiah* 51:39. However, in one of the manuscripts used by *Shoham Yakar,* as well as in some later printed editions, the comment reads שְׁנוֹת עוֹלָם, *the years of eternity.*

62. See *Mechilta* to 16:13, cited by *Rashi* to 11:20 above; see also *Yoma* 75b.

63. In all other editions, this comment appears either at the beginning of verse 5 or at the end of verse 8 or at verse 12 above. The confusion stems from the fact that the early printed editions mistakenly have the wrong key word (see note 65 below). We have taken the liberty of moving this comment to verse 25, for that is where מִקְלָטוֹ first appears.

64. The reading מִגְרָשׁ follows the early printed editions, and that is how it reads in *Shoham Yakar's* manuscript edition. Many later printed editions read מִקְלָט, [*cities of*] *refuge,* in place of מִגְרָשׁ, *open cities.* In either case, it refers to the same verses.

65. The reading מִקְלָטוֹ follows *Ittur Bikkurim's* emendation. The early printed editions read לְמִקְלָט, but that cannot be the Baal HaTurim's intention, for that word appears only twice (vv. 12,15) in this passage.

66. In verses 25,26,27,28 and 32.

67. *Bereishis Rabbah* 14:9 lists the five names as

אֲשֶׁר־נָס שָׁמָּה וְיָשַׁב בָּהּ עַד־מוֹת הַכֹּהֵן הַגָּדֹל
כו אֲשֶׁר־מָשַׁח אֹתוֹ בְּשֶׁמֶן הַקֹּדֶשׁ: וְאִם־יָצֹא יֵצֵא
הָרֹצֵחַ אֶת־גְּבוּל עִיר מִקְלָטוֹ אֲשֶׁר יָנוּס שָׁמָּה:
כז וּמָצָא אֹתוֹ גֹּאֵל הַדָּם מִחוּץ לִגְבוּל עִיר מִקְלָטוֹ
כח וְרָצַח גֹּאֵל הַדָּם אֶת־הָרֹצֵחַ אֵין לוֹ דָּם: כִּי בְעִיר
מִקְלָטוֹ יֵשֵׁב עַד־מוֹת הַכֹּהֵן הַגָּדֹל וְאַחֲרֵי מוֹת
כט הַכֹּהֵן הַגָּדֹל יָשׁוּב הָרֹצֵחַ אֶל־אֶרֶץ אֲחֻזָּתוֹ: וְהָיוּ
אֵלֶּה לָכֶם לְחֻקַּת מִשְׁפָּט לְדֹרֹתֵיכֶם בְּכֹל
ל מוֹשְׁבֹתֵיכֶם: כָּל־מַכֵּה־נֶפֶשׁ לְפִי עֵדִים יִרְצַח אֶת־
לא הָרֹצֵחַ וְעֵד אֶחָד לֹא־יַעֲנֶה בְנֶפֶשׁ לָמוּת: וְלֹא־
תִקְחוּ כֹפֶר לְנֶפֶשׁ רֹצֵחַ אֲשֶׁר־הוּא רָשָׁע לָמוּת כִּי־
לב מוֹת יוּמָת: וְלֹא־תִקְחוּ כֹפֶר לָנוּס אֶל־עִיר מִקְלָטוֹ
לג לָשׁוּב לָשֶׁבֶת בָּאָרֶץ עַד־מוֹת הַכֹּהֵן: וְלֹא־תַחֲנִיפוּ
אֶת־הָאָרֶץ אֲשֶׁר אַתֶּם בָּהּ כִּי הַדָּם הוּא יַחֲנִיף
אֶת־הָאָרֶץ וְלָאָרֶץ לֹא־יְכֻפַּר לַדָּם אֲשֶׁר שֻׁפַּךְ־בָּהּ

בעל הטורים

❑ **עַד מוֹת הַכֹּהֵן הַגָּדֹל.** שָׁלֹשׁ פְּעָמִים כֹּהֵן גָּדוֹל בַּפָּרָשָׁה. לוֹמַר, אֶחָד כֹּהֵן גָּדוֹל שֶׁנִּמְשַׁח וְאֶחָד מְרֻבֵּה בְגָדִים וְאֶחָד כֹּהֵן גָּדוֹל שֶׁעָבַר, כֻּלָּם מְשִׁיבִים אֶת הָרוֹצֵחַ בְּמִיתָתָן:

(לג) **יְכֻפַּר.** ד׳ — ״וְלָאָרֶץ לֹא יְכֻפַּר לַדָּם״; וְאִידָךְ ״אִם יְכֻפַּר הֶעָוֹן הַזֶּה לָכֶם עַד תְּמֻתוּן״; ״לָכֵן בְּזֹאת יְכֻפַּר עֲוֹן יַעֲקֹב״; ״בְּחֶסֶד וֶאֱמֶת יְכֻפַּר עָוֹן״. שֶׁתְּשׁוּבָה וְיוֹם הַכִּפּוּרִים תּוֹלִים

BAAL HATURIM ELUCIDATED

❑ **עַד מוֹת הַכֹּהֵן הַגָּדֹל** — UNTIL THE DEATH OF THE KOHEN GADOL. The term הַכֹּהֵן הַגָּדֹל appears three times in this passage.[68] This is to indicate that [it speaks of three classes of *Kohen Gadol*] — (i) a *Kohen Gadol* [installed in his office] by means of the anointment oil;[69] (ii) one [installed in his office] through donning the added

נֶפֶשׁ רוּחַ נְשָׁמָה יְחִידָה חַיָּה. The Midrash there adduces Scriptural verses containing those terms and discusses the reasons for and implications of each name. The Baal HaTurim also speaks of the five names of the soul in his comments to *Exodus* 29:40; *Leviticus* 16:14, s.v., וְחָמֵשׁ טְבִילוֹת, and 23:27; and *Deuteronomy* 21:7.

68. Once in verse 25 and twice in verse 28.

69. Aaron and his sons and all subsequent *Kohanim Gedolim* were installed into their office by being anointed with the sacred anointment oil (see *Exodus* 30:30). Miraculously, the twelve *log* (about one or two gallons) of anointment oil compounded by Moses lasted through the generations, until the time of King Josiah. During his reign, Josiah hid various sacred articles of the *Beis HaMikdash* to prevent them from falling into the hands of idolatrous gentiles (see *Yoma* 52a). Among the articles hidden were the *Aron* [Ark] and the cruse of anointment oil. Thus, from the time of Josiah until the destruction of the First Temple and during the entire Second Temple era, the *Kohanim Gedolim*

where he had fled; he shall dwell in it until the death of the
Kohen Gadol, whom one had anointed with the sacred oil.
26 *But if the murderer will ever leave the border of the city of*
refuge to which he had fled, 27 *and the avenger of the blood*
shall find him outside of the border of his city of refuge, and
the avenger of the blood will kill the murderer — he has no
blood-guilt. 28 *For he must dwell in his city of refuge until the*
death of the Kohen Gadol, and after the death of the Kohen
Gadol the murderer shall return to the land of his possession.
29 *These shall be for you a decree of justice for your*
generations, in all your dwelling places. 30 *Whoever smites a*
person, according to the testimony of witnesses shall one kill
the murderer, but a single witness shall not testify against a
person regarding death.
31 *You shall not accept ransom for the life of a murderer*
who is worthy of death, for he shall surely be put to death.
32 *You shall not accept ransom for one who fled to his city of*
refuge to return to dwell in the land, before the death of the
Kohen.
33 *You shall not bring guilt upon the land in which you*
are, for the blood will bring guilt upon the land; the land will
not be atoned for regarding the blood that was spilled in it,

BAAL HATURIM ELUCIDATED

vestments [of that office];[70] (iii) one who has stepped down[71] — the death of any one of these three returns the unintentional killer [to his home].[72]

33. יְכֻפַּר — WILL BE ATONED FOR. The masoretic note, ד׳, means that this word appears four times in the *Tanach:* (i) here, וְלָאָרֶץ לֹא יְכֻפַּר לַדָּם, *the land will not be atoned for regarding the blood;* (ii) אִם יְכֻפַּר הֶעָוֹן הַזֶּה לָכֶם עַד תְּמֻתוּן, *This sin will not be atoned for you until you die* (*Isaiah* 22:14); (iii) לָכֵן בְּזֹאת יְכֻפַּר עֲוֹן יַעֲקֹב, *Therefore, through this Jacob's iniquity shall be atoned for* (*Isaiah* 27:9); and (iv) בְּחֶסֶד וֶאֱמֶת יְכֻפַּר עָוֹן, *Through kindness and truth iniquity will be atoned for* (*Proverbs* 16:6). [The similarity of expression alludes to the Talmudic teaching:] *Teshuvah* (repentance) and Yom Kippur hold [the effects of sin] in check, while

could not be anointed (see note 70).

70. After Josiah hid the cruse of anointment oil, *Kohanim Gedolim* were installed into their office by donning the eight vestments of the *Kohen Gadol,* in accord with *Leviticus* 16:32 (*Rashi* to *Makkos* 11a).

71. This refers to a Kohen who had served in place of a *Kohen Gadol* who had become temporarily disqualified or incapacitated. When the first *Kohen Gadol* is able to resume the duties of his office, the replacement *Kohen* "steps down" (*Rashi* to *Makkos* 11a). Nevertheless, he retains his *Kohen Gadol* status in certain respects, including with regard to the laws of releasing the unintentional killer from exile, upon his death.

72. *Makkos* 11a.

לה/לד־לו/ו לד כִּי־אִם בְּדַם שֹׁפְכוֹ: וְלֹא תְטַמֵּא אֶת־הָאָרֶץ אֲשֶׁר
אַתֶּם יֹשְׁבִים בָּהּ אֲשֶׁר אֲנִי שֹׁכֵן בְּתוֹכָהּ כִּי אֲנִי
יהוה שֹׁכֵן בְּתוֹךְ בְּנֵי יִשְׂרָאֵל:

לו שביעי א וַיִּקְרְבוּ רָאשֵׁי הָאָבוֹת לְמִשְׁפַּחַת בְּנֵי־גִלְעָד בֶּן־
מָכִיר בֶּן־מְנַשֶּׁה מִמִּשְׁפְּחֹת בְּנֵי יוֹסֵף וַיְדַבְּרוּ לִפְנֵי
מֹשֶׁה וְלִפְנֵי הַנְּשִׂאִים רָאשֵׁי אָבוֹת לִבְנֵי יִשְׂרָאֵל:
ב וַיֹּאמְרוּ אֶת־אֲדֹנִי צִוָּה יהוה לָתֵת אֶת־הָאָרֶץ
בְּנַחֲלָה בְּגוֹרָל לִבְנֵי יִשְׂרָאֵל וַאדֹנִי צֻוָּה בַיהוה
ג לָתֵת אֶת־נַחֲלַת צְלָפְחָד אָחִינוּ לִבְנֹתָיו: וְהָיוּ
לְאֶחָד מִבְּנֵי שִׁבְטֵי בְנֵי־יִשְׂרָאֵל לְנָשִׁים וְנִגְרְעָה
נַחֲלָתָן מִנַּחֲלַת אֲבֹתֵינוּ וְנוֹסַף עַל נַחֲלַת הַמַּטֶּה
ד אֲשֶׁר תִּהְיֶינָה לָהֶם וּמִגֹּרַל נַחֲלָתֵנוּ יִגָּרֵעַ: וְאִם־
יִהְיֶה הַיֹּבֵל לִבְנֵי יִשְׂרָאֵל וְנוֹסְפָה נַחֲלָתָן עַל נַחֲלַת
הַמַּטֶּה אֲשֶׁר תִּהְיֶינָה לָהֶם וּמִנַּחֲלַת מַטֵּה אֲבֹתֵינוּ
ה יִגָּרַע נַחֲלָתָן: וַיְצַו מֹשֶׁה אֶת־בְּנֵי יִשְׂרָאֵל עַל־פִּי
ו יהוה לֵאמֹר כֵּן מַטֵּה בְנֵי־יוֹסֵף דֹּבְרִים: זֶה הַדָּבָר

בעל הטורים

וּמִיתָה מְמָרֶקֶת, שֶׁנֶּאֱמַר "אִם יְכֻפַּר הֶעָוֹן . . . עַד תְּמֻתוּן". "לָכֵן בְּזֹאת יְכֻפַּר עֲוֹן יַעֲקֹב". בַּמֶּה? בְּחֶסֶד, שֶׁנֶּאֱמַר "בְּחֶסֶד וֶאֱמֶת יְכֻפַּר עָוֹן". כִּדְאָמְרִינַן, רַבָּה דְּעָסֵק בִּגְמִילוּת חֲסָדִים חָיָה שִׁתִּין שְׁנִין:

לו (ג) וְנוֹסַף. ג' בַּמָּסוֹרֶת — ב' "וְאֵלֶּה שְׁמוֹת":

(ו) זֶה הַדָּבָר. בְּגִימַטְרִיָּא בְּדוֹר זֶה. שֶׁלֹּא נָהַג אֶלָּא בְּאוֹתוֹ הַדּוֹר:

BAAL HATURIM ELUCIDATED

death wipes [them] away,[72a] as it is stated, *This sin will not be atoned for . . . until you die.* Nevertheless, לָכֵן, *For this reason,* בְּזֹאת, *through this,* יְכֻפַּר עֲוֹן יַעֲקֹב, *Jacob's iniquity shall be atoned for.* But with what?[73] With kindness, as it is written, *Through kindness and truth iniquity will be atoned for.* This is in accordance with what the Sages have said: Rabbah, who involved himself with deeds of kindness, lived sixty years.[74,74a]

72a. *Yoma* 86a. Some sins are so severe that repentance alone cannot suspend the full punishment, Yom Kippur cannot atone, and suffering cannot purge. Rather, the three together — repentance, Yom Kippur, suffering — suspend the full brunt of the punishment and the sinner's death purges him of the sin.

73. That is, to what does בְּזֹאת, *with this,* refer?

74. *Rosh Hashanah* 18a [where the extant version differs from that of the Baal HaTurim]: Because of the misdeeds of the sons of Eli the *Kohen Gadol,* God sent a prophet to announce that a decree had been promulgated in heaven that every male descendant of Eli would die

except through the blood of the one who spilled it. 34 *You*
shall not contaminate the land in which you dwell, in whose
midst I rest, for I am HASHEM *Who rests among the Children*
of Israel.

36 1 *The heads of the fathers of the family of the children of*
Gilead, son of Machir son of Manasseh, of the families of the
children of Joseph, approached and spoke before Moses and
before the leaders, the heads of the fathers of the Children of
Israel. 2 *They said, "*HASHEM *has commanded my master to*
give the land as an inheritance by lot to the Children of Israel,
and My master has been commanded by HASHEM *to give the*
inheritance of Zelophehad our brother to his daughters. 3 *If*
they become wives of one of the sons of the tribes of the
Children of Israel, then their inheritance will be subtracted
from the inheritance of our fathers and be added to the
inheritance of the tribe into which they will marry, and it will
be subtracted from the lot of our inheritance. 4 *And when the*
Jubilee will arrive for the Children of Israel, their inheritance
will be added to the inheritance of the tribe into which they
will marry; and from the inheritance of the tribe of our fathers
will their inheritance be subtracted."

5 *Moses commanded the Children of Israel according*
to the word of HASHEM, *saying, "Correctly does the tribe*
of the children of Joseph speak. 6 *This is the word that*

BAAL HATURIM ELUCIDATED

XXXVI.

3. וְנוֹסַף — AND BE ADDED. The masoretic note, ג׳, means that this word appears three times in the *Tanach* [as explained in the commentary] at *Exodus* (1:10).

6. זֶה הַדָּבָר — THIS IS THE WORD. The *gematria* of this phrase (223) is equivalent[75] to that of בְּדוֹר זֶה, *in this generation.* For this commandment was specifically for that generation only.[76]

---

young [by age twenty (*R' Chananel*)]. Nevertheless, Rabbah [some read Rava (see *Rashi* and *Tosafos*)] and Abaye were descended from Eli, yet Rabbah, because he engaged primarily in Torah study, lived forty years, and Abaye, because he engaged primarily in both acts of kindness and Torah study, lived sixty years. [See *Doros HaRishonim* (Vol. 2, Frankfort ed.; Vol. 5, "*Yemai HaAmoraim*" Ch. 49, new format) regarding the correct text of that Talmudic passage.]

74a. Strangely, the Baal HaTurim's allusion incorporates the other three verses cited in the masoretic note, but does not include our verse.

75. The principle of *im hakollel* allows 223 to be considered equivalent to 224, the *gematria* of the Baal HaTurim's phrase.

76. *Peirush HaRokeach;* see *Bava Basra* 120a — The Talmud there infers from the term זֶה הַדָּבָר that the law under discussion was given specifically בְּדוֹר זֶה. That is, during the generation of the wilderness, a girl without brothers who was

אֲשֶׁר־צִוָּה יהוה לִבְנוֹת צְלָפְחָד לֵאמֹר לַטּוֹב
בְּעֵינֵיהֶם תִּהְיֶינָה לְנָשִׁים אַךְ לְמִשְׁפַּחַת מַטֵּה
ז אֲבִיהֶם תִּהְיֶינָה לְנָשִׁים: וְלֹא־תִסֹּב נַחֲלָה לִבְנֵי
יִשְׂרָאֵל מִמַּטֶּה אֶל־מַטֶּה כִּי אִישׁ בְּנַחֲלַת מַטֵּה
ח אֲבֹתָיו יִדְבְּקוּ בְּנֵי יִשְׂרָאֵל: וְכָל־בַּת יֹרֶשֶׁת נַחֲלָה
מִמַּטּוֹת בְּנֵי יִשְׂרָאֵל לְאֶחָד מִמִּשְׁפַּחַת מַטֵּה אָבִיהָ
תִּהְיֶה לְאִשָּׁה לְמַעַן יִירְשׁוּ בְּנֵי יִשְׂרָאֵל אִישׁ נַחֲלַת
ט אֲבֹתָיו: וְלֹא־תִסֹּב נַחֲלָה מִמַּטֶּה לְמַטֶּה אַחֵר
י כִּי־אִישׁ בְּנַחֲלָתוֹ יִדְבְּקוּ מַטּוֹת בְּנֵי יִשְׂרָאֵל: כַּאֲשֶׁר
צִוָּה יהוה אֶת־מֹשֶׁה כֵּן עָשׂוּ בְּנוֹת צְלָפְחָד:
מפטיר יא וַתִּהְיֶינָה מַחְלָה תִרְצָה וְחָגְלָה וּמִלְכָּה וְנֹעָה בְּנוֹת
יב צְלָפְחָד לִבְנֵי דֹדֵיהֶן לְנָשִׁים: מִמִּשְׁפְּחֹת בְּנֵי־
מְנַשֶּׁה בֶן־יוֹסֵף הָיוּ לְנָשִׁים וַתְּהִי נַחֲלָתָן עַל־מַטֵּה

בעל הטורים

(ז) **תִסֹּב נַחֲלָה.** בְּגִימַטְרִיָּא זוֹ הִיא בַהֲסָבַת הַבֵּן. לוֹמַר שֶׁהַבֵּן יוֹרֵשׁ אֶת אִמּוֹ:

❑ **וְלֹא תִסֹּב נַחֲלָה.** בְּגִימַטְרִיָּא זוֹ הִיא הֲסָבַת בַּעַל:

(יא) **לִבְנֵי דֹדֵיהֶן.** בְּגִימַטְרִיָּא לְהָגוּן לָהֶם:

BAAL HATURIM ELUCIDATED

7. [76a]**תִסֹּב נַחֲלָה** — **AN INHERITANCE SHALL [NOT] GO ROUND.**[76a] The *gematria* of this phrase (555) is equal to that of זוֹ הִיא בַהֲסָבַת הַבֵּן, *This refers to the son causing the inheritance to go round.* This indicates that the son inherits his mother's[77] estate.[78]

due to inherit her father's not-yet-received portion of the Land of Israel was enjoined from marrying outside of her father's tribe. Once the land had been apportioned, however, that law was no longer binding.

Alternatively: *Rashi* (30:2 above, s.v., זֶה הַדָּבָר) states that Moses prophesied using the expression כֹּה אָמַר ה׳, *so said HASHEM* (e.g., *Exodus* 11:4), and the other prophets did the same (e.g., *Joshua* 24:2; *I Samuel* 10:18; *Isaiah* 7:7; *Jeremiah* 2:2; *Ezekiel* 2:4; and more than 400 other times). Moses was superior to them, for he also prophesied with the wording זֶה הַדָּבָר, *this is the word.* Accordingly, the Baal HaTurim states that [a prophecy with the wording] זֶה הַדָּבָר was practiced only בְּדוֹר זֶה, *in this generation,* of Moses (*Atros Addar*).

76a. These words appear in the verse as part of a negative statement that begins with וְלֹא, *and not.* Nevertheless, in the realm of *remez* (allusion), phrases are often taken out of their textual context for the sake of the allusion. In his next comment, the Baal HaTurim uses the full comment for another allusion.

77. The reading אֶת אִמּוֹ, *his mother,* follows *Shoham Yakar's* manuscript edition. The early printed editions read אֶת אָבִיו, *his father,* a reading that does not make sense, for a son is always of the same tribe as his father and does not cause his father's portion to go round to another tribe.

78. *Peirush HaRokeach.* If a woman marries a man from another tribe, her son will be of her husband's tribe, not her father's. If she has inherited her father's portion and her husband

HASHEM has commanded regarding the daughters of
Zelophehad, saying: Let them be wives to whomever is
good in their eyes, but only to the family of their father's
tribe shall they become wives. [7] *An inheritance of the*
Children of Israel shall not go round from tribe to tribe;
rather the Children of Israel shall cleave every man to the
inheritance of the tribe of his fathers. [8] *Every daughter who*
inherits an inheritance of the tribes of the Children of Israel
shall become the wife of someone from a family of her
father's tribe, so that everyone of the Children of Israel will
inherit the inheritance of his fathers. [9] *An inheritance shall*
not go round from a tribe to another tribe, for the tribes of
the Children of Israel shall cleave every man to his own
inheritance.
[10] *As HASHEM commanded Moses, so did the daughters*
of Zelophehad do. [11] *Mahlah, Tirzah, Hoglah, Milcah and*
Noah, the daughters of Zelophehad, became wives to sons
of their uncles. [12] *[To cousins] from the families of the*
children of Manasseh son of Joseph did they become
wives, and their inheritance remained with the tribe of the

BAAL HATURIM ELUCIDATED

❑ וְלֹא תִסֹּב נַחֲלָה — AN INHERITANCE SHALL NOT GO ROUND. The *gematria* of this phrase (592) is equivalent[79] to that of זו הִיא הֲסִבַּת בַּעַל, *This refers to the husband causing the inheritance to go round.*[80]

11. לִבְנֵי דֹדֵיהֶן — TO SONS OF THEIR UNCLES. The *gematria* of this phrase (165) is equivalent[81] to לְהָגוּן לָהֶם, *to [those] appropriate for them.*[82]

---

died before she did, when she dies, that portion will be inherited by her son, thus moving from her father's tribe to her son's.

79. The *gematria* of the Baal HaTurim's phrase is 598, six more than that of the Scriptural phrase. The numbers can be reconciled by using the full spelling תִּסוֹב, instead of the defective spelling תִסֹּב used by the Torah. This is a common practice in the realm of *gematria* (*VeChur LaZahav*).

Alternatively: The Baal HaTurim's phrase should be emended to הִיא בַּהֲסִבַּת הַבַּעַל, which has a *gematria* of 592 (*VeChur LaZahav*).

80. If a woman who has inherited her father's portion were to marry a man from another tribe and were to predecease him, he would inherit her estate (see the Baal HaTurim to 27:11 above) and it would move from her father's tribe to her husband's.

81. The *gematria* of לְהָגוּן לָהֶם is 169, four more than that of the Scriptural phrase. The two *gematriaos* can be reconciled by using the full spelling of דוֹדֵיהֶן, with a ו, thus bringing the *gematria* to 171; the principle of *im hamillim* then allows two to be added to the Baal HaTurim's phrase, bringing its *gematria* to 171 (*Matzreif LaKesef; Yad Aharon*).

82. See *Bava Basra* 120a; the Talmud there reads לְהָגוּן לָהֶן, *to [those] appropriate for them,* using the feminine form לָהֶן for *for them.* The Baal HaTurim's comment ungrammatically uses the masculine form לָהֶם. In the realm of *remez* (allusion), grammatical rules are often suspended for the sake of a *gematria.*

לו/יג יג מִשְׁפַּ֥חַת אֲבִיהֶֽן׃ אֵ֣לֶּה הַמִּצְוֺ֞ת וְהַמִּשְׁפָּטִ֗ים אֲשֶׁ֨ר
צִוָּ֧ה יהוָ֛ה בְּיַד־מֹשֶׁ֖ה אֶל־בְּנֵ֣י יִשְׂרָאֵ֑ל בְּעַֽרְבֹ֣ת
מוֹאָ֔ב עַ֖ל יַרְדֵּ֥ן יְרֵחֽוֹ׃

It is customary for the congregation followed by the reader to proclaim:

חֲזַק! חֲזַק! וְנִתְחַזֵּק!

קל״ב פסוקים. מחל״ה חול״ה סימן. סכום פסוקי דספר במדבר אלף ומאתים ושמנים ושמנה. ארפ״ח (אפר״ח) סימן.

36/13 *family of their father.*

[13] *These are the commandments and the ordinances that HASHEM commanded through Moses to the Children of Israel in the Plains of Moab, at the Jordan, by Jericho.*

It is customary for the congregation followed by the reader to proclaim:

"Chazak! Chazak! Venischazeik!
(Be strong! Be strong! And may we be strengthened!)"

ההפטרות

The Haftaros

BLESSINGS OF THE HAFTARAH / ברכות ההפטרה

After the Torah Scroll has been tied and covered, the *Maftir* recites the *Haftarah* blessings.

בָּרוּךְ אַתָּה יהוה אֱלֹהֵינוּ מֶלֶךְ הָעוֹלָם, אֲשֶׁר בָּחַר בִּנְבִיאִים טוֹבִים, וְרָצָה בְדִבְרֵיהֶם הַנֶּאֱמָרִים בֶּאֱמֶת, בָּרוּךְ אַתָּה יהוה, הַבּוֹחֵר בַּתּוֹרָה וּבְמֹשֶׁה עַבְדּוֹ, וּבְיִשְׂרָאֵל עַמּוֹ, וּבִנְבִיאֵי הָאֱמֶת וָצֶדֶק. (קהל – אָמֵן)

Blessed are You, HASHEM, our God, King of the universe, Who has chosen good prophets and was pleased with their words that were uttered with truth. Blessed are You, HASHEM, Who chooses the Torah; Moses, His servant; Israel, His nation; and the prophets of truth and righteousness. (Cong. – *Amen.*)

The *Haftarah* is read, after which the *Maftir* recites the following blessings.

בָּרוּךְ אַתָּה יהוה אֱלֹהֵינוּ מֶלֶךְ הָעוֹלָם, צוּר כָּל הָעוֹלָמִים, צַדִּיק בְּכָל הַדּוֹרוֹת, הָאֵל הַנֶּאֱמָן הָאוֹמֵר וְעֹשֶׂה, הַמְּדַבֵּר וּמְקַיֵּם, שֶׁכָּל דְּבָרָיו אֱמֶת וָצֶדֶק. נֶאֱמָן אַתָּה הוּא יהוה אֱלֹהֵינוּ, וְנֶאֱמָנִים דְּבָרֶיךָ, וְדָבָר אֶחָד מִדְּבָרֶיךָ אָחוֹר לֹא יָשׁוּב רֵיקָם, כִּי אֵל מֶלֶךְ נֶאֱמָן (וְרַחֲמָן) אָתָּה. בָּרוּךְ אַתָּה יהוה, הָאֵל הַנֶּאֱמָן בְּכָל דְּבָרָיו. (קהל – אָמֵן)

Blessed are You, HASHEM, our God, King of the universe, Rock of all eternities, Righteous in all generations, the trustworthy God, Who says and does, Who speaks and fulfills, all of Whose words are true and righteous. Trustworthy are You, HASHEM, our God, and trustworthy are Your words, not one of Your words is turned back to its origin unfulfilled, for You are God, trustworthy (and compassionate) King. Blessed are You, HASHEM, the God Who is trustworthy in all His words. (Cong. – *Amen.*)

רַחֵם עַל צִיּוֹן כִּי הִיא בֵּית חַיֵּינוּ, וְלַעֲלוּבַת נֶפֶשׁ תּוֹשִׁיעַ בִּמְהֵרָה בְיָמֵינוּ. בָּרוּךְ אַתָּה יהוה, מְשַׂמֵּחַ צִיּוֹן בְּבָנֶיהָ. (קהל – אָמֵן)

Have mercy on Zion for it is the source of our life; to the one who is deeply humiliated bring salvation speedily, in our days. Blessed are You, HASHEM, Who gladdens Zion through her children. (Cong. – *Amen.*)

שַׂמְּחֵנוּ יהוה אֱלֹהֵינוּ בְּאֵלִיָּהוּ הַנָּבִיא עַבְדֶּךָ, וּבְמַלְכוּת בֵּית דָּוִד מְשִׁיחֶךָ, בִּמְהֵרָה יָבֹא וְיָגֵל לִבֵּנוּ, עַל כִּסְאוֹ לֹא יֵשֶׁב זָר וְלֹא יִנְחֲלוּ עוֹד אֲחֵרִים אֶת כְּבוֹדוֹ, כִּי בְשֵׁם קָדְשְׁךָ נִשְׁבַּעְתָּ לּוֹ, שֶׁלֹּא יִכְבֶּה נֵרוֹ לְעוֹלָם וָעֶד. בָּרוּךְ אַתָּה יהוה, מָגֵן דָּוִד. (קהל – אָמֵן)

Gladden us, HASHEM, our God, with Elijah the prophet Your servant, and with the kingdom of the House of David, Your anointed, may he come speedily and cause our heart to exult. On his throne let no stranger sit nor let others continue to inherit his honor, for by Your holy Name You swore to him that his lamp will not be extinguished forever and ever. Blessed are You, HASHEM, Shield of David. (Cong. – *Amen.*)

עַל הַתּוֹרָה, וְעַל הָעֲבוֹדָה, וְעַל הַנְּבִיאִים, וְעַל יוֹם הַשַּׁבָּת הַזֶּה, שֶׁנָּתַתָּ לָּנוּ יהוה אֱלֹהֵינוּ, לִקְדֻשָּׁה וְלִמְנוּחָה, לְכָבוֹד וּלְתִפְאָרֶת. עַל הַכֹּל יהוה אֱלֹהֵינוּ, אֲנַחְנוּ מוֹדִים לָךְ, וּמְבָרְכִים אוֹתָךְ, יִתְבָּרַךְ שִׁמְךָ בְּפִי כָּל חַי תָּמִיד לְעוֹלָם וָעֶד. בָּרוּךְ אַתָּה יהוה, מְקַדֵּשׁ הַשַּׁבָּת. (קהל – אָמֵן)

For the Torah reading, for the prayer service, for the reading from the Prophets and for this Sabbath day that You, HASHEM, our God, have given us for holiness and contentment, for glory and splendor — for all this, HASHEM, our God, we gratefully thank You and bless You. May Your Name be blessed by the mouth of all the living always, for all eternity. Blessed are You, HASHEM, Who sanctifies the Sabbath. (Cong. – *Amen.*)

HAFTARAS BAMIDBAR / הפטרת במדבר

Hosea 2:1-22 / הושע ב:א־כב

2 1 *The number of the Children of Israel shall be like the sand of the sea, which can neither be measured nor counted; and it shall be that instead of it being said about them, "You are not My people," it shall be said of them, "the children of the living God."* 2 *The Children of Judah and the Children of Israel shall be assembled together, and they shall appoint for themselves a single leader and ascend from the land — great is the day of Jezreel.* 3 *Say to your brothers, "My People!" and to your sisters, "Object of Mercy!"*

4 *Bear a grievance against your mother, bear a grievance, for she is not my wife and I am not her husband; let her remove her harlotry from before her face and her adulteries from between her breasts.* 5 *Lest I strip her bare and stand her up as on the day she was born; and I shall set her like a wilderness and place her like a parched land, and I will kill her with thirst.* 6 *I shall not have mercy on her children, for they are children of harlotry.* 7 *For their mother has been promiscuous; she who conceived them has shamed herself, for she said, "I shall go after my lovers, those who provide my bread and my water, my wool and my flax, my oil and my drink."*

8 *Therefore, behold! — I shall hedge your way with thorns and build up its fence, so that she will not find her paths.* 9 *She will pursue her lovers, but she shall not reach them; she will seek them, but she shall not find them; then she will say, "I shall go and return to my first Husband, for it was better for me then than now."* 10 *She did not realize that it was I Who gave her the grain, and the wine, and the oil, and that I lavished silver upon her, and gold; but they used it for the Baal.* 11 *Therefore I shall return and take My grain in its time and My wine in its season, and I shall remove My wool and flax for covering her nakedness.* 12 *Now I shall reveal her degradation before the eyes of her lovers, and no man shall save her from My hand.* 13 *I shall make an end of her rejoicing, her celebration, her New Moon, and her Sabbath, and her every Festival.* 14 *I shall lay waste her vine and her fig tree, of which she said, "They are my fee that my lovers gave me"; I shall make them a forest, and the beast of the field shall devour them.* 15 *I shall visit upon her the day of the Baal-idols when she burned incense to them, and when she adorned herself with her earrings and her jewelry and went after her lovers; and she forgot Me — the words of* H*ASHEM.*

16 *Therefore, behold! — I shall seduce her and lead her to the wilderness, and speak to her heart.* 17 *I shall give her vineyards from there and the desolate valley will be a portal of hope; and she will call out there as in the days of her youth and as on the day of her ascent from the land of Egypt.*

18 *It shall be on that day — the words of* H*ASHEM —*

ב א וְהָיָה מִסְפַּר בְּנֵי־יִשְׂרָאֵל כְּחוֹל הַיָּם אֲשֶׁר לֹא־יִמַּד וְלֹא יִסָּפֵר וְהָיָה בִּמְקוֹם אֲשֶׁר־יֵאָמֵר לָהֶם לֹא־עַמִּי אַתֶּם יֵאָמֵר לָהֶם בְּנֵי אֵל־חָי׃ ב וְנִקְבְּצוּ בְּנֵי־יְהוּדָה וּבְנֵי־יִשְׂרָאֵל יַחְדָּו וְשָׂמוּ לָהֶם רֹאשׁ אֶחָד וְעָלוּ מִן־הָאָרֶץ כִּי גָדוֹל יוֹם יִזְרְעֶאל׃ ג אִמְרוּ לַאֲחֵיכֶם עַמִּי וְלַאֲחוֹתֵיכֶם רֻחָמָה׃ ד רִיבוּ בְאִמְּכֶם רִיבוּ כִּי־הִיא לֹא אִשְׁתִּי וְאָנֹכִי לֹא אִישָׁהּ וְתָסֵר זְנוּנֶיהָ מִפָּנֶיהָ וְנַאֲפוּפֶיהָ מִבֵּין שָׁדֶיהָ׃ ה פֶּן־אַפְשִׁיטֶנָּה עֲרֻמָּה וְהִצַּגְתִּיהָ כְּיוֹם הִוָּלְדָהּ וְשַׂמְתִּיהָ כַמִּדְבָּר וְשַׁתִּהָ כְּאֶרֶץ צִיָּה וַהֲמִתִּיהָ בַּצָּמָא׃ ו וְאֶת־בָּנֶיהָ לֹא אֲרַחֵם כִּי־בְנֵי זְנוּנִים הֵמָּה׃ ז כִּי זָנְתָה אִמָּם הֹבִישָׁה הוֹרָתָם כִּי אָמְרָה אֵלְכָה אַחֲרֵי מְאַהֲבַי נֹתְנֵי לַחְמִי וּמֵימַי צַמְרִי וּפִשְׁתִּי שַׁמְנִי וְשִׁקּוּיָי׃ ח לָכֵן הִנְנִי־שָׂךְ אֶת־דַּרְכֵּךְ בַּסִּירִים וְגָדַרְתִּי אֶת־גְּדֵרָהּ וּנְתִיבוֹתֶיהָ לֹא תִמְצָא׃ ט וְרִדְּפָה אֶת־מְאַהֲבֶיהָ וְלֹא־תַשִּׂיג אֹתָם וּבִקְשָׁתַם וְלֹא תִמְצָא וְאָמְרָה אֵלְכָה וְאָשׁוּבָה אֶל־אִישִׁי הָרִאשׁוֹן כִּי טוֹב לִי אָז מֵעָתָּה׃ י וְהִיא לֹא יָדְעָה כִּי אָנֹכִי נָתַתִּי לָהּ הַדָּגָן וְהַתִּירוֹשׁ וְהַיִּצְהָר וְכֶסֶף הִרְבֵּיתִי לָהּ וְזָהָב עָשׂוּ לַבָּעַל׃ יא לָכֵן אָשׁוּב וְלָקַחְתִּי דְגָנִי בְּעִתּוֹ וְתִירוֹשִׁי בְּמוֹעֲדוֹ וְהִצַּלְתִּי צַמְרִי וּפִשְׁתִּי לְכַסּוֹת אֶת־עֶרְוָתָהּ׃ יב וְעַתָּה אֲגַלֶּה אֶת־נַבְלֻתָהּ לְעֵינֵי מְאַהֲבֶיהָ וְאִישׁ לֹא־יַצִּילֶנָּה מִיָּדִי׃ יג וְהִשְׁבַּתִּי כָּל־מְשׂוֹשָׂהּ חַגָּהּ חָדְשָׁהּ וְשַׁבַּתָּהּ וְכֹל מוֹעֲדָהּ׃ יד וַהֲשִׁמֹּתִי גַּפְנָהּ וּתְאֵנָתָהּ אֲשֶׁר אָמְרָה אֶתְנָה הֵמָּה לִי אֲשֶׁר נָתְנוּ־לִי מְאַהֲבָי וְשַׂמְתִּים לְיַעַר וַאֲכָלָתַם חַיַּת הַשָּׂדֶה׃ טו וּפָקַדְתִּי עָלֶיהָ אֶת־יְמֵי הַבְּעָלִים אֲשֶׁר תַּקְטִיר לָהֶם וַתַּעַד נִזְמָהּ וְחֶלְיָתָהּ וַתֵּלֶךְ אַחֲרֵי מְאַהֲבֶיהָ וְאֹתִי שָׁכְחָה נְאֻם־יהוה׃ טז לָכֵן הִנֵּה אָנֹכִי מְפַתֶּיהָ וְהֹלַכְתִּיהָ הַמִּדְבָּר וְדִבַּרְתִּי עַל־לִבָּהּ׃ יז וְנָתַתִּי לָהּ אֶת־כְּרָמֶיהָ מִשָּׁם וְאֶת־עֵמֶק עָכוֹר לְפֶתַח תִּקְוָה וְעָנְתָה שָׁמָּה כִּימֵי נְעוּרֶיהָ וּכְיוֹם עֲלוֹתָהּ מֵאֶרֶץ־מִצְרָיִם׃ יח וְהָיָה בַיּוֹם־הַהוּא נְאֻם־יהוה

תִּקְרְאִי אִישִׁי וְלֹא־תִקְרְאִי־לִי עוֹד בַּעְלִי:
יט וַהֲסִרֹתִי אֶת־שְׁמוֹת הַבְּעָלִים מִפִּיהָ וְלֹא־
יִזָּכְרוּ עוֹד בִּשְׁמָם: כ וְכָרַתִּי לָהֶם בְּרִית בַּיּוֹם
הַהוּא עִם־חַיַּת הַשָּׂדֶה וְעִם־עוֹף הַשָּׁמַיִם
וְרֶמֶשׂ הָאֲדָמָה וְקֶשֶׁת וְחֶרֶב וּמִלְחָמָה
אֶשְׁבּוֹר מִן־הָאָרֶץ וְהִשְׁכַּבְתִּים לָבֶטַח:
כא וְאֵרַשְׂתִּיךְ לִי לְעוֹלָם וְאֵרַשְׂתִּיךְ לִי בְּצֶדֶק
וּבְמִשְׁפָּט וּבְחֶסֶד וּבְרַחֲמִים: כב וְאֵרַשְׂתִּיךְ לִי
בֶּאֱמוּנָה וְיָדַעַתְּ אֶת־יְהוָה:

you will call [Me] "my Husband," and you will no
longer call Me "my Master." [19] I shall remove the
names of the Baal-idols from her mouth, and they
shall no longer be mentioned by their name. [20] I
shall seal for them a covenant on that day with the
beast of the field, and with the bird of the sky and the
creeping creature of the earth; bow, and sword, and
war shall I destroy from the land, and I shall let them
lie securely.
[21] I shall marry you to Me forever; I shall marry you
to Me with righteousness, and with justice, and with
kindness, and with mercy. [22] I shall marry you to Me
with fidelity; and you shall know HASHEM.

HAFTARAS NASSO / הפטרת נשא

Judges 13:2-25 / שופטים יג:ב־כה

יג ב וַיְהִי אִישׁ אֶחָד מִצָּרְעָה מִמִּשְׁפַּחַת הַדָּנִי
וּשְׁמוֹ מָנוֹחַ וְאִשְׁתּוֹ עֲקָרָה וְלֹא יָלָדָה: ג וַיֵּרָא
מַלְאַךְ־יְהוָה אֶל־הָאִשָּׁה וַיֹּאמֶר אֵלֶיהָ הִנֵּה־
נָא אַתְּ־עֲקָרָה וְלֹא יָלַדְתְּ וְהָרִית וְיָלַדְתְּ בֵּן:
ד וְעַתָּה הִשָּׁמְרִי נָא וְאַל־תִּשְׁתִּי יַיִן וְשֵׁכָר
וְאַל־תֹּאכְלִי כָּל־טָמֵא: ה כִּי הִנָּךְ הָרָה וְיֹלַדְתְּ
בֵּן וּמוֹרָה לֹא־יַעֲלֶה עַל־רֹאשׁוֹ כִּי־נְזִיר
אֱלֹהִים יִהְיֶה הַנַּעַר מִן־הַבָּטֶן וְהוּא יָחֵל
לְהוֹשִׁיעַ אֶת־יִשְׂרָאֵל מִיַּד פְּלִשְׁתִּים: ו וַתָּבֹא
הָאִשָּׁה וַתֹּאמֶר לְאִישָׁהּ לֵאמֹר אִישׁ הָאֱלֹהִים
בָּא אֵלַי וּמַרְאֵהוּ כְּמַרְאֵה מַלְאַךְ הָאֱלֹהִים
נוֹרָא מְאֹד וְלֹא שְׁאִלְתִּיהוּ אֵי־מִזֶּה הוּא
וְאֶת־שְׁמוֹ לֹא־הִגִּיד לִי: ז וַיֹּאמֶר לִי הִנָּךְ הָרָה
וְיֹלַדְתְּ בֵּן וְעַתָּה אַל־תִּשְׁתִּי | יַיִן וְשֵׁכָר וְאַל־
תֹּאכְלִי כָּל־טֻמְאָה כִּי־נְזִיר אֱלֹהִים יִהְיֶה
הַנַּעַר מִן־הַבֶּטֶן עַד־יוֹם מוֹתוֹ: ח וַיֶּעְתַּר מָנוֹחַ
אֶל־יְהוָה וַיֹּאמַר בִּי אֲדוֹנָי אִישׁ הָאֱלֹהִים
אֲשֶׁר שָׁלַחְתָּ יָבוֹא־נָא עוֹד אֵלֵינוּ וְיוֹרֵנוּ מַה־
נַּעֲשֶׂה לַנַּעַר הַיּוּלָּד: ט וַיִּשְׁמַע הָאֱלֹהִים בְּקוֹל
מָנוֹחַ וַיָּבֹא מַלְאַךְ הָאֱלֹהִים עוֹד אֶל־הָאִשָּׁה
וְהִיא יוֹשֶׁבֶת בַּשָּׂדֶה וּמָנוֹחַ אִישָׁהּ אֵין עִמָּהּ:
י וַתְּמַהֵר הָאִשָּׁה וַתָּרָץ וַתַּגֵּד לְאִישָׁהּ וַתֹּאמֶר
אֵלָיו הִנֵּה נִרְאָה אֵלַי הָאִישׁ אֲשֶׁר־בָּא בַיּוֹם
אֵלָי: יא וַיָּקָם וַיֵּלֶךְ מָנוֹחַ אַחֲרֵי אִשְׁתּוֹ וַיָּבֹא
אֶל־הָאִישׁ וַיֹּאמֶר לוֹ הַאַתָּה הָאִישׁ אֲשֶׁר־
דִּבַּרְתָּ אֶל־הָאִשָּׁה וַיֹּאמֶר אָנִי: יב וַיֹּאמֶר מָנוֹחַ
עַתָּה יָבֹא דְבָרֶיךָ מַה־יִּהְיֶה מִשְׁפַּט הַנַּעַר
וּמַעֲשֵׂהוּ: יג וַיֹּאמֶר מַלְאַךְ יְהוָה אֶל־מָנוֹחַ
מִכֹּל אֲשֶׁר־אָמַרְתִּי אֶל־הָאִשָּׁה תִּשָּׁמֵר:

13 [2] There was a certain man of Zorah, of the Danite
family, whose name was Manoah; his wife
was barren and had not given birth. [3] An angel of God
appeared to the woman and said to her, "Behold now!
— you are barren and have not given birth, but you
shall conceive and give birth to a son. [4] And now, be
careful not to drink wine or intoxicant, and not to eat
anything prohibited [to a nazirite]. [5] For you shall con-
ceive and give birth to a son; a razor shall not come
upon his head for the lad shall be a nazirite of God
from the womb, and he will begin to save Israel from
the hand of the Philistines."
[6] The woman came and told her husband, saying:
"A man of God came to me, and his appearance
was like the appearance of an angel of God —
very awesome! I did not ask him where he was from
and he did not tell me his name. [7] He said to me,
'Behold! you shall conceive and give birth to a son;
and now, do not drink wine or intoxicant, and do not
eat anything prohibited [to a nazirite], for the lad shall
be a nazirite of God from the womb until the day of his
death.' "
[8] Manoah prayed to HASHEM and said, "Please, my
Lord, may the man of God whom You sent come now
again to us and teach us what we should do to the lad
who will be born."
[9] God heeded the call of Manoah and the angel of
God came again to the woman when she was sitting
in the field, but Manoah her husband was not with her.
[10] The woman hastened and ran and told her hus-
band; she said to him, "Behold! — the man who came
to me that day appeared to me."
[11] Manoah stood up and went after his wife; he
came to the man and said to him, "Are you the man
who spoke to the woman?"
He said, "I am."
[12] Manoah said, "Now — your words shall come
true; what should be the conduct of the lad and his
behavior?"
[13] The angel of God said to Manoah, "Of every-
thing that I spoke to the woman let her beware.

יד מִכֹּל אֲשֶׁר־יֵצֵא מִגֶּפֶן הַיַּיִן לֹא תֹאכַל
וְיַיִן וְשֵׁכָר אַל־תֵּשְׁתְּ וְכָל־טֻמְאָה אַל־תֹּאכַל
כֹּל אֲשֶׁר־צִוִּיתִיהָ תִּשְׁמֹר: טו וַיֹּאמֶר מָנוֹחַ
אֶל־מַלְאַךְ יהוה נַעְצְרָה־נָּא אוֹתָךְ וְנַעֲשֶׂה
לְפָנֶיךָ גְּדִי עִזִּים: טז וַיֹּאמֶר מַלְאַךְ יהוה אֶל־
מָנוֹחַ אִם־תַּעְצְרֵנִי לֹא־אֹכַל בְּלַחְמֶךָ וְאִם־
תַּעֲשֶׂה עֹלָה לַיהוה תַּעֲלֶנָּה כִּי לֹא־יָדַע
מָנוֹחַ כִּי־מַלְאַךְ יהוה הוּא: יז וַיֹּאמֶר מָנוֹחַ
אֶל־מַלְאַךְ יהוה מִי שְׁמֶךָ כִּי־יָבֹא דְבָרְךָ
[דבריך כ׳] וְכִבַּדְנוּךָ: יח וַיֹּאמֶר לוֹ מַלְאַךְ יהוה
לָמָּה זֶּה תִּשְׁאַל לִשְׁמִי וְהוּא־פֶלִאי: יט וַיִּקַּח
מָנוֹחַ אֶת־גְּדִי הָעִזִּים וְאֶת־הַמִּנְחָה וַיַּעַל
עַל־הַצּוּר לַיהוה וּמַפְלִא לַעֲשׂוֹת וּמָנוֹחַ
וְאִשְׁתּוֹ רֹאִים: כ וַיְהִי בַעֲלוֹת הַלַּהַב מֵעַל
הַמִּזְבֵּחַ הַשָּׁמַיְמָה וַיַּעַל מַלְאַךְ־יהוה בְּלַהַב
הַמִּזְבֵּחַ וּמָנוֹחַ וְאִשְׁתּוֹ רֹאִים וַיִּפְּלוּ עַל־
פְּנֵיהֶם אָרְצָה: כא וְלֹא־יָסַף עוֹד מַלְאַךְ יהוה
לְהֵרָאֹה אֶל־מָנוֹחַ וְאֶל־אִשְׁתּוֹ אָז יָדַע מָנוֹחַ
כִּי־מַלְאַךְ יהוה הוּא: כב וַיֹּאמֶר מָנוֹחַ אֶל־
אִשְׁתּוֹ מוֹת נָמוּת כִּי אֱלֹהִים רָאִינוּ:
כג וַתֹּאמֶר לוֹ אִשְׁתּוֹ לוּ חָפֵץ יהוה לַהֲמִיתֵנוּ
לֹא־לָקַח מִיָּדֵנוּ עֹלָה וּמִנְחָה וְלֹא הֶרְאָנוּ
אֶת־כָּל־אֵלֶּה וְכָעֵת לֹא הִשְׁמִיעָנוּ כָּזֹאת:
כד וַתֵּלֶד הָאִשָּׁה בֵּן וַתִּקְרָא אֶת־שְׁמוֹ שִׁמְשׁוֹן
וַיִּגְדַּל הַנַּעַר וַיְבָרְכֵהוּ יהוה: כה וַתָּחֶל רוּחַ
יהוה לְפַעֲמוֹ בְּמַחֲנֵה־דָן בֵּין צָרְעָה וּבֵין
אֶשְׁתָּאֹל:

14 *Of anything that comes from the grapevine she shall not eat; wine or intoxicant she shall not drink; and anything prohibited [to a nazirite] she shall not eat — everything that I commanded her she shall observe."*

15 *Manoah said to the angel of* HASHEM, *"Please let us detain you, and we shall prepare for you a kid of the goats."*

16 *The angel of* HASHEM *said to Manoah, "If you detain me, I shall not eat from your food, but if you would bring up an elevation-offering, bring it up to* HASHEM,*" — for Manoah did not know that he was an angel of* HASHEM.

17 *Manoah said to the angel of* HASHEM, *"What is your name, so that when your words come about we may honor you?"*

18 *The angel of* HASHEM *said to him, "Why is it that you ask for my name? It is hidden."*

19 *Manoah took the kid of the goats and the meal-offering and brought them up on the rock to* HASHEM; *and he [the angel] performed a miracle as Manoah and his wife watched.* 20 *It happened that as the flame rose up from atop the altar toward the heavens, the angel of* HASHEM *went up in the flame of the altar; Manoah and his wife were watching and they fell upon their faces to the ground.*

21 *The angel of* HASHEM *did not continue anymore to appear to Manoah and his wife; then Manoah realized that he was an angel of* HASHEM. 22 *So Manoah said to his wife, "We shall surely die, for we have seen a Godly angel!"*

23 *His wife said to him, "Had* HASHEM *wanted to put us to death He would not have accepted from our hand an elevation-offering and a meal-offering, nor would He have shown us all this, nor would He let us hear such news at this time."*

24 *The woman gave birth to a son, and she called his name Samson; the lad grew and* HASHEM *blessed him.* 25 *The spirit of* HASHEM *began to resound in the camp of Dan, between Zorah and Eshtaol.*

HAFTARAS BEHA'ALOSCHA / הפטרת בהעלותך

Zechariah 2:14 — 4:7 / זכריה ב:יד — ד:ז

ב יד רָנִּי וְשִׂמְחִי בַּת־צִיּוֹן כִּי הִנְנִי־בָא
וְשָׁכַנְתִּי בְתוֹכֵךְ נְאֻם־יהוה: טו וְנִלְווּ גוֹיִם
רַבִּים אֶל־יהוה בַּיּוֹם הַהוּא וְהָיוּ לִי לְעָם
וְשָׁכַנְתִּי בְתוֹכֵךְ וְיָדַעַתְּ כִּי־יהוה צְבָאוֹת
שְׁלָחַנִי אֵלָיִךְ: טז וְנָחַל יהוה אֶת־יְהוּדָה
חֶלְקוֹ עַל אַדְמַת הַקֹּדֶשׁ וּבָחַר עוֹד
בִּירוּשָׁלָם: יז הַס כָּל־בָּשָׂר מִפְּנֵי יהוה כִּי
נֵעוֹר מִמְּעוֹן קָדְשׁוֹ: ג א וַיַּרְאֵנִי אֶת־
יְהוֹשֻׁעַ הַכֹּהֵן הַגָּדוֹל עֹמֵד לִפְנֵי מַלְאַךְ
יהוה וְהַשָּׂטָן עֹמֵד עַל־יְמִינוֹ לְשִׂטְנוֹ: ב וַיֹּאמֶר
יהוה אֶל־הַשָּׂטָן יִגְעַר יהוה בְּךָ הַשָּׂטָן

2 14 *Sing and be glad, O daughter of Zion, for behold! — I come and I will dwell among you — the words of* HASHEM. 15 *Many nations will attach themselves to* HASHEM *on that day, and they shall become a people unto Me, but I will dwell among you — then you will realize that* HASHEM, *Master of Legions, has sent me to you.* 16 HASHEM *shall take Judah as a heritage to Himself for His portion upon the Holy Land, and He shall choose Jerusalem again.* 17 *Be silent, all flesh, before* HASHEM, *for He is aroused from His holy habitation!*

3 1 *He showed me Joshua the Kohen Gadol standing before an angel of* HASHEM, *and the Satan standing at his right to accuse him.* 2 *And* HASHEM *said to the Satan, "*HASHEM *shall denounce you, O Satan,*

וְיִגְעַר יהוה בְּךָ הַבֹּחֵר בִּירוּשָׁלָ͏ִם הֲלוֹא זֶה
אוּד מֻצָּל מֵאֵשׁ: ג וִיהוֹשֻׁעַ הָיָה לָבֻשׁ בְּגָדִים
צוֹאִים וְעֹמֵד לִפְנֵי הַמַּלְאָךְ: ד וַיַּעַן וַיֹּאמֶר אֶל־
הָעֹמְדִים לְפָנָיו לֵאמֹר הָסִירוּ הַבְּגָדִים הַצֹּאִים
מֵעָלָיו וַיֹּאמֶר אֵלָיו רְאֵה הֶעֱבַרְתִּי מֵעָלֶיךָ
עֲוֺנֶךָ וְהַלְבֵּשׁ אֹתְךָ מַחֲלָצוֹת: ה וָאֹמַר יָשִׂימוּ
צָנִיף טָהוֹר עַל־רֹאשׁוֹ וַיָּשִׂימוּ הַצָּנִיף הַטָּהוֹר
עַל־רֹאשׁוֹ וַיַּלְבִּשֻׁהוּ בְּגָדִים וּמַלְאַךְ יהוה עֹמֵד:
ו וַיָּעַד מַלְאַךְ יהוה בִּיהוֹשֻׁעַ לֵאמֹר: ז כֹּה־
אָמַר יהוה צְבָאוֹת אִם־בִּדְרָכַי תֵּלֵךְ וְאִם אֶת־
מִשְׁמַרְתִּי תִשְׁמֹר וְגַם־אַתָּה תָּדִין אֶת־בֵּיתִי
וְגַם תִּשְׁמֹר אֶת־חֲצֵרָי וְנָתַתִּי לְךָ מַהְלְכִים בֵּין
הָעֹמְדִים הָאֵלֶּה: ח שְׁמַע־נָא יְהוֹשֻׁעַ ׀ הַכֹּהֵן
הַגָּדוֹל אַתָּה וְרֵעֶיךָ הַיֹּשְׁבִים לְפָנֶיךָ כִּי־אַנְשֵׁי
מוֹפֵת הֵמָּה כִּי־הִנְנִי מֵבִיא אֶת־עַבְדִּי צֶמַח:
ט כִּי ׀ הִנֵּה הָאֶבֶן אֲשֶׁר נָתַתִּי לִפְנֵי יְהוֹשֻׁעַ עַל־
אֶבֶן אַחַת שִׁבְעָה עֵינָיִם הִנְנִי מְפַתֵּחַ פִּתֻּחָהּ
נְאֻם יהוה צְבָאוֹת וּמַשְׁתִּי אֶת־עֲוֺן הָאָרֶץ־
הַהִיא בְּיוֹם אֶחָד: י בַּיּוֹם הַהוּא נְאֻם יהוה
צְבָאוֹת תִּקְרְאוּ אִישׁ לְרֵעֵהוּ אֶל־תַּחַת גֶּפֶן
וְאֶל־תַּחַת תְּאֵנָה: ד א וַיָּשָׁב הַמַּלְאָךְ הַדֹּבֵר
בִּי וַיְעִירֵנִי כְּאִישׁ אֲשֶׁר־יֵעוֹר מִשְּׁנָתוֹ: ב וַיֹּאמֶר
אֵלַי מָה אַתָּה רֹאֶה וָאֹמַר [ויאמר כ׳] רָאִיתִי
וְהִנֵּה מְנוֹרַת זָהָב כֻּלָּהּ וְגֻלָּהּ עַל־רֹאשָׁהּ
וְשִׁבְעָה נֵרֹתֶיהָ עָלֶיהָ שִׁבְעָה וְשִׁבְעָה מוּצָקוֹת
לַנֵּרוֹת אֲשֶׁר עַל־רֹאשָׁהּ: ג וּשְׁנַיִם זֵיתִים עָלֶיהָ
אֶחָד מִימִין הַגֻּלָּה וְאֶחָד עַל־שְׂמֹאלָהּ: ד וָאַעַן
וָאֹמַר אֶל־הַמַּלְאָךְ הַדֹּבֵר בִּי לֵאמֹר מָה אֵלֶּה
אֲדֹנִי: ה וַיַּעַן הַמַּלְאָךְ הַדֹּבֵר בִּי וַיֹּאמֶר אֵלַי
הֲלוֹא יָדַעְתָּ מָה־הֵמָּה אֵלֶּה וָאֹמַר לֹא אֲדֹנִי:
ו וַיַּעַן וַיֹּאמֶר אֵלַי לֵאמֹר זֶה דְּבַר־יהוה אֶל־
זְרֻבָּבֶל לֵאמֹר לֹא בְחַיִל וְלֹא בְכֹחַ כִּי אִם־
בְּרוּחִי אָמַר יהוה צְבָאוֹת: ז מִי־אַתָּה הַר־
הַגָּדוֹל לִפְנֵי זְרֻבָּבֶל לְמִישֹׁר וְהוֹצִיא אֶת־
הָאֶבֶן הָרֹאשָׁה תְּשֻׁאוֹת חֵן ׀ חֵן לָהּ:

and HASHEM Who chooses Jerusalem shall denounce you again; this is indeed a firebrand rescued from the flames." 3 Joshua was dressed in soiled garments as he stood before the angel. 4 *[The angel]* spoke up and said to those standing before him, saying, "Remove the soiled garments from upon him." Then he said to him, "See, I have removed your iniquity from upon you and had you clothed in fresh garments."

5 Then I said, "Let them place a pure turban on his head"; and they placed the pure turban on his head and they dressed him in garments; and the angel of HASHEM remained standing.

6 Then the angel of HASHEM warned Joshua, saying, 7 "So said HASHEM, Master of Legions: If you walk in My ways and safeguard My charge, then you shall administer My Temple and safeguard My courtyards, and I shall permit you movement among these immobile *[angels]*. 8 Listen now, O Joshua the Kohen Gadol — you and your fellows sitting before you, for they are miracle workers — for behold I bring My servant, the flourishing one. 9 For behold! — the stone that I have placed before Joshua, seven eyes toward one stone; behold I am engraving its adornment, the words of HASHEM, Master of Legions, and I have removed the sin of that land in one day. 10 On that day, the words of HASHEM, Master of Legions, each man will invite his fellow beneath the vine and beneath the fig tree."

4 1 The angel who spoke with me returned and woke me, as a man is awakened from his sleep. 2 He said to me, "What do you see?"

I said, "I see, and behold! — there is a Menorah made entirely of gold with its bowl on its top, and its seven lamps are upon it and there are seven tubes to each of the lamps that are on its top. 3 And two olive trees are near it, one to the right of the bowl and one to its left."

4 And I spoke up and said to the angel that was speaking to me, saying, "What are these, my lord?"

5 The angel who was speaking to me spoke up and said to me, "Do you not know what they are?"

I said, "No, my lord."

6 He spoke up and said to me, saying, "This is the word of HASHEM to Zerubbabel, saying, 'Not through armies and not through might, but through My spirit,' says HASHEM, Master of Legions. 7 Who are you, O great mountain — before Zerubbabel *[you shall become]* a plain! He shall bring forth the main stone to shouts of, 'Beauty, beauty to it!' "

HAFTARAS SHELACH / הפטרת שלח

Joshua 2:1-24 / יהושע ב:א־כד

ב א וַיִּשְׁלַח יְהוֹשֻׁעַ בִּן־נוּן מִן־הַשִּׁטִּים
שְׁנַיִם אֲנָשִׁים מְרַגְּלִים חֶרֶשׁ לֵאמֹר לְכוּ
רְאוּ אֶת־הָאָרֶץ וְאֶת־יְרִיחוֹ וַיֵּלְכוּ וַיָּבֹאוּ
בֵּית אִשָּׁה זוֹנָה וּשְׁמָהּ רָחָב וַיִּשְׁכְּבוּ־שָׁמָּה:

2 1 Joshua son of Nun dispatched from Shittim two men, spies, secretly saying, "Go observe the Land and Jericho." So they traveled and came to the house of a woman innkeeper whose name was Rahab, and they slept there.

2 *It was told to the king of Jericho saying, "Behold! — men have come here tonight from the Children of Israel to search out the Land."*

3 *The king of Jericho then sent to Rahab, saying, "Bring out the men who have come to you, who have entered your house, for they have come to search out the entire Land."*

4 *The woman had taken the two men and had hidden them; so she said, "True, the men did come to me, but I did not know from where they were.* 5 *When the [city] gate was to close at dark, the men left; I do not know where the men went; chase after them quickly for you can overtake them."* 6 *But she had brought them up to the roof and had hidden them in the stalks of flax that she had arranged on the roof.* 7 *So the men chased after them in the direction of the Jordan to the fords; they closed the gate soon after the pursuers had gone out after them.*

8 *They had not yet gone to sleep when she came up to them on the roof.* 9 *And she said to the men, "I know that HASHEM has given you the Land, and that your terror has fallen upon us, and that all the inhabitants of the Land have melted because of you.* 10 *For we have heard how HASHEM dried up the water of the Sea of Reeds before you when you came out of Egypt, and what you did to the two Amorite kings across the Jordan — to Sihon and to Og — whom you utterly destroyed.* 11 *When we heard, our hearts melted — no spirit is left in man because of you, for HASHEM, your God, He is God in the heavens above and on the earth below.* 12 *And now, please swear to me by HASHEM — since I have done kindness with you — that you too will do kindness with my father's house and give me an authentic countersign.* 13 *Keep alive my father, and my mother, and my brothers, and my sisters, and all that they have, and rescue our souls from death."*

14 *The men said to her, "Our soul is in your place to die, if you do not reveal this discussion of ours; then it will be when HASHEM gives us the Land, we will deal with you in kindness and truth."*

15 *And she lowered them by the rope through the window, for her house was in a wall of the fortification and in the fortification she lived.* 16 *She said to them, "Go to the mountain lest your pursuers meet you; hide there for a three-day period until the pursuers return; then you may go on your way."*

17 *The men said to her, "We shall be clean from this oath of yours which you made us swear.* 18 *Behold! — when we come into the Land this scarlet cord shall you bind in the window from which you lowered us;*

ב וַיֵּאָמַר לְמֶלֶךְ יְרִיחוֹ לֵאמֹר הִנֵּה אֲנָשִׁים בָּאוּ
הֵנָּה הַלַּיְלָה מִבְּנֵי יִשְׂרָאֵל לַחְפֹּר אֶת־הָאָרֶץ:
ג וַיִּשְׁלַח מֶלֶךְ יְרִיחוֹ אֶל־רָחָב לֵאמֹר הוֹצִיאִי
הָאֲנָשִׁים הַבָּאִים אֵלַיִךְ אֲשֶׁר־בָּאוּ לְבֵיתֵךְ כִּי
לַחְפֹּר אֶת־כָּל־הָאָרֶץ בָּאוּ: ד וַתִּקַּח הָאִשָּׁה
אֶת־שְׁנֵי הָאֲנָשִׁים וַתִּצְפְּנוֹ וַתֹּאמֶר כֵּן בָּאוּ
אֵלַי הָאֲנָשִׁים וְלֹא יָדַעְתִּי מֵאַיִן הֵמָּה: ה וַיְהִי
הַשַּׁעַר לִסְגּוֹר בַּחֹשֶׁךְ וְהָאֲנָשִׁים יָצָאוּ לֹא
יָדַעְתִּי אָנָה הָלְכוּ הָאֲנָשִׁים רִדְפוּ מַהֵר
אַחֲרֵיהֶם כִּי תַשִּׂיגוּם: ו וְהִיא הֶעֱלָתַם הַגָּגָה
וַתִּטְמְנֵם בְּפִשְׁתֵּי הָעֵץ הָעֲרֻכוֹת לָהּ עַל־הַגָּג:
ז וְהָאֲנָשִׁים רָדְפוּ אַחֲרֵיהֶם דֶּרֶךְ הַיַּרְדֵּן עַל
הַמַּעְבְּרוֹת וְהַשַּׁעַר סָגָרוּ אַחֲרֵי כַּאֲשֶׁר יָצְאוּ
הָרֹדְפִים אַחֲרֵיהֶם: ח וְהֵמָּה טֶרֶם יִשְׁכָּבוּן
וְהִיא עָלְתָה עֲלֵיהֶם עַל־הַגָּג: ט וַתֹּאמֶר אֶל־
הָאֲנָשִׁים יָדַעְתִּי כִּי־נָתַן יהוה לָכֶם אֶת־
הָאָרֶץ וְכִי־נָפְלָה אֵימַתְכֶם עָלֵינוּ וְכִי נָמֹגוּ
כָּל־יֹשְׁבֵי הָאָרֶץ מִפְּנֵיכֶם: י כִּי שָׁמַעְנוּ אֵת
אֲשֶׁר־הוֹבִישׁ יהוה אֶת־מֵי יַם־סוּף מִפְּנֵיכֶם
בְּצֵאתְכֶם מִמִּצְרָיִם וַאֲשֶׁר עֲשִׂיתֶם לִשְׁנֵי
מַלְכֵי הָאֱמֹרִי אֲשֶׁר בְּעֵבֶר הַיַּרְדֵּן לְסִיחֹן וּלְעוֹג
אֲשֶׁר הֶחֱרַמְתֶּם אוֹתָם: יא וַנִּשְׁמַע וַיִּמַּס לְבָבֵנוּ
וְלֹא־קָמָה עוֹד רוּחַ בְּאִישׁ מִפְּנֵיכֶם כִּי יהוה
אֱלֹהֵיכֶם הוּא אֱלֹהִים בַּשָּׁמַיִם מִמַּעַל וְעַל־
הָאָרֶץ מִתָּחַת: יב וְעַתָּה הִשָּׁבְעוּ־נָא לִי בַּיהוה
כִּי־עָשִׂיתִי עִמָּכֶם חָסֶד וַעֲשִׂיתֶם גַּם־אַתֶּם
עִם־בֵּית אָבִי חֶסֶד וּנְתַתֶּם לִי אוֹת אֱמֶת:
יג וְהַחֲיִתֶם אֶת־אָבִי וְאֶת־אִמִּי וְאֶת־אַחַי
וְאֶת־אַחְיוֹתַי [ואת־אחותי כ׳] וְאֵת כָּל־אֲשֶׁר
לָהֶם וְהִצַּלְתֶּם אֶת־נַפְשֹׁתֵינוּ מִמָּוֶת: יד וַיֹּאמְרוּ
לָהּ הָאֲנָשִׁים נַפְשֵׁנוּ תַחְתֵּיכֶם לָמוּת אִם לֹא
תַגִּידוּ אֶת־דְּבָרֵנוּ זֶה וְהָיָה בְּתֵת־יהוה לָנוּ
אֶת־הָאָרֶץ וְעָשִׂינוּ עִמָּךְ חֶסֶד וֶאֱמֶת:
טו וַתּוֹרִדֵם בַּחֶבֶל בְּעַד הַחַלּוֹן כִּי בֵיתָהּ בְּקִיר
הַחוֹמָה וּבַחוֹמָה הִיא יוֹשָׁבֶת: טז וַתֹּאמֶר לָהֶם
הָהָרָה לֵּכוּ פֶּן־יִפְגְּעוּ בָכֶם הָרֹדְפִים וְנַחְבֵּתֶם
שָׁמָּה שְׁלֹשֶׁת יָמִים עַד שׁוֹב הָרֹדְפִים וְאַחַר
תֵּלְכוּ לְדַרְכְּכֶם: יז וַיֹּאמְרוּ אֵלֶיהָ הָאֲנָשִׁים
נְקִיִּם אֲנַחְנוּ מִשְּׁבֻעָתֵךְ הַזֶּה אֲשֶׁר הִשְׁבַּעְתָּנוּ:
יח הִנֵּה אֲנַחְנוּ בָאִים בָּאָרֶץ אֶת־תִּקְוַת חוּט
הַשָּׁנִי הַזֶּה תִּקְשְׁרִי בַּחַלּוֹן אֲשֶׁר הוֹרַדְתֵּנוּ בוֹ

and your father, and your mother, and your brothers, and all your father's household shall you gather to you in the house. 19 *Then it will be that anyone who leaves the doors of your house for the outside, his blood guilt shall be upon his own head; we will be clean; but anyone who will be with you inside the house, his blood guilt shall be on our head, if a hand is upon him.* 20 *And if you will tell of this discussion of ours, we will be clean from your oath that you have made us swear."*

21 *She said, "Like your words, so it is," and she sent them away, and they went; and she tied the scarlet cord to the window.*

22 *And they went, and they came to the mountain and stayed there for a three-day period, until the pursuers returned; the pursuers sought along the entire way but they did not find.*

23 *The two men returned and descended from the mountain; they crossed over [the Jordan] and came to Joshua son of Nun and told him all that happened to them.* 24 *They said to Joshua, "For* HASHEM *has given all the Land into our hands; also, all the inhabitants of the Land have melted before us."*

וְאֶת־אָבִיךְ וְאֶת־אִמֵּךְ וְאֶת־אַחַיִךְ וְאֵת כָּל־
בֵּית אָבִיךְ תַּאַסְפִי אֵלַיִךְ הַבָּיְתָה׃ יט וְהָיָה כֹּל
אֲשֶׁר־יֵצֵא מִדַּלְתֵי בֵיתֵךְ ׀ הַחוּצָה דָּמוֹ
בְרֹאשׁוֹ וַאֲנַחְנוּ נְקִיִּם וְכֹל אֲשֶׁר יִהְיֶה אִתָּךְ
בַּבַּיִת דָּמוֹ בְרֹאשֵׁנוּ אִם־יָד תִּהְיֶה־בּוֹ׃ כ וְאִם־
תַּגִּידִי אֶת־דְּבָרֵנוּ זֶה וְהָיִינוּ נְקִיִּם מִשְּׁבֻעָתֵךְ
אֲשֶׁר הִשְׁבַּעְתָּנוּ׃ כא וַתֹּאמֶר כְּדִבְרֵיכֶם כֶּן־
הוּא וַתְּשַׁלְּחֵם וַיֵּלֵכוּ וַתִּקְשֹׁר אֶת־תִּקְוַת הַשָּׁנִי
בַּחַלּוֹן׃ כב וַיֵּלְכוּ וַיָּבֹאוּ הָהָרָה וַיֵּשְׁבוּ שָׁם
שְׁלֹשֶׁת יָמִים עַד־שָׁבוּ הָרֹדְפִים וַיְבַקְשׁוּ
הָרֹדְפִים בְּכָל־הַדֶּרֶךְ וְלֹא מָצָאוּ׃ כג וַיָּשֻׁבוּ
שְׁנֵי הָאֲנָשִׁים וַיֵּרְדוּ מֵהָהָר וַיַּעַבְרוּ וַיָּבֹאוּ אֶל־
יְהוֹשֻׁעַ בִּן־נוּן וַיְסַפְּרוּ־לוֹ אֵת כָּל־הַמֹּצְאוֹת
אוֹתָם׃ כד וַיֹּאמְרוּ אֶל־יְהוֹשֻׁעַ כִּי־נָתַן יהוה
בְּיָדֵנוּ אֶת־כָּל־הָאָרֶץ וְגַם־נָמֹגוּ כָּל־יֹשְׁבֵי
הָאָרֶץ מִפָּנֵינוּ׃

HAFTARAS KORACH / הפטרת קרח

I Samuel 11:14 — 12:22 / שמואל א יא:יד – יב:כב

11 14 *Then Samuel said to the people, "Come and let us go to the Gilgal, and let us renew the kingdom there."*

15 *So all the people went to the Gilgal: There they made Saul king before* HASHEM *in the Gilgal; and there they slaughtered feast peace-offerings before* HASHEM*; and there Saul, as well as all the men of Israel, rejoiced exceedingly.*

12 1 *Then Samuel said to all of Israel, "Behold! I have hearkened to your voice, to everything that you have said to me, and I have crowned a king over you.* 2 *And now, behold! — the king walks before you, but I have aged and become gray; and, my sons, here they are with you; and as for me, I have walked before you from my youth until this day.* 3 *Here I am; testify about me in the presence of* HASHEM *and in the presence of His anointed: Whose ox have I taken? — or whose donkey have I taken? — or whom have I robbed? — whom have I coerced? — or from whose hand have I taken redemption-money that I close my eyes to him? — and I shall return [it] to you."*

4 *And they said, "You have not robbed us, and you have not coerced us, nor have you taken anything from anyone's hand."*

5 *So he said to them, "*HASHEM *is a witness about you, and His anointed is a witness this day, that you have not found anything in my hand. . . "*

And He said, "[I am] a witness!"

6 *And Samuel said to the people, ". . .* HASHEM *Who worked through Moses and Aaron, and Who brought your forefathers up from the land of Egypt.* 7 *And now,*

יא יד וַיֹּאמֶר שְׁמוּאֵל אֶל־הָעָם לְכוּ וְנֵלְכָה
הַגִּלְגָּל וּנְחַדֵּשׁ שָׁם הַמְּלוּכָה׃ טו וַיֵּלְכוּ כָל־
הָעָם הַגִּלְגָּל וַיַּמְלִכוּ שָׁם אֶת־שָׁאוּל לִפְנֵי
יהוה בַּגִּלְגָּל וַיִּזְבְּחוּ־שָׁם זְבָחִים שְׁלָמִים
לִפְנֵי יהוה וַיִּשְׂמַח שָׁם שָׁאוּל וְכָל־אַנְשֵׁי
יִשְׂרָאֵל עַד־מְאֹד׃ **יב** א וַיֹּאמֶר שְׁמוּאֵל אֶל־
כָּל־יִשְׂרָאֵל הִנֵּה שָׁמַעְתִּי בְקֹלְכֶם לְכֹל אֲשֶׁר־
אֲמַרְתֶּם לִי וָאַמְלִיךְ עֲלֵיכֶם מֶלֶךְ׃ ב וְעַתָּה
הִנֵּה הַמֶּלֶךְ ׀ מִתְהַלֵּךְ לִפְנֵיכֶם וַאֲנִי זָקַנְתִּי
וָשַׂבְתִּי וּבָנַי הִנָּם אִתְּכֶם וַאֲנִי הִתְהַלַּכְתִּי
לִפְנֵיכֶם מִנְּעֻרַי עַד־הַיּוֹם הַזֶּה׃ ג הִנְנִי עֲנוּ בִי
נֶגֶד יהוה וְנֶגֶד מְשִׁיחוֹ אֶת־שׁוֹר ׀ מִי לָקַחְתִּי
וַחֲמוֹר מִי לָקַחְתִּי וְאֶת־מִי עָשַׁקְתִּי אֶת־מִי
רַצּוֹתִי וּמִיַּד־מִי לָקַחְתִּי כֹפֶר וְאַעְלִים עֵינַי
בּוֹ וְאָשִׁיב לָכֶם׃ ד וַיֹּאמְרוּ לֹא עֲשַׁקְתָּנוּ וְלֹא
רַצּוֹתָנוּ וְלֹא־לָקַחְתָּ מִיַּד־אִישׁ מְאוּמָה׃
ה וַיֹּאמֶר אֲלֵיהֶם עֵד יהוה בָּכֶם וְעֵד מְשִׁיחוֹ
הַיּוֹם הַזֶּה כִּי לֹא מְצָאתֶם בְּיָדִי מְאוּמָה
וַיֹּאמֶר עֵד׃ ו וַיֹּאמֶר שְׁמוּאֵל אֶל־הָעָם יהוה
אֲשֶׁר עָשָׂה אֶת־מֹשֶׁה וְאֶת־אַהֲרֹן וַאֲשֶׁר
הֶעֱלָה אֶת־אֲבוֹתֵיכֶם מֵאֶרֶץ מִצְרָיִם׃ ז וְעַתָּה

stand yourselves erect, and I shall be judged with you before HASHEM *with regard to all the righteous deeds that He has done with you and with your forefathers.* 8 *When Jacob had come to Egypt and your forefathers cried out to* HASHEM, HASHEM *sent Moses and Aaron, and they brought your forefathers out of Egypt, and settled them in this place.* 9 *But they forgot* HASHEM, *their God, Who [in turn] gave them over into the hand of Sisera, general of the army of Hazor, and into the hand of the Philistines, and into the hand of the king of Moab, and they did battle with them.* 10 *Then they cried out to* HASHEM, *and said, 'We have sinned! For we have forsaken* HASHEM *and we have worshiped the Baal idols and the Ashtaroth idols; but now, rescue us from the hand of our enemy, and we will worship You.'* 11 *So* HASHEM *sent Jerubbaal (Gideon) and Bedan (Samson) and Jephthah and Samuel, and He rescued you from the hand of your enemies from all around, so that you dwelt in safety.* 12 *And when you saw that Nahash, king of the children of Ammon, came upon you, you said to me, 'No! For a king shall reign over us!' but* HASHEM, *your God, is your King.*

13 *"And now, behold! — the king whom you have chosen, whom you have requested; and, behold! —* HASHEM *has set a king over you.* 14 *If you will fear* HASHEM, *and worship Him, and hearken to His voice, and you will not rebel against the word of* HASHEM, *but you and the king who reigns over you will follow after* HASHEM, *your God . . .* 15 *But if you will not hearken to the voice of* HASHEM, *and you will rebel against the word of* HASHEM, *then* HASHEM*'s hand will be against you and against your fathers.* 16 *Even now, stand yourselves erect and see this great thing that* HASHEM *will do before your eyes.* 17 *Is not the harvest of the wheat today? — yet I shall call to* HASHEM *and He will set forth thunder and rain, then you shall recognize and see that great is your wickedness that you have perpetrated before the eyes of* HASHEM, *to request for yourselves a king."*

18 *Then Samuel called to* HASHEM, *and* HASHEM *set forth thunder and rain on that day; and all the people greatly feared* HASHEM *and Samuel.* 19 *All the people said to Samuel, "Pray on behalf of your servants to* HASHEM, *your God, that we not die; for we have added wickedness upon all of our sins, to request for ourselves a king."*

20 *So Samuel said to the people, "Fear not; [though] you have done all this wickedness, nevertheless, do not turn away from following after* HASHEM, *but serve* HASHEM *with all your heart.* 21 *And you shall not turn away to follow after the futility which cannot avail and cannot rescue, for they are futile.* 22 *For* HASHEM *shall not cast off his people for the sake of His great Name; for* HASHEM *has sworn to make you for a people unto Him."*

הִתְיַצְּבוּ וְאִשָּׁפְטָה אִתְּכֶם לִפְנֵי יְהֹוָה אֵת כָּל־
צִדְקוֹת יְהֹוָה אֲשֶׁר־עָשָׂה אִתְּכֶם וְאֶת־
אֲבֹתֵיכֶם: ח כַּאֲשֶׁר־בָּא יַעֲקֹב מִצְרָיִם וַיִּזְעֲקוּ
אֲבֹתֵיכֶם אֶל־יְהֹוָה וַיִּשְׁלַח יְהֹוָה אֶת־מֹשֶׁה
וְאֶת־אַהֲרֹן וַיּוֹצִיאוּ אֶת־אֲבֹתֵיכֶם מִמִּצְרַיִם
וַיֹּשִׁבוּם בַּמָּקוֹם הַזֶּה: ט וַיִּשְׁכְּחוּ אֶת־יְהֹוָה
אֱלֹהֵיהֶם וַיִּמְכֹּר אֹתָם בְּיַד סִיסְרָא שַׂר־צְבָא
חָצוֹר וּבְיַד־פְּלִשְׁתִּים וּבְיַד מֶלֶךְ מוֹאָב וַיִּלָּחֲמוּ
בָּם: י וַיִּזְעֲקוּ אֶל־יְהֹוָה וַיֹּאמְרוּ [ויאמר כ׳]
חָטָאנוּ כִּי עָזַבְנוּ אֶת־יְהֹוָה וַנַּעֲבֹד אֶת־
הַבְּעָלִים וְאֶת־הָעַשְׁתָּרוֹת וְעַתָּה הַצִּילֵנוּ מִיַּד
אֹיְבֵינוּ וְנַעַבְדֶךָּ: יא וַיִּשְׁלַח יְהֹוָה אֶת־יְרֻבַּעַל
וְאֶת־בְּדָן וְאֶת־יִפְתָּח וְאֶת־שְׁמוּאֵל וַיַּצֵּל
אֶתְכֶם מִיַּד אֹיְבֵיכֶם מִסָּבִיב וַתֵּשְׁבוּ בֶּטַח:
יב וַתִּרְאוּ כִּי נָחָשׁ מֶלֶךְ בְּנֵי־עַמּוֹן בָּא עֲלֵיכֶם
וַתֹּאמְרוּ לִי לֹא כִּי־מֶלֶךְ יִמְלֹךְ עָלֵינוּ וַיהֹוָה
אֱלֹהֵיכֶם מַלְכְּכֶם: יג וְעַתָּה הִנֵּה הַמֶּלֶךְ אֲשֶׁר
בְּחַרְתֶּם אֲשֶׁר שְׁאֶלְתֶּם וְהִנֵּה נָתַן יְהֹוָה
עֲלֵיכֶם מֶלֶךְ: יד אִם־תִּירְאוּ אֶת־יְהֹוָה וַעֲבַדְתֶּם
אֹתוֹ וּשְׁמַעְתֶּם בְּקֹלוֹ וְלֹא תַמְרוּ אֶת־פִּי יְהֹוָה
וִהְיִתֶם גַּם־אַתֶּם וְגַם־הַמֶּלֶךְ אֲשֶׁר־מָלַךְ עֲלֵיכֶם
אַחַר יְהֹוָה אֱלֹהֵיכֶם: טו וְאִם־לֹא תִשְׁמְעוּ
בְּקוֹל יְהֹוָה וּמְרִיתֶם אֶת־פִּי יְהֹוָה וְהָיְתָה יַד־
יְהֹוָה בָּכֶם וּבַאֲבֹתֵיכֶם: טז גַּם־עַתָּה הִתְיַצְּבוּ
וּרְאוּ אֶת־הַדָּבָר הַגָּדוֹל הַזֶּה אֲשֶׁר יְהֹוָה עֹשֶׂה
לְעֵינֵיכֶם: יז הֲלוֹא קְצִיר־חִטִּים הַיּוֹם אֶקְרָא
אֶל־יְהֹוָה וְיִתֵּן קֹלוֹת וּמָטָר וּדְעוּ וּרְאוּ כִּי־
רָעַתְכֶם רַבָּה אֲשֶׁר עֲשִׂיתֶם בְּעֵינֵי יְהֹוָה
לִשְׁאוֹל לָכֶם מֶלֶךְ: יח וַיִּקְרָא שְׁמוּאֵל אֶל־יְהֹוָה
וַיִּתֵּן יְהֹוָה קֹלֹת וּמָטָר בַּיּוֹם הַהוּא וַיִּירָא כָל־
הָעָם מְאֹד אֶת־יְהֹוָה וְאֶת־שְׁמוּאֵל: יט וַיֹּאמְרוּ
כָל־הָעָם אֶל־שְׁמוּאֵל הִתְפַּלֵּל בְּעַד־עֲבָדֶיךָ
אֶל־יְהֹוָה אֱלֹהֶיךָ וְאַל־נָמוּת כִּי־יָסַפְנוּ עַל־
כָּל־חַטֹּאתֵינוּ רָעָה לִשְׁאֹל לָנוּ מֶלֶךְ: כ וַיֹּאמֶר
שְׁמוּאֵל אֶל־הָעָם אַל־תִּירָאוּ אַתֶּם עֲשִׂיתֶם
אֵת כָּל־הָרָעָה הַזֹּאת אַךְ אַל־תָּסוּרוּ מֵאַחֲרֵי
יְהֹוָה וַעֲבַדְתֶּם אֶת־יְהֹוָה בְּכָל־לְבַבְכֶם:
כא וְלֹא תָּסוּרוּ כִּי ׀ אַחֲרֵי הַתֹּהוּ אֲשֶׁר לֹא־
יוֹעִילוּ וְלֹא יַצִּילוּ כִּי־תֹהוּ הֵמָּה: כב כִּי לֹא־
יִטֹּשׁ יְהֹוָה אֶת־עַמּוֹ בַּעֲבוּר שְׁמוֹ הַגָּדוֹל כִּי
הוֹאִיל יְהֹוָה לַעֲשׂוֹת אֶתְכֶם לוֹ לְעָם:

HAFTARAS CHUKAS / הפטרת חקת

When the *Sidros* of *Chukas* and *Balak* are read on the same Sabbath,
this *Haftarah* is omitted, and the *Haftarah* of *Balak* is read.

Judges 11:1-33 / שופטים יא:א-לג

11 1 *Jephthah the Gileadite was a mighty man of valor, and he was the son of a concubine, and Gilead begot Jephthah.* 2 *And Gilead's wife bore him sons, and when the wife's sons grew up they drove Jephthah away and said to him, "You shall not inherit in our father's house, for you are the son of another woman."*

3 *So Jephthah fled because of his brothers and settled in the land of Tob; empty-handed men gathered themselves about Jephthah and ventured forth with him.*

4 *After a period of time, the children of Ammon made war with Israel.* 5 *And it happened when the children of Ammon made war with Israel that the Gileadite elders went to fetch Jephthah from the land of Tob.* 6 *They said to Jephthah, "Go forth and become our chief and we will do battle with the children of Ammon."*

7 *But Jephthah said to the Gileadite elders, "Was it not you who hated me and who drove me away from my father's house? — so why have you come to me now when you are in distress?"*

8 *The Gileadite elders said to Jephthah, "For this have we now returned to you, that you go with us and we will do battle with the children of Ammon, and that you shall become a leader unto us, unto all the inhabitants of Gilead."*

9 *So Jephthah said to the Gileadite elders, "If you return me to do battle with the children of Ammon and* HASHEM *delivers them before me, I will become your leader."*

10 *The Gileadite leaders said to Jephthah, "*HASHEM *shall be witness between us if it is not according to your word that we do."* 11 *So Jephthah went with the Gileadite elders, and the people set him as a leader and a chief over them; then Jephthah spoke all his words before* HASHEM *in Mizpah.*

12 *Jephthah sent emissaries to the king of the children of Ammon saying, "What is unto you and unto me that you have come to me to make war in my land?"*

13 *The king of the children of Ammon said to Jephthah's emissaries, "Because Israel took my land when it ascended from Egypt, from Arnon until the Jabbok until the Jordan, so now return them in peace."*

14 *And Jephthah once again sent emissaries to the king of the children of Ammon.*

15 *He said to him, "Thus said Jephthah: Israel did not take the land of Moab and the land of the children of Ammon.* 16 *For when Israel ascended from Egypt, Israel went in the wilderness until the Sea of Reeds and they arrived at Kadesh.* 17 *Israel sent emissaries to the king of Edom saying, 'Let me please pass through*

יא א וְיִפְתָּח הַגִּלְעָדִי הָיָה גִּבּוֹר חַיִל וְהוּא בֶּן־
אִשָּׁה זוֹנָה וַיּוֹלֶד גִּלְעָד אֶת־יִפְתָּח: ב וַתֵּלֶד
אֵשֶׁת־גִּלְעָד לוֹ בָּנִים וַיִּגְדְּלוּ בְנֵי־הָאִשָּׁה
וַיְגָרְשׁוּ אֶת־יִפְתָּח וַיֹּאמְרוּ לוֹ לֹא־תִנְחַל
בְּבֵית־אָבִינוּ כִּי בֶּן־אִשָּׁה אַחֶרֶת אָתָּה:
ג וַיִּבְרַח יִפְתָּח מִפְּנֵי אֶחָיו וַיֵּשֶׁב בְּאֶרֶץ טוֹב
וַיִּתְלַקְּטוּ אֶל־יִפְתָּח אֲנָשִׁים רֵיקִים וַיֵּצְאוּ
עִמּוֹ: ד וַיְהִי מִיָּמִים וַיִּלָּחֲמוּ בְנֵי־עַמּוֹן עִם־
יִשְׂרָאֵל: ה וַיְהִי כַּאֲשֶׁר־נִלְחֲמוּ בְנֵי־עַמּוֹן עִם־
יִשְׂרָאֵל וַיֵּלְכוּ זִקְנֵי גִלְעָד לָקַחַת אֶת־יִפְתָּח
מֵאֶרֶץ טוֹב: ו וַיֹּאמְרוּ לְיִפְתָּח לְכָה וְהָיִיתָה לָּנוּ
לְקָצִין וְנִלָּחֲמָה בִּבְנֵי עַמּוֹן: ז וַיֹּאמֶר יִפְתָּח
לְזִקְנֵי גִלְעָד הֲלֹא אַתֶּם שְׂנֵאתֶם אוֹתִי
וַתְּגָרְשׁוּנִי מִבֵּית אָבִי וּמַדּוּעַ בָּאתֶם אֵלַי עַתָּה
כַּאֲשֶׁר צַר לָכֶם: ח וַיֹּאמְרוּ זִקְנֵי גִלְעָד אֶל־
יִפְתָּח לָכֵן עַתָּה שַׁבְנוּ אֵלֶיךָ וְהָלַכְתָּ עִמָּנוּ
וְנִלְחַמְתָּ בִּבְנֵי עַמּוֹן וְהָיִיתָ לָּנוּ לְרֹאשׁ לְכֹל
יֹשְׁבֵי גִלְעָד: ט וַיֹּאמֶר יִפְתָּח אֶל־זִקְנֵי גִלְעָד
אִם־מְשִׁיבִים אַתֶּם אוֹתִי לְהִלָּחֵם בִּבְנֵי עַמּוֹן
וְנָתַן יהוה אוֹתָם לְפָנָי אָנֹכִי אֶהְיֶה לָכֶם
לְרֹאשׁ: י וַיֹּאמְרוּ זִקְנֵי־גִלְעָד אֶל־יִפְתָּח יהוה
יִהְיֶה שֹׁמֵעַ בֵּינוֹתֵינוּ אִם־לֹא כִדְבָרְךָ כֵּן
נַעֲשֶׂה: יא וַיֵּלֶךְ יִפְתָּח עִם־זִקְנֵי גִלְעָד וַיָּשִׂימוּ
הָעָם אוֹתוֹ עֲלֵיהֶם לְרֹאשׁ וּלְקָצִין וַיְדַבֵּר
יִפְתָּח אֶת־כָּל־דְּבָרָיו לִפְנֵי יהוה בַּמִּצְפָּה:
יב וַיִּשְׁלַח יִפְתָּח מַלְאָכִים אֶל־מֶלֶךְ בְּנֵי־עַמּוֹן
לֵאמֹר מַה־לִּי וָלָךְ כִּי־בָאתָ אֵלַי לְהִלָּחֵם
בְּאַרְצִי: יג וַיֹּאמֶר מֶלֶךְ בְּנֵי־עַמּוֹן אֶל־מַלְאֲכֵי
יִפְתָּח כִּי־לָקַח יִשְׂרָאֵל אֶת־אַרְצִי בַּעֲלוֹתוֹ
מִמִּצְרַיִם מֵאַרְנוֹן וְעַד־הַיַּבֹּק וְעַד־הַיַּרְדֵּן
וְעַתָּה הָשִׁיבָה אֶתְהֶן בְּשָׁלוֹם: יד וַיּוֹסֶף עוֹד
יִפְתָּח וַיִּשְׁלַח מַלְאָכִים אֶל־מֶלֶךְ בְּנֵי עַמּוֹן:
טו וַיֹּאמֶר לוֹ כֹּה אָמַר יִפְתָּח לֹא־לָקַח יִשְׂרָאֵל
אֶת־אֶרֶץ מוֹאָב וְאֶת־אֶרֶץ בְּנֵי עַמּוֹן: טז כִּי
בַּעֲלוֹתָם מִמִּצְרָיִם וַיֵּלֶךְ יִשְׂרָאֵל בַּמִּדְבָּר עַד־
יַם־סוּף וַיָּבֹא קָדֵשָׁה: יז וַיִּשְׁלַח יִשְׂרָאֵל
מַלְאָכִים | אֶל־מֶלֶךְ אֱדוֹם | לֵאמֹר אֶעְבְּרָה

נָּא בְאַרְצֶךָ וְלֹא שָׁמַע מֶלֶךְ אֱדוֹם וְגַם אֶל־
מֶלֶךְ מוֹאָב שָׁלַח וְלֹא אָבָה וַיֵּשֶׁב יִשְׂרָאֵל
בְּקָדֵשׁ: יח וַיֵּלֶךְ בַּמִּדְבָּר וַיָּסָב אֶת־אֶרֶץ אֱדוֹם
וְאֶת־אֶרֶץ מוֹאָב וַיָּבֹא מִמִּזְרַח־שֶׁמֶשׁ לְאֶרֶץ
מוֹאָב וַיַּחֲנוּן בְּעֵבֶר אַרְנוֹן וְלֹא־בָאוּ בִּגְבוּל
מוֹאָב כִּי אַרְנוֹן גְּבוּל מוֹאָב: יט וַיִּשְׁלַח יִשְׂרָאֵל
מַלְאָכִים אֶל־סִיחוֹן מֶלֶךְ־הָאֱמֹרִי מֶלֶךְ חֶשְׁבּוֹן
וַיֹּאמֶר לוֹ יִשְׂרָאֵל נַעְבְּרָה־נָּא בְאַרְצְךָ עַד־
מְקוֹמִי: כ וְלֹא־הֶאֱמִין סִיחוֹן אֶת־יִשְׂרָאֵל
עֲבֹר בִּגְבֻלוֹ וַיֶּאֱסֹף סִיחוֹן אֶת־כָּל־עַמּוֹ וַיַּחֲנוּ
בְּיָהְצָה וַיִּלָּחֶם עִם־יִשְׂרָאֵל: כא וַיִּתֵּן יהוה
אֱלֹהֵי־יִשְׂרָאֵל אֶת־סִיחוֹן וְאֶת־כָּל־עַמּוֹ בְּיַד
יִשְׂרָאֵל וַיַּכּוּם וַיִּירַשׁ יִשְׂרָאֵל אֵת כָּל־אֶרֶץ
הָאֱמֹרִי יוֹשֵׁב הָאָרֶץ הַהִיא: כב וַיִּירְשׁוּ אֵת
כָּל־גְּבוּל הָאֱמֹרִי מֵאַרְנוֹן וְעַד־הַיַּבֹּק וּמִן־
הַמִּדְבָּר וְעַד־הַיַּרְדֵּן: כג וְעַתָּה יהוה | אֱלֹהֵי
יִשְׂרָאֵל הוֹרִישׁ אֶת־הָאֱמֹרִי מִפְּנֵי עַמּוֹ
יִשְׂרָאֵל וְאַתָּה תִּירָשֶׁנּוּ: כד הֲלֹא אֵת אֲשֶׁר
יוֹרִישְׁךָ כְּמוֹשׁ אֱלֹהֶיךָ אוֹתוֹ תִירָשׁ וְאֵת כָּל־
אֲשֶׁר הוֹרִישׁ יהוה אֱלֹהֵינוּ מִפָּנֵינוּ אוֹתוֹ
נִירָשׁ: כה וְעַתָּה הֲטוֹב טוֹב אַתָּה מִבָּלָק בֶּן־
צִפּוֹר מֶלֶךְ מוֹאָב הֲרוֹב רָב עִם־יִשְׂרָאֵל אִם־
נִלְחֹם נִלְחַם בָּם: כו בְּשֶׁבֶת יִשְׂרָאֵל בְּחֶשְׁבּוֹן
וּבִבְנוֹתֶיהָ וּבְעַרְעוֹר וּבִבְנוֹתֶיהָ וּבְכָל־הֶעָרִים
אֲשֶׁר עַל־יְדֵי אַרְנוֹן שְׁלֹשׁ מֵאוֹת שָׁנָה וּמַדּוּעַ
לֹא־הִצַּלְתֶּם בָּעֵת הַהִיא: כז וְאָנֹכִי לֹא־
חָטָאתִי לָךְ וְאַתָּה עֹשֶׂה אִתִּי רָעָה לְהִלָּחֶם בִּי
יִשְׁפֹּט יהוה הַשֹּׁפֵט הַיּוֹם בֵּין בְּנֵי יִשְׂרָאֵל וּבֵין
בְּנֵי עַמּוֹן: כח וְלֹא שָׁמַע מֶלֶךְ בְּנֵי עַמּוֹן אֶל־
דִּבְרֵי יִפְתָּח אֲשֶׁר שָׁלַח אֵלָיו: כט וַתְּהִי עַל־
יִפְתָּח רוּחַ יהוה וַיַּעֲבֹר אֶת־הַגִּלְעָד וְאֶת־
מְנַשֶּׁה וַיַּעֲבֹר אֶת־מִצְפֵּה גִלְעָד וּמִמִּצְפֵּה
גִלְעָד עָבַר בְּנֵי עַמּוֹן: ל וַיִּדַּר יִפְתָּח נֶדֶר
לַיהוה וַיֹּאמַר אִם־נָתוֹן תִּתֵּן אֶת־בְּנֵי עַמּוֹן
בְּיָדִי: לא וְהָיָה הַיּוֹצֵא אֲשֶׁר יֵצֵא מִדַּלְתֵי בֵיתִי
לִקְרָאתִי בְּשׁוּבִי בְשָׁלוֹם מִבְּנֵי עַמּוֹן וְהָיָה
לַיהוה וְהַעֲלִיתִיהוּ עוֹלָה: לב וַיַּעֲבֹר יִפְתָּח
אֶל־בְּנֵי עַמּוֹן לְהִלָּחֶם בָּם וַיִּתְּנֵם יהוה בְּיָדוֹ:
לג וַיַּכֵּם מֵעֲרוֹעֵר וְעַד־בּוֹאֲךָ מִנִּית עֶשְׂרִים
עִיר וְעַד אָבֵל כְּרָמִים מַכָּה גְּדוֹלָה מְאֹד
וַיִּכָּנְעוּ בְּנֵי עַמּוֹן מִפְּנֵי בְּנֵי יִשְׂרָאֵל:

*your land,' but the king of Edom did not listen; and also
to the king of Moab did [Israel] send, but he was [also]
not willing; so Israel sojourned in Kadesh. 18 It went
through the wilderness, and went around the land of
Edom and the land of Moab and came to the eastern
side of the land of Moab where they encamped across
the Arnon; but they did not enter the border of Moab,
for Arnon is the border of Moab. 19 Then Israel sent
emissaries to Sihon king of the Amorite, king of Hesh-
bon, and Israel said to him, 'Let us please pass through
your land until my place.' 20 But Sihon did not trust
Israel to pass through his border, rather Sihon assem-
bled all his people and they encamped in Jahaz; and he
made war against Israel. 21 Then HASHEM, God of Is-
rael, delivered Sihon and all his people into the hand of
Israel, and He struck them; and Israel took possession
of the entire land of the Amorite, the inhabitant of that
land.*

*22 They took possession of the entire border of the
Amorite, from Arnon to the Jabbok, and from the
wilderness to the Jordan. 23 And now HASHEM, God of
Israel, has driven out the Amorite from before His peo-
ple Israel, and you would possess it? 24 Do you not
take into your possession that which your god
Chemosh bequeaths to you? — that may you pos-
sess; but all that HASHEM our God drives out from be-
fore us, we shall take possession of it. 25 And now, are
you much better than Balak son of Zippor, king of
Moab? — did he ever strive against Israel? — Did he
ever do battle with them? 26 When Israel dwelled in
Heshbon and its villages and in Aroer and its villages
and in all the cities that are alongside Arnon for three
hundred years, why did you not recover them during
that time? 27 I have not sinned against you; but you do
me wrong to make war against me; may HASHEM the
Judge judge today between the Children of Israel and
the Children of Ammon."*

*28 But the king of the children of Ammon did not
listen to the words of Jephthah that he had sent to him.*

*29 A spirit of HASHEM was upon Jephthah: He passed
through Gilead and through Manasseh, and he passed
through Mizpeh of Gilead, and from Mizpeh of Gilead
he passed through [to] the children of Ammon. 30 Then
Jephthah declared a vow unto HASHEM, and he said, "If
You will indeed deliver the children of Ammon into my
hand, 31 then it will be that whatever emerges, what
will emerge from the doors of my house to greet me
when I return in peace from the children of Ammon, it
shall be unto HASHEM, and I will offer it up as an eleva-
tion-offering."*

*32 Then Jephthah passed through to the children of
Ammon to do battle against them, and HASHEM deliv-
ered them into his hand. 33 And he struck them from
Aroer until you come to Minnith, twenty cities, until the
Plain of Cheramim, a very great slaughter; and the
children of Ammon were subdued before the Children
of Israel.*

HAFTARAS BALAK / הפטרת בלק

Micah 5:6 – 6:8 / מיכה ה:ו – ו:ח

ה ו וְהָיָה ׀ שְׁאֵרִית יַעֲקֹב בְּקֶרֶב עַמִּים
רַבִּים כְּטַל מֵאֵת יהוה כִּרְבִיבִים עֲלֵי־
עֵשֶׂב אֲשֶׁר לֹא־יְקַוֶּה לְאִישׁ וְלֹא יְיַחֵל
לִבְנֵי אָדָם: ז וְהָיָה שְׁאֵרִית יַעֲקֹב בַּגּוֹיִם
בְּקֶרֶב עַמִּים רַבִּים כְּאַרְיֵה בְּבַהֲמוֹת יַעַר
כִּכְפִיר בְּעֶדְרֵי־צֹאן אֲשֶׁר אִם־עָבַר וְרָמַס
וְטָרַף וְאֵין מַצִּיל: ח תָּרֹם יָדְךָ עַל־צָרֶיךָ
וְכָל־אֹיְבֶיךָ יִכָּרֵתוּ: ט וְהָיָה בַיּוֹם־הַהוּא
נְאֻם־יהוה וְהִכְרַתִּי סוּסֶיךָ מִקִּרְבֶּךָ
וְהַאֲבַדְתִּי מַרְכְּבֹתֶיךָ: י וְהִכְרַתִּי עָרֵי אַרְצֶךָ
וְהָרַסְתִּי כָּל־מִבְצָרֶיךָ: יא וְהִכְרַתִּי כְשָׁפִים
מִיָּדֶךָ וּמְעוֹנְנִים לֹא יִהְיוּ־לָךְ: יב וְהִכְרַתִּי
פְסִילֶיךָ וּמַצֵּבוֹתֶיךָ מִקִּרְבֶּךָ וְלֹא־תִשְׁתַּחֲוֶה
עוֹד לְמַעֲשֵׂה יָדֶיךָ: יג וְנָתַשְׁתִּי אֲשֵׁירֶיךָ
מִקִּרְבֶּךָ וְהִשְׁמַדְתִּי עָרֶיךָ: יד וְעָשִׂיתִי בְּאַף
וּבְחֵמָה נָקָם אֶת־הַגּוֹיִם אֲשֶׁר לֹא שָׁמֵעוּ:
ו א שִׁמְעוּ־נָא אֵת אֲשֶׁר־יהוה אֹמֵר קוּם
רִיב אֶת־הֶהָרִים וְתִשְׁמַעְנָה הַגְּבָעוֹת קוֹלֶךָ:
ב שִׁמְעוּ הָרִים אֶת־רִיב יהוה וְהָאֵתָנִים
מֹסְדֵי אָרֶץ כִּי רִיב לַיהוה עִם־עַמּוֹ וְעִם־
יִשְׂרָאֵל יִתְוַכָּח: ג עַמִּי מֶה־עָשִׂיתִי לְךָ וּמָה
הֶלְאֵתִיךָ עֲנֵה בִי: ד כִּי הֶעֱלִתִיךָ מֵאֶרֶץ
מִצְרַיִם וּמִבֵּית עֲבָדִים פְּדִיתִיךָ וָאֶשְׁלַח
לְפָנֶיךָ אֶת־מֹשֶׁה אַהֲרֹן וּמִרְיָם: ה עַמִּי
זְכָר־נָא מַה־יָּעַץ בָּלָק מֶלֶךְ מוֹאָב וּמֶה־
עָנָה אֹתוֹ בִּלְעָם בֶּן־בְּעוֹר מִן־הַשִּׁטִּים עַד־
הַגִּלְגָּל לְמַעַן דַּעַת צִדְקוֹת יהוה: ו בַּמָּה
אֲקַדֵּם יהוה אִכַּף לֵאלֹהֵי מָרוֹם הַאֲקַדְּמֶנּוּ
בְעוֹלוֹת בַּעֲגָלִים בְּנֵי שָׁנָה: ז הֲיִרְצֶה יהוה
בְּאַלְפֵי אֵילִים בְּרִבְבוֹת נַחֲלֵי־שָׁמֶן הַאֶתֵּן
בְּכוֹרִי פִּשְׁעִי פְּרִי בִטְנִי חַטַּאת נַפְשִׁי: ח הִגִּיד
לְךָ אָדָם מַה־טּוֹב וּמָה־יהוה דּוֹרֵשׁ מִמְּךָ כִּי
אִם־עֲשׂוֹת מִשְׁפָּט וְאַהֲבַת חֶסֶד וְהַצְנֵעַ לֶכֶת
עִם־אֱלֹהֶיךָ:

5 6 *And the remnant of Jacob shall be in the midst of many peoples — like dew from HASHEM, like raindrops upon grass, that hopes not for a man and anticipates not the soul of a man.* 7 *And the remnant of Jacob shall be among the nations, in the midst of many peoples — like a lion among the forest animals, like a lion cub among the flocks of sheep, which, if it passes through, tramples and sunders, and there is no rescuer.* 8 *Your hand shall be raised over your adversaries, and all your enemies shall be cut down.*

9 *And it shall be on that day — the word of HASHEM — I will cut down your horses from your midst, and I will cause your chariots to be lost;* 10 *and I will cut down the cities of your land; and I will raze all your strongholds;* 11 *and I will cut out wizardry from your hand; and soothsayers there will not be for you;* 12 *and I will cut down your graven idols and your pillars from your midst; and you shall never again prostrate yourself to your handiwork;* 13 *and I will uproot your idol-trees from your midst; and I will destroy your cities;* 14 *in anger and fury will I inflict vengeance upon the nations that do not listen.*

6 1 *Listen now to what HASHEM says: "Arise! Contend with the mountains, and let the hills hear your voice.* 2 *Listen, O mountains, to HASHEM's argument, and the mighty ones, the foundations of the earth; for HASHEM has an argument against His people, and He shall contend with Israel.* 3 *O My people, what have I done to you? How have I wearied you? Testify against Me.* 4 *When I brought you up from the land of Egypt and redeemed you from the house of slavery, I sent before you Moses, Aaron, and Miriam.* 5 *O My people, remember now what Balak king of Moab plotted and what Balaam son of Beor answered him; [despite the sin of the spies dispatched] from the Shittim, [I nevertheless split the Jordan for you when I brought you] to the Gilgal; that you may know the righteous acts of HASHEM."*

6 *With what shall I approach HASHEM, shall I humble myself before God of the heavens? — shall I approach Him with burnt-offerings, with calves in their first year?* 7 *Will HASHEM find favor in thousands of rams, in tens of thousands of streams of oil? — shall I give over my firstborn [to atone for] my transgression, the fruit of my womb [for] the sin of my soul?* 8 *He has told you, O man, what is good, and what HASHEM seeks from you: only the performance of justice, the love of kindness, and walking humbly with your God.*

HAFTARAS PINCHAS / הפטרת פינחס

During most years, *Parashas Pinchas* is read after the Seventeenth of Tammuz. In those years, the two *Parashiyos Mattos* and *Masei* are read on the Sabbath after *Parashas Pinchas*. The *Haftarah* of *Parashas Pinchas* is then omitted, and the *Haftarah* of *Parashas Mattos* (p. 448) is read in its place. In those years when *Parashas Pinchas* is read before the Seventeenth of Tammuz, the following *Haftarah* is read.

I Kings 18:46 — 19:21 / מלכים א יח:מו — יט:כא

18 [46] *And the hand of HASHEM was upon Elijah, so he girded his loins and ran before Ahab until the approach to Jezreel.*

19 [1] *Then Ahab told Jezebel all that Elijah had done and all that he had slain — all the [false] prophets — with the sword.*

[2] *Jezebel sent an emissary to Elijah saying, "Thus may the gods do [to me] and thus may they increase [upon me], unless at this time tomorrow I shall set your soul as the soul of one of them."*

[3] *When he saw [the danger], he arose and went for his life; he came to Beer-sheba, which belongs to Judah, and left his servant there.* [4] *But as for himself, he went a day's journey into the wilderness; he came [there], sat under a rosem-bush, and requested for his soul to die; and he said, "It is enough! — now, HASHEM, take my soul, for I am not better than my forefathers."*

[5] *Then he lay down and slept under a rosem-bush, and, behold this! — an angel touched him and said to him, "Arise! Eat!"*

[6] *So he looked, and, behold! — near his head, a coal-baked cake and a container of water; he ate and drank, then he went back and lay down.*

[7] *The angel of HASHEM returned to him a second time, touched him and said, "Arise! Eat! for the road will be long for you."*

[8] *So he arose, and ate and drank; then he went, on the strength of that meal, forty days and forty nights, until the Mountain of God, [until] Horeb.* [9] *He came there to the cave and spent the night there; and, behold! — the word of HASHEM came to him and said to him, "Why are you here, Elijah?"*

[10] *And he said, "I have been exceedingly zealous for HASHEM, God of Legions, for the Children of Israel have abandoned Your covenant; they have razed Your Altars; they have killed Your prophets with the sword, so that I alone have remained, and they seek my soul to take it."*

[11] *And He said, "Go forth and stand on the mountain before HASHEM; and, behold! — HASHEM is passing, and a great, powerful wind is smashing mountains and breaking rocks before HASHEM — but not in the wind is HASHEM; and after the wind an earthquake — but not in the earthquake is HASHEM;* [12] *and after the earthquake a fire — but not in the fire is HASHEM; and after the fire a still, thin sound."*

[13] *And it happened when Elijah heard, he bound his face in his mantle, went out, and stood by the cave's entrance; and, behold! — a voice came unto him and it said, "Why are you here, Elijah?"*

יח מו וְיַד־יהוה הָיְתָה אֶל־אֵלִיָּהוּ וַיְשַׁנֵּס
מָתְנָיו וַיָּרָץ לִפְנֵי אַחְאָב עַד־בֹּאֲכָה
יִזְרְעֶאלָה: יט א וַיַּגֵּד אַחְאָב לְאִיזֶבֶל אֵת כָּל־
אֲשֶׁר עָשָׂה אֵלִיָּהוּ וְאֵת כָּל־אֲשֶׁר הָרַג אֶת־
כָּל־הַנְּבִיאִים בֶּחָרֶב: ב וַתִּשְׁלַח אִיזֶבֶל
מַלְאָךְ אֶל־אֵלִיָּהוּ לֵאמֹר כֹּה־יַעֲשׂוּן אֱלֹהִים
וְכֹה יוֹסִפוּן כִּי־כָעֵת מָחָר אָשִׂים אֶת־נַפְשְׁךָ
כְּנֶפֶשׁ אַחַד מֵהֶם: ג וַיַּרְא וַיָּקָם וַיֵּלֶךְ אֶל־
נַפְשׁוֹ וַיָּבֹא בְּאֵר שֶׁבַע אֲשֶׁר לִיהוּדָה וַיַּנַּח
אֶת־נַעֲרוֹ שָׁם: ד וְהוּא־הָלַךְ בַּמִּדְבָּר דֶּרֶךְ יוֹם
וַיָּבֹא וַיֵּשֶׁב תַּחַת רֹתֶם אֶחָד [אחת כ׳] וַיִּשְׁאַל
אֶת־נַפְשׁוֹ לָמוּת וַיֹּאמֶר | רַב עַתָּה יהוה קַח
נַפְשִׁי כִּי לֹא־טוֹב אָנֹכִי מֵאֲבֹתָי: ה וַיִּשְׁכַּב
וַיִּישַׁן תַּחַת רֹתֶם אֶחָד וְהִנֵּה־זֶה מַלְאָךְ נֹגֵעַ
בּוֹ וַיֹּאמֶר לוֹ קוּם אֱכוֹל: ו וַיַּבֵּט וְהִנֵּה
מְרַאֲשֹׁתָיו עֻגַת רְצָפִים וְצַפַּחַת מָיִם וַיֹּאכַל
וַיֵּשְׁתְּ וַיָּשָׁב וַיִּשְׁכָּב: ז וַיָּשָׁב מַלְאַךְ יהוה |
שֵׁנִית וַיִּגַּע־בּוֹ וַיֹּאמֶר קוּם אֱכֹל כִּי רַב מִמְּךָ
הַדָּרֶךְ: ח וַיָּקָם וַיֹּאכַל וַיִּשְׁתֶּה וַיֵּלֶךְ בְּכֹחַ |
הָאֲכִילָה הַהִיא אַרְבָּעִים יוֹם וְאַרְבָּעִים לַיְלָה
עַד הַר הָאֱלֹהִים חֹרֵב: ט וַיָּבֹא־שָׁם אֶל־
הַמְּעָרָה וַיָּלֶן שָׁם וְהִנֵּה דְבַר־יהוה אֵלָיו
וַיֹּאמֶר לוֹ מַה־לְּךָ פֹה אֵלִיָּהוּ: י וַיֹּאמֶר קַנֹּא
קִנֵּאתִי לַיהוה | אֱלֹהֵי צְבָאוֹת כִּי־עָזְבוּ
בְרִיתְךָ בְּנֵי יִשְׂרָאֵל אֶת־מִזְבְּחֹתֶיךָ הָרָסוּ
וְאֶת־נְבִיאֶיךָ הָרְגוּ בֶחָרֶב וָאִוָּתֵר אֲנִי לְבַדִּי
וַיְבַקְשׁוּ אֶת־נַפְשִׁי לְקַחְתָּהּ: יא וַיֹּאמֶר צֵא
וְעָמַדְתָּ בָהָר לִפְנֵי יהוה וְהִנֵּה יהוה עֹבֵר
וְרוּחַ גְּדוֹלָה וְחָזָק מְפָרֵק הָרִים וּמְשַׁבֵּר
סְלָעִים לִפְנֵי יהוה לֹא בָרוּחַ יהוה וְאַחַר
הָרוּחַ רַעַשׁ לֹא בָרַעַשׁ יהוה: יב וְאַחַר הָרַעַשׁ
אֵשׁ לֹא בָאֵשׁ יהוה וְאַחַר הָאֵשׁ קוֹל דְּמָמָה
דַקָּה: יג וַיְהִי | כִּשְׁמֹעַ אֵלִיָּהוּ וַיָּלֶט פָּנָיו
בְּאַדַּרְתּוֹ וַיֵּצֵא וַיַּעֲמֹד פֶּתַח הַמְּעָרָה וְהִנֵּה
אֵלָיו קוֹל וַיֹּאמֶר מַה־לְּךָ פֹּה אֵלִיָּהוּ:

יד ויאמר קנא קנאתי ליהוה | אלהי צבאות
כי־עזבו בריתך בני ישראל את־מזבחתיך
הרסו ואת־נביאיך הרגו בחרב ואותר אני
לבדי ויבקשו את־נפשי לקחתה: טו ויאמר
יהוה אליו לך שוב לדרכך מדברה דמשק
ובאת ומשחת את־חזאל למלך על־ארם:
טז ואת יהוא בן־נמשי תמשח למלך על־
ישראל ואת־אלישע בן־שפט מאבל
מחולה תמשח לנביא תחתיך: יז והיה
הנמלט מחרב חזאל ימית יהוא והנמלט
מחרב יהוא ימית אלישע: יח והשארתי
בישראל שבעת אלפים כל־הברכים אשר
לא־כרעו לבעל וכל־הפה אשר לא־נשק
לו: יט וילך משם וימצא את־אלישע בן־
שפט והוא חרש שנים־עשר צמדים לפניו
והוא בשנים העשר ויעבר אליהו אליו
וישלך אדרתו אליו: כ ויעזב את־הבקר
וירץ אחרי אליהו ויאמר אשקה־נא לאבי
ולאמי ואלכה אחריך ויאמר לו לך שוב כי
מה־עשיתי לך: כא וישב מאחריו ויקח את־
צמד הבקר ויזבחהו ובכלי הבקר בשלם
הבשר ויתן לעם ויאכלו ויקם וילך אחרי
אליהו וישרתהו:

14 *And he said, "I have been exceedingly zealous for HASHEM, God of Legions, for the Children of Israel have abandoned Your covenant; they have razed Your Altars; they have killed Your prophets with the sword, so that I alone have remained, and they seek my soul, to take it."*

15 *Then HASHEM said to him, "Go, return to your way, to the Wilderness of Damascus; and when you arrive, you shall anoint Hazael as king over Aram.*

16 *"And Jehu son of Nimshi shall you anoint as king over Israel; and Elisha son of Shaphat from the Plain of Meholah shall you anoint as prophet in your stead.* 17 *And it shall happen that whoever escapes the sword of Hazael, Jehu will kill; and whoever escapes the sword of Jehu, Elisha will kill.* 18 *But I will allow to remain in Israel seven thousand, all the knees that did not kneel to the Baal-idol and every mouth that did not kiss it."*

19 *Then he went from there and found Elisha son of Shaphat while he was plowing, twelve span [of oxen] before him and he with the twelfth; so Elijah passed across to him and cast his mantle upon him.*

20 *And he left the oxen and ran after Elijah and said, "Let me kiss, please, my father and my mother, then I shall go after you."*

But he said to him, "Go, return, for what have I done to you?"

21 *So he turned back from following him; and he took the span of oxen and slaughtered it; with the implements of the oxen he cooked the meat and gave it to the people, and they ate; then he rose and went after Elijah and ministered unto him.*

HAFTARAS MATTOS / הפטרת מטות

During most years, *Parashiyos Mattos* and *Masei* are read together. In those years, the *Haftarah* of *Parashas Pinchas* is omitted and the following *Haftarah* is read in its place. When *Mattos* and *Masei* are read on different *Shabbosos*, the following *Haftarah* is read after *Parashas Mattos.*

Jeremiah 1:1 – 2:3 / ירמיה א:א – ב:ג

א א דברי ירמיהו בן־חלקיהו מן־הכהנים
אשר בענתות בארץ בנימן: ב אשר היה
דבר־יהוה אליו בימי יאשיהו בן־אמון
מלך יהודה בשלש־עשרה שנה למלכו:
ג ויהי בימי יהויקים בן־יאשיהו מלך
יהודה עד־תם עשתי־עשרה שנה לצדקיהו
בן־יאשיהו מלך יהודה עד־גלות ירושלם
בחדש החמישי: ד ויהי דבר־יהוה אלי
לאמר: ה בטרם אצרך [אצורך כ׳] בבטן
ידעתיך ובטרם תצא מרחם הקדשתיך
נביא לגוים נתתיך: ו ואמר אהה אדני
יהוה הנה לא־ידעתי דבר כי־נער אנכי:
ז ויאמר יהוה אלי אל־תאמר נער אנכי

1 1 *The words of Jeremiah son of Hilkiah, of the Kohanim who were in Anathoth in the land of Benjamin.* 2 *With whom the word of HASHEM was during the days of Josiah son of Amon king of Judah, in the thirteenth year of his reign.* 3 *And he was [prophet] in the days of Jehoiakim son of Josiah king of Judah, until the eleventh year of Zedekiah son of Josiah king of Judah, until the exile of Jerusalem in the fifth month.*

4 *And the word of HASHEM was upon me, saying,* 5 *"When I had not yet formed you in the belly, I [already] recognized you; and when you had not yet come forth from the womb, I sanctified you; a prophet to the nations have I made you."*

6 *And I said, "Aha! My Lord HASHEM/ELOHIM, behold! — I know not how to speak, for I am [but] a lad."*

7 *Then HASHEM said to me, "Do not say, 'I am [but]*

כִּי עַל־כָּל־אֲשֶׁר אֶשְׁלָחֲךָ תֵּלֵךְ וְאֵת כָּל־
אֲשֶׁר אֲצַוְּךָ תְּדַבֵּר: ח אַל־תִּירָא מִפְּנֵיהֶם כִּי־
אִתְּךָ אֲנִי לְהַצִּלֶךָ נְאֻם־יהוה: ט וַיִּשְׁלַח יהוה
אֶת־יָדוֹ וַיַּגַּע עַל־פִּי וַיֹּאמֶר יהוה אֵלַי הִנֵּה
נָתַתִּי דְבָרַי בְּפִיךָ: י רְאֵה הִפְקַדְתִּיךָ | הַיּוֹם
הַזֶּה עַל־הַגּוֹיִם וְעַל־הַמַּמְלָכוֹת לִנְתוֹשׁ
וְלִנְתוֹץ וּלְהַאֲבִיד וְלַהֲרוֹס לִבְנוֹת וְלִנְטוֹעַ:
יא וַיְהִי דְבַר־יהוה אֵלַי לֵאמֹר מָה־אַתָּה רֹאֶה
יִרְמְיָהוּ וָאֹמַר מַקֵּל שָׁקֵד אֲנִי רֹאֶה: יב וַיֹּאמֶר
יהוה אֵלַי הֵיטַבְתָּ לִרְאוֹת כִּי־שֹׁקֵד אֲנִי עַל־
דְּבָרִי לַעֲשֹׂתוֹ: יג וַיְהִי דְבַר־יהוה | אֵלַי שֵׁנִית
לֵאמֹר מָה אַתָּה רֹאֶה וָאֹמַר סִיר נָפוּחַ אֲנִי
רֹאֶה וּפָנָיו מִפְּנֵי צָפוֹנָה: יד וַיֹּאמֶר יהוה אֵלָי
מִצָּפוֹן תִּפָּתַח הָרָעָה עַל כָּל־יֹשְׁבֵי הָאָרֶץ:
טו כִּי | הִנְנִי קֹרֵא לְכָל־מִשְׁפְּחוֹת מַמְלְכוֹת
צָפוֹנָה נְאֻם־יהוה וּבָאוּ וְנָתְנוּ אִישׁ כִּסְאוֹ
פֶּתַח | שַׁעֲרֵי יְרוּשָׁלִַם וְעַל כָּל־חוֹמֹתֶיהָ
סָבִיב וְעַל כָּל־עָרֵי יְהוּדָה: טז וְדִבַּרְתִּי מִשְׁפָּטַי
אוֹתָם עַל כָּל־רָעָתָם אֲשֶׁר עֲזָבוּנִי וַיְקַטְּרוּ
לֵאלֹהִים אֲחֵרִים וַיִּשְׁתַּחֲווּ לְמַעֲשֵׂי יְדֵיהֶם:
יז וְאַתָּה תֶּאְזֹר מָתְנֶיךָ וְקַמְתָּ וְדִבַּרְתָּ אֲלֵיהֶם
אֵת כָּל־אֲשֶׁר אָנֹכִי אֲצַוֶּךָּ אַל־תֵּחַת מִפְּנֵיהֶם
פֶּן־אֲחִתְּךָ לִפְנֵיהֶם: יח וַאֲנִי הִנֵּה נְתַתִּיךָ הַיּוֹם
לְעִיר מִבְצָר וּלְעַמּוּד בַּרְזֶל וּלְחֹמוֹת נְחֹשֶׁת
עַל־כָּל־הָאָרֶץ לְמַלְכֵי יְהוּדָה לְשָׂרֶיהָ
לְכֹהֲנֶיהָ וּלְעַם הָאָרֶץ: יט וְנִלְחֲמוּ אֵלֶיךָ וְלֹא־
יוּכְלוּ לָךְ כִּי־אִתְּךָ אֲנִי נְאֻם־יהוה לְהַצִּילֶךָ:
ב א וַיְהִי דְבַר־יהוה אֵלַי לֵאמֹר: ב הָלֹךְ
וְקָרָאתָ בְאָזְנֵי יְרוּשָׁלִַם לֵאמֹר כֹּה אָמַר יהוה
זָכַרְתִּי לָךְ חֶסֶד נְעוּרַיִךְ אַהֲבַת כְּלוּלֹתָיִךְ
לֶכְתֵּךְ אַחֲרַי בַּמִּדְבָּר בְּאֶרֶץ לֹא זְרוּעָה:
ג קֹדֶשׁ יִשְׂרָאֵל לַיהוה רֵאשִׁית תְּבוּאָתֹה כָּל־
אֹכְלָיו יֶאְשָׁמוּ רָעָה תָּבֹא אֲלֵיהֶם נְאֻם־יהוה:

a lad,' rather to wherever I send you shall you go, and whatever I command you shall you speak. 8 *Fear not before them, for I am with you, to rescue you — the word of HASHEM."*

9 *And HASHEM sent forth His hand and made it touch my mouth; and HASHEM said to me, "Behold! I have placed My words in your mouth.* 10 *See, I have appointed you this day over the nations and over the kingdoms, to uproot and to smash and to destroy and to raze; to build and to plant."*

11 *And the word of HASHEM was upon me, saying, "What do you see, Jeremiah?"*

And I said, "An almond-wood staff do I see."

12 *And HASHEM said to me, "You have seen well, for I shall hasten regarding My word, to fulfill it."*

13 *Then the word of HASHEM was upon me a second time, saying, "What do you see?"*

And I said, "A boiling pot do I see; and its bubbling is from the northern side."

14 *And HASHEM said to me, "From the north shall the evil loose itself upon all the inhabitants of the Land.* 15 *For, behold! — I will call all the families of the kingdoms of the North — the word of HASHEM — and they shall come and each of them shall place his throne at the entranceway of the gates of Jerusalem, and against all its walls, and against all the cities of Judah.* 16 *Then I will speak My judgments against them for all their evil; for they have forsaken Me, and they have censed to the gods of others, and they have prostrated themselves to their handiwork.* 17 *But as for you, you shall gird your loins and arise and speak to them all that I shall command you; do not tremble before them lest I cause you dismay before them.* 18 *And as for Me, behold! — I have set you today as a fortified city and as an iron pillar and as copper walls over the entire land; against the kings of Judah, against her princes, against her Kohanim, and against the people of the Land.* 19 *And they will do battle against you, but they shall not prevail over you, for with you am I — the word of HASHEM — to rescue you."*

2 1 *And the word of HASHEM was upon me, saying,* 2 *"Go and proclaim in the ears of Jerusalem, saying, 'Thus said HASHEM: I remember for your sake the kindness of your youth, the love of your bridal days, your following after Me in the wilderness, in a land not sown.'* 3 *Israel is sacred unto HASHEM, the first of His grain; all who devour him shall bear guilt, evil shall come upon them — the word of HASHEM."*

HAFTARAS MASEI / הפטרת מסעי

Jeremiah 2:4-28; 3:4; 4:1-2 / ירמיה ב:ד־כח; ג:ד; ד:א־ב

ב ד שִׁמְעוּ דְבַר־יהוה בֵּית יַעֲקֹב וְכָל־
מִשְׁפְּחוֹת בֵּית יִשְׂרָאֵל: ה כֹּה | אָמַר יהוה
מַה־מָּצְאוּ אֲבוֹתֵיכֶם בִּי עָוֶל כִּי רָחֲקוּ מֵעָלָי
וַיֵּלְכוּ אַחֲרֵי הַהֶבֶל וַיֶּהְבָּלוּ: ו וְלֹא אָמְרוּ
אַיֵּה יהוה הַמַּעֲלֶה אֹתָנוּ מֵאֶרֶץ מִצְרָיִם

2 4 *Hear the word of HASHEM, O House of Jacob and all families of the House of Israel.* 5 *Thus said HASHEM, "What did your forefathers find in Me that is a wrong, that they distanced themselves from me and went after nothingness, and have turned into nothingness?* 6 *But they did not say, 'Where is HASHEM, Who brought us up from the land of Egypt,*

הַמּוֹלִיךְ אֹתָנוּ בַּמִּדְבָּר בְּאֶרֶץ עֲרָבָה וְשׁוּחָה
בְּאֶרֶץ צִיָּה וְצַלְמָוֶת בְּאֶרֶץ לֹא־עָבַר בָּהּ
אִישׁ וְלֹא־יָשַׁב אָדָם שָׁם: ז וָאָבִיא אֶתְכֶם
אֶל־אֶרֶץ הַכַּרְמֶל לֶאֱכֹל פִּרְיָהּ וְטוּבָהּ וַתָּבֹאוּ
וַתְּטַמְּאוּ אֶת־אַרְצִי וְנַחֲלָתִי שַׂמְתֶּם
לְתוֹעֵבָה: ח הַכֹּהֲנִים לֹא אָמְרוּ אַיֵּה יהוה
וְתֹפְשֵׂי הַתּוֹרָה לֹא יְדָעוּנִי וְהָרֹעִים פָּשְׁעוּ בִי
וְהַנְּבִיאִים נִבְּאוּ בַבַּעַל וְאַחֲרֵי לֹא־יוֹעִלוּ
הָלָכוּ: ט לָכֵן עֹד אָרִיב אִתְּכֶם נְאֻם־יהוה
וְאֶת־בְּנֵי בְנֵיכֶם אָרִיב: י כִּי עִבְרוּ אִיֵּי כִתִּיִּים
וּרְאוּ וְקֵדָר שִׁלְחוּ וְהִתְבּוֹנְנוּ מְאֹד וּרְאוּ הֵן
הָיְתָה כָּזֹאת: יא הַהֵימִיר גּוֹי אֱלֹהִים וְהֵמָּה
לֹא אֱלֹהִים וְעַמִּי הֵמִיר כְּבוֹדוֹ בְּלוֹא יוֹעִיל:
יב שֹׁמּוּ שָׁמַיִם עַל־זֹאת וְשַׂעֲרוּ חָרְבוּ מְאֹד
נְאֻם־יהוה: יג כִּי־שְׁתַּיִם רָעוֹת עָשָׂה עַמִּי
אֹתִי עָזְבוּ מְקוֹר | מַיִם חַיִּים לַחְצֹב לָהֶם
בֹּארוֹת בֹּארֹת נִשְׁבָּרִים אֲשֶׁר לֹא־יָכִלוּ
הַמָּיִם: יד הַעֶבֶד יִשְׂרָאֵל אִם־יְלִיד בַּיִת הוּא
מַדּוּעַ הָיָה לָבַז: טו עָלָיו יִשְׁאֲגוּ כְפִרִים נָתְנוּ
קוֹלָם וַיָּשִׁיתוּ אַרְצוֹ לְשַׁמָּה עָרָיו נִצְּתוּ
[נצתה כ׳] מִבְּלִי יֹשֵׁב: טז גַּם־בְּנֵי־נֹף
וְתַחְפַּנְחֵס [ותחפנס כ׳] יִרְעוּךְ קָדְקֹד:
יז הֲלוֹא־זֹאת תַּעֲשֶׂה־לָּךְ עָזְבֵךְ אֶת־יהוה
אֱלֹהַיִךְ בְּעֵת מוֹלִכֵךְ בַּדָּרֶךְ: יח וְעַתָּה מַה־לָּךְ
לְדֶרֶךְ מִצְרַיִם לִשְׁתּוֹת מֵי שִׁחוֹר וּמַה־לָּךְ
לְדֶרֶךְ אַשּׁוּר לִשְׁתּוֹת מֵי נָהָר: יט תְּיַסְּרֵךְ
רָעָתֵךְ וּמְשֻׁבוֹתַיִךְ תּוֹכִחֻךְ וּדְעִי וּרְאִי כִּי־רַע
וָמָר עָזְבֵךְ אֶת־יהוה אֱלֹהָיִךְ וְלֹא פַחְדָּתִי
אֵלַיִךְ נְאֻם־אֲדֹנָי יֱהוִֹה צְבָאוֹת: כ כִּי מֵעוֹלָם
שָׁבַרְתִּי עֻלֵּךְ נִתַּקְתִּי מוֹסְרוֹתַיִךְ וַתֹּאמְרִי לֹא
אֶעֱבוֹר [אעבוד כ׳] כִּי עַל־כָּל־גִּבְעָה גְּבֹהָה
וְתַחַת כָּל־עֵץ רַעֲנָן אַתְּ צֹעָה זֹנָה:
כא וְאָנֹכִי נְטַעְתִּיךְ שׂוֹרֵק כֻּלֹּה זֶרַע אֱמֶת
וְאֵיךְ נֶהְפַּכְתְּ לִי סוּרֵי הַגֶּפֶן נָכְרִיָּה: כב כִּי
אִם־תְּכַבְּסִי בַּנֶּתֶר וְתַרְבִּי־לָךְ בֹּרִית נִכְתָּם
עֲוֹנֵךְ לְפָנַי נְאֻם אֲדֹנָי יֱהוִֹה: כג אֵיךְ
תֹּאמְרִי לֹא נִטְמֵאתִי אַחֲרֵי הַבְּעָלִים לֹא
הָלַכְתִּי רְאִי דַרְכֵּךְ בַּגַּיְא דְּעִי מֶה עָשִׂית
בִּכְרָה קַלָּה מְשָׂרֶכֶת דְּרָכֶיהָ: כד פֶּרֶה | לִמֻּד

Who led us in the Wilderness, in a land of plain and pit,
in a land of waste and the shadow of death, in a land
through which no man has passed and where no man
has settled.'
7 *"Yet I brought you to a fruitful Land, to eat its fruit*
and its goodness; but when you came, you contami-
nated My Land, and made My heritage into an
abomination. 8 *The Kohanim did not say, 'Where is*
HASHEM?'; — even those charged with teaching the
Torah did not know Me; the shepherd-kings rebelled
against Me; and the prophets prophesied in the name
of the Baal-idols; and they went after that which
cannot avail.
9 *"Therefore I will again contend with you — the*
word of HASHEM — and with your children's children
will I contend. 10 *Traverse the isles of the Kittites and*
see, send forth unto Kedar and consider deeply, and
see whether there has occurred such as this. 11 *Has a*
nation exchanged its gods — though they be not gods;
yet My people has exchanged its Glory for that which
cannot avail. 12 *Mourn, O heavens, over this; rage*
forth in storm, send forth great devastation — the word
of HASHEM. 13 *For My people has perpetrated two evils:*
Me have they forsaken, the Source of living waters; to
dig for themselves cisterns, broken cisterns that
cannot hold water.
14 *"Is Israel a slave? Is he born to a housemaid? Why*
has he become prey? 15 *Young lions have roared at*
him, they have given out their voice; they have laid his
land a waste, devastated his cities, without inhabitant.
16 *Even the people of Noph and Tahpanhes smash*
your skull. 17 *Is this not what you do to yourself; by*
forsaking HASHEM, your God, when He leads you on
the way?
18 *"And now, what is there for you on the road to*
Egypt — to drink the water of Shihor? And what is
there for you on the road to Assyria — to drink the
water of the [Euphrates] River? 19 *Your evil shall*
castigate you; your waywardness shall chasten you;
know and see that evil and bitter is your forsaking of
HASHEM, your God, and that awe of Me was not upon
you — the word of my Lord, HASHEM/ELOHIM, Master
of Legions.
20 *"For from of old have I broken your yoke, I have*
removed your reins, and you said, 'I will not trans-
gress!' — yet upon every lofty hill, and under every
vigorous tree, you wander like a harlot. 21 *I had planted*
you a noble vine, full of true seed; how, then, have you
transformed yourself before Me into a degenerate alien
vine? 22 *Even were you to wash yourself with natron,*
and use much soap upon yourself, your iniquity is as
the mark of a stain before Me — the word of my Lord,
HASHEM/ELOHIM.
23 *"How can you say, 'I have not become con-*
taminated; after the Baal-idols have I not gone?'
See your way in the Valley [of Peor]; know what you
have done [to this day], like a fleet dromedary bound
in her ways. 24 *Like a wild-donkey well acquainted*

מִדְבָּר בְּאַוַּת נַפְשָׁהּ [נפשו כ׳] שָׁאֲפָה רוּחַ
תַּאֲנָתָהּ מִי יְשִׁיבֶנָּה כָּל־מְבַקְשֶׁיהָ לֹא יִיעָפוּ
בְּחָדְשָׁהּ יִמְצָאוּנְהָ׃ כה מִנְעִי רַגְלֵךְ מִיָּחֵף
וּגְרוֹנֵךְ [וגורנך כ׳] מִצִּמְאָה וַתֹּאמְרִי נוֹאָשׁ
לוֹא כִּי־אָהַבְתִּי זָרִים וְאַחֲרֵיהֶם אֵלֵךְ׃
כו כְּבֹשֶׁת גַּנָּב כִּי יִמָּצֵא כֵּן הֹבִישׁוּ בֵּית
יִשְׂרָאֵל הֵמָּה מַלְכֵיהֶם שָׂרֵיהֶם וְכֹהֲנֵיהֶם
וּנְבִיאֵיהֶם׃ כז אֹמְרִים לָעֵץ אָבִי אַתָּה וְלָאֶבֶן
אַתְּ יְלִדְתָּנוּ [ילדתני כ׳] כִּי־פָנוּ אֵלַי עֹרֶף וְלֹא
פָנִים וּבְעֵת רָעָתָם יֹאמְרוּ קוּמָה וְהוֹשִׁיעֵנוּ׃
כח וְאַיֵּה אֱלֹהֶיךָ אֲשֶׁר עָשִׂיתָ לָּךְ יָקוּמוּ אִם־
יוֹשִׁיעוּךָ בְּעֵת רָעָתֶךָ כִּי מִסְפַּר עָרֶיךָ הָיוּ
אֱלֹהֶיךָ יְהוּדָה׃

with the wilderness, that in the passion of her soul inhales the wind; [when] her lust [overwhelms her], who can reform her? Those who seek her should not weary themselves for in her [final] month [of pregnancy] they will find her. 25 *[The prophets told you that by remaining faithful you would] withhold your foot from barefooted [exile], and your throat from thirst; but you said, 'I do not care! No! For I have loved strangers and after them will I go.'* 26 *As the shame of a thief when he is discovered, so has the House of Israel been shamed — they, their kings, their princes, and their [idolatrous] priests and their [false] prophets.* 27 *They say to the wood, 'You are my father,' and to the stone, 'You gave birth to us'; for they have turned unto Me their back and not their face; yet in the time of their distress, they will say, 'Arise and save us!'* 28 *So where are your gods that you made for yourself? Let them arise, if they can save you in the time of your distress; for as the number of your cities was [the number of] your gods, O Judah."*

Some congregations conclude the *Haftarah* here. *Ashkenazim* recite one more verse (3:4):

ג ד הֲלוֹא מֵעַתָּה קָרָאת [קראתי כ׳] לִי אָבִי
אַלּוּף נְעֻרַי אָתָּה׃

3 4 *Will you not from this time call to Me, "My Father! Master of my youth are You?"*

Sephardim recite two more verses (4:1-2):

ד א אִם־תָּשׁוּב יִשְׂרָאֵל | נְאֻם־יְהוָה אֵלַי
תָּשׁוּב וְאִם־תָּסִיר שִׁקּוּצֶיךָ מִפָּנַי וְלֹא
תָנוּד׃ ב וְנִשְׁבַּעְתָּ חַי־יְהוָה בֶּאֱמֶת
בְּמִשְׁפָּט וּבִצְדָקָה וְהִתְבָּרְכוּ בוֹ גּוֹיִם וּבוֹ
יִתְהַלָּלוּ׃

4 1 *If you will return, O Israel — the word of* H*ASHEM — to Me shall you return; and if you will remove your abominations from before Me and you will not stray;* 2 *but you will swear, "As* H*ASHEM lives!" in truth, in justice, and in righteousness, then shall the nations bless themselves in Him, and in Him shall they praise themselves.*

When Rosh Chodesh Av falls on *Shabbos*, some congregations add the first and last verses of the *Haftarah* for *Shabbas* Rosh Chodesh (*Isaiah* 66:1;23):

כֹּה אָמַר יְהוָה הַשָּׁמַיִם כִּסְאִי וְהָאָרֶץ הֲדֹם רַגְלָי
אֵי־זֶה בַיִת אֲשֶׁר תִּבְנוּ־לִי וְאֵי־זֶה מָקוֹם מְנוּחָתִי׃
וְהָיָה מִדֵּי־חֹדֶשׁ בְּחָדְשׁוֹ וּמִדֵּי שַׁבָּת בְּשַׁבַּתּוֹ יָבוֹא
כָל־בָּשָׂר לְהִשְׁתַּחֲוֹת לְפָנַי אָמַר יְהוָה׃

So said H*ASHEM: The heaven is My throne and the earth is My footstool; what House could you build for Me, and what could be My resting place? And it shall be that, from New Moon to New Moon, and from Sabbath to Sabbath, all flesh shall come to prostrate themselves before Me, said* H*ASHEM.*

HAFTARAS SHABBAS EREV ROSH CHODESH / הפטרת שבת ערב ראש חודש

I Samuel 20:18-42 / שמואל א כ:יח-מב

כ יח וַיֹּאמֶר־לוֹ יְהוֹנָתָן מָחָר חֹדֶשׁ וְנִפְקַדְתָּ כִּי
יִפָּקֵד מוֹשָׁבֶךָ׃ יט וְשִׁלַּשְׁתָּ תֵּרֵד מְאֹד וּבָאתָ
אֶל־הַמָּקוֹם אֲשֶׁר־נִסְתַּרְתָּ שָּׁם בְּיוֹם הַמַּעֲשֶׂה
וְיָשַׁבְתָּ אֵצֶל הָאֶבֶן הָאָזֶל׃ כ וַאֲנִי שְׁלֹשֶׁת
הַחִצִּים צִדָּה אוֹרֶה לְשַׁלַּח־לִי לְמַטָּרָה׃
כא וְהִנֵּה אֶשְׁלַח אֶת־הַנַּעַר לֵךְ מְצָא אֶת־
הַחִצִּים אִם־אָמֹר אֹמַר לַנַּעַר הִנֵּה הַחִצִּים |
מִמְּךָ וָהֵנָּה קָחֶנּוּ וָבֹאָה כִּי־שָׁלוֹם לְךָ וְאֵין
דָּבָר חַי־יְהוָה׃ כב וְאִם־כֹּה אֹמַר לָעֶלֶם הִנֵּה
הַחִצִּים מִמְּךָ וָהָלְאָה לֵךְ כִּי שִׁלַּחֲךָ יְהוָה׃

20 18 *Jonathan said to [David], "Tomorrow is the New Moon, and you will be missed because your seat will be empty.* 19 *For three days you are to go far down and come to the place where you hid on the day of the deed, and remain near the marker stone.* 20 *I will shoot three arrows in that direction as if I were shooting at a target.* 21 *Behold! — I will then send the lad, 'Go, find the arrows.' If I call out to the lad, 'Behold! — the arrows are on this side of you!' then you should take them and return, for it is well with you and there is no concern, as* H*ASHEM lives.* 22 *But if I say this to the boy, 'Behold! — the arrows are beyond you!' then go, for* H*ASHEM will have sent you away.*

כג וְהַדָּבָר אֲשֶׁר דִּבַּרְנוּ אֲנִי וָאָתָּה הִנֵּה יְהוָה
בֵּינִי וּבֵינְךָ עַד־עוֹלָם: כד וַיִּסָּתֵר דָּוִד בַּשָּׂדֶה
וַיְהִי הַחֹדֶשׁ וַיֵּשֶׁב הַמֶּלֶךְ אֶל־ [על־ כ׳] הַלֶּחֶם
לֶאֱכוֹל: כה וַיֵּשֶׁב הַמֶּלֶךְ עַל־מוֹשָׁבוֹ כְּפַעַם ׀
בְּפַעַם אֶל־מוֹשַׁב הַקִּיר וַיָּקָם יְהוֹנָתָן וַיֵּשֶׁב
אַבְנֵר מִצַּד שָׁאוּל וַיִּפָּקֵד מְקוֹם דָּוִד: כו וְלֹא־
דִבֶּר שָׁאוּל מְאוּמָה בַּיּוֹם הַהוּא כִּי אָמַר מִקְרֶה
הוּא בִּלְתִּי טָהוֹר הוּא כִּי־לֹא טָהוֹר: כז וַיְהִי
מִמָּחֳרַת הַחֹדֶשׁ הַשֵּׁנִי וַיִּפָּקֵד מְקוֹם דָּוִד
וַיֹּאמֶר שָׁאוּל אֶל־יְהוֹנָתָן בְּנוֹ מַדּוּעַ לֹא־בָא
בֶן־יִשַׁי גַּם־תְּמוֹל גַּם־הַיּוֹם אֶל־הַלָּחֶם:
כח וַיַּעַן יְהוֹנָתָן אֶת־שָׁאוּל נִשְׁאֹל נִשְׁאַל דָּוִד
מֵעִמָּדִי עַד־בֵּית לָחֶם: כט וַיֹּאמֶר שַׁלְּחֵנִי נָא
כִּי זֶבַח מִשְׁפָּחָה לָנוּ בָּעִיר וְהוּא צִוָּה־לִי אָחִי
וְעַתָּה אִם־מָצָאתִי חֵן בְּעֵינֶיךָ אִמָּלְטָה נָּא
וְאֶרְאֶה אֶת־אֶחָי עַל־כֵּן לֹא־בָא אֶל־שֻׁלְחַן
הַמֶּלֶךְ: ל וַיִּחַר־אַף שָׁאוּל בִּיהוֹנָתָן וַיֹּאמֶר לוֹ
בֶּן־נַעֲוַת הַמַּרְדּוּת הֲלוֹא יָדַעְתִּי כִּי־בֹחֵר
אַתָּה לְבֶן־יִשַׁי לְבָשְׁתְּךָ וּלְבֹשֶׁת עֶרְוַת אִמֶּךָ:
לא כִּי כָל־הַיָּמִים אֲשֶׁר בֶּן־יִשַׁי חַי עַל־
הָאֲדָמָה לֹא תִכּוֹן אַתָּה וּמַלְכוּתֶךָ וְעַתָּה
שְׁלַח וְקַח אֹתוֹ אֵלַי כִּי בֶן־מָוֶת הוּא: לב וַיַּעַן
יְהוֹנָתָן אֶת־שָׁאוּל אָבִיו וַיֹּאמֶר אֵלָיו לָמָּה
יוּמַת מֶה עָשָׂה: לג וַיָּטֶל שָׁאוּל אֶת־הַחֲנִית
עָלָיו לְהַכֹּתוֹ וַיֵּדַע יְהוֹנָתָן כִּי־כָלָה הִיא מֵעִם
אָבִיו לְהָמִית אֶת־דָּוִד: לד וַיָּקָם יְהוֹנָתָן מֵעִם
הַשֻּׁלְחָן בָּחֳרִי־אָף וְלֹא־אָכַל בְּיוֹם־הַחֹדֶשׁ
הַשֵּׁנִי לֶחֶם כִּי נֶעְצַב אֶל־דָּוִד כִּי הִכְלִמוֹ אָבִיו:
לה וַיְהִי בַבֹּקֶר וַיֵּצֵא יְהוֹנָתָן הַשָּׂדֶה לְמוֹעֵד דָּוִד
וְנַעַר קָטֹן עִמּוֹ: לו וַיֹּאמֶר לְנַעֲרוֹ רֻץ מְצָא־נָא
אֶת־הַחִצִּים אֲשֶׁר אָנֹכִי מוֹרֶה הַנַּעַר רָץ
וְהוּא־יָרָה הַחֵצִי לְהַעֲבִרוֹ: לז וַיָּבֹא הַנַּעַר עַד־
מְקוֹם הַחֵצִי אֲשֶׁר יָרָה יְהוֹנָתָן וַיִּקְרָא יְהוֹנָתָן
אַחֲרֵי הַנַּעַר וַיֹּאמֶר הֲלוֹא הַחֵצִי מִמְּךָ
וָהָלְאָה: לח וַיִּקְרָא יְהוֹנָתָן אַחֲרֵי הַנַּעַר מְהֵרָה
חוּשָׁה אַל־תַּעֲמֹד וַיְלַקֵּט נַעַר יְהוֹנָתָן אֶת־
הַחִצִּים [החצי כ׳] וַיָּבֹא אֶל־אֲדֹנָיו: לט וְהַנַּעַר
לֹא־יָדַע מְאוּמָה אַךְ יְהוֹנָתָן וְדָוִד יָדְעוּ אֶת־
הַדָּבָר: מ וַיִּתֵּן יְהוֹנָתָן אֶת־כֵּלָיו אֶל־הַנַּעַר
אֲשֶׁר־לוֹ וַיֹּאמֶר לוֹ לֵךְ הָבֵיא הָעִיר: מא הַנַּעַר
בָּא וְדָוִד קָם מֵאֵצֶל הַנֶּגֶב וַיִּפֹּל לְאַפָּיו

23 *This matter of which we have spoken, I and you, behold! — HASHEM remains [witness] between me and you forever."*

24 *David concealed himself in the field. It was the New Moon and the king sat at the feast to eat.* 25 *The king sat on his seat as usual, on the seat by the wall; and Jonathan stood up so that Abner could sit at Saul's side, and David's seat was empty.* 26 *Saul said nothing on that day, for he thought, "It is a coincidence, he must be impure, for he has not been cleansed."*

27 *It was the day after the New Moon, the second day, and David's place was empty; Saul said to Jonathan, his son, "Why did the son of Jesse not come to the feast yesterday or today?"*

28 *Jonathan answered Saul, "David asked me for permission to go Bethlehem.* 29 *He said, 'Please send me away, for we have a family feast in the city, and he, my brother, ordered me [to come]; so now, if I have found favor in your eyes, excuse me, please, and let me see my brothers.' Therefore, he has not come to the king's table."*

30 *Saul's anger flared up at Jonathan, and he said to him, "Son of a pervertedly rebellious woman, do I not know that you prefer the son of Jesse, for your own shame and the shame of your mother's nakedness!* 31 *For all the days that the son of Jesse is alive on the earth, you and your kingdom will not be secure! And now send and bring him to me, for he is deserving of death."*

32 *Jonathan answered his father Saul and he said to him, "Why should he die; what has he done?"*

33 *Saul hurled his spear at him to strike him; so Jonathan realized that it was decided by his father to kill David.* 34 *Jonathan arose from the table in a burning anger; he did not partake of food on that second day of the month, for he was saddened over David because his father had humiliated him.*

35 *It happened in the morning that Jonathan went out to the field for the meeting with David, and a young lad was with him.* 36 *He said to his lad, "Run — please find the arrows that I shoot." The lad ran, and he shot the arrow to make it go further.* 37 *The lad arrived at the place of the arrow that Jonathan had shot, and Jonathan called out after the lad, and he said, "Is not the arrow beyond you?"*

38 *And Jonathan called out after the lad, "Quickly, hurry, do not stand still!" The lad gathered the arrows and came to his master.* 39 *The lad knew nothing, only Jonathan and David understood the matter.* 40 *Jonathan gave his equipment to his lad and said to him, "Go bring it to the city."*

41 *The lad went and David stood up from near the south [side of the stone], and he fell on his face*

*to the ground and prostrated himself three times.
They kissed one another and they wept with one
another, until David [wept] greatly.*
*42 Jonathan said to David, "Go to peace. What the
two of us have sworn in the Name of HASHEM —
saying, 'HASHEM shall be between me and you, and
between my children and your children' — shall be
forever!"*

אַ֫רְצָה וַיִּשְׁתַּחוּ שָׁלֹשׁ פְּעָמִים וַיִּשְׁקוּ ׀ אִישׁ
אֶת־רֵעֵהוּ וַיִּבְכּוּ אִישׁ אֶת־רֵעֵהוּ עַד־דָּוִד
הִגְדִּיל: מב וַיֹּאמֶר יְהוֹנָתָן לְדָוִד לֵךְ לְשָׁלוֹם
אֲשֶׁר נִשְׁבַּעְנוּ שְׁנֵינוּ אֲנַחְנוּ בְּשֵׁם יהוה
לֵאמֹר יהוה יִהְיֶה ׀ בֵּינִי וּבֵינֶךָ וּבֵין זַרְעִי וּבֵין
זַרְעֲךָ עַד־עוֹלָם:

MAFTIR SHABBAS ROSH CHODESH / מפטיר לשבת ראש חודש

Numbers 28:9-15 / במדבר כח:ט-טו

28 9 *And on the Sabbath day: two male lambs in
their first year, unblemished, two tenth-
ephah of fine flour for a meal-offering, mixed with oil,
and its libation.* 10 *The olah-offering of each Sabbath
on its own Sabbath, in addition to the continual
olah-offering and its libation.*
11 *On your New Moons, you shall bring an olah-
offering to HASHEM: two young bulls, one ram, seven
male lambs in their first year, unblemished.* 12 *And
three tenth-ephah of fine flour for a meal-offering
mixed with oil, for each bull; and two tenth-ephah of
fine flour mixed with oil, for each ram;* 13 *and a
tenth-ephah of fine flour for a meal-offering, mixed
with oil, for each lamb — an olah-offering, a satisfy-
ing aroma, a fire-offering to HASHEM.* 14 *And their
libations: a half-hin for a bull, a third-hin for a ram, a
quarter-hin for a lamb — of wine. This is the
olah-offering of each month in its own month for
the months of the year.* 15 *And one male of the goats
for a sin-offering to HASHEM. In addition to the
continual olah-offering, shall it be made, and its
libation.*

כח ט וּבְיוֹם הַשַּׁבָּת שְׁנֵי־כְבָשִׂים בְּנֵי־שָׁנָה
תְּמִימִם וּשְׁנֵי עֶשְׂרֹנִים סֹלֶת מִנְחָה בְּלוּלָה
בַשֶּׁמֶן וְנִסְכּוֹ: י עֹלַת שַׁבַּת בְּשַׁבַּתּוֹ עַל־עֹלַת
הַתָּמִיד וְנִסְכָּהּ: יא וּבְרָאשֵׁי חָדְשֵׁיכֶם תַּקְרִיבוּ
עֹלָה לַיהוה פָּרִים בְּנֵי־בָקָר שְׁנַיִם וְאַיִל אֶחָד
כְּבָשִׂים בְּנֵי־שָׁנָה שִׁבְעָה תְּמִימִם: יב וּשְׁלֹשָׁה
עֶשְׂרֹנִים סֹלֶת מִנְחָה בְּלוּלָה בַשֶּׁמֶן לַפָּר
הָאֶחָד וּשְׁנֵי עֶשְׂרֹנִים סֹלֶת מִנְחָה בְּלוּלָה
בַשֶּׁמֶן לָאַיִל הָאֶחָד: יג וְעִשָּׂרֹן עִשָּׂרוֹן סֹלֶת
מִנְחָה בְּלוּלָה בַשֶּׁמֶן לַכֶּבֶשׂ הָאֶחָד עֹלָה
רֵיחַ נִיחֹחַ אִשֶּׁה לַיהוה: יד וְנִסְכֵּיהֶם חֲצִי
הַהִין יִהְיֶה לַפָּר וּשְׁלִישִׁת הַהִין לָאַיִל
וּרְבִיעִת הַהִין לַכֶּבֶשׂ יָיִן זֹאת עֹלַת חֹדֶשׁ
בְּחָדְשׁוֹ לְחָדְשֵׁי הַשָּׁנָה: טו וּשְׂעִיר עִזִּים אֶחָד
לְחַטָּאת לַיהוה עַל־עֹלַת הַתָּמִיד יֵעָשֶׂה
וְנִסְכּוֹ:

HAFTARAS SHABBAS ROSH CHODESH / הפטרת שבת ראש חודש

Isaiah 66:1-24 / ישעיה סו:א-כד

66 1 *So said HASHEM: The heaven is My throne and
the earth is My footstool; what House could
you build for Me, and what could be My resting
place?* 2 *My hand made all these and thus they came
into being, the words of HASHEM — but it is to this that
I look: to the poor and broken-spirited person who is
zealous regarding My Word.*
3 *He who slaughters an ox is as if he slays a man;
he who offers a sheep is as if he breaks a dog's neck;
he who brings up a meal-offering is as if he offers a
swine's blood; one who brings a frankincense re-
membrance is as if he brings a gift of extortion; they
have even chosen their ways, and their souls have
desired their abominations.*
4 *I, too, will choose to mock them and what they
dread I will bring upon them — because I have called,
but no one responded; I have spoken, but they did
not hear; they did what is evil in My eyes and what I
did not desire they chose.*
5 *Listen to the Word of HASHEM, those who are zeal-
ous regarding His Word; your brethren who hate you*

סו א כֹּה אָמַר יהוה הַשָּׁמַיִם כִּסְאִי וְהָאָרֶץ
הֲדֹם רַגְלָי אֵי־זֶה בַיִת אֲשֶׁר תִּבְנוּ־לִי וְאֵי־
זֶה מָקוֹם מְנוּחָתִי: ב וְאֶת־כָּל־אֵלֶּה יָדִי
עָשָׂתָה וַיִּהְיוּ כָל־אֵלֶּה נְאֻם־יהוה וְאֶל־
זֶה אַבִּיט אֶל־עָנִי וּנְכֵה־רוּחַ וְחָרֵד עַל־
דְּבָרִי: ג שׁוֹחֵט הַשּׁוֹר מַכֵּה־אִישׁ זוֹבֵחַ
הַשֶּׂה עֹרֵף כֶּלֶב מַעֲלֵה מִנְחָה דַּם־חֲזִיר
מַזְכִּיר לְבֹנָה מְבָרֵךְ אָוֶן גַּם־הֵמָּה בָּחֲרוּ
בְּדַרְכֵיהֶם וּבְשִׁקּוּצֵיהֶם נַפְשָׁם חָפֵצָה: ד גַּם־
אֲנִי אֶבְחַר בְּתַעֲלֻלֵיהֶם וּמְגוּרֹתָם אָבִיא
לָהֶם יַעַן קָרָאתִי וְאֵין עוֹנֶה דִּבַּרְתִּי
וְלֹא שָׁמֵעוּ וַיַּעֲשׂוּ הָרַע בְּעֵינַי וּבַאֲשֶׁר
לֹא־חָפַצְתִּי בָּחָרוּ: ה שִׁמְעוּ דְּבַר־יהוה
הַחֲרֵדִים אֶל־דְּבָרוֹ אָמְרוּ אֲחֵיכֶם שֹׂנְאֵיכֶם

מְנַדֵּיכֶם לְמַעַן שְׁמִי יִכְבַּד יהוה וְנִרְאֶה
בְשִׂמְחַתְכֶם וְהֵם יֵבֹשׁוּ: ו קוֹל שָׁאוֹן מֵעִיר קוֹל
מֵהֵיכָל קוֹל יהוה מְשַׁלֵּם גְּמוּל לְאֹיְבָיו:
ז בְּטֶרֶם תָּחִיל יָלָדָה בְּטֶרֶם יָבוֹא חֵבֶל לָהּ
וְהִמְלִיטָה זָכָר: ח מִי־שָׁמַע כָּזֹאת מִי רָאָה
כָּאֵלֶּה הֲיוּחַל אֶרֶץ בְּיוֹם אֶחָד אִם־יִוָּלֵד גּוֹי
פַּעַם אֶחָת כִּי־חָלָה גַּם־יָלְדָה צִיּוֹן אֶת־בָּנֶיהָ:
ט הַאֲנִי אַשְׁבִּיר וְלֹא אוֹלִיד יֹאמַר יהוה אִם־
אֲנִי הַמּוֹלִיד וְעָצַרְתִּי אָמַר אֱלֹהָיִךְ: י שִׂמְחוּ
אֶת־יְרוּשָׁלַםִ וְגִילוּ בָהּ כָּל־אֹהֲבֶיהָ שִׂישׂוּ
אִתָּהּ מָשׂוֹשׂ כָּל־הַמִּתְאַבְּלִים עָלֶיהָ: יא לְמַעַן
תִּינְקוּ וּשְׂבַעְתֶּם מִשֹּׁד תַּנְחֻמֶיהָ לְמַעַן תָּמֹצּוּ
וְהִתְעַנַּגְתֶּם מִזִּיז כְּבוֹדָהּ: יב כִּי־כֹה | אָמַר יהוה
הִנְנִי נֹטֶה־אֵלֶיהָ כְּנָהָר שָׁלוֹם וּכְנַחַל שׁוֹטֵף
כְּבוֹד גּוֹיִם וִינַקְתֶּם עַל־צַד תִּנָּשֵׂאוּ וְעַל־
בִּרְכַּיִם תְּשָׁעֳשָׁעוּ: יג כְּאִישׁ אֲשֶׁר אִמּוֹ
תְּנַחֲמֶנּוּ כֵּן אָנֹכִי אֲנַחֶמְכֶם וּבִירוּשָׁלַםִ
תְּנֻחָמוּ: יד וּרְאִיתֶם וְשָׂשׂ לִבְּכֶם וְעַצְמוֹתֵיכֶם
כַּדֶּשֶׁא תִפְרַחְנָה וְנוֹדְעָה יַד־יהוה אֶת־עֲבָדָיו
וְזָעַם אֶת־אֹיְבָיו: טו כִּי־הִנֵּה יהוה בָּאֵשׁ יָבוֹא
וְכַסּוּפָה מַרְכְּבֹתָיו לְהָשִׁיב בְּחֵמָה אַפּוֹ
וְגַעֲרָתוֹ בְּלַהֲבֵי־אֵשׁ: טז כִּי בָאֵשׁ יהוה נִשְׁפָּט
וּבְחַרְבּוֹ אֶת־כָּל־בָּשָׂר וְרַבּוּ חַלְלֵי יהוה:
יז הַמִּתְקַדְּשִׁים וְהַמִּטַּהֲרִים אֶל־הַגַּנּוֹת אַחַר
אַחַת [אחד כ׳] בַּתָּוֶךְ אֹכְלֵי בְּשַׂר הַחֲזִיר
וְהַשֶּׁקֶץ וְהָעַכְבָּר יַחְדָּו יָסֻפוּ נְאֻם־יהוה:
יח וְאָנֹכִי מַעֲשֵׂיהֶם וּמַחְשְׁבֹתֵיהֶם בָּאָה לְקַבֵּץ
אֶת־כָּל־הַגּוֹיִם וְהַלְּשֹׁנוֹת וּבָאוּ וְרָאוּ אֶת־
כְּבוֹדִי: יט וְשַׂמְתִּי בָהֶם אוֹת וְשִׁלַּחְתִּי מֵהֶם |
פְּלֵיטִים אֶל־הַגּוֹיִם תַּרְשִׁישׁ פּוּל וְלוּד מֹשְׁכֵי
קֶשֶׁת תֻּבַל וְיָוָן הָאִיִּים הָרְחֹקִים אֲשֶׁר לֹא־
שָׁמְעוּ אֶת־שִׁמְעִי וְלֹא־רָאוּ אֶת־כְּבוֹדִי
וְהִגִּידוּ אֶת־כְּבוֹדִי בַּגּוֹיִם: כ וְהֵבִיאוּ אֶת־כָּל־
אֲחֵיכֶם מִכָּל־הַגּוֹיִם | מִנְחָה | לַיהוה בַּסּוּסִים
וּבָרֶכֶב וּבַצַּבִּים וּבַפְּרָדִים וּבַכִּרְכָּרוֹת עַל הַר
קָדְשִׁי יְרוּשָׁלַםִ אָמַר יהוה כַּאֲשֶׁר יָבִיאוּ בְנֵי
יִשְׂרָאֵל אֶת־הַמִּנְחָה בִּכְלִי טָהוֹר בֵּית יהוה:
כא וְגַם־מֵהֶם אֶקַּח לַכֹּהֲנִים לַלְוִיִּם אָמַר יהוה:
כב כִּי כַאֲשֶׁר הַשָּׁמַיִם הַחֲדָשִׁים וְהָאָרֶץ
הַחֲדָשָׁה אֲשֶׁר אֲנִי עֹשֶׂה עֹמְדִים לְפָנַי נְאֻם־

and distance themselves from you say, "HASHEM is glorified because of my reputation" — but we shall see your gladness and they will be shamed. 6 A tumultuous sound comes from the city, a sound from the Sanctuary, the sound of HASHEM dealing retribution to His enemies. 7 When she has not yet felt her labor, she will have given birth! When the pain has not yet come to her, she will have delivered a son! 8 Who has heard such a thing? Who has seen its like? Has a land gone through its labor in one day? Has a nation been born at one time, as Zion went through labor and gave birth to her children? 9 Shall I bring [a woman] to the birthstool and not have her give birth? says HASHEM. Shall I, Who causes birth, hold it back? says your God.

10 Be glad with Jerusalem and rejoice in her, all who love her; exult with her exultation, all who mourned for her; 11 so that you may nurse and be sated from the breast of her consolations; so that you may suck and delight from the glow of her glory. 12 For so said HASHEM, Behold! — I shall direct peace to her like a river, and the honor of nations like a surging stream and you shall suckle; you will be carried on a shoulder and dandled on knees. 13 Like a man whose mother consoled him, so will I console you, and in Jerusalem will you be consoled. 14 You shall see and your heart will exult, and your bones will flourish like grass; the hand of HASHEM will be known to His servants, and He will be angry with His enemies. 15 For behold! — HASHEM will arrive in fire and His chariots like the whirlwind, to requite His anger with wrath, and His rebuke with flaming fire. 16 For with fire HASHEM will judge, and with His sword against all flesh; many will be those slain by HASHEM.

17 Those who prepare and purify themselves [to storm] the gardens go one after another to the midst [of the fray]; together will be consumed those who eat the flesh of swine, of abominable creatures and rodents — the words of HASHEM. 18 I [am aware of] their deeds and their thoughts; [the time] has come to gather in all the nations and tongues; they shall come and see My glory.

19 I shall put a sign upon them and send some as survivors to the nations: Tarshish, Pul and, Lud, the bow-drawers, Tubal, and Yavan; the distant islands, who have not heard of My fame and not seen My glory, and they will declare My glory among the nations. 20 They will bring all your brethren from all the nations as an offering to HASHEM, on horses, on chariot, on covered wagons, on mules, and with joyful dances upon My holy mountain, Jerusalem, said HASHEM; just as the Children of Israel bring their offering in a pure vessel to the House of HASHEM. 21 From them, too, will I take to be Kohanim and Levites, said HASHEM.

22 For just as the new heavens and the new earth that I will make will endure before Me — the words of

יְהֹוָה כֵּן יַעֲמֹד זַרְעֲכֶם וְשִׁמְכֶם: כג וְהָיָה מִדֵּי־
חֹדֶשׁ בְּחָדְשׁוֹ וּמִדֵּי שַׁבָּת בְּשַׁבַּתּוֹ יָבוֹא כָל־
בָּשָׂר לְהִשְׁתַּחֲוֹת לְפָנַי אָמַר יְהֹוָה: כד וְיָצְאוּ
וְרָאוּ בְּפִגְרֵי הָאֲנָשִׁים הַפֹּשְׁעִים בִּי כִּי
תוֹלַעְתָּם לֹא תָמוּת וְאִשָּׁם לֹא תִכְבֶּה וְהָיוּ
דֵרָאוֹן לְכָל־בָּשָׂר:
וְהָיָה מִדֵּי־חֹדֶשׁ בְּחָדְשׁוֹ וּמִדֵּי שַׁבָּת בְּשַׁבַּתּוֹ
יָבוֹא כָל־בָּשָׂר לְהִשְׁתַּחֲוֹת לְפָנַי אָמַר יְהֹוָה:

HASHEM — so will your offspring and your name endure. 23 *And it shall be that, from New Moon to New Moon, and from Sabbath to Sabbath, all flesh shall come to prostrate themselves before Me, said HASHEM.*

24 *They shall go out and see the corpses of those who rebel against Me, for their worms will not die and their fire will not go out, and they shall be a disgrace for all flesh.*

And it shall be that, from New Moon to New Moon, and from Sabbath to Sabbath, all flesh shall come to prostrate themselves before Me, said HASHEM.

When the second day Rosh Chodesh falls on Sunday, some congregations add the first and last verses of the *Haftarah* for *Shabbas* Erev Rosh Chodesh (*I Samuel* 20-18;42):

וַיֹּאמֶר־לוֹ יְהוֹנָתָן מָחָר חֹדֶשׁ וְנִפְקַדְתָּ כִּי
יִפָּקֵד מוֹשָׁבֶךָ: וַיֹּאמֶר יְהוֹנָתָן לְדָוִד לֵךְ לְשָׁלוֹם
אֲשֶׁר נִשְׁבַּעְנוּ שְׁנֵינוּ אֲנַחְנוּ בְּשֵׁם יהוה לֵאמֹר
יהוה יִהְיֶה | בֵּינִי וּבֵינֶךָ וּבֵין זַרְעִי וּבֵין זַרְעֲךָ
עַד־עוֹלָם:

Jonathan said to [David], "Tomorrow is the New Moon, and you will be missed because your seat will be empty." Jonathan said to David, "Go to peace. What the two of us have sworn in the Name of HASHEM — saying, 'HASHEM shall be between me and you, and between my children and your children' — shall be forever!"

This volume is part of
THE ARTSCROLL SERIES®
an ongoing project of
translations, commentaries and expositions
on Scripture, Mishnah, Talmud, Halachah,
liturgy, history, the classic Rabbinic writings,
biographies and thought.

For a brochure of current publications
visit your local Hebrew bookseller
or contact the publisher:

Mesorah Publications, ltd

4401 Second Avenue
Brooklyn, New York 11232
(718) 921-9000
www.artscroll.com